ESSENTIALS OF AMATEUR SPORTS LAW

ESSENTIALS OF AMATEUR SPORTS LAW

Second Edition

GLENN M. WONG

Westport, Connecticut
London

Library of Congress Cataloging-in-Publication Data

Wong, Glenn M.
    Essentials of amateur sports law / Glenn M. Wong.—2nd ed.
      p. cm.
    Includes index.
    ISBN 0–275–94810–2 (alk. paper)
      1. School sports—Law and legislation—United States. 2. Sports—
Law and legislation—United States. I. Title.
    KF4166.W66   1994
    344.73'077–dc20   93–32899
    [347.30477]

British Library Cataloguing in Publication Data is available.

Copyright © 1994 by Greenwood Publishing Group, Inc.

Library of Congress Catalog Card Number: 93–32899
ISBN: 0–275–94810–2

First published in 1994

Praeger Publishers, 88 Post Road West, Westport, CT 06881
An imprint of Greenwood Publishing Group, Inc.

Printed in the United States of America

∞

The paper used in this book complies with the
Permanent Paper Standard issued by the National
Information Standards Organization (Z39.48–1984).

10 9 8 7 6 5 4 3 2 1

CONTENTS

CHAPTER 3
Contract Law Applications to Amateur Athletics   63

CHAPTER 9
Television and Media Broadcasting   565

CHAPTER 10
Trademark Law   597

CHAPTER 11
Professional Careers and Player Agents   629

PREFACE TO THE FIRST EDITION

In my several professional roles as attorney, teacher, and consultant, I meet frequently with individuals and groups active in amateur sports. Athletic administrators and others around the country have repeatedly expressed a need for a "practitioner's" book because sports law has become such an integral part of their day-to-day operation. They want to have a background on sports law before they deal with attorneys on legal issues. Even more important, they want to attempt to avoid litigation. The interest and concerns of these people motivated the writing of this book.

I started with the concept that the book should be written for those affected by sport law issues who are not necessarily lawyers, including college or high school athletic administrators or coaches, student-athletes, school board members, institutional representatives, and those involved in amateur sports organizations. There is, for example, a chapter on the court system, a glossary, and an appendix of sample forms that can be used by practitioners as starting points for developing their own forms. The major intercollegiate and interscholastic amateur sports organizations, such as the U.S. Olympic Committee and the National Collegiate Athletic Association, are described in detail. All new legal concepts and issues are discussed, as are basic tort law, contract law, trademark law, and constitutional law. Each of the chapters has been designed as a self-contained unit that can be used as a quick reference. Case citations and brief summaries of cases (rather than lengthy discussions) have been included in the notes. The notes also include law review articles, names and addresses of relevant organizations, and other information which can lead the reader to additional sources of information.

I would like to thank some of the many people who have been instrumental in assisting me with *Essentials of Amateur Sports Law*. First, Margaret M. Kearney, the editor, helped express the thoughts and principles in this book. In addition, she kept the project moving and made sure that legalese was eliminated. As for research and writing, I would like to thank and acknowledge the work of Professor Richard J. Ensor of the University of Massachusetts, Amherst. He co-authored Chapter 9 (sports broadcasting) and Chapter 10 (trademark law). His numerous reviews of the manuscript and comments were invaluable in that he provided the perspectives of a sports lawyer and of an experienced athletic administrator. I also acknowledge the contributions of several research assistants: David Knopp, William Hubbard, Scott Proefrock, and Scott Zuffelato. The many drafts of the manuscript were typed by Susan McBride, to whom I am grateful. Several others, too numerous to mention individually, also contributed in various ways to this project. And, finally, I would like to thank Professor Robert Berry of Boston College Law School for getting me started in sports law.

PREFACE TO THE SECOND EDITION

How much has changed since 1988, when the first edition of *Essentials of Amateur Sports Law* was published? The Knight Commission has been formed, disbanded, and reinstated; Dick Shultz has resigned as Executive Director of the NCAA; and the impact of the passage of the Civil Rights Restoration Act is being felt and has even spawned a new term—*gender equity*. The first edition of this book does not mention idiopathic cardiomyopathy (Hank Gathers' heart disease); Jerry Tarkanian was still Head Basketball Coach at the University of Nevada, Las Vegas; and there is another new term—*ambush marketing*. The first Proposition 48 (now Propositions 48/42/26) student-athletes have graduated, but it has not stopped the debate over academic requirements for NCAA initial eligibility. Butch Reynolds has a judgment in hand for $27.3 million dollars and a new law is coming into place—Americans with Disabilities Act.

These are only some of the significant changes in the constantly changing area of sports law. Many of the changes since 1988 have further clouded the line between professional and amateur athletics: a case-decision ruling that a college football player was an employee of the university, the 1992 Men's Olympic basketball team dominated by professional basketball players from the NBA, and a proposal to pay Olympic athletes for performance in the 1994 Olympics.

As you can see from this brief overview, there have been significant changes and important litigation that continue to shape athletics. Some will be discussed in a global manner in Chapter 1 and then discussed in more detail throughout the book. In all, there are approximately 165 new cases in this edition. The title of the book, however, remains the same. The reason for this is analogous to baseball's antitrust exemption, it is done for precedent reasons and not because it is the most appropriate title in 1994. The number of chapters and major topical areas covered in the book have not changed, but they have been updated.

For me, a major reason for putting together a second edition was the positive, strong, and encouraging responses I received from the audience. I would like to thank them. Many of these people have provided comments which have been incorporated into the second edition.

The second edition has been a challenge. While trying to finish the revision, I served for several months in 1992–93 as Director of Athletics and Dean of the School of Physical Education at the University of Massachusetts. Also, I was appointed as Faculty Athletics Representative to the NCAA. While these positions made completion of the second edition more difficult, it also served to provide me with different insights and to confirm on a first-hand basis some of my thoughts and ideas. In addition, a second son, Gary, arrived. I dedicate the second edition to him, to my first son, Glenn, and to my wife, Paula.

There were many people who assisted in seeing this project through. Carol Barr, my research assistant, kept this project going and my colleague, Lisa Pike, Assistant Professor, provided invaluable assistance with the manuscript, including feedback from the use of the book in her Sports Law course.

Other students and research assistants who assisted in the production of this second edition include Jack Woodbury, Jesse Wilde, Peter Carton, Leslie Keast, Margaret Driscoll, Steve Hilliard, Jeff Craig, and Burke Magnus. All of these students and research assistants have already moved on to their careers in the sports industry.

For those of you who know publishing, you are well aware that there are several months' lag time between submission of the final manuscript and the published book. By the time you read this, my files will already include cases for the third edition. I anticipate many new cases involving discrimination issues (and also reverse discrimination), litigation or arbitration regarding eligibility for the Olympics, changes in NCAA enforcement procedures, drug testing and contractual rights, conference contract issues, additional litigation relative to medical issues, and a host of new issues which no one can predict. These new issues will continue to make sports law a constantly changing, interesting, and varied discipline, and will certainly provide cause for a third edition of *Essentials of Amateur Sports Law.*

Chapter 1

OVERVIEW OF AMATEUR ATHLETICS AND SPORTS LAW

INTRODUCTION

Amateur athletic organizations have grown tremendously over the last quarter century in terms of their scope, power, and financial status. In the United States alone, amateur athletics encompass organizations that involve the lives and athletic experiences of people from their childhoods (e.g., Pop Warner Football and Little League) through high school years (e.g., the National Federation of State High School Associations) through college (e.g., the National Collegiate Athletic Association) and beyond (e.g., the United States Olympic Committee). The purpose of this chapter is to give the reader an overview of the structure and involvement of amateur athletic organizations, and to show how the constituencies involved in these organizations—the athlete, the coach, the administrator, the referee, and others—are involved in rule making and litigation involving these amateur athletic organizations. The first sections will provide information on the structure and authority these amateur athletic organizations possess starting off with an introduction to the sports industry and introducing the various segments that are investigated in this chapter. Next, information on intercollegiate athletics, Olympic sports, and interscholastic athletics is discussed. The last section of the chapter addresses the constituencies—the athlete, the coach, the administrator, the referee, and others—and shows how the rules and regulations of these organizations affect these constituencies including the types of litigation that have resulted.

THE SPORTS INDUSTRY

This chapter will first explore the various industry segments or organizations of the sports industry, including the structure, rules, and procedures, and the power and authority relationships within the sport organization itself and with other amateur sport organizations. The sport industry segments have been broken into three main categories: college (which will focus on the National Collegiate Athletic Association), Olympics (which will investigate the United States Olympic Committee, the International Olympic Committee, the international federations for sports, and the National Governing Body for sports), and high school (which will look at the National Federation of State High Schools Association and the Massachusetts Interscholastic Athletic Association).

INTERCOLLEGIATE ATHLETICS

The collegiate athletic industry segment comprises a number of different national organizations: the National Collegiate Athletic Association (NCAA), the National Junior College Athletic Association, and the National Association of Intercollegiate Athletics, to name a few. These associations have organizational power over those colleges and universities which have joined the national association. The NCAA, though, is the primary rules-governing organization within the college sport industry segment, which contains 847 member institutions, and is used in this section as an example of how these collegiate athletic industry segment organizations function. The NCAA was founded in the early 1900s and states its purpose today to be "to maintain intercollegiate athletics as an integral part of the educational program and the athlete as an integral part of the student body and, by so doing, retain a clear line of demarcation between intercollegiate athletics and professional sports" (*1993–94 NCAA Manual*, Constitution, Art. 1.3.1). Membership of the association consists of four-year colleges and universities and two-year upper-level collegiate institutions in the United States. The more than 1,000 members agree to be bound by NCAA rules and regulations and are obligated to administer their athletic programs in accordance with NCAA rules.

The NCAA administrative structure is composed of five groups: (1) the NCAA Council, consisting of forty-six members including the president and secretary-treasurer of the NCAA and forty-four members selected from Division I, II, and III members, which directs the general policy of the organization between conventions; (2) the NCAA Executive Committee, consisting of the NCAA president and secretary-treasurer and the division vice presidents as well as nine members selected from the membership, which handles the financial aspects of the organization; (3) the NCAA Administrative Committee, consisting of the officers of the NCAA and the executive director, which conducts business between meetings of the Council and Executive Committee; (4) the Presidents Commission, consisting of forty-four members selected from the three divisions of the membership, which nominates candidates for office, places topics on the agenda of the council and convention, proposes legislation, and sponsors studies related to intercollegiate athletics; and (5) the Joint Policy Board consisting of the officers of the NCAA, the executive director, and the officers of the Presidents Commission. This Board reviews the NCAA's budget, the NCAA's legislative process and agenda, evaluates and supervises the executive director, and reviews other nonlegislative policies (see Exhibit 1–1). In addition, the NCAA has various committees assigned to oversee playing rules and championship administration responsibilities, nomination procedures, convention arrangements, eligibility, enforcement, and legislative committees, to name a few.

The NCAA controls virtually all areas of collegiate athletics; in-

Exhibit 1–1
NCAA Organizational Structure

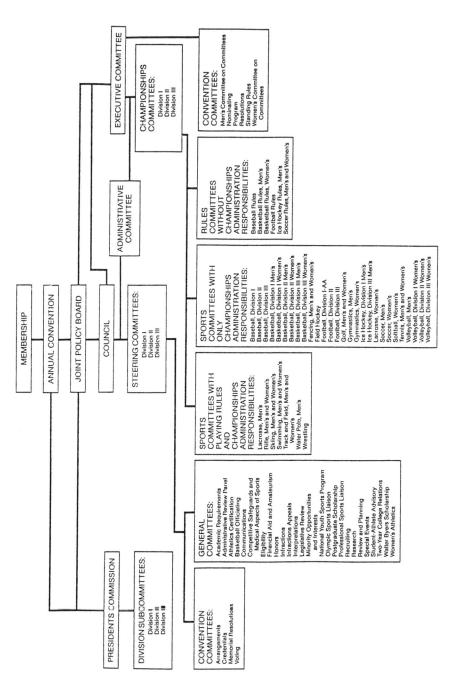

cluded in its bylaws are rules and regulations concerning amateurism, recruiting of student-athletes, eligibility requirements, playing and practice seasons, financial aid, championship events, and enforcement procedures. Legislation is presented and voted upon at an annual convention by the membership (each school receives one vote). This legislation is then published in the *NCAA Manual*, approximately four hundred pages long, and sent to all member schools, which must comply with it. The membership, in essence, has the power to control the enactment of rules and regulations; the NCAA administrative structure consists of the national office, which carries out and enforces legislation passed by the membership. The colleges and universities, the same schools constituting the membership that pass legislation, put the enforcement power and control into the hands of the NCAA national office legislative and enforcement staff. The NCAA maintains, though, that institutional control must also lie in the colleges and universities, which must play a role in enforcing the NCAA legislation. In other words, the NCAA staff still serves the membership and must act and enforce rules in accordance with the policies and procedures mandated by the membership, but the membership gives power to the NCAA national office staff to oversee the rules and regulations set forth by the membership regarding a school's awarding of scholarships, monitor a coach's recruiting efforts, enforce allowable practice and playing dates for teams, organize and run championship events, and conduct the NCAA drug testing program. The institution must be involved through its own institutional control; the NCAA becomes involved in investigating and enforcing legislative rules and regulations in accordance with the membership's wishes.

This enforcement structure and the idea of institutional control were aspects of an interesting event in 1991–93, when the University of Virginia was being investigated by the NCAA enforcement staff for providing extra benefits to student-athletes and graduate assistant coaches through the issuance of interest-free loans. The notable aspect of this case was that these improprieties occurred during the tenure of a former director of athletics who was at the time of the investigation the current executive director of the NCAA, Richard D. Schultz. An independent fact-finder, James Park, Jr., was hired by the NCAA to conduct the investigation as it pertained to the NCAA executive director. This independent fact-finder reached the conclusion that Schultz had actual knowledge of at least some of the loans made to student-athletes. Although maintaining his innocence and reiterating that he knew nothing about the loans, Schultz resigned as executive director of the NCAA in May 1993. Schultz, in his resignation statement, said that he had worked hard to establish a high level of credibility for the NCAA and to strengthen the NCAA's enforcement program and he didn't want that compromised by critics' stating that he had received favored treatment during the infractions process.

Recently, the NCAA has encountered scrutiny over the abundance of recruiting violations that have been taking place in college athletics, in addition to the poor academic progress and graduation rates of collegiate student-athletes. Public awareness and concern regarding these issues have increased to the point that state and federal governments are getting involved by proposing legislation which addresses these areas of concern. A bill, sponsored by Senator Bill Bradley (D-N.J.), former Representative Tom McMillen (D-Md.), and Representative Ed Towns (D-N.Y.), called the "Student Athlete Right to Know Act" (S.580), was approved by Congress and signed into law by President Bush on November 8, 1990. This bill, effective in 1993, requires colleges and universities that receive federal financial assistance to report graduation rates, itemized by race and sex, annually to the secretary of education. The act also calls for reporting the proportion of students who earn a degree within six years. The information is to be made available to high school student-athletes and their families and to high school guidance counselors and principals in order to aid the student-athletes as they choose the school they will attend.

A significant move toward introducing reform to fight the financial, recruiting, and academic abuses prevalent in collegiate athletics was taken on October 19, 1989, when the Trustees of the Knight Foundation created the Knight Commission to study collegiate athletics and devise a proposal for reform. The commission, in more than a year of meetings, held discussions with athletics directors, faculty representatives, coaches, athletes, conference leaders, television officials, and accrediting associations. It was concluded that the larger problem is not that of curbing particular abuses but of having academic administrators define the terms under which athletics will be conducted in the university's name. The main difficulty does not lie in creating a "level playing field" but, rather, ensuring that those on the field are students as well as athletes. The commission proposed a new structure of reform in its report, "Keeping Faith with the Student-Athlete," which was released in March 1991. This structure of reform is called the "one-plus-three" model, in which the "one" (presidential control) is directed toward the "three" (academic integrity, financial integrity, and independent certification). The Knight Commission states in its report that with such a model in place, higher education could address all of the subordinate difficulties, such as athletic dorms, freshman eligibility, length of playing seasons, and recruiting policies in college sports. Without such a model, "athletics reform will continue in fits and starts, its energy squandered on symptoms, the underlying problems ignored."

In March 1992, the Knight Commission published a follow-up report, "A Solid Start: A Report on Reform of Intercollegiate Athletics." In this report, the Knight Commission states that the reform of college athletics has certainly started to take place as seen through the enactment at the 1992 NCAA Convention of a number of important reform measures (see Exhibit 1–2). These measures are a start, but the commission states that more needs to be done. The NCAA will be concentrating on major structural considerations in athletics, including a certification program; presidential authority at the institutional, conference, and national levels; and financial control and integrity. The Knight Commission warns that many detours exist on this road to reform. These potential detours include legislative efforts at the federal level to impose reform, which in the Knight Commission's mind would create more harm than good, and legislation being enacted by states over existing NCAA enforcement rules. The Knight Commission believes that academic and athletic administrators are showing that they can meet the challenge of reform in college athletics and they have asked in their report that the people involved in public policy and legislation, that is, government officials and elected representatives, stand aside while college and university leaders complete the job. The Knight Commission endorses the position that government legislation is not the appropriate method to use in reforming athletics; instead reform should be left up to the academic and athletic people themselves.

In March 1993, the Knight Commission published its final report, "A New Beginning for a New Century." In this report the commission reviewed the changes that have occurred in the years since they first addressed the problems inherent in college athletics and discussed the reform movement that must take place. In the forefront of these changes were cost reductions, new academic standards, and an athletics certification program. In its 1993 report, the Knight Commission stated that two great issues still dominate athletics policy discussions: cost containment and gender equity. The commission stated that athletics programs will not disarm, in order to decrease expenses, unilaterally, and therefore conferences and the NCAA must support cost containment unanimously in order for it to be effective. The commission also stated that the unfinished agenda of equity for women also demands attention. Comparable opportunities for both sexes must be offered while also keeping in mind the objective of controlling costs. Although the Knight Commission was supposed to end its three-year study of college athletics in March 1993, the commission offered its

Exhibit 1–2
NCAA Legislative Proposals Approved at the 1992 Convention

1.   Effective in 1992:

> • **Satisfactory Progress in Degree Requirements.** "Majoring in eligibility" is a thing of the past. Division I student-athletes must have completed 25 percent, 50 percent and 75 percent of the program course requirements for their specific degree in order to compete in their third, fourth and fifth years of enrollment, respectively.
>
> • **Satisfactory Progress in Grade Point Average.** Student-athletes cannot compete with little chance of graduating. Entering their third and fourth years of enrollment, Division I student-athletes must have a GPA of 90 and 95 percent, respectively, of the minimum cumulative GPA required to graduate.
>
> • **Satisfactory Progress in School Year.** Student-athletes can no longer slide by during the academic year. Division I and II student-athletes will have to take three-quarters of their courses during the regular academic year, instead of relying on summer school to make up credits.
>
> • **Coaches' Income.** It is clear who employs the coaches. All coaches in Divisions I and II are now required to obtain prior, annual, written approval from university presidents for all athletically related income, the use of the institution's name, and outside compensation from shoe and apparel companies.
>
> • **Official Visits.** High school athletes will understand that reform is real. Prospects cannot accept official visits to Division I schools prior to the "early signing period" unless they present minimum SAT results of 700 (ACT results of 17) and a GPA of 2.0 in seven core courses.
>
> • **Transfer Students.** Mid-year transfer students (including junior college transfers) at all Division I and II institutions must meet satisfactory progress requirements the following fall, not one year later.

2.   Effective in 1993:

> • **Presidential Control.** University presidents and the NCAA Council will have in hand a major examination of the role of presidents at the institutional, conference and national levels.
>
> • **Certification.** The proposals of the NCAA Subcommittee on Certification, which encompass the "one-plus-three" model, will be considered at the 1993 convention.

Exhibit 1–2 (Continued)

    • **Gender Equity.** A study of gender equity in intercollegiate athletics will be completed, including consideration of equity in grants-in-aid for women's sports.

    • **Cost Containment.** Grants-in-aid for Division II programs will be reduced by 10 percent, matching cost reductions enacted in 1991 for Division I.

3.   Effective in 1994:

    • **Financial Integrity.** University presidents and the NCAA Council will have access to a comprehensive examination of financial issues (including sources of financial assistance for student-athletes; the influence of athletics foundations, booster clubs and media revenues; and gender equity).

4.   Effective by 1995:

    • **Initial Eligibility.** New initial-eligibility rules will ensure that prospective student-athletes have a reasonable chance of completing college. By August 1995, prospects will be required to present a 2.5 grade point average (out of a possible 4.0) in 13 core high school units, along with a combined SAT score of 700 (ACT score of 17) in order to compete in their first year of enrollment.

services, in the wake of NCAA Executive Director Dick Schultz's resignation in May 1993, in order to keep the reform movement moving forward.

More work has been conducted in the area of cost containment and gender equity by the NCAA. The NCAA formed two committees to study these issues: the NCAA's Special Committee to Review Financial Conditions in Intercollegiate Athletics, and the NCAA Gender-Equity Task Force. Both of these committees during the spring of 1993 issued preliminary reports containing proposed legislative changes to be voted on by the NCAA membership. Regarding cost containment, some of the proposals consisted of decreasing squad sizes at both Division I-A and I-AA football programs. Other proposed changes included an end to team getaways in local hotels the night before home games, elimination of offseason training-table meals for athletes, cutbacks in the number of visits by recruits and the number of coaches who recruit off campus, an end to off-campus scouting of football and basketball opponents, and scheduling of the NCAA convention every two years rather than annually. This committee also recommended that individual schools and conferences look into the possibility of decreasing the number of officials used in basketball and perhaps other sports.

The NCAA Gender-Equity Task Force proposals consisted of recommending a list of emerging sports for women that should be acceptable in meeting the minimum sports-sponsorship requirements of the NCAA. Also, this committee recommended an increase in the maximum number of financial aid awards allowed for Divisions I and II women's sports. In another recommendation, the Committee on Women's Athletics explored the addition of one graduate assistant or volunteer coach, who must be a female, to the numbers of allowable coaches in men's and women's sports, not including football and basketball. The committee also stated that the comparison of the numbers of male and female athletes with their proportions in the undergraduate student population should be the benchmark in assessing equal opportunity and should be the goal toward which each institution is moving.

The college sport industry segment also includes schools and conferences that determine their own rules and regulations in terms of eligibility, playing and practice seasons, drug testing, financial aid, and so on. In most instances, these rules are adopted by the schools and conferences because they are stricter than the NCAA regulations or because the area is not covered by NCAA rules and regulations. The athletic programs and the coaches need to comply not only with NCAA rules but also with individual school and conference rules. These rules may vary, so that the school and/or conference may have a higher GPA requirement, for instance, than the NCAA for incoming freshmen. In these situations, the athletic program and coach must comply with the tougher standard, even though in the NCAA's eyes only compliance with NCAA rules and standards is required. A second reason for schools and conferences to adopt their own rules is that the NCAA does not have any regulations governing the athletes and athletic department in a particular area. For example, the Southwest Athletic Conference (SWC) conducts steroid testing for all sports during the fall semester. Although the NCAA conducts drug testing during NCAA championship events and conducts random steroid testing for the sport of football, the SWC has decided to enforce a stricter drug testing program. Thirty student-athletes in the sport of football and twenty "top" returning athletes in all other sports are selected to undergo this test. In addition, the SWC conducts a spring steroid testing program with twenty-four athletes from all sports selected to be tested during the spring semester. These two drug testing programs are examples of conference regulations which are more strict than the NCAA regulations governing drug testing.

Another example pertains to how schools and conferences may be affected by different policies and regulations depending on the area involved and the organization that is the authority in that area. For instance, schools and conferences must abide by the Collegiate Commissioners Association (CCA) rules surrounding the signing of incoming freshmen student-athletes to a letter of intent. The letter of intent form is prepared and administered by the CCA. The NCAA is not involved in the promulgation of rules or the enforcement of the letter of intent; thus an athlete who wants to nullify his or her letter of intent with a particular institution must pursue this with the CCA. The schools and conferences are affected by these different rules and regulations and must submit to the authority of these different organizations or groups.

The college sport industry segment has seen the member organizations—the NCAA, colleges and universities, and conferences—become involved in litigation concerning their rules and regulations. This litigation has involved complaints by athletes surrounding eligibility rules, drug testing, and academic preparation. For instance, Braxston Banks and Brad Gaines were declared ineligible by the NCAA for their senior football seasons after entering the NFL draft. The two filed separate suits against the NCAA, claiming the NCAA was boycotting them and other athletes and violation of antitrust laws by the NCAA in declaring an athlete ineligible for further intercollegiate play once the athlete asks that his or her name be placed into the professional draft, even if he or she is not drafted or signs a professional contract, or once the athlete retains an agent or attorney to represent him or her. The courts applied an antitrust analysis to this argument and in *Banks v. NCAA*, Cause No. S90-394 (Ind. Dist. Ct. 1990), found that the NCAA eligibility rules were subject to antitrust law, but that the NCAA bylaws at issue were reasonable in respect to the NCAA's purpose of defining and maintaining amateurism in college athletics (see note 1). In *Gaines v. NCAA*, Civil Docket No. 3-90-0773 (Tenn. Dist. Ct. 1990), however, the court found that although the NCAA is engaged in a business venture and thus subject to antitrust legislation, the eligibility rules of the NCAA are not economic and therefore not subject to antitrust scrutiny. The NCAA has experienced an increase in the amount of court decisions and interpretations finding that it is in fact a trade or business, such as in *Gaines v. NCAA* and *NCAA v. Board of Regents of University of Oklahoma and University of Georgia Athletic Association*, 104 S. Ct. 2948 (U.S. 1984), and therefore should be subject to antitrust legislation. These results may have an impact on future litigation brought against the NCAA.

The courts have also looked at the rights of the student-athlete in these cases and have ruled for the athlete if, in the court's opinion, his or her rights were violated. This particular argument has been used in drug testing cases. Athletes have argued that the procedure followed for conducting a drug test, with a witness present at all times when the athlete is supplying a urine sample, is a violation of their constitutional right to privacy. Other arguments athletes have used involve the drug testing procedure, such as capping of the specimen bottles, which, if not performed accurately, may have allowed the bottles to be tampered with and produced an erroneous test result. Athletes have argued that the tests constitute unreasonable search and seizure in that they are singled out because of their athletic status and forced to undergo drug testing whereas other students are not subject to compliance with this program. The courts have found in some situations that the athlete's constitutional right supersedes the school or organization's reason for the drug testing program and have revoked the power of the NCAA or the school to conduct the program.

NOTE _____

1. Under NCAA Rule 12.2.4.2, "An individual loses amateur status in a particular sport when the individual asks to be placed on the draft list or supplemental draft list of a professional league in that sport, even though

(a) The individual asks that his or her name be withdrawn from the list prior to the actual draft;

(b) The individual's name remains on the list but he or she is not drafted, or

(c) The individual is drafted but does not sign an agreement with any professional athletics team." (*1993–94 NCAA Manual*)

At the heart of the case of *Braxton Banks v. NCAA*, Case No. S90-394 (Ind. Dist. Ct. 1990), are the circumstances discussed in 12.2.4.2(b). Braxton Banks began attending Notre Dame in September 1986 on a full athletic scholarship. He played running back on Notre Dame's football team for three years and sat out a fourth year because of a knee injury. He had a fourth year of eligibility remaining. In March 1990, Banks decided to enter the National Football League draft and declared himself eligible to be drafted. Banks, however, was not selected, and after failing to catch on with any clubs as a free agent, he sought to return to Notre Dame.

In August 1990, Banks filed a class action lawsuit in U.S. district court attacking the NCAA rule on antitrust grounds, claiming it had an anticompetitive effect and constituted illegal restraint of trade by preventing players from freely testing their worth in the professional marketplace. Banks's hopes of being able to return to the playing field immediately ended on August 17, 1990, when a request for a temporary injunction was denied and the lawsuit dismissed.

The 7th U.S. Circuit Court of Appeals agreed with the lower court by upholding the dismissal of Banks's claim. At issue in this case is essentially whether the NCAA should be considered a "big business" and therefore be held to the same standards as other industries, or an overseer of amateur athletics.

Banks's case reached a conclusion in May 1993, when the U.S. Supreme Court rejected a request to reopen the case. The appeals court's decision, therefore, in effect bars all future student-athletes from raising antitrust challenges to NCAA eligibility rules.

OLYMPIC SPORT

The Olympic sport industry segment comprises a number of organizations each responsible for various segments of the Olympic sport competitions. The International Olympic Committee (IOC) is the head of all of these organizations in respect to Olympic competition. Each sport is also represented by its own International Federation (IF), which has authority over determining eligibility regulations for athletes competing in the Olympic Games. In order to participate in the Olympic Games, each country must be represented by a National Olympic Committee (NOC). This organization is responsible for overseeing the training, preparation, and eligibility of all athletes and teams who will represent the country in Olympic competition. Within each country's NOC, each sport is represented by its own National Governing Body (NGB). The NGBs are in charge of determining and regulating the eligibility of each individual athlete training and competing within that sport for the Olympic Games. Each of these organizations is addressed in more detail in the following sections.

International Olympic Committee

The International Olympic Committee (IOC) is responsible for overseeing the organization of the Olympic Games. To this extent, any organization or country that wishes to participate in the Olympic Games must be bound to the rules set forth by the IOC. The IOC is responsible for eligibility rules in setting regulations stipulating the standards used for athletes and countries to be recognized as eligible to compete in the Olympic Games. The strict IOC eligibility rules regarding amateurism have recently been relaxed through the institution of Rule 26 of the IOC amateur code. This rule places the power of athlete eligibility decision making in the hands of the individual international sport federations. The international federations devise their own eligibility rules; the athlete is responsible for abiding by not only the IOC rules but also the federation rules, even if they are more strict than the IOC rules. An athlete is allowed to receive only the financial rewards and material deemed allowable by the international federation.

In 1985, the IOC, after receiving pressure from several international federations, relaxed its eligibility rules by voting to allow professionals under the age of twenty-three in the sports of tennis, ice hockey, and soccer to participate in the 1988 Winter and Summer Olympic Games. Since that time, the decision of whether to allow professionals to compete in the Olympic Games has been left up to the international federations. For example, in 1989 the international federation governing basketball (FIBA) voted overwhelmingly to allow professionals to compete in the Olympics, and USA Basketball, the U.S. National Governing Body for the sport, allowed professional players from the National Basketball Association to play. Not all international federations, however, allow professionals to compete (for example, baseball).

The IOC is also responsible for selecting sites where the Winter and Summer Olympic Games will be held. National Olympic Committees from various countries submit proposals to host these Games. The IOC reviews all of the proposals and then makes a decision on which site will host the Games. In selecting sites for the Games, the IOC has come under criticism for taking into consideration the wishes of the U.S. television networks. Because of the large amount of television rights fees the IOC is paid by the U.S. network, the IOC takes into consideration the network's interest before selecting Olympic sites and allows the network to have input in the scheduling of events. The influence of these U.S. networks can also be seen in the IOC's decision to move the Winter Olympics out of the same year as the Summer Olympics, with the Games to alternate every two years (1992 Summer Olympics, 1994 Winter Olympics, 1996 Summer Olympics, etc.). This allows both events to fit more comfortably into a network's budget.

The IOC also conducts and enforces the drug testing of athletes at the Olympic Games. During the Olympic Games, the IOC is directly responsible for all drug testing procedures and tests conducted in connection with this event. The international sport federations, which run the qualifying events for the Olympic Games, conduct the drug testing program at these events. The international federations may implement their own drug testing program or may use the IOC drug testing procedures and IOC approved drug testing centers.

Various potential areas of litigation for the IOC involve the drug testing program. If the test is not conducted in the appropriate manner, an athlete may argue that the specimen was tampered with or that the tests were conducted improperly. The IOC sets out a defined procedure that must be followed from the initial notification of the athlete that he or she is to be drug tested, through the specimen collection period, through the transportation of the specimen to the drug testing lab, through the testing procedure, and through the potential for an appeal with a retest of the sample being performed. If at any time this procedure is broken, the test may be deemed to have been conducted improperly and thus invalid. In addition, there is always the possibility that the testing conducted at the drug testing lab was performed inadequately, contributing to the inaccuracy of the results. When a test result is positive, an athlete may experience serious repercussions such as forfeiting a medal and harm to sponsorship and endorsement contracts. Athletes may insist that they have never taken any of the IOC banned drugs and argue that the drug testing procedure or the tests themselves were conducted improperly. The athlete will have a potential cause of action, arguing loss of revenue and employment through the harm done to the athlete's sponsorship and endorsement contracts, because of the IOC drug testing program and the announced positive results.

An additional area where litigation is possible revolves around the issue of boycotting of the Olympic Games. The problem facing the IOC is that participation in the Olympic Games is voluntary and not compulsory, and a country has every right to refuse to participate. When that country happens to be the United States, as happened in 1980 at the Moscow Summer Olympics, or the former USSR, as in the 1984 Los Angeles Summer Olympics, the financial and public relations impacts to the IOC can be extremely harmful. The U.S. networks contribute a tremendous amount of money to the IOC for television rights to the Olympic Games. When the U.S. team refuses to participate, or when the most interesting competition, such as the former USSR, does not attend the Games, the effect on the television revenue can be dramatic. It has been proposed that the IOC should penalize countries which boycott the Olympic Games by restricting future participation. The IOC has adopted Rule 25, which forbids a competitor, team, or delegation to withdraw from the Games once final entries have been made. The IOC has stated that certain penalties and sanctions will take place against such a competitor, team, or delegation if such a withdrawal does take place without just reason, such as illness.

International Federation

Each sport that is included in the Olympic Games competition must have an IOC-recognized international federation. The international federation (IF) for each sport sets its own rules and regulations governing eligibility of athletes for international competitions. As mentioned earlier, the IOC recently has relinquished a portion of its authority on eligibility of athletes for Olympic competition to the international federations. The IFs set rules on their definition of "amateur" and whether a "professional" athlete will be allowed to compete in international competition events, including the Olympic Games. In determining their definition of amateurism and eligibility of athletes, IFs set regulations on the amount of money an athlete can earn while competing in the sport.

The sports' IFs may set different eligibility standards for the athletes. For instance, the international federation for figure skating (ISU) recently reviewed their eligibility rules and decided to allow professional figure skaters to compete in the Olympic Games. This decision follows the decisions made in the sports of basketball, ice hockey, soccer, and tennis, in which the international federations' eligibility rules have been changed to allow professionals to compete. The international federation for baseball (AINBA), however, will not allow professional players to compete in Olympic or Pan American Games competition. This issue of professionalism and eligibility for Olympic Games participation has been litigated before in the courts. For example, in 1984 Willie Gault, a wide receiver for the Chicago Bears, sued for the right to run the hurdles in the 1984 Summer Games. Gault lost in court and was declared ineligible because according to rules of the international federation for track and field (IAAF) a professional in one sport was still considered a professional for purposes of track and field. In 1988, however, Gault was allowed to win a spot on the U.S. Olympic Bobsled team. This was because of the different rules regarding eligibility set forth by the IAAF, the international federation for track and field, and the FIBT, the international federation for bobsled.

International federations have also been the subject of litigation over their involvement in drug testing. The following example provides a good description as to the procedures that must be followed by an athlete who wishes to fight a drug testing ruling by an international federation. Butch Reynolds is a track and field record holder who won a silver medal at the 1988 Olympic Games in Seoul, South Korea. During the month of August 1990, Reynolds was competing at a meet in Monte Carlo when he tested positive for steroids. In November 1990, the international federation, the IAAF, announced a two-year suspension for Reynolds because of the positive drug test results. Reynolds had the option of appealing to his NGB, the TAC, regarding these IAAF suspensions. If this process is followed, the athlete is presumed guilty, in accordance with the procedures followed by the NGB, unless he or she can prove his innocence, thereby placing the burden on the athlete. If the NGB appeal is denied, the athlete has the option of then appealing to the USOC. If the athlete is exonerated by either TAC or the USOC appeal panel, the IAAF's next course of action is to seek independent arbitration. Reynolds, though, avoided appeals to TAC and the IAAF and took advantage of a USOC rule which provides for arbitration if a suspended athlete is banned from a national meet. Reynolds won a temporary lifting of the suspension in June 1991 through a ruling by an American Arbitration Association arbitrator which found that the drug testing was sloppy and very incomplete. TAC's Doping Control Board then reviewed the case and in October 1991 reinstated Reynolds, finding that the IOC-accredited Paris drug testing lab did not carry out adequate procedures and conducted the drug tests in an inappropriate way. The next step for Reynolds was an appeal before the IAAF to lift the suspension. TAC, through the Doping Control Board's findings, supported Reynolds through this appeal process. Reynolds was allowed to compete in American meets while awaiting appeal of his suspension by the IAAF but was still ineligible for the 1992 Olympic Games. The IAAF's arbitration panel heard Reynolds's appeal but ruled in May 1992 that the weight of evidence was not great enough to overturn the suspension. Reynolds then filed a civil lawsuit in the United States. The district court found that Reynolds had established a likelihood of success on the merits of his case and therefore issued a preliminary injunction on June 19, 1992, which allowed Reynolds to compete in all track and field competitions including the Olympic trials and Games. TAC appealed the decision to the U.S. Sixth Circuit Court of Appeals, which overturned the lower court's decision ruling that no U.S. court had the jurisdiction to allow Reynolds to compete in Barcelona. In addition, the court ruled that granting Reynolds an injunction would harm other athletes through the IAAF's threat to invoke their "contamination rule," which would bar any athlete from the Olympic Games should he or she compete against Reynolds. Reynolds then appealed to the U.S. Supreme Court, and on June 20, 1992, Justice John Paul Stevens reinstated the injunction, claiming that the IAAF's threatened harm to other athletes could not dictate the disposition of Reynolds's claim. The issue of whether Butch Reynolds would have been allowed to compete in the Olympic Games in Barcelona was rendered moot on June 26, when he finished fifth in the 400-meter final and failed to qualify for the Olympics.

On December 3, 1992, a U.S. District Court in Ohio awarded Reynolds $27.3 million ($6.8 million in compensatory damages and $20.5 million in punitive damages) from the IAAF as a result of the civil lawsuit Reynolds filed against TAC and the IAAF citing lost earnings and personal anguish. Judge Joseph P. Kinneary stated in his ruling that the IAAF had "defamed" Reynolds, had acted with "malice" and "a spirit of revenge," and had "purposefully avoided the truth" in the case. The IAAF has maintained from the beginning of this dispute that no court in the United States holds any legal jurisdiction over the federation and has thus far been unwilling to recognize any ruling by any U.S. court. The IAAF, therefore, has refused to pay Reynolds any money. Reynolds has begun to collect some of the award after a U.S. District Court judge in Virginia in August of 1993 ruled that sponsorship money from the Mobil Corp. owed to the IAAF should instead be paid into an escrow account for Reynolds as partial payment of the $27.3 million owed to Reynolds by the IAAF.

An alternative method for deciding appeals has been used by three international federations in addition to their internal system. The three international federations—for rowing, wrestling, and swimming— have selected the Court of Arbitration for Sport (CAS) as the body of appeal outside the federation's own internal bodies. When all internal methods of appeal within the IF have been exhausted, the athlete or organization may submit an appeal to the CAS. The CAS serves as the final judicial body and is a legitimate substitute for a civil court judge. The CAS satisfies the requirements of statutory law, and there-fore its verdicts are definitive and executory and have the same effects as those determined by a civil judge. More international federations may turn to this method in an attempt to avoid potential civil lawsuits.

United States Olympic Committee

The United States Olympic Committee (USOC) is the National Olym-pic Committee (NOC) recognized by the IOC to represent the interest of the United States in participation in the Olympic Games. Each country's NOC is responsible for enforcing the rules and bylaws of the IOC. The United States Congress in 1978 enacted legislation, The Amateur Sports Act of 1978 P.L. 95-606 (95th Cong. 2d Sess.), which defined the objectives, purposes, and authority of the USOC. This governmental legislation put the authority and enforcement power governing international amateur athletic competition into the hands of the USOC. Prior to this legislation, the USOC structure in the United States was composed primarily of two powerful amateur ath-letic organizations at the time, the Amateur Athletic Union (AAU) and the National Collegiate Athletic Association (NCAA). The AAU was the organization which controlled many of the National Governing Bodies, while the NCAA maintained control over collegiate athletics, which supplied many of the athletes who participated in the Olympic Games and international competition. The USOC's authority rested in these two organizations. After the 1972 Summer Olympic Games in Munich, in which the USOC was blamed for a number of mishaps, a flurry of federal legislation was filed to reform the USOC. The Am-ateur Sports Act of 1978 was a result of this suggested legislation, along with a President's Commission on Olympic Sports report which suggested that a vertical structure for the amateur sport sector with the USOC as the coordinating body was needed. The authority over international amateur sport competition was thus granted to the USOC.

The USOC states as its purpose and goals that it is "dedicated to providing opportunities for American athletes at all age and skill lev-els, and to preparing and training those athletes for their challenges that range from domestic competitions to the Olympic Games themselves" (1992 U.S. Olympic Committee Financial Report). As part of this purpose, the USOC oversees development, promotion, and coordination of amateur athletic competition in the United States and fields and finances the teams for the Olympic and Pan American Games. In an attempt to fulfill its purpose and goals, the USOC operates Olympic training centers in Colorado Springs, Colorado, and Lake Placid, New York. A third training center is being built in San Diego, California, with projected completion expected in late 1994. In addition, the USOC supports a U.S. Olympic education center at Northern Michigan University in Marquette, Michigan. The education center is designed to assist athletes who are in training and are also interested in pursuing an education. Athletes who participate in this program pay in-state tuition rates and are allowed to use the facilities on the Northern Michigan University campus.

The organizational structure of the USOC consists of a two-tiered governance structure with a 101-member board of directors, which handles legislative and constitutional matters, and the sixteen-member executive committee, which formulates and implements policy and oversees the USOC's day-to-day business. The officers of the USOC include a president, three vice presidents, a secretary, and a treasurer. The board of directors, executive committee, and officers are volunteers. The USOC employs an executive director, a paid employee, who is responsible for the daily operation of the USOC national office (located in Colorado Springs, Colorado).

Each country's National Olympic Committee (NOC) is responsible for naming the athletes and teams who will represent that country in the Olympic Games. The USOC, as the NOC for the United States to the IOC, therefore must approve all athletes and teams named by the individual sport NGBs before they are allowed to attend and participate in the Olympic Games. Each NGB submits their criteria for selection of their Olympic athletes and teams, including eligibility requirements as set forth by the IOC and the individual sport's international federation (IF). The USOC must make sure that the selection procedures are appropriate and are followed by the NGB and must approve the eligibility of the athletes prior to their participation in the Olympic Games. This area, because of the prestige and money potential of a future professional career and/or sponsorship contract, has become increasingly more important and the subject of increased litigation.

The USOC also oversees funding of the NGBs and national-caliber athletes. The NGBs receive funding from the USOC to support their developmental, training, and international competition programs. Individual athletes, through their NGB, can also apply for financial assistance to help to offset expenses incurred while training for their national and Olympic teams.

As another measure for financial support of Olympic athletes, the USOC Executive Committee in 1993 approved a program called Operation Gold which guarantees each Olympic fourth-place finisher or better and each World championship eighth-place finisher or better a monetary bonus. Under this program a gold medalist at the Olympic Games will receive $15,000, a silver medal is worth $10,000, a bronze medal worth $7,500, and a fourth-place finish worth $5,000. At World championships a gold medal is worth $5,000, silver worth $4,000, bronze worth $3,500, fourth-place finish worth $3,000, fifth/sixth place finish worth $2,500, seventh/eighth-place finish worth $2,000. For world championships held the year before the Olympics, the monetary bonuses increase by anywhere from $500 to $1,000 depending on the placement. The USOC's intent in this program is to provide additional funding to amateur athletes, thereby reducing the financial burdens that training and competition can place upon them. Because this program revolves around amateur athletes who need the additional financial support, the USOC has recommended that all professional athletes competing in the Olympic or world championship games donate any bonus money they earn to youth sports development.

The USOC is also involved in drug testing and drug education of athletes. The USOC has established a drug testing program which tests for drugs at every major athletic competition it sanctions, such as the United States Olympic Festival. In addition, the USOC has worked closely with individual NGBs in the implementation of their own individual drug testing programs at their own events, such as the U.S. Olympic Boxing Trials, and in relation to the USOC's drug testing and education policies.

The USOC can be named in litigation by athletes, coaches, or National Governing Bodies involving such issues as eligibility and drug testing at USOC-sanctioned events. When the United States boycotted the 1980 Olympic Games in Moscow, a group of twenty-five Olympic athletes filed suit (*DeFranz v. United States Olympic Committee*, 492 F. Supp. 1181 [D.D.C. 1980]), seeking an injunction barring the USOC from carrying out the boycott (see Chapter 5). The court denied the injunction, stating that the USOC had the authority to decide on this action. The court also found that this boycott did not infringe upon the athletes' constitutional rights.

National Governing Body

The international federations elect one amateur organization from each nation as their affiliate member for that nation. This organization

Exhibit 1–3
Relationship of NGBs to NOCs and IFs

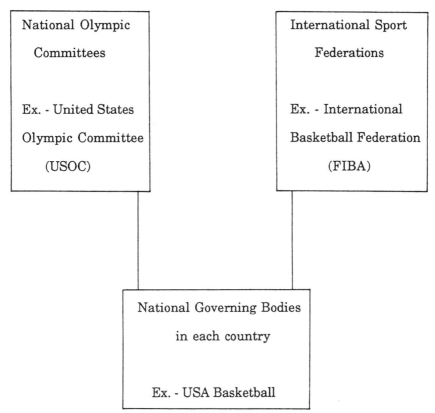

is the National Governing Body (NGB) for that sport in each individual
country. The National Governing Body, therefore, not only must be
accepted by the international federation, but also must be recognized
by the NOC within that country as the organization governing Olympic
and international competition for that particular sport (see Exhibit 1–
3). Under Section 203 of the Amateur Sports Act (36 U.S.C. section
393), each USOC-recognized NGB is authorized to exercise certain
powers, including representing the United States without limitation
in the international sports federation for its particular sport.

Some NGBs have also become involved in the drug testing of athletes and have organized their own programs for this purpose. For
example, The Athletics Congress (TAC), the national governing body
for track and field in the United States, conducts its own drug testing
program. Under this program, an athlete is randomly selected and
notified forty-eight hours prior to when the drug test will take place.

It is then the athlete's responsibility to make immediate contact with TAC if there is a problem in appearing for the drug test or to show up at the designated location for the drug test. An athlete who fails to appear may be assessed a suspension by TAC. This program came under fire in 1990 when Henry Marsh, a steeplechase Olympic athlete, was notified for drug testing. Marsh did not appear at the designated location for the drug test and was subsequently suspended by TAC. Marsh appealed the suspension and went to arbitration claiming that he was out of town when the notification arrived at his house, and when he finally received the notification later that day he asked his secretary to change the location of the drug testing to a city where he was going to be on business the following day. TAC claims they were never notified by Marsh or his secretary of this location change request. Marsh appealed to TAC; a three-member TAC doping control review board panel rejected the appeal because Marsh failed to make immediate contact and the panel did not find his circumstances extenuating enough to miss the test. Marsh then appealed to the United States Olympic Committee, and the USOC arbitration panel exonerated him and overturned TAC's suspension of Marsh. This example shows the process an athlete may use in appealing a decision made by a national governing body. Although this decision in the end was favorable for Marsh, TAC's drug testing program and procedures have been adhered to by numerous athletes and have not changed much since the Henry Marsh incident.

INTERSCHOLASTIC ATHLETICS

The National Federation of State High School Associations (NFSHSA) is the organization which oversees interscholastic activities. The NFSHSA differs from the other amateur athletic organizations discussed thus far in this chapter in that they are an advisory federation lacking the power and authority that governing organizations, such as the NCAA and the USOC, have. The power and authority in high school athletics are in the individual state organizations, which determine the rules and regulations for the sport programs and high schools within that state. The NFSHSA provides guidelines for regulations to be followed by these state associations. The association's purpose is to help coordinate the efforts of the state associations to help pursue and fulfill the objectives of interscholastic activities. The National Council of the NFSHSA is the legislative body which votes on legislation affecting the NFSHSA. The council has one representative from each member state association (see Exhibit 1–4). The membership of the NFSHSA consists of fifty individual state high school

Exhibit 1–4
National Federation of State High School Associations Organization Structure

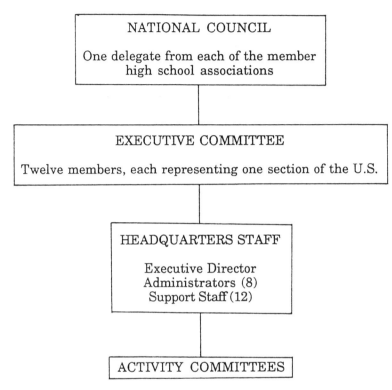

NATIONAL COUNCIL

One delegate from each of the member high school associations

EXECUTIVE COMMITTEE

Twelve members, each representing one section of the U.S.

HEADQUARTERS STAFF

Executive Director
Administrators (8)
Support Staff (12)

ACTIVITY COMMITTEES

athletic and/or activities associations and the association of the District of Columbia.

The NFSHSA is both a service and a regulatory organization. The services it provides to its members include conferences for high school directors of athletics, national associations for coaches and officials, a national resource center, a chemical health program, a high school sports hall of fame, and a newsletter published ten times a year. The NFSHSA also serves as a regulatory organization by enacting and monitoring playing rules for sports, eligibility rules for high school athletes, sanctioning of athletic contests, and athletic safety and protection regulations.

The NFSHSA has cooperated with the United States Olympic Committee and individual NGBs in regard to high school athletes and their high school eligibility status when they participate in a national or international athletic competition. The National Federation Competition Committee has recommended procedures to be followed when a high school athlete participates in Olympic Development Programs. The committee recommended that students should be permitted to participate in such programs without loss of interscholastic eligibility, provided they inform the high school principal within thirty days of the start of the program; make prior arrangements to complete missed academic lessons, assignments, and tests before the last days of classes of the semester; and miss no school-sponsored or state high school association–sponsored athletic event involving the team in that sport. These recommendations were adopted by the Federation's Executive Committee in 1979.

The state high school athletic association is the primary governing body in regard to the rules and regulations overseeing high school athletics. For example, the Massachusetts Interscholastic Athletic Association (MIAA), formed in 1978, is responsible for the organization, regulation, and promotion of interscholastic athletics for secondary schools of Massachusetts. The Board of Control is the ultimate authority for approving policies and regulations. The board consists of members elected annually by the different committees and subunits of the MIAA along with representatives from the athletic districts. The board also hears appeals of decisions administered by administrative and sport committees.

The MIAA is in charge of such areas as athlete eligibility, tournament proceedings and participation requirements, season schedule limitations, out of state competition, all-star games, coach activities and code of conduct, game official policies and penalties, and sport participation rules. Any public or private secondary school or any trade or vocational school in Massachusetts is eligible to be a member of the MIAA, providing it is approved by the Board of Control, agrees to abide by the MIAA rules and regulations, and pays a membership service fee, consisting of an annual fee and a per sport assessment, to the MIAA.

State athletic associations, because they are governing organizations and most rule making for the state high school athletic programs is done at the state level by these associations, come under attack from litigation rather than the NFSHSA. This litigation has resulted from complaints arguing the authority of the state high school association. Authority to formulate and enforce rules is fundamental to the power that the state high school athletic association has. This authority has been repeatedly upheld by the courts as long as the rule in question is reasonable. Key facts that the courts have looked at and interpreted include the following: (1) that the high school is a member of the state association and therefore voluntarily became subject to the association's rules and regulations; (2) that the association is acting in good faith in formulating and enforcing its rules; (3) that the association's rules do not violate state law; and (4) that participation on an interscholastic athletic team is a privilege to be earned by meeting certain criteria and adhering to certain rules and regulations. There has been an increasing amount of litigation on the high school level, and it has been directed at the state associations and schools, not the national federation, the NFSHSA.

CONSTITUENCY GROUPS

The following sections contain information on the various constituencies that are a part of the various amateur athletic organizations that have been discussed thus far. These constituency groups include the athlete, the coach, the administrator, the referee, the medical personnel, the organization, and a variety of miscellaneous additional groups such as sporting equipment manufacturers, facility operators, broadcasters, agents, boosters, the government (state and federal), and spectators. All of these constituency groups are involved in athletics and are makers and enforcers of the rules or are affected by the rules and regulations. These constituency groups may end up as plaintiffs or defendants in lawsuits, depending on the circumstances in each case. This section will look at these constituencies and investigate how they are affected by the rules and regulations carried out by these organizations. In addition, potential litigation areas involving the athlete or coach and the amateur athletic organization are discussed.

The Athlete

When reviewing the information on the various amateur athletic organizations presented earlier in this chapter a common area of regulations is evident, that of eligibility. All of these organizations deal to a certain extent with determining eligibility rules and regulations for the athlete. The athlete must be aware of these eligibility rules and in particular know of any differences that might exist between organizations if the athlete is a member of and competes in events sanctioned by different organizations.

An example of eligibility rules which an Olympic athlete has to abide by is provided in the 1993 United States Ski Association's *Alpine Competition Guide,* which is given to all athletes, coaches, and administrators. In the section "Athlete Rights, Responsibilities and Regulations," the guidebook provides information on Olympic eligibility rules and International Ski Federation (FIS) eligibility rules.

The Charter of the IOC, in Rule 26, states that to be eligible for participation in the Olympic Games, a competitor must

- observe and abide by the Rules of the IOC and, in addition, abide by the rules of his or her IF (International Federation), as approved by the IOC, even if the Federation's rules are more strict than those of the IOC;
- not have received any financial rewards or material benefit in connection with his or her sports participation, except as permitted in the by-laws to this rule.

These eligibility rules are IOC rules; the international federation for the United States Ski Association enforces their own set of eligibility rules. The FIS Rules are contained in Section 209 of the ICR, "Qualification of Competitors." Section 209, in its entirety, states the following:

209.1	A national association shall not enter a competitor for any international competition nor shall it issue a license to any competitor who:
209.1.1	has been guilty of improper or unsportsmanlike conduct;
209.1.2	accepts or has accepted, directly or indirectly, a money payment as an inducement to take part in a ski competition except as stated in these rules;
209.1.3	competes or has competed for a cash prize or has accepted a prize of higher value than approved from time to time by the FIS Council;
209.1.4	permits his name, title or individual picture to be used for advertising except when the national association concerned enters into the contract for sponsorship, equipment or advertisements;
209.1.5	knowingly competes or has competed against any skier not eligible according to the FIS Rules, except if:
209.1.5.1	the competition concerned is approved by the FIS Council, is directly controlled by the FIS or by a national ski association, and the competition is announced "open."

A skier who has been declared ineligible by the U.S. Ski Association for USSA competition can be reinstated by appealing to the Eligibility Committee and showing intent never to commit further action which would result in future loss of eligibility. The athlete can be reinstated by the Board of Directors upon recommendation from the Eligibility Committee but only after a period of at least six months has elapsed.

The athlete may have reason to seek an appeal or a civil lawsuit if declared ineligible by the NGB or the international sport federation. When an athlete decides on this course of action, certain procedures must be followed. For instance, if the NGB is involved and the suspension or ineligibility is only for NGB-sanctioned events, the athlete must initiate an internal appeal. This process consists of first appealing the decision to the NGB itself; if the suspension is upheld, the athlete can then appeal to the USOC. The USOC will usually only hear appeals after all avenues of internal NGB appeal have been exhausted. If this route proves fruitless for the athlete and the USOC upholds the decision by the NGB, the athlete can then seek the last recourse— a civil lawsuit. This is the procedure followed by most NGBs although variations may occur in the NGB's approach to hearing the athlete's appeal. Some NGBs have an appeal board which will hear the appeal and rule; other NGBs provide for an independent arbitrator to hear the appeal and to issue a decision.

If the suspension or declaration of ineligibility occurs at an international competition and/or by the international federation, a different procedure for appeal must be taken. The athlete will usually first appeal to the IF. If the appeal is rejected on the basis of the IF's interpretation of the situation and the facts presented to it, the athlete may then appeal to his or her NGB (although some athletes have appealed directly to the NGB first). If the appeal is denied because of the NGB's interpretation of the situation and the facts, the athlete may have to begin a civil lawsuit. If the appeal is supported by the NGB and the NGB sides with the athlete and disagrees with the suspension brought down by the IF, a second appeal may be placed with the IF, with the athlete receiving the NGB's support in the appeal. The support from the NGB may or may not play any part in the IF's handling and discussion of the second appeal. If the IF refuses the appeal, the athlete can then introduce a civil lawsuit in an attempt to seek redemption. This process may be a long, drawn out procedure causing the athlete to be suspended and ineligible for competition for a number of years. In addition, it can be quite expensive and the athlete assumes the costs involved in the litigation and appeals procedures.

Most litigation involving athletes and the NGB, IF, or IOC has occurred in the area of drug testing. The athlete has argued that the procedures involved in the drug test were not carried out properly, causing the sample to test positive but maintains he or she never used the drug(s). As a result of the positive drug test result, the athlete may have been suspended from further competition. The procedure the athlete must take to appeal the suspension will depend on the organization that was in charge of the drug testing and who enacted the suspension. The athlete will usually fulfill all organizational appeal procedures (i.e., exhaust administrative procedures) before filing a civil lawsuit. When a civil lawsuit is filed, the questions always remain as to whether the court has jurisdiction to hear the case and how the decision of the court will be enforced. These questions can be complicated when an international federation, whose national office is in another country, or the IOC, which is based in Switzerland, is involved; it can even become an item of debate when a United States NGB, located in Indiana for example, and the USOC, headquartered in Colorado, are involved.

Athletes may find themselves defendants in lawsuits in situations such as breach of contract with an agent. As the prospect of a professional career becomes more likely to a particularly talented athlete, a number of player-agents may try to persuade the athlete to sign a representation contract with them. In some situations, agents have approached college student-athletes prior to expiration of their eligibility in an attempt to get a jump on the rest of the player-agents by getting this athlete to sign with them before any other agent has an opportunity to approach the athlete. In these situations, though, the athlete may enter an agreement without fully understanding its implications and may later want to get out of the contract. These situations have led to litigation in several situations.

The Coach

The coach finds himself or herself in the same position as the athlete in terms of determining which eligibility rules he or she must abide by or may be affected by a number of different rules because of the different roles a coach may play. For instance, a college coach must be aware of and abide by athletic department rules, university rules, conference rules, NCAA rules, and, potentially, Olympic sport rules. These rules may all be different or vary to some degree from one another. For example, when a coach is recruiting a high school senior who is known to have academic difficulties, the coach's institution follows a rule which states that the incoming student must have a minimum high school GPA of 1.5. The conference rule is the same as the NCAA rule, which states that an incoming freshman student-athlete must have a 2.5 GPA and a 700 SAT score or a 2.0 GPA and a 900 SAT score or a sliding scale score between these two standards (revised Proposition 48 standards to take effect in 1995) in order to receive an athletic scholarship and be able to participate in college athletics. To complicate matters further, the coach's athletic department has a policy that they do not want any Proposition 48 athletes (those athletes who do not meet the minimum standards set forth by the NCAA must sit out a year before they are allowed to participate). The coach must be aware of all of these rules and policies and abide by them. In these situations, the coach must adhere to the more severe or restrictive of these rules, which in this example means the coach should not be recruiting this particular student-athlete.

The coach can be involved in litigation in a variety of different areas. With the emphasis college sports places on win-loss record and the implications on a coach's employment that this factor can have, coaches may find themselves plaintiffs filing a lawsuit against their institution regarding a breach of an employment contract. The coach may have signed with an institution for a specific number of years in his or her contract, but after a poor couple of years in terms of win-loss record the institution may decide to release the coach prior to the expiration of the contract. The coach may then file suit against the institution for breach of contract, releasing the coach before the expiration of the contract. A coach may also file a lawsuit if he or she feels that due process rights have been violated in the release from the contract. This has occurred when an athletic conference and the NCAA were investigating a coach for improprieties committed with a sport program. The conference wanted to invoke sanctions including prohibiting the coach from coaching at any of the conference member institutions and the NCAA wanted effectively to "blackball" the coach from coaching at any of its member institutions. The coach filed suit claiming that the investigative procedures, which included a hearing in which the coach was not allowed to cross-examine those making allegations against him, violated his due process rights. The court ruled in favor of the coach, stating that because the coach had spent his entire adult life as a head or assistant coach, he had a protectable liberty interest and due process guarantees could be invoked.

Coaches can also find themselves named as defendants in a lawsuit. Litigation where this situation can occur includes tort cases in which the coach is named as a defendant responsible for an incident. If an athlete is injured during the course of practice or a game, the coach may be accused of not taking proper medical precautions. The coach may be sued in negligence cases for failure to supervise and instruct properly as well. The improper supervision and instruction may have been contributing factors in the injury that the athlete sustained. The coach may be sued for negligence for proximately causing the athlete's injury.

A coach may also be sued for breach of contract when he or she leaves a job for another one with time remaining on his or her original contract. A coach may also be involved in defending his or her actions in an investigation by a governing organization. It should be noted that this is an administrative hearing in which the institution is being reviewed. For example, when the NCAA investigates a school for potential recruiting violations, a coach will be asked to justify and document his/her actions. The nature of the coaching profession, in which coaches are likely to move around from job to job, causes these situations. In addition, the emphasis being placed on organizational and institutional control over athletics may cause an increase in the amount of investigations of the behavior of coaches.

The Administrator

Administrators in college athletic departments are another constituency involved in the eligibility questions surrounding athletes and coaches. The administrator may have direct responsibility over monitoring of an athlete's progress and compliance with eligibility rules that the athlete and coach need to follow. For these reasons, the administrator is also impacted by the number and different kinds of eligibility rules that may be in place. It is the administrator's responsibility to know these rules, communicate them to the coach and athlete, and make sure they are being followed within the athletic department.

Athletic administrators have been involved in litigation as both plaintiffs and defendants. Lawsuits involving the administrator as plaintiff have involved breach of contract cases. The administrator might be held responsible for NCAA rule violations or improprieties conducted by a particular coach or sport program and might lose his or her job as a result. This may be due to the increasing pressure put on college and university presidents by the NCAA regarding presidential control over athletics. An administrator may initiate a breach of contract suit arguing that he or she should not be released because of being held accountable for another person's actions. It was not the administrator who violated NCAA rules and therefore he or she should not be punished for the actions of the coach merely because he or she is in charge of the coach.

The administrator may also be named as a defendant in a tort lawsuit involving an injury to an athlete. The argument behind these complaints revolves around the issue of the administrator's maintaining control of or overseeing the coach and the sport program. The injury sustained by the athlete is argued to be a result of negligence. This negligence is attributed in the athlete's argument to negligence of the coach, the trainer and/or team doctor, or the administrator. The administrator's potential negligence is due to staffing these positions with unqualified people whose incompetence caused the injury to occur, or failing to supervise the coach and others involved, and that as a result of this lack of supervision the coach, trainer, or doctor employed inappropriate methods which caused or contributed to the injury. The administrator may also be named as vicariously liable for the coach, trainer, or doctor by being the employer of these people, although the institution is normally named because it has the deeper pockets. Vicarious liability imposes liability for a tortious act upon a person who is not personally negligent, but is held liable because of the relationship between the parties (i.e., employer-employee relationship). The administrator needs to be aware of all these legal ramifications and be sure to take appropriate precautions in order to prevent such a situation.

The Referee

Another constituency group in the college athletic setting which doesn't receive much notice but is certainly a major component of college athletics is referees. The referee, although not a member of the athletic department and usually employed as an independent contractor, can be involved in litigation in a number of different ways. Referees have been named as defendants in tort cases involving injury to an athlete. They have been held responsible to an extent for the athlete's injury if they employed improper rule enforcement methods or did not stop the contest when inclement weather caused the field conditions to be poor. If it is determined that the athlete would not have sustained the injury if proper procedures had been followed, the referee may be held accountable. The issue revolves around the extent to which the referee in an athletic contest should be held responsible for the injuries that may occur. If an injury is due to an improper technique which the referee should have noticed and prevented, then the referee may be negligent and will be held accountable for the injury. Another question surrounding this issue is whether the referee should be classified as an independent contractor or whether the institution, conference, or athletic organization is the referee's employer, making that organization vicariously liable for the referee's actions. This is an important question in terms of vicarious liability of an employer for hiring a referee and of worker's compensation issues. These are all issues that need to be considered when a referee finds himself/herself the subject of litigation.

The referee may also take the role of plaintiff in litigation cases. A situation when this might occur involves the referee's being forced into retirement or prohibited from working any games because of an age limit set by the athletic conference or organization. This type of incident has occurred a couple of times, when a referee brought litigation against an athletic conference or organization over an age discrimination complaint. Also, the referee may take action against his or her employer or against a private citizen when he or she is battered and/or assaulted on the playing field. The employer may be held responsible for not taking the proper precautions to prevent such a situation, and the private citizen may be held accountable for any injuries the referee may have sustained in the attack.

Medical Personnel

Medical personnel include team doctors, trainers, and other medical specialists who may be involved with an amateur athletic team, organization, or event. Through their involvement with the athletes, coaches, spectators, and other people involved in the sporting event, the medical personnel can find themselves dealing with a variety of medical issues. In these situations, medical personnel can be named as defendants in a lawsuit in a number of different ways. For example, a spectator injured at a baseball game by a foul ball may claim that the medical attention he or she received from the personnel at the stadium was inappropriate or improper. Another potential lawsuit may involve an athlete who feels the team doctor and/or trainer did not treat an injury properly or did not hold them out of a game when this precaution should have been taken as a result of the injury. Another example involves a team doctor or trainer who withholds information on the injury to the athlete and allows the athlete out on the field when further damage or injury can result.

The potential for litigation involving medical personnel can be seen when examining the Hank Gathers situation that occurred at Loyola Marymount University. Hank Gathers was a star basketball player at Loyola Marymount University, finishing out his college career before turning pro. On December 9, 1989, Gathers passed out in a basketball game. He was treated by the team trainer and doctor at the university's health services. Gathers was later admitted to a hospital to undergo tests, where it was found that he suffered from an irregular heartbeat and abnormalities in his heart. Gathers was put on medication and released to participate in practices again. Gathers eventually returned to competition with the team trainer and doctors keeping a close eye on him. In March 1990, Gathers was playing in a game against the University of Portland when he collapsed to the gym floor. A short time later, Gathers was pronounced dead. The medical personnel involved—the team trainer, the cardiologist, the doctor from the health services, and another doctor from the hospital who examined Gathers and treated him when he first collapsed—were named in a lawsuit brought by the family. The lawsuit alleged that the team trainer and doctors were negligent in the treatment of Gathers when he collapsed in March 1990, the doctors withheld information on his condition from Gathers, and the doctors decreased his medication because of outside pressures to keep him playing. This lawsuit has since been settled out of court, but the potential for a similar situation in the future remains. The medical personnel involved in treating an athlete need to be aware of their duty and responsibility to treat the athlete and resist pressures such as getting the athlete out on the field in order that the team may win.

Medical personnel, if employed by an institution or team, may involve their institution or team in the lawsuit through vicarious liability. If a team doctor or trainer is employed by the school team, the school or team may find itself held liable for the doctor's or trainer's actions. This situation occurred in the Hank Gathers incident, as Loyola Marymount was named to the lawsuit as vicariously liable for the actions of the team trainer and health services doctor. Institutions and organizations need to be aware of this and use proper screening and hiring methods when employing medical personnel. If the medical personnel are independent contractors, not employees of the institution or organization, then they will be held personally liable for their negligent actions.

Amateur Athletic Organizations

Amateur athletic organizations, such as the NCAA, collegiate conference, NGB, or school, can become involved in litigation because they are the decision makers in a number of organizational areas. The type of litigation that such organizations experience has been discussed. Organizations can also be involved with litigation because of open meeting laws. States may have laws that require organizations to fulfill certain public duties, including opening their meetings to the public through open meeting laws. An organization that does not comply with these laws may find itself a defendant in a litigation case. Any amateur athletic organization that is considered public or is ruled by the courts to have public interests and responsibilities will be held to the state's open meeting laws.

Additional Constituencies

The preceding sections have discussed various constituencies of the sports industry and how these constituencies may find themselves involved in litigation. There are, of course, many additional constituencies which may also be involved in litigation.

Equipment manufacturers have found themselves defendants in

lawsuits concerning the safety or proper use of their equipment. Injuries that have occurred among athletes or spectators have been
blamed on the improper manufacturing or safety features of the equipment. Virtually every athletic event uses some type of equipment or
instrument produced by an equipment manufacturer. The equipment
manufacturer is responsible for making sure the item has been produced in the proper way, it is safe, and the proper instructions for use
have been provided to the consumer. A company that fails in any way
to ensure that these steps have been taken appropriately may be sued
for negligence. An equipment manufacturer also runs the risk of being
held responsible for equipment that does not meet performance standards. For example, if a trampoline is promoted as being safe up to a
200-pound limit and yet a 150-pound student is injured when the
trampoline collapses under his or her weight, the student has a potential cause of action against the equipment manufacturer because
the equipment did not measure up to the advertised performance
standards. The equipment manufacturer must be sure that the equipment has been produced correctly, has been tested for safety, and
carries the appropriate instructions for usage. When accomplished,
these steps will not totally eliminate all litigation but is certainly
helpful in preventing these situations from occurring.

Facility owners and managers are another constituency group who
through their involvement with sports and sporting events may encounter litigation. Much as the equipment manufacturers must ensure
that their equipment is safe and not dangerous to the consumers of
the product, facility owners and managers must assure that facilities
are safe for the spectators and participants. Specific examples in which
facility owners and managers may be held negligent if an injury occurs
are hallways that are not well lit, bleachers or seats in the stands that
are not safely set up or secured, or playing surfaces for participants
that are not appropriate for the event. Owners and managers have a
duty to provide a certain standard of care to the users of their facility;
when this standard of care is not followed and an injury results, facility
owners may be held negligent and be named in litigation.

Broadcasters are involved in the promotion and coverage of sporting
events. Through this arrangement the broadcaster has responsibility
to cover the events, relaying information to the spectators watching.
Broadcasters must be careful, though, not to defame athletes or public
figures they are discussing. In covering a story or promoting an event,
broadcasters must make sure what they are communicating to the
spectators are indeed the facts. A broadcaster who supplies erroneous
information on an athlete or sponsor may be accused of defamation.
Broadcasters may also find themselves on the other end of a lawsuit,
suing their employer over a breach of contract. In an effort to increase

television viewer ratings, a network may make a change in the broadcasters scheduled to cover an event or season. This may cause the broadcaster to be reassigned or let go before the expiration of his/her contract. When this occurs, the broadcaster may bring a breach of contract suit against the network.

Agents for players have found their way into the sports industry not only in the professional ranks but in the collegiate ranks. Occasions when an agent may be involved in litigation are numerous; they usually revolve around the negotiations performed on behalf of an athlete the agent is representing. In professional sports, the agent can be sued by the player for not fully disclosing to the player all the information surrounding the negotiations that the agent is conducting on behalf of the player. The agent may not be representing the athlete's best interests, but instead trying to enter into a contract for the athlete which is in the best interests of the agent. The college athletic arena has seen an influx of agents trying to sign athletes prior to the expiration of their collegiate eligibility. In this situation, the athlete may be declared ineligible by the NCAA for having signed an athlete-agent contract before the eligibility expired, the school may have to forfeit games and revenue by using this ineligible player, but the agent is virtually untouched. The NCAA does not have jurisdiction over these player agents. A school, however, may attempt to sue an agent for the loss of revenue that it incurred as a result of the agent's actions in signing the player and causing him or her to be declared ineligible. In addition, an athlete may find cause to sue an agent when trying to get out of an athlete-agent contract. An agent can also have cause of litigation if he or she believes an athlete terminated their agreement unfairly or did not pay the agent appropriate compensation set forth in the agreement with the athlete.

Boosters, through their involvement with a college's athletic teams and athletes, can also cause problems for the school. The NCAA has certain requirements limiting the way a booster can be associated with an athletic program or team. On numerous occasions, though, the booster does not adhere to these requirements. Because boosters are not regulated by the NCAA, the NCAA has no enforcement power over their actions. The school, however, is under the authority of the NCAA and incurs the penalties from the NCAA for boosters' actions. As in the agent scenario, the school itself may attempt to sue the booster, but there is not much cause of action that the school can undertake unless the activities or actions by the booster are illegal.

Federal and state governments have become involved in the sports industry and are therefore a constituency that very much needs to be addressed. Federal and state governments have proposed and even approved legislation which specifies how certain sporting events or situations will be carried out. For instance, numerous states have passed due process legislation which stipulates how the NCAA must conduct their investigations into schools, coaches, and athletes accused of violating their rules. This legislation has a dramatic impact on the enforcement powers of this collegiate athletic governing body. The federal government has become involved in the educational aspect of athletics, passing a bill requiring each institution to monitor the graduation rates of their student-athletes. If state and federal governments feel that the NCAA, conferences, or institutions themselves are not running college athletics effectively, they may continue to propose legislation which will affect these other constituencies and their governing power over collegiate athletics.

Spectators are also a major constituency group in the sports industry. At virtually all sporting events or activities spectators are in attendance. Through their presence at these events, spectators may find themselves involved in injury-causing situations such as when a baseball is hit into the stands and injures a spectator. In situations such as this, the spectator may claim that the injury was due to the negligence of the facility owner or even the player involved. The spectator will then become the plaintiff of a lawsuit and bring the case to court. The spectator is not protected from being named as a defendant in litigation as well; this can occur when a spectator becomes excited during an event and rushes onto the field of play, causing injury to another spectator or player. Another example can involve a spectator's becoming enraged over a referee's call, approaching the referee after the game, and attacking the referee, causing injury.

SUMMARY

This chapter has provided background on the organizations involved in the sports industry. Information on the structure, rules and procedures, power and authority, and types of litigation areas these organizations can be involved in were discussed. The focus of the chapter then switched to the constituencies of the sports industry. The sections on these constituencies discussed the role each of these groups plays in the sports industry and also provided a brief discussion of ways that these constituencies can be involved in litigation.

The rest of the chapters provide further detail on areas of the law and types of litigation that have occurred. The types of cases will be discussed in more detail with additional description of the constituency group involved and the type of complaint, the legal arguments, and the court decisions. The reader should refer to Chapter 1 if any questions should arise about the various organizations and constituencies involved in the litigation discussions presented in the rest of the chapters.

Chapter 2

THE COURT AND LEGAL SYSTEM IN THE UNITED STATES

INTRODUCTION

Directors of amateur athletic organizations need a fundamental understanding of the legal system in the United States to deal effectively with the wide variety of legal matters they face today. The overview given in this chapter is brief and general in nature, but the reader can consult the Notes for source materials that provide greater detail.

The American legal system is based primarily on the common law tradition established in England. *Common law* is to be distinguished from *statutory law* in that it is based on legal custom and precedent. The influence of English common law in our American legal system goes back to colonial America, with its English laws, customs, and language.

Two fundamental concepts, precedent and stare decisis, are associated with the common law tradition. *Precedent* is the example established in an earlier case decision that is followed by the courts in future cases that arise under similar circumstances. *Stare decisis* is the following by the court of a principle of law established previously. Understanding these two concepts will help amateur athletic administrators and coaches to avoid mistakes made in the past by other administrators and coaches which have been litigated in the courts.

The legal system in the United States is generally viewed as having three functions: (1) administering state and national laws, (2) resolving private civil suits among parties, and (3) interpreting the legislative intent of a law in deciding a case.

There are two basic legal systems in the United States: the federal system and the state system. Chapter 2 begins with a description of the federal court system, which includes the U.S. Supreme Court, U.S. courts of appeals, U.S. district courts, and several administrative agencies. The chapter next discusses the state legal system, which consists of the primary sources of law in each state's constitution and court decisions in each state. Naturally, there is variation among state legal systems.

Just as important as understanding the legal system in the United States is knowing how to find legal information. The next section identifies and describes numerous legal sources that coaches and administrators may find useful. The last section of Chapter 2 describes the ten steps in the trial system—information that will reduce the fear often associated with "going to court."

THE FEDERAL COURT SYSTEM

The federal court system in the United States consists of the Supreme Court, thirteen courts of appeals, ninety-four district courts, certain specialized courts, and administrative agencies (Exhibit 2–1). Federal cases usually are first heard in a district court, although certain cases are initiated in the higher courts of appeals or in the Supreme Court. Cases that are appealed after being heard in the district courts usually go to a court of appeals, or in rare cases, directly to the Supreme Court. The thirteen courts of appeals (representing eleven judicial circuits, the District of Columbia, and the Federal Circuit) also review orders issued by administrative agencies such as the Securities and Exchange Commission, the Federal Trade Commission, the Internal Revenue Service, and the National Labor Relations Board.

The special federal courts include the U.S. Claims Court, the U.S. Court of International Trade, the U.S. Court of Military Appeals, the U.S. Tax Court, the U.S. Bankruptcy Court, and the Temporary Emergency Court of Appeals. The jurisdiction of these courts is rather narrow. For example, the U.S. Claims Court only hears cases in which individuals have a claim against the federal government, and the Court of International Trade hears civil actions against the United States arising from federal laws governing import and trade transactions. These courts, generally, are not of concern to athletic administrators.

The U.S. Supreme Court

The U.S. Supreme Court is the highest court in the nation and the ultimate dispute arbitrator. Once the Supreme Court decides an issue, all other federal courts must interpret the law by its lead. The Supreme Court has two types of jurisdiction: original and appellate. *Original jurisdiction* covers two types of cases: those involving ambassadors, ministers, and consuls, and those involving a state as one of the parties to a lawsuit. The Supreme Court hears very few cases under original jurisdiction. *Appellate jurisdiction* covers cases tried or reviewed by the individual state's highest court involving federal questions, including those bearing on the U.S. Constitution, congressional acts, or foreign treaties. It also covers cases tried or reviewed by the U.S. courts of appeals or the U.S. district courts.

A chief justice and eight associate justices sit on the U.S. Supreme Court. The nine Supreme Court justices are appointed by the President of the United States and confirmed by the United States Senate. They serve lifetime tenures. The chief justice receives a salary of $160,600, and the associate justices receive $153,600 each (1992).

The Supreme Court generally reviews cases brought before it by writ of appeal or writ of certiorari. A *writ of appeal* applies when:

1. A state supreme court has held a federal act to be unconstitutional.

Exhibit 2–1
The United States Court System

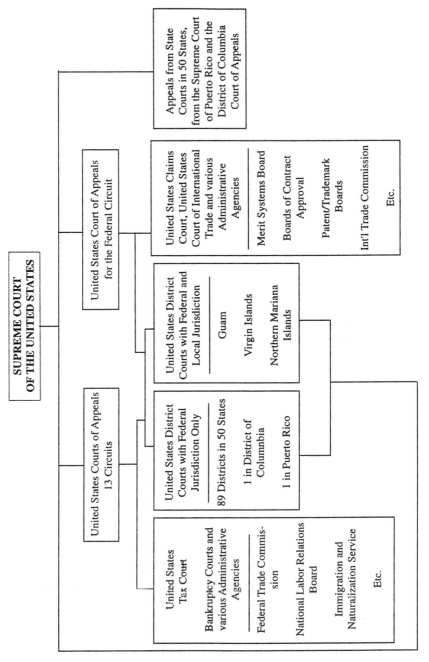

2. A state supreme court has held a state action to be constitutional.
3. A lower federal court has decided against the United States in a criminal case.
4. The United States has brought suit under the Interstate Commerce Act.
5. A federal district court has heard a suit that involves a restraint on enforcement of a state or federal statute on the grounds that it is unconstitutional.

A *writ of certiorari* allows the Court to hear cases not covered by the writ of appeal. It is a written order to call up for review a case from a lower court. Four of the nine Supreme Court justices have to vote to review a case under a writ of certiorari. Certiorari gives the Supreme Court broad discretion in deciding which cases to review. It can be employed by the Court to review:

1. Any civil or criminal case in the federal court of appeals, no matter which party petitions the Court.
2. Any state court decision in which a federal statute or treaty is questioned.
3. Any state court decision that rules a state statute unconstitutional under the federal Constitution.

The Supreme Court hears oral arguments from the attorneys for the parties when it decides to hear a case. The parties also submit *briefs,* or written arguments, to the Court. Sometimes the Court allows a brief termed *amicus curiae,* or "friend of the court," to be submitted by third parties who believe that they (or the organization they represent) may be affected by the Court's decision in a case. For instance, in a 1984 Supreme Court case not directly involving athletics, *Grove City College v. Bell* (see Chapter 8), the Council of Collegiate Women's Athletic Administrators submitted an *amicus curiae* brief because it feared that opportunities for women in intercollegiate athletics would be diminished if an adverse Court decision was made.

Supreme Court decisions are made after the justices have heard the oral presentations and reviewed the briefs from both parties. Each justice renders an opinion on why a certain decision should be made, and then the justices vote in order of seniority. After a decision has been reached by majority vote, a justice is chosen to write the *opinion of the Court.* A justice who disagrees with the opinion and who did not vote with the majority may write a *dissenting opinion.* A justice who agrees with the majority opinion but not with the reasoning by which it was reached may write a *concurring opinion.* All opinions that result from a case are reported in the following publications:

1. *United States Reports* (official edition), cited U.S.
2. *United States Supreme Court Reports* (Lawyers Co-operative Publishing Company), cited L. Ed. or L. Ed. 2d.
3. *Supreme Court Reporter* (West Publishing Company), cited S. Ct.; the *United States Reports* (official edition), the *United States Supreme Court Reports* (Lawyers Co-operative Publishing Company), cited L. Ed. 2d; and the *Supreme Court Reporter,* cited S. Ct., are published in order to publicize the opinions of the Supreme Court. The *United States Reports* is the official set of the three and is cited by the *United States Supreme Court Reports* and the *Supreme Court Reporter.* Most lawyers and researchers use the unofficial sets because they include editorial features, known as annotations, which make the opinions easier to read.
4. *United States Supreme Court Bulletin* (Commerce Clearing House), cited S. Ct. Bull. (CCH), provides the reader with the Court's decisions during the current term.
5. *United States Law Week* (Bureau of National Affairs), cited U.S.L.W. The *United States Law Week* is published by the Bureau of National Affairs in Washington, D.C. The publication is composed of two looseleaf volumes; one contains the current opinions of the United States Supreme Court, and the other volume deals with matters that do not relate to the United States Supreme Court.

Only a small percentage of cases that are filed on the trial level ever reach the Supreme Court for the following reasons: cases are settled, parties do not believe they will be successful on appeal, costs can be prohibitive, and appellate courts can refuse to hear an appeal. Cases that the appellate courts do review are those in which there may have been an error at the trial court level or ones that may involve important questions of law. Even so, Warren Berger, Chief Justice from 1969 to 1986, often complained that the U.S. court system does not filter out enough cases and that the Supreme Court is overburdened. Some critics of the judicial system believe an additional level of judicial review between the courts of appeals and the Supreme Court is needed.

U.S. Courts of Appeals

There are thirteen United States Courts of Appeals. In addition to the eleven judicial districts, there are the District of Columbia and the United States Court of Appeals for the Federal Circuit (Exhibit 2–2). The appeals courts have one type of jurisdiction, *appellate.* That

Exhibit 2–2
U.S. Courts of Appeals Locations

The Thirteen Federal Judicial Circuits

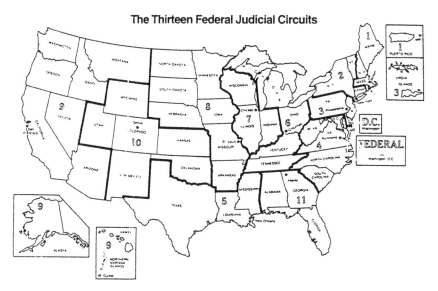

Circuits	Location
District of Columbia	Washington, D.C.
First	Boston
Second	New York
Third	Philadelphia
Fourth	New Orleans, Forth Worth, Jackson
Sixth	Cincinnati
Seventh	Chicago
Eighth	St. Louis, Kansas City, Omaha, St. Paul
Ninth	San Francisco, Los Angeles, Portland, Seattle
Tenth	Denver, Wichita, Oklahoma City
Eleventh	Atlanta, Jacksonville, Montgomery
Federal	Washington, D.C.

7 5th

Note: If there is more than one city listed for the circuit, the one listed first is the primary location for the circuit.

Reprinted with permission from West's National Reporter System, Copyright © by West Publishing Company.

means they review cases tried in the federal district courts and cases heard and decided by the federal regulatory commissions mentioned earlier. Decisions of the appeals courts (also called appellate courts) are reported in the *Federal Reporter* (West Publishing Company) and are cited F. or F. 2d, depending on the date of the court decision. The *Federal Reporter* has now limited the number of published opinions because of the caseload. Additional cases for the athletic administrator to review would be found in the Temporary Emergency Court of Appeals, which are published in the *Federal Reporter.*

U.S. District Courts

The district courts are the trial courts of the federal court system. Each state has at least one district court, and some of the larger states have as many as four. A total of ninety-four district courts cover the fifty states, the District of Columbia, the Commonwealth of Puerto Rico, Guam, the Virgin Islands, and the Northern Mariana Islands (see Exhibit 2–3). Each district court has at least one federal district judge, and some have as many as twenty-seven federal judges.

The decisions of the district courts are reported in the *Federal Supplement* (West Publishing Company) and are cited F. Supp. In a district court opinion, the district involved is always included as a part of the citation. For example, D.N.J. 1992 is the citation for District of New Jersey, 1992. When there is more than one federal district court in a state, the particular district involved in the decision is cited. For example, S.D.N.Y. 1992 is the citation for Southern District of New York, 1992 which differentiates it from the Northern District of New York, 1992, or N.D.N.Y. 1992.

Administrative Agencies

Rulings made by federal agencies such as the Federal Trade Commission, the Internal Revenue Service, and the National Labor Relations Board fall into the category of administrative law. For a number of reasons, notably specialization, efficiency, and flexibility, Congress and the state legislatures decided to grant certain judicial powers to administrative agencies such as those named in Exhibit 2–1. These agencies are authorized to formulate rules for the administrative area they regulate, enforce the rules, hold hearings on any violations, and issue decisions, including penalties. This delegation of power to adjudicate controversies has been generally held to be constitutional, although the agencies must follow specific guidelines in their administration of these delegated powers. On the federal level, Congress has enacted the Administrative Procedure Act, which sets guidelines

Exhibit 2–3
U.S. District Court Locations

Alabama	3 districts (Northern, Middle, and Southern)
Alaska	1 district
Arizona	1 district
Arkansas	2 districts (Eastern and Western)
California	4 districts (Northern, Eastern, Central, and Southern)
Colorado	1 district
Connecticut	1 district
Delaware	1 district
District of Columbia	1 district
Florida	3 districts (Northern, Middle, and Southern)
Georgia	3 districts (Northern, Middle, and Southern)
Guam	1 district
Hawaii	1 district
Idaho	1 district
Illinois	3 districts (Northern, Central, and Southern)
Indiana	2 districts (Northern and Southern)
Iowa	2 districts (Northern and Southern)
Kansas	1 district
Kentucky	2 districts (Eastern and Western)
Louisiana	3 districts (Eastern, Middle, and Western)
Maine	1 district
Maryland	1 district
Massachusetts	1 district
Michigan	2 districts (Eastern and Western)
Minnesota	1 district
Mississippi	2 districts (Northern and Southern)
Missouri	2 districts (Eastern and Western)
Montana	1 district
Nebraska	1 district
Nevada	1 district
New Hampshire	1 district
New Jersey	1 district
New Mexico	1 district
New York	4 districts (Northern, Southern, Eastern, and Western)
North Carolina	3 districts (Eastern, Middle, and Western)
North Dakota	1 district
Northern Mariana Islands	1 district
Ohio	2 districts (Northern and Southern)
Oklahoma	3 districts (Northern, Eastern, and Western)
Oregon	1 district
Pennsylvania	3 districts (Eastern, Middle, and Western)
Puerto Rico	1 district
Rhode Island	1 district
South Carolina	1 district
South Dakota	1 district
Tennessee	3 districts (Eastern, Middle, and Western)
Texas	4 districts (Northern, Southern, Eastern, and Western)
Utah	1 district
Vermont	1 district
Virgin Islands	1 district
Virginia	2 districts (Eastern and Western)
Washington	2 districts (Eastern and Western)
West Virginia	2 districts (Northern and Southern)
Wisconsin	2 districts (Eastern and Western)
Wyoming	1 district

Exhibit 2–4
A Typical State Court System

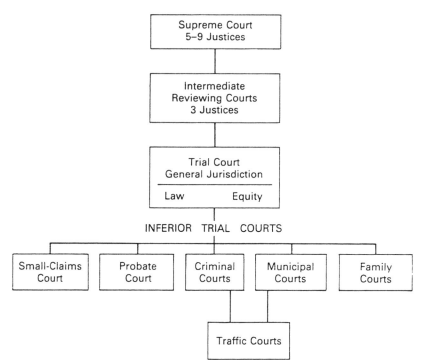

for the agencies to follow. Many states have similar state statutes. A party to an administrative law decision can appeal such decisions and sometimes obtain judicial review, depending on the nature of the dispute and whether all administrative remedies have been exhausted.

THE STATE COURT SYSTEM

Generally, each of the fifty states has a three-tiered court system, with a trial court level, appellate level, and supreme court level of review. Each state judicial system hears cases and reviews the law, on the basis of its state constitution, state statutes, and court decisions. In addition, a state court must often interpret the federal constitution and/or federal statutes, in terms of how they impact on state criminal or civil laws that are reviewed under its jurisdiction. The structure of the state court system, in which the more important the court the fewer they are in number, is very similar to the federal court structure (see Exhibit 2–4).

State court decisions can be reported (although only a small per-

Exhibit 2–5
Regional Reporters

Pacific Reporter (P. or P.2d)	Alaska, Arizona, California to 1960, Colorado, Hawaii, Idaho, Kansas, Montana, Nevada, New Mexico, Oklahoma, Oregon, Utah, Washington, and Wyoming
North Western Reporter (N.W. or N.W.2d)	Michigan, Minnesota, Nebraska, North Dakota, South Dakota, and Wisconsin
South Western Reporter (S.W. or S.W.2d)	Arkansas, Kentucky, Missouri, Tennessee, and Texas
North Eastern Reporter (N.E. or N.E.2d)	Illinois, Indiana, Massachusetts, New York, and Ohio
Atlantic Reporter (A. or A.2d)	Connecticut, Delaware, Maine, Maryland, New Hampshire, New Jersey, Pennsylvania, Rhode Island, Vermont, and District of Columbia Municipal Court of Appeals
South Eastern Reporter (S.E. or S.E.2d)	Georgia, North Carolina, South Carolina, Virginia, and West Virginia
Southern Reporter (So. or So. 2d)	Alabama, Florida, Louisiana, and Mississippi

centage are) in a state or regional collection of reports called a *reporter*. A regional reporter groups decisions from a number of states in one publication. The regional reporters as a group are termed the *National Reporter System*, which is published by the West Publishing Company and includes West's federal law reports and some additional special court reporters. The *National Reporter System* provides a quick method of making the opinions of the state courts known to the public. The seven regional reporters are listed in Exhibit 2–5.

SOURCES OF LEGAL INFORMATION

The athletic administrator should know how to locate legal information. Sources include legal dictionaries, directories, encyclopedias, indexes, treatises, guides, and law reviews; state and federal constitutions and legislation; federal administrative rules and regulations; and case law.

Legal Reference Materials

Legal Dictionaries

Legal dictionaries contain definitions of words and functions that are commonly used in the legal system in the United States and other common law jurisdictions, such as Great Britain, Canada, and Australia. The following are four of the best and most popular legal dictionaries:

1. *Black's Law Dictionary*, 6th ed. (St. Paul, Minn.: West Publishing Company, 1990).
2. *Ballentine's Law Dictionary*, 3d ed. (Rochester, N.Y.: Lawyers Cooperative Publishing Company, 1969).
3. *Modern Legal Glossary* (Charlottesville, Va.: Michie Company, 1980).
4. D. Oran, *Law Dictionary for Non-Lawyers*, 2d ed. (St. Paul, Minn.: West Publishing Company, 1985), is an excellent small dictionary for nonlawyers.

Lawyer Directories

Lawyer directories are published lists of lawyers by states or regions. The *Martindale-Hubbell Law Directory*, published by Martindale-Hubbell, Summit, New Jersey, is an annual publication that lists all the lawyers in the United States. Another useful directory is published by Legal Directories Publishing Company, Los Angeles, California. It publishes many state directories (e.g., the *Texas Legal Directory*) and regional directories (e.g., the *New England Legal Directory*).

Legal Research Guides

Legal research guides are texts that explain how to conduct legal research. They include instruction on different sources of law and how best to utilize the sources. The athletic administrator will find the following guides most helpful:

1. Price and Bitner, *Effective Legal Research*, 4th ed. (Boston, Mass.: Little, Brown, 1979). A guide that gives the athletic administrator an in-depth description of the types of sources available for law research by providing separate chapters geared to the individual source.
2. Jacobstein and Mersky, *Fundamentals of Legal Research*, 3d ed. (Mineola, N.Y.: Foundation Press, 1987). An excellent guide to legal research. This book is very well organized for the person who is learning how to conduct legal research.
3. Cohen, *How to Find the Law*, 9th ed. (St. Paul, Minn.: West Publishing Company, 1989). A guide that trains the student and nonlawyer to research law.
4. Cohen, *Legal Research in a Nutshell*, 4th ed. (St. Paul, Minn.: West Publishing Company, 1985). A condensed guide that briefs the reader on how to perform legal research. This book may be

most appropriate for the athletic administrator's introduction to legal research material.

5. Uberstine, Bronstein, and Grad, *Covering All the Bases: A Comprehensive Research Guide to Sports Law*, 2d ed. (Buffalo: William S. Hein Company, 1988). A good research source for sports law issues that an athletic coach or administrator might wish to review.

Annotated Law Reports

The *American Law Reports* (ALR) gives comprehensive annotations on legal subject matters. It consists of five series. An *annotation* is a commentary on how a particular legal subject developed and the current status of the law on that subject. The annotations in the *ALR* often include a list of cases that have discussed the point of law that the annotation explains. For a good example of an *ALR* annotation, see "Tort Liability of Public Schools and Institutions for Accidents Occurring During School Athletic Events," 35 *ALR* 3d 725.

Legal Encyclopedias

Legal encyclopedias are texts designed to give the reader a broad view of the law on any given legal subject. The following are two of the best:

1. *Corpus Juris Secundum (C.J.S.)* (St. Paul, Minn.: West Publishing Company, 1936–current date). This encyclopedia is a compilation of the entire body of American law from the first case to present cases. There are approximately 150 volumes of this text.

2. *American Jurisprudence (Am. Jur. 2d)* (Summit, N.J.: Lawyers Cooperative Publishing Company and Bancroft-Whitney Company, 1962–current data). *American Jurisprudence* differs from *Corpus Juris Secundum* in that it publishes only selected court decisions; it provides quick answers to problems that can then be explored more fully.

Restatements of the Law

The *Restatements of the Law* are produced by committees of distinguished judges, law professors, and lawyers and provide the reader with a "black letter" rule in specific legal areas, such as torts, agency, contract, trusts, and property. In addition, The *Restatements* provide case authority and cross-reference to *ALR* annotations.

Treatises

Treatises are texts designed to give the user legal information on one particular legal subject. Treatises can be in the form of casebooks, textbooks, or hornbooks. *Casebooks* are compilations of cases and narrative on a particular subject (see, for example, Berry and Wong, *Law and Business of the Sports Industries,* Vols. 1 and 2 [Westport, Conn.: Praeger Publishers, 1993]). *Textbooks* are narratives on a particular area of law (see, for example, Weistart and Lowell, *The Law of Sports* [Indianapolis, Ind.: Bobbs-Merrill, 1979]). *Hornbooks* are texts designed to produce rudimentary knowledge on a particular subject of law (see, for example, Schubert, Smith, and Trentadue, *Sports Law* [St. Paul, Minn.: West Publishing Company, 1986]).

Legal Indexes

Legal indexes are lists of articles that contain information on legal subjects, case decisions, and general legal information that has been published in law reviews and other legal periodicals. The following are legal indexes:

1. *Index to Legal Periodicals* (Bronx, N.Y.: H. W. Wilson Company, 1908–current date). Includes periodicals published in the United States, Canada, Great Britain, Ireland, Australia, and New Zealand and is therefore comprehensive in nature.
2. *Index to Periodical Articles Related to Law* (Dobbs Ferry, N.Y.: Glanville Publishers, 1958–1988, Vols. 1–30). Contains articles that appear to be of value and are not covered by the *Index to Legal Periodicals.* This index is useful in locating newly developing areas of law.
3. *Current Law Index* (CLI) (Foster City, Calif.: Information Access Company, 1980–current date). This index is issued monthly and provides access to over 700 legal and law related periodicals.
4. *Wilsondisc,* H. W. Wilson Company, Bronx, New York, is a computer service which indexes 476 legal periodicals, case law, and statutory law and is updated quarterly.
5. *Infotrac,* Information Access Company, Foster City, Calif., is a computer service which indexes over 800 of the major legal publications and is updated monthly.

Law Review Articles

Law reviews, published by law schools and administered by a student editorial board, contain current or historical articles that relate to the study of law and lawmaking (for example, legal, legislative, entertainment, and sport law). A school usually publishes a general law review, and many opt to publish additional reviews of specific areas of the law.

Law reviews are designed to add to the process of developing a better understanding of law and the legal process. This is accomplished by reviewing cases and the impact of decisions, analyzing the legal reasoning behind court decisions, reviewing legislative enactments, proposing reforms, and reviewing legal writings through book reviews.

Shepard's Citations

Shepard's Citations is a system that is used to research reported case decisions to see whether the case being researched has been cited as authority by another court, or whether a reported case has been overruled, modified, or questioned in a later decision. *Shepard's*, or "shepardizing," provides a complete history of any case since it was first reported. *Shepard's* is available in hard copies in all law libraries and is also incorporated into the two major legal computer services described next.

Legal Computer Services

Legal computer services offer subscribers access through remote terminals to federal and state court decisions, annotated reports, statutes, law reviews, and so forth, stored within their systems. They generally are the most up-to-date source for legal information, but unfortunately they are not readily available to the lay person. Further, they are expensive and require some training to use.

The two major legal computer services are *Lexis*, Mead Data Central, New York, New York, and *Westlaw*, West Publishing Company, St. Paul, Minnesota.

Constitutions

A constitution is the written instrument that serves as the ultimate source of legal authority by which a government and the courts derive their power to govern and adjudicate. The courts in the United States use the federal Constitution or a state constitution as the source for interpreting whether enacted laws are constitutional and whether individual rights granted to citizens are legal. The laws and actions of a government must be consistent with the constitution of that government to be considered legal. A constitution may not always contain language that specifically covers every governmental action, and in such instances the courts must interpret the constitution broadly to include certain governmental actions that are not specifically covered in the constitution. Constitutions can be amended.

Legislation

Legislation is the process by which laws are enacted. Laws are also referred to as *statutes*. Federal legislation is enacted by the U.S. Congress. Very little federal legislation is geared specifically to amateur athletics. One notable exception is the Amateur Sports Act of 1978 (36 U.S.C. §§ 371–396), which governs some of the operation of amateur athletics, especially the U.S. Olympic efforts, in the United States. It should be noted that non-sport-specific legislation may be applied to athletics. An example is Title IX, which governs education and applies to athletics as athletics pertains to the educational mission of an institution. Bills can be introduced by individual representatives or senators or groups of commissioned representatives or senators. Copies of pending legislation can be obtained by writing to the following addresses (enclose a self-addressed gummed return label):

Senate Document Room	House Document Room
B-04, Hart Senate Office Bldg.	H-226, U.S. Capitol
Washington, D.C. 20510	Washington, D.C. 20515
(202) 224-7860	(202) 225-3456

The public may receive up to six different items per request, but only one request per day will be filled. Also, only one copy of an individual item will be distributed at a time.

When legislation is enacted and first issued, it is called a *slip law.* Once a session of Congress ends, all the slips laws are published as a group and called *U.S. Statutes at Large.* This is a chronological list of legislation that has been enacted. Every six years, the *U.S. Statutes at Large* is codified—that is, arranged by subject—and published as the *United States Code* (U.S.C.). The *United States Code* includes the public and permanent laws in effect, arranged alphabetically under fifty different titles. The annotated codes are also published by private firms; for example, the *United States Code Annotated* (U.S.C.A.) is published by West Publishing Company, and the *United States Code Service* (U.S.C.S.), *Lawyers Edition*, is published by the Lawyers Cooperative Publishing Company and the Bancroft-Whitney Company.

State legislation is enacted by the legislature in each state. As with federal legislation, very little state legislation is geared specifically to athletics. However, one example is Louisiana's Bribery of Sports Participants Law (L.S.A.—R.S. 14: 118.1), which concerns gambling on sports events. On the state level, bills are also introduced by individual legislators or groups of legislators. Copies of legislation can usually be obtained from the legislators or from the state office that handles legislative services. Each state publishes all the laws that it has passed in a given year. These are called *session laws.* Session laws are compiled into statutes, which may be single or multivolume editions. Annotated editions are usually available from private publishing companies.

Federal Administrative Rules and Regulations

Federal administrative rules and regulations attempt to translate enacted laws into practices that must be followed in order to comply with the law. For instance, when Congress enacted Title IX of the Education Amendments of 1972—a federal statute which prohibited sex discrimination in education (see Chapter 8)—the Department of Health, Education and Welfare had to develop rules and regulations to be followed in order to comply with the new law. An administrative agency which promulgates rules and regulations publishes them in the *Federal Register* (Fed. Reg.). This information is periodically organized by subject (codified) and published in the *Code of Federal Regulations* (C.F.R.).

Citation Form

One of the most intimidating tasks for any student of the legal system is learning how to cite a case properly. Probably the best reference for checking the correct citation form for legal decisions or writings is the "Blue Book," *A Uniform System of Citation,* 15th ed. (Cambridge, Mass.: Harvard Law Review Association, 1991). Two alternatives to the Blue Book are *The University of Chicago Manual of Legal Citation,* 53 U. Chi. L. Rev. 1353 (1986) and *Bieber's Dictionary of Legal Citations,* 3d ed. (Buffalo, N.Y.: William S. Hein Company, 1988).

Case Law

Although this book is not written as a case law text, case law is often cited to give the athletic administrator a better understanding of a legal point in amateur sports law by providing an actual set of circumstances tried before a court. In the Notes sections, case law is provided to give the athletic administrator a source for further information on a sports law subject. A case law citation consists of a case title and case citation, which includes the court reporter in which the decision can be found, the court which made the decision, the year of the decision, the volume, and the page number. For example, *Shelton v. National Collegiate Athletic Ass'n,* 539 F.2d 1179 (9th Cir. 1976) was a case decided in the federal court of appeals (denoted by F.2d, which is the *Federal Reporter,* Second Series), volume 539, page 1179; the case was heard in the Ninth Circuit Court of Appeals and was decided in 1976.

Often a case is reported in more than one court reporter. A case may be reported in a state reporter and/or a regional reporter. In the case of the U.S. Supreme Court, a case *can be* reported in as many as five reporters. When a case is reported in more than one court reporter, the multiple cites are termed *parallel citations.* For example, *University of Nevada-Las Vegas v. Tarkanian,* 95 Nev. 389, 594 P.2d 1159 (1979) was a case heard in the state court system in Nevada. The case is reported in two different places. The first is the *Nevada State Reporter* (denoted by Nev.), volume 594, page 1159; the case was decided in 1979. The *Pacific Reporter* (denoted by P.2d) contains appellate-level decisions of several states, including Nevada; it is the second place this case was reported.

Sometimes a case citation will involve multiple courts and explain how the case fared through judicial review. For example, in *Parish v. National Collegiate Athletic Ass'n,* 361 F. Supp. 1214 (N.D. La. 1973), *aff'd,* 506 F.2d 1028 (5th Cir. 1973), this district court decision was affirmed by the court of appeals.

Depending on the nature of the trial—that is, whether it is a civil or a criminal trial—a citation's case name will reflect the type of case involved. For example, the case names in a civil case would look like this:

1. *Jones v. Smith* (individual suing another individual)
2. *Jones v. NCAA* (individual suing an organization)

In a criminal case, the case names will look like this:

1. *State v. Smith* (state criminal law case)
2. *U.S. v. Jones* (federal criminal law case)

Most case decisions can be broken down into the following parts:

1. Case title and citation.
2. Case summary. Gives brief synopsis of the case and decisions.
3. The facts. Gives the facts of the case, identifies the parties involved, and reviews any case history, including the lower court decisions.
4. The issues. Presents the issue or issues before the court to be decided.
5. The reasoning. Gives the explanation of the court for its decisions on the issues presented by the parties.
6. Conclusion. A case may contain a final conclusion by the court, which may include the disposition of the case.
7. Majority, dissenting, or concurring opinions. A case on the appellate or supreme court level may contain the majority (the deciding opinion), concurring (in agreement with decision but on different or additional reasoning), or dissenting (does not agree with majority decision) opinions.

THE TRIAL SYSTEM

For many nonlawyers, a group which includes most amateur athletic administrators, the threat of litigation, including the possibility of having to go to trial, is a very upsetting proposition, with the potential of great expense. However, with some basic information about how the trial system works, the athletic administrator will realize that dealing with the trial system is not so difficult after all.

An athletic administrator should follow these basic rules when there is a possibility of a lawsuit:

1. Know your organization's attorney and insurance carrier. If some event occurs that may lead to litigation, inform them immediately so that they can take steps to protect your organization's interests.
2. In preparing for litigation, do not hide from your attorney. Be honest and open about the facts of the case and be prepared to supply any information or records that are needed for trial.
3. Do not talk to outsiders, especially the media, about the pending litigation.
4. If possible, review any alternatives for possible settlement of the litigation before it goes to trial.

The steps in the trial system can be broken down into ten parts:

1. The complaint
2. The summons
3. The answer
4. Court jurisdiction
5. Discovery
6. The parties
7. The type of court
8. The trial
9. The judgment
10. The appeals process

The Complaint

The *complaint,* the initial pleading in a trial, is filed by the plaintiff in a civil case and the prosecutor (e.g., attorney general, district attorney) in a criminal case. *DeFrantz v. United States Olympic Committee,* 492 F. Supp. 1181 (D.D.C. 1980), is an example of a *civil case.* The plaintiffs, twenty-five athletes who wished to participate in the 1980 Summer Olympic Games in Moscow, filed a civil complaint against the U.S. Olympic Committee for its participation in a boycott of the Olympics. To illustrate an example of a *criminal case,* in 1985, the Orleans Parish district attorney's office issued criminal complaints against Tulane University basketball players for allegedly fixing games ("point shaving") for gambling purposes.

The Summons

When filing a complaint, the plaintiff must make sure that notice of the legal action being instituted against the defendant is served. The *summons* is the actual serving of notice. The plaintiff (or prosecutor) serves a summons on the defendant ordering the defendant to "answer" the charge by a certain date. Often the summons is served by a process server or officer of the court, such as a sheriff. Until a complaint is lawfully served to the defendant, a court has no jurisdiction to review the dispute.

The Answer

The *answer* is the defendant's initial pleading on the alleged violation of criminal or civil law. The defendant may deny or admit to the allegations made by the plaintiff and state his or her own facts about the matter in dispute. In some instances, a defendant may also file a *counterclaim* against the plaintiff, which essentially means the defendant admits no guilt and, in fact, has been injured by the plaintiff.

Court Jurisdiction

Two types of jurisdiction must be satisfied before a court can hear a case: personal and subject matter. *Personal jurisdiction* means that a court must have sufficient contact with the defendant to bring the defendant into its jurisdiction. Simply stated, the defendant must have some contact within the boundaries of that court's jurisdiction to be eligible to be brought into it for a trial. Some criteria that would be considered by a court to establish personal jurisdiction would be residency, voter registration, driver's license, or business activity. *Subject matter jurisdiction* means that the court must have authority to hear the subject matter that is being tried. For instance, a state court would not be the correct jurisdiction in which to bring a suit involving a federal law, which is within the subject matter jurisdiction of the federal courts.

Discovery

Discovery is a pretrial procedure by which each party to a lawsuit obtains facts and information about the case from the other parties in the case in order to assist the party's preparation for trial. Discovery is designed to:

1. Discover facts and evidence concerning the case. It apprises the parties to the lawsuit of the nature of the claim to be litigated.
2. Bind the other party to a legal position. It is advantageous for the litigant to have the other party's legal position clearly stated in advance, so as to anticipate what legal arguments are likely to be argued and what witnesses and evidence will be introduced at the trial.
3. Seek out weaknesses in the other party's legal position.
4. Preserve testimony that may become unavailable at trial.
5. Narrow the issues in contention.

A party can ascertain information about the case being litigated from the other party to the lawsuit using a number of methods. The three most common discovery techniques are depositions, interrogatories, and requests for production of documents. A *deposition* is an out-of-court examination of a witness to a lawsuit, under oath, during which questions and answers are recorded by a notary public or court official. An *interrogatory* is a set of written questions sent by one party involved in a lawsuit to another party involved in the litigation. The questions must be answered under oath and must be returned within a specific period. A *request for production of documents* is a request by one party involved in a lawsuit to the other to produce and allow for the inspection of any designated documents. The documents produced must be returned within a specific period.

The Parties

The *plaintiff* is a person or party that initiates a legal action by bringing a lawsuit against another person or party. The *defendant is* the person or party against whom relief or recovery is sought in a legal action or lawsuit. The defendant does the defending or denying of the charges brought by the plaintiff.

On the trial level of review, a case citation usually notes the plaintiff first and the defendant second. For example, in *Kupec v. Atlantic Coast Conference*, 399 F. Supp. 1377 (M.D.N.C. 1975), Kupec is the plaintiff and the Atlantic Coast Conference is the defendant. Sometimes another party will be joined in litigation as a *third-party defendant* when its involvement is such as to make its presence at trial imperative. Athletic associations such as the National Collegiate Athletic Association (NCAA) are often named as third-party defendants. For instance, a student-athlete who is suing the school over an eligibility matter as a third-party defendant often names the NCAA (or athletic governing organization), because the NCAA implements or oversees the regulations being enforced by the school against the student-athlete.

The Type of Court

The *trial court* is the court of original jurisdiction where all issues are brought forth, argued, and decided on by either a judge or a jury. The *appeals court* is the court of review where issues decided at trial are reviewed for error. No new evidence or issues may be entered. Generally, in order to be reviewed, an issue must have been objected to and put on the record at trial.

In the federal court system, original jurisdiction is limited to all criminal cases involving a federal law and civil cases that fall into the following categories:

1. A suit brought by the United States against a citizen or group of citizens.
2. Litigation between citizens of the same state in which the amount in controversy is over $50,000 (designed to prevent the use of federal courts for frivolous lawsuits).
3. A lawsuit between citizens who reside in two different states.
4. A case brought by a citizen of one state against a foreign nation or citizen of a foreign nation.

In the state court system, original jurisdiction exists for all state law matters, including disputes among the state's citizens and disputes between one of its citizens and a citizen of another state when the out-of-state party has made itself amenable to the jurisdiction of the suing party's state courts. For example, the NCAA, which is located in Kansas, is often a party in state court actions because it is a national organization with members in all the states and therefore has the requisite contact with each state to make it amenable to each state's jurisdiction.

The Trial

Trials can involve a jury or they can take place without a jury present. Whether a trial will be a jury or a nonjury trial depends on the nature of the trial. Federal criminal cases require a trial by a jury of twelve persons. State criminal cases generally require a jury of no less than six persons. If a defendant pleads guilty, a jury is not required. In civil cases a trial by jury is not always required and may be waived. Jury size in civil cases may also vary.

Pretrial motions are proposed by either side concerning any number of legalities—for example, a motion to dismiss. In a motion, one of the parties to the suit is attempting to gain a better strategic position for the upcoming trial, or trying to have certain procedural matters settled prior to trial. For instance, a defendant may try to make a motion to dismiss because of a lack of sufficient grounds for the suit. Often, a judge will hold a pretrial conference in the judge's chambers in an effort to attempt to resolve the dispute or elements of the dispute before trial.

The state prosecutor in a criminal case or the plaintiff in a civil suit gives the _opening statement_ to the court; then the defendant may do the same. The opening statement is designed to alert the triers of fact (either the judge or the jury, depending on the type of trial) to the nature of the case and to the types of evidence that will be presented during trial. Such statements set expectations and when delivered correctly can serve as the basis for a persuasive argument that will be presented during the trial.

After the opening statements have been made, the plaintiff (or the prosecutor) presents the case first. The plaintiff calls witnesses and examines them; the witnesses are cross-examined by the defendant (or the defense attorney), redirected by the plaintiff, and recrossed by the defendant. The defendant then repeats the whole process—that is, the defendant calls and examines witnesses, and these witnesses are cross-examined by the plaintiff. After the witnesses are redirected by the defendant and recrossed by the plaintiff, both parties are allowed to call rebuttal witnesses.

At the conclusion of the trial, the defendant (or defense attorney) gives a closing statement first. Then the plaintiff (or prosecutor) gives a closing statement.

The Judgment

After the closing statements when a trial is being argued before a jury, the judge instructs the members of the jury on their options in reaching a decision based on the applicable state and/or federal law or laws. These instructions can be quite involved and are often a subject of appeal by the losing party. Case law and precedent are noted in the instructions. If any statutes are involved, they are read to the jury. After deliberation, the jury renders a decision.

In a trial without a jury, the judge can either recess the court while reaching a decision or render a decision immediately on completion of closing statements. Some decisions are given orally; others are written. In rendering a decision, the judge will often cite case law or statutes.

The Appeals Process

Many judgments by trial courts are *appealed*—that is, the party who lost the case requests that the trial proceedings be reviewed by a higher court in the hope that the decision will be reversed. Among the reasons allowed for an appeal are the following:

1. The plaintiff did not have an opportunity to state his or her case at trial.
2. Evidence was incorrectly allowed into or disallowed at the trial.
3. The judge interpreted the law incorrectly.

The party who takes an appeal from one court to another—the losing party at trial—is called the *appellant*. The party in a case against whom an appeal is taken—the winning party at trial—is called the *appellee.*

In an appeals procedure, no new jury, no new witnesses, and no new facts are allowed to be introduced. The basis for appeal is the record, which may include copies of the testimony, exhibits, and any other evidence introduced at trial. Attorneys for the appellant and the appellee may appear before the court, argue their cases, and submit briefs.

An appeals court may *reverse* (disagree with) a lower court's ruling totally or in part. It may *remand* (return) the case back to the lower court for further proceeding, or it may *affirm* (agree with) the lower court's decision. After a decision has been rendered, the case may be appealed again, to either a state supreme court or the U.S. Supreme Court, depending on what court system is involved. (State supreme court cases involving a federal question—for example, a constitutional law claim—may also in some circumstances be appealed to the U.S. Supreme Court.)

NOTES _____

1. Exhibit 2–6 contains a list of some of the legal and sports-related abbreviations used frequently in this text and in reported case decisions.

2. A good research source about governmental policy toward sports issues and potential legislative issues involving amateur athletics is Johnson and Frey, *Government and Sports* (Totowa, N.J.: Rowman and Allanheld Publishers, 1985).

3. In any research involving a legal issue, or in preparation for litigation, an athletic administrator should attempt to answer some basic questions, including the following:

- Who are the plaintiffs in the case?
- Who are the defendants in the case?
- What are the legal theories of the plaintiffs?
- What are the defenses raised by the defendants?
- Is it state or federal court?
- Is it an administrative agency?
- Is it a decision on a pretrial motion?
- Is it a trial or appellate level decision?
- What issue or issues did the judge have to decide in the case?
- For whom did the judge rule?
- What was the rationale for the judge's ruling?
- What is the impact of the case?
- Does the decision set any case precedent?

Exhibit 2–6
Glossary of Legal and Sports-Related Abbreviations

AAU	Amateur Athletic Union	LPGA	Ladies Professional Golf Association
ABA	American Bar Association	maj	majority view
ABA	American Basketball Association	min	minority view
AE	assignee	MISL	Major Indoor Soccer League
aff'd	affirm(ed)	MLB	Major League Baseball
AFL	American Football League	MLBPA	MLB Players Association
agt	agent	n/a	not applicable
AIAW	Association of Intercollegiate Athletics for Women	NAIA	National Association of Intercollegiate Athletics
ans	answer	NASL	North American Soccer League
AR	assignor	NBA	National Basketball Association
a/r	assumption of risk	NBPA	National Basketball Players Assn.
b/c	because	NCAA	National Collegiate Athletic Assn.
b/p	burden of proof	NFHSAA	National Federation of High School Athletic Associations
br/K	breach of contract		
c/a	cause of action	NFL	National Football League
CBA	Continental Basketball Association	NFLPA	NFL Players Association
c/c	counterclaim	NGB	National Governing Bodies
c/d	corpus delicti	NHL	National Hockey League
c/l	common law	NHLPA	NHL Players Association
c/n	contributory negligence	NJCAA	National Junior College Athletic Association
c/p	condition precedent		
c/s	condition subsequent	neg	negligence
c/x	cross examination	OE	offeree
Con	constitutional(ity)	OR	offeror
corp	corporation	P	plaintiff
ct	court	PE	promisee
d>	distinguish (compare)	PGA	Professional Golf Association
d/x	direct examination	PR	promisor
D	defendant	p/f	prima facie or partner(ship)
dem	demurrer	Q	question (or issue)
eq	equity	R	rule (or holding)
ev	evidence	rd/x	redirect examination
g/r	general rule	rem	remanded
int	interest	rev'd	reversed
IOC	International Olympic Committee	RIL	res ipsa loquitur
J	judgment	RS	restatement
J/D	judgment for defendant	S	statute
J/P	judgment for plaintiff	S/F	statute of frauds
J/aff'd	judgment affirmed	TC	trial court
J/rev'd	judgment reversed	TP	third party
K	contract	TPB	third party beneficiary
LBA	Liberty Basketball Association	UCC	Uniform Commercial Code
lcc	last clear chance	USBL	United States Basketball League
USFL	United States Football League	WFL	World Football League
USOC	United States Olympic Committee	WHL	World Hockey League
v	versus	WLAF	World League of American Football
w	with	w/i	within
w/a	weight of authority	w/o	without
WBL	World Basketball League	xn	action

Chapter 3

CONTRACT LAW APPLICATIONS TO AMATEUR ATHLETICS

INTRODUCTION

Amateur athletic administrators are likely to have regular dealings with contract law when they handle game contracts, officiating contracts, personnel contracts, television and radio contracts (see Chapter 9), facility lease agreements, and scholarships. For this reason, athletic administrators should have a working knowledge of contract law terminology and its many applications in sports law. Athletic administrators who do not pay careful attention to the contracts they enter into on behalf of the amateur organization they represent can anticipate potentially disastrous results. For instance, contracts can help safeguard against events such as teams not showing up for scheduled games, referees not showing up to officiate athletic events, insurance premiums not being paid, and injury claims not being paid. The problems can be endless.

Contract law forms the basis for many of the daily activities of an athletic organization. This chapter begins with an introduction to contract law. It then provides a checklist of information the person preparing the contract should consider and a checklist of typical clauses that are included in most contracts. The last section examines the different types of contracts an athletic administrator may need to review. Examples are included of each type of contract discussed.

NOTE ──

1. Although athletic scholarships are viewed as financial aid, they possess many features similar to those of contracts, as shown in Chapter 5. For further information, see the following law review articles.

(a) M. J. Cozillio, "The Athletic Scholarship and the College National Letter of Intent: A Contract by Any Other Name," 35 Wayne L. Rev. 1275 (1989).

(b) Note, "Educating Misguided Student Athletes: An Application of Contract Theory," 85 Colum. L. Rev. 96 (1985).

CONTRACT LAW

The simplest way for an amateur athletic administrator to consider a contract is as an agreement between parties which is enforceable under the law. A contract can be either written or oral, and it must contain a promise to do something. There are three major sources of contract law:

1. *Common law.* Common law is based on previous court decisions regarding fact situations not specifically dealt with by statute. These previous court decisions provide guidelines in determining the legality of a contract.

2. *Restatement of Contracts.* The American Law Institute (ALI) first published *Restatement of Contracts* in 1932; the most recent edition (2nd) was published in 1979. It has organized and summarized this country's common law concerning contracts. Attorneys and the judiciary rely on it for precedent.

3. *Uniform Commercial Code* (U.C.C.). The U.C.C., a uniform statute that every state except Louisiana has enacted, involves commercial transactions (not land or services). Athletic administrators most often would deal with the U.C.C. art. 2 when dealing with contracts which specifically cover the sale of goods— for example, of sporting goods and game tickets.

Formation of a Contract

The major legal concepts involved in the formation of a contract are offer, acceptance, consideration, legality, and capacity.

Offer

For a contract to come into existence, the parties must agree on terms. To reach the stage at which there is mutual assent, the parties must go through a process of offering terms and accepting terms. To form a contract the parties must not necessarily agree on all the terms of a contract, but only on the major or essential terms. The terms of a contract are interpreted objectively, and questions concerning the terms are often answered in keeping with the intent of the parties forming the contract.

An *offer* is a conditional promise made by the offeror to the offeree. It is conditional because the offeror will not be bound by the promise unless the offeree responds to the offer in the proper fashion. *The Second Restatement of Contracts* defines an offer as "the manifestation of willingness to enter into a bargain, so made as to justify another person in understanding that his assent to that bargain is invited." An offer usually includes the following essential terms: (1) the parties involved, (2) the subject matter, (3) the time (and place) for the subject matter to be performed, and (4) the price to be paid. For example, School A offers to play at School B in football on January 1, 1994 at 2 P.M. for the sum of $100 plus complimentary tickets. School B accepts the offer and signs a written contract with School A. Here, an exchange of promises has been made, and the essential terms of parties, time, place, performance, and price have been incorporated. Note, however, that the number of complimentary tickets has not been specified. By itself this would not void a contract; rather, it would be expected that this number would be the number of tickets usually given to the opposing team as a standard practice in football games.

Most offers contain a pair of promises—a conditional promise made by one party that is premised on the second party's promising to do some act in return. This exchange of promises is categorized as a *bilateral contract.* When an offer is made by one party to a proposed contract to the second party to the contract, it creates a *power of acceptance*, because if the second party accepts the offer, a contract is formed. For example, A promises to pay B $100 if B promises to officiate a basketball game for A. This would be a bilateral contract.

A *unilateral contract* is a contract that does not involve an exchange of promises. It instead involves an exchange of a promise in return for an act by a second party. The second party is not bound to do anything, but if the second party chooses to do the requested act, the first party is bound to the terms of his or her promise. For example, a promoter promises Fighter A that if he will box Fighter B, the promoter will pay A $100. A has not agreed to fight B, but if A does fight B, then the promoter is bound to pay A $100.

An *option contract* involves an offer by one party to keep an offer open exclusively to a second party, for a stated period of time, if the second party pays a fee (or some consideration) to the first party for keeping the offer open. For example, A offers B the opportunity to buy 100 baseball bats at $10 each and also offers that if B will pay A $1, the price quote will remain fixed at $10 per bat (up to 100 bats) for six months.

An offer made in jest is not a valid offer and creates no power of acceptance in the second party. Similarly, an offer is not made if it is just an expression of opinion. It is also important to distinguish preliminary negotiations from an offer that creates a power of acceptance. Consider the following situation: The athletic director of School A calls the athletic director of School B and says School A would be interested in playing School B in men's basketball during the 1992 season. School B's athletic director then sends out a game contract to School A's athletic director which states, "I accept your offer and will play you on December 1, 1992 at 8 P.M. at Madison Square Garden for $1,000." School A has not entered into the contract since its athletic director's call was only a solicitation of a contest and not an offer creating the power of acceptance in School B's athletic director. School A may still agree to the date, but it is under no obligation to do so.

Advertisements are generally not considered offers to sell but rather are viewed as an invitation to the public to buy. For example, a school advertises an upcoming football game in the town newspaper. The game is a sellout. A fan wants to buy a ticket to the game. The school is under no obligation to sell the fan a ticket since its advertisement was just an invitation for the public to buy tickets—not a specific offer to sell the fan a ticket. However, an advertisement which includes the phrase "First come, first served" is considered an offer. Thus, the first person to respond to the advertisement accepts the offer, creating a binding contract with the advertiser. A valid offer is created only with the first person to respond to the offer.

In addition, price quotes and estimates are not considered offers, as the person making the quote or estimate is only stating an opinion and does not have the intent to create an offer. Similarly, inquiries or invitations to make an offer are not considered offers, as the one making the statement does not possess the intent to create a valid offer.

Acceptance

An *acceptance* can only be made by the party to whom the offer was made. For example, a school's equipment manager offers to buy ten football helmets from Manufacturer A for $100 each. Unknown to the equipment manager, Manufacturer B has bought Manufacturer A's business. The equipment manager has dealt with Manufacturer B's company before and does not like its warranty policy. Manufacturer B accepts the order from the equipment manager. However, the equipment manager refuses to accept delivery from Manufacturer B and does not have to do so since the offer to purchase was made to Manufacturer A and does not create a power of acceptance in Manufacturer B.

The party accepting the offer, the *offeree*, may be required to accept the offer from the party making it, the *offeror*, in a certain specified manner (e.g., by letter). In some instances, which may depend in part on the past practice between the parties, an offer may be accepted in silence (offeree makes no response to offeror). This is why athletic administrators should always respond to any offer made, whether to reject or accept, in writing or by telephone, and keep a record of the response made.

One major problem that often arises in athletic administration is when an acceptance varies in its terms from the initial offer. Historically, the acceptance had to be a mirror image of the offer (common law). However, under the U.C.C. provisions for the sale of goods an acceptance that differs from the offer will be enforceable as long as the acceptance is not expressly conditioned on the offeror's accepting the new terms. This is provided that one party to the contract is not a merchant. This example illustrates the problems: an equipment manager orders two dozen football helmets with face guards and chin straps attached for $100 each. The manufacturer accepts the order but notes on its order acknowledgment form that chin straps are not usually included but that they will be included in this sale for an additional $1 per helmet. Under U.C.C. art. 2-207, this is considered "a proposal for addition to the contract" because the equipment manager is not a merchant. It may not become part of the contract unless the equipment manager agrees to it. If the question of chin straps is essential to the formation of the entire contract, then a contract may be deemed not to have come into existence at all.

The offeree's power of acceptance can be terminated in four ways:

1. By rejection or counteroffer by the offeree.
2. By the lapse of time.
3. By revocation by the offeror.
4. By death or incapacity of either party to the contract.

The following examples illustrate these reasons for termination:

- School A offers to play School B in field hockey on October 15, 1992. School B rejects the October 15 date and instead offers to play on October 16. The offer by A is terminated by B's rejection and counteroffer.
- School A sends a letter of intent to a proposed scholarship student-athlete, which notes that if the letter of intent is not signed by a certain date, it is no longer valid. Student-athlete is considering a number of other scholarships and allows School A's letter of intent to lapse. Student-athlete later reconsiders and requests a new letter to be sent. School A has subsequently offered the scholarship to another individual and notifies the initial offeree that its offer of a scholarship has lapsed because of time.
- The Meadowlands Arena contacts School A and offers to schedule the school to play there on June 1, 1992 at 8 P.M. for $1,000 against a specified school. School A says it is interested but wants to think it over. While School A is considering the offer, its seven-foot All-American center declares his intent to play in the NBA for the upcoming season. The Meadowlands immediately calls up School A upon hearing the news of the student-athlete's decision and revokes its offer.
- Smith, a sole proprietor, offers to print all the tickets for Home State University's athletic contests for the upcoming school year in exchange for $500. Smith dies before Home State can accept the offer. Home State's power of acceptance is terminated because Smith's death makes the performance of a contract impossible.

Consideration

In addition to mutual assent, the offer, and acceptance, it is essential for the formation of most contracts that there be some form of consideration. *Consideration* is defined abstractly, and there are various definitions of the term. It is often described as a "legal detriment." It involves an exchange of value wherein one party agrees through a bargaining process to give up or do something in return for another party's doing the same. For example, Bob offers Scott a book in exchange for $25. Scott accepts. This is a binding contract. Bob is giving up his book in exchange for Scott's giving up $25. Each party has pledged to give up something to benefit the other. An example in athletic administration would involve a coach who agrees to work at School A, to the exclusion of all other schools, for a period of two years; in return, School A agrees to pay the coach the sum of $100,000 per year. Consideration is often viewed as the essential term needed in a contract to make it legally enforceable. Without consideration, there may be a promise to do an act, but it may not be legally enforceable as a contract.

Consideration can be contrasted to the giving of a gift, which may involve a promise to give something of value but involves no promise to do anything in return for receiving it. Generally, past consideration cannot be a basis for enacting a legally binding current contract. Past consideration is an act that could have served as consideration if it had been bargained for at the time the contract was formed. Since consideration involves an exchange, parties cannot bargain (or exchange) for something which has already occurred. The following situation illustrates this point: School A played School B at School A's home court in basketball the previous season under a single game contract. The following year School A agrees to a return game at School B under a separate game contract. There is no further remuneration or benefit accrued to School A for returning the date. Subsequently, School A decides to cancel the game with School B. School B will not be able to have the game contract legally enforced if it was not receiving any consideration for playing at School B. The previous year's game will not be deemed to be consideration, since it occurred in the past and was not part of the current contract with School B.

In discussing consideration, there are a few related concepts which need be recognized. First is the doctrine of *mutuality of obligation*, which states that the consideration given by both parties to the contract must be equivalent. The consideration, however, need not be identically matched for a contract to be upheld.

Second, one must recognize the *preexisting duty rule*. This rule states that duties imposed by law or by a prior contract will not serve as adequate consideration. For example, a school promises to pay its tennis team's bus driver an additional sum of money if the driver does not speed with the team van. This is inadequate consideration because the driver is already obligated to drive the speed limit, and legal detriment involves the doing of something that one is not legally obligated to do.

Third is the doctrine of *promissory estoppel*, which allows the enforcement of a contract which is not supported by consideration. Under the doctrine of promissory estoppel, a court will enforce a contract with inadequate consideration if a promise is made which the promisor should reasonably expect would and which does induce forbearance or reliance on the part of the promisee. The court honors such a contract in this situation to prevent an injustice to the promisee. An example would be if an athletic director tells an employee that since she has been such a dedicated and hardworking worker when she retires the athletic department will give her $500 per month for the rest of her life. Relying on this statement, the employee does not purchase an additional retirement plan. While there is no valid consideration given, the court may choose to enforce a contract here because the employee relied on the statement of the athletic director.

Legality

Another requirement for an enforceable contract is the *legality* of the underlying bargain. The general rule is that the courts will not enforce an illegal contract. The courts hope that by not enforcing illegal contracts they will discourage unlawful behavior. In addition, the honoring of such contracts would be demeaning to the judiciary. The courts are concerned with two types of illegalities: statutory violations and violations of public policy not expressly declared unlawful by statute. The former include gambling contracts, contracts with unlicensed professionals (doctors, lawyers, accountants, etc.), and a variety of contracts that violate laws regulating consumer credit transactions ("loan sharks," etc.). Contracts that violate public policy include many types of "covenants not to compete," provisions that waive tort liability (discussed in Chapters 6 and 7), and contracts that interfere with family relationships.

With these contracts, no general rule for determining their legality can be given, except to say that the harsher the restrictions or interference the less likely they will withstand judicial scrutiny. Although both types of illegal contracts are generally unenforceable, the severity of this approach has led courts to seek ways to moderate the impact. The principle of restitution has been used to accomplish this moderation. *Restitution* requires that no one who has conferred a benefit or suffered a loss should unfairly be denied compensation. In a case where the underlying bargain of the contract is illegal, the court may find it appropriate to reimburse or "make whole" a party who unfairly suffered a loss.

Capacity

In addition to the offer and the acceptance, the capacity of a party to make or accept an offer is an important factor in the formation of a valid contract. *Capacity* is defined as the ability to understand the nature and effects of one's acts. In regard to contracts, the general rule is that anyone who has reached the age of majority (18 in most states) and is mentally competent has the capacity to enter into a contract. A contract entered into by a *minor,* or one who has not yet reached the age of majority, is considered voidable. In other words, the minor may disaffirm the contract anytime before reaching majority and for a reasonable time after reaching majority. Although minors have the right to disaffirm a contract, they are liable for any tangible benefits they have received or still possess. Generally, a contract entered into by one who is mentally incompetent is also considered voidable because of a lack of capacity. Like minors, incompetents may, however, be liable for the value of tangible benefits received. However, if one has been adjudicated mentally incompetent and a guardian has been appointed, the contract is void. Finally, one who is intoxicated with drugs or alcohol may not have the capacity to enter into an agreement. A person who is so drugged or drunk that he or she has no awareness of his or her acts and the other party knows this, there will be no contract.

In addition to individual capacity, members of organizations can have the capacity to bind a corporation to a contract. A corporate agent can be a natural person or another corporation that is authorized to act for the corporation, as for example, in accepting a summons. An athletic director is authorized to bind the school in certain areas; thus the athletic director has corporate capacity to act on behalf of the athletic department and/or the school.

Mistakes in Contracts

Mistakes frequently occur in the contracting process. In fact, much litigation surrounds contractual mistakes. The claim of a mistake is raised by one seeking to rescind the contract or is raised as a defense to avoid liability under the contract. In the past, courts focused on whether a contractual mistake was unilateral or mutual. *Unilateral mistakes,* or those made by one party, were often denied relief, unless the other party to the contract knew of the mistake, creating a fraudulent disclosure. Enforcing such a contract would be unconscionable. For example, Powerhouse University is eager to schedule its junior varsity basketball team and sends a game contract to Pushover University seeking to schedule Pushover's varsity team. Pushover, eager to play Powerhouse to gain prestige for its program, readily accepts by signing the game contract without reading it. Pushover believes it will be playing Powerhouse's varsity team. When Pushover's mistake is discovered, Pushover will not be able to avoid the contract. Pushover is bound to play Powerhouse's junior varsity, because it did not read the contract before signing it.

Mutual mistakes occur when both parties make a mistake about a basic assumption of the contract. The contract is voidable by the party that is adversely affected. For example, Wahoo University entered into an agreement to purchase 125 football helmets from Tribex Corporation made of a compound called "plastex." Unbeknown to the buyer and the seller, two different compounds called "plastex" could be used to make football helmets. Wahoo University thought it was ordering one form of the compound, while Tribex made the helmet out of the only form of the compound it knew of, the other form. There would be no contract upon discovery of the mutual mistake; since neither party was aware of the ambiguity, and there was no common assent to the terms of the agreement. Today, courts tend to examine the underlying merits of any litigation involving contractual mistakes.

The Parol Evidence Rule

When a written contract is finalized and the parties agree that it represents the final expression of their agreement, the contract may be considered to be an *integration of the agreement*. Often a contract will contain an integration clause that stipulates that the written document represents the total agreement between the parties. When this occurs, the contract is considered the *total expression of the agreement*.

The *parol evidence rule* prohibits the admission of oral statements, preliminary agreements, or writings made prior to or at the time of signing that would in any way alter, contradict, or change the written contract. However, any evidence may be introduced to show the intention of the parties whenever the object of the contract cannot be ascertained from the language employed. In its strictest form, the parol evidence rule bars any evidence of preliminary agreements, writings, or oral understandings between the parties to an agreement from being introduced in court when the contract was considered integrated at its signing. For example, School A negotiates with School B to have School B play a soccer match at School A. In preliminary negotiations, there was some discussion that School A would return the match at School B for the season following the year School B plays at School A. The final contract makes no mention of a return match. The final contract contains an integration clause. School B is barred under the parol evidence rule from introducing any evidence in court about any oral negotiations concerning a return of the match by School A.

Conditions of a Contract

Usually in a contract one or more conditions must be met by each of the parties in order for each party to be in compliance with the contract. The nonoccurrence of a condition by either party operates to discharge a contractual duty by the other party. Consider the following situation. School A has a medical insurance policy that covers injury to its student-athletes. Payment of medical expenses by the insurance company is conditioned on an accident's being reported within thirty days of its occurrence. If a claim is not filed within that period, the insurance company is discharged from its duty to pay the medical expenses incurred by the student-athlete.

Generally there are two types of conditions: a condition precedent and a condition subsequent. A *condition precedent* is one which must occur before a contract will be considered binding on the parties. For example, an athletic director's signature may be a condition precedent to all university athletic contracts. Before an athletic department contract will be binding, the contract may require the athletic director's signature. A *condition subsequent* occurs when the parties condition a contract on an event's not occurring. For example, assume a school decides to open a health and fitness center on campus and decides to install Nautilus equipment. However, the supplier of the equipment may not be sure the Nautilus machines will be available in time to meet the deadline for the club's opening. The school may decide to make a second contract with a hydraulic weight machine manufacturer and condition that contract on the Nautilus equipment's not arriving on time.

Conditions may be expressed, stated directly in the agreement, implied (tacitly understood between the parties as part of the agreement), or constructive (not agreed upon at all by the parties but imposed by a court in order to ensure fairness).

The Statute of Frauds

Certain types of contracts are unenforceable under the statute of frauds unless they are in writing. The statute of frauds has its roots in English common law. Certain types of contracts were required to be in writing to prevent injustices resulting from fraudulent claims or promises that were never kept. The U.C.C. in art. 2–201 states that a contract for the sale of goods over $500 is not enforceable by way of either action or defense unless there is some writing sufficient to indicate that there was a contract for sale between the parties now contesting the arrangement. Contracts involving an "interest" in land are also subject to the statute of frauds and must be in writing. An "interest" in land includes the sale, mortgaging, and leasing of real property and the creation of easements. Additionally, any contract that cannot be fully performed within one year shall not be enforceable unless it is in writing.

Two types of contracts athletic administrators might enter into that would fall under this statute would be a contract that is not to be performed within one year from the making (e.g., future game contracts or coaches' contracts) and land contracts that involve the sale of an interest in land (e.g., facility site land purchases).

Breach of Contract

A *breach of contract* is a failure to perform a duty imposed under the contract. A contract may be totally or partially breached by a party to it. A total breach discharges the aggrieved party of any duty to perform, and the aggrieved party may immediately file suit. A partial breach may not discharge the aggrieved party from a duty to perform, but the aggrieved party may file suit immediately to collect any damages that are due. The following two situations illustrate breach of contract:

- State U agrees in 1988 to play Private U in a home-and-away series of football games, with State U playing at Private U in September 1990 and Private U returning the game the following year at State U. In June 1990, State U informs Private U that it cannot afford to travel to Private U and cancels the game set for September. The total breach by State U discharges Private U from any duty to play at State U in 1991, and Private U may immediately sue for any damages it may have suffered because of State U's actions (lost ticket revenue, concession revenue, television revenue, parking revenue, etc.).
- Pushover University agrees in 1988 to play Powerhouse University in a home-and-away series of football games, with Pushover hosting Powerhouse in 1990 and paying Powerhouse a $500,000 guarantee within a year of the contest, and with Powerhouse hosting Pushover in 1991 but paying no guarantee. (Powerhouse is a national football power, while Pushover is trying to develop such a program.) Powerhouse travels in 1990 to Pushover and trounces them in a game that sports writers considered amateurish. Two weeks after the first game, Powerhouse cancels its home game with Pushover in 1991 but will play in 1995 or sooner if Pushover becomes ranked in the top

twenty. Pushover, which has not yet paid Powerhouse its guarantee for the game played in 1990, may still have to do so despite the partial breach of contract. However, Pushover can immediately file suit for any damages it suffered because of the partial breach by Powerhouse.

Assignment and Delegation of a Contract

Rights and obligations of a contract may be assigned and duties under a contract may be delegated without nullifying the contract. Generally all rights under a contract may be assigned to another party. When one assigns a contract to another party, he or she gives up all claims under the contract as well. A trade of a professional athlete to another team would be an example of an assignment of a contract. All rights of the trading team under the contract with the player, unless otherwise specified in the contract, will be assigned to the player's new team when the player is traded. One cannot, however, assign an offer to contract to another party. The reason for this is that offers are made to a particular party so that only that party may accept or the offer is terminated.

Delegation of duties under a contract does not create a transfer in the same sense as an assignment, as the original party is not relieved of all obligations under the contract. The delegating party may be held liable for any breaches of the contract. For example, assume a university has a contract with sporting goods supplier A for the purchase of ten cases of tennis balls. If supplier A will not be able to fulfill the agreement on time, it may delegate its duties for the supply of tennis balls to supplier B. While this delegation is valid, supplier A will still be liable for any breach in the original contract with the university if supplier B does not properly fulfill the duties under the contract.

Defenses to a Breach of Contract

There are three possible defenses to a breach of contract suit. The first, *impossibility of performance,* occurs when a party to the contract promises something that becomes impossible to perform through no fault of his or her own. Generally this defense is used when the subject matter of the contract is destroyed, the action required under the contract becomes illegal, or there is death or incapacity of one of the parties to the contract. For example, the impossibility of performance defense would be used if a state university had a contract with a company to supply beer at their football stadium and if the legislature outlawed the sale of alcohol at all public school and college events. The action under the contract would then be illegal and the university could use impossibility of performance as a defense to a breach of the contract.

The second defense available is the *frustration of purpose*. This defense occurs when the value of performance to be obtained becomes useless to a party because of an *unforeseen* change in circumstances. For example, assume a school contracted with a landscaping company to landscape the college's golf course. If a week later the state decided to take the land by eminent domain to build a highway through it, the purpose for which the university contracted would be frustrated and therefore, it might use this defense.

Impracticability is the final defense available to a breach of contract. It occurs when the cost of performance is greatly increased as the result of an unforeseen occurrence. This is a narrowly interpreted defense and is rarely used. The courts will allow performance to be excused under this defense in cases of war, embargo, or crop failure.

Remedies for a Breach of Contract

Remedies for a breach of contract usually entail monetary damages awarded by the court to the aggrieved party. The philosophy of monetary damages is to compensate the injured party for economic losses. The problem with monetary damages is that the aggrieved party must be able to translate the injury into a financial sum and be able to justify that amount to the court.

With the exception of some land sale contracts, the courts are extremely reluctant to require specific performance of a contract. *Specific performance* requires the performance of a contract in the specific form in which it was made. It is generally invoked by the courts when damages would be an inadequate compensation for the breach of an agreement—for example, a specific piece of land is ordered to be conveyed under the terms of the original agreement. The court rarely requires a contract for personal services, like a coach's contract, to be specifically performed. The courts usually reason that this would be a form of involuntary servitude.

Courts will usually award contract damages based in whole or in part on three legal economic interests: expectation, reliance, and restitution. An *expectation interest* is the benefit that was bargained, and the remedy is to put the party breached in a position equal to his or her position had the contract been performed. A *reliance interest* is the loss suffered by relying on the contract and taking actions consistent with the expectation that the other party will abide by it; the remedy is reimbursement that restores the promisee to his or her position before the contract was made. A *restitution interest* is that which restores to the promisee any benefit the promisee conferred on the promisor.

PREPARING AND REVIEWING A CONTRACT

In many athletic organizations an administrator may routinely draft and/or review documents such as game contracts or facility leases. It is suggested that an attorney always review such documents to see whether they would withstand legal review. At a minimum all standard form contracts should be reviewed at least once annually. In preparing a contract it is critical for the athletic administrator to provide the attorney drafting the contract with as many pertinent facts as possible so that the attorney can fully protect the amateur athletic organization's rights under the agreement. Since many of the contracts used in amateur athletics are unique to the industry, the attorney will require significant input from the athletic administrator in order to draw up a proper contract. Athletic administrators should be prepared to provide such data and to review drafts of contracts to check for errors. The following is a checklist of information that an amateur athletic organization should consider when developing contracts for use by the organization.

1. If there have been prior dealings between the parties, the lawyer drafting the new contract should be informed of the nature of these dealings in order to decide whether they have any bearing on the new contract.
2. If the contract can only be performed by the original parties to the contract, the lawyer should be informed so as to state in the contract that it will not be assignable.
3. If any party is to be required to furnish a bond or to make a deposit, this information needs to be incorporated into the agreement.
4. If the parties have agreed to any special conditions, the lawyer drafting the contract must know of the conditions in order to include them in the agreement.
5. The consideration for the contract needs to be identified.
6. A description of the subject matter of the contract should be provided. If property is the subject matter, then a description of the property should be furnished.
7. If there are any circumstances that would excuse either party from performing the contract, these circumstances should be explained in detail and included in the agreement.
8. The lawyer must be informed if the parties to the agreement need to view each other's books and records.

9. The attorney should know the means of payment agreed to between the parties for the subject matter of the contract, any agreement as to the payment of attorney's fees should a breach occur, and any agreement as to the payment of any resulting taxes.

10. The attorney should have the name, capacity, and residence of all parties to the agreement and information regarding their ability to sign the contract and bind themselves or the organization they represent.

11. The effective date of the contract, the duration of the contract, and how the contract can be terminated before it runs its stated length all need to be incorporated into the agreements.

12. The attorney must be informed of the liabilities of both parties to the agreement and whether the liability of either party is to be limited under the agreement.

With all of the preceding information in hand, the attorney can proceed with drafting the contract document. The following is a general checklist of typical clauses that are included in most sports contracts (see Exhibit 3–1):

1. *Opening.* Identifies the parties to the agreement and also the date of the contract and its effective date.

2. *Representations and warranties.* Contains information regarding the rights and qualifications of the parties to enter into an agreement and also any express or implied warranties regarding the subject matter of the contract.

3. *Operational language.* Contains the subject matter of the contract. The precise rights and duties of the parties under the contract are explained.

4. *Other clauses.* Certain other clauses may be included, depending on the nature of the contract. Compensation, rights to arbitration for any disagreements, and the right to assign the contract are typical examples of other clauses.

5. *Termination.* Discusses the length of the contract and the means of ending the agreement.

6. *Entire agreement and amendments.* Details the comprehensiveness of the contract and its relation to other agreements and also the methods by which the contract can be amended.

7. *Closing.* Contains the signatures of the parties to the contract, any acknowledgments, and the signatures of any witnesses.

Exhibit 3-1
Typical Clauses in a Sports Contract

CONTRACT

Opening

This Agreement made and entered into this __1st__ day __September__, 19 __XX__, by and between the athletic authorities of the Powerhouse University and the athletic authorities of __Anyschool University__, stipulates:

Representations & Warranties

First: Whereas, Powerhouse University and Anyschool University are the owners to the rights for their individual basketball teams to compete in NCAA intercollegiate competition.

Second: That the __basketball (men's)__ teams representing the above named institutions shall

__meet and play__ at _____ (site)

on _____ (date), 19____, and at _____

_____ on _____, 19____.

Operational Language

Third: That in consideration of playing this game,

(1) That the Host Team shall provide the Visiting Team one rights-free radio outlet for the broadcast of the game by its designated radio station and or network.

(2) That television rights to the game remain the property of the Big Time Conference and the Powerhouse University.

(3) That the Host Team shall provide the Visiting Team with forty (40) complimentary tickets.

(4) That a minimum of 200 tickets shall be made available for sale to the Visiting Team, but that unsold tickets be returned to the Home Team no later than 72 hours prior to the game.

Other Clauses

Fourth: That officials for the game shall be provided by the conference.

Fifth: That the game shall be played under the eligibility rules of the respective institutions.

Termination

Sixth: Either party failing to comply with condition of Article One, either by cancellation or failure to appear, shall forfeit money in the amount of __Big $$__ unless such cancellation shall be by mutual consent, in which case this agreement shall be null and void.

Entire Agreement and Amendments

Seventh: This agreement constitutes the entire agreement and understanding between Powerhouse University and Anyschool University and cancels, terminates and supersedes any prior agreement or understanding relating to the game contest. There are no representations, agreements, warranties, covenants or undertakings other than those contained herein. None of the provisions of this Agreement may be waived or modified except expressly in writing signed by both parties. However, failure of either party to require the performance of any term in this Agreement or the waiver by either party of any breach

Exhibit 3–1 continued

thereof shall not prevent subsequent enforcement of such term nor be deemed a waiver of any subsequent breach.

Closing

Witnessed by: Powerhouse University

_____   _____
Business Manager   Director of Athletics
of Athletics

_____   Anyschool University
Witnessed by: (Visiting Institution)

_____   _____
Business Manager   Director of Athletics
of Athletics

TYPES OF ATHLETIC CONTRACTS

Typically, an athletic administrator will be routinely involved with the negotiation and execution of a wide variety of contractual agreements, from personnel contracts involving coaches to event-related contracts encompassing media, officials, physicians, or facility lease agreements. The following sections include examples of various types of contracts which may confront an athletic administrator. Examples of contracts are provided for informational purposes only. An administrator should consult the organization's attorney before utilizing any of the language described in the examples to ensure that the language adequately covers the organization's legal needs.

Coaches' Contracts

Major college and university athletic coaches in the revenue-producing sports (basketball and football) are changing the face of contracts between institutions and the coaches who work for them. Recent lawsuits and the resulting out-of-court settlements should have placed athletic directors across the country on notice. The negotiation of a coaching contract is a serious business. Coaching is a profession, and the men and women who pursue it as such may be formidable opponents at the negotiating table. Several coaches at the intercollegiate level hire attorneys to represent them in contract negotiations. Great care should be taken in drafting the agreement to protect the school's best interest.

Basically, a coach's contract is similar to any other employment contract. It sets forth the nature and duration of the employment, the compensation to be paid to the employee, and any other terms and conditions of the employment (see Exhibit 3–2).

The employer-employee relationship between the institution and the coach is similar to the typical employer-employee relationship found in the business world; nevertheless, some unique aspects of the coach's employment should be considered before an institution signs a coach to an employment contract. Coaches at all levels of competition are under tremendous pressure to win. The pressure to win at the high school level may not be as great as at a major university, but it exists nonetheless.

Like it or not, the standard evaluative measure of a coach is his or her ability to produce a winner. A coach who is not successful in producing a winning program is often a likely candidate for termination. The termination of a coaching contract constitutes a breach for which an institution can be held liable in damages. Traditionally, this liability has been discharged by an institution by either making a lump sum payment based on the dollar value of the remaining years of the contract to the coach or simply continuing periodic payments to the coach for the remaining term of his or her contract as if he or she were still employed. However, a 1983 decision by the Georgia Court of Appeals in *Rodgers v. Georgia Tech Athletic Ass'n*, 303 S.E. 2d 467 (Ga. Ct. App. 1983), suggests that an institution may be liable to its former coach for more than the salary stated in the contract. Pepper Rodgers, the head coach of the Georgia Tech football team at the time he was fired, sued the school for damages relating to the perquisites he had lost as a result of his termination. The parties settled out of court prior to trial on the issue after the Georgia court ruled that the inclusion of the word *perquisite* in Rodgers's contract might permit a jury to award Rodgers some of the damages he was claiming (see Exhibit 3–3).

Aside from liability for damages for the face value of the contract and other perquisites, institutions should be also be aware of the potential liability to a coach in defamation. The high visibility of a coach and the tremendous publicity surrounding a football or basketball team at a major university magnify this problem. The institution must be careful in announcing the firing and in disclosing the reasons for the termination. Even though the firing is often a result of the coach's inability to perform his or her responsibilities adequately, the institution must be careful not to convey this message as the reason for termination unless it is satisfied that the truth of this allegation can be easily established as a defense to an anticipated claim of defamation by the former coach.

In addition to the damage issues associated with termination, the

Exhibit 3–2
A Coach's Contract

EMPLOYMENT CONTRACT

Agreement made this_____day of_____, 19   , by and between _____ *University* and _____, supersedes a contract agreement dated November 22, 1982, a copy of which is attached hereto.

The University hereby continues the employment of _____ as Head Coach of Football for the period beginning this date and ending on the 30th day of June, 19   . The Coach hereby agrees to and does accept paid employment for the designated period, subject to the provisos below. The termination date of this agreement may be exended on a year-to-year basis at the agreement of the University and Head Coach, in accordance with Paragraph 6.

The University may suspend the Head Coach for a reasonable period of time without compensation, or terminate his employment, if he is found to be in deliberate or serious violation of NCAA regulations.

The Head Coach agrees that he will devote full time to his football responsibilities during the practice and game seasons. The Head Coach agrees that he will undertake no paid public speaking engagements during the fall practice and game seasons, unless specifically authorized to do so by the Director of Athletics, whose permission shall not be unreasonably withheld.

If the University ceases to engage in Intercollegiate Football through its own election, or chooses to terminate the Coach's coaching responsibilities prior to the expiration of the Contract, the University will provide a responsible administrative position to the Coach for the duration of the Contract. If the Coach desires to leave under these circumstances for another assignment which does not offer the salary compensation at the same level as the University does, then the University will provide the financial difference during the length of the Contract.

The University shall have the ability to extend this Contract for a period of one year, and for additional one year periods thereafter, provided the University gives the Coach written notice of its desire to extend the Contract at least 19 months in advance of the termination date of this Contract. The Coach shall then either accept or reject in writing the extension of this Contract within four weeks after receipt of the University's intent to extend this Contract, or two weeks after the completion of the football game season, whichever is later.

The Coach agrees that he will not seek, negotiate for or discuss other full time employment of any nature during the football game season, without the express written permission of the Executive Vice President or his designee prior to the expiration of this Contract, whose permission shall not be unreasonably withheld.

The parties agree that in the event of the death or disability of the Head Coach rendering it impossible for him to perform his duties as set forth herein, but not including any disability arising out of or in the course of his employment, _____ *University* shall be entitled to cancel this Agreement or suspend the operations of this Agreement for the duration of said disability. However, the employee will be eligible to apply for and receive disability payments through the University's normal disability insurance plan.

In witness whereof, the parties have caused this Contract to be signed and sealed by their respective officers hereunto duly authorized the _____ day of _____, 19

For the University   *Coach*

_____   _____
Executive Vice President   **Head Coach-Football**

Exhibit 3–3
Perquisites in Pepper Rodgers's Georgia Tech Coaching Contract

Pepper Rodgers was fired in December, 1979 with two years of his contract remaining. Rodgers received his salary through December 1981 but sued for his perquisites. They included the following:

A. benefits and perquisites received by Rodgers directly from the Georgia Tech Athletic Association:
(1) gas, oil, maintenance, repairs, other automobile expenses;
(2) automobile liability and collision insurance;
(3) general expense money;
(4) meals available at the Georgia Tech training table;
(5) eight season tickets to Georgia Tech home football games during fall of 1980 and 1981;
(6) two reserved booths, consisting of approximately forty seats at Georgia Tech home football games during the fall of 1980 and 1981;
(7) five season tickets to Georgia Tech home basketball games for 1980 and 1981;
(8) four season tickets to Atlanta Falcon home football games for 1980 and 1981;
(9) four game tickets to each out-of-town Georgia Tech football game during fall of 1980 and 1981;
(10) pocket money at each home football game during fall of 1980 and 1981;
(11) pocket money at each out-of-town Georgia Tech football game during fall of 1980–1981;
(12) parking privileges at all Georgia Tech home sporting events;
(13) the services of a secretary;
(14) the services of an administrative assistant;
(15) the cost of admission to Georgia Tech home baseball games during the spring of 1980–1981;
(16) the cost of trips to football coaches' conventions, clinics, and meetings and to observe football practice sessions of professional and college football teams;
(17) initiation fee, dues, monthly bills, and cost of memberhip at the Capital City Club;
(18) initiation fee, dues, monthly bills, and cost of membership at the Cherokee Country Club;
(19) initiation fee and dues at the East Lake Country Club.

B. benefits and perquisites received by Rodgers from sources other than the Georgia Tech Athletic Association by virtue of being head coach of football:
(1) profits from Rodgers' television football show, "The Pepper Rodgers Show," on Station WSB-TV in Atlanta for the fall of 1980–1981;
(2) profits from Rodgers' radio football show on Station WGST in Atlanta for the fall of 1980 and 1981;
(3) use of a new Cadillac automobile during 1980–1981;
(4) profits from Rodgers' summer football camp, known as the "Pepper Rodgers Football School," for June 1980 and June 1981;
(5) financial gifts from alumni and supporters of Georgia Tech for 1980–1981;
(6) lodging at any of the Holiday Inns owned by Topeka Inn Management, Inc. of Topeka, Kansas, for the time period from December 18, 1979 through December 31, 1981;
(7) the cost of membership in Terminus International Tennis Club in Atlanta for 1980 and 1981;
(8) individual game tickets to Hawks basketball and Braves baseball games during 1980–1981 seasons;
(9) housing for Rodgers and his family in Atlanta for the period from December 18, 1979 through December 31, 1981;
(10) the cost of premiums of a $400,000.00 policy on the life of Rodgers for the time period from December 18, 1979 through December 31, 1981.

Rodgers v. Georgia Tech Athletic Ass'n, 303 S.E. 2d 467 (6A. App 1983).

institution may also encounter procedural problems in attempting to rid itself of its coach prior to the expiration of his or her contract. In *Yukica v. Leland*, No. 85-E-191 (N.H. Super. Ct. 1985), the New Hampshire Superior Court granted the Dartmouth College head football coach an order restraining the college's athletic director from terminating his coaching contract or from taking steps to appoint another to his position. The court granted the order on the basis of the wording of the coaching contract, which, as interpreted by the court, provided that notice of termination was to be given twelve months prior to actual termination.

Termination of a coaching contract is, of course, not solely an institutional concern. A coach may wish to leave the institution before the end of his or her contract term. It is not uncommon for coaches at various levels of competition to aspire to "career enhancement" and higher-profile positions which offer more pay, increased exposure, and greater benefits. As these positions become available, the coach may leave his or her current coaching position to assume similar responsibilities at another institution. This departure before the end of the contract term also constitutes a breach, for which a coach can be held liable.

Unlike coaches, however, institutions have been reluctant to pursue legal remedies against the departed coach. If the coach is leaving for a better position, it would be bad publicity for the school to hold the individual back. It may be problematic to have a coach at the institution if he or she really does not want to be there. Also, finding a replacement for the departed coach may be more difficult if it appears that the university is not willing to allow its personnel to advance to better positions. In addition, it is difficult for the university to prove monetary damages. The most the university could hope for would be the cost of searching for a new coach. The loss of revenue for the school due to the loss of a successful coach is very difficult to quantify and prove.

Institutions, however, are not without recourse in attempting to retain coaches. Although the case involved a professional football team's attempt to retain a coach, *New England Patriots Football Club, Inc. v. University of Colorado*, 592 F.2d 1196 (1st Cir. 1979), illustrates one potential remedy available to an employer. In this decision, the U.S. Court of Appeals held that a clause in Chuck Fairbanks's coaching contract with the Patriots, which required him to refrain from contracting elsewhere for his coaching services, was a proper basis for a preliminary injunction to enjoin the University of Colorado from employing Fairbanks while he was under contract with the Patriots.

Another potential solution to either party's desire for an early termination of a coaching contract is to provide for buy-out clauses at some agreed amount. Under a mutual buy-out clause, either the institution or the coach may unilaterally and prematurely terminate the contract during its term and be responsible only for damages in the agreed amount. This was the status of Jim Valvano's coaching contract with North Carolina State University, which reportedly provided for a mutual buy-out in the sum of $575,000.

Occasionally institutions hire coaches as "at-will employees," where no contract exists. In these cases, the courts have given the institutions complete discretion to terminate contracts at will. *Frazier v. University of the District of Columbia*, 742 F. Supp. 28 (D.D.C. 1990), provides an example of an at-will employee who unsuccessfully challenged his dismissal.

In another case, *Parker v. Graves*, 340 F. Supp. 586 (D.C. Fla. 1972), a coach was dismissed for conduct that he claimed was guaranteed under the First Amendment. The coach sued the University of Florida for wrongful discharge. In denying plaintiff's First Amendment claim, the court balanced the coach's rights against his responsibility as a public school employee to provide orderly administration.

It is important to note, however, that the doctrine of wrongful termination may bring relief to an "at-will" employee who is wrongfully terminated. As many athletic administrators are at-will employees (working without a written, signed contract), a wrongful termination claim may provide recovery when they are discharged from employment. In many states wrongful termination claims have been successful when an attorney could show that certain practices, promises made by the employer, or set forth in an employee handbook caused an employee to rely on an employment relationship and the court implies a contract. Many courts have disregarded the employer's rights under the employment at-will doctrine by finding implied contract terms that restrict an employer's right to discharge employees. In practice, wrongful termination law varies by state, and court decisions in a particular state must be examined to estimate one's possibility of success in such a suit.

NOTES ————————————————————————————

1. For further information, see Graves "Coaches in the Courtroom: Recovery in Actions for Breach of Employment Contracts," 12 *J.C. & U.L.* 545 (1986).

2. For a review of a model university coaching contract, athletic administrators would be well advised to consult Stoner and Nogay, "The Model University Coaching Contract: A Better Starting Point for Your Next Negotiation," 16 *J.C. & U.L.* 43 (Summer 1989). This article reviews a number of key issues relevant to the negotiation of coaching contracts, including the following:

   (a) Position responsibilities.
   (b) Term of employment.

(c) Coaching compensation, including guaranteed base salary, merit increases, fringe benefits, and opportunities to earn outside income.

(d) Termination of contract by university for just cause.

(e) Liquidated damages payable upon termination of contract by university without just cause.

(f) Liquidated damages payable upon termination of contract by coach.

(g) Restrictive covenant not to compete.

(h) Responsibility for violations of NCAA rules and regulations.

3. In *Stanley v. Big Eight Conference*, 463 F. Supp. 920 (D.Mo. 1978), a collegiate football coach brought action against a collegiate athletic conference, seeking to enjoin the conference from proceeding in an investigation without complying with due process. In granting the injunction, the court reasoned that the coach's reputation and prospect of future employment were a liberty interest (the right to live and work where one wants to) which conference investigation could alter, and therefore due process was required.

Coaches' Contracts—High School

High school coaches, unlike their collegiate brethren, are generally teachers first and coaches second. Most have separate *divisible* contracts involving the two jobs. As a teacher, the high school coach is usually eligible to gain tenure after a specified number of years of teaching. For a coach, however, this is not usually the case. Most states do not grant tenure for coaches. A practical problem arises when a coach is dismissed from his or her job as coach but has tenure as a teacher and decides to remain at the school in that capacity. Unless there is another teacher already in the school system who can take over the coaching duties, it may not be feasible to go out and hire another coach other than on a part-time basis, because there will not be a teaching position to go along with the coaching job. In addition, depending on the circumstances surrounding the dismissal, it may be awkward to have the ex-coach continue to teach at the school.

In coaching contract disputes, the question frequently arises as to whether coaches can resign their coaching positions without affecting their teaching positions. The court must consider whether the duties are under a single contract, and whether that contract is divisible. Often the coaching contract is a supplemental contract, which avoids this type of dispute. However, when the duties appear on a single contract, the courts have been split as to whether these contracts are divisible. In *Brown v. Board of Education* (see note 1), the court ruled that the plaintiff was hired as a teacher-coach and not as either one, and therefore plaintiff could not resign from one without resigning from the other. On the other hand, in *Swager v. Board of Education* (see note 2), the court ruled that plaintiff could resign from his coaching duties without affecting his position as math teacher.

In order to address the problem of divisible teaching-coaching contracts, many school districts require the individual to sign an ~~*indivi-sible contract*~~. Under this type of an agreement, the loss of either position results in the loss of both positions. The indivisible contract may solve the problem of having a teaching position available for the new coach and also may reduce the potential for ill will as discussed earlier. The issue of tenure and its relationship to coaching in secondary schools has resulted in some litigation, and athletic administrators should be aware of their school district's policies before entering into any coaching agreement.

NOTES ───

1. In *Brown v. Board of Education of Morgan County School District*, 560 P.2d 1129 (Utah Sup. Ct. 1977), a teacher who was also a coach resigned from his coaching duties. The school district, claiming that he could not resign from his coaching duties without also resigning from his teaching duties because they were not separate contracts, treated the resignation as a resignation from both duties. The issue in this case was whether the contract to coach and teach was a divisible contract, thus permitting the teacher to resign from one of his duties without affecting the other. The court ruled that the contract was not divisible and thus the plaintiff's resignation was a resignation from both duties.

2. In *Swager v. Board of Education*, 688 P.2d 270 (Kan. Ct. App. 1984) a teacher brought an action against the Board of Education to reinstate him as a math teacher after the Board of Education had misinterpreted his resignation as basketball coach as a resignation from teaching and coaching. In ruling for the teacher, the appellate court reasoned that were his position as teacher not renewed, he would be entitled to certain due process requirements, including a hearing, that the Board never provided.

3. In *George v. School District No. 8R of Umatilla County*, 490 P.2d 1009 (Or. Ct. App. 1971), a teacher who had a three-year contract to teach and to coach was dismissed from his coaching duties after one year and his salary was reduced accordingly. Teacher brought action claiming that he was entitled to his full contract for three years. The appellate court found that under the three- year contract, the coaching portion and the teaching portion were not divisible, and therefore the teacher was entitled to the full contract for all three years. The teacher was awarded back pay.

4. In *Cruciotti v. McNeel*, 396 S.E.2d 191 (W.Va. Sup. Ct. 1990), an unsuccessful applicant for position of physical education teacher brought action against school district alleging that job posting, which described the opening as "physical education teacher and athletic trainer," constituted an improper joining of employment positions. In affirming the lower court's decision, the Supreme Court of Appeals held that position of athletic trainer was "extracurricular" and therefore required a separate contract for employment.

5. In *School Directors of District U-46 v. Kosoff*, 419 N.E.2d 658 (Ill. Ct. App. 1981), three physical education teachers, who were also athletic coaches, were suspended. The hearing officer decided that they were improperly suspended. He ordered reinstatement of the teachers with back pay to their

tenured teaching positions but failed to reinstate the teachers to their coaching positions. The teachers appealed. In affirming the circuit court's decision, the appellate court held that coaches were not tenured under the school code and therefore were not entitled to reinstatement following improper suspension under the code.

The following sections address some of the most common areas for litigation in high school coaches' contracts. As opposed to college coaches, high school teachers and coaches are generally governed by a collective bargaining agreement. Consequently, coaches must file for grievance arbitration rather than go through the court system. *Grievance arbitration* is the submission of the parties' grievance to a private unofficial person(s) who listens to the disputed question and contentions and then gives a decision regarding the dispute. The cases presented in this chapter are limited to the court cases, but it should be noted that there are many published and unpublished arbitration decisions which also address the issues set forth in this chapter.

Contract and Statutory Interpretation

In cases where the interpretation of a contract is questioned, the judge must carefully scrutinize the wording of the contract to determine its precise meaning. As in *Trevino v. Board of Trustees* (see note 1), the judge often has to decide whether the action of a certain party to the contract is allowed under the terms of the contract. In *Trevino,* the school district assigned additional duties to the athletic director. The judge had to decide whether these duties were permitted under the terms of the contract. In other cases (see notes 2–7, *infra*) the interpretation of a statute is debated and the court must look at the underlying intent of the statute.

NOTES ─────────────────────────────────────

1. In *Trevino v. Board of Trustees of West Oso Independent School District,* 783 S.W.2d 806 (Tex. Ct. App. 1990), a high school football coach and athletic director was assigned duties to teach two history classes per day. The coach filed a breach of contract suit against the school district seeking an injunction to prevent the school district from assigning him the teaching duties. In examining the terms of the contract, the court ruled for the school district, upholding the trial court's decision.

2. In *Neal v. School Dist. of York,* 288 N.W.2d 725 (Neb. Sup. Ct. 1980), a schoolteacher brought an action alleging that the school district was contractually obligated to pay him for his services as varsity head basketball coach. In ruling for defendants, the Supreme Court of Nebraska held that the coaching contract was not subject to procedural and substantive requirements that the contract must remain in effect until terminated for just cause.

3. In *Stang v. Independent Sch. Dist. No. 191,* 256 N.W.2d 82 (Minn. Sup. Ct. 1977), a high school basketball coach brought action against the school

district alleging that he was entitled to written notice and hearing before his termination. The Minnesota Supreme Court held for the defendant, stating that a coach is not held to the same standard as a teacher.

4. In *School Directors of District U-46 v. Kosoff*, 419 N.E.2d 658 (Ill. Ct. App. 1981), three physical education teachers, who were also athletic coaches, were suspended. The hearing officer decided that they were improperly suspended. He ordered reinstatement of the teachers to their tenured teaching positions with back pay but failed to reinstate the teachers to their coaching positions. The teachers appealed. In affirming the circuit court's decision, the appellate court held that coaches were not tenured under the school code and therefore were not entitled to reinstatement following improper suspension under the code.

5. In *Tate v. Livingston Parish School Board*, 444 So. 2d 219 (La. Ct. App. 1983), a teacher brought due process action against the school board when his coaching contract was not renewed. The court found that a high school athletic coach is not a "teacher" within the meaning of Teacher Tenure Act, and thus due process allowances in this act did not apply to coaches.

6. In *Leone v. Kimmell*, 335 A.2d 290 (Del. Super. Ct. 1975), an assistant football coach brought action against the school board to nullify the board's decision not to award him a contract. In ruling for the defendant school board, the court held that the school district's failure to grant a new contract was not a matter within the coverage of the professional negotiations agreement. Thus, the school district was not required to establish just cause, and the plaintiff was not permitted to pursue grievance procedures.

7. In *Chiodo v. Board of Education*, 215 N.W.2d 806 (Minn. Sup. Ct. 1974), a high school basketball coach brought action against the Board of Education for declaratory judgment that he had acquired tenure status as a coach pursuant to relevant statute. After reviewing said statute, the Minnesota Supreme Court held that although the plaintiff was certified to teach, he was not a "teacher" and therefore the statute did not apply to plaintiff basketball coach.

Dismissal—Procedural

In *procedural dismissal* cases, the reason for dismissal is not challenged, but the procedure followed by the employer to dismiss the employee is challenged. Cases are often brought by a coach who is dismissed without proper notice or hearing. In *Smith v. Board of Education* (see note 1), no prior notice was given to a coach whose contract was not renewed. Further, no reason was provided for his dismissal. The judge had to determine whether under state statute, a coach's contract was under the same procedural requirements as a teacher's contract. In *State Ex. Rel. Dennis v. Board of Education* (see note 1b), a teacher was given written notice that his duties to coach football and basketball would not be renewed. His other duties to substitute teach and coach track were also not renewed, but he received no notice regarding these duties. He brought a lawsuit contending that the proper procedures were not followed with respect to his dismissal to substitute teach and coach track.

NOTES _____

1. In the following cases the court found procedural safeguards were required:

(a) In *Smith v. Board of Education of County of Logan*, 341 S.E.2d 685 (W. Va. Sup. Ct. 1985), a teacher and football coach was dismissed from his coaching duties without prior notice and without any explanation. The issue before the court was whether a coach was entitled to the same procedural rights that a teacher was under the West Virginia code. The court concluded that a coach was entitled to the procedural rights. The court reversed the trial court's decision and ordered reinstatement of coach's position.

(b) In *State Ex. Rel. Dennis v. Board of Education*, 529 N.E.2d 1248 (Ohio Sup. Ct. 1988), a substitute teacher, who was also a football, basketball and track coach, was given written notice that his contracts to coach football and basketball would not be renewed. He was not, however, given notice that his substitute teaching and track coaching contracts would not be renewed, but they too were not renewed. The coach brought action claiming a procedural violation against the Board of Education for not giving him notice of his nonrenewal of contracts to substitute teach and coach track. The court of appeals upheld the lower court's decision to reinstate plaintiff as substitute teacher and track coach.

2. In the following cases, procedural safeguards were not required.

(a) In *Stang v. Independent School District No. 191*, 256 N.W.2d 82 (Minn. Sup. Ct. 1977), high school basketball coach brought action against school district alleging school district had failed to give him proper written notice and a hearing prior to his termination as coach. In ruling for the defendant school district, the judge held that the coach was not a teacher within the meaning of the Teacher Tenure Act, and thus was not entitled to a written notice and hearing.

(b) In *Matter of Hahn*, 386 N.W.2d. 789 (Minn. Ct. App. 1986), girls' basketball coach challenged the hearing officer's conclusion that school board properly refused to renew her coaching contract. The court of appeals held that the notice and hearing requirement was not necessary, and that the school district established adequate reasons for not renewing the coaching contract.

(c) In *Reid v. Huron Bd. of Educ.*, 449 N.W.2d 240 (S.D. 1989), a teacher brought suit against school board when his basketball coaching job was not renewed. The Supreme Court held that continuing contract law did apply to coaching portions of teacher's contract, and thus plaintiff should be reinstated as basketball coach.

Dismissal—Substantive

In a substantive dismissal case, the court must assess whether the reason for the dismissal is valid under the terms of the contract. For example, in *McLaughlin v. Machias School Committee* (see note 1), the court had to decide whether a coach's contract permitted the dismissal of the coach after the coach punched a student. In substantive dismissal cases, courts must determine whether there is just cause for the termination.

NOTES _____

1. In *McLaughlin v. Machias School Committee*, 385 A.2d. 53 (Me. Sup. Ct. 1978), a teacher who struck a student in the face during a "pick-up" basketball game was dismissed as "unfit to teach." The teacher challenged the dismissal. In affirming the lower court's decision, the Maine Supreme Court ruled that the school committee was acting within its rights when it dismissed the teacher.

2. In *Albert Lea Educational Ass'n v. Independent School Dist.*, 284 N.W.2d 1 (Minn. Sup. Ct. 1979), teacher and union brought action against the school district seeking court order to compel the issue of the teacher's dismissal as wrestling coach into grievance arbitration. The Minnesota Supreme Court held that nonrenewal of coaching assignment was not a condition of employment under the teaching contract and thus was not an arbitrable grievance.

3. In *Bd. of Ed. of Fort Madison Community v. Youel*, 282 N.W.2d 677 (Iowa Sup. Ct. 1979), a nonprobational teacher challenged the termination of his contract. In ruling for the board of education, the Iowa Supreme Court found a preponderance of competent evidence supporting board's claim that the teacher improperly handled the football program, and such evidence amounted to just cause for termination of the teacher's contract.

4. In *Matter of Hahn*, 386 N.W.2d. 789 (Minn Ct. App. 1986), a girls' basketball coach challenged the hearing officer's conclusion that the school board properly refused to renew her coaching contract. The court of appeals held that the notice and hearing requirement was not necessary, and that the school district established adequate reasons for not renewing the coaching contract.

Due Process

Coaches whose contracts are not renewed occasionally bring due process claims against the school district. These claims often fail because coaches are not entitled to the same due process requirements as teachers are under the Teacher Tenure Act. In *Hachiya v. Board of Education* (see note 1), however, the court ruled in favor of the plaintiff on a due process claim, but that was because plaintiff's claim related to his position as a teacher and not as a coach.

The Fourteenth Amendment guarantees that no person can be deprived of liberty or property interest without due process of law. All people are guaranteed proper notice and a hearing. Coaches have occasionally been unsuccessful in litigation, because the court has ruled that they were not deprived of a liberty and thus due process is not applicable. In *Richards v. Board of Ed. Jt. Sch. Dist. No. 1*,

Sheboygan (see note 6), the court ruled that a coach was not guaranteed due process because he was not deprived of a liberty or property right secured by the Fourteenth Amendment.

NOTES

1. In *Hachiya v. Board of Educ. Sch. Dist. 307*, 750 P.2d 383 (Kan. Sup. Ct. 1988), a dispute arose whether coaching duties were part of a teacher's primary contract. In this case, two teachers resigned their duties as athletics coaches, and the school board subsequently reduced the salary of their primary contracts by a certain amount. The Supreme Court of Kansas ruled for the teachers, stating that the resignation from the coaching positions did not affect the primary teaching contracts of the plaintiffs.

2. In *Williams v. Day*, 412 F. Supp. 336 (D.Ark. 1976), a teacher brought a civil rights action, alleging that school district had unlawfully failed to renew his coaching and teaching contract for constitutionally impermissible reasons. He also claimed that he was denied due process. Two years prior to the teacher's dismissal, he had become unhappy at not being named athletic director, and from that time until his dismissal, he reportedly had often failed to cooperate with the administration. The U.S. District Court held that non-renewal was due to personnel considerations and in no way based on the teacher's exercise of his First Amendment rights. The court further concluded that the school board had not prejudiced future employment opportunities for the teacher and thus did not deprive him of a constitutionally protected interest in liberty. The court also held that due process procedures had been followed.

3. In *Neal v. School Dist. of York*, 288 N.W.2d 725 (Neb. Sup. Ct. 1980), a school teacher brought action alleging that school district was contractually obligated to pay him for his services as varsity head basketball coach for a certain year. In ruling for defendants, the Supreme Court of Nebraska held that coaching contract was not subject to procedural and substantive requirements and that contract must remain in effect until terminated for just cause.

4. In *Diehl v. Albany County School District No. 1*, 694 F. Supp. 1534 (D. Wyo. 1988), a high school basketball coach whose contract was not renewed brought action against school district, claiming he was deprived of liberty without due process of law. The district court held that coach did not establish a liberty interest claim.

5. In *Swager v. Board of Education*, 688 P.2d 270 (Kan. Ct. App. 1984), a teacher brought an action against the defendant Board of Education to reinstate him as math teacher after the Board of Education had misinterpreted his resignation as basketball coach as a resignation from teaching and coaching. In ruling for the teacher, the appellate court reasoned that were his position as teacher not renewed, he would be entitled certain due process requirements, including a hearing, that the Board never provided.

6. In *Richards v. Board of Ed. Jt. Sch. Dist. No. 1, Sheboygan*, 206 N.W.2d 597 (Wis. Sup. Ct. 1973), a high school basketball coach brought due process action against school district when his contract was not renewed. The Wisconsin Supreme Court held that the school board's refusal to rehire the coach

did not deprive him of a liberty or property right secured by the Fourteenth Amendment.

Breach of Contract

Breach of contract claims have been filed by coaches against schools, as well as cases in which school boards have sued coaches. These cases occur when one of the parties to a contract believes the other party is failing to fulfill the terms of the contract. In *Unified School District v. Swanson* (see note 1), a school district brought a breach of contract action against a coach for refusing to accept supplemental teaching duties. The appellate court ruled against the school district, determining that the supplemental duties in question, although required under the contract, were unenforceable under Kansas law. See *Trevino v. Board of Trustees of West Oso Independent School District* (see note 2) for an example of a situation where a coach sued the school district regarding the terms of a contract.

NOTES

1. In *Unified School District No. 241, Wallace County v. Swanson*, 717 P.2d 526 (Kan. Ct. App. 1988), a school district brought a breach of contract action against a teacher who refused to accept extra duties. In reversing the lower court's decision, the appellate court ruled for the teacher, stating that teacher's contract could not be terminated for refusal of teacher to accept supplemental duties.

2. In *Trevino v. Board of Trustees of West Oso Independent School District*, 783 S.W.2d 806 (Tex. Ct. App. 1990), a high school football coach and athletic director was assigned duties to teach two history classes per day. The coach filed a breach of contract suit against the school district seeking an injunction to prevent the school district from assigning him the teaching duties. In examining the terms of the contract, the court ruled for the school district, upholding the trial court's decision.

Contracts Involving Student-Athletes

Even though NCAA regulations prohibit the payment of student-athletes for their athletic participation, some courts have concluded that the offer of an athletic scholarship by an institution and its acceptance by a student-athlete constitute a contractual relationship between the parties. The issue of an athletic scholarship as a contract is but one of many contractual issues that may arise during the course of the relationship between a student-athlete and his or her institution. The reader should also be aware of other contractual issues involving student-athletes, which include letter of intent, NCAA student-athlete statement of eligibility, student-athlete consent-disclosure statements, student-athlete drug-testing consent forms, and contractual failure to provide an education.

Scheduling

Traditionally, scheduling of athletic events on the intercollegiate level has been free of litigation. If for some reason—for example, a change of coaches—an institution wanted to drop a contracted commitment to play against another institution, the contest has up until now generally been dropped without much difficulty. Recently, however, some scheduling problems have resulted in threats of litigation.

In 1982 the University of Missouri bought its way out of its contract with San Diego State for $50,000. It did so by exercising the contract's forfeiture clause, because Missouri felt that the revenue received would not have justified travel expenses. Exhibit 3–4 provides an example of a game contract.

NOTES _____

1. *University of Washington v. Ingram,* No. C811426 (W.D. Wash.), a case involving football schedules, was dismissed by the district court because it lacked jurisdiction in a suit between states. Washington sued Florida State when defendant institution, citing rising travel costs, canceled a scheduled football game (the 1982 season opener at Washington). Washington sought damages of $350,000 for losses in tickets, programs, concessions, parking, and other revenues. In addition, it sought $400,000 for lost opportunity of television coverage and loss of prestige, recruiting opportunities, and early season national rankings. The plaintiff went on to argue, "If two institutions enter into a contract and one institution says twelve months before the game that it is not going to play, it's not reasonable or responsible to expect the other institution to readjust its schedule. A school needs three or four years to readjust its schedule, and if there is mutual consent, then there is no problem. But there is a terrible problem if mutual consent does not exist."

Texas El Paso agreed to play plaintiff in place of Florida State for a guarantee of $100,000. Florida State, meanwhile, juggled its schedule and played the University of Cincinnati for its season opener. Florida State argued that travel expenses forced the cancellation of the game after Washington refused a Florida State proposal to include travel costs as part of expenses. "People have to cooperate to keep intercollegiate athletics going," stated Florida State. "Football is our biggest money-making sport. If we have a loss, it's hard to meet our athletic budget. You've got to respect other universities, and you've got to understand their difficulties and try to be as flexible and cooperative as possible." The case was dismissed by the District Court because it lacked jurisdiction in a suit between states.

2. The NCAA has specific limitations on the number of contests, including scrimmages, that a member can play. The limitations in Division I are 27 basketball games, 11 football games, and 20 soccer games. Games played in Hawaii, Alaska, or Puerto Rico do not count toward this number (see 1993–94 *NCAA Manual,* figures 17-1 and 17-2).

3. In *Sult v. Gilbert,* 148 Fla. 31, 3 So. 2d 729 (Fla. Sup. Ct. 1941), two schools had agreed to play a football game. Later, one of the schools refused

Exhibit 3–4
Game Contract

 PENNSTATE　　　　**Intercollegiate Athletics Contract**

This agreement is made and entered into this _____ day of _____, 19 _____,
by and between The·Pennsylvania State University and _____
_____.

The parties agree to the following conditions:

(1) To participate in _____ competition:

　　　on _____, 19 _____, at _____ at _____ p.m.
　　　on _____, 19 _____, at _____ at _____ p.m.
　　　on _____, 19 _____, at _____ at _____ p.m.
　　　on _____, 19 _____, at _____ at _____ p.m.

(2) The financial arrangements shall be _____
_____.

(3) The contest(s) shall be governed in all respects, including the eligibility of the participants and the number of
participants, by rules and regulations of the National Collegiate Athletic Association and the Big Ten Conference,
or any conference or association to which either or both of the parties may belong.

(4) Officials shall be _____
_____.

(5) The visiting team shall be allowed _____ complimentary tickets.

(6) All radio rights shall be the property of the home team, except reciprocal rights for the visiting team for one free outlet.

(7) The over-the-air broadcast and cable television rights for Penn State's men's basketball games have been assigned to
the Big Ten Conference, Inc., which in turn has contracted with certain television networks and cable broadcasters
("Conference Contracts"). Conditions in the Conference Contracts relating to television exposure and/or exclusivity shall
apply to Penn State's participation in the Games. Any discussion regarding the conditions of the Conference Contracts
should be directed to the Big Ten Conference office. The following principles shall regulate television revenue
distribution:

(a) CBS Sports: payment, if any, to opponent is the responsibility of the network; (b) Raycom: payment, if any, is the
responsibility of Raycom; (c) ESPN: payment to opponent governed by existing crossover agreement with 1.) Big East
Conference, or 2.)Atlantic Coast Conference, or 3.)Western Athletic Conference, or 4.)Southeastern Conference, or
5.)Southwest Conference. Payment, if any, to a team not covered by these crossover agreements should be negotiated
with the Big Ten Conference office.

(8) Other conditions shall include _____
_____
_____.

For The Pennsylvania State University　　　　　　For _____

Name: _____　　　　Name: _____
Position: _____　　　　Position: _____

Signature: _____　　　　Signature: _____
Date: _____　　　　Date: _____

Signature: _____　　　　Signature: _____
Position: _____　　　　Position: _____
Date: _____　　　　Date: _____

Please return signed contract to Penn State Intercollegiate Athletics, Athletic Business Office,
237 Recreation Building, University Park, PA 16802. Retain WHITE copy for your files.

Distribution: White-Visiting AD, Yellow-Home Business Office, Pink-Home AD, Blue-Home Events to play the game, and a controversy arose as to whether the game would be played. The Florida High School Athletic Association ruled that the contract did not require a game between the schools. On appeal, the Florida Supreme Court decided that the athletic association's settlement was sufficient review and it would not interfere with their decision.

Physicians' Contracts

The need to have a physician on duty at athletic events is obvious. Injuries are a possibility in all athletic contests, and immediate treatment and diagnosis of an injury by a qualified doctor are desirable and often critical. The presence of a physician at certain athletic contests may be a requirement of most schools' insurance policies. However, it is important from the standpoint of the school to acquire the doctor's services as an independent contractor and not as an employee. If the doctor is an employee of the institution or school district, the school could be held vicariously liable for a tort (discussed in Chapters 6 and 7) committed by the doctor in the performance of medical duties for the school. If the doctor is an independent contractor, however, the school will not be at risk.

The key difference between an employee and an independent contractor is the degree of control and direction exercised over the individual worker by the institution. An employee is subject to a much higher degree of control than an independent contractor. Because of the high degree of control, the employer can be held responsible for the acts of the employee in the performance of the employee's assigned duties. The independent contractor's actions generally cannot be attributed to the institution that contracted for his or her services (see Exhibit 3–5).

Officials' Contracts

As with physicians, the need to have officials at athletic events is obvious. There has to be someone present to enforce the rules of the game—someone who is independent of the participants. The referee or official can be involved in two distinct areas where tort liability can arise: personal injury of participants and/or spectators and judicial review of a decision of an official. (Both are discussed in Chapters 6 and 7.) In order to protect the school or college from being held vicariously liable for the actions of officials, it is important that the officials be deemed independent contractors. Exhibit 3–6 is an example of a model contract between schools and sports officials. Particular attention should be given to clause 3, "official's status," which clearly states that the official has agreed to work as an independent

Exhibit 3–5
A Physician's Contract

AGREEMENT

STATE_____

COUNTY_____

THIS AGREEMENT made and entered into the _____day of _____, 19xx, by and between _____, a college having its principal place of business in ____ _____ (hereinafter referred to as "College"), and DR. _____, a citizen and resident of _____, (hereinafter referred to as "Physician").

WITNESSETH:

WHEREAS, College is desirous of obtaining the services of Physician in connection with its intercollegiate sports program, and

WHEREAS, Physician is skilled in the practice of medicine and is willing to assist College with its medical programs in its intercollegiate sports program,

NOW THEREFORE, in consideration of the convenants and promises contained herein, the parties agree as follows:

1. College hereby retains and Physician agrees to be retained by College as College's consultant in College's intercollegiate sports program for the school year 1985–86.

2. Physician will act as a consultant with the College's coaches, trainers, athletes and other personnel with regard to medical problems incurred by athletes in the College's intercollegiate sports program. Physician's consulting services shall include attendance at home football games whenever possible. In Physician's absence, he will attempt to find qualified medical help to attend. Physician will be available for consultation one day per week.

3. Physician agrees to review participation medical records on a yearly basis.

4. Physician shall make recommendations to the coaching staff, trainers, and other personnel as to the handling of all medical matters with regards to the athletes in the College's intercollegiate sports program. Such recommendations shall include prescribing treatment for injuries and other medical problems, and recommendations for surgical and other hospital procedures when necessary. All physician charges for such surgery and other hospital procedures are not covered under the terms of this agreement.

5. Physician shall make decisions on athletes practicing, returning to practice or playing in athletic contests. In absence of Physician, he will delegate authority to another physician, head trainer or sports medicine coordinator.

6. Physician will supervise student trainers and graduate assistants through the head athletic trainer and sports medicine coordinator.

7. Physician will make the decision to send an athlete to another physician or delegate that decision to another individual.

8. If an athlete seeks a second opinion without consent of team physician, payment is not guaranteed.

9. As compensation for all consulting services rendered hereunder, College agrees to pay to Physician the sum of $_____ to be paid upon execution of this agreement.

10. It is understood and agreed that Physician is an independent contractor with regard to all consulting services to be rendered hereunder, and is not acting as College's agent, employee or servant. It is also understood that Physician is not an insurer of results in any medical treatment rendered under the terms of this agreement.

11. This agreement is to be construed under and governed by the laws of the State of ____.

IN WITNESS WHEREOF, the parties hereto have executed this agreement in duplicate originals on the day and year first above written.

_____COLLEGE

By: _____

DR: _____

By: _____

Exhibit 3–6
An Official's Contract

MODEL CONTRACT BETWEEN
SCHOOLS AND SPORTS OFFICIALS

Please note that this is a "Model" and may have to be modified to fit the particular circumstances of your local association and/or schools at which you officiate. Also, it is based upon general principles of law; therefore, you should review it with a local attorney prior to using it due to differences of state law.

The _____ (home school) [hereinafter "School"] of _____ (city and state) and _____ (official's name) of _____ (of- ficial's address) [hereinafter "Official"] enter into the following Agreement:

1. CONTEST. The Official agrees to officiate a _____ (level) _____ (sport) contest between _____ (home school) and _____ (visitor school) at _____ (place) _____ (city and state) on _____ (date) at _____ (time). The other official(s) is/are _____ _____.

2. PAYMENT. In consideration of such services, the _____ (home school) will pay the Official within _____ days of the game date a fee of _____ (amount), plus mileage at the rate of 20 cents/mile for _____ miles, in the amount of $_____.

3. OFFICIAL'S STATUS. The Official agrees to work this game as an independent contractor.

4. OFFICIAL'S REPRESENTATION. The Official represents that he/she is, or will be by the date of the contest, a duly licensed official in this state authorized to officiate this contest. If it is found to be otherwise, this Agreement shall become null and void.

5. INTERPRETATION. The Constitution, By-Laws and rules and regulations of the ____ (state association) and of the _____ (local association) are consid- ered a part of this Agreement and shall govern, except as modified by this Agreement, any disputes arising out of this Agreement. Both parties to this Agreement agree to be so bound.

6. VOIDING OF CONTRACT. This contract shall become null and void upon probation or suspension of either the School or the Official by the _____ (state association).

7. CANCELLATION/POSTPONEMENT. This contract may be canceled at any time by the mutual written consent of both parties. This contract is voidable if either party cannot comply with its terms for any sufficient reason.

A. Sufficient Reason. If the contest is canceled by mutual written consent or for sufficient reason (including, but not limited to, unfavorable weather, illness, accident, or injury) and the Official is not notified in time to prevent travel to the game site, the Official shall be paid the round-trip mileage at the rate of 20 cents/mile. If the contest begins, but is then canceled due to unfavorable weather, the Official shall be paid the fee and mileage expenses set forth in Paragraph 2.

B. Insufficient Reason. If the game is canceled for any insufficient reason, or if either school participating in the contest no longer desires the Official to officiate, the Official shall be paid the fee.

C. Rescheduling. If the contest is postponed and rescheduled, the Official shall be paid the fee set forth in Paragraph 2. If the agreed time of the contest is changed, the Official will be given the first opportunity to officiate at the new time, but if the Official is unable to do so, the Official shall be paid the fee set forth in Paragraph 2.

D. Official's Failure To Officiate. If the Official fails to officiate the game for a reason other than a sufficient reason, then the Official shall pay the school an amount equal to the fee within _____ days of the game date.

E. Payment. Payment of the fee and/or mileage as a result of cancellation, resched- uling, or postponement shall be made by the School and received by the Official within _____days after the original date set for the game.

Exhibit 3–6 continued

> **F. Notification.** All notification concerning the provisions of this paragraph shall be in writing to the below address. If initial notification is by phone then a written confirmation shall thereafter be sent within seven days.
>
> **8. ACCEPTANCE.** This contract is void if not signed by the Official and the School on or before _____ (date).

Date: _____	Date: _____
School: _____	Official: _____
By: _____	Address: _____
(Name), (Title)	_____
Address: _____	Business Phone: _____
_____	Home Phone: _____
School Phone: _____	
Home Phone: _____	

> *Copyright © 1985 by Melvin S. Narol, Esquire. Jamieson, Moore, Peskin, and Spicer, Princeton, New Jersey. Permission to use and reproduce this Model Contract is hereby granted provided the above copyright notice is set forth on the document.*
>
> **National Association of Sports Officials, 2017 Lathrop Avenue, Racine, WI 53405.**
> **Phone (414) 632-5448.**

Copyright 1985 by Mel Narol, Esquire, Pellettieri, Rabstein and Altman, Princeton, NJ.

contractor. The independent contractor status is beneficial for the school because it shields it from attempts to hold the school liable for improper actions of the official and avoids any liability for workers' compensation should the official be injured.

Facility Contracts

When an institution competing in athletics does not own an arena or a stadium, it is necessary to enter into agreements for the use of these facilities. In reaching an agreement for the use of a facility, the athletic administrator should take great care in detailing the responsibilities and duties of both parties to the contract. In addition to the use of the facility, consideration should be given to the amount of rent charged, the method of payment, and the specific services provided for the rent. The responsibility for the promotion of the event, the setting up of the arena for the event, and the provision of personnel to run the arena (such as a security force, ticket takers, a public address announcer, and various work crews) need to be addressed in the contract. The time of the event itself and the availability of the arena for warm-ups before the event should also be explicity stated in the contract. In addition, any potential conflicts between multiple lessees should be addressed in the drawing of an agreement.

Third-party agreements, such as radio or television contracts between the institution and the media, also need to be considered in the drafting of a contract for the use of a facility in case certain accommodations are necessary. Insurance requirements must also be considered. Generally, facilities require specific types of insurance coverage to be carried by the institution before they will allow it to use their facilities for a particular event. A review of the insurance carried by the institution should be carried out before an agreement is reached. Exhibit 3–7 is an example of a facility contract.

NOTE ───

1. For further information, see the following law review article: Graves, "Coaches in the Courtroom: Recovery in Actions for Breach of Employment Contracts," 12 *J.C. & U.L.* 545 (1986).

Marketing, Promotional Contracts

One of the more recent developments in the sports industry has been the arrival of the sports marketing firm. Sports marketing firms offer a variety of services to sports organizations, including market research, event promotion, and consulting. Many of these firms specialize in intercollegiate and Olympic sport, which presents another area of contract negotiation between the sports marketing firm and the institution. These contracts vary considerably, depending on the requirements of the university, the services provided, and the individuals negotiating the contract.

As yet, there is no published decision relevant to a contract dispute between a sports marketer and an institution. Litigation has, however, been filed involving a contractual relationship between Raycom, Inc., a sports marketing firm, and U.S.A. Sports International Inc. (see *Raycom v. Aebli*, Docket No. C-C-84-29M (D.N.C. 1989). This case was settled prior to being heard before the court. The complaint filed by Raycom and a counterclaim filed by USA Sports International dealt with an agreement between the two to produce and promote the Glasnost Bowl, a football game in Russia between American college teams. In the counterclaim, USA Sports International alleged that Raycom breached their contract with USA Sports International by failing to provide funds to the joint venture and by executing contracts with the University of Southern California, the University of Illinois, and ABC in its own name rather than the joint venture name. The case is waiting to be heard.

Exhibit 3–8 provides an example of a contract between a college athletic conference and a marketing firm. The contract outlines the requirements of the conference and the services to be provided by the marketing firm.

Exhibit 3–7
A Facility Contract

MULLINS CENTER

contract # _____

WILLIAM D. MULLINS MEMORIAL CENTER
FACILITY AGREEMENT

This agreement, entered into this _____ day of_____
199__ ,by and between Ogden Entertainment Services, an independent
contractor retained by the University of Massachusetts Amherst
and the University of Massachusetts Building Authority to manage
the William D. Mullins Memorial Center. (hereinafter referred to
as CENTER) and:

```
    Name:_____
     Org:_____
 Address:_____
    City: _____ State: _____ Zip:_____
   Phone: _____ Fax: _____
```

(hereinafter referred to as CONTRACTOR).

        Rent Category: ____University ____Non-University

It is understood and agreed that the term CENTER will, throughout
the conditions of this agreement, refer to the duly appointed
manager of the Mullins Center, Ogden Entertainment Services.

CONTRACTOR Warrants that said use is for the following and no
other purpose:

_____
_____
_____
_____

Spaces utilized for the above stated purpose will be as follows:

_____
_____
_____

Payment for spaces utilized for the above stated purpose will be
as follows:

_____
_____
_____

Exhibit 3–7 continued

CONTRACTOR also shall pay CENTER $_____ for rehearsal
day(s), and $_____ for move-in and $_____ for
move-out.

CONTRACTOR agrees to pay all reimbursable expenses required for
the completion of this event according to the Schedule of User
Fees in force on the date of this event.

CONTRACTOR is required to provide, on demand of the CENTER,
documentation of qualification for NON-PROFIT status as it may
relate to this agreement.

Through the conditions of this agreement, "gross ticket sales"
will be total ticket sales less any applicable federal, state,
and local admission taxes and Mullins Center Facility Charge when
applicable.

CONTRACTOR agrees to pay $_____ with the return of this
signed agreement as DEPOSIT. Thereafter, CONTRACTOR agrees to
make additional deposit with CENTER at address on this agreement,
of such sums as CENTER feels are necessary to cover those costs
which the CENTER would encounter on behalf of CONTRACTOR in
relation to the event, and to make such payment by certified
check payable to the Mullins Center. CENTER agrees that such
demand will not be made more than twenty days prior to the first
date of the event described herein.

CONTRACTOR agrees to provide prior to_____, a public
liability INSURANCE policy in which the CENTER, The University of
Massachusetts Amherst, its trustees, officers, employees and
agents, Ogden Entertainment Services, and CONTRACTOR are named as
insureds, of an acceptable certificate of insurance, with minimum
policy limits of:

- $1,000,000 for injuries, including death, sustained by
  one person.
- $5,000.000 for injuries, including death, sustained by
  two or more persons from a single occurrence.
- $100,000 for property damage.

The terms of such coverage to coincide with the dates of this
agreement, including move-in and move-out. Insurance policy
shall contain provisions that prevent the policy from being
materially changed or cancelled without prior ten (10) day
written notice to CENTER. Aggregate limits as they relate to the
insurance requirements here stated shall be on a per event basis.
All coverage and limits shall be on an occurrence basis, not on a
claims made basis.

Exhibit 3–7 continued

CONTRACTOR agrees to provide CENTER with _____
COMPLIMENTARY TICKETS for each performance covered by this
agreement.

It is agreed that the on-sale date for the event covered by this
agreement will be _____.

Upon CONTRACTOR request and upon receipt of specific event
information from CONTRACTOR, CENTER will provide an event cost
estimate. This cost estimate is a good faith attempt to identify
event costs. However, an event cost estimate is not a price
quotation, and CONTRACTOR is responsible to CENTER for full
payment of the actual costs billed to the event.

This agreement pertains to the main arena only. The Rink and
Link are separate and exempt from this agreement unless otherwise
noted. The Mullins Center reserves the right to program
simultaneous activities in all the facilities as long as in the
CENTER'S judgement, the activities do not interfere with each
other.

ADDITIONAL COVENANTS AND AGREEMENTS:
_____
_____
_____
_____
_____

Attachments hereby incorporated as part of this agreement:

_____Terms and Conditions _____Schedule of User Fees
_____Ticket Office Rider _____Catering Quotation
_____Explanation of Fees _____ _____

All conditions and regulations set forth on the attached
documents are hereby incorporated as a part of this agreement.

             For Ogden Entertainment   For CONTRACTOR:
             Services:

             BY_____   BY_____
               Lee A. Esckilsen,   _____
               Executive Director   Title_____

             DATE_____   DATE_____

                                             FEDERAL ID#_____

                            iii

Exhibit 3–7 continued

WILLIAM D. MULLINS MEMORIAL CENTER
FACILITY AGREEMENT
Terms and Conditions

For the purposes of these terms and conditions, "CENTER" shall mean Ogden
Entertainment Services, an independent contractor retained by the University
of Massachusetts Amherst and the University of Massachusetts Building
Authority to manage the William D. Mullins Memorial Center.

I.   BUILDING CONTROL

A.   CONTROL OF FACILITY: In occupying the building, property and/or grounds
at CENTER the CONTRACTOR understands that CENTER does not relinquish the right
to control the management thereof, and to enforce all necessary laws, rules,
and regulations.

B.   RIGHT OF ENTRY: Duly authorized representatives of CENTER may enter
and/or be present within the CENTER premises, including those areas to be used
for the event described herein at any time and on any occasion without any
restrictions whatsoever. All facilities, including the area which is the
subject of this permit, and all parking areas shall at all times be under the
charge and control of CENTER.

C.   NON-EXCLUSIVE RIGHT: CENTER shall retain the right to use any portion
of its facility not covered by this agreement. CENTER also retains the right
to re-enter or use any portion of its facility which becomes vacant for
sufficient time to warrant doing so. CENTER shall retain the proceeds from
all such actions.

D.   INTERRUPTION OR TERMINATION OF EVENT: CENTER shall retain the right to
cause the interruption of any performance in the interest of public safety,
and to likewise cause the termination of such performance when in the sole
judgement of CENTER such act is necessary in the interest of public safety.

E.   EVACUATION OF FACILITY: Should it become necessary in the judgement of
CENTER to evacuate the premises because of a bomb threat or for other reasons
of public safety, the CONTRACTOR will retain possession of the premises for
sufficient time to complete presentation of activity without additional rental
charge providing such time does not interfere with another building
commitment. If it is not possible to complete presentation of the activity,
CENTER charges shall be forfeited, prorated, or adjusted at the discretion of
the CENTER based on the situation, and the CONTRACTOR hereby waives any claim
for damages or compensation from the CENTER.

F.   PROGRAM APPROVAL: CENTER reserves the right of approval for any
performance, exhibition, or entertainment to be offered under this agreement,
and CONTRACTOR agrees that no such activity or part thereof shall be given or
held if CENTER presents written objection on the grounds of character
offensive to public morals, failure to uphold event advertising claims, or
violations of agreed event content restrictions agreed to by both parties at
the time of the completion of this agreement.

G.   DEFACEMENT OF FACILITY: CONTRACTOR shall not alter, add to, deface,
repair, and/or change CENTER facilities and grounds in any manner whatsoever,
except with the prior written consent of CENTER. The facilities and grounds
shall be maintained and vacated, as and when required, in as good condition as
they were upon entry of CONTRACTOR therein, reasonable wear and tear accepted.
If CENTER and CONTRACTOR agree to alter any CENTER facilities in any way,
CONTRACTOR shall be solely responsible for the cost of restoration.

Exhibit 3–7 continued

H.   DAMAGES: CONTRACTOR agrees to pay upon demand for all damages and or injury done to CENTER facilities and personnel by CONTRACTOR, by CONTRACTOR'S associated staff and crew, by CONTRACTOR'S artist(s) and client(s), and by CONTRACTOR'S patrons. CENTER reserves the right to retain and apply the deposit and box office receipts (if deposit is not sufficient) for such damage and/or injury, notice thereof having been given to CONTRACTOR. CENTER will provide detailed billing and accounting to CONTRACTOR when needed restoration or replacement of damaged items is completed; or, in the case of injuries to personnel, when the total cost associated with the injury is compiled.

I.   LOST ARTICLES: CENTER shall have the sole right to collect and have the custody of articles left in the premises by persons attending any performance, exhibition, or entertainment given or held on the premises, and the CONTRACTOR or any person in the CONTRACTOR'S employ shall not interfere with the collection or custody of such articles.

J.   ANNOUNCEMENTS: CENTER reserves the right to make announcements or display signage during the period of this agreement which would relate to future attractions and commercial messages. CENTER is also entitled to make such announcements as CENTER may deem necessary at any time in the interest of public safety. CONTRACTOR agrees that it will cooperate and will cause its agents and performers to cooperate with the delivery of such announcements for public safety, including, but not limited to, announcements to require patrons to return to their seats, and/or "No Smoking" announcements. CENTER reserves the right to display posters, banners, and announcements, and to distribute literature concerning any activity it deems worthy.

K.   SIGNS AND POSTERS: CONTRACTOR will not post or allow to be posted, any signs, cards or posters except upon such display areas as CENTER may provide. Use of such areas in a nonexclusive right. All material is subject to approval by CENTER. By such approval, however, CENTER does not accept any responsibility in any manner for content. CENTER will remove any unauthorized signs at the CONTRACTOR'S expense.

L.   OPEN HOURS: Doors shall be opened for event in accordance with advertised times, CENTER policy, and Massachusetts Law.

M.   INTERMISSIONS: CONTRACTOR agrees that every public performance which is not staged within a single hour, will have an intermission period of not less than ten (10) minutes, excepting religious services or other engagements specifically excluded. CENTER reserves the right to assess a fee in advance, or a penalty after the fact, if an intermission is not held due to act or omission of CONTRACTOR, CONTRACTOR'S associated staff, crew, artists, clients, or patrons.

N.   OBJECTIONABLE PERSONS: CENTER reserves the right to refuse admission to, eject or cause to be ejected from the premises, any objectionable person or persons; and neither the CENTER nor any of its officers, agents, or employees shall be liable to CONTRACTOR for any damages that may be sustained by CONTRACTOR through the exercise by CENTER of such right.

O.   SECURITY: CENTER will exercise all reasonable care to safeguard property of the CONTRACTOR while in the facilities. However, CENTER shall assume no responsibility whatsoever, for any property placed in CENTER facilities and is hereby expressly relieved and discharged from any and all liability for any loss, injury, or damage to persons or property that may be sustained by reason of the occupancy of CENTER facilities or any part thereof under this agreement. All security or other protective services desired by CONTRACTOR must be arranged for and by special agreement with CENTER.

Exhibit 3–7 continued

II.   SERVICES PROVIDED

A.   HEAT, LIGHT, UTILITIES: During the period of this agreement, CENTER
will provide ventilation, air conditioning or heat, and overhead light for
ordinary use, subject to a utility charge as outlined in the Schedule of User
Fees in force on the date of the event. CENTER will provide at CONTRACTOR'S
expense and at its discretion, continuous cleaning of corridors, public
lobbies, and restrooms with necessary equipment, materials, supplies, labor,
and supervision.

B.   ADDITIONAL SPACE: Available dressing rooms, office space and storage
space will be provided by CENTER at the sole discretion of CENTER, at no cost
to CONTRACTOR. All other services or conditions will be at the expense of
CONTRACTOR.

C.   ADDITIONAL SERVICES AND STAFFING: All labor and services not
specifically mentioned above (see Services Provided) but required for the
execution of CONTRACTOR'S event, shall be secured by CENTER and be considered
reimbursable costs payable to the CENTER by the CONTRACTOR, according to rates
set down in the Schedule of User Fees in force on the date of the event. Such
services shall include, but are not limited to, those performed by
technicians, laborers, security guards, ushers, house manager, traffic
personnel, paramedics, stage manager, technical director, house electricians
and cashiers.

In cases of special custodial services necessitated by an event, CONTRACTOR
shall pay costs of these services as a reimbursable expense to CENTER. CENTER
retains the right to determine the appropriate number of personnel necessary
to properly serve and protect the public. All personnel provided by the
CENTER shall remain employees of the CENTER and will be under direct CENTER
staff supervision.

D.   CONTRACT SERVICES: CENTER reserves the exclusive right to furnish,
install or provide electricity, gas, water, waste water, compressed air and
steam services. Such services shall be provided on written order at the then
prevailing published rates for such services. CONTRACTOR may contract with
persons approved by CENTER for services not available from CENTER, provided
however, that such approval shall not be unreasonably withheld.

E.   CATERING: All catering must be performed by CENTER'S contracted caterer
unless agreement to the contrary is reached in writing no fewer than ten (10)
days prior to event.

III. EVENT REQUIREMENTS

A.   TALENT CONTRACT: The CONTRACTOR certifies and attests that CONTRACTOR
has a valid, properly executed, and compatible contract with the performers
whose services form the basis for the desire to rent the facility. The
CONTRACTOR shall submit to CENTER upon demand, a copy of said contract with
the performers.

B.   PRODUCTION REQUIREMENTS: CONTRACTOR agrees to furnish CENTER with
detailed production and house requirements and/or information for CONTRACTOR'S
use of space(s) no later than four (4) weeks prior to the beginning of the use
period. The intent of the foregoing is to enable both parties of this
agreement to anticipate and work out in advance, any problems that might or
can occur, relating to CONTRACTOR'S use of space(s). CENTER requires advance
information in order to schedule the appropriate personnel and equipment for
CONTRACTOR'S use of space(s) and to compile expense estimates.

Exhibit 3-7 continued

C.   EQUIPMENT AND UTILITIES: CENTER will provide equipment and utilities presently owned by CENTER at CONTRACTOR'S expense as listed in the Schedule of User Fees in force on the date of the event. Additional equipment or utilities required shall be provided and paid for by CONTRACTOR. CENTER reserves the right to operate/control all equipment and utilities used for CONTRACTOR'S event.

D.   CONTRACTOR PROVIDED EQUIPMENT: CONTRACTOR warrants that all equipment brought into CENTER shall be in good working order and meets applicable safety regulations. CONTRACTOR accepts responsibility for proper and safe operation, supervision and guarding of its equipment.

E.   PRODUCTION CONSULTING: CENTER will provide a reasonable amount of complimentary production consulting; however, a charge will be levied for any excessive demands placed upon CENTER employees.

F.   SCHEDULE CONSULTING: CENTER agrees that all load-ins, set-ups, strikes, load-outs, and any other work calls shall be scheduled at times specified by CENTER unless CONTRACTOR has specific schedule obligations from other contract agreements that may pertain to CONTRACTOR'S use of CENTER. In the absence of any such obligations and/or waivers, all strikes and load-outs shall take place immediately following CONTRACTOR'S use of space(s). Should CONTRACTOR fail to fulfill the obligations of the schedule as specified, then CENTER may remove and store all equipment and/or property belonging to CONTRACTOR at CONTRACTOR'S expense and risk.

G.   AUTHORIZED AGENT: An authorized representative of CONTRACTOR with decision making capabilities must be on the premises, in and/or available to the space(s) being used by CONTRACTOR for the duration of any load-in, set-up, rehearsal(s), performance(s), strike, and load-out of all scheduled events, unless prior arrangements have been made with the appropriate staff of CENTER.

H.   PUBLIC ADDRESS SYSTEM: CENTER shall furnish at CONTRACTOR expense, the facility's public address system as needed. This system shall be operated according to rules and regulations established by CENTER.

I.   ADDITIONAL EQUIPMENT: If CONTRACTOR requires additional production, stage, shop, house, and other building equipment beyond that which is considered "in-house" then CENTER can and/or will rent or procure such equipment and charge to CONTRACTOR, any cost associated with obtaining such equipment with an added 15% service charge. If CONTRACTOR declines to have CENTER obtain such equipment, then CONTRACTOR must coordinate the use of any outside services with CENTER. The intent of the foregoing is to insure both parties, that outside services are compatible with CENTER policies and facilities.

J.   TRANSPORTATION: All transportation of CONTRACTOR equipment and personnel required for this event, shall be the responsibility of the CONTRACTOR.

K.   CLOSED CIRCUIT TELEVISION EQUIPMENT: CONTRACTOR agrees to provide primary and back up projection units for all closed circuit television events, said units to be in place and tested in the facility no less than four (4) hours before the scheduled event time.

L.   NOTIFICATION: It is the obligation and responsibility of CONTRACTOR to timely inform the artist's management and/or client(s) contracted with CONTRACTOR, of any and all general conditions, restrictions, and policies specified in this agreement. CENTER shall not be held responsible for any discrepancies, difficulties, and/or charges that might occur if CONTRACTOR'S artist and/or client(s) is or was not aware of CENTER restrictions and policies.

Exhibit 3–7 continued

IV.   CONCESSIONS AND NOVELTIES

A.   CONCESSIONS: CONTRACTOR shall not sell or serve any concessions
including, but not limited to, cigarettes, cigars, beverages, food, gum or
refreshments of any kind, within the leased space except with prior written
permission from CENTER. Programs and novelties may be offered for sale in
leased space during period of this agreement with approval in advance from
CENTER. CENTER shall designate stand locations for merchandising such items.

B.   SALES BY LESSEE: CENTER shall receive a 40% commission on all items
sold by CONTRACTOR inclusive of the cost of CENTER'S sellers. CENTER will
provide all sellers for all sales. CONTRACTOR is responsible for payment of
all appropriate taxes including Massachusetts state sales tax. CONTRACTOR
warrants that it has all necessary rights and permission to sell its
novelties, and shall hold CENTER, the University of Massachusetts Amherst, its
trustees, officers, employees, and agents, and the University of Massachusetts
Building Authority (UMBA), harmless from any and all disputes arising from
these sales. CENTER reserves the right to prevent the sale of any item in
CENTER facilities.

C.   SALES BY CENTER: CENTER reserves the right to sell, at its discretion,
any of its concession items that are appropriate to this event. All proceeds
from sale of CENTER concession items will remain with CENTER.

D.   FREE SAMPLES: No free samples of food, beverage, or any product, may be
given away or otherwise distributed without prior written approval of CENTER.

V.   SHIPPING AND STORAGE

A.   SHIPMENTS: CONTRACTOR shall not direct shipments to CENTER prior to the
first set up day as listed on the face of this agreement, without advance
written permission of CENTER. CENTER reserves the right to refuse
CONTRACTOR'S shipments prior to said date.

B.   STORAGE: CONTRACTOR assumes all responsibility for any goods or
materials which may be placed in storage with CENTER before, during, or after
event.

C.   CONTRACTOR PROPERTY: CENTER will accept delivery of property addressed
to CONTRACTOR only as a courtesy to CONTRACTOR, and CONTRACTOR hereby releases
and agrees to hold harmless and indemnify, the William D. Mullins Memorial
Center, the University of Massachusetts Amherst, its trusteess, officers,
employees and agents, the University of Massachusetts Building Authority
(UMBA), and Ogden Entertainment Services for loss of or damage to, including,
but not limited to, destruction of such property in the receipt, handling,
care or custody of such property at any time. CONTRACTOR further agrees to
indemnify and hold harmless, all of the aforesaid indemnities from all claims,
lawsuits, litigation, judgements, damages, and costs arising out of loss of or
damage to, including, but not limited to, destruction of such property on the
premises of CENTER. Under no circumstances shall the CENTER or any of the
aforesaid indemnities be considered a bailee of such property at any time, for
any reason.

VI.   SETTLEMENT

A.   SETTLEMENT DATE AND TIME: Settlement shall occur on the final day of
this agreement or no later than thirty (30) days following presentation of the
final billing, and shall consist of CENTER remission to CONTRACTOR, all ticket
office receipts, less CENTER charges, ticket office labor and equipment fees,
all reimbursable expenses, and other appropriate fees as allowed for in this
agreement. If not all of the reimbursable expenses are known at the time of
settlement, CENTER shall withhold an estimate, plus ten percent (10%) as a

Exhibit 3–7 continued

contingency, unused portion to be returned to CONTRACTOR with final settlement statement as soon thereafter as possible. CONTRACTOR waives all rights to that portion of the ticket office receipts necessary to pay ACTUAL costs accrued by CENTER. Where no ticket office receipts are involved, CENTER shall present to CONTRACTOR, a statement of expenses and either: (a) collect payment of expenses beyond sum of advance payments; or (b) return to CONTRACTOR the unused portion of advance payment.

B.   METHOD OF PAYMENT: All CENTER payments of ticket proceeds will be made by CENTER check. If cash is required as a part of the settlement, requests must be made to CENTER at least three (3) working days before the event.

C.   DEDUCTIONS: CONTRACTOR shall be responsible for payment of any federal, state, and local taxes which may be levied against the entertainment and/or activity being presented or on the admissions to such entertainment and/or activity provided, however, that CENTER may withhold and pay any taxes collected on behalf of CONTRACTOR which CENTER deems its responsibility to collect and pay, including but not limited to Massachusetts state sales tax.

D.   COPYRIGHTS: CONTRACTOR will assume all costs arising from the use of patented, trademarked, franchised or copyrighted music, materials, devices, processes or dramatic rights used on, or incorporated in, the entertainment and/or activity being presented. CONTRACTOR shall obtain and pay for all appropriate American Society of Composers, Authors, and Publishers (ASCAP), Broadcast Music, Inc. (BMI), SESAC and other similar licenses for the entertainment and/or activity, CONTRACTOR agrees to indemnify, defend, and hold harmless CENTER, the University of Massachusetts Amherst, its trustees, officers, employees and agents, the University of Massachusetts Building Authority (UMBA), and Ogden Entertainment Services from any and all claims, lawsuits, litigation, costs, royalties, or damages, including but not limited to legal fees which might arise from use or proposed use of any such material described above.

E.   CONTRACTOR agrees that CONTRACTOR and all CONTRACTOR'S associated staff, crew, artists, agents, and clients connected with CONTRACTOR'S use of CENTER building and/or grounds, shall abide by, and conform to, all federal, state, and local laws, rules, and regulations and by all facility rules and regulations as provided by CENTER and CENTER will require that its agents or employees likewise so comply. CONTRACTOR agrees to acquire and pay for all necessary licenses and permits.

F.   ADA: CONTRACTOR agrees to abide by, and conform to, the Americans With Disabilities Act. CONTRACTOR shall be responsible for ensuring that all services for individuals with disabilities, as outlined in this act, are fulfilled in relation to the show and performance.

G.   AGREEMENT TO QUIT PREMISES: CONTRACTOR agrees to quit premises no later than the end term of this agreement and further agrees to leave premises in condition equal to that at the commencement date of this agreement, ordinary wear and use thereof only excepted. CONTRACTOR agrees that all materials pertinent to the event which are not the possession of CENTER will be removed from premises before the expiration date of this agreement. The CENTER shall be authorized to remove, at the expense of the CONTRACTOR, all material remaining on premises on the termination date of this agreement. CONTRACTOR shall be responsible for payment of storage costs for such materials and CONTRACTOR agrees CENTER shall in no way, be responsible for loss, damage, or claims for material removed or stored under the provision. CONTRACTOR agrees that CENTER will have first lien on such materials for payment of costs accrued for removal and storage.

Exhibit 3–7 continued

VII. ADVERTISING

A.   LOGO: The Mullins Center logo and name must appear in all print event advertising.

B.   HONEST AND TRUE: CONTRACTOR agrees that all advertising of this event will be honest and true and will include correct information on event times, ticket prices and place of event.

C.   EVENT ADVERTISING: CONTRACTOR shall provide CENTER with copies of all advertising and media releases relating to the event(s) described herein, at least 48 hours in advance of the placement or release of said materials. CONTRACTOR agrees to discontinue and/or correct any advertising and announcements of the entertainment and/or activity being presented by CONTRACTOR which CENTER determines, in its sole discretion, to be dishonest, misleading, untruthful, containing incomplete information, damaging to the reputation of CENTER, or which does not accurately convey the date(s) of such entertainment and/or activity, the type of admission (general or reserved seating), and the correct ticket price(s). CENTER reserves the right to determine the time at which CONTRACTOR'S event will be announced and/or released to the public.

D.   SALES AND USE OF ADVERTISING SPACE: All advertising space on CENTER premises is the exclusive property of and subject to control by CENTER, and all receipts therefrom shall accrue to CENTER. No advertising by CONTRACTOR shall be permitted, except by prior written permission of CENTER.

E.   ADVERTISING BILLING: The CENTER will charge CONTRACTOR gross rate less any applicable discount according to the Schedule of User Fees in force on the date of the event covered by this agreement for advertising placed by CENTER Marketing Department. The CENTER will not pay for advertising of an event which has been placed directly by CONTRACTOR without prior approval by CENTER Marketing Department and written authorization from CONTRACTOR.

F.   STATEMENT OF EVENT SPONSORSHIP: The use of University of Massachusetts Amherst facilities by any organization, individual or group of individuals does not in itself constitute endorsement by the University of that organization, individual or group of individuals, nor of any product, service, precept or tense of any kind. Those using University of Massachusetts Amherst facilities are forbidden to express or imply such endorsement in any of the programs or performances carried on in the facilities or in advertising or promotion associated with such events. A statement of true event sponsorship must appear in all advertisement of this event. The CENTER reserves the right to withhold its name or logo from any advertisement, if used in any way other than for place of event.

VIII.   BROADCAST RIGHTS

The CENTER reserves all rights and privileges for radio broadcasting, televising, filming, videotaping, sound recording, photographing, or any kind of reproduction of whatever nature originating from the CENTER facility during the term of this agreement. Should the CENTER grant to CONTRACTOR such privilege, CENTER has the right to require payment for said privilege in addition to rental fee. Such permission must be obtained in writing in advance of broadcast date.

IX.   MEDIA COVERAGE

A.   The CENTER will honor requests from working media and University photographers to photograph portions of the CONTRACTOR'S event, subject to reasonable and proper restrictions, unless specifically prohibited by the CONTRACTOR.

Exhibit 3–7 continued

B.   The CENTER reserves the right to use photographs of, and references to, event subject to reasonable and proper restrictions for promotion of CENTER and/or University archival purposes.

X.   PUBLIC SAFETY

A.   CONTRACTOR shall at all times conduct activities with full regard to public safety and will observe and abide by all applicable regulations and requests by duly authorized governmental agencies responsible for public safety and with CENTER to ensure such safety.

B.   All portions of the sidewalks, entries, doors, passages, vestibules, halls, corridors, stairways, passageways, and all ways of access to public utilities on premises shall be kept unobstructed by the CONTRACTOR and shall not be used for any purpose other than ingress or egress to and from the premises by the CONTRACTOR.

C.   CONTRACTOR agrees not to bring onto the premises any material, substance, equipment, or object which is likely to endanger the life of, or cause bodily injury to, any person on the premises, or which is likely to constitute hazard to property thereon, without the prior approval of CENTER. CENTER shall have the right to refuse to allow such material, substance, equipment, or object to be brought onto the premises and further right to require its immediate removal therefrom if found thereon.

XI.   CANCELLATION

A.   RIGHT TO CANCEL: CENTER reserves the right to terminate this agreement for good cause which shall not include subsequent scheduling of a preferred event.

1.   Should CONTRACTOR default in the performance of any of the terms and conditions of this agreement, CENTER at its option may terminate the same.

2.   CENTER reserves the right to cancel this agreement if it receives evidence that the artist(s) and/or client(s) named in the contract or audiences of the named artist(s) and/or client(s) have violated laws, caused disturbances, and/or taken any action resulting in injury at any performance and/or activity prior to the proposed appearance at CENTER.

3.   In the event CENTER does terminate this agreement, the CONTRACTOR shall be liable for full payment of the rental fees accrued to point of termination and for all reimbursable expenses.   Should CENTER exercise said right to terminate this agreement, CONTRACTOR agrees to forego any and all claims which might arise by reason of the terms of this agreement and CONTRACTOR shall have no recourse of any kind against CENTER.

B.   CANCELLATION BY CONTRACTOR: If CONTRACTOR shall cancel for any reason other than those set forth in section XII, paragraph H, or fails to take possession of or to use the facilities substantially in accordance with this agreement, unless otherwise agreed to in writing, then CENTER shall be entitled to liquidated damages equal to the minimum daily base rental, 100% of applicable ticket handling fees on the sale of tickets up to the time of cancellation, plus any other disbursement or expenses incurred by CENTER in connection with the event.

C.   CANCELLATION: In the case of cancellation of any performance and/or activity, the CONTRACTOR shall have the obligation, at its own expense, to inform the public of such cancellation through regular information media.   In

Exhibit 3–7 continued

the event of default of such obligation by CONTRACTOR as determined by CENTER in its reasonable discretion, CENTER reserves the right to make such announcements at the expense of CONTRACTOR.

XII.   ADHERENCE TO CONTRACT TERMS

A.   ALTERATION: Any alterations to this agreement must be agreed to prior to signing and must be initialized by both parties.

B.   RETENTION OF CENTER PRIVILEGES: Failure of CENTER to insist upon strict and prompt performance of the covenants and agreements hereunder, shall not constitute or be construed as a relinquishment of CENTER'S right thereafter to enforce the same strictly.

C.   NON-ASSIGNMENT: CONTRACTOR will not assign, transfer or subject this agreement or its right, title or interest therein without CENTER'S prior written approval.

D.   SUIT TO ENFORCE: Should CENTER institute a suit or other action against CONTRACTOR as a result of CONTRACTOR failure to comply with any terms of this agreement, CENTER shall recover all damages provided by law, all costs and disbursements provided by statute, and all costs actually incurred including reasonable attorney's fees.

E.   COURT ACTION: If any portion of this agreement shall be found invalid by any court having jurisdiction thereof, such invalidity shall not affect any other section or provision or portion of this agreement. The parties agree that the provisions of this agreement are to be deemed severable in the event of any judicial determination of partial invalidity.

F.   INTERRUPTIONS AND CANCELLATIONS: CENTER may, without liability, refuse to perform any obligation(s) otherwise arising under this agreement if performance of such obligation(s) would in any way violate or result in conflict, on the part of the CENTER or CONTRACTOR, with federal, state and/or local laws, or if performance of such obligation(s) is found to be objectionable or contrary to public interests. All such judgements to be made by CENTER in its sole, reasonable discretion.

G.   APPROVAL OF CONTRACT: It is agreed that this agreement will not be in force until it has been signed by both parties and approval has been given by a designated authorized agent of the University of Massachusetts Amherst. In the event approval is denied, deposit will be returned to CONTRACTOR.

H.   UNAVOIDABLE HAPPENING: In the event that; (a) CENTER or any portion thereof shall be destroyed or damaged by fire or any other cause so as to prevent the use of the premises for the purposes and during the periods specified herein; or (b) if the premises cannot be so used because of strikes, acts of God, national emergency or other cause beyond the control of CENTER, then this lease shall terminate and the CONTRACTOR hereby waives any claim against CENTER, the University of Massachusetts Amherst, its trustees, officers, employees and agents, the University of Massachusetts Building Authority (UMBA), and Ogden Entertainment Services for damages or compensation by reason of such termination except that any unearned portion of the rent due hereunder shall abate, or if previously paid, shall be refunded by CENTER to CONTRACTOR. This clause shall be invoked at the sole discretion of CENTER.

I.   INDEMNITY: CONTRACTOR agrees to indemnify, defend and hold harmless, CENTER, the University of Massachusetts Amherst, its trustees, officers, employees and agents, the Massachusetts Higher Education Coordinating Council, the University of Massachusetts Building Authority (UMBA), Ogden Entertainment Services, and the Commonwealth of Massachusetts from any and all demands, claims, suits, actions or liabilities resulting from injuries or death to any

Exhibit 3–7 continued

persons, or damage or loss of any property prior to, during, or subsequent to the period covered by this agreement arising from any activity undertaken by CONTRACTOR or by CENTER or their employees or agents in performance of any terms, conditions, or promises under this agreement for the use of facilities leased or services obligated hereunder, except with respect to any such demand, claim, suit, action or liability proven to be due solely to the willing act of CENTER for which CENTER similarly agrees to indemnify CONTRACTOR. No claim or litigation shall be settled without prior written approval of CENTER. CENTER'S agreement to indemnify shall be in an amount not to exceed that set forth in Massachusetts General Laws, Chapter 258, Sec.2 as amended.

J.   DISCRETIONARY MATTERS: It is agreed that any matters not expressly incorporated in this agreement will be at the reasonable discretion of CENTER.

K.   MASSACHUSETTS LAW: The validity, construction and effect of this contract shall be governed by the laws of the State of Massachusetts.

XIII. CIVIL RIGHTS

CONTRACTOR agrees not to discriminate against any employee or any applicant because of race, religion, sex, marital status, age, or national origin, and further agrees to likewise not discriminate for those same reasons against any persons relative to admission, services or privileges offered to or enjoyed by the general public.

XIV. COMPLETE AGREEMENT

All terms and conditions of this written contract shall be binding upon the parties, their heirs or representatives, and assigns, and cannot be waived by any oral representation of promise of any of the parties hereto unless the same be in writing and signed by the duly authorized agent or agents who executed this contract.

XV. RELEASE

CONTRACTOR hereby releases the Commonwealth of Massachusetts, the Massachusetts Higher Education Coordinating Council established under Massachusetts General Laws, Chapter 1142 of the Acts of 1991 of the Commonwealth, the University of Massachusetts Building Authority (UMBA), and the University of Massachusetts, its trustees, officers, employees and agents, from all claims, legal actions, suits, judgements, expenses, and costs arising out of the acts or failure to act of Ogden Entertainment Services, its directors, employees, agents and subcontractors.

Exhibit 3–7 continued

WILLIAM D. MULLINS MEMORIAL CENTER
FACILITY AGREEMENT
Ticket Office Rider

A.   In the handling, control and custody of ticket receipts, whether received through the Box Office or otherwise, CENTER is acting for the accommodation and sole benefit of the CONTRACTOR and, as to such receipts, CENTER shall be responsible only for gross neglect or bad faith.

B.   Tickets will not be put on sale until after receipt of the signed contract and any advance rental deposit required by the contract.

C.   CENTER has a contract with TicketMaster to provide computerized ticketing services.

D.   Tickets for events occurring in the CENTER facilities must be ordered through the Mullins Center Box Office.

   1.   Ticket copy, prices, discounts, date(s) and time(s), and any notification of tickets to be withheld from sale by CONTRACTOR, must be submitted to the CENTER no less than three (3) working days prior to the on-sale date of event.

   2.   CONTRACTOR agrees to sell all tickets at the prices as advertised and any deviations must be approved in writing by CENTER.

   3.   In no event shall tickets to any concert, entertainment or other use being made of facility by CONTRACTOR, be sold or disposed of in excess of seating capacity of the house. CONTRACTOR shall not admit to the facility, a greater number of persons than can safely and freely move about, and the decision of the CENTER management in this respect will be final. CONTRACTOR agrees that any seats with limited or impaired vision or any behind stage seats will be sold, only if the limitation is clearly marked. CENTER will have the right to retain a certain number of seats as backup for sound console and problem seat locations.

   4.   CONTRACTOR shall provide the CENTER Box Office with written notification of any discount and/or special ticket offers, and supply sample copies of all coupons and/or printed materials relating to the discounts. CONTRACTOR will provide complete information pertaining to disclaimers, availability of discount seats and necessary identification required, no later than forty-eight (48) hours prior to their availability to the general public.

   5.   CONTRACTOR will designate to the CENTER Box Office a representative who is authorized to approve requests for complimentary tickets. No requests for complimentary tickets will be processed without approval of this authorized representative.

E.   CENTER shall offer tickets for sale in the following manner.

   1.   CENTER will provide staff to handle sales in person at the CENTER Box Office during normal business hours, during the on-sale period, and at the event venue the day(s) of the performance(s). Cash, check, Visa, MasterCard and American Express will be accepted.

   2.   Phone sales will be through the TicketMaster phone room. Visa, MasterCard and American Express will be accepted.

Exhibit 3–7 continued

3. Outlet sales will be through TicketMaster outlets. Cash, checks and charge cards honored by the individual outlet will be accepted.

4. All tickets sold for the engagement covered by the terms of this agreement, are subject to convenience surcharges. Convenience surcharges will be considered as monies due to TicketMaster over which CONTRACTOR shall have no claim.

5. All tickets sold for the engagement covered by the terms of this agreement, shall be subject to a parking, transportation, and traffic surcharge (P.T.T.) which shall be considered as monies due to the University of Massachusetts Amherst to cover services rendered in these areas, and shall not be considered as part of the ticket price and over which the CONTRACTOR shall have no claim. For the event described herein, the per ticket P.T.T. surcharge will be $

6. CENTER Box Office will provide at settlement, a manifest indicating total inventory of tickets that were available for sale and a statement listing tickets sold, discounted tickets sold, and complimentary tickets processed.

F. CENTER retains the right to make determination of ticket refunds for cause, in keeping with the CENTER policy of retaining public faith. Cause for refund shall include, but not be limited to, seats blocked by equipment when exchange for comparable locations is not possible; failure of projection equipment; postponement or change of date or time; or failure of advertised act to show or to go on stage within reasonable time of schedule provided by CONTRACTOR.

G. CENTER shall have the first lien against Box Office receipts and all property of CONTRACTOR upon the premises of the CENTER for all unpaid rental fees, reimbursable expenses, and appropriate taxes due for the event covered by this agreement. CENTER is empowered to withhold from Box Office receipts all such items, and if such funds are not available at the conclusion of the event, to impound CONTRACTOR property. Should such unpaid charges remain unpaid, CENTER shall have the power to sell such property at public auction to the retirement of these unpaid charges.

H. CENTER shall, at all times, maintain control and direction of Box Office, ticket personnel, and ticket sales revenue until settlement. Only employees under the direct control and supervision of CENTER shall be permitted use of the CENTER box office facilities or otherwise be engaged as admissions control personnel.

I. CONSIGNMENT OF TICKETS:

1. CONTRACTOR must designate one individual to pick up and return tickets to CENTER Box Office. The Box Office cannot be responsible for the pick up and return of tickets for more than one individual.

2. Tickets can be issued on consignment only after a release is signed relieving CENTER Box Office of all responsibility for those tickets released.

3. CONTRACTOR will be responsible for the monies collected for consignment tickets. Monies for sold consignment tickets and unsold consignment tickets must be delivered to CENTER Box Office from designated sales outlets outside the CENTER, no later than 24 hours prior to the start of the event. CONTRACTOR will be responsible for delivery to CENTER Box Office of all said tickets. CENTER Box Office reserves the right to refuse to sell tickets not delivered in accordance with the above stated deadline. Unsold consignment tickets

Exhibit 3–7 continued

can be returned only if they are whole, complete tickets. These will
be accepted for resale only after a signed release has been presented.
This must be done twenty-four (24) hours in advance of the first
performance covered by this agreement.

4. CONTRACTOR will be responsible for collection of the P.T.T. surcharge
on each ticket sold from a consignment.

5. CENTER reserves the right to dictate the means of payment in settling
consignments.

6. A representative from the CONTRACTOR organization is required to be
available to the CENTER Box Office on the date of the event to handle
problems with consignment tickets sold.

J. CENTER Box Office will provide ticket counts for CONTRACTOR daily or as
needed during box office business hours.

K. Fees for Box Office services will be consistent with the Schedule of User
Fees in force on the date of the event covered by this agreement.

L. In the event that the event(s) covered by this agreement is cancelled,
CONTRACTOR shall permit the CENTER to reimburse any amount due ticket holders.
CONTRACTOR shall pay the CENTER the computer set-up fee plus the ticket
handling charge on tickets sold up to the time of cancellation as
compensation for the task of refunding tickets to the cancelled event.

Ogden Management Services Contract for usage of the University of Massachusetts'
Mullins Center used with permission of Lee A. Esckilsen, Executive Director,
Ogden Entertainment Services.

Exhibit 3–8
Marketing Contract

AGREEMENT made this August 1, 1988, between ("Representative/ Consultant") and _____

WITNESSETH:

WHEREAS, Representative/Consultant is engaged in the business of managing and advising its clients in the pursuit of developing marketing strategy, and commercial opportunities and in seeking and negotiating agreements on their behalf defined hereinafter; and

WHEREAS, _____ wishes to engage Representative/Consultant's services for the purpose of managing and advising and assisting _____ in the development of commercial opportunities for the _____, as hereinafter defined,

NOW, THEREFORE, in consideration of the mutual promises exchanged below, the parties agree as follows:

1. _____ hereby engages Representative/Consultant to act as _____'s sole and exclusive manager, representative and advisor for the purpose of supervising and guiding _____ in the "Entertainment Field" (as defined below), including but not limited to the following services:

(a) Conferring with _____ in connection with all matters concerning _____;

(b) Representing _____ and consulting with _____ for the purpose of reviewing and evaluating the terms of all agreements for _____ with any third party;

(c) Supervising _____'s contractual obligations and, on _____'s behalf, consulting with employers to assure the proper use of _____'s services;

For the purposes of this agreement, the term "Entertainment Field" shall be defined as all activities in the sports marketing, corporate sponsorship, broadcasting and merchandising industries with a view toward the commercial exploitation of the _____.

2. (a) The term of this agreement shall be a period of one year from the date hereof.

(b) Prior to the expiration of the initial one year term hereof, should both parties mutually agree, in writing, this agreement may be terminated, provided, however, that all compensation due from any agreements or extensions as set out in paragraph 7 (b) below shall be payable to Representative/Consultant as if this agreement was not so terminated.

Exhibit 3–8 continued

(c) 30 days prior to the expiration of the initial one year term hereof, should both parties agree, in writing, this agreement may be extended in accordance with the wish of the parties.

3. _____ shall not engage any other individual or entity as _____'s Representative/Consultant.

4. _____ agrees to consult with Representative/Consultant with respect to every engagement, performance or contract offered to _____ in any marketing or broadcasting field.

5. Representative/Consultant's services to _____ hereunder are not exclusive to _____ and Representative/Consultant shall have the right to perform the same or similar services for others, as well as to engage in other business activities. Representative/Consultant is engaged hereunder as an independent contractor. Representative/Consultant shall have the right to publicize Representative/Consultant's role as _____'s personal Representative/Consultant.

6. _____ hereby appoints Representative/Consultant as _____'s lawful attorney-in-fact to collect and receive sums, as well as endorse _____'s name on all checks payable to _____ for _____'s services, and retain therefrom all sums owing to Representative/Consultant. All proceeds due _____ shall be remitted on a monthly basis.

7. (a) As compensation for Representative/Consultant's services hereunder, _____ agrees to pay Representative/Consultant a sum (the "Representative/Consultant's Fee") equal to twenty percent (20%) of any "gross monies or other considerations" (as defined below) paid or payable to _____ as set forth herein, as and when received by _____ or by any person, firm or corporation on _____'s behalf or by any entity owned or controlled by _____, for services rendered by _____ in the commercial or marketing field or for the use of _____'s name, likeness or endorsement.

(b) As compensation for Representative/Consultant's services hereunder, _____ agrees to pay Representative/Consultant a sum (the "Representative/Consultant's Fee") equal to ten percent (10%) of any "gross monies or other considerations" paid or payable to _____, as and when received by _____ or by any person, firm or corporation on _____'s behalf or by any entity owned or controlled by _____, for all television rights fees pertaining to conference or inter-conference games. _____ agrees to waive any rights fee pertaining to the 1988 (TV) agreement. This waiving of rights fees for the 1988 (TV) agreement does not include the selling of commercial time which would be part of an overall marketing program. Any monies generated by

Exhibit 3–8 continued

the selling of commercial time by _____ during a telecast of any _____ game would fall under section 7(a).

(c) The Representative/Consultant's Fee shall be payable to Representative/Consultant with respect to all engagements, contracts and agreements entered into by _____ during the term hereof or substantially negotiated during the term hereof and executed within six (6) months thereafter, and upon any extensions or renewals thereof and substitutions therefor, and upon any resumption of any engagements, contracts and agreements which may have been discontinued during the term hereof and resumed within one (1) year thereafter. For the purposes hereof, the term "substitutions" shall include without limitation, any engagement, contract or agreement entered into with any entity within three (3) months after the expiration or termination of any previous engagement, contract or agreement for services of the same or similar nature entered into during the term hereof with the same entity.

(d) The term "gross monies or other considerations" shall include all salaries, earnings, fees, royalties, residuals, repeat and/or rerun fees, bonuses, shares or profits, shares of stock, partnership interests, earned or received directly or indirectly by _____ .

(e) As part of this agreement, _____ shall pay _____ _____ a fee of $1,500 per month, for ten months total, for representation/consulting commencing as of August 1, 1988.

8. All office and other expenses incurred by _____, in connection with its obligations hereunder shall be submitted by _____ to _____ for its approval.

9. Any controversy or claim arising out of or relating to this agreement, or the breach thereof, shall be submitted to arbitration in New York, New York, in accordance with the Commercial Arbitration Rules of the American Arbitration Association, and judgement upon the award rendered by the Arbitrator(s) (including, without limitation, interests, costs, expenses and attorneys fees as the Arbitrator(s) may award in his/their discretion) may be entered in any court having jurisdiction thereof.

10. This agreement shall be governed by the laws of the State of New York applicable to agreements wholly performed within said State.

11. _____ agrees that Representative/Consultant's services as _____'s sole and exclusive representative hereunder are unique and irreplaceable and that any breach or threatened breach by _____ would cause Representative/Consultant immediate and unavoidable damages which could not be adequately compensated for by a money judgment.

Exhibit 3–8 continued

12. This agreement shall not be construed to create a partnership or joint venture between _____ and Representative/Consultant.

13. Any waiver by Representative/Consultant of any breach hereof by _____ shall not be considered a waiver of any subsequent breach.

BY:_____

Television Contracts

In recent years, more and more colleges are having to negotiate television contracts; thus it is very important for athletic administrators to be familiar with the issues in these contracts. While television contracts are often similar to marketing and promotional contracts, they may differ, depending on the particular sport, the level of competition, and the type of broadcaster. The types of broadcaster include cable, national, regional, local, and pay-per-view.

Although television contracts in college athletics are relatively new, they are subject to rapid changes in technology. Such changes often lead to the implementation of new rules and regulations by the Federal Communications Commission (FCC). In light of such rapid changes, college administrators must constantly review contracts to ensure compliance with these factors. A further discussion on sports broadcasting issues is presented in Chapter 9. Exhibit 3–9 is an example of a contract between a collegiate athletic conference and ESPN, which gives ESPN the exclusive right to broadcast certain sporting events.

Failure to Hire and Failure to Renew Contracts

Failure to hire and failure to renew a contract are other areas of litigation where coaches have filed claims. *Cruciotti v. McNeel* (see note 1) is an example of a failure to hire case, where the plaintiff claimed that grouping the positions of physical education teacher and athletic trainer into one position, which he could not qualify for, was unlawful. The plaintiff, who unsuccessfully sought only the physical education position, won the case. Coaches who bring an action against a school district for failure to renew a contract use a variety of legal principles ranging from denial of constitutional rights to procedural claims. Many of these cases overlap with cases and issues discussed in other subsections in this chapter. In *Williams v. Day* (see note 2), a coach

Exhibit 3–9
Television Contract

<u>ESPN, INC.</u>

<u>RIGHTS AGREEMENT</u>

This Agreement, dated as of _____ , is between _____ ("Institution") and ESPN, Inc., a Delaware corporation with offices at ESPN Plaza, Bristol, Connecticut 06010-7454 ("ESPN").

<u>WITNESSETH</u>:

1. <u>GRANT OF RIGHTS</u>

   Institution hereby grants to ESPN exclusive rights to produce and to distribute one or more programs based on each sporting event described in paragraph 2, below (an "Event"), all subject to the terms and conditions of this Agreement.

2. <u>EVENT(S); RIGHTS FEE(S)</u>

   (a) Each Event, the participants in the Event, its site(s), the date(s) and starting time(s) of the Event, and the consideration payable by ESPN to Institution for all rights granted herein with respect to the Event (the "Rights Fee") are as follows:

EVENT(S), PARTICIPANTS, and SITE(S)	DATE(S)/STARTING TIME(S)	RIGHTS FEE(S)
_____	_____	_____
_____	_____	_____
_____	_____	_____
_____	_____	_____
_____	_____	_____
_____		

   The Rights Fee for each Event shall be due and payable within fifteen days from the later of the execution and delivery of this Agreement or the occurrence of the Event in accordance with the terms and conditions of this Agreement.

   (b) Institution shall be solely responsible for all arrangements (including any compensation) for the holding of each Event and with all participants and any officials involved in the Event, and such arrangements shall accord to ESPN all rights and consents required or contemplated with respect to ESPN's rights hereunder. Institution shall use its best efforts to make available to ESPN such participants, officials and other persons connected with the Event as ESPN may request for purposes of interviews and discussion. For Event(s) which ESPN intends to distribute as Program(s) on a live basis, Institution shall (i) consult and coordinate with ESPN's producer prior to the Event to integrate the Event format with ESPN's commercial format, and (ii) appoint at Institution's sole expense a

Exhibit 3–9 continued

liaison officer to be responsible for and cooperate in calling time-outs or other structured interruptions so that ESPN's commercial format is reasonably satisfied and commercial and promotional announcements are properly spaced.

3.   PROGRAM(S)

(a) It is contemplated by the parties that the Event, together with any interviews, films and discussion which ESPN may incorporate into its coverage of such Event as provided above shall serve as the basis of one or more audio-video programs (the "Program(s)").

(b) ESPN shall select such announcers, commentators, technical and other personnel for the Programs as ESPN shall determine and Institution shall have no rights of approval over such personnel.

(c) Institution shall provide to ESPN, without charge, suitable space and locations, as ESPN may determine at the time of its advance technical survey of the site of the Event, for its announcers and for the installation and operation of all microphones, television cameras and related equipment to be used by ESPN in connection with the production and transmission (including satellite uplink) of its Program of such Event. Institution will assure the availability of such electrical power as is necessary to operate such equipment and all necessary lighting for a first-quality television production in color, all free of charge to ESPN. ESPN shall have the right to install, maintain in and remove from the site and the surrounding premises such wires, cables and equipment as may be necessary for the Program of the Event; provided, however, that such facilities shall not substantially interfere with the use of the site or with any of the means of ingress or egress. ESPN shall have the right to bring into or adjacent to the site such equipment as it deems necessary for the Program of the Event including mobile units for the transportation of equipment and personnel. Employees and agents of ESPN shall be admitted to the site free of charge to the extent necessary to accomplish the Program of the Event and Institution will provide ESPN gratis with the necessary credentials for such purposes. Except as otherwise specifically provided herein, Institution will not grant access to the Event to any other videotape or film crew without ESPN's prior written consent.

(d) ESPN shall have complete control over the production and format of the Programs and shall have the right to present commercial and other promotional material in the Programs as it may determine or authorize.

(e) ESPN shall have the right to display its name and trademark on banners, on its equipment and on any platform or broadcasting booth used at the site in such a manner and location as to be reasonably and readily apparent to both the spectators at the Site and the viewers watching the Programs as distributed by ESPN.

(f) Institution represents that, unless ESPN consents thereto in advance in writing, no billboards, display or public announcements for any product or service will be visible or heard at the site during ESPN's coverage of any Event except such advertising which is permanently affixed at the site (i.e., advertising intended for spectators at the Event and not for the television audience).

Exhibit 3–9 continued

(g) At ESPN's request, Institution shall furnish ESPN a reasonable number of choice complimentary tickets to the Event.

4. DISTRIBUTION AND EXHIBITION

(a) Except as expressly limited below, Institution hereby grants to ESPN the exclusive right in perpetuity to distribute, transmit, exhibit, license, advertise, promote, publicize and perform (hereinafter "distribute") the Event(s) as incorporated by ESPN in the Program and any constituent element thereof throughout the universe by any and all means, uses, and media now known or hereafter developed without limitation as to the number of exhibitions.

(b) ESPN shall have the right to make a recording of any Program for distribution on a delayed basis. As used herein the term "recording" shall mean and include any recording by tape, wire, film, disc or any other similar or dissimilar method of recording television programs, whether now known or hereafter developed. ESPN (or such party as it may designate) shall have the right to copyright such recording and ESPN (and its designee) may use such recording for but not limited to the following:

> (i)   use in distributing the Program embodied thereon pursuant to subsection 4(a), above;
>
> (ii) file, reference and publicity purposes; and
>
> (iii) distribution of excerpts of the Program embodied thereon as part of television news and for highlights purposes in other programs.

(c) Notwithstanding the foregoing or any other provision of this Agreement, ESPN may use, and ESPN or Institution may permit any television broadcaster or cablecaster to use in the television market of the participating teams (provided that ESPN receives an appropriate audio/video courtesy announcement) extracts of the Program not to exceed two (2) minutes in running time, at any time other than on a live basis for telecasts or cablecasts within the framework of general newscasts and sports newscasts and such use shall not be a violation of ESPN's right of exclusivity or any other right of ESPN or Institution under this Agreement. In addition, provided that no interference with ESPN's television production of the Event occurs as a result thereof, Institution may itself or permit others to film or videotape the Event for the following purposes:

> (i)   use of no more than two minutes of action footage in the general newscasts and sports newscasts of local broadcast television stations provided that such stations agree in writing that such material will not be used before the conclusion of ESPN's first distribution of its Program of the affected Event in their market(s) nor after forty-eight hours following the conclusion of such distribution, and that they will not furnish such material to any regional or national newsfeed or network;
>
> (ii) production of Institution's own game and coaching films for use in pursuance of its tax-exempt activities; and

Exhibit 3–9 continued

(iii) production of a coach's television program for distribution in the television market or markets of Institution's local and regional areas of natural interest.

5. PROMOTION AND PUBLICITY

(a) ESPN shall have the right, and may grant others the right, to reproduce, print, publish or disseminate in any medium, the name and likeness and voice of each person appearing in or connected with the Program(s) and biographical material concerning such persons as well as Institution's name, trademarks, service marks and logos, and the names of and any trademarks, service marks and logos associated with the Event(s) and the Site(s) for information purposes and to advertise, promote, publicize and distribute the Program(s) and the ESPN Service, but not as a direct endorsement of any product or other services.

(b) Institution will use its best efforts generally to promote its relationship with ESPN as contemplated hereby, and will afford ESPN such promotional services as are usually afforded the broadcast networks and stations which televise Institution's events.

6. MUSIC

At least thirty days before the Event, Institution shall send to ESPN a list naming all musical compositions scheduled to be played during the Event which list shall include as to each composition the name of the composer, publisher, copyright holder and performing rights owner. If ESPN notifies Institution that it is unable to clear any such composition for use in connection with its distribution of the Program of the Event, such composition will not be played.

7. FORCE MAJEURE

If the holding or the coverage of any Event should be prevented or cancelled due to an act of God, inevitable accident, strike or other labor dispute, fire, riot or civil commotion, government action or decree, inclement weather, failure of technical, production or television equipment, or for any other reason beyond the control of Institution or ESPN, then neither Institution nor ESPN shall be obligated in any manner to the other with respect to the Event (including for payment of the Rights Fee for the Event), but all other rights ESPN may have in this Agreement shall remain in effect and shall not be affected in any manner. If, however, the Event should be postponed or delayed, then ESPN shall have the right to elect to cover the Event on its rescheduled date in accordance with all the terms hereof or to not cover the rescheduled Event, in which case ESPN shall not be obligated in any manner to Institution therefor (including for payment), but all ESPN's other rights herein shall survive.

8. WARRANTIES

(a) Institution warrants and represents to ESPN that (i) it is free to enter into and perform this Agreement; (ii) it has all rights necessary to its grant of rights to ESPN hereunder; (iii) the rights ESPN has acquired, and its use of such rights, will not infringe upon or violate the rights of any third party; and (iv) it will not do

Exhibit 3–9 continued

anything which might tend to interfere with or impair the rights which ESPN has acquired in this Agreement.

(b) Institution acknowledges that ESPN's rights in this Agreement are valuable and unique. Except as expressly provided in this Agreement, Institution warrants that it will not authorize or permit any other exhibition or distribution of any Event by any television medium in any manner or by any means whatsoever for the Program of the Event and that it will not grant any rights inconsistent with the rights granted ESPN herein.

9. INDEMNIFICATION

(a) ESPN and Institution will each indemnify, defend and hold the other harmless from any and all claims, costs, liabilities, judgments, expenses or damages (including reasonable attorney's fees) arising out of any breach or alleged breach of this Agreement or any representation made by it herein.

(b) In any case in which indemnification is sought hereunder:

(i) the party seeking indemnification shall promptly notify the other of any claim or litigation to which the indemnification relates; and

(ii) the party seeking indemnification shall afford the other the opportunity to participate in and, at the other party's option, fully control any compromise, settlement, litigation or other resolution or disposition of such claim or litigation.

10. INDEPENDENT CONTRACTORS

Institution and ESPN are independent contractors with respect to each other, and nothing herein shall create any association, partnership, joint venture or agency relationship between them. All persons employed by Institution in connection with its performance hereunder shall be Institution's employees and Institution shall be fully responsible for them, except as otherwise specifically and explicitly provided herein.

11. FINANCIAL DISCLOSURE

In conformity with Section 507 of the U.S. Federal Communications Act concerning broadcasting matters and disclosure required thereunder, Institution warrants and represents that it has not accepted or agreed to accept, and will not permit its employees, agents, representatives, contractors, or affiliate entities to accept any monies, services, or other consideration for the inclusion of any commercial material or matter in or as part of the Program(s).

12. MISCELLANEOUS

(a) All notices and other communications from either party to the other hereunder shall, unless otherwise specifically provided herein, be given in writing at the respective addresses of Institution and ESPN set forth above, unless either party at any time or times designates another address for itself by notifying the other party

Exhibit 3–9 continued

thereof by certified mail, in which case all notices to such party shall thereafter be given at its most recently so designated address. Notice shall be deemed given: when delivered in person, or on the date of dispatch by commercial courier or private messenger; upon deposit in the United States mails, postage prepaid; on delivery of a telegram to a telegraph office with charges therefor prepaid or to be billed to the sender thereof; or on the sending of a private wire, including by facsimile machine or by telex. Notice shall be deemed received when given except that notice given by commercial courier or private messenger shall be deemed received when delivered and notice given by mail shall be deemed received five days after deposit in the United States mails, postage prepaid.

(b) Each party hereto shall execute any and all further documents or amendments which either party hereto may deem necessary and proper to carry out the purposes of this Agreement.

(c) This Agreement contains the full and complete understanding among the parties hereto, supersedes all prior agreements and understandings, whether written or oral, pertaining thereto and cannot be modified except by a written instrument signed by each party hereto. The language of all parts of this Agreement shall in all cases be construed as a whole according to its fair meaning and not strictly for or against any of the parties.

(d) The descriptive headings of the several sections and paragraphs of this Agreement are inserted for convenience only and do not constitute a part of this Agreement.

(e) This Agreement is to be governed by and construed in accordance with the laws of the State of New York, applicable to contracts entered into and to be fully performed therein.

(f) Institution shall not assign any of its rights or obligations hereunder without the prior written consent of ESPN, and any purported assignment without such prior written consent, shall be null and void and of no force and effect.

(g) Any provisions herein found by a court to be void or unenforceable shall not affect the validity or enforceability of any other provisions.

IN WITNESS WHEREOF, the parties have executed this Agreement as of the day and year first above written.

ESPN, INC.

By _____   By_____
                                                  Loren E. Matthews
                                                  Senior Vice President
                                                  Programming

brought an action against the school district, claiming that the district's failure to renew his contract was for constitutionally impermissible reasons. *Diehl v. Albany County School District No. 1* (see note 3) provides an example of an unsuccessful due process claim against a school district for nonrenewal of a coach's contract. In *Leone v. Kimmell* (see note 4), the court determined that the school board's nonrenewal of a coach's contract was not covered by the professional negotiations agreement between the teachers and school board.

NOTES ———————————————————————————————

1. In *Cruciotti v. McNeel*, 396 S.E.2d 191 (W. Va. Sup. Ct. 1990), an unsuccessful applicant for position of physical education teacher brought an action against the school district alleging that a job posting, which described the opening as "physical education teacher and athletic trainer," constituted an improper joinder of employment positions. In affirming the lower court's decision, the Supreme Court of Appeals of West Virginia held that position of athletic trainer was "extracurricular" and therefore required a separate contract for employment.

2. In *Williams v. Day*, 412 F. Supp. 336 (D.C. Ark. 1976), a teacher brought a civil rights action, alleging that the school district had unlawfully failed to renew his coaching and teaching contract for constitutionally impermissible reasons. He also claimed that he was denied due process. Two years prior to the teacher's dismissal, he had become unhappy at not being named athletic director, and from that time until his dismissal, he reportedly had often failed to cooperate with the administration. The U.S. District Court held that nonrenewal was due to personnel considerations and in no way based on the teacher's First Amendment rights. The court further concluded that the school board had not prejudiced future employment opportunities for the teacher, and thus did not deprive him of a constitutionally protected interest in liberty. The court also held that due process procedures had been followed.

3. In *Diehl v. Albany County School District No. 1*, 694 F. Supp. 1534 (D.C. Wyo. 1988), a high school basketball coach whose contract was not renewed brought action against the school district, claiming he was deprived of liberty without due process of law. The district court held that coach did not establish a liberty interest claim.

4. In *Leone v. Kimmell*, 335 A.2d 290 (Del. Super. Ct. 1975), an assistant football coach brought action against the school board to nullify board's decision not to award him a contract. In ruling for defendant school board, the court held that the school district's failure to grant a new contract was not a matter within the coverage of the professional negotiations agreement. If it had been, the school board would have to establish just cause for the nonrenewal, and the coach would be permitted to pursue grievance procedures.

Chapter 4

AMATEUR ATHLETIC ASSOCIATIONS

INTRODUCTION

Amateur athletics are an integral part of American life both inside and outside educational institutions. They have, over time, become complex. Increasingly, certain amateur athletics bear a resemblance to big business, and the ineligibility or unavailability of an individual athlete or program can result in a large financial loss for the institution or the forfeiture of a chance to pursue a sports career for the athlete.

The organizations that govern amateur athletics are collectively referred to in this chapter as amateur athletic associations. For our purposes, amateur athletic associations include high school and college athletic associations such as the National Federation of State High School Associations (NFSHSA), the National Collegiate Athletic Association (NCAA), the National Association of Intercollegiate Athletics (NAIA), and the National Junior College Athletic Association (NJCAA); high school and college athletic conferences such as the Big Ten and the Pac-10; and national and international governing bodies such as the United States Olympic Committee (USOC), the Amateur Athletic Union (AAU), the International Amateur Athletic Federation (IAAF), and USA Track & Field.

Besides these organizations, interscholastic and intercollegiate athletics are governed in this country by three other groups: the educational institutions, athletic directors, and coaches. These groups, together with amateur athletic associations, operate in a pyramidlike fashion: athletic associations set certain minimum standards and requirements for participation, conferences and educational institutions may impose stricter obligations on their student-athletes, and athletic directors and coaches may further demand stringent requirements that they judge to be necessary for successful performance in their individual sport or for proper functioning of the educational department as a whole. Since educational institutions and coaches must act within the scope of association and conference regulations, our focus will be primarily on the activities, rules, and governance of amateur athletic associations and conferences.

Chapter 4 analyzes the impact of the law on amateur athletics and notes the growing power of organizations that govern amateur athletics. Traditionally, these organizations have not been challenged in terms of legal accountability, but their pervasive influence has recently led to increasing legal scrutiny. Some argue that this has resulted in better protection of individual rights from arbitrary or unfair actions of governing organizations, institutions, schools, or coaches and teachers. Others argue that this increased judicial presence is an unwarranted intrusion into amateur athletics.

The chapter begins with a discussion of the various definitions of an amateur athlete. While the amateur athlete is the topic of Chapter 5, the definitions of *amateur* are discussed here because the various definitions and interpretations of an amateur athlete have sparked controversy among the many amateur athletic associations that promulgate, interpret, and enforce the eligibility rules and regulations affecting amateur athletes.

The chapter then discusses three basic legal principles that often are the focus of court rulings and decisions concerning amateur athletic associations: judicial review, standing, and injunctive relief. This section is followed by information about major categories of voluntary amateur athletic organizations: the U.S. Olympic Committee, collegiate athletic associations such as the NCAA, and high school athletic associations. The public responsibilities of these categories of amateur athletic organizations are also discussed.

The chapter continues with the constitutional law aspects of athletics. The focus is on the amateur organization as a defendant or potential defendant in a court case. The last section of Chapter 4 discusses association authority with respect to promulgating and enforcing rules and regulations. The NCAA is used as the primary example of an amateur association's authority in this area.

The material covered in Chapter 4 is very important to athletic administrators. High school and college athletic administrators must deal with amateur athletic associations on a frequent basis, covering topics such as eligibility requirements, rule interpretations, student-athlete rights, and compliance and enforcement processes and procedures. Increasingly, athletic administrators have also become involved with athletic associations in a record number of lawsuits. Consequently, it has become essential for these administrators to understand as much about sports law and athletic associations as possible. The information in this chapter and in Chapter 5 can assist high school and college administrators to eliminate or minimize potential litigation by sensitizing them to the manner in which the courts view certain athletic organizations, their rules, and their authority to establish regulations on various topics. In addition, for the athletic administrator who becomes involved in a lawsuit as a representative of the student-athlete or the institution, familiarity with the legal terms and concepts introduced in the chapter is essential.

NOTE _____

1. For further information concerning the emergence of intercollegiate athletics as big business and the treatment of athletes, see the following:

(a) Hofman, D., Greenberg, M. J. (1989). *Sport Biz*. Champaign, Ill.: Human Kinetics Publishers.

(b) Klatell, D. A., Marcus, N. (1988). *Sports for Sale*. New York: Oxford University Press.

(c) Lawrence, P. R. (1987). *Unsportsmanlike Conduct.* New York: Praeger Publishers.

(d) Sperber, M. (1990) *College Sports Inc.* New York: Henry Holt and Company.

(e) Thelin, J. R., Wiseman, L. L. (1989). *The Old College Try: Balancing Athletics and Academics in Higher Education.* Report No. 4. Washington, D.C.: School of Education and Human Development, The George Washington University.

(f) Wolff, A., Keteyian, A. (1990). *Raw Recruits.* New York: Pocket Books.

DEFINITIONS OF "AMATEUR"

Each individual amateur athletic association has developed its own definition of an amateur athlete. Because the line between professional and amateur is difficult to draw, these definitions overlap to some extent.

In times past, most amateur athletic organizations refused to allow amateur athletes to receive any money at all in compensation for their time or expenses. In fact, this restriction was the basis for distinguishing the amateur from the professional athlete. Increasingly, however, amateur athletes are receiving compensation for certain living, training, and competition expenses. The amount and type of reimbursement allowed are determined by the governing athletic organization. For example, USA Track & Field, track and field's national governing body, has established a direct payment program to enable registered athletes to receive fees for product endorsements or expenses from event promoters and still maintain their amateur track eligibility (see note 1, and Exhibit 4–1).

The compensation issue has made the line between professional and amateur more difficult to draw. While the definitions of "amateur athlete" offered by various amateur athletic associations have not changed much over the years, the interpretations of these definitions have become more liberal to allow reimbursement of expenses. The following are several examples of the definitions of "amateur":

- National Collegiate Athletic Association: "An amateur student-athlete is one who engages in a particular sport for the educational, physical, mental and social benefits derived therefrom and for whom participation in that sport is an avocation." (*1993–94 NCAA Manual,* Bylaw 12.02.1)
- International Olympic Committee: "To be eligible for participation in the Olympic Games a competitor must comply with the Olympic Charter as well as with the rules of the IF concerned as approved by the IOC, and must be entered by his NOC. . . . The entry or participation of a competitor in the Olym-

pic Games shall not be conditional on any financial consideration." (1992 IOC Olympic Charter, Rule 45)

⊘United States Olympic Committee: "Amateur athlete means any athlete who meets the eligibility standards established by the national governing body for the sport in which the athlete competes." (Chapter 17, U.S.C.A. sec. 373 [1]) (See note 2.)

⊘Amateur Athletic Union: "Amateur" is one who engages in athletic competition or exhibition solely for the pleasure and physical, mental, or social benefits derived therefrom and to whom the sport in which the athlete is engaged is nothing more than an avocation. (1993 Code/Art. I, sec. 100.3.3)

• Massachusetts Interscholastic Athletic Association:

58.1	A student who represents a school in an interscholastic sport shall be an amateur in that sport. An athlete forfeits amateur status in a sport by:
58.1.1	Competing for money or other monetary compensation (allowable travel, meals, and lodging expenses may be accepted);
58.1.2	Receiving any award or prize of monetary value which has not been approved by the MIAA;
58.1.3	Capitalizing on athletic fame by receiving money or gifts of monetary value (scholarships to institutions of higher learning are specifically exempted); or
58.1.4	Signing a professional playing contract in that sport.
58.2	Accepting a nominal standard fee or salary for instructing or officiating in an organized sports program or recreation, playground or camp activity shall not jeopardize amateur status....
58.3	Only awards of no intrinsic value and approved by MIAA may be accepted by a high school student-athlete as a result of participation in school or non-school competition in any sport recognized by the Association. . . .
58.4	Participating under an assumed name in any athletic contest shall make the student ineligible for one year. (*1991–93 MIAA Blue Book,* Rule 58)

☉USA Hockey: "An amateur hockey player is one who is registered with the national association governing amateur hockey and is not engaged in playing organized professional hockey under contract to a professional club. Any player having completed his/her contractual obligations to a professional club may apply to USA Hockey for reinstatement of his/her amateur status. Fee—$100.00." (*1992–93 Official Guide,* Operating Procedures No. C[IX])

☉ United States Tennis Association: "Any tennis player is an Amateur if he does not receive and has not received, directly or indirectly, pecuniary advantage by the playing, teaching, demonstrating or pursuit of the game except as expressly permitted by the USTA." (*1993 Official USTA Yearbook: Standing Orders of the USTA*, art. II [A1])

These definitions have sparked a lively controversy because of the serious consequences of defining an amateur athlete. At the international level, the International Olympic Committee in 1986 endorsed a proposed rule change to eliminate the distinction between amateur and professional athletes. Although the individual international sports federations retain the power to say who can compete in the Olympic Games, the Games are now open to professional athletes, at least in some sports. In 1987, for example, the International Tennis Federation (ITF) and the IOC approved a code of tennis eligibility that permitted the sport's millionaire stars to play in the 1988 Games. The IOC also allowed former World Hockey Association (WHA) players to compete at Sarajevo in 1984, and the International Hockey Federation (IHF) already allows NHL players to compete in its annual world championships. In soccer, a professional can compete unless he has played in the World Cup for a European or South American nation according to the Federation Internationale de Football Association (FIFA). In 1985, as an experiment, the International Olympic Committee voted to allow professionals under the age of twenty-three to participate in the 1988 Winter and Summer Games in the sports of ice hockey, tennis, and soccer. In 1989 the International Federation for Basketball (FIBA) voted to allow professional basketball players to compete in the 1992 Summer Olympics.

High school and collegiate athletic administrators must be familiar with these definitions because student-athletes who receive money or products related to a USA Track & Field approved competition, or compete with professionals on a team in an IHF annual world championship, may lose their eligibility under NCAA or high school regulations. Athletic administrators should also be aware that professionalism in one sport may impact amateur status in another sport. A case in point is that of Renaldo Nehemiah, a former world-class hurdler who joined the San Francisco Forty-Niners of the National Football League. Nehemiah lost his amateur track status for several years as a result of his pro football affiliation but was later reinstated after he retired from football. More recently, Willie Gault, a professional on the Chicago Bears National Football League team, also competed as an amateur, in this case in the sport of bobsledding.

Athletic administrators would be wise to explore the details and the interpretations of the definitions of "amateur" for those associations with which their student-athletes become involved. The definitions can be found in association bylaws or constitutions, and interpretations can be obtained by contacting the organization's rule interpretation department or attorney. Again, it is important to emphasize that the definitions of "amateur" have not changed as much as the interpretations of those definitions.

NOTES _____

1. USA Track & Field, America's national governing body for track, operates a Direct Payment License program (see Exhibit 4–1) from which athletes licensed according to this program can receive appearance fees, prize money, and endorsement fees directly from the event or sponsor. Any U.S. citizen or resident alien who is eligible for international competition and does not have collegiate eligibility, or is willing to give up their collegiate eligibility, may apply for a Direct Payment License from USA Track & Field. This new program became effective in 1993 replacing the TACTRUST agreement which allowed athletes to deposit athletic funds and earnings and withdraw money to pay for living, training expenses while still maintaining his or her amateur eligibility.

2. The United States Olympic Committee operates the Olympic Job Opportunities Program (OJOP) for amateur athletes with high Olympic potential. The program is designed to provide athletes with a high degree of financial security, an opportunity to progress toward a productive career, as well as the necessary time off for physical training and competitions. The job-matching program has served over 400 athletes since 1977. More than $1.3 million of the USOC's 1989–92 quadrennial budget is devoted to the OJOP.

3. For further information concerning the governance of amateur athletic associations, see Note, "Government of Amateur Athletics: The NCAA-AAU Dispute," 41 *S. Cal. L. Rev.* 464 (1968).

LEGAL PRINCIPLES PERTAINING TO AMATEUR ATHLETIC ASSOCIATIONS

Amateur athletic associations are a pervasive part of American society. Individuals in the United States begin participating in such organizations at an early age (Pop Warner Football, Biddy Basketball, etc.) and can continue to do so through adulthood (NFSHSA, NCAA, AAU Master's Program, etc.). This section explores the mechanisms and principles of law as they pertain to amateur athletic associations, examines the structure of some of the organizations, and reviews litigation involving these organizations. A listing of various athletic organizations appears in Exhibit 4–2.

As college and high school athletics administration becomes increasingly complex and accountable with regard to legal issues, a basic knowledge of law becomes a necessary tool for all athletic administrators. For example, when revoking a student-athlete's scholarship, an administrator must be attentive to due process considerations. Or, when an interscholastic eligibility rule must be established with re-

Exhibit 4–1
USA Track & Field Direct Payment License Agreement

PRESIDENT
Larry T. Ellis

VICE PRESIDENTS
Herman Frazier
Darlene Hickman
Patricia Rico

SECRETARY
Bill Roe

TREASURER
Steven K. Busley

EXECUTIVE DIRECTOR
Ollan C. Cassell

November 11, 1993

Dear Athlete:

In 1993, track and field made a major stride forward in allowing athletes of all abilities to receive directly any appearance, prize or endorsement monies earned. This great step for our sport took over a decade to achieve.

Before 1980, no track and field athlete could receive financial rewards. But 13 years ago, Frank Shorter put his career and eligibility on the line by entering into a corporate sponsorship -- thereby helping pull the sport away from previous definitions of amateurism. In 1981, The Athletics Congress introduced legislation and led the IAAF to change its rules with TACTRUST, which was designed to allow athletes to benefit monetarily from their hard work and effort. The TACTRUST system allowed athletes to draw out living and training expenses, lengthen their competitive careers, and put the USA on a more equal footing with the state-sponsored systems of the Eastern Bloc.

The new world order of 1990 allowed USA Track & Field to again take the initiative and propose to the IAAF a DIRECT payment arrangement to pass on these monies directly to the athletes. The direct payment system was passed at the IAAF Congress meeting in Stuttgart in August 1993.

The USA Track & Field Direct Payment License is a lifetime tool that allows money to go immediately and directly to the athlete. The license represents tremendous progress in modernizing our sport and helping support the unique athletic legacy and talent that makes up track and field today.

What follows is a complete description of USATF's Direct Payment program, inclusive of a license application. Please direct any questions regarding the program to USATF's Chief Financial Officer Barbara Rush.

Best regards,

USA TRACK & FIELD

Ollan C. Cassell

Ollan C. Cassell
Executive Director

Exhibit 4–1 continued

USA TRACK & FIELD
DIRECT PAYMENT LICENSE
PROGRAM

Effective with the IAAF Congress in August, 1993, athletes may receive appearance fees, prize money, and endorsement fees directly from the event or sponsor provided that the athlete has obtained a Direct Payment License from USA Track & Field.

Any U.S. citizen or resident alien who is eligible for international competition and does not have collegiate eligibility may apply for a Direct Payment License from USA Track & Field. A credit card style license will be issued to those whose application is approved. An athlete only needs to apply for the license once in his or her lifetime. However, it must be validated each year by the purchase of a USA Track & Field Membership card.

The athlete must make the following representations:

> Eligible to compete in accordance with USATF & IAAF Rules
> Abide by all applicable doping rules and comply with drug testing regulations
> Abide by all rules and regulations governing the sport including but not limited to:
>> IAAF Rule 12 regarding International Meetings
>> IAAF Rule 18 regarding Advertising and Displays during competition
>> IAAF Rule 53 regarding Ineligibility for International Competition
> Will only use an Athlete Representative registered with USATF
> Is a U.S. Citizen or a bona fide resident alien
> Does not have collegiate eligibility

All applications and appropriate fees will be forwarded to the USA Track & Field national office for processing. Athletes whose applications are accepted will be sent a letter notifying them of acceptance. The letter will incorporate a temporary Direct Payment License to be replaced with a permanent license in approximately three weeks.

Athletes who are registered by a National Club for individual athlete membership cards will be sent the annual validation stamp with a USATF Membership card. Athletes who receive their membership cards through a local Association must notify USATF by telephone or letter of their USATF membership card number and will be sent an annual validation stamp upon such notification.

The athlete's name and license number will be entered into a computer data base. A computer diskette and appropriate instructions will be sent to directors of Regulation 14 sanctioned events approximately one week before the date of the event. Hard copy print-outs will be available upon request if the computer diskette is not acceptable.

Event directors may only directly pay funds to those athletes who present a validated Direct Payment License or whose names appear on the list provided by USATF. An athlete's license is only valid if the athlete has renewed his or her USATF Membership Card. **The athlete's card is valid only if it has the current year's sticker on it or if his or her name appears on the USATF list.**

Exhibit 4–1 continued

If an athlete has a Direct Payment License, but has not validated it for the current year or if an athlete does not have a Direct Payment License, the event director may provide the athlete with an application. The athlete will complete the application and send appropriate fees to the USATF national office which will provide the appropriate numbers. The event director may contact USATF subsequent to the event to determine if the athlete has a valid licenses. The event director must withhold payment if the athlete does not obtain a license.

Only U.S. citizens and bona fide resident foreign athletes are eligible for Direct Payment Licenses. Details of payments to non-resident foreign athletes will be set forth during the formal invitation process with that athlete's Federation. The event director will be responsible for appropriate Federal income tax withholding on all such payments. USA Track & Field has produced a brochure on the issue of the Federal income tax requirements for non-resident foreign athletes. This brochure is available upon request from the USATF national office.

Event directors will continue to file a special sanction application if they are planning to pay appearance fees or award prize money. After the event, the event director will file a report on the payment of funds, including the Direct Payment License number of each athlete paid or a Direct Payment License application and appropriate fees.

Each event director will also receive notification regarding athletes whose direct payment license applications have been rejected or whose licenses have been revoked. Athletes on this list may not be paid by the event director.

Athletes who compete **only** at the Masters level are exempt from the Direct Payment License requirement. Athletes who qualify as Masters but wish continue in open competition must have a Direct Payment License.

Athletes with a valid Direct Payment License may also receive sponsor and endorsement fees directly from the sponsor or its agent. Such fees no longer need to be paid to USA Track & Field. However, the sponsorship or endorsement contract must still be between USATF and the sponsor. The athlete signs a release for use of his or her name by the sponsor. Athletes who receive sponsor fees directly without an agreement with USA Track & Field may be subject to disciplinary action.

Applications for a Direct Payment License may be accepted by Regulation 14 Sanctioned event directors, USATF Association Representatives or the USATF national office. Direct Payment Licenses are only issued by the USATF national office.

Athlete Representatives are expected to ensure that all of their athletes have Direct Payment Licenses and have current USATF athlete membership cards. All USATF membership cards expire as of December 31. Athlete representatives may apply for athlete membership cards through the USATF National Office or through any USATF local Association.

Questions from athletes regarding this program may be directed to Barbara Rush, Chief Financial Officer of USA Track & Field. Race and Meet Directors should direct their questions to USATF's Director of Operations.

Exhibit 4–1 continued

Rule 12

International Meetings - Competitors Competing Abroad - Qualifications of Competitors

1. At the following International Meetings, the rules and regulations of the I.A.A.F. must apply:

    (a)   Olympic Games, World Championships and World Cups.
    (b)   Continental, Regional or Area Championships or Cups open to all I.A.A.F. Members in the Area or Region (i.e. Championships over which the I.A.A.F. has exclusive control, comprising only athletics events).
    (c)   Group Games (i.e. Area or Group Games at which competition in several sports is to take place, and over which therefore, the I.A.A.F. has no exclusive control).
    (d)   Matches between two or more Members, or combination of Members.
    (e)   International Invitation meetings specifically sanctioned by the I.A.A.F.
          See Rule 13.3 (b).
    (f)   International Invitation Meetings specifically sanctioned by an Area Group Association.
    (g)   Other meetings specifically sanctioned by a Member so that foreign athletes may take part.

2. All International Meetings or any meetings in which any foreign athlete takes part must be sanctioned by the I.A.A.F. or by a Member. In order to obtain the sanction referred to in 12, 1 (e), a Member must apply on behalf of the meeting organizer to the I.A.A.F. for a permit.
    See Rule 13.3 (b).

    Before sanctioning any International Meeting under Rule 12, 1 (e), 1 (f) or 1 (g) above, the I.A.A.F., Area Group Association or Member must obtain from the promoter an undertaking in writing:

    (a)   that all I.A.A.F. Rules and Regulations will be observed;
    (b)   that in particular, the Rules relating to expenses will be strictly followed;
    (c)   that all prizes should be intended for the athlete and should not exceed the value of US 250 or its equivalent in the currency of the organizing country;
    Note - *A prize is defined as an object which is neither cash nor marketable security.*
    (d)   that an account of all such expenses paid will be forwarded within 30 days to the Member sanctioning such a meeting, if requested by that Member.

Exhibit 4–1 continued

3.   No member may grant its sanction for a meeting under I.A.A.F. Rule
      12.1 (g), being a meeting which extends invitations to athletes from
      more than 5 (five) members other than the host Member, taking place
      during the period May 1st to September 30th, unless the meeting has
      had its date reserved in the Athletic Calendar by 30th November of the
      year preceding the intended date of the meeting.

      In the exceptional circumstances, however, a Meeting Organizer who
      has not reserved a date may apply to the Council for permission to add
      a meeting to the Athletic calendar.

4.   No athlete or club may take part in an athletic meeting in a foreign
      country without the written approval of his governing body, and no
      Member shall allow any foreign athlete to enter any competition
      without such permit certifying that he is eligible and permitted to
      compete in the country concerned.

      No athlete may have affiliation abroad, without previous authorization
      from his original Federation.

      Even then, the Federation of the country in which the athlete is
      residing, cannot enter any athlete's name for meetings in another
      country without previous authorization from the original Federation.

5.   In approving the participation of an athlete at an athletic meeting in a
      foreign country, the Member should specify the number of days for
      which the athlete and any accompanying manager or coach is
      permitted to receive expenses and the daily allowances detailed in
      Rule 14 "Expenses", paragraphs 1 and 2.

      After the meeting, the Member may request an account of expenses
      paid.

6.   Any athlete competing in any foreign country (other than in
      international meetings as above defined) shall, in respect of that
      competition, be subject to the athletic laws of that country.

7.   All negotiations for the participation of an athlete in another country
      shall be carried on through the Members concerned or through the
      relevant Athletes' Representatives, or directly with athletes. Formal
      invitations shall not be extended directly or indirectly to an athlete by
      any individual, club, college, university or other organization.

      However, a Member may authorize one of its member clubs to
      communicate with the club of another country concerning the
      participation of one or more of its athletes, subject to the expressed
      condition that the Member concerned is kept informed as to the
      content of any communications.

Exhibit 4–1 continued

8. Where an athlete of any member country receives a scholarship from an institution in another country, then as a condition to and before the athlete's governing body shall grant the permission to compete referred to in Rule 12(4), the President of the institution granting the scholarship shall first submit to the Member, in whose country the educational institution is located, full and detailed information of the nature and extent of the scholarship aid furnished to the athlete, for transmission to the Member for the athlete's country.

9. In International meetings under categories 1(a) and 1(b) of Rule 12, Members shall be represented only by citizens (by birth or naturalization or registration) of the country which the affiliated Member represents, or by athletes otherwise acquiring citizenship by the procedure legally recognized in that country, except in the case of citizens of a colony, when they shall be eligible to represent the mother country in any such meeting, if such colony is not represented by membership of the I.A.A.F. having once represented any Member in a Meeting which comes within the categories defined in 1(a) and 1(b), no contestant may thereafter represent any other member in such a meeting except in the following circumstances:

    (a) The incorporation of one country in another.
    (b) The creation of a new country ratified by Treaty.
    (c) The election to membership off the I.A.A.F. of the national governing body of a colony not previously directly represented by a Member.
    (d) A change of citizenship by marriage.
    (e) Residence in a country for at least three years since the date when the athlete last represented another Member in a Meeting under Rule 12,1(a) or (b), and, if there are legal provisions for acquiring citizenship of that country, compliance with such provisions. The period of residence may be reduced to one year, if the two Members concerned agree, and if the Council of the I.A.A.F. approves.
    (f) Where an athlete holds, or is legally entitled to hold citizenship of two or more countries, provided that it is at least three years since the athlete las represented the first Member in any competition under Rule 12, paragraphs 1(a) and (b). The period of residence may be reduced to one year, if the two Members concerned agree, and if the Council of the I.A.A.F. approves.

10. Athletes from a National Federation or some other athletics organization which is not an affiliated Member of the I.A.A.F. may compete in any competition except for meetings listed under paragraph 1(a) and (b) of Rule 12 against athletes under the jurisdiction of a Member, provided:

Exhibit 4–1 continued

 (a) that the Federation or Organization concerned is not at that time suspended by the I.A.A.F. or excluded from particular categories of competition;

 (b) that the athletes concerned are amateurs;

 (c) that the prior permission of the Council is given upon the application of the Member in the country or territory where the competition is to take place, or of the Member wishing to send athletes to compete in a non-Member country or territory;

 (d) that where the competition is held in a non-Member country or territory, the member must obtain an undertaking from the organizing body that in all other respects, the rules of the I.A.A.F. will be observed.

11. (a) When a citizen from a country which is suspended from the I.A.A.F. is seeking to become a national of an eligible country, he may compete in domestic competition on condition that:

  (i) he renounces his former nationality in the process of applying for citizenship of an eligible country and publicly states this fact by advising the Members concerned;

  (ii) he completes at least one year's continuous residence in his new country;

  (iii) the domestic competition in which he participates does not include athletes from other Federations.

 (b) An athlete who has complied with the requirements of 11(a) above may compete in international meetings, under Rules 12.1(e), (f) and (g) after completing **two years'** continuous residence in the new country.

 (c) An athlete who has complied with the requirements of 11(a) above may represent his new Federation in international competitions under Rule 12.1 (a) to (d) only after completing a period of **three years** continuous residence in, and after he has acquired citizenship of, his new country.

 (d) The period of continuous residence shall be computed on the basis of a year of 365 days, starting from the day after a person lands in the country where he/she seeks to gain nationality.

 (e) In any continuous 365 day period, an athlete may not spend more than a total of 90 days in the territory of a suspended country.

 (f) Any athlete seeking to qualify under this Rule must refrain from any athletic activities, which shall include, but not be restricted to, exhibition races, training, coaching, officiating, lecturing, giving interviews and publicity interviews, with any members of an athletic federation which is under suspension.

Exhibit 4–1 continued

12. I.A.A.F. Members and their officials, coaches and athletes, are not to conduct any activities, as defined in paragraph 12.11(f) above, associated with athletes of a suspended Member, their officials, coaches, judges, athletes, etc. In case of any infringement of this Rule, the provisions for suspensions and sanction laid down in Rule 2 shall apply.

Rule 18
Advertising and Displays during Competition

General

1. Advertising and displays of a promotional nature shall be permitted in all events held under I.A.A.F. Rule 12.1 (a)-(g), provided such advertising and displays comply with the terms of this Rule and any Regulations made under it. In addition all advertising and displays must comply with the local legal requirements and in meetings held under I.A.A.F. Rule 12.1(g) must be consistent with the Rules of the Member in whose territory the competition is taking place.

2. The Council may pass Regulations giving detailed guidance as to the form advertising may take and the manner in which promotional or other material may be displayed during competitions. These Regulations may be amended by the Council. Any such amendment shall come into force immediately after the Council meeting making any such decision.

3. The advertising of tobacco products is prohibited. The advertising of alcohol products is prohibited unless expressly permitted by the Council.

4. Only advertising of a commercial or charitable nature shall be allowed at meetings conducted under I.A.A.F. Rules. No advertising which has as its objective the advancement of any political cause of the interests of any pressure group, whether domestic or international, shall be allowed.

5. No advertising may appear which is in the opinion of the I.A.A.F., tasteless, distracting, offensive, defamatory or unsuitable bearing in mind the nature of the event. No advertising may appear which obscures, either partially or otherwise, the television camera's view of a competition. All advertising must comply with any applicable safety regulations.

6. Meeting organizers may only acknowledge sponsors during the competition as permitted in Regulations made under this Rule.

Exhibit 4–1 continued

7.   No identification of sponsors of individual athletes may appear on advertising inside the competition arena. For the purposes of these Rules and any Regulations made hereunder references to the competition shall include where relevant all activity within the competition arena.

8.   The I.A.A.F. shall have the right to review any contract entered into by any Member to ensure compliance with all applicable I.A.A.F. Rules and regulations. Members should insert a provision in their constitution which allows them to review any advertising contracts entered into by an individual athlete or by a club. In appropriate cases, the I.A.A.F. may ask members for copies of contracts between advertisers and athletes or clubs within their jurisdiction.

9.   Members must ensure that no contract between a sponsor or advertiser and an athlete contains a provision obliging the athlete either to organize his competition schedule in accordance with directions given by the sponsor or advertiser, or obliging the athlete to appear at meetings designated by the sponsor or advertiser, other than those meetings at which the sponsor or advertiser is also sponsor of the meeting.

Advertising Boards

10.   Advertising material may appear on boards outside or inside the competition arena, on notices or posters at the meeting or in programs relating to the meeting, as provided in the Regulations.

11.   All advertising boards must be solidly attached to supporting structures and, other than in exceptional circumstances, may not be moved from the time the competition starts to its finish. The advertising on such boards must remain the same throughout each day of competition. It may, however, be changed after each day's competition.

Technical Equipment

12.   Technical equipment for use in competition may carry the manufacturers name, label or trademark, or the name of the competition or competition venue, or the name or logo of the Member under whose jurisdiction the competition is organized. The number, size and combination of the markings allowed to be placed on each specific piece of equipment is to be found in the Regulations. However, other than as provided in the Regulations, no more than one brand name, label or trademark or other identification may appear on any one piece of equipment.

Exhibit 4–1 continued

Clothing

13. All clothing worn by competitors in the competition arena must conform to these Rules and any Regulations made hereunder. All Members must submit to the I.A.A.F. for central registration purposes details of all sponsorship agreements entered into by the national team in consequence of which advertising will appear on national team competition clothing. Members should also keep a register of all approved club sponsor identification, which must be made available to the I.A.A.F. These details should include a photograph of the complete uniform including the marks of recognition of any sponsor.

14. In meetings held under I.A.A.F. Rules 12.1(a), (b) and (c), no sponsor identification, other than that of the manufacturer of the clothing, may appear on any clothing worn by an athlete. In competitions held under I.A.A.F. Rule 12.1 (d) one mark of sponsor identification of the national team, as registered with the I.A.A.F. may appear on any clothing worn by any athlete, provided that the Member hosting the event agrees. In meetings held under I.A.A.F. Rule 12.1 (e), (f) and (g) athletes may wear clothing displaying either national team or club identification, provided this has been registered in accordance with the Rule.

15. No competitor, official or any other person wearing any clothing in breach of these Rules or any Regulations made hereunder will be allowed into the competition arena. It is a condition of the grant of a permit by the I.A.A.F. that the Meeting Organizer ensures compliance with these Rules and Regulations made hereunder.

Other Equipment taken into the Competition Arena

16. Any other equipment taken into the competition arena (for example bags) shall also be subject to Regulations made under this Rule.

Athletes Number Cards

17. Athletes number cards must comply with the technical requirements laid down in the Regulations. These cards must be worn as issued and may not be cut, folded or obscured in any way. In long distance events these cards may be perforated to assist the circulation of air, but the perforation must not be made on any of the lettering or numerals which appear on them.

Exhibit 4–1 continued

Clubs Sponsored by Commercial Enterprises

18.   If the Member for the territory in which a club is based agrees, a commercially sponsored club may be registered in the name of a sponsor. With the agreement of such Member, the name of not more than one sponsor may be added to, or incorporated in, the existing club name.

19.   Each member should submit, if requested, to the I.A.A.F. for central registration, any sponsor identification which is to appear on commercially sponsored club vests, or other clothing as permitted by these Rules. This information should include a photograph of the club uniform.

20.   International Commercial Clubs, i.e. clubs consisting of athletes who are not normally resident in the territory of the Member under whose jurisdiction the club is organized, shall not be permitted.

Enforcement and Sanctions

21.   The I.A.A.F. council may appoint one or more designated individuals to act as I.A.A.F. Advertising Commissioners. The powers and duties of such Commissioners are more clearly expressed in the Regulations made pursuant to this Rule. In the event of a conflict between the decision of the Advertising Commissioner and that of a competition official, the view of the Advertising Commissioner will prevail.

22.   Where a breach of these Rules or any Regulations made hereunder have taken place, the designated I.A.A.F. Advertising Commissioner may impose sanctions which may include a period of ineligibility or a fine. Details of the sanctions which may be imposed, and of the relevant disciplinary procedures, are to be found in the Regulations made hereunder.

Rule 53
Ineligibility for International and Domestic Competition

1.   The following persons are ineligible to take part in competitions, whether held under I.A.A.F. Rules or the domestic Rules of the Member.

   Any person:
   (i)   whose National Federation is currently suspended by the I.A.A.F.;
   (ii)   who has taken part in any athletic meeting or event in which any of the competitors were, to his knowledge, ineligible for compete under I.A.A.F. Rules, or which takes place in the territory of a suspended Member. This does not apply to any athletic meeting which is restricted to the Veteran age groups (40 years or over for men and 35 years and over for women);

Exhibit 4–1 continued

(iii)   who takes part in an athletic meeting which is not sanctioned, recognized or certified by the member in the country in which the event is held;

(iv)   who is ineligible to compete in competitions under the jurisdiction of his National Federation, in so far as such ineligibility is consistent with the I.A.A.F. Rules;

(v)   who contravenes Rules 55 to 61. ("Control of Drug Abuse");

(vi)   who has competed, or is competing in any sport for pecuniary reward, other than as permitted by I.A.A.F. Rules or by special sanction of the council;

Note - No person shall be declared ineligible who prior to August 21st, 1991, has (i) competed for pecuniary reward in a sport other than athletics or (ii) entered into a contract or agreement to compete as a professional in any sport other than athletics. Any person who, prior to August 21st, 1991, has been declared ineligible by virtue of having (i) competed for pecuniary reward in a sport other than athletics or (ii) entered into a contract or agreement to compete as a professional in any sport other than athletics shall be deemed eligible after September 15th, 1991, without further action of the Council or the Athlete's Federation.

(vii)   accepts directly or indirectly any money or other consideration for expenses or loss of earnings, other than what is permitted under Rules 14, 15 and 16;

(viii)   who has committed any act or made any statement either verbally or in writing, or has been responsible for any breaches of the Rules or other conduct which in the opinion of the I.A.A.F. Council is considered to be insulting or improper or likely to bring the sport into disrepute;

(ix)   who contravenes Rule 17 (Athletic Funds) or any Regulations made thereunder;

(x)   who contravenes Rule 18 (Advertising and Displays during Competition) or any Regulations made thereunder;

(xi)   who uses the services of an Athlete's Representative, other than one approved by the relevant Member under Rule 19;

(xii)   who has been declared ineligible by virtue of a breach of any Regulations made under I.A.A.F. Rules.

2.   Unless the period of such ineligibility is stated in the relevant I.A.A.F. rule or Regulations, those ineligible under this Rule shall be ineligible for a period set down in guidelines produced by the Council. In the absence of such guidelines, the Council may decide upon the appropriate period of ineligibility.

Reprinted from 1992-1993 IAAF Handbook

Exhibit 4–1 continued

QUESTIONS AND ANSWERS

ATHLETES

When do I need to have a Direct Payment License?
Athletes must obtain a Direct Payment License to accept prize money or appearance fees or to receive stipend funds and prize money from USA Track & Field, or to participate in the Athlete Sponsorship Program.

What is the fee for a Direct Payment License?
There is a one time application fee of $25.00. However, the athlete must validate his or her license annually by obtaining a USATF Athlete Membership card.

How does USATF know that I have purchased my Membership Card?
Athletes who are registered by National Clubs will have their records automatically up-dated. Other athletes should call the USATF national office DPL Department and report their new membership number.

What if I win prize money and don't have a Direct Payment License?
The meet or race director can provide you with an application for a license. After completing the application, send it with payment to the USATF national office to process your license.

What if I don't have my license with me?
USATF provides each meet and race director with a current list of licensed athletes approximately one week prior to the meet. The event director will also receive a list of athletes who may not receive direct payment in cases where a license has been revoked or an application has been rejected.

Why might a license be revoked or application rejected?
Licenses will be revoked if an athlete becomes ineligible for competition. Applications will be rejected if not filled out completely or if deletions or modifications have been made to the certifications and representations on the application.

The application states that I must use a USATF authorized athlete representative. What does that mean?
If you choose to use an athlete represenative, that representative must be registered with USATF. It does not require an athlete to have representative.

What if I lose my license?
You can request a replacement card for a modest fee.

I am a Masters athlete -- do I need a Direct Payment License?
You only need a Direct Payment License if you are also planning to continue to compete at the elite senior level. If you compete exclusively in Masters competition, you do not need a license.

How does the Direct Payment License affect the Athlete Sponsorship Program?
With the Direct Payment License, you still must have the agreement signed by USATF and the sponsor in accordance with IAAF Rule 17. However, all fees may be paid directly to you, if you have a Direct Payment License. Payments no longer need to be made to USATF and then forwarded to you.

Do I need a Direct Payment License to receive stipend payments?
Yes, you will need a Direct Payment License to receive stipend payments.

Exhibit 4–1 continued

I still have funds in my TACTRUST account. What happens to those funds?
Those funds belong to you and may be withdrawn immediately once you have your Direct Payment License. All Trustees will be notified of the change in the program and the terms under which athletes may withdraw remaining balances.

What if I would like to maintain my TACTRUST account?
If it is acceptable to your trustee, you may maintain your account. However, it will not replace a Direct Payment License if you need one. If you maintain your TACTRUST account and have a Direct Payment License, you do not need USATF's approval to withdraw funds.

MEET AND RACE DIRECTORS

Do I need to obtain a special sanction if I award prize money and appearance fees?
Yes, you still need to complete a "Regulation 14" Sanction if you plan to award prize money or appearance fees. We need to have a special identification for these sanctions so that we can inform you of athletes who may and may not receive direct payments.

How will I know who can receive Direct Payments?
Approximately one week before your event, you will receive a diskette that contains an ASCII file of the athletes who have valid licenses and the athletes whose licenses have been revoked or denied. The diskette will contain a program that will allow you to search the file by name. You will also be able to print the file.

What if an athlete's name does not appear on the list?
You may give a Direct Payment License application from the athlete, provided he or she is a U.S. Citizen or Resident Alien. The athlete will complete the application and mail all applicable fees to the USATF national office. The athlete will be notified of his or her USATF membership card and license number and may give you this information. Or you may call the national office directly to follow up on unlicensed athletes. Under no circumstances may you pay athletes who do not hold valid licenses.

How do I know if an athlete has been suspended or had a license revoked?
The diskette will specifically identify athletes who may not receive direct payments if they have been suspended, declared ineligible, or have not met all of the provisions of the application.

What about non-resident foreign athletes?
Since the new IAAF rules allow each country to establish its own method of monitoring payments to its athletes. In cases where foreign athletes are invited to compete in your event, payment terms will be detailed by the athlete's Federation.

What if the athlete has a license, but does not have a current USATF Membership?
You may accept the membership application and $12.00 fee from the athlete and forward that to the USATF national office with your report.

What if the athlete says he or she already has a USATF member number, but doesn't know it?
Give the athlete the option of filling out a new application to receive the money immediately and you'll return the $12.00 when the athlete gives you the USATF number, within a reasonable time period or hold the funds until the athlete calls or presents the number. Do not accept "applied for" in lieu of a USATF membership number.

REV. 11/93

Exhibit 4–1 continued

USA TRACK & FIELD

APPLICATION FOR DIRECT PAYMENT LICENSE

Please return to:
USA TRACK & FIELD
P.O. BOX 120
INDIANAPOLIS, IN 46206

The USA Track & Field Direct Payment License allows U.S. and resident foreign athletes to receive appearance fees, prize money, and endorsement fees directly from the event or sponsor. U.S. Athletes may apply for a lifetime or annual card while resident foreign athletes may only apply for an annual card. All license holders must hold current USATF membership cards for their license to be valid. License holders must renew USATF membership cards on an annual basis and will be sent validation sticker for their license.

Name _____

Address _____

_____

Daytime Phone _____

Country of Citizenship _____

Social Security Number _____

Date of application _____   Date of Birth_____

Age _____   Male ___   Female ___   U.S. Citizen   Yes ___ No ___

I compete in: Track & Field ___   Long Distance Running ___   Race Walking ___

Club Number _____ Club Name _____

If you have a valid USATF membership card enter the number here _____. If not, please enclose an additional $12.00 for your membership card.

I certify and represent that:

I am eligible to compete in accordance with the rules of USA Track & Field and the IAAF
I will abide by all applicable doping rules and comply with drug testing regulations
I will abide by all rules and regulations governing the sport including but not limited to:
    IAAF Rule 12 regarding International Meetings
    IAAF Rule 18 regarding Advertising and Displays during Competition
    IAAF Rule 53 regarding Ineligibility for International Competition
If I elect to use an agent or athlete representative, that individual will be registered with USATF
I am a U.S. Citizen or a resident alien
I do not have collegiate or high school athletic eligibility under NCAA or NAIA rules

_____
Signature

REQUIRED FEES:

Direct Payment License	$25.00	_____
USATF Membership Card	$12.00	_____

Rev. 11/93

Exhibit 4–2
Amateur Athletic Associations and Organizations

Council of Ivy Group Presidents
70 Washington Road, Princeton, NJ 08544. (609) 452-6426
Strives to provide sound and balanced athletic programs within an academic framework.

National Association of Intercollegiate Athletics (NAIA)
1221 Baltimore St., Kansas City, MO 64105. (816) 842-5050
Formed in 1940, the NAIA administers programs of intercollegiate athletes for over 500 member institutions.

National Christian College Athletic Association (NCCAA)
1815 Union Ave., Chattanooga, TN 37404. (615) 698-6021
Formed in 1966, the NCCAA provides Christian athletes in Christian colleges an opportunity to be a national champion.

National Collegiate Athletic Association (NCAA)
6201 College Blvd., Overland Park, KS 66211-2422. (913) 339-1906
Formed in 1905, the NCAA is the premier governing body of intercollegiate athletics.

National Collegiate Football Association (NCFA)
15 Tulipwood Drive, Commack, NY 11725. (516) 543-0730
Founded in 1976, the NCFA sponsors and encourages intercollegiate competititon in nonvarsity football programs.

National Junior Colleges Athletic Association (NJCAA)
12 East 2nd, Hutchinson, KS 67501. (316) 663- 5445
Formed in 1937, the NJCAA promotes and supervises a national program of junior college sports and activities.

National Little College Athletic Association (NLCAA)
R.R. #1, Princeton, IN 47670. (812) 385-5757
Formed in 1966, the NLCAA sponsors intercollegiate competition for smaller schools (fewer than 500).

United States Olympic Committee (USOC)
1750 East Boulder St., Colorado Springs, CO 80909. (719) 632-5551
Coordinates U.S. participation in Olympics.

International Olympic Committee (IOC)
Chateau de Bidy CH-1007, Lausanne, Switzerland. Phone: 41-21-54-25-55
Governs the Olympic movement and exercises all rights over the Olympic Games.

U.S.A. Basketball
1750 East Boulder St., Colorado Springs, CO 80909. (303) 632-7687
Founded 1975; serves as a class A member of the United States Olympic Committee

American Baseball Coaches Association (ABCA)
605 Hamilton Drive, Champion, IL 61820. (217) 371-6000
Founded in 1945, the ABCA furthers the game of baseball in schools and colleges.

American Football Coaches Association (AFCA)
7758 Wallace Road, Suite I, Orlando, FL 32819. (305) 351-6113
Founded in 1922, the AFCA promotes the sport of football through the exchange of information among coaches.

College Sports Information Directors of America
Campus Box 114, Kingsville, TX 78363.
Founded in 1955; provides the exchange of ideas among members of the sports information profession.

gard to married student-athletes or transfer student-athletes, the high school administrator should be aware of the potential for claims of equal protection violations.

Three legal concepts that are particularly important in the application of the law to the areas of amateur athletics are limited judicial review, standing, and injunctive relief. The concept of *limited judicial review* derives from a theory that courts should not review every legislative judgment of an organization but rather defer to the organization's decisions. The legal system intervenes as a general rule through judicial review only when legislative actions violate rights guaranteed by the Constitution, rights granted by the institution concerned, or basic notions of fairness. It should be noted that federal courts possess a more limited power of review than do state courts. This means that only cases involving certain constitutional issues will be heard at the federal level, while most others are deferred to the state level. The federal courts may thus be prevented from reviewing cases that might be subject to review at the state court level. A case in which an action by the state violates a federal constitutional right is, however, usually subject to judicial review at the federal level.

Standing is a procedural device that must be demonstrated prior to the initiation of any lawsuit. The requirement of standing is based on the theory that all cases brought before the legal system must be part of a current or an ongoing controversy. Academic curiosity or contrived situations are not sufficient requisites for a plaintiff to demonstrate standing.

The type of relief to be granted is the third important legal concept. Two types of relief are commonly sought: *monetary damages* and *injunctive relief.* Since monetary damages do not always give the plaintiff appropriate or adequate relief, the equitable remedy of injunctive relief is available. Injunctive relief is a fair, nonmonetary form of compensation to redress a wrong or an injury. This type of relief is particularly important in amateur sports during the period in which legal action involving that participation is being tried in the courts. Time often is of the essence, and injunctive relief may be crucial to the student-athlete, since it allows him or her to continue competing.

These three concepts—limited judicial review, standing, and injunctive relief—are examined in greater detail in the following subsections.

Judicial Review

College and high school athletic administrators make decisions and take actions regarding rules and regulations every day. Yet athletic administrators must realize that as decision makers they do not possess uncontroverted control over student-athletes. Some decisions may be reviewed by the courts. Historically, courts have refused to intervene in the internal affairs of organizations that govern any aspect of a school's athletic program. However, beginning in the 1960s, student-athletes began to challenge the authority that was delegated to directors of athletic programs, because these administrators had begun to regulate personal behavior, including marriage and physical appearance. Courts accepted jurisdiction over these cases and invalidated rules that interfered with the constitutional rights of individual participants.

Private voluntary associations such as the National Collegiate Athletic Association (NCAA), the National Junior College Athletic Association (NJCAA), USA Track & Field, and state high school athletic associations and conferences are ordinarily allowed to make and enforce their own rules without interference from the courts. By becoming a member of such an organization, an individual and/or an institution agrees to be bound by the athletic association's existing rules as well as any others subsequently passed.

As a general rule, the courts will review a voluntary association's rules only if one of the following conditions is present:

1. The rules violate public policy because they are fraudulent or unreasonable.
2. The rules exceed the scope of the association's authority.
3. The organization violates one of its own rules.
4. The rules are applied unreasonably or arbitrarily.
5. The rules violate an individual's constitutional rights.

For example, in one high school case, the courts determined that if a rule regulating either hair length or facial hair was reasonable and was advancing an educational purpose, it should be obeyed. Thus, the federal court decided to defer to the judgment of school officials. Yet, in another case, a court struck down a good-conduct rule on due process and equal protection grounds because it was too broad and attempted to regulate a student-athlete's conduct during the off-season (*Bunger v. Iowa High School Athletic Ass'n*, 197 N.W.2d 555 [Iowa Sup. Ct. 1972]) (see note 1d). The harshness of a rule is not by itself grounds for judicial relief. Relief is granted only for those rules found to be in violation of one of the above conditions.

Even if the rule is subject to review, the role of a court is very limited. A court will not review the merits of the rule involved. It will only determine whether the rule is invalid by virtue of one of the five standards listed. If a violation is found, the case is remanded or deferred back to the athletic association for further consideration based on directions from the court.

Constitutional violations that require judicial intervention are often based on either due process or equal protection considerations. Due process involves infringements on life, liberty, or property, and equal protection involves the fair application of laws to individuals. Both of these constitutional standards require that state action be present prior to judicial review (state action is discussed later in the chapter).

Amateur athletic associations can guard against judicial scrutiny by reviewing and updating rules and regulations so that they (1) protect the health and welfare of athletes and serve to protect a justifiable public interest and (2) are consistent with court decisions in the state, region, or nation regarding similar rules. If a case is brought, the court is then more likely to show great deference to the judgment of the athletic administrators who created these rules and are best equipped to decide controversies concerning them. Only evidence of fraud, collusion, or unreasonable, arbitrary, or capricious action will cause a court to intervene on behalf of an athlete concerning the interpretation of a rule.

NOTES ───

   1. The courts *granted* review in the following cases.

     (a) In *California State University, Hayward v. National Collegiate Athletic Ass'n*, 47 Cal. App. 3d 533, 121 Cal. Rptr. 85 (Cal. Ct. App. 1975), a university filed a request for an injunction to prevent the NCAA from designating the entire intercollegiate athletic program as indefinitely ineligible for postseason play. The court ruled that when a voluntary association such as the NCAA clearly violates one of its own rules, its decision is subject to judicial review.

     (b) In *Estay v. LaFourche Parish School Board*, 230 So. 2d 443 (La. Ct. App. 1969), a rule prohibiting athletic participation for married students was held to be invalid because it exceeded the scope of the school board's authority and was therefore unreasonable.

     (c) In *Dunham v. Pulsifer*, 312 F. Supp. 411 (D. Vt. 1970), a rule requiring short hair for male student-athletes was held to be invalid because it was beyond the school board's authority to make such a rule. Athletic safety was not the issue, and even if it were, the problem could be solved by a much less intrusive measure such as requiring the wearing of headbands. (See Chapter 5.)

     (d) In *Bunger v. Iowa School Athletic Ass'n*, 197 N.W.2d 555 (Iowa Sup. Ct. 1972), a rule that denied eligibility to any student-athlete found in a car that also carried alcohol was held to be invalid. The rule was judged to be too far removed from the problem of high school drinking to be a reasonable exercise of authority. (See Chapter 5.)

   2. The courts *denied* review in the following cases.

     (a) In *Kentucky High School Athletic Ass'n v. Hopkins County Board of Education*, 552 S.W.2d 685 (Ky. Ct. App. 1977), a high school transfer student-athlete sought to prohibit the school from enforcing the state high school athletic association bylaw under which he was declared ineligible. The court held that the bylaw was valid and that it had not been arbitrarily applied. The court reasoned as follows: "It is not the responsibility of the courts to inquire into the expediency, practicality, or wisdom of the bylaws and regulations of voluntary associations. Furthermore, the courts will not substitute their interpretation of the bylaws ... so long as [the association's] interpretation is fair and reasonable."

(b) In *State ex rel. National Junior College Athletic Ass'n v. Luten,* 492 S.W.2d 404 (Mo. Ct. App. 1973), a junior college filed a request for equitable relief, alleging that the NJCAA had misinterpreted one of its rules. The court ruled that "the interpretation [of the NJCAA] being a reasonable and permissible one, and no other basis for the court's interference being present, the trial court lacked the jurisdiction to prohibit the implementation of the NJCAA ruling."

(c) In *Tennessee Secondary School Ass'n v. Cox,* 425 S.W.2d 597 (Tenn. Sup. Ct. 1968), a lower court's review of a transfer rule based on a violation of public policy and due process was ruled invalid because of lack of jurisdiction. The court held that participation in high school athletics is a privilege, not a legally cognizable right.

(d) In *Sanders v. Louisiana High School Athletic Ass'n,* 242 So.2d 19 (La. Ct. App. 1970), a high school student-athlete was ruled ineligible by the high school athletic association under the transfer rule, because he had been "enrolled" for a period of one year. The court held that it will not ordinarily interfere with a voluntary association unless the association deprives an individual of a property right or its actions are capricious, arbitrary, or unjustly discriminatory.

(e) In *Albach v. Odle,* 531 F.2d 983 (10th Cir. 1976), a high school student-athlete challenged the athletic association's transfer rule. The court held that unless the regulation denied the student-athlete a constitutionally protected right, the rules regarding transfer would remain within the discretion of the appropriate state board and would not be within federal jurisdiction.

(f) In *Colorado Seminary v. National Collegiate Athletic Ass'n,* 417 F. Supp. 885 (D. Colo. 1976), the court held that it should not act as arbiter of disputes between an athletic association and its member institutions.

3. For the proposition that harshness by itself is not grounds for judicial review, see the following cases.

(a) In *State v. Judges of Court of Common Pleas* 181 N.E.2d 261 (Ohio Sup. Ct. 1962), the state high school athletic association suspended a member high school from participating in athletics for one year and declared two boys from the high school ineligible for interscholastic athletics for failure to abide by association rules. The court held that this action should not be prohibited when, although harsh, determination was not the result of mistake, fraud, collusion, or arbitrariness.

(b) In *Shelton v. National Collegiate Athletic Ass'n,* 539 F.2d 1179 (9th Cir. 1976), the court found no violation of equal protection of an NCAA eligibility rule as applied to a college basketball player. The court did admit that "the application of such [eligibility] rules may produce unreasonable results in certain situations." Although the court recognized that the eligibility rule and its means of enforcement may not be the best way to achieve the objective of ensuring amateurism, it stated: "It is not judicial business to tell a voluntary athletic association how best to formulate or enforce its rules." (See Chapter 5.)

(c) In *Marino v. Waters*, 220 So. 2d 802 (La. Ct. App. 1969), a high school student-athlete who had transferred to another school because of his marriage, violated a policy of the private school he had originally attended. The court held that the rule was not arbitrary because it was promulgated for a legitimate purpose and was not applied in a discriminatory manner. Again, the mere harshness of a rule in its application to an individual does not make it subject to proper judicial review.

4. For further information, see the following law review articles.

(a) Note, "Judicial Control of Actions of Private Associations," 76 *Harv. L. Rev.* 983 (1963).

(b) Shuck, "Administration of Amateur Athletes." 48 *Fordham L. Rev.* 53 (1979).

(c) Lowell, "Federal Administrative Intervention in Amateur Athletics," 43 *Geo. Wash. L. Rev.* 729 (March 1975).

(d) Lowell, "Judicial Review of Rule Making in Amateur Athletics," 5 *J. C. & U. L.* 11 (1977).

5. Certain federal statutes are commonly cited in an effort to obtain federal court jurisdiction in athletic cases. Among them are the following:

28 U.S.C. section 1343—Civil Rights and Elective Franchise.

The district courts shall have original jurisdiction of any civil action authorized by law to be commenced by any person:

(1) To recover damages for injury to his person or property, or because of the deprivation of any right or privilege of a citizen of the United States, by any act done in furtherance of any conspiracy mentioned in section 1985 of Title 42;

(2) To recover damages from any person who fails to prevent or to aid in preventing any wrongs mentioned in section 1985 of Title 42 which he had knowledge were about to occur and power to prevent;

(3) To redress the deprivation, under color of any State law, statute, ordinance, regulation, custom or usage, of any right, privilege or immunity secured by the Constitution of the United States or by any Act of Congress providing for equal rights of citizens or of all persons within the jurisdiction of the United States;

(4) To recover damages or to secure equitable or other relief under any Act of Congress providing for the protection of civil rights, including the right to vote.

For purposes of this section—

(1) the District of Columbia shall be considered to be a State; and

(2) any Act of Congress applicable exclusively to the District of Columbia shall be considered to be a statute of the District of Columbia.

(b) 42 U.S.C. section 1983—Civil Action for Deprivation of Rights: "Every person who, under color of any statute, ordinance, regulation, custom, or usage, of any State or Territory or the District of Columbia, subjects, or causes to be subjected, any citizen of the United States or other person within the jurisdiction thereof to the deprivation of any rights, privileges, or immunities secured by the Constitution and laws, shall be liable to the party injured in an action at law, suit in equity, or other proper proceeding for redress. For the purposes of this section, any Act of Congress applicable exclusively to the District of Columbia shall be considered to be a statute of the District of Columbia."

Standing

In spite of safeguards designed to prevent judicial review, college and high school administrators may become involved in court cases. The athletic administrator may represent the school or the conference against a student-athlete's challenge, the student-athlete's interest against a larger association such as the NCAA, or the school in relation to a student-athlete's challenge of an NCAA rule. To proceed in these situations, the student-athlete and/or the school must first justify, to the satisfaction of the court, bringing the complaint to a court of law. If successful, the party bringing the suit is said to have established *standing.*

In order to establish standing in court, the plaintiff must meet three criteria. First, the plaintiff must demonstrate that the action in question did in fact cause an injury. Second, the plaintiff must establish that the interest to be protected is at least arguably within the zone of interests protected by the Constitution, legislative enactments, or judicial principles. This criterion is often labeled by the phrase "substantiality of federal question." Finally, the plaintiff must be the party whose interest was infringed upon. That is, the plaintiff must be an interested party or be otherwise directly involved. If the plaintiff has only a peripheral interest, there may be no standing. This often applies to an amateur association and one of its member institutions. An individual student-athlete therefore is not directly involved in the controversy because the individual is not a member of the amateur association. Consequently, the student-athlete who brings suit may be deemed to lack the necessary standing. An example is the NCAA, whose membership consists of colleges and universities and not of individual student-athletes.

NOTE

1. The following cases discuss the substantiality of federal question required for federal court jurisdiction in athletic association cases.
(a) In *Fluitt v. University of Nebraska*, 489 F. Supp. 1194 (D. Neb. 1980), the court found that there was a substantial federal question for two reasons: (1) the Supreme Court had not, in prior decisions, spoken clearly enough on the issues raised by the college student-athlete—in this case to render the claims frivolous or the subject foreclosed—and

(2) the student-athlete's claim alleged that two people in the identical situation are treated differently solely on the basis of their sex, and sex discrimination is one of the categories the tenth circuit court has held as presenting a substantial federal question. (See the section Substantive Due Process in this chapter.)

(b) In *Parish v. National Collegiate Athletic Ass'n*, 361 F. Supp. 1214 (W.D. La. 1973), *aff'd*, 506 F.2d 1028 (5th Cir. 1975), the court held that the NCAA's imposition of a rule requiring a grade point average of 1.600 for athletic eligibility does not raise a substantial federal question under the Civil Rights Act such that federal court jurisdiction would be appropriate. (See Chapter 5.)

(c) In *National Collegiate Athletic Ass'n v. Califano*, 444 F. Supp. 425 (D. Kan. 1978), *rev'd*, 622 F.2d 1382 (10th Cir. 1980), the NCAA challenged the Department of Health, Education and Welfare's jurisdiction with regard to Title IX. On appeal, the Tenth Circuit ruled that the NCAA had standing to challenge the application of Title IX legislation to intercollegiate athletic programs. The court based its decision on the fact that individual NCAA member institutions have the necessary standing to test the validity of Title IX regulations. The court stated that the NCAA could bring suit on behalf of its member institutions if it could show that it had their support. (See Chapter 8.)

(d) In *Georgia High School Athletic Ass'n v. Waddell*, 285 S.E.2d 7 (Ga. Sup. Ct. 1981), the court held that appeals of decisions made by football officials in game conditions are not subject to judicial review. The court ruled that were the decision to be otherwise, every error in the trial courts would constitute a denial of equal protection. The court further held that courts of equity in Georgia do not have authority to review decisions of football referees because they do not present judicial controversies.

(e) In *Watkins v. Louisiana High School Athletic Ass'n*, 301 So. 2d 695 (La. Ct. App. 1974), a spectator sought an injunction preventing an association from enforcing a ruling that prohibited her high school team from playing any athletic contests for one year if she was in attendance as a fan because of a dispute she had had with a referee. The Louisiana Court of Appeals held that the spectator had a sufficient legal interest to institute the suit, assuming a valid cause of action was alleged.

(f) In *Florida High School Activities Ass'n v. Bradshaw*, 369 So. 2d 398 (Fla. Dist. Ct. App. 1979), the court held that neither the coach nor team players had standing to assert a denial of equal protection to an individual player.

(g) In *Assmus v. Little League Baseball, Inc.*, 334 N.Y.S.2d 982 (N.Y. Sup. Ct. 1972), the court held that players who were not members of a baseball corporation did not have standing to attack the alleged illegality of the corporation's rule.

(h) In *Peebles v. National Collegiate Athletic Ass'n*, 723 F. Supp. 1155 (E.D. Va. 1988), the plaintiff brought action against the NCAA after his son was denied admission to the University of Georgia. The court ruled that the plaintiff failed to state any legally cognizable claim against the NCAA and therefore lacked standing to bring this lawsuit.

Injunctive Relief

Providing the plaintiff has been successful on the issues of limited judicial review and standing, the next step for the plaintiff is to request relief. Because enforcement of the rules and regulations of amateur athletic associations frequently prohibits athletes from competing, student-athletes and their schools often bring lawsuits to obtain relief in the form of injunctions that force the associations to allow the student-athlete to participate. These attempts to keep the student-athlete eligible are critical to the high school athlete hoping to obtain a college scholarship and to the collegiate athletic program striving for a profitable and prestigious winning team.

An *injunction is* a court order for one of the parties to a lawsuit to behave in a certain manner. Injunctive relief is designed to prevent future wrongs—not to punish past acts. It is only used to prevent an irreparable injury, which is suffered when monetary damages cannot be calculated or when money will not adequately compensate the injured party. An injury is considered irreparable when it involves the risk of physical harm and death, the loss of some special opportunity, or the deprivation of unique, irreplaceable property. For example, a high school football star may be granted an injunction to compete in an all-star game since an inability to do so may jeopardize his chances of obtaining a college scholarship.

The injunction is a form of equitable relief that can be used to force an athletic association to engage in or refrain from an action that affects an institution, an individual student-athlete, or a staff member. There are three types of injunctive relief: a temporary restraining order (TRO), a preliminary injunction, and a permanent injunction.

A *temporary restraining order* is issued to the defendant without notice and is usually effective for a maximum of ten days. The defendant is not bound by the TRO until actual notice is received. After receiving notice, the defendant can immediately ask the court for a review. A *preliminary injunction* is granted prior to a full hearing and disposition of a case. The plaintiff is obligated to give the defendant notice and also to post a bond. The defendant is usually present at the preliminary injunction hearing. The hearing on the issuance of a preliminary injunction is granted only in an apparent emergency and only if the plaintiff shows a likelihood of success for winning the case on the merits. Temporary restraining orders and preliminary injunctions are also granted during the course of a trial to preserve the status quo until the rights of the litigants can be determined. A *permanent injunction* may be issued after a full hearing, and if it is issued, it remains in force until the termination of the particular suit.

The issuance of any injunctive relief requires the exercise of sound judicial discretion. A judge generally considers three factors before granting or denying any form of equitable relief: the nature of the controversy, the objective of the injunction, and the comparative hardship or inconvenience to both parties. The judge then weighs these factors on a sliding scale before making a determination; the more likely a plaintiff is to succeed on the merits at trial, the less harm need be shown to obtain relief. However, if the prospects of success are bleak, a plaintiff would have to show a far greater degree of potential harm before relief would be granted.

An excellent example of the use of a preliminary injunction may be found in the case of Greg Kite, a high school basketball player (who later played several years in the NBA). Kite was declared ineligible for his senior year after attending a basketball camp, which was against state interscholastic association rules. Kite sued and was granted a preliminary injunction to prevent the high school athletic association from enforcing its training camp rule against him. The court maintained that Kite had a strong likelihood of winning the case, that he would suffer irreparable harm if he lost his senior year of competition, that it served the public interest to have Kite eligible, and that when the hardships were balanced, he would suffer more material harm if the injunction were denied than the association would suffer in having Kite compete until the matter came to trial (*Kite v. Marshall*, 454 F. Supp. 1347 [S. D. Tex. 1978]). Two years after Kite graduated, the trial concluded, with the Houston district court ruling for Kite. The court found that the parents' decision to send their child to summer basketball camp was important enough to warrant constitutional protection under the family's fundamental right of personal privacy, and that the interscholastic rule forbidding such summer camp participation was a violation of this privacy and therefore unconstitutional (*Kite v. Marshall*, 494 F. Supp. 227 [S.D. Tex. 1980]). On appeal, the interscholastic association was successful in reversing the lower court decision. The Court of Appeals found that the interscholastic league's summer camp rule did not violate either the due process or equal protection clauses of the Fourteenth Amendment (*Kite v. Marshall*, 661 F. 2d 1027 [5th Cir. 1981]).

NOTES ————————————————————————————————

1. Injunctions were *denied* in the following cases.
   (a) In *Samara v. National Collegiate Athletic Ass'n*, 1973 Trade Cases (CCH) ¶74,536 (E.D. Va.), two track athletes, students at NCAA schools,

wished to participate in a Russian-American meet sponsored by the Amateur Athletic Union. Under NCAA bylaws, this meet was an "extra event" that must be certified by the NCAA or the participating student-athletes would lose their NCAA eligibility. The plaintiffs sought injunctive and declaratory relief on the basis of the Sherman Act to prevent the NCAA from imposing sanctions due to their participation. Equitable relief was denied because the plaintiffs only faced a threat; they had not suffered any injury.

(b) In *Thompson v. Barnes*, 200 N.W.2d 921 (Minn. Sup. Ct. 1972), a student-athlete had been suspended for one year from participating in interscholastic athletics because of a second violation of the alcohol rule of the league to which his high school belonged. The student-athlete requested a temporary injunction staying his suspension until his motion for a permanent injunction could be heard. The request was denied because the student-athlete failed to show that he would have competed during the period of the suspension, that the suspension would cause irreparable injury pending trial, or that the permanent injunction sought in the main action would be insufficient relief.

(c) In *Kupec v. Atlantic Coast Conference*, 399 F. Supp. 1377 (M.D.N.C. 1975), a student-athlete's request for a preliminary injunction was ruled improper when the student-athlete did not show actual harm, when harm would be done to the college athletic conference by granting an injunction, and when the student-athlete did not seem likely to succeed on the merits of his claim.

(d) In *Florida High School Activities Ass'n v. Bradshaw*, 369 So. 2d 398 (Fla. Ct. App. 1979), an injunction was denied as improper when the student-athlete failed to show personal injury.

2. Injunctions were *granted* in the following cases.

(a) In *University of Nevada-Las Vegas v. Tarkanian*, 594 P.2d 1159 (Nev. Sup. Ct. 1979), University of Nevada at Las Vegas (UNLV) basketball coach Jerry Tarkanian was granted a temporary restraining order and then a permanent injunction barring UNLV from suspending him from his coaching duties for two years. UNLV was directed to impose the suspension by the NCAA Committee on Infractions under the show-cause provisions of the NCAA's enforcement procedures. On appeal to the Nevada Supreme Court, the permanent injunction was reversed and sent back to the Clark County District Court for further proceedings. (See the section Funding of Public Facilities, note 2.)

(b) In *Hall v. University of Minnesota*, 530 F. Supp. 104 (D. Minn. 1982), the court looked to four factors to determine whether a preliminary injunction should be issued: (1) the threat of irreparable harm to the moving party, (2) the state of balance between that harm and the injury that granting the injunction would inflict on other parties, (3) the public interest, and (4) the probability that the moving party would succeed on the merits of the claim. (See Chapter 5.) On the basis of all of these factors the Court issued an injunction requiring the university to admit the plaintiff into a degree program.

VOLUNTARY ATHLETIC ASSOCIATIONS

All amateur athletic organizations are subject to fundamental legal principles. Athletic associations and conferences, such as the National Federation of State High School Associations (NFSHSA), the NCAA, and the Big Ten, although private and voluntary organizations, are nevertheless scrutinized. The courts have begun to question these supposedly "private" athletic associations and conferences for two reasons: (1) large numbers of public institutions form the membership of these organizations, and (2) these organizations are performing a traditional government or public function.

In this public function vein, a number of organizations have been created to serve different groups of individuals in a variety of athletic activities. The Amateur Athletic Union (AAU) has, for almost 100 years, dedicated itself to the development of amateur sports and physical fitness for amateur athletes of all ages (e.g., the AAU Junior Olympics and the AAU Masters Program for adults age twenty-five and over). The NCAA has taken upon itself the role of a coordinator and overseer of college athletics, in the interest of individuals and their educational institutions. As these organizations become more and more a part of the public domain in the eyes of the judicial system, it becomes crucial for college and high school athletic administrators to understand their nature, their composition, and their operation.

Amateur athletic organizations are often distinguished on the basis of the sport (e.g., USA Track & Field, the national governing body for track and field), educational level (e.g., National Junior College Athletic Association [NJCAA]), or geographical location (e.g., a state high school athletic association). Some amateur sports organizations govern institutions (e.g., the NCAA governs colleges and universities), and some govern individual athletes (e.g., NGBs). Belonging to one such organization does not preclude membership in another. In fact, most educational institutions belong to an allied conference (e.g., Pacific-10 Conference or Big East Conference) in addition to being a member of a national association with a broader constituency (e.g., NCAA). Allied conferences, a subset of the larger amateur sports associations, usually consist of a number of schools in a geographic area that have similar institutional goals and interests. These schools compete against each other in a number of sports and often compete for conference championships in each of the sports.

In many ways, the NCAA's functions and its relationship with its members are analogous to the federal government's relationship with the state governments. For example, the NCAA promulgates rules regarding minimum standards that must be followed by all of its members. These rules do not, however, preclude its membership from creating a stricter rule on any subject already covered by an NCAA regulation. In addition, the membership can also make and enforce any rule that does not conflict with a stated rule or policy of the NCAA.

The courts, in recent years, have allowed this two-tier system of authority to exist with few intrusions. Despite claims that organizations like the NCAA should be considered state actors and thus subject to constitutional limitations like any other federal or state government agency, the courts have been deciding against this argument. In no case is this more apparent than in *National Collegiate Athletic Ass'n v. Tarkanian*, 109 S. Ct. 454 (1988). In this case the U.S. Supreme Court examined the role of the NCAA in threatening the University of Nevada-Las Vegas with additional sanctions when it failed to suspend its basketball coach, Jerry Tarkanian. Tarkanian brought suit against the NCAA alleging due process violations, but in examining the role of the NCAA, the Court found that the organization's actions were not under the color of state law.

NOTES

1. In *Santee v. Amateur Athletic Union of the U.S.*, 153 N.Y.S.2d 465 (N.Y. Sup. Ct. 1956), a track athlete sought an injunction against the AAU to prevent that voluntary organization from suspending him from competition. The court found that the AAU did, indeed, have the power to suspend athletes who violate its rules, since when the athlete took out his athletic membership in AAU, he agreed to abide by the rules and regulations of the union.

2. The National Association of Intercollegiate Athletes (NAIA) is composed of approximately 500 small four-year colleges and universities.

3. The National Junior College Athletic Association (NJCAA) is composed of approximately 600 two-year colleges.

The United States Olympic Committee

The Amateur Sports Act of 1978 (36 U.S.C. § 371–396) was passed by the United States Congress to reorganize and coordinate amateur athletics in the United States and to encourage and strengthen participation of U.S. amateurs in international competition. The act concerns itself with two major areas: (1) the relationship between athletes eligible for international amateur competition and the ruling bodies that govern those competitions and (2) the relationship between the ruling bodies themselves. The act establishes the United States Olympic Committee (USOC) as the principal mechanism for attaining these goals and assigns the USOC the following fourteen objects and purposes as guidelines for its operation:

1. Establish national goals for amateur athletic activities and encourage the attainment of those goals.

2. Coordinate and develop amateur athletic activity in the United States directly relating to international amateur athletic competition, so as to foster productive working relationships among sports-related organizations.

3. Exercise exclusive jurisdiction, either directly or through its constituent members of committees, over all matters pertaining to the participation of the United States in the Olympic Games and in the Pan-American Games when held in the United States.

4. Obtain for the United States, either directly or by delegation to the appropriate national governing body, the most competent amateur representation possible in each competition and event of the Olympic Games and of the Pan-American Games.

5. Promote and support amateur athletic activities involving the United States and foreign nations.

6. Promote and encourage physical fitness and public participation in amateur athletic activities.

7. Assist organizations and persons concerned with sports in the development of amateur athletes.

8. Provide for the swift resolution of conflicts and disputes involving amateur athletes, national governing bodies, and amateur sports organizations, and protect the opportunity of any amateur athlete, coach, trainer, manager, administrator, or official to participate in amateur athletic competition.

9. Foster the development of amateur athletic facilities for use by amateur athletes and assist in making existing amateur athletic facilities available for use by amateur athletes.

10. Provide and coordinate technical information on physical training, equipment design, coaching, and performance analysis.

11. Encourage and support research, development, and dissemination of information in the areas of sports medicine and sports safety.

12. Encourage and provide assistance to amateur athletic activities for women.

13. Encourage and provide assistance to amateur athletic programs and competition for handicapped individuals, including, when feasible, the expansion of opportunities for meaningful participation by handicapped individuals in programs of athletic competition for able-bodied individuals.

14. Encourage and provide assistance to amateur athletes of racial and ethnic minorities for the purpose of eliciting the participation of such minorities in amateur athletic activities in which they are underrepresented.

The Amateur Sports Act creates a governing structure for the USOC by empowering it to select one national governing body (NGB) for each Olympic or Pan-American sport. The act enumerates specific responsibilities for an NGB, including the definition of an "amateur athlete" and the determination of eligibility of each athlete for competition in that particular sport. The NGBs do the actual organizational work of developing athletes, organizing teams, instructing coaches and officials, and scheduling events. The act details explicit requirements for amateur sports organizations to become NGBs and provides a mechanism for resolution of disputes between individual organizations wishing to be recognized as the sole NGB. One important requirement of NGBs is that they have the backing of the sport's participants in the United States; they must also be recognized by international governing bodies.

Interestingly, provisions in the Amateur Sports Act call for the encouragement and assistance to "amateur athletic programs and competition for handicapped individuals" and the promotion of "physical fitness and public participation in amateur athletic activities." This language would seem to warrant the inclusion of non-Olympic or Pan-American sports in its realm of responsibility. In the past, however, the USOC has chosen to reject this broader interpretation and has instead directed its efforts through the NGBs toward Olympic/Pan-American sports. Nevertheless, USOC membership remains open to any sport not falling into the Olympic or Pan-American classification.

Although the USOC has chosen to concentrate on Olympic and Pan-American sports, its jurisdiction in this area is not exclusive. Not only must the NGBs be approved by an international governing body, but the USOC itself must contend with and conform to the policies and regulations of the International Olympic Committee (IOC) (see Exhibits 4–3 and 4–4). Furthermore, the Amateur Sports Act specifies that "any amateur sports organization which conducts amateur athletic competition, participation in which is restricted to a specific class of amateur athletes (such as high school students, college students, members of the Armed Forces or similar groups or categories), shall have exclusive jurisdiction over such competition." It is only when that group wishes to become involved in international competition that the USOC may play a role through the granting of a sanction or "certificate of approval issued by an NGB," which is required for such international competition. Even here, the USOC does not have exclusive control. For instance, when the United States hosts the Olympic or Pan-American Games, the USOC must work in concert with local and state governments and also with the organizing committee of the host city.

Exhibit 4–3
Organizational Chart Showing Regulatory Power of Amateur Sport
Governing Bodies

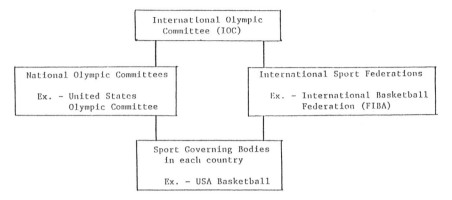

Exhibit 4–4
United States Olympic Committee Organizational Structure

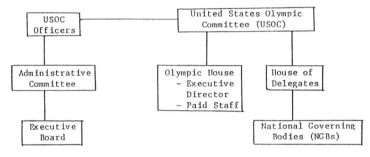

The Amateur Sports Act defines an "amateur sports organization" as a "not-for-profit corporation, club, federation, union, association or other group organized in the United States which sponsors or arranges any amateur athletic competition." This broad definition, when taken together with the specification regarding exclusive jurisdiction over amateur athletic competition referred to above, limits the jurisdiction of the USOC by delegating the jurisdiction over competitions to any sports body that meets the definition. Yet, this broad definition also allows for a comprehensive structure of many organizations which assume a role in the regulation of amateur athletics in the United States. Exhibit 4–5 lists the various groups that compose the USOC membership. Particular note should be given to Group B members— the NCAA, NFSHSA, NAIA, and NJCAA. Exhibit 4–6 lists the inter-

Exhibit 4–5
Membership of the United States Olympic Committee

Group A, National Governing Bodies

Archery	National Archery Association (NAA)
Athletics	The Athletics Congress of the USA (TAC)
Baseball	U.S. Baseball Federation (USBF)
Basketball	Amateur Basketball Association of the USA (ABAUSA)
Biathlon	U.S. Biathlon Association (USBA)
Bobsledding	U.S. Bobsled and Skeleton Association
Boxing	USA Amateur Boxing Federation (USA/ABF)
Canoeing	American Canoe Association (ACA)
Cycling	U.S. Cycling Federation (USCF)
Diving	U.S. Diving (USD)
Equestrian	American Horse Shows Association (AHSA)
Fencing	U.S. Fencing Association (USFA)
Field Hockey	(Men) Field Hockey Association of America (FHAA)
	(Women) U.S. Field Hockey Association (USFHA)
Figure Skating	U.S. Figure Skating Association (USFSA)
Gymnastics	U.S. Gymnastics Federation (USGF)
Ice Hockey	Amateur Hockey Association of the U.S. (AHAUS)
Judo	U.S. Judo (USJ)
Luge	U.S. Luge Association (USLA)
Modern Pentathlon	U.S. Modern Pentathlon Association (USMPA)
Roller Skating	U.S. Amateur Confederation of Roller Skating (USAC/RS)
Rowing	U.S. Rowing Association (USRA)
Shooting	National Rifle Association of America (NRA)
Skiing	U.S. Ski Association (USSA)
Soccer	U.S. Soccer Federation (USSF)
Softball	Amateur Softball Association of America (ASA)
Speedskating	U.S. International Speedskating Association (USISA)
Swimming	U.S. Swimming (USS)
Synchronized Swimming	U.S. Synchronized Swimming (USSS)
Table Tennis	U.S. Table Tennis Association (USTTA)
Taekwondo	U.S. Tae Kwon Do Union (USTU)
Team Handball	U.S. Team Handball Federation (USTHF)
Tennis	U.S. Tennis Association (USTA)
Volleyball	U.S. Volleyball Association (USVBA)
Water Polo	U.S. Water Polo (USWP)
Weightlifting	U.S. Weightlifting Federation (USWF)
Wrestling	USA Wrestling (USAW)
Yachting	U.S. Yacht Racing Union (USYRU)

Group B, National Multi-Sport Organizations

Amateur Atlantic Union of the U.S. (AAU)
American Alliance for Health, Physical Education,
   Recreation, and Dance (AAHPERD)
Catholic Youth Organization (CYO)
Jewish Welfare Board (JWB)
National Association of Intercollegiate Athletics (NAIA)
National Collegiate Athletic Association (NCAA)
National Exploring Division, Boy Scouts of America
National Federation of State High School Associations (NFSHSA)
National Junior College Athletic Association (NJCAA)
U.S. Armed Forces
Young Men's Christian Association of the USA (YMCA)

Exhibit 4–5 continued

Group C, Affiliated Sports Organizations
American Amateur Racquetball Association (AARA)
(Men) American Bowling Congress (ABC),
(Women) Women's International Bowling
  Congress (WIBC)

Group D, U.S. Olympic Committee State Fundraising Organizations
There are 54 state/area organizations in the U.S.

Group E, Handicapped in Sports
American Athletic Association of the Deaf
National Association of Sports For Cerebral Palsy
National Wheelchair Athletic Association
Special Olympics
United States Amputee Athletic Association
U.S. Association for Blind Athletes

national sports federations that are recognized by the International Olympic Committee.

For high school and college administrators, the Amateur Sports Act represents the foundation upon which their athletic associations are based. Through this foundation, the various athletic associations (NCAA, NJCAA, NFSHSA, etc.) are interrelated with the USOC and the Amateur Sports Act. As athletes bring lawsuits against their governing associations, this relationship can be analyzed by the courts. Consequently, being familiar with this relationship prepares the administrator for these situations.

NOTES

1. For further information on the USOC and its powers, see in *DeFrantz v. United States Olympic Committee*, 492 F. Supp. 1181 (D.D.C. 1980), *aff'd without opinion*, 701 F.2d 221 (D.C. Cir. 1980). The federal district court held that the Amateur Sports Act of 1978 did not establish a cause of action for 25 designated Olympic athletes who sought to prohibit the USOC from barring these American athletes from participating in the 1980 Olympic Games in Moscow. The court noted:

> We ... conclude that the USOC not only had the authority to decide not to send an American team to the summer Olympics, but also that it could do so for reasons not directly related to sports considerations.
> We ... find that the decision of the USOC not to send an American team to the summer Olympics was not state action, and therefore, does not give rise to an actionable claim for the infringements of the constitutional rights alleged.

2. In *Michels v. United States Olympic Committee*, 741 F.2d 155 (7th Cir. 1984), a weightlifter was suspended by the International Weightlifting Federation for two years after showing an impermissible testosterone level during a drug test. The weightlifter brought suit against the USOC claiming a violation of the Amateur Sports Act in not conducting a hearing on his behalf.

Exhibit 4–6
International Sports Federations Recognized by the International Olympic
Committee and U.S. Members of the International Federations

INTERNATIONAL FEDERATION
For Olympic Sports

IAAF International Amateur Athletic Federation (track and field)

FITA International Archery Federation

FIBA International Amateur Basketball Federation

FIBT International Bobsleigh and Tobogganing Federation

AIBA International Amateur Boxing Association

FIAC International Amateur Cyclists Federation

FIE International Fencing Federation

FIFA International Association Football Federation (soccer)

FEI International Equestrian Federation

FIG International Gymnastics Federation

IHF International Handball Federation

FIH International Hockey Federation (field hockey)

IFWHA International Federation of Women's Hockey Associations

IIHF International Ice Hockey Federation

IJF International Judo Federation

FIL International Luge Federation

IUPMB International Union of Modern Pentathlon and Biathlon

FISA International Federation of Rowing Societies

UIT International Shooting Union

ISU International Skating Union (figure skating and speed skating)

FIS International Ski Federation

FINA International Amateur Swimming Federation (also diving and water polo)

FIVB International Volleyball Federation

IWF International Weightlifting Federation

FILA International Amateur Wrestling Federation

IYRU International Yacht Racing Union

FIC International Canoe Federation

For Pan American Games Sports

AINBA The International Baseball Association

FIRS International Roller Skating Federation

FIS International Softball Association

ITF International Tennis Federation

UNITED STATES MEMBER

NAA National Archery Association

ABAUSA Amateur Basketball Association of the USA

USCF U.S. Cycling Federation

USSF U.S. Soccer Federation

AHSA American Horse Shows Association

USGF U.S. Gymnastics Federation

USTHBF U.S. Team Handball Federation

FHAA Field Hockey Association of America (men's)

USFHA U.S. Field Hockey Association, Inc. (women's)

AHAUS Amateur Hockey Association of the U.S.

AAU Judo Div.

AAU Luge Div.

USMPBA U.S. Modern Pentathlon and Biathlon Association

NAAO National Association of Amateur Oarsmen

NRA National Rifle Association of America

USFSA U.S. Figure Skating Association

USISA U.S. International Skating Association

USSA U.S. Ski Association

AAU Aquatics Div.

USVBA U.S. Volleyball Association

AAU Weightlifting Div.

AAU Wrestling Div.

USYRU U.S. Yacht Racing Union

ACA American Canoe Association

USBF U.S. Baseball Federation

USACRS U.S. Amateur Confederation of Roller Skating

A.S.A. Amateur Softball Association of America

USTA U.S. Tennis Association

The Court of Appeals held that the weightlifter had no private cause of action under the Amateur Sports Act and thus the USOC was not required to fulfill his demand of providing a hearing on the validity of the test results.

3. Additional cases involving the interpretation of the Amateur Sports Act include the following.

(a) In *Oldfield v. The Athletic Congress*, 779 F.2d 505 (9th Cir. 1985), the plaintiff was disallowed by TAC from competing in the 1980 Olympic Trials on the ground that he signed a professional performance contract with the International Track Association in 1972 and was therefore, according to an IOC rule, not an amateur anymore. The Court of Appeals concluded that TAC and the USOC, under the Amateur Sports Act of 1978, had acted appropriately and therefore affirmed the summary judgment granted by the district court for the defendants.

(b) In *Martinez v. United States Olympic Committee*, 802 F.2d 1275 (10th Cir. 1986), the plaintiff filed a wrongful death action as representative of the estate of a boxer killed during an amateur match. The Court of Appeals agreed with the district court ruling that the plaintiff showed no cause of action under the Amateur Sports Act.

4. For further information on national governing bodies, review *United States Wrestling Federation v. Wrestling Division of the AAU, Inc.*, 545 F. Supp. 1053 (N.D. Ohio, 1982), *aff'd*, 711 F.2d 1060 (4th Cir. 1983). The federal court prohibited one national athletic organization from being the designated NGB over another organization pursuant to the Amateur Sports Act of 1978. (See Chapter 5.)

5. For information on how the federal courts interpret IOC decisions, see *Martin v. International Olympic Committee*, 740 F.2d 670 (9th Cir. 1984). The U.S. Court of Appeals for the Ninth Circuit turned down a request by 82 women athletes from twenty-seven countries for an injunction that would order the IOC to let women compete in the 5,000-meter and 10,000-meter races at the 1984 Los Angeles Olympics. The court held that California civil rights law does not authorize the establishment of "separate but equal" events for men and women and that the IOC rule which governed the addition of new events to the games was applied equally to men and women and thus was not discriminatory.

6. For further information on the Amateur Sports Act, see Nafzinger, "The Amateur Sports Act of 1978," 1983 *B.Y.U. L. Rev.* 47 (1983), and Nafzinger, *International Sports Law*, New York: Transnational Publishers, 1988.

The National Collegiate Athletic Association

Although not every athletic administrator may be directly involved with the National Collegiate Athletic Association (NCAA), administrators of all types of amateur athletic associations should be familiar with its characteristics. Because of the NCAA's breadth and influence, it affects athletes from grade school to the professional level. In addition, the way the courts approach a voluntary athletic association such as the NCAA can serve as a good indicator of how the courts may deal with other organizations that embrace principles and goals similar to those of the NCAA.

The NCAA was formed in the early 1900s in response to the rugged nature of football. The flying wedge, football's major offense in 1905, and other mass formations and gang tackling led to many injuries and even deaths. As a result, many institutions discontinued football and others urged that it be reformed or abolished from intercollegiate athletics. President Theodore Roosevelt reacted by holding two White House conferences with college athletic leaders to encourage such reform. In early December 1905, Chancellor Henry M. MacCracken of New York University brought thirteen institutions together to propose changes in football playing rules. At a subsequent meeting held on December 28, the Intercollegiate Athletic Association of the United States (IAAUS) was founded. When the IAAUS was officially constituted on March 31, 1906, it had sixty-two members. It took its present name—the National Collegiate Athletic Association—in 1910.

Initially, the NCAA was a discussion group and rules-making body. In 1921, the first NCAA national championship was held: the National Track and Field Championships. Over the years, more rules committees were formed and more championships in other athletic events were held. After World War II, the NCAA adopted the "Sanity Code," which established guidelines for recruiting and granting financial aid. Unfortunately, the code failed to curb abuses involving student-athletes. The number of postseason football games began to increase, and member institutions became more concerned about the effects of unrestricted television coverage on football attendance. As the complexity and scope of these problems and the growth in membership and championships multiplied, the need for full-time professional leadership became apparent.

In 1951, Walter Byers, a former part-time executive assistant, was named executive director of the NCAA. In 1952, a national headquarters was established in Kansas City. In addition, a program to control live television coverage of football games was approved, the annual convention delegated enforcement powers to the association's council, and legislation governing postseason bowl games was adopted. By 1988, a national staff of approximately 147 employees occupied two NCAA buildings in Mission, Kansas. Dick Schultz, former athletic director at the University of Virginia was selected to replace Walter Byers as executive director beginning in October 1987. In 1990 the NCAA moved into its new office complex located in Overland Park, Kansas.

At the first special convention in 1973, the NCAA's membership was divided into three legislative and competitive divisions (referred to as Division I, Division II, and Division III). Subdivisions I-A and

I-AA were created in the sport of football by Division I members five years later. Women joined the NCAA's activities in 1980 when Divisions II and III established ten championships for 1981–82. At the historic seventy-fifth convention a year later, an extensive governance plan was adopted to include women's athletic programs, services, and representation. The women's championships program was expanded with the addition of nineteen more events.

In 1984, the President's Commission was created in a special convention. This decisive step was taken to strengthen the association's compliance and enforcement efforts. With this presidential involvement, the NCAA has come full circle since its beginnings in 1905.

The NCAA's current voluntary membership consists of over 1,000 four-year colleges and universities and two-year upper-level collegiate institutions located throughout the United States. Member schools agree to be bound by NCAA rules and regulations and are obligated to administer their athletic programs in accordance with NCAA rules. Over half of the NCAA's members are state-subsidized universities, and most receive some form of federal financial assistance. Operating funds for the NCAA are in part accumulated through membership dues that are figured on a sliding scale based on the type of membership held. The annual dues range from $225 to $1,800 (*1993–94 NCAA Manual,* Bylaw 3.6.3). If a school's dues are not paid, the school is denied a chance to vote at the annual convention and cannot enter teams in NCAA-sponsored competitions. In addition, if the dues are not paid within one year, the membership automatically terminates.

The NCAA does not offer membership to individual student-athletes. Instead, it uses the principle of institutional control. In essence, this means that the NCAA deals only with school administrations and not with individual student-athletes. When a violation that concerns a student-athlete is discovered, the NCAA informs the school of its findings and request that the school declare the student-athlete ineligible. If the school does not comply with the request, the NCAA may invoke sanctions against all or any part of the institution's athletic program.

The purposes of the NCAA are stated in its constitution:

(a) To initiate, stimulate and improve intercollegiate athletic programs for student-athletes and to promote and develop educational leadership, physical fitness, athletics excellence and athletics participation as a recreational pursuit;
(b) To uphold the principle of institutional control of, and responsibility for, all intercollegiate sports in conformity with the constitution and bylaws of this Association;
(c) To encourage its members to adopt eligibility rules to comply

with satisfactory standards of scholarship, sportsmanship and amateurism;

(d) To formulate, copyright and publish rules of play governing intercollegiate athletics;

(e) To preserve intercollegiate athletics records;

(f) To supervise the conduct of, and to establish eligibility standards for, regional and national athletic events under the auspices of this Association;

(g) To cooperate with other amateur athletics organizations in promoting and conducting national and international athletics events;

(h) To legislate, through bylaws or by resolutions of a Convention, upon any subject of general concern to the members related to the administration of intercollegiate athletics; and,

(i) To study in general all phases of competitive intercollegiate athletics and establish standards whereby the colleges and universities of the United States can maintain their athletic programs on a high level. (*1998–94 NCAA Manual*, Bylaw 1.2)

In addition, the fundamental policy upon which the NCAA is based is as follows:

The competitive athletics programs of member institutions are designed to be a vital part of the educational system. A basic purpose of this Association is to maintain intercollegiate athletics as an integral part of the educational program and the athlete an as integral part of the student body and, by so doing, retain a clear line of demarcation between intercollegiate athletics and professional sports. (*1993–94 NCAA Manual*, Bylaw 1.3.1)

Although all members can propose new rules and revisions of old rules, the NCAA administration has overall organizational responsibility and often initiates legislation on matters of general interest to all its members. The administrative body of the NCAA consists of a forty-six-member Council. The Council is elected at the annual convention of the association. At least four Council seats are reserved for women. Between annual meetings, the Council is empowered to interpret the NCAA constitution and bylaws. Between Council meetings, this is done by the Legislation and Interpretation Committee. These interpretations are binding after they are published and circulated to the membership via the NCAA's weekly publication (biweekly in the summer), *NCAA News.* Any member can request affirmation of a Council decision at the next annual convention as a check on the Council's power. Approval of a bylaw can be obtained by a simple majority vote of the delegates. The Council is also responsible for facilitating cooperation with other amateur organizations, such as the National Association of Intercollegiate Athletics (NAIA) and USA Track Field in promoting and conducting national or international events.

Historically, the NCAA has tried to balance the distribution of athletic talent among member institutions. It has also acted as a bargaining agent for its members in matters that concern commercial opportunity such as television telecasts (see Chapter 9), and arranged postseason play in intercollegiate athletics. The revenue from postseason games is distributed among eligible member institutions.

Although the NCAA's major purposes include creating, administering, and enforcing rules regarding intercollegiate athletics, these purposes are not beyond judicial review. An example of how the courts may view the NCAA's rule-making authority can be seen in the case of *Justice v. National Collegiate Athletic Ass'n*, 577 F. Supp. 356 (D. Ariz. 1983). In the *Justice* case, four members of the University of Arizona's football team sought a preliminary injunction to prevent enforcement of the NCAA's sanctions against the team that would prohibit postseason play in 1983 and 1984 and television appearances in 1984 and 1985. The U.S. District Court held that:

1. The student-athletes in this case have been deprived neither of their scholarships nor their right to participate in intercollegiate athletics.
2. Whatever oral representations that were made by university coaches to the student-athletes regarding participation in postseason and televised athletic contests created a mere expectation or desire rather than a legitimate claim of entitlement based on contract.
3. A distinction must be drawn between actions that constitute punishment without personal guilt for substantive due process purposes and actions which merely affect innocent persons adversely.
4. The student-athletes' loss of the opportunity to participate in post-season and televised competition, however, unfortunate and personally undeserved, does not constitute a deprivation of their due process rights.

Prior to the 1984–85 academic year, the NCAA was funded in part by its percentage share of the national television contracts for intercollegiate football. However, on June 27, 1984, the Supreme Court in a 7–2 decision in *National Collegiate Athletic Ass'n v. Board of Regents of University of Oklahoma and University of Georgia Athletic*

Ass'n, 468 U.S. 85 (1984), struck down the NCAA's 1982–85 Football Television Plan because it violated the Sherman Antitrust Act (see Chapters 9 and 13). The effect of this ruling on the NCAA's budget was immediate. Estimates were that the NCAA would lose about $5 million in football television revenues, or 14 percent of its budget. In January 1985, the NCAA Executive Committee in its report to the membership reported an actual loss of $4.7 million. Fortunately for the organization, a $14 million increase in the CBS-TV fee to telecast the 1985 NCAA Basketball Championship covered the loss. A portion of this increase also went to teams in the NCAA Basketball Tournament.

In 1989 the NCAA signed a seven-year television contract with CBS which generated $1 billion in revenue for the NCAA. While a percentage of this revenue is kept by the NCAA to cover expenses, the majority is distributed to NCAA-member institutions. The NCAA moved away from their traditional system of paying basketball teams a certain monetary amount depending on how far they advanced in the tournament and instead initiated a new revenue-distribution plan for this excess revenue. This revenue-distribution plan includes $25,000 paid to each Division I institution to be used for student-athlete academic enhancement programs; a certain amount paid to conferences to be used as a needy student-athlete fund; a certain payout to Division I institutions dependent on the number of varsity sports sponsored and the number of athletics grants-in-aid awarded; and a certain amount paid to Division I conferences on the basis of past performances in the men's basketball championship. In addition, funds were provided to Division II institutions and conferences.

Intercollegiate football provides its own method of financial payouts to participating schools. In 1990, football bowl games ranged from a payout of $250,000 per team competing in the California Raisin Bowl to $5.5 million per team competing in the Rose Bowl. These large stakes have put enormous pressure on coaches to succeed and, as some believe, may be the root cause of many of the rules violations that occur.

In addition to the financial issues, a major problem facing the NCAA in recent years has been in the area of recruiting violations by member schools. "I believe there is a growing acceptance of the belief that the conditions of intercollegiate athletics are such that you have to cut corners, you have to circumvent the rules," stated Walter Byers in 1984. Byers added: "There seems to be a growing number of coaches and administrators who look upon NCAA penalties as the price of doing business: If you get punished, that's unfortunate, but that's part of the cost of getting along." As of April 1991, thirty-four institutions were under NCAA sanctions. The NCAA has an enforcement division which investigates and punishes schools that are in violation of NCAA rules.

Other Collegiate Athletic Associations

In addition to the NCAA, several other athletic organizations govern collegiate sports participation. One of these is the National Association of Intercollegiate Athletics (NAIA), an intercollegiate athletic governing organization composed of four-year institutions. The NAIA was formed in 1940 as the National Association of Intercollegiate Basketball. The association changed its name to the NAIA in 1952 as it expanded into sports other than basketball. The NAIA quickly grew from a small organization and had 411 member institutions as of July 1993.

A good description of the NAIA is contained in *Williams v. Hamilton*, 497 F. Supp. 641 (D.N.H. 1980):

[The] NAIA is a voluntary association of 512 four-year colleges ranging in size from small (500) to moderate (1100), whose primary purpose as set forth in its constitution is "to promote the development of athletics as a sound part of the educational offerings of member institutions." The member institutions of NAIA pay dues to the Association, which are scaled by enrollment. Among other things, NAIA sets standards for recruiting and eligibility, and it sponsors post-season national championships in various collegiate sports, including soccer.

NAIA is divided into several districts, each of which is governed by a "District Executive Committee." Each district has voting representation at NAIA's Annual National Convention, at which time policy decisions are made. Also at the National Convention delegates vote for new members of the National Executive Committee, the overall governing body of NAIA.

The NAIA is open to any four-year, degree-granting college or university in the United States or Canada that is fully accredited by accrediting agencies or commissions of the Council on Postsecondary Accreditation. Those institutions belonging to the NAIA must operate their intercollegiate athletic programs according to the association's regulations and rules. Of course, member institutions can establish even stricter standards than those of the association. The NAIA's eligibility regulations are very similar to those of the NCAA, except that the NAIA's eligibility rules govern all play in sports recognized by the association, whereas the NCAA has special rules for postseason tournaments.

Like the NCAA, the NAIA has specific rules relating to transfer student-athlete eligibility and hardship regulations. The NAIA's eligibility regulations typically contain the following provisions:

1. Beginning the fall term of 1989 YOU MUST, if a first-time entering freshman, meet two of three entry level requirements:
   a. A minimum score of 18 on the ACT or 740 on the SAT (740 SAT effective August 1, 1993. Prior to August 1 enrollment, a 700 or better SAT is acceptable). Tests must be taken on a national testing date. Scores must be achieved on a single test (residual tests are not acceptable).
   b. Achieve an overall high school grade point average of 2.000 on a 4.000 scale, or
   c. Graduate in the top half of your high school graduating class. The ACT/SAT test must be taken on a national testing date and certified to the institution prior to the beginning of the term in which the student initially participates.

A first-time entering Freshman is defined as a student who upon becoming identified with an NAIA institution has not been previously identified with another institution of higher learning for two semesters or three quarters (or equivalent).

2. YOU MUST be making normal progress toward a recognized baccalaureate degree and maintain the grade points required to remain a student in good standing, as defined by the institution you are attending.
3. YOU MUST be enrolled in 12 institutionally-approved, or required, credit hours at the time of participation. Should participation take place between terms, you must have been enrolled and in attendance the term immediately preceding the date of participation.
4. YOU MUST have accumulated a minimum total of twenty-four (24) institutional, or required, credit hours the two immediately previous terms of attendance. Up to 12 institutional credit hours earned during the summer and/or non-term may be applied to meet the 24 credit hour rule, provided such credit is earned AFTER one of the two immediately previous terms of attendance.
5. YOU MUST, if a second term freshman, have accumulated nine degree or required credit hours **before** identification for the second term of attendance.
6. YOU MAY NOT count repeat courses previously passed in ANY term toward the 24-hour rule.
7. YOU MUST be eligible in your own conference.
8. YOU MUST, if a transfer student from a four-year institution, have eligibility remaining at the institution from which you are

transferring to be eligible for further intercollegiate competition.

9. YOU MUST, if a transfer student having ever attended a four-year institution, reside for 16 consecutive calendar weeks (112 calendar days), not including summer sessions, at the transferred institution before becoming eligible for intercollegiate competition in any sport in which you participated at the previous four-year institution. Exceptions to the 16 calendar weeks residency will be explained by the institution's faculty athletics representative.

10. YOU MUST be within your first 10 semesters, 12 trimesters, or 15 quarters of attendance as a regularly enrolled student.
    A term of attendance is any semester, trimester, or quarter in which you initially enrolled for nine or more institutional credit hours and attended any class. (Summer sessions are not included, but night school, extension, or correspondence courses are applicable to this ruling.)

11. YOU MUST, upon reaching junior academic standing as defined by the identified institution, have a cumulative grade point average of at least 2.000 on a 4.000 scale as certified by the institutional registrar.

12. YOU MUST, to participate the second season in a sport, accumulate at least 24 semester/36 quarter institutional credit hours (effective for all new students enrolling Fall 1989 or later).

13. YOU MUST, to participate the third season in a sport, accumulate at least 48 semester/72 quarter institutional credit hours (effective for all new students enrolling Fall 1989 or later).

14. YOU MUST, to participate the fourth season in a sport, accumulate at least 72 semester/108 quarter institutional credit hours. These hours include at least 48 semester/72 quarter hours in general education and/or your major field of study (effective for all new students enrolling Fall 1989 or later).

15. YOU MUST, to participate the third and/or fourth season in a sport, have and maintain a total cumulative grade point average of at least 2.000 on a 4.000 scale (effective for all new students enrolling Fall 1989 or later).

16. YOU MAY NOT participate for more than four seasons in any one sport. A season of competition is defined as participation in one or more intercollegiate contests, whether a freshman, junior varsity, or varsity participant or in any other athletic competition in which the institution, as such, is represented during a sport season.

17. Should you participate for two different institutions in the same

sport, in the same academic year (example—basketball or fall basketball at a junior college and then transfer to an NAIA school and participate in basketball or spring baseball), you shall be charged with a second season of competition in that sport unless you earned an associate degree at a junior college the immediately previous term to transferring.

18. YOU MUST be an amateur, as defined by the NAIA, in the sport(s) in which you participate. See your athletics director or faculty athletics representative for all amateur regulations as printed in the NAIA Bylaws. (1992 NAIA "A Guide for the College Board Student")

Another athletic organization that governs amateur sports participation is the National Small College Athletic Association (NSCAA). Four-year colleges with enrollments of less than 500 male and/or female undergraduate students qualify for membership. The National Christian College Athletic Association (NCCAA) offers championships to both sexes and governs athletics in four-year institutions. The NCCAA, which is composed of 104 members, is only open to four-year Christian institutions that are willing to subscribe to a "Statement of Faith."

The National Junior College Athletic Association (NJCAA) is another intercollegiate organization that performs functions similar to those of the NSCAA and NCCAA, except that it encompasses men's and women's junior college athletic programs. It was described in *State ex rel. National Junior College Athletic Ass'n v. Luten*, 492 S.W.2d 404 (Mo. Ct. App. 1973) as a

> not-for-profit corporation which coordinates the scheduling and playing of intercollegiate athletics among its member schools. In 1971–72 it had 513 member schools who agree to "supervise and to control athletics sponsored by this corporation so that they will be administered in accordance with the eligibility rules...set forth in the...Bylaws." Among its functions it issues and enforces rules relating to the eligibility of students at its member schools participating in intercollegiate athletics.

The NCAA, NAIA, and the other intercollegiate athletic organizations already mentioned perform a regulatory function at the national level. However, there are other organizations that govern amateur athletics at a regional level. These regional governing bodies are typically leagues and conferences to which members belong. Regional leagues and conferences can make and enforce their own rules and regulations for the governance of athletics among themselves, but those rules and regulations must also comply and not conflict with the standards created by the national organization to which they belong. In addition to the right to establish and create separate rules and regulations, these leagues and conferences have enforcement authority to sanction and reprimand member institutions. The most notable difference between national association and league or conference rules is that league or conference rules impose more restrictive standards.

Intercollegiate athletics also has what are known as allied conferences. Allied conferences are associations of NCAA member schools that agree to participate against each other to determine a champion in any number of sports. These allied conferences can have significant financial resources of their own and have detailed revenue distribution requirements as noted in the following excerpt from the 1992–93 *Pacific 10 Conference Handbook*, Administrative Rules, Chapter 1, Financial Distribution:

1. Football Ticket Settlement.
Financial settlement of traditional rival football games shall consist of a 50-50 split of the net receipts with no minimum guarantee or maximum payout. Financial settlement of all other Conference football games shall consist of a 50-50 split of the net receipts with a minimum guarantee of $125,000 and a maximum payout of $200,000.

2. Men's Basketball Ticket Settlement.
Financial settlement of traditional rival basketball games shall consist of a 50-50 split of the net receipts with no minimum guarantee or maximum payout. Financial settlement of all other Conference basketball games shall consist of a 50-50 split of the net receipts with a minimum guarantee of $12,500 and a maximum payout of $20,000.

3. Football Bowl Games and Preseason Classics Income.
Revenue from participation in postseason football bowl games and preseason contests (i.e., NACDA Kickoff Classic, Disneyland Pigskin Classic) shall be divided equally among the Conference's ten members after the participating institution receives the following expenses:

	Travel Party (Airline Tickets)	Expense Budget
Rose Bowl	400	$800,000 (plus CPI ≤ 5%)
Tier I Bowls (min. $3 million)	325	$750,000
Tier II Bowls (min. $1 million)	325	$650,000
Freedom Bowl	150	$650,000

| Other Bowls (min. $650,000) | 0 | $650,000 |
| Preseason Game | 150 | $550,000 |

Expenses for the travel party shall consist of actual transportation expenses not to exceed coach air fare. In no case shall the total expense (travel party plus expense budget) exceed the actual game payout.

4. Men's Basketball Postseason Income.

a. NCAA Tournament.

A member institution which participates in the NCAA men's basketball tournament shall submit detailed expenses on the Conference's approved budget form to receive reimbursement for those specified expenses not covered by its NCAA reimbursement. The applicable expense form is contained in Appendix C. The participating institution may retain all expense monies provided by the NCAA.

b. Tip-off Classic and NIT.

All revenue derived from the Tip-off Classic and the NIT preseason or postseason basketball tournaments shall be retained by the participating institution.

NOTES ————————————————————————————

1. The organizational structure of the NCAA is briefly described in the following excerpts from the 1993–94 *NCAA Manual:*

(a) President's Commission: Was created at the 1984 NCAA Convention to give the chief executive officers of NCAA member institutions a greater input into Association operations. It is composed of a board of 44 college presidents; 22 Division I, 11 Division II, and 11 Division III members, with at least 3 women, who will be chosen by the NCAA. The board can propose legislation but it cannot enact it without approval of the annual Convention delegates.

(b) NCAA Council: Includes 46 members; 22 from Division I, 11 from Division II and 11 from Division III, with the NCAA president and secretary-treasurer as ex officio members. Members are elected by their respective division round tables at the annual Convention. The president and secretary-treasurer are elected by the full Convention. Geographical and conference representation requirements are the same as for the President's Commission.

The Council establishes and directs the general policy of the Association in the interim between NCAA Conventions. In effect, the Convention establishes Association law and policy, and the Council implements and applies the Convention's decisions, with day-to-day administration provided by the staff. The Council is arguably the most powerful entity in the NCAA governance structure as it currently exists.

(c) Division Steering Committees: The 44 elected members of the Council represent their respective divisions as members of Council subcommittees identified as Division I, Division II and Division III Steering Committees. Each meeting of the Council includes separate meetings of the three steering committees, as well as sessions involving the entire Council.

The steering committees consider and act upon matters relating to their respective divisions, while the Council acts as one body to deal with matters of overall Association policy and interdivision interests. The steering committees report their actions to the full Council, and any division decision stands unless overruled by a two-thirds vote of the Council members present and voting.

The steering committees also plan and conduct the division meetings, review legislative proposals of interest to their divisions, and encourage communication between division members and the steering committee and Council.

(d) NCAA Executive Committee: Includes fourteen members, including at least 3 women, with the NCAA president and secretary-treasurer as ex officio members. Of the remaining twelve members, three shall be the division vice presidents and the remaining nine represented as follows:

(1) seven shall represent Division I members,

(2) one shall represent Division II members, and

(3) one shall represent Division III members.

The five officers are elected by the Convention; the other nine members are elected by the NCAA Council.

The Executive Committee transacts the business and administers the financial and championship affairs of the Association, including employment of an executive director (with approval of the Council) and such other staff as necessary for conduct of the Association's business.

(e) At the 1993 NCAA Convention, member institutions approved legislation establishing a new committee of five members, the Infractions Appeals Committee. This committee, which replaces the NCAA Council steering committees, now serves as the appellate body for findings of major violations by the Committee on Infractions. Of the five members of the committee, at least one is designated to be part of the general public, who is not associated with a collegiate institution, conference, or professional or similar sports organization and does not represent coaches or athletes in any capacity. The remaining members must presently or previously be on the staff of any active member institution or member conference but not currently on the NCAA Council, Executive Committee, or President's Commission.

(f) Other Committees: The other standing committees of the Association are in three general categories: Convention committees, Council-appointed (sometimes called general) committees and sports committees (some with rules-making responsibilities and some without). The size of the respective committees is specified in NCAA Bylaw 12. In most cases, each division is represented on a committee, unless it deals specifically with a matter involving only one division. In addition, ad hoc committees frequently are appointed to deal with specific assignments.

In general, such committees report to the NCAA Council and/or the Executive Committee. Actions of any committee are subject to review by the annual Convention.

(g) Staff: The NCAA employs a staff of approximately 225 (as of 1992), including clerical personnel. The staff administers the policies and decisions approved by the Association through the annual Convention or by the Council and Executive Committee. It also serves all NCAA committees by providing administrative services, including necessary record-keeping and continuing communications.

Operating under the executive director, the national office staff is organized in nine departments: administration, business, championships, communications, compliance, enforcement, publishing, legislative services, and visitors center/special projects.

2. For further information on how the NAIA's governing authority is viewed by the courts, see *Williams v. Hamilton*, 497 F. Supp. 641 (D.N.H. 1980), in which a college student-athlete challenged the NAIA transfer rule requiring him to be in residence at his new college for sixteen weeks before becoming eligible for intercollegiate athletics. The rule was imposed, in part, to prevent "tramp athletes" from transferring from school to school for the sole purpose of participating in sports. The court held that the transfer rule was valid and did not deny due process or equal protection guarantees.

3. The National Junior College Athletic Association (NJCAA) is a nonprofit corporation with 544 (5/93) junior colleges (two-year programs of study) as member institutions. For further information on the NJCAA's governing authority as viewed by the courts, see *State ex rel. National Junior College Athletic Ass'n v. Luten*, 492 S.W.2d 404 (Mo. Ct. App. 1973).

4. In addition to the NCAA, intercollegiate athletics has what are known as allied conferences. These are associations of NCAA member schools that agree to participate against each other to determine a champion in any number of sports. These allied conferences can have significant financial resources of their own and have detailed revenue distribution requirements. Examples are the Pacific-10 Conference, the Big East Conference, the Atlantic Ten Conference, and the Southwest Athletic Conference.

5. The 1992–93 NCAA budget was $179,427,000. Exhibit 4–7 shows how the budget breaks down.

6. Exhibit 4–8 is a flowchart of the NCAA organization structure.

7. For further information on the governing structure of the NCAA, see the following law review articles:

(a) Philpot & Mackall, "Judicial Review of Disputes Between Athletes and the NCAA," 24 *Stan. L. Rev.* 903 (1972).
(b) Weistart, "Legal Accountability and the NCAA," 10 *J. C. & U. L.* 167 (1983–84).
(c) Greene, "The New NCAA Rules of the Game: Academic Integrity or Racism?," 28 *St. Louis U. L. J.* 101 (1984).

High School Athletic Associations

Having some knowledge of the structure and nature of high school athletic associations can help college athletic administrators as well

Exhibit 4–7
NCAA Operating Budgets from 1991–92 and 1992–93

REVENUE

	1991-92 Budget	1992-93 Budget
NCAA operating revenue		
Television	$ 124,705,500	$ 133,505,500
Royalties	5,963,000	7,049,000
Division I men's basketball	11,567,900	12,945,000
Other Division I championships	5,728,000	5,935,500
Division II championships	856,000	949,750
Division III championships	439,500	447,950
Publishing	1,414,000	1,484,000
Communications	707,600	596,600
Visitors Center	680,000	305,000
Investments	2,000,000	1,750,000
Membership fees	878,400	870,000
General	635,800	470,000
Transfers from reserves	1,386,000	
Total NCAA operating revenue	156,961,700	166,308,300
Associated organizations		
National Youth Sports Program	10,831,800	12,000,000
NCAA Foundation	948,500	1,118,700
Total associated organizations	11,780,300	13,118,700
TOTAL REVENUE	$ 168,742,000	$ 179,427,000

EXPENSE

NCAA operating expense		
Distributions to members:		
Division I men's basketball fund	$ 31,500,000	$ 31,500,000
Division I grants-in-aid fund	21,000,000	21,000,000
Division I sports-sponsorship fund	10,500,000	10,500,000
Division I academic-enhancement fund	7,425,000	8,940,000
Division I conference grants	3,856,000	4,103,000
Division I special-assistance fund	3,000,000	3,000,000
Division I membership trust	1,228,500	2,637,000
Royalties to members	1,075,500	989,000
Division II enhancement fund	2,000,000	3,000,000
Grants to affiliated organizations	105,000	115,400
Total distributions to members	81,690,000	85,784,400
Division I men's basketball expense	9,799,500	9,909,000
Other Division I championships expense	13,398,000	13,835,150
Division II championships expense	4,426,500	4,824,710
Division III championships expense	4,845,800	5,097,920
Sports sciences expense	4,131,000	3,877,500
Publications expense	1,680,000	1,824,500
Catastrophic injury insurance expense	3,528,800	2,832,500
Legal services/govt. affairs expense	2,500,000	2,500,000

Exhibit 4–7 continued

Scholarships expense	1,290,000	1,350,000
Youth clinics	735,000	678,100
Convention and honors banquet	661,500	705,000
General expense	1,442,600	1,760,600
Promotion and public relations expense...	2,553,500	2,397,000
Visitors Center expense	1,105,000	1,052,000
Committee expense	1,665,000	2,100,000
National office operations expense	6,386,600	5,890,700
Administration and finance group expense		2,560,600
Championships and event management group expense		2,146,900
Membership services group expense:		
Compliance services	1,135,000	1,309,200
Enforcement services	2,366,000	2,466,400
Legislative services	1,376,000	1,419,900
Public affairs group expense:		
Communications expense	1,768,000	1,674,400
Publishing expense	1,325,000	1,309,200
Visitors Center expense	484,000	493,700
Executive expense	2,432,000	2,648,800
Administration department expense	1,747,000	
Business department expense	1,509,000	
Championships department expense	1,753,000	
Total NCAA operating expense	157,733,800	162,448,180
Championships reserve		4,360,120
Associated organizations		
National Youth Sports Program	10,831,800	12,000,000
NCAA Foundation	176,400	618,700
Total associated organizations	11,008,200	12,618,700
TOTAL EXPENSE	$ 168,742,000	$ 179,427,000

as high school athletic administrators better analyze the courts' conclusions regarding various interscholastic rules for comparison to intercollegiate situations and circumstances. Furthermore, an understanding of high school athletic associations can assist college athletic administrators in facilitating the transition of the student-athlete from the high school to the college ranks by creating a heightened level of awareness and possibly opening lines of communication.

High school athletic associations are voluntary associations consisting of all the high schools within a state that wish to participate in association events, agree to abide by the rules of the association, and are accepted as members. High school associations are often given authority to organize through enabling legislation, which in effect creates a private corporation to perform a quasi-public function.

Each of the fifty states has its own high school athletic association

Exhibit 4–8
NCAA Organizational Structure

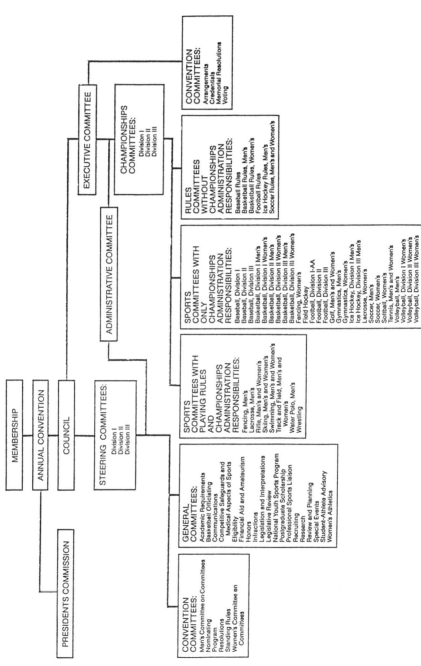

Source: 1990–91 NCAA Manual, p. 18.

to govern interscholastic athletics. Generally, membership in the association is open to all high schools in the state approved by the appropriate state department of education, secondary education, or public instruction. The association's purpose is to promote, develop, direct, protect, and regulate amateur interscholastic athletic relationships among member schools and to stimulate fair play, friendly rivalry, and good sportsmanship among contestants, schools, and communities throughout the state.

Interscholastic state athletic associations have had litigation brought against them because of a claim that the rules of the association were unconstitutional or a complaint about the sanctions imposed on the school and/or student-athlete. In the majority of these cases, the courts have found that the state athletic association has the responsibility to enforce its rules, and that the student-athlete's participation in interscholastic athletics is a privilege more than a right. The courts have found, though, that the association's rules still cannot be arbitrary or irrational and deny the student-athlete the exercise of a privilege; otherwise the rules will be declared unconstitutional.

NOTES ————————————————————————————

1. In *Florida High School Activities Ass'n v. Thomas*, 409 So. 2d 245 (Fla. Dist. Ct. App. 1982), the court found that the association's rule regarding limitation of a football player roster prior to the championships created two disparately treated classes, those who practiced and were eligible to play during both the regular season and the playoff games and those who practiced and were eligible only for regular season play. The courts thus stated that this rule was a violation of student-athletes' constitutional rights and declared it to be unconstitutional.

2. In *School District of the City of Harrisburg v. Pa. Interscholastic Athletic Ass'n*, 309 A.2d 353 (Pa. Sup. Ct. 1973), the school principal's admission of responsibility with respect to culpability for incidents of fighting among spectators following a football game was sufficient to sustain a finding that the school had violated athletic association rules and that sanctions then imposed were therefore justified.

3. In *Kelley v. Metropolitan County Board of Education of Nashville, Etc.*, 293 F. Supp. 485 (M.D. Tenn. 1968), a school board and an athletic association attempted to suspend an all-black high school's athletic program for one year. The district court granted injunctive relief to the student-athletes and held that procedural due process was violated because there was a lack of preexisting standards and regulations by which the school board could take disciplinary actions, and there was a conspicuous lack of formal charges or hearings in regard to the individual student-athletes that the school suspended.

4. In *Florida High School Activities Ass'n v. Bradshaw*, 369 So. 2d 398 (Fla. Dist. Ct. App. 1979), plaintiff high school football player sought to enjoin state high school activities association from imposing a forfeiture for two games

in which plaintiff participated while ineligible. The court held that in the absence of actual harm to the plaintiff and because of a lack of standing for the coach and other team members to assert denial of equal protection, the injunction was valid. The court also held that the opportunity to participate is a constitutionally protected right; therefore, the court will not intervene in an association's discipline or sanction of its members.

The National Federation of State High School Associations (NFSHSA) is the governing body for high school athletics. Founded in 1920, the federation was based on the belief that strong state and national high school organizations are necessary to protect the integrity of interscholastic programs and to promote healthy growth of those programs. The NFSHSA as a federation has much less power than the NCAA (which has national authority). Instead, the high school athletic associations are established on an insular, state-by-state basis. Like the NCAA, they are usually funded by membership dues. Many associations charge a flat fee for each school, which includes such items as entry fees and transportation costs to association tournaments, although some states have sliding fee scales.

NFSHSA services include a press service subscribed to by editors of local, state, and national publications; a national film library; national federation publications for thirteen sports; national records for more than 40,000 performances as listed in the *National Interscholastic Record Book;* sanctioning of applications for interstate and international events among schools; athletic directors conferences; printed proceedings; and a quarterly magazine. The NFSHSA membership serves over 20,000 high schools, 500,000 coaches and sponsors, and 500,000 officials and judges. Its structure is shown in Exhibit 4–9.

The Massachusetts Interscholastic Athletic Association (MIAA) is an example of a high school association. Its members include public and private secondary schools, as well as technical and vocational schools. Prior to membership, an applicant school must be approved by the Board of Directors, which administers the rules and enforces the discipline with the association. Upon acceptance of membership, the approved school agrees to be bound by the requirements set forth in the MIAA eligibility rules. Each school is free, however, to make any other rules, including ones that are stricter than MIAA rules, as long as the school's rules do not conflict with those of the association.

The purpose of the MIAA is clearly set forth in the MIAA constitution:

> The purpose of the Association shall be to organize, regulate and promote interscholastic athletics for secondary schools of Massachusetts. In pursuing this commitment the Association shall:

Exhibit 4–9
Organizational Structure of the NFSHSA

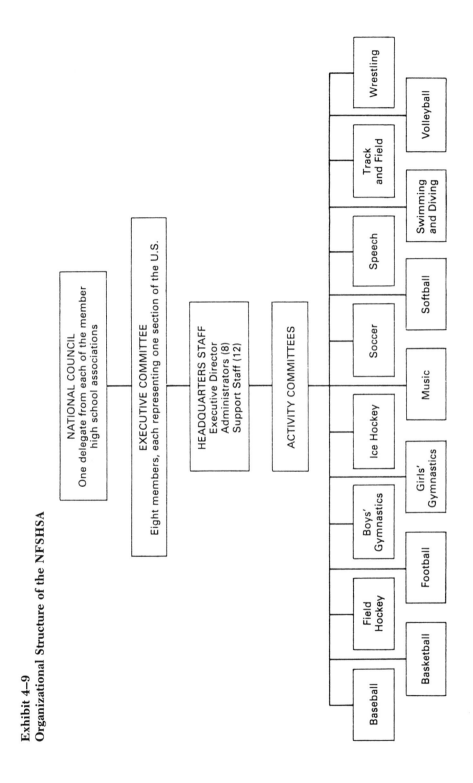

A. Provide leadership and service designed to improve interschool relations in athletics.
B. Foster cooperation among voluntary institutional members and the Massachusetts Secondary School Administrators Association, the Massachusetts Department of Education, Massachusetts Association of School Committees, Massachusetts Association of School Superintendents, Massachusetts Secondary School Athletic Directors Association, Massachusetts State Coaches' Association, and with professional organizations interested in attaining common goals.
C. Secure uniform regulations and control of interscholastic participation in athletics throughout the state to provide equitable competition for students as an integral part of the education of secondary school students.
D. Promote safety and health of participants in interscholastic athletics.
E. Develop and channel the force of opinion to keep interscholastic athletics within reasonable bounds so that it will expressly encourage all that is honorable and sportsmanlike in all branches of sports for secondary youth.
F. Provide a forum for concerns related to interscholastic athletics for institutions which become voluntary members of the Association.
G. Develop uniform standards and procedures for determining championships at the end of the season. [Article II—Purpose, 1991–93]

Note that sections D and E expressly designate areas of concern not explicit in NCAA policies. Here, the MIAA expresses its concern for the health and safety of participating student-athletes. It also recognizes the particular problem of the effect of public opinion on presumably unsophisticated high school student-athletes.

The rule-making body of the MIAA is an assembly composed of the principals of the member schools. The assembly meets annually and is empowered with the authority to organize administrative committees as they are deemed necessary.

There are two administrative bodies of the MIAA—the Board of Directors and the Eligibility Review Board (ERB). The Board of Directors is composed of seventeen members elected from various professional, educational, and athletic associations within the state. It is authorized to hear appeals of decisions, decide the time and place of meetings, create and appoint special committees, interpret rules and fix penalties, and issue and revise rules as necessary. The Board of Directors also has the power to warn, censure, or place on probation any school, player, team, coach, or game or school official who violates any rule.

The second administrative body is the Eligibility Review Board. The board is composed of six high school principals—one assistant principal, two athletic directors, one superintendent, one school committee member, and one coach—who are appointed by, but are not members of, the Board of Directors. It has the authority, when validated by a majority vote of its members, to set aside any rules. This action is permitted when the rule clearly fails to accomplish the purpose for which it is intended or when the application of the rule causes an undue hardship to an individual student-athlete. The granting of a waiver must not, however, result in an unfair advantage to the school or to the particular competitor seeking the waiver.

Using Massachusetts as an example, it is possible to generalize that high school associations often have a great deal of power to make decisions in the following areas: creation of rules, interpretation of rules, handling of alleged violations, eligibility of individual student-athletes, and administering tournaments.

A leading case in the area of governing authority of high school athletic associations is *Denis J. O'Connell High School v. The Virginia High School League*, 581 F.2d 81 (4th Cir. 1978), *cert. denied*, 440 U.S. 936 (1979). The case involved the league's denial of membership to a private high school. The federal appeals court ruled that a state is justified in taking any reasonable step to prevent actual or potential abuse of student-athletes. The league had defended its policy of exclusion of private schools as members because it was rationally related to the league's interest in enforcing its eligibility rules concerning transfer student-athletes. The league presented evidence that because public schools draw students from strictly defined areas while private schools are not so limited, it would be difficult to enforce transfer rules with respect to private schools.

The question of whether to allow private schools to compete against public schools is one that is drawing increasing attention. The proponents of allowing private and public school competition claim that it saves travel costs through scheduling in a smaller geographic area, and it furthermore provides a clear-cut state champion as opposed to having two teams who do not compete lay claim to a state title. Opponents argue that since private schools recruit their students (and athletes), they will have an unfair advantage against the public schools on the playing field.

The majority of states have one state high school association, which is open to private, public, and parochial schools for membership. Some states have three or four different governing associations defined by geographic boundaries. For example, the cities of New York and Philadelphia have separate associations that govern the city schools, and they do not compete for state titles.

Another area of high school athletic association authority that may come under increasing judicial scrutiny is academic requirements (see also Chapter 5). For instance, the New Jersey State Interscholastic Athletic Association (NJSIAA) has minimum academic standards for student-athletes. Under the NJSIAA rule, a student-athlete must have passed courses totaling 27.5 credits the last school year to be eligible to play sports. In addition, the student-athlete needs to pass 13.75 credits at the end of the first semester to be eligible for the second semester.

Some New Jersey schools maintain higher standards than the NJSIAA requires. In Newark, for instance, a 1983 regulation requires that in addition to meeting NJSIAA standards, student-athletes must maintain a cumulative 2.0 or "C" average to be eligible for athletic competition.

In 1984, the Texas Legislature promulgated a "no pass, no play" rule, which was adopted by the State Board of Education in March 1985. Under the tough new academic standard a student must have a passing grade of at least 70 in all courses to participate in sports and other extracurricular activities. Students who fail even one course in the six-week grading period must sit out the next six-week grading period. Texas Governor Mark White noted in 1985: "We in Texas don't tell our students it's OK to flunk one course.... We're going to put winners in the classroom.... And it's going to make Texas the big winner." (See Chapter 5.)

NOTES _____

1. High school athletic association governance authority was *upheld* in the following cases.

(a) In *State v. Judges of Court of Common Pleas*, 181 N.E.2d 261 (Ohio Sup. Ct. 1962), the state high school athletic association suspended a member high school from participating in athletics for one year and declared two boys from the high school ineligible for interscholastic athletics for failure to abide by association rules. The court held that this action should not be prohibited when the determination, although harsh, was not the result of mistake, fraud, collusion, or arbitrariness.

(b) In *Mitchell v. Louisiana High School Athletic Ass'n*, 430 F.2d 1155 (5th Cir. 1970), a redshirt rule restricting all incoming high school students who voluntarily repeat eighth grade to six semesters of competition rather than to the normal eight semesters was held to be rationally related to a legitimate state interest and was declared valid.

(c) In *Walsh v. Louisiana High School Athletic Ass'n*, 428 F. Supp. 1261 (E.D. La. 1977), the court upheld the constitutional validity of a transfer rule governing high school athletics. The transfer rule was found to be rationally related to the state's valid and legitimate interest in deterring or eliminating the recruitment of promising young student-athletes by overzealous coaches, fans, and faculty members.

(d) In *Guelker v. Evans*, 602 S.W.2d 756 (Mo. Ct. App. 1980), a high school soccer player violated Missouri State High School Activities Association rules concerning school competition, the eleven-day rule, and international competition when he missed twenty-nine school days and a major part of the soccer season while participating in a tournament sponsored by the United States Soccer Federation in Puerto Rico. The court concluded that the student-athlete failed to meet requirements for a class action and thus ruled in favor of the high school activities association.

(e) In *Christian Brothers Institute v. North New Jersey Interscholastic League*, 86 N.J. 409 (N.J. 1981), a suit was brought by a private high school against a high school athletic league for alleged unlawful discrimination in evaluating a membership application. The court held that a rational basis can exist for interscholastic leagues to be limited to public schools and that such a limitation does not result per se in a denial of equal protection under the federal constitution.

(f) In *Snow v. New Hampshire Interscholastic Athletic Ass'n*, 449 A.2d 1223 (N.H. Sup. Ct. 1982), a high school track athlete claimed he would have qualified for a "Meet of Champions" if he had not been fouled in a qualified meet and finished seventh. The court supported the state association's ruling denying the student's appeal to compete in the championship meet, stating that the court was extremely limited in deciding such matters as fouls in track meets.

(g) In *Board of Education v. Anderson*, 532 N.Y.S.2d 330 (N.Y. Sup. Ct. 1988), the Board of Education and superintendent of school district brought action seeking to enjoin the president of a nonprofit, voluntary, unincorporated association of school superintendents from placing the school district in a certain athletic league. The supreme court ruled that the commissioner of education had primary jurisdiction over the dispute and therefore dismissed the case.

2. The courts ruled *against* high school athletic association governance authority in the following cases.

(a) In *Alabama High School Athletic Ass'n v. Rose*, 446 So. 2d 1 (Ala. Sup. Ct. 1984), a high school football player was granted a preliminary injunction to compete despite an Alabama High School Athletic Association (AHSAA) declaration of ineligibility. The court found clear and convincing evidence of collusion perpetrated upon the student-athlete by AHSAA and its executive director.

(b) In *Florida High School Activities Ass'n v. Bryant*, 313 So. 2d 57 (Fla. Dist. Ct. App. 1975), a high school basketball player was declared eligible to play more than four years of interscholastic basketball after presenting an adequate case of undue hardship, meriting a waiver of the four-year rule. The court reasoned that basketball was vital to this student-athlete because it provided the impetus for his general scholastic and social development, and rehabilitation from prior problems of juvenile delinquency.

(c) In *Bunger v. Iowa High School Athletic Ass'n*, 197 N.W.2d 555 (Iowa Sup. Ct. 1972), a high school football player brought a suit against a high school athletic association to determine the validity of a good conduct rule. The student-athlete was declared ineligible for athletics when it was discovered that he had ridden in a car that contained a case of beer. The court stated that "school authorities may make reasonable beer rules, but we think this rule is too extreme. Some closer relationship between the student-athlete and the beer is required than mere knowledge that the beer is there."

(d) In *Dunham v. Pulsifer*, 312 F. Supp. 411 (D. Vt. 1970), a high school tennis player requested an injunction to stop his high school from enforcing an athletic grooming code. The court found that there was no reasonable relationship between the rule and the asserted justifications for imposing the restriction on hair length. The court stated that when there was not even a reasonable relationship, "the code falls far short of substantial justification. It is not essential to any compelling interest ...and its enforcement cannot be upheld."

(e) In *Hartzell v. Connell*, 186 Cal. Rptr. 852 (Cal. Ct. App. 1982), high school parents successfully challenged a school board's attempt to levy a fee upon students participating in extracurricular activities (including interscholastic athletics). The court determined that since the fees were not authorized by the California Constitution, they were unlawful, and thus the school district could not levy a fee on extracurricular activities at will.

3. For further information, see the following law review article: Weistart, "Rule-making in Interscholastic Sports: The Bases of Judicial Review," 11 *J. L. & Educ.* 291 (1982).

PUBLIC RESPONSIBILITIES OF AMATEUR ATHLETIC ASSOCIATIONS

As legal bodies, amateur athletic associations may have certain duties to fulfill for the public at large as a condition of their corporate existence. Public responsibilities can include broadcast rights (see Chapter 9), antitrust liabilities (see Chapter 13), opening of records, and disclosure and funding of public facilities (see later discussion). Even a voluntary association that considers itself a private organization may have a responsibility to the general public. For instance, the NCAA is responsible to the public for maintaining amateurism in college athletics, providing competition in intercollegiate sports for both men and women student-athletes, and, most recently, allowing greater access to televised football.

Generally, any amateur athletic organization that is public or quasi-public in nature is a potential defendant in a public responsibility case. A case that dealt with the public responsibilities of amateur athletic associations was *Greene v. Athletic Council of Iowa State University*, 251 N.W.2d 559 (Iowa Sup. Ct. 1977). In *Greene*, the Iowa Superior Court ruled that an amateur college association, although private in name, is "quasi-public" in character. The Iowa court discussed the specific statute and decided that the controlling issue was "whether the athletic council was a 'council' as authorized by the laws of the state." The record showed that the Iowa State University (ISU) athletic council was an entity established by officials of ISU to manage and control its intercollegiate athletic program. After a discussion of specific powers, the court found that the athletic council exercised powers that clearly made it a governmental entity. The court went on to decide that the athletic council was granted authorization under the laws of the state, which allowed the board of regents of the university to delegate responsibility to it. In conclusion, the court held that since this body was a council as authorized by the laws of the state, it was subject to the Iowa open-meeting law.

NOTE _____

1. For further information on the public responsibilities of amateur athletic associations, see Wong and Ensor, "Recent Developments in Amateur Athletics: The Organization's Responsibility to the Public," 2 *Enter. & Sports L. J.* 123 (Fall 1985). The article discusses in detail amateur athletic organizations as legal entities and the duties they must fulfill as a condition for retaining their nonprofit corporate status. It includes discussion on access to public records, public access to televised sporting events, public funding of athletic facilities, and delegation of public-entrusted responsibilities.

Disclosure Cases

Disclosure cases involve the argument that certain information possessed by associations or meetings held by organizations should be a matter of public record and therefore open to the public. Disclosure cases are brought on arguments ranging from open-meeting and "sunshine" laws, to Freedom of Information Acts within individual states. Designation as a governmental or other public body may require an organization to be subject to these laws. Thus, a quasi-public association may be subject to restrictions differing from those placed on a private organization. For instance, the quasi-public association may have to open its records for public inspection, while a private association would not have this obligation.

The degree of disclosure that a quasi-public association, conference, or institution may be required to give varies from state to state. Some state laws are more restrictive than others regarding state universities and colleges under their jurisdiction. Under the state of Florida's public records law, for example, interviews related to searches for new coaches or athletic directors are open to the media when state institutions are involved with such searches. In fact, reporters are permitted to sit in on every interview session, as was the case, for example, when Louisiana State University coach Bill Arnsparger was interviewed for the University of Florida's athletic director position in 1985.

For the media and the public, such laws provide factual accounts of who is actually in the running for the job, where the interviews are conducted, what is being asked, and how those being interviewed are responding. For athletic administrators and institutions, these laws put pressure on them to be unbiased, fair, evaluative, and accurate in selecting candidates for vacant positions. Athletic administrators may have to be more specific in identifying job qualifications and characteristics and the means of measuring those characteristics, in defining job responsibilities, and in establishing or refining methods of evaluating and distinguishing candidates' backgrounds and credentials.

Disclosure cases illustrate conflicts that arise concerning the right of the public to be accurately informed by athletic organizations against the need of the organization to protect the confidentiality of its files. In *Kneeland v. National Collegiate Athletic Ass'n*, 850 F.2d 224 (5th Cir. 1988), a reporter sought to gain disclosure of information from the NCAA and the Southwest Conference about the recruiting scandal at Southern Methodist University. The U.S. court of appeals for the Fifth Circuit concluded that the NCAA and Southwest Conference were not government bodies and thus were not subject to the Texas Open Records Act.

The NCAA has argued that only through confidentiality can it investigate itself properly and thereby maintain its amateur integrity and fulfill this additional public responsibility.

The NCAA argues that opening confidential investigation files compromises the NCAA's cooperative principles, to which all member institutions agree to adhere when they join the association. The NCAA, as previously discussed, is a voluntary association whose members, by joining the organization, agree to follow certain conditions and obligations of membership, including the obligation to conduct their individual institutional athletic programs in a manner consistent with NCAA legislation. In addition, member institutions agree to be policed in regard to the organization's rule by the NCAA's enforcement staff. The key to the NCAA investigative process is the cooperative principle—that is, the accused member institution and the NCAA's enforcement staff work together to ascertain the truth of alleged infractions.

NOTES _____

1. In 1984, the Miami Herald Publishing Company, the *St. Petersburg Times,* and Campus Communications, publisher of the University of Florida student newspaper *The Gator,* had a declaratory suit filed against them in

Florida State District Court by the University of Florida. The university asked the court to decide what information the university could reveal to the newspapers in response to their request that files pertaining to an NCAA preliminary investigation into the school's football program be opened to the media. The University of Florida said that strict federal and state laws involving the confidentiality of student and employee records led to the decision to file the suit.

The University of Florida subsequently decided to release the requested information. The information released included the seventy-five-page official letter of inquiry from the NCAA that listed 107 violations by Florida's football program, as well as 1,700 pages of documents about the violations. These included transcripts of interviews with a number of witnesses.

2. In *Re Subpoena To Testify Before Grand Jury*, 864 F.2d 1559 (11th Cir. 1989), four Florida newspapers sought to overrule a district court ruling which restrained counsel and parties from disclosing content of pleadings and memoranda in connection with a grand jury investigation into the University of Florida Athletic Program. The district court ordered this closure to stop the publication of sensitive information in regard to the investigation. The U.S. Court of Appeals affirmed the district court ruling, stating that the newspapers had no right of access to grand jury proceedings under the First Amendment.

3. In the following cases, the courts required amateur athletic associations to open their records to the public under the individual states' Freedom of Information Act.

(a) In *Arkansas Gazette Company v. Southern State College*, 620 S.W.2d 258 (Ark. Sup. Ct. 1981), the newspaper brought suit against the Arkansas Intercollegiate Athletic Conference, seeking to compel it to disclose the amount of money member institutions dispensed to student-athletes during the school year. The court held that the records were not protected by the federal Family Education Rights Privacy Act of 1974, disclosure was allowed under the Arkansas Freedom of Information Act, and such disclosure did not violate student-athletes' reasonable expectation of privacy.

(b) In *Palladrium Publishing Co. v. River Valley School District*, 321 N.W.2d 705 (Mich. Ct. App. 1982), a newspaper sought declaration that the school district and board of education were required to disclose names of students suspended for alleged drug-related activities on school property. The court held that minutes of a school board must identify any student suspended by board action by name rather than student number and that the Freedom of Information Act did not prevent disclosure of this information.

(c) In *Pooler v. Nyquist*, 392 N.Y.S.2d 948 (N.Y. Sup. Ct. 1976), the court ruled that according to the Freedom of Information Act, dropout rates are subject to disclosure after an investigation of a complaint.

(d) In *Depoyster v. Cole*, 766 S.W.2d 606 (Ark. Sup. Ct. 1989), the court ruled that the use of unsigned paper ballots that were not retained in selecting sites for state high school basketball tournaments was in violation of the Arkansas Freedom of Information Act. The ballots constitute "public records" that should have been retained and made available for public inspection.

4. In the following cases, the courts required amateur athletic associations to open their records to the public under state sunshine or disclosure laws other than the Freedom of Information Act:

(a) In *Seal v. Birmingham Post*, 8 Med. L. Rptr. 1633 (Kan. Dist. Ct. 1982), the newspaper sought issuance of subpoenas for NCAA files for use in its defense of a libel suit concerning a published news story. The court ruled that the interests of the newspaper in defending itself far outweighed the NCAA's need to keep such information confidential.

(b) In *Berst v. Chipman*, 653 P.2d 106 (Kan. Sup. Ct. 1982), the state supreme court ruled to overturn the decision in *Seal v. Birmingham Post*. After reviewing the file, the court declared that only certain specific materials, not the entire file, were discoverable by the *Birmingham Post*.

(c) In *Berst v. Chipman*, 653 P.2d 107 (Kan. Sup. Ct. 1982), the state supreme court reiterated its opinion in *Berst v. Chipman* and affirmed the decision in *Seal v. Birmingham Post*, reasoning that the needs of the newspaper outweighed those of the NCAA.

(d) In *Citizens for Better Education v. Board of Education*, 308 A.2d 35 (N.J. Super. Ct. 1973), the court held that citywide standardized achievement tests by grade and school were subject to public inspection. Such reports were ruled to be "public records" within provision of the state Right-to-Know Law, which states that every citizen of the state shall have the right to inspect and copy or purchase copies of public records.

(e) In *Guy Gannett Publishing Co. v. University of Maine*, 555 A.2d 470 (Me. Sup. Ct. 1989), the court ruled that under the Maine Freedom of Access Act, a settlement agreement between the University of Maine and a former basketball coach was subject to disclosure.

(f) In *Guard Publishing Company v. Lane County School District*, 791 P.2d 854 (Or. Sup. Ct. 1990), the court held that under the Oregon Inspection of Public Records Law, the school district was required to release the names and addresses of replacement teachers serving as coaches during a teachers' strike.

(g) In *Dooley, et al. v. Davidson, et al.*, 397 S.E.2d 922 (Ga. Sup. Ct. 1990), the Georgia Supreme Court held that certain athletic department records relating to athletic coaches' income were subject to the Georgia Open Records Act.

5. In the following cases, the courts ruled that amateur athletic associations do *not* have to open their records to the public.

(a) *McMahon v. Board of Trustees of University of Arkansas*, 499 S.W.2d 56 (Ark. Sup. Ct. 1973), was a suit brought to obtain the names of those persons who were given complimentary tickets and the number of tickets each person received for all University of Arkansas football games held in the state of Arkansas. The court held that such information lists are not public records under the Freedom of Information Act and dismissed the petition.

(b) In *Athens Newspaper, Inc. v. Board of Regents*, No. 42,571 (Ga. Sup.

Ct. Jan. 25, 1985) and *Cox Enterprises, Inc. v. Board of Regents*, No. 42,577 (Ga. Sup. Ct. Jan. 25, 1985), the University of Georgia in December 1984 had agreed to release documents pertaining to an NCAA investigation of its football program, but it refused to do so in regard to an investigation of its men's basketball program. Georgia was under pressure to do so because of suits filed by Morris Communications Corp., which publishes newspapers in Georgia and Florida, including the *Athens Georgia Daily News*, and Cox Enterprises, which publishes the *Atlanta Journal* and the *Atlanta Constitution*.

In January 1985, a Georgia Superior Court refused to release the information requested by the newspaper concerning the men's basketball program because:

> the ongoing investigation ... would be impeded if statements of witnesses become available to the public before the investigation was completed or that (a) some witnesses ... would be reluctant to furnish information if they were aware that their identity and the substance of the information they furnished would immediately become hot news; or (b) if they were aware they might be immediately subject to contact by the news media.

After the completion of the investigation, the records were released by the University of Georgia.

6. For further information on public disclosure cases and intercollegiate athletics, see Wong and Ensor, "The NCAA's Enforcement Procedure—Erosion of Confidentiality," 4 *The Entertainment and Sports Lawyer* 1 (1985).

7. Mr. Michael J. Davis, general counsel for the University of Kansas, requested an opinion of the attorney general of the state of Kansas regarding whether certain records (vouchers, invoices, expense claims, purchase orders, and other supporting documents for checks) of the University of Kansas Athletic Corporation (KUAC) should be made available for public inspection upon request.

In the Slip Opinion dated June 5, 1980, No. 80-118, the attorney general found that the University of Kansas substantially controlled the KUAC; therefore, the KUAC fell within the public records law. The attorney general then had to determine what qualified as "public records." Using corporation (non-sports) cases as precedent, the attorney general interpreted "public records" broadly and held that they must be available to the public.

Funding of Public Facilities

A recent development with respect to public responsibilities of an amateur organization is the challenge to the use of public funds. Challenges have been made to the building of sports facilities by faculty governing bodies who have been concerned that funds would be diverted from other educational areas. In *Lester v. Public Building Authority of County of Knox*, No. 78491, (1983), Chancery Court for Knox County, Tenn, a case settled out of court, the issues raised shed light on potential problem areas in financing athletic facilities. This suit was brought by faculty members of the University of Tennessee against the university in order to block its planned funding and construction of a $30-million assembly center and sports arena. University faculty members in forcing a settlement were successful in placing pressure on school officials by commencing litigation to allow some controls and approve projects with which faculty were involved in return for the promise not to delay the financing for the assembly center and arena.

NOTES

1. The courts will often be very protective of a perceived public interest. A key question is how much of the amateur athletic organization's power can be delegated. For an examination of this subject in regard to the Boston Marathon, see the following cases.

(a) In *Boston Athletic Ass'n v. International Marathons, Inc.*, 467 N.E.2d 58 (Mass. 1984), the board of directors of the Boston Athletic Association (BAA) brought a lawsuit against International Marathons, Inc. (IMI) to prevent it from representing itself to the public as the association's agent. The hearing examiner found that the contract which set up the agency relationship and was signed by the president of the BAA violated state law and that the president had exceeded his authority in entering into the agreement.

(b) In *International Marathons, Inc. v. Attorney General*, 467 N.E.2d 55 (Mass. 1984), IMI appealed the hearing examiner's decision in *BAA v. IMI*, but the court refused to review the decision because it was a moot question. The hearing examiner had disapproved the contract between IMI and BAA because it was violative of state law.

2. Individuals involved with a public athletic organization (administrators, coaches, and others) should be aware that such involvement may come under a high degree of scrutiny by a court because of the "public trust" issue. For an examination of the strict standards of ethics the courts expect from an organization such as the NCAA, see *Tarkanian v. University of Nevada, Las Vegas*, Case No. A173498, 8th Judicial District Court of the State of Nevada (June 25, 1984). The University of Nevada, Las Vegas (UNLV), basketball coach successfully brought this suit to prohibit the enforcement of an NCAA-mandated sanction, which required UNLV to sever all ties with coach Tarkanian. The court held that the NCAA and UNLV acted arbitrarily and with prejudice in accepting investigative information and reaching its decisions. The injunction was affirmed by the Supreme Court of Nevada (*Tarkanian v. National Collegiate Athletic Ass'n*, 741 P.2d 1345 [Nev. Sup. Ct. 1987]). However, the United States Supreme Court later reversed this decision, finding that the acts of the NCAA were not under color of state law and thus not subject to the same standards as those set forth in the lower court's decision (*Tarkanian v. National Collegiate Athletic Ass'n*, 488 U.S. 179 [1988]).

CONSTITUTIONAL LAW ASPECTS OF AMATEUR ATHLETICS

Athletic administrators at the high school and college level are beginning to question the frequency of claims directed against them alleging that certain penalties are violations of student-athletes' constitutional rights. Judicial decisions indicate that those administrators who seek to impose severe penalties that impair or jeopardize an individual's career should be aware of the correct procedures and limitations as imposed by law. Consequently, athletic administrators initiating disciplinary action against a coach or student-athlete must proceed in a fair and legal manner. This does not mean that an athletic administrator, athletic association, or conference cannot impose penalties. The implication is clear, however, that failure to proceed in a fair, reasonable, and constitutional manner may result in litigation brought by the student-athlete or coach.

A student-athlete involved in a dispute with an amateur organization may decide to initiate a lawsuit based on the theory that a constitutional right has been violated. In light of the problems of limited judicial review and standing, the constitutionally based claims of due process and equal protection may be the only avenues available. In addition, the constitutional law approach has other advantages. Most important, it enables the student-athlete to bring the case to a federal court, thereby utilizing the federal jurisdiction statutes of due process and equal protection. To succeed on a federal constitutional claim, however, one must show (1) that state action exists, (2) that the claim is not frivolous, and (3) that the claim concerns a right of sufficient importance to be litigated in federal court. If these three points can be established, the student-athlete can then proceed generally on an equal protection and/or a due process theory. The student-athlete may also pursue state constitutional arguments.

State Action Requirement

The constitutional safeguards of the Fifth and Fourteenth Amendments of the United States Constitution apply only when state action is present. Any action taken directly or indirectly by a state, local, or federal government is *state action* for constitutional purposes. In addition, action by any public school, state college, or state university or any of their officials is construed as state action. The issue of state action arises only when alleged wrongdoers argue that they are not acting directly on behalf of the government. In order to subject voluntary, private associations to constitutional limitations, some degree of state action must be present. Of course, actions by private organizations that are deemed to be performing a public function or are authorized under the laws of the state (quasi-public institutions) are also construed as state action.

Beyond the fact that the actions taken by high school and college athletic associations are generally considered state action, it may be argued that private institutions acting in compliance with these organizations are also engaging in state action. Action by strictly private individuals does not constitute state action. Three common methods of analysis used to determine whether or not state action exists in particular circumstances are the public function theory, the entanglement theory, and the balancing approach theory.

The *public function theory* is somewhat limited and is traditionally confined to essential governmental services that have no counterparts in the public sector. A good example is American Telephone and Telegraph Company, which is a private company performing an essentially public function. The NCAA has, in at least one case, been deemed a public functionary on the basis of its comprehensive regulation of an area that would otherwise have to be regulated by the states. The alternatives—having each state regulate college athletic programs without the existence of the NCAA—would be extremely inefficient and not viable. High school athletic association activities have also been found to be state action under the public function theory. In one case, the functions served by the high school athletic association were deemed to be so similar to the functions of the state in providing education that the association's rules were judged to be state action (see note 3a).

In the second method of analysis, commonly known as the *entanglement theory,* the usual focal point is the amount of state and/or federal aid directly or indirectly given to the private organization. Under this view, state action issues involve a conflict between rights, and the court must balance these rights in determining whether the Constitution mandates a preference for one right over another. The receipt of such aid may subject a recipient's action to constitutional review. For this theory to be used by the court, total state and/or federal control over the organization need not exist. Instead, the state or federal government must only have substantial influence over the association's activities. State and association actions must be intertwined to the extent that the organization's actions are supported or sanctioned by the government. State action is found on the basis of the relationship of the association to the government.

During the 1970s, case law had held the NCAA's actions to be the equivalent of state action under this theory. In these cases, the rationale typically had been that over half of the NCAA's members were state-supported schools. In addition, most NCAA member schools received federal aid, and their students received federal financial aid (work-study, National Defense loans). Therefore, albeit indirectly, the NCAA was supported by state and federal governments. The NCAA also provided a service that was beyond the competence or authority of any one state.

In the 1980s, court decisions began to change as the NCAA was seen as not a state actor. Courts began to take a narrower interpretation of what was a state actor (see *Arlosoroff v. National Collegiate Athletic Ass'n*, note 2b).

In 1988, the U.S. Supreme Court decision in *NCAA v. Tarkanian*, 109 S. Ct. 454 (1988), found that the NCAA was not a state actor. The NCAA's policies are determined by several hundred public and private member institutions independent of any particular state, and the NCAA enjoyed no governmental powers to facilitate its investigation of UNLV and Tarkanian; therefore, no state action existed.

High school athletic associations similarly have had their actions scrutinized under the entanglement theory. Many times high schools and their associations receive financial assistance from the state, public school or state officials may have a say in the association's policies and actions, and/or a portion of the association's membership may consist of public schools. These circumstances are sufficient to constitute state action.

The *balancing approach theory* is more general and not widely accepted. Here, if the merits of allowing the organizational practice are outweighed by the limitations on asserted/protected rights, courts have found state action which allows judicial intervention for the protection of individual constitutional rights.

In the past few years the courts have moved away from all three of these methods, finding that the decisions of the NCAA do not constitute state action. In *Tarkanian v. NCAA*, 488 U.S. 179 (1988), the Supreme Court found that even when the organization may have threatened a university with further sanctions if it did not suspend its basketball coach, neither the percentage of public members nor the organization's function was sufficient to find state action. In *Hawkins v. National Collegiate Athletic Ass'n*, 652 F. Supp. 602 (Ill. C.D. 1987), the court ruled that the NCAA is a voluntary association of public and private institutions and although the NCAA may perform a public function in overseeing the nation's intercollegiate athletics, it remains a private institution.

As far as state action at the high school level is concerned, when an alleged state or federal statute violation involves a public high school, state action is obvious. The rights and liberties of the public high school students are therefore protected by the federal Constitution. However, when a private school is involved, the courts have looked for sufficient ties between the alleged wrongful activity and the state to justify intervention. If no state influence related to the wrongful activity is found, no state action will be present and the federal Constitution will not protect the rights and liberties of the students.

NOTES

1. In the following cases, the NCAA's decisions were found to have constituted state action.

(a) In *Howard University v. National Collegiate Athletic Ass'n*, 510 F.2d 213 (D.C. Cir. 1975), the court noted that state-supported educational institutions and their members and officers play a substantial role in the NCAA's program, and that such state participation is a basis for finding state action (entanglement theory).

(b) In *Parish v. National Collegiate Athletic Ass'n*, 361 F. Supp. 1220 (W.D. La. 1973), *aff'd.*, 506 F.2d 1251 (9th Cir. 1974), the court found state action, since over half of the NCAA's members are state-supported schools and the NCAA performs a public function by regulating intercollegiate athletics (entanglement theory).

(c) *Buckton v. National Collegiate Athletic Ass'n*, 366 F. Supp. 1152 (D. Mass. 1973), was the first case to declare the NCAA to be engaged in state action (public function theory). The public function theory has since been supplanted by other theories. (See Chapter 5.)

(d) In *Regents of the University of Minnesota v. National Collegiate Athletic Ass'n*, 422 F. Supp. 1158 (D. Minn. 1976), the court acknowledged that the action taken by the NCAA has generally been accepted as the equivalent of state action. (See Chapter 5.)

(e) In *Associated Students, Inc. v. National Collegiate Athletic Ass'n*, 493 F.2d 1251 (9th Cir. 1974), the court determined that the actions of the NCAA did constitute state action since the NCAA regulates schools and universities, at least half of which are public.

2. In the following cases, the NCAA's decisions were found to have *not* constituted state action.

(a) In *McDonald v. National Collegiate Athletic Ass'n*, 370 F. Supp. 625 (C.D. Calif. 1974), the court concluded that the NCAA is not sufficiently state supported to be considered state action, and it has an existence separate and apart from the educational system of any state. In the court's words, "if an institution is unable to concur with a voluntary organization without contravening the constitutional rights of its students, it must withdraw from the organization."

(b) In *Arlosoroff v. National Collegiate Athletic Ass'n*, 746 F.2d 1019 (4th Cir. 1984), the court stated that the "fact that NCAA's regulatory function may be of some public service lends no support to the finding of state action, for the function is not one traditionally reserved to the state."

(c) In *Graham v. NCAA*, 804 F.2d 953 (6th Cir. 1986), a football player in his fifth year at the University of Louisville attempted to transfer to Western Kentucky University but was declared ineligible as a result of the one-year transfer rule. Plaintiff claimed he was denied procedural due process rights in not being able to challenge the rule itself. The court held that there was no state action by the NCAA and thus no violation of due process. Only when a voluntary organization undertakes to regulate a function traditionally and exclusively reserved to the state, or when there is a showing that the state-supported universities caused or procured the adoption of the rules, will the acts of the NCAA be held to be "under the color of state action."

(d) In *Karmanos v. Baker*, 816 F.2d 258 (6th Cir. 1987), the circuit court followed the reasoning in *Graham v. NCAA* and found that the NCAA ruling that the plaintiff was ineligible for intercollegiate hockey because he played for a professional Canadian league was not state action.

3. The court ruled in the following cases that high school athletic associations *were acting* under color of state action.

(a) In *Barnhorst v. Missouri State High School Athletic Ass'n*, 504 F. Supp. 449 (W.D. Mo. 1980), the court found that the close identification of the functions served by the state high school athletic association with the state's provision of education (including extracurricular activities) to all children of school age is a sufficient link to transmute into state action the challenged association rule forbidding any student-athlete transferring from one member school to another member school from participating in interscholastic athletic competition for 365 days.

(b) In *Yellow Springs Exempted School District v. Ohio High School Athletic Ass'n*, 443 F. Supp. 753 (S.D. Ohio 1978), *rev.'d on other grounds*, 647 F.2d 651 (6th Cir. 1981), the court found that the OHSAA's conduct constituted state action because (1) the association depended on the state for operating revenue, (2) school officials were involved in the decision-making process, (3) public schools were predominant within the association membership, and (4) the association had the ability to impose sanctions upon state schools.

(c) In *Wright v. Arkansas Activities Ass'n*, 501 F.2d 25 (8th Cir. 1974), even though a voluntary athletic association of public and parochial schools was not a state agency, its actions in regulating public school athletic activities and imposing a sanction for rule violations were found to constitute state action. The athletic association, having found a violation of "offseason" football practice rules, gave the school or school district a choice of suspending the high school from participation in association football games or not employing a particular coach as head football coach. The coach was accordingly requested to resign his coaching and teaching position and later sued the association.

4. For a case in which the court ruled that an Olympic organization was not acting under color of state action, see *DeFrantz v. United States Olympic Committee*, 492 F. Supp. 1181 (D.D.C. 1980), *aff'd. without decision*, 701 F.2d 221 (D.C. Cir. 1980). Twenty-five athletes sought an injunction to bar the USOC from boycotting the 1980 Moscow Olympics. Emphasizing that the USOC receives no federal funding and that it operates and exists independently of the federal government, the court found that the state was not in a position of interdependence with the USOC. The court also stated that the plaintiffs failed to prove that some form of control, or governmental persuasion or pressure, was behind the challenged action. (See Chapter 1.)

5. For further information, see the following law review articles:

(a) Docrhoff, "State High School Athletic Associations: When Will a Court Interfere?" 36 *Mo. L. Rev.* 400 (1971).

(b) Martin, "The NCAA and Its Student-Athletes: Is There Still State Action?" 21 *New Eng. L. Rev.* 49 (1985–86).

(c) Note, "Constitutional Law: Is the NCAA Eligible for a New Interpretation of State Action?" 7 *Loy. Enter. L. J.* 337 (1987).

(d) K. M. McKenna, "The Tarkanian [National Collegiate Athletic Association v. Tarkanian, 109 S.Ct. 454] Decision: The State of College Athletics Is Everything but State Action," 40 *De Paul L. Rev.* 459 (Winter 1991).

(e) Note, "National Collegiate Athletic Association v. Tarkanian [109 S.Ct. 454]: A Death Knell for the Symbiotic Relationship Test," 18 *Hastings Const. L. Q.* 237 (Fall 1990).

Due Process

Constitutional guarantees afforded citizens in general apply equally to educational institutions, administrators, coaches, and student-athletes. The courts are reviewing with less hesitancy cases claiming a violation of protected rights. In light of this legal development, a primary concern of athletic administrators when imposing penalties which jeopardize an individual's career should be minimum standards of "due process of law."

Due process is an elusive concept. One definition for the term *due process* is "a course of legal proceedings which have been established in our system of jurisprudence for the protection and enforcement of private rights" (*Pennoyer v. Neff,* 95 U.S. 714 [1877]). The concept may vary, depending on three basic considerations: (1) the seriousness of the infraction, (2) the possible consequences to the institution or individual in question, and (3) the degree of sanction or penalty imposed.

The constitutional guarantee of due process is found in both the Fifth and Fourteenth Amendments to the U.S. Constitution. The Fifth Amendment, enacted in 1791, is applicable to the federal government. It states that "no person . . . shall be deprived of life, liberty, or property without due process of law." In 1886, the Fourteenth Amendment was ratified, reading, "nor shall any state deprive any person of life, liberty, or property without due process of law. . . ." This amendment extended the applicability of the due process doctrine to the states. Both amendments apply only to federal or state governmental action and not to the conduct of purely private entities. While the Constitution extends these liberties to all persons, it is also limiting in that a person must demonstrate deprivation of life, liberty, or property to claim a violation of due process guarantees.

Since athletic associations and conferences rarely deprive a person of life, the major interests that trigger application of the due process clause in the athletic context are deprivations of liberty and property.

Unless an athlete or other party can establish that he or she has been deprived of liberty or property, he or she will not be able to establish a deprivation of due process.

The due process doctrine presses two inquiries. The first is *procedural due process,* which refers to the procedures required to ensure fairness. The second is *substantive due process,* which guarantees basic rights that cannot be denied by governmental action. Procedural due process has as its focal point the questioning of the decision-making process which is followed in determining whether the rule or regulation has been violated and the penalty, if any, that is imposed. Was the decision made in an arbitrary, capricious, or collusive manner? Was the accused given the opportunity to know what to defend against and to know reasonably well in advance what is thought to have been violated? Substantive due process involves the rule, regulation, or legislation being violated—namely, is it fair and reasonable? In other words, when measuring substantive due process, does the rule or legislation have a purpose and is it clearly related to the accomplishment of that purpose?

Claims to due process protection may be based not only on protections guaranteed by state constitutions and by federal and state statutes, but also on the regulations and constitutions of athletic institutions, conferences, and other athletic governing organizations.

Procedural Due Process

The two minimum requirements of procedural due process are the right to a hearing and notice of the hearing's time, date, and content. The requirements are flexible, and the degree of formality depends on the nature of the right involved as well as on the circumstances surrounding the situation. If the deprivation concerned is not that of a fundamental right or is a right marginally affected by the challenged rule, only the minimal due process requirements may be necessary (see Exhibit 4–10).

On the other hand, when a fundamental right is involved or when an infringement on personal freedom is present, the hearing must be more formal, with additional safeguards. The full protections of due process include notice and the right to a hearing in front of a neutral decision maker, with an opportunity to make an oral presentation, to present favorable evidence, and to confront and cross-examine adverse witnesses. In addition, there may also be a right to have an attorney present during the proceedings, a right to receive a copy of the transcript of the hearing, and a right to a written decision based on the record (see Exhibit 4–11).

Although an individual may enjoy the guarantee of due process, the actual process is rarely spelled out. The type of due process protections

Exhibit 4–10
Minimal Due Process Checklist

General Considerations
- The special requirements or procedures imposed by state law, association policy, conference policy, institution policy, or board policy regarding the declaration of student-athlete ineligibility should be determined and followed.
- The person or persons who have authority to declare a student-athlete ineligible should be identified.
- Whether the matter requires rudimentary due process or formal due process should be decided.

Due Process Procedures
- A determination should be made as to whether the alleged violation, unfulfilled requirement, or ruling is a proper basis for the proposed regulatory action.
- The person dealing with the student-athlete should promptly give the student-athlete oral or written notice of the specific violation or ruling and the proposed regulatory measure.
- If the student-athlete denies the violation or disagrees with the ruling, the individual should be provided with an explanation of the evidence which the athletic department has in its possession.
- The student-athlete should be allowed to present his or her side of the story.
- The proposed regulatory action should be imposed unless the student-athlete adequately refutes the violation or the ruling.
- The student-athlete's parents or guardian should be notified, if appropriate, of the regulatory measure being imposed.
- If requested by the student-athlete or parent, the ruling and action taken under applicable procedures should be reviewed. This may entail a verification of the ruling and action with the institution's athletic conference and/or association.

guaranteed in a given situation are determined by a consideration of the importance of the right involved, the degree of the infringement, and the potential harm of the violation. As a general rule, the more an individual has at stake, the more extensive and formal are the due process requirements. Since a number of factors are involved, administrative agencies must examine the merits of each case to determine the required procedures on a case-by-case basis.

The Supreme Court has further applied a three-pronged inquiry to determine what is due process: the private interest that will be affected

Exhibit 4–11
Full Due Process Checklist

General Considerations
- The special requirements or procedures imposed by state law, association policy, conference policy, institution policy, or board policy regarding the declaration of student-athlete ineligibility should be determined and followed.
- The person or persons who have authority to declare a student-athlete ineligible should be identified.
- Whether the matter requires rudimentary due process or formal due process should be decided.

Preliminary Due Process Procedures
- A determination should be made as to whether proper grounds exist for the proposed regulatory action and, if appropriate, charges consistent with applicable procedures should be initiated.
- The student-athlete, and if a minor, the individual's parents or guardian, should be notified in writing, of the violation or ruling, the factual basis for the charges, the specific provisions of any student-athlete code, the right of the student-athlete to a hearing and the procedures to be followed at that hearing, the right of the student-athlete to be represented by an attorney or other counsel, and whether a hearing must be requested or whether one will be scheduled automatically. Also, the student-athlete, and if a minor, the individual's parents or guardian, should be given a copy of any applicable rules governing the violation or ruling and the regulatory proceedings.
- If appropriate, the written notice should be preceded or followed by a telephone or personal conference with the student-athlete or, if a minor, the parents or guardian.
- If requested or required automatically under applicable regulatory procedures, a hearing should be scheduled.
- If requested, the student-athlete or the individual's counsel should be given the names of witnesses against him and an oral or written report of the facts to which each witness will testify, unless such disclosures may result in reprisals against the witnesses.
- A transcript or record of the hearing should be arranged for if required or desired by the student-athlete.
- All steps necessary to assure fairness and impartiality of the parties involved in the hearing should be taken.

Conduct of the Hearing
- To open the hearing, the presiding officer should declare the hearing convened, state the matter under consideration, take a roll call of the members of the board or panel, and confirm the existence of a quorum.
- All persons present should be identified and their interest in the matter verified. The meeting may be closed to the public and those without a proper interest in the matter.

Exhibit 4–11 continued

- The presiding officer should summarize the procedures to be followed.
- The student-athlete or the individual's counsel should be asked whether any objections exist with regard to the time, place, or procedures of the hearing.
- The student-athlete or his counsel should be allowed the opportunity to raise any questions regarding the impartiality of any member of the tribunal or the hearer.
- The charges or ruling against the student-athlete should then be read and the student-athlete requested to confirm that he or she has received a copy of the charges.
- If the parties to the matter have stipulated or agreed on any facts or exhibits in the case, they should be requested to present them.
- Each party should be provided an opportunity to make opening statements.
- Subject to the applicable rules of evidence, the person bringing the charges or ruling and, thereafter, the student-athlete, should be allowed to present any relevant material and reliable evidence, generally subject to a right of cross-examination by the other.
- Following the initial presentation of evidence, the parties should be allowed to present rebuttal and surrebuttal evidence.
- At the close of all the evidence, the parties should be invited to make closing statements or arguments.
- The hearing should then be closed with an explanation of the timetable and procedures to be used for rendering a decision.

Posthearing Procedures
- Deliberations of the case should commence.
- Only the members of the tribunal or hearer and their attorneys or advisers should be allowed to participate in or attend the deliberations.
- Once decision is reached, it should be reduced to writing, setting forth findings of fact, the basis of the decision, and the regulatory measure imposed.
- The student-athlete and, if a minor, the individual's parents or guardian, should be notified of the decision.
- Consistent with applicable procedures, the student-athlete should be advised of any available administrative review and provided that review.
- All parties should realize that the student-athlete may always seek appropriate judicial relief.

by the official action; the risk of an erroneous deprivation of such interest through the procedures used and the probable value, if any, of additional or substitute procedural safeguards; and the government's interest, including the function involved and the fiscal and administrative burdens that the additional or substitute procedural requirement would entail (*Mathews v. Eldridge*, 424 U.S. 319 [1976]). Some have suggested that athletic organizations fashion a set of notice and hearing procedures that will withstand constitutional scrutiny. The benefits to establishing a set of procedures include the following:

1. Establishing procedures may be fairer to student-athletes, thereby building goodwill.
2. Courts, which are already inclined to defer to athletic decision makers, will in most cases find the procedures adequate, particularly if the procedures are originally fashioned in light of the *Mathews* case.
3. Provided that the procedures are basically fair and balance the factors outlined in *Mathews*, they are less likely to be challenged by the student-athletes themselves because some due process will already have been afforded the aggrieved party.
4. Establishing procedures would contribute some certainty to an area otherwise fraught with ambiguity.

Having a set of notice and hearing procedures would benefit the organization as well as the athlete, thereby reducing the role of the courts in fashioning and implementing required procedures.

NOTES _____

1. In the following cases the courts ruled that there was no violation of due process rights:

(a) In *Southern Methodist University v. Smith*, 515 S.W.2d 63 (Tex. Civ. App. 1974), the court held that no due process is required if the facts are not disputed, or if the issues have already been resolved (see *Graesen v. Pasquale*, 200 N.W.2d 842 [1978]).

(b) In *Pegram v. Nelson*, 469 F. Supp. 1134 (M.D.N.C. 1979), the court held that a short suspension (less than ten days) from participation in after-school extracurricular activities requires only an informal hearing.

(c) In *Mitchell v. Louisiana High School Athletic Ass'n*, 430 F.2d 1155 (5th Cir. 1970), the court of appeals ruled that the association's eligibility rules did not violate students' rights under due process and equal protection clauses of the Fourteenth Amendment, since a substantial federal question was not raised.

(d) In *Hamilton v. Tennessee Secondary Athletic Ass'n*, 552 F.2d 681 (6th Cir. 1976), the court of appeals ruled that the privilege of participating in interscholastic athletics is outside the protection of due process.

(e) In *Marcum v. Dahl,* 658 F.2d 731 (10th Cir. 1981), college basketball student-athletes claimed their right to due process had been violated when they were dropped from the team for disciplinary reasons without a hearing. The court held that the college had offered the opportunity for a hearing, but the student-athletes had failed to take advantage of it, thus freeing the college of any further due process responsibilities.

(f) In *Spring Branch I.S.D. v. Stamos,* 695 S.W.2d 556 (Tex. Sup. Ct. 1985), an action was brought on behalf of several students, seeking a permanent injunction to bar the enforcement of a rule requiring students to maintain a 70 average in all classes to be eligible for participation in extracurricular activities. The lower court held the rule unconstitutional and issued an order enjoining its enforcement. On appeal, the Supreme Court of Texas held that the rule was rationally related to a legitimate state interest in providing high-quality education to public school students and thus was not violative of constitutional equal protection guarantees. Further, the court held that the students did not possess a constitutionally protected interest in their participation in extracurricular activities and, therefore, the rule was not violative of due process rights.

(g) In *Brands v. Sheldon Community School,* 671 F. Supp. 627 (N.D. Iowa 1987), the plaintiff, a high school athlete, brought an action challenging the school board's decision declaring him ineligible to compete on his high school wrestling team. On the plaintiff's motion for a temporary restraining order or preliminary injunction, the court held that the athlete was not deprived of a liberty or property right when the school declared him ineligible; therefore, procedural due process rights did not apply.

(h) In *Palmer v. Merluzzi,* 868 F.2d 90 (3rd Cir. 1989), the plaintiff argued that he should be given additional procedural due process rights after the imposition of additional penalties, after he was caught smoking marijuana and drinking beer. The court of appeals concluded that the single proceeding which resulted in two sanctions being imposed was enough to satisfy the due process rights of the plaintiff.

2. In the following cases the courts ruled that there was a violation of due process rights:

(a) In *Behagen v. Intercollegiate Conference of Faculty Representatives,* 346 F. Supp. 602 (D. Minn. 1972), two college basketball players who had been suspended for the season sought to prohibit the ICFR (also known as the Big Ten Conference) from enforcing their suspension until they were granted due process. The court found it consistent with the powers of the commissioner to suspend the players temporarily pending a hearing, if such action was not arbitrary or capricious and was done to protect the interest of the conference. However, due process could not be denied since the suspensions bordered on punitive action, with a notable concern being that the players were prevented from displaying skills that could lead to future economic rewards as professionals.

(b) In *Regents of University of Minnesota v. National Collegiate Athletic*

Ass'n, 560 F.2d 352 (8th Cir. 1977), the court held that due process requires notice and a hearing.

(c) In *Kelley v. Metropolitan County Board of Education of Nashville*, 293 F. Supp. 485 (M.D. Tenn. 1968), plaintiff high school student-athlete was suspended from athletic competition by the board of education without being formally charged with a rule violation. The court held that due process involves the right to be heard before being condemned. Due process requires published standards, formal charges, notice, and a hearing. The court granted an injunction that prevented the enforcement of the suspension.

(d) In *O'Connor v. Board of Education*, 316 N.Y.S.2d 799 (N.Y. Sup. Ct. 1970), a high school student-athlete was deprived of his athletic award (letter) after his coach turned him in for allegedly violating a "no drinking" rule. The court held that the process required a hearing prior to revocation of a high school athlete's letter.

(e) In *Taylor v. Alabama High School Athletic Ass'n*, 336 F. Supp. 54 (M.D. Ala. 1972), plaintiff high school was prohibited from hosting or participating in invitational basketball tournaments for one year because of the "misconduct and unruliness" of spectators at one of its games. The Alabama High School Athletic Association violated the plaintiff's due process rights for the following reasons:

(1) There were no preexisting standards.
(2) No punishments were provided for violation of the rules.
(3) No specific charge was made.
(4) No notice was given.
(5) There was no opportunity for an adequate hearing.
(6) The hearing was not convened as required by the association's rules.

The court also found that the penalty imposed exceeded any other previously imposed penalty.

(f) In *Duffley v. New Hampshire Interscholastic Athletic Ass'n*, 446 A.2d 462 (N.H. Sup. Ct. 1982), the New Hampshire Supreme Court ruled that plaintiff student-athlete had been denied procedural due process because the New Hampshire Interscholastic Athletic Association failed to state the reasons for denial of eligibility.

(g) In *Wright v. Arkansas Activities Ass'n*, 501 F.2d 25 (8th Cir. 1974), the court of appeals ruled that a rule prohibiting football practice prior to a certain date may provide fair notice that a school may be sanctioned. However, imposition of a sanction resulting in the loss of a coaching/ teaching position denied the coach due process. The rule gave no notice of the fact that the coach could be subject to a sanction resulting in unemployment.

3. In *Stone v. Kansas State High School Activities Ass'n*, 761 P.2d 1255 (Kan. App. 1988), the Kansas Court of Appeals took a unique position by declaring that even though participation in extracurricular school activities is not a fundamental right, a student's interest in participating in such activities should still be constitutionally protected with due process of the law. The court went on to state that even though participation in such activities may

not be a fundamental right, an athletic association may not enact and enforce, free of judicial review, rules that are arbitrary and capricious.

4. An example of a hearing and appeal process which can be made available to an athlete by an amateur sports organization is the following process implemented by the United States Swimming Association.

Article 401: Hearings and Appeals

401.1 General—As hereinafter set forth, the Corporation may censure, suspend for a definite or indefinite period of time with or without terms of probation, fine, or expel any member of the Corporation, including any athlete, coach, manager, official, member of any committee, or any person participating in any capacity whatsoever in the affairs of the Corporation, who has violated any of its rules or regulations, or who aids, abets, and encourages another to violate any of its rules or regulations, or who has acted in a manner which brings disrepute upon the Corporation or upon the sport of swimming. The Corporation may also conduct hearings on any matter affecting the Corporation as the national governing body for swimming.

401.2 Jurisdiction of the LSC—In those matters involving only a member or members of one LSC, the procedure to be taken and the rules to be followed for hearing shall be as set forth in Part Six, Article 611. (For guide to hearings and appeals, and form for notice of hearing, see Appendix 6-A.)

401.3 Jurisdiction of the Corporation—In those matters in which athletes or other members of the Corporation from more than one LSC are involved, or in matters involving such persons during a national or international event, an investigation and report of the facts shall be made to the General Chairman of the National Board of Review and to the officers of the Corporation. If in the opinion of a majority of the officers, a hearing or further investigation is then warranted, the matter shall be submitted to a National Board of Review for hearing and decision.

.1 Where persons or entities from more than one LSC are involved, the investigation and report shall be made by the Executive Director or his designee.

.2 In those matters occurring during the course of a national, regional or zone event, the Vice President of Program Operations, or his designee, shall make the investigation and report.

.3 In those matters occurring during the course of an international event, Olympic International Operations Committee Coordinator, or his designee, shall make the investigation and report.

401.4 National Board of Review—The Board shall be comprised of the General Counsel of the Corporation, all associate counsel, one or more athlete representatives, and such other members as may be appointed from time to time by the President and approved by the Executive Committee. The President shall appoint the chairman and shall designate a panel of no less than three members, one of whom shall be an athlete representative, to hear and decide any case before the Board of Review.

401.5 Authority of National Board of Review

The National Board of Review has the authority to:

.1 Impose and enforce penalties for any violation of the rules and regulations, administrative or technical, of the Corporation;

.2 Determine the eligibility and right to compete of any athlete;

.3 Vacate, modify, sustain, reverse or stay any decision or order properly submitted for review, or remand the matter for further action;

.4 Investigate any election impropriety or cause for removal of a national committeeman or national officer and take corrective action;

.5 Interpret any provision of the rules and regulations of the Corporation with the exception of the technical rules (Part One);

.6 Review any revocation, suspension or reinstatement of membership to assure due process; and

.7 Issue such interim orders, prohibitory or mandatory in nature, as may be necessary pending a final decision of the Board.

.8 Reinstate any athlete to amateur status. (Note: This relates only to USS domestic competition and NOT international competition. It must be read in light of current FINA rules on requalification.)

401.6 Exclusive Authority of National Board of Review

The National Board of Review has exclusive authority to hear any complaint against any members of the Corporation, including any athlete, coach, manager, official member of any committee, or any person participating in any capacity whatsoever in the affair of the Corporation, who is the subject of a current law enforcement agency investigation alleging a crime involving moral turpitude or has been charged with a crime involving moral turpitude, which alleged misconduct may relate to that member's involvement in the sport of swimming.

401.7 Procedure for Review

.1 Every appeal to the Board of Review shall be instituted by a petition served upon the Executive Director and shall be accompanied by a $50 filing fee payable to the Corporation. The petition for review shall set forth the grounds for appeal, citing factual and legal issues in as much detail as possible. The filing fee shall be returned if the appeal is upheld, but forfeited if it is rejected, modified or abandoned. The Board of Review may assess costs against any party.

.2 The Executive Director shall send a copy of the petition for review to the respondent and chairman of the Board of Review immediately upon receipt. The respondent shall within 30 days following receipt of the petition file a written response with the Executive Director, the petitioner and the chairman. The petitioner may within 10 days following receipt of a copy of the response file a written rebuttal with the Executive Director, the respondent and the chairman. The chairman may decrease or increase the time limits for any of the foregoing upon request of either party and if circumstances should warrant it.

.3 A final and binding decision shall be rendered within 75 days from date of filing of the petition by a majority of the acting panel based on the record submitted for review and on evidence submitted at such hearing as may be required by the panel. A written decision shall be sent to all parties. Petitions once reviewed and decided shall not be reopened for consideration by the Board of Review, except by direction of the Board of Directors of the Corporation, or upon showing of sufficient cause to the chairman of the Board of Review.

.4 In all matters where a decision is sought under Section 401.6 the request for review shall be submitted directly to the Chairman of the National Board of Review or his designee ("Chairman"). The Chairman shall consider the request and conduct such investigation as he considers appropriate. If the Chairman considers the allegations serious enough to warrant consideration of an immediate suspension before any judicial determination of the matter under investigation has been made, the Chairman may refer the matter to the National Board of Review. The member who is the subject of the complaint shall be notified of such action when the matter is referred to the National Board of Review. The review process shall then proceed as outlined in the foregoing sections. Until such time as the National Board of Review makes a decision all proceedings under Rule 401.6 shall be confidential and not subject to disclosure to anyone other than the parties to the review and/or witness.

401.8 Appeal to the Board of Directors—Any real party in interest may appeal to the Board of Directors for review of any decision of the National Board of Review within thirty (30) days of the postmark date of the mailing of its written decision. The petition on appeal is to be served upon the Executive Director and shall be accompanied by a $50.00 filing fee payable to USS. The petition shall set forth the grounds for appeal, citing factual and legal issues in as much detail as possible. The Board of Directors may assess fees and costs against the losing party.

401.9 Exclusive Jurisdiction—After an LSC that is a real party in interest is given such notice and hearing as time and circumstances may reasonably dictate, and upon a majority vote of the officers of USS, the USS Board of Directors or the USS National Board of Review may be assigned exclusive jurisdiction at any stage of any matter within the purview of this Article 401 when the best interests of the Corporation will be served thereby, or when compliance with regular LSC procedures would not be likely to produce a sufficiently early decision to do justice to the affected parties. If exclusive jurisdiction is so assigned compliance shall be made in every instance with all requirements of procedural due process as set forth in this Article 401. In either case the reviewing body may assess fees and costs against any party.

401.10 Full Faith and Credit—Final decisions rendered by any LSC shall, when applicable, be recognized and fully enforced in all other LSCs of the Corporation. (1993 Code)

5. As a result of actions taken by the NCAA, numerous politicians have complained that the NCAA does not provide due process in their investigations and enforcement procedures. As a result of the U.S. Supreme Court's decision in *National Collegiate Athletic Association v. Tarkanian*, 488 U.S. 179 (1988), stating that the NCAA was not a state actor, the NCAA has no duty to provide due process protections. Therefore, a number of bills have been proposed in Congress and in numerous states which would guarantee that an institution, coach, or athlete would receive proper due process rights. Due process legislation has passed in Nevada, Nebraska, Florida, and Illinois. Legislation that used to be currently pending in South Carolina, Minnesota, Kansas, Iowa, New York, and California has all been defeated either in Committee or on the floor.

6. For further information, see Lowell, "Federal Administrative Intervention in Amateur Athletes," 43 *Geo. Wash. L. Rev.* 729 (1975).

Substantive Due Process

If the court finds that the right deprived involves life, liberty, or property, then full due process rights may be granted to the individual (see Exhibit 4–10). In sports cases, the interest most commonly cited is the property interest, although in some instances the personal liberty interest is involved (see hair length cases in Chapter 5). For the purposes of the due process clause, types of property are not distinguished. Therefore, the first problem encountered in many of these cases is a determination of whether the interest involved constitutes property.

Traditionally, *property* has been defined as all valuable interests that can be possessed outside oneself, which have an exchangeable value or which add to an individual's wealth or estate. Since 1972 in the Supreme Court's decision in *Board of Regents v. Roth*, 408 U.S. 564, (1972), property has been defined as all interests to which an individual could be deemed "entitled." Entitlements occur only if there is some form of current interest in or current use of the property. For example, a holder of a scholarship has a property right because he is currently entitled to benefits derived from it. Once this entitlement is established, there is a property right. Due process protections are triggered only when there is an actual deprivation of the entitled rights. This "entitlement" standard does not encompass wishes that do not come true or expectations that fail to materialize; an entitlement to property must be more than an abstract need or desire for it.

The property right involved in amateur sports is the right to participate in athletic activities. The major controversy revolves around the question of whether participation is an individual protectable right or a privilege that is unprotected. This question is analyzed differently depending on whether the athletic activity is on the high school or college level. On both levels defendants have argued that participation in athletics is a privilege and therefore falls outside the parameters of the due process clause.

In the collegiate area, however, plaintiffs have been successful in claiming a property interest based on the proximity of monetary benefits currently or potentially available to the student-athlete. A property interest has been found in athletic participation because there exists a potential economic benefit to the student-athlete in the form of either a scholarship or a future professional contract. A current holder of a scholarship who would be deprived of that scholarship has a well-defined property interest based on the present economic value of the award.

A college student-athlete may also have a protectable interest in a future professional contract, as in *Behagen v. Intercollegiate Conference of Faculty Representatives*, 346 F. Supp. 602 (D. Minn. 1972) (see note 4d). Some courts, however, by looking at a statistical analysis of the percentage of people who successfully enter professional sports, have discounted a legitimate property interest in a future professional contract as being too speculative. Also, at least one court has indicated that it would find a protectable property interest only if there were a professional league in that particular sport. (See *Fluitt v. University of Nebraska*, note 1.)

In the interscholastic area, the right or privilege dichotomy is analyzed differently. A high school student-athlete with only the possibility of obtaining a scholarship generally has no present economic interest, and the possibility of obtaining a scholarship is too speculative an interest to receive protection. Similarly, a high school student-athlete is usually considered to have an entirely speculative interest in a future professional contract.

In high school cases, the right versus the privilege controversy involves the student-athlete's argument that he or she has a right to an education and that participation in interscholastic athletics is included in that right. The threshold issue is whether there is a right to an education. The Supreme Court has specifically denied a general constitutional right to education (see *San Antonio Independent School Dist. v. Rodriguez,* 411 U.S. 1 [1973]). Even though the right to an education is not grounded in federal law, a state may grant a right to an education either explicitly or implicitly by requiring school attendance. Through this measure, the state effectively gives each child within its boundaries an interest in the education provided. This interest has been held to be a type of property interest protected by the due process clause. (See *Pegram v. Nelson,* 469 F. Supp. 1134 [M.D.N.C. 1979] and *Goss v. Lopez,* 419 U.S. 565 [1974].) Whether a right is stated explicitly or implicitly, once it has been established, it cannot be limited or removed without due process protections.

After finding a right to education based on statutory attendance requirements, a determination must then be made as to whether or not that right includes participation in extracurricular activities. If the right to education means a right to the "total" educational process provided by a school, the courts may find participation in athletic competition to be a right. The right to participate would then be protected by due process considerations. Many courts, however, interpret educational rights as encompassing only classroom learning and view all other activities as unprotected privileges.

NOTES ───

1. In *Fluitt v. University of Nebraska,* 489 F. Supp. 1194 (D. Neb. 1980), a fifth-year college student-athlete requested one additional year of eligibility because an injury had terminated his freshman season but was denied. The court reasoned that the Faculty Committee was solely responsible for all determinations of hardship, a procedure that had been followed for at least twenty-five years. Any denial of due process at a first hearing was remedied at the second hearing, and thus no violation of due process occurred.

2. In the following cases the court decided that there was not a property interest in intercollegiate athletics.

    (a) In *National Collegiate Athletic Ass'n v. Gillard,* 352 So. 2d 1072 (Miss. 1977), the court ruled that a player's right to play intercollegiate football was not a property right to be protected by due process guarantees. The court ruled that the denial of a player's eligibility to compete for having accepted clothing at a discount did not infringe on the plaintiff's constitutional rights to due process.

(b) In *Karmanos v. Baker*, 816 F. 2d 258 (6th Cir. 1987), a college hockey player was declared ineligible because he played in a professional league in Canada. The court denied the due process claim brought by him and his father on the grounds that his father's "right to direct the upbringing and education [of his son] does not extend so far as to give [him] the right to direct his child to play hockey on a professional team without losing his amateur status."

(c) In *McHale v. Cornell Univ.*, 620 F. Supp. 67 (N.D.N.Y. 1985), a student-athlete transferred for "academic reasons alone" and opposed a loss of eligibility as it infringed upon his right to play football. The court found, once again, that the NCAA was not a state actor and thus there was no due process violation.

(d) In *Weiss v. Eastern College Athletic Conference*, 563 F. Supp. 192 (E.D. Pa. 1983), a student who challenged the transfer rule when it deprived him of a year of eligibility to play tennis at the University of Pennsylvania was unsuccessful in his due process claim, as the court did not find sufficient evidence of irreparable harm to grant an injunction.

3. In the following cases the court decided that there was not a property interest in interscholastic athletics.

(a) In *Stock v. Texas Catholic Interscholastic League*, 364 F. Supp. 362 (N.D. Tex. 1973), the court held that the plaintiff high school student's interest in playing interscholastic football was too insignificant to justify federal court jurisdiction. The plaintiff failed to show that he had been deprived of a right under color of state law such that jurisdiction under 42 U.S.C. section 1983 should be granted. The court held, "Nowhere in the Constitution is there any guarantee of a right to play football.... Even if the participation was thwarted under color of state law, the interest at stake was still too insignificant to justify jurisdiction."

(b) In *Robinson v. Illinois High School Ass'n*, 195 N.E. 2d 38 (Ill. App. Ct. 1963), plaintiff high school student was denied eligibility because he was over the age limit set by the defendant association. The court held that no property interest was sufficient to justify judicial intervention when the association's determination of eligibility did not show fraud, collusion, or unreasonable or arbitrary acts.

(c) In *Taylor v. Alabama High School Athletic Ass'n*, 336 F. Supp. 54 (M.D. Ala. 1972), the district court held that participation in interscholastic athletics is a privilege. The mere chance of receiving a college scholarship based on display of athletic ability at tournaments is not a protectable property right.

(d) In *Palmer by Palmer v. Merluzzi*, 868 F.2d 90 (3rd Cir. 1989), the court of appeals concluded that participation in extracurricular activities is not a fundamental right under the Constitution.

4. In the following cases the court determined that there was a property interest in interscholastic or intercollegiate athletics.

(a) In *Moran v. School District #7, Yellowstone County*, 350 F. Supp.

1180 (D. Mont. 1972), the court held that the right to attend school includes the right to participate in extracurricular activities. The court reasoned that sports are an integral part of the total educational process. This educational process is extremely important, and sport participation may not be denied when there is no reasonable basis upon which to distinguish among the various parts of the educational process.

(b) In *Gulf South Conference v. Boyd*, 369 So. 2d 553 (Ala. Sup. Ct. 1979), "the Supreme Court of Alabama held that the right to participate in college athletics is a property right of present economic value. The case was distinguished from *Scott v. Kilpatrick* [at note 3(e)] as a college athlete receives a scholarship for his efforts and a high school athlete only receives an opportunity to try for a scholarship. Thus, the college athlete may place a dollar value on his efforts, whereas the high school athlete's interest is only speculative."

(c) In *Hall v. University of Minnesota*, 530 F. Supp. 104 (D. Minn 1982), in granting an injunction for the plaintiff, the court found that a property interest existed in the plaintiff's ability to remain eligible for college basketball. The court recognized Hall's need to play college basketball his senior year and possibly to land an NBA contract. Although the court found it difficult to place a definite dollar value on the loss of eligibility, it looked to the value of a professional contract and stated that because the exceptionally talented student-athlete is led to perceive college athletic programs as farm systems for the professional ranks, Hall did deserve at least minimal due process protection.

(d) In *Behagen v. Intercollegiate Conference of Faculty Representatives*, 346 F. Supp. 602 (D. Minn. 1972), the court noted that although "big time" college athletics may not be a total part of the educational experience as athletics is in high schools, nonetheless the ability to participate is of substantial economic value to some students. Further, the court recognized that the opportunity to display one's talents may be of greater economic value than the opportunity to receive an education.

(e) In *Scott v. Kilpatrick*, 237 So. 2d 652 (Ala. Sup. Ct. 1970), the Supreme Court of Alabama held that the "speculative possibility" of receiving a college football scholarship was not a sufficient basis for finding that a student was deprived of a property right when he was declared ineligible to participate for one year.

5. In *Behagen v. Amateur Basketball Association of the United States*, 884 F. 2d 524 (10th Cir. 1989), the court of appeals ruled that the district court erred when they allowed the due process claim of the plaintiff to go to jury and be decided in favor of the plaintiff. The court of appeals ruled that the plaintiff's claim that he had been denied a "property right" by being declared ineligible to play basketball in Italy after competing in professional basketball in the United States was inadmissible because the Amateur Basketball Association was a private rather than a governmental actor and thus not subject to due process requirements.

6. For further information, see the following law review articles:

(a) Philpot and Mackall, "Judicial Review of Disputes Between Athletes and the National Collegiate Athletic Association," 24 *Stan. L. Rev.* 903 (1972).

(b) Comment, "A Student-Athlete's Interest in Eligibility: Its Context and Constitutional Dimensions," 10 *Conn. L. Rev.* 318 (1975).

(c) Martin, "Due Process and Its Future Within the NCAA," 10 *Conn. L. Rev.* 290 (1978).

(d) Keyes, "NCAA, Amateurism and Student-Athletes' Constitutional Rights," 15 *New Eng. L. Rev.* 597 (1978).

(e) Monaghan, "Of Liberty and Property," 62 *Cornell L. Rev.* 405 (1977).

(f) Carrafiello, "Jocks Are People Too," 13 *Creighton L. Rev.* 843 (1979).

(g) Verling, "High School Athletics and Due Process Notice of Eligibility Rules," 57 *Neb. L. Rev.* 877 (1978).

(h) Riegel and Hanley, "Judicial Review of NCAA Decisions: Does the College Athlete Have a Property Interest in Interscholastic Athletics?" 10 *Stetson L. Rev.* 483 (1981).

Equal Protection

Through the equal protection clause of the Fourteenth Amendment of the U.S. Constitution, student-athletes and coaches are provided with the means to challenge certain rules and regulations that are of a discriminatory nature. This source of law forbids discrimination of one form or another in various contexts and thus serves to limit the regulatory power of amateur athletic organizations controlling sports activities.

Equal protection is the constitutional method of checking on the fairness of the application of any law. This independent constitutional guarantee governs all federal, state, and local laws which classify individuals or which impact on individual rights. The equal protection guarantee is found in the Fourteenth Amendment of the U.S. Constitution. It reads: "No state shall ... deny to any person within its jurisdiction the equal protection of the laws." It is specifically applicable only to the states, but the federal government is held to similar standards under the due process clause of the Fifth Amendment. Equal protection requires that no person be singled out from similarly situated people, or have different benefits bestowed or burdens imposed, unless a constitutionally permissible reason for doing so exists.

Three standards of review are used under equal protection analysis. The highest standard of review is that of *strict scrutiny*. Application of the strict scrutiny standard by the court means that the rule challenged will be invalidated unless the defendant can demonstrate that the rule is supported by a compelling state interest. When a rule abridges a fundamental right or makes a distinction based on suspect criteria, the defendant has the burden of proof. This standard tests only whether a classification is properly drawn, not whether an individual is properly placed within that classification. This type of review is triggered by the use of either a suspect class or a fundamental interest.

The Supreme Court has found three suspect classes: alienage, race, and national origin. Any time a rule discriminates directly or indirectly on the basis of these suspect classifications, the strict scrutiny standard will be applied.

There are a number of fundamental interests, and the vast majority of these rights arise expressly from the U.S. Constitution. They include the First Amendment guarantees, such as the right to freedom of religion, speech, and press, as well as the right to assemble peaceably and to petition the government for redress of grievances. In addition to these specific rights, the Supreme Court has found three other fundamental rights: the right to travel, the right to vote, and the right to privacy (which involves decisions about marriage, abortion, and other family choices).

Some interests have been specifically found to be nonfundamental; these include subsistence and welfare payments, housing, government employment, and education. The fact that education has been deemed a nonfundamental interest is particularly important in cases involving high school or college athletic associations. This designation makes it difficult for the student-athlete plaintiff to establish athletic participation as a fundamental interest.

The second standard of review under the equal protection guarantee is that of *rational basis*. This standard requires only that the rule have some rational relationship to a legitimate organizational purpose. It is used in the absence of a classification defined as suspect or as a fundamental right. Rules reviewed under this standard are difficult for a plaintiff to challenge successfully since the defendant is generally able to present some rational relationship between the restriction and a legitimate governmental objective. The rational basis test is the most commonly applied constitutional standard.

The third standard of review or category of classes imposes an *intermediate test*, which falls between the strict scrutiny and rational basis tests. It requires that rules classifying certain groups satisfy an "important" but not necessarily a "compelling" interest. Two "quasi-suspect" classifications have been established: gender and legitimacy. Use of either gender- or legitimacy-based classifications will trigger this intermediate standard of review. To date, the difference between a "compelling" versus an "important" interest has not been made explicit and remains the subject of much examination and speculation when argued before the courts.

Equal protection does not bar states from creating classifications.

Instead, it requires that classifications not be predicated on race, alienage, or national origin. It also requires that the criteria bear a reasonable relationship to the purpose of the law. Otherwise, the distinction is automatically suspect. Once a law is suspect, it will be held valid only if a compelling interest is established and there is no less intrusive means by which the same end may be achieved. The burden of proof is on the states to establish the compelling nature of the interest. The same analysis is used when a fundamental interest is infringed upon by a state law. In summary, the theory of equal protection is used to protect individuals by ensuring that they are fairly treated in the exercise of their fundamental rights and by assuring the elimination of distinctions based on constitutionally impermissible criteria.

The equal protection guarantee relates to classes and distinctions inevitably drawn whenever a legislative body makes rules relating to specific groups. One method typically employed to challenge a rule under the equal protection clause is that which claims either under- or overinclusiveness. Under- or overinclusiveness can make a rule impermissibly discriminatory. *Overinclusiveness* means that the legislative class includes many people to whom the rule in question lacks a rational relationship. In other words, at least some of the class of affected individuals are not part of the problem addressed by the rule, and the rule as applied to these people has no relationship to its purpose. A rule's validity depends not on whether classes differ but on whether differences between the classes are pertinent to the subject with respect to which the classification is made. Whereas overinclusiveness exists when a rule creates a class more extensive than necessary to effectuate the purpose of the rule, *underinclusiveness* exists when a class does not contain all the members necessary to effectuate the rule's purpose.

It is possible for a rule to be both over- and underinclusive. For example, consider the following rule: "All transfer students from public high schools will not be eligible for interscholastic play for one year from date of entry." This rule is overinclusive with respect to public school transfers that were made for reasons unrelated to athletics. It would be underinclusive, however, if it permitted immediate eligibility for transfer students from private schools who might be transferring for solely athletic reasons.

To draw perfect classifications that are neither over- nor underinclusive is extremely difficult. In light of this, when no important constitutional rights are involved, the courts can and do uphold both over- and underinclusive categories as long as they can find a rational relationship between the rule and its purpose. For example, only when an athletic association cannot demonstrate the connection between the rule and its purpose will the court find that an equal protection violation has occurred.

Another reason why the court will uphold rules that do not make perfect classifications is to allow athletic associations to deal with problems on an individual basis. Associations or legislatures do not have to create perfect solutions prior to attacking specific problems. In many cases, the court will not decide whether the rule itself is invalid but may conclude that its application to a specific individual violates the person's constitutional rights. The court can therefore pay deference to the legislative judgment initiating the rule while upholding the rights of the individual.

Technically, there is a two-tiered system for equal protection analysis; however, the trend may be toward a sliding scale that would dissolve the absolute categories of fundamental rights and interests. The advantage of a sliding-scale approach is that it is much more flexible and would in effect create a flexible scale of rights and/or classes that would be directly compared with the governmental interest involved.

NOTES _____

1. In the following cases, violations of equal protection were found in the application of an athletic association's rules or decisions.

(a) In *Buckton v. National Collegiate Athletic Ass'n*, 366 F. Supp. 1152 (D. Mass. 1973), Canadian ice hockey players were denied eligibility because they had received funding from junior league hockey teams in Canada rather than from high schools, as is the custom in the United States. The court prohibited the NCAA from enforcing ineligibility, because the rule in effect discriminated against plaintiffs on the basis of the suspect class of national origin.

(b) In *Indiana High School v. Raike*, 329 N.E.2d 66 (Ind. Ct. App. 1975), a public high school rule which prohibited married students from participating in any extracurricular activities was held invalid, even though the court decided the right to marry was not a fundamental right. The court, in using a sliding-scale approach, held that the rule denied equal protection because there was no fair and substantial relationship between the classification (married students) and the objective sought (preventing dropouts).

(c) In *Rivas Tenorio v. Liga Atletica Interuniversitaria*, 554 F.2d 492 (1st Cir. 1977), the trial court, in dismissing the complaint which questioned the constitutionality of an athletic association's regulation banning non-Puerto Ricans from competing in intercollegiate athletics if they enrolled in member institutions after their twenty-first birthday, erred in failing to subject the regulation to strict constitutional scrutiny in view of the fact that it discriminated, on its face, against aliens. The case was reversed and sent back to the district court.

(d) In *Howard University v. National Collegiate Athletic Ass'n*, 510 F.2d 213 (D.C. Cir. 1975), the court applied strict scrutiny in striking down the NCAA's "Foreign Student Rule" because the classification was based on alienage. Even though the court accepted the purpose of the rule, it held that the rule was not closely tailored to achieve its goal, since it penalized foreign student-athletes for activities that citizens participated in without penalty.

2. In the following cases, violations of equal protection were *not* found in the application of an athletic association's rules or decisions.

(a) *Mitchell v. Louisiana High School Athletic Ass'n*, 430 F.2d 1155 (5th Cir. 1970), was a case litigated on the theory that there was discrimination against students who chose to repeat a junior high school grade for academic or personal reasons. The court held that allowing those who failed a year still to have four years of high school eligibility, while reducing eligibility to three years for those who chose to repeat a year, had a rational relationship with regard to the problem of redshirting (see Chapter 5). Therefore, it was not appropriate for the judiciary to intervene, even when the rule was unduly harsh on the individual.

(b) In *Moreland v. Western Pennsylvania Interscholastic Athletic League*, 572 F.2d 121 (3rd Cir. 1978), a high school basketball player claimed denial of equal protection when he was prohibited from competing in postseason play because he was absent from school for more than twenty days, a violation of a league rule. The court held that the rule was rationally related to the purpose of safeguarding educational values, cultivating high ideals of good sportsmanship, and promoting uniformity of standards in athletic competition.

(c) In *Graham v. NCAA*, 804 F.2d 953 (6th Cir. 1986), a football player challenged the NCAA transfer rules on an equal protection basis. The court, however, found that no state action was present and thus it was unnecessary to address claims of due process or equal protection.

(d) In *McHale v. Cornell Univ.*, 620 F. Supp. 67 (N.D.N.Y. 1985), a student who transferred for academic reasons unsuccessfully challenged the loss of athletic eligibility on equal protection grounds, because his was not the type of transfer the NCAA rules were intended to curtail.

(e) In *Spath v. NCAA*, 728 F.2d (1st Cir. 1984), a student at the University of Lowell lost a year of eligibility because he played a year of organized hockey in Canada after his twentieth birthday. His claim of a denial of equal protection for aliens failed, as the court found no discriminatory intent in the legislative history of the NCAA rule.

(f) In *Jones v. Wichita State Univ.*, 698 F.2d. 1082 (10th Cir. 1983), a student failed to meet the NCAA minimum of 2.00 grade point average for an incoming freshman, because his school did not calculate physical education grades in determining the grade point average. His equal protection claim failed because the court said it did not entail a substantial federal question.

(g) In *Weiss v. Eastern College Athletic Conference*, 563 F. Supp. 192 (E.D. Pa. 1983), a tennis player who had transferred from Arizona State to the University of Pennsylvania challenged the loss of eligibility on an equal protection basis, in that the transfer rule was overinclusive when it included student-athletes like him who were not recruited or given a scholarship by the new school. His attempt to obtain an injunction allowing him to play was denied because he did not offer sufficient evidence of potential harm.

(h) In *Giannattasio v. Stamford Youth Hockey Ass'n, Inc.*, 621 F. Supp. 825 (D.C. Conn. 1985), the parents of minors suspended from participation in a hockey program brought an action against the association and its officers and the superintendent of the city board of recreation. In granting the defendants' motion to dismiss, the court held that the conduct of the hockey association, its officers, and the superintendent did not constitute state action. The court also found that the minors did not enjoy liberty or property interests in participation in the hockey program so as to invoke due process protection. Further, the disciplinary rules of the association were rationally and logically related to a valid and legitimate interest and did not violate equal protection.

(i) In *Zuments v. Colorado High School Activities Ass'n*, 737 P.2d 1113 (Colo. Ct. App. 1987), student-athletes enrolled in various Colorado public high schools sued to enjoin the defendant from enforcing its "outside competition" rule, which prevented students from practicing with nonschool teams while participating in interscholastic athletics. The lower court granted a preliminary injunction to the students. On appeal the Court of Appeals held that the association's enforcement of the "outside competition" rule was not arbitrary, capricious, or haphazard and that it rationally furthered legitimate state purposes without violating the students' right to equal protection. Further, the "outside competition" rule did not impermissibly infringe the students' constitutional right of free association.

(j) In *Stone v. Kansas State High School Activities Ass'n*, 761 P.2d 1255 (Kan. App. 1988), the plaintiff challenged a no-make-up rule which prevented a student from making up work after the end of the semester for the purpose of regaining eligibility. The court used the rational basis test and determined that the rule had a rational basis and therefore the plaintiff's equal protection rights had not been denied.

ASSOCIATION ENFORCEMENT AUTHORITY

The authority for amateur athletic associations to regulate their membership originates from two sources. First, as corporate bodies, amateur athletic organizations must be recognized as entities by the state. Second, in order for the association to govern, the membership must have agreed to be so regulated. Most high school athletic associations and conferences do not have the resources to enforce and review compliance of rules and regulations of their organization on a first-hand basis. They rely primarily on the concept of institutional control. However, on the collegiate level, the large stakes of revenue-producing sports such as football and basketball have made it necessary to police a university's athletic program for rules violations more stringently. In this section, the legal relationships among the state government, the intercollegiate association, and the membership are examined, using the NCAA as an example.

The NCAA, as described earlier in this chapter, is a voluntary association whose members agree to honor certain conditions and obligations of membership, including the obligation to conduct their individual institutional athletic programs in a manner consistent with NCAA legislation. This legislation is enacted by a majority vote of delegates at either the annual convention, held each January, or special conventions called by the NCAA Council. The rules of the organization are published annually in the *NCAA Manual*, which is available to every member of the organization.

Member institutions agree when they join the NCAA to be policed in regard to the organization's rules by the NCAA's enforcement staff, which is given policy guidance by the NCAA's Committee on Infractions. The committee is composed of six members, one of whom serves as chair. Committee members may serve for a period not to exceed nine years. The enforcement staff conducts all NCAA investigations on the basis of allegations of infractions by a member institution. Some investigations may involve only one or two allegations, while others may include 100 or more.

The first NCAA enforcement program was enacted by the association in 1948. Called the "Sanity Code," it was designed to correct recruiting abuses. In addition, the NCAA created a Constitutional Compliance Committee, which was designed to interpret the new code and investigate violations.

The Constitutional Compliance Committee was replaced in 1951 by the Committee on Infractions. This committee was given broader investigative powers. In 1973, the NCAA membership voted to divide investigative and hearing duties so that the NCAA assumed investigation responsibilities and the Committee on Infractions handled hearings. This remains the basic structure of today's enforcement programs.

In response to increasing criticism of its enforcement procedures, the NCAA in the last few years has taken steps to improve its procedures. These steps have included expanding its staff of professional investigators (who are often former FBI agents) and interviewing highly recruited student-athletes in an attempt to uncover possible recruiting violations. Investigators attempt to develop close relationships with highly recruited "blue chip" student-athletes in hopes that they will inform them of any illegal offers they receive from recruiters.

As a result of the "integrity crisis," the NCAA called a special summer convention in 1985 (only the fifth in its history) and enacted stronger enforcement and penalty procedures for member schools that violate NCAA regulations. The so-called death penalty includes suspension of an athletic team for as long as two seasons if it is found guilty of major NCAA rule infractions twice in a five-year period (retroactive to September 1980) and sanctions against student-athletes who knowingly violate NCAA rules.

Southern Methodist University (SMU), whose football program has been on probation six times—the most of any school in the United States—became the first victim of the death penalty in 1987. Shortly after allegations of NCAA violations surfaced in November 1986, SMU's president, athletic director, and football coach all resigned.

The NCAA also instituted mandatory reporting requirements for member institutions in regard to student-athlete academic progress and independent financial audits of athletic department budgets. As Dr. John W. Ryan, president of Indiana University and past chairman of the NCAA's President's Commission, noted at the special convention that enacted the new enforcement rules, "The nation's presidents and chancellors are going to determine the direction and major policies of college athletics and . . . we are not going to condone any failure to comply with these policies."

In conjunction with the programs approved by the June 1985 NCAA special summer convention, the Executive Committee expanded the previous NCAA enforcement department and renamed it the Compliance and Enforcement Department. A compliance services staff has also been created to assist chief executive officers in compliance matters such as (1) questions and problems encountered in completing the self-study, financial audit, and academic-reporting requirements; (2) provision of compliance models in such key areas as financial aid, eligibility, and recruiting to assist member institutions in confronting problems that may arise; (3) organization of campus visits to aid in analyzing the structure and administration of the athletics program; (4) assistance to member institutions that have been penalized under the association's enforcement procedures in correcting the problems that resulted in rules violations; and (5) cooperation with member conferences with full-time administrators in the development of conference compliance programs.

The new NCAA legislation also calls for an "institutional self-study to enhance integrity in intercollegiate athletics." Each member institution is required to undertake the self-study at least once every five years. By means of the candid self-examination, the chief executive officer and athletic administrators will be alerted to a broad spectrum of measurable indicators designed to minimize and perhaps eliminate the potential for rules violations.

The constitution also requires an annual independent financial audit to provide detailed information concerning revenues and expenditures for or on behalf of an intercollegiate athletic program, including funds received and expended by outside organizations in support of intercollegiate athletics. This requirement is designed to assist chief executive officers in determining the extent to which their athletic programs rely on outside financial support and in assuring that such support does not compromise the premise or the fact of institutional control.

An NCAA bylaw also requires Division I members to compile and report data concerning admissions standards, the academic qualifications of entering recruited student-athletes, academic progress, and the graduation rate of student-athletes. All data are compiled across member institutions and then distributed to all Division I members to permit comparisons with similar institutions.

The key to the NCAA investigative process is the cooperative principle, whereby the accused member institution and the NCAA's enforcement staff work together to ascertain the truth of alleged infractions. An NCAA enforcement program consists of the following six steps:

1. *A preliminary inquiry.* A preliminary inquiry is initiated by the NCAA enforcement staff if alleged violations seem serious and plausible. A preliminary inquiry letter notifies the school that enforcement staff members will be on campus in the near future investigating alleged infractions of the NCAA's rules. This preliminary inquiry letter does not specify the nature of the allegations. In response to a school's request for further information, allegations will be made specific as to time, place, and personnel; however, at no time will the source of these allegations be revealed. In some cases the source becomes obvious and may involve one of the school's own student-athletes. Additional sources of information are other institutions and coaches.

If the preliminary inquiry indicates that allegations of wrongdoing may be valid, the enforcement staff will elect either to deal with the issue using a summary procedure before the committee on Infractions or undertake an official inquiry.

2. *Official inquiry (OI).* An official inquiry is authorized by the NCAA's Committee on Infractions on the basis of the results of the enforcement staff's preliminary inquiry. The OI is primarily a second letter to the institution listing specific allegations of infractions and directing the school, under obligation of NCAA membership, to conduct its own investigation immediately. Initially, the school has sixty days to respond, although extensions are frequently granted.

The OI breaks down into three parts: the overture, the allegations, and the coda. The *overture* consists of four questions requesting information about how the athletic programs are organized and administered at the accused institution. The *allegations*, the heart of the OI, list the specific charges. They also cite the rules that have been violated and identify those believed to be involved. An allegation might take the following form:

> It is alleged that in January 1979, through the arrangements of head football coach Neils Thompson, student-athlete Charles Wright received the benefit of one-way commercial airline transportation at no cost to him between Ardmore, Pennsylvania, and Austin, Texas, in order to travel to the University following a visit to his home. Please indicate whether this information is substantially correct and submit evidence to support your response.
>
> Also provide the following:
> a. The actual date of this transportation.
> b. The reasons Wright was provided commercial airline transportation at no personal expense to him on this occasion.
> c. A statement indicating the actual cost of this transportation and the source of funds utilized to pay the resultant cost.
> d. The identity of all athletic department staff members involved in or knowledgeable of these arrangements for Wright, and a description of such involvement or knowledge prior to, at the time of, and subsequent to this trip.

There may be one or many of these allegations. They can name student-athletes, potential recruits, coaches, alumni, and boosters.

The *coda*, the third part of an OI, is directed at the president of the institution. Since 1974, the NCAA has required the chief executive officer of each member institution to certify through a signed statement that the institution is complying with NCAA rules. In addition, since 1975, all members of an institution's athletic department staff have been required to sign a statement that they have reported their knowledge of and involvement in any violation of NCAA legislation. The coda comprises both of these statements—the institutional and the athletic department certifications of compliance.

The NCAA has a gag rule in effect on its involvement in an investigation. It remains in effect throughout the entire procedure (see *1993–94 NCAA Manual*, Bylaw 32.1.1). The NCAA will not even comment on the existence of an investigation unless it is in response to information released by the institution (see *1993–94 NCAA Manual*, Bylaw 32.1.2).

The enforcement procedures also provide that the NCAA's primary investigator will be available to meet with the institution to discuss the development of its response and to assist in the case (see *1993–94 NCAA Manual*, Bylaw 32.5.3). The two parties attempt to reach agreement on certain facts of the case in order to streamline the hearing process. Statements of persons interviewed on behalf of the institution by the NCAA investigator will be presented as part of the institution's response to the OI.

The institution must then carry out its own investigation and draft its response to the NCAA allegations. This response, which may be hundreds of pages long, is sent to the NCAA and to the members of the Committee on Infractions.

3. *Committee on Infractions hearings.* Committee on Infractions hearings are usually held at the NCAA offices in Overland Park, Kansas. These meetings are closed and confidential. Present at the hearings are members of the Committee on Infractions, the delegation from the institution, and the NCAA enforcement staff members. The procedure begins with opening statements by a spokesperson from the institution, often an attorney, who is then followed by a spokesperson for the enforcement staff. These opening statements express the overall position of the university and of the enforcement staff. The heart of the official inquiry is a detailed review of the allegations, which includes determining which allegations are and are not in dispute. The enforcement staff presents all evidence it has, regardless of whether it supports or refutes the allegations. The institution's spokesperson then responds and may wish to refer to or add to the school's written response. This is an informal procedure, with frequent verbal exchanges between committee members and the university. Rigid rules of evidence are not enforced at these hearings, which may proceed for several days until all allegations have been covered. After the closing statements, the chairman of the committee advises the university of the next steps in the case, including the university's opportunity to appeal to the NCAA Council if it is dissatisfied with the committee's findings, its penalty, or both. After this, the hearing is adjourned.

4. *Findings.* Findings are made after the members of the Committee on Infractions have deliberated over the case on an individual basis, reviewing each allegation. Sometimes additional information is needed, often from previous cases. The NCAA has charged the committee to base its findings on information it determines to be "credible, persuasive and of a kind on which reasonably prudent persons rely in the conduct of serious affairs" (*1993–94 NCAA Manual,* Bylaw 32.76.2). Once the members of the committee reach a consensus, all findings are compiled into a confidential report. The report is then sent to the institution's president.

5. *Penalties.* If warranted, penalties are included in the Committee on Infraction's final report. These may include prohibiting an institution's team or teams from television appearances, taking away athletic scholarships, and barring teams from postseason play. Such

actions are often referred to as being put on probation. There is a trend toward making individual coaches accountable when rule violations are discovered. Possible penalties may include freezing salary levels, limiting expense accounts, and restricting recruitment travel. At its 1983 convention, the NCAA passed a requirement that all coaches' contracts include a stipulation that the coach can be suspended without pay or fired if he or she is involved in "deliberate and serious violations of NCAA regulations." The proposal was submitted by the College Football Association and was sponsored by Georgia, Nebraska, North Carolina, Penn State, Rutgers, and Tulane.

In some cases when violations are deemed to be less severe, the penalty imposed by the NCAA may take the form of a private reproach.

6. *Appeal (optional).* An institution has an automatic right of appeal to the NCAA Council. It is heard "de novo"—that is, the matter is heard as if for the first time. The Council can reverse, expand, contract, or completely change the finding of the Infractions Committee. The option of appealing to the courts also remains.

After the appeals process has been exhausted, the NCAA will issue an expanded infractions report, with names of individuals deleted, announcing any allegations found to be true and that penalties that have been imposed (see *1993–94 NCAA Manual*, Bylaw 32.9.6).

NOTES _____

1. For a case that examines the NCAA enforcement procedures, see *Trustees of the State Colleges and Universities v. National Collegiate Athletic Ass'n*, 147 Cal. Rptr. 187 (Cal. Ct. App. 1978). Although a university's NCAA appeal involved only the penalty imposed and not the findings for an alleged failure to comply with a decision regarding the eligibility of two student-athletes, this did not bar relief on the grounds of failure to exhaust administrative remedies. The court's reasoning was that the internal appeal presented all circumstances of the university's reliance on a letter of the executive director of the NCAA and afforded the NCAA full opportunity to review the merits of its proposed disciplinary action in light thereof.

2. For further information of association enforcement authority, see the following law review articles.

(a) Wright, "Responding to an NCAA Investigation, or What to Do When an Official Inquiry Comes," 1 *Enter. & Sports L. J.* (1984).

(b) Gaona, "The NCAA: Fundamental Fairness and the Enforcement Program," 23 *Ariz. L. Rev.* 1065 (1981).

(c) Miller, "The Enforcement Procedures of the NCAA: An Abuse of the Student-Athlete's Right to Reasonable Discovery," *Ariz. L. Rev.* 133 (1982).

(d) Remington, "NCAA Enforcement Procedures Including the Role of the Committee on Infractions," 10 *J. C. & U. L.* 8 (1983–84).

3. In the National Association of Intercollegiate Athletics (NAIA), procedures for rules infractions are much simpler than in the NCAA. Each of the

NAIA's thirty-two districts has an eligibility committee, usually composed of faculty members of member association schools. Most infractions involve satisfaction of academic requirements or improper institution eligibility certificates. District officials settle most cases on that level, usually by asking for an explanation from the student-athlete or athletic director from the involved college. The district eligibility committee (three members) then makes a recommendation to a national panel, which makes its decision to the NAIA's executive committee. Standard penalties include forfeiture of games, loss of student-athletes eligibility, and probation and suspension of athletic programs from participation in NAIA competition.

The NCAA, Conferences, and Member Institutions

Occasionally, the NCAA will become involved in litigation with one of its member institutions over the imposition of sanctions against the member institution, one of the member institution's athletes, or personnel of the member institution. Often this litigation will center around a challenge to sanctions or penalties imposed by the NCAA. In *California State University, Hayward v. National Collegiate Athletic Ass'n*, 121 Cal. Rptr. 85 (Cal. Ct. App. 1975), the court of appeals upheld a superior court ruling which granted an injunction against the NCAA preventing the NCAA from imposing any penalties against the institution. The NCAA wanted the institution to declare two student-athletes ineligible under an NCAA academic rule, but the court stated that the NCAA rule did not have a retroactive effect and thus the student-athletes, who were eligible under NCAA rules at the time they competed, could not after the fact be declared ineligible.

In addition to the individual member institutions and the institution's student-athletes, the NCAA regulates the activity of an institution's coaching personnel. In these cases, the NCAA holds an institution responsible for the enforcement of NCAA regulations against the institution's coaching personnel. In *Tarkanian v. National Collegiate Athletic Ass'n*, 741 P.2d 1345 (Nev. Sup. Ct.), Jerry Tarkanian, the men's basketball coach at the University of Nevada-Las Vegas (UNLV), argued that he was being deprived of a protected property interest without due process of the law by being suspended by UNLV in response to an NCAA ruling regarding rule violations by Tarkanian. Tarkanian was promised tenure when he arrived to coach and teach at UNLV. The Nevada Supreme Court ruled that, if suspended, Tarkanian would have been deprived of a property right and thus the NCAA could not suspend Tarkanian.

The NCAA, however, appealed this decision to the U.S. Supreme Court and found a more favorable outcome. In *National Collegiate Athletic Ass'n v. Tarkanian*, 488 U.S. 179 (1988), the Supreme Court held that the NCAA's participation in UNLV's suspension of Jerry

Tarkanian did not constitute state action and thus the coach was not deprived of his constitutional rights. (See note 5.)

NOTES _____

1. The following excerpt, from the *1990–91 NCAA Manual,* Bylaw 19.4.2.1, concerns NCAA penalties for major violations:

Among the disciplinary measures, singly or in combination, that may be adopted by the committee (or the Infractions Appeals Committee) and imposed against an institution for major violations are:

(a) Reprimand and censure.

(b) Probation for one year.

(c) Probation for more than one year.

(d) Ineligibility for one or more NCAA championship events.

(e) Ineligibility for invitational and postseason meets and tournaments.

(f) Ineligibility for any television programs involving coverage of the institution's intercollegiate athletics team or teams in the sport or sports in which the violations occurred.

(g) Ineligibility of the member to vote or its personnel to serve on committees of the Association, or both.

(h) Prohibition against an intercollegiate sports team or teams participating against outside competition for a specified period.

(i) Prohibition against the recruitment of prospective student-athletes for a sport or sports for a specified period.

(j) A reduction in the number of financial aid awards (as defined in 15.02.3.1) that may be awarded during a specified period.

(k) Forfeiture of all or a portion of the institution's share of the broad-based revenue distribution monies for a specified period.

(l) All or any combination of the following penalties:

(1) requirement that an institution that has been represented in an NCAA championship by a student-athlete who was recruited or who received improper benefits (which would not necessarily render the student-athlete ineligible) in violation of NCAA legislation shall return 90 percent of its share of net receipts from such competition in excess of the regular expense reimbursement. If such funds have not been distributed, they shall be withheld by the NCAA executive director; or

(2) individual or team records and performances shall be vacated or stricken; or

(3) individual or team awards shall be returned to the Association.

(m) Requirement that a member institution that has been found in violation, or that has an athletics department staff member who has been found in violation of the provisions of NCAA legislation while representing another institution, show cause why:

(1) a penalty or an additional penalty should not be imposed if, in the opinion of the committee (or Infractions Appeals Committee), it does not take appropriate disciplinary or corrective action against athletics department personnel involved in the infractions case, any other institutional employee if the circumstances warrant or representatives of the institution's athletics interests; or

(2) a recommendation should not be made to the membership that the institution's membership in the Association be suspended or terminated if, in the opinion of the committee (or Infractions Appeals Committee), it does not take appropriate disciplinary or corrective action against the head

coach of the sport involved, any other institutional employee if the circumstances warrant, or representatives of the institution's athletics interests;

(3) "Appropriate disciplinary or corrective action" as specified in subparagraphs (1) and (2) above may include, for example, termination of the coaching contract of the head coach and any assistants involved; suspension or termination of the employment status of any other institutional employee who may be involved; severance of relations with any representative of the institution's athletics interests who may be involved; the debarment of the head or assistant coach from any coaching, recruiting, or speaking engagements for a specified period, and the prohibition of all recruiting in a specified sport for a specified period;

(4) The nature and extent of such action shall be the determination of the institution after due notice and hearing to the individuals concerned, but the determination of whether or not the action is appropriate in the fulfillment of NCAA policies and principles, and its resulting effect on any institutional penalty, shall be solely that of the committee (or Infractions Appeals Committee);

(5) Where this requirement is made, the institution shall show cause or, in the alternative, shall show the appropriate disciplinary or corrective action taken, in writing, to the committee (or Infractions Appeals Committee) within 15 days thereafter. The committee (or Infractions Appeals Committee) may, without further hearing, determine on the basis of such writing whether or not in its opinion appropriate disciplinary or corrective action has been taken and may impose a penalty or additional penalty; take no further action; or, by notice to the institution, conduct a further hearing at a later date before making a final determination.

2. In *Board of Regents, University of Oklahoma v. National Collegiate Athletic Ass'n*, 561 P.2d 499 (Okla. Sup. Ct. 1977), the Oklahoma Supreme Court overruled the trial court's granting of a temporary injunction against the NCAA regarding an NCAA bylaw which limited the number of football coaches a Division I member school could employ. The Supreme Court concluded that the NCAA's rule appeared to be a reasonable one and did not prevent coaches from exercising their lawful profession.

3. In *Hennessey v. National Collegiate Athletic Ass'n*, 564 F.2d 1136 (5th Cir. 1977), a limitation on the size of a school's coaching staff was upheld as an "economy measure" designed to maintain athletic balance and preserve amateurism.

4. In *Stanley v. Big Eight Conference*, 463 F. Supp. 920 (W.D. Mo. 1978), a former Oklahoma State University football coach was granted an injunction which prevented the conference and the NCAA from conducting an infractions hearing because the procedure violated his due process rights.

5. In *National Collegiate Athletic Ass'n v. Tarkanian*, 488 U.S. 179 (1988), the Supreme Court held that the NCAA's participation in UNLV's suspension of Jerry Tarkanian did not constitute state action prohibited by the Fourteenth Amendment and was not performed "under color of" state law within the meaning of 42 U.S.C. sec. 1983. The NCAA could not be deemed a state actor solely because UNLV's decision to suspend Tarkanian was made in compliance with NCAA rules and recommendations. In addition, UNLV's decision to adopt the NCAA's rules and recommendations does not make them action-

able under color of Nevada law, as UNLV retained plenary power to withdraw from the NCAA and establish its own standards. Finally, the Supreme Court noted that the NCAA did not and could not discipline Tarkanian directly, but could only threaten further sanctions against UNLV if it chose not to suspend their coach. The suspension of Tarkanian then was an action taken by UNLV and not the NCAA.

Chapter 5

THE AMATEUR ATHLETE

INTRODUCTION

The athletic associations define "amateur athlete" and then interpret and enforce the definitions (see Chapter 4), but the rules and regulations are what most directly impact the student-athlete and are the subject of this chapter. Chapter 5 first discusses individual eligibility requirements for the student-athlete. Many of the requirements, such as academic progress, redshirting, and pay, are problems and thus the NCAA is often used as an example. However, other eligibility requirements—grade point average, transfer rules, scholarship and financial aid, and professional contracts—concern college, high school, and other amateur athletes.

Although this chapter primarily examines individual eligibility requirements for participation at the high school and college level, a brief section is devoted to the eligibility requirements for Olympic competition. The significance of this topic is not confined to the Olympic arena, because participation in Olympic competition may affect a student-athlete's participation in interscholastic or intercollegiate competition.

The next major section of Chapter 5 covers freedom of expression, hair length, rules relating to high school marriages, and alcohol and drug rules. It focuses on the coach-athlete relationship in high schools and colleges. The courts have attempted to balance the rights of the individual student-athlete with the right of the coach to instruct and supervise the student-athlete.

In some cases, student-athletes do not always meet the individual eligibility requirements that are established for them by high school and college amateur athletic conferences and associations. Student-athletes may knowingly or unknowingly violate eligibility rules and regulations, and it is the responsibility of the institution and/or governing athletic association to take appropriate disciplinary action. The next section of Chapter 5 examines the penalties or sanctions levied against the student-athlete, and in some cases the institution. These penalties and sanctions may be reviewed by the courts if the student-athlete challenges the decision.

Of course, before a student-athlete can be disciplined, a violation must be found. At the collegiate level, the NCAA has established an enforcement program designed to produce compliance with its complex set of rules and regulations—the next topic of Chapter 5. The chapter then discusses the Buckley Amendment. Athletic administrators should be aware of the Buckley Amendment and its restrictions because the investigation of alleged violations may require review of student-athletes' records.

The final sections of this chapter involve two areas in which student-athletes have brought lawsuits against their high schools and colleges. Both of these areas—failure to provide an education and participation in summer camps and on independent teams—portray activities that exist on the perimeter of the amateur athletic sphere but remain within the realm of high school and college athletic governance.

INDIVIDUAL ELIGIBILITY REQUIREMENTS: COLLEGE AND HIGH SCHOOL

For athletic administrators individual eligibility requirements are a major area of concern because they impact both the student-athlete and the institution. For instance, intercollegiate athletics, primarily football and basketball, may be financially lucrative and lead to career advancement for the individual. The monetary rewards to the institution are also great for the successful programs. To capture these financial benefits, there are several different ways an athletic department can be set up. Some departments operate under the university budget, with revenues going directly to the general fund and expenses covered as line items; others are operated like businesses; still others are separately incorporated and are responsible for covering the expenses of the department solely with revenues taken in by the department. As football and basketball have become more lucrative, the stakes in intercollegiate athletics have become higher, and the pressure to be successful and to attract the top-notch student-athlete has increased. Consequently, athletic excellence has been pursued in several instances at the expense of academic performance. College and high school athletic associations have tried to address this problem by establishing academic eligibility requirements.

Many standards must be maintained by individual student-athletes in order for them to be eligible for intercollegiate and interscholastic practice and/or competition. Each school, conference, or association such as the NCAA has rules and regulations that extend its authority to various areas surrounding sports activities. For collegiate and high school student-athletes there are usually academic standards, rules governing personal conduct, and rules for each individual sport. Individual institutions on the collegiate and scholastic level may also establish eligibility requirements that are stricter than the minimum standards imposed by that institution's conference or association. In addition, a conference may impose a stricter rule than its association.

Under the principle of *institutional control,* it is the institution's responsibility to determine which of its student-athletes meet, and do not meet, the eligibility standards. The process of determining eligibility for each student-athlete may be very time-consuming for an institution's athletic department, depending on the number of student-athletes participating, the number of sports offered by the institution, and the complexity of institutional, conference, and association rules, regulations, and interpretations.

In some cases, an institution's conference may assist member institutions in keeping track of the eligibility status of every student-athlete. The most a conference might do in this area is to recheck, confirm, and correct, when necessary, all institutional information. Conferences may aid in the complex process of eligibility determination because correct eligibility status may be the best, if not the first, preventative to rules violations.

An institution's athletic association is usually the primary governing body, and it is responsible for enforcing the rules and regulations relative to the eligibility of student-athletes. Penalties or sanctions may be levied against a student-athlete and the team and/or institution for knowingly or unknowingly competing despite the student-athlete's ineligible status. In addition to enforcement, college and high school athletic associations recommend changes in rules, make policy decisions, and render interpretations of the eligibility rules and regulations.

Eligibility rules that are enacted by a college or high school athletic association are instituted to protect student-athletes and institutions and to promote amateur athletics. Consistent with these objectives, individual eligibility requirements are established with regard to grade point average, academic progress, transferring, age restrictions, years of athletic participation, professional pay, drug use, and full-time student status among others.

The grade point average requirement is one method used by the NCAA to ensure that entering student-athletes are academically qualified to participate. The grade point average is also used by some conferences to determine a student-athlete's eligibility to participate while enrolled at the university or the high school. Rules regarding grade point average requirements have been subject to judicial review. One issue before the courts is which types of courses should be included in the computation of the grade point average. For example, should physical education courses involving athletic skills be included? Another issue is whether each university or high school should be allowed to compute grade point averages according to its own guidelines or whether the computation should be standardized according to rules promulgated by athletic associations.

In 1983, the NCAA passed Proposition 48, which requires that an incoming freshman student-athlete achieve both a certain grade point average, 2.0 in a core curriculum of at least eleven academic courses, and a certain score on standardized examinations, at least 700 on the SAT test or an 18 composite score on the ACT. Proponents of Prop

48 saw the core curriculum requirement as providing an athlete exposure to a solid base of academic work. The test score requirement would also provide some uniformity in standards among institutions. Prop 48 was a signal to high school athletes that they needed to pay close attention to their academic preparation if they planned to participate in college athletics. It was designed to give them a better chance of obtaining a college degree and to end the exploitation of talented athletes that had been commonplace at many Division I institutions.

Prop 48 went into effect in August 1986, but not without severe dissent from several universities whose enrollments have historically been composed of black students. Prop 48's test score standard was criticized as being discriminatory against certain minority groups, because standardized tests have been accused of being culturally biased toward white, middle-class American males. Criticism was also aimed at the use of specific standards or cut-off points for eligibility and the failure of Prop 48 to take into account the vast differences among colleges and universities across the nation.

In an attempt to ease the criticism of Prop 48, the concept of the "partial qualifier" was introduced (see Chapter 3). A *partial qualifier* was a student-athlete who met some, but not all of the requirements for first-year eligibility under Prop 48. A partial qualifier could still receive institutional financial aid, including an athletic scholarship, but could not play or practice with the team as a freshman. The student-athlete would then only have three years of eligibility remaining.

On January 11, 1989, the NCAA passed Proposition 42, an amendment to Proposition 48. The main emphasis of Proposition 42 was on the elimination of the partial qualifier under Prop 48. In other words, schools would be allowed to grant athletic scholarships only to incoming freshmen who met all of the requirements of Prop 48. This meant that nonqualifiers would have to pay their own way as freshmen, or go to a junior college, which would leave them with as few as two years of eligibility at a four-year school. A nonqualifier could still receive nonathletic financial aid but would be entitled to only three seasons of eligibility.

Not surprisingly, the passage of Prop 42 caused immediate public debate. Proponents of the rule argued that eliminating the partial qualifier would send a strong message to high school students and teachers that emphasis must be placed on academic achievement as a prerequisite to athletic participation at NCAA schools. Many opponents of the rule, however, criticized the elimination of the partial qualifier. Opponents argued that by denying the athletes financial aid, the rule was especially detrimental to blacks and those from disadvantaged backgrounds, since it relied too heavily on the results of standardized tests and cut off the financial aid that many needed to attend college. John Thompson, the men's basketball coach at George-town University, focused public interest on the issue three days after the January 1989 convention vote, when he protested the rule by walking off the basketball court before a game against Boston College, vowing not to return until he was satisfied that something would be done to provide disadvantaged student-athletes with appropriate op-portunity and hope for access to a college education. Thompson, who criticized Prop 42 as being biased against minority students, returned to courtside after a two-game boycott, having received assurances from the NCAA and the organization's President's Commission that they would at least recommend postponing enactment of the new rule.

Soon after the 1989 convention, it became clear that public opinion was shifting regarding the merits of Proposal 42. In February 1989, the *New York Times* reported that less than 40 percent of NCAA delegates sup-ported the rule. As public opinion shifted, the NCAA reacted. At the 1990 convention, the NCAA adopted Proposal 26, which gave new life to the partial qualifier. Under this new proposal, freshman student-athletes who failed to meet minimum academic standards would be permitted to receive institutional, non-sports financial aid based on their family in-come. The athletes would remain ineligible for an athletic scholarship during their first year of college. Further, as with previous rules, the ath-letes who failed to meet both the grade point average and test score min-imums would be banned from practicing or competing as freshmen.

In August 1994, the NCAA's Initial Eligibility Clearinghouse be-came effective. This central clearinghouse determines the initial el-igibility of all incoming freshman student-athletes.

A second individual eligibility requirement used by the NCAA is the rule requiring sufficient academic progress by the student-athlete. The rule was promulgated when it was discovered that a number of student-athletes maintained their eligibility with respect to grade point average by taking introductory level courses in a number of areas in the university. While this strategy enabled the student-athletes to maintain academic eligibility in accordance with grade point average requirements, it often left the student three or four semesters short of graduation after the individual's playing eligibility expired, because many upper-level course requirements in the student-athlete's major had not been fulfilled before athletic eligibility and scholarship funds ceased. Interestingly, the NCAA is not the only organization to have promulgated academic progress rules; many individual intercollegiate and interscholastic conferences have also instituted such rules—sev-eral of them more rigorous than the NCAA rules.

The third eligibility requirement deals with transfer rules that place restrictions on certain student-athletes who transfer from one school to another. The reasons behind the transfer rules are twofold: first, to discourage coaches from recruiting student-athletes who are enrolled in another school; and second, to prevent student-athletes from jumping from school to school primarily for athletic reasons. Many transfer student-athletes have sued their high school or college athletic associations in an attempt to obtain immediate playing eligibility at their new school. The result of such litigation is that many amateur athletic associations have redefined transfer rules more narrowly. While the revised rules may still be overinclusive in that the rule makes ineligible certain student-athletes who were not recruited and who did not transfer for athletic reasons, they usually allow immediate athletic eligibility for student-athletes who meet certain objective criteria.

The fourth individual eligibility requirement is the practice of redshirting. "Redshirting" is a term used to describe the practice of extending the playing career of a student-athlete by postponing or passing over a year of interscholastic or intercollegiate competition, and thus not affecting the student-athlete's maximum number of eligible seasons in high school or college athletics. The reasons for redshirting are varied and include medical, academic, and coaching factors. Many of the legal challenges on the intercollegiate level deal with situations in which the student-athlete is requesting an additional year of competition (hardship year) for a season in which he or she has already participated to some degree (less than 20 percent of the season).

The fifth area of individual eligibility requirements concerns financial considerations for the NCAA student-athlete. The NCAA has promulgated guidelines concerning scholarships and financial aid and pay. If the university is found to be in violation of any of these rules, it may forfeit games and/or face NCAA sanctions and penalties. On the other hand, if the student-athlete has violated the rules, he or she may be ruled ineligible for NCAA competition by the university or the NCAA. Furthermore, violations of certain NCAA rules while the student-athlete was in high school can make the student-athlete ineligible when he or she is in college. For example, an individual who is deemed to have received pay from a professional team is considered a professional and is not eligible for intercollegiate athletics in that particular sport. If a student-athlete participates in NCAA games after receipt of money from a professional team, the NCAA may ask the university to forfeit those games. Thus, it is very important for the athletic administrator to police the program in order to escape potential association sanctions and to maintain the eligibility of the student-athlete.

A key legal issue with respect to athletic scholarships is whether they are to be construed as employment contracts. The ramifications of such a determination are potentially great: the value of the scholarship becomes taxable income for the student-athlete, and as a result of receiving income, the student-athlete may no longer be deemed an amateur athlete in accordance with NCAA regulations. In addition, the student-athlete may be eligible for workers' compensation benefits, and the university athletic departments may be responsible for obtaining workers' compensation insurance.

The sixth individual eligibility requirement deals with student-athletes who have signed professional contracts. In addition to the aforementioned increased stake in a successful intercollegiate athletic program, there has been a concomitant rise in professional sports salaries. Larger television contracts, cable television, increased attendance, increased ticket prices, and competing leagues have all contributed to the pressure of placing a successful professional team on the field while leading to increased salaries. Therefore, the teams, leagues, and player agents who compete for these athletes may sign student-athletes before their college eligibility has expired. This practice is in violation of the NCAA rules governing amateurism, since the student-athlete, at the time of commitment, in effect becomes a paid professional. (See Chapter 11 for a discussion of professional careers, drafts, contracts, and player representatives.)

The seventh individual eligibility requirement deals with a student-athlete's contact with player agents (see Chapter 11). The representation of athletes has become a very lucrative area and the competition among player agents for student-athletes has become extremely intense. As a result, some player agents are signing student-athletes before their intercollegiate eligibility has expired, thus rendering them ineligible for future NCAA competition and possibly causing forfeiture of past school victories and/or loss of financial receipts from NCAA-sponsored championships.

NOTES ———————————————————————————————————

1. For further information, see the following law review articles:

   (a) Solar, "Collegiate Athletic Participation: A Property or Liberty Interest?" 15 *Pac. L. J.* 1203 (July 1984).

   (b) Waicukauski, "The Regulation of Academic Standards in Intercollegiate Athletics," 1982 *Ariz. St. L. J.* 79 (1982).

   (c) Riegel and Hanley, "Judicial Review of NCAA Decisions: Does the College Athlete Have a Property Interest in Interscholastic Athletics?" 10 *Stetson L. Rev.* 483 (1981).

   (d) Springer, "A Student-Athlete's Interest in Eligibility: Its Context and Constitutional Dimensions," 10 *Conn. L. Rev.* 318 (1977).

   (e) Philpot and Mackall, "Judicial Review of Disputes Between Athletes and the National Collegiate Athletic Association," 24 *Stanford L. Rev.* 903 (1972).

2. See Exhibit 5–1 for the NCAA form for the student-athlete statement of eligibility.

Exhibit 5–1
NCAA Student-Athlete Eligibility Form

	Form 93-3a	**Academic Year 1993-94**
	Student-Athlete Statement—Division I	

	For:	All student-athletes
	Action:	Sign and return to your director of athletics
	Due date:	Before you first compete each year
	Required by:	NCAA Constitution 3.2.4.5 and Bylaws 14.01.3, 14.1.3.1 and 30.11
To Student-Athlete	Purpose:	To assist in certifying eligibility

Name of your institution: _____

This form has two parts: a statement concerning eligibility and a Buckley Amendment consent. You must sign both parts to participate in intercollegiate competition.

Before you sign this form, you should read the Summary of NCAA Regulations provided by your director of athletics or read the bylaws of the NCAA Manual that deal with your eligibility. If you have any questions, you should discuss them with your director of athletics.

The conditions that you must meet to be eligible and the requirement that you sign this form are spelled out in the following articles and bylaws of the NCAA Manual:

- Articles 10, 12, 13, 14, 15 and 16 • Bylaws 14.01.3, 14.1.3.1, 18.4 and 31.2.3

Part I: Statement Concerning Eligibility

By signing this part of the form, you affirm that, to the best of your knowledge, you are eligible to compete in intercollegiate competition.

You affirm that you have read the Summary of NCAA Regulations or the relevant sections of the NCAA Manual, and that your director of athletics (or his or her designee) gave you the opportunity to ask questions about them.

You affirm that you meet the NCAA regulations for student-athletes regarding eligibility, recruitment, financial aid, amateur status and involvement in organized gambling.

You affirm that you are aware of the NCAA drug-testing program and that you have signed the 1993-94 Drug-Testing Consent (Form 93-3d).

You affirm that you have reported to the director of athletics of your institution any violations of NCAA regulations involving you and your institution.

You affirm that you understand that if you sign this statement falsely or erroneously, you violate NCAA legislation on ethical conduct and you will further jeopardize your eligibility.

_____   _____
Name (please print)   Date of Birth

_____   _____
Signature of Student-Athlete   Home Address

_____
Date

_____
Sport(s)

Part II: Buckley Amendment Consent

By signing this part of the form, you certify that you agree to disclose your education records.

You understand that this entire form and the results of any NCAA drug test you may take are part of your education records. These records are protected by the Family Educational Rights and Privacy Act of 1974, and they may not be disclosed without your consent.

See other side

Exhibit 5–1 continued

Student-Athlete Statement—Division I
Page 2

You give your consent to disclose only to authorized representatives of this institution, its athletics conference (if any) and the NCAA, the following documents:

- This form;

- Results of NCAA drug tests;

- Any transcript from your high school, this institution, or any junior college or any other four-year institutions you have attended;

- Precollege test scores and appropriately related information and correspondence (e.g., testing sites and dates, and letters of test-score certification or appeal);

- Records concerning your financial aid, and

- Any other papers or information obtained by this institution pertaining to your NCAA eligibility.

You agree to disclose these records only to determine your eligibility for intercollegiate athletics, your eligibility for athletically related financial aid, for purposes of inclusion in summary institutional information reported to the NCAA (and which may be publicly released by it), for NCAA longitudinal research studies and for activities related to the NCAA's institutional athletics certification program and NCAA compliance reviews.

_____   _____
Date   Signature of Student-Athlete

What to do with this form: Sign and return it to your director of athletics before you first compete. This form is to be kept in the director of athletics' office for six years.

Exhibit 5–1 continued

Academic Year 1993-94

Summary of NCAA Regulations—Division I

For:	All student-athletes
Action:	Read and then sign Form 93-3a
Purpose:	To summarize NCAA regulations regarding eligibility of student-athletes to compete

To Student-Athlete

This summary of NCAA regulations contains information about your eligibility to compete in intercollegiate athletics. Scan the headings and read carefully the sections that apply to you, then sign the Student-Athlete Statement (Form 93-3a).

This summary has two parts:

- Part I is for **all** student-athletes.

- Part II is for **new** student-athletes only (those who are signing the Student-Athlete Statement for the first time).

If you have questions, ask your director of athletics (or his or her official designee) or look at the 1993-94 NCAA Manual. The references in brackets after each summarized regulation show you where to find the regulation in the NCAA Manual.

Part I: For All Student-Athletes

This part of the summary discusses ethical conduct, amateurism, financial aid, academic standards and other regulations concerning your eligibility for intercollegiate competition.

Ethical conduct

All sports:

You must compete with honesty and sportsmanship at all times so that you represent the honor and dignity of fair play. [Bylaw 10.01.1]

You are **not eligible** to compete if you knowingly: provide information to individuals involved in organized gambling activities concerning intercollegiate athletics competition; solicit a bet on any intercollegiate team; accept a bet on any team representing the institution or participate in any gambling activity that involves intercollegiate athletics through a bookmaker, a parlay card or any other method employed by organized gambling. [Bylaw 10.3]

You are **not eligible** to compete if you have shown dishonesty in evading or violating NCAA regulations. [Bylaw 14.01.5.3]

Amateurism

All sports:

You are **not eligible** for participation in a sport if you have ever

- Taken pay, or the promise of pay, for competing in that sport;

- Agreed to compete in professional athletics in that sport;

- Played on any professional athletics team as defined by the NCAA in that sport, or

- Used your athletics skill for pay in any form in that sport.

(The NCAA Manual describes the various forms of pay, as well as acceptable forms of financial assistance from and contact with professional athletics teams.) [Bylaws 12.1 and 12.2]

You are **not eligible** in a sport if you have ever accepted money, transportation or other benefits from an agent or agreed to have an agent market your athletics ability or reputation in that sport. [Bylaw 12.3]

Exhibit 5–1 continued

Summary of NCAA Regulations—Division I
Page 2

You are **not eligible** in any sport if, since you became a student-athlete, you have accepted any pay for promoting a commercial product or service or allowed your name or picture to be used for promoting a commercial product or service. [Bylaw 12.5.2]

You are **not eligible** in any sport if, because of your athletics ability, you were paid for work you did not perform, paid at a rate higher than the going rate or were paid for the value an employer placed on your reputation, fame or personal following. [Bylaw 12.4]

Financial aid

All sports:

You are **not eligible** if you receive financial aid other than the financial aid that your institution distributes. However, it is all right to receive

- Money from anyone upon whom you are naturally or legally dependent.

- Financial aid that has been awarded to you on a basis other than athletics ability.

- Financial aid from a program outside your institution that meets the requirements specified in the NCAA Manual. [Bylaw 15.01.3]

You must report to your institution any financial aid that you receive from a source other than your institution, except that you do not need to report financial aid received from anyone upon whom you are naturally or legally dependent.

Academic standards

All sports:

To be **eligible** to compete, you must

- Have been admitted as a regular student seeking a degree according to the published entrance requirements of your institution;

- Be in good academic standing according to the standards of your institution, and

- Be enrolled in at least a minimum full-time program (not less than 12 semester or quarter hours) and maintain satisfactory progress toward a baccalaureate degree at your institution.

If you are enrolled in less than a full-time program, you are **eligible** to compete only if you are enrolled in the last term of your degree program and are carrying credits necessary to finish your degree. [Bylaws 14.01.1, 14.1.5.1 and 14.1.6.2]

You are **not eligible** to participate in organized practice sessions in a sport unless you are enrolled in at least a minimum full-time program of studies leading to a baccalaureate or equivalent degree. Your institution determines what is a minimum full-time program to be eligible to practice. [Bylaw 14.1.6.1]

You are **eligible** to practice during the official vacation period immediately preceding initial enrollment, provided you have been accepted by your institution for enrollment in a regular, full-time program of studies at the time of your initial participation; you are no longer enrolled in your previous educational institution, and you are eligible under all institutional and NCAA requirements. [Bylaw 14.1.6.1.1]

You also are **eligible** to participate in practice sessions if you are enrolled in the final semester or quarter of a baccalaureate program while enrolled in less than a minimum full-time program of studies and your institution certifies that you are carrying (for credit) the courses necessary to complete the degree requirements, as determined by the faculty of the institution. [Bylaw 14.1.6.1.3]

If you have transferred to your current institution midyear, or you have completed one academic year in residence at your current institution or used one season of eligibility in a sport at your current institution, your eligibility shall be determined by your academic record in existence at the beginning of the fall term of the regular academic year, and you must satisfy the following requirements for academic progress to be **eligible** to compete:

- You must have satisfactorily completed at least an average of 12 semester or quarter hours of

Exhibit 5–1 continued

academic credit during each of the terms in academic years in which you have been enrolled, or you must have satisfactorily completed 24 semester hours or 36 quarter hours of academic credit since the beginning of the previous fall term. If you are **ineligible** based on your record in existence at the beginning of the fall term, you may regain your eligibility at the beginning of any other regular term in that academic year by satisfactorily completing at least an average of 12 semester or quarter hours of academic credit during each of the terms in academic years in which you have been enrolled, or by satisfactorily completing 24 semester or 36 quarter hours of academic credit during your school's preceding regular two semesters or three quarters.

- You must choose a major that leads toward a specific baccalaureate degree by the beginning of your third year of enrollment. (This includes transfer students who have not yet completed an academic year in residence or utilized one season of eligibility in a sport at their current institution.) [Bylaw 14.5.4.3]

- If you are entering your third year of collegiate enrollment, you must have completed successfully at least 25 percent of the course requirements in your specific degree program, and you must present a cumulative minimum grade-point average (based upon a maximum of 4.000) that equals at least 90 percent of the cumulative minimum grade-point average required for graduation.

- If you are entering your fourth year of collegiate enrollment, you must have completed successfully at least 50 percent of the course requirements in your specific degree program, and you must present a cumulative minimum grade-point average (based upon a maximum of 4.000) that equals 95 percent of the cumulative minimum grade-point average required for graduation.

- If you are entering your fifth year of collegiate enrollment, you must have completed successfully at least 75 percent of the course requirements in your specific degree program, and you must present a cumulative minimum grade-point average (based upon a maximum of 4.000) that equals 95 percent of the cumulative minimum grade-point average required for graduation. [Bylaws 14.5.2 and 14.5.3]

- You must earn at least 75 percent of the semester or quarter hours required for satisfactory progress during the regular academic year, and you may not earn more than 25 percent of the semester or quarter hours required for satisfactory progress during the summer. This applies only for credit hours earned during the 1992-93 academic year and thereafter. [Bylaw 14.5.4.1]

Freshmen:

You are called a qualifier and are permitted to receive institutional and athletically related financial aid, practice and compete in your sport under Bylaw 14.02.9.1 if you:

- Graduate from high school;

- Attain a minimum high-school grade-point average of 2.000 in the core curriculum as specified in Bylaw 14.3.1.1, and

- Achieve the required ACT (17) or SAT (700) score as specified in Bylaw 14.3.1.1.

You are called a partial qualifier and are permitted to receive nonathletics institutional need-based financial aid only (but cannot practice or compete in your sport) if you were recruited and fail to meet the criteria above but have achieved an overall 2.000 grade-point average in high school and you graduated. [Bylaws 14.02.9.2 and 14.3.2.1]

You are called a nonqualifier if you fail to meet the criteria above and do not have an overall 2.000 grade-point average in high school. [Bylaw 14.02.9.4] In addition to being ineligible for practice and competition, the nonqualifier is not permitted to receive any institutional financial aid, except as stated below.

You are eligible to receive nonathletics institutional financial aid as a nonqualifier or partial qualifier only if:

- You were not recruited by the institution;

- You were admitted to the institution without regard to athletics ability;

- Your financial aid was awarded without regard to athletics ability, and

- Written certification from the faculty athletics representative, admissions officer and the chair of the financial-aid committee is on file in the office of the director of athletics stating that admission and financial aid was granted according to regulation. [Bylaws 14.3.2.1 and 14.3.2.2]

  If you are a nonqualifier or partial qualifier, you will have three seasons of eligibility after your first academic year in residence.

Exhibit 5–1 continued

Other regulations concerning eligibility

All sports:

You are **not eligible** to participate in more than four seasons of intercollegiate competition, except for extensions that have been approved in accordance with NCAA legislation. [Bylaw 14.2]

You are **not eligible** if you have received or satisfied the requirements for a baccalaureate degree or an equivalent degree, unless you have eligibility remaining while seeking a second baccalaureate degree, a graduate degree at the same institution you attended as an undergraduate, or you are taking course work that leads to the equivalent of another major or degree as defined and documented by the institution. You are **eligible**, however, for championships that occur within 60 days of the date you complete the requirements for your degree. [Bylaw 14.1.8.2]

All sports other than basketball:

You are **not eligible** in your sport for the remainder of the year and the next academic year if, during the academic year, you competed as a member of any outside team in any noncollegiate, amateur competition. Competing in the Olympic Games tryouts and competition and other specified Council-approved competition is permitted. [Bylaw 14.8.1.1]

All-star football and basketball only:

You are **not eligible** if, after you completed your high-school eligibility in your sport and before your high-school graduation, you participated in more than two high-school all-star football or basketball games. [Bylaw 14.7]

Basketball only:

You are **not eligible** if you have played in any organized, outside basketball competition after you became a candidate for an intercollegiate basketball team at an institution that is a member of the NCAA, or after you enrolled at a member institution that recruited you to play on its intercollegiate basketball team. Competing in the Olympic Games tryouts and competition and other specified NCAA Council-approved competition is permitted. [Bylaw 14.8.2]

It is all right to have played on a basketball team in a summer basketball league that the NCAA approved. [Bylaw 14.8.5.2-(a)]

Transfer students only:

You are a transfer student if

- The registrar or admissions officer from your former college certified that you were officially registered and enrolled at that college in any term in a minimum full-time load and you were present on the opening day of classes, **or**

- The director of athletics from your former college certified that you reported for the regular squad practice that any staff member of the athletics department of your former college announced before the beginning of any term. [Bylaw 14.6.2]

If you are a transfer student from a four-year institution, you are **not eligible** during your first academic year in residence unless you meet the provisions of one of the exceptions specified in Bylaw 14.6.5.3 or 14.9.1.2.

If you are a transfer student from a two-year institution, you are **not eligible** during your first academic year in residence at your new institution unless you meet the academic and residence requirements specified in Bylaw 14.6.4 or the exceptions specified in Bylaw 14.6.4.5.

If you transferred from a four-year college to a two-year college and then to your new institution, you are **not eligible** during your first academic year in residence at your new institution unless you meet the requirements specified in Bylaw 14.6.6.

You are **not eligible** if five calendar years have passed from the date you first registered as a full-time student at college and attended your first day of classes for that term, except for time spent in the armed services, on official church missions or with recognized foreign-aid services of the U.S. government. [Bylaw 14.2.1]

Exhibit 5–1 continued

Drugs

All sports:

If the NCAA tests you for the banned drugs listed in Bylaw 31.2.3.1 and you test positive (consistent with NCAA drug-testing protocol), you will be **ineligible** to participate in regular-season and postseason competition during the time period ending one calendar year after your positive drug test, and you will be charged with the loss of a minimum of one season of competition in all sports if the season of competition has not yet begun or a minimum of the equivalent of one full season of competition in all sports if you test positive during the season of competition (i.e., the remainder of contests in the current season and contests in the subsequent season up to the period of time in which you were declared ineligible during the previous year). You will remain ineligible until you retest negative and your eligibility has been restored by the NCAA Eligibility Committee. [Bylaw 18.4.1.5.1]

If you test positive for the use of any drug, other than a "street drug" as defined in Bylaw 31.2.3.1, after your eligibility has been restored, you will lose all remaining regular-season and postseason eligibility in all sports. If you test positive for the use of a "street drug" after being restored to eligibility, you shall be charged with the loss of one additional season of competition in all sports and also shall remain ineligible for regular-season and postseason competition at least through the next calendar year. [Bylaw 18.4.1.5.1]

Part II: For New Student-Athletes Only

This part of the summary contains information about your recruitment, which is governed by Article 13 of the NCAA Manual.

Recruitment

Offers

All sports:

You are **not eligible** if, before you enrolled at your institution, any staff member of your institution or any other representative of your institution's athletics interests offered to you, your relatives or your friends any financial aid or other benefits that NCAA legislation does not permit. It is all right if your summer employment was arranged or you accepted loans from a regular lending agency as long as you did not receive the job or loan before the end of your senior year in high school. [Bylaws 13.2.1, 13.2.4 and 13.2.5]

Contacts

All sports:

You are **not eligible** if, while you were being recruited, any staff member of your institution or any other representative of your institution's athletics interests, contacted you during the day or days of competition at the site of any athletics competition in which you were competing. It is okay for such contact to occur (during the permissible period) after the competition if you are released by the high-school authority. [Bylaw 13.1.6.2]

You are **not eligible** if any staff member of your institution

- Contacted you, your relatives or your legal guardians in person off your institution's campus before you completed your junior year in high school (except for students at military academies) as described in Bylaw 13.1.1.1, or

- Contacted you in person off your institution's campus more than the number of times specified in Bylaw 13.1.5, or

- Contacted you in person off your institution's campus outside the time periods specified in Bylaw 13.1.3 for the sports of football and basketball.

You are **not eligible** if, before you enrolled at your institution, a coach from your institution contacted you in person on or off your institution's campus while you were practicing or competing in football or basketball outside the permissible contact periods. [Bylaw 13.1.6.2.2]

You are **not eligible** if any staff member of your institution contacted you, your relatives or your legal

Exhibit 5–1 continued

guardians on or off your institution's campus and you were not a qualifier according to Bylaw 14.3.1.1 and you were enrolled in your first year at a junior college. [Bylaw 13.1.1.2]

You are **not eligible** if anyone other than a staff member of your institution contacted you on or off your institution's campus, your relatives or your legal guardian in person in order to recruit you. You also are **not eligible** if you received recruiting letters or telephone calls from any representative of your institution's athletics interests. [Bylaw 13.1.2.1]

[Note: For purposes of the sections above, contact means "any face-to-face encounter between a prospect or the prospect's parent or legal guardian and an institutional staff member or athletics representative during which any dialogue occurs in excess of an exchange of a greeting. Any such face-to-face encounter that is prearranged or that takes place on the grounds of the prospect's educational institution or at the site of organized competition or practice involving the prospect or the prospect's high-school, preparatory school, two-year college or all-star team shall be considered a contact, regardless of the conversation that occurs."] [Bylaw 13.02.3]

Publicity

All sports:

You are **not eligible** if, before you enrolled at your institution, your institution publicized any visit that you made to its campus. [Bylaw 13.11.3]

You are **not eligible** if, before you enrolled at your institution, you appeared on a radio or television program that involved a coach or another member of the staff of the athletics department at your institution. [Bylaw 13.11.2]

Division I-A football only:

You are **not eligible** if your institution's head football coach was present while you were signing, at an off-campus site, a National Letter of Intent or an acceptance of a financial-aid offer from your institution or your conference. [Bylaw 13.1.2.7.2]

Source of funds

All sports:

You are **not eligible** if any organization or group of people outside your institution spent money recruiting you, including entertaining, giving gifts or services and providing transportation to you or your relatives or friends. [Bylaw 13.15.4]

Tryouts

You are **not eligible** if, after starting classes for the ninth grade, you displayed your abilities in any phase of any sport in a tryout conducted by or for your institution. [Bylaw 13.12.1]

Football, basketball, volleyball and gymnastics only:

You are **not eligible** if, after starting classes for the ninth grade, you participated in a high-school competition that was run in conjunction with a college competition. [Bylaw 13.12.1.3]

Basketball only:

You are **not eligible** if a member of your institution's coaching staff participated in coaching activities involving an AAU basketball team of which you were a member. [Bylaw 13.12.1.4]

Sports camps

You are **not eligible** if, before you enrolled at your institution, the institution, a member of its staff or a representative of its athletics interests employed you at a sports camp it operates or gave you free or reduced admission to a sports camp and you were a winner of any athletics participation award in high school (includes ninth-grade level) or junior college. [Bylaw 13.13.1.5.1]

Visits, transportation and entertainment

All sports:

You are **not eligible** under Bylaw 13.7 if, before you enrolled at your institution, any of the following happened to you:

• Your institution paid for you to visit its campus more than once.

• Your one expense-paid visit to the campus lasted longer than 48 hours.

• Your institution paid more than the actual round-trip cost by direct route between your home and

Exhibit 5–1 continued

the campus when you made your one expense-paid visit.

- Your institution paid for you to visit during your first year in a junior college, and you are not a qualifier. [Bylaw 13.7.1.3.1]

You are **not eligible** if you accepted expense-paid visits to more than five NCAA member institutions or more than one expense-paid visit to one NCAA member institution. [Bylaws 13.7.1.1 and 13.7.1.2]

You are **not eligible** if, before you enrolled at your institution, your institution

- Entertained you outside a 30-mile radius of the campus. [Bylaw 13.5.1]
- Entertained you excessively at any site. [Bylaw 13.5.2]

You are **not eligible** if your institution paid for you to visit its campus before the first day of classes of your senior year in high school. [Bylaw 13.7.1.2.2]

You are **not eligible** if your institution paid for you to visit its campus before you presented the institution with a score from a PSAT, an SAT, a PACT Plus or an ACT test taken on a national testing date under national testing conditions. (A foreign or learning-disabled prospective student-athlete who requires a special administration of the PSAT, SAT, PACT Plus or ACT may present such a score upon the approval of the NCAA Academic Requirements Committee or the Council Subcommittee on Initial-Eligibility Waivers.) [Bylaw 13.7.1.2.3]

You are **not eligible** if your institution paid for you to visit its campus before you presented the institution with a high-school (or college) academic transcript. The transcript may be an unofficial photocopy of an official document from the prospective student-athlete's high school (or collegiate institution). [Bylaw 13.7.1.2.3.2]

You are **not eligible** if your institution paid for you to visit its campus before the initial early signing date in sports that have an early signing period for the National Letter of Intent before you presented the institution with a minimum combined SAT score of 700 or PSAT score of 70 or a minimum composite ACT or PACT Plus score of 17, and also presented a minimum 2.000 grade-point average in at least seven core courses specified in Bylaw 14.3.1.1.1. If you do not present these academic credentials you may not begin an official visit until 24 hours after the last day of the early signing period in that sport. [Bylaw 13.7.1.2.4]

You are **not eligible** if, at any time that you were visiting your institution's campus at your own expense, your institution paid for anything more than the following:

- Three free passes, for you and those people who came with you, to an athletics event on campus in which your institution's team competed. [Bylaw 13.8.2.1]
- Transportation, when accompanied by a staff member, to see off-campus practice and competition sites and other institutional facilities located within a 30-mile radius of the campus. [Bylaw 13.6.3]

You are **not eligible** if, when you were being recruited, staff members of your institution or any representatives of its athletics interests paid the transportation costs for your relatives or friends to visit the campus or elsewhere. [Bylaw 13.6.2.9]

You are **not eligible** if, when you were being recruited, a staff member of your institution entertained your parents (or legal guardians) or spouse at any site other than your institution's campus (or, on an official visit, within 30 miles of the institution's campus) or entertained your friends or other relatives at any site. [Bylaw 13.5.1]

You are **not eligible** if, when you were being recruited, your institution gave you free passes to more than one regular-season home game scheduled outside your institution's community or gave you more than three free passes to that one regular-season home game scheduled outside your institution's community. [Bylaw 13.8.2.2]

You are **not eligible** if, when you were being recruited, a staff member of your institution's athletics department spent money other than what was necessary for the staff member's (or representative's) personal expense during an off-campus visit with you. [Bylaw 13.15.2]

Precollege or postgraduate expense

All sports:

You are **not eligible** if your institution or any representative of its athletics interests offered you money, directly or indirectly, to pay for any part of your educational expenses or other expenses during any period of time before you enrolled at your institution. This applies to your postgraduate education as well. [Bylaw 13.16.1]

Grade Point Average

The grade point average, or GPA, has long been used and recognized as a measure of a student's academic achievement. To compute a student's GPA, each letter grade in a course is converted to the 4.000 scale (A = 4, B = 3, C = 2, D = 1, F = 0). If a different number of credits are issued for some of the courses, the letter grades and resulting grade points must be weighted according to the proportion of credits issued in the course to the number of credits granted for a normal course. The points are then totaled for the courses to be included in the computation, and that total is divided by the number of courses. A student's GPA is usually calculated for each academic term, each year, and cumulatively for the student's entire high school or college career. The method and the subjects to be considered in the computation of a student's GPA vary from school to school. The GPA is used both as a measure of initial eligibility when the athlete enters college and as an indicator of progress to maintain the athlete's eligibility at both the collegiate and scholastic levels.

In an attempt to guarantee academic achievement for their student-athletes, a number of high schools have adopted grade point average standards. These rules serve the dual purpose of assuring that their student-athletes make sufficient academic progress during high school and that they are eligible for participation in intercollegiate athletics as incoming freshmen. It is important to realize that this dual purpose contains two separate requirements, since freshman intercollegiate eligibility in the NCAA is dependent on both standardized test scores and grade point average.

Certain states have proposed or established academic standards governing eligibility for high school sports and other extracurricular activities. Texas legislators in 1985, for example, passed such a "no pass, no play" rule requiring all students involved in extracurricular activities to maintain a minimum grade of 70 in each class to retain eligibility. A score below 70 during a six-week grading period will result in ineligibility during the next six-week grading period. The state association in Tennessee has proposed increasing the number of subjects passed from four to five, and Mississippi has considered changing to a Texas-like law requiring a C average. Exhibit 5–2 is a state-by-state summary of academic requirements for high school athletes.

The courts have generally upheld "no pass, no play" rules as students have been found to have no right or property interest in participating in extracurricular activities. Extracurricular activities are defined to include all those activities for students that are sponsored or sanctioned by an educational institution that supplement or complement, but are not a part of, the institution's required academic

Exhibit 5–2
State Academic Standards Governing Eligibility for High School Athletes

Alabama: Minimum 70 average in previous school year.

Alaska: Must pass four subjects in previous semester, be enrolled in four subjects in current semester. Fifty of 56 school districts have more stringent rules, some requiring weekly C average or weekly no pass-no play.

Arizona: No pass-no play but passing grade (minimum five classes each semester through junior year, maintain graduation progress as senior) and grading interval (maximum of nine weeks) set by local districts.

Arkansas: Beginning in September, a 1.3 grade-point average in four academic courses counted toward graduation the previous school year. Minimum goes to 1.6 for 1991-92. Some districts are more strict.

California: State law requires C average, but each district may establish a probation period in which athlete remains eligible. Several parochial and public school systems have more stringent rules.

Colorado: Must be enrolled in five classes and passing at least four in current semester. Some districts have weekly requirements.

Connecticut: Must be enrolled in and passing four classes. Some districts have more stringent rules.

Delaware: Must be enrolled in and passing four classes, two of which must be in English, science, mathematics or social studies. Seniors must be passing all classes needed for graduation. Some districts have more stringent rules.

District of Columbia: Must have 2.0 grade-point average in previous grading period.

Florida: Must have 1.5 grade-point average in previous school year and have passed five classes in previous grading period.

Georgia: Minimum 70 average in each of five classes in previous semester and currently must be maintaining 70 average. Must complete five classes each school year to be eligible following year. Grades evaluated quarterly.

Hawaii: Must have 2.0 grade-point average and passing grades in required subjects—English, science, mathematics, social studies—in quarter preceding eligibility. A 1.6 GPA creates three-week probation period to reach 2.0 to maintain eligibility.

Idaho: No pass-no play based on receiving full credit for five full-credit classes in previous semester.

Illinois: Must pass 20 credit hours in previous semester (equivalent to four full-credit classes) and have cumulative passing grades weekly to maintain eligibility. About 30 percent of state schools have more stringent rules.

Indiana: No pass-no play based on five full-credit subjects in current grading period.

Iowa: Must have passed 15 hours (three classes meeting five times a week) in previous semester and be passing 15 hours during participation. Nearly half the school districts have more stringent rules.

Kansas: No pass-no play based on five classes in previous grading period and be current in at least five unrepeated classes during current grading period.

Kentucky: Must have been enrolled at proper grade level in previous semester and currently passing four subjects. Freshmen must have passed 80 percent of classes in eighth grade.

Louisiana: No pass-no play based on five classes and have current 1.5 grade-point average. Some districts have more stringent rules.

Maine: No pass-no play based on four current classes offering credit toward graduation. Most districts have more stringent rules.

Maryland: No statewide rules. Each district sets standards.

Massachusetts: No pass-no play based on four classes in previous grading period or previous school year. Some districts have more stringent rules.

Exhibit 5–2 continued

Michigan: No pass-no play based on four classes. Some districts have more stringent rules.

Minnesota: Must be making satisfactory progress toward graduation as determined by local districts.

Mississippi: Must pass 4.5 class/semesters toward graduation in previous year and currently.

Missouri: No pass-no play based on five classes in previous semester. About 40 percent of districts have more stringent rules.

Montana: No pass-no play based on four classes in previous semester.

Nebraska: No pass-no play based on 20 semester hours and currently enrolled in 20 semester hours.

Nevada: No pass-no play based on four classes in previous semester. Some districts have more stringent rules.

New Hampshire: No pass-no play based on four classes in current grading period. About 20 percent of districts have more stringent rules.

New Jersey: Requirements being changed. Beginning in September, freshmen and sophomores will need 110 credits for graduation and must pass 27.5 credits each school year to be eligible in following year. Juniors and seniors will need 92 credits and must pass 23 each year. Eligibility determined by semesters.

New Mexico: Must be passing four classes, failing no more than one and have 2.0 grade-point average in previous period. Some districts have more stringent rules.

New York: Must be enrolled in at least four classes, including physical education. Some districts have more stringent rules.

North Carolina: Must pass five courses each semester and attend 75 percent of class days.

North Dakota: Must be currently passing four credits. If fail a semester, ineligible for four weeks, then reinstated if passing. Some districts have more stringent rules.

Ohio: No pass-no play based on four classes in previous grading period.

Oklahoma: No pass-no play based on five classes in semester previous to competition, then must pass all classes on weekly basis. Local districts set criteria.

Oregon: No pass-no play based on five class in previous and current semesters. Local districts set criteria.

Pennsylvania: No pass-no play based on four classes. Some districts have more stringent rules.

Rhode Island: No pass-no play based on three classes, not counting physical education, in previous grading period.

South Carolina: No pass-no play based on five classes each semester, with four in English, social science, mathematics, science and physical education.

South Dakota: Must pass four full-time classes in previous and current semesters. Some districts have more stringent rules.

Tennessee: No pass-no play based on five classes in preceding semester. May average a class grade for two semesters to achieve eligibility for following school year.

Texas: No pass-no play based on all classes each grading period. State law: Sophomores, juniors and seniors must be on graduation rate of five credits a school year or have earned five credits in previous 12 months.

Utah: No more than one failing grade each grading period. Some districts have more stringent rules.

Vermont: No state rules. Each district sets standards.

Virginia: No pass-no play based on five classes in preceding semester. Must be enrolled in five classes in current semester.

Washington: No pass-no play based on four full-time classes in current grading period. Some districts have more stringent rules.

West Virginia: Must have 2.0 grade-point average and pass at least four classes in pre-

Exhibit 5–2 continued

ceding semester. Two of the four must be in English, mathematics, science, or social studies.

Wisconsin: Public schools—No pass-no play based on four full-credit classes or equivalent in preceding semester. Private schools—No pass-no play based on three full-credit classes or equivalent in preceding semester

and must be enrolled in four full-credit classes in current grading period. Most schools have higher criteria.

Wyoming: Must be enrolled in at least 20 hours of class each week and be passing four five-day classes. Criteria for passing set by local districts.

program or curriculum. Consequently, the courts have usually reasoned that participation is a privilege which may be granted or withdrawn at the discretion of the school board. The board, furthermore, has the discretion to set the qualifications necessary for students to participate when participation in extracurricular activities is considered a privilege. In reviewing such eligibility requirements, the courts will not consider whether the qualifications are wise or expedient, but only whether they are a reasonable exercise of the power and discretion of the board. As a general rule, eligibility requirements will be upheld if they are rationally related to the purpose of the extracurricular activity involved and are not arbitrary, capricious, or unjustly discriminatory. Also, as previously mentioned, a student-athlete's high school grade point average is also important for participation in intercollegiate athletics.

There are two special situations in which a student-athlete's high school grades are considered differently for admission to college. The first situation involves a student-athlete who enters a junior college without having graduated from high school and then subsequently transfers to an NCAA Division I institution. Under this circumstance, the student's junior college course grades cannot be calculated in the student's high school GPA for purposes of meeting the NCAA core requirement for freshmen, even though the junior college courses transfer to the student-athlete's high school record and satisfy requirements toward high school graduation. Upon matriculation at a four-year NCAA Division I member institution, the student-athlete is considered a junior college transfer as opposed to an incoming freshman. The prospective student-athlete must then meet the transfer requirement that applies to junior college transfer student-athletes who do not graduate from high school (and are nonqualifiers) in order to be eligible to participate at a Division I institution during the first academic year in residence.

The second situation involves the student-athlete who does not graduate from high school but later obtains a state high school equivalency diploma by passing the General Educational Development

(GED) test. The student-athlete's GED scores are treated as a substitute for the high school graduation and GPA. In this situation, the NCAA applies an NCAA-approved table that converts the average of the five GED scores to the high school GPA with four stipulations: (1) the scores have to have been obtained more than one calendar year from the date the student-athlete would have graduated had the student-athlete remained in high school, (2) the student-athlete must present the state high school equivalency diploma prior to initial enrollment in a collegiate institution, (3) the prospect may qualify for financial aid but not for practice or competition by presenting a minimum average score of 45 on the GED test, and (4) to qualify for financial aid, practice, and competition, the prospect must meet the core-curriculum GPA and test score requirements in addition to the minimum score of 45 on the GED test (*1993–94 NCAA Manual*, Bylaw 14.3.5.3.4).

An NCAA member institution can permit a recruited student-athlete whose high school GPA and test scores have not been certified by the high school to practice, but not compete, for a maximum of two weeks. If the student-athlete's 2.0 GPA has not been certified after two weeks, the student-athlete is barred from both practice and competition. The nonrecruited student-athlete receives a "grace period" of forty-five days in these circumstances (*1993–94 NCAA Manual*, Bylaw 14.3.5.1). In those instances when a high school or preparatory school notifies the institution in writing that it will not provide the student-athlete's GPA or convert the GPA to a 4.0 scale, the NCAA member institution may submit the student-athlete's transcript to the NCAA Academic Requirements Committee for certification or conversion (*1993–94 NCAA Manual*, Bylaw 14.3.5.2).

A leading case in the area of academic requirements for intercollegiate participation is *Parish v. National Collegiate Athletic Ass'n*, 361 F. Supp. 1220 (W.D. La. 1973), *aff'd*, 506 F.2d 1028 (5th Cir. 1975). Parish and some fellow basketball players sought injunctive relief in this litigation to prevent member institutions from enforcing an NCAA rule that declared players ineligible if they did not predict a grade point average of 1.6 when entering college. (The 1.6 rule was the predecessor of the current 2.0 rule, and it was stricter.) The court held that the 1.6 rule limiting eligibility did not raise a federal question since there was no restriction of constitutional rights. The court ruled that judicial intervention was not required for a rule that was enacted and implemented by a private, voluntary organization. This case and several others indicate that courts will allow amateur athletic organizations to make reasonable rules related to academic requirements.

NOTES _____

1. For cases in which academic requirements for *interscholastic* athletic participation were upheld, see *Bailey v. Truby* and *Myles v. Board of Edu-*

cation of the County of Kanawha, 321 S.E.2d 302 (W. Va. 1984). The court stated that the State Board of Education's rule requiring a 2.000 grade point average for participation in nonacademic extracurricular activities was valid since the rule was a legitimate exercise of its power of "general supervision" over the state's educational system (*Bailey*). The Kanawha County Board of Education's rule requiring students to receive passing grades in all of their classes in order to participate in nonacademic extracurricular activities was also found to be valid (*Myles*). The county board was judged to have a legitimate concern in the encouragement of academic excellence, and regulation of such extracurricular activity was a common and accepted method of achieving that fundamental goal.

2. In *Associated Students Inc. v. National Collegiate Athletic Ass'n,* 493 F.2d 1251 (9th Cir. 1974), the court held that the purpose of the 1.6 GPA rule was to guarantee that only bona fide students would be eligible to participate in intercollegiate athletics in their first year, to help discourage recruiting violations, and to encourage weak students to concentrate on developing proper study skills prior to being involved in time-consuming intercollegiate athletics. The court found that the rule was reasonably related to its purposes, even as applied to students who had earned a 1.6 GPA after the first year but had failed to predict a 1.6 GPA prior to being admitted to college.

3. In *Thompson v. Fayette County Public Schools,* 786 S.W.2d 879 (Ky. Ct. App. 1990), the plaintiff sued the school district claiming a violation of his high school son's civil rights because he was excluded from the wrestling team for failure to maintain a satisfactory grade point average. The court of appeals affirmed the trial court ruling by stating there was no violation of the student's rights since he had neither a property interest nor any fundamental right to participate in extracurricular activities.

4. In *Bartmess v. Board of Trustees,* 726 P.2d 801 (Mont. Sup. Ct. 1986), the plaintiff challenged the enforcement of a school district's eligibility rule which required a student to maintain a 2.0 GPA for the preceding nine-week period as a prerequisite to participate in any extracurricular activities in the following nine-week period. The interesting aspect of this case is that the school district's 2.0 rule was more stringent than the 1.0 GPA required by the Montana High School Association. The Court held that the school district's no-pass rule had a rational relation to the state's legitimate goal and therefore ruled in favor of the school district.

5. In *Manuel v. Oklahoma City University,* No. CJ-90-7020 (Okla. Dist. Ct. 1990), the plaintiff sought an injunction against Oklahoma City University (OCU) and the NAIA after being ruled ineligible to compete. Manuel played basketball at the University of Kentucky (UK) in 1987–89. During the 1988–89 NCAA investigation into UK, it was found that Manuel committed academic fraud by cheating on a precollege entrance examination. The NCAA declared Manuel ineligible to participate in varsity athletics at any NCAA-affiliated college or university. After attending a junior college, Manuel signed a scholarship contract with OCU. OCU was informed by the NAIA that Manuel was ineligible to compete because of an NAIA rule which stated, "A student who has completed eligibility at a four year institution is ineligible for further intercollegiate participation." On receiving proof from Manuel that he had not used up his four years of eligibility and he would be harmed if the in-

junction were not issued, the district court awarded a permanent injunction against OCU and the NAIA from prohibiting Manuel from participating and finishing up his remaining eligibility.

6. For further information, see the following law review articles:

(a) Green, "The New NCAA Rules of the Game: Academic Integrity or Racism?" 28 *St. Louis U. L. J.* 101 (February 1984).

(b) Yasser, "The Black Athletes' Equal Protection Case Against the NCAA's New Academic Standards," 19 (1) *Gonz. L. Rev.* 83 (1983/1984).

(c) McKenna, "A Proposition with a Powerful Punch: The Legality and Constitutionality of NCAA Proposition 48," 28 *Duq. L. Rev.* 43 (1987).

(d) Note, "Balancing Due Process and Academic Integrity in Intercollegiate Athletics: The Scholarship Athlete's Limited Property Interest in Eligibility," 62 *Ind. L. J.* 1151 (1986–87).

7. See Exhibit 5–3 for the NCAA's requirements regarding a recruited student-athlete's GPA.

Academic Progress

Academic progress rules are designed to ensure that student-athletes enroll in the type of courses required to obtain a high school diploma or college degree. At the interscholastic level, most state athletic associations do not have any academic progress rules, per se. The Massachusetts Interscholastic Athletic Association (MIAA), for example, has the following regulations:

62. Academic Requirements:

62.1 A student must secure during the last marking period preceding the contest (e.g. second quarter marks and not semester grades determine third quarter eligibility) a passing grade in the equivalent of four major subjects. To satisfy this requirement, a student must have passed sufficient courses for that marking period which carry credits totalling the equivalent of four 1-year major English courses....

62.6 A student who repeats work upon which he/she has once received credit cannot count that subject a second time for eligibility. *(1991–93 MIAA Rules and Regulations Governing Athletics, Part IV, Rule 62)*

Therefore, a student-athlete who repeats a grade remains ineligible for athletic participation during that period.

A case in which the academic progress rules of an interscholastic state association were addressed is *Stone v. Kansas State High School Activities Association*, 761 P.2d 1255 (Kan. App. Div. 1988). The plaintiff, Stone, was declared ineligible for the 1987 fall semester because he had passed only four classes the previous semester, not the Kansas State High School Activities Association (KSHSAA) requirement of

Exhibit 5–3
**Relationships Between Academic Requirements, Recruitment, Financial
Aid, and Eligibility in Division I for High School Graduates**

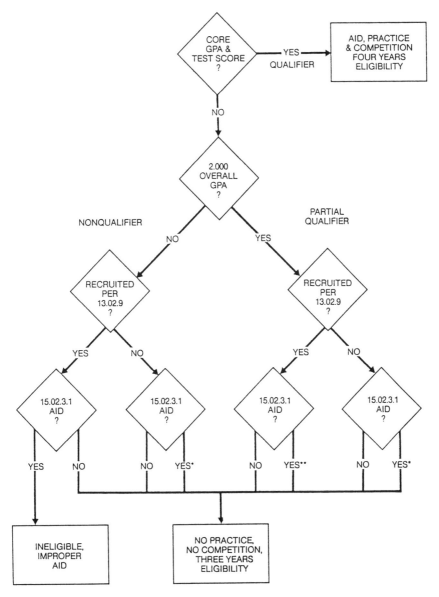

*Must be certified as not related to athletics ability.

**Must be need-based, nonathletically related financial aid that is available on the same basis to students in general.

Source: 1993–94 NCAA Manual

five classes. During the summer of 1987, Stone was tutored by his teacher of English, the class he failed during the 1987 spring semester. During September 1987, Stone and his parents asked for his eligibility to be restored because he had made up the fifth class requirement over the summer. The KSHSAA executive board denied this request because of a rule which prevents a student from making up work after the end of the semester for the purpose of regaining eligibility. Stone challenged this rule on due process and equal protection grounds.

In October 1987, Stone sought and was granted a temporary restraining order prohibiting KSHSAA and the school district from preventing his participation in interscholastic and interschool activity during the 1987 fall semester. The KSHSAA appealed this decision. The court ruled that the no-make-up rule has a rational basis and its application to Stone did not violate his due process rights. Stone also argued the rule on equal protection grounds because of another student who had transferred from the state of Iowa to Kansas. This student did not pass the required number of classes in Iowa but was allowed to make up the coursework during the summer. Upon transferring to Kansas for the fall semester, the student was declared eligible. Stone argued that if this student was allowed to make up work during the summer and then transfer to Kansas and be eligible for participation, not allowing Stone the same opportunity to make up coursework during the summer was a violation of his equal protection rights. The court determined that Iowa allows classes to be made up during the summer; therefore, when the student transferred to Kansas he had already completed the necessary requirements to restore his eligibility in Iowa. Because he was eligible in Iowa, he was therefore eligible for participation in Kansas. The court ruled that the difference between these two students' situations was not based on a suspect classification and therefore Stone's equal protection rights were not violated. The Appellate court reversed the district court's granting of a temporary restraining order to Stone.

At the intercollegiate level, the general rule for continued academic eligibility under NCAA rules (Divisions I and II) is that a student-athlete, after the first academic year, must maintain satisfactory progress toward a degree based on the member institution's academic rules of eligibility for *all* students, those specific academic eligibility rules adopted by the NCAA, and those of the athletic conference to which the institution belongs (*1993–94 NCAA Manual,* Bylaw 14.5.1). The NCAA requires that a student-athlete satisfactorily complete an average of at least 12 semester or quarter hours of coursework for all regular terms or satisfactorily complete 24 semester or 36 quarter hours. In addition, a student-athlete must have completed successfully at least 25 percent of the course requirements in the student's degree program when entering his or her third year of enrollment, 50 percent by the fourth year, and 75 percent by the fifth year (*1993–94 NCAA Manual*, Bylaw 14.5.2.1). In addition, academic progress in college also requires that a student-athlete be accepted into a degree-granting program by the beginning of the third year of enrollment and thereafter make satisfactory progress toward that specific degree (*1993–94 NCAA Manual*, Bylaw 14.5.4.3).

The NCAA academic progress requirement was adopted in August 1981 in an effort to fight the major problem of student-athletes' taking the required number of credit hours necessary to maintain eligibility but not enrolling in the type of courses necessary to satisfy degree requirements. The NCAA rule is general in nature, and many individual conferences have established stricter academic guidelines to deal with this problem at their member institutions.

Allied conferences may decide their own eligibility standards as long as they satisfy the NCAA's minimum requirements. For example, even before it became an NCAA requirement, the Big Ten Conference Committee on Academic Progress and Eligibility declared that a student-athlete "must have earned at least 24 semester hours or 36 quarter hours which are acceptable toward meeting requirements for the student-athlete's baccalaureate degree objective and maintain a 1.8 GPA" to be eligible for competition during the student-athlete's second school year of residence. (See *1992–93 Handbook of Intercollegiate [Big Ten] Conference*, Rules 14.5.3[B] and 14.5.4[A].) In addition, on entering the third year, the Big Ten requires 51 semester hours or 77 quarter hours with a 1.9 GPA; in the fourth year, at least 78 semester hours or 117 quarter hours with a 2.0 GPA is required to maintain athletic eligibility. In the fifth year, at least 105 semester hours or 158 quarter hours with a 2.0 GPA is required. (See *1992–93 Handbook of Intercollegiate [Big Ten] Conference*, Rules 14.5.3[B] and 14.5.4[A].)

A leading case in the area of academic progress is *Wilson v. Intercollegiate (Big Ten) Conference*, 668 F.2d 962 (7th Cir. 1982). Dave Wilson was injured for the entire season in his first football game at Fullerton Junior College in 1977 prior to the beginning of classes. Wilson was advised to drop out of Fullerton for the year to retain four years of playing eligibility. Wilson then enrolled at Fullerton the following year, playing football and attending classes in 1978–79 and 1979–80.

After the 1979–80 season, Wilson transferred to the University of Illinois, where he was told that he would have only one year of eligibility because he had played in a game during the 1977 season. He was also informed that he would have to earn senior academic year status before playing. Under Big Ten Conference rules, because he had not received a hardship waiver after being injured in the first game of the 1977–78 season, he had used three years of playing eligibility while playing at Fullerton. Since he had completed only two years of school, Wilson was subject to the Big Ten's "insufficient academic progress rule," which requires that a specific number of credits be accumulated in order for a student-athlete to be eligible for each successive playing season. Because of those alleged rule violations, the conference's faculty representatives who govern Big Ten athletics ruled that Wilson would be eligible for one season only.

In response, Wilson brought suit against the NCAA, the Big Ten, and the University of Illinois. He charged that the faculty representatives had illegally overruled their own eligibility committee, which had originally determined that he would be eligible for two seasons at Illinois. Wilson also contended that he should have been granted a hearing regarding the determination of his eligibility.

In addressing the alleged academic progress violations, Wilson argued that NCAA eligibility requirements regarding academic progress are intended to ensure a level of academic achievement for all student-athletes. In this case, considering the circumstances and the fact that he had submitted transcripts and records of his academic performance which demonstrated that he was a "serious student," the application of the rule was unnecessary.

Under several temporary court injunctions, Wilson was allowed to play football for the 1980 season, but not for the 1981 season, even though he ultimately won the case on an appeal. The Big Ten held fast to its decision to grant Wilson only one full year of eligibility, so Wilson left Illinois to pursue a career in professional football.

In addition to the *Wilson* type of case, there are the "educational exploitation" cases like *Hall* (see note 1). The threat of litigation in this area may cause educators and athletic administrators to right many of the existing wrongs that border on unfair educational abuses. Such litigation may force the minority of educationally unsound programs to join the majority of programs, whose academic standards are above reproach.

NOTES ————————————————————————————

1. For a case in which the academic progress rule was challenged, see *Hall v. University of Minnesota*, 530 F. Supp. 104 (D. Minn. 1982). Hall, a former basketball player, brought suit against the University of Minnesota for its failure to admit him to a degree-granting program, which resulted in his being declared ineligible to play basketball for his senior year. Big Ten Conference rules require a student-athlete to be enrolled in such a degree-granting program to maintain eligibility. The court found in favor of Hall, stating that a constitutionally protected property interest in a potential professional basketball contract was involved; therefore, Hall's due process rights had been violated.

2. In *Stone v. Kansas State High School Activities Association, Inc.*, 761 P.2d 1255 (Kan. Ct. App. 1988), the plaintiff, a high school student, challenged the constitutionality of the defendant's academic eligibility rule. The district court held that the rule was unconstitutional. On appeal, the court of appeals held that the rule prohibiting high school students from making up failed classes in order to regain academic eligibility was constitutional.

3. For an example of an academic progress form used at the collegiate level, see Exhibit 5–4.

Transfer Rules

On both the intercollegiate and interscholastic levels of athletic competition, the issue of student-athletes transferring from one institution to another is often troublesome and controversial. For the student-athlete, the issue centers on the individual's right to attend school and compete in athletics wherever he or she wishes. For the institution, allied conference, and national association, the issues revolve around illegal recruitment, stability of programs, and a desire to avoid an image of student-athletes being recruited from one program to another.

Transfer rules were created to deter: (1) the recruiting of student-athletes by colleges or high schools that the student-athlete does not attend and (2) the shopping around by student-athletes for institutions that seem to offer them the best opportunities for advancing their athletic careers. The courts have generally upheld transfer rules, basing their decisions on the fact that neither has a suspect class been established nor has a fundamental right been violated. The transfer rule needs only to be rationally related to the legitimate state interest or purpose of preventing recruitment and school hopping. The exception to this general rule is when substantial hardship or other mitigating circumstances can be shown to require judicial intervention. The following sections discuss in detail the problems and litigation associated with the transfer of student-athletes.

College Transfer Rules

Under NCAA Division I and II regulations, a "transfer student" is one who: (1) officially registers and enrolls at one institution in any quarter or semester with a minimum full-time academic load and was present at the institution on the opening day of classes; (2) attends one or more classes, in any quarter or semester in which the student-athlete was enrolled in a minimum full-time program; (3) reports for regular squad practice; (4) enrolls in an institution in a minimum full-time program of studies in a night school and is considered a regularly matriculated student; (5) attends a branch school that conducted an intercollegiate athletics program and transfers to an institution other than the parent institution; (6) practices or competes in a given sport

Exhibit 5–4
College Academic Progress Form

UNIVERSITY OF MASSACHUSETTS   Department of Athletics/Intramurals
AT AMHERST
Amherst, MA 01003
                                          1992-93
                            Satisfactory   Progress   Form

To: Chief Undergraduate Advisor

From: Glenn Wong, Interim Athletic Director

Subject: DECLARATION OF MAJOR AND ACADEMIC PROGRESS FORM FOR STUDENT-ATHLETES

Printed Name:_____ Student Signature: _____

Sport: _____ Academic Major: _____

Date of Request: _____

Legislation by the National Collegiate Athletic Association (NCAA) governing the eligibility
of student-athletes requires that in order to remain eligible in the fifth and subsequent
semesters of enrollment, a student must designate in writing the specific baccalaureate
degree program he/she will pursue. Further, once the student-athlete has designated
a program of study, the student's satisfactory progress shall be based upon the satisfactory
completion of courses in the designated program, as well as the student's overall academic
record at the Institution. Written verification of the academic progress is required
in the designated program and must be affirmed annually by an academic official in
the major program of study.

Satisfactory Progress - "Student is completing, will complete, or has the potential
to complete academic course work that would allow him/her to graduate within in total
of five years (10 semesters) in college" NOTE: This definition is consistent with
both the University of Massachusetts/Amherst and NCAA Satisfactory Progress criteria
requirements.

By completing this required form two weeks from the above date, you will be assisting
the Department of Athletics to comply with these NCAA regulations concerning academic
eligibility. This student-athlete will not be declared eligible and may not participate
without this form on file with Athletics.

Thank you in advance for your assistance. If you have any questions, please call my
office (545-2460)

                  DECLARATION OF MAJOR AND ACADEMIC PROGRESS FORM FOR STUDENT-ATHLETES

ACADEMIC OFFICIAL:

By signing this form you will be affirming that:
a. The above named student is a declared major as listed above ____   ____
                                                                  yes   no
b. He/She is making satisfactory academic progress toward the designated program of
    studies and is satisfying program or institutional requirements leading to the
    baccalaureate degree.   ____   ____
                                                                  yes   no

_____   _____   _____
Chief Undergraduate Advisor   Campus Address   Department
     Signature
           Office Phone Number _____   Date _____
                                                              August, 1992

even though enrolled in less than a minimum full-time program; (7) attends a branch school that does not conduct an intercollegiate athletics program, but the student had been enrolled in another collegiate institution prior to attendance at the branch school; or (8) receives institutional financial aid while attending a summer term, summer school, or summer orientation program (*1993–94 NCAA Manual*, Bylaw 14.6.2). A student-athlete who meets any or all of these criteria and then desires to change schools is considered by the NCAA to be a "transfer student."

Generally, as a transfer, the student-athlete must forego intercollegiate athletic competition for one full academic year, regardless of the reason for changing schools. Additionally, the student-athlete must be enrolled full-time at the new institution for the duration of that year. There are many exceptions to this rule, too numerous to detail, with the exception of the two discussed below. One exception to this rule occurs when a student-athlete who meets the 2.0 qualifier rule transfers from a two-year to a four-year college. To qualify for this exception, a student-athlete must have either graduated from the two-year institution and satisfactorily completed a minimum of 48 semester or 72 quarter hours of transferrable degree credit, with a minimum GPA of 2.0 for all transferrable degree credits, or completed a minimum of 24 semester or 36 quarter hours of transferrable degree credits, with a minimum GPA of 2.0 and an average of 12 semester or 18 quarter hours of transferrable degree credit for each term of attendance at the two-year college (*1993–94 NCAA Manual*, Bylaw 14.6.4.1.1).

A second exception to the rule occurs when a student-athlete transfers from one four-year to another four-year institution in order to continue participation in a sport that has been dropped by the original institution, has been reclassified from Division I to Division III, or was never sponsored on the intercollegiate level while the student-athlete was in attendance at the institution, provided the student-athlete had never attended any other institution that offered intercollegiate competition in that sport (*1993–94 NCAA Manual*, Bylaw 14.6.5.3.6). Of course, athletic conferences may establish stricter transfer rules than those of the NCAA, such as requiring a student-athlete to forego athletic competition for two full academic years. However, these stricter conference eligibility rules may be subject to challenge (see note 1a).

A leading case in the area of student-athlete transfer rules is *English v. National Collegiate Athletic Ass'n*, 439 So. 2d 1218 (La. App. 4th Cir. 1983). The *English* case is very important because it upholds the authority of the NCAA to regulate the very type of activity transfer rules are designed to prevent. English was an outstanding high school quarterback who entered Michigan State University in the fall of 1979 on a football scholarship. Realizing that his prospects for playing at Michigan State were poor, in part because of an injury, he enrolled at Allegheny Junior College in Pittsburgh, Pennsylvania. English attended Allegheny during the 1980–81 school year and graduated in the spring. English did not play football for Allegheny during the year he attended. In the fall of 1981, English enrolled at Iowa State University and was on the football team there during the 1981 and 1982 seasons. Once again deciding that his prospects were poor, he enrolled at Delgado Junior College in New Orleans, where his family resided and where his father had recently taken the position as head football coach at Tulane. English graduated from Delgado in the spring, and in August 1983 he enrolled in Tulane, where he sought to play football immediately but was told he was ineligible because he was a transfer.

English brought suit, contending that he was denied due process and that the NCAA's actions were arbitrary, capricious, unfair, and discriminatory. The court found from the testimony of his father that there was a question in English's mind from the very beginning about his eligibility, notwithstanding the way he wanted to read the rule. The NCAA rule in question stated that a student-athlete from a junior college who had transferred from a four-year college must complete a one-year residency requirement to be eligible for NCAA postseason competition unless the student-athlete completed 24 semester hours (credits) and graduated from the junior college, and one calendar year had elapsed since the transfer from the first four-year college. English was aware of the NCAA policy of preventing a student-athlete from playing for different colleges in successive years. Since there was a question in his mind, English was also obliged to contact the NCAA national office for answers but failed to avail himself of this opportunity and instead embarked on a course he knew was perilous; therefore, he was not deprived of due process.

The court found that the NCAA rule contemplated two colleges, the first and second. A student-athlete who plays for a college one year cannot play for another college the following year. The rule does not and need not concern itself with what the court described as "the bizarre situation where one had played for yet a third college in the distant past." The court ruled that the NCAA, in adopting and implementing the transfer rule, acted reasonably in its efforts to prevent players from jumping from one school to another.

NOTES _____

1. In the following cases, the courts *struck down* intercollegiate transfer rules.

(a) In *Gulf South Conference v. Boyd*, 369 So. 2d 553 (Ala. Sup. Ct.

1979), a full-scholarship football player decided not to renew his football scholarship for his second year at one Gulf South Conference (GSC) institution and instead transferred to a junior college. After completing his degree at the junior college a year later, Boyd wanted to attend a second Gulf South Conference institution and play football. The Commissioner of the GSC informed him that he had been ruled ineligible. The court of appeals affirmed the district court ruling, which granted the student-athlete eligibility to participate since he had refused the scholarship for a second year at the first GSC institution and had not played football for two years. The court rejected the interpretation of the conference that the school must not offer to renew the scholarship, instead of the athlete's refusing to renew, for the athlete to remain eligible. In addition, the court found that Boyd was eligible to compete because he fulfilled a GSC bylaw which stated that "a prospective athlete who does not accept the grant-in-aid at that school or participate becomes a free agent at the end of two years and can be signed by any GSC school."

(b) In *Cabrillo Community College District of Santa Cruz County v. California Junior College Ass'n,* 44 Cal. App. 3d 367, 118 Cal. Rptr. 708 (Cal. Ct. App. 1975), the court held that a community college may not prevent a student from trying out for an interscholastic athletic program merely because that student had not lived in a college district for a particular period of time. The court stated that such athletic residency requirements were violative of state law since they imposed additional residency requirements upon students who wish to participate in community college athletic programs after they had already been duly admitted to an institution.

(c) In *McHale v. Cornell University,* 620 F. Supp. 67 (N.D.N.Y. 1985), McHale played football at the University of Maryland in 1982–84 and then transferred to Cornell in January 1985. The NCAA's transfer rule stated that a student who transfers to a Division I school must complete one year at the new institution before establishing eligibility to compete. McHale argued that he was not recruited but transferred to Cornell solely for academic reasons and thus the transfer rule should not apply to him because his competing would not subvert the purposes of the rule. The court did not grant McHale a preliminary injunction, stating that the plaintiff had failed to show a likelihood of success on the merits.

2. In the following cases the courts *upheld* an intercollegiate transfer rule.

(a) In *Weiss v. National Collegiate Athletic Ass'n and Eastern Collegiate Athletic Conference,* 563 F. Supp. 192 (E.D. Pa. 1983), a college tennis player who had transferred from Arizona State to the University of Pennsylvania brought suit claiming the one-year-loss-of-eligibility transfer rule violated antitrust law because the practice constituted a group boycott and that the rule did not fulfill its intended purpose of preventing the exploitation of college athletes by coaches attempting to raid other institutions of athletes. Weiss was neither recruited by the University of Pennsylvania nor given an athletic scholarship. The court denied the request for an injunction, finding that Weiss had not offered sufficient evidence that he would be irreparably harmed if the injunction were denied.

(b) In *Williams v. Hamilton,* 497 F. Supp. 641 (D.N.H. 1980), a college student-athlete challenged the National Association of Intercollegiate Athletics (NAIA) transfer rule requiring him to be in residence at his new college for sixteen weeks before becoming eligible for intercollegiate athletics. The court held that the transfer rule was valid and did not deny due process or equal protection guarantees.

3. For further information concerning the increase in the number of student-athletes who are transferring from colleges and the attendant problems involved, see the following law review article: Comment, "Williams v. Hamilton: Constitutional Protection of the Student-Athlete," 8 *J. C. & U. L.* 399 (1982).

High School Transfer Rules

High school athletic associations usually restrict eligibility for student-athlete transfers in one of three ways. Some schools, in an effort to limit abuse, apply blanket restrictions on all students who change schools, regardless of their reason. This approach is often overrestrictive and unduly harsh. Even so, such rules are often upheld by the courts, and those bringing suit have failed to gain monetary or equitable relief. The rules are said to be reasonably related to alleviating recruiting problems, and courts have been reluctant to get involved with private voluntary association matters.

In other high school athletic associations, exceptions are provided to allow students who transfer to schools for reasons unrelated to athletics to have immediate athletic eligibility upon enrollment at the new school. Inherent in any rule which restricts eligibility with specific exceptions is the potential for inconsistency and abuse in the decision-making process. That is why many high school athletic associations simply find it easier to require all new students to meet a residency period (usually one year) before participating in athletics.

Since there are problems with both blanket restrictions and exceptions on a case-by-case basis, some high school athletic associations have taken a third approach, which allows transfer student-athletes to be eligible immediately if certain objective criteria are met. The Massachusetts Interscholastic Athletic Association, for instance, has taken this third approach. To qualify for immediate athletic eligibility, the student-athlete must not have participated on the varsity level of that sport at the previous school, and the transfer must occur prior to the start of practice in the sport. If a student-athlete fails to meet these criteria, he or she must forfeit athletic eligibility for one year.

Interscholastic transfer rules have come under scrutiny when the transfer is due to the movement of school boundaries or religious reasons. Two noteworthy cases in this area are *Alabama High School Athletic Ass'n v. Scaffidi*, 564 So. 2d 910 (Ala. Sup. Ct. 1990), and *Walsh v. Louisiana High School Athletic Ass'n*, 616 F.2d 152 (5th Cir. 1980). In *Alabama High School Athletic Ass'n v. Scaffidi*, John Scaffidi was a ninth grade student at a private school in Mobile, Alabama. During this school year a federal court order in a school desegregation case redrew school lines. Under the new order John's house was in the Davidson public school district rather than the Baker public school district. John and his parents decided he should attend the Davidson public school and he transferred. The Alabama High School Athletic Association (AHSAA) decided that all students attending public schools in the Baker school district would not lose any eligibility because of their transfer to Davidson public schools as a result of the federal court order. John, however, was declared ineligible by the AHSAA because he had voluntary transferred from a private school to the public school. The Alabama Supreme Court reversed the circuit court's decision of granting John injunctive relief. The Supreme Court stated that the federal court order applied exclusively to public school students and John Scaffidi had voluntarily transferred and thus was subject to the transfer rule or sitting out one year before being eligible to compete.

In *Walsh v. Louisiana High School Athletic Ass'n*, the parents of student-athletes brought an action on behalf of their children against the Louisiana High School Athletic Association (LSHAA). The suit alleged that the LSHAA's transfer rule unduly burdened their First Amendment right to the free exercise of their religion and deprived them of their Fourteenth Amendment right of equal protection. Several student-athletes wanted to attend a Lutheran school outside their home district, but enrollment in any high school other than a school in their home district could have resulted in their ineligibility. The appeals court held that the transfer rule was rationally related to the state's valid interest in elementary recruitment of interscholastic athletes.

Many court cases have challenged high school transfer rules on equal protection, freedom of religion, right to travel, and due process grounds. Yet, in most instances, the courts have upheld such rules unless the student-athlete established a violation of a constitutionally protected right, or if fraud, collusion, or arbitrariness was found. Exceptions to the general rule may be found when regulations presume that all transfers are made for improper reasons (see note 3a), and when a student-athlete moves from one state to another by virtue of change in a parent's employment (see note 3b).

States may also adopt a statute or rule preventing implementation of a transfer rule, as Oregon did in response to a suit in which it was determined that transfer rules did not violate any statutory or constitutional restrictions (see note 2c). According to such a statute, the student who moved with his or her parents may not be declared ineligible to participate in athletics as a result of the transfer. On the other hand, the student who moved just to live with friends of the family could be declared ineligible as a result of the transfer. In addition, such a statute prohibits the declaration of ineligibility when the declaration is based solely on the fact that the student-athlete formerly participated in a given sport at another school.

NOTES _____

1. In *Kentucky High School Athletic Ass'n v. Hopkins County Board of Education*, 552 S.W.2d 685 (Ky. Ct. App. 1977), a high school student-athlete sought a permanent injunction to stop the Kentucky High School Athletic Association (KHSAA) from denying him eligibility to participate in interscholastic athletics. The student-athlete's parents were divorced, with legal custody awarded to the mother. After living with his mother and playing varsity sports at the high school where he was enrolled, the student-athlete decided to move to his father's home and enrolled in another school. The court of appeals found that the student-athlete was not compelled to change his residence, but did so because of his own wishes and therefore the transfer was not involuntary. The appeals court also found that the association did not act arbitrarily in applying the transfer rule to the student-athlete. The district court's issuance of an injunction was therefore reversed.

After deciding the essential issue, the court in *Kentucky High School Athletic Ass'n v. Hopkins County Board of Education* discussed at length a particular problem illustrated by this appeal:

> In the court's mind, this case demonstrates why courts are a very poor place in which to settle interscholastic athletic disputes, especially since this type of litigation is most likely to arise at playoff or tournament time. If an injunction or restraining order is granted erroneously, it will be practically impossible to unscramble the tournament results to reflect the ultimate outcome of the case. In almost every instance, the possible benefits flowing from a temporary restraining order or injunction are far outweighed by the potential detriment to the Association, as well as to its member schools who are not before the court. Only in a rare instance should a temporary restraining order or preliminary injunction be granted.

2. The courts *upheld* interscholastic transfer rules in the following cases.
   (a) In *Scott v. Kilpatrick*, 286 Ala. 129, 237 So. 2d 652 (Ala. Sup. Ct. 1970), a student-athlete contended that the transfer rule of the high school athletic association was unconstitutional, since the student-athlete's desire to compete in high school football involved a property right. The denied property right was alleged to be the opportunity for the student-athlete to compete for a college football scholarship. The court found that participation in high school athletics was a privilege and not a property right.
   (b) In *Bruce v. South Carolina High School League*, 258 S.C. 546, 189

S.E.2d 817 (S.C. S. Ct. 1972), student-athletes who transferred voluntarily contended that, since they were not recruited and the transfer rule
was designed to prevent recruiting, it should not apply to them. The
court held that given the prohibitive administrative difficulties of administering such rules, the court should not question the merits or wisdom of their adoption. The court also ruled that the student-athletes had
no constitutionally protected right to participate in athletics, and therefore, the court had no right to prohibit enforcement of the transfer rule.
(c) In *Cooper v. Oregon School Activities Ass'n,* and *Faherty v. Oregon
School Activities Ass'n,* 52 Or. App. 425, 629 P.2d 386 (Or. Ct. App.
1981), student-athletes who transferred from a parochial to a public high
school were barred from competition for a year. The court held that
since the rule did not treat parochial schools differently from other
schools and did not prevent parents from sending their children to parochial schools, the rule did not violate their free exercise of religion.
The burden imposed on the parents and student-athletes was constitutionally permissible and justified by the state's interest in deterring
the recruitment of high school athletes and the lack of an effective,
workable alternative.
(d) In *Albach v. Odle,* 531 F.2d 983 (10th Cir. 1976), a federal appeals
court held that a high school transfer rule was not within federal court
jurisdiction. Athletic governance, supervision, and regulation were
within the discretion of state boards, unless a substantial federal question was involved.
(e) In *Marino v. Waters,* 220 So. 2d 802 (La. Ct. App. 1969), a public
school transfer rule which excluded from athletic competition student-
athletes who transferred between schools because of marriage was upheld because it was applied in a nondiscriminatory manner and did not
deny due process.
(f) In *Dallam v. Cumberland Valley School District,* 391 F. Supp. 358
(M.D. Pa. 1975), the court held that a transfer rule is not in violation of
a recognized right or privilege protected by the Constitution.
(g) In *Chabert v. Louisiana High School Athletic Ass'n,* 323 So. 2d 774
(La. Sup. Ct. 1975), the court upheld the association transfer rule. The
court reasoned that in view of the avowed purpose of the rule—to prevent recruiting abuses—the rule should be upheld. Plaintiff student-
athlete lost one year's eligibility by enrolling in a parochial school located within a public school district other than the one in which he
resided. If he had enrolled in a parochial school within the same public
school district in which he resided, he would have been eligible immediately. The court held that the rule was not arbitrary and did not
abridge religious freedom, even though there was only one parochial
high school in the public high school district.
(h) In *Kulovitz v. Illinois High School Ass'n,* 462 F. Supp. 875 (N.D.
Ill. 1978), a rule mandating a one-year loss of eligibility due to a transfer
was held constitutional when the court rejected the student-athlete's
claim that such a rule deprived him of a college scholarship. The court
held that expectation of an athletic scholarship is not a constitutionally

protected right. In addition, the court held that the right to interstate travel is not implicitly or expressly guaranteed by the Constitution, and therefore, equal protection claims were not applicable to this case.

(i) In *Niles v. University Interscholastic League*, 715 F.2d 1027 (5th Cir. 1983), the University Interscholastic League declared a student-athlete football player ineligible to compete after he moved out of state to live with his mother during the spring term and then returned to his original school in the subsequent fall semester to participate in football. The student-athlete contended that the decision was a denial of freedom of travel and freedom of familial choice. The U.S. Circuit Court of Appeals ruled that there was no constitutional violation on which the student-athlete could base a suit.

(j) In *Kriss v. Brown*, 390 N.E.2d 193 (Ind. Ct. App. 1979), the Indiana Court of Appeals held that a high school basketball player was ineligible for competition after transferring to another school district because there was substantial evidence that a guardianship was created primarily to make him eligible and because the move was a result of undue influence. The court added that a determination of the Indiana High School Athletic Association that a student-athlete's desire for a scholarship was not a sufficient reason to excuse him from operation of the rules was neither arbitrary, capricious, nor unreasonable.

(k) In *re U.S. ex rel. Missouri State High Sch., etc.*, 682 F.2d 147 (8th Cir. 1982), the United States Court of Appeals held that a Missouri State High School Activities Association transfer rule did not violate the federal Constitution. It noted that the minimal impact on interstate travel of the transfer rule did not require strict judicial scrutiny normally applied to classifications that penalize exercise of the right to travel.

(l) In *Crandall v. North Dakota High School Activities Ass'n*, 261 N.W.2d 921 (N.D. Sup. Ct. 1978), a transfer rule which declared a transferring student-athlete ineligible unless the student-athlete's parents had been residents of the new high school district for eighteen weeks was held not arbitrary or unreasonable. The rule was found to be reasonably related to a legitimate purpose, even though no exception was made for student-athletes who transferred solely for academic reasons.

(m) In *Simkins v. South Dakota High School Activities Ass'n*, 434 N.W.2d 367 (S.D. Sup. Ct. 1989), the South Dakota Supreme Court upheld the state association's transfer rule. Plaintiff claimed the rule was overinclusive in that he was denied participation in athletics, even though his reasons for transfer were not related to athletics. The court held that the transfer rule was rationally related to the purpose of discouraging recruiting by schools and switching by student-athletes for athletic purposes.

(n) In *ABC League v. Missouri State High School Activities Ass'n*, 682 F.2d 147 (8th Cir. 1982), the student and the league sought an injunction stopping the Missouri State High School Activities Association (MSHSAA) from enforcing a rule that prevented students who transferred to private schools, which form the ABC league, from participating in athletic competition when their schools played against members of the MSHSAA. The Court of Appeals ruled for the defendants, stating that the transfer rule was not arbitrary and did not violate the equal protection rights of the students.

3. The courts *struck down* transfer rules in the following cases.

(a) In *Sturrup v. Mahon*, 305 N.E.2d 877 (Ind. 1974), the court held that a transfer rule violated equal protection because it was overinclusive. The rule denied participation to a student-athlete who moved for reasons unrelated to athletics. The student-athlete moved to escape detrimental conditions at home and heavy drug use at his former school. The rule as applied was not rationally related to its stated goal.

(b) In *Sullivan v. University Interscholastic League*, 616 S.W.2d 170 (Tex. Sup. Ct. 1981), the court held that a rule providing that a student-athlete who had represented a high school other than his present school in football or basketball was ineligible to participate for one calendar year was found to be overbroad, overinclusive, harsh, and not rationally related to the purpose of deterring high school athletic recruitment. The student-athlete had changed high schools because his father had received a job transfer.

(c) In *Anderson v. Indiana High School Athletic Ass'n*, 669 F. Supp. 719 (S.D. Ind. 1988), the plaintiff sought an injunction against the defendant high school athletic association, its commissioner, and the principal of her high school to prevent the association from declaring her ineligible for participation in interscholastic athletics. In allowing the defendant's motion for summary judgment, the court held that while the association's regulation imposing a 365-day suspension from athletics upon certain transferring students was arbitrary and capricious, the association's conduct was not "state action" as required for the injunction.

Redshirting and Longevity

Redshirting

Redshirting is a term used to describe the practice of extending the playing career of a student-athlete by postponing or passing over a year of interscholastic or intercollegiate participation, while not affecting the student-athlete's maximum allowable time for participating in high school or college athletics. Redshirting rules are designed to allow delaying a student-athlete's eligibility on the basis of legitimate factors such as injury or academic difficulty, while preventing abuse by coaches and student-athletes seeking to gain a competitive advantage through an extension of a student athlete's career. High school athletic associations and conferences, which do not allow redshirting, employ a four-year eligibility rule. Under most high school association rules, a student-athlete has eight consecutive semesters in which to participate in interscholastic competition, beginning with the student-athlete's entry into the ninth grade.

Colleges competing under NCAA governance, on the other hand, are allowed to have their student-athletes compete in four complete seasons of play within five calendar years (in Division I) from the beginning of the semester or quarter in which the student-athlete first registers in a minimum full-time program of studies in a collegiate institution (*1993–94 NCAA Manual*, Bylaw 14.2.1). Any participation during a season in an intercollegiate sport, including a scrimmage with an outside opponent, counts as a season of competition toward the four-year total, as does any season of competition at the junior college level (*1993–94 NCAA Manual*, Bylaw 14.2.4.1). The only exceptions to the five-year limit are for time spent in the armed services, on official and required church missions, or with recognized foreign aid services of the United States government—for example, the Peace Corps (*1993–94 NCAA Manual*, Bylaw 14.2.1.2).

Designed to give student-athletes flexibility in completing their four seasons of eligible collegiate playing time, the five-year rule gives the student-athlete the option to postpone his or her playing career any one of the five years during which he or she has eligibility. The year postponed is commonly referred to as "redshirting." The practice of redshirting may be initiated for a number of reasons, including the following:

1. *Medical reasons.* Includes a serious injury or illness occurring in the off-season or before the start of the season. The student-athlete might consider it advantageous to recover fully from such a problem by postponing for a year the resumption of athletic competition.
2. *Academic reasons.* Includes a student-athlete's becoming ineligible for play because of low grades or wishing to study abroad for a year of college education.
3. *Transfers.* The five-year rule also protects the playing career of first-time transfer students, allowing them the opportunity to switch schools once without eliminating one of their four seasons of playing time. The student-athlete must complete one full year of academic residence at the institution before being eligible to compete (Division I) (*1993–94 NCAA Manual*, Bylaw 14.6.1).
4. *Coaching strategy.* The coach might ask a student-athlete to redshirt a season because the coach wants to use and schedule the player's eligibility to fit the long-term needs and requirements of the team.

In some instances, an athlete may argue for an extra year of eligibility on the grounds of an injury, but this is denied if the athlete participated in more than the allotted number of games allowed in order to receive a medical redshirt. In this case, the athlete loses that year of eligibility.

A case involving this type of situation is *Kupec v. Atlantic Coast Conference*, 399 F. Supp. 1377 (M.D. N.C. 1975), in which a football player sought an injunction from enforcement of the Atlantic Coast Conference (ACC) eligibility rule which allows a medical redshirt if a student-athlete incurs an injury or illness which prevents him or her from participating in more than one football game or more than three contests in other sports. Kupec played during the 1971, 1972, and 1974 seasons. During 1973, Kupec played in two games before being injured and missing the rest of the season. The court found that the ACC was not in error in ruling Kupec ineligible because he participated in two games during the 1973 season, and that participation constituted a loss of eligibility for that year.

In part to curb the allure of redshirting players for coaching reasons (and to reduce expenses), the NCAA membership imposed limitations on financial aid awards, including maximum (allowable) awards (*1993–94 NCAA Manual*, Bylaw 15.5). Reducing the number of scholarships a program can award has the effect of making it less advantageous for coaches to redshirt student-athletes for reasons other than those necessitated by academics or injury. The NCAA membership has also voted to allow certain graduate student-athletes to be eligible for competition if they have playing eligibility remaining (*1993–94 NCAA Manual*, Bylaw 14.1.8.2).

At the interscholastic level, the practice of redshirting is not as commonplace as on the intercollegiate level, primarily because the rules do not allow the flexibility provided at the intercollegiate level. Therefore, the only alternative at the high school level in many states may be keeping back a student-athlete for an extra year before the student-athlete enters high school. This allows a student-athlete another year to develop his or her body and playing skills before entering high school competition. However, the student-athlete who does this must be careful about maximum age restrictions. For instance, the Massachusetts Interscholastic Athletic Association (MIAA) does not allow students aged nineteen and above to compete in high school athletics unless they turn nineteen after September 1 of the school year (*MIAA Rules and Regulations Governing Athletics 1991–93*, Part IV [64]). The MIAA also restricts competition to twelve consecutive athletic seasons (fall, winter, and spring grading semesters for four years) past the eighth grade. However, an MIAA Eligibility Review Board can authorize exceptions to the twelve-consecutive-season rule because of injury or illness.

High school regulations prohibiting the practice of redshirting have been justified on the basis of preventing competition between individuals with vast differences in strength, speed, and experience. Such rules are designed to promote equitable competition and player safety as well as to prevent schools from abusing athletes by holding them back a grade or "redshirting" them to allow them to mature and develop athletically. However, high school rules may make exceptions for students who academically fail a grade, enabling the student to maintain athletic eligibility since the retention was not related to athletics. Therefore, the student-athlete is allowed to compete in the fifth year but cannot compete for more than four seasons.

In *Clay v. Arizona Interscholastic Ass'n*, 779 P.2d 349 (Ariz. Sup. Ct. 1989), a student-athlete dropped out of school after the basketball season of his sophomore year after he became dependent on alcohol, cocaine, and marijuana. After committing a burglary to satisfy drug debts, Clay underwent extensive rehabilitation while incarcerated at Catalina Mountain School. Upon his release, he returned to his previous high school and joined the basketball team. Because Clay had only participated in three seasons of basketball, he sought an exemption to the Arizona Interscholastic Association's eight consecutive semester rule of athletic eligibility so that he might participate in a fourth season. The AIA ruled that Clay's alcohol and drug dependence was not an illness which would qualify him for an exemption. The Supreme Court of Arizona held that the state interscholastic association abused its discretion in determining that the student did not suffer from "disabling illness or injury." A preliminary injunction enabling Clay to qualify for an exemption of the eight consecutive semester rule was granted.

These rules have often been upheld by the courts when the student-athlete's delay in school was unrelated to athletics or even academic failure (see note 2c). A few courts, however, have placed restrictions on the use of such rules when the reasons for the student's ineligibility were clearly unrelated to athletics (see note 3b). Furthermore, at least one court has intervened to overturn an association's refusal to grant a hardship exception, since allowing a particular student to participate in basketball was crucial to his rehabilitation from juvenile delinquency (see note 3a).

NOTES ⎯⎯⎯

1. The NCAA has what it terms a "hardship exception," which is often confused with redshirting. A student-athlete may be granted an additional year of competition by the conference of the Eligibility Committee for reasons of *hardship*, which is defined as an incapacity resulting from an injury or illness that has occurred under all of the following conditions:

(a) The incapacitating injury or illness occurs in one of the four seasons of intercollegiate competition at any two-year or four-year collegiate institution;

(b) The injury or illness occurs prior to the completion of the first half of the traditional playing season in that sport (measured by the number of contests or dates of competition rather than calendar days) and results in incapacity to compete for the remainder of the traditional playing season;

(c) The injury or illness occurs when the student-athlete has not participated in more than two events or 20 percent (whichever number is greater) of the institution's completed events in his or her sport for student-athletes in Divisions I and II or three events or one-third (whichever number is greater) of the institution's completed events in his or her sport for student-athletes in Division III. Only competition (excluding scrimmages and exhibition contests in Divisions I and II, but including such contests in Division III) against outside participants during the traditional playing season, or, if so designated, during the official NCAA championship playing season in that sport (e.g., spring baseball, fall soccer), shall be countable under this limitation in calculating both the number of events in which the student-athlete has participated and the number of completed events during that season in the sport (*1993–94 NCAA Manual*, Bylaw 14.2.5).

2. In the following cases the courts *upheld* redshirt rules.

(a) In *Mitchell v. Louisiana High School Athletic Ass'n*, 430 F.2d 1155 (5th Cir. 1970), a redshirt rule which restricted all incoming high school students who voluntarily repeated eighth grade to six semesters of competition rather than the normal eight semesters was held valid because it was rationally related to a legitimate state interest.

(b) In *David v. Louisiana High School Athletic Ass'n*, 244 So. 2d 292 (La. Ct. App. 1971), a student who repeats a grade for reasons unrelated to athletics may still be validly restricted to six semesters (three years) of athletic eligibility rather than the normal eight semesters (four years).

(c) In *Smith v. Crim*, 240 Ga. 390, 240 S.E.2d 884 (Ga. 1977), a student challenged the application of a rule that counted his absence against his four-year limit of eligibility after he dropped out of school for a year to care for his invalid mother. The court, however, upheld the rule because it was rationally related to the goals of assuring fair competition and preventing redshirting.

(d) In *Alabama High School Athletic Ass'n v. Medders*, 456 So. 2d 284, 20 Educ. L. Rep. 797 (Ala. Sup. Ct. 1984), a student who had successfully completed eighth grade but voluntarily repeated eighth grade was declared ineligible to play football on the high school team during his senior year under the eight-semester rule. The court held that although the rule was susceptible to two interpretations, it had been interpreted in the same way as in the student's case for thirty-five years, and that interpretation fell short of fraud, collusion, or arbitrariness.

(e) In *Maroney v. University Interscholastic League*, 764 F.2d 403, 25 Educ. L. Rep. 765 (5th Cir. 1985), an eighteen-year-old high school football player was declared ineligible under a five-year rule which provided that students may participate in interscholastic athletics for only five years after their first enrollment in eighth grade. The court dismissed the claim for lack of a substantial federal question because the claim had no plausible foundation in law and participation in interscholastic athletics was not an interest protected by the due process clause.

(f) In *Pratt v. New York State Public High School Athletic Ass'n*, 507 N.Y.S.2d 793 (N.Y. Sup. Ct. 1986), the parents of a student brought suit to vacate a high school athletic association's denial to extend student's eligibility to participate in athletics for one additional year. The court ruled that the high school athletic association was correct in holding that the decision of the parents to withdraw the student from athletics for one year to help him mature and focus on academics was not a proper basis for granting him an additional year of eligibility once his original four-year period of eligibility expired.

3. In the following cases the courts *struck down* redshirt rules.

(a) In *Florida High School Activities Ass'n v. Bryant*, 313 So. 2d 57 (Fla. Dist. Ct. App. 1975), an association sought reversal of a final judgment which found a student eligible to play more than four years of inter-scholastic basketball. Affirming the judgment, the court of appeals held that for this student, basketball was vital because it provided the impetus for his general scholastic and social development and rehabilitation from prior problems of juvenile delinquency. The student had presented an adequate case of undue hardship, meriting a waiver of the four-year rule.

(b) In *Lee v. Florida High School Activities Ass'n*, 291 So. 2d 636 (Fla. Dist. Ct. App. 1974), the student stayed out of school for ten months to help alleviate his family's troubled financial situation. Upon returning to school, he sought a waiver of the four-year (successive) rule to par-ticipate in athletics. It was denied by the association. The court found his participation in athletics would have enhanced his chances of being admitted to college and of winning a scholarship. Except for the four-year rule, the student would have been eligible. Therefore, the court found that the denial of a waiver was a violation of due process because no justification had been given for denying eligibility in such extreme circumstances. The rule was held unconstitutional as it applied to the student.

(c) In *Duffley v. New Hampshire Interscholastic Athletic Ass'n*, 446 A.2d 462 (N.H. S. Ct. 1982), the court held that a student-athlete must be given procedural due process when he or she is denied a waiver of the four-year eligibility rule.

Longevity

In 1980, the NCAA enacted a new Division I bylaw designed to ad-dress problems concerning the increasing number of older athletes being recruited, especially in the sports of track and soccer. Some member institutions believed that athletes were entering intercolle-giate athletics after excessive experience in amateur leagues in the United States and more frequently in foreign countries. The "longev-ity" rule was initiated because it was believed that these older, more experienced athletes would place younger and more inexperienced athletes at a disadvantage in competition and when trying to gain scholarship monies.

A leading case in this area, *Butts v. National Collegiate Athletic Ass'n*, 751 F.2d 609 (3d Cir. 1984), shows how the courts view the purpose of the NCAA rule. Butts had played for the Frederick Military Academy basketball team after reaching the age of twenty. When Butts entered LaSalle, a private university, it was feared that under NCAA Bylaw 5-1-(d)-(3) his post–high school experience would be counted against his four years of college eligibility. Bylaw 5-1-(d)-(3) stated that "any participation by a student as an individual or as a representative of any team in organized competition in a sport during each 12-month period after his 20th birthday and prior to his matriculation at a member institution shall count as one year of varsity competition in that sport." When the NCAA indicated that Butts would be ineligible to play basketball during his senior year, he filed suit against the NCAA and LaSalle, seeking declaratory and injunctive relief. Butts alleged constitutional and statutory defects in Bylaw 5-1-(d)-(3). He claimed that the bylaw violated 42 U.S.C. § 6102 (1982), which states, "[N]o person in the United States shall, on the basis of age, be excluded from participation in, be denied the benefits of, or be subjected to discrimination under, any program or activity receiving Federal financial assistance." He also claimed that the bylaw violated 42 U.S.C. § 2000d (1982), which states, "No person in the United States shall, on the grounds of race, color, or national origin, be excluded from participation in, be denied the benefits of, or be subjected to discrimination under any program or activity receiving Federal financial assistance."

The district court concluded that Butts had shown a strong likelihood that the bylaw had a racially disparate impact (affected some races more than others even though unintentionally); however, it also concluded that the NCAA had advanced a legitimate, nondiscriminatory reason for the bylaw:

> [T]he bylaw is designed and intended to promote equality of competition among its members at each level so as to prevent college athletics and access to athletic scholarships from being dominated by more mature, older, more experienced players, and to discourage high school students from delaying their entrance into college in order to develop and mature their athletic skills.

The district court held that Butts had the burden of showing that the bylaw was pretextual or that "some other, less intrusive, rule would accomplish the stated objects of the present rule." The district court found that Butts had not shown a reasonable likelihood of being able to meet this burden, and it upheld the rule and the NCAA's position and denied a preliminary injunction.

The current NCAA bylaw, commonly called the "twentieth birthday rule," states that any student-athlete who participates in any organized athletic competition during any twelve-month period after his or her twentieth birthday and before matriculation at an NCAA member institution shall have that participation counted as one season of varsity competition in that sport (*1993–94 NCAA Manual*, Bylaw 14.2.4.5).

Most state high school athletic associations have rules governing the age of participants. Often students who are nineteen years old or older are prohibited from participating in interscholastic athletics. These rules have been established and promulgated for a number of reasons. First, older and mature student-athletes could constitute a danger to the health and safety of younger competitors. Second, these older student-athletes are also not the typical high school student-athlete, since many college players are nineteen years of age. Third, longevity rules eliminate the possibility of "redshirting" student-athletes through voluntary repetition of grades to gain advantage in competition. Last, the older student-athletes are prevented from precluding from competition the younger athletes who might otherwise be bumped from a squad with a limited size.

The courts have generally ruled that these reasons are legitimate goals for state high school athletic associations. Thus, rules excluding student-athletes from participation in interscholastic competition because of age are commonly upheld since they only need to meet a rational basis test. Challenges based on constitutional claims have been countered by the courts' rulings that athletic participation is not a property right, only a privilege; that regulations do not create a suspect class; and that age restrictions are rationally related to assuring the legitimate state interests of fair competition and student-athlete safety.

In *Nichols v. Farmington Public Schools*, 389 N.W.2d 480 (Mich. App. 1986), the plaintiff had a hearing impairment which caused him to be placed in special education classes. When he was mainstreamed into regular classes the plaintiff was placed in a grade one level below that which his age would normally warrant. During plaintiff's senior year in high school he was declared ineligible to compete in varsity basketball because he had reached his nineteenth birthday prior to September 1 of his senior academic year. The court found that the age rule had a rational basis and thus the plaintiff was declared ineligible and unable to compete.

NOTE _____

1. Additional cases on longevity rules include the following.
   (a) In *Blue v. University Interscholastic League*, 503 F. Supp. 1030 (N.D.

Tex. 1980), a nineteen-year-old high school football player sought to enjoin the University Interscholastic League from enforcing the nineteen-year-old eligibility rule. The U.S. District Court held that the rule did not violate due process or equal protection guarantees of the Constitution.

(b) In *State ex rel. Missouri State High School Activities Ass'n v. Schoenlaub,* 507 S.W.2d 354 (Mo. Sup. Ct. 1974), an age rule was found reasonable, even though no hardship exception existed. The court held that an association's refusal to grant an exception was not an arbitrary or unreasonable act since the fact that this may be a hardship case did not diminish the danger to younger participants if an older athlete was allowed to compete.

(c) In *Howard University v. National Collegiate Athletic Ass'n,* 510 F.2d 213 (D.C. Cir. 1975), the court ruled as invalid the NCAA's "Foreign Student Rule," NCAA Bylaw 4-(1)-(f)-(2), which provides that if an alien participated in organized athletics in a foreign country, after his nineteenth birthday the time spent doing so counts against the athlete's period of collegiate eligibility. Even though the court accepted the rule's purpose, it held that the rule was not closely tailored to achieving its goal because foreigners were penalized for activities that citizens participated in without penalty.

(d) In *Murtaugh v. Nyquist,* 78 Misc. 2d 876, 358 N.Y.S.2d 595 (N.Y. Sup. Ct. 1974), a longevity rule was held not arbitrary or unreasonable when a rational basis for the rule existed. Reasons such as the prevention of delay in the educational process and the prevention of injuries to younger, less developed student-athletes were adequate to support a longevity rule. The court found this to be true even in the case of a rule which denied eligibility to students held back for academic reasons.

(e) In *Spath v. National Collegiate Athletic Ass'n,* 728 F.2d 25 (1st Cir. 1984), the plaintiff was a Canadian citizen who had played after his twentieth birthday for a team in Canada prior to entering college in the United States. The plaintiff filed suit after he was deemed ineligible for his fourth season after playing three years of intercollegiate hockey. The court found that the rule was reasonable and the plaintiff's due process rights had not been violated.

(f) In *Mahan v. Agee,* 652 P.2d 765 (Okl. Sup. Ct. 1982), the plaintiff argued that he had to be held back in the fourth grade because of the learning disability dyslexia and the school did not provide him with the special education and training that he needed. As a result, he was a nineteen-year-old senior who was declared ineligible to participate in interscholastic track events. The Supreme Court held that the school's activities association's nineteen-year-old eligibility rule was reasonable and fair and related to the purposes it was intended to serve.

(g) In *Booth v. University Interscholastic League,* No. A-90-CA-764 (Tex. Dist. Ct. 1990), the court granted a preliminary injunction which stated the University Interscholastic League (UIL) could not prevent the plaintiff from participating in interscholastic athletics because of the UIL nineteen-year-old eligibility rule. The plaintiff had turned nineteen before his senior year but had been held back in school because of a debilitating childhood illness. In its ruling the court cited the Rehabilitation Act, which states that any individual with handicaps who is otherwise qualified may not be excluded from participation in a federally assisted program solely on the basis of the handicap.

(h) In *Tiffany v. The Arizona Interscholastic Ass'n*, Inc., 726 P.2d 231 (Ariz. App. 1986), the plaintiff brought suit requesting that the defendant be enjoined from disqualifying him from interscholastic athletic competition. He requested that the defendant's actions be declared unconstitutional as a denial of due process. The trial court granted a preliminary injunction allowing the plaintiff to play during the 1983–84 school year. A final judgment was awarded in favor of the plaintiff in 1985. On appeal, the court held that the plaintiff did not have a constitutional right to participate in interscholastic athletic competition, and therefore the refusal of the defendant to grant a hardship waiver from the nineteen-year-old eligibility rule was not unconstitutional.

Scholarships and Financial Aid

In intercollegiate competition, financial matters such as scholarships and financial aid are often sources of dispute and litigation regarding an individual's athletic eligibility. In this section, these considerations are examined, as well as the concept of scholarships as contracts, letters of intent, and excess financial aid.

The cardinal rule concerning financial aid to a student-athlete for programs within the NCAA is that the aid *must*, in most cases, be administered by the school. If it is administered by an outside source, such as an alumnus of the university, it jeopardizes intercollegiate eligibility. The school is required to distribute athletic scholarships through its regular financial aid channels. Donors are prohibited from making contributions to finance a scholarship or grant-in-aid for a particular student-athlete, although the individual may contribute funds to finance a scholarship or grant-in-aid for a particular sport. No financial aid from an outside source can be based solely on athletic ability. Student-athletes, however, are permitted to receive aid from persons on whom they are naturally or legally dependent (i.e., family) (*1993–94 NCAA Manual*, Bylaw 15.2.5.1).

Institutions may not pay certain preenrollment fees, application processing fees, room deposits, or dormitory damage deposits, unless such benefits conform to the institutional policy as it applies to other prospective student grantees. The student-athlete, however, can be reimbursed after payment, as part of the institution's regular fees as long as the prospect enrolls and is awarded financial aid covering institutional fees. If such expenses are covered, the student-athlete can be reimbursed after payment, or the fees may be paid by the school as long as these are the policies that apply to the entire student population.

The school financial aid mechanism is required to provide the athletic scholarship recipient with an officially signed document that stipulates the amount, duration, terms, and conditions to which the parties must adhere.

Certain features, among them the following, make athletic scholarships different from other types of financial aid:

1. The amount of aid granted in an athletic scholarship is not dependent on need.
2. The scholarship may be withdrawn for nonacademic reasons.
3. The recipients need no special academic qualifications other than qualifications required for entering freshmen under NCAA Bylaw 14.3.1.
4. The athlete is expected to compete in the sports program that is granting the scholarship.

Thus, some view an athletic scholarship as payment for athletic performance.

The topic of athletic scholarships marks an area of disagreement between the NCAA and the International Olympic Committee (IOC). In its regulations the IOC states that scholarships are permitted but must be "dependent upon the fulfillment of scholastic obligations and not athletic prowess." The NCAA, on the other hand, does permit athletic ability as a determining factor in the awarding of scholarship aid. The IOC also states that "individuals subsidized by governments, educational institutions, or business concerns because of their athletic ability are not amateurs." Consequently, if the athletic scholarship continues to be part of higher educational aid, litigation related to the definition of "amateur" between these athletic organizations may result.

Athletic scholarships are technically renewable each year, but after being granted, they cannot be increased, reduced, or canceled during the period of the award on the basis of the student-athlete's ability or contribution to the team. In addition, athletic scholarships cannot be withdrawn during the period of the award because of an injury to a student-athlete or for any other athletically related reasons (*1993–94 NCAA Manual*, Bylaw 15.3.4.2). NCAA rules do not, however, prohibit all types of scholarship revision or rescission. Scholarship aid may be canceled or reduced during the period of the award for any of the following reasons:

1. The student-athlete's rendering himself/herself ineligible for competition.
2. Fraudulent misrepresentation by the student-athlete on an application, letter of intent, or financial aid agreement.
3. Serious misconduct by the student-athlete warranting substantial disciplinary penalty.
4. Voluntary withdrawal by the student-athlete from a sport for personal reasons, although aid cannot be reduced prior to the conclusion of that semester or quarter provided that withdrawal takes place subsequent to the institution's first competition in that sport (*1993–94 NCAA Manual*, Article 15.3.4.1 [a–d]).

Any gradation or cancellation of aid per 15.3.4.1 is permissible only if such action is taken for proper cause by the regular disciplinary or financial aid authorities of the institution and the student athlete has had an opportunity for a hearing. (*1993–94 NCAA Manual*, Bylaw 15.3.4.1.3)

As indicated by the preceding NCAA rule, the renewal or nonrenewal of a scholarship award is the responsibility of the institution (usually the head coach of the specific sport). When a scholarship is not renewed, care should be taken to provide due process in case the student-athlete chooses to request a hearing or file suit. The nonrenewal letter sent to the student-athlete should include the reasons for the action and a statement informing the athlete that he or she is entitled to a hearing on the nonrenewal of the scholarship. This letter should be kept on file in the athletic director's office and be available upon request to the student-athlete.

In the case of a scholarship revocation, the student-athlete must be given the opportunity for a hearing. Again, according to due process considerations, a written notice of the action, containing specific time and place, should be given to the student-athlete. The hearing, depending on the formality required, may include a presentation of statements from both parties, cross-examination of witnesses, and the right to legal counsel.

Other suggestions that might serve to defuse the potentially explosive situation surrounding a scholarship revocation or nonrenewal include the following:

1. The student-athlete's parents should be contacted by telephone before notifying them or the student-athlete by letter.
2. The student-athlete should be told in person what the impending action is and the reasons for the action before being notified in writing.
3. The student-athlete's high school coach should be contacted in

some cases to be told of the reasoning behind the action before the student-athlete has an opportunity to do so.
4. A meeting should be arranged in some cases with the assistant coach or the person who recruited the student-athlete to ensure that care is used in future recruiting in order to prevent such a situation from recurring.

These steps can serve several useful purposes. First, they allow a coach and athletic administrators the opportunity to assess, and prepare for, the possibility that the student-athlete will use the appeal process. Second, these steps may prevent an appeal by informing all interested parties of the justification for the action. Last, these steps may reduce friction with the high school coach (for recruiting purposes) and with the student-athlete's parents. These parties may be less likely to bring the matter to public attention, and the student-athlete may be less likely to pursue litigation.

Letter of Intent

The national letter of intent was developed to regulate the intense competition surrounding the recruitment of talented student-athletes, commonly referred to as "blue-chippers," to play college athletics. Letters of intent first were developed on the conference level in the late 1940s during a period when intercollegiate athletics first gained national prominence.

The guiding principle behind the letter of intent or preenrollment application is that there is agreement among member institutions that subscribe to the letter of intent to place a time limit on recruiting. Yet, once the recruited student-athlete signs a national letter of intent, there are no further limits on contacting the student-athlete by the signing institution. On a specific date, high school student-athletes can sign a letter of intent, and after the signing no member institution subscribing to the letter will make any effort to recruit the student-athlete. NCAA regulations, however, prohibit the use of press conferences, receptions, and dinners to announce the fact that an athlete has signed a letter of intent. A student who signs the letter, whether or not the athlete actually enrolls at the institution, is not eligible to compete at any other institution subscribing to the letter-of-intent plan for two calendar years of intercollegiate competition with certain exceptions. However, the student-athlete is free to enroll at any member institution to pursue his or her academic interests. The letter of intent also contains some strict regulations; for example, an athlete will lose one year of eligibility if he/she transfers within the first year of attendance at an institution.

A letter of intent becomes invalid if any of the following circumstances exists:

1. The player does not meet minimum academic standards to play as a freshman.
2. The player attends and graduates from a junior college.
3. The player does not enroll and the institution withdraws its scholarship offer the next year.
4. The player serves in the armed forces or a church mission for at least eighteen months.
5. The institution discontinues the sport.

The letter of intent is administered by the Collegiate Commissioners Association (CCA) through the commissioners of allied athletic conferences. Exhibit 5–5 is a CCA national letter of intent form, which also lists policies and interpretations concerning letters of intent. An institution must be an NCAA member to belong to the program, and the national letter of intent applies only to four-year member institutions. Independent institutions that belong to the letter-of-intent program file all necessary paperwork through an allied athletic conference of their choice. The program in its present form was started in 1964 with seven conferences and eight independent institutions joining for a total of sixty-eight schools. In 1982 a women's letter of intent was added. Today, twenty-seven conferences and nearly 300 institutions belong to the program.

The letter of intent is considered a preenrollment application by the CCA, although much of the language creates the possibility that it may be construed as a contract. The men's and women's letters of intent contain identical regulations and procedures; only the membership differs. Both have four signing dates based on sport categories of (1) midyear junior college transfer, (2) football, (3) basketball (basketball has two signing dates—an early signing period in November and the traditional period beginning in April), and (4) all other sports.

Excess Financial Aid

The amount of financial aid a student-athlete may receive from the institution or from outside sources is strictly regulated under NCAA guidelines. Student-athletes may lose their eligibility if their financial aid exceeds a certain limit. Scholarships may not exceed commonly accepted educational expenses (*1993–94 NCAA Manual*, Bylaw 15.01.7). These expenses are limited in Divisions I and II to tuition and fees, room and board, and books. A school or other donor is not allowed to pay expenses exceeding these, and the student-athlete is

Exhibit 5-5
National Letter of Intent

Administered by the Collegiate Commissioners Association (CCA)

Do not sign prior to 8:00 a.m. on the following initial signing dates, or after the final date listed for each sport.

	Sport	Initial Signing Date	Final Signing Date
____	Basketball (Early Period)	November 14, 1990	November 21, 1990
____	Basketball (Late Period)	April 10, 1991	May 15, 1991
____	Football, Midyear JC Transfer	December 12, 1990	January 15, 1991
____	Football (Regular Period)	February 6, 1991	April 1, 1991
____	Women's Volleyball, Field Hockey	February 13, 1991	April 1, 1991
____	Soccer, Water Polo	February 13, 1991	August 1, 1991
____	All Other Sports (Early Period)	November 14, 1990	November 21, 1990
____	All Other Sports (Late Period)	April 10, 1991	August 1, 1991

(Place an "x" on the proper line above.)

Name of student _____
          Type Proper Name, Including Middle Name or Initial

Address _____
          Street Number   City, State, Zip Code

Submission of this NLI has been authorized by:

SIGNED _____   _____   _____
          Director of Athletics   Date Issued to Student   Sport

This is to certify my decision to enroll at _____
                              Name of Institution

IMPORTANT - READ CAREFULLY

It is important to read carefully this entire document before signing it in triplicate. One copy is to be retained by you and two copies are to be returned to the institution, one of which will be filed with the appropriate conference commissioner.

1. **Initial Enrollment In Four-Year Institution.** This NLI is applicable only to prospective student-athletes who will be entering four-year institutions for the first time as fulltime students, except for "4-2-4" college transfers who are graduating from junior college as outlined in paragraph 7-b.

Exhibit 5–5 continued

2. **Basic Penalty.** I understand that if I do not attend the institution named on page 1 for one full academic year, and enroll in another institution participating in the NLI program, I may not represent the latter institution in intercollegiate athletics competition until I have completed two full academic years of residence at the latter institution. Further, I understand that I will forfeit eligibility for two seasons of intercollegiate athletics competition in all sports except as otherwise provided in this Letter. This is in addition to any eligibility expended at the institution at which I initially enrolled.

    a. **Early Signing Period Penalties.** A prospective student-athlete who signs a National Letter of Intent during the early signing period (November 14-21, 1990) will be ineligible for practice and competition in football for a two-year period. A violation of this provision shall result in the loss of two seasons of competition in the sport of football.

3. **Financial Aid Requirement.** I must receive in writing an award or recommendation for athletics financial aid from the institution named on page 1 at the time of my signing for this NLI to be valid. The offer or recommendation shall list the terms and conditions of the award, including the amount and duration of the financial aid. If such recommended financial aid is not approved within the institution's normal time period for awarding financial aid, this NLI shall be invalid.

    a. **Professional Sports Contract.** If I sign a professional sports contract, I will remain bound by the provisions of this NLI even if the institution named on page 1 is prohibited from making athletically related financial aid available to me under NCAA rules.

4. Provisions of Letter Satisfied.

    a. **One-Year Attendance Requirement Met.** The terms of this NLI shall be satisfied if I attend the institution named on page 1 for at least one academic year (i.e., two full regular semesters or three full regular quarters).

    b. **Junior College Graduation.** The terms of this NLI shall be satisfied if I graduate from junior college after signing a NLI while in high school or during my first year in junior college.

5. Letter Becomes Null and Void. This NLI shall be declared null and void if any of the following occurs:

    a. **Admissions and Eligibility Requirements.** This NLI shall be declared null and void if the institution with which I signed notifies me in writing that I have been denied admission, or if I have not, by the institution's opening day of classes in the fall of 1991 (or, for a midyear junior college football signee, the opening day of its classes of the winter or spring term of 1991), met the institution's requirements for admission, its academic requirements for financial aid to athletes, the NCAA requirement for freshman financial aid (NCAA Bylaw 14.3) or the NCAA junior college transfer rule.

        (1) It is presumed that I am eligible for admission and financial aid until information is submitted to the contrary. Thus, it is mandatory for me to provide a transcript of my previous academic record and an application for admission to the institution named on page 1.

        (2) If I am eligible for admission, but the institution named on page 1 defers admission to a subsequent term, this NLI shall be rendered null and void. However, if I defer my admission, the NLI remains binding.

        (3) If I become a nonqualifier (applicable to NCAA Division I or II signees) or a partial qualifier (applicable only to NCAA Division I signees) as per NCAA Bylaw 14.3, this NLI shall be rendered null and void.

        (4) For a Midyear Junior College Football Transfer signee, the NLI remains binding for the following fall term if the prospect was eligible for admission and financial aid, and met the NCAA junior college transfer requirements for competition, for the winter or spring term, but chose to delay his admission.

Exhibit 5–5 continued

b. **One-Year Absence.** This NLI shall be null and void if I have not attended any institution (or attended an institution, including a junior college, that does not participate in the NLI Program) for at least one academic year after signing this NLI, provided my request for athletics financial aid for a subsequent fall term is not approved by the institution with which I signed. To receive this waiver, I must file with the appropriate conference commissioner a statement from the Director of Athletics at the institution named on page 1 that such financial aid will not be available to me for the requested fall term.

c. **Service in U. S. Armed Forces, Church Mission.** This NLI will be null and void if I serve on active duty with the armed forces of the United States or on an official church mission for at least eighteen (18) months.

d. **Discontinued Sport.** This NLI shall be null and void if my sport is discontinued by the institution named on page 1.

e. **Recruiting Rules Violation.** If the institution (or a representative of its athletics interests) named on page 1 violates NCAA or conference rules while recruiting me, as found through the NCAA or conference enforcement process or acknowledged by the institution, this NLI shall be declared null and void. Such declaration shall not take place until all appeals to the NCAA or conference for restoration of eligibility have been concluded.

6. **Mutual Release Agreement.** A release procedure shall be provided in the event the institution and I mutually agree to release each other from any obligations to the NLI. If I receive a formal release, I shall not be eligible for competition at a second institution during my first academic year of residence there and shall lose one season of competition. The form must be approved by me, my parent or legal guardian, and the Director of Athletics of the institution named on page 1. A copy of the release form shall be filed with the conference which processes this NLI.

a. **Authority to Release.** A coach is not authorized to void, cancel or give a release to this NLI.

b. **Extent of Release.** A release from this NLI shall apply to all participating institutions and shall not be conditional or selective by institution.

7. **Only One Valid NLI Permitted.** I understand that I may sign only one valid NLI, except as listed below.

a. **Subsequent Signing Year.** If this NLI is rendered null and void under Item 5, I remain free to enroll in any institution of my choice where I am admissible and shall be permitted to sign another NLI in a subsequent signing year.

b. **Junior College Exception.** If I signed a NLI while in high school or during my first year in junior college, I may sign another NLI in the signing year in which I am scheduled to graduate from junior college. If I graduate, the second NLI shall be binding on me; otherwise, the original NLI I signed shall remain valid.

8. **Recruiting Ban After Signing.** I understand that all participating conferences and institutions are obligated to respect my signing and shall cease to recruit me upon my signing this NLI. I shall notify any recruiter who contacts me that I have signed.

9. **Institutional Signatures Required Prior to Submission.** This NLI must be signed and dated by the Director of Athletics or his/her authorized representative before submission to me and my parents (or legal guardian) for our signatures. This NLI may be mailed prior to the initial signing date. When a NLI is issued prior to the initial signing date, the "date of issuance" shall be considered to be the initial signing date and not the date that the NLI was signed or mailed by the institution.

Exhibit 5–5 continued

10. **Parent/Guardian Signature Required.** My parent or legal guardian is required to sign this NLI regardless of my age or marital status. If I do not have a living parent or a legal guardian, this NLI may be signed by the person who is acting in the capacity of a guardian. An explanation of the circumstances shall accompany this NLI.

11. **Falsification of NLI.** If I falsify any part of this NLI, or if I have knowledge that my parent or guardian falsified any part of this NLI, I understand that I shall forfeit the first two years of my eligibility at any NLI participating institution as outlined in Item 2.

12. **14-Day Signing Deadline.** If my parent or legal guardian and I fail to sign this NLI within 14 days after it has been issued to me, it will be invalid. In that event, another NLI may be issued within the appropriate signing period.

13. **Institutional Filing Deadline.** This NLI must be filed with the appropriate conference by the institution named on page 1 within 21 days after the date of final signature or it will be invalid. In that event, another NLI may be issued within the appropriate signing period.

14. **No Additions or Deletions Allowed to NLI.** No additions or deletions may be made to this NLI or the Mutual Release Agreement.

15. **Appeal Process.** I understand that the NLI Steering Committee has been authorized to issue interpretations, settle disputes and consider petitions for release from the provisions of this NLI where there are extenuating circumstances. I further understand its decision may be appealed to the Collegiate Commissioners Association, whose decision shall be final and binding.

16. **Official Time for Validity.** This NLI shall be considered to be officially signed on the final date of signature by myself or my parent (or guardian). If no time of day is listed, an 11:59 p.m. time is presumed.

17. **Statute of Limitations.** This NLI shall carry a four-year statute of limitations.

18. **Nullification of Other Agreements.** My signature on this NLI nullifies any agreements, oral or otherwise, which would release me from the conditions stated on this NLI.

19. **If Coach Leaves.** I understand that I have signed this NLI with the institution and not for a particular sport or individual. For example, if the coach leaves the institution or the sports program, I remain bound by the provisions of this NLI.

I certify that I have read all terms and conditions in this document, and fully understand, accept and agree to be bound by them. (*All three copies of this NLI must be signed individually.*)

SIGNED_____   _____   _____
                        Student   Date   Time

          _____
                Student's Social Security Number

SIGNED_____   _____   _____
                Parent or Legal Guardian   Date   Time

7/9/90

not allowed to have any other benefits generally unavailable to all members of the student body.

In addition, a team is limited to a certain number of full scholarships or value of the financial aid awards (equivalents) that can be in effect at one time in a given sport (*1993–94 NCAA Manual*, Bylaw 15.5.3). A team may forfeit games or an entire season if the number of full scholarships or equivalents exceeds the limits established by the NCAA for that particular sport. Other sports, referred to as "head-count sports," are limited to a total number of student-athletes who may be receiving any portion of a scholarship (*1993–94 NCAA Manual*, Bylaw 15.5.2). Thus, collegiate athletic administrators and coaches must be aware of the number and levels of financial aid for their student-athletes.

Other situations that might raise the excess financial aid issue involve cases in which a former professional athlete returns to participate in another NCAA sport. Under NCAA rules, a former professional athlete may receive institutional financial aid, but not athletically related aid, provided all the following conditions are met:

1. The student-athlete no longer is involved in professional athletics;
2. The student-athlete is not receiving any remuneration from a professional sports organization, and
3. The student-athlete has no active contractual relationship with any professional athletics team, although the student-athlete may remain bound by an option clause (i.e., a clause in the contract that requires assignment to a particular team if the student-athlete's professional athletics career is resumed). (*1993–94 NCAA Manual*, Bylaw 15.3.1.4.1)

Acceptance of either payment or the promise of money for participation, with few exceptions, in a sport at the collegiate level automatically categorizes the student-athlete as a professional and thus erases his or her amateur status. The student-athlete is also not entitled to be paid or sponsored in sporting events even though he or she may not be representing the collegiate institution (unless by his or her natural or legal guardian). Also, the student-athlete may not receive special treatment because of his or her athletic prowess (e.g., loans on a deferred pay-back basis, automobiles, or special living quarters (*1993–94 NCAA Manual*, Bylaw 12.1.2[m]).

Student-athletes may not participate in any competition for cash or prizes, either for themselves or for a donation on their behalf, unless they are eligible to receive such monies under the NCAA guidelines (*1993–94 NCAA Manual*, Bylaw 12.1.2.[r]). For example, the NCAA does not approve of the granting of scholarship funds in a student-athlete's name if the person was selected as a most valuable player by a national advertiser or sponsor of an event. Further, the NCAA has not approved a student-athlete's participation in the "Superstars" competition or similar staged sporting events. A student-athlete would also jeopardize eligibility if he or she received, for example, a country-club membership as a prize or compensation.

The rule of thumb regarding payment/receipt of expenses provides that an individual, including a student-athlete, may not receive money for expenses that are in excess of the actual and necessary expenses involved in an activity authorized by the NCAA. Examples of prohibited expense payments include travel expenses to a special location for an article on and/or photographs of a student-athlete (unless in conjunction with the receipt of an established/authorized award at that location) and expenses from an agent seeking to represent the student-athlete in the marketing of his or her athletic skills (*1993–94 NCAA Manual*, Bylaw 12.3.1.2). The courts have historically upheld the NCAA rules restricting excess pay or financial aid unless the regulations violate constitutionally protected rights (see notes 1 and 2).

A leading case in the area of excess financial aid is *Wiley v. National Collegiate Athletic Ass'n*, 612 F.2d 473 (10th Cir. 1979), *cert. denied*, 446 U.S. 943 (1980). An action was brought by Wiley, a student-athlete who was declared ineligible to compete because his financial aid exceeded the amount allowed by the NCAA. Wiley had been awarded a full Basic Educational Opportunity Grant (BEOG) in addition to an athletic scholarship. Taken together, these exceeded the financial limitations imposed by the institutions under NCAA regulations and made the student ineligible to compete. Wiley filed suit, and the court applied a rational basis analysis rejecting a strict scrutiny approach because poverty or wealth is not a suspect classification (see Chapter 4). The court refused to prohibit the NCAA from enforcing its regulations on the grounds that "unless clearly defined constitutional principles are at issue, suits by student-athletes against high school athletic associations or NCAA rules do not present a substantial federal question."

Under NCAA rules, a member school may allow a student-athlete a maximum of four complimentary admissions for each contest in his or her particular sport. However, in Division I the student-athlete's guest must sign for the admission and receive no hard tickets (*1993–94 NCAA Manual*, Bylaw 16.2.1.2). Tickets are prohibited (Division I) as a result of previous abuses by student-athletes who received compensation by scalping the tickets.

NOTES

1. A case in which a court *denied* a student-athlete's eligibility on the basis of his receipt of excess financial aid is *Jones v. National Collegiate Athletic*

Ass'n, 392 F. Supp. 295 (D. Mass. 1975). An American ice hockey player brought an action against the NCAA for a preliminary injunction to prohibit the NCAA from declaring him ineligible to compete and from imposing sanctions against his college if they allowed him to play because of excess financial aid he received. Prior to entering college, the student-athlete had been compensated for five years while playing junior hockey in Canada. During one of those three years, he was paid a weekly salary and received a signing bonus. The court denied Jones injunctive relief, finding that the NCAA's rules on financial aid were reasonable.

2. A court *granted* eligibility to a student-athlete in *Buckton v. National Collegiate Athletic Ass'n*, 366 F. Supp. 1158 (D. Mass 1973), despite the NCAA's contention that the student-athlete received excess financial aid. Buckton and other Canadian ice hockey players were denied eligibility because they had received funding from Junior League Hockey teams in Canada rather than from high schools, as is the custom in the United States. The court prohibited the NCAA from enforcing ineligibility because the rule, in effect, discriminated against individuals on the basis of national origin.

Pay/Employment/Marketing/Expenses

Pay

The NCAA defines pay as "the receipt of funds, awards, or benefits not permitted by the governing legislation of the Association for participation in athletics" (*1993–94 NCAA Manual*, Bylaw 12.02.3). Under NCAA regulations, student-athletes may not receive pay without jeopardizing their eligibility. The concept of pay is directly related to the concept of amateurism and should not be confused with employment, which is permitted under NCAA regulations.

The NCAA considers an individual ineligible for competition if he or she has received pay. The following are examples of forms of pay under NCAA regulations (*1993–94 NCAA Manual*, Bylaw 12.1.2):

1. Educational expenses not permitted by the governing legislation of this Association;
2. Any direct or indirect salary, gratuity, or comparable compensation;
3. Any division or split of surplus (bonuses, games receipts, etc.);
4. Excessive or improper expenses, awards, and benefits;
5. Expenses received from an outside amateur sports team or organization in excess of actual and necessary travel, room and board expenses, and apparel and equipment;
6. Actual and necessary expenses or any other form of compensation to participate in athletics competition from a sponsor other than an individual upon whom the athlete is naturally or legally dependent or the nonprofessional organization that is sponsoring the competition;

7. Expenses received by the parents or legal guardians of a participant in athletics competition from a nonprofessional organization sponsoring the competition in excess of actual and necessary travel, room, and board expenses;
8. Payment to individual team members or individual competitors for unspecified or unitemized expenses;
9. Expenses incurred or awards received by an individual that are prohibited by the rules governing an amateur, noncollegiate event;
10. Any payment, including actual and necessary expenses, conditioned on the individual's or team's place finish or performance or given on an incentive basis;
11. Educational expenses provided to an individual by an outside sports team or organization that are based in any degree upon the recipient's athletic ability;
12. Cash, or the equivalent thereof, as an award for participation in competition at any time;
13. Preferential treatment, benefits, or services awarded because of the individual's athletics reputation or skill or pay-back potential as a professional athlete;
14. Receipt of a prize for participation (involving the utilization of athletics ability) in a member institution's promotional activity.

The NCAA rules concerning pay were challenged in *Shelton v. National Collegiate Athletic Ass'n,* 539 F.2d 1197 (9th Cir. 1976). Lonnie Shelton, a student-athlete at the time, was allegedly persuaded to sign a professional contract by the use of fraud and undue influence by an agent. After being declared ineligible by the NCAA, Shelton sued the NCAA, claiming that the rule should not be enforced against him since the misconduct of the agent rendered the contract voidable.

The court, however, after examining the rule, upheld it because the NCAA goals of protecting and promoting amateurism, which were incorporated into the rule, were legitimate. Therefore, although the rule might, when applied in certain situations, produce unreasonable results, it did not violate the U.S. Constitution because the rule was rationally related to its goals.

USA Track & Field was one of the first NGBs to start a trust fund program, TACTRUST, which was implemented in 1982 and allowed track and field athletes to accept corporate sponsorship monies by putting them into a trust fund with the NGB. The athlete could then draw out living and training expenses from these monies while still maintaining amateur eligibility. TACTRUST-authorized withdrawals were permitted for: (1) training, coaching, travel, lodging, equipment, and educational expenses; (2) taxes on athletic earnings; (3) professional fees; and (4) medical and dental bills. The balance of the trust could then be withdrawn by the athlete upon the completion of the athlete's amateur career.

USA Track & Field again took the initiative by proposing and getting passed at a 1993 IAAF Congress meeting the Direct Payment License (see Exhibit 4–1). The Direct Payment License Program replaced the TACTRUST. This program allows appearance fees, prize money, and endorsement fees to go directly from the event or sponsor to the athlete. The athlete needs to obtain a Direct Payment License from USA Track & Field in order to receive this money directly. Any U.S. citizen or resident alien who is eligible for international competition and does not have collegiate eligibility may apply for a Direct Payment License. Sponsorship and endorsement contracts must still be between USA Track & Field and the sponsor, however, the athlete can receive the sponsorship or endorsement fees involved directly from the sponsor. This program is a more liberal approach to the "payment" of amateur athletes shifting from an expense reimbursement program, such as the TACTRUST program, to a payment-oriented program. Other NGBs are following USA Track & Field's model moving away from the trust fund accounts to these payment-oriented types of programs.

NOTES ───

1. The New Jersey Interscholastic Athletic Association has the following policy on pay and employment of high school student-athletes:

Section 2. Amateur-Athlete—An amateur-athlete is one who participates in athletics solely for the physical, mental, social, and educational benefits derived from such participation. The amateur-athlete treats all athletic activities in which he/she participates as an avocational endeavor. One who takes or has taken pay, or has accepted the promise of pay, in any form, for participation in athletics or has directly or indirectly used his/her athletic skill for pay in any form shall not be considered an amateur and will not be eligible for high school interscholastic athletics in the State of New Jersey.

The following are the basic interpretations of the principles involved in the amateur code which may lead to the loss of an athlete's eligibility: . . .

B. Accepting pay or material remuneration for a display of athletic ability.

C. Any student who signs or has ever signed a contract to play professional athletics (whether for a money consideration or not); plays or has ever played on any professional team in any sport; receives or has ever received, directly or indirectly, a salary or any other form of financial assistance from a professional sports organization or any of his/her expenses for reporting to or visiting a professional team is no longer an amateur as defined by this code.

D. A Student-Athlete may participate as an individual, or as a member of a team against professional athletes, or as a member of a team on which there are some professionals who are not currently under contract with a professional team and are not receiving payment for their participation; but he/she may not participate on a professional team. (*1992–93 NJSIAA Handbook,* Article V. Sec. 2 B-D

2. The U.S. Amateur Boxing Federation has the following policy concerning pay and continued eligibility:

219.7 Receiving compensation for athletic services.

(a) Any school or college teacher, including physical education teacher, whose work is educational or who is not paid more than 20 percent of his or her total salary or compensation directly or indirectly for coaching of athletes for competition is eligible to compete as an amateur boxer.

(b) Any person receiving compensation for officiating in boxing renders himself ineligible for further amateur competition in boxing contests sanctioned by the Corporation. The Registration Committee of the local boxing committee in which such person is or was registered is empowered to approve registration or reinstatement of such person whose compensation was or is not in excess of allowable expenses under the Corporation regulations and who has not otherwise rendered himself ineligible.

(c) An athlete who for gain solicits publicly the employment of his athletic services shall automatically disqualify himself from further competition....

(*1991–93 USA Boxing Official Rules*)

Outside Employment

A student-athlete who is receiving a full athletic scholarship from an institution is not eligible for employment during the academic year except during the institution's official vacation periods and then only until the first day of class. The student-athlete is not eligible for employment, because under NCAA Division I and II regulations, any monies or financial assistance which exceeds commonly accepted educational expenses (i.e., tuition and fees, room and board, and required course-related books) is classified as pay and renders the student ineligible to compete in NCAA athletics (*1993–94 NCAA Manual*, Bylaw 15.1).

A student-athlete who is receiving only partial financial assistance from an institution, including a partial athletic scholarship, is allowed to receive employment compensation from work-study on campus or employment off campus, up to the limit established by the institution as the cost of attendance. This employment compensation also counts toward the value of the total financial aid awards in effect at one time for each sport (*1993–94 NCAA Manual*, Bylaw 15.02.3.1).

Student-athletes can hold campus jobs or employment through alumni of the institution, but they must be paid only for the work actually done. Student-athletes who receive remuneration for work not performed are no longer eligible for participation in intercollegiate athletics. Furthermore, student-athletes must be paid at a rate commensurate with the going rate in the particular locality for services of a similar character (*1993–94 NCAA Manual*, Bylaw 12.4.1).

With some exceptions (see note 1), any compensation received over commonly accepted educational expenses as set by the individual institution must be deducted from the financial assistance package received by the student-athlete (including athletic scholarships), or else the student-athlete will be ineligible to compete for the institution.

There are limits to the types of employment a student-athlete can consider to maintain amateur status and collegiate eligibility. For example, student-athletes are not permitted to be employed by their institutions as teachers or coaches in any sport for which they wish to remain eligible and may only be employed by other organizations as teachers or coaches in their particular sport under certain circumstances (see note 2).

Monitoring a student-athlete's employment activities during the academic year can be a difficult endeavor for an athletic administrator. Weekend jobs, jobs with friends, or odd jobs on and off campus, while seemingly insignificant to the casual bystander or to the student-athlete, may in fact be a threat to retaining eligibility to compete in intercollegiate athletics.

NOTES ———————————————————————————————

1. The student-athlete who is preparing to compete or has competed in the Olympic Games is entitled to recover any financial loss occurring as a result of absence from employment that is authorized by the United States Olympic Committee. The period involved in recovering the losses must "immediately" precede and/or include actual Olympic competition (*1993–94 NCAA Manual,* Bylaws 12.4.2.4 and 16.11.2.3).

2. Under NCAA regulations, a student-athlete may serve as a coach or as an instructor for compensation in a physical education class outside the student-athlete's institution in which he or she teaches sports techniques or skills or both, but a student-athlete shall not be so employed if the employment is arranged by the student-athlete's institution or a representative of its athletics interests (*1993–94 NCAA Manual,* Bylaw 12.4.2.1).

Marketing the Athlete with Remaining Eligibility

A particularly challenging task for athletic directors, coaches, and other athletic administrators is to police the contracts between marketing organizations and student-athletes. As an aid to assist athletic administrators, the NCAA regulations in this area are very strict. Basically, the rules state that a student-athlete who contracts (orally or in writing) to be represented by an agent in the marketing of his or her athletic skills or reputation in a particular sport is ineligible in that sport. Contracts with scouting services that distribute personal information for high school prospects to NCAA member institutions are deemed not to be marketing of the student-athlete's ability unless the company receives remuneration for placing the student-athlete in an institution as a recipient of athletically related financial aid (*1993–94 NCAA Manual,* Bylaw 12.3.3.1). A marketing contract that is not limited to a particular sport is considered applicable to all sports. More specifically, once enrolled in an NCAA member institution, student-athletes cannot consent to the use of their name or picture in promoting commercial products. Doing so results in the loss of eligibility. Such activities prior to enrollment in a member institution, however, generally do not violate NCAA rules provided no compensation is received for one's athletic ability (*1993–94 NCAA Manual*, Bylaws 12.5.2.1 and 12.5.2.1.1).

Certain activities in the realm of advertising will not jeopardize the student-athlete's eligibility. For example, athletic equipment manufacturers can donate equipment to member institutions and publicize the school's use of it without endangering any student-athlete's eligibility, provided that no names or pictures of team members are used.

When a student-athlete's name or picture is used for commercial purposes without his or her knowledge or permission, the student-athlete or his or her institution is required to take action to stop the activity in order to preserve eligibility. An individual or team picture can be used in an advertisement only if the primary purpose is to congratulate the athlete or athletes on an achievement. There must be no indication that it is an endorsement of the advertiser's product.

Student-athletes may appear on radio or television because of their athletic abilities or performance but may not receive compensation or endorse a product or service. Student-athletes are allowed, however, to receive legitimate and necessary expenses related to the appearance, provided it occurs within a thirty-mile radius of the institution's main campus. The institution may also provide such expenses for such an appearance in the general locale of an institution's away-from-home competition (*1993–94 NCAA Manual*, Bylaw 12.5.3).

NOTES

1. The NCAA is not alone among athletic organizations that limit their athletes' involvement in marketing in order to remain eligible for competition. The United States Tennis Association (USTA) has a detailed rule for marketing amateur players who wish to retain their eligibility. According to the USTA rule, an amateur is prohibited from the following:

C. Acts That Will Cause the Loss of Amateur Status

(1) *Prize money.* An Amateur may not play for a money prize or any other prohibited prize, nor may he sell a prize or transfer his right to a prize to another person.

(2) *Teaching and coaching.* An Amateur may not teach, coach, instruct or demonstrate the game except as authorized in Standing Order II. D.

(3) *Films and books.* An Amateur may not accept money or gain pecuniary advantage by permitting the taking of tennis action films or television pictures of himself or by permitting the use of his name as the author of any book or article on tennis of which he is not the actual author.

(4) *Services.* An Amateur may not accept money for services which he does not actually render.

(5) *Endorsements.* An Amateur may not permit his name, initials, or likeness to be placed on tennis equipment or apparel of which he is not the actual manufacturer, wholesaler, retailer or other seller. He may not permit the use of his name, initials, or likeness in the advertising or other sales promotion of any goods of any manufacturer, wholesaler, retailer or other seller.

2. The New Jersey Interscholastic Athletic Association has the following policy concerning the marketing of a high school athlete, which, if violated, results in the student-athlete's being declared ineligible:

F. If a Student-Athlete's appearance on radio or television is related in any way to his/her athletic ability or prestige, the athlete may not under any circumstances receive remuneration for his/her appearance. Under such circumstances, however, an athlete may appear on a sponsored radio or television program or have his or her name appear in newsprint ads or in player of the week, month or year advertisement promoting products provided he or she does not endorse or imply endorsement of any commercial product. (*1992–93 NJSIAA Handbook,* Article V. Sec. 2. F)

3. The U.S. Amateur Boxing Federation has the following policy concerning marketing of amateurs and continued eligibility:

219.8 Capitalizing on athletic fame is:

(a) Granting or sanctioning the use of one's name to advertise, recommend or promote the sale of the goods or apparatus of any person, firm, manufacturer or agent, or by accepting compensation, directly or indirectly, for using the goods or apparatus of any person, firm, manufacturer or agent unless it is in accordance with the AIBA eligibility code and approved and handled through an escrow account supervised by the Corporation.

(b) Participating in radio broadcast or telecast either directly or indirectly connected with an advertisement unless special permission in writing is granted by USA Boxing's Registration Committee. The advertising of any current athletic event or any civic, charitable or educational enterprise by an athlete shall not be considered a violation of the foregoing. However, the approval of the LBC Registration Committee must be obtained.

(c) Allowing his photograph to be taken and used for advertising or motion picture purposes (other than a news picture which may or may not be used on sponsored programs) whether or not he has received or is to receive compensation of any kind, directly from the use of such photograph, unless special written permission be granted by USA Boxing's Registration Committee; provided, however, if such photograph or motion picture is in connection with regular gainful employment and not directly related to or identified with any athletic fame, then it is not a violation of this section, but the LBC's Registration Committee should be informed of such occupational intent for record purposes prior to the first acceptance of such employment. The use of an athlete's photograph in so-called loop films or similar films for training or coaching purposes only is not prohibited by this section, provided the athlete receives no compensation of any kind, directly or indirectly for or in connection with its use. However, before such films may be sold or offered for sale, written permission must first be obtained from USA Boxing's Registration Committee.

(d) Writing, lecturing or broadcasting for payment upon any athletic event, competition or sport without the prior permission of USA Boxing's Registration Committee. Such permission may be given only to a person who is genuinely making his main career in one or another of such activities; shall not extend to any amateur boxing contest in which the athlete himself participates as a competitor or otherwise. It shall be effective provided the athlete does not violate any of the other provisions of this Article, and is in accordance with the rules and regulations of the Corporation. (*1991–93 USA Boxing Official Rules*)

Expenses

The issue of expense can provide a unique source of trouble for the amateur athlete. In general, any amateur in a position to receive compensation for expenses, regardless of the source and prior to receiving the expenses, should distinguish between those that are permissible to receive under the athletic governing body, and more importantly, those that are not. This approach is the safest way for the amateur athlete to safeguard eligibility as an amateur and as a member of a particular athletic association (see notes 1–3).

In the NCAA, expenses are limited to those that are actual and necessary. Actual and necessary expenses are defined by the NCAA as amounts received for reasonable travel and meals associated with practice and game competition. The NCAA considers any expenses in excess of "reasonable" to be compensation for athletic ability and warns that receipt of same can lead to a loss of eligibility. Expenses are to be paid on a regular basis and must not be determined by performance or any other incentive plan (see note 2).

NOTES _____

1. The approaches to expense reimbursement vary among other governing bodies, as can be seen in the following examples.

   (a) The United States Soccer Federation (USSF) requires that amateur players may not receive and retain any remuneration for playing, except expenses that have actually been incurred by the player and that are directly related to a game or games (*1992–93 Official Administrative Rule Book*, Rule 3012, Section 3).

   (b) The United States Tennis Association (USTA) allows an amateur reasonable expenses actually incurred in connection with participation in a tournament, match, or exhibition (*1993 Official USTA Yearbook*, Article II, Section E-1).

2. The NCAA allows very minimal expenses, such as actual and necessary travel expenses while representing an institution in competition, a per diem for foreign-tour expenses, and other actual and necessary expenses associated with the student-athlete's participation (*1993–94 NCAA Manual*, Bylaw 16.8).

3. Under NCAA regulations, a student-athlete remains eligible in a sport even though, prior to enrollment in a collegiate institution, he or she may have tried out with a professional athletics team in a sport or received not more than one expense-paid visit from each professional team (or a combine including that team), provided such a visit did not exceed forty-eight hours and any payment or compensation associated with the visit did not exceed

actual and necessary expenses. A self-financed tryout may be for any length of time (*1993–94 NCAA Manual,* Bylaw 12.2.1.1).

4. For further information see the following law review article: Histrop, "The Taxation of Amateur Athlete 'Reserve Funds,' " 33 *Canadian L. J.* 1123.

Professional Contracts

A student-athlete who agrees either orally or in writing to play for a professional sports team loses his or her eligibility to participate in that intercollegiate sport (*1993–94 NCAA Manual,* Bylaw 12.2.5.1). The professed goal of the NCAA is the promotion and preservation of amateurism in college athletics. The reasoning behind these eligibility rules is that if the NCAA is realistically to supervise and regulate amateur status, absolute rules are more administratively efficient than those that require a consideration of mitigating factors. The contract itself does not compromise amateur status; it is the act of signing that is the prohibited first step toward professionalism.

For the purposes of this rule, it does not matter whether the contract is legally enforceable. A student-athlete should be wary of a professional team or agent who attempts to circumvent this rule by first indicating that a contract signed by the student-athlete is only legally binding when also signed by a team representative or agent, and then, second, that the team representative or agent promises not to sign the contract until after the student-athlete's college eligibility has expired. Under NCAA rules, legal enforceability is irrelevant; *merely signing or verbally agreeing to the contract terminates the student-athlete's eligibility.*

The courts have upheld rules similar to the NCAA rules on professionalism that have been promulgated by private voluntary associations as long as they do not violate the constitutional guarantees of due process or equal protection. The courts have said they cannot determine the validity of a rule simply because of its unfortunate effects on particular individuals.

The leading case in the area of intercollegiate athletic eligibility and professional contracts is *Shelton v. National Collegiate Athletic Ass'n,* 539 F.2d 1197 (9th Cir. 1976). This case involved an appeal by the NCAA from a grant of preliminary injunction which suspended enforcement of its amateur eligibility rule. The rule stated that a college student-athlete who signed a professional contract was ineligible to participate in intercollegiate athletics for the sport involved.

Shelton had signed a professional contract with an American Basketball Association (ABA) team and was declared ineligible by Oregon State University. He claimed that the contract was unenforceable because he had been induced to sign it by fraud and undue influence.

He argued that the NCAA rule which made him ineligible, despite the alleged defects of the contract, created an impermissible, over-inclusive classification and was thus violative of equal protection.

The appeals court reversed the decision of the lower court, dissolving the preliminary injunction, and thus rendered Shelton ineligible. The court decided that in the *Shelton* case, the NCAA rule on eligibility was not in violation of equal protection because the rule rationally furthered a legitimate purpose. The NCAA's goal of preserving amateurism in intercollegiate athletics legitimized the rule.

NOTES

1. In the 1971 NCAA Basketball Tournament, Villanova University finished second and received a tournament share of $68,318.84. After the tournament, it was discovered that one of Villanova's players, Howard Porter, had signed a contract with an agent and also a contract with a professional team. The NCAA ruled that Villanova had to forfeit its second-place finish and return its tournament share of the winnings.

2. Student-athletes can compete against professional athletes but not as members of a professional team. If a student-athlete played on a professional team, eligibility is lost only if the student-athlete knew or should have reasonably known he or she was playing on such a team (1993–94 *NCAA Manual*, Bylaws 12.2.3.1 and 12.2.3.2).

A team is professional if it is recognized as a member of an organized professional league or is supported or sponsored by a professional organization or team (e.g., minor league baseball). The team that the student-athlete plays on, however, can have a coach who also coaches a professional team (e.g., U.S. Olympic Hockey Team).

The NCAA specifically permits the student-athlete to compete in tennis or golf with persons competing for money, but the student-athlete cannot receive compensation of any kind (e.g., PGA tournaments or Pro-Am tournaments).

Teams supported by a national amateur sports administrative organization that is using developmental funds received from professional teams or organizations are not considered to be professional (1993–94 *NCAA Manual*, Bylaw 12.6.1.1).

3. The student-athlete does not lose eligibility if, prior to enrollment in college, he or she had a tryout with a professional team, provided it was either at the athlete's own expense or consisted of one visit, expenses paid, lasting no longer than forty-eight hours. The expenses paid must be for actual and necessary expenditures. The student-athlete enrolled in a full-time course of studies cannot try out for a professional team during the academic year, unless his or her eligibility has been exhausted. Part-time student-athletes are permitted to try out during the academic year. It is permissible for the student-athlete to be observed by a professional team representative during normally scheduled practice sessions, provided the activities observed to evaluate the student-athlete are a normal part of the practice session and not conducted specifically for the observer's benefit. Special workouts after the student-athlete's eligibility has expired are permissible and are common practice

among potential professional football players (*1993–94 NCAA Manual*, Bylaw 12.2.1.2).

4. The U.S. Amateur Boxing Federation has the following policies about becoming a professional and continued eligibility:

219.10 Becoming a professional.

(a) When an athlete receives compensation to compete or participate in any professional competition or exhibition in any sport, he shall thereafter be ineligible to compete as an amateur boxer.

(b) An athlete who has entered into a tryout agreement or contract or participates in a professional training camp and who does not receive any compensation, either directly or indirectly, beyond actual expenses not in excess of the sum permitted by Corporation rules may be reinstated by his local boxing committee Registration Committee upon proper application therefore at any time after 30 days from the date of his first appearance with the professional group.

(c) A competitor must not:

(1) Be, or have ever been, a professional athlete in any sport, or have entered into a contract to that end prior to the official closure of the Olympic Games.

(2) Have allowed his person, name, picture or sports performance to be used for advertising, except when AIBA, the U.S. Olympic Committee, or USA Boxing enters into a contract for sponsorship or equipment. All payments must be made to AIBA, the U.S. Olympic Committee, or USA Boxing and not to the athlete.

(3) Carry advertising material on his person or clothing in the Olympic Games, world or continental championships and Games under patronage of the IOC, other than trade marks on technical equipment or clothing as agreed by the IOC with AIBA. (*1991–93 USA Boxing Official Rules*)

5. The NCAA ruled that the University of Alabama must forfeit 90 percent ($253,447) of its net receipts from the 1987 NCAA Division I Basketball Championship as a result of using two student-athletes who agreed to be represented by an agent. Terry Coner and Derrick McKey had contracts with player agents Lloyd Bloom and Norby Walters. In addition to the penalty levied against the university, McKey lost his final year of eligibility; he subsequently entered into the June NBA draft and was selected by the Seattle Supersonics in the first round.

6. The following rule was passed by the NCAA in 1985 to allow athletes to borrow money against a potential professional contract for the purpose of purchasing a professional disability insurance policy. The purpose behind the rule was to provide an incentive for underclass student-athletes to remain in college and complete their eligibility, while protecting their potential income as a professional. Under the rule,

An individual may borrow against his or her future earnings potential from an established, accredited commercial lending institution exclusively for the purpose of purchasing insurance (with no cash surrender value) against a disabling injury or illness that would prevent the individual from pursuing a chosen career, provided a third party (including a member institution's athletics department staff members, its professional sports counseling panel, or representatives of its athletics interests) is not involved in arrangements for securing the loan. The student-athlete shall report all such transactions and shall file copies of the loan documents and insurance policy with the member institution. (*1993–94 NCAA Manual*, Bylaw 12.1.2.1)

7. In *Karmanos v. Baker*, 617 F. Supp. 809 (D.C. Mich. 1985), the plaintiff, his father, and the father's company brought suit against the University of Michigan, its officials, and the NCAA, challenging the legality of a ruling determining that the plaintiff was ineligible to play amateur intercollegiate hockey because he had played, albeit without compensation, for a professional team in Canada. In allowing the defendants' motion for summary judgment, the court held that the defendants did not deprive the plaintiff of any property or liberty interest by ruling that he was ineligible to play intercollegiate hockey.

INDIVIDUAL ELIGIBILITY REQUIREMENTS: OLYMPIC ATHLETES

Olympic-caliber athletes are quite scarce. Not many high schools or colleges are fortunate to have a student-athlete of Olympic quality as a member of their athletic program. Yet, the infrequency of this occurrence does not diminish the significance of being informed as to the relationship between Olympic governing bodies and amateur athletes. High school and college athletic administrators need to know how these governing bodies view the student-athletes and their eligibility, as well as how the courts view the governing bodies and their rules and regulations. The consequences of not understanding these relationships may affect a student-athlete's eligibility for interscholastic, intercollegiate, or Olympic athletic participation.

The Olympic Games have been run by the International Olympic Committee (IOC) since 1896. Located in Lausanne, Switzerland, the IOC controls all aspects of the Olympic operation, including eligibility to participate. The determination and enforcement of eligibility of individual athletes are delegated by the IOC to each participating country's National Olympic Committee (NOC), pursuant to IOC Rule 24, which stipulates that each NOC must enforce the rules and bylaws of the IOC.

The IOC recognizes the United States Olympic Committee (USOC) as the NOC for the United States. (The objects and purposes of the USOC are discussed in Chapter 4.) The USOC is a corporation chartered by Congress in 1950 (Pub. L. No. 81–805 [81st Cong., 2d Sess.], September 21, 1950; 64 Stat. 889). This charter was amended in 1978 by enactment of the Amateur Sports Act of 1978 (Pub. L. 95–606 [95th Cong., 2d Sess.], November 8, 1978; 92 Stat. 3045). One of the principal purposes of the Amateur Sports Act was to establish a means of resolving disputes between American sports organizations seeking to become the national governing body (NGB) for a sport as recognized by the USOC. The congressional intent was to shield amateur athletes from being harmed by these disputes.

The IOC also designates one international federation for each Olympic sport. The international federations are responsible for setting worldwide eligibility rules for each of their sports. The reason for this rule is that each sport has different circumstances, and the federations are in the best position to interpret amateur status. However, this has also had a confusing effect since there exists no uniformity among the different international federations as to what constitutes an amateur and an eligible athlete (for example, the international federation for basketball, FIBA, allows professional athletes to participate in the Olympic Games, while AINBA, the baseball international federation, does not). Furthermore, as was discussed at the beginning of Chapter 4, the lack of consistency among Olympic governing bodies and domestic governing associations (such as the NCAA) as to the definition and interpretation of an amateur athlete further complicates the issue.

The USOC has specific regulations that govern the eligibility of athletes who try out for a spot on the U.S. Olympic team. Any athlete who is a U.S. citizen at the time the team is selected and is eligible under the international rules of the IOC for selection for membership on the U.S. Olympic or Pan American team is allowed to try out directly or indirectly under the authority of any national governing body. All members qualifying for the Olympic or Pan American teams must pass the USOC medical examination before being accepted on the team, as well as sign an oath attesting to their eligibility (*USOC Constitution*, Chapter XL, XLI). Although the specific eligibility rules and regulations are determined by the IOC and the International Federations for each sport, the USOC does play an important role in serving to reconcile differences in eligibility requirements that exist among the various amateur and Olympic governing bodies.

A leading case on amateur athletic eligibility involved Renaldo Nehemiah, who attempted to participate in amateur track and field events after he had signed a contract to play professional football with the San Francisco 49ers of the National Football League. Despite Nehemiah's arguments that his profession of football did not give him a competitive advantage in track and field, and despite numerous appeals to the USOC, TAC and IAAF, and the judicial system, Nehemiah was unsuccessful in obtaining eligibility. Nehemiah finally had his amateur eligibility reinstated after he retired from football.

This situation is indicative of the way the courts have viewed the authority of Olympic governing bodies. Generally, the courts have deferred to the powers of these governing bodies and to their authority when dealing with controversies involving Olympic athletes (see note 1).

NOTES _____

1. The following cases deal with the relationship between the athlete and Olympic governing bodies.

(a) In *Martin v. International Olympic Committee*, 740 F.2d 670 (9th Cir. 1984), women runners and runners' organizations filed suit against the IOC and sought to require the IOC to institute 5,000-meter and 10,000-meter track events for women at the 1984 Summer Olympic Games in Los Angeles. The U.S. District Court (C.D. Cal.) denied a request for a preliminary injunction, and the U.S. Court of Appeals affirmed this decision. The two courts reasoned that the IOC's Rule 32, which was the process for adding new events, was not arbitrary. In addition, it was reasoned that state law should not be applied to alter the structure of Olympic events.

(b) In *Michels v. United States Olympic Committee*, 741 F.2d 155 (7th Cir. 1984), a federal appeals court found that an individual athlete had no private cause of action (a reason or means by which to challenge the USOC's authority) against the USOC, under the Amateur Sports Act of 1978. In reversing a district court decision, the appeals court noted that the Supreme Court has emphasized congressional intent in ruling on cause of action suits and that "the legislative history of the Act clearly reveals that Congress intended not to create a private cause of action under the Act."

(c) In *DeFrantz v. United States Olympic Committee*, 492 F. Supp. 1181 (D.D.C. 1980), *aff'd without opinion*, 701 F.2d 221 (D.C. Cir. 1980), the district court held that the Amateur Sports Act of 1978 did not establish a cause of action for twenty-five designated Olympic athletes who sought to prohibit the USOC from barring these American athletes from participating in the 1980 Olympic Games in Moscow because of an American boycott of the event. The court concluded "that the USOC not only had the authority to decide not to send an American team to the summer Olympics, but also . . . could do so for reasons not directly related to sports considerations."

(d) In *Oldfield v. The Athletics Congress*, 779 F.2d 505 (9th Cir. 1985), the plaintiff was a world-class athlete in the shot put competition. After the 1972 Olympics, Oldfield signed a professional performance contract with the International Track Association and competed for them for four years. He then wished to reestablish his standing as an amateur and participate in the 1980 Olympic Trials. The Athletics Congress sought to exclude Oldfield from these trials on the grounds that he was ineligible to participate in the Olympics because he had been registered as a professional. The Court of Appeals affirmed the district court awarding of a summary judgment for the defendants based on the fact that the plaintiff had no private right of action under the Amateur Sports Act.

(e) In *Behagen v. Amateur Basketball Association of the United States*, 884 F.2d 524 (10th Cir. 1989), the plaintiff, after having played professional basketball in the NBA, wanted to return to Italy and play for an amateur team he had played for the year before. The Amateur Basketball

Association had informed the International Basketball Association (FIBA) of Behagen's professional playing career; thus FIBA declared Behagen ineligible to compete for the Italian team. Behagen filed suit, claiming a violation of antitrust laws, through the formation of a boycott preventing him from competing in Italy, and a violation of his due process rights. The Court of Appeals held for the defendants, stating that the actions of the amateur basketball association, in refusing to reinstate plaintiff's amateur status, were exempt from the federal antitrust laws, and that the association was a private rather than a governmental actor and thus not subject to due process requirements.

2. For a fuller discussion on the roles of the different governing bodies in the Olympic Games organization, see *United States v. Wrestling Division of the AAU*, 545 F. Supp. 1053 (N.D. Ohio 1982), in which the federal court prohibited one national sports organization (the Amateur Athletic Union) from exercising any of the national governing body (NGB) powers and ordered it to sever all ties with the international governing body for that sport pursuant to the Amateur Sports Act of 1978, since the United States Olympic Committee had selected a competing national sports organization to be the NGB. The USOC was also ordered to terminate its recognition of the AAU group as the NGB and the United States representative to the international federation. See also the companion case of *United States Wrestling Federation v. United States Olympic Committee*, Civil Action No. 13460-78, Superior Court, District of Columbia (1978), in which the USWF successfully filed suit against the USOC to compel it to recognize it as its NGB and Group A member for amateur Olympic wrestling.

3. Another major purpose of the Amateur Sports Act of 1978 was to protect the USOC's ability to raise financial revenues to field American Olympic teams which receive no direct government funding. In *United States Olympic Committee v. Intelicense Corporation*, 737 F.2d 263 (2nd Cir. 1984), the United States Court of Appeals affirmed the judgment of the district court, which ruled that pursuant to the Amateur Sports Act the USOC's consent is a prerequisite to marketing the Olympic Symbol (five interlocking rings) in the United States.

4. While Olympic symbols and trademarks may be protected by the Olympic Symbol protection provision of the Amateur Sports Act of 1978, they may also be protected under the Federal Trademark Act (Lanham Act) (15 U.S.C. § 114) or individual state trademark statutes. The following cases deal with trademark law:

(a) In *Stop the Olympic Prison v. United States Olympic Committee*, 489 F. Supp. 1112 (S.D.N.Y. 1980), an organization opposed to the postgames' use of the Lake Placid Olympic Village for a prison filed suit to protect its First Amendment right to print and distribute a "Stop the Olympic Prison" poster. The court held that the poster did not violate the Amateur Sports Act of 1978, since the poster was not used "for the purpose of trade," or "to induce the sale of any goods or services, or to promote any theatrical exhibition, athletic performance, or competition"; nor was the poster sold or distributed commercially.

(b) In *San Francisco Arts & Athletics, Inc. v. United States Olympic*

Committee, 483 U.S. 522 (1987), the Supreme Court ruled for the defendants and prevented the plaintiffs from using the term *Olympics* in the special event called the Gay Olympics. The court stated that the word *Olympics* may not be used if the ultimate purpose is trade or promotion of some other exhibition.

INDIVIDUAL RIGHTS OF THE STUDENT-ATHLETE

The authority of an athletic association or a coach to make rules regarding a student-athlete's private life is limited. As in the case of the rules of athletic associations and conferences, the rules of coaches and their institutions are held to the same standards of reasonableness and rational relationship to a legitimate purpose. Generally, the purpose of the rules created and enforced must be reasonably related to the pursuit of the sport itself. Without this relationship, the rule may be deemed impermissible on constitutional grounds by the courts. Even when a rational relationship to the association's or coach's purpose does exist, a rule may be impermissible if it infringes on the constitutional rights of life, liberty, and property, which are protected by due process guarantees (see Chapter 4). In other words, rules have been struck down when they deal with areas that might be loosely termed "personal choice" or "preference." In these cases, the courts have to weigh the personal freedoms of the student-athlete against the institution's or coach's regulation of athletics in the name of character building, fair play, and esprit de corps.

The personal freedoms of student-athletes that may be infringed upon by an institution's or coach's athletic rules concern the areas of freedom of expression, hair length, high school marriages, alcohol and drugs, and handicaps. In these individual rights areas, the student-athlete often challenges the alleged deprivatory athletic rule by challenging the authority of the coach to enforce such a regulation. To understand these challenges, the basis for a coach's authority should be examined.

Basically, the authority of a coach is limited to the coach's position within the institution's administration. The first possible legal basis for a coach's authority within the institution is in loco parentis. This means that the relationship between the coach or institution and the student-athlete is analogous to that of a parent and child. Although this principle would seem to give a coach virtual free reign in disciplining players, its validity, particularly as it applies to college student-athletes, many of whom are adults in the eyes of the law, has been held suspect.

The second basis for a coach's authority is the proposition that a contract exist between the student-athlete and the institution. This notion rests on the belief that education, at least at the college level, is a privilege, not a right, and that the student has access to that privilege through compliance with an institution's regulations. This doctrine has also lost favor as a college education has come to be viewed as a benefit and vital interest. However, the doctrine applies to the scholarship student-athlete if the scholarship is deemed to be a contract. Yet, if the student-athlete is perceived to be primarily a student rather than an athlete, this contract analysis will most likely be invalid.

The final possibility that might be used to justify a coach's legal authority is the argument that the coach is part of an administrative agency of the state. Educational institutions and athletic associations have in many cases been found to be engaged in state action. By extension, the authority of a department in a school or college is granted and limited by the rationale for and functions of that department. Consequently, a coach's source of authority is derived from having a role as part of the "faculty" of an athletic department, and that authority is limited to those activities of the student-athletes which are related to the purposes and goals of the department.

Freedom of Expression

Freedom-of-expression issues can often be raised in the amateur athletics context whenever the athlete's or coach's right to speak is impeded. Student-athletes, coaches, and others have brought claims alleging that they lost their scholarships or jobs for engaging in expressive activity or speech that was unacceptable to their superiors. If the superior who is limiting the right to free expression is found to be engaged in state action, the student-athlete or coach may have grounds to sue the superior, using a constitutional law argument.

Freedom of expression is the cornerstone of the Bill of Rights and individual liberty under the U.S. Constitution. Freedom of expression is a broad term describing the right to free "speech." The term *freedom of expression* is used rather than *free speech* because certain nonverbal types of communication are protected under the First Amendment—for example, carrying a sign with a written message. Therefore, while the First Amendment uses the words "Congress shall make no law . . . abridging the freedom of *speech*" (emphasis added), a broader range of expression is protected.

For purposes of analysis, expression must be broken down into two component parts. First is the element of conduct or physical action, which is a necessary part of communicating a message. For example, a demonstration requires conduct by the demonstrators which can be either peaceful or violent. Violence is a noncommunicative aspect of speech that may be regulated since there are compelling government interests in peace and order involved. Second is the component that is the actual message or content of speech. This communicative aspect of speech, consisting of the thoughts or informational content of the communication, may be regulated if there is a clear and present danger of imminent lawless action—for example, shouting "fire" in a crowded theater.

Some student-athletes, coaches, and athletic personnel have been successful in challenging their termination of scholarships or suspension from their jobs on freedom-of-expression grounds (see notes 1c and d). In analyzing these situations, the courts have examined whether or not the individual's communication involved a public or private concern. Only if the matter is of public concern have the courts been inclined to protect the individual's right to express his or her views, but this protection is not absolute. The courts must balance the speaker's interest against the other party's interest. As a general rule, the courts have favored the speaker's interest over that of the other party. However, the courts also seem ready to allow restrictions on student-athletes' speech by deciding that players' comments (as opposed to those of students and coaches) are not matters of public concern. However, student-athletes have, on occasion, received some protection of First Amendment rights.

A leading case in the area of freedom of expression concerning athletics is *Williams v. Eaton,* 468 F.2d 1079 (10th Cir. 1972). The plaintiffs were a group of fourteen black football players for the University of Wyoming. In October 1969, prior to a game against Brigham Young University, the players had approached head football coach Lloyd Eaton wearing black armbands to protest the beliefs of the Mormon Church. Coach Eaton dismissed them from the team for violating team discipline rules, which did not allow protests or demonstrations by players.

The players brought suit in district court, but their action was dismissed. The players appealed, and the court of appeals affirmed the decision in part, while sending the case back for further proceedings. Upon the second hearing, the lower court held that the players had been given a full and impartial hearing before their suspensions and that their procedural due process rights had not been violated. The court reasoned that coach Eaton's rule had not been arbitrary or capricious, and up until their action, there had been no complaint concerning the rule by any of the players. In addition, Coach Eaton, acting as an agent of the University of Wyoming and the state of Wyoming, was compelled not to allow the players, under the guise of the First Amendment rights of freedom of speech, to undertake a planned protest demonstration against the religious beliefs of the Mormon Church and Brigham Young University. The demonstration would have taken place in a tax-supported facility, and had the officials of the university acceded to the demands of the players, such action would have been violative of Brigham Young University's First Amendment rights. The court held that the rights of the players to freedom of speech as guaranteed by the First Amendment could not be held paramount to the rights of others under the same amendment to practice their religion free from state-supported protest or demonstration.

NOTE _____

1. The following cases also involve freedom of expression.

(a) In *Menora v. Illinois High School Ass'n*, 527 F. Supp. 637 (N.D. Ill. 1981), *vacated*, 683 F.2d 1030 (7th Cir. 1982), *cert. denied*, 103 S. Ct. 801 (1983), a federal district court ruled that an Illinois High School Association (IHSA) rule that prohibited student-athletes from wearing soft barrettes or yarmulkes during basketball games violated their right to freedom of religion guaranteed by the First Amendment. Orthodox Jewish students are required by their religion to keep their head covered at all times except when unconscious, immersed in water, or in imminent danger of loss of life.

On appeal to the court of appeals, the decision was overturned. The court ruled that the students have no constitutional right to wear yarmulkes during the basketball games. It noted that Jewish religious law requires that the head only be covered, not specifically by yarmulkes.

(b) In *Marcum v. Dahl*, 658 F.2d 731 (10th Cir. 1981), two members of the University of Oklahoma women's basketball team had their scholarships terminated after publicly voicing opposition to the renewal of the head coach's contract. The student-athletes contended that such an action, in response to their comments, was a violation of their right to free speech under the First Amendment. The court disagreed and held that the termination of the scholarships was a result of months of dissension, and not solely a product of the players' comments.

(c) In *Pickering v. Board of Education of Township High School District 205, Will County, Illinois*, 225 N.E.2d 1, *rev'd*, 391 U.S. 563 (1968), the Supreme Court held that the dismissal of a high school teacher for openly criticizing the school board's allocation of funds between athletics and education was unconstitutional on First Amendment grounds. The court reasoned that because Pickering's criticism was a matter of public concern necessary for the free and open debate which was vital to the decision-making process, it was constitutionally protected.

(d) In *Tinker v. Des Moines Independent School District*, 383 F.2d 988, *rev'd*, 393 U.S. 503 (1969), student-athletes wearing politically motivated black armbands in a public high school were found to have a constitutionally protected right of expression. The court recognized that the student-athletes' First Amendment rights do not stop at the schoolhouse or gym door, and that constitutional protection extends to forms of expression other than speech or written communication.

(e) In *Hall v. Ford*, 856 F.2d 255 (D.C. Cir. 1988), the plaintiff, a former athletic director, brought action against University of the District of Columbia officials, challenging his termination. The lower court dismissed the action, and the plaintiff appealed. The court of appeals held that the plaintiff occupied a position from which he could be discharged for the exercise of the right to free speech with respect to matters of university policy, and that he did not have a property interest in continued employment. Further, the plaintiff's discharge did not violate his liberty interest, and a memorandum written by another university officer was not libelous per se.

Hair Length

Rules regulating the length of hair for males have often led to lawsuits, especially on the high school level. Most litigation of athletic rules on constitutional grounds is based on allegations of infringement of a property interest; however, hair-length regulations have also been attacked for being infringements of personal liberty interests. Since these cases present constitutional issues, they are usually litigated in federal court. Some of the circuit courts have recognized a student-athlete's right to govern his or her personal appearance while attending public school, while other circuit courts see this liberty interest as too insubstantial to create the threshold controversy (a substantial enough federal question) necessary to attain federal jurisdiction. The courts that have upheld such rules have determined that if a rule regulating either hair length or facial hair is reasonable and advances an educational purpose, the court should defer to the judgment of school officials.

One case in which the courts viewed hair length as a constitutional issue was *Dunham v. Pulsifer*, 312 F. Supp. 411 (D. Vt. 1970). In *Dunham*, a high school student-athlete requested an injunction to stop Brattleboro (Vermont) High School from enforcing an athletic grooming code. Alleged violations of this code had resulted in dismissal of the student-athlete from the school tennis team. The court noted that although one of the asserted justifications for these rules was the promotion of closer team work and discipline, the tennis team had no such problems prior to the enactment of the dress code. "Outside of uniformity in appearance, no evidence was introduced as to advantages to be derived from the athletic code except the question of discipline for the sake of discipline."

The court reasoned that

> there are few individual characteristics more basic to one's personality and image than the manner in which one wears his hair.... The cut of one's hair style is more fundamental to personal appearance than the

type of clothing he wears. Garments can be changed at will whereas hair, once it is cut, has to remain constant for substantial periods of time. Hair style has been shadowed with political, philosophical and ideological overtones.

The court held that the enforcement of the hair code could not be upheld.

An opposite result was reached in *Zeller v. Donegal School Dist.*, 517 F.2d 600 (3rd Cir. 1975). In *Zeller*, a high school soccer player sought an injunction and monetary damages under the Civil Rights Act for his dismissal from the soccer team for noncompliance with the athletic grooming code regulating length of hair. The district court dismissed the complaint, and the student-athlete appealed. The court of appeals held that the nature of constitutional interpretation calls for the making of a value judgment in areas that are regulated by the state and in which federal courts should not intrude, and it stated: "We hold that plaintiff's contention does not rise to the dignity of a protectible constitutional interest." The court based its decision on the concept that a student-athlete's liberties and freedoms are not absolute and stated: "We determine today that the Federal System is ill-equipped to make value judgments on hair-lengths in terms of the Constitution." The court concluded that student-athlete hair-length cases should be left to school regulation, "where the wisdom and experience of school authorities must be deemed superior and preferable to the federal judiciary's."

NOTES ───

1. The following cases also hold that hair-length rules *warrant* constitutional review.

    (a) In *Dostert v. Berthold Public School Dist. No. 54*, 391 F. Supp. 876 (D.N.Dak. 1975), a student-athlete sought relief from a rule regulating hair length. The court held that the school's interest in requiring uniformity was such a compelling part of its public educational mission as to outweigh the constitutionally protected interest of student-athletes in regard to personal appearance.

    (b) In *Long v. Zopp*, 476 F.2d 180 (4th Cir. 1973), a high school football player challenged the denial of his football letter because of his hair length. The court held unlawful the coach's regulation of the hair length of his players after the end of the football season. The holding was based on the analysis that it was reasonable for a coach to require short hair during a playing season for health and safety reasons. However, it was not reasonable to deny an athletic award or an invitation to a sports banquet when a student-athlete allowed his hair to grow long after the season.

2. For another case in which a court found hair length as *insubstantial* for constitutional review, see *Davenport v. Randolph County Bd. of Education*,

730 F.2d 1395 (11th Cir. 1984). High school football student-athletes sought an injunction from the school board's decision that refused them participation in athletics unless they complied with the coach's "clean shaven" policy for football and basketball team members. The district court denied the injunction. The court of appeals affirmed the decision.

3. The following rules are from the dress code of the United States of America Amateur Boxing Federation:

> (1) Hair shall be cut in such a manner as not to interfere with his vision....
>
> (2) Contestants shall not wear contact lenses or eye glasses during competition.
>
> (3) The use of any type of grease/Vaseline or other substance on the body is prohibited....
>
> (4) All contestants must be clean, present a tidy appearance, and be clean-shaven, with no goatee or beard. A thin-line mustache on the lip to the edge of the outer corners of the mouth is authorized.... (*1991–93 USA Boxing Official Rules*, Technical Rules, Article III).

High School Marriages

Rules that relate to high school marriages have also resulted in much litigation. In the early cases, rules excluding married student-athletes from interscholastic competition were upheld under the rational relationship standard (i.e., they bore a reasonable relationship to a legitimate objective). These rules were considered reasonable because it was believed that exclusion of married students from athletics was necessary to (1) protect unmarried students from bad influences, (2) encourage students to finish high school before marriage, and (3) give married students the opportunity for more time together to develop their family life. Such exclusion from athletic participation was not considered an infringement of a constitutionally protected right since participation in extracurricular activities was not viewed as a property right but as a privilege.

More recently, however, such rules have been struck down as invalid and improper invasions of the right to marital property (i.e., the right to be married). Marriage rules have also been overturned on the basis of a property interest. In other words, the courts have reasoned that such rules deprive student-athletes of a chance for a college scholarship and therefore infringe upon their property interest of obtaining a free education (see note 2 for the *Moran* case). Most courts have refused to accept the property interest found by *Moran*, noting that such an interest is too speculative at the high school level to merit legal protection as a property interest. However, the courts now typically hold that marital classifications are unconstitutional on equal protection grounds.

A leading case in the area of interscholastic athletic eligibility and marriage is *Estay v. La Fourche Parish School Board*, 230 So. 2d 443 (La. Ct. App. 1969). In *Estay*, a married high school student challenged his exclusion from all extracurricular participation based on a school board regulation. The court of appeals held that the school board had the authority to adopt the regulation. It found the regulation to be reasonable—not arbitrary or capricious—and concluded that enforcement of the rule did not deprive the student of any constitutional rights. The court reasoned that there was a rational relationship between the rule and its stated objective of promoting completion of high school education prior to marriage. The court held that the classification rested on a sound and reasonable basis and that the criteria were applied uniformly and impartially.

A different result was reached in *Davis v. Meek*, 344 F. Supp. 298 (N.D. Ohio 1972). In *Davis*, a married high school baseball player challenged his exclusion from the baseball team and all other extracurricular activities. The student-athlete was aware of the rule prior to his marriage and had been informed that it would be enforced against him.

The court held that extracurricular activities are an integral part of the total educational program. Therefore, the rule denied the student-athlete an opportunity which, under Ohio statutes, he had a right to receive. The issue therefore was whether the school board could enforce against the student-athlete "a rule which will in effect punish him by depriving him of a part of his education." The court held that the school board should be precluded from imposing this restriction because the deterrent effect the rule had was minimal.

NOTES ───

1. Rules barring married student-athletes from participation in extracurricular activities were held constitutionally *permissible* in the following cases.

(a) In *Kissick v. Garland Independent School District*, 330 S.W.2d 708 (Tex. Civ. App. 1959), the court of appeals held that the "resolution of school district providing that married students or previously married students should be restricted wholly to classroom work and barring them from participation in athletics or other exhibitions and prohibiting them from holding class offices or other positions of honor other than academic honor—was not arbitrary, capricious, discriminatory, or unreasonable."

(b) In *Starkey v. Board of Education*, 14 Utah 2d 227, 381 P.2d 718 (Utah Sup. Ct. 1963), the Utah Supreme Court held that the "rule against participation in extracurricular activities by married students bore a reasonable relationship to the problem of 'dropouts' and did not constitute an abuse of school board's discretion."

(c) In *Cochrane v. Board of Education of Mesick Consol. School Dist.*, 360 Mich. 390, 103 N.W.2d 569 (Mich. Sup. Ct. 1960), proceedings were held to compel the board of education to allow married high school student-athletes to play football during the 1958 school year. On appeal, the Michigan Supreme Court affirmed the circuit court's decision and held that the "school district did not violate the statute guaranteeing to all students an equal right to public educational facilities by excluding married high school students from participation in co-curricular activities."

(d) In *State ex. rel. Baker v. Stevenson*, 270 Ohio Ap. 223, 189 N.E.2d 181 (Ohio C.P. 1962), the Court of Common Pleas held that the rule precluding married high school students from participating in extracurricular activities was valid.

(e) In *Board of Directors of the Independent School District of Waterloo v. Green*, 259 Iowa 260, 147 N.W.2d 854 (Iowa Sup. Ct. 1967), an action was brought to prohibit enforcement of a school board rule barring participation in extracurricular activities by married pupils. Upon appeal, the Iowa Supreme Court held that engaging in extracurricular activities, such as basketball, is a privilege which may be enjoyed only in accordance with standards set by the school district. The student did not have a "right" to participate; therefore, no violation of the equal protection clause occurred.

2. Rules barring married students from participation in extracurricular activities were held *impermissible* in the absence of a finding of a rational basis for the rules in *Moran v. School District #7, Yellowstone County*, 350 F. Supp. 1180 (D. Mont. 1972). A marriage rule was held invalid because it deprived a student-athlete of the chance for a college scholarship without showing any evidence that the presence of married students would result in a reasonable likelihood of imposing moral pollution on unmarried students. No rational basis on which to restrict participation existed.

3. Rules barring married students from participation in extracurricular activities were held *impermissible* as violative of equal protection standards in the following cases.

(a) In *Hollon v. Mathis Independent School District*, 358 F. Supp. 1269 (S.D. Tex. 1973), the plaintiff sought a temporary injunction against the enforcement of a school district policy which prohibited married students from engaging in interscholastic league activities. The district court held that the policy was unconstitutional. The court decided "there was no justifiable relationship between the marriage of high school athletes and the overall drop-out problem; nor does it appear that preventing a good athlete, although married, from continuing to play ... would in any way deter marriages or otherwise enhance the dropout problem."

(b) In *Romans v. Crenshaw*, 354 F. Supp. 868 (S.D. Tex. 1971), a student challenged a public high school regulation which prohibited any married or previously married student from participating in any extracurricular activity. The district court held that "absent factual support for considerations urged by the school district to sustain its regulation, the same denied equal protection"; the court granted judgment for the student.

(c) In *Indiana High School v. Raike*, 164 Ind. App. 169, 329 N.E.2d 66 (Ind. Ct. App. 1975), a public high school rule which prohibited married students from participating in any extracurricular activities was held invalid. The court found the rule both overinclusive because it barred married students of good moral character and underinclusive because it did not bar unmarried students of questionable character. The court concluded, therefore, that the rule did not have a substantial relationship to its goal, and thus it violated the equal protection clause.

(d) In *Beeson v. Kiowa County School District*, 567 P.2d 801 (Colo. Ct. App. 1977), the court of appeals ruled for the plaintiff, stating that the student had a fundamental right to marry and reasons given by the school board regarding a policy which prohibited married students from participating in extracurricular activities did not establish compelling state interest to justify violation of the plaintiff's fundamental right.

(e) In *Bell v. Lone Oak Independent School District*, 507 S.W.2d 636 (Tex. Ct. App. 1974), the court of appeals reversed a district court decision and held that a regulation prohibiting married high school students from participating in extracurricular activities was a violation of the equal protection clause of the Fourteenth Amendment.

Alcohol and Drugs

Another set of rules frequently contested in the courts are those regulating the use and abuse of alcohol and other drugs. While acknowledging that a school and its coaches have a strong interest in the prevention of drug abuse (see Chapter 12), the courts have consistently required that any rule established in this area be closely related to the problem of drug abuse.

Many high schools and high school athletic associations also have "good conduct" rules. These rules can be general in nature, as opposed to specific alcohol and drug rules. These good conduct rules usually require the student-athlete to adhere to some standard of conduct. If these rules, like the alcohol and drug rules, extend to a legitimate sports-related purpose, they will most likely be upheld. If, on the other hand, the rule is too broad and attempts to regulate an athlete's conduct during the off-season or conduct not related to athletics, it will probably be struck down by the courts on due process or equal protection grounds.

A leading case in the area of alcohol and drug rules is *Bunger v. Iowa High School Athletic Ass'n*, 197 N.W.2d 555 (Iowa Sup. Ct. 1972). In *Bunger,* a high school football player brought an action to determine the validity of a good conduct rule promulgated by the state high school athletic association which prohibited the use of alcoholic beverages. In 1971, Bunger and three other minors were riding in a car which contained a case of beer. Bunger knew that the beer was in the car. The car was stopped by a state police officer, who discovered the beer and issued summonses to all four occupants for possession of beer as minors. Bunger reported the incident to his school, whereupon he was declared ineligible for athletics.

The Supreme Court of Iowa decided that based on state law, the ability to enact eligibility rules rested with the State Board of Education, not with the Iowa High School Athletic Association. Therefore, the rule was invalid because the association had no authority to make an eligibility determination. The court noted in this case that

> we are inclined to think the nexus between the school and a situation like the present one is simply too tenuous: outside of football season, beyond the school year, no illegal or even improper use of beer. We cannot find a "direct" effect upon the school here. School authorities in reaching out to control beer in cases like this are entering the sphere of the civil authorities. We hold that the rule in question is invalid as beyond the permissible scope of school rules.

NOTE ───

1. Alcohol rules have been *upheld* by the courts in the following cases.
    (a) In *Braesch v. DePasquale*, 200 Neb. 726, 265 N.W.2d 842 (Neb. Sup. Ct. 1978), the court ruled that a drinking rule served a legitimate rational interest and directly affected the discipline of a student-athlete. Such a rule was held not an arbitrary and unreasonable means to attain the legitimate end of deterrence of alcohol use.
    (b) In *French v. Cornwell*, 202 Neb. 569, 276 N.W.2d 216 (Neb. Sup. Ct. 1979), a rule that allowed a school official to suspend a student for six weeks after the student admitted being arrested for intoxication was constitutionally acceptable. The court found that suspension of the student was not in violation of due process, as the student had been aware of the rule providing for the suspension and admitted his own violation of the rule.
    (c) In *Palmer v. Merluzzi*, 868 F.2d 90 (3rd Cir. 1989), the plaintiff, a high school student, brought an action challenging on equal protection and due process grounds the imposition of a sixty-day suspension, in addition to a ten-day academic suspension, imposed against him for smoking marijuana and consuming beer at a school radio station. The district court entered summary judgment in favor of the superintendent, school district and board of education. The plaintiff appealed. The court of appeals held that the plaintiff had received all process that was due to him, and that the disciplinary action taken by the school was rationally related to a valid state interest in preserving a drug-free environment.
    (d) In *Clements v. Board of Education of Decatur Public School District No. 61*, 478 N.E.2d 1209 (Ill. Ct. App. 1985), a student brought action against school officials seeking injunctive relief against enforcement of a suspension she received as a result of her presence at a party where minors were drinking beer. The appellate court upheld the district court decision and stated that the school principal, by giving the student the suspension, did not act arbitrarily or capriciously, justifying intervention by the court, and injunctive relief against the suspension was denied.

Disabled Student-Athletes

A policy at some high schools and colleges is to prohibit students with physical disabilities from participating in athletic activities. The rationale for this policy, which is often based on American Medical Association (AMA) guidelines that recommend barring students with particular disabilities from participating in certain interscholastic and intercollegiate sports, is that the physical requirements of certain athletic activities pose a significant degree of physical risk to the student-athlete's safety. School boards have established such rules in the face of higher injury risks to decrease the likelihood of the injured athlete suing the school for failure to take reasonable care.

The extent of a school's or association's ability to restrict the availability of athletic participation/opportunities for disabled students is a problem which can lead to litigation by the disabled individual seeking athletic participation. It is crucial, then, for athletic administrators to analyze the legal aspects of the legislation that applies to disabled students in high schools and colleges in order to facilitate the making of legally sound decisions and policies.

The courts often refer to three pieces of legislation concerning physically disabled student-athletes: the Education for All Handicapped Children Act; Section 504 of the Rehabilitation Act; and the Amateur Sports Act. These pieces of legislation serve three basic functions in the sports context:

1. To ensure equal opportunities in athletic programs for participants of all ages.
2. To search out methods of organizing sports activities in order to integrate the disabled into regular programs.
3. To provide special athletic opportunities for those unable to participate in regular athletic programs.

The Education for All Handicapped Children Act guarantees a free public education for every disabled child up to twenty-one years of age (twenty-five in some states), including physical education, extracurricular activities, and interscholastic sports. The Rehabilitation Act goes even further in prohibiting discrimination against any disabled individual in any program or activity sponsored by a recipient of federal funds. The Amateur Sports Act names the USOC as the coordinator of amateur athletics in the United States (see Chapter 4). This responsibility for coordinating athletic activities includes sports participation for individuals with disabilities. The USOC fulfills this responsibility through the Committee on Sports for the Disabled. The committee helps disabled athletes by breaking down unnecessary barriers to competition and supporting organizations that provide sports experiences for the blind, deaf, amputee, paralyzed, cerebral palsied, or mentally retarded. Other amateur athletic associations have also been involved in lawsuits as a result of their treatment of disabled athletes.

Although these legislative mandates have led to significant gains for disabled student-athletes, certain problems continue to frustrate individuals with disabilities. Two types of problems commonly arise with disabled student-athletes. First, many organizations have rules that prohibit the participation of athletes who have either lost the use of a sense (e.g., hearing or sight), or of a limb or organs. Such rules are justified on the theory that a loss of this sort creates a hazard for the affected student as well as for the other participants in that sport.

Second, a problem stems from a rule common to most high school athletic associations—limiting participation to students *nineteen years old or under*. Disabled students often do not finish high school until after age nineteen, because of the extended period they may need to complete a basic education. Age limit rules are designed to prevent the deliberate retention of students to increase a varsity team's advantage and to equalize physical size and maturity of participants in contact sports such as football. These rules, however, may seem unreasonable when applied to older disabled students, especially in some sports like wrestling, where competitors are matched by weight.

When a student-athlete brings suit involving one of these problem areas, the courts have generally deferred to the judgment of the educational institution in upholding the disqualification from athletic participation unless the school's actions were arbitrary or capricious (see note 1). The courts, however, have begun to recognize the rights of disabled student-athletes on the grounds of Section 504 of the Rehabilitation Act. The Rehabilitation Act argument was used in *Booth v. University Interscholastic League*, Civil No. A-90-CA-764 (Tex. Dist. Ct. 1990), in which the plaintiff argued a debilitating illness he suffered as a child, which set him back a year in school, should be considered a handicap and provide him with an exemption to the University Interscholastic League's (UIL) nineteen-year-old eligibility rule. The court found that the UIL was inflexible in its enforcement of the nineteen-year-old eligibility rule and should have taken into consideration the illness suffered by the plaintiff. The court stated this illness should have been looked upon as a handicap and therefore granted an injunction to the plaintiff against the enforcement of the UIL's nineteen-year-old eligibility rule.

Basically, the lawmakers and the courts want to assure that extracurricular activities are made available to disabled students on an equal basis with nondisabled students. Yet, as the *Rettig v. Kent City*

School District, 539 F. Supp. 768 (N.D. Ohio 1981), case showed, even though equal opportunities must be provided, extracurricular activities generally may be separate or different from those offered to nondisabled students, provided disabled students are allowed to participate with nondisabled students to the maximum extent appropriate to the needs of the disabled person.

A leading case concerning the rights of disabled athletes is *New York Roadrunners Club v. State Division of Human Rights*, 432 N.E.2d 780 (N.Y. Ct. App. 1982). This case involved an appeal by the State Division of Human Rights to allow disabled persons in wheelchairs to participate in the New York City Marathon. The court of appeals reasoned that, "The record reveals no proof to support the Human Rights Division's finding that the respondents, New York Roadrunners Club...discriminated against the disabled..., in organizing and promoting the 1978 New York City Marathon, when it required participants to use only their feet, and not wheelchairs, skateboards, bicycles or other extraneous aids."

The court noted that the Roadrunners Club had decided to run a "traditional" marathon footrace. The club could have laid down guidelines for other competitors, but as a private, though not-for-profit organization, it was under no legal compulsion to do so. The court further stated:

> In making these observations, we, of course, are not insensitive to the role athletic activity may play in the rehabilitation and in the lives of the handicapped. Nor do we depart from our appreciation of the special concerns committed to the expertise of the Human Rights Division to combat discrimination in the first instance.... Rather, we simply hold that, under the circumstances, the acts on which the complaint here was posited did not constitute an unlawful discriminatory practice.

Another piece of legislation, the Americans with Disabilities Act, contains two provisions which affect sports and recreation facility management at the high school, college, and professional sport organization levels (see note 6). This act, passed in 1991, prohibits discrimination in public accommodations by requiring facilities to be accessible to disabled patrons and employees, as well as prohibiting discrimination against any employee on the basis of a disability. In particular, compliance with this piece of legislation requires sports facilities to provide auxiliary aids and services and remove architectural barriers when readily achievable (for example, providing curb cuts, installing ramps and rest room grab bars, repositioning shelves, and installing wider doors). While employing disabled personnel, an employer must attempt reasonably to accommodate the individual's functional limitation unless doing so would cause an undue hardship. Accepted reasonable accommodations include restructuring jobs through modified work schedules, providing qualified interpreters, modifying equipment or devices, and modifying entrance exams, training materials, and policies. When interviewing an applicant, an employer may not question a disabled individual about the specific nature of his or her disability or require medical records during the screening process. The employer may, however, prepare a list of essential functions required to perform a job adequately and ask an applicant whether he or she is able to perform the tasks.

NOTES _____

1. In the following cases the courts *upheld* athletic eligibility rules that barred participation by disabled students.

(a) In *Colombo v. Sewanhaka Central High School Dist.*, 383 N.Y.S.2d 518 (N.Y. Sup. Ct. 1976), a high school student-athlete sought to overturn a school district directive which prevented him from participating in football, lacrosse, and soccer. In granting judgment for the school district, the court held that the decision of the school district to follow the advice of its medical director and American Medical Association guidelines and prohibit the fifteen-year-old student with a hearing deficiency from athletic participation was justified. The court believed there existed a risk of further injury to the ear in which there was only partial hearing and to which additional injury could result in irreversible and permanent damage. The court held that the prohibition was neither arbitrary nor capricious.

(b) In *Cavallaro by Cavallaro v. Ambach*, 575 F. Supp. 171 (W.D.N.Y. 1983), a disabled nineteen-year-old wrestler, with neurological problems that kept him behind in school, sought a waiver of the interscholastic conference's age rule so that he could participate on the wrestling team in his senior year. After denial of the waiver by the conference's eligibility committee, the plaintiff sought judicial relief, arguing that the age rule violated his rights under the Fourteenth Amendment's equal protection clause. In denying his claim, the court noted that the student was not physically impaired and had physical skills superior to most other nineteen-year-old students. It noted that the age rule was designed to prevent more mature students with experience from injuring younger student-athletes in contact sports such as wrestling.

(c) In *Spitaleri v. Nyquist*, 345 N.Y.S.2d 878 (N.Y. Sup. Ct. 1973), the court upheld the disqualification of a disabled student-athlete, which was based on the American Medical Association recommendation that students with the loss of one paired organ be barred from contact sports.

(d) In *Kampmeier v. Nyquist*, 553 F.2d 296 (2nd Cir. 1977), two visually impaired junior high school students brought a claim against school officials for refusing to allow them to participate in contact sports. The court permitted enforcement of the rule because testimony indicated a high risk to their good eyes. The students ultimately won their suit under state law in the state courts, even though their federal suit was unsuccessful.

(e) In *Mahan v. Agee*, 652 P.2d 765 (Okla. Sup. Ct. 1982), the plaintiff was barred from participating in interscholastic track events because he had turned nineteen years of age. The plaintiff's parents sought injunctive relief against the Oklahoma Secondary Schools Activities Association because the plaintiff was forced to repeat a grade because he suffered from a learning disability, dyslexia. The district court granted the injunction, but the Supreme Court overruled this decision, stating that the nineteen-year-old eligibility rule was reasonable and fair and related to purposes it was intended to serve, and there was nothing presented to the trial court which showed that the association had acted unreasonably, arbitrarily, or capriciously in enforcing this eligibility rule against the plaintiff.

2. In the following cases the courts *struck down* eligibility rules that barred participation by disabled students.

(a) In *Wright v. Columbia University*, 520 F. Supp. 789 (E.D. Pa. 1981), a college student with vision in only one eye sued his university to play football. The district court granted a temporary restraining order forbidding the university from barring the student's participation in intercollegiate football. The court concluded that federal funds do not need to go specifically to the football program to bring it under Section 504 of the Rehabilitation Act. The court also noted that the college student was an adult who decided for himself whether to assume the risks of participation.

(b) In *Poole v. South Plainfield Board of Education*, 490 F. Supp. 948 (D.N.J. 1980), the court ruled that a student who had been born with one kidney should be permitted to participate in interscholastic wrestling. The court stated that the school board's only duty was to advise the family of the risks (the student and his parents signed a waiver releasing the school from liability) and not to impose its own view of proper action on the family.

(c) In *Grube v. Bethlehem Area School District*, 550 F. Supp. 418 (E.D. Pa. 1982), the court ruled that under Section 504 of the Rehabilitation Act, a high school student with one kidney should be allowed to play football if his parents signed a waiver.

(d) In *Southeastern Community College v. Davis*, 442 U.S. 397 (1979), the Supreme Court stated that Section 504 requires only that a person who is able to meet all of a program's requirements in spite of his handicap not be excluded from participation in a federally funded program "solely by reason of his handicap." This indicates that the "mere possession of a handicap is not a permissible ground for assuming an inability to function in a particular context."

(e) In *Crocker v. Tennessee Secondary School Athletic Ass'n*, 735 F. Supp. 753 (Tenn. Dist. Ct. 1990), the plaintiff sought an injunction against the high school athletic association to prevent them from enforcing their transfer rule, which would prohibit him from participation for a year after transferring from a private religious school to a public school. The plaintiff was a certified disabled student under the Education of the Handicapped Act. The court ruled that the athletic association discriminated against the plaintiff by failing to grant him a special hardship exception to the transfer rule. The court thus issued the preliminary injunction against the athletic association.

3. See Education of the Handicapped Act, Pub. L. 91–230, Title VI Sec. 601, Apr. 13, 1970, 84 Stat. 175, amended Pub. L. 94–142 Sec. 3-(a), Nov. 29, 1975, 89 Stat. 774, which guarantees that all disabled children be provided a free public education and emphasizes special education and special services designed to meet their unique needs. It also guarantees the rights of these children and parents or guardians and, while assisting states with the provision of such an educational experience, is designed to aid in the assessment of these programs.

4. Section 504 of the Rehabilitation Act of 1973 (Pub. L. 93–112), 29 U.S.C. 706, provides that "no otherwise qualified handicapped individual . . . shall, solely by reason of his handicap, be excluded from the participation in, be denied the benefits of, or be subjected to discrimination under any program or activity receiving federal financial assistance." The regulation defines and forbids acts of discrimination against qualified disabled persons in employment and in the operation of programs and activities receiving assistance from the Department of Health, Education and Welfare (HEW). The regulation, which applies to all recipients of federal assistance from HEW, is intended to ensure that their federally assisted programs and activities are operated without discrimination on the basis of handicap. Since HEW was split, the Department of Education now has jurisdiction.

5. The New Jersey State Interscholastic Athletic Association (NJSIAA) has a policy for the use of a prosthesis (artificial limb) in high school athletic competition. The policy states

> Federal legislation which prohibits discrimination on the basis of a physical handicap, makes it difficult for state associations to defend the former blanket prohibition of the use of a prosthesis when challenged in the courts. Many sports now have revised rules to provide "*artificial* limbs which, in *the judgment of the rules administering officials, are no more dangerous players than the corresponding human limb and do not place an opponent at a disadvantage may be permitted*" (italics in original). The NJSIAA endorses this policy so long as it is not in conflict with the rules for a specific sport.

The NJSIAA procedure for approving the wearing of a prosthesis by a student-athlete will be as follows:

> 1. The member school must notify the NJSIAA and arrange for a meeting to determine the legality of the prosthesis; present at this meeting must be the school physician, athletic director, principal, coach, a representative from NJSIAA, and the player who must be fully equipped as he/she will be when competing; an athletic trainer or other school representative may also be present.
> 2. The criteria recommended as a guideline to follow in determining the legality and suitability of wearing a prosthesis in a contact sport are:
>   (a) The prosthesis should be approved at any Juvenile Amputee Clinic listed in the National Directory. Kessler Institute for Rehabilitation, 1199 Pleas-

ant Valley Way, West Orange, New Jersey 07052 is the only New Jersey clinic listed.

(b) Prosthesis should be properly padded.

(c) Signed approval by an orthopedic surgeon or physician associated with a juvenile amputee clinic and the school physician. Such approval must be presented to the officials before each game for the officials final inspection and approval of proper padding.

NOTE: Member schools are given this advance notice to allay the possibility of having a prosthesis declared illegal, thereby preventing the player from participating until approval is granted (*1992–93 NJSIAA Handbook*).

6. For more information on the Americans with Disabilities Act and the specific requirements set forth in the legislation see, Americans with Disabilities Act, Public Law 101–336, or *The ADA Handbook,* published by the Equal Employment Opportunities Commission and the U.S. Department of Justice.

DISCIPLINE OF INDIVIDUAL STUDENT-ATHLETES

The topic of discipline of individual student-athletes is particularly important and sensitive, since the act of disciplining a student-athlete is usually the precipitating event in the decision-making process of an athlete contemplating litigation as a recourse to redress a potential wrong. The high school or college that fails to carry out a disciplinary action against a student-athlete, as prescribed by an association or conference, risks forfeiting games, championships, returning television and championship money, and possibly losing its membership in the governing athletic organization. This unpleasant alternative often places the high school or college athletic administrator in a precarious position between the student-athlete and the athletic association or conference.

The NCAA has very specific sanctions for rule violations by individual student-athletes. The association has set strict and often complicated guidelines that student-athletes *must* follow if they are to maintain eligibility for NCAA competition. Deviation from these guidelines may result in sanctions against the student-athlete, and/or the team, and/or the institution's athletic program (see discussion on NCAA enforcement program in Chapter 4).

The major and most common disciplinary action that the NCAA takes against individual student-athletes is to declare them ineligible for intercollegiate competition for a stated period of time. This action is enforced by the individual institution as part of its responsibilities of membership in the NCAA (*1993–94 NCAA Manual*, Bylaw 14.13.1). A recent trend has been for the NCAA to take disciplinary action against the student-athletes and coaches in conjunction with imposing sanctions imposed on the institution.

At the high school level, student-athletes must also conform to rules and regulations as established by the institution, its athletic conference, and its athletic association. High school athletic associations often possess fairly broad disciplinary powers. For example, in the Massachusetts Interscholastic Athletic Association the Board of Directors is authorized to "warn, censure, place on probation or suspend any player, team, coach, game official, school official or school which violates any MIAA rule regarding interscholastic athletics" (*Rules and Regulations Governing Athletics MIAA 1991–93*, Part VI 86.1). High school athletic associations may also prohibit a school from participating in league championships or association-sponsored tournaments.

Other amateur athletic organizations, like national governing bodies, discipline athletes in a very similar manner. For example, the U.S. Amateur Boxing Federation states:

> 230.1 As hereinafter set forth, the Corporation and LBC may censure, suspend for a definite or indefinite period of time with or without terms of probation, or expel any member defined under Article III, Membership, of the Corporation or LBC, who has violated any of the rules/regulations of the Corporation or LBC, or who aids, abets or encourages another to violate any of the rules/regulations of the Corporation or LBC, or who has acted in a manner which brings disrepute upon the Corporation, LBC or upon the sport of amateur boxing. The Corporation may also conduct hearings on any matter affecting the Corporation as the national governing body for amateur boxing. (*1991–93 USA Boxing Official Rules*, sec. 230.1)

Probably the best way to illustrate the issues involved in disciplining athletes is to examine a few situations that have been litigated in the courts. In the case of the *Regents of University of Minnesota v. National Collegiate Athletic Ass'n*, 422 F. Supp. 1158 (D. Minn. 1976), the University of Minnesota challenged an NCAA sanction that placed all the university's athletic teams on indefinite probation when the university refused to declare three student-athletes ineligible for intercollegiate competition.

The student-athletes had admitted to the NCAA violations, which consisted of (1) selling complimentary season tickets; (2) accepting an invitation to stay at a cabin with all meals, lodging, and entertainment provided by a member of the booster club; and (3) using a private WATS line to place long-distance calls. After admitting to the violations, the student-athletes donated the proceeds from the sale of the tickets to charity and satisfied a university committee's punishment. However, the NCAA was not satisfied. The NCAA's proposed penalty for Minnesota's not declaring the student-athletes ineligible to compete was a three-year probation and a two-year ban on postseason play and televised games. Additionally, the NCAA imposed a two-year restriction on the granting of athletic scholarships for basketball.

Minnesota, as was its policy for all students, had afforded the three basketball players a hearing before the Campus Committee on Student Behaviors and the Assembly Committee on Intercollegiate Athletics. These committees voted not to declare the student-athletes ineligible, despite the findings of the NCAA's Committee on Infractions.

The court found that participation in intercollegiate athletics was a substantial property right entitled to due process guarantees. Thus, a student-athlete had to be afforded due process rights before the right to an education or any substantial element of it could be adversely affected. The court reasoned that the NCAA's action transgressed on the university's legal duty to afford due process hearings to student-athletes and to abide by the results of the hearing.

The court concluded that the plaintiffs had demonstrated a strong possibility of success on the merits and that Minnesota would be irreparably harmed if a preliminary injunction was not issued while the NCAA would not be harmed. The court directed the NCAA to lift the probation and temporarily prohibited the NCAA from imposing further sanctions pending a hearing on the merits of the case.

The NCAA appealed the district court's decision in *Regents of University of Minnesota v. National Collegiate Athletic Ass'n*, 560 F.2d 352 (8th Cir. 1977). The appeals court dissolved the preliminary injunction. The court noted that, as a voluntary member of the NCAA, the university agreed to adhere to association rules, including Constitution 4-2-(a), which required Minnesota "[t]o administer their athletic programs in accordance with the Constitution, the Bylaws and other legislation of the Association."

In another discipline case, *Southern Methodist University v. Smith*, 515 S.W.2d 63 (Tex. Civ. App. 1974), Southern Methodist University (SMU) appealed an order which temporarily prohibited the university from declaring student-athlete Smith ineligible to play intercollegiate football. Smith admitted to receiving financial aid in excess of the amounts allowed under NCAA rules. The NCAA ordered SMU to declare Smith ineligible. Faced with the possibility of losing its membership in the NCAA, SMU notified Smith of his ineligibility after it protested the sanction and exhausted its appeals to the NCAA Council.

Smith filed suit and claimed that he was deprived of due process when he was denied notice and a hearing concerning his violations and penalty. The court held that Smith had no legal right to a hearing by SMU. In addition, he failed to establish a constitutional or contractual right to claim a benefit or privilege from playing football. The court reasoned that the NCAA had sole authority over the eligibility decision, and its rules did not provide for the type of hearing that Smith had requested. An SMU hearing on the issues could not have declared him eligible to compete in the NCAA. Moreover, a hearing could not have afforded any relief in light of Smith's admission that he had violated the rule.

In the case of *Carlton Walker v. National Collegiate Athletic Ass'n and Officials at the University of Wisconsin*, Madison Case No. El-C-916 (W.D. Wis. 1981), Walker, a starting guard for the University of Wisconsin football team, was declared ineligible to participate in a postseason football game (the Garden State Bowl) as a result of an investigation of recruiting violations. Previously, in July 1981, the NCAA had officially charged the university and its alumni with twenty violations of NCAA regulations and bylaws in connection with Walker's recruitment. Neither the NCAA nor the university charged Walker with any violation.

Walker immediately filed a motion for a preliminary injunction to gain eligibility for the postseason bowl game. Walker contended that he was not afforded due process in connection with the declaration of ineligibility since athletic participation was a property right protected by the Constitution. The district court denied Walker's motion on the grounds that he failed to establish a reasonable likelihood of success on the merits and a degree of irreparable harm necessary to afford the requested relief.

Walker, who attended the University of Wisconsin from the fall of 1980 to the spring of 1982, then transferred to the University of Utah and enrolled as a full-time student. In August 1982, pursuant to NCAA Bylaw 5-3-(3), the University of Utah requested a waiver of Walker's one-year loss of eligibility due to his transfer (NCAA Bylaw 5-1-[j]-[7]).

The NCAA Committee on Infractions reviewed the waiver request by Utah. The committee determined from the available evidence that Walker's involvement in the Wisconsin recruiting violations was not inadvertent or innocent. The waiver was denied.

Walker amended his initial complaint in November 1982, and claimed that the NCAA had tortiously and arbitrarily interfered with the contractual relations between Walker and the universities of Wisconsin and Utah, thereby depriving him of the opportunity to compete in collegiate athletics and damaging his ability to secure a professional contract.

The NCAA filed a brief in support of a motion to dismiss, or in the alternative for summary judgment. Regarding Walker's due process claims, the NCAA stated that it was well settled that a student possesses no liberty or property interest in intercollegiate athletics. Therefore, the NCAA argued, the privilege of participating in intercollegiate athletics falls outside the parameters of the due process clause.

Of course, the situations exhibited in these cases will not arise if the student-athlete can avoid being declared ineligible. This, obviously, can be accomplished if the athlete obeys the rules and regulations of the associations and conferences to which the institution belongs. This, however, is not as easy as it sounds. An athlete may unknowingly violate eligibility rules or be deceived or coerced into rules violations by a third party. Other athletes may be declared ineligible as part of a larger sanction against their high school or college, as when a football team is placed on probation and suspension of postseason competition for recruiting violations.

A student-athlete who is declared ineligible can follow a number of steps in response to such a disciplinary action. First, the athlete should exhaust all remedies available under the school's or association's policies. These remedies may include the opportunity to appeal the decision, ask for a reconsideration, or initiate other procedures for reevaluating the initial ruling of ineligibility. For example, the United States Amateur Boxing Federation, Inc. has the following appeals procedure:

220.6 Procedure. The procedure for reinstatement is as follows:
  (a) Application in writing shall be made to the chairperson of the Registration Committee where the athlete is registered or, in the case of other members, the chairperson of the local boxing committee's Registration Committee, stating the act or acts which caused the disqualification, when and where the last act was committed.
  (b) When given authority, the local boxing committee Registration Committee shall render its opinion and inform the applicant in writing of its decision, forwarding a copy of the application and the committee's actions to USA Boxing's Registration Committee chairperson.
  (c) In cases requiring action by the national Registration Committee or by the Board of Governors, the LBC Registration Committee will forward its recommendations to the chairperson of USA Boxing's Registration Committee with a copy to the applicant.
  (d) USA Boxing's Registration Committee shall give its findings and/ or recommendations to the Board of Governors at the Corporation's annual meeting whose actions shall be final and binding on all parties. (*1991–93 USA Boxing Official Rules*, sec. 220.6)

If these procedures prove fruitless, the athlete may then resort to bringing a lawsuit against the governing body. Even though most claims against the NCAA or other amateur athletic association rules have ended in unsuccessful challenges by the student-athletes involved, it is still possible for student-athletes to obtain their objective—another season of competition, in some cases. The student-athlete achieves this objective by asking the court for a preliminary injunction in response to a ruling that the particular rule violated by the student-athlete is unenforceable. To declare an eligibility rule unenforceable, the student-athlete must argue that the rule violates due process or equal protection clauses of the state and federal constitutions, or that it violates federal antitrust and other federal laws, or that it represents breach of contract. Together with this attack on the rule, the student-athlete asks for a court order to prohibit the enforcement of the rule as it is applied to his or her individual case until the case goes to trial. Since this may be months and years later, the student-athlete can compete in the interim. (These and other legal principles are discussed in Chapters 3, 4, and 13.)

NOTES ————————————————————————————————

1. The discipline decisions of intercollegiate athlete associations were *upheld* in the following cases.
    (a) In *Samara v. National Collegiate Athletic Ass'n*, 1973 Trade Cases (CCH) 74,536 (E.D. Va.), the court upheld an NCAA decision that participation by a student-athlete in a noncertified track and field event resulted in ineligibility for further NCAA competition. The court stated that the NCAA rule and its subsequent sanctions were not illegal. This was true even though the event would have been certified if the Amateur Athletic Union (AAU) had requested the NCAA to provide such authorization.
    (b) In *National Collegiate Athletic Ass'n v. Gillard*, 352 So. 2d 1072 (Miss. Sup. Ct. 1977), sanctions were imposed against a non-NCAA member player who accepted a 20 percent clothing discount. There was some evidence that this discount policy was not limited to student-athletes. The NCAA decided there was a rule transgression. The Mississippi Supreme Court held that the player's rights were adequately protected by the NCAA's procedures and that the player's right to play intercollegiate football was not a property right protected by due process guarantees.
    (c) In *McDonald v. National Collegiate Athletic Ass'n*, 370 F. Supp. 625 (C.D. Cal. 1974), the court ruled that student-athletes had no due process rights infringed when the NCAA imposed sanctions against their school for bylaw violations that affected their opportunity to compete.
2. For a case in which discipline decisions of intercollegiate athletic associations have been *struck down*, see *Hall v. University of Minnesota*, 530 F. Supp. 104 (D. Minn. 1982). This case, also discussed in note 1 in the Academic Progress section of this chapter, concerned a conference academic progress rule. The court was quick to point out that the student-athlete had been recruited as "a basketball player and not a scholar" and that "his aca-

demic record reflects that he has lived up to those expectations as do the academic records of many of the athletes presented to this court." The court ruled that a constitutionally protected interest was involved and that Hall's due process rights had been violated. The court ordered the restoration of Hall's scholarship money and mandated his acceptance into a degree-granting program.

3. A case that involves discipline issues relating to student-athletes in interscholastic athletics is *Florida High School Activities Ass'n v. Bradshaw,* 369 So. 2d 398 (Fla. Dist. Ct. App. 1979). A high school football player sought to prohibit the state high school activities association from imposing a forfeiture of two of his team's games in which an ineligible player competed. The court upheld the penalty, reasoning that there was an absence of actual harm to the player and that the coach and other team members lacked standing to assert a claim of denial of equal protection. The court also held that the opportunity to participate is a privilege, not a constitutionally protected right; therefore, the court would not intervene in an association's discipline of its members.

4. A case that involves discipline issues relating to the Amateur Athletic Union is *Santee v. Amateur Athletic Union of the U.S.,* 153 N.Y.S.2d 465 (N.Y. Sup. Ct. 1956). The court ruled that the Amateur Athletic Union (AAU) had the authority and the jurisdiction to determine the eligibility of athletes who wished to participate in its sanctioned events. This included selection of squads for the Olympic Games, which were held under the auspices of the International Amateur Athletic Federation, from which the AAU received its sanctioning authority.

5. The New Jersey State Interscholastic Athletic Association (NJSIAA) has the following policy on reinstatement of eligibility:

> Section 3. Reinstatement of Amateur Eligibility—The Executive Committee of the NJSIAA is the only body that may reinstate a Student-Athlete of a member school to eligibility status under the provisions of the organization's Constitution, Bylaws, and Rules and Regulations. In cases where the Executive Committee has determined that a Student-Athlete inadvertently participated in an activity that has caused his/her loss of eligibility, the Executive Committee may reinstate said athlete after a period of not less than one year. An application for reinstatement must be made in writing by the high school Principal to the Executive Committee and shall include all data pertinent to the case. (*1992–93 NJSIAA Handbook,* Article V. Sec. 3)

6. In 1984 a Louisiana state court dismissed a case involving Bruce Smith of Virginia Polytechnic Institute because the eligibility issue involved was moot. Smith had been declared ineligible to participate by the NCAA in the 1984 Independence Bowl under Bylaws 5-1-(i) and 5-6-(e) (which apply to postseason bowl-game eligibility per Bylaw 2-2-(f)), because of infractions of violations in his recruitment. After his ineligibility was affirmed by the NCAA on appeal, Smith sought and received temporary restraining orders from state courts in Virginia and Louisiana to allow him to compete in the bowl game. See "Smith Eligibility Case Dismissed," *NCAA News,* March 26, 1984, p. 1.

7. An example of disciplinary actions taken by the NCAA against student-athletes occurred in May 1989, when the NCAA sanctioned the University of

Kentucky for numerous rule violations by its basketball program. First, Eric Manuel, a sophomore, was barred from NCAA competition for life when the NCAA found that he had committed academic fraud by cheating on his college entrance exam. Second, as a result of Kentucky Assistant Coach Dwayne Casey's sending $1,000 to Chris Mills's father, the freshman Mills was declared ineligible to play because he took the cash payments. Mills was, however, given the opportunity to transfer to another institution, sit out one year, and have three years of eligibility remaining (see Kirkpatrick, "Dodging a Bullet," *Sports Illustrated*, May 29, 1989, p. 24).

THE BUCKLEY AMENDMENT

An integral aspect of the NCAA's enforcement program is the compilation of information regarding the alleged infraction and also the operation of the institution's athletic department. Access to student-athletes' records concerning academic and financial aid information may be critical in the investigation. In order to protect against an invasion of a student's privacy and to prevent the likelihood that such information may be used in a way that hurts the student, Congress enacted the Family Educational Rights and Privacy Act (FERPA), which regulates the release and review of such records. Consequently, the NCAA and other third parties can be restricted and sometimes prevented from access to or publication of certain types of student-athlete information. The Family Educational Rights and Privacy Act of 1974 is often referred to as the Buckley Amendment.

The Buckley Amendment was designed to enhance comprehensive civil rights protections, with two objectives in mind: (1) to assure parents of students, and students themselves if they are attending an institution of postsecondary education or are eighteen years old, access to their education records; and (2) to protect the students' right to privacy by restricting the transferability and disclosure of information in their records without prior consent. The procedures established by the Buckley Amendment for accomplishing these two objectives apply only to public or private educational agencies or institutions that receive funds, directly or indirectly, from a program which is administered by the secretary of education (e.g., Basic Educational Opportunity Grant [BEOG], Guaranteed Student Loan [GSL], or National Direct Student Loans [NDSL]). The agency or institution is also obligated to establish a written policy and procedures for the access, disclosure, and challenge of education records. The secretary of education has the power to withdraw federal funding from any educational agency or institution that does not comply with the Buckley Amendment.

This amendment to the General Education Provisions Act primarily involves release of information concerning a student-athlete's education records, including academic rank, biographical material, and injury and health records. This type of information is often used in athletic department publications and media releases. Sports information directors, especially, should be aware of the provisions and limitations enacted by the Buckley Amendment.

Two basic rights created under the Buckley Amendment are particularly important to athletic administrators. First, students have the right to challenge any information in their education record which they or their parents believe to be inaccurate, misleading, or in violation of the student's rights. The student can bring the challenge in a hearing, or, if the institution still refuses the challenge, the student can note his or her concerns on the education record. Second, the Buckley Amendment also protects the right to prevent personally identifiable information from being disclosed, with some exceptions, in the absence of a prior written consent of the parent or student. A school official with a "legitimate educational interest" may have access without consent.

As a general rule, information concerning student-athletes should not be disclosed unless the student has filled out and signed a consent-disclosure statement form. These consent-disclosure statements are intended to protect both the student-athlete and the institution. The NCAA has a student-athlete sign a Buckley Amendment consent disclosure statement as part of the student-athlete statement (see Exhibit 5–1, Part II). Written consent-disclosure statements must include the following information:

1. A specification of the records to be disclosed.
2. The purpose or purposes of the disclosure.
3. The party or class of parties to whom the disclosure may be made.

In addition, the form should contain language that allows for the disclosure of unforeseen events, such as academic ineligibility, injury reports, and sudden illness affecting athletic involvement.

Another section of the Buckley Amendment deals with specific parties who do not have to receive a prior written authorization from the student to see the student's education files. Athletic department personnel fall into the school official exemption category and can review student-athlete files as needed to evaluate grade point average qualifiers, academic eligibility, and other matters which affect eligibility.

Athletic administrators should also be aware that some states impose additional and sometimes more restrictive requirements regarding the privacy of education records. However, these state statutes may not preempt the Buckley Amendment.

High school student-athletes' education records are also covered under the Buckley Amendment. A potential problem often may arise when members of a community desire access to student records to determine the effectiveness of their educational system.

NOTES _____

1. The Buckley Amendment, introduced by Senator James Buckley, appeared as an amendment to the Family Educational Rights and Privacy Act of 1974. The bill extended the Elementary and Secondary Education Act of 1965, Pub. L. No. 93-380, 20 U.S.C. §1232g(a)(4)(A).

2. A case that involves access to student records is *Arkansas Gazette Co. v. Southern State College*, 620 S.W.2d 258 (Ark. Sup. Ct. 1981). A newspaper publisher brought suit against an intercollegiate athletic conference seeking to compel it to disclose the amount of money its member institutions dispersed to student-athletes during the school year. The court held that records of disbursements to student-athletes by member institutions were subject to public inspection. The court reasoned that no one has a reasonable expectation of privacy concerning the amount of public funds distributed to him unless that person clearly comes within a specific exception of law, which in this case does not under the Arkansas Freedom of Information Act. The court also ruled that such records maintained by an intercollegiate athletic conference were "educational records" required to be closed under Family Education Rights Privacy Act of 1974. (See also Chapter 4.)

LITIGATION FOR FAILURE TO PROVIDE AN EDUCATION

A more recent area of litigation is one in which former student-athletes have sued institutions for failing to provide an education. The student-athletes in such cases are claiming that they failed to receive a proper education from the college or university in exchange for their athletic participation and competition. The alleged educational exploitation of student-athletes has resulted in increasing litigation and an equal number of tragedies. The courts appear to be concerned with the problem of educational exploitation of athletes. In *Sturrup v. Mahan*, 290 N.E.2d 64 (Ind. App. 1972), the court expressed its opinion on the importance of education:

> Schools are for education. There is no doubt that extracurricular athletic competition may add to the educational process, but the extracurricular activities should not take precedence over the curricular activities of the school. The sideshow may not consume the circus.

Echols v. Board of Trustees of the California State University and Colleges, (Cal. Super. Ct.) County of Los Angeles, No. C266 777 (Settled), is another example of an educational exploitation case. Randall Echols and six other former student-athletes of California State University at Los Angeles (CSULA) brought suit against the board of trustees of CSULA, the president, the athletic director, and the basketball coach of the school. The students claimed they attended CSULA with the understanding, based upon claims by university officials, that they would receive a tuition- and cost-free college education in exchange for their participation in the basketball program. All the athletes were admitted into a special program for minority students, which they claim wasted four to six years of their lives. The students were enrolled in courses such as backpacking that were designed to keep them eligible for varsity basketball.

The suit also included a claim that the university did specifically breach its portion of the athletic scholarship contracts by not providing education-related services such as adequate counseling. The students were denied access to university counselors and directed by coaches in the athletic department to enroll in courses that did not satisfy degree requirements. They were never informed of various academic and course requirements as were other CSULA students and as a result were unaware of them. The students claimed they were instructed to accept grades for courses they had never attended and were therefore deprived of educational opportunities. Last, the students claimed the defendants were at all times "agents and employees" of CSULA and at all times were acting "within the course and scope of such agency and with the permission and consent" of the university. A settlement was reached with six of the seven athletes. It awarded them $10,000 each and payment of loans that ranged from $2,100 to $6,000. The university also agreed "to issue a public statement expressing regret for what happened and guaranteeing that such a situation will not recur." In addition, the university established a scholarship fund for any of the plaintiffs who desired to continue their studies.

Legal experts predict that plaintiffs in future educational exploitation cases will win if "proximate cause" can be established. If this occurs, educational institutions may be besieged by countless claims which could amount to great losses of time and money.

With the increasing threat of litigation in the area of educational exploitation, it is important to look at the related area of educational malpractice. In one highly publicized case, Kevin Ross, a former Creighton University basketball star, who played there for three years, returned to the seventh grade in a Chicago preparatory school to improve his reading skills, which were reportedly at a second-grade level. Creighton University agreed to provide Ross with the financial help necessary for this education. Ross decided, however, to sue Creighton University for educational malpractice. In *Ross v. Creighton University*, 740 F. Supp. 1319 (Ill. Dist. Ct. 1990), the court found no contractual agreement between Ross and Creighton University for which a case could be argued. In finding for Creighton University, the court stated that the supervision of college athletics should be left to private regulatory groups, such as the NCAA.

In March 1992, a federal appeals court ruled that Ross, who claimed that the university exploited his athletic ability while failing to educate him, may sue the school for breach of contract but not for negligence. The negligent-admission claim, which alleged that Creighton had a duty to "recruit and enroll only those students reasonably qualified and able to academically perform," along with the claim of educational malpractice were thrown out by the court.

The lawsuit has since been settled out of court. Creighton agreed to pay Ross a sum of $30,000, while admitting no liability to the claims of educational exploitation. The impact of the court of appeals decision is that future plaintiffs will have the opportunity to have their cases heard on breach of contract grounds. For colleges and universities, on the other hand, the decision to deny the negligent-admission and educational malpractice claims makes it easier to defend against future litigation in situations similar to the *Ross* case.

Educational exploitation and malpractice lawsuits have been increasing and present a threat to both the education profession and athletics. Although no appellate court has awarded damages to the plaintiffs, the increase in litigation has not been stemmed. In the present environment of academic abuses involving many student-athletes at the NCAA Division I-A level, a decision by the courts to award damages to a plaintiff in a malpractice case may lead to additional claims brought by scholarship athletes who feel they may have been held back academically because of their athletic talent.

In a case related to the educational exploitation of student-athletes, Jan Kemp, a former University of Georgia remedial studies instructor, successfully sued the university's vice president for academic affairs and the assistant vice president in charge of Georgia's developmental studies program, after Kemp was first demoted and then dismissed for speaking out against preferential academic treatment for student-athletes, in *Kemp v. University of Georgia*, Case No. C83-330A (N.D. Ga. 1986). One of Kemp's protests involved the changing of failing grades of nine football players so that they could remain eligible for the 1982 Sugar Bowl. The court, in agreeing with Kemp, who charged that her constitutional rights to free speech had been violated, awarded her $2.5 million for lost wages, mental anguish, and punitive damages. One of the issues discussed in the case was whether a university should have a responsibility to graduate its student-athletes or just teach them to read, write, and communicate better.

NOTES ───

1. *Apuna v. Arizona State University* (pending 1984), involves claims of failure to provide an athlete with an education. A football player charges an academic adviser, the president of Arizona State University, and a former football coach with fraud, negligence, and interference with a professional contract as a result of their inducement of the student to enroll in and accept credit for a "bogus correspondence course." Apuna claims that the resulting scandal, adverse publicity, and his subsequent loss of eligibility caused him to lose his bid to play in three college all-star games and undermined his negotiating position with the National Football League. The suit also charges the university with invasion of privacy in the institution's public disclosure of plaintiff's academic records.

2. For a case involving alleged educational exploitation, see *Jones v. Snowdon* (Wayne Co. Cir. Ct., N. Mich. Cir. Ct. 81-131648). A former high school basketball star sued his high school coaches and the University of Michigan for $15 million for exploitation of his athletic ability. Alleged learning disabilities prevented him from keeping pace academically with his classmates, but word of his outstanding athletic talent moved him from school to school to capitalize on his basketball skills. "Thoughtless and unrelenting criticism, taunts and insults" from fellow students at his junior college led to humiliation, emotional pressure, and severe psychological illness. A Michigan district court held that the University of Michigan was a governmental agency and therefore immune from lawsuit. The Michigan Court of Appeals overturned the decision and ordered a trial on the merits.

3. The following nonsport cases are suits that involve alleged educational malpractice.

    (a) In *Donohue v. Copiague Union Free School District*, 418 N.Y.S.2d 375 (N.Y. Ct. App. 1979), the court reasoned that judicial interference would disrupt the administration of the schools involved. In the court's words: "Recognition in the courts of this cause of action would constitute blatant interference with the responsibility for the administration of the public school system lodged by Constitution and statute in school administrative agencies."

    (b) In *Hoffman v. Board of Education of the City of New York*, 424 N.Y.S.2d 376 (N.Y. Ct. App. 1979), a student of normal intelligence was placed in classes for the mentally retarded for the majority of his schooling because of a faulty diagnosis. The court awarded him $750,000 in damages, but later the court of appeals reversed this decision, denying any reward.

4. For further information, see the following law review articles: (a) Norton, "No Time for Classes: Many Athletes Go to College Hoping to Play Professionally . . . but Now They Are Suing Because They Failed to Get an Education," 4(7) *California Lawyer* 44 (1984). (b) Stokes, "The Jan Kemp Case: No Penalty for Pass Interference," 16 *Journal of Law and Education* 257 (1987).

SUMMER CAMPS, PARTICIPATION ON
INDEPENDENT TEAMS, AND OUTSIDE ACTIVITIES

One of the more recent trends in amateur sports litigation involves high school athletes and their parents challenging rules that prohibit student-athlete participation and attendance at camps that specialize in teaching the skills of a particular sport. The rules prohibiting such attendance are relatively new. They were instituted to control overzealous coaches and parents and to equalize interscholastic competition.

One of the first rules to be challenged was one promulgated by the University Interscholastic League in Texas in the case of *Kite v. Marshall*, 494 F. Supp. 227 (S.D. Tex. 1980). The plaintiffs attacked the rule on constitutional grounds, claiming that it violated the constitutional rights of parents to make decisions for their children. The district court treated the rule as an infringement of a protected right and overturned it. However, the court of appeals reversed and held that the right, although important, was not a fundamental one and that the rule need only meet a rational basis test (see the later discussion in this chapter).

The NCAA has many regulations involving summer camps. These rules involve participation by prospective student-athletes, current student-athletes, and coaching staffs. For example, in drawing up their regulations for Division I football and basketball the NCAA divides summer camps into two categories: specialized sport camps and diversified sport camps. The specialized camps, which place special emphasis on a particular sport or sports, provide specialized instruction, practice, and usually competition. Diversified camps offer a balanced camping experience, including participation in seasonal summer sports and recreational activities, without emphasis on instruction, practice, or competition in any one sport.

Prospective student-athletes are not allowed to enroll, participate, or be employed at camps, schools, and clinics that are run by a member institution, either on or off campus, since this would be considered by the association as a tryout (*1993–94 NCAA Manual*, Bylaw 13.13.1.2). In Division I it is permissible to employ a prospective student-athlete at a reasonable rate, provided the prospect is not a high school or junior college athletics award winner (*1993–94 NCAA Manual*, Bylaw 13.13.1.5.1). The NCAA defines a prospective student-athlete, in terms of summer camp participation, as one who is eligible for admission to a member institution or who has started classes for the senior year in high school. Junior college student-athletes also are eligible for employment, provided they are not athletics award winners. Prospective student-athletes who are high school or junior college athletics awards winners are not allowed to receive free or reduced admission to a camp, school, or clinic (*1993–94 NCAA Manual*, Bylaw 13.13.1.5.1).

In the case of specialized camps in the sports of Division I basketball and football, an institution cannot hire one of its own student-athletes with eligibility remaining in those sports to work at the camp (*1993–94 NCAA Manual*, Bylaw 13.13.2.1.2.1.1.1). Under special regulations, a specialized camp can hire one student-athlete from another institution from the previous year's football or basketball squad (*1993–94 NCAA Manual*, Bylaw 13.13.2.1.2.1.2). Diversified camps, run at a member institution, can employ one student-athlete, with eligibility remaining, from the basketball and football squads. Private camps may employ student-athletes under more stringent regulations (*1993–94 NCAA Manual*, Bylaw 13.13.2.1.2.1.3).

Many high school and college athletic associations establish rules that prohibit student-athletes from participating on independent teams (YMCA, church leagues) while the student-athlete is participating in the same sport as a member of a high school or college team. The rules are intended to prevent players from obtaining unfair additional training and competition and to keep overzealous coaches from involving student-athletes in excessive athletic participation. Not all sports are subject to these rules; golf, tennis, and swimming are often exempt.

The courts have generally upheld independent team participation rules on the grounds that the restrictions do not violate any constitutionally protected rights. In one case the court dismissed a student-athlete's complaint because the limitation on the student-athlete's participation created no circumstances violative of either state or federal constitutions (see note 3a).

There has been one successful challenge to an independent team rule in the case of *Buckton v. NCAA*, 366 F. Supp. 1152, 1155 (D. Mass. 1973). Two resident alien college hockey players brought suit against the Eastern College Athletic Conference (ECAC) and the NCAA to challenge an ECAC and NCAA regulation which declared them ineligible because they had competed as members of the Canadian Amateur Hockey Association's major junior A classification. The challenge independent team rule stated: "Any student-athlete who participated as a member of the Canadian Amateur Hockey Association's major junior A hockey classification shall not be eligible for intercollegiate athletics" (NCAA Constitution, Article 3, Section 1, 0.I.5. [1973–74]; ECAC Bylaws, Article 3, Section 1, 0.I.5. [1972]). The court struck down the rule after finding that it violated the equal protection clause of the Fourteenth Amendment since resident aliens were granted the same constitutional right of equal protection as American citizens. The court ruled that the university must declare the student-athletes eligible, and the NCAA was prohibited from bringing sanctions against the university.

In the case of *Kite v. Marshall*, 454 F. Supp. 1347 (Tex. Dist. Ct. 1978), parents of high school student-athletes brought an action which challenged the constitutionality of the "summer camp rule," which was adopted by the defendant University Interscholastic League (UIL), the high school athletic association in Texas. The rationale underlying the rule's adoption was that it ensured that high school athletes would compete on a relatively equal basis. The court decided that

> the decision to send a child to summer basketball camp is important enough to warrant constitutional protection under the family's funda- mental right of personal privacy....
>
> Having found a fundamental constitutional right, the remaining in- quiries are whether or not the UIL rule in question infringes the right and if so, whether the rule is motivated by compelling state interest and has been narrowly drawn to express only those interests.

In deciding the degree of infringement, the court stated:

> The summer camp rule is, however, directly and purposefully aimed at discouraging a specific parental decision made during the summer months when the school is not acting *in loco parentis.* The interference posed by the UIL rule... is neither indirect nor incidental.

The court reasoned, "As it presently reads, the summer camp rule constitutes an overbroad and unreasonable infringement on the right of a family to make decisions concerning the education of its children."

In *Kite v. Marshall*, 661 F.2d 1027 (5th Cir. 1981), UIL appealed the lower court ruling striking down its "summer camp rule." The court of appeals held that the "summer camp rule" did not violate either the due process or the equal protection clauses of the Consti- tution. It reversed the opinion of the district court. The court of appeals found that, "this case implicates no fundamental constitutional right." The court subjected the rule to the rational basis analysis.

The court also upheld a similar high school rule in *Texas High School Gymnastics Coaches Ass'n v. Andrews*, 532 S.W.2d 142 (Tex. Civ. App. 1975). This suit was brought by parents and coaches of gymnasts who sought to overturn a Texas High School Gymnastics Coaches Association rule that governed dual membership. The asso- ciation rule read as follows:

> A Texas high school gymnast must not work out with, practice with, take

lessons with, or compete with a private club, and be eligible for dual regional or state competition during the school calendar year of their school district.

The complaint alleged that the rule was an "unfair, unlawful and unconstitutional restriction upon the individual rights of high school students who... desire to compete in high school gymnastic competition." The trial court granted an injunction which temporarily prohibited the association from enforcing the rule. The association appealed.

The appeals court noted that there was not sufficient evidence to support the conclusion that the rule is unreasonable, capricious, or arbitrary. The court held that the rule must be upheld unless it could be shown that the rule bears no rational relationship to the achievement of a legitimate purpose. The court found that the purpose of the rule was valid since it prevented inequality and unfair advantage between students of different economic means and schools located in different areas of economic wealth.

These cases show the reluctance of the court to overturn association rules which are reasonably related to a legitimate purpose.

NOTES ───

1. At the 1983 NCAA convention, the membership enacted legislation that prohibits a member of a Division I basketball coaching staff from being employed by a basketball camp that has been established, sponsored, or conducted by an individual or organization that provides recruiting or scouting services. Since the 1983 convention, this legislation has been updated to restrict Division I football coaches in the same way and has added the restriction that a coach is also not allowed to lecture at a noninstitutional (i.e., privately owned) football or basketball camp or clinic in which prospective student-athletes of either gender participate (*1993–94 NCAA Manual*, Bylaw 13.13.2.3.2).

2. In the initial district court decision of *Kite v. Marshall*, 454 F. Supp. 1347 (Tex. Dist. Ct. 1978), the court determined that the plaintiff was entitled to a preliminary injunction which prohibited the interscholastic league from enforcing a rule which stated that students who play in special basketball training camps are ineligible for one year for any athletic contest in the league. The court stated that the rule was overbroad and the player would suffer material harm if relief was denied.

3. The following cases also involve camp participation.

(a) In *Art Gaines Baseball Camp, Inc. v. Houston*, 500 S.W.2d 735 (Mo. Ct. App. 1973), a camp sought to restrain the Missouri High School Activities Association from enforcing a rule which stated that a student-athlete who attended a camp specializing in one sport for more than two weeks during a summer would lose eligibility to represent his or her school in that particular sport the following school year. In affirming judgment for the high school athletic association, the court of appeals held that the rule did not infringe on public policy or law and was not unreasonable or arbitrary.

(b) In *Brown v. Wells*, 284 Minn. 468, 181 N.W.2d 708 (1970), a hockey player challenged rules excluding his participation on the high school hockey team if he participated in nonschool hockey, including hockey schools or camps. The court held that when rules are adopted for the purpose of deemphasizing extracurricular athletics that may detract from student interest in education, the court cannot deem such rules arbitrary or unreasonable. The court found that the school board had the discretion to deal with the issue as it thought best. The courts should not attempt to control the discretion of the school board.

4. The following cases deal with participation on independent teams.

(a) In *Kubiszyn v. Alabama High School Athletic Ass'n*, 374 So. 2d 256 (Ala. Sup. Ct. 1979), members of a high school basketball team were declared ineligible after playing on YMCA and church basketball teams at the same time they were playing for their high school team. The high school athletic association rule provided that any member of a high school athletic team who participated in an athletic contest as a member of a similar team during the same season was ineligible to play for the high school team for the remainder of the season. The court found that the rule did not violate the state or federal constitution, in absence of some evidence that the student-athlete suffered some impairment of a property right, or that the acts of the athletic association were the result of fraud or collusion.

(b) In *Dumez v. Louisiana High School Athletic Ass'n*, 334 So. 2d 494 (La. Ct. App. 1976), parents of high school student-athletes who were declared ineligible to participate in interscholastic baseball athletics by an athletic association sought a permanent injunction to prohibit enforcement of the ruling. In reversing judgment for the parents, the court of appeals held that determination by the association to declare the students ineligible because they violated the "independent team rule" by participating in practice sessions held by the Babe Ruth Baseball League was not subject to judicial rescission or modification on the grounds that it constituted a serious "inequity" to the students when similar action was not taken against coaches or schools.

(c) In *Texas High School Gymnastics Coaches Association v. Andrews*, 532 S.W.2d 142 (Tex. Civ. App. 1975), the court considered the appeal of a temporary injunction forbidding the association from applying its dual membership rule. The rule prohibited gymnasts from competing on the high school team as well as for a private club during the school calendar year. The court reversed the judgment of the trial court and dissolved the temporary injunction, finding that there was no basis at all for finding the rule to be invalid.

(d) In *University Interscholastic League v. North Dallas Chamber of Commerce Soccer Association*, 693 S.W.2d 513 (Tex. Ct. App. 1985), the lower court had granted a permanent injunction prohibiting enforcement of a rule restricting club soccer activities of varsity school athletes. The rule declared public high school contestants who had previously played on their high school varsity soccer team ineligible for participation on their high school soccer team, in the event that they had played or practiced with nonschool soccer teams between the first day of school and November 12. On appeal, the court reversed the decision, holding that the rule was reasonably related, for equal protection purposes, to its objectives, which were the prevention of competitive advantage and coaching pressure, and the encouragement of participation by student-athletes in activities other than competitive soccer. Further, the soccer association had failed to establish a fundamental right to participation in varsity school athletics, so as to invoke the protection of the due process clause.

(e) In *Burrows, et al. v. Ohio High School Athletic Ass'n.* 712 F. Supp. 620 (S.D. Ohio 1988), the plaintiffs brought action challenging the constitutionality of the defendant's bylaw, which provided that no soccer squad member could participate in independent soccer and maintain eligibility for interscholastic soccer without approval of the commissioner of the association. The court held that high school students' association with others for the purpose of participating in independent spring soccer and out-of-season instruction was not private association or expressive association within the constitutional protection of freedom of association. Further, the bylaw did not violate the equal protection guarantee because it did not apply to students who had not played interscholastic soccer the previous fall, or because it did not apply to certain sports involving primarily individual rather than team competition.

(f) In *Zuments v. Colorado High School Activities Ass'n* 737 P.2d 1113 (Colo. Ct. App. 1987), student-athletes enrolled in various Colorado public high schools sued to enjoin the defendant from enforcing its "outside competition" rule, which prevented students from practicing with nonschool teams while participating in interscholastic athletics. The lower court granted a preliminary injunction to the students. On appeal, the court of appeals held that the association's enforcement of the "outside competition" rule was not arbitrary, capricious, or haphazard and that it rationally furthered legitimate state purposes, so as not to violate the students' right to equal protection. Further, the outside competition rule did not impermissibly burden the students' constitutional right of free association.

5. The New Jersey State Interscholastic Athletic Association (NJSIAA) has the following regulation regarding high school student-athletes who work at summer camps or recreational programs:

E. A Student-Athlete may work as a counselor in a summer camp, life guard, swimming pool attendant and swimming instructor for children without affecting his/her eligibility under the terms of this principle; he/she may work in a tennis or golf shop provided he/she does not give instruction for compensation, and he/she may obtain employment with a recreation department, his/her duties to include some officiating and coaching responsibilities; however, he/she may not be employed as an athletic coach. (*1992–93 NJSIAA Handbook*, Art. V, sec. 2E)

Chapter 6

LEGAL PRINCIPLES IN TORT LAW

INTRODUCTION

Tort law is an important area of sports law. There has been an increase in the number of cases filed based on intentional or unintentional tort theories. There are many reasons for this increase, including the astronomical rise in medical costs that injured athletes or other plaintiffs are unable to meet, along with a prevailing notion that one who injures deliberately or negligently should pay for such actions when they create serious consequences.

Civil law provides injured individuals with a cause of action by which they may be compensated or "made whole" through the recovery of damages. This cause of action comes under the general heading of torts. A *tort* is a private (or civil) wrong or injury, other than a breach of contract, suffered by an individual as the result of another person's conduct. The law of torts deals with the allocation of losses arising from human activities and provides for the adjustment of these losses via the monetary compensation of the individual for injuries sustained as a result of another's conduct.

Civil law and criminal law share the common end of inducing people to act for the benefit of society by preventing behavior that negatively affects society and by encouraging behavior that has a positive effect. Civil law and criminal law differ, however, in their means of achieving this common end. Criminal law is designed to protect the public from harm through the punishment of conduct likely to cause harm. Civil law, on the other hand, aims to compensate (to make whole) an injured party for the harm suffered as a result of another person's conduct.

Varying interpretations of criminal and civil offenses lead to divergent methods of action in these two areas of law. Criminal actions emphasize the immorality or bad intentions of the defendants. Tort actions, on the other hand, seek to achieve desirable social results by resolving the conflicting interests of individuals. Society tends to distinguish criminal wrongs by condemning or judging the morality of the criminal more severely than that of the tortious wrongdoer. Once a crime has been discovered, the state or a subdivision of the state (e.g., county), in its capacity as protector of the public interest, brings an action against the accused. In a tort action, however, the injured party institutes the action as an individual in an effort to recover damages as compensation for the injury received.

It is important to distinguish between intentional and unintentional torts. The responsibility of distinguishing between intentional and unintentional tort lies with the court because the court determines the manner in which it will assess the case. The degree of the defendant's intent toward the plaintiff (intent to harm) can be differentiated on the following three levels:

1. Intentional tort (e.g., assault and battery): Intent to commit the act and intent to harm the plaintiff.
2. Reckless misconduct or gross negligence: Intent to commit the act, but no intent to harm the plaintiff.
3. Unintentional tort or negligence: No intent to commit the act and no intent to harm the plaintiff, but a failure to exercise reasonable care.

Reckless misconduct (also called gross negligence) falls somewhere between intentional torts and mere ordinary negligence. It differs from negligence in degree rather than in substance. The court may view one single act either as negligent or grossly negligent, depending on the state of mind of the actor.

Intentional and unintentional torts are the most common tort actions in the sports setting. *Assault and battery,* an intentional tort; *reckless misconduct,* somewhere between intentional and unintentional torts; and *negligence,* an unintentional tort, are therefore emphasized in the first part of Chapter 6. The doctrine of *vicarious liability,* often used in tort cases to sue an employer for the negligence of employees, is presented next. A discussion of defamation law and the issues of libel and slander follows. The less common torts of *invasion of privacy* and *intentional infliction of emotional distress* are described. *Products liability law,* a growth area in sports because it allows a party who has been injured by a product (e.g., sports equipment) that is defectively designed, manufactured, or distributed to recover damages follows. The next section involves a discussion of *tortious interference with contractual relations,* a tort which recognizes a cause of action against one who intentionally induces another to breach a contract. The chapter concludes with an examination of *workers' compensation* issues present in amateur athletics.

Several common problems are involved in the majority of sports-related tort cases. The first is the difficulty of determining exactly what a tort is in an athletic context. There is also a public policy consideration involved in that it has been suggested in several court decisions that court interference with sports will destroy amateur athletics and unreasonably restrict the free play of sports. The third common problem is that litigation may discourage participation in the more dangerous sports. For these reasons, athletic administrators must be aware of the legal principles involved in tort liability relating to sports so that they can be better prepared to take preventive measures that will minimize the adverse effects of such litigation.

NOTES ――――――――――――――――――――――――――――――――――――

1. The legal ramifications concerning tort liability are similar for amateur and professional athletics. Thus, for further information, see the following law review articles, which involve professional sports.

(a) Note, "Compensating Injured Professional Athletes: The Mystique of Sport Versus Traditional Tort Principles," 55 *N.Y.U. L. Rev.* 971 (1980).

(b) Comment, "A Proposed Legislative Solution to the Problem of Violent Acts by Participants During Professional Sporting Events," 7 *U. Dayton L. Rev.* 91 (1981).

(c) Hayes, "Professional Sports and Tort Liability: A Victory for the Intentionally Injured Player," 1980 *Det. C. L. Rev.* 687 (1980).

(d) Gulotta, "Torts in Sports: Deterring Violence in Professional Athletics," 48 *Fordham L. Rev.* 764 (1980).

2. For further information, see the following texts:

(a) Weistart and Lowell, *The Law of Sports* (Indianapolis, Ind.: Bobbs-Merrill, 1979). Supplement (Charlottesville, Va.: The Michie Company, 1985).

(b) Sobel, *Professional Sports and the Law* (New York: Law Arts Publishers, 1977). Supplement, 1981.

(c) Appenzeller, *Sports and the Courts* (Charlottesville, Va.: The Michie Company, 1980).

(d) Yasser, *Torts and Sports: Legal Liability in Professional and Amateur Athletics* (Westport, Conn.: Quorum Books, 1985).

(e) Schubert, Smith, and Trentadue, *Sports Law* (St. Paul, Minn.: West Publishing Company, 1986).

(f) Boone and Nygaard, *Coaches' Guide to Sport Law* (Champaign, Ill.: Human Kinetics Publishers, 1985).

(g) Berry and Wong, *Law and Business of the Sports Industries*, Vols. I and II (Dover, Mass.: Auburn House, 1986).

THE TORTS OF ASSAULT AND BATTERY

Assault and battery can be both a criminal and a civil case; however, most people associate assault and battery with criminal law. Most state statues broadly define criminal assault to include both attempted and actual battery. Such is not the case in civil law, where assault and battery are more specifically and narrowly defined, and where the two actions constitute separate and distinct torts. Further elaboration will clarify the distinction between the criminal and civil law definitions of assault and battery. A *civil law battery* is an unpermitted actual touching of another person, and a *civil law assault* is the apprehension of imminent harmful contact. For civil assault and battery, as for all intentional torts, there does not have to be harm to the plaintiff to establish a claim of assault and/or battery. The mere fact that a person has done and intended to do a proscribed action will suffice to provide at least nominal damages, but the degree of harm will be important in assessing monetary damages.

In torts involving intentional harm to the person, the plaintiff may recover for lost earning capacity, medical expenses, pain and suffering, and for the loss of consortium, affection, assistance, and martial fellowship. These are termed *actual damages*. Unlike negligence, however, it is not necessary in an intentional tort case to prove actual damages to recover; the plaintiff may recover substantial damages without proving specific bodily injuries. Torts involving intentional harm allow for recovery of damages for emotional suffering (i.e., humiliation, indignity, injury to feelings), as long as this suffering was proximately caused by the defendant's conduct. Certain conduct on the part of the plaintiff that is not sufficient to constitute a defense to the action may be considered in mitigation of damages. For example, although provocative words by the plaintiff do not justify the defendant's use of force, these words may be considered to mitigate the amount of damages awarded to the plaintiff.

In addition to actual damages, a plaintiff may recover *punitive damages* when the defendant has acted willfully or has exhibited outrageous conduct. These damages are awarded on the theory that they may help to deter future wrongful conduct. They have also been justified on the theory that they help remedy the lack of money available to pay litigation expenses, which are usually not recoverable under American civil procedure. Punitive damages are awarded not according to the tort committed, although they are often given for assault and battery, but for the defendant's intentional conduct. This is usually a matter of degree, and punitive damages are awarded when the defendant's conduct is particularly reprehensible. Punitive damages are available only for intentional tort cases and are not awarded in negligence cases.

Assault

For an action to constitute assault, the following three elements must be present:

1. Intent to cause harm by the defendant.
2. Apprehension of immediate harm by the plaintiff.
3. Lack of consent by the plaintiff.

With the first element, the plaintiff does not have to prove that the defendant intended to inflict bodily harm. With the second element, the apprehension of immediate harm by the plaintiff must be reasonable, and claims that a plaintiff is extraordinarily timid will not lower the court's standard of reasonable apprehension. However, the defendant will be held responsible if the defendant knows of the plaintiff's timidness. The *apparent* ability to carry out a threat as opposed to *actual* ability is what the court relies on in determining assault. The defendant who claims that he or she had no intention of carrying out a threat will not be successful. For example, for a defendant to claim that the gun was not loaded is not a successful defense against the reasonable person's being placed in apprehension of immediate harm by the defendant because the plaintiff had no way of knowing whether or not the gun was loaded.

The third element, lack of consent by the plaintiff to the alleged assault, is extremely important in sports cases in which the court has difficulty distinguishing among consented to contact, apprehension, and intimidation, as opposed to unconsented to activities. Actual contact between the defendant and the plaintiff need not have occurred for assault to have been committed; however, the plaintiff must be aware of the possibility of contact. The distinction between actual physical contact and the mere apprehension of it marks the dividing line between assault and battery. For example, in a high school baseball game, Freddy Fastball threw a pitch that unintentionally got away from him and passed dangerously close to Harry Hothead's head. Harry took offense at the closeness of the pitch and charged the mound and threw his bat in the direction of Freddy. The bat missed Freddy. Nevertheless, Freddy could bring suit against Harry for assault.

Battery

For an action to constitute battery, three elements must be present:

1. The intent to touch by the defendant.
2. Actual touching.
3. The lack of consent to the contact by the plaintiff.

With the first element, the plaintiff does not have to prove that the defendant intended the specific harm that the victim incurred. The rationale is that the defendant is presumed to have intended the natural and probable consequences of the act. However, a touching that results from a reflex action is not considered intentional.

With the second element, the mere apprehension of contact is not sufficient; actual contact must occur for a plaintiff to prove that a defendant's action constituted battery. The plaintiff's awareness of the contact at the time of the battery is not essential. Plaintiffs have made successful battery claims in cases in which the contact occurred when they were asleep or under anesthesia. Contact does not necessarily have to be harmful but may instead be offensive, such as spitting at another person. The act must cause and be intended to cause an unconsented contact by the defendant.

The third element required in a battery action is lack of consent to the contact by the plaintiff. The determination of whether or not consent existed is often difficult; factors such as the time of the act and the place in which it occurred must be considered. The element of consent is crucial to both assault and battery, especially in the sports setting. In contact sports, force is expected to be used by the participants because it is one of the necessary terms and conditions of the game. The contact is justified if it is reasonable under the circumstances. Many of the contacts that occur in the sports setting would be considered batteries in a nonsports setting. However, the key distinction in sports battery cases is the determination of whether a particular contact has been consented to by the participant. If the court concludes that consent was given and the contact was reasonable, a plaintiff will not be successful in a battery case. For example, during a basketball game, Bully Smith was guarding Tommy Timid as Tommy was about to receive a pass. Without provocation, Bully intentionally pushed Tommy from behind and punched him in the back of the head. As Tommy fell, Bully hit him again, knocking Tommy unconscious. The acts of Bully were not of the type to which Tommy would consent in a game of basketball. Thus, Tommy can bring suit against Bully for battery, because there was intention to harm. However, Tommy cannot bring an action for assault, because there was no apprehension of harm since Tommy did not see the punch coming.

If consent was not given or if the contact was unreasonable, then the type of contact initiated by the defendant will determine the type of damages available to the plaintiff. Any proven intentional tort provides at least nominal damages. Outrageous or extremely offensive contact will, in addition to the nominal damages, provide a basis on which to support punitive damages that may greatly increase the plaintiff's award.

NOTES ───

1. In *Bourque v. Duplechin*, 331 So. 2d 40 (La. Ct. App. 1976), the plaintiff sued defendant for an intentional battery that occurred during a softball game. Defendant ran into plaintiff after plaintiff second baseman had completed his throw to first base. On appeal, the court held that it was not an intentional tort because the defendant had no intent to harm the plaintiff.

2. In *Griggas v. Clauson*, 128 N.E.2d 363 (Ill. App. Ct. 1955), Griggas sued Clauson for assault and battery for injuries received when the defendant struck the plaintiff in the face several times in a basketball game. The court found that Griggas was subjected to wanton, unprovoked, and unanticipated assault and battery and held for Griggas.

3. In *Averill v. Luttrell*, 311 S.W.2d 812 (Tenn. Ct. App. 1957), plaintiff batter, angered by the pitcher's intentionally thrown beanball, which struck him, threw his bat in the direction of the mound. The defendant catcher then stepped behind the batter and hit him with his fist. The batter sued both the

catcher and the catcher's club. The court held for the plaintiff batter and found that the defendant catcher had committed assault and battery.

4. In *Manning v. Grimsley*, 643 F.2d 20 (1st Cir. 1981), defendant pitcher was sued for assault and battery for throwing a baseball from the bullpen into the stands and hitting a spectator.

5. In *Hackbart v. Cincinnati Bengals*, 435 F. Supp. 352 (D. Colo. 1977), *rev'd*, 601 F.2d 516 (10th Cir. 1979), plaintiff football player was precluded from suing for assault and battery by the statute of limitations.

6. For further information, see the following articles:

(a) Note, "Professional Sports and Tort Liability: A Victory for the Intentionally Injured Player," 1980 *Det. C. L. Rev.* 687 (Summer 1980).

(b) Note, "Torts in Sports—Deterring Violence in Professional Athletics," 48 *Fordham L. Rev.* 764 (April 1980).

(c) Narol, "Protecting the Rights of Sports Officials: Cases of Personal Injury and Damages to Reputation," 23 *Trial* 64 (January 1987).

(d) Narol, "Sports Participation with Limited Litigation: The Emerging Reckless Disregard Standard," 1 *Seton Hall Journal of Sport Law* 29 (1991).

Defenses for Assault and Battery

The three defenses available to the defendant in an intentional harm-to-the-person action such as assault or battery are consent, privilege, and immunity. Consent, when given by a plaintiff, does not excuse a tort. However, because its absence is an essential element of an intentional tort, its presence will totally negate the claim of liability in that the plaintiff will not be able to establish the three required elements. On the other hand, both privilege and immunity, in effect, excuse the commission of a tort after its occurrence.

Consent

Consent is a voluntary yielding of one's will to the dictates of another. It is an act of reason, accompanied by deliberation, which is made by an individual possessed of sufficient mental capacity to make an intelligent choice. To be effective, consent must be an act unclouded by fraud or duress. Consent may be expressed, or it may be reasonably implied by the circumstances surrounding the situation.

The element of consent presents a special problem in the realm of sports in general and for athletic participants in particular. The traditional interpretation in many assault and battery cases in the sports setting has been that the athlete, by participating in a given event, consents to the degree of contact commonly found within the rules of the sport. A special problem arises in the area of sports because it is often difficult to determine the extent or scope of the implied consent given. Consent implied from participation in athletic events is not a blanket consent that protects athletes from the consequences of their actions under all circumstances. Instead, many plaintiffs argue that the scope of consent is limited to acts that occur in the ordinary and normal conduct of the game.

The difficulty arises from the determination of what is "ordinary and normal conduct" in a particular game. For example, the consent defense might be employed in a sports-related assault and battery action. The defendant could claim that no tort was committed on the basis of the nature of the relationship between him or her and the plaintiff, who by his or her very participation in the contest consents to a certain degree of contact. Indeed, a problem in maintaining a tort action in a sports case is the difficulty of ascertaining, in the context of a game in which physical contact is allowed, exactly when or how a tort occurs.

NOTE _____

1. In *Tavernier v. Maes*, 51 Cal. Rptr. 575 (Cal. Ct. App. 1966), plaintiff sought recovery for injuries sustained during a family softball game. Plaintiff alleged defendant deliberately slid into him in an attempt to break up a double play. The court held that the scope of the implied consent created by plaintiff's participation, as well as the question of whether the defendant's conduct exceeded the scope of the consent given, was a matter for the jury to decide.

Privilege

A *privilege* is a particular, limited benefit enjoyed by an individual or class that extends beyond the common advantages of other citizens. In certain situations a privilege is more appropriately classified as an exemption from a burden rather than as a benefit to be enjoyed. A privilege is commonly enjoyed in situations in which the defendant has acted in defense of his or her person or property. The defendant bears the burden of proof to establish that a privilege existed and that the force used pursuant to the privilege was reasonable under the circumstances. The defense is denied, and the defendant will be held liable if the force used is found to be excessive or unreasonable. The defense of privilege commonly encompasses six types of behavior:

1. Self-defense
2. Defense of third persons
3. Corporal punishment
4. Defense of property
5. Effecting an arrest
6. Arrest without a warrant

The privilege most commonly utilized in sports cases is that of self-defense. To argue self-defense successfully, the defendant must prove that no more force than was reasonably necessary was used to repel an attack.

The self-defense privilege rests on the policy that allows a person being attacked to come to his or her own defense. The privilege extends to the use of all reasonable force needed to prevent harmful bodily contact. The privilege arises when danger exists or there is a reasonable belief that danger is imminent. It is limited to the use of force that is necessary or that appears to be necessary for adequate protection. There is never any privilege to use force when the immediate danger is past.

The defense of third persons is also a potentially viable legal argument for defending against an action for assault or battery. In order for the defense to be effective, certain requirements must be met. First, the privilege extends only to the reasonable force necessary to defend another from imminent harm. Second, the defense must occur in reaction to events as they exist at the time of the threat. There is no privilege for physical reactions to future threats or past attacks.

The privilege of third-person defense is available to anyone who reasonably defends another. There does not have to be any special relationship between the two. Some courts require that the third party take the risk that the person being defended would not be privileged to defend himself or herself. The preferred view, however, is that an honest mistake as to the necessity for the defensive action will relieve the defendant of liability.

Immunity

Immunity is a condition that protects against a tort action. It exists because of the position of the defendant, and not because of any action taken by the defendant. This defense may exist either because of a relationship between the plaintiff and the defendant, or because of the capacity of the defendant. Examples of relationships that in some states permit a defense of immunity in intentional torts include those between husband and wife or between parent and child. Charitable corporations; federal, state, and municipal governments; and public officials may use this defense because of their role as protectors and defenders of the public welfare under the doctrine of charitable or sovereign immunity. (See Chapter 7.)

THE TORT OF RECKLESS MISCONDUCT

Reckless misconduct or gross negligence falls between the unintentional tort of negligence and the intentional torts of assault and battery. Behavior constituting reckless misconduct is characterized by intent on the part of the defendant to commit the act, but no intent to harm the plaintiff by this act. Reckless misconduct occurs when the actor has intentionally performed an act in disregard of a risk known to him where the risk is so great as to make the harm highly probable. It must usually be accompanied by a conscious disregard of the circumstances. For example, Frankie Fieldevent, after a high school track practice, was throwing the javelin at some of his teammates who were running around the track. He had no intention of hitting any of his friends, but Mikey Marathon fell while running, and the javelin pierced him in the shoulder. Mikey successfully brought suit against Frankie for reckless misconduct.

Reckless misconduct is particularly important in the area of participant-against-participant tort cases. Only recently have courts found a duty between sports participants to refrain from reckless misconduct toward another player.

To find reckless misconduct, an action must be more than ordinary inadvertence or inattention but less than conscious indifference to the consequences. It is defined as an action that is willful, wanton, or reckless; while reckless misconduct is not an intentional action, the degree of the care exercised is so far below the usual standard that, in effect, it is treated as intentional action. Reckless misconduct encompasses action which evidences an extreme departure from the ordinary degree of care required from the actor in the particular circumstances. However, the damages awarded, especially in the area of punitive damages, may be greater if the defendant's action is deemed grossly negligent.

NOTES

1. For further information, see the following law review article: "Note, Compensating Injured Professional Athletes: The Mystique of Sport Versus Traditional Tort Principles," 55 *N.Y.U. L. Rev.* 971 (1980).

2. for a case in which the reckless misconduct theory was successfully applied, see *Nabozny v. Barnhill*, 334 N.E.2d 258 (Ill. App. 1975) in Chapter 7.

THE TORT OF NEGLIGENCE

Negligence is an unintentional tort which focuses on an individual's conduct or actions. Negligence must be distinguished from intentional torts such as assault and battery which revolve around the individual's state of mind or intent. *Negligent conduct* is defined as that which falls below the standard established by law for the protection of others against an unreasonably great risk of harm. The ability of the injured party to sue and to recover damages for negligence is based on the idea that one who acts should anticipate the consequences which might involve unreasonable danger to others.

A person must take precautions only against unreasonable risks of harm. Unreasonable risks are those whose danger is apparent or should be apparent to one in the position of the actor. The law, however, does not seek to burden the freedom of human action with excessive or unreasonable demands and restraints. Therefore, one is not expected to guard against situations or occurrences that are unlikely to happen. The standard of care required is measured by the *reasonable person standard*. The reasonable person is one who selects a course of action that would be selected by an ordinary, prudent person residing in the affected community under the same conditions. The law excuses all persons from liability for accidents that are either unavoidable or unforeseeable.

Determining Negligence

The court commonly examines three factors to aid in its determination of whether or not a defendant's action constitutes negligence:

1. The extent and nature of the risk involved.
2. The social value and utility of the interest advanced.
3. The availability of an alternative course of action.

With the first factor, the greater the risk of a particular action (e.g., the risk of death), the greater the extent of precautions required by the actor. Acknowledgment that as the gravity of the potential harm of a given action increases, the apparent likelihood of the occurrence lessens, does not preclude precaution regarding an action that involves great risk. In other words, if the potential risk is significant—if death is likely to occur—the court will weigh less heavily the rarity of the event and will demand a higher degree of precaution despite the low probability of the particular harm in question. For example, a school bus carrying student-athletes to a game may be required to stop at all railroad crossings. The chance that the bus will be hit is extremely small, yet if a collision were to occur, the consequences could be devastating. Thus, the court would demand a high degree of precaution, even if this standard were not set by state statute. In sports, the degree of care required for archery might exceed the degree required for softball. Even though there might be the same likelihood of injury, the potential gravity of the harm in archery (death) is so much greater than for softball (broken bones) that the degree of care required may be greater.

In examining the second factor, the court will balance a consideration of the potential harm of an action and the probability of its occurrence against social value or utility in the interest which the actor seeks to advance. Swimming pools, for example, pose significant potential harm to the people who use them. Their introduction or continued use, however, may be justified in the public interest because of the tremendous amount of use and enjoyment they provide. Instead of banning swimming pools, federal and state governments may enact and impose safety regulations for their use. If the safety regulations are met and an injury occurs, the defendant will not be found negligent. In the same vein, sports will be found to have some social value or utility which will permit their continuance despite the potential for serious injury, although in theory the degree of social utility may vary from sport to sport. Thus, one issue is that of defining the extent or existence of a social value for a sport such as football which causes catastrophic injuries.

The third factor the court uses to determine whether or not an act is negligent is the availability to the actor of alternative courses of action. Different persons in the same situation may have a variety of courses of action available based on their age, knowledge, and/or experience. Acts will be negligent if the action taken is not one which is acceptable under a "reasonable person standard" and if there is an alternative available. For example, when confronted with a serious injury to an athlete, an athletic trainer may call for an ambulance or attempt to administer medical treatment without help. It may not always be reasonable to attempt to treat the injury without help. The athletic trainer may be negligent in failing to call for help if treating the serious injury (e.g., a spinal injury) is beyond his or her capability. This point leads to a discussion of the various elements and standards involved in the theory of negligence.

The following four elements must be proved by the plaintiff in order for an action to be considered negligence:

1. Duty of care owed
2. Breach of duty
3. Actual and proximate causation
4. Damages

Duty of Care Owed

The plaintiff in a negligence case must initially establish the duty of care owed to him or her by the defendant. Duty is divided into two categories: a duty to act and a duty not to act in an unreasonable manner. A *duty of care* is an obligation, recognized by law, which requires an individual or a group to conform to a particular standard of conduct toward another. The duty of care required of an individual is established by reference to any special qualifications. In the case of a professional (doctor, trainer), a duty of care is determined by uniform requirements that establish minimum standards of behavior. All professionals are judged not as individuals in society at large, but as members of a specified class. When acting in a professional capacity, the professional person will be judged by the standards of the profession in existence at the time.

The concept of *legal duty* is based on the relationship that exists between the parties involved. Certain relationships, such as employer-employee, principal-agent, teacher-student, and coach-athlete, establish a legal duty to act. An employer, for example, has the duty to render aid and assistance to an employee who is injured during the course of employment. However, absent a duty-imposing relationship, an individual is not liable for an omission to act. A moral obligation to act does not create a legal duty to act, and hence the individual who failed to act cannot be held liable in negligence. If one without a duty to act does undertake to act, however, that person may be held liable if he or she acts negligently. By acting, one can create a duty between oneself and another that may not have previously existed. For example, a person who undertakes to rescue another may not abandon that rescue attempt if it becomes inconvenient. By acting, the would-be rescuer has created a duty to continue to aid the person in trouble. In sports cases, the duty is often described as the "reasonable care" necessary to avoid creating risks that may result in injuries to players or spectators. For example, Peter Perry suffered a serious neck injury in a high school football practice. Coach Foot attempted to provide medical assistance. In doing so, he became responsible for causing further damage which left Peter paralyzed. Peter has grounds for a suit because the coach was negligent in acting as he did if the court finds that Coach Foot did not act as a "reasonable football coach" would act in this situation.

Often liability will rest on whether the court designates the act or nonact as misfeasance, nonfeasance, or malfeasance. *Misfeasance* is the term applied to lawful conduct that is improperly done. *Nonfeasance* is an omission of an action that ought to be taken. *Malfeasance* is the doing of an act that is wholly wrongful and unlawful.

NOTES ───

1. For a sports case in which a court decided that a legal duty was present, see *Berman v. Philadelphia Board of Education*, 456 A.2d 545 (Pa. Super. Ct. 1983). The plaintiff-student was injured during a school-sponsored floor hockey game supervised by a physical education instructor. A mouth guard would have prevented the injury, but Amateur Hockey Association rules did not require them at the time. The court, however, held that the board of education could not escape its duty of care for the welfare of students because of a lack of rules and standards.

2. For a sports case in which a court decided that no legal duty was required,

see *Scaduto v. State*, 446 N.Y.S.2d 529 (N.Y. App. Div. 1982), plaintiff was injured when he fell, after tripping on a drainage ditch while participating in an intramural softball game on a makeshift field usually reserved for soccer. The court held that the college breached no duty owed to the plaintiff. There was no duty to provide a perfectly level terrain, and the plaintiff assumed the dangers of the game, one of which was tripping in an attempt to catch a fly ball.

3. In *Fox, et al. v. Board of Supervisors of Louisiana State University and Agricultural and Mechanical College, et al.*, 76 So. 2d 978 (La. 1991), the plaintiff was a member of the St. Olaf rugby club team who broke his neck while participating in a rugby club tournament hosted by the Louisiana State University's rugby club team. The plaintiff filed suit against LSU and St. Olaf College arguing that LSU was negligent because it failed to ensure that the tournament was run safely and it was vicariously liable for the negligent conduct of the LSU rugby club, and that St. Olaf was liable for the actions of its rugby club team. Fox claimed that the LSU rugby club was negligent for having hosted a cocktail party the night before the tournament, scheduling two matches on the same day, and failing to determine whether the clubs participating in the tournament were properly trained or supervised. In order to recover for claims that LSU was negligent, Fox had to first prove that there is a relationship between the two parties that warranted a duty owed. The court found that no relationship existed between LSU and Fox which would have required LSU to owe a duty of care to Fox. The court also found that Fox's participation was voluntary and that he knew the dangers involved in the sport.

On the issue of vicarious liability, the court found that although LSU provided the LSU rugby club with office space, equipment, financial assistance, and a faculty adviser, the rugby club was not part of the university. LSU was not accountable, therefore, for the actions of the LSU rugby team. The court also accepted St. Olaf's argument along these same lines. St. Olaf argued, and the court agreed, it was not liable for the actions of its rugby team because it had no control over the rugby club; it did not provide the club with coaches, equipment, or uniforms; and, therefore, the club was not part of the school's athletic department. Control is the key determinant in these cases, and if the plaintiff can establish that the university has control over a club program, then the university may be held vicariously liable.

4. In *Wicina, By and Through Wicina v. Strecker*, 747 P.2d 167 (Kan. Sup. Ct. 1987), a private high school student injured during a football game filed a negligence action against his high school and other school officials for failure to provide disability insurance and failure to advise and inform the student of the extent of the insurance coverage provided. The district court sustained the defendant's motion to dismiss, and the student appealed. The Kansas Supreme Court affirmed the lower court decision and held that there was no duty by the private high school or its officials to provide disability insurance or to inform students of the extent of insurance coverage provided.

5. For further information, see the following law review article: Harty, "School Liability for Athletic Injuries: Duty, Causation and Defense," 21 *Washburn L. J.* 315 (1982).

Breach of Duty

Once a plaintiff has demonstrated that a duty of care was owed by the defendant, the plaintiff must prove that the defendant violated this duty. In other words, the burden of proof requires that the party on whom it rests establish the validity of the claim. There are three methods by which the plaintiff may sustain this burden of proof:

1. Direct evidence of negligence
2. Violation of a statute
3. Res ipsa loquitur

Direct evidence of negligence is evidence that tends to establish negligence through direct proof that actual factual occurrences happened. An example of direct evidence is eyewitness testimony. For instance, Larry Lacroix suffered an injury to his back in a high school lacrosse game. The athletic trainer told Coach Winatallcosts not to allow Larry to play and later served as an eyewitness against the coach at the trial. Coach Winatallcosts, ignoring the trainer's warning, coerced Larry to play the last ten minutes because the state championship was on the line. As a result of further play, Larry was more severely injured. Coach Winatallcosts breached the duty of care he owed Larry. The trainer's testimony and the injury constituted the direct evidence.

When direct evidence is not available, certain procedural devices are used to enable a plaintiff to prove his or her case. One of these is presumptions. A *presumption* is a legal fiction which requires the judge or jury to assume the existence of one fact on the basis of the existence of another fact or group of facts. It is used in the absence of sufficient evidence to prove the fact itself. The classic example is the presumption that a person who has been gone seven years without explanation is dead. Another type of presumption involves an individual who violates a valid statute.

Violation of a statute is sometimes referred to as *negligence per se*. Negligence per se means that upon finding a violation of an applicable statute, there is a conclusive presumption of negligence. This conclusive presumption requires that a jury find for the plaintiff. It does not allow the jury to weigh all the evidence and independently determine the relative liabilities of the parties. Although in some states the violation of a valid statute may be considered negligence per se, in other states, the violation of a statute, ordinance, or even an administrative regulation is deemed only evidence of negligence. The current trend is away from viewing violations of statutes as negligence per se. When a violation is treated as evidence of negligence, it is accorded a different weight. A jury will not be required to draw any specific conclusion from the violation. Instead, a violation merely establishes an inference of negligence that may or may not be accepted by the jury.

In order for a statutory violation to provide evidence of negligence, the complaining party must establish two points. First, the statutory violation must be causally related to the plaintiff's harm. If an individual's taillights are out in violation of a statute, that violation may only be used to establish negligence when the failure of the taillights causes an accident. The second factor to be considered is that the harm must be the sort sought to be prevented by the statute. If the driver of one car pushes another car into a wall, the fact that the pusher's car taillights do not work in violation of a motor vehicle safety statute is of little or no significance.

The last method of establishing the negligence of the defendant is through the use of the legal doctrine of *res ipsa loquitur*. Res ipsa loquitur permits the fact finder to infer both negligence and causation from circumstantial evidence. It is, in effect, another type of presumption. The plaintiff must establish that more likely than not, the harm to the plaintiff was a result of the defendant's negligence. In order to defeat the application of this doctrine, the defendant must establish that there is another, equally believable explanation of the injury to the plaintiff.

Res ipsa loquitur is strictly a procedural device designed to allow a plaintiff to establish an otherwise unprovable case. In negligence cases, direct evidence of the defendant's negligence may not be available. This doctrine allows a plaintiff to recover on the basis of what probably happened.

Presumptions may be rebuttable, depending on the situation. If rebuttable, the defendant or plaintiff may counter the presumption raised by the opposition through the introduction of alternative evidence tending to dispute the validity of the presumption.

NOTES ───

1. The doctrine of res ipsa loquitur was successfully raised in the following cases:

(a) *Parker v. Warren*, 503 S. W.2d 938 (Tenn. App. 1973). (See Chapter 7.)

(b) *Grauer v. State of New York*, 181 N.Y.S.2d 994 (N.Y. Ct. Cl. 1959). (See Chapter 7.)

2. For a case in which a court decided *not* to apply the doctrine of res ipsa loquitur, see *Jordan v. Loveland Skiing Corp.*, 503 P.2d 1034 (Colo. App. 1972). Plaintiff skier sought recovery for injuries sustained in a fall from defendant's ski lift. In ruling in favor of the defendant, the court of appeals held that the issues of the lift operator's negligence and proximate cause were

properly submitted to the jury and the doctrine of res ipsa loquitur did not apply.

Actual and Proximate Causation

The primary issue in the area of causation is that of *proximate cause*— that is, whether the defendant's negligent act was connected to the plaintiff's harm to such an extent as to be considered the legal cause of the harm. Before any determination of proximate cause, however, the defendant's conduct must be shown to be the actual cause of the plaintiff's harm. If the same harm would have resulted if the negligent act had never occurred, then the act is not the actual cause of the harm. This is sometimes referred to as the "but for" test; the particular harm in question would not have been suffered "but for" the negligent act of the defendant.

After the existence of actual causation between the plaintiff's harm and the defendant's act has been established, recovery requires that it be demonstrated that the latter is also the proximate cause of the former. Proximate cause is tested by determining whether or not the harm which resulted to the plaintiff was a reasonable, foreseeable consequence of the defendant's act. To demonstrate proximate cause, it is sufficient to show that the probable consequence of the defendant's act was harm of the same general character as that which befell the plaintiff. It is not necessary to show that the harm to the plaintiff in its precise form or particular manner should have been foreseen by the defendant. For example, Jerry Janitor, in cleaning a spot off the basketball court, used a cleaning substance that left the floor extremely slippery. During the game later that day, Ralph Rocket slipped on the spot and seriously injured his knee. Jerry's use of the improper cleaning substance was the proximate cause of Ralph's injury.

One last problem of determining causation occurs when there is more than one cause of injury. When a combination of causes leads to the damage, a defendant can defeat claims of liability by showing that there was an unforeseeable intervening cause. An *intervening cause* is one which comes into existence after the negligent action of the defendant and somehow affects the "result."

Often there may be more than one cause for any given injury. In such cases, no liability will be assigned to individual causes unless the individual cause was a "substantial factor" in the creation of the ultimate result. This substantial factor test precludes liability for inadvertent or minor causational factors. The test is predicated on the theory that any cause should not be held partly or totally liable for the injury unless it substantially causes the harm.

NOTES _____

1. For a case involving intervening negligence in which the court did *not* relieve the original wrongdoer of liability, see *Freeman v. United States*, 509

F.2d 626 (6th Cir. 1975). Plaintiff brought an action against the United States for wrongful death of parachutists. In affirming judgment for the plaintiff, the court of appeals held that the air controller owed a duty of care to the parachutists, that they were not contributorily negligent in jumping through the cloud cover into Lake Erie, and that the intervening negligence of the pilot and jump master in directing a jump through a cloud cover did not relieve the government of liability.

2. For cases in which the court decided that *no* proximate cause existed, see the following.

(a) In *Kallish v. American Baseball Club of Philadelphia*, 10 A.2d 831 (Pa. Super. Ct. 1940), plaintiff spectator sought recovery for injuries sustained by his four-year-old son when the boy fell from an overcrowded parapet in defendant's ballpark. In ruling in favor of the defendant, the superior court held that there was no circumstance from which it could have been foreseen and controlled by the club or that the club had knowledge or constructive notice that patrons were standing on the parapet or that their conduct was disorderly and that such conduct was the proximate cause of injury to the patron.

(b) In *Burkart v. Health and Tennis Corporation of America, Inc.*, 730 S.W.2d 367 (Tex. Ct. App. 1987), plaintiff brought suit against a health club for injuries received when he fell from a machine (Gravity Gym) which allows its user to hang upside down. Plaintiff alleged that the club failed to supervise his activities properly, that the club failed to inspect the Gravity Gym properly, and that the club's negligent failure to instruct its employees in the correct manner of using the Gravity Gym was the proximate cause of his injuries. The Texas Court of Appeals affirmed the lower court's decision in favor of the defendant, stating that the club's actions were not the proximate cause of the plaintiff's injuries.

(c) *In Allen v. Rutgers State University*, 523 A.2d 262 (N.J. Super. Ct. 1987), a student patron at a football game at the university brought negligence action against the university after suffering injuries at the game. The plaintiff was injured when he vaulted over a four-foot wall and fell approximately thirty feet. The plaintiff had been drinking although the university had a no alcohol policy in its stadium. The superior court entered judgment on a jury verdict in favor of the defendant, and the plaintiff appealed. The appellate court affirmed the lower court's decision and held that the lower court jury could properly find that the plaintiff had failed to establish that his injuries were proximately related to negligence of the university.

(d) In *Gehling v. St. George Univ. School of Medicine*, 705 F. Supp. 761 (E.D.N.Y. 1989), plaintiff's family sued the medical school for his death, which resulted from his running in a student-sponsored road race. The school was found not to be the proximate cause of the plaintiff's death, because the participant, a medical student, was aware of the dangers of running the race in tropical weather, being seventy-five pounds overweight, suffering from high blood pressure, and having ingested an amphetamine-like drug prior to the race.

(e) In *Wertheim v. U.S. Tennis Ass'n Inc.*, 540 N.Y.S.2d 443 (N.Y. Ct.

App. Div. 1989), the New York Supreme Court Appellate Division reversed the lower court finding for the plaintiff who sought recovery for the wrongful death of a tennis umpire who died after being hit in the groin by a served tennis ball. The court ruled that even if the tennis tournament operator breached a duty of care owed to the umpire, it was unlikely that this breach of duty was the proximate cause of the umpire's death. The umpire had chronic cardiovascular disease and eyewitness testimony was consistent with the opinion of appellant's expert that the umpire suffered a stroke upon being hit by the ball.

3. For cases in which the court decided that proximate cause *did* exist, see the following.

(a) In *Schofield v. Wood,* 49 N.E. 636 (Mass. S.J.C. 1898), plaintiff spectator sought recovery for injuries sustained when the rail he was leaning on gave way. Plaintiff contended that the rail had been negligently maintained. In affirming a jury verdict for the plaintiff, the Supreme Judicial Court held that the fact that other spectators pushed the plaintiff did not relieve defendant of liability for negligent maintenance of the rail.

(b) In *Locilento v. Coleman Catholic High School,* 523 N.Y.S.2d 198 (N.Y. Ct. App. 1987), the court found in favor of a student injured in an intramural football game in a suit against the school. The court held that the evidence sustained a finding that the school's failure to provide the student with proper equipment during an intramural tackle football game was a proximate cause of the shoulder injury and that the student's voluntary participation was merely an implied assumption of risk which did not preclude all recovery.

4. For further information, see the following law review article: Harty, "School Liability for Athletic Injuries: Duty, Causation and Defense," 21 *Washburn L. J.* 315 (Winter 1982).

Damages

Damages are a pecuniary compensation given by courts to any person who suffers an injury through the unlawful act, omission, or negligence of another. Damages may be either compensatory or punitive. *Compensatory damages* consist of money given to the injured party that is measured by the amount of actual injury incurred. For example, Suzie Slowpitch suffered an injury as a result of the negligence of the school district in not properly maintaining the softball field. She was hospitalized and missed work at her part-time job for three weeks. The court instructed the school district to compensate her for hospital costs and lost wages. In intentional tort actions, when no actual injury has occurred, nominal damages may still be awarded. These damages are a minimum amount given when no real loss or injury can be proved but when a right has been infringed. Generally, they are $1 or less.

Punitive damages are awarded to an injured party as punishment for outrageous conduct inflicted on the party and to deter future transgressions. They are awarded to a plaintiff in an amount over and above the amount given to compensate for the actual loss, where the wrong done was aggravated by violence, oppression, malice, fraud, or excessively wicked conduct. Punitive damages are intended to comfort the plaintiff for mental anguish, shame, or degradation suffered. In addition, punitive damages also serve to punish the defendant and to set an example for other wrongdoers. They are based on entirely different policy considerations than are compensatory damages, which merely reimburse a plaintiff for any actual loss suffered. For example, Kenny Kicker, after failing to complete a football drill successfully, in practice, was forced by Coach Haze to push a football back and forth in front of the school fifty times with his nose during school hours. Kenny sued Coach Haze and the school and was awarded punitive damages for suffering mental anguish, shame, and degradation.

Unlike intentional tort actions in which the plaintiff need not prove actual damages in order to recover, negligence actions require that the plaintiff establish that he or she suffered damage as a result of the defendant's conduct. In a negligence action, the plaintiff may seek recovery of damages in any or all of the following four areas:

1. Pain and suffering—past, present, and future
2. Medical expenses—past, present, and future
3. Diminution of earning capacity—past, present, and future
4. Loss of consortium (right to a spouse's companionship)

NOTES

1. In *Lynch v. Board of Education of Collingsville Community School District*, 390 N.E.2d 526 (Ill. Ct. App. 1979), the court awarded $600,000 in damages to the plaintiff because of a dramatic personality change caused by injuries received in a powderpuff football game that was authorized by the school. The school had failed to provide adequate protective equipment. (See Chapter 7.)

2. In *Benjamin v. State*, 453 N.Y.S.2d 329 (N.Y. Ct. Cl. 1982), the court awarded compensatory damages for reimbursement of medical expenses incurred by the plaintiff spectator as a result of injuries sustained when a hockey puck left the rink. (See Chapter 7.)

Wrongful Death Statutes

Wrongful death statutes exist in all states. They provide a statutory cause of action in favor of the decedent's (person who died) personal representative for the benefit of certain beneficiaries (e.g., a spouse, parent, or child) against the person who negligently caused the death of the spouse, parent, or child. The provision changes the common law rule that the cause of the action died (ended) with the death of the person. The cause of action is for the wrong to the beneficiaries and for their loss of companionship and suffering—not for the harm done to the decedent.

The majority of the statutes award compensatory damages. These damages attempt to evaluate the monetary worth of the individual and award money based on that determination. In a minority of jurisdictions, the statutes measure damages by the level of culpability shown by the negligent party. The damages awarded are greater for injuries inflicted intentionally than for those inflicted negligently. Additionally, a few states employ a combination of the two methods to determine damages.

NOTES

1. For a case in which the court decided that a wrongful death statute was not applicable, see *Truelove v. Wilson*, 285 S.E.2d 556 (Ga. Ct. App. 1981). An action was brought for wrongful death of a student who was fatally injured when struck by a metal soccer goalpost during a physical education class. Punitive damages and damages for maintenance of a nuisance were also sought. The DeKalb Superior Court decided in favor of the defendants and held that (1) punitive damages were not available in wrongful death actions; (2) the county board of education and the county school district were entitled to a defense of sovereign immunity; and (3) individual defendants who were school employees and members of the county board of education were entitled to the defense of sovereign immunity.

2. In *Fish v. Los Angeles Dodgers Baseball Club*, 128 Cal. Rptr. 807 (Cal. Ct. App. 1976), a wrongful death action was brought by parents whose son died after being struck in the head by a line-drive foul ball. The baseball club and its agent-doctor operating its emergency medical station were found liable. Experts testified that the doctor was negligent in treating decedent, because of his failure to immobilize decedent immediately after his injury, which probably prevented the hemorrhage from stopping by the normal healing process. While experts also testified that decedent could have been saved by emergency surgery which the hospital never performed, the court ruled that as a concurrent cause of the boy's death, the hospital's negligence was no defense to the defendant's negligence.

3. For other cases in which the court decided that a wrongful death statute was applicable, see the following.

    (a) *Mogabgab v. Orleans Parish School Board*, 239 So. 2d 456 (La. Ct. App. 1970). (See Chapter 7.)

    (b) *Woodring v. Board of Education of Manhasset*, 435 N.Y.S.2d 52 (N.Y. App. Div. 1981). (See Chapter 7.)

Reasonable Person Standard

Even if a particular relationship does not exist between parties, a person owes to others the duty of exercising reasonable care in his or her activities. The courts "measure" the conduct in each negligence case against the "reasonable person" standard—that is, how a person of ordinary sense using ordinary care and skill would react under similar circumstances. It is important to note that the conduct of the "reasonable person" is not necessarily "perfect" conduct but is that of a prudent and careful individual. As employed by the courts, the standard of reasonableness takes into account the risk apparent to an actor, the capacity of the actor to meet the risk, and the circumstances under which the person must act.

The reasonable person is held to possess a minimum level of knowledge common to the community in which the injury occurs. A negligent defendant who possesses superior knowledge, skill, or intelligence, however, will be held to a greater degree of care—that is, conduct which conforms to that of others with similar knowledge and/or skills. For example, a team doctor performing a procedure on an athlete on the playing field would be held to the same standard of skill and conduct exhibited by other team doctors in the same specialty performing a similar procedure. When the reasonable person standard entails a degree of skill or knowledge higher than that of a judge or the lay person sitting on a jury, qualified expert testimony is utilized to establish the proper standard of care for the defendant. Again, using the case of a team doctor sued for negligence, both parties would probably call as witnesses other qualified team doctors to testify as to how the procedure is usually performed and what precautions or steps are taken under normal circumstances. This expert testimony would help establish the standard of care for the situation. The jury would then determine whether the defendant surgeon met the standard of care.

The reasonable person is deemed to possess physical characteristics identical to those of the defendant. If the actor is exceptionally strong, for example, the standard of care demands that the person exhibit conduct which parallels that of a reasonably prudent person of like strength under similar circumstances. The reasonable person standard does not take into account the temperament or emotions of the individual actor. The law seeks an objective standard, not a subjective one based on a person's mental attributes. There are several reasons for this. First, it would be extremely difficult, if not impossible, to prove what was in an individual's mind at the time of the particular conduct. Second, the harm caused by a negligent act is not changed by the actor's particular thoughts or feelings. Finally, the courts have determined that a person must learn to conform to the standards of the community or to pay for violating those standards.

It is argued that in extreme cases of mental deficiency the actor cannot comprehend the danger inherent in certain conduct. The courts, however, have still applied the reasonable person standard when dealing with insane defendants. This is based on the public policy consideration of promoting the responsibility of guardians for those in their care. The sanction for civil liability involves monetary compensation and not personal liberty. Therefore, courts and legislatures have determined that protecting the public from harm, or at least requiring those responsible to pay for their own harm, justifies distinguishing between civil liability and moral culpability.

A "greater degree of care" standard may be applicable when dealing with an inherently dangerous object or an activity in which it is reasonably foreseeable that an accident or injury may occur.

NOTE ───

1. The courts found that a reasonable care standard was exercised by a defendant in the following cases.

(a) In *Johnson v. Krueger*, 539 P.2d 1296 (Colo. Ct. App. 1975), plaintiff sought recovery in negligence for injuries sustained when, while playing football, he ran onto defendant's land and fell on a stump ten inches high and six inches in diameter. In ruling in favor of the landowner, the Court of Appeals held that the landowner did not act unreasonably in leaving the stump on his land. It was not reasonably foreseeable that a child would run from a football game onto an adjacent lot, a considerable distance onto landowner's property, and fall on the stump, which was clearly visible, even when the owner knew children often played football on the adjacent lot.

(b) In *Rabiner v. Rosenberg*, 28 N.Y.S.2d 533 (N.Y. City Civ. Ct. 1941), plaintiff spectator sued for damages sustained when a fish slipped off defendant fisherman's hook, causing the hook to snap back and become embedded in the plaintiff's eye. The trial court, in ruling in favor of the defendant, held that the fisherman acted as any prudent fisherman would have and was not liable.

(c) In *Reddick v. Lindquist*, 484 S.W.2d 441 (Tex. Civ. App. 1972), plaintiff widow sued in wrongful death for the loss of her husband, who was killed when defendant's boat ran over him after he fell while water skiing. In ruling in favor of the defendant, the Court of Civil Appeals held that the deceased's negligence in attempting a maneuver which an ordinarily prudent skier would not have tried was the proximate cause of the fatal accident.

(d) In *Smith v. Vernon Parish School Bd.*, 442 So.2d 1319 (La. Ct. App. 1983), plaintiff sued the school board, the physical education teacher, and the insurer of the teacher for damages suffered in a trampoline activity during a physical education class at a high school. The court held that the teacher exercised reasonable supervision and that the "greater degree of care" standard was not applicable.

(e) In *Tiemann v. Independent School Dist.*, 331 N.W.2d 250 (Minn. Sup. Ct. 1983), plaintiff was injured during a physical education class taught by defendant teacher while undertaking a vault over a vaulting horse. Plaintiff claimed that injury occurred because of exposed holes from the removal of "pommels," or handles, which left two half-inch holes; and one finger got stuck, causing the plaintiff to fall to the floor. The court held for the plaintiff and found that the exposed-hole horses fell below the requirements of reasonable care regardless of the prevailing custom, which was to use vaulting horses with exposed holes where the pommels were removed.

(f) In *Robitaille et al. v. Vancouver Hockey Club Ltd.*, 124 D.L.R.3d 228 (B.C. Ct. App. 1981), plaintiff hockey player sought to recover for damages sustained after suffering a permanent spinal cord injury in a hockey game. The plaintiff had suffered a minor injury to the spinal cord in two hockey games, prior to the one in which he was injured. The club doctors failed to examine him after the first two injuries. The court held that the club was negligent in failing to subject the player to a thorough medical examination after the earlier injuries and in failing to prevent him from playing in the final game. In holding for the plaintiff, the court said that the club breached its duty to exercise reasonable care to ensure the safety, fitness, and health of its players.

Standard of Care for Children

Children as defendants in a negligence case present an important exception to the reasonable person standard. Children are not held to the same objective standard of duty that is applied to adults. The courts recognize that at young age levels there exists a wide range of mental capabilities and experiences. The law attempts to accommodate this variety by viewing the reasonable child as one who exercises in his or her actions a degree of care that is reasonably to be expected of children of like age, intelligence, and experience. For example, in a baseball game an eleven-year-old boy swung at a pitched ball and missed it; the bat slipped from his hands, struck his teammate in the head, and caused serious injuries. The court held that there was no negligence because the youngster exercised a reasonable degree of care for a person of his age, intelligence, and experience. However, under this more subjective standard, it follows that if a six-year-old boy has intelligence vastly superior to that of his peers, the child will be held to that standard of care encompassing his superior knowledge. Several states have established age brackets which purport to distinguish childhood from adulthood. This method has been criticized, however, because of the problems inherent in setting an accurate age-level guideline regarding mental capabilities.

An exception to the application of this subjective standard for children occurs when a child engages in an activity normally reserved for adults, such as driving an automobile or hunting with a gun. In cases such as these, the courts in many jurisdictions will apply the reasonable standard for adults without any special consideration of the fact that the individual is a child.

Defenses for Negligence

Once the four elements essential to a negligence action have been presented by the plaintiff, the defendants in such lawsuits can employ a number of defenses. The following are the most common defenses employed by defendants in tort actions for negligence:

1. No negligence
2. Contributory negligence
3. Comparative negligence
4. Assumption of risk
5. Immunity, statute of limitations, and Good Samaritan statutes

No Negligence

The defendant usually attempts to prove first that his or her behavior did not constitute negligence. This can be approached in two ways. The defendant can dispute the negligence claim by either attacking one or more of the four previously discussed requirements for negligence or by proving that he exercised reasonable care in his or her actions. Thus a defendant may defend a claim of negligence by asserting that he or she had no duty toward the plaintiff. Even if a defendant had a duty toward the plaintiff, (s)he would not be liable if (s)he did not breach that duty. Therefore, if the defendant owed the plaintiff a duty of reasonable care and properly discharged that duty, any harm to the plaintiff would not be actionable negligence on the part of the defendant.

NOTE _____

1. For a case in which the plaintiff was precluded from recovery because the defendant was not negligent, see *Cramer v. Hoffman*, 390 F.2d 19 (2d Cir. 1968). The court found, on the basis of New York law, that an institution was not liable for the negligence of a physician who was an independent contractor exercising his own discretion. The court concluded that there was not an automatic agency relationship established between the university and its physician.

2. In *Gehling v. St. George Univ. School of Medicine*, 705 F. Supp. 761 (E.D.N.Y. 1989), the court held that defendant medical school was not negligent in the death of a participant in a student-sponsored road race. The court found that although the school knew of the race, it did not control, monitor, or supervise it and, thus, did not have sufficient control to be in a position to prevent negligence.

Contributory Negligence

Any act of the plaintiff which amounts to a lack of ordinary care and contributes to the proximate cause of the injury is contributory negligence. Contributory negligence is, in essence, a departure from the standard of reasonableness required of all people, including plaintiffs. There does not have to be an actual appreciation of the risk involved. There need only be a risk that is known or would be known and avoided by a reasonable person. A plaintiff also has a duty to exercise ordinary care. Without such care, the plaintiff is at least to some degree contributorily negligent.

In a jurisdiction that recognizes the defense of contributory negligence, a finding of contributory negligence effectively bars the plaintiff from any recovery from the defendant. The success of the defense of contributory negligence rests on the defendant's ability to prove that the plaintiff failed to exercise due care for his or her own safety and that this lack of due care was the proximate cause of the plaintiff's injury. In contributory negligence theory, as in negligence theory, the standard of care for children is reasonable care. The child's age, intelligence, and experience, however, are relevant to the issue of whether reasonable care was exercised. With respect to both negligence and contributory negligence, there are situations in which the negligent conduct of one party may be imputed to a second party under the doctrine of respondeat superior, which means "let the superior reply."

NOTES ──

1. In the following cases the plaintiff was precluded from recovery because of a successful contributory negligence defense.

(a) In *Juntila v. Everett School Dist. #24*, 48 P.2d 613 (Wash. Sup. Ct. 1935), plaintiff spectator sought recovery for injuries sustained when the guard railing on which he was seated while watching a football game collapsed. In ruling for the defendant, the Washington Supreme Court held that the plaintiff, who sat on the railing knowing it was not intended as a seat, was contributorily negligent.

(b) In *Powless v. Milwaukee Co.*, 94 N.W.2d 187 (Wis. Sup. Ct. 1959), plaintiff spectator sought recovery for injuries suffered because she was struck by a foul ball. In ruling for the defendant, the Wisconsin Supreme Court held that even if owners were negligent under the "safe-place" statute, the plaintiff's choice of seat and failure to react to the noise and excitement around her after hearing the bat hit the ball made her contributorily negligent.

(c) In *Shields v. Van Kelton Amusement Corp.*, 127 N.E. 261 (N.Y. Ct. App. 1920), plaintiff ice skater sought recovery for injuries sustained when she fell as a result of a soft spot on defendant's outdoor skating rink. In ruling against the plaintiff, the court of appeals held that the plaintiff, an experienced skater, was aware that the ice was getting soft and that defendant's placement of benches near the soft spot to prevent access was sufficient to notify patrons of dangerous areas. Therefore, the court found that the plaintiff was contributorily negligent.

(d) In *Pierce v. Murnick*, 145 S.E.2d 11 (N.C. Sup. Ct. 1965), plaintiff, a ringside spectator at defendant promoter's wrestling match, sought recovery for injuries sustained when a wrestler fell on him from the ring. In ruling for the defendant, the North Carolina Supreme Court held that the promoter was not required to take steps for the safety of invitees which would reasonably impair enjoyment of the exhibition by the usual patrons, and that even if defendant were negligent in failing to take precautions to protect the plaintiff, the plaintiff was barred by contributory negligence in choosing the ringside seat.

(e) In *Polsky v. Levine*, 243 N.W.2d 503 (Wis. Sup. Ct. 1976), plaintiff, a minor, sought recovery for injuries sustained while water skiing on defendant camp operator's lake. In ruling for the defendant, the Wisconsin Supreme Court held that since plaintiff could have kicked the rope and tow bar free and avoided injury, but did not do so because he would have fallen and received unsuccessful marks, he failed to exercise ordinary care for his own safety and could not recover.

2. For a case in which the defense of contributory negligence was *not* successful, see *Harrison v. Montgomery County Board of Education*, 456 A.2d 894 (Md. Ct. App. 1983). A suit was brought by an eighth grader who was rendered a quadriplegic while attempting a running front flip during a "free exercise" day in the gymnasium. The Maryland court refused to abandon the doctrine of contributory negligence in favor of comparative negligence. The court found dissatisfaction with the doctrine in Maryland case law; however, the court said that a change should be left to the legislature.

3. In *Richardson v. Clayton & Lambert Manufacturing Co.*, 657 F. Supp. 751 (N.D. Mo. 1987), a swimmer brought suit against the manufacturer of a pool for injuries sustained when he dove into the pool and struck the bottom. The manufacturer alleged that the swimmer assumed the risk of injury when he dove into shallow water. The court disagreed, claiming the issue was one of contributory negligence. Thus, the negligence of both parties was considered.

4. In *Wilkinson v. Hartford Accident and Indemnity Co.*, 411 So. 2d 22 (La. Sup. Ct. 1982), plaintiff sued the athletic coach, school board, and school's liability insurer to recover for injuries which his son sustained when he crashed through a glass panel of the gymnasium foyer while engaging in an unsupervised race during physical education class. The Louisiana Supreme Court reversed a lower court's decision and held that the minor plaintiff was not contributorily negligent because the race in the foyer was simply an unsupervised extension of the races on the basketball court and the plaintiff had no reason to know that the panel was not of safety glass.

Comparative Negligence

Comparative negligence is a statutory rule adopted in many states in an effort to alleviate the harshness of the contributory negligence doctrine. Where both the plaintiff and the defendant are negligent, comparative negligence statutes seek to divide the responsibility between the two negligent parties. Under a comparative negligence statute, the jury or fact finder determines the proportionate degree of negligence that will be attributed to all parties involved. The damages are then assessed pro rata.

In states that have adopted the doctrine of comparative negligence, contributory negligence on the part of the plaintiff is not necessarily a complete bar to recovery. Generally, one of two rules is applied under the theory of comparative negligence in most states:

1. If the plaintiff's negligence as compared with total negligence of all defendants is greater than 50 percent, plaintiff is totally barred from recovery. For example, a plaintiff who is determined to be 60 percent at fault will not be able to recover against the defendant, or
2. If the plaintiff's negligence as compared with the total negligence of all defendants is 50 percent or less, plaintiff's damages are reduced in proportion to his or her negligence. For example, a plaintiff who suffers $100,000 in damages and whose negligence is determined to be 40 percent recovers $100,000 minus 40 percent of $100,000, or $60,000.

NOTE

1. *Ford v. Gouin,* 266 Cal. Rptr. 87 (Cal. Ct. App. 1990) discusses the relationship of the defense of assumption of risk to comparative negligence.

Assumption of Risk

Assumption of risk means that the plaintiff has given prior consent to what would normally be an unpermitted, potentially injury-causing action. This consent effectively relieves a defendant's obligation to a certain standard of conduct toward the plaintiff. There is no longer any legal duty existing between the two. When there is no duty, there is no negligence.

There are three types of assumption of risk. The first, express assumption of risk, arises when a plaintiff gives advance consent to relieve a defendant of a legal duty and to take his or her chances from a known risk. The second, unreasonable implied assumption of risk, arises when a plaintiff negligently chooses to encounter a known risk. The third, reasonable implied assumption of risk, arises when a plaintiff's reasonable conduct in encountering a known risk creates an inference that he or she has agreed to relieve the defendant's duty of care.

Assumption of risk requires that the plaintiff know and fully appreciate the risks involved in pursuing the course of action to which he or she is committed. In addition to knowing and appreciating the risk, the plaintiff must also carefully and reasonably agree to assume whatever risk is involved.

The defense of assumption of risk may be utilized in those states that have not passed a comparative negligence statute to supplement the contributory negligence statute. In such states, the defendant may claim that the plaintiff, by assuming the risk of injury, is barred from any recovery. Under the comparative negligence statute, however, partial recovery is allowed in many situations in which the plaintiff's contributory negligence proximately contributed to his injury. This did not reconcile with the previous legal interpretation under which no recovery was allowed to a plaintiff who was found to have assumed the risk, even when such assumption of risk was considered reasonable under the circumstances. In states in which assumption of risk has been abolished as a defense in negligence actions, a plaintiff is entitled to full recovery if his or her assumption of risk was reasonable. In sports cases, assumption of risk is an important concept because its action may negate a plaintiff's case. If the plaintiff is deemed to have assumed the risk, there may be a valid excuse for a tort that may have been committed.

NOTES _____

1. The plaintiff was precluded from recovery because of a successful assumption of risk defense in the following cases.

(a) In *Schentzel v. Philadelphia Nat'l League Club,* 96 A.2d 181 (Sup. Ct. Pa. 1953), plaintiff, a woman spectator viewing a baseball game for the first time, sought recovery for injuries sustained when she was struck by a foul ball while seated in the upper deck near first base. The court held that the plaintiff knew or should have known that foul balls sometimes go astray, that she had assumed the risk, and that the defendant was not negligent in failing to provide screens for the upper deck.

(b) In *Richmond v. Employers' Fire Insurance Co.,* 298 So. 2d 118 (La. Ct. App. 1974), plaintiff, a college baseball player, sought recovery from the defendant college coach and insurance company for injuries sustained during practice in which the coach was allegedly negligent in allowing a bat to fly from his hands. In ruling for the defendants, the court of appeals held that the coach was not negligent and that the player had assumed the risk of injury inherent in a baseball practice session.

(c) *Ordway v. Superior Court,* 243 Cal. Rptr. 536 (Cal. Ct. App. 1988), involved a professional jockey's claim for damages for injuries sustained when thrown from his horse in a race as a result of another jockey's rule violation. The court found that when the plaintiff raced, he voluntarily and reasonably assumed the risk of injury, thereby reducing the defendant's duty of care.

(d) In *Turcotte v. Fell,* 502 N.E.2d 964 (N.Y. Ct. App. 1986), a jockey was permanently injured when an opponent who was riding carelessly caused him to be thrown from his horse. The court found that horse racing is an inherently dangerous sport and, as such, a jockey assumes the risk of injury caused by an opponent's careless riding.

(e) In *Kuehner v. Green*, 436 So. 2d 78 (Fla. Sup. Ct. 1983), plaintiff sued defendant for injuries incurred in a karate sparring match. Finding for the defendant, the court held that where plaintiff was familiar with the dangers associated with karate and decided to participate in the competition, he waived his right to be free from bodily contacts inherent in the chance taken.

(f) In *Ford v. Gouin*, 266 Cal. Rptr. 87 (Cal. Ct. App. 1990), plaintiff was injured when, while waterskiing on a narrow river channel, he collided with a tree limb overhanging the waterway. As a result, plaintiff suffered severe head injuries. At the time of the accident plaintiff was skiing backward and barefoot and the boat towing the plaintiff was driven by the defendant. Evidence showed the plaintiff had skied in this area over fifty times before and was well aware of the channel and branches hanging over the waterway. Thus, the court held that the plaintiff reasonably assumed the risks inherent in the activity because of his extensive experience as a water skier in the area where his injuries occurred.

(g) In *Novak v. Lamar Ins. Co.*, 488 So. 2d 739 (La. Cir. Ct. App. 1986), plaintiff softball player brought action against a second softball player, the homeowner's insurer of that player's father, and the insurer of the church which sponsored the defendant softball player's team. Plaintiff sought recovery for injuries sustained when the two collided as defendant softball player ran to first base. The court held that the defendant softball player was not acting in a reckless or unsportsmanlike manner. The court reasoned that the risk of collision was a foreseeable risk which the plaintiff had assumed.

(h) In *Wertheim v. U.S. Tennis Ass'n Inc.*, 540 N.Y.S.2d 443 (N.Y. App. Div. 1989), plaintiff executrix sought recovery for the wrongful death of a tennis umpire who died after being hit in the groin by a served tennis ball. In reversing the lower court finding for the plaintiff, the New York Supreme Court held that the umpire had assumed the risk of being struck by a served tennis ball.

(i) In *Benitez v. New York City Bd. of Educ.*, 541 N.E.2d (N.Y. Ct. App. 1989), plaintiff high school football player brought personal injury action against the board of education and the city public school athletic league. The plaintiff alleged negligence of the coach and principal in permitting him to play in a mismatched game in a fatigued condition. In reversing the lower court's decision, the appeals court ruled in favor of the defendants and held that the board of education and its organized athletic counsels must exercise ordinary reasonable care to protect student-athletes voluntarily involved in extracurricular sports from unassumed, concealed, or unreasonably increased risks. In this case, the school district was not liable to the player because player assumed the risks of injury in competition and was not under inherent compulsion to play.

(j) In *Breheny v. The Catholic University of America*, 1989 U.S. District

Lexis 14029, plaintiff brought action against defendant school after fracturing her ankle in an intramural touch football game on a wet field. The court ruled in favor of defendant and reasoned that the plaintiff had knowledge of the risk involved in playing under such conditions. Therefore, plaintiff's claim was barred by the doctrine of assumption of risk.

2. The defense of assumption of risk was *not* successful in the following cases.

(a) In *Rutter v. Northeastern Beaver County School District*, 437 A.2d 1198 (Pa. Sup. Ct. 1981), the plaintiff lost an eye as a result of an injury which occurred during a summer football practice supervised by the high school coaches. The plaintiff was playing a type of touch football known as "jungle football" when he was injured. The court abolished the doctrine of assumption of risk because of the extreme difficulty in applying the doctrine and because the doctrine is duplicative of two other concepts—the scope of the defendant's duty and the plaintiff's contributory negligence.

(b) In *Stevens v. Central School District*, 270 N.Y.S.2d 23 (N.Y. App. Div. 1966), plaintiff sought recovery for injuries sustained when, while playing basketball in defendant's school building, his momentum carried him through a glass window in a door just behind the basket. In ruling for the plaintiff, the court held the plaintiff had not assumed the risk of the dangerous condition caused by use of ordinary window glass in the door. The court ruled that the defendant was negligent in not using safety glass in the doors.

(c) In *Codd v. Stevens Pass, Inc.*, 725 P.2d 1008 (Wash. Ct. App. 1986), a skier chose to ski an "ungroomed area" between two "groomed" trails and fell, struck his head, and was killed. The decedent's wife brought suit against the ski area, claiming that it had not met the duty of care owed the decedent. The court found that as an invitee, the decedent was owed by the ski operator an affirmative duty of care for the "area of invitation." The defendant claimed that an ungroomed trail was an unimproved area and that, under Washington statute, the decedent assumed the risk of such injury. The court disagreed and extended the area of invitation to encompass the entire area serviced by the chair lifts.

3. In *Kelleher v. Big Sky of Montana*, 642 F. Supp. 1128 (D.C. Mont. 1986), a skier injured in an avalanche brought an action against the ski area for damages. The defendant contended that the plaintiff's recovery was barred under the Montana statute which provides that "skier[s] assume the risk and all legal responsibility for injury...." Plaintiff then contended that the statute was unconstitutional, for it would bar his opportunity to recover. The court disagreed, however, finding that because the statute defined the risks of skiing, and that negligence was not such a risk, recovery was possible under a valid negligence theory.

4. In *King v. Kayak Manufacturing Corp.* 688 F. Supp. 227 (D.C. W. Va. 1989), the plaintiff sued a manufacturer of an aboveground swimming pool under a product liability claim when he was rendered quadraplegic after diving into four feet of water. The trial court held the manufacturer strictly

liable and directed the verdict for the plaintiff. The appellate court reversed and remanded the case to resolve the issues of whether the plaintiff was contributorily negligent and assumed the risk of injury on the dive.

5. In *Locilento v. Coleman Catholic High School*, 523 N.Y.S.2d 198 (N.Y. App. Div. 1987), the court found in favor of a student injured in an intramural football game in a suit against the school. The court held that evidence sustained a finding that the school's failure to provide the student with proper equipment during an intramural tackle football game was a proximate cause of the shoulder injury and that the student's voluntary participation was merely an implied assumption of risk which did not preclude all recovery.

6. For more information on the *Rutter* decision, see the following law review article: Comment, *"Rutter v. Northeastern Beaver County School District,"* 21 *Duq. L. Rev.* 815 (1983).

Immunity, Statute of Limitations, Good Samaritan Statutes

Other defenses that may be raised when appropriate are those of immunity, expiration of the statute of limitations, and Good Samaritan statutes. The same type of immunity that can be raised in assault and battery cases—that stemming from relationships between the parties or the capacity of the parties—can also be applied to negligence actions. The trend, however, is to move away from an immunity defense based solely on the relationship of the parties.

Most states have sovereign immunity statutes which protect the government from tort liability. In addition, there is a developing trend to enact immunity legislation to protect those involved in amateur athletics from civil liability (see the section Civil Liability Immunity Legislation). Individual states establish statutory periods for maintaining a tort action, and a plaintiff filing an action after the expiration of the state's statute of limitations is completely barred from recovery. (See *Hackbart v. Cincinnati Bengals*, 435 F. Supp. 352 [D. Colo. 1977], *rev'd*, 601 F.2d 516 [10th Cir. 1979], on the issue of assault and battery.)

Another statutory defense involves the Good Samaritan doctrine. Good Samaritan statutes, as a matter of law, preclude negligence liability for one who sees and attempts to aid another person who has been placed in imminent and serious peril through the negligence of a third person. States that have adopted Good Samaritan statutes will impose a lesser standard of care for doctors and other individuals trained in first aid who gratuitously render medical assistance to a sick or injured person. Good Samaritan statutes generally protect medical personnel rendering aid from liability, unless the treatment provided is grossly negligent or actually worsens the condition of the person in need of treatment.

NOTES ⎯⎯⎯⎯⎯⎯⎯⎯⎯⎯⎯⎯⎯⎯⎯⎯⎯⎯⎯⎯⎯⎯⎯⎯⎯⎯⎯

1. New York has a Good Samaritan statute that applies to dentists:

Notwithstanding any inconsistent provision of any general, special or local law, any licensed dentist who voluntarily and without the expectation of monetary compensation renders first aid or emergency treatment at the scene of an accident or other emergency, outside of a hospital or any other place having proper and necessary medical equipment, to a person who is unconscious, ill or injured shall not be liable for damages for injuries alleged to have been sustained by such person or for damages for the death of such person alleged to have occurred by reason of an act or omission in the rendering of such first aid or emergency treatment unless it is established that such injuries were or such death was caused by gross negligence on the part of such dentist. Nothing in this subdivision shall be deemed or construed to relieve a licensed dentist from liability for damages for injuries or death caused by an act or omission on the part of a dentist while rendering professional services in the normal and ordinary course of practice. (Title 8 Art. 133 Education Law, Section 6611)

2. The following examples of Good Samaritan statutes are from the Massachusetts General Laws.

Ch. 111C Sec. 13. Liability of doctors, nurses, hospitals, ambulance operators and attendants:

No physician duly registered ... and no hospital shall be liable in a suit for damages as a result of acts or omissions related to advice, consultation or orders given in good faith to ambulance operators and attendants who ... under emergency conditions and prior to arrival of the patient at the hospital, clinic, office or other health facility from which the emergency communication to the ambulance operators or attendant is made shall be liable in a suit for damages as result of his said acts or omissions based upon said advice, consultations or orders....

Ch. 71, Sec. 54A. Physician or person trained in emergency medical care; assignment to interscholastic football games:

A physician employed by a school committee or a person who has completed a full course in emergency medical care as provided in section six of chapter one hundred and eleven C shall be assigned to every interscholastic football game played by any team representing a public secondary school in the commonwealth, and the expenses of such physician or person shall be paid by the school committee of the city, town or district wherein such football game is played.

Ch. 71, Sec. 55A. Sick, injured or incapacitated pupils; procedure for handling; emergency first aid or transportation; teachers, et al. exempted from civil liability.

No public school teacher and no collaborative school teacher, no principal, secretary to the principal, nurse or other public school or collaborative school employee who, in good faith, renders emergency first aid or transportation to a student who has become injured or incapacitated in a public school or collaborative school building or on the grounds thereof shall be liable in a suit for damages as a result of his acts or omissions either for such first aid or as a result of providing such emergency transportation to a place of safety, nor shall such person be liable to a hospital for its expenses if under such emergency conditions he causes the admission of such injured or incapacitated student, nor shall such person be subject to any disciplinary action by the school committee, or collaborative board of such collaborative for such emergency first aid or transportation.

Ch. 231. Sec. 85I. Emergency care, etc. of injured persons by members of ski patrols; exemption from civil liability:

No member of a ski patrol duly registered in the National Ski Patrol system, who, in good faith, renders emergency care or treatment to a person who has become injured or incapacitated at a place or in an area where an emergency rescue can be best accomplished by the members of such a ski patrol together with their special equipment, shall be liable in a suit for damages as a result of his acts or omissions, either for such care or treatment or as a result of providing emergency transportation to a place of safety, nor shall he be liable to a hospital for its expenses if, under such emergency conditions, he causes the admission of such injured or incapacitated person.

3. In *Ramos v. Waukegan Community Unit School District No. 60,* 544 N.E.2d 1302 (Ill. App. Ct. 1989), the court found the school district immune from liability for ordinary negligence under the Tort Claims Act. Because the plaintiff showed no evidence of willful and wanton misconduct, the court denied recovery for injuries sustained while jumping rope on a cracked sidewalk.

4. In *Kirschner v. Carney-Nadeau Public Schools,* 436 N.W.2d. 416 (Mich. Ct. App. 1989), plaintiff suffered near-fatal injuries on the school playground during a tackling game and sued the school, its superintendent, and principal. The court held that the superintendent and principal were entitled to limited governmental immunity because setting policy to supervise the playground was a discretionary duty.

5. See Chapter 7 for a discussion of sovereign immunity and a discussion of civil liability immunity, including examples of proposed and enacted legislation.

THE DOCTRINE OF VICARIOUS LIABILITY

The doctrine of vicarious liability imposes liability for a tortious act upon a person who is not personally negligent but is held liable because of the relationship between the parties. The most typical relationships which give rise to vicarious liability are master-servant (employer-employee) and principal-agent. Vicarious liability is also known as the doctrine of respondeat superior.

Vicarious liability imposes liability for a negligent act by A upon C, because of some legal relationship between A and B, such as employer-employee. Under the doctrine of vicarious liability, B is liable to C, the party injured by A, even though B was not himself negligent, did not aid or encourage the negligence of A, and did everything he could to prevent harm to C. For example, if the groundskeeper of a stadium fails to fix a hole on the front of the pitcher's mound and an injury results to a player, the owner of the stadium and the employer of the groundskeeper may be held vicariously liable to the injured player.

The justification for the doctrine of vicarious liability has been a topic of debate since the doctrine first appeared in the mid-1700s. The catalyst for the introduction of vicarious liability was the industrial revolution, which complicated commerce and industry. The rationale behind the doctrine is based on public policy considerations. Since the servant is furthering the master's employment, the master should be responsible for the servant's actions. This places an increased burden on the master, but the master is in a better position to bear the risks of injuries to others. A master is in a better position to cover risks by insuring himself. In addition, this doctrine allows an innocent plaintiff to recover from a "deep pocket."

In sports-related cases under vicarious liability, the employer may be held responsible when the employer exercises control and direction over the employee, and the employee is negligent while acting within the scope of his employment. Vicarious liability is usually imposed when an employee has been involved in unreasonable or grossly negligent conduct. Liability is usually not imposed on the employer for intentional torts committed by the employee. An intentional tort is usually considered beyond the scope of authority and control of the employer, and not in the furtherance of the employer's business. For example, if a coach assaults a bartender after work, the school district will not be held liable under a vicarious liability theory. However, an employer may be held responsible for an intentional tort committed by an employee if the employee was under the authority and control of the employer and the employee is in a position where such torts may be encouraged or expected in furtherance of the employer's business. These same general rules apply to principal-agent vicarious liability situations in sports-related cases.

The doctrine of vicarious liability is widely applicable to tort actions for negligence in the sports setting. For example, a coach may be held liable for the actions of his players, a school district may be held liable for the actions of a coach or a teacher, or an athletic administrator may be held liable for the actions of a coach. In order for an employer to be held liable in these situations, the employee must first be found negligent under the primary standard of reasonable care, and then the action must be determined to have been within the scope of the defendant's employment.

In a case (sport or nonsport) involving a monetary award for damages, it is common practice to sue in the alternative—that is, to sue each party involved in the alleged incident of negligence. This practice serves three primary purposes:

1. It allows the plaintiff to determine exactly who is liable for the particular injury.
2. It allows the plaintiff to determine which party involved in the suit has money sufficient to pay the damages award ("deep pocket").
3. It prevents multiple suits on the same cause of action directed against the various defendants.

NOTES ——

1. For a case in which a promoter of athletic events was held liable for negligent actions of his supervisory personnel, see *Rosenberger v. Central La. District Livestock Show, Inc.*, 312 So. 2d 300 (La. Sup. Ct. 1975). Plaintiff bareback bronco rider sought recovery from defendant rodeo promoters and defendant employees for injuries sustained at the rodeo. In ruling for the plaintiff, the Louisiana Supreme Court held that the negligence of the rodeo supervisor in failing to check whether the gate of the rodeo facility was closed resulted in plaintiff's injuries and that promoters were liable under the doctrine of respondeat superior.

2. For a case in which an owner of a facility could be held liable for the negligence of an employee if the employee is acting within the scope of his job, see *Johnson v. County Arena*, 349 A.2d 643 (Md. Ct. App. 1976). Plaintiff sought recovery in wrongful death for a roller skater who was struck from behind and knocked down by a skating guard while the guards were playing tag. In ruling against the defendant arena owner, the court of special appeals held that the evidence on the issue of whether the guard had exercised the amount of care and prudence in the performance of his duties commensurate with his relationship with the patron required submission to the jury.

3. In *Fustin v. Board of Education of Community Unit Dist. No. 2*, 242 N.E.2d 308 (Ill. App. 1968), plaintiff, a high school basketball player, sought recovery for injuries sustained when struck in the face by the fist of an opposing player. In ruling for the defendant school board, the court of appeals held that the employer's lack of negligence prevented application of respondeat superior and the fact that the board had taken out liability insurance did not in any way make the board liable.

4. In *Hackbart v. Cincinnati Bengals*, 435 F. Supp. 352 (D. Colo. 1977), *rev'd.*, 601 F.2d 516 (10th Cir. 1979), a team was sued under the doctrine of respondeat superior for the alleged reckless misconduct of one of its players.

5. In *Mogabgab v. Orleans Parish School Board*, 239 So. 2d 456 (La. Ct. App. 1970), the school district and principal were held not liable for the death of a football player who died from heat exhaustion, although the coach had actively denied medical assistance to the player for over two hours.

6. In *Toone v. Adams*, 137 S.E.2d 132 (N.C. Sup. Ct. 1964), a coach was not held responsible for the action of a fan since he had not directly incited the fan to a violent act.

7. In *Averill v. Luttrell*, 311 S.W.2d 812 (Tenn. Ct. App. 1957), a club was not held liable for an intentional tort committed by its employee since the employee's action was not within the scope of his employment or working to further his employer's business.

8. In *Domino v. Mercurio*, 234 N.Y.S.2d 1011 (1962), *aff'd*, 193 N.E.2d 893 (N.Y. 1963), a school district was held liable under the doctrine of respondeat superior for the negligence of its employees who allowed spectators at a softball game to push a bench too close to the playing surface. Therefore, the school district was held responsible for the injuries caused to a player who fell over the bench.

9. In *Welch v. Dunsmuir Joint Union High School District*, 326 P.2d 633 (Cal. Ct. App. 1958), the doctor was held to be an independent contractor.

10. In *Morris v. Union High School District A, King County*, 294 P. 998 (Wash. Sup. Ct. 1931), and *Vargo v. Svitchan*, 301 N.W.2d 1 (Mich. Ct. App. 1980), both school districts were held vicariously liable for the negligence of their employee, the football coach.

11. In *Tomjanovich v. California Sports*, No. H-78-243 (S.D. Tex. 1979), the defendant basketball team was held vicariously liable for the actions of one of its players.

12. In *Simmons v. Baltimore Orioles, Inc.*, 712 F. Supp. 79 (W.D. Va. 1989), a fan brought an action against an owner of a minor league baseball team to recover damages incurred when he was assaulted in the stadium parking lot. The court held that the owner did not negligently hire baseball players and was under no duty to instruct players how to deal with hecklers.

13. In *Hanson v. Kynast*, 494 N.E.2d 1091 (Ohio Sup. Ct. 1986), the Ohio Supreme Court held that defendant university lacrosse player, who received no scholarship or compensation but joined the team voluntarily, provided his own equipment, and received instructions but was not otherwise controlled by his coach, was not an agent of the university. Therefore, the university could not be held liable for the defendant's actions in injuring the plaintiff opponent.

Exception: Independent Contractors

The problems raised by the existence of independent contractors are important in understanding the scope of the doctrine of vicarious liability. An independent contractor is a person who, although in some way is connected to the employer, is not under the employer's control, and, as such, no vicarious liability may be imposed.

To determine the status of any person, the degree of control that the employer has over the employee's actions must be examined. The person who was hired for a specific, limited purpose, with no direct supervision, and who works without allowing the employer to have control over his or her actions is most likely an independent contractor. Once a determination has been made that the person is an independent contractor, the employer may not be held liable for negligence committed by that independent contractor. As a general rule, a doctor who is provided by a school that is hosting a football game is considered to be an independent contractor. Here, although paid by the school district, the doctor is not in any way under its control when making medical decisions. Thus, the doctrine of vicarious liability would not be applicable, and the school would not be liable for the doctor's medical negligence.

Another group that is classified as independent contractors are officials and referees. In most cases the referee has been determined by the courts to be an independent contractor. (See Exhibit 3–6 in Chapter 3 and the section Liability of Officials, Referees, and Umpires in Chapter 7.)

NOTES _____

1. A plaintiff's recovery against an employer is based on the defendant's being found to be an employee rather than an independent contractor. In *Gross v. Pellicane*, 167 A.2d 838 (N.J. Super. Ct. App. Div. 1961), petitioner, a free-lance jockey, sought workers' compensation for injuries sustained while riding defendant's horse in a race. In affirming the award, the trial court held that petitioner was an employee of the horse trainer, because of the control the trainer exercised over his duties, rather than an independent contractor.

2. In *Classen v. Izquierdo*, 520 N.Y.S.2d 999 (N.Y. County Sup. Ct. 1987), plaintiff widow brought action against ringside physicians and the proprietor of the sports facility to recover damages for the death of her husband, a boxer. The proprietor did not participate in the selection of the referee or ringside physicians and did not provide them with training, instruction, or supervision. Consequently, the court held that the proprietor was not vicariously liable for any negligence of the referee in the boxing match for allowing the contest to continue since the referee was an independent contractor.

3. In *Harvey v. Ouachita Parish School Board*, 545 So. 2d 1241 (La. Ct. App. 1989), an injured football player sued the state high school athletic association for negligence for injuries suffered as a result of excessively rough behavior. The court held for the defendant on the basis that the association was not responsible for the referees' failure to remove football players who were displaying excessively rough behavior. The court reasoned that though the association had registered the referees, the referees were neither agents nor servants of the association.

4. In *Wilson, et al. v. Vancouver Hockey Club*, 5 D.L.R. (4th) 282 (B.C. Sup. Ct. 1983), a doctor employed by the hockey club to treat players for hockey injuries failed to refer plaintiff hockey player to a specialist for a biopsy on a mole on plaintiff's arm. The plaintiff claimed that the doctor negligently failed to tell the player that he suspected cancer. Evidence indicated that the doctor made the final decision as to what treatment an injured player would have and whether an injured player would play, without advice from the management of the club; therefore, the doctor acted as an independent contractor and not as a servant of the hockey club. The court held that the club was not vicariously liable for the negligence of the doctor because he was an independent contractor.

DEFAMATION LAW

Sports are played in public settings and are coached and administered in what often seems like "the heat of battle." As such, amateur athletic administrators have to be extremely cautious that what begins as a sporting event does not erupt into litigation involving defamation-- either libel or slander. The passions of the contest should not be allowed to evolve into inappropriate statements about an individual to the media or the general public. Athletic administrators have to always be on guard for such eventualities and must instruct their staff about the potential litigation any such statement could cause for the organization or individuals involved.

Defamation law protects a person's reputation. The focus of a defamation action is on the alleged defamatory statement and its impact on third persons. *The Restatement (Second) of Torts*, section 559, defines a defamatory communication as one which "tends to harm the reputation of another as to lower him in the estimation of the community or to deter third persons from associating or dealing with him."

The elements which establish liability for defamation are (1) a false and defamatory statement concerning another, (2) publication to a third person, (3) some degree of fault on the defendant's part, and (4) damages. A defamatory statement is also one that exposes the plaintiff to public hatred, shame, contempt, or ridicule. A statement may be oral, written, a photograph, a cartoon, or any other form of communication. The reputation protected by the law of defamation is the opinion of others. The plaintiff must show that his or her reputation was injured in the eyes of a respectable group of the community.

Defamation is an intentional tort in that the defendant need only intend to make the publication of the statement or material. It matters not that the defendant did not intend to harm the reputation of the plaintiff. The defendant will still be accountable if he or she intended to make the defamatory statement.

Defamation is divided into libel and slander. *Libel* is the publication of defamatory matter by writing. There are three classes of libel: (1) libel per se, which includes materials that are obviously defamatory; (2) materials that could be taken as defamatory or as not defamatory; and (3) materials that are not by themselves defamatory but when combined with other facts become libelous. *Slander* is the publication of defamatory matter through spoken words.

Libel

The basic elements of libel are a defamatory statement, publication, and damages. Truth is a defense to a libel action; however, it is only a qualified defense—not an absolute defense. The defendant has the burden of proving the truth of the communication if his defense is truth. If the libel is true, the plaintiff has the burden of proving that it was published with malice. To prove malice the plaintiff must prove that the statement was made with hatred, ill will, or malevolent intent. The plaintiff must also prove that a third person was exposed to the publication. Finally, the plaintiff must prove actual damages. There are two basic forms of damages in this context—general and special damages. *General damages* include humiliation and mental and physical suffering. *Special damages* are those damages that are the natural, but not the necessary, result of the alleged wrong. The defendant may be able to mitigate damages by making a retraction or taking some other measure.

Slander

Slander is publication of defamatory matter by spoken words. There must be a publication, and the plaintiff must be held up to scorn and ridicule as a result of the defamatory statement. A statement is slanderous per se if it falls into one of the following categories:

1. Accuses the plaintiff of criminal conduct.
2. Accuses the plaintiff of having a loathsome disease.
3. Accuses the plaintiff of being unchaste.
4. Accuses the plaintiff of misconduct in public office.
5. Injures plaintiff's profession, business, or trade.

Truth is an absolute defense to a slander action. Again, however, the plaintiff must show that the statement was heard and understood by a third person. To show damages, the plaintiff must prove that it was slanderous per se or must prove special damages.

The United States Supreme Court has established standards that apply in libel and slander situations. In its decisions the Court balanced the competing interests of protecting the reputation of an individual against freedom of the press. In the first of its decisions in 1964 the Court held that the constitutional guarantee of a free press requires a public official to prove actual malice in the publication of a defamatory falsehood in order to recover for defamation (*New York Times Company v. Sullivan*, 376 U.S. 254 [1964]). In 1967 the Court extended the constitutional privilege to public figures as well as public officials. Finally in *Gertz v. Robert Welch Inc.*, 418 U.S. 323, the Court extended the "actual malice" standard. A public official or public figure who has been defamed must prove that the defendant published the statement with actual malice—that is, knowing that the material was false or in reckless disregard as to whether it was false or not.

Defamation should be distinguished from both intentional infliction of emotional distress and invasion of privacy. *Intentional infliction of emotional distress* is classified as an intentional tort and is concerned with the impact on the individual plaintiff without regard to third persons. *Defamation* involves the element of publication to third persons, as well as the requirement that the material be taken by these third persons as damaging. Defamation must also be distinguished from the tort of invasion of privacy. An action for *invasion of privacy* concerns one's right to peace of mind and comfort, while an action for defamation involves the plaintiff's character or reputation. Invasion of privacy can also be distinguished from defamation in that truth is an absolute defense to the defamation action, but truth is not a defense to an invasion of privacy action.

A leading sports case in the area of defamation law is *Curtis Publishing Co. v. Butts*, 388 U.S. 130 (1967). Curtis Publishing Company had printed an article alleging that Wallace Butts, while the athletic director at the University of Georgia, had supplied to Paul Bryant, the head football coach at Alabama, information concerning Georgia's game plan for an upcoming game against Alabama. The article was based on a phone conversation between Butts and Bryant, supposedly overheard by an insurance salesman. Butts brought action for libel against Curtis in federal court and was awarded compensatory and punitive damages. Curtis appealed the decision to the Supreme Court, arguing that Butts was a public figure and as such needed to prove the article was written with actual malice. The Supreme Court held that a public figure who is not a public official may recover damages for a defamatory falsehood which is obviously damaging to his reputation, on a showing that the conduct of the publisher was highly unreasonable and constituted an extreme departure from the standards of investigation and reporting ordinarily adhered to by responsible publishers.

NOTES ───

1. The following cases involve individuals in sports who were sued or brought suit for defamation.

(a) In *Chuy v. Philadelphia Eagles Football Club*, 431 F. Supp. 254 (E.D. Pa., 1977), *aff'd*, 595 F.2d 1265 (3d Cir. 1979), a pro football player brought an action against his team, the Philadelphia Eagles, based on breach of contract, intentional infliction of emotional distress, and defamation. Chuy's defamation claim was founded on an allegedly false statement made by a team physician which was reported to the press. The court found that Chuy was a public figure. He was a prominent starting player on a pro team, and he had voluntarily placed himself in the public eye. Once it was established that Chuy was a public figure, in order to succeed Chuy had to meet the "actual malice" test established in *New York Times Company v. Sullivan*, 376 U.S. 254 (1964). Although the evidence showed that the doctor knew that the statement was false, Chuy was not allowed to recover.

The court held for the Eagles on the defamation claim because Pennsylvania law provided that the newspaper columnist had to understand the statement as defamatory for there to be liability. Since Chuy could not show that the reporter took the statement in a defamatory way, Chuy was barred from recovery. In a different case arising out of the same incident, Chuy also sued for intentional infliction of emotional distress.

(b) In *Rutledge v. Arizona Board of Regents*, 660 F.2d 1345 (9th Cir. 1981), a football coach was sued for defamation by one of his players.

(c) In *Carlen v. University of South Carolina*, No. 83-379-0 (U.S.D.C., Dist. S. Carolina, February 11, 1983), plaintiff, former head football coach at the University of South Carolina, sued the university, in part, under a defamation theory. He alleged that his termination in breach of his contract permanently damaged his reputation as a major college football coach, irreparably impairing his ability to obtain another position. The case was settled.

(d) In *Parks v. Steinbrenner*, 520 N.Y.S.2d 374 (N.Y. App. Div. 1987), plaintiff Parks, a baseball umpire, filed a libel and slander suit against New York Yankees owner George Steinbrenner. Steinbrenner issued a press release which criticized Parks's capabilities as an umpire and accused him of "having it out" for the Yankees. The court found that it was questionable whether the statements could be construed as defamatory, since "razzing of the umpire" is used to inspire baseball fans and participants.

2. In *Stepien v. Franklin*, 528 N.E.2d 1324 (Ohio Ct. App. 1988), plaintiff, owner of professional basketball team, brought a suit for slander and intentional infliction of emotional distress against a radio talk show host for harsh and insulting criticism of him. The Court of Appeals affirmed a lower court's decision for the defendant, stating that plaintiff, a public figure, failed to show clear and convincing proof of actual malice by the talk show host.

3. In *Langston v. ACT*, 890 F.2d 380 (U.S. Cir. 1989), a student whose college test scores were cancelled as a result of suspected cheating, brought action against a national testing company for violation of his civil rights, breach of contract, and defamation. The court of appeals affirmed the lower court's decision in favor of the testing company and held that communications between college testing service and student's high school faculty, regarding validity of student's test scores, were privileged, and thus could not be subject to defamation claim without showing malice of testing service.

4. In *Warford v. Lexington Herald-Leader Co.*, 789 S.W.2d 758 (Ky. Sup. Ct. 1990), assistant college basketball coach brought defamation action against newspaper which had printed a story of alleged recruiting violations. The Kentucky Supreme Court held that the assistant coach was a private, rather than a public figure at the time of the alleged defamation. The assistant coach, as a private figure, was not required to show actual malice in order to establish the newspaper's liability.

5. In *Brooks v. Paige*, 773 P.2d 1098 (Colo. Ct. App. 1989), soccer player brought suit against television station and sports commentator, claiming defamation with regard to statements of the sports commentator about the soccer player. The court of appeals upheld a lower court's decision in favor of defendants, reasoning that statements made on the television talk show were opinions meriting constitutional protection and were not deliberate or reckless falsehoods.

THE TORT OF INVASION OF PRIVACY

An action for invasion of privacy is designed to protect a person's mental peace and/or comfort. Invasion of privacy is an intentional tort.

The laws prohibiting invasion of privacy are intended to protect the purely private matters of a person. Although some intrusions into a person's life are expected and must be tolerated in society, when the intrusions become excessive or unjustified, then a cause of action will exist for invasion of privacy.

The *Restatement (Second) of Torts*, § 652, determines the ways in which one may tortiously invade the privacy of another. That section provides:

> One who gives publicity to a matter concerning the private life of another is subject to liability to the other for invasion of his privacy, if the matter publicized is of a kind that
> (a) would be highly offensive to a reasonable person; and
> (b) is not of legitimate concern to the public.

As set forth in William L. Prosser, *Law of Torts*, § 117 (1971), one can invade the privacy of another in four distinct ways:

1. Intruding upon one's physical solitude.
2. Publicly disclosing private facts.
3. Putting one in a false light in the public eye.
4. Appropriating some element of another's personality for commercial gain.

In an action for invasion of privacy, the intrusion must be substantial and must be into an area for which there is an expectation of privacy. For example, simply staring at a person would not generally amount to an intrusion; wiretapping, on the other hand, would amount to an intrusion.

The plaintiff must also show that the publication of private matters involved a matter which in fact was truly private. Newsworthy public interest matters or public facts are not considered to be of a purely private nature. Court records, for example, are open to the public and are therefore not viewed as private facts.

The United States Supreme Court in *Time, Inc. v. Hill*, 385 U.S. 374, (1967), held that the First Amendment to the United States Constitution protects reports of newsworthy matters. These matters can be publicized unless, as was discussed in the previous section, actual malice is shown. The actual malice standard may be applied, even though a plaintiff was a private person who did not want the publicity.

In *Bilney v. Evening Star Newspaper Co.*, 406 A.2d 652 (Md. Ct. App. 1979), a leading case in the area, members of the University of Maryland basketball team brought suit against two newspapers. The newspapers published an article concerning certain players whose academic standing was threatening their eligibility. The players based their action, in part, on the theory of invasion of privacy. The court, basing its decision on the *Restatement (Second) of Torts*, § 652, held that the players were public figures. The court found that there was widespread public interest in Maryland basketball. When the players' academic standing threatened their eligibility, then the privacy of those facts lessened. The court stated that "the publication of their eligibility-threatening status was not unreasonable and did not trample community mores" of what is legitimate public interest.

The court relied primarily on the reasoning of the *Restatement (Second) of Torts*, § 652D. Under this section a public figure cannot complain when given publicity that was sought, even though it may be unfavorable. The *Restatement (Second) of Torts* also states that the publicity of public figures "is not limited to the particular events that arouse the interests of the public" (§ 652D, comment). The legitimate public interest of these figures extends into some of their private matters. The court also held that the right to make public the private facts of a public figure is not an unlimited right. The court held that what is allowable is determined by community mores: "The line is to be drawn when the publicity ceases to be the giving of information to which the public is entitled and becomes a morbid and sensational prying into private lives" (§ 652, comment).

The *Bilney* case typifies the difficult burden an athlete has in winning an invasion of privacy action. The Maryland players were unsuccessful because the news article did not invade a "private" area. The opinion reflects how difficult it is for a person classified as a public figure to recover for invasion of privacy. Public figures must put up with more publicity concerning their private lives than one who is not a public figure. Since most pro athletes and the majority of big-time college student-athletes would probably be classified as public figures, it would be difficult for them to recover under the theory of invasion of privacy.

NOTES

1. In Massachusetts, for example, there is a statute governing invasion of privacy (Mass. G.L.A. 214, § 1B). It provides: "A person shall have a right against unreasonable, substantial or serious interference with his privacy." This section allows for legal as well as equitable relief. It also appears broad enough to cover the four distinct ways to invade the privacy of another as discussed above and mentioned in Prosser, *Law of Torts* (1971).

2. For further information, review the discussion on the Buckley Amendment in Chapter 5.

THE TORT OF INTENTIONAL INFLICTION OF
EMOTIONAL DISTRESS

The tort of intentional infliction of emotional distress protects a person's emotional tranquility. Simple minor disturbances and infringements are not actionable. The provoking conduct must be outrageous for the plaintiff to have an action for intentional infliction of emotional distress. An increasing number of states are recognizing intentional infliction of emotional distress as an independent tort. The recent trend of states recognizing this tort has been to adopt principles of the *Restatement (Second) of Torts*, § 46. Section 46 sets forth the following four requirements:

1. There must be extreme and outrageous conduct.
2. The conduct must be intentional or reckless.
3. The conduct must cause emotional distress.
4. The distress must be severe.

The intent required under § 46(2) is simply the intent to engage in the conduct; that is what is meant by intentional. Section 46, however, does not require that the defendant have a criminal or tortious intent, or even an intent to cause emotional distress. It is enough if the conduct:

> has been so outrageous in character and so extreme in degree as to go beyond all possible bounds of decency and to be regarded as atrocious, and utterly intolerable in a civilized community. (*Restatement (Second) of Torts*, § 46, comment [d])

For example, if the defendant is joking and informs the plaintiff that her son has been killed and the plaintiff suffers emotional distress, the defendant will be liable. Or, if a doctor falsely or recklessly makes it known to a person that he is suffering from a fatal disease, then the doctor will be liable.

The conduct required by § 46 is outrageous and extreme. The plaintiff has an initial burden of showing enough evidence for reasonable persons to find extreme and outrageous conduct. Section 46 also requires that the plaintiff actually suffer severe emotional distress. Comment (j) to § 46 requires that the plaintiff prove that he suffered severe distress and that this distress was not unreasonable, exaggerated, or unjustified.

A leading case in the area of intentional infliction of emotional distress is *Chuy v. Philadelphia Eagles Football Club*, 431 F. Supp. 254 (E.D. Pa. 1977), *aff'd*, 595 F.2d 1265 (3d Cir. 1979). Chuy, a professional football player, brought suit against the Eagles and the National Football League seeking to recover the balance of his salary allegedly due on his contract and for damages for defamation and intentional infliction of emotional distress. Chuy had suffered a serious injury while playing football.

Chuy's claims for emotional distress were based on a statement made by a team physician who was being interviewed by the press. The doctor reported that Chuy had contracted a rare blood disease which would prevent him from ever playing football again. Chuy, having no prior knowledge of the existence of such a condition, claimed that upon hearing the report he was put under incredible emotional anguish and he anticipated death.

The court held that the doctor's conduct was sufficiently outrageous. The court found that the doctor intentionally told news reporters that Chuy was suffering from a blood disease, knowing that this was in fact not true. Chuy recovered $10,000 in compensatory damages for this intentional infliction of emotional distress. Chuy also recovered $60,000 in punitive damages, which was affirmed on appeal as not being excessive.

Amateur athletic administrators must also be on their guard about statements made by members of an organization's staff that could lead to litigation such as that in *Chuy*. The following are examples of potential instances in which such statements to the media could lead to similar litigation:

- A coach's statement about the playing ability of a student-athlete, including professional career aspirations.
- An administration's statement about the employment tenure of a coach.
- A trainer's announcement about the playing ability or injury of a student-athlete.
- A sports information director's comments about student-athletes and coaches.

In any of these situations, if the statement was "extremely outrageous" and injured the individual about whom it was made, an athletic administrator might anticipate that litigation will be filed.

NOTE

1. In *Stepien v. Franklin*, 528 N.E.2d 1324 (Ohio Ct. App. 1988), plaintiff, owner of professional basketball team, brought action for slander and intentional infliction of emotional distress a against radio talk show host for harsh and insulting criticism of him. The court of appeals affirmed a lower court's decision for the defendant, stating that the comments were statements of

opinion which were constitutionally protected. Plaintiff was not able to show that alleged conduct so exceeded bounds of decency as to be considered atrocious, completely outrageous, and utterly intolerable in a civilized community.

PRODUCTS LIABILITY LAW

Products liability is an expansive area of tort law which allows a party who has been injured by a product defectively designed, manufactured, or distributed to recover under one of several possible causes of action. The causes of action in products liability cases are negligence, strict liability, and breach of warranty.

The class of possible defendants in a products liability action is broad. Everyone in the chain of distribution of a product is potentially liable, from the manufacturer to the seller or lessor to those who service or install the product. A product is any item of personal property, most commonly consumer goods, and includes the container in which it is sold. Even vacant land that has been altered by earth-moving equipment to be made into a baseball diamond can be a "product," so that the manufacturer (earth mover) could be liable for injuries caused by holes or bumps in the surface.

The plaintiff in a products liability case must show that a defect existed at the time the product left the control of the defendant and that the injury was caused by the defect. Courts have most frequently applied a definition of defect from the *Restatement (Second) of Torts,* § 402A, which says a product is in a defective condition if it is "unreasonably dangerous to the user." Comment (i) of section 401A further defines a defect:

> The article sold must be dangerous to the extent beyond that which would be contemplated by the ordinary consumer who purchases it, with the knowledge common to the community as to its characteristics.

In the amateur sports setting an athletic administrator has to be particularly aware of potential product liability problems. Sports involve the participation of individuals and the use of equipment by those individuals, and both factors are the basis for any product liability lawsuit. Ultimately, such litigation leads to increases in a sports organization's insurance premiums, a subject discussed in Chapter 7.

The Sporting Goods Manufacturers Association has been lobbying for liability relief from Congress and the state legislatures, because it contends that product liability litigation and other tort lawsuits are making sports unaffordable in the United States. The association in 1986–87 made this statement:

The sporting goods industry concludes that liability relief is imperative to maintaining affordable and available recreational products and sports programs. For American sports, the two minute warning is sounding. The time for debate and study is over. Public officials need to stop the bleeding if the U.S. sporting goods industry and amateur sports in America are to survive. We have no more "deep pockets."

In reviewing this problem area, the association notes further:

Sporting goods manufacturers, retailers, schools, amateur sports groups, municipalities, and private providers of recreation services are suffering from:
1. a panoply of frivolous suits.
2. extravagant awards for injury predicated on the "deep pocket" theory.
3. insurance that is either unavailable or unaffordable.
4. erosion of contributory negligence and assumption of risk defenses.

The result:

1. U.S. companies, large and small, are dropping product lines or going bare.
2. U.S. jobs are lost or never created.
3. U.S. sporting goods manufacturers' competitive position is being further eroded.
4. less sporting goods product is available to consumers and at higher cost.
5. injured parties are compensated in some states and victimized in others.
6. schools are dropping their sports programs.
7. amateur sports groups are disbanding leagues or hiking dues to where they may be unaffordable to participants.
8. volunteer coaches, refs, and other league officials are refusing their services out of fear of being sued.
9. municipalities are closing facilities or dropping recreational activities.
10. private providers of services at campgrounds and marinas, on rivers and at water sports sites, or gymnastic and health clubs are abandoning their services.

In 1993, the association further noted:

Sporting goods manufacturers, retailers, schools, amateur sports groups, municipalities, and private providers of recreation services are suffering from frivolous lawsuit abuse. Our legal system is an adversarial system. Once you are named as a defendant in a sports-related lawsuit, you have already lost, regardless of the outcome of the case. What are the immediate losses? The loss of your time and energy that the case will require... the negative publicity the case may encourage.... The money in defense costs—win, lose, or draw.

While the association's position represents only one side of the situation, there is no doubt that product liability lawsuits remain a big problem for equipment manufacturers and amateur athletic administrators.

NOTES _____

1. For further information, see the following law articles.
    (a) "Sports Products Liability: 'It's All Part of the Game—Or Is It?' " 17 *Trial* 58 (1981).
    (b) Coben, "Sports Helmets: More Harm Than Protection?" 25 *Trial* 74 (1989).
    (c) Houser, Ashworth, and Clark, "Products Liability in the Sports Industry," 23 *Tort & Insurance L. J.* 44 (1987).
2. For further information, see the following text: Wittenberg, *Products Liability: Recreation and Sports Equipment* (New York: Law Journal Seminars Press, 1987).
3. The Sporting Goods Manufacturers Association can be contacted at:

> *Palm Beach Headquarters:*
> 200 Castlewood Drive
> N. Palm Beach, FL 33408
> (305) 842-4100

> *Washington Office:*
> 1625 K Street, N.W., Ste. 900
> Washington, DC 20006
> (202) 775-1762

Negligence as a Cause of Action

In products liability law, a manufacturer of a product has the duty to meet legal standards of safety and care in the product's design, manufacture, and use. In addition, the supplier of the product and the seller may be liable for negligence if they have not exercised reasonable care. The courts generally balance the probability and gravity of the potential harm against the social value of the product and the inconvenience of taking precautions in determining whether or not a duty of care has been breached.

The standard of care involved in manufacturing is one of reasonable care in both the manufacture and design of the product to ensure that it will be reasonably safe when used in the manner in which it was intended. In addition, when a product may be dangerous even when properly used, a manufacturer may have a duty to warn users of the product about the hazard. However, the manufacturer is not required to make the safest or best possible product, although the product will be compared to similar products. The similar products will be used to help determine what is a "reasonably" safe product.

Suppliers, the wholesalers of a product, must also exercise reasonable care. First, a supplier has a duty to use reasonable care to make a product safe. In addition, if the supplier knows or has reason to know that the product is dangerous and that the user is not likely to realize the danger, the supplier must exercise reasonable care to notify the user of the potential danger. For example, the Flybynight Company was contracted to replace a drainage system at a high school soccer field. After completion of the job, the ground around one of the drain-pipes settled, leaving the pipe exposed. Kenny Keeper dove to make a save; he fell on the pipe and suffered severe injuries. The Flybynight Company was negligent for its failure to insure the safety of the field. The school would also be a potential defendant for failing to hire a competent contractor to install the new drainage system.

Sellers, the retailers of a product, are also subject to liability for negligence under some circumstances. A seller of a product which the seller knows to be dangerous has a duty to warn a purchaser who has no knowledge of the dangerous nature of the product. A seller may also have a duty to inspect a product manufactured by another if the seller knows or has reason to know that it is likely to be hazardous.

Advertisers and marketers of a product also have a duty to exercise reasonable care. When a product appears on the market, a warning about the dangers associated with the product must accompany it. This warning must be adequate and disclose the dangers from an improper design as well as dangers that are possible even when the product is properly used. The warning must also be sufficient to protect third parties who might reasonably be expected to come into contact with the product.

NOTE ───

1. In *Rawlings Sporting Goods Co. Inc., v. Daniels*, 619 S.W.2d 435 (Tex. Ct. App. 1981), a high school football player, who sustained severe brain damage due to injury when his helmet caved in as a result of a collision in practice, brought a products liability and negligence cause of action against the manufacturer of the helmet. The court of appeals affirmed a lower court's decision in favor of the high school football player and reasoned that the helmet was defectively manufactured and that the defective condition was a producing cause of the player's injuries.

Strict Liability as a Cause of Action

The strict liability cause of action requires that one who sells a product which is unreasonably dangerous because of a defect—whether in design or manufacture—be held liable for any physical harm proximately caused by use of the product. The seller will be liable to the ultimate user or customer, provided that the product has not been changed from its initial state or condition. Liability can be found only if the product has been used in the manner and for the purposes intended by the sellers; therefore, a seller will not be liable for harm resulting from unforeseeable, abnormal use of the product. This strict liability standard applies despite the fact that a seller may have exercised all the care necessary in, and appropriate for, the preparation and sale of the product.

The theory behind strict liability is that when the seller markets its product for use and consumption by the public, it assumes a special responsibility to any member of the public for any injury caused by the product. The public has the right to expect that the seller will provide a reasonably safe product. There is a strong public policy supporting the demand that the burden of accidental injuries caused by a seller's products be placed on those who marketed them. The theory is that the cost inherent in the assumption of responsibility can be insured; it will be treated as a cost of production and added to the cost of the item. Therefore, the consumer is given the maximum possible protection from unreasonably dangerous products in that the people in the best position to provide this protection are those who market and profit from the products.

Most courts have applied the *Restatement (Second) of Torts*, §402A definition of strict tort liability, which states:

1. One who sells any product in a defective condition unreasonably dangerous to the user or consumer or to his property is subject to liability for physical harm thereby caused to the ultimate user or consumer, or to his property; if:
   (a) the seller is engaged in the business of selling such a product, and
   (b) it is expected to and does reach the user or consumer without substantial change in the condition in which it is sold.
2. The rule stated in subsection (1) applies although:
   (a) the seller has exercised all possible care in the preparation and sale of his product, and
   (b) the user or consumer has not bought the product from or entered into any contractual relation with the seller.

NOTES _____

1. In *Hemphill v. Sayers*, 552 F. Supp. 685 (Ill. D. 1982), a university football player who sustained injury to his cervical spine as a result of an allegedly defective football helmet brought action against the university's

athletic director, football coach, athletic trainer, and helmet manufacturer. The court held, *inter alia,* that the claim be dismissed as to the defendant helmet manufacturer because the plaintiff failed to show (1) what made the product's condition unreasonably dangerous and (2) that this allegedly dangerous condition existed at the time it left the manufacturer.

2. In *Breeden v. Valencia, Inc.,* 557 So. 2d 302 (La. Ct. App. 1990), a twelve-year-old injured while riding a jet ski at camp claimed that a jet ski was unreasonably dangerous and contained inadequate warnings. The court found no evidence that a defect existed in the design or manufacture of the steering mechanism. It further found that warnings contained in the instruction manual were adequate to inform riders about the turning ability of the jet ski.

Breach of Warranty as a Cause of Action

A cause of action for products liability may be based on a breach of warranty claim against a manufacturer. This is basically an adaption of contract law to torts problems. First, the plaintiff must establish that there was an express or implied warranty. Then the plaintiff must prove that the warranty was breached by the defendant. The advantage to a claim based on warranty principles is that the plaintiff does not have to prove that the product was defective in its design.

An *express warranty* is an affirmation of material fact concerning the nature and fitness of a particular product upon which the buyer might reasonably rely. An *implied warranty* does not arise from any words of the seller, either oral or in writing, but is a rule of law in every state. The rule is embodied in § 2-314 of the Uniform Commercial Code, which states, "A warranty that the goods shall be merchantable is implied in a contract for their sale if the seller is a merchant with respect to goods of that kind."

NOTE ───

1. In *Hauter v. Zogarts,* 534 P.2d 377 (Cal. Sup. Ct. 1975), plaintiff filed action to recover for injuries received when he was hit on the head by a golf ball after a practice swing with a golf training device. The device was described by the manufacturer as a completely equipped backyard driving range and carried the label "completely safe ball will not hit player" on the shipping carton and on the cover of the instruction booklet. The superior court granted the plaintiff's motion for judgment notwithstanding the verdict, and defendants appealed. The California Supreme Court held that the plaintiff was entitled to recover on the theories of false representation, breach of express and implied warranties, and strict liability in tort based on defective design.

TORTIOUS INTERFERENCE WITH CONTRACTUAL RELATIONS

Tortious interference with contractual relations occurs where a third party, without justification, intentionally induces one not to perform a contract with another person. The third party is liable to the person with whom the original contract was going to be signed. This type of tort liability protects the rights of a party to a contract from third-party interference. The plaintiff in such a suit bears the burden of proving that the defendant intentionally interfered with the plaintiff's contractual relationship such that the performance of the contract was either prevented or made difficult. The defendant must have actual knowledge of the contract and have the intent to interfere with it. The defendant can rebut or justify the interference by showing that the conduct was not "improper." The *Restatement (Second) of Torts* sets forth the following seven factors to be considered in determining whether the conduct was improper:

1. The nature of the actor's conduct.
2. The actor's motive.
3. The interests of the other with which the actor's conduct interferes.
4. The interests sought to be advanced by the actor.
5. The social interests in protecting the freedom of the action of the actor and the contractual interests of others.
6. The proximity or remoteness of the actor's conduct to the interference.
7. The relations between the parties.

This theory has been used when a player or coach signs a contract with a rival team while already under contract with his or her present team. Often, the temptation to obtain a player or a coach already obligated to another team is too difficult to resist, and a player or coach will be induced to breach a current contract to sign with a new employer. In such a situation, the party injured by the breach of the contract may sue the new party for intentionally interfering with the previous contract. Recently, universities have used the doctrine of tortious interference with contractual relations against agents who have interfered with their players' eligibility.

In *National Collegiate Athletic Ass'n v. Hornung*, 754 S.W.2d 855 (Ky. Sup. Ct. 1988), a leading case in this area, the NCAA appealed a judgment that it intentionally interfered with Paul Hornung's signing of a contract as a college football color analyst for WTBS. Since the college football games televised were NCAA-sanctioned games, the NCAA retained the right to approve or disapprove any announcer or analyst chosen by WTBS. Hornung, a former Green Bay Packer star and Heisman Trophy winner, had an extensive sports broadcasting career and was under contract with WTBS for a college football weekly. WTBS had therefore chosen Hornung as one of four persons proposed for approval by the NCAA. The NCAA, however, disapproved of Hornung because of his identification with professional football and his Miller Lite Beer commercials, which portrayed him as a playboy. The Supreme Court of Kentucky found that the NCAA's disapproval was justified under its agreement with WTBS, even though it's effect was to the detriment of Hornung's prospective contractual relation. Thus, the court found that Hornung did not prove that the NCAA's action was improper.

NOTES ⸻

1. In *Lindsey* v. *Dempsey*, 735 P.2d 840 (Ariz. Ct. App. 1987), a head basketball coach at a university brought an action against the university's athletic director and president for intentional interference with contractual relations. The court found that in recommending that the coach not be rehired, the athletic director did not interfere with the coach's contract because the coach was hired for only a one-year term, which had expired, and the university was free to hire someone else.

2. In *Walters* v. *Fullwood*, 675 F. Supp. 155 (S.D.N.Y. 1987), plaintiffs brought suit against a professional football player and his agent for tortious interference with contractual relations. The plaintiffs alleged that the agent tortiously induced Fullwood to breach an earlier signed agreement with them. They further alleged that the two defendants tortiously interfered with their prospective contractual relations with other players by breaching or inducing the breach between their agency and Fullwood. The court rejected the plaintiffs' claims and further found that, since the agreement between Walters and Fullwood was violative of NCAA rules, it was unenforceable under New York law.

3. In *New England Patriots Football Club, Inc.* v. *University of Colorado*, 592 F.2d 1196 (1st Cir. 1979), plaintiff professional football team sought a preliminary injunction enjoining defendant university's regents, president, athletic director, and alumni from tortiously interfering with Head Coach Chuck Fairbanks's contract with the New England Patriots. Fairbanks had signed a contract for employment with the Patriots through January 1983. In November 1978 the defendants, officially and sentimentally attached to the university, attempted to persuade him to quit the Patriots and become football coach at Colorado. While the university argued that the Patriots were barred from relief because of the doctrine of unclean hands, the court found that the allegations that the Patriots lured Fairbanks from the University of Oklahoma in 1973 had no effect on the controversy at hand. Thus, the injunction was granted. The parties later settled the issue out of court as the university bought out Fairbanks' contract with the Patriots.

4. For further reading on the application of tortious interference with contractual relations in the sports context, see Woods and Mills, "Tortious Interference with an Athletic Scholarship: A University's Remedy for the Unscrupulous Sports Agent," 40 *Ala. L. Rev.* 141 (1988).

WORKERS' COMPENSATION

Workers' compensation is a statutorily created method for providing cash benefits and medical care to employees and their dependents when the employee has suffered personal injuries or death in the course of employment. The purpose of the benefits is to provide employees and their dependents with greater protection than they are afforded by the common law remedy of a suit for damages. Each state has its own workers' compensation act that provides a system of monetary payments for the loss of earning capacity to an employee, according to a scale established by the state. The act may also have provisions for furnishing burial, medical, or other expenses incurred by the employee.

Workers' compensation acts differ as to where the funds are derived and the method of payment used in compensating claims. Some acts require the employer to make payment directly to the employee. Other acts provide payment out of a fund from which many different employers contribute. In still other acts, the employer's private insurer makes payments.

The primary reason for passage of workers' compensation statutes was to eliminate the inadequacies of the common law remedies that resulted from the injured party having to show that the employer was negligent. Proving negligence was often difficult for the employee because of defenses available to the employer, such as contributory negligence, assumption of the risk, and co-worker negligence. Under a workers' compensation act the injured employee need only show that the employer was subject to the act, that he or she was an employee under the act's definition, and that the injury occurred during the course of employment. Fault or employer negligence is not a prerequisite to receiving workers' compensation benefits. Payments are made in intervals, when the injured party and his or her dependents need money most, instead of waiting until the completion of costly litigation. To claim a right to compensation, an employee need only fall within the terms of the statute.

This theory of compensation shifts the burden of economic loss from the employee and the employee's dependents under the common law to the employer under the act. While the employer considers workers' compensation benefits part of the production cost, it is the consumer who will most likely bear the economic burden of the cost of the benefits, since the employer adds the costs to his products or services.

Every state's workers' compensation act has the same fundamental principle—the worker's right to benefit payments for injuries arising out of the worker's employment. Although each jurisdiction varies in the details of its act, the various acts have some general similarities.

For example, in all jurisdictions there is a short waiting period during which the employee must be either totally or partially incapacitated. This is to avoid small and insignificant claims. When the period ends, the worker is eligible for compensation beginning from the date of the injury. Every jurisdiction sets its own rate schedule prescribing minimum and maximum compensation amounts for either total disability, partial disability, or permanent and total disability. These amounts are determined by each state's legislature and may be revised yearly. An additional benefit, separate from weekly compensation, is added for every person wholly dependent on the injured provider. An additional sum may be awarded for certain specific injuries, such as the loss of eyesight. Each state may have its own procedure for arriving at dollar amounts depending on that state's average wage or its economy.

Workers' compensation eligibility issues are of particular significance to amateur athletic administrators for three reasons: (1) a determination that scholarship athletes are employees of their institutions will allow injured student-athletes to collect workers' compensation benefits in some circumstances, increasing insurance costs for institutions and their athletic departments; (2) injured student-athletes, if found to be employees, may bring more workers' compensation claims or costly tort actions against institutions and their personnel in order to collect workers' compensation benefits; and (3) an athletic department or institution employee injured in an employer-sponsored athletic event may be found to be acting within the scope of employment and thus eligible for workers' compensation benefits.

Workers' compensation claims filed by injured student-athletes against their institutions increased during the early 1980s. In response to this trend the NCAA in 1985 instituted a catastrophic injury protection insurance plan that could be purchased by member institutions. The NCAA's insurance policy provides benefits to catastrophically injured student-athletes regardless of fault. In many cases, the NCAA program may be more attractive than a successful workers' compensation claim, as the student-athlete may obtain benefits immediately and avoid the time delays, costs, and uncertainties of litigation involved in filing for workers' compensation benefits. Yet, because the scholarship athlete/employee issue has not been firmly resolved, workers' compensation cases may still be brought by injured student-athletes. The NCAA would rather have the costs of the benefits to the injured student-athlete covered by an insurance policy than paid for through the more costly and more tenuous method of workers' compensation. The catastrophic injury protection plan is paid for by the NCAA and its member institutions and benefits the institutions by protecting them against the sudden and substantial costs of injury benefits. The student-athlete also benefits from the plan, as it provides immediate benefits without depending on a workers' compensation board or judge's opinion on the issue.

Student-athletes receiving some form of compensation for athletic activities, including athletic scholarships, have at times been considered employees by the courts and thus entitled to workers' compensation benefits for sports injuries. This view is, however, a minority position.

This issue was raised in *Rensing v. Indiana State University Board of Trustees* (see notes 1a and 2a) and in *University of Denver v. Nemeth* (see note 1b). In these cases the courts were divided as to whether the student-athlete was eligible to receive workers' compensation benefits.

In finding that the student-athlete was an employee of the institution and thus eligible for benefits, one court ruled that the continued receipt of a job, free meals, or scholarship money was conditioned on the student-athlete's participation in football, thereby creating a contract for employment. With the employment contract established, workers' compensation benefits were then paid to the employee-athletes injured or killed during the course of their employment. (See notes 1b, c, and d).

In other cases, however, courts did not find that the proper employment contract existed and benefits were denied. In two such cases it was found that football was not an integral money-making part of the university's educational function. Therefore, while the student-athlete was employed because of the receipt of an athletic scholarship, that employment was not in the institution's usual trade or business. (See notes 2a, b, and c.)

When considering the issue of whether an athletic department or institution's employee was injured while participating in employer-sponsored athletic activities is entitled to workers' compensation benefits, the courts attempt to determine whether the injury occurred in the course of employment. Factors the courts will consider include whether the event occurred on the employer's property and during working hours; whether the employer provided financial support, awards, and/or equipment; the level of encouragement to participate expressed by the employer; and any benefits derived by the employer as a result of the employee's participation in the event. For instance, if the employer required employees to participate in athletic activities with prospective clients as a means of increasing business and income, an employee injured in such activities may prove that the injury occurred while he or she was acting in the course of his or her employment. In addition, injuries sustained while participating in employee golf outings during a workday and participating in a local school system's basketball league to promote better public relations have both been found compensable under workers' compensation statutes. (See notes 3[a] and [b].)

NOTES ————————————————————————————————

1. The courts *granted* workers' compensation benefits to intercollegiate student-athletes in the following cases.

(a) In *Rensing v. Indiana State University*, 437 N.E.2d 78 (Ind. Ct. App. 1982), plaintiff football player filed a workers' compensation claim to recover for injuries and medical expenses. The court found that Rensing's athletic scholarship created employment with the university that was "periodically regular and not casual" and that maintaining a football team was in fact "an important aspect of the university's overall business or profession of educating students, even if it may not be said that athletic endeavors themselves are the university's 'principal' occupation." However, this decision was reversed; see note 2a.

(b) In *University of Denver v. Nemeth*, 257 P.2d 423 (Colo. Sup. Ct. 1953), Nemeth, a student-athlete injured during football practice, was found eligible for workers' compensation. Since Nemeth was given meal money and a job on campus only if he performed well on the football field, he fulfilled the workers' compensation act's requirement that the "injury aris[e] out of and in the course of employment."

(c) In *Van Horn v. Industrial Accident Comm'n*, 33 Cal. Rptr. 169 (Cal Dist. Ct. App. 1963), Van Horn, who received a football scholarship from California State Polytechnic College, was killed in a plane crash while returning from a game. The Industrial Accident Commission ruled that there was no contract of employment between the school and Van Horn and that his scholarship did not depend on his playing football. The district court of appeals overruled the commission's findings and found a contract of employment did exist, dependent on Van Horn's athletic prowess, which entitled his dependents to compensation. The court stressed that his scholarship alone could be construed as an employment contract.

(d) In 1974, Kent Waldrep, a third-year football player for Texas Christian University (TCU), was injured during a game against the University of Alabama. During that game, Waldrep, a running back, was flipped into the air on a play and landed head first on the artificial turf. Waldrep's fifth cervical vertebra was crushed, and he was immediately paralyzed. Because Waldrep was unable to satisfy his athletic commitment to TCU, TCU withdrew his scholarship for the next school year and Waldrep was forced to withdraw from school. In 1991, after incurring an estimated $500,000 in medical expenses, Waldrep filed a workers' compensation claim with the Texas Workers Compensation Commission. After reviewing his claim, the commission ruled that Waldrep was an employee of TCU and that his injury occurred in the course of his employment. The commission ruled that as an employee Waldrep was entitled to future medical expenses, $500,000 in past medical expenses, and a weekly salary, retroactive to 1974, for the rest of his life. In determining the value of Waldrep's salary, the commission assigned a value to Waldrep's scholarship of $115 a week. The injured employee is then entitled to two-thirds of his or her weekly wage.

2. The courts *denied* workers' compensation to intercollegiate student-athletes in the following cases.

(a) In *Rensing v. Indiana State University Board of Trustees*, 444 N.E.2d 1170 (Ind. Sup. Ct. 1983), the court noted a number of factors that suggested that the scholarship did not constitute an employment contract: (1) Rensing had not reported his benefits on his income tax returns; (2) NCAA regulations are incorporated by reference into the scholarship agreement, and since these regulations prohibit payment for athletic participation, the scholarship cannot be a job contract; and (3) the employer's right to dismiss Rensing on the basis of poor performance was conspicuously absent. Finally, the court also found that neither of the parties had the intent to enter into an employment contract.

(b) In *Cheatham v. Workers' Compensation Appeals Board*, 3 Civ. 21975 (Cal. Ct. App. 1984), Cheatham, a wrestler who was recruited and awarded an athletic scholarship by California Polytechnic, suffered a career-ending injury during a team scrimmage. He applied for workers' compensation. In denying his request, the court noted that the state legislature had amended the California Labor Code to specifically exclude student-athletes from the definition of employee.

(c) In *State Compensation Ins. Fund v. Industrial Commission*, 135 Colo. 570, 314 P. 2d 288 (Colo. Sup. Ct. 1957), Ray Dennison left his job at a gas station to play football for Fort Lewis A & M College after the Fort Lewis coach offered him a job and scholarship. Dennison received a fatal head injury in a game, and the Industrial Commission of Colorado awarded death benefits to his widow. The Colorado Supreme Court reversed this decision, however, because it found that no evidence existed that Dennison's employment was dependent upon his playing football. The court also found it significant that the school did not produce a profit from its football program.

3. The following cases are examples of workers' compensation claims made by employees injured while participating in athletic activities.

(a) In *Malan v. Town of Yorktown*, 448 N.Y.S.2d 100 (1985), an off-duty police officer was injured during a basketball practice organized by local schools. He was allowed to receive workers' compensation benefits since the employer benefited from the development of good public relations by officers participating in the league.

(b) In *Lybrand, Ross Brothers, and Montgomery v. Industrial Comm'n*, 223 N.E.2d 150 (Ill. Ct. App. 1967), an employee was killed while driving home from an all-expense-paid employer-sponsored golf outing. The outing occurred on a business day, and all employees were paid if they chose to participate but were required to work if they chose not to participate. Therefore, workers' compensation benefits were awarded.

(c) However, in *Kemp's Case*, 437 N.E.2d 526 (Mass. S.J.C. 1982), *reversing* 428 N.E.2d 326 (Mass. App. Ct. 1981), an employee's claim was denied after he was injured while participating in a company-sponsored softball game. While the employees could change into uniforms on company premises, the games were played after work and on public fields. Even though the employer furnished uniforms with the company logo and posted game scores on the company bulletin board, it did not give awards nor a banquet for employees. Therefore, the activity was not considered to be in the course of employment for workers' compensation purposes.

(d) In *De Carr v. N.Y. State Workers' Compensation Board*, 543 N.Y.S.2d 206 (N.Y. App. Div. 1989), the court found that where there was insufficient evidence to support a finding that the employer sponsored the postwork softball game, the injured employee was therefore not entitled to benefits. But see *Diem v. Diem & Burger Ins. Co.*, 536 N.Y.S.2d 246 (N.Y. App. Div. 1989), where the court upheld a finding that the employee's injury was compensable because participation in the insurance softball league sponsored by his employer was supported by evidence that the employer's president encouraged him to participate in the league because it was good for business and for enhancing contact with employees of major insurance carriers.

(e) In *Seiber v. Moog Auto. Inc.*, 773 S.W.2d 161 (Mo. Ct. App. 1989) the court held that injuries sustained by an employee during an uncompensated lunch-hour basketball game on the employer's premises are compensable where the employer acquiesced to activity to the extent that the activity became a regular incident of employment. But see *Todd v. Workers' Compensation Appeals Board*, 243 Cal. Rptr. 925 (1988), in which an employee was not entitled to benefits for injuries sustained while voluntarily playing basketball during his uncompensated lunch break on the employer's premises. Also, in *Taylor v. Workers' Compensation Appeals Board*, 244 Cal. Rptr. 643 (1988), the court held that a police officer injured while playing basketball during his lunch hour was not entitled to benefits, because his job required him to keep himself in good physical condition.

4. For further information, see the following law review articles:
   (a) Steinbach, "Workmen's Compensation and the Scholarship Athlete," 19 *Clev. St. L. Rev.*
   (b) Note, "Workers' Compensation and College Athletes: Should Universities Be Responsible for Athletes Who Incur Serious Injuries?" 10 *J. C. & U. L.* 197 (1983).

Chapter 7

APPLICATION OF TORT LAW

INTRODUCTION

Chapter 7 is organized according to possible defendants in sports tort cases. The chapter begins with a discussion of the potential liabilities of a participant in a sporting event. It then focuses on the potential liabilities of coaches and teachers in the areas of supervision, instruction and training, medical assistance, and vicarious liability for actions of fans and players. The legal theory most commonly used in this area is negligence. The chapter next covers the potential liabilities of administrators, schools, and universities. Administrators may be found negligent in hiring personnel (an employee such as a coach or teacher) or in supervising personnel. Administrators may also be found vicariously liable for the negligence of an employee in rendering medical assistance. Finally, administrators may be found negligent for not providing equipment, or vicariously liable if an employee did not furnish equipment or furnished ill-fitting or defective equipment. Schools and universities may also be sued under a vicarious liability theory for the negligence of any of their employees in the area of supervision and personnel, medical assistance, and equipment.

A defense for the administrator, school, or university may be the doctrine of sovereign immunity, the next topic presented in Chapter 7. Charitable immunity and civil liability immunity legislation are also discussed in this section. The next sections of Chapter 7 cover the liability of facility owners and possessors, which may include defects in a building or negligent supervision of a crowd, and the liability of medical personnel for negligent treatment of an injured athlete or fan.

The chapter continues with a discussion of a developing area of sports torts—the potential liabilities of officials, referees, and umpires. Some officials have been sued for injuries to athletes that have allegedly resulted from a failure to take corrective action to remedy the injury-causing situation. Examples include failing to stop a game during inclement weather conditions or allowing objects or spectators to be too close to the playing area. Officials, referees, and umpires have also been sued for the incorrect application of game rules and making incorrect judgment calls. The next section sets forth cases involving defects in equipment.

The final section in Chapter 7 discusses liability insurance and how high school athletic associations and high schools are purchasing insurance to combat the rising number of tort claims being made by those associated with sports activities. The National Collegiate Athletic Association implemented a liability insurance program, which began in the 1985–86 academic year. This last section also includes a discussion on the waiver and release of liability.

LIABILITY OF PARTICIPANTS

The liability stemming most directly from sports activity is that for injuries to participants. Until recently, most sports-related injuries were viewed as a natural outgrowth of the competitive and physical nature of sports. This attitude was supported by the traditional belief that a participant assumes the dangers inherent in the sport and is therefore precluded from recovery for an injury caused by another participant. Although this theory has some merit, it fails to address injuries that occur during a game that are not necessarily an outgrowth of competitive spirit.

This traditional attitude has been strictly scrutinized in recent decisions which clearly establish that a player does not necessarily assume the risk of all injuries resulting from the gross recklessness of another player. Nor does the player necessarily consent to intentional attacks falling outside the recognized rules of the sport. Thus, the defenses of assumption of the risk or of consent must be reviewed on a case-by-case basis to determine whether or not they are applicable in a particular instance (see Chapter 6).

This change in attitude has occurred in part because of the increasing number of serious injuries to sports participants. The increased volume of sports participation resulting from the involvement of boys and girls, and men and women, in unprecedented numbers has produced a corresponding increase in the number of sports-related injuries. The NCAA estimates that in football, basketball, and wrestling seasons alone there are approximately 1.3 million injuries at 32,650 high schools and 70,000 injuries at 900 colleges and universities (78 per institution). On the average, there is one injury per player per year in the National Football League (NFL).

A second reason for the change in attitude is that professional sports, and to some extent, intercollegiate and amateur athletics, are now viewed as businesses. Because of this, people are more inclined to see the situation as one in which a lawsuit is a viable option. In addition, amateur athletic associations have increased revenues and may have deep pockets to pay large awards. A third reason is that legal precedents have been established which allow injured athletes to recover. Finally, the rise in sports-related lawsuits is a result of society becoming increasingly reliant on the judicial system for the resolution of disputes.

An increase in claims of negligence and other tortious conduct has paralleled the rising number of sports injuries in recent years. One factor behind the rise in participant-versus-participant lawsuits is the steady erosion of the athlete's traditional reluctance to sue fellow participants. The increasing recognition of the dangers involved in playing a game against an opponent who does not follow an accepted safety rule has increased the likelihood of a lawsuit. Players are refusing to accept injury-provoking actions of opponents when the actions are not sanctioned by the rules of the game. There is some legal precedent which recognizes that each player has a legal duty to refrain from unreasonably dangerous acts (See notes 1b and c and note 2.)

Courts have found that many sports, including soccer, softball, and football, have created safety rules to help define the often unclear line between legal and illegal behavior on the field. A safety rule is one that is initiated to protect players and to prevent injuries. The existence of safety rules mandates that in many situations a player be charged with a legal duty to every other player involved in the activity. In cases involving the alleged violation of a safety rule, the courts have held that a player is liable for tort action only if his or her conduct displays deliberate, willful, or reckless disregard for the safety of other participants and results in injury to another participant (see note 1g and 1h).

Thus, a participant may recover for either intentional torts or for gross negligence (see Chapter 6). Actions based on ordinary negligence are still difficult to establish in athletic participant cases (see note 1a). However, case law indicates that there are situations in sports for which the commonly accepted defenses of assumption of risk and contributory negligence are not adequate to bar recovery by the plaintiff (see Chapter 6).

NOTES ⎯⎯⎯⎯⎯⎯⎯⎯⎯⎯⎯⎯⎯⎯⎯⎯⎯⎯⎯⎯⎯⎯⎯⎯⎯⎯⎯⎯⎯⎯⎯⎯⎯⎯⎯⎯⎯⎯

1. The courts discussed the liability of participants in sports in the following cases.

(a) In *Gaspard v. Grain Dealers Mutual Insurance Co.*, 131 So. 2d. 831 (La. 1961), Andrus Gaspard brought suit for damages for personal injuries on behalf of his son, Ronnie, after an injury to the boy in a playground baseball game. Defendant, Grain Dealers Mutual Insurance Company, had issued a comprehensive liability policy to Alfred Viator, the father of the boy responsible for the plaintiff's injury. At the trial court level, the defendant denied any negligence on the part of Ronald Viator and pleaded assumption of risk as a bar to plaintiff's recovery. In the alternative, the defendant alleged contributory negligence of Ronnie Gaspard. After a decision in the defendant's favor, the plaintiff filed this appeal. The appeals court found that young Viator's action did not constitute negligence because he exercised a reasonable degree of care. Gaspard assumed the risk as he "knew of the danger and clearly acquiesced or proceeded in the face of danger by voluntarily playing the game." Accordingly, the court denied Gaspard's appeal.

(b) In *Bourque v. Duplechin*, 331 So. 2d 40 (La. 1976), plaintiff brought suit for injuries he received in a softball game. In 1974, Jerome Bourque played second base on an amateur softball team sponsored by Boo Boo's

Lounge. Adrien Duplechin was a member of the opposing team. During the game, Duplechin was on first base when a teammate hit a ground ball. Duplechin started for second base as the shortstop threw the ball to Bourque. Bourque caught the ball, stepped on second base, and then stepped away from second base to throw the ball to first and complete a double play. After Bourque had thrown the ball to first base, Duplechin ran full speed into Bourque and brought his left arm up under Bourque's chin. When Duplechin made contact with Bourque, Bourque was standing five feet outside the base path. The umpire ejected Duplechin from the game for his conduct.

Bourque brought suit against Duplechin and his liability insurer. The lower court found for Bourque.

The court of appeals rejected Duplechin's argument that when Bourque voluntarily participated in the softball game, he assumed the risk of injury. The court stated that while Bourque did assume the risk of those injuries, which were common incidents of baseball and softball, he did not assume the risk of Duplechin breaching his duty to play softball in the ordinary fashion without unsportsmanlike conduct and inflicting wanton injury to his fellow players.

Allstate Insurance Company claimed on appeal that there was no coverage under its policy because Duplechin's actions were an intentional tort and he should have expected injury to occur. On this issue, the court quoted William Prosser from the *Law of Torts*, 4th edition:

> ...The mere knowledge and appreciation of a risk, short of substantial certainty, is not the equivalent of intent. The defendant who acts in the belief or consciousness that he is causing an appreciable risk of harm to another may be negligent, and if the risk is great his conduct may be characterized as reckless or wanton, but it is not classed as an intentional wrong.

Thus, in the court's opinion, Duplechin did not commit an intentional tort because he was not motivated by a desire to injure Bourque. Duplechin's conduct was negligent and was thus covered under the Allstate policy. The judgment of the trial court was affirmed.

(c) In *Griggas v. Clauson*, 128 N.E.2d 363 (Ill. App. ct. 1955), Griggas, a nineteen-year-old member of an amateur basketball team, brought suit for injuries received during a game. During that game he was guarded by La Verne Clauson. While Griggas had his back to Clauson and was about to receive a pass from a teammate, Clauson pushed him and then struck him in the face with his fist. As Griggas fell, Clauson struck him again and knocked him unconscious. Clauson began to swear profusely and made statements to the effect that he was going to teach Griggas a lesson and that one of the two was going to play in the city and the other was not. Griggas was hospitalized for about three weeks. The Appellate Court of Illinois supported a trial court decision for Griggas. It held that the evidence in the record supported the finding that Griggas was subjected to a wanton and unprovoked battery.

(d) In *Nabozny v. Barnhill*, 334 N.E.2d 258 (Ill. App. Ct. 1975), plaintiff soccer player filed suit for injuries received when he was kicked in the head by an opponent during an amateur soccer game involving two teams composed of high school age players. The defendant, David Barnhill, was playing a forward position for one team, and the plaintiff, Julian Nabozny, was the goaltender for the other team. Barnhill kicked Nabozny in the head while Nabozny was in possession of the ball. Contact with the goaltender while he is in possession of the ball is a violation of FIFA (International Association Football Federation—soccer's international governing body) rules which governed the contest. The resultant injury left the plaintiff with permanent skull and brain damage. Nabozny brought suit, and the trial court directed a verdict in favor of the defendant.

On appeal, the court noted that it did not wish to "place unreasonable burdens on the free and vigorous participation in sports by our youth," but also stated that "athletic competition does not exist in a vacuum." Therefore, in reversing the trial court decision, the court held that a player is charged with a legal duty to every other player on the field to refrain from conduct proscribed by a safety rule. The court held that when athletes are engaged in athletic competition, all teams involved are trained and coached by knowledgeable personnel; a recognized set of rules governs the conduct of the competition; and a safety rule is contained therein which is primarily designed to protect players from serious injury. Thus, a reckless disregard for the safety of other players cannot be excused.

(e) In *Barrett v. Phillips*, 223 S.E.2d 918 (N.C. 1976), a wrongful death suit against a high school and an athletic association was brought when Barrett's son was killed in a collision during a high school football game with a player over twenty years old. The defendants were in violation of a rule prohibiting players over age nineteen from playing. The court reasoned that the purpose of the rule was not for the safety of the players, and there was no actionable negligence because there was no causal connection between the death and the violation of the rule.

(f) In *Osborne v. Sprowls*, 419 N.E.2d (Ill. 1981), a bystander sued a participant for injuries incurred during a "tackle-the-football" game. This game is a combination of football, keep-away, and soccer in which all players chase the person with the football until he or she is tackled or kicks or throws the ball away. The Supreme Court of Illinois determined that an ordinary negligence standard would apply because Osborne was neither a participant nor was he located in an area where the game was or could be in progress. The court determined the defendant owed the plaintiff the duty to select an area free from the presence of nonparticipating individuals.

(g) In *Dotzler v. Tuttle*, 449 N.W.2d 774 (Neb. Sup. Ct. 1990), plaintiff sued defendant for injuries arising out of a collision between them during a "pick-up" basketball game. The trial court found for the defendant and the plaintiff appealed. The supreme court held that a participant in a contact sport is liable for tortious conduct only if he acts willfully or with reckless disregard for the safety of the plaintiff, but is not liable for ordinary negligence. The case, however, was reversed and remanded on the issue of the plaintiff's contributory negligence, which was improperly submitted to the jury.

(h) In *Gauvin v. Clark*, 537 N.E.2d 94 (Mass. S.J.C. 1989), plaintiff hockey player sued the defendant for injuries sustained when the defendant "butt-ended" the plaintiff in the abdomen with his stick. The supreme judicial court held that the defendant was not liable for injuries caused by his violation of a safety rule where he did not act in reckless disregard of the plaintiff's safety.

(i) In *Novak v. Lamar Ins. Co.*, 488 So. 2d 739 (La. Ct. App. 1986), plaintiff softball player brought action against a second softball player, the homeowner's insurer of that player's father, and the insurer of the church which sponsored the defendant softball player's team. Plaintiff sought recovery for injuries sustained when the two collided as defendant softball player ran to first base. The court held that the defendant softball player was not acting in a reckless or unsportsmanlike manner. The court reasoned that the risk of collision was a foreseeable risk which the plaintiff had assumed.

(j) In *Picou v. Hartford Ins. Co.*, 558 So. 2d 787 (La. Ct. App. 1990), the court of appeals held that a softball base runner could not be held liable for negligence toward the second base player who suffered an ankle injury in a collision. The court held that the defendant did not act in an unreasonable or unsportsmanlike manner and thus could not be held liable in negligence.

2. The liability of participants has also been a subject of much judicial scrutiny on the professional sports level. The following cases examine this area of sports law.

(a) In *Hackbart v. Cincinnati Bengals*, 435 F. Supp. 352 (D. Colo. 1977), *rev'd*, 601 F.2d 516 (10th Cir. 1979), Charles Clark, a running back with the Cincinnati Bengals, was sued for reckless misconduct by Dale Hackbart, a defensive back for the Denver Broncos. Clark had struck Hackbart in the head, an action outside the rules of the game of football. The trial court had ruled that there was no duty between the players. However, the appeals court found enough justification for a retrial on a reckless misconduct theory before a jury to determine the liability of defendant Charles Clark. The case was settled before trial for a reported $200,000.

(b) In *Manning v. Grimsley*, 643 F.2d 20 (1st Cir. 1981), Ross Grimsley, a pitcher for the Baltimore Orioles, was upset at the heckling fans at Fenway Park and upon finishing his warmups, threw a ball through a protective screen and hit the plaintiff. The plaintiff sued the pitcher and his employer for battery and negligence. The district court ruled for the defendant on both counts. The court of appeals, however, vacated and remanded the decision regarding the battery charge, holding that the jury verdict on the negligence claim did not preclude the plaintiff from maintaining the battery claim.

3. For further information on participant liability in sports, see the following law review articles.

(a) Lazaroff, "Torts and Sports: Participant Liability to Co-Participants for Injuries Sustained During Competition," 7 *U. of Miami Ent. & Sports L. Rev.* 191 (1990).

(b) Ranii, "Sports Violence Lawsuits Erupt," *National L. J.*, February 9, 1981, p. 1.

(c) Carroll, "Torts in Sports—I'll See You in Court," 16 *Akron L. Rev.* 537 (1983).

(d) Comment, "A Proposed Legislative Solution to the Problem of Violent Acts by Participants During Professional Sporting Events," 7 *U. Dayton L. Rev.* 91 (1981).

(e) Hayes, "Professional Sports and Tort Liability: A Victory for the Intentionally Injured Player," 1980 *Det. C. L. Rev.* 687 (1980).

(f) Gulotta, "Torts in Sports: Deterring Violence in Professional Athletics," 48 *Fordham L. Rev.* 764 (1980).

LIABILITY OF COACHES AND TEACHERS

Coaches or teachers, as individuals, are always responsible for any intentional torts they commit in their capacity as coaches or physical education teachers. They are generally not shielded by the defenses of consent, privilege, and immunity from liability by virtue of their positions. (See Chapter 6.)

The coach is judged by the standard of a "reasonable coach" and the teacher by the standard of a "reasonable teacher." There are some limited exceptions in which coaches and teachers are held to a lower standard of care and will not be held liable unless they are deemed to be grossly negligent. One situation involves coaches or teachers who are given the status "in loco parentis"—that is, the coach or teacher is placed in the position of the parents of the student-athlete (see note 1d in the section entitled Failure to Provide Proper Instruction and Training). A coach or teacher may, however, have a number of defenses available (see Chapter 6).

Since a minor is often involved in this area, note should be taken that certain defenses such as contributory negligence, comparative negligence, and assumption of the risk may be affected by the different standard of care for children (see Chapter 6). The defense of sovereign immunity is a particularly important one for coaches and teachers. As a general rule, the coach or teacher cannot be sued individually when the school district is protected under sovereign immunity (discussed later in this chapter). However, this protection is limited and may not cover the coach who is not acting within the scope of employment or who has been misfeasant.

Until recently, very little litigation was brought against coaches and teachers as a result of the sovereign immunity protection and the reluctance by potential plaintiffs to bring lawsuits. This was especially true in the case of coaches and teachers who were often members of the community and highly respected for their work. However, the coach and teacher are increasingly likely to be sued today, because injured student-athletes are more likely to bring suit and the sovereign immunity doctrine is being eroded (as discussed later in this chapter).

In many of the cases, the institution has been sued under the doctrine of respondeat superior (also called the doctrine of vicarious liability) for the coach's or teacher's negligence and the coach has not been a named defendant. However, the basis for the litigation is the negligence of the coach or teacher, and in future cases the coach or teacher may be sued individually. The areas of responsibility for which a coach or teacher may be sued include supervision, instruction and training, medical assistance, and vicarious liability for actions of fans and players.

Failure to Provide Adequate Supervision

The coach and teacher are responsible for providing reasonable supervision to the student-athletes under their direction. However, they are not insurers of the safety of everyone under their supervision.

Examples of failure to provide adequate supervision include negligent supervision at a football game or failure to provide the proper equipment for the game. It would also include improperly supervising an off-season weight training program or encouraging an injured student-athlete to play. An additional responsibility for the coach and teacher is to check the playing area to make sure it is in proper playing condition and that nothing is on or near the playing area that could cause injury; such obstructions include benches, other students, and spectators.

Finally, the coach and teacher also may be sued for nonplaying field activities, such as supervising student-athletes who are going to or from the playing field. The coach and teacher are responsible for providing reasonable supervision. Any supervisory capacity carries with it the responsibility to exercise due care—that is, the care of a "reasonable supervisor" (see Chapter 6). This due care must be provided for the safety of anyone who is likely to or actually does come into contact with the area under supervision. The duty entails using reasonable care in either rectifying dangerous situations or warning those who may encounter them of the possible hazards. A supervisor generally is not liable for any intentional acts of his employees unless it can be proved that he or she was negligent in choosing or supervising the employee(s) involved. A school district or supervisor is liable in such instances only if the institution, or one to whom the district or supervisor is legally responsible, breaches the requisite standard of reasonable care. If the supervisor is not negligent himself, liability will be assessed only if the employee and the action taken satisfy the requirements of respondeat superior (see Chapter 5). Also, the doctrine of sovereign immunity (discussed later in this chapter in the section Failure to Provide Safe Equipment) may bar the action unless the state involved has specifically eliminated its immunity under this doctrine.

A supervisor is not, however, an insurer of everyone's safety; rather, the supervisor needs only to exercise reasonable care. Unless there is information or notice to the contrary, the supervisor is entitled to assume that all under his or her supervision will also be exercising due care. Thus, a spectator who is injured by another spectator may not enforce a claim against a school district or its administrators unless the school district or administrator, having had notice that the other spectator was likely to cause an unreasonably dangerous condition, failed to take steps to prevent the injury. Past experience, moreover, will be considered when assessing liability. For example, if the same spectator appeared at another contest and injured a fellow spectator, the school district might be held liable because the first situation provided warning of the person's potentially dangerous nature. The duty of care required may depend on the type of event. Hockey games, for instance, may require more security and precautions than do track and field events.

NOTE ———————————————————————————————

1. The following cases deal with supervision of student-athletes by the coach or teacher.

(a) *Morris v. Union High School District A, King County,* 294 P. 998 (Wash. Sup. Ct. 1931), was a suit brought by a high school athlete who injured his back during football practice. The coach, who was well aware of the injury, or should have become aware of it in the exercise of reasonable care, "permitted, persuaded and coerced" the athlete to play in a game. As a result of the athlete's participation, he suffered more serious injuries to his back and spine. The athlete brought suit against the school district alleging that the school district was liable for the negligence of its coach, who negligently coerced him to play. The court ruled in favor of the plaintiff and held that the school district was liable.

(b) *Vargo v. Svitchan,* 301 N.W.2d 1 (Mich. Ct. App. 1980), was a suit brought by a high school athlete who, while participating in a summer weight training program at the high school gymnasium, attempted to lift a 250- to 300-pound weight, fell, and received injuries resulting in paraplegia. The plaintiff's lawsuit charged the school's athletic director, principal, and superintendent with negligent supervision of the football coach. The court of appeals held that the school's principal and athletic director were sued for "personal neglect" in maintaining inadequate school facilities, in allowing an illegal summer weight-lifting program and providing insufficient supervision. Therefore, they were not entitled to the protection of the governmental immunity statute. The school superintendent was entitled to protection under the governmental immunity standard because there was no "personal neglect" on his part.

(c) In *Lynch v. Board of Education of Collingsville Community School District*, 390 N.E.2d 526 (Ill. 1979), parents of a junior in high school brought a negligence suit on her behalf against the school district for damages she received as a result of an injury suffered in a "powderpuff" intramural football game. Plaintiffs alleged ordinary negligence on the part of the defendant in failing to provide adequate equipment and willful and wanton misconduct in failing to adequately supervise the game. An appeals court, in affirming the trial court's decision for the parents, held that since the teams' coaches were teachers and the field on which the contest was played was fenced and could have been locked to keep students out, there was sufficient evidence for the jury to conclude that the game was authorized by the school. The court also held that the presence of the plaintiff's parents at the game site did not obviate the school's duty to provide adequate equipment.

(d) In *Domino v. Mercurio*, 234 N.Y.S.2d 1011 (N.Y. App. Div. 1962), *aff'd*, 193 N.E.2d 893 (N.Y. Ct. App. 1963), a negligence suit was brought by plaintiff father against the local board of education and playground supervisors who were employees of the board for injuries sustained by his son, who, while playing softball on the school playground, fell over a bench that was too close to the base path. The court held that the board could be held liable for the negligence of the playground supervisors who allowed spectators to congregate too close to the third base line and moved a bench into a dangerous position near that line. It was not necessary that the board itself be found guilty of negligence in selecting playground supervisors.

(e) *Foster v. Houston General Insurance Company*, 407 So. 2d 759 (La. Ct. App. 1981), was a suit for the wrongful death of a mentally retarded student-athlete. A member of his school's Special Olympics basketball team, plaintiff was en route to basketball practice at an off-campus facility when he dashed in front of a car and was struck and killed while under the supervision of one teacher. The teacher had assumed responsibility for eleven players because the other teacher involved was detained in class. The trial and appeals courts ruled that the defendant teachers owed the deceased a legal duty and breached their duty by failing to act reasonably under the circumstances. They did not provide an adequate number of supervisory personnel, and they were negligent in the selection of the safest possible walk route. The defendant school board was not liable for independent negligence.

(f) In *Kersey v. Harbin*, 591 S.W.2d 745 (Mo. Ct. App. 1979), a negligence suit was filed against school officials for fatal injuries sustained by plaintiff's son during gym class. Decedent engaged in a brief scuffle after a fellow student deliberately and persistently stepped on decedent's heels. Decedent sustained a skull fracture during the scuffle, which occurred on the stairway leading from the locker room to the gymnasium. The plaintiff alleged that the school authorities had possessed actual and/or constructive knowledge of quarrelsome propensities on the part of the fellow student and, despite such knowledge, had failed to take "appropriate measures to prevent injury ... by exercising ordinary care." The appeals court held that "supervisory public school employees and teachers are not immune from tort liability for inadequate supervision of their students but that such liability is highly subjective and the scope of their duties extremely narrow." The case was remanded to the trial court for a factual determination.

(g) In *Childress by Childress v. Madison County,* 777 S.W.2d 1 (Tenn. Ct. App. 1989), a severely retarded student and his parents sued the county and its board of education, alleging negligence in supervision of the student, who was taken to a public pool for training for the Special Olympics. The court found the county negligent in failing to supervise the student adequately, as neither teacher, aide, nor lifeguard was watching the student after he was told to get out of the pool. As a result, student wandered into deep end of the pool and was found on the pool's floor. In addition, the court found that the release signed by student's mother relieved the county of liability to the mother, but not to the student.

(h) In *Locilento v. Coleman Catholic High School,* 523 N.Y.S.2d 198 (N.Y. App. Div. 1987), the court found in favor of a student injured during intramural football game in a suit against the school. The court held that the evidence sustained a finding that the school's failure to provide the student with proper equipment during an intramural tackle football game was a proximate cause of the shoulder injury and that the student's voluntary participation was merely an implied assumption of risk which did not preclude all recovery.

(i) In *Best v. Houtz,* 541 So.2d 8 (Ala. 1989), a student who broke his elbow when he slipped in a puddle of water during a physical education class sued his two teachers for negligent supervision. The court found for the teachers because neither was aware of the puddle or any tendency of the vents to leak water onto the floor.

(j) In *Lentz v. Morris,* 372 S.E.2d 608 (Va. Sup. Ct. 1988), a minor who was injured playing tackle football sued his physical education teacher for negligent supervision. The Virginia Supreme Court affirmed the lower court's decision in favor of the defendant. The court concluded that since the defendant was acting within the scope of his employment at the time of the injury, he was immune from suit as an employee of a governmental entity.

Failure to Provide Proper Instruction and Training

The coach and teacher are responsible for providing proper instruction and training to the student-athletes; they should be qualified to teach the particular activity involved. In addition, the coach must properly instruct the student-athletes on the activity, the safety rules, and the proper method of playing. In a number of cases, the injured player alleged that the coach or teacher did not provide proper instruction and training. In addition, a proper preseason conditioning program should be provided, although such programs become an issue where football practice is started in August and some players experience fatal injuries related to heat exhaustion.

Coaches and teachers should keep detailed records of their instruction and training sessions. They should also be aware of any new developments in their sport. Some companies have started producing instruction and training films to assist coaches and teachers in preparing their student-athletes.

Another area of potential liability for the coach or teacher is a claim by a student-athlete of assault and battery. Several issues are raised in this area. Is there a defense of privilege? Is the standard of care "reasonable care" or "gross negligence"? Does sovereign immunity protect the coach and teacher? Can force be used to bring about compliance with commands and punishment for prohibited conduct? Can force be used when the player has not performed adequately? There has not been a great deal of litigation in this area, but coaches and teachers should be aware that cases may be brought (see notes 1b and d).

NOTE _____

1. The following cases deal with the instruction and training of student-athletes by coaches and teachers.

(a) In *Vendrell v. School District No. 26C, Malheur County,* 233 Or. 1, 376 P.2d 406 (Or. Sup. Ct. 1962), plaintiff, a freshman football player who had played two years of junior high football, brought suit against the school district for damages for the neck injury he sustained while playing in a high school game. The plaintiff suffered a fractured neck when he lowered his head and collided with two opposing players. The plaintiff contended that he was an inexperienced player and had been improperly trained. The court of appeals ruled against the plaintiff, holding that the plaintiff was not inexperienced in that he had played for two years in junior high school and during those years had received substantial football training from competent coaches. The court held that the game of football is an inherently rough sport in which body contact and some degree of injury are inevitable and that no player should need to have this explained.

(b) In *Rutledge v. Arizona Board of Regents,* 660 F.2d 1345 (9th Cir. 1981), *aff'd,* 103 S. Ct. 148 (1983), plaintiff student-athlete sued his college football coach for assault and battery, demotion, harassment, embarrassment, defamation, and deprivation of his scholarship. Plaintiff claimed that in October 1978, the coach took his helmeted head between his hands, shook it from side to side, yelled obscenities, and then struck his mouth with his fist. Plaintiff filed suit in Arizona state court but was denied relief. He then filed suit in federal district court. The court dismissed the complaint, and Rutledge appealed. On appeal, the 9th Circuit Court of Appeals held that the university, the board of regents, and the athletic director were entitled to at least partial immunity. The coaches were not entitled to immunity, and the athletic director was not immune on the claim he failed to supervise the coach properly. However, the court dismissed Rutledge's assault and battery complaint because it had been previously litigated in state court.

(c) In *Pirkle v. Oakdale Union Grammer School Dist.*, 253 P.2d 1 (Cal. Sup. Ct. 1953), an eighth grade student brought an action against the school district for injuries received from being blocked during a touch football game that was played without supervision. The court held for the defendant on appeal, ruling that the players had been properly selected and instructed. The court also held that plaintiff's injuries could not have been readily apparent to a lay person and that no further damage resulted from a delay in receiving medical treatment.

(d) In *Hogenson v. Williams*, 542 S.W.2d 456 (Tex. 1976), an action for assault was brought when the coach, displeased with the blocking of a seventh grade player, grabbed him by the face mask and knocked him to the ground. The player received a severe cervical sprain. The jury found for the defendant, but the appeals court held the trial judge had improperly interpreted the rule of "privileged force" granted a teacher when he instructed the jury that "intent to injure is the gist of an assault." Rather, a teacher or coach can use force necessary to invoke compliance with his commands or to punish the child for prohibited conduct. A coach cannot use force merely because the student's performance is inadequate, even though the coach may consider such violence to be constructive. The jury verdict was reversed and remanded.

(e) In *Kluka v. Livingston Parish School District*, 433 So. 2d 302 (La. 1983), a basketball coach was held not liable for injuries to a student who caught his foot between two mats while wrestling the coach in a friendly match. The court held that the student initiated the match and knew that wrestling could lead to injury.

(f) In *Thompson v. Seattle Public School District* (unpublished decision 1985), plaintiff high school football player sought to recover damages for injuries sustained during high school football game. The plaintiff was injured after lowering his head to ward off tacklers. The court decided in favor of the plaintiff on the basis that the player was not properly warned of the dangers of lowering his head while carrying the football.

Failure to Provide Prompt and Capable Medical Assistance

A common risk encountered in the area of sports is the risk of serious injury. When an injury to an athlete or spectator appears to be serious, those in charge of the activity are under a duty to use reasonable efforts to obtain reasonably prompt and capable medical assistance. At the same time, there is a duty to refrain from actions that might aggravate an injury, when a reasonable person would know of the risk.

The coach and teacher are held to a standard of "reasonable care" when rendering medical assistance to an injured student-athlete. They are not expected to provide the assistance of a doctor or one with medical training. In fact, some of the obligations of the coach and teacher have been shifted to others. For example, many states have passed statutes requiring that medical personnel be in attendance at games (see Chapter 6). Such laws may reduce the liability exposure for the coach and teacher.

The institution may be the responsible party if medical personnel have not been provided. In addition, the institution may be responsible for having medical personnel "reasonably" available, even when it is not statutorily mandated. With medical personnel available, the care of the injured student-athlete may not have to be undertaken by the coach or teacher.

Therefore, in most situations, the main responsibilities of the coach and teacher are twofold. First, they may have to render assistance before the medical personnel arrive. First-aid training may be helpful to prevent a situation in which, for example, the coach improperly moves an injured student-athlete. The second responsibility is to exercise reasonable care in sending an injured athlete for medical treatment.

NOTE _____

1. The following cases deal with the duties of amateur athletic programs and personnel in regards to medical assistance.

(a) In *Welch v. Dunsmuir Joint Union High School District*, 326 P.2d 633 (Cal. Ct. App. 1958), plaintiff high school football player was injured during a scrimmage between two high school teams and brought suit against the school district. The player was lying on the ground unable to get to his feet. One coach suspected the player might have a serious neck injury and had him take hold of his hands to see whether they could grip. The evidence was conflicting as to whether or not the team physician, who was present at the scrimmage, examined the player before he was moved to the sidelines. Evidence indicated, however, that plaintiff was carried from the field without the aid of a stretcher or board or any other solid structure beneath him. Medical testimony established that the plaintiff became a permanent quadriplegic as a result of damage to the spinal cord. The jury ruled for the plaintiff and the appeals court held that from the evidence presented the jury could have reasonably inferred that both the doctor and the coach were negligent in the removal of the plaintiff from the field—the coach for failing to wait for the doctor and allowing the plaintiff to be moved, and the doctor for failing to act promptly after the injury.

(b) *Mogabgab v. Orleans Parish School Board*, 239 So. 2d 456 (La. 1970), was an action brought by parents for the wrongful death of their son, a high school football player who died as a result of heatstroke and exhaustion following a practice. The plaintiffs sued the coach, the school principal, and the school district on the theory that the school was negligent in not making sure the coach was properly trained. They argued also that the school was negligent in making arrangements for the proper care of sick and injured players. The court held that the coach who actively denied the student-athlete access to medical treatment for two hours after symptoms of heatstroke and shock appeared was guilty of negligence. However, the court did not find negligence attributable to the principal, school district, physical education supervisor, or school superintendent because they were unaware of the events.

(c) In *Stineman v. Fontbonne College,* 664 F.2d 1082 (8th Cir. 1981), plaintiff was a deaf student-athlete whose softball coaches were aware of her handicap. Plaintiff had signed an authorization for emergency medical treatment in the event of an injury. During the course of practice plaintiff was struck in the eye with a ball. A coach applied ice and advised her, despite the great amount of pain she was experiencing, to go to her room and rest and she would be all right. Neither coach who was present suggested that she seek medical attention. No immediate professional medical attention was given, even though the school infirmary was across the street. Permanent eye damage resulted from the injury. The trial court found negligence of the college in failing to provide the proper medical assistance. The appeals court affirmed the decision; however, it reduced the damages from $800,000 to $600,000.

Vicarious Liability for Actions of Fans and Players

The coach and teacher may be sued under a vicarious liability theory for either an unintentional or an intentional tort. However, plaintiffs generally have difficulty in winning cases based on a vicarious liability theory. For instance, in *Toone v. Adams,* an umpire was injured by a fan, and the umpire sued, among others, the manager for inciting the fan to act. The court held for the manager and found that the manager's actions were not the proximate cause of the umpire's injuries (see note 1).

The nexus between the coach and the injury may be more easily established in other fact situations which have occurred but have not resulted in litigation. For example, a coach who orders a player to fight or to attempt to injure an opposing player may be liable under the vicarious liability theory if injuries occur.

NOTE _____

1. For a case involving coaches' vicarious liability for the actions of fans and players, see *Toone v. Adams,* 262 N.C. 403, 137 S.E.2nd 132 (N.C. Sup. Ct. 1964). A baseball umpire brought suit against the manager and the owner of the team after being assaulted by a fan after a game. The umpire contended that the conduct of the manager, who had been ejected from the game, and the lack of adequate protection were the proximate causes of his injury. The court found that umpires are used to having their calls disputed and that

disagreements, as such, are not a major problem. The plaintiff was well escorted on his way to the dressing room, and though the guards themselves could have been more diligent, lack of protection was not the proximate cause of the plaintiff's injury. The court asserted that the club and its manager did not actually intend or could not have reasonably anticipated that one or more persons would assault the plaintiff as a result of the manager's conduct.

LIABILITY OF ADMINISTRATORS, SCHOOLS, AND UNIVERSITIES

Sports-related injuries that occur within the confines of an educational institution raise the issue of legal accountability of the institution itself. From the perspective of the seriously injured plaintiff, it may be more desirable to obtain a judgment against an institution rather than an individual coach or instructor because the institution is much more likely to have a "deep pocket" from which the plaintiff bringing suit can receive monetary damage awards.

If an administrator or institution is subject to liability, the standards to which it will be held are the same as in similar areas of tort law. The administrator and institution are required to exercise reasonable care to prevent reasonably foreseeable risks and to make safe foreseeably dangerous conditions by repairing or warning. If the institution fails to maintain a reasonable standard of care, it may be sued for negligence (see Chapter 6). For example, the administrator or institution should establish rules for the safe use of facilities, provide supervision of athletic activities and hire qualified personnel; provide proper medical assistance; and provide proper equipment. Institutions cannot guarantee the safety of students, but they are subject to liability when the institution or someone for whom the institution is legally responsible does not meet the standard of care required by the law.

The administrator, school, or university may also be sued under the theory of vicarious liability for the alleged negligence of an employee (see Chapter 6). An administrator may be sued in his or her role as the supervisor of a coach or teacher. The institution may also be sued in its role as the employer of the administrator, coach, teacher, referee, doctor, or as the owner or possessor of a facility.

One roadblock in the path of the potential plaintiff, however, is the sovereign immunity doctrine. This doctrine is a rule of law, which in many states exempts public schools and universities from private suit. Sovereign immunity has been around for centuries, but more recently the doctrine has eroded in fairness to injured plaintiffs, who previously could not collect when injured. In states where sovereign immunity has been partially eliminated, there are usually special rules of procedure which the plaintiff must carefully follow. (See the section Sovereign Immunity.)

1. For further information on liability of sports administrators, see the following law review article: Note, "The Student-Athlete and the NCAA: The Need for a Prima Facie Tort Doctrine," 9 *Suffolk U. L. Rev.* 1340 (1975).

Failure to Provide Supervision of Athletic Activities and to Hire Qualified Personnel

The administrator is the supervisor of the coach or teacher, and as such may be held liable in negligence for failing to exercise reasonable care in fulfilling this responsibility. Many of the administrator's duties and responsibilities are similar to the supervisory duties of the coach or teacher in dealing with student-athletes. In dealing with personnel, administrators may be held liable if they have not exercised reasonable care in hiring coaches and teachers with proper skills and qualifications and in insuring that properly qualified personnel are supervising.

Schools and universities are generally sued on a vicarious liability theory, meaning that the negligence of their employee is imputed to the employer. The negligent individual may be an administrator, a teacher, a coach, a substitute teacher, a student teacher, or a referee. Any of these individuals, and the school or university, may be immune from lawsuit based on sovereign immunity (discussed later in this chapter).

NOTES _____

1. The following cases discuss the liability of the sports administrator and personnel in the area of supervision.

    (a) In *Carabba v. Anacortes School District No. 103*, 435 P.2d 936 (Wash. 1967), the plaintiff, a high school wrestler, brought suit against the defendant school district to recover injuries sustained in a match. The plaintiff was injured when the referee's attention was diverted and his opponent applied an illegal "full nelson" hold. The plaintiff was paralyzed below the neck due to substantial severance of his spinal cord. The court held that because the referee was an agent for the school district, the school could be held vicariously liable for the referee's negligence.

    (b) In *Cook v. Bennett*, 288 N.W.2d 609 (Mich. 1979), plaintiff elementary school student brought suit after being seriously injured while playing "kill" during recess. In the game of "kill" all participants attempt to obtain the ball by tackling the lone participant who has it. In regards to the school's principal, the appeals court reversed the trial court's decision and held that "the extent to which a school principal is protected by immunity is dependent on whether the act complained of falls within the principal's discretionary or ministerial powers." The court held that inadequate supervision is not a discretionary function and is not protected by governmental immunity.

(c) In *DeMauro v. Tusculum College, Inc.*, 603 S.W.2d 115 (Tenn. Sup. Ct. 1980), plaintiff brought suit for injuries he received in a golf class. Plaintiff was injured when a teaching assistant, an inexperienced golfer who was assigned to supervise plaintiff's class, was attempting to demonstrate how to hit a golf ball. The teaching assistant "shanked" the shot, which struck the plaintiff in the face. The court allowed the plaintiff to sue the college under the doctrine of vicarious liability.

(d) In *Germond v. Board of Education of Central School District No. 1*, 197 N.Y.S.2d 548 (N.Y. App. Div. 1960), plaintiff student sought recovery from defendant school board and teacher for injuries sustained when struck in the face by a bat swung by an older student during a softball game on the school's playground. A trial court's decision against the board was affirmed by the court of appeals. The court held that the board assumed responsibility for the individual negligence of the teacher. The board's failure to reasonably enforce adequate rules with respect to playing games on the playground and its failure to provide adequate supervision was sufficient evidence to justify a verdict against the board. The evidence presented sustained a finding of no cause of action against the school teacher who had been supervising play. The appellate court ruled that "the mere presence of the older girls would not necessarily alert a reasonable and careful teacher of young children to danger."

(e) *Brahatcek v. Millard School District #17*, N.W.2d 680 (Neb. Sup. Ct. 1979), was a suit involving an action for the death of a ninth-grade student who was accidently struck by a golf club during physical education class. The court held that the school district and instructors were negligent in not providing supervision and that the lack of supervision was the proximate cause of the student's death. It held that the instructors should have foreseen the intervening negligent act of the student who fatally struck the other student. If there had been proper supervision, the death would not have occurred, and therefore, intervening negligence of the classmate did not preclude the district from liability for the death.

(f) In *Larson v. Independent School District #314*, 289 N.W.2d 112 (Minn. Sup. Ct. 1979), plaintiff sued the superintendent of the school district, the principal of the high school, a physical education teacher, and the school district, charging them with negligence in improper teaching and supervision. The plaintiff became a quadriplegic as a result of an injury suffered while performing a "headspring over a rolled mat" in a physical education class. The court held that the superintendent was not sufficiently involved to be found negligent, but the teacher was personally liable for negligent spotting and teaching of the exercise and the principal was negligent for not supervising the physical education curriculum more closely.

(g) In *Benitez v. New York City Bd. of Educ.*, 541 N.E.2d (N.Y. Ct. App.

1989), plaintiff high school football player brought personal injury action against the board of education and the city public school athletic league. The plaintiff alleged negligence of the coach and principal in permitting him to play in a fatigued condition in a mismatched game. In reversing the lower court's decision, the appeals court ruled in favor of the defendants and held that the player assumed the risks of injury in competition and was not under inherent compulsion to play.

(h) In *Hemphill v. Sayers*, 552 F. Supp. 685 (Ill. D. 1982), university football player, who sustained an injury to his cervical spine as a result of an allegedly defective football helmet, brought an action against the university's athletic director, football coach, athletic trainer, and helmet manufacturer. The court denied the motion by the defendants to dismiss. The court held, *inter alia*, that the university athletic director, football coach, and athletic trainer were not immune under the Eleventh Amendment from liability for negligence in failing to warn of dangers of a football helmet because they were being sued in their individual capacities.

(i) In *Montgomery v. City of Detroit*, 448 N.W.2d 822 (Mich. Ct. App. 1989), the mother of a student who died of a heart attack after collapsing on a school's athletic field sued the principal, the teacher, and the operator of the emergency medical service telephone. The court found for the defendants, holding that (1) the principal was immune from liability; (2) the alleged failure of the teacher to learn to make emergency calls was an immune discretionary decision; (3) the telephone operator was not negligent; (4) the statute which provided that school officials could be sued for discretionary acts constituting gross negligence did not apply; (5) the student's civil rights were not violated by schoolteacher's acts, which allegedly delayed student's arrival at hospital.

2. For further information on the liability of sports administrators and personnel in the area of supervision, see the following legal articles.

(a) Cohen, "Gymnastics Litigation: Meeting the Defenses," 16 *Trial* 34 (August 1980).

(b) Greenwald, "Gymnastics Litigation: The Standard of Care," 16 *Trial* 24 (August 1980).

(c) Fidel and Langerman, "Responsibility Is Also a Part of the Game," 13 *Trial* 22 (January 1977).

Failure to Provide Proper Medical Assistance

Administrators, schools, and universities are generally not responsible for providing direct medical treatment to an injured student, student-athlete, or spectator. However, the administrator, school, or university may be sued on the doctrine of vicarious liability if the coach improperly provided medical treatment. The administrator, school, or university generally will not be held responsible for the medical malpractice of a doctor, since in most cases the doctor is held to be an independent contractor and not an employee. However, the administrator, school, or university may be held responsible for the negligent selection, supervision, or hiring of medical personnel. There may also be potential liability if the administrator, school, or university was negligent in not providing medical personnel at a game or practice. Many schools and universities have rules that require medical personnel at certain events, such as football or basketball games. And finally, the school or university may be held responsible on the theory of vicarious liability if the administrator is found to be negligent.

NOTES ───

1. The following cases deal with the alleged liability of sports administrators and personnel in the area of medical assistance.

(a) In *O'Brien v. Township High School District #214*, 392 N.E.2d 615 (Ill. 1979), plaintiff student-athlete brought a suit which alleged negligence by the school district for permitting an incompetent and untrained student to administer medical and surgical treatment, for failing to carry out treatment properly, and for failing to secure parental consent. On appeal, the court found that an educator's immunity under the Illinois School Code should not bar plaintiff's complaint. The court held that the treatment of injuries or medical conditions does not fall into the realm of action "necessary for the orderly conduct of schools and maintenance of a sound learning atmosphere" and as such was subject to ordinary negligence claims: "To hold school districts to an ordinary care standard in this area does not appear unduly burdensome." The court did affirm the trial court's opinion that the facts of the case did not represent a "reckless disregard for the safety of others" and thus did not constitute willful and wanton misconduct.

(b) In *Cramer v. Hoffman*, 390 F.2d 19 (2nd Cir. 1968), plaintiff brought suit after being seriously injured while making a tackle during football practice. Plaintiff alleged that the cervical injuries and paralysis which he received were a consequence of negligence in moving him and in treatment. The action was brought against the university, the coach, and the treating physician. The plaintiff in his suit sought to hold the university liable for any negligence of the doctor under an agency theory. The trial judge ruled as a matter of law that the alleged negligence of the doctor could not be imputed to the university. The court held that the plaintiff failed to set forth any substantial facts to prove an agency relationship between the doctor and the university. The Circuit Court of Appeals agreed and noted that under New York law an institution is not responsible for the negligence of physicians who are independent contractors exercising their own discretion.

(c) In *Kleinknecht v. Gettysburg College*, CA 3, No. 92-7160 (3rd Cir. 1993), a twenty-year-old student-athlete died of cardiac arrest while participating in a practice session of the intercollegiate lacrosse team at Gettysburg College. His parents brought a wrongful death suit against Gettysburg College, claiming that the school breached the duty of care it owed their son by failing to provide proper medical services at the time of his death.

The student-athlete was participating in a drill when suddenly he stepped away from the play and dropped to the ground. There was no trainer on the field during the practice because the practice session was held during the nontraditional fall practice season and the school did not require trainers to be at these practices. The practices were being held on the softball fields outside the football stadium. The nearest telephone was in the football stadium's training room, which required scaling an eight-foot fence in order to get inside the stadium. The head trainer was the first to administer CPR, but five to twelve minutes passed before he was summoned and arrived on the field. It was also estimated that another ten minutes elapsed before the first ambulance arrived at the scene.

The district court ruled for the defendant, stating that even though the parents had presented evidence showing that severe and life-threatening injuries can occur and are not out of the question during contact sports, the college still had no duty to the student-athlete because it could not foresee that a young athlete who had no previous history of medical trouble was likely to suffer cardiac arrest during a practice or game. The court of appeals, however, ruled that the district court's definition of foreseeability was too narrow and felt that the parents had produced ample evidence that a life-threatening injury occurring during participation in an athletic event such as lacrosse was reasonably foreseeable. The college, therefore, owed the student-athlete a duty, which required the college to have measures in place at the lacrosse team's practice in order to provide prompt treatment in the event that any member of the lacrosse team suffered a life-threatening injury.

2. Many states, including Massachusetts, require a physician or person trained in emergency medical care to be assigned to all interscholastic football games. See Mass. Gen. Laws Ann. ch. 71, § 54A and § 10.12-5(e). (See Chapter 6.)

Failure to Provide Safe Equipment

The failure to provide equipment or the failure to provide satisfactory equipment has been the basis for a number of lawsuits brought against administrators, schools, and universities. The individuals who are involved with equipment vary from institution to institution. They include the coach, the teacher, an equipment manager, a business manager who purchases the equipment, an athletic director, and/or other administrators. All of these individuals are employees of the institution, and the institution may be responsible for their negligent acts under the theory of vicarious liability.

Although many lawsuits filed against institutions regarding equipment have been unsuccessful, they indicate potential liability areas. The first consideration is the purchase of appropriate equipment for the athletic activities offered. The second consideration is the purchase of equipment that is of satisfactory quality. For example, with respect to football helmets, the institution should adhere to guidelines established by the National Operating Committee on Standards for Athletic Equipment (NOCSAE) (see note 8 in the section entitled Application of Legal Principles to Defects in Equipment). The third consideration is the provision of equipment for the athletic activities in which equipment is necessary. For example, plaintiffs may allege that a defendant school or a school district was negligent in not providing equipment for a tackle football game. The fourth consideration is the provision of properly fitting equipment. For example, plaintiffs may allege that football equipment did not fit properly and that it was the proximate cause of the resulting injuries. The fifth and last consideration is the periodic inspection of the equipment and reconditioning when necessary. The NOCSAE guidelines will again be useful.

NOTE ───

1. The following cases deal with the liability of sports administrators and personnel in the area of equipment.

    (a) In *Gerrity v. Beatty*, 373 N.E.2d 1323 (Ill. Sup. Ct. 1978), plaintiff alleged that the school district provided unsatisfactory equipment, which resulted in a severe injury. The plaintiff had complained about the ill-fitting equipment but no replacement equipment was provided. The court held the school district negligent for failing to ensure that equipment provided for student-athletes was fit for the purpose intended.

    (b) In *Turner v. Caddo Parish School Board*, 214 So. 2d 153 (La. Sup. Ct. 1968), plaintiff spectator grandmother sued defendant school authorities for negligence when she was injured by a football player who intentionally ran out of bounds. The Louisiana Supreme Court, in reinstating the trial court's dismissal, held that defendant was not negligent in failing to anticipate spectators who do not know plays are often designed to carry the ball out of bounds. The court also held that defendant was not negligent in its failure to provide a barricade.

    (c) In *Tiemann v. Independent School Dist.*, 331 N.W.2d 250 (Minn. Sup. Ct. 1983), plaintiff was injured during a physical education class taught by defendent teacher while performing a vault over a vaulting horse. Plaintiff claimed that the injury occurred because of exposed holes from the removal of "pommels," or handles, which left two half-inch holes, whereby one finger became stuck, causing the plaintiff to fall to the floor. The court held for the plaintiff and found that the exposed-hole horses fell below the requirements of reasonable care regardless of the prevailing custom, which was to use vaulting horses with exposed holes where the pommels were removed.

THE DEFENSE OF IMMUNITY

An *immunity* is a condition which protects against tort liability regardless of the circumstances. An immunity is to be distinguished from a *privilege*, which operates to excuse the commission of an intentional tort under specific conditions.

Sovereign Immunity

Sovereign immunity is the type of immunity most often encountered in a sports setting, although charitable immunity may, in some instances, be a consideration. Historically, all states had sovereign immunity laws. Recently, however, some state courts and state legislatures have determined that the state can be sued in certain situations for certain activities. To determine if an entity is immune from legal recourse, one must first determine whether it is a governmental entity. Governmental entities may be federal, state, or local governments, municipalities, or any activity that is under the control of any of the aforementioned.

Certain public policy considerations underlie the establishment of sovereign immunity. One rationale is that public agencies have limited funds and should expend them only for public purposes. To allow an individual to sue a public entity unfairly restricts the amount of funds that should be devoted to the public welfare. Another rationale for sovereign immunity is the idea that the state can do no wrong. This is a vestige of the historical policy that a king could do no wrong and was the original basis for the establishment of sovereign immunity. Other reasons include the idea that the public cannot be held responsible for the torts of their government employees and that public bodies themselves have no authority to commit torts. Many believe that the aforementioned policy considerations are not compelling, and the trend in several jurisdictions is to repeal or limit the immunity granted to governments.

Sovereign immunity rests on the concept that a state must give consent to be sued. Most states have given such consent, either in the form of a statute which authorizes an individual to sue or by providing special courts and procedures to be followed when an instrumentality of the state is responsible for an injury (i.e., court of claims). In addition, these statutes generally limit the amount a tort claimant may recover in an action against the government. These statutes are generally narrowly interpreted, but they have been extended to agencies related to but not part of the actual state government. Public high schools and high school athletic associations are usually included as part of the list of agencies whose traditional sovereign immunity may be eliminated by statutes of this kind.

In those states governed by a sovereign immunity statute, the distinction between governmental and proprietary activities presents an important legal issue. A *governmental activity* is one that can be performed only by the state and as such is commonly protected from lawsuits on the grounds of sovereign immunity. Education is a governmental activity. A *proprietary activity* is one that is done by the state but that could be undertaken by the private sector and is therefore not given the protection of sovereign immunity. An example is when a town leases a facility for a professional sporting event.

In any lawsuit brought against a government entity, it must first be determined whether the activity on which the plaintiff's case against the state entity is based is a governmental or proprietary activity. If the activity is found to be a governmental one, the action brought by the plaintiff is automatically dismissed on the basis of the sovereign immunity statute that protects the governmental body. A determination that the activity is proprietary in nature, however, permits continuation of the case and possible recovery of damages by the plaintiff. Naturally, then, in the initial stages of a case involving the state, the defendant commonly argues that the activity in question was governmental and the plaintiff claims it was proprietary.

The distinction between governmental and proprietary functions is very difficult to make. A sports facility may be conducting either a proprietary or a governmental function. In the case of a public school using its own sports facility, the courts have usually found that the holding of athletic contests is part of the educational function of the state and is therefore a governmental function protected by the sovereign immunity doctrine. If the facility is leased for use by the private sector, the courts have concluded that the school will be conducting a proprietary activity (by leasing) and will therefore be liable for injuries sustained as a result of the negligent maintenance or construction of the facility.

NOTES ——

1. The liability of sports administrators and personnel and the concept of sovereign immunity are discussed in *Cantwell v. University of Massachusetts,* 551 F.2d 879 (1st Cir. 1977). Plaintiff gymnast was hurt as a result of the negligence of an assistant coach. She sued the coach and the university. The district court dismissed the action against both the coach and university on the basis of sovereign immunity. The court of appeals agreed, except for stating that if the coach's act was misfeasance instead of nonfeasance, he would be subject to personal liability and sovereign immunity would not protect him.

2. Generally, liability of school districts and colleges for tortious acts or omissions of its officers, agents, or servants shall be determined according to

the normal rules of tort law. Some states by statute have made their public agencies immune to suits in tort. See, for example, the following cases.

(a) In *Clary v. Alexander County Board of Education*, 203 S.E.2d 820 (N.C. Sup. Ct. 1974), a North Carolina student who was injured when he crashed into glass panel doors placed at the end of a basketball court was denied any recovery for his injuries. The doors did not have safety glass, and as evidence of the unsafe structure, there was shown to have been several previous collisions with the doors. However, the court found statutory immunity and stated that the purchase of liability insurance was not enough to abrogate the immunity.

(b) In *Zawadzki v. Taylor*, 246 N.W.2d 161 (Mich. 1976), the court denied recovery to a student who sustained eye injuries when struck by a tennis ball in physical education class. The court reasoned that the school district was protected by a statute granting immunity from tort liability for government agencies.

(c) In *Holzer v. Oakland University Academy of Dramatic Arts*, 313 N.W.2d 124 (Mich. 1981), plaintiff brought suit against the university seeking to recover damages based on an injury sustained while attempting to perform an exercise in a "movement" class. The Oakland County Circuit Court entered a summary judgment for the defendant. On appeal it was held that the operation of a state university was a governmental function immune from tort liability.

(d) In *Lentz v. Morris*, 372 S.E.2d 608 (Va. Sup. Ct. 1988), a minor who was injured playing tackle football sued his physical education teacher for negligent supervision. The Virginia Supreme Court affirmed the lower court's decision in favor of the defendant. The court concluded that since the defendant was acting within the scope of his employment at the time of the injury, he was immune from suit as an employee of a governmental entity.

3. The liability of a school district will not be sustained in the absence of a statute imposing such liability. See, for instance, *Perkins v. Trask*, 23 P.2d 982 (Mont. Sup. Ct. 1933). Plaintiff parent sued defendant school district for negligence in the drowning of her son in defendant's swimming pool. In affirming the trial court's dismissal, the Montana Supreme Court held that school districts are not liable for injuries caused by negligence of officers, agents, or employees unless liability is imposed by statute.

4. Sovereign immunity, even if not expressly abrogated, will not protect a state from all liability. See, for instance, *Johnson v. Municipal University of Omaha*, 187 N.W.2d 102 (Neb. Sup. Ct. 1971). Plaintiff, a pole vaulter, brought a personal injury action against Municipal University of Omaha to recover damages for injuries he sustained while attempting a vault during a track meet in the university's stadium. Plaintiff had landed during a vault on one of the wooden boxes used to support the uprights. The uprights hold the crossbar which measures the height of the vault. The Nebraska Supreme Court affirmed the trial court's decision and held that where a reasonable person would perceive an act to involve risk of harm to another, such risk will be negligent and unreasonable only when the risk is so great it outweighs the utility of the act or the manner in which it is performed. The court found that

the wooden boxes used by the university to hold the uprights served a useful purpose in that they expedited the event, made officiating easier, and did not restrict the level of the crossbar to a maximum height of fifteen feet.

5. A school will not be liable if its exercise of a governmental function causes any injury. See, for instance, *Rhoades v. School District #9*, 142 P.2d 890 (Mont. Sup. Ct. 1943). Plaintiff, a visiting spectator at defendant school's basketball game, sought recovery for injuries sustained when an improperly maintained stairway collapsed. In ruling in favor of the school district, the Montana Supreme Court held that the school district was exercising a "government function" so that it could not be held liable. See also, *Fetzer v. Minor Park District*, 138 N.W.2d 601 (N.D. Sup. Ct. 1965).

6. When a school district is immune as a governmental agency, its employees will avoid liability if they are performing discretionary duties. See, for instance, *Hall v. Columbus Board of Education*, 290 N.E.2d 580 (Ohio Ct. App. 1972). Plaintiff elementary school student sought recovery from the board of education and school officials for an injury sustained in a fall from a sliding board on the school playground. In ruling in favor of the board of education, the court of appeals held that the board of education was immune as a governmental agency of the state and that school officials were not liable for torts committed by them in performance of duties involving judgment and discretion.

7. Immunity for a school board will not guarantee immunity for individuals. See, for example, *Short v. Griffiths*, 255 S.E.2d 479 (Va. Sup. Ct. 1979). Plaintiff sued the school board, athletic director, baseball coach, and buildings and grounds supervisor for injuries sustained by falling on broken glass while running laps around the school's outdoor track facility. The court held that the athletic director and the buildings and grounds supervisor were not entitled to immunity, even though their employer (school board) had immunity. The court reasoned that the employees of a local government agency should be answerable for their own acts of simple negligence, even though they are engaged in working for an immune employer, because to hold otherwise would be to unacceptably widen the role of sovereign immunity.

8. In *Robinson v. Central Texas MHMR Center*, 780 S.W.2d 169 (Tex. Sup. Ct. 1989), the plaintiff sued a state mental health center for the drowning of her adopted son and biological grandson. While the trial court found for the plaintiff, the court of appeals reversed on the basis of governmental immunity. The Supreme Court of Texas recognized that the failure to provide a patient prone to epileptic seizures with a life preserver while swimming fell within the purview of the statutory waiver of immunity under the Tort Claims Act. Thus, the case was reversed and remanded for a decision not inconsitent with its findings.

9. In *Gasper v. Friedel*, 450 N.W.2d 226 (S.D. Sup. Ct. 1990), a student injured during summer weight training was unsuccessful in his suit against the school board, the superintendent, and his coaches. The court found that the failure of the school board to take formal action initiating the use of the school for the athletes' summer conditioning program deprived neither the school board nor the superintendent of sovereign immunity. Further, in conducting the program, the coaches were found to be acting within the scope

of their employment, and, as such, their actions were discretionary for purposes of immunity.

10. In *Wilson v. Miladin,* 553 A.2d 535 (Pa. Sup. Ct. 1989), the plaintiff, who was a spectator at a high school football game, brought action against a high school football player after the football player knocked her to the ground while leading his team from the locker room after halftime. The Pennsylvania Supreme Court affirmed a lower court's decision for the defendant and held that since defendant was an "employee" of the school district he was immune from action.

11. For a case in which the court found no liability for a sports administrator's discretionary decision, see *Brown v. Wichita State University,* 547 P.2d 1015 (Kan. Sup. Ct. 1976). Plaintiffs sought to recover as third-party beneficiaries after a charter airplane carrying the school football team crashed. The Kansas Supreme Court made the distinction between a governmental function and proprietary function. The court found the carrying of the football team to be a proprietary function and held the action could be maintained. See also, *Shriver v. Athletic Commission of Kansas State University,* 222 Kan. 216 (1977).

12. The availability of insurance will not eliminate immunity as a defense. See, for example, the following cases.

> (a) In *Weinstein v. Evanston Township Community,* 40 Ill. App. 3d 6, 351 N.E.2d 236 (Ill. App. Ct. 1976), the court held that the purchase of liability insurance did not waive general immunity of the school district, and no damages were awarded to a junior high school student who was injured while exercising on the parallel bars.
>
> (b) In *Merrill v. Birhanzel,* 310 N.W.2d 522 (S.D. Sup. Ct. 1981), plaintiff sued the teacher who was in charge of a required wrestling class at the time of plaintiff's injury. During the match, the plaintiff was thrown to the ground and his left ankle was broken. The court failed to find any grounds for the district to be sued given its sovereign immunity. It noted that the "authority to purchase, and the purchase of liability insurance does not provide that permission. . . . We have consistently held that if there is to be a departure from the immunity rule, the policy must be declared and the extent of liability fixed by the legislature."

13. For further information on the doctrine of sovereign immunity and schools see Note, "Liability of Schools and Coaches: The Current Status of Sovereign Immunity and Assumption of Risk," 39 *Drake L. Rev.* 759 (1989–90).

Charitable Immunity

Charitable immunity was developed to limit the liabilities of charitable organizations. The justifications for applying the charitable immunity laws are based on the following reasons:

1. Donations to charitable organizations constitute a trust fund which may not be used for an unintended purpose.

2. No profits have been accumulated, so the doctrine of vicarious liability cannot apply.
3. Charities perform governmental or public duties and therefore should be immune.
4. The overall good of a charity is protected by not diverting its money to pay damage claims.

The doctrine of charitable immunity, similar to sovereign immunity, has been eliminated in many jurisdictions.

NOTE _____

1. The following cases discuss the liability of sports administrators and personnel and the concept of charitable immunity.

(a) In *Southern Methodist University v. Clayton*, 176 S.W.2d 749 (Tex. Sup. Ct. 1943), plaintiff spectator sought recovery from Southern Methodist University (SMU) for injuries sustained when a temporary bleacher collapsed during the SMU-Texas A&M football game in 1940. The court held that SMU, a charitable institution, was immune from liability for torts of its agents unless the injured party was an employee of the charity. The Supreme Court of Texas reasoned, in affirming a trial court decision: "It is better for the individual to suffer injury without compensation than for the public to be deprived of the benefit of the charity."

(b) In *Pomeroy v. Little League Baseball of Collingswood*, 362 A.2d 39 (N.J. Super. Ct. App. Div. 1976), plaintiff spectator at a Little League game sought to recover for injuries sustained when a bleacher collapsed. In affirming judgment for the defendant, the court held that the league had been established for purely educational purposes—that is, to build character and sportsmanship—and that the charitable immunity statute prevented the plaintiff from recovery from the defendant.

Civil Liability Immunity Legislation

Increasingly, and for a number of reasons, governmental bodies have seen a need to institute regulations that govern certain aspects of sports. An area that has undergone particular legislative scrutiny is liability for sports coaches, administrators, and officials, especially in regards to youth sports organizations. Legislation has been proposed on both the federal and state levels of government and has been enacted in New Jersey, Pennsylvania, and Delaware.

Proponents of civil liability immunity legislation contend that it is needed because of a proliferation of civil lawsuits that threaten to force many of those involved in sports, especially volunteers, from participating in sports organizations. It is reasoned that coaches and managers of youth sport organizations and other like groups cannot carry out their roles without fear of being sued for damages. For instance, during consideration of the New Jersey legislation, the most frequently cited case involving Little League lawsuits was a complaint filed by a Camden County mother against the Runnemede Youth Athletic Association seeking $750,000 in damages after her son misjudged a fly ball and was struck in the eye. The mother had claimed that her son usually played second base but was put in the outfield, a position for which he was not properly trained. After the case was settled out of court for $25,000, the league encountered problems obtaining insurance.

In response to the liability crisis facing youth sports, a Youth Sports Volunteer Coalition (YSVC) was established. It is composed of some twenty-two amateur organizations, including Little League Baseball, Pop Warner Football, and the United States Olympic Committee. The coalition notes:

> Each year millions of volunteers, mostly mothers and fathers who consider youth athletic activity as a vehicle for family togetherness and development, give freely of their time to provide wholesome recreational programs for our nation's youth. Much of what is good in our country is the result of volunteerism. To let the volunteer element of our society erode or be eliminated by frivolous lawsuits would be a grave injustice to the present and future generations.

The YSVC particularly favors legislation such as the Nonprofit Sports Liability Limitation Act (H.R. 3756), which was first introduced in Congress on November 13, 1985, by Congressman George Gekas (R. Penn.) but was defeated in Congress. The legislation's purpose, as noted in H.R. 3756, was "to limit the civil liability of certain persons associated with nonprofit sports programs." H.R. 3756 specifically proposed:

Sec. 2. Limitation on Liability of Nonprofit Sports Programs
(a) Uncompensated Qualified Staff—Any person who renders services without compensation as a member of the qualified staff of a nonprofit sports program shall not be liable under the laws of the United States or of any State for civil damages resulting from any negligent act or omission of such qualified member occurring in the performance of any duty of such qualified member.
(b) Sponsors and Operators—Any person who sponsors or operates a nonprofit sports program shall not be liable under the laws of the United States or of any State for civil damages resulting from any negligent act or omission—
   (1) of any person who renders services without compensation as a member of the qualified staff of a nonprofit sports program; and
   (2) occurring in the performance of any duty of such qualified member.

For the purpose of the legislation, H.R. 3756 defined a "nonprofit sports program" as

> any program (whether or not it is registered with or recognized by any State or any political subdivision of any State)—
> (A) that is in a competitive sport formally recognized as a sport, on the date the cause of action to which this Act applies arises, by the Amateur Athletic Union or the National Collegiate Athletic Association;
> (B) that is organized for recreational purposes and whose activities are substantially for such purposes; and
> (C) no part of whose net earnings inures to the benefit of any private person.

The YSVC made these comments about the Gekas bill:

> The Youth Sports Volunteer Coalition, an organization of nonprofit youth sports programs, has come together to focus national attention on this critical liability problem and to generate support for legislative reform as stated in House Bill 3756, the "Nonprofit Sports Liability Limitation Act." For this bill to become law, and allow volunteerism to remain a steady and positive influence on our nation's youth, we need your support. Millions of kids are counting on us.

NOTES _____

1. For further information about government's increasing regulation of sports in the United States, see Johnson and Frey, *Government and Sport: The Public Policy Issues*. Totowa, N.J.: Rowman and Allanheld Publishers, 1985.

2. For further information about civil liability of volunteer coaches, contact the Youth Sports Volunteer Coalition, P.O. Box 3485, Williamsport, Pennsylvania 17701.

3. The following states enacted legislation to deal with the civil liability immunity crisis for those involved in sports:

> (a) The State of New Jersey enacted Senate Bill No. 1678 in 1986 to provide immunity for volunteer athletic coaches and officials. The legislation stated in part:
> 1.a. Notwithstanding any provisions of law to the contrary, no person who provides services or assistance free of charge, except for reimbursement of expenses, as an athletic coach, manager, or official for a sports team which is organized or performing pursuant to a nonprofit or similar charter shall be liable in any civil action for damages to a player or participant as a result of his acts of commission or omission arising out of and in the course of his rendering that service or assistance.
> b. The provisions of subsection a. of this section shall apply not only to organized sports competitions, but shall also apply to practice and instruction in that sport.
> c. Nothing in this section shall be deemed to grant immunity to any person causing damage by his willful, wanton, or grossly negligent act of

commission or omission, nor to any coach, manager, or official who has not participated in a safety orientation and training program established by the league or team with which he is affiliated.

d. Nothing in this section shall be deemed to grant immunity to any person causing damage as the result of his negligent operation of a motor vehicle.

(b) The state of Pennsylvania enacted House Bill No. 1625 in 1986. The legislation, which provided a negligence standard in the conduct of certain sports programs, stated in part:

Sec. 8332.1. Manager, Coach, Umpire or Referee and Nonprofit Association Negligence Standard

(a) General rule—Except as provided otherwise in this section, no person who, without compensation and as a volunteer, renders services as a manager, coach, instructor, umpire or referee or who, without compensation and as a volunteer assists a manager, coach, instructor, umpire or referee in a sports program of a nonprofit association, and no nonprofit association, or any officer or employee thereof, conducting or sponsoring a sports program, shall be liable to any person for any civil damages as a result of any acts or omissions in rendering such services or in conducting or sponsoring such sports program unless the conduct of such person or nonprofit association falls substantially below the standards generally practiced and accepted in like circumstances by similar persons or similar nonprofit associations rendering such services or conducting or sponsoring such sports programs and unless it is shown that such person or nonprofit association did an act or omitted the doing of an act which such person or nonprofit association was under a recognized duty to another to do, knowing or having reason to know that such act or omission created a substantial risk of actual harm to the person or property of another. It shall be insufficient to impose liability to establish only that the conduct of such person or nonprofit association fell below ordinary standards of care.

(b) Exceptions—

(1) Nothing in this section shall be construed as affecting or modifying the liability of such person or nonprofit association for any of the following:

(i) Acts or omissions relating to the transportation of participants in a sports program or others to or from a game, event or practice.

(ii) Acts or omissions relating to the care and maintenance of real estate unrelated to the practice or playing areas which such persons or nonprofit associations own, possess or control.

(c) The state of Delaware enacted House Bill No. 411 in 1986, which related to exemptions from civil liability of certain persons associated with nonprofit sports programs. The legislation stated in part:

Sec. 6836. Limitation on Liability of Non-profit Programs

(a) Uncompensated qualified staff—Any person who renders services without compensation as a member of the qualified staff of a non-profit sports program shall not be liable under the laws of this State for civil damages resulting from any negligent act or omission of such qualified member occurring in the performance of any duty of such qualified member.

(b) Sponsors and operators—Any person who sponsors or operates a

non-profit sports program shall not be liable under the laws of this State
for civil damages resulting from any negligent act or omission:
(1) of any person who renders services without compensation as a member
of the qualified staff of a non-profit sports program; and
(2) occurring in the performance of any duty of such qualified member.

LIABILITY OF FACILITY OWNERS AND POSSESSORS

The duty that the owner or possessor of a facility owes varies, depending on the characterization of the party who was injured while
on the premises. To establish a duty for owners, operators, supervisors,
or possessors of land, the status of the person injured must be determined. Generally, there are two classes of persons: licensees and
invitees. A *licensee* is one who enters the property of another, with
the owner's consent, for the licensee's own purposes. The occupier
of the property owes only a duty of ordinary care. There is no obligation to inspect the area to discover dangers currently unknown, or
to warn of conditions which should be obvious to the licensee. The
occupier of the property owes a licensee a duty to warn only when a
risk is known or should have been known under the reasonable person
standard, which the licensee is unaware of.

An *invitee* is owed a greater degree of care by the owner, operator,
supervisor, or occupier of the property. There is an affirmative duty
to be free from known defects as well as from defects which should
have been discovered by the exercise of reasonable care. The basis
of liability is the implied representation at the time of the invitation
that the premises are safe to enter. The invitation does not have to be
extended personally for an individual to be classified as an invitee.
The invitation implies that reasonable care has been exercised for the
safety of the invitee. The owner or possessor of the property is not,
however, an insurer of the safety of the invitee. That is, the owner
does not guarantee safety under all possible circumstance. Instead,
the owner or possessor must only exercise reasonable care for the
invitee's protection.

The distinction between licensee and invitee is important because
the different standards of care that may be applied can be decisive in
determining the outcome of a lawsuit. An athlete or a spectator at a
sports event is characterized as a business invitee. A *business invitee*
is a visitor who brings a monetary benefit to the person in possession
of the property. The business invitee is also a person whom the possessor encourages to enter onto the property. By such encouragement
the possessor implicitly represents that the premises are safe to enter.

The distinction between patent and latent defects is also important
in any discussion of the liability of owners and possessors of sports
facilities. Both types of defects are potentially injury causing, but an

owner or operator cannot be held liable for undiscovered and undiscoverable defects.

A *patent defect* is one that is plainly visible or that could easily be discovered upon inspection. A facility owner or a lessee is liable for obvious defects, such as old debris on steps that create a hazard, if they cause an injury. A *latent defect* is a hidden or concealed defect that could not be discovered by reasonable inspection. It is a defect of which the owner has no knowledge, or of which, in the exercise of reasonable care, the owner should not have knowledge. Owners and lessees are generally not liable for injuries caused by latent defects.

In the eyes of the law, when a facility is leased, it is, in effect, sold for a period of time. Thus, the lessee—the person taking control of the property—assumes the responsibilities of the lessor—the person giving up control of the property—toward those who enter the property. The lessor still has a duty, however, to disclose any concealed or dangerous conditions—any latent defects—to lessees, their guests, and others reasonably expected to be on the premises. For this duty to attach, the lessor does not have to believe that the condition is dangerous or to have definite knowledge of the defect. Instead, it is sufficient that the lessor be informed of facts from which a reasonable person would conclude that there is a possible danger. The lessor has no duty to warn about patent defects, which are defined as known, open, or obvious conditions. When a property is leased for a purpose that includes admission to the public, the lessor has an affirmative duty to exercise reasonable care to inspect and repair the leased property. This duty is imposed to prevent an unreasonable risk to the public. Liability will extend only to parts of the premises open to the public and to invitees who enter for the purpose for which the place was leased.

Facility owners and possessors have a duty to exercise reasonable care in maintaining the premises and in supervising the conduct of others at the facility. They are, however, entitled to assume that participants will obey the rules and that employees will not be negligent, absent notice to the contrary. Thus, their duty does not include protecting consumers from unreasonable risks. An unreasonable risk is one such that the probability of injury outweighs the burden of taking adequate precautions (see Chapter 6).

The general rule is that facility owners and possessors are liable for conditions on their premises which cause physical harm if they know or should reasonably have known about the existence of the dangerous condition when such a condition poses an unreasonable risk to an invitee. The requirement of reasonable care is supported by the assumption that a spectator or a participant assumes all the ordinary and inherent risks of the particular sport (see Chapter 6). These inherent risks are those commonly associated with the sport. The application of this common knowledge rule will depend on the circumstances. No invitee, whether a player or a spectator, assumes the risk that an owner will fail to meet his or her duty of reasonable care.

A facility owner and possessor's duty of reasonable care can be divided into three areas. First is the duty to protect invitees from injurious or defective products. An owner and possessor must exercise reasonable care in the selection of equipment necessary for the operation of the facility. Second, owners and possessors must exercise reasonable care in the maintenance of the facility itself and any equipment in the facility. Standards of safety, suitability, and sanitation must be maintained. In addition, if an invitee uses any of the equipment and the facility owner or possessor supervises, then the facility owner or possessor is held to a standard of reasonable care. Third, an owner and possessor must guard against foreseeable harmful risks caused by other invitees. A breach of any of these duties may subject a facility owner or operator to liability for negligence.

Promoters and other sports event organizers often use the facility only for a day or a few days. They do not own the facility, and they are not in a long-term lease situation; therefore, they cannot be considered a permanent tenant. Some examples are a boxing match, the Harlem Globetrotters, and the Ice Capades. The promoter owes a duty of reasonable care in the maintenance and supervision of the facility. With respect to maintenance, the owner is more likely to be responsible for patent defects that are uncorrected. With respect to supervision, the promoter is responsible for reasonable care in the running of the event, although the determination of reasonable care may differ depending on the type of event. For example, the amount and type of security may differ for a family event as opposed to a rock concert. The promoter, however, is not responsible for unique or unforeseeable events causing injury in the absence of notice that an injury is apt to occur. Therefore, courts have often refused to find liability for patrons' injuries caused by other spectators. Promoters are required only to exercise reasonable precautions. However, to protect themselves in the event that an invitee is successful in a claim against a promoter, facility owners or possessors may require a promoter to execute a lease agreement (see Exhibit 3–7 in Chapter 3). An agreement will usually require the promoter to obtain general liability insurance and agree to indemnify and hold harmless the facility owner or possessor.

Owners of facilities that allow alcoholic drinks to be consumed at athletic events have instituted some of the following procedures:

- To purchase beer, customers must go to the concession stand. Beer vendors no longer are allowed to sell beer to customers in their seats. In addition, low-alcohol (3.2 beer) and no-alcohol beer are offered for sale.

- At football games, the sale of beer is discontinued at the beginning of the third quarter.
- The largest capacity beer sold is twenty ounces, instead of the thirty-two ounce "big beers."
- Season ticket holders can lose their ticket rights for subsequent seasons if they become involved in fights or other such rowdy behavior.
- No-alcohol seating sections are designated.

Generally, a facility operator is not responsible for all injuries that occur at its stadium or arena; it only needs to take reasonable precautions. Control of alcoholic beverage sales in the facility, limiting or supervising the practice of tailgating in pregame and postgame situations, and ensuring that security is present inside and outside the facility would seem to address these concerns. At a minimum, sponsored activities require some type of increased safety measures, especially if there have been incidents of rowdiness or other disruptive behavior in the past. If such measures are undertaken, liability should be greatly reduced.

Another potential problem area for facility owners is tailgating, which has become a standard component of the traditional college football weekend. In fact, many colleges and universities have actively promoted the concept, seeking to capitalize on its popularity to market their intercollegiate athletic programs. In most cases, tailgating is a harmless afternoon's pleasure for fans, but on occasion it can lead to excessive drinking and rowdy behavior. It is this aspect of tailgating that must concern facility administrators.

In general, the last few years have seen an increasing concern by society about excessive drinking and its impact on public safety. Some states have acted on these concerns by raising the drinking age and eliminating "happy hours," and in addition there have been toughening attitudes about alcohol-related crimes among the judiciary.

Sports administrators have also been concerned about drinking at intercollegiate events. The National Collegiate Athletic Association has long banned the sale of alcoholic beverages at NCAA tournaments and postseason championship events, and many campuses have policies that limit consumption of alcoholic beverages at on-campus athletic events. The University of Massachusetts at Amherst, for example, banned pregame "keg" parties in the stadium parking lot, beginning with the 1984 football season.

As a general summary, the following checklist will help facility owners protect themselves against possible litigation:

1. Anticipate any potentially injurious situations in the facility (stadium, arena, pool, etc.) or event site (baseball field, soccer field, etc.).
2. Ensure that the facility is adequately maintained, and perform regular inspections (with written reports) on the condition of the facility.
3. In designing a facility, make safety a top concern of the architects and planning committee. Ensure that safe materials are used throughout the facility (glass, padding, mats, etc.).
4. Designate an individual on the staff to serve as the safety expert.
5. Develop a clear, written policy concerning safety in the facility, institute a reporting procedure for potential problems, and document any mishaps in detail.
6. Develop policies for alcoholic consumption at the facility.

NOTES _____

1. The following lawsuits were brought against facility owners and possessors by participants.

(a) In *Kaiser v. State*, 285 N.Y.S.2d 874(N.Y. Ct. Cl. 1967), plaintiff bobsledders sought recovery for injuries sustained when their bobsled crashed on the state's bobsled run. In granting summary judgment for the plaintiffs, the court of claims held that evidence established that the state was negligent in failing to close the run, when it had actual notice of a gash in the wall in sufficient time to suspend operation before bobsledders were injured.

(b) In *Praetorius v. Shell Oil Co.*, 207 So. 2d 872 (La. Ct. App. 1968), plaintiff baseball player sought recovery from a defendant baseball field owner for injuries sustained when he stepped into a hole while running from home to first. In reversing the trial court's judgment for the plaintiff, the court of appeals held that the defendants were not negligent in failing to properly maintain the area in the batter's box where small holes and depressions were dug by batters' cleats during the course of a softball game. Defendants cannot be held negligent for lack of reasonable care because of holes made inadvertently by participants during the course of a game.

(c) In *Ardoin v. Evangeline Parish School Board*, 376 So. 2d 372 (La. Ct. App. 1979), plaintiff student, while playing softball during a physical education class at his elementary school, tripped over a twelve-inch square piece of concrete embedded in the base path between second and third base. His father brought a negligence suit against the school, alleging that the concrete slab, which protruded at least half an inch above ground, constituted such a hazardous condition that it was a breach of the required standard of care on the part of the school board to fail to remove it from the playing field. The school district argued that no evidence had been presented that it had actual knowledge of the concrete slab. In affirming the trial court's finding of negligence of the school authorities, the appeals court held that the school board had constructive knowledge of the hazardous condition since it should have anticipated and discovered the potential danger and eliminated it before allowing students to use the field during physical education classes.

(d) In *Sykes v. Bensinger Recreation Corp.*, 117 F.2d 964 (7th Cir. 1941), plaintiff bowler sought recovery under the Wisconsin "safe place" statute for injuries sustained as a result of catching his foot in a two-inch space between the floor of the alley and the bottom of a return, through which he slipped and fell on the alley. In reversing judgment for the plaintiff, the court of appeals held that a proprietor is not an insurer of bowlers' safety and that the mere fact that such an accident happened does not prove the place was not safe. "Safe" is a relative term, and what is safe depends on the facts and conditions of each case.

(e) In *Clary v. Alexander County Board of Education*, 199 S.E.2d 738 (N.C. Ct. App. 1973), aff'd, 203 S.E.2d 820 (N.C. Sup. Ct. 1974), plaintiff senior student on a high school basketball team brought suit after suffering severe lacerations when he collided with some glass panels along one wall of the gymnasium while running wind sprints. Plaintiff alleged negligence on the part of the school board for permitting breakable glass to be used in the gym and in permitting the coaches to direct the players to run wind sprints toward the glass panels. An appeals court affirmed a trial court decision and held that the evidence indicated the plaintiff was contributorily negligent. The court reasoned that the plaintiff had run similar wind sprints in the gym during his three previous years in the basketball program. "Yet he chose to run at the panel at full speed without slowing down until he was within three feet of the glass. Anyone [doing such] . . . would be compelled by his momentum to crash into the wall and suffer injury." Plaintiff contended he was excused from contributory negligence because he was acting under the instructions of his coach. The court disagreed and held that a reasonable person disregards orders when compliance with such orders could result in injury.

(f) In *Friedman v. State*, 282 N.Y.S.2d 858 (N.Y. Ct. Cl. 1967), plaintiff skier sought recovery for injuries sustained in a fall from an aerial ski lift at a ski center owned by the state. In granting judgment for the plaintiff, the court of claims held that the state was negligent in its placement of signs relating to the time of chair lift operation, size of signs, and failure to use a loudspeaker to announce that the lift was closed for the night and that such negligence was the proximate cause of injuries sustained when the plaintiff fell from the lift after it had stopped for the night while she was descending.

(g) In *Ragni v. Lincoln-Devon Bounceland, Inc.*, 234 N.E.2d 168 (Ill. App. Ct. 1968), plaintiff trampoline user sought recovery for injuries sustained in landing on the frame of defendant's trampoline. In affirming a lower court verdict, the appellate court held that owner had no duty to warn plaintiff, who had received instruction on indoor trampolines in college, that the mat in the middle of the trampoline was the only safe place to land.

(h) In *Maddox v. City of New York, et al.*, 455 N.Y.S.2d 102 (Sup. Ct.

A.D. 1982), 487 N.Y.S.2d 354 (A.D.2d Dept. 1985), a former New York Yankee center fielder brought suit against the owner, maintenance company, and designer of Shea Stadium for an injury that occurred when he slipped on the wet field in Shea Stadium. In ruling for the plaintiff on defendant's motion for a summary judgment, the court found that Maddox did not assume the risk of playing on a dangerous field in that, as an employee, he was under the orders of his superiors. The appeals court reversed the lower court decision and held (1) that the doctrine of assumption of risk completely barred recovery; (2) that a professional baseball player did not fall within protected individuals under the statute governing general duty of the employer to protect health and safety of employees; (3) that even if eligible under the statute, the ballplayer failed to allege any fault by employer which resulted in the wet condition of the playing field; and (4) that player was not acting within the confines of the superior's instructions when he was injured.

(i) In *Eddy v. Syracuse University*, 433 N.Y.S.2d 923 (N.Y. App. Div. 1980), plaintiff sought recovery for injuries he received during a frisbee game. Plaintiff was an "ultimate frisbee" player for a team of college students. In March 1977, the team traveled to Syracuse University to play against a group of Syracuse students, although the latter team was neither officially recognized nor sponsored by the defendant. During the course of an "ultimate frisbee" game played in the basketball gymnasium, the plaintiff crashed through a glass window in one door, severely lacerating his arm. The plaintiff sued the university for negligence in a personal injury action. The defendant argued that since it did not authorize use of the gym, had no foreknowledge of plaintiff's use, could not have foreseen that students would use the basketball courts for an "ultimate frisbee" game, and that the gym was not defective in design or construction for its ordinary purposes, there was lack of evidence to even submit the issue of negligence. The trial court ruled for the plaintiff. In affirming the trial court verdict, the appeals court held: "Surely the jury could have concluded that... on the campus of a large university... some of its students, and their guests, might use the facility without express permission... (in novel games)." Also properly left to the jury were the questions of whether the glass doors, located as they were in a building intended to be used for strenuous physical activity, constituted a dangerous condition and whether the risk presented by the glass doors could have been alleviated without imposing an undue burden on the university.

(j) In *Graver v. State of New York*, 181 N.Y.S.2d 994 (N.Y. App. Div. 1959), plaintiff sought recovery for personal injuries sustained when the chair he was to sit in on the lift at Belleayre State Park swung or was tipped such that it struck the back of his right leg, fracturing it. The trial court found the evidence sufficient, based on the doctrine of res ipsa loquitur, to establish that the state was negligent in permitting the accident to happen. The court found that the state was a common carrier in the operation of the chair lift, stating that "the degree of care to be exercised should be commensurate with the danger to be avoided."

2. The following lawsuits involved actions of other spectators, and were brought against facility owners and possessors by spectators.

(a) In *Weldy v. Oakland H.S. District*, 65 P.2d 851 (Cal. Ct. App. 1937), plaintiff, a spectator at a football game supervised by agents of defendant school district, sued for negligence for injuries sustained when struck by a bottle thrown by a fellow student. The appeals court held that the plaintiff had failed to state a cause of action. The complaint did not allege that defendant should have foreseen the rowdyism of the student nor that the defendant's servants were responsible for some act or omission amounting to negligence.

(b) In *Porter v. California Jockey Club*, 285 P.2d 60 (Cal. Ct. App. 1955), plaintiff, a race track spectator, sought recovery from defendant track operator for injuries sustained when she was violently knocked down by another spectator. The appeals court, in ruling for the defendant, held that in the absence of facts which would reasonably put defendant on notice that one spectator would run violently into another so as to put the duty on defendant to guard against it, there was no question of negligence.

(c) In *Townsley v. Cincinnati Gardens, Inc.*, 314 N.E.2d 409 (Ohio Ct. App. 1974), plaintiff, a minor, brought suit after being assaulted in a washroom by a group of boys while he was attending a Harlem Globetrotters exhibition at Cincinnati Gardens. The plaintiff, as a business invitee of the facility owner, sought damages for negligence on the part of the facility. The trial court held for the plaintiff, stating that "the defendant either knew, or, in the exercise of ordinary care, should have known of the danger which victimized the plaintiff." On appeal, the decision of the trial court was reversed. The appeals court ruled that there was no evidence to indicate that the defendant could have anticipated, or reasonably have known of, the danger to the plaintiff.

(d) In *Bearman v. University of Notre Dame*, 453 N.E.2d 1196 (Ind. Ct. App. 1983), plaintiff sued the University of Notre Dame for injuries she suffered as she left a Notre Dame home football game. The injury occurred in the stadium's parking lot when a third party, who was tailgating and became involved in a fight, fell onto the plaintiff and broke her leg. Plaintiff claimed that the school had "a duty to protect her from injury caused by the acts of other persons on the premises" since she was a business invitee. The university argued that it could not be held liable for the act of a third person since it had no knowledge or notice of any danger to the woman. The Court of Appeals of Indiana, Third District, noted that the issue involved two different factors: An operator of a place of public entertainment generally "owes a duty to keep the premises safe for its invitees"; on the other hand, "an invitor is not the insurer of invitee's safety and before liability may be imposed on invitor, it must have actual or constructive knowledge of the danger." The court reasoned that Notre Dame was aware of the tailgate parties in the parking areas around the stadium and the fact that drinking occurs. It recognized that while Notre Dame did not have particular knowledge of any danger for the plaintiff, it was aware that intoxicated people pose a threat to the safety of patrons at the games. The appeals court therefore reversed the lower court's decision and held that Notre Dame had a duty to do all it could reasonably do to protect those people who attend the games from injury inflicted by the acts of third parties.

(e) In *Whitfield v. Cox,* 52 S.E.2d 72 (Va. 1949), plaintiff spectator, at defendant promoter's wrestling match, sought recovery in negligence for injuries sustained when she was struck by a whiskey bottle thrown by another spectator. The supreme court of appeals held that defendant was not required to search patrons for objects which could be used to injure other patrons.

(f) In *Philpot v. Brooklyn Nat'l League Baseball Club,* 100 N.E.2d 164 (N.Y. 1951), plaintiff spectator sought recovery for injuries sustained when she was struck by a broken bottle in defendant's ballpark. In reversing judgment for defendants, the court of appeals held that whether defendant provided a sufficient means of protecting plaintiff from reasonably foreseeable risk of harm from a bottle where no waste receptacles were provided and where the park seats were slanted so as to allow bottles to spill, was a question for the jury to decide.

3. The following lawsuits involving actions of participants were brought against facility owners and possessors by spectators.

(a) In *Wiersma v. Long Beach,* 106 P.2d 45 (Cal. Ct. App. 1940), plaintiff, who purchased a ticket to watch a wrestling match held in defendant's municipal auditorium, sought recovery for injuries sustained when one of the wrestlers deliberately hit him with a chair. The district court of appeals held that, since the city had leased the auditorium to a promoter, it was not responsible to the plaintiff for the misconduct of its tenant.

(b) In *Silvia v. Woodhouse,* 248 N.E.2d 260 (Mass. Sup. Jud. Ct. 1960), plaintiff wrestling spectator sought recovery for injuries sustained when wrestler, who had been ejected from the ring, was knocked back into him while trying to reenter. The supreme judicial court held that the defendant, who had seen such jostling before, was negligent in either failing to warn patrons or for failing to move seats back to a safer distance.

(c) In *Turner v. Caddo Parish School Board,* 214 So. 2d 153 (La. Sup. Ct. 1968), plaintiff spectator grandmother sued defendant school authorities in negligence when she was run down on a football play that was intended to carry the ball out of bounds. The Louisiana Supreme Court held that defendant was not negligent in failing to anticipate spectators who did not know that plays are often carried out of bounds or for failing to have a barricade.

(d) In *Rich v. Madison Square Garden,* 266 N.Y.S. 288 (N.Y. Sup. Ct. 1933) *aff'd* 270 N.Y.S. 915 (N.Y. App. Div. 1934), plaintiff spectator sought recovery for injuries sustained when struck by a hockey stick during a game at defendant's rink. The trial court held that the defendant was not required to foresee that a hockey stick would fly into the stands and was therefore not liable for failure to have constructed protective screens.

(e) In *Ramsey v. Kallio,* 62 So. 2d 146 (La. 1952), plaintiff spectators sought recovery from the operator of a wrestling arena for damages incurred when a wrestler jumped out of the ring and assaulted them. The court of appeals held that the operator had no reason to expect that the wrestler would jump from the ring and assault spectators and therefore was not liable.

(f) *Ratcliff v. San Diego Baseball Club of the Pacific Coast League*, 81 P.2d 625 (Cal. Ct. App. 1938), was an action for injuries sustained when a bat slipped out of baseball player's hands and flew into the stands. The district court of appeals held that, while screens for all seats are not required, those in charge of professional baseball games are required to exercise ordinary care to protect patrons from injuries, and the question of whether the defendant exercised such care where plaintiff was struck with a bat in the aisle on the way to a seat was for a jury to decide.

(g) In *Iervolino v. Pittsburgh Athletic Co.*, 243 A.2d 490 (Super. Pa. 1968), plaintiff spectator sought recovery for injuries sustained after being struck by a foul ball. In reversing the trial court's judgment for the plaintiff, the superior court held that, in absence of proof that the operator of game had deviated from ordinary standards in erection or maintenance of the ballpark, it was an error to permit a jury to determine what safety measures, if any, the operator should have taken for protection of its customers and that plaintiff assumed the risk of injury from foul balls.

(h) In *Guttenplan v. Boston Professional Hockey Ass'n, Inc.*, No. 80-415 (S.D.N.Y. 1981), four hockey fans sued nine individual Boston Bruin hockey players, the Bruins, the New York Rangers, Madison Square Garden, Inc., the National Hockey League, and the city of New York for $7 million in damages for injuries suffered when a players' brawl on the ice spilled over into the stands in December 1979. The suit charged that the plaintiffs were "stomped" by the Bruins players while league and arena security personnel "merely observed and made no attempt to prevent or stop" the altercation. Criminal charges against individual Bruin players were dropped due to conflicting evidence and testimony that indicated fans had provoked the players. A federal judge dismissed the civil damage suit on jurisdictional grounds.

(i) In *Duffy v. Midlothian Country Club, et al.*, No. 75 L 12096 (Cook County Cir. Ct. 1982), plaintiff spectator sought recovery after being struck by a golf ball at the 1972 Western Open and losing an eye. She was standing in the rough between the first and 18th holes, watching play on the first hole. She was hit by a golfer playing the 18th hole, 200 to 250 yards away. Duffy was found 10 percent at fault when her negligence was compared to the tournament sponsors', but was awarded compensation. The court barred the assumption-of-risk defense.

(j) In *Johnson v. Houston Sports Ass'n*, 615 S.W.2d 781 (Tex. Civ. App. 1980), plaintiff spectator filed a personal injury action after being struck in the face by a baseball during pregame batting practice. In affirming the trial court decision, the court of civil appeals held that it was not an error to give an instruction on an unavoidable accident when there was evidence (1) that the spectator saw the screened area behind home plate even though the seats in that area were not filled, made no attempt to sit in the protected area; (2) that the screened-in seats were visible from all over the field; (3) that the screens were the same or similar to those used in stadiums all over the country; and (4) that the area offered more protection than the same area in other stadiums. The court of civil appeals also held that it was not an error to refuse to submit the spectator's requested special issue on whether the ball was negligently knocked into the stands on the occasion in question when there was no evidence that the batter who struck the ball that hit the spectator committed any negligent act in striking the ball or that the batter conducted himself differently from the practices of other baseball players in the same situation.

(k) In *Knebel v. Jones*, 266 S.W.2d 470 (Tex. Civ. App. 1954), plaintiff spectator brought suit against defendant's park for injuries sustained when she was struck by a foul ball. The district court entered judgment for the plaintiff. The court of civil appeals reversed and held that when the patron could have observed, by mere ordinary observation, that she was not sitting in an area protected by a screen, she was negligent in not so observing, and she was not entitled to recover from defendant, as owner of ballpark, for injuries sustained by her when a foul ball struck her in the face.

(l) *Benjamin v. State*, 453 N.Y.S.2d 329 (Ct. Cl. 1982), was an action brought by an eleven-year-old spectator, who in November 1979 was injured in a college hockey doubleheader at Romney Arena, a state facility on the campus of the State University of New York at Oswego. Plaintiff was seated behind the protective fence, ten to fifteen feet north of the nearest players' bench. While there, an errant puck found its way through the open area in front of the players' bench, passed behind the protective fence, and struck plaintiff on the left side of the forehead. Plaintiff brought action against the state alleging that the state failed to provide adequate protection for the safety of spectators seated in the arena. At the trial an expert testified that in similar facilities it was the usual and customary practice to protect the area around the players' bench. Absent such protection, it was the usual and customary practice to restrict seating in an arena without protection from the zone of danger. Since neither course of action was chosen, the court held that the state failed to provide plaintiff with adequate protection that evening. The court found that the failure of the state to provide for the safety of its patrons in the protected seating area constituted negligence and that such negligence was a substantial factor in bringing about the injuries.

(m) In *Wilkinson v. Hartford Accident and Indemnity Co.*, 411 So. 2d 22 (La. Sup. Ct. 1982), plaintiff sued athletic coach, school board, and school's liability insurer to recover for injuries son sustained when he crashed through a glass panel of the gymnasium foyer while engaging in an unsupervised race during physical education class. The Louisiana Supreme Court reversed a lower court's decision and held for the plaintiff, reasoning that the school board was negligent because several years previous a visiting coach had broken the glass panel when he walked into it. The glass panel was so close to spectator traffic that school authorities should have known of the hazard it created.

(n) In *Drew v. State of New York*, 536 N.Y.S.2d 252 (N.Y. Ct. App. 1989), a student who injured his knee while playing touch football during a recreational period in the orientation program for freshmen at the state university brought a negligence suit against the state. The court of appeals upheld a lower court's decision for defendant and reasoned that the state did not breach any duty of care to the student. The state's duty was not to provide a perfectly level playing field, but only to use reasonable care under the circumstances to prevent injury to participating students.

4. The following lawsuits involving the equipment in facilities and buildings were brought against facility owners and possessors.

(a) In *Taylor v. Hardee*, 102 S.E.2d 218 (S.C. Sup. Ct. 1958), plaintiff spectator sought recovery for injuries sustained when a bleacher, negligently constructed by defendant speedway owner, collapsed under him. The supreme court held that evidence of how the bleachers were constructed was sufficient on the issue of the race track owner's negligence to send the question to the jury.

(b) In *Rockwell v. Hillcrest Country Club*, 181 N.W.2d 290 (Mich. Ct. App. 1970), plaintiffs, golf spectators, sought recovery for injuries sustained when, while watching a golf tournament, a suspension bridge collapsed and dropped plaintiffs into the river below. The court of appeals held that plaintiffs had established a prima facie case of negligence because the bridge capacity was twenty-five people, that eighty to one hundred people were on the bridge when it collapsed, and that no warning signs or supervisors were present.

(c) In *Woodring v. Board of Education of Manhasset*, 435 N.Y.S.2d 52 (N.Y. App. Div. 1981), plaintiff brought a wrongful death suit against the school district after a platform railing in the gymnasium gave way, throwing decedent to his death. In affirming the $1,400,000 award to plaintiff, the appeals court found evidence that the school district (1) lacked a preventive maintenance program, (2) improperly constructed the platforms, (3) failed to inspect its gymnasium facilities regularly, and (4) should have known—given the extensive use of the platforms by students—that injury was foreseeable if the railings were not properly maintained or constructed. The appeals court thus sustained the jury's determination of the defendant's negligence.

(d) In *Novak v. City of Delavan*, 143 N.W.2d 6 (Wis. 1966), plaintiff spectator brought an action against the city and the school district for injuries sustained as a result of a bleacher collapse at an athletic event. The court held that because the only use the school district made of the facility was for seven football games, since the school district did not purport to inspect the bleachers or perform any maintenance services, and because it was the city, not the school employees, who attended to any bleacher problems, the school district could not be held liable when a footboard gave way; the school district had no control or custody and thus no obligation to repair the bleachers. However, the city was found to be negligent for failing to properly maintain its property.

(e) In *Witherspoon v. Haft,* 106 N.E.2d 296 (Ohio Sup. Ct. 1952), plaintiff spectator sued defendant, who had installed temporary bleachers at a football game, for injuries sustained when the plaintiff fell from the last row of bleachers, which were negligently fastened. The Ohio Supreme Court held that reasonable minds could conclude that failure of defendants to fasten the top plant seat securely resulted in serious hazard to the plaintiff.

(f) In *Williams v. Strickland,* 112 S.E.2d 533 (N.C. Sup. Ct. 1960), plaintiff race track patron sued defendant race track owner in negligence for injuries sustained when a wheel came off a race car and struck her. The North Carolina Supreme Court held that the operators of the race track could be held liable for failure to exercise care commensurate with known or reasonably foreseeable dangers incident to motor vehicles racing at high speed, because no seats were provided and no ropes strung to indicate where patrons could stand to view the races safely.

(g) In *Parker v. Warren,* 503 S.W.2d 938 (Tenn. Ct. App. 1973), plaintiff spectator sued defendant promoter when the bleacher on which she was to view a wrestling match collapsed. In affirming a verdict for the plaintiff, the court of appeals held that the evidence made a submissible case for res ipsa loquitur, that the promoter was required to use ordinary care with respect to the bleacher conditions and had a duty to inspect, and that patrons were entitled to assume that premises were in safe condition.

(h) In *Brown v. Racquetball Centers, Inc.,* 534 A.2d 842 (Sup. Ct. Pa. 1987), a fitness club member sued his club to recover for injuries caused when he slipped on a wet tile floor. The court held that the release he signed, stating that fitness club member assumed all risks of injury sustained in connection with activities in and about the premises, did not absolve the fitness center of liability for its negligence.

5. In 1985, New York State Senator Dunne introduced legislation to mandate nonalcohol seating sections for sporting events. The legislation mandated:

Section 1. The alcoholic beverage control law is amended by adding a new section one hundred six-b to read as follows:

106-b. Nonalcohol seating section at spectator events. 1.(a) Every person who operates a facility for the performance of spectator events on the premises of which facility alcoholic beverages are sold or otherwise furnished for consumption on such premises shall establish, separate from other seating accommodations, nonalcohol seating accommodations within such premises wherein the possession or consumption of alcoholic beverages shall not be permitted. At least twenty-five per cent of the seating accommodations of each separately designated ticket price at such facilities shall be segregated contiguously to the maximum extent feasible for the purpose of constituting nonalcohol seating accommodations.

The legislation is indicative of the type that governing bodies might begin instituting if sports administrators fail to regulate the problem of alcohol at sporting events. (S. 5690 and A. 7502, New York State Senate Assembly, introduced May 7, 1985.)

6. For further information on facility liability, see the following law review articles.

(a) Note, "Tort Liability and the Recreational Use of Land," 28 *Buff. L. Rev.* 767 (1979).

(b) Note, "Owner Liability for International Torts Committed by Professional Athletes Against Spectators," 30 *Buff. L. Rev.* 565 (1981).

(c) Wong and Ensor, "Torts and Tailgates," 9 *Athletic Business* 46 (May 1985).

(d) "Facility Liability: Spotting Danger Before It Strikes," 10 *Athletic Business* 106 (June 1986).

(e) Fisher and Single, "Beer in the Ballpark: Recommendations to the Liquor License Board of Ontario Concerning the Renewal of Beer Sales at Sporting Events," Document No. 39, Alcoholism and Drug Research Foundation, Toronto, Ontario (1983).

(f) "Sports Liability Insurance," 10 *Athletic Business* 12 (May 1986).

(g) "A Payoff for Prevention," 11 *Athletic Business* 36 (March 1987).

LIABILITY OF MEDICAL PERSONNEL

A person or an organization in charge of a sports activity has a duty to provide reasonable medical assistance to participants as well as to spectators. To determine if this duty has been met, both the quality of care and the speed of the treatment must be considered. The quality of the treatment will be assessed by looking at the qualifications of the provider and the type of treatment offered. The speed of the treatment may be determined by the response time and availability of medical personnel.

There are many different levels of health care providers within the American medical system. With respect to athletic events, these providers may be doctors or nurses; more often they are trainers or emergency medical technicians (EMTs). The standard of care required of each medical provider is based on the person's training and qualifications (see Chapter 6). A higher standard of care is established if the class of medical personnel can perform skills and training beyond what is expected of the reasonable lay person. For example, the standard of care imposed on the medical profession is that the doctor must have met the level of skill and knowledge common to the profession in adherence to a uniform standard of conduct.

In the case of a specialist, however, the duty has increasingly become more stringent. A specialist must act with the skill and knowledge reasonable within that specialty. Thus, while in the past, little has distinguished medical malpractice cases involving athletes from other cases, the growing ranks of doctors practicing sports medicine will certainly lead to a higher standard of care for doctors specializing in sports injuries in negligence lawsuits brought by injured athletes.

The standard of care is usually established by expert testimony. For example, a doctor may be negligent while others of lesser skill and expertise would not be. The standard for any other member of the medical system would be applied in a similar fashion.

Generally, medical personnel are considered independent contractors rather than employees (see Chapter 6), even though they may be paid by a school district, facility owner, or other supervisory body. As independent contractors, even if they are found to have been negligent, their employers cannot be held liable under the doctrine of vicarious liability (see Chapter 6). To determine if a doctor or other medical person is an independent contractor, the court considers the degree of control exercised by the employee's supervisor over actual medical decisions. Although the general rule is that medical personnel are independent contractors, there have been cases in which the employer has been held liable under the doctrine of vicarious liability. In these cases, courts have found that the employer exercised control and direction over the medical personnel. (See the discussion of the *Chuy* case, Chapter 6.)

There are some special considerations for a doctor involved in the area of athletics. The first concerns the relationship between a doctor and patient. Typically, the doctor is paid by the patient. However, in sports, the doctor is hired and paid by the amateur athletic organization. Usually, there is a confidential relationship between doctor and patient. When the doctor is employed by a third party, however, the normal relationship is not established. In effect, then, team doctors have two masters to serve: the athletic organization for which they work and the player they treat. In addition, while both the organization and player are concerned with restoring the player to full health, there are potential situations in which the team may seek a shorter rehabilitation program while the player may favor a more cautious time frame for recovery. The team doctor is placed in the middle. The doctor's dilemma is highlighted by suits involving the team doctor if the player believes the doctor has not placed his or her long-term recovery before the program's wishes.

In one case, a team doctor and athletic trainer allowed a college football player to play with a sprained neck. The doctor altered the player's equipment to restrict movement. The player was injured during the game and rendered a quadriplegic (see note 8). Such a case also raises the issue of the duty of a player to refuse to play with an injury after a team doctor has declared him or her healthy enough to participate.

In addition to this potential conflict, the normal confidential relationship between a doctor and patient (the athlete) changes when a third party, the athletic organization, pays the doctor. The athletic organization typically has full access to the athlete's medical records and often discusses the appropriate treatment for the injured athlete with the doctor and patient.

The potential for abuse in this situation was demonstrated in *Kreuger v. San Francisco Forty-Niners* (note 14). Kreuger, a player with the Forty-Niners, sued the team personnel for fraudulent concealment of medical information. The court found that due to the team's interest in keeping Kreuger on the field, he never received a full disclosure of the extent of his knee injury and thus continued to play when he should have retired from the game. In some situations, the athletic organization has access to the medical records and the athlete does not. As an example, Rafael Septien, a placekicker formerly with the Dallas Cowboys, sued the Cowboys for full access to his medical records. The confidential relationship between a doctor and a patient may also preclude a doctor's release of information to the athletic organization or anyone else without permission from the patient.

Another consideration concerns the prescribing of pain-killing drugs to enable the athlete to continue playing for the benefit of the team but to the potential detriment of the player's career. There have been situations on the professional level in which athletes—for example, Bill Walton and Dick Butkus—have brought lawsuits against their employers and team physicians for prescribing pain-killing drugs that allowed them to play without informing them of the potential harm to their long-term careers. These cases could be applicable at the collegiate level given similar circumstances. Furthermore, they raise the issue of the responsibility a doctor has to his patient—the injured player—and the responsibility the doctor has to his or her employer—the team.

One final consideration is that even though doctors may be negligent in their handling of an injured player, they may not be legally liable under normal tort analysis. When a player is injured through intentional or negligent actions on the part of a coach, referee, player, spectator, or anyone else, subsequent negligent action will not usually relieve the original negligent party from liability created by the original action. Doctors may, however, be liable as an additional defendant if their conduct is found to be a substantial factor in the injury or if additional injuries occurred because of their negligence. Subsequent medical negligence is generally not an unforeseeable and unreasonable cause which would relieve the original party from liability.

NOTES _____

1. For a case in which a team physician was sued for failure to provide good, sound, reasonable medical care, see *Bayless v. Philadelphia National*

League Club, 472 F. Supp. 625 (E.D. Pa. 1979). Plaintiff baseball player argued that he had been given pain-killing drugs without knowledge of their potential side effects. The court determined that the plaintiff's exclusive remedy for the action lay under the state workers' compensation act, not under legal jurisdiction.

2. For a case in which a professional sports team could have been held liable for the negligence of its medical staff and its assistance provided for the spectators, see *Fish v. L.A. Dodgers Baseball Club,* 128 Cal. Rptr. 807 (Cal. Ct. App. 1976). Plaintiffs sought recovery from defendant club and defendant physician for the death of their son, who died as a result of an allegedly negligent diagnosis after being struck by a foul ball. In reversing judgment, the court of appeals held for the plaintiffs, finding that negligence of the ballpark doctor in failing to ascertain decedent's symptoms necessitated the emergency surgery which resulted in death. This converted decedent from a patient who probably would have survived without emergency surgery to a patient who had little hope of recovery. The trial court's verdict in favor of the club was also reversed for consideration of the issue of the agency relationship between the parties.

3. For a case in which the court ruled that the school district was immune from tort liability, see *Deaner v. Utica Community School District,* 297 N.W.2d 625 (Mich. Ct. App. 1980), an action brought for damages suffered by plaintiff student during wrestling class when a vertebrae injury resulted in his quadriplegia. The appeals court held that summary judgment could not be granted to the doctor who had examined and approved the student's participation because issues of fact had to be decided.

4. For a case in which a professional hockey team was found to be liable for the team doctors' actions, see *Robitaille v. Vancouver Hockey Club,* 3 W.W.R. 481 (Ct. App. B.C. 1981). Plaintiff professional hockey player brought suit against his club for injuries incurred while playing. A shoulder injury caused the plaintiff recurring problems, which the club's management and physicians attributed to mental rather than physical causes. The plaintiff was ordered to play while injured and sustained a minor spinal cord injury during a game. He requested medical attention but was ignored, because he was perceived as having mental problems. Further play aggravated the minor injury, and the plaintiff suffered a spinal cord injury which left him permanently disabled. The appeals court upheld the award of damages to the plaintiff and held that the club had breached its duty to ensure the fitness, health, and safety of its player. The club was also found to have exercised sufficient control over the doctors to make the doctors employees of the club. Therefore, the club was liable for the acts of the doctors.

5. For a case in which the athletic trainer was found to not be liable for negligent treatment, see *Gillespie v. Southern Utah State College,* 669 P.2d 861 (Utah Sup. Ct. 1983). Plaintiff sought recovery against the college for its trainer's negligence in treating a sprained ankle. The court held that the trainer is not a "guarantor" of good results because that standard would result in anyone treating an injury to be "strictly" liable for any adverse consequences resulting from the treatment.

6. In *Walton v. Cook,* Civil Case No. A8003-0165 (Or. 1981), professional

basketball player Bill Walton filed suit against Robert Cook, the team doctor of the Portland Trail Blazers, and twenty other unnamed physicians of the Oregon City Orthopedic Clinic, for $632,000 in lost income and medical expenses and $5 million in general damages. The complaint alleged negligence in the examination, diagnosis, and treatment of his left foot, along with failure to provide him with accurate information concerning the true nature of the injury. Drugs were prescribed and shots of steroids were given Walton and he was advised to play in games. Three months later, Walton consulted other physicians and discovered that he had actually fractured a bone in his foot, which caused damage to the nerves, muscles, and tissues of the left foot, as well a permanent weakness in that foot and an increased chance of subsequent fractures. Further, Walton could not continue to play basketball. The case was settled for an undisclosed amount prior to the trial.

7. In *Martin v. Casagrande*, 559 N.Y.S.2d 68 (N.Y. App. Div. 1990), plaintiff hockey player brought personal injury action against the hockey team, the team's general manager, and the team doctor for allegedly conspiring to withhold information regarding the extent of injury and deciding to play him even though he was hurt. The trial court entered an order dismissing the causes of action, and the plaintiff appealed. The N.Y. Supreme Court affirmed the lower court's decision and held that the plaintiff's claims of intentional concealment and fraud lacked merit because the initial X-rays and arthrograms by the defendant did not indicate the specific damage to the plaintiff's knee that was later discovered by a second doctor.

8. Former Citadel football, player Marc Buoniconti sued Citadel team doctor E. K. Wallace, Jr., Citadel athletic trainer, Andy Clawson, and Citadel, as employer, for injuries which rendered him a quadriplegic after he tackled an opponent in a football game. Buoniconti alleged that the doctor should not have allowed him to play in the game with a sprained neck. A major issue in the trial was the doctor's addition of a ten-inch fitted strap to Buoniconti's uniform, running from the face mask and hooked to the shoulder pads. Plaintiff's experts testified that the strap restricted movement and contributed to the injury, whereas the defense experts stated that the strap prevented hyperextension of the neck and did not cause the injury. The jury raised a question: If helmet manufacturers are held liable for faulty design or construction, should not the team doctor also be liable for a fault in the design or construction of his alteration of that equipment? The jury found no liability for the doctor. The athletic trainer and Citadel settled out of court for $800,000.

9. In *Wilson et al. v. Vancouver Hockey Club*, 5 D.L.R. (4th), a doctor employed by the hockey club to treat players for hockey injuries failed to refer plaintiff hockey player to a specialist for a biopsy on a mole on plaintiff's arm. The plaintiff claimed that the doctor negligently failed to tell the player that he suspected cancer. Evidence indicated that the doctor made the final decision as to what treatment an injured player would have and whether an injured player would play, without advice from the management of the club, and, therefore, the doctor acted as an independent contractor and not as a servant of the hockey club. The court held that the club was not vicariously liable for the negligence of the doctor because he was an independent contractor.

10. In *Classen v. Izquierdo*, 520 N.Y.S.2d 999 (N.Y. County Sup. Ct. 1987), plaintiff widow brought action against ringside physicians and the proprietor of the sports facility to recover damages for the death of her husband, a boxer. The court ruled for the plaintiff and held that the risks of professional boxing do not include negligent medical care rendered by physicians who have independently contracted to provide medical services. Therefore, ringside physicians could be held liable in action arising from the boxer's death, for any deviation from good and accepted standards of medical care.

11. In *Kleinknecht v. Gettysburg College*, CA 3, No. 92-7160 (3rd Cir. 1993), a twenty-year old student-athlete died of cardiac arrest while participating in a practice session of the intercollegiate lacrosse team at Gettysburg College. There was no trainer on the field during the practice because the session was held during the nontraditional fall practice season and the school did not require trainers to be at these practices. When the student-athlete collapsed during the practice, a trainer had to be summoned from one of the on-campus training facilities. The head trainer was the first to administer CPR, but five to twelve minutes passed before he arrived at the field. It was also estimated that another ten minutes elapsed before the first ambulance arrived at the scene.

This decision is based on the appeal after the trial court had ruled that the college had no duty to the student-athlete because the school could not foresee that a young athlete who had no previous history of medical trouble was likely to suffer a cardiac arrest during a practice or game. The court of appeals ruled that the parents of the student-athlete had provided ample evidence showing that a life-threatening injury occurring during participation in an athletic event such as lacrosse was reasonably foreseeable. The college, therefore, owed the student-athlete a duty which required the college to have measures in place at the lacrosse team's practice in order to provide prompt treatment in the event that any member of the lacrosse team suffered a life-threatening injury. The court of appeals ruled only on the duty issue and sent the case back to trial court to determine whether there was a breach of this duty.

12. On March 4, 1990, during an intercollegiate basketball game between Loyola Marymount University and the University of Portland, Hank Gathers, star of the Loyola Marymount team, collapsed and died as a result of a heart disorder known as cardiomyopathy. Shortly after his death, several members of Gathers's family filed suit claiming that Gathers's death was a result of negligence of Gathers's physicians, the Loyola Marymount trainer, the head basketball coach, the athletic director, and the university itself.

The lawsuit revolved around allegations made by the family about the treatment and information Gathers was given prior to his death. After passing out during a game earlier in the season, Gathers was examined by a number of doctors and underwent tests to discover the nature of his illness. Gathers was diagnosed with a syncope, a temporary suspension of respiration and circulation due to an obstructed flow of blood to the brain, and cardiac arrhythmia, an alteration in the normal rhythm of the heartbeat.

Gathers was started on medication to help regulate his heartbeat and cleared to rejoin the basketball team. The lawsuit claims, however, that doctors decreased the dosage of the medication because of its effect on Gathers's on-court performance. In addition, the school purchased a defibrillator, a machine used to help restore the rhythm of the heart, and kept it courtside during practices and games. The family alleged, however, that the defibrillator was not used within the required timeframe after Gathers had collapsed.

In settlements reached with Loyola Marymount and Dr. Vernon Hattori, a cardiologist who treated Gathers, Lucille Gathers, Hank's mother, received $545,000 from the university and $350,000 from Hattori, while Aaron Crump, Gathers's eight-year-old son, received $855,000 from the school and $650,000 from Hattori. These settlements were a result of the wrongful death claims made against the involved parties. Earlier in the proceedings, Loyola Marymount athletics director Brian Quinn, head basketball coach Paul Westhead, former trainer Chip Schaefer, and four of the five named physicians were dismissed from the suit.

The final lawsuit, a civil action brought by the family against two doctors who attended Gathers on the night he collapsed, was dismissed September 9, 1992, after the plaintiffs did not appear in court to testify. The family members had contended that the doctors were negligent and caused the family emotional distress in the way they treated Gathers at courtside and outside the gym.

13. For further information on liability of medical personnel, see the following law review articles.

(a) Pitt, "Malpractice on the Sidelines: Developing a Standard of Care for Team Sports Physicians," 2 *J. Comm. & Enter. L.* 579 (1980).

(b) King, "Duty and Standard of Care for Team Physicians," 18 *Hous. L. Rev.* 657 (1981).

(c) Russell, "Legal and Ethical Conflicts Arising from the Team Physician's Dual Obligations to the Athlete and Management," 10 *Seton Hall Legis. J.* 299 (1987).

14. In *Krueger v. San Francisco Forty-Niners*, 234 Cal. Rptr. 579 (Cal. App. 1st Dist. 1987), the court ruled in favor of a retired professional football player and held that he might be entitled to damages for fraudulent concealment of medical information by team personnel.

LIABILITY OF OFFICIALS, REFEREES, AND UMPIRES

Officials, referees, and umpires have sought recovery in civil litigation for injuries suffered in the course of employment. Officials, referees, and umpires may also be protected against violence in certain states, by criminal statutes.

Officials, referees, and umpires of athletic contests may incur tort liability as a result of their actions or inactions on the playing field. There have been two distinct areas in which suits against officials, referees, and umpires have been filed: the personal injury area, in which the official, referee, or umpire is sued for negligence, and the judicial review of an official's, referee's, or umpire's decision. There have been few reported cases in either of these areas, since few cases have been filed and many of those have been settled. However, this area has the potential for increased litigation.

In the personal injury area, the official, referee, or umpire may be sued for negligence in a number of different situations. The first is when there has been a failure to inspect the premises. For instance, a plaintiff may contend that a referee should have inspected the field for holes or other dangerous conditions that could cause injury to players. In the second situation the official, referee, or umpire fails to keep the playing area free of equipment and/or spectators. For example, a ball or bat may be left on the playing field, and a player trips, falls, and is injured by the equipment. With respect to spectators, an injured spectator might contend that the official, umpire, or referee should have stopped play on the field and warned the spectators to move from the playing area. A player who is injured by running into a spectator might contend that the official, referee, or umpire should have moved the spectator away from the playing area. The third situation involves weather conditions; an injured player may contend that the official, referee, or umpire should not have started the game or that the game should have been stopped. The fourth situation involves equipment which causes injury to a player. It could be argued that the official, referee, or umpire has the responsibility to prevent a player from participating if the player's equipment is obviously ill-fitting. A situation that may be more likely to result in successful litigation is when a referee does not enforce a rule, especially a safety rule such as the "no jewelry" rule in basketball. The fifth and final situation involves a potential claim that the official, referee, or umpire did not properly enforce the rules of the games. For example, the plaintiff may allege that the basketball referees failed to control the game by not calling fouls or technical fouls and that this resulted in a much rougher game, which was the proximate cause of the injuries suffered by the plaintiff.

The area of judicial review of an official's, referee's, or umpire's decision is one that has been infrequently litigated. Generally, courts are reluctant to review playing field decisions, whether they have been judgmental errors or a misapplication of a rule. Plaintiffs have not been successful in this area, and the courts will continue to show their reluctance to become involved in decisions on the playing field unless fraud or corruption can be found.

A problem not related to the liability of referees, officials, and umpires but one that an athletic administrator and the official should be aware of is the type of relationship created by the association of referees, officials, and umpires. The official may be classified as an independent contractor or an employee. This distinction becomes important if an official is injured in the course of performing his or her duties. If acting as an independent contractor, the official will not be eligible for workers' compensation. If classified as an employee, the official would be entitled to receive those benefits (see Chapter 6). In addition, the athletic administrator could be held liable for the actions of the referee under the legal theory of vicarious liability if the referee is deemed to be an employee. The athletic administrator will generally not be held responsible for the actions of the official if he or she is an independent contractor (see Chapter 6). The interpretation of a referee's status differs from state to state, on the basis of state laws and the legal relationship between the referees and the hiring institution. An examination of legal cases involving the question to determine a particular state's interpretation of the relationship is advised (see note 4).

The following liability checklist will help officials, referees, and umpires protect themselves against possible litigation.

1. Inspect playing surface, including sidelines and endlines, for visible and potential hazards.
2. Determine if weather conditions are appropriate for competition and do not allow coaches or other athletic officials to influence the decision.
3. Inspect game equipment, such as bases and goalposts.
4. Inspect players' equipment for safety and make sure that players are not wearing any potentially dangerous jewelry or accessories.

NOTES

1. The following cases involve intentional and negligent injury of officials.
   (a) In *Dillard v. Little League Baseball Inc.*, 390 N.Y.S.2d 735 (N.Y. App. Div. 1977), plaintiff umpire sued Little League for negligence in failing to provide him with a cup which provides groin protection after he was seriously injured when struck by a pitched ball in the groin area during a game. The court dismissed the case on the grounds that plaintiff had assumed the risks of such injury when he volunteered to umpire the game. The court based its decision on the fact that it was not customary for Little League to provide such equipment, as it is personal to the wearer. Additionally, the plaintiff could have provided it himself at little expense.
   (b) In *Carroll v. State of Oklahoma*, 620 P.2d 416 (Okla. Crim. App. 1980), appellant challenged an Arizona statute under which he was convicted for assault. Appellant was an assistant coach for the losing team at a baseball tournament. After the game, the home plate umpire was at the trunk of his car in the parking lot changing uniforms in preparation for the next game. He was surrounded by a group of players from the losing team who were criticizing his calls. The assistant coach approached the group, exchanged words with the umpire, and struck

the umpire on the jaw with his fist. The assistant coach was convicted of "assault upon a sports officiary" under Oklahoma law.

The appellant challenged the statute on the grounds that it was unconstitutionally vague. The court of criminal appeals, however, held that the statute clearly indicated which persons were covered and also apprised the public of what particular conduct was deemed punishable, for which reasons the court found the statute neither unconstitutionally vague and indefinite, nor void for uncertainty.

(c) In *McGee v. Board of Education of the City of New York*, 226 N.Y.S.2d 329 (N.Y. App. Div. 1962), plaintiff sought recovery for injuries suffered while coaching. The plaintiff was a high school teacher employed by defendant, board of education, and was assigned by the school principal to assist the regular coach of the student baseball team. While conducting a practice session on fielding bunts, the plaintiff stood behind the pitcher's mound and advised the pitcher what to do. The practice session was conducted on a temporary diamond, and the bases were only about eighty feet apart instead of the regulation ninety feet. As a result, the pitcher stood on a direct line between first and third bases. McGee was hit in the face by a ball thrown to third base by the first baseman, who made the throw when the head coach called out for him to "get the man at third." The first baseman had not on previous occasions during the practice routine thrown the ball to third base, but rather had returned the ball to home plate for the next bunt. Plaintiff brought suit against the board of education on the grounds that their employee, the head coach, was negligent in conducting the practice session on a diamond of nonregulation size, without making adjusting precautions, and in suddenly directing a departure from the practice routine while plaintiff's attention was distracted, thereby exposing him to the hazard of being hit by a thrown ball. The appeals court held that, generally, players, coaches, managers, referees and others who voluntarily participate in an athletic event must accept the risks to which their roles expose them. Though there may be occasions when a participant's conduct amounts to such careless disregard for the safety of others as to create risks not fairly assumed, what the scorekeeper may regard as an "error" was not, according to the court, the equivalent, in law, of negligence.

(d) In *McHugh v. Hackensack Public Schools*, N.J. Sup. Ct., Mercer Co., Docket No. 1-2542-81 (1983), plaintiff high school basketball referee was attacked by an unknown fan after a state tournament game and sought damages from the public school system because it did not provide a safe place to work, safe entry and exit before and at the conclusion of the game, or proper supervision of the crowd. The trial court granted summary judgment in favor of the school since the school was immune under the New Jersey Tort Claims Act.

(e) For another case involving intentional and negligent injury of officials, see *Toone v. Adams* in the section Vicarious Liability for Actions of Fans and Players, note 1, earlier in this chapter.

2. The cases in this section raise various concerns for officials, referees,

and umpires being sued for negligence when a participant in a sporting event is injured because of action or inaction by the official.

(a) In *Cap v. Bound Brook Board of Education,* N.J. Sup. Ct., Cape May Co., Somerset City (Settled 1984), New Jersey high school football officials were sued for permitting a game to be played on a field that was in an unsafe and unplayable condition, which allegedly was a factor in a player's becoming paralyzed after an injury suffered during the contest. The case was dismissed against the officials and settled with the other co-defendants.

(b) In *Nash v. Borough of Wildwood Crest,* Docket No. 1-662477, Cape May Co., (N.J. Sup. Ct., 1983), a recreational softball catcher sought recovery for injuries suffered when he was struck in the eye by a softball while catching without wearing a protective mask. In slo-pitch softball, a catcher is not required to wear a mask. The player sued and alleged that the umpire should have given him his mask and then officiated from behind the pitcher's position rather than from behind home plate. The case was settled prior to trial, with the plaintiff receiving $24,000.

(c) In *Pantalone v. Lenape Valley Regional High School,* Docket No. L-40828-26, Sussex Co. (N.J. Sup. Ct. 1976), a New Jersey high school wrestling referee was sued for allegedly allowing a wrestler to continue an illegal hold on his opponent, which resulted in a paralyzing injury. The case was settled by monetary damages.

(d) In *Smith v. National Football League,* No. 74-418 Civ. T-K (U.S. Dist. Ct. Fla. 1974), plaintiff, an All-Pro and National Football League (NFL) Lineman of the Year, sued the head linesman and one of the attendants of the down markers, along with the Tampa Bay Sports Authority and the NFL for $2.5 million. The plaintiff alleged that a collision he had with the down marker caused a serious knee injury that ended his career. He claimed that the collision was a result of neglect on the part of the defendants, including the failure of the sports official to properly supervise and move the markers and the use of dangerous equipment. The jury in the case's second trial found no liability on the part of the defendants.

(e) In *Pape v. State of New York,* 456 N.Y.S.2d 863 (N.Y. App. Div. 1982), plaintiff brought action to recover for personal injuries sustained during intramural floor hockey game played in the gym of a state university. It was the plaintiff's contention that the proximate cause of his injuries was attributable to the state for failing to instruct and supervise the intramural referees who officiated the game adequately. The court of appeals ruled in favor of defendant and held that plaintiff's injuries were not attributable to a lack of supervision and training by New York State relative to the referee's officiating.

(f) In *Harvey v. Ouachita Parish School Board,* 545 So. 2d 1241 (La. Ct. App. 1989), an injured football player sued the state high school athletic association under negligence for injuries suffered as a result of excessively rough behavior. The court held for the defendant on the basis that the association was not responsible for the referees' failure to remove football players who were displaying excessively rough behavior. The court reasoned that though the association had registered the referees, the referees were neither agents or servants of the association.

3. Officials' decisions have been reviewed in the following cases.

(a) In *Georgia High School Ass'n v. Waddell*, 285 S.E.2d 7 (Ga. Sup. Ct. 1981), the Georgia Supreme Court ruled that it does not possess authority to review the decision of a high school football referee. The high school referee admitted that he made the error—not awarding an automatic first down on a roughing-the-kicker penalty—which might have been determinative of the final outcome for the game. The trial court had overturned the referee's ruling based on a school's property right in the game of football being played according to the rules. The court ordered the game to be replayed from the point of the referee's error. The Georgia Supreme Court reversed, stating: "We now go further and hold that courts for equality in this state are without authority to review decisions of football referees because those decisions do not present judicial controversies."

(b) In *Tilelli v. Christenbery*, 120 N.Y.S.2d 697 (N.Y. Sup. Ct. 1953), a New York court upheld the decision of a boxing referee and a ringside judge. The New York Athletic Commission had ordered that the voting card of the judge, who they suspected was involved in an illegal gambling scheme, be changed. The court overruled the commission and held that the suspicion of illegality was not sufficient enough grounds for the court to intercede in the decision and substitute its judgment for that of the assigned judge.

(c) In *State ex rel. Durando v. State Athletic Commission*, 75 N.W.2d 451 (Wis. Sup. Ct. 1956), a court upheld the State Athletic Commission's decision that under its rules it had no authority to reverse a boxing referee's alleged failure to properly administer the "knock-down" rule.

(d) In *Wellsville-Middleton School District v. Miles*, Docket No. 406570 (Mo. Cir. Ct. 1982) (unreported), a court dismissed for failure to state a claim a lawsuit filed by the plaintiff school district against the Missouri State High School Activities Association. The plaintiff claimed that the official scorer in a state tournament basketball game had made a scoring mistake which ultimately led to plaintiff's team's losing the contest. The plaintiff had challenged the correctness of the final score.

(e) *Wellsville-Middleton School District v. Miles*, Docket No. 406570 (Mo. Cir. Ct. 1982) (unreported), a companion case to the *Wellsville-Middleton* case above, was filed by three student-athletes on the affected high school team. The plaintiffs alleged that the referee negligently failed to follow proper procedures, which ultimately affected their opportunity to secure college athletic scholarships. The plaintiffs dropped their suit after dismissal of the companion suit.

(f) In *Bain v. Gillespie*, 357 N.W.2d 47 (Iowa Ct. App. 1984), plaintiff, a Big-10 basketball referee, filed suit for injunctive relief and damages against defendants who produced T-shirts with his likeness in a noose imprinted on them. Defendants had produced the T-shirts after a controversial call by the referee at an intercollegiate basketball game. Injunctive relief was granted to the referee.

4. The following cases involve officials and workers' compensation issues:

(a) In *Gale v. Greater Washington, D.C. Softball Umpires Ass'n*, 311 A.2d 817 (Md. Ct. Spec. App. 1973), the court ruled that an umpire is not an employee of an umpire association, but an "independent contractor," thereby precluding the umpire from receiving workers' compensation under Maryland law.

(b) In *Ehehalt v. Livingston Board of Education*, 371 A.2d 752 (N.J. App. Div. 1977), the court ruled that a basketball official is not an employee of the school for which he or she officiates regularly but an "independent contractor," thereby precluding the official from recovering workers' compensation under New Jersey law.

(c) In *Ford v. Bonner County School District*, 612 P.2d 557 (Idaho Sup. Ct. 1980), the Idaho Supreme Court found that a high school football official injured while officiating is an employee of the school district and entitled to workers' compensation under Idaho law.

(d) In *Daniels v. Gates Rubber Co.*, 479 P.2d 983 (Colo. Ct. App. 1970), the court found that a member of the Umpires Association of Colorado, who was struck in the eye by a softball while umpiring a corporate recreational league game, was not an employee of the corporation for purposes of the Colorado workers' compensation statute.

(e) In *Warthen v. Southeast Oklahoma State University*, 641 P.2d 1125 (Okla. Ct. App. 1981), the court ruled that a university drama professor, who was also a licensed basketball referee and was asked by a dean to referee an intramural fraternity game, sustained a compensable injury when he died while officiating the game.

5. For a case in which a court found that an umpire might be liable for allowing a game to proceed on an unfit playing surface, see *Forkash v. New York*, 227 N.Y.S.2d 827 (N.Y. App. Div. 1966). The plaintiffs sought recovery for injuries sustained in a collision in the outfield during a city-sponsored softball game. In reversing the trial court's dismissal, the appellate division court held that whether the players could recover was a question for a jury to determine. The evidence presented proved that the collision took place after one plaintiff tripped over a piece of glass. The umpire furnished by the city had been advised that the outfield was not in playing condition but had directed that the game proceed.

6. For a case in which a promoter was held not liable for all actions of a referee employed by him, see *Ulrich v. Minneapolis Boxing and Wrestling Club, Inc.*, 129 N.W.2d 288 (Minn. 1964). The plaintiff, a seventy-seven-year-old wrestling spectator, sought recovery from defendant promoter for injuries sustained when a referee, hired by the defendant, whirled about, striking him. The Minnesota Supreme Court held that the injury was not proximately caused by the promoter's alleged failure to provide adequate crowd supervision, exposure of the referee to the plaintiff when he left the ring, or employment of a referee with dangerous propensities.

7. The following cases also involve officials, and their duties and liabilities.

(a) *Agnew v. City of Los Angeles*, 82 Cal. App. 2d 616, 186 P.2d 450 (Cal. Ct. App. 1947), details duties of officials.

(b) *Wilhelm v. San Diego United School Dist.*, No. N29412 (Cal. Super. Ct., filed July, 1985), involves an attack on an official at a high school basketball game.

(c) *Banfield v. George Junior Republic, Inc.*, (N.Y. Sup. Ct., filed 1983), involves a negligence claim by a basketball official against a private school.

(d) *Frazier v. Rutherford Board of Education*, No. L-05689-83 (N.J. Super. Ct. Law Div., filed Jan. 1983), involves a long-jump official and an injury to a high school track athlete.

8. For further information on the subject of sports officiating and the law, see the following law articles:

(a) Dedopoulos and Narol, "A Guide to Referees' Rights and Potential Liability," 16 *Trial* 18 (March 1980).

(b) Dedopoulos and Narol, "Kill the Umpire: A Guide to Referee's Rights," 15 *Trial* 32 (March 1979).

(c) Ranii, "Sports Violence Lawsuits Erupt," *National L. J.* February 9, 1981, p. 1.

(d) Narol and Dedopoulos, "The Official's Right to Sue for Game-Related Injuries," *National L. J.* June 7, 1982, p. 26.

(e) "A Workers' Compensation Casebook," *Referee*, September 1983.

(f) Narol and Dedopoulos, "The Official's Potential Liability for Injuries in Sporting Events," *National L. J.* September 6, 1982, p. 20.

(g) Davis, "Sports Liability: Blowing the Whistle on the Referees," 12 *Pac. L. J.* 937 (1981).

(h) Narol, "Player Injuries: Baseball Umps' Potential Liability," *Referee*, February 1984.

(i) Annotation, "Liability for Injury to or Death of Umpire, Referee, or Judge of Game or Contest," 10 *A. L. R.* 3d 446.

(j) Annotation, "Tort Liability of Public Schools and Institutions of Higher Education for Injuries Resulting from Lack or Insufficiency of Supervision," 38 *A. L. R.* 3d 830.

(k) Annotation, "Tort Liability of Public Schools and Institutions of Higher Education for Accident Occurring During School Athletic Events," 35 *A. L. R.* 3d 725.

(l) Annotation, "Modern Status of Doctrine of Sovereign Immunity as Applied to Public Schools and Institutions of Higher Learning," 33 *A. L. R.* 3d 703.

(m) Carpenter, "Decreasing Sports Violence Equals Increasing Official's Liability," 3 *Loyola Entertainment L. J.* 127 (1983).

(n) Narol, "The Legal Chalkboard," 67 *Athletic Journal* 42 (January 1987).

(o) Narol, "Protecting the Rights of Sports Officials," 23 *Trial* 64 (January 1987).

APPLICATION OF LEGAL PRINCIPLES TO DEFECTS IN EQUIPMENT

The "failure to warn" theory is established upon the finding of a manufacturer's duty to warn of known latent and potential injury-causing defects in the design of equipment. The extent of the duty is based on the age and experience of the reasonably foreseeable users of the product.

In order to maintain a suit based on a theory of a "failure to warn," the plaintiff must prove that the product is defective in design. The test used by courts has two distinct prongs. The first prong involves looking at the product to see if it has failed to perform as safely as an ordinary consumer would expect. Whether it was used as intended, or was misused or tampered with, will be considered in making the determination of safety. If the plaintiff cannot directly establish that the product failed to perform adequately, this part of the test may be satisfied by the second prong, which involves proving that the product's defective design proximately caused the injury and that the benefits of the challenged design do not outweigh the inherent risk of danger created by the design. To aid in its determination as to both defectiveness and resultant liability, the court will also consider factors such as the nature of the sport, the type of injury, the amount of use or foreseeable misuse, the degree to which the particular risk is greater due to the defect, and the current state of the art in designing an absolutely safe product. (See also the section Products Liability Law in Chapter 6.)

NOTES ───

1. The following cases involve the application of legal principles to defects in equipment.
   (a) In *Dudley Sports Co. v. Schmitt*, 279 N.E.2d 266 (Ind. Ct. App. 1972), a sixteen-year-old high school boy sought recovery for injuries received when he was struck in the face by the throwing arm of an automatic baseball pitching machine, which was purchased in March 1965 by Danville High School. Designed and manufactured by Dudley, the machine consisted of a frame and an open extended metal throwing arm. No protective shield guarded the throwing arm. When the arm reached a ten o'clock energized position and it received a ball, energy was released from the coiled spring and transmitted to the arm; the arm passed through a clockwise pitching cycle at a high rate of speed and came to rest in a four o'clock position. The machine was capable of delivering a powerful blow in the ten o'clock position, even if it was unplugged.

   When the machine was uncrated, it came with a parts list, assembly instructions, and a tool to deactivate the spring. The only warning instruction contained in the crate was a general warning tag which said:

"Warning! *Safety First* STAY CLEAR OF THROWING ARM AT ALL TIMES." No operating instructions were included in the crate. The machine was stored, unplugged, behind locked doors in locker room no. 2. However, the two adjoining locker rooms, with inside entrances to locker room no. 2, were not locked from the outside hallway entrance. On the day he was injured, plaintiff student was sweeping in locker room no. 2, as he had done in the past at the request of the coaching staff. He said that as he approached the front of the machine he heard a whistling noise and a pop. He was hit in the face by the throwing arm and received extensive facial injuries.

Plaintiff brought this action alleging negligence against the high school, the sporting goods company, and Dudley. The appeals court held that Dudley was negligent in the design, manufacture, and sale of the machine. The ability of the machine to operate while unplugged as a result of even a slight vibration was considered a latent danger, which could only be discovered through an examination of the machine combined with knowledge of the engineering principles which produce the action of the machine. Such knowledge is not ordinarily possessed by a sixteen-year-old high school boy who had never seen the machine before.

(b) In *Heldman v. Uniroyal, Inc.*, 371 N.E.2d 557 (Ohio Ct. App. 1977), a professional tennis player injured her knee during a tennis championship and brought suit for damages against Uniroyal, Inc., which supplied the tennis court surface for the matches. Plaintiff claimed that the defendant made certain representations and warranties, both expressed and implied, concerning its court surface. An appeals court ruled that there was sufficient evidence to raise a jury question as to whether plaintiff assumed the risk by playing in the match. The court reached its conclusion based on the reasons that the plaintiff told all the members of her team that the court was in a dangerous condition, that she was a professional tennis player and is presumed to know the various risks attendant with playing on different types of surfaces, and that a higher degree of knowledge and awareness is imputed to professional tennis players than to average nonprofessional tennis players as to the dangers of playing on a synthetic tennis court having obvious bubbles on the playing surface.

(c) In *Byrns v. Riddell, Inc.*, 550 P.2d 1065 (Ariz. Sup. Ct. 1976), plaintiff student-athlete brought a products liability action against Riddell, Inc., a manufacturer of football helmets, after he had sustained a head injury in an interscholastic football contest in October 1970. Plaintiff was injured in a play in which he received an "on-side" kick. The supreme court examined evidence relating to proof of strict liability in tort to determine whether the trial court properly found for Riddell. The Arizona Supreme Court reversed on the basis of doubts raised as to the possibility of a defect in the design of the helmet, the place of impact, and the presence of the defect at the time the helmet left the seller's hands. The case was remanded to the trial court to make these determinations.

(d) In _Everett v. Bucky Warren, Inc._, 380 N.E.2d 653 (Mass. Sup. Jud. Ct. 1978), plaintiff hockey player claimed that his serious head injury resulted from the defective design of the helmet he wore. The team's hockey coach distributed to the team helmets which were of a three-piece design, consisting of three plastic pieces. One piece covered the back of the head, one the forehead, and one the top of the head. The pieces were attached to each other by elastic straps. The straps expanded, depending on the size of the wearer's head, leaving gaps as large as three-fourths of an inch. This design was somewhat unique; however, there were also available on the market helmets which were of a one-piece design with no gaps.

During a game with the Brown University freshman team, plaintiff threw himself in front of a Brown player's shot in an attempt to block it. The puck struck Everett above the right ear, penetrating a gap in the helmet and causing a skull fracture. The injury required that a steel plate be inserted in his skull and caused recurring headaches. Everett then brought suit against the school, the manufacturer, and the retailer on the grounds of strict liability.

The appeals court held that the manufacturer could be found strictly liable for producing a helmet with an "unreasonably dangerous design." Factors that the court weighed when determining whether a particular design is reasonably safe included "the gravity of the danger posed by the challenged design, the likelihood that such danger would occur, the mechanical feasibility of a safer alternative design, the ... cost of an improved design, and the adverse consequences to the product and the consumer that would result from an alternative design." The court held that the gravity of the danger was demonstrated by the injuries, that helmets of the one-piece design were safer than the model used and were in manufacture prior to the injury, and that, while more expensive than the helmets used, the one-piece helmets were not economically unfeasible.

(e) _Halbrook v. Oregon State University_, Case No. 16-83-04631, Circuit Court of the State of Oregon for Lane County, (1983) (pending), was an action brought by the family of a boy who died from injuries received during baseball practice. In March 1982, the student-athlete was participating in an Oregon State University baseball practice on an Astroturf field when he collided with another player, fell to the ground, and struck his head. As a result of the injuries, Halbrook died. Plaintiff-estate alleges that the university and the Oregon State Board of Higher Education were responsible for the proper selection, installation, maintenance, and repair of the athletic field surface. More specifically, the university and state board of higher education failed to hire a competent and qualified installer for the Astroturf, they failed to adequately supervise the activities of the installer they had hired, and they failed to perform adequate shock absorbency tests upon the Astroturf when they knew or should have known that continued use would diminish its shock absorbency characteristics. Plaintiff alleged that the Astroturf sold by defendant Monsanto was in a defective condition, was unreasonably dangerous, and created an unreasonable risk of harm because it was too hard and without adequate cushioning. In addition, plaintiff claims that Monsanto marketed the Astroturf without adequate warnings to the average user. Plaintiff also sued Matrecon, the company which sold the asphalt that was placed under the Astroturf, under many of the same theories that were alleged against Monsanto.

(f) In *Breeden v. Valencia, Inc.*, 557 So. 2d 302 (La. Ct. App. 1990), a twelve-year-old injured while riding a jet ski at camp claimed that the jet ski was unreasonably dangerous and contained inadequate warnings. The court found no evidence that a defect existed in the design or manufacture of the steering mechanism. It further found that warnings contained in the instruction manual were adequate to inform riders about the turning ability of the jet ski.

(g) In *King v. Kayak Manufacturing Corp.*, unpublished decision (W. Va. 1989), the plaintiff sued a manufacturer of an aboveground swimming pool under a product liability claim when he was rendered quadriplegic after diving into four feet of water. The trial court held the manufacturer strictly liable and directed the verdict for the plaintiff. The appellate court reversed and remanded the case to resolve the issues of whether the plaintiff was contributorily negligent and assumed the risk of injury on the dive. The court recognized that the defense of assumption of risk is available in a strict product liability case where there is evidence that the plaintiff had actual knowledge of the risk and accepted the chance of injury.

2. For a case in which liability for failure to warn was based on constructive knowledge, see *Filler v. Rayex Corp.*, 435 F.2d 336 (7th Cir. 1970). Plaintiff baseball player sued defendant sunglass manufacturer for negligence, strict liability, and breach of implied warranty of fitness for a particular purpose when the glasses shattered into his eye. The court of appeals, in affirming the district court in favor of the plaintiff, held that defendant, which advertised the glasses as providing protection against baseballs, had constructive knowledge of the danger and was liable for failure to warn and liable for breach of warranty of fitness for a particular purpose.

3. For a case in which the court held there is no duty to warn of known dangers, see *Garrett v. Nissen Corp.*, 498 P.2d 1359 (N.M. Sup. Ct. 1972). Plaintiff, an experienced trampoline user, sued defendant trampoline manufacturer for negligence for failure to warn of the danger involved in landing incorrectly. The New Mexico Supreme Court held there is no duty to warn of dangers known to user of the product, either under strict liability or negligence theories.

4. For a case in which the court warned that there was a duty to warn of known dangerous conditions, see *Pleasant v. Blue Mound Swim Club*, 262 N.E.2d 107 (Ill. App. Ct. 1970). Plaintiff diver sought recovery from defendant pool owner for injuries sustained when he hit the pool bottom after diving off the board. The appellate court held for the plaintiff and found that the evidence would support a finding that the water level of the pool had been lowered to the extent that it constituted a dangerous condition, which was

brought about by defendant by a back flushing process, and that the manager and lifeguards were negligent for failure to warn swimmers of the danger.

5. The following cases involve negligent design.

    (a) In *Standard v. Meadors*, 347 F. Supp. 908 (N.D. Ga. 1972), plaintiff water skier sought recovery from defendant designer and manufacturer of a speed boat for injuries sustained when the boat propeller severed her leg while she was in the water waiting to be towed. The district court held that the allegation that the boat was negligently designed so that the prow (front of the boat) obscured the forward view of the operator and that the propeller was manufactured so that it would not stop upon contacting a person in water, stated a claim upon which relief could be granted under Georgia law.

    (b) In *Hauter v. Zogarts*, 120 Cal. Rptr. 681 (Cal. Sup. Ct. 1975), plaintiff sought recovery for injuries sustained when he was hit on the head by a golf ball following a practice swing with a golf training device that was described by manufacturer as "completely safe, ball will not hit player." The California Supreme Court held that the plaintiff was entitled to recover on the theories of false representation, breach of express and implied warranties, and strict liability in tort based on defective design.

6. For a case that held that a mere change in design is not sufficient to establish the existence of a defect and that misuse of a product may preclude liability, see *Gentemen v. Saunders Archery Co.*, 355 N.E.2d 647 (Ill. App. Ct. 1976). Plaintiff archer sought recovery in strict products liability against the manufacturer of "string silencers," which broke when he used them and injured him. In affirming a jury verdict for the defendant, the appellate court held that the evidence was sufficient to warrant a reasonable belief that the change in design did not establish the existence of a defect in the product and that the plaintiff had misused it.

7. For a case in which it was held that a breach of warranty will cause liability, see *Salk v. Alpine Ski Shop*, 342 A.2d 622 (R.I. Supp. Ct. 1975). Plaintiff skier sought recovery from defendant ski manufacturers for injuries sustained in a fall. The Rhode Island Supreme Court held that there was no jury question presented as to the negligence of the ski manufacturer in that there was no competent evidence that the failure of the bindings to release actually caused the injury. Furthermore, the plaintiff failed to show a breach of express warranty in that the skier did not establish that the advertisement of the manufacturer warranted that the bindings would release in every situation presenting a danger to the user's limbs.

8. The National Operating Committee on Standards for Athletic Equipment (NOCSAE) was organized to research and test equipment to develop new standards and improve existing ones. NOCSAE was founded in 1969 in an effort to reduce death and injuries through the adoption of standards and certification for athletic equipment. Fatalities decreased by more than 50 percent by 1977, after a thirty-seven-year high of thirty-six deaths in 1968. The number of cases of permanent quadriplegia from neck injuries in the early 1970s averaged thirty-five per year; these were reduced to seven in 1977, nine in 1978, and seven in 1979. NOCSAE published helmet standards

in 1973, and manufacturers and reconditioners have improved their equipment to meet those standards. An area of recent study was face masks for ice hockey helmets. Research in the future may result in helmets for lacrosse and equestrian competition.

9. For further information on the application of legal principles to defects in equipment, see the following.

(a) Levin and Bortz, "Torts on the Courts," 14 *Trial* 28 (June 1978).

(b) Wilkinson, "It's All Part of the Game—Or Is It?" 17 *Trial* 58 (November 1981).

(c) Coben, "Sports Helmets: More Harm Than Protection?" 25 *Trial* 74 (1989).

(d) Houser, Ashworth, and Clark, "Products Liability in the Sports Industry," 23 *Tort & Insurance L. J.* 44 (1987).

(e) Wittenberg, *Products Liability: Recreation and Sports Equipment* (New York: Law Journal Seminars Press, 1987).

LIABILITY INSURANCE

Liability insurance is a form of indemnity whereby the insurer undertakes to indemnify or pay the insured for a loss resulting from legal liability to a third person. It is based on contract law principles. Liability insurance protects an insured against financial loss resulting from lawsuits brought against him or her for negligent behavior. Common subjects for liability insurance in athletics are risks from use of the premises, from faulty products, from use of vehicles, and from the practice of professions.

Insurance is effective even if the insured has committed a minor violation of the criminal law. A minor violation will not invalidate the insurance or deprive the defendant of protection. An insurance policy may be invalidated, however, if the insured's conduct was so outrageous that it would be against public policy to indemnify it. The policy may also be invalidated if the insured misrepresented a material fact at the time of the application for the policy.

One of the standard provisions in any insurance policy requires the insured to cooperate fully with the insurance company by providing full and accurate information about the accident. It may also require the insured to attend the trial, to take part in it if required, and to do nothing for the injured party that would harm the insurance company. A violation of any of the above requirements would relieve the insurance company of liability to the injured third party.

The term "subrogation" is often times found in tort cases involving insurance claims. *Subrogation* is the right of the insurance company who has paid the legal obligation of the insured party to recover payment from the third party who was negligent. For example, a fan is injured at a baseball stadium by a foul ball that passed through a hole in the netting behind home plate, and that the hole was there because of the negligence of a third-party contractor who damaged the screen during installation. If the liability insurer for the stadium pays the injured fan, it has a right, under subrogation, to sue the installer for negligence, just as its insured, the stadium owner, had.

Typically, insurance policies contain a clause which entitles the insurer to be subrogated to his insured cause of action against any party who caused a loss which the insurer paid. The insurer can also be entitled to subrogation in the absence of an express contractual provision. This is called *equitable subrogation.* In some states, however, an insurance company must prove it was not a gratuitous payment in order to recover under equitable subrogation.

One response by institutions and sports associations to the increasing number of lawsuits brought under a tort liability theory is to use insurance. The National Federation of High School Associations and many state high school athletic associations and their member schools have adopted a liability/lifetime catastrophe medical plan. The plan covers the National Federation of State High School Associations, the state high school athletic/activity association, their member schools and school districts, and member school administrators, athletic directors, coaches, and trainers. This type of insurance allows the student-athlete who suffers a catastrophic injury to waive suit and opt for medical, rehabilitation, and work-loss benefits for the rest of his or her life. The philosophy behind the insurance plan is to provide needed benefits to the injured student-athlete, without the time, costs, and risks involved in litigation. If the injured student-athlete opts for the benefits provided by the insurance policy, the institution saves time, expense, and a possible award in favor of the plaintiff.

The NCAA has instituted a similar catastrophic injury protection plan. The NCAA's plan, which can be adopted by institutions on an individual basis, should accomplish two important objectives. First, by having this type of plan, it should reduce—if not eliminate—the number of workers' compensation cases filed against NCAA member institutions. The NCAA policy is similar to workers' compensation in that it provides benefits to catastrophically injured student-athletes regardless of fault. And the benefits offered by the NCAA program may be more attractive than a successful workers' compensation claim. For instance, a student-athlete's claim for workers' compensation benefits may have to be litigated. Second, the NCAA insurance policy assists the catastrophically injured student-athlete by providing benefits immediately, without time delays, without the costs of litigation, and without the uncertainties involved in litigation. The benefits are provided for the lifetime of the student-athlete, and the plan is extremely helpful to the student-athlete who is injured without fault.

The student-athlete who is catastrophically injured as a result of negligence of an institution or one of its employees still has the alternative of litigating the case and not collecting the benefits provided by the NCAA policy.

NOTES ⎯⎯⎯⎯⎯⎯⎯⎯⎯⎯⎯⎯⎯⎯⎯⎯⎯⎯⎯⎯⎯⎯⎯⎯⎯⎯⎯⎯⎯⎯⎯⎯

1. For a case involving liability insurance and sports, see *Strong v. Curators of University of Missouri,* 575 S.W.2d 812 (Mo. 1979). Plaintiffs sued for the death of their six-year-old child in a swimming pool run by defendant university. The defense of sovereign immunity was raised, and the plaintiffs countered with the argument that insurance precluded the necessity for and therefore abrogated the doctrine of sovereign immunity. The court held that the purchase of liability insurance will not, by itself, abrogate the doctrine.

2. For further information on liability insurance, see the following articles.
    (a) Quinn, "Litigating Youth Sports Injuries," 22 *Trial* 76 (March 1986).
    (b) "Sports Liability Insurance," 10 *Athletic Business* 12 (May 1986).
    (c) "Cancelling the Quality of Life," 10 *Athletic Business* 12 (June 1986).

WAIVER AND RELEASE OF LIABILITY

In the law, there are often competing legal theories in a given situation. The resolution of this type of situation is usually based on the preeminent public policies existing at the time the conflict arises. In the area of waivers and releases of liability, the underlying principles of tort law and contract law conflict. *Waivers* or *exculpatory agreements* are contracts that alter the ordinary negligence principles of tort law. *Contract law* is based on the idea that any competent party should have the absolute right to make a binding agreement with any other competent party. The only limit to this right to make such agreements is that a contract is invalid if it violates public policy. For example, a contract in which the parties agree to commit a crime would violate an important public policy of preventing crime.

Tort law, on the other hand, is based on the idea that a party should be responsible for negligent or intentional actions that cause injury to another person. Waivers, then, create a conflict between the right to enter into contracts and the policy that one should be held responsible for injury-causing negligent actions. The conflict between contract and tort law principles has been resolved in favor of the general rule that waivers and releases of liability will be enforceable unless they frustrate an important public policy or unless the party getting the waiver is unfairly dominant in the bargaining process. This resolution is based on the general contract law principle that a party is bound by the signing of a contract unless there is evidence of fraud, misrepresentation, or duress.

In order to determine if fraud, misrepresentation, or duress exists, a court will consider whether the party waiving its rights knew or had an opportunity to know the terms. This does not mean that merely failing to read or to understand a waiver and release of liability will invalidate it. It must be conspicuous and not be hidden in fine print so that a careful reader is unlikely to see it. The waiver and release of liability must also result from a free and open bargaining process. If one party forces the other to agree to a waiver, it may not be enforceable. The last consideration is whether the express terms of the waiver and release of liability are applicable to the particular conduct of the party whose potential liability is being waived. In other words, the language of the waiver must be clear, detailed, and specific. A waiver and release of liability will not be enforceable if it attempts to insulate one party from wanton, intentional, or reckless misconduct. Therefore, only liability for negligent actions can be waived (see Exhibit 7–1).

If the person signing the waiver and release of liability is a minor, other issues are raised. Under basic contract principles, a minor may repudiate an otherwise valid contract. A problem may also arise when parents sign waivers for their children. Courts are struggling with the issue of the rights of minors that may be waived by their parents (see Exhibit 7–2).

For competent adult participants in sports activities, waivers and releases of liability are generally upheld unless the waiver or release of liability violates public policy. However, questions are frequently litigated in the area of auto racing. Courts have reasoned that a driver is under no compulsion to race; therefore, a driver has the ability to make a decision whether to race and to assume all the risks inherent in auto racing. This may include risks that arise as a result of negligence on the part of the event's promoters. Courts are generally more reluctant to enforce a waiver and release of liability signed by spectators based on the theory that they may not be as familiar with the risks of auto racing or that they are entitled to assume that the premises are reasonably safe.

NOTES _____

1. The following cases involve waiver and release of liability in sports.
   (a) *Doyle v. Bowdoin College v. Cooper International, Inc.*, 403 A.2d 1206 (Me. Sup. Jud. Ct. 1979), was an action brought by plaintiffs on behalf of their son Brian, who was injured while playing floor hockey at a clinic sponsored by defendant college and directed by the school's agents. Plaintiffs alleged that the defendant's negligence resulted in their son's injury when a plastic hockey blade flew off the end of another boy's stick, hitting Brian in the eye, shattering his glasses, and damaging his retina so as to leave him partially blind.
   The case was tried before a jury which concluded that the negligent

Exhibit 7–1
NCAA Ticket Release of Liability Statement

Dear College Basketball Season Ticket Holder:

Enclosed are your NCAA tickets. Please safeguard your tickets; lost tickets will not be replaced.

**Please note there will be no drop-off of tickets at the Reservations Window for the rest of the season or NCAA games. Tickets *Will Not Be Accepted* under any circumstances. Please distribute any tickets prior to day of game.

THIS TICKET IS A REVOCABLE LICENSE
USER ACCEPTS RISK OF INJURY

The holder of this ticket voluntarily assumes all risks of property loss and personal injury arising during its use. Management may revoke the license and eject or refuse entry to the holder by refunding the stated purchase price. Tickets reported as lost or stolen may not be honored. If lost or stolen, this ticket will not be replaced nor the price refunded. Holder may not solicit contributions or distribute literature on the premises. Every person, regardless of age, must have a ticket to enter the facility. Holder may not bring alcoholic beverages, bottles, cans or containers, irritants (e.g., noise makers), videotape cameras, cups, shakers or strobe lights onto the premises without the written permission of the NCAA. Large signs, flags or banners are not permitted. It is the tournament manager's responsibility to confiscate all prohibited articles. No signs, flags or banners of any size may be affixed to the facility. Items that reflect good sportsmanship that can be held by one individual and do not block the view of other ticket patrons may be permitted. Unless specifically authorized in advance by the NCAA, this ticket may not be offered as a prize in a sweepstakes or contest. No readmittance.

conduct of defendants Bowdoin College and its agents proximately caused plaintiffs' son's injuries. The defendants appealed this judgment, contending that the trial court erred in holding (1) that certain documents were *not* releases relieving defendants of all liability for future injuries Brian might suffer as a result of defendants' negligent conduct and (2) that another document was not a contract of indemnification obligating the injured child's mother to reimburse defendants for any liability they might incur regarding injuries sustained by him at the clinic.

The appeals court denied the defendants' appeal. It noted that courts have traditionally disfavored contractual exclusions of negligence liability. The court found that the documents executed by the child's parents contained no express reference to defendants' liability for their own negligence: "Though the documents state that Bowdoin College will not 'assume' or 'accept' any 'responsibility' for injuries sustained by

Exhibit 7–2
Waiver and Release of Liability Form

SEATTLE PUBLIC SCHOOLS
1982–83 STUDENT INFORMATION AND PARENTAL APPROVAL FORM

A. **STUDENT INFORMATION**

    1. Student's Name _____ Birth Date _____ Age _____

    2. Name of Parent(s) _____

    3. Address of Parent(s) _____

    4. Name of Person(s) with whom Student Resides _____

    5. Address of Person(s) with whom Student Resides _____

    6. If this student does not reside with a parent, supply the following information:

        (a) How long has the student resided with this person(s)? _____

        (b) Has a legal guardianship been appointed by the courts? Yes ____ No ____
        (If the answer is "yes", submit a certified copy of the court order or letter of guardianship.)

    7. School attended last year _____ City _____

    8. Grade level completed last June _____

    9. Did student pass in at least four (4) full-time subjects in the immediately preceding semester/trimester and receive the maximum credit given? Yes ____ No ____

   10. Describe any physical limitations or problems that should be known by the coach: _____
_____

B. **STUDENT RIGHTS**

Students participating in the Interscholastic Athletic program are governed by the rights, protection and responsibilities as prescribed by the Washington Interscholastic Activities Association Handbook, the Metropolitan League By-Laws, and their respective schools.

Students and/or their parent(s)/guardians may make application for exceptions to League and WIAA eligibility regulations and may appeal any decisions relative to such request through their school principal.

C. **STUDENT RESPONSIBILITIES**

Participants are required to conform to the rules and regulations of their school, Metropolitan League, and the WIAA, and to conduct themselves in a safe and sportsmanlike manner. Violators are subject to probation, suspension or expulsion.

D. **STUDENT ELIGIBILITY REQUIREMENTS**

    1. Prior to participation in practice of athletic contests a student must:

        (a) PHYSICAL EXAMINATION—During the 12-month period prior to first participation in interscholastic athletics in a middle school, a junior high school, and prior to participation in a high school, a student shall undergo a medical examination and be approved for interscholastic athletic competition by a medical authority licensed to perform a physical examination. Prior to each subsequent year of participation, a student shall furnish a statement, signed by a medical authority licensed to perform a physical examination, which provides clearance for continued athletic participation.

        The school in which this student is enrolled must have on file a statement (or prepared form) from a medical authority licensed to give a physical examination, certifying that his/her physical condition is adequate for the activity or activities in which he/she participates.

Exhibit 7–2 continued

We have read, understand, and agree to abide by the Student Rights and Responsibilities and Student Eligibility listed in this form.

Date: _____, 19_____ Signed _____
                                            Parent or Guadian

                                  Signed _____
                                            Student

WARNING, AGREEMENT TO OBEY INSTRUCTIONS, RELEASE, ASSUMPTION OF RISK, AND AGREEMENT TO HOLD HARMLESS

(Both the applicant student and a parent or guardian must read carefully and sign.)

SPORT (check applicable box):

- ☐ Football   ☐ Basketball   ☐ Track
- ☐ Volleyball   ☐ Wrestling   ☐ Baseball
- ☐ Cross-Country   ☐ Gymnastics   ☐ Softball
- ☐ Soccer   ☐ Swimming   ☐ Tennis
- ☐ Golf

STUDENT

I am aware playing or practicing to play/participate in any sport can be a dangerous activity involving MANY RISKS OF INJURY. I understand that the dangers and risks of playing or practicing to play/participate in the above sport include, but are not limited to, death, serious neck and spinal injuries which may result in complete or partial paralysis, brain damage, serious injury to virtually all internal organs, serious injury to virtually all bones, joints, ligaments, muscles, tendons, and other aspects of the muscular skeletal system, and serious injury or impairment to other aspects of my body, general health and well-being. I understand that the dangers and risks of playing or practicing to play/participate in the above sport may result not only in serious injury, but in a serious impairment of my future abilities to earn a living, to engage in other business, social and recreational activities, and generally to enjoy life.

Because of the dangers of participating in the above sport, I recognize the importance of following coaches' instructions regarding playing techniques, training and other team rules, etc., and to agree to obey such instructions.

In consideration of the Seattle School District permitting me to try out for the _____ High School _____ team and to engage in all activities
                                  (indicate sport)
related to the team, including, but not limited to, trying out, practicing or playing/participating in that sport, I hereby assume all the risks associated with participation and agree to hold the Seattle School District, its employees, agents, representatives, coaches, and volunteers harmless from any and all liability, actions, causes of action, debts, claims, or demands of any kind and nature whatsoever which may arise by or in connection with my participation in any activities related to the _____ High School _____ team. The terms hereof shall serve as a release and
        (indicate sport)
assumption of risk for my heirs, estate, executor, administrator, assignees, and for all members of my family.

> The following to be completed only if sport is *football, wrestling, gymnastics,* or *baseball*:
>
> I specifically acknowledge that _____ is a VIOLENT CONTACT SPORT involving even greater risk of injury. _____
>   (initial)

Date: _____, 19 _____   _____
                                         Signature of Student

Exhibit 7–2 continued

> To resume participation following an illness and/or injury serious enough
> to require medical care, a participating student must present to the school
> officials a physican's written release.

- (b) be covered by the school's athletic injury insurance or have on file in the school office a properly signed League Insurance Waiver form.
- (c) Seattle school students must have paid for the school's Catastrophic Insurance coverage.
- (d) have on file in the school office a signed Student Information and Parental Approval form.

2. To be eligible to participate in an Interscholastic contest a student must:
   - (a) be under twenty (20) years of age on September 1 for the Fall sport season; on December 1 for the Winter sport season; and March 1 for the Spring sport season.
   - (b) have passed in at least four (4) full-time subjects in the immediately preceding semester/trimester and earned the maximum credit given for each subject.
   - (c) be enrolled in and currently passing at least four full credit subjects.
   - (d) reside with their parents, the parent with legal custody, or a court appointed guardian who has acted in such a capacity for a period of one year or more.
   - (e) not miss practices or games for the purpose of participating in non-school athletic activities.
   - (f) not accept cash awards in any amount or merchandise of more than $100.00 in value, or have ever signed a contract with or played for a professional athletic organization.

3. Students shall be entitled to four consecutive years of participation after entering the ninth (9th) grade.

4. A student completing the highest grade offered in an elementary or middle-school is eligible for athletic participation upon entering a public or non-public high school. After starting his/her attendance in a high school, a student who transfers voluntarily or involuntarily to another high school shall become ineligible unless he/she obtains a signed Transfer Form from the principal of the high school from which he/she transfers, indicating that the transfer was not for athletic or disciplinary reasons.

5. Be in attendance a full day of school on any game date which falls on a school day.

6. Your athletic eligibility can be adversely affected by:
   - (a) Providing misleading or false information relative to factors which affect your eligibility. (Loss of minimum of one year of eligibility.)
   - (b) Missing a game or practice to participate in an out-of-school athletic activity.
   - (c) Participating in an athletic activity under a false name.
   - (d) Disruptive behavior during practice and/or contests.
   - (e) Irregular attendance at school or practice.
   - (f) Committing and/or aiding or abetting in the commission of any physical abuse or attack upon any person associated with athletic practices or contests.
   - (g) Using a school uniform in a non-school athletic event or failure to maintain proper care or return of athletic equipment.

Exhibit 7–2 continued

PARENT/GUARDIAN

I, _____, am the parent/legal guardian of _____ (student). I have read the above warning and release and understand its terms. I understand that all sports can involve many RISKS OF INJURY, including, but not limited to, those risks outlined above.

In consideration of the Seattle School District permitting my child/ward to try out for the _____ High School _____ team and to engage in all ac-
(indicate sport)

tivities related to the team, including, but not limited to, trying out, practicing, or play-ing/participating in _____ I hereby agree to hold the Seattle School District,
(indicate sport)

its employees, agents, representatives, coaches, and volunteers harmless from any and all liability, actions, causes of action, debts, claims, or demands of every kind and na-ture whatsoever which may arise by or in connection with participation of my child/ward in any activities related to the _____ High School _____
(indicate sport)

team. The terms hereof shall serve as a release for my heirs, estate, executor, adminis-trator, assignees, and for all members of my family.

> The following to be completed only if sport is *football, wrestling, gymnastics,* or *baseball*:
>
> I specifically acknowledge that _____ is a VIOLENT CONTACT SPORT involving even greater risk of injury than other sports. _____
> (initial)

Date: _____, 19 _____

_____
Signature of Parent or Legal Guardian

10/82

Brian . . . whether 'assumed' or 'accepted,' or not, Bowdoin College has such responsibility in any event because the *law* had imposed it."

(b) In *Williams v. Cox Enterprises, Inc.*, 283 S.E.2d 367 (Ga. Ct. App. 1981), plaintiff, who had participated in the 10,000-meter Georgia Peach-tree Road Race, brought a class action lawsuit charging sponsors of the event with negligence in failing to adequately warn participants of the inherent dangers involved in running the race. In the 1977 race, plaintiff suffered heat stroke, heat prostration, renal failure, and other disorders, which resulted in the permanent impairment of some motor functions. Cox Enterprises argued in the trial court that plaintiff had assumed the risk of injury and that he had signed a required waiver-of-liability form. Plaintiff argued that the waiver was invalid because given the size of the event and the fact that the race was so well publicized, it was the public duty of the sponsor to provide and ensure the safety of the par-ticipants. Plaintiff also contended that the waiver was invalid due to the disparity in bargaining positions between the runners and the race of-ficials. Plaintiff claimed that because running had become so popular and because the Peachtree Road Race was "the only road race of its kind in the Atlanta area," he and other athletes were under "enormous pressure to enter it on whatever terms were offered to them."

An appeals court held that the contractual waiver of liability is valid unless the waiver violates public policy. The court held that the contract signed by the plaintiff was valid. It also held that plaintiff signed the waiver without duress; thus his claim of disparity in bargaining positions was not valid. The court further held that the application signed by plaintiff described the race as "grueling" due to heat and humidity. Since plaintiff admitted having read the warning and being aware of the danger, recovery was precluded under the assumption-of-risk doctrine.

(c) In *Garretson v. United States*, 456 F.2d 1017 (9th Cir. 1972), a federal court held that a release was valid when plaintiffs had read conspicuous language and previously signed similar forms.

(d) In *Winterstein v. Wilcom*, 293 A.2d 821 (Md. 1972), a release was held valid because it had been freely entered into and bargained for by two equal parties.

2. Releases are not valid if they are not clearly stated. For example, in *Hertzog v. Harrison Island Shores Inc.*, 251 N.Y.S.2d 164 (N.Y. App. Div. 1964), plaintiff beach and yacht club member sought recovery for injuries received in a fall from the gangplank leading to the dock on club premises. The court held for the plaintiff, despite the fact that the plaintiff signed a release of liability. The court reasoned that a provision of the membership application, providing that, if accepted as a member, plaintiff would waive his claim for any loss to personality or for personal injury while a member of club, was not sufficiently clear or explicit to absolve club of its own negligence in regard to the plaintiff's fall.

3. In *Wagenblast v. Odessa School District No. 105-157-166J*, 758 P.2d 968 (Wash. Sup. Ct. 1988), the court did not decide the question presented as to whether the standardized release of liability forms used for athletics could stand as an express assumption of the risk. The court said that in order to determine that question an actual lawsuit with facts on which to base the conclusion was required.

4. In *Brown v. Racquetball Centers, Inc.*, 534 A.2d 842 (Sup. Ct. Pa. 1987), a fitness club member sued his club to recover injuries caused when he slipped on a wet tile floor. The court held that the release he signed stating that fitness club member assumed all risks of injury sustained in connection with activities in and about the premises did not absolve the fitness center of liability for its negligence.

5. In *Childress by Childress v. Madison County*, 777 S.W.2d 1 (Tenn. Ct. App. 1989), a severely retarded student and his parents sued a county and its board of education, alleging negligence in supervision of the student, who was taken to a public pool for training for Special Olympics. The court found the county negligent in failing to supervise the student adequately and also found that the release signed by the student's mother relieved the county of liability to the mother, but in no way waived the rights of the student or the father to sue the county for negligence.

6. In *Hiett v. Lake Barcroft Community Association, Inc., et al.*, 1992 WL 120775 (Va. 1992), the plaintiff was competing in a triathlon when he dove into the water during the swim portion and struck his head on the bottom or some unseen object beneath the surface. The injury left Hiett a quadriplegic.

Prior to competing in the triathlon, each participant had been required to sign an entry form which included a waiver releasing the event's organizers and sponsors from liability "for any and all injuries" suffered in the event. Hiett cited a Virginia Supreme Court decision from 1890, *Johnson's Adm'x v. Rich Danville R.R. Co.* (86 VA. 975 [1890]), in which the court found that an agreement with the railroad company excusing them from liability for any injuries or death resulting from any cause whatsoever was in violation of public policy and therefore invalid. Hiett argued that this precedent still stands and Virginia law has voided any preinjury agreement releasing a party from liability for negligence. The Supreme Court agreed with this argument and found that the release of liability on the entry form for the triathlon violated public policy and was therefore invalid.

Chapter 8

SEX DISCRIMINATION ISSUES

INTRODUCTION

As women's athletic programs enter a midlife growth pattern after the initial explosion in women's intercollegiate participation in the 1970s and early 1980s, they face great uncertainties. The absorption of the now-defunct Association of Intercollegiate Athletics for Women (AIAW) by the NCAA, the decrease in the percentages of women coaches and administrators leading women's programs, and the failure of attempts to ratify the Equal Rights Amendment as a federal constitutional amendment all pose serious concerns for those attempting to promote the development of women's athletic programs. In contrast, the possibilities generated by the passage of the Civil Rights Restoration Act, the settlement of entire programmatic sex discrimination complaints in several cases, the hiring of six female athletic directors (in combined men and women's athletic departments), and the evolution of state legislation specifically designed to fund women's athletics are all positive steps which should serve to advance the interests of women.

The initial development of athletic opportunities for women may be attributed, to a large extent, to Title IX of the Education Amendments of 1972, a federal statute which prohibits sex discrimination.

During the 1970s and early 1980s, Title IX and other legislation were in the vanguard of changed societal attitudes, as well as legal factors, that helped bring about substantial reduction in sex discrimination in the United States. The availability of legal options brought about an increased reliance on the legal system to redress sex discrimination. Women brought complaints about unequal treatment to court and they were often successful in their litigation.

Throughout the mid-1980s, however, a trend of setbacks besieged the women's movement. The failure to enact the Equal Rights Amendment and limitations imposed on Title IX enforcement by the Supreme Court's *Grove City College* decision left the situation at a virtual standstill throughout much of this period. Only recently, with the passage of the Civil Rights Restoration Act by Congress in 1988 and the settlement of entire programmatic sex equity complaints against Temple University, Washington State University, and the Montana High School Association, have the prospects for continued movement toward equality in athletics regained momentum.

Before the passage of Title IX, women composed only 5 percent of the total number of athletic participants in high school and 15 percent in college. By 1992, 36 percent of all interscholastic participants and 34 percent of all NCAA intercollegiate participants were women. The number of women's varsity programs offered by NCAA member institutions has also continued to rise, from 5.61 women's programs per school in 1977 to 7.09 in 1992.

Participation in women's athletics has increased for many reasons. A major factor is the drastic change in social attitudes about women, including a new perception among women of their own athletic capabilities and interest in participation. According to a 1985 comprehensive survey commissioned by the Miller Brewing Company in cooperation with the Women's Sports Foundation, the transformation of attitudes is due, in the opinion of women, to three developments:

1. Women believe they have something to teach men about humane competition.
2. Women are seeking sports partners of equal skill, regardless of gender.
3. Women have strong self-confidence and a clear conviction that sports participation does not diminish femininity.

Another investigation, commissioned by the Wilson Sporting Goods Company and the Women's Sports Foundation in 1987, revealed other important intergenerational attitudes relating the influence of parents and family to girls' participation in sports. The Wilson Report showed that 87 percent of today's parents "generally accept the idea that sports are equally important for boys and girls." The findings also acknowledged that 97 percent of the parents surveyed think that sports and other fitness-related activities are beneficial to girls who participate. These attitudinal changes have helped increase athletic opportunities for women.

In 1987 the President's Commission of the NCAA sponsored a series of studies to help identify the effects of participation in intercollegiate athletics on student-athletes. The results of the fourth study in this series, released in 1989, focused upon the special circumstances of women student-athletes at NCAA Division I colleges and universities. Among the key findings were the following:

1. On the Division I level, 78 percent of women basketball players report GPAs in high school of B or better.
2. During the season, women basketball players report spending an average of 26 hours per week in their sport, the same amount of time reported by men basketball players.
3. Some 65 percent of women basketball players say that it is easier for them to take on leadership responsibility as a result of their intercollegiate participation.

While the growth in participation in women's sports has increased dramatically since the onset of Title IX, other problems have emerged. According to a report by R. Vivian Acosta and Linda Carpenter of Brooklyn College, "The positive/negative pattern of the last 18 years can be summarized as: An increase in sports participation by girls and women and a decrease in women in leadership positions."

The Acosta-Carpenter study reveals that in 1972, 90 percent of women's athletic programs were run by female administrators, compared with only 16.8 percent in 1992. The report also states that while the average number of administrators of athletics per institution (for all divisions) in 1992 was 2.7, the average number of women administrators was only 0.83. Among the intercollegiate coaching ranks, the percentage of women coaching women's teams steadily dropped from 1978 to 1992. In three of the most popular sports, women have seen reductions in the percentage of basketball coaches, from 79.4 to 63.5 percent; of softball coaches, from 83.5 to 63.7 percent; and of track coaches, from 52.3 to 20.4 percent—all in that 14-year period. While this problem may be, in part, a reflection of the limited experience of women in the coaching ranks, some also claim it is because women have a limited role in the governing procedures of the NCAA.

Another area of concern to high school and college athletic administrators is the funding of women's programs. On the intercollegiate level, some worry that the NCAA made commitments to attract women's athletic programs into the association in the early 1980s that it will find hard to continue.

Faced with the often difficult fiscal dilemmas associated with supporting athletic programs, some states and administrators have looked to innovative alternatives in order to fund women's athletics effectively. Both the Minnesota and Washington (state) legislatures have passed specific legislation addressing this issue. House Bill 2020, the Washington legislation that passed in 1989, serves to redress inequities in intercollegiate athletics throughout Washington's higher education system by creating additional tuition and fee waivers for women's programs.

As women reach the competitive level of men's athletics, they also begin to face the same pressures to succeed, market, and control corruption in their programs. Merrily Dean Baker, former assistant executive director of the NCAA, noted that the potential for corruption exists, and that corruption may already have occurred in some places. She thinks that women athletes' greatest challenge will be to avoid the pitfalls of men into which athletes have fallen. The NCAA's director of enforcement, David Berst, has acknowledged that the worst examples exist in men's programs. He hopes that women will conclude that it would be intolerable to end up in the same situation. Berst added that cheating in women's athletics has not reached the same proportions as in men's basketball and football, "but there are apparently some abuses that are intentional in nature."

When charges of sex discrimination are filed, the plaintiffs usually base their arguments on the equal protection laws, Title IX, and/or state equal rights amendments. Therefore, Chapter 8 begins with a discussion of the various legal theories and principles utilized in sex discrimination cases in high school and intercollegiate athletics. The chapter next focuses on the legality of and the scope and applicability of Title IX, and how the Office of Civil Rights conducts compliance reviews of alleged Title IX violations. The chapter then discusses sex discrimination cases involving individual athletes. The cases have been grouped according to the presence or absence of teams available to either sex and according to whether the sport involved is a contact or noncontact sport. The final section of Chapter 8 focuses on sex discrimination in the area of athletic employment. The Equal Pay Act and Title VII, federal statutes that specifically pertain to discrimination in employment, are discussed. Employment discrimination in the area of coaching, officiating, refereeing, and media coverage is also examined.

NOTES ──

1. For further information on sex discrimination in women's athletics, see Tokarz, *Women, Sports and the Law: A Comprehensive Research Guide to Sex Discrimination in Sports* (Buffalo: William S. Hein Company, 1987).

2. For further information on the survey by Miller Brewing Company and the Women's Sports Foundation, see "Miller Lite Report on Women in Sports: Summary," copyright 1985 by Miller Brewing Company, 3939 West Highland Boulevard, Milwaukee, Wisconsin 53208.

3. For further information on the NCAA Presidents Commission report, see *Report No. 4: Women in Intercollegiate Athletics at NCAA Division I Institutions,* Center for the Study of Athletics, American Institutes for Research, Palo Alto, Calif., July 1989.

4. For further information on sex discrimination in athletics, see the following law review articles.

(a) Note, "Sex Discrimination in High School Athletics: An Examination of Applicable Legal Doctrines," 66 *Minn. L. Rev.* 1115 (1982).

(b) Nelson, "Title IX: Women's Collegiate Athletics in Limbo," 40 *Wash. & Lee L. Rev.* 297 (1983).

(c) Wien, "The Case for Equality in Athletics," 22 *Cleve. St. L. Rev.* 570 (fall 1973).

(d) Hawley, "The Legal Problems of Sex Discrimination," 15 *Alberta Law Review* 122 (1977).

(e) Note, "Sex Discrimination and Intercollegiate Athletics," 61 *Iowa L. Rev.* 420 (1975).

(f) Note, "Sex Discrimination and Intercollegiate Athletics: Putting Some Muscle on Title IX," 88 *Yale L. J.* 1254 (May 1979).

(g) Skilton, "The Emergent Law of Women and Amateur Sports: Recent Developments," 28 *Wayne L. Rev.* 1701 (1982).

(h) McNamara, "Sex Discrimination in High School Athletics," 47 *U. M.-Kansas City L. Rev.* 109 (1978).

(i) Rubin, "Sex Discrimination in Interscholastic High School Athletics," 25 *Syracuse L. Rev.* 535 (1974).

(j) Ingram and Bellaver, "Sex Discrimination in Park District Athletic Programs," 64 *Women's L. Jour.* 33 (1978).

(k) Wong and Ensor, "Sex Discrimination in Athletics: A Review of Two Decades of Accomplishments and Defeats," 21 *Gonz. L. Rev.* 345 (1985/86).

5. At NCAA member institutions, the number of female participants in intercollegiate athletics increased from 32,000 in 1971–72 to 64,000 in 1976–77, to 80,000 in 1982–83, and then rose to 91,000 by 1988–89, a 184 percent increase in seventeen years. During that period, 1971–88, the number of NCAA member institutions that sponsored women's intercollegiate sports increased as follows:

	1971	1988	1991–92
Basketball	307	764	810
Cross Country	10	638	677
Softball	147	549	605
Swimming	140	397	394
Tennis	243	691	723
Track and Field	78	540	561
Volleyball	208	719	762

6. On the high school level, prior to the enactment of Title IX in 1972, fewer than 300,000 girls took part in high school athletics. In 1992, this figure rose to 1.9 million (compared with 3.4 million boys participating).

7. Administrators and coaches will find the following organizations useful resources.

(a) Women's Sports Foundation, 342 Madison Ave., Suite 728, New York, NY 10173. This organization publishes *Women's Sports and Fitness*, a monthly magazine. The foundation also created the Women's Sports Hall of Fame, a traveling exhibit.

(b) Women's Equity Action League, 805 Fifteenth Street, N.W., Washington, DC 20005. This organization established the project SPRINT, whose major purpose is to promote equal opportunity for women in sports. The organization also publishes *In the Running*.

(c) National Association for Girls and Women in Sport, 1900 Association Drive, Reston, VA 22091. The association regularly publishes official rulebooks for many women's sports.

(d) Center for Women and Sport, White Building, Pennsylvania State University, University Park, PA 16802.

(e) NOW Task Force on Women Sports, National NOW Action Center, 425 Thirteenth Street, N.W., Suite 1001, Washington, DC 20004.

LEGAL PRINCIPLES UTILIZED IN SEX DISCRIMINATION CASES

Sex discrimination in high school and intercollegiate athletics has been challenged using a variety of legal arguments, including equal protection laws, Title IX of the Education Amendment of 1972, state equal rights amendments, and the Equal Pay Act. Most challenges have been based on either the equal protection laws or Title IX, or both. For example, in *Pavey v. University of Alaska v. National Collegiate Athletic Ass'n*, 490 F. Supp. 1011 (D. Alaska 1980), an action was brought against the University of Alaska charging it with discrimination against female student-athletes in the operation of its athletic program in violation of Title IX and the Fourteenth Amendment's due process and equal protection clauses. The university filed a third-party suit against the NCAA and the AIAW, which charged that the two associations' inconsistent rules required the university to discriminate in its athletic program in violation of federal laws. The NCAA and AIAW made motions for dismissal of the suit. In denying the motions, the district court held that the university's suit stated a valid claim, that the university was reasonably trying to avoid a confrontation with the two associations' rules that could cause a disruption in the participation of student-athletes in intercollegiate athletics, and that the facial neutrality of the associations' rules did not negate the university's claim that those rules, in combined effect, forced the university to discriminate in its athletic programs.

Equal protection arguments are based on the Fifth Amendment of the U.S. Constitution, which guarantees equal protection of the law to all persons found within the United States. (See Chapter 4 for a further discussion of equal protection.)

Title IX is a relatively recent method of attacking sex discrimination. Although the original legislation was passed in 1972, implementation was delayed for the promulgation of regulations and policy interpretations. Even with the delay, many have claimed that the rise in participation by women in athletics was directly related to the passage of Title IX. A state equal rights amendment can also be used to attack alleged sex discrimination; however, not all states have passed such legislation. The fourth argument concerns two separate statutes: the Equal Pay Act and Title VII of the Civil Rights Act of 1964. Although neither statute was passed to deal specifically with sex discrimination, both have been used to challenge employment discrimination.

In a sex discrimination case, the plaintiff usually contends that there is a fundamental inequality, regardless of whether a plaintiff employs an equal protection or Title IX approach. In attempting to deal with these claims, the court considers three factors. The first is whether or not the sport from which women are excluded is one involving physical contact. Total exclusion from all sports or from any noncontact sport is considered a violation of equal educational opportunity. The second factor is the quality and quantity of opportunities available to each sex. The courts compare the number of athletic opportunities available to each sex as well as the amount of money spent on equipment, the type of coaches provided, and the access to school-owned facilities. The third factor the courts consider is age and level of competition involved in the dispute. The younger the athletes involved, the fewer the actual physiological differences that exist. Without demonstrable physiological differences, the justification of inherent biological differences as a rational basis for the exclusion of one sex from athletic participation is negated.

Equal Protection Laws

The basic analysis utilized for equal protection questions is discussed in Chapter 4. Here we examine more closely the effects of using gender to classify persons for different athletic opportunities.

Historically, sex has been an acceptable category for classifying persons for different benefits and burdens under any given law. In 1872 the Supreme Court, in *Bradwell v. State*, 83 U.S. (16 Wall) 130 (1873), opened with the statement that a woman's place was in the home. The Court went on to say that this was part of a "divinely ordained law of nature." In 1908, the Court stated in *Muller v. Oregon*, 208 U.S. 412 (1908), that a classification based on gender was a valid constitutional classification. Such a classification was not considered to be a violation of equal protection, regardless of whether it was based on actual or imagined physical differences between men and women. Modern equal protection theories have now gained preeminence, and the use of gender to classify persons is considered less acceptable.

A school's, conference's, or athletic association's rules prohibiting mixed-gender competition have typically been challenged on equal protection grounds. As women's rights have been gaining importance and attracting attention in all areas, so too have women begun to assert their right to participate in athletics free from sex discrimination. In a number of cases, women have been successful in asserting their right to participate on an equal basis with men, and one legal theory they have utilized on these occasions has been the equal protection clause.

Under traditional equal protection analysis, the legislative gender-based classification must be sustained unless it is found to be patently arbitrary and/or if it bears absolutely no rational relationship to a legitimate governmental interest. Under this traditional rational basis analysis, overturning discriminatory laws is extremely difficult. The implication for sex discrimination sports litigation in high schools and colleges is such that women may be excluded from athletic participation upon a showing of a rational reason for their exclusion and by providing comparable options for those who are excluded. The rational reason must be factually supported and may not be based on mere presumptions about the relative physical and athletic capabilities of women and men. It remains, however, a relatively easy standard for the defendant to meet, as it invokes only the lowest standard of scrutiny by the court.

The court will apply its highest standard, that of strict scrutiny, if it finds that the classification restricts a "fundamental right" or if the rule involves a "suspect" classification. Under the standard of strict scrutiny, the party seeking to enforce the regulation must show that the rule's classification is necessary to promote a compelling governmental purpose or interest. To date the courts have not found sex to be a suspect class, which would elevate it to the status held by race, national origin, and alienage. Sex and other classifications may, however, be deemed "suspect" under a state equal protection clause. In addition, the courts have generally ruled that participation in interscholastic and intercollegiate sports is not a fundamental right under the equal protection clause. Consequently, this participation interest alone does not warrant the application of strict scrutiny in evaluating a classification.

If the courts were, however, to decide that sex is a suspect class or athletic participation is a fundamental right, all rules that classify on the basis of gender would become subject to strict scrutiny analysis. If this were the standard, the rule makers would have to prove that there are compelling reasons for the classification and that there is no less restrictive alternative. They would also have to prove that the classification was directly related to the constitutional purpose of the legislation and that this purpose could not have been achieved by any less objectionable means. Many rules and laws would fail to meet this high standard, and hence would be judged to be discriminatory.

The Supreme Court has moved away from the broad interpretation of the rational relationship test by increasing the burden on the defendant. This intermediate test, between the rational basis and strict scrutiny test, was first established in *Reed v. Reed,* 404 U.S. 71 (1971). The Supreme Court established therein that sex-based classifications must be "reasonable, not arbitrary, and must rest upon some ground of difference having a fair and substantial relation to the object of the legislation, so that all persons similarly circumstanced shall be treated alike." The Supreme Court again addressed this issue in *Frontiero v. Richardson,* 411 U.S. 677 (1973); in a plurality opinion, Justice Brennan stated, "what differentiates sex from such nonsuspect statuses as intelligence or physical disability . . . is that the sex characteristic frequently bears no relation to ability to perform or contribute to society." Finally in *Craig v. Boren,* 429 U.S. 190 (1976), and again in *Mississippi University for Women v. Hogan,* 458 U.S. 718 (1982), the Supreme Court held that a gender classification will fail unless it is substantially related to a sufficiently important governmental interest. Thus, the Supreme Court has established the intermediate level of scrutiny to apply in gender-based discrimination cases.

A factual basis for any gender classification must exist. Mere preferences or assumptions concerning the ability of one sex to perform adequately are not acceptable bases for a discriminatory classification. The intermediate standard requires more than an easily achieved rational relationship but less than a strict scrutiny standard would demand. The class must bear a substantial relationship to an important but not compelling governmental interest. Also, the relationship between a classification and a law's purpose must now be founded on fact, not on general legislative views of the relative strengths and/or abilities of the two sexes.

Three key factors commonly are considered in an equal protection analysis of athletic discrimination cases. The first factor is state action. Before any claim can be successfully litigated, a sufficient amount of state action must be present. Without state action, an equal protection argument under the U.S. Constitution is not applicable. This factor has significant ramifications in cases in which the athletic activity is conducted outside the auspices of a state or municipal entity or a public educational institution. Examples include youth sport leagues such as Little League Baseball, Pop Warner Football, and the YMCA's Youth Basketball Association.

The second factor is whether the sport involves physical contact. In contact sports the courts have allowed separate men's and women's teams. This "separate but equal" doctrine is based on considerations of the physical health and safety of the participants. When separate teams do not exist, however, both sexes may have an opportunity to try out and to meet the necessary physical requirements on an individual basis. A complete ban on the participation of one sex will not be upheld if it is based on generalizations about characteristics of an entire sex rather than on a reasonable consideration of individual characteristics. (See *Clinton v. Nagy* later in this chapter.)

The third factor to be considered is whether both sexes have equal opportunities to participate. This "equal opportunity" usually requires the existence of completely separate teams or an opportunity to try out for the one available team. If there are separate teams, however, it is permissible for the governing organization to prohibit co-ed participation. Unlike classifications based on race, when gender is a determining factor, "separate but equal" doctrines may be acceptable. The issue then often becomes whether the teams are indeed equal (see *O'Connor v. Board of Education of School District No. 23* and *Ritacco v. Norwin School District* later in this chapter). Other factors that have been taken into consideration are the age of the participant and the level of the competition. Physical differences between boys and girls below the age of 12 are minimal. Therefore, health and safety considerations that might be applicable to older athletes have not constituted legitimate reasons for restricting young athletes' access to participation (see *Bednar v. Nebraska School Activities Ass'n* later in this chapter).

The legal analysis of any particular case, however, will depend on the philosophy of the court and the particular factual circumstances presented (see *Brenden v. Independent School District 742* later in this chapter). Some courts are reluctant to intervene in discretionary decisions made by an association governing athletic events unless there are obvious abuses. (See Chapter 4 for a discussion of judicial review.) Other courts have been reluctant to intervene in discretionary decisions because they do not believe they are equipped with the administrative knowledge or time necessary to oversee the administration of sport programs effectively.

Historically, challenging sex discrimination based on the equal protection laws has not been totally effective. The constitutional standard of rational relationship has been a very difficult one for a plaintiff to challenge alleged sex discrimination successfully. The use of the intermediate standard, a more stringent test, is partly attributable to some of the recent successful challenges of alleged sex discrimination.

Another disadvantage of the equal protection laws is that they constitute a private remedy. Therefore, the plaintiff must be in a position to absorb the costs of litigation. This reduces the number of complaints filed and encourages settlement before final resolution of a number of equal protection claims.

NOTES ──

1. In *Ridgefield Women's Political Caucus, Inc. v. Fossi*, 458 F. Supp. 117 (D. Conn. 1978), girls and taxpayer parents brought claims against town selectmen seeking to prohibit the town from offering public property at a nominal price to a private organization that restricted membership to boys. The district court found for the girls and parents, ruling that the town selectmen had no right to offer land at less than fair value to the private organization in question as long as this organization restricted membership and the town failed to offer to girls comparable recreational opportunities equivalent to those provided by the organization in question. Until such services are offered, any conveyance of the property at a nominal fee would constitute govern-

mental support of sex discrimination in violation of the equal protection clause of the Fourteenth Amendment.

2. In *Kelly v. Wisconsin Interscholastic Athletic Ass'n*, 367 F. Supp. 1388 (E.D. Wis. 1973), the court held that the claim of female students excluded from participation on the male varsity swimming teams because of an association rule stated a constitutional claim under the Fourteenth Amendment against the high school association officials who, either directly or in their official capacities, allowed enforcement of such rule. The court held that the female students failed to state a cause of action on which relief could be granted (a) against the association because they failed to allege the necessary "state action"; (b) against the state superintenent of schools because they failed to allege any facts to support failure to provide due process; or (c) against the board of school directors because actions may not be maintained against municipal corporations.

3. The California Supreme Court ruled in October 1985 that "Ladies Night" discounts must be banned because they discriminate against men. The state's high court unanimously found that sex-based price discounts violate "clear and unambiguous" language of the state's civil rights act. One chief justice believed that the discount, designed to attract more female patrons, may in fact hurt both men and women, "because it reinforces harmful stereotypes ("California Bans Sex-Based Discounts," *Boston Globe*, October 18, 1985, p. 18, col. 6).

4. In *Richards v. United States Tennis Ass'n*, 400 N.Y.S.2d 267 (Sup. Ct. N.Y. County 1977), an action was brought by a professional tennis player, who had undergone a sex-change operation, against a professional tennis association which sought a preliminary injunction against the organization to prevent it from requiring the tennis player to undergo a sex-chromatin test to prove she was a female and eligible to participate in a women's tournament. The court granted the injunction and held the test was grossly unfair, discriminatory, and inequitable, and violated the tennis player's rights under the New York Human Rights Law.

Title IX

Section 901 (a) of Title IX of the Education Amendments of 1972 contains the following language:

> No person in the United States shall, on the basis of sex, be excluded from participation in, be denied the benefits of, or be subjected to discrimination under any education program or activity receiving Federal financial assistance.

Title IX became law on July 1, 1972, as Public Law 92-318. It specifically and clearly recognizes the problems of sex discrimination and forbids such discrimination in any program, organization, or agency that receives federal funds. A long process of citizen involvement preceded the first set of regulations. In July 1975, the Department of

Health, Education and Welfare (HEW) issued the regulations designed to implement Title IX.

These regulations are found in Title 45, Code of Federal Regulations (C.F.R.), section 86 A-F. The regulations were criticized by many as being vague and inadequate. In December 1978, HEW attempted to alleviate the criticism by releasing a proposed policy interpretation, which attempted to explain but did not change the 1975 requirements. However, not until December 1979, seven years after the original passage of Title IX, did the Office of Civil Rights (OCR), the successor to HEW, release the policy interpretation for Title IX. These final guidelines specifically included interscholastic and intercollegiate athletics. Developed after numerous meetings and countless revisions, they reflected comments from universities, legislative sources, and the public.

The policy interpretation focused on three areas which the OCR evaluates to determine whether an institution is in compliance with Title IX regulations with regards to athletics. First, the OCR assesses whether an institution's athletic scholarships are awarded on a "substantially proportional" basis. To determine this, the amount of scholarship money available for each sex is divided by the number of male or female participants in the athletic program and results are compared. If comparison shows "substantially equal amounts" of money spent per athlete, or if a disparity is explained by legitimate and nondiscriminatory factors, the OCR will find compliance.

The second area of assessment under the policy interpretation is the degree to which the institution provides equal treatment, benefits, and opportunities in certain program areas. The areas considered by the OCR in evaluating equal treatment include equipment, coaching, and facilities.

The final area the OCR assesses is the extent to which the institution has met the interests and abilities of male and female students. The policy interpretation requires that the school "equally and effectively" accommodate the athletic interest and abilities of both men and women. This determination requires an examination of the institution's assessment of the athletic interest and abilities of its students, its selection of offered sports, and its available competitive opportunities. The OCR evaluates the level of competitive opportunities in one of three ways:

1. Are intercollegiate competitive opportunities provided in numbers substantially proportionate to the respective enrollments of each sex?
2. Is the institution's current and historical practice of program

expansion responsive to the athletic interests of the underrepresented sex?
3. Does the institution accommodate the abilities and the interests
   of the underrepresented sex in the current program?

If the OCR determines that an institution complies with any one of
these tests, the institution is judged to have effectively accommodated
the interest and the abilities of its student-athletes.

The policy interpretation developed by the OCR contained some
strict guidelines for assessing Title IX compliance, including the
following:

1. The inclusion of football and other revenue-providing sports.
2. "Sport-specifics" comparisons as the basis for assessing compliance.
3. "Team-based" comparisons (grouping sports by levels of development) as the basis for compliance assessments.
4. Institutional planning that does not meet the provisions of the
   policy interpretation as applied by the OCR.

The policy interpretation also outlined certain "nondiscriminatory
factors" to be considered when assessing Title IX compliance. These
factors include differences that may result from the unique nature of
particular sports, special circumstances of a temporary nature, the need
for greater funding for crowd control at more popular athletic events,
and differences that have not yet been remedied but which an institution is voluntarily working to correct. In the area of compensation
for men's and women's coaches, HEW assessed rates of compensation,
length of contracts, experience, and other factors, while taking into
account mitigating conditions such as nature of duties, number of
assistants to be supervised, number of participants, and level of
competition.

The major issues raised regarding Title IX revolve around the scope
of the legislation and the programs to which it is applicable. The July
1975 policy regulations issued by HEW covered three areas of activity
within educational institutions: employment, treatment of students,
and admissions. Several sections of the regulations concerned with
the treatment of students included specific requirements for interscholastic, intercollegiate, intramural, and club athletic programs.

Athletics and athletics programs were not specifically mentioned in
Title IX when it first became law in 1972. Congress was generally
opposed to placing athletics programs under the realm of Title IX.
However, HEW, taking the position that sports and physical education
are an integral part of education, specifically included athletics, de-

spite strong lobbying efforts to exempt revenue-producing intercollegiate sports from the Title IX requirements. This specific inclusion of athletics occurred in 1974 and extended from general athletic opportunities to athletic scholarships. The principles governing athletic scholarships included the idea that all recipients of federal aid must provide *"reasonable opportunities"* for both sexes to receive scholarship aid. The existence of *"reasonable opportunities"* is determined by examining the ratio of male to female participants. Scholarship aid must then be distributed according to this participation ratio (see Title 45, *Code of Federal Regulations,* Section 86.13[c]).

Another section of the HEW Title IX regulations specifies requirements for athletic programs (see 45 C.F.R. sec. 86.41[c]). Contact sports are subject to regulations distinct from those governing non-contact sports. The regulations in this section state that separate teams are acceptable for contact sports and for teams in either contact or noncontact sports in which selection is based on competitive skill. There is one exception to the rule forbidding separate teams when selection is based on competitive skill: If a school sponsors a team in a particular sport for one sex but not for the other, and if athletic opportunities for the excluded sex have been historically more restricted than athletic opportunities for the other sex, members of the excluded sex must be allowed to try out for the team. The exception does not apply if the sport is a contact sport. For noncontact sports, if only one team exists, both sexes must be allowed to compete for positions on the team.

In assessing compliance with Title IX the OCR looks at several factors, including athletic expenditures and program components. Athletic expenditures need not be equal, but the pattern of expenditures must not result in a disparate effect on opportunity. Institutions may not discriminate in the provision of necessary equipment, supplies, facilities, and publicity for sports programs.

The OCR may use additional factors in determining whether an institution is providing equal opportunity for members of both sexes in its sports program. However, some of these factors (publicity, academic tutoring, housing, and dining services) are relevant in intercollegiate programs but are not generally relevant in assessing a sports program in a secondary school.

The procedures for Title IX analysis are established in special administrative guidelines, which list specific factors that should be examined in determining whether or not equality in athletics exists. The number of sports, the type of arrangements, and benefits offered to women competing in athletics are reviewed. When teams of one sex are favored in such areas as funding, coaching, and facilities, resulting in severely reduced opportunities for the other sex to compete, the courts will closely examine program expenditures, number of teams, and access to facilities to determine if the school is fulfilling the requirements of Title IX. As a general rule, although Title IX does not require the adoption of programs or equivalent funding, increases in either or both may be necessary to redress past discrimination.

The final area of coverage in the regulations is the method of enforcement of Title IX. Compliance with the dictates of the law is monitored by the OCR in the Department of Education (formerly part of the Department of Health, Education and Welfare). The procedure to be followed is initiated by the OCR, which makes random compliance reviews and also investigates complaints submitted by individuals. The first step in the process is to examine the records kept by the institution under investigation to review its attempted compliance with Title IX. Each institution must adopt and publish complaint procedures and designate one employee to carry out its Title IX responsibilities, including investigation of complaints. The institution must notify all students and employees of the designated employee's name, office address, and telephone number. After a preliminary review, the OCR has the option to conduct a full hearing or to drop the case.

If the OCR calls a full hearing, the institution has the right to have counsel present and to appeal an adverse decision; the complainant has neither of these rights. The affected individual is not a party involved in the hearing. Instead, the OCR becomes the complainant and pursues the claim. If the OCR finds that there has not been substantial compliance, it may turn its finding over to federal or local authorities for prosecution under the appropriate statutes (discussed in the section OCR Title IX Compliance Reviews and Enforcement later on in this chapter).

In 1990, the OCR published the *Title IX Athletics Investigator's Manual*, which is designed to assist OCR in Title IX investigations of interscholastic and intercollegiate athletics programs. This manual updates and supersedes *The Interim Title IX Intercollegiate Athletics Manual* issued July 28, 1980, and the memorandum "Guidance for Writing Title IX Intercollegiate Athletics Letters of Findings," issued March 26, 1982.

NOTES ————————————————————————————————

1. In *Lieberman v. University of Chicago*, 660 F.2d 1185 (7th Cir. 1981), *cert. denied*, 456 U.S. 937 (1982), the court held that Title IX does not provide a damages remedy, citing *Pennhurst State School and Hospital v. Halderman*, 451 U.S. 1 (1981), a case in which the Court had declined to impose upon the states as a condition of receiving federal funding the obligation to comply with the "bill of rights" section of the Developmentally Disabled Assistance

and Bill of Rights Act. An individual Title IX plaintiff is entitled only to injunctive and declaratory relief. The court reasoned that the imposition of a damages remedy might give rise to "a potentially massive financial liability" upon an institution, which could theoretically exceed the amount of the federal funds received. (Compare *Guardians Association v. Civil Service Commissioner of the City of New York*, 463 U.S. 1228 [1983], which cited *Lieberman* with approval and concluded compensatory relief is not available as a private remedy for Title VI violations not involving intentional discrimination.)

2. In *Alexander v. Yale University*, 631 F.2d 178 (2nd Cir. 1978), the court held that a party seeking relief under Title IX must demonstrate a personal "distinct and palpable injury," and the relief requested must "redound to that party's personal benefit." Former students lacked standing to get any relief from sexual harassment charges.

3. For an examination of the legislative history of Title IX in respect to athletics, see the following law review articles.

(a) Johnson, "The Evolution of Title IX: Prospects for Equality in Intercollegiate Athletics," 11 *Golden Gate U. L. Rev.* 759 (1981).

(b) Note, "Title IX and Intercollegiate Athletics: Adducing Congressional Intent," 24 *B. C. L. Rev.* 1243 (1983).

4. For further information on Title IX, see the following law review articles.

(a) Gaal, DiLorenzo and Evans, "HEW's Final 'Policy Interpretation' of Title IX and Intercollegiate Athletics," 6 *J. C. & U. L.* 345 (1980).

(b) Note, "Implementing Title IX: The HEW Regulations," 124 *U. Pa. L. Rev.* 806 (1976).

(c) Cox, "Intercollegiate Athletics and Title IX," 46 *Geo. Wash. L. Rev.* 34 (1977).

(d) Gaal and DiLorenzo, "The Legality and Requirements of HEW's Proposed 'Policy Interpretation' of Title IX and Intercollegiate Athletics," 6 *J. C. & U. L.* 161 (1980).

(e) Kadzielski, "Postsecondary Athletics in an Era of Equality: An Appraisal of the Effect of Title IX," 5 *J. C. & U. L.* 123 (1979).

(f) Comment, "Sex Discrimination in Athletics," 21 *Vill. L. Rev.* 876 (1976).

(g) Commentary, "Sex Discrimination in Athletics: Conflicting Legislative and Judicial Approaches," 29 *Ala. L. Rev.* 390 (1978).

(h) Note, "Title IX and Intercollegiate Athletics: Scoring Points for Women," 8 *Ohio N. U. L. Rev.* 481 (Summer 1981).

(i) Kadzielski, "Title IX of the Education Amendments of 1972: Change or Continuity?" 6 *J. L. & Educ.* 183 (April 1977).

(j) Comment, "Title IX's Promise of Equality of Opportunity in Athletics: Does It Cover the Bases?" 64 *Ky. L. J.* 432 (1975–76).

(k) Note, "Judicial Deference to Legislative Reality: The Interpretation of Title IX in the Context of Collegiate Athletics," 14 *N. C. Cent. L. J.* 601 (1984).

The ERA and State Equal Rights Amendments

Although there are many legal alternatives to allegations of sex discrimination, to date there has been no nationwide comprehensive prohibition of sex discrimination. Supporters of the Equal Rights Amendment (ERA) argued that passage of a constitutional amendment would remedy the lack of such a general prohibition. In order to amend the United States Constitution, the proposed amendment must first be passed by a three-fourths vote of both the United States Senate and the House of Representatives. Then it must be ratified by at least thirty-eight state legislatures. The ERA was passed in both Houses of Congress in 1972, but it did not receive the necessary thirty-eight ratifications from state legislatures by the required deadline of July 1, 1982.

While uniform prohibition of sex discrimination has not material-ized, states and the District of Columbia have enacted their own equal rights amendments. Thus, equal rights amendments have impacted on athletics at the state level but not at the federal level. Several cases have been decided in favor of the complainant on the basis of a state ERA. All of these cases, however, could have been decided on other arguments in states without ERAs.

In general, the proposed federal ERA absolutely prohibited dis-crimination based on gender and required that any law using gender as a basis for classification be subject to a strict scrutiny analysis by the courts. Opponents of the ERA claimed that this prohibition was an unnecessary step. They believed that women's rights are suffi-ciently protected by the U.S. Constitution, state equal protection laws, and other federal legislation such as the Equal Pay Act, Title VII, and Title IX.

Supporters of the ERA argued that without proper enforcement, neither Title IX nor Title VII can alleviate the basic problems of sex discrimination. The weakness of Title IX in particular is its depen-dence on federal funding, since a reduction in funding can effectively diminish the OCR's enforcement capabilities. In addition to this fi-nancial vulnerability, sex discrimination statutes are also subject to congressional revisions, which may lessen or even negate much of the available protection. It has been argued that a constitutional amend-ment would be more sheltered from fluctuating political interests.

Supporters of a constitutional amendment continue to argue that the effectiveness and importance of an equal rights amendment can be demonstrated in *Darrin v. Gould* (see note 1). In *Darrin*, the lower court considered the equal protection argument and ruled in favor of the defendant. The Washington Supreme Court, however, reversed the decision in favor of the plaintiffs, based on the state's equal rights argument. As such, the court's decision may be effectively down-graded with the subsequent passage of limiting legislation to the state ERA. Regardless of the precarious position in which protection against sex discrimination exists, the existence of an equal rights amendment on the state level is often helpful and may even be crucial to the success of sex discrimination cases.

NOTES —————————————————————————————————————

1. In *Darrin v. Gould*, 85 Wash. 2d 859, 540 P.2d 882 (1975), an action was brought by the parents of high school students Carol and Delores Darrin, who appealed a Washington Superior Court decision denying them relief in their class action claim of illegal discrimination against females in interscholastic football competition. The Washington Supreme Court found that the school board's denial of permission for the girls to compete on the boys' interscholastic contact football team constituted "a discrimination by state action based on ability to play." Under the due process clause of the Fourteenth Amendment, "performers are entitled to an individualized determination of their qualifications, not a determination based on the qualifications of a majority of the broader class of which the individual is a member." The Supreme Court decided that the Darrin girls could participate, based on the provision of Washington's Equal Rights Amendment, which stated: "Equality of rights and responsibility under the law shall not be denied or abridged on account of sex."

2. In *MacLean v. First Northwest Industries of America, Inc.*, 600 P.2d 1027 (Wash. Ct. App. 1979), a class action was brought against the city of Seattle and the corporation operating a professional basketball team that alleged "Ladies Night" price-ticketing policies were violative of the state's equal rights amendment that prohibited sex discrimination. The court of appeals reversed a lower court decision and found the ticket practice a violation of the amendment.

3. In *Commonwealth, Packal v. Pennsylvania Interscholastic Athletic Ass'n*, 18 Pa. Commw. Ct. 45, 334 A.2d 839 (1975), the state of Pennsylvania, acting through its attorney general, filed suit against the Pennsylvania Interscholastic Athletic Association (PIAA), charging that Article XIX, Section 38 of the PIAA bylaws, which states that "girls shall not compete or practice against boys in any athletic contest," was in violation of both the Fourteenth Amendment of the U.S. Constitution and Pennsylvania's equal rights amendment. Plaintiff claimed that the association's rule denied to female athletes the same opportunities to practice and compete in interscholastic sports that were afforded male athletes. Pennsylvania's ERA provides that "equality of rights under law shall not be denied or abridged in the Commonwealth of Pennsylvania because of the sex of the individual." The court found the association's rule to be "unconstitutional on its face under the ERA" and proclaimed that "none of the justifications for it offered by the PIAA, even if proved, could sustain its legality." The court found it unnecessary to consider whether or not the rule also violated the Fourteenth Amendment.

4. In *Blair v. Washington State University*, 740 P.2d 1379 (Wash. Sup. Ct. 1987), female athletes and coaches of female athletes brought a sex discrimination action under the State Equal Rights Amendment. The trial court ruled for plaintiffs and awarded damages, injunctive relief, attorney fees, and costs. On appeal, the Washington Supreme Court affirmed the lower court's con-

clusion of sex discrimation but modified the lower court's calculations of comparative scholarships for male and female athletes and attorney fees.

5. For further information on individual states' ERAs, see the following law review articles.

    (a) Broder and Wee, "Hawaii's Equal Rights Amendment: Its Impact on Athletic Opportunities and Competition for Women," 2 *U. Haw. L. Rev.* 97 (1979).

    (b) Jacklin, "Sexual Equality in High School Athletics: The Approach of *Darrin v. Gould*," 12 *Gonz. L. Rev.* 691 (Summer 1977).

6. As of 1991, the following 19 states had enacted their own individual equal rights amendments: Alaska, Arizona, California, Colorado, Connecticut, Hawaii, Illinois, Louisiana, Maryland, Massachusetts, Montana, New Hampshire, New Mexico, Pennsylvania, Texas, Utah, Virginia, Washington, and Wyoming.

An example of an equal rights amendment is Massachusetts Constitution Pt. I, Art. I, Amend. Art. 106:

> Art. CVI. Article I of Part the First of the Constitution is hereby annulled and the following is adopted:—
>
> All people are born free and equal and have certain natural, essential and unalienable rights; among which may be reckoned the right of enjoying and defending their lives and liberties; that of acquiring, possessing and protecting property; in fine, that of seeking and obtaining their safety and happiness. Equality under the law shall not be denied or abridged because of sex, race, color, creed or national origin.

7. Title IX and educational equity laws which have been passed on the state level parallel the intent and coverage of the federal Title IX legislation; thirteen states (Alaska, California, Florida, Illinois, Maine, Montana, Massachusetts, Nebraska, New Jersey, Oregon, Rhode Island, Washington, and Wisconsin) have each enacted state laws which closely mirror the federal regulation. Another eighteen states (Arizona, Colorado, Connecticut, Hawaii, Idaho, Indiana, Iowa, Kansas, Maryland, Michigan, Minnesota, New Hampshire, New York, North Carolina, Pennsylvania, South Dakota, Vermont, and Wyoming) have enacted fragmented sex equity laws which incorporate various aspects of the federal regulation.

8. The State of Florida adopted legislation to take effect January 1, 1994, which consisted of a number of gender-equity issues. This specific "gender-equity" state legislation is the first of its type. Some of the issues presented in this legislation are the following:

    (1) Membership of each statutorily created decision-making or regulatory board, commission, council, and committee of the state shall be balanced by gender (50/50 proportion).

    (2) If a district school board sponsors an athletic activity or sport that is similar to a sport for which a university in the State University System or a Florida public community college offers an athletic scholarship, it must sponsor the athletic activity or sport for which a scholarship is offered.

    (3) By July 1, 1994, the Task Force on Gender Equity in Education will have defined equity in athletics at all levels of public education and

shall recommend to the Commissioner of Education rules for appropriate enforcement mechanisms to ensure equity.

(4) An equitable portion of all separate athletics fees shall be designated for women's intercollegiate athletics. In addition, an amount equal to the sales taxes collected from admission to athletic events sponsored by an institution within the State University System shall be retained and utilized by each institution to support women's athletics.

(5) Each state university shall develop a gender equity plan which shall include consideration of equity in sports offerings, participation, availability of facilities, scholarship offerings, and funds allocated for administration, recruitment, comparable coaching, publicity and promotion, and other support costs.

(6) Any public community college or school district found to be out of compliance with the rules of gender equity, can be penalized by: declaring the educational agency ineligible for competitive state grants; and, directing the Comptroller to withhold general revenue funds.

LEGAL CHALLENGES TO TITLE IX

Legality of Title IX

The Title IX regulations and accompanying policy interpretations were promulgated by the Department of Health, Education and Welfare (HEW) and were not finalized until July 1979 after many revisions and despite remaining ambiguities. Many of the remaining questions may eventually be decided by the courts in any future interpretations of Title IX.

The first legal challenge to Title IX was brought by the NCAA. The NCAA sought declaratory and injunctive relief for the invalidation of the Title IX regulations promulgated by HEW in *National Collegiate Athletic Ass'n v. Califano*, 444 F. Supp. 425 (D. Kan. 1978), *rev'd*, 622 F.2d 1382 (10th Cir. 1980). The NCAA specifically sought relief for the invalidation of the Title IX regulations promulgated by HEW with respect to sex discrimination in athletics. Summary judgment was granted to HEW, as the district court held that the NCAA did not have standing as an association representing its member schools to pursue the suit. The NCAA appealed the district court decision. The appeals court reversed the lower court ruling and held that while the NCAA does not have standing to sue in its own right, it does have standing to sue on behalf of its members. (See the section Standing in Chapter 4, for further discussion.)

NOTE _____

1. For further information, see the following law review articles.
    (a) Cox, "Intercollegiate Athletics and Title IX," 46 *Geo. Wash. L. Rev.* 34 (1977).

(b) Note, "Sex Discrimination in High School Athletics," 47 *UMKC L. Rev.* 109 (1978).
(c) Note, "Sex Discrimination and Intercollegiate Athletics: Putting Some Muscle in Title IX," 88 *Yale L. J.* 1254 (1979).

Scope and Applicability of Title IX

Since the inception of Title IX in 1972, a major point of contention had been whether the legislation applied only to the specific departments which received direct funding (commonly referred to as the "programmatic approach") or was extended to any department within an institution that benefited from federal assistance (commonly referred to as the "institutional approach"). This dilemma had often been expressed in a debate as to whether Title IX was, or was not, program-specific.

An integral factor in the resultant litigation had been the determination of what constituted qualifying federal assistance. In some cases, it had been argued that federal student loan programs constitute federal aid to an institution, while other interpretations defined federal aid as only those funds specifically earmarked or directly given to a particular program. Therefore, in terms of the scope of Title IX, the questions became very complex: What constituted federal aid? Was indirect aid or direct aid required by the statute? Once federal assistance was found, was only the particular program that benefitted from the aid or the entire institution subject to Title IX regulation?

In March 1988 the United States Congress acted to clarify this issue when it voted overwhelmingly to override President Ronald Reagan's veto of the Civil Rights Restoration Act of 1987 (see note 9). Enactment of this legislation served, "to restore the broad scope of coverage and clarify the application of Title IX of the Education Amendments of 1972." Thus, Congress returned Title IX applicability to the "institutional approach"; accordingly, athletic departments within institutions benefitting from federal assistance are subject to the Title IX strictures.

Passage of the Civil Rights Restoration Act counteracted the effects of the Supreme Court's decision in *Grove City College v. Bell (infra)*. In this 1984 ruling, the issue of "programmatic" versus "institutional" had been decided by the highest court in favor of the "programmatic approach." Judgments in many of the cases preceding *Grove City College* had been contradictory. A programmatic approach was taken by the courts in *Othen v. Ann Arbor School Board, Bennett v. West Texas State, Hillsdale College v. Department of Health, Education, and Welfare*, and *University of Richmond v. Bell*. An institutional approach was taken by the courts in *Haffer v. Temple University*, and by the court of appeals in *Grove City College v. Bell* (see notes 4, 5, and 8).

The emergence of the Civil Rights Restoration Act has also restored strength to the administrative enforcement of Title IX. The ability of OCR to investigate effectively possible Title IX violations by institutions has always been contingent upon the prevailing judicial sentiments and legislative enactments regarding Title IX at a particular time.

After *Grove City*, OCR had to drop cases against athletic departments if it could not be established that the athletic departments or programs were direct recipients of federal funds. Cases against the University of Maryland, Auburn University, the New York School System, and at least twenty other institutions were discontinued or severely narrowed when no such connection could be found. For example, in the case of Auburn University, OCR decided it would still seek to pursue enforcement through the student financial aid program at the university, since that program did receive federal aid. Financial aid was involved in the Auburn case because OCR charged that Auburn failed "to award athletic scholarships and grants-in-aid so as to provide reasonable opportunity for such awards for students of each sex in proportion to the number of students of each sex participating in intercollegiate athletics." At the time, this strategy seemed indicative of the approach the OCR would take, because it no longer had jurisdiction over the athletic department.

Within the first year after the passage of the Restoration Act in 1988, several institutions had been named in sex-discrimination complaints. While some proponents of sex equity believed a flood of new complaints would be initiated after the passage of this legislation, it has at least created a new wave of OCR investigations after an extended period of dormancy following *Grove City College.*

While Title IX does not require the creation of athletic programs or the same sport offerings to both sexes—for example, a football program for women or a volleyball program for men—it does require equality of opportunity in accomodation of interests and abilities, in athletic scholarships, and in other benefits and opportunities.

NOTES ————————————————————————————

1. In *Yellow Springs Exempted Village School District Board of Education v. Ohio High School Athletic Ass'n*, 443 F. Supp. 753 (S.D. Ohio 1978), *aff'd*, 647 F.2d 651 (6th Cir. 1981), a suit was brought against the Ohio High School Athletic Association (OHSAA) and the Ohio Board of Education challenging the association's rule excluding girls from participation in contact sports. In 1974, two female students competed for and earned positions on the Morgan Middle School's interscholastic basketball team. The board excluded them from the team and then created a separate girls' basketball team. This action

was taken to comply with OHSAA Rule 1, section 6, which prohibited mixed-gender interscholastic athletic competition in contact sports such as basketball. Failure to exclude the girls from the team would have jeopardized the school district's membership in the association. The district court held that the "Association's exclusionary rule deprives school girls of liberty without due process of law. Freedom of personal choice in matters of 'education and acquisition of knowledge' is a liberty interest protected by the due process clause of the Fourteenth Amendment." The appeals court upheld portions of the district court's decision and ruled that Title IX focuses on "recipients" of federal aid. Since OHSAA was not itself a recipient of federal aid and does not bear the burden of noncompliance, it may not adopt a rule that limits the abilities of recipient schools to furnish equal athletic opportunities for girls and boys.

2. In *Othen v. Ann Arbor School Board*, 507 F. Supp. 1376 (E.D. Mich., 1981), *aff'd* 699 F.2d 309 (6th Cir. 1983), a complaint was filed on behalf of female student-athletes charging the Ann Arbor school board and its golf coach with sex discrimination in violation of Title IX. The father of the girls sought a temporary restraining order immediately restoring his daughters to the 1979 golf team and prohibiting discrimination "against women who want to play on the Pioneer golf team." The district court denied the motion for an injunction and found the father/daughters failed to demonstrate a likelihood of success on the merits.

The school board responded to the amended complaint with a motion for summary judgment, stating that none of the athletic programs at Pioneer received federal financial assistance and therefore were not covered by the provisions of Title IX. A school official testified that the only federal financial aid that the board received was "impact aid" in the form of payments to the school systems to compensate for increased enrollments caused by the proximity of federal facilities and the loss of tax revenue resulting from these tax-exempt federal properties. This money was channeled through the Ann Arbor school system's general fund and indirectly aided athletic programs. The school board also asserted that the golf team had always been open to both men and women, and students were accepted "as their abilities warranted."

The district court found the athletic programs at Pioneer received no direct federal assistance and the indirect federal assistance from "impact aid" was "de minimus." The court's finding that "the clear language of Title IX and the intent of Congress requires that the Act [Title IX] be applied programmatically" had important ramifications in the case. Since it was determined that the athletic programs and activities under the jurisdiction of the Ann Arbor School Board received no direct federal financial assistance, the school board was not obligated under the law to establish a golf team for girls. Therefore, the daughters were not excluded from participation, denied, or discriminated against in violation of Title IX.

3. In *Bennett v. West Texas State University*, 525 F. Supp. 77 (N.D. Tex. 1981), plaintiffs, six female athletes, filed a class action suit charging West Texas State University (WTSU) with sex discrimination, based on their denial of equal opportunity in the institution's intercollegiate athletic program. The

athletes contended that WTSU had intentionally discriminated against female athletes in the following areas:

(a) The allocation of athletic scholarship money

(b) Travel allowances, allocations, and expenditures

(c) Scheduling of games and practice times

(d) The compensation and treatment of coaches

(e) The provision of supplies, equipment, and laundry facilities

(f) The provision of support staff

(g) The provision of locker room, practice, and office facilities

(h) Authority to spend in excess of budget allocations

(i) The provision of publicity, promotion, and awards

(j) Perpetuating and aiding assistance to organizations and persons who discriminate on the basis of sex in providing aid, benefit, and service to students and employees

The athletes stated that the effect of these policies has been to exclude them from full participation and benefits thereof and subject them to sex discrimination in violation of Title IX. The district court rejected the athletes' contentions, finding that the athletic department of WTSU was not subject to Title IX regulation. The court ruled that the language of Title IX showed "the clear intent of Congress" in that the terms "recipient" and "programs" limited Title IX application to only specific programs or activities that receive direct financial assistance.

This decision was reversed without opinion after the *Grove City College* decision (see 698 F.2d 1215 [5th Cir. 1983]).

4. *Haffer v. Temple University,* 524 F. Supp. 531 (E.D. Pa. 1981), *aff'd,* 688 F.2d 14 (3rd Cir. 1982), was an appeal of the district court decision denying summary judgment to Temple University on the basis that its athletic department was not exempt from Title IX regulation. Eight women undergraduates had filed a class action suit charging Temple University with sex discrimination in its intercollegiate athletic program in violation of Title IX. Temple had requested summary judgment arguing that Title IX applied only to those educational programs or activities which received direct federal funding and that the athletic department at Temple had received no such assistance.

After an extensive examination of the federal funding received by the institution, the district court rejected Temple's request for summary judgment. The court held that "Title IX coverage is not limited to educational programs and activities that receive *earmarked* federal dollars, but also includes any program that *indirectly* benefits from the receipt of federal funds; because Temple's athletic program indirectly benefits from the large amounts of federal financial assistance furnished to the University in the form of grants and contracts, Title IX is applicable to Temple's athletic program." In addition, the court held that "even if Title IX is construed to require direct federal financing, the Temple athletic program receives and benefits from several hundred thousand dollars worth of annual federal aid, and therefore is covered under Title IX."

Temple appealed, questioning whether the court's inclusion of the athletic program under Title IX jurisdiction was consistent with the wording of the statute, which required that the education program or activity receive "federal financial assistance" as a prerequisite for its inclusion in the realm of Title IX authority. The appeals court affirmed the lower court's opinion, and rejected the "program-specific" interpretation put forth by Temple, claiming that the entire institution should be considered the "program." In referring to *Grove City College* (appellate court decision), the court suggested that "the legislators (who enacted Title IX) did not contemplate that separate, discrete and distinct components or functions of an integrated educational institution would be regarded as the individual program to which section 901 . . . refer(s)." The court added that "if Temple University as a whole is to be considered the program or activity" for Title IX purposes, it follows that because the university as a whole receives federal monies, its intercollegiate athletic department is governed by Title IX. The court held that the district court's theory that federal monies received by the institution benefited the athletic program because it freed other university money for athletic program-related purposes was consistent with its finding that Title IX was applicable.

5. In *Haffer v. Temple University*, Consent Decree, Rollin Haffer, *et al.*, filed this lawsuit against Temple University ("Temple"), complaining that Temple has violated the Equal Protection Clause of the Fourteenth Amendment of the United States Constitution, the Pennsylvania Equal Rights Amendment, and Title IX of the Education Amendments of 1972 by discriminating against women student-athletes and potential student-athletes at Temple on the basis of gender in the provision of opportunities to participate in intercollegiate athletics, athletic financial aid, and athletic resources.

While denying allegations, Temple entered into a consent decree dated June 9, 1988, settling the case of *Haffer v. Temple*, 524 F. Supp. 531 (E.D. Pa. 1981), *aff'd* 688 F.2d 14 (3rd Cir. 1982). The parties agreed to the following conditions.

1. An increase in opportunities for women to participate in intercollegiate athletics that are comparable to the opportunities provided its men students.

a. Temple will provide sufficient resources for its women's intercollegiate athletic crew team.

b. Temple will establish a women's intercollegiate athletic swimming team.

c. With respect to Temple's intercollegiate athletic teams which were in place during the 1986–87 academic year (that is, not including women's crew and swimming), certain other guidelines were established to deal with:

(1) Increases or decreases in participation.

(2) Discontinuance of teams.

d. Temple will maintain the overall percentage of women participating in intercollegiate athletics equal to the percentage of men participating if a men's team is added.

e. For the purposes of subparagraphs c and d, to determine the percentage of women and men participating in the overall intercollegiate athletic program, women and men student-athletes who participate on more than one team will be counted separately for each team on which they participate.

2. Temple will provide to its women student-athletes a percentage of athletic financial aid that, in the aggregate and averaged over three years, will not be less than two percentage points below the participation rate of women student-athletes in the overall intercollegiate athletic program, also averaged over those same three years, with certain other provisions.

3. The percentage of money that Temple will spend on its women's intercollegiate athletic teams each year, in the aggregate, will be within 10 percentage points of the participation rate of women student-athletes in the overall intercollegiate athletic program in that year, provided that expenditures on home game events, coaches' salaries and benefits, and post season competition will be excluded from the aggregate percentage requirement (these will be treated under specified guidelines agreed to by the two parties).

4. Temple will hire an additional full-time weight-training coach by February 1, 1989. Temple will provide to its women student-athletes weight-training coaching, facilities, and equipment comparable to the weight-training coaching, facilities, and equipment that it provides to its men student-athletes, consistent with the needs of each sport.

5. Temple will hire a full-time employee to promote Temple's women's intercollegiate athletics by February 1, 1989.

6. Temple continues to recognize that its women student-athletes are entitled to treatment that is comparable to the treatment provided to its men student-athletes in the remaining aspects of the intercollegiate athletic program beyond those addressed in paragraphs 1 through 5 of this Consent Decree.

a. Subject to the steps set forth in subparagraph b below, Temple will continue to provide treatment to its women student-athletes that is comparable to the treatment it provides to its men student-athletes in the following areas:

(1) Athletic administration, including the assignment of support staff.

(2) Locker rooms and practice, competitive, and other facilities.

(3) Athletic medicine, including medical and training services and facilities.

(4) Uniform and equipment managers and other uniform and equipment-related support, including laundry.

(5) Academic advising, including the provision of tutors to accompany teams on trips when both the academic advisor and head coach determine that it is necessary.

(6) Awards and honors.

(7) Practice and competitive scheduling.

(8) Sports information.

(9) Fundraising.

(10) Cheerleaders, band(s), and mascot(s).

b. Temple will:

(1) By November 1, 1988, carpet the women's locker room at Temple Stadium.

(2) Rearrange the awards in the intercollegiate athletic award display cases so that the women's awards are exhibited in a manner comparable to that of the men's awards.

7. By October 1, 1989, and by October 1 of each year thereafter, Temple will file with the Court and serve on plaintiffs' counsel reports setting forth Temple's compliance with the terms of this Consent Decree for the immediately preceding academic year (these reports have extensive requirements which are outlined in detail in the Consent Decree).

6. In *Hillsdale College v. Department of Health, Education and Welfare,* 696 F.2d 418 (6th Cir. 1982), HEW issued an order disqualifying students from participation in federal aid programs in response to the refusal of Hillsdale's officials to sign an "assurance of compliance" with Title IX. Hillsdale appealed the HEW order. The court reversed and held for Hillsdale, reasoning that because Congress failed to adopt proposals that would have prohibited

all discriminatory practices of an institution that receives federal funds, it was clear that, as enacted, Title IX adopts a "programmatic as opposed to institutional approach to discrimination on the basis of sex in education." Even though the court found that Hillsdale was subject to Title IX regulations in those programs receiving federal financial assistance, the court believed that while HEW had been given the authority to promulgate regulations for Title IX enforcement, in this case, the order imposed was in excess of statutory authority in that it would subject the entire college, rather than any one program, to the strictures of Title IX.

7. In *North Haven Board of Education v. Bell*, 456 U.S. 512 (1982), a tenured teacher in the North Haven public school district filed a complaint on her behalf and others with HEW and its secretary, Bell, alleging that North Haven had violated Title IX by refusing to rehire her after a one-year maternity leave. The district court agreed with the defendant's claim that Title IX was not intended to apply to employment practices. The U.S. Supreme Court, however, affirmed a Second Circuit Court of Appeals decision which examined Title IX's legislative history and concluded that it was intended to prohibit employment discrimination.

8. In *Grove City College v. Bell*, 465 U.S. 555, (1984), a private, liberal arts college refused to execute an "assurance of compliance" with Title IX. The Department of Education initiated proceedings to declare the college and its students ineligible to receive basic educational opportunity grants (BEOGs), and the college and four of its students filed suit after an administrative law judge ordered federal financial assistance terminated until Grove City met the requirements of Title IX. The U.S. Supreme Court ruled that the language of Title IX made it program-specific, that only those programs directly receiving federal funds were subject to the regulations of Title IX. This ruling applies to schools that participate in the BEOG program. Otherwise, one student receiving federal aid would trigger Title IX coverage of the entire institution. This does not square with the program-specific language of the legislation.

9. The following is language from the Civil Rights Restoration Act of 1987 which restores the impact of Title IX on athletic departments:

PUBLIC LAW 100–259—MAR. 22, 1988

Public Law 100–259
100th Congress

An Act

To restore the broad scope of coverage and to clarify the application of title IX of the Education Amendments of 1972, section 504 of the Rehabilitation Act of 1973, the Age Discrimination Act of 1975, and title VI of the Civil Rights Act of 1964.

Be it enacted by the Senate and House of Representatives of the United States of America in Congress assembled,

SHORT TITLE

SECTION 1. This Act may be cited as the "Civil Rights Restoration Act of 1987".

FINDINGS OF CONGRESS

SEC. 2. The Congress finds that—

(1) certain aspects of recent decisions and opinions of the Supreme Court have unduly narrowed or cast doubt upon the broad application of title IX of the Education Amendments of 1972, section 504 of the Rehabilitation Act of 1973, the Age Discrimination Act of 1975, and title VI of the Civil Rights Act of 1964; and

(2) legislative action is necessary to restore the prior consistent and long-standing executive branch interpretation and broad, institution-wide application of those laws as previously administered.

EDUCATION AMENDMENTS AMENDMENTS

SEC. 3. (a) Title IX of the Education Amendments of 1972 is amended by adding at the end the following new sections:

"INTERPRETATION OF 'PROGRAM OR ACTIVITY'"

"SEC. 908. For the purposes of this title, the term 'program or activity' and 'program' mean all of the operations of—

"(1)(A) a department, agency, special purpose district, or other instrumentality of a State or of a local government; or

"(B) the entity of such State or local government that distributes such assistance and each such department or agency (and each other State or local government entity) to which the assistance is extended, in the case of assistance to a State or local government;

"(2)(A) a college, university, or other post-secondary institution, or a public system of higher education; or

"(B) a local educational agency (as defined in section 198(a)(10) of the Elementary and Secondary Education Act of 1965), system of vocational education, or other school system;

"(3)(A) an entire corporation, partnership, or other private organization, or an entire sole proprietorship—

"(i) if assistance is extended to such corporation, partnership, private organization, or sole proprietorship as a whole; or

"(ii) which is principally engaged in the business of providing education, health care, housing, social services, or parks and recreation; or

"(B) the entire plant or other comparable, geographically separate facility to which Federal financial assistance is extended, in the case of any other corporation, partnership, private organization, or sole proprietorship; or

"(4) any other entity which is established by two or more of the entities described in paragraph (1), (2), or (3);

any part of which is extended Federal financial assistance, except that such term does not include any operation of an entity which is controlled by a religious organization if the application of section 901 to such operation would not be consistent with the religious tenets of such organization."

Post-Civil Rights Restoration Act Litigation

The passage of the Civil Rights Restoration Act in 1988 restored the power to Title IX legislation in its applicability to athletic programs across the country. Another step that also was crucial to providing clear guidelines in the interpretation of Title IX legislation and what Title IX compliance involves was the publication of the *Title IX Ath-*

letics Investigator's Manual in 1990 by the Office for Civil Rights. This manual supersedes the *Interim Title IX Intercollegiate Athletics Manual 1980,* and the memorandum "Guidance for Writing Title IX Intercollegiate Athletics Letters of Findings," issued in 1982. This recent manual set out three main areas that are involved in Title IX compliance and would be investigated by the OCR and the courts when ruling on whether an institution is complying with Title IX.

The first area that is investigated is that of financial assistance. This area determines whether athletics scholarships are awarded on a "substantially proportional" basis between the sexes. In analyzing this area, the OCR and the courts determine the proportion of scholarship dollars that are spent on male and female athletes and compare this proportion to the proportion of athletes of each sex. These proportions should be equivalent when an institution is complying with Title IX.

For example, compare schools A, B, and C. At school A, 50 percent of the athletes are female, but only 25 percent of the total financial assistance goes to females. At school B, 50 percent of the athletes are female, and 45 percent of the financial assistance goes to females. At school C, 50 percent of the athletes are female and 50 percent of the financial assistance goes to females. School A would not be in compliance with Title IX because the 25 percent assistance to females is significantly below the 50 percent participation rate. School C is clearly in compliance because the proportion of financial assistance equals the proportion of participation to females. School B's situation requires further analysis. When the proportions are not exactly equal, but close, the OCR applies certain statistical tests to determine whether the proportions are substantially equal.

The policy manual also suggests certain nondiscriminatory factors that may explain disparities in financial assistance to men's and women's athletic programs. An example of a nondiscriminatory factor would be the difference between in-state and out-of-state tuition. Two students may both have a tuition waiver for one year, but since one of the students is from out of state his or her waiver has a much higher price tag.

The second area that is investigated concerns the benefits and opportunities that the athletes of each sex receive. The OCR has distinguished eleven program component areas that have been targeted when investigating this area:

- Provision of equipment and supplies
- Scheduling of games and practice times
- Travel and per diem allowances
- Opportunity to receive academic tutoring, assignment, and compensation of tutors

- Opportunity to receive coaching, assignment, and compensation of coaches
- Provision of locker rooms, practice, and competitive facilities
- Provision of medical and training facilities and services
- Provision of housing and dining facilities and services
- Publicity
- Provision of support services
- Recruitment of student-athletes

Title IX requires that both sexes receive comparable or equivalent services in each of these program component areas. The *Investigator's Manual* identifies, though, some potential differences that do not cause the institution to be out of compliance with Title IX. These differences are allowed if they are based on certain factors the OCR has identified as nondiscriminatory:

- Unique nature of particular sports
- Special circumstances of a temporary nature
- The need for greater funding for crowd control at more popular athletic events
- Differences that have not yet been remedied but which an institution is voluntarily working to correct

As long as these differences in the program component areas are based on one of the previous nondiscriminatory factors, the OCR and the courts have not found noncompliance with Title IX.

The third area that is identified in the *Investigator's Manual* and is analyzed by the OCR and the courts regarding Title IX compliance is that of accommodation of student interests and abilities. In analyzing this area, the OCR and the courts must determine the extent to which the institution has met the interests and abilities of male and female students. In other words, a determination must be made as to whether there are equal opportunities to compete for both men and women, and whether the opportunities to compete are at equivalent levels of competition. In analyzing this particular area, the OCR and the courts compare the ratio of male and female athletes to the ratio of undergraduate full-time students for each sex. The ratios should be equivalent.

Of the three areas discussed previously; financial assistance, athletic benefits and opportunities, and effective accommodation of athletic interests and abilities, that are used when investigating Title IX compliance at institutions, cases subsequent to the passage of the Civil Rights Restoration Act have focused on the analysis of the accommodation of interests and abilities area. This type of analysis is evident in *Cohen, et al. v. Brown University, et al.*, Case No. 92-2483 (1st Cir. 1993), *infra; Favia, et al. v. Indiana University of Pennsylvania, et al.*, C.A. No. 92-2045 (W.D. Pa. 1992) (see note 1); *Roberts, et al. v. Colorado State University*, C.A. No. 92-A-1310 (Colo. Dist. Ct. 1993) (see note 2); and *Cook, et al. v. Colgate University*, Case No. 90-CV-411 (N.D. N.Y. 1992) (in the section Varsity Sport Versus Club Sport). In the *Brown University* case, plaintiff female student-athletes brought a Title IX compliant against the university after the sports of women's gymnastics and women's volleyball, along with men's golf and men's water polo, were dropped to club status in the spring of 1991 because of financial difficulties the university was experiencing. The plaintiffs claimed that Brown violated the "equal opportunity" provision of Title IX and that the interests and abilities of the female student-athletes were not being effectively accommodated.

The district court, 809 F. Supp. 978 (D.R.I. 1992), granted a preliminary injunction against Brown University ordering the immediate restoration of the women's gymnastics and women's volleyball team to their former status as fully funded intercollegiate varsity teams. The First Circuit Court of Appeals upheld the district court's preliminary injunction, stating that the ordering of Brown University to return the two women's sport programs to varsity status was a fair and lawful solution. Both of these courts applied a three-part test in determining the accommodation of interests and abilities issue:

1. Whether intercollegiate level participation opportunities for male and female students are provided in numbers substantially proportionate to their respective enrollments; or
2. Where the members of one sex have been and are underrepresented among intercollegiate athletes, whether the institution can show a history and continuing practice of program expansion which is demonstrably responsive to the developing interest and abilities of the members of that sex; or
3. Where the members of one sex are underererepresented among intercollegiate athletes, and the institution cannot show a continuing practice of program expansion such as that cited, whether it can be demonstrated that the interests and abilities of the members of that sex have been fully and effectively accommodated by the present program.

The plaintiffs argued that Brown University did not meet any of these requirements because the female athlete proportion stood at 39 percent compared to an undergraduate female enrollment of 48 percent to 49 percent, and no women's varsity sport had been added since 1982. The university failed to meet the third part of the three-part test because they refused on a couple of occasions to elevate the women's fencing team to varsity status.

Brown University argued that the plaintiffs were not interpreting Title IX legislation accurately. Brown asserted that Title IX provisions explicitly recognize that equal opportunity does not require proportionality, and that the interests and abilities of the students, not the relative proportion of the sexes, determine what participation opportunities must be offered to each sex. Brown stated that the 60 percent male to 40 percent female athletic participation ratio was merely a reflection of the interests and abilities of the students. Therefore, Brown was effectively accommodating the interests and abilities of the students through the participation opportunities they were providing. Brown University also argued that if Title IX required full and effective accommodation of the underrepresented gender, then this requirement would violate the Fifth Amendment's equal protection clause by putting male athletes at a disadvantage.

The district court and court of appeals, in addressing both the plaintiff's and defendant's arguments, found that with the demotion of the four sports, two women's teams and two men's teams, from varsity to club status, the percentage of male and female athletes did not change. Thus, women athletes at Brown still constituted 39 percent of the total number of student-athletes. The courts went on to say that this was not an example of effectively accommodating the interests and abilities of the underrepresented sex because women were interested in competing and participating in additional activities, as the interest and talent on campus sufficient to support the women's gymnastics and volleyball teams show. This was a critical ruling by the court which sets a standard for women in that full accommodation of the interests and abilities of the underrepresented gender must be met and that Brown's argument regarding their 60/40 participation proportion as being appropriate will not hold when analyzing Title IX compliance. In addition, keeping the percentage of female athletes at 39 percent does not effectively accommodate the equitable proportion of athletic opportunities available to each sex requirement of Title IX. The full accommodation test was not met by Brown and therefore a violation of Title IX was occurring. The court of appeals discussed the Fifth Amendment argument and ruled that Brown supplied no evidence that showed men were more likely to engage in athletics than women. In addition, the court stated that in view of congressional and administrative urging that women, if given the opportunity, will naturally participate in athletics in numbers equal to those of men, the court did not find that the regulation offended the Fifth Amendment.

The court of appeals upheld the district court's granting of a preliminary injunction which ordered Brown University to restore the women's gymnastics and women's volleyball teams to their previous varsity status. These rulings were based on analysis of one part, effectively accommodating the interests and abilities of the underrepresented sex, of the three areas the Title IX Policy Interpretations state should be used when investigating Title IX compliance. Other Title IX cases and court decisions have also used the analysis of the interests and abilities component to rule on Title IX compliance cases (see notes 1 and 2).

NOTES _____

1. In *Favia, et al. v. Indiana University of Pennsylvania, et al.*, C.A. No. 92-2045 (W.D. Pa. 1992), Indiana University of Pennsylvania announced in August 1991 that the women's gymnastics and field hockey teams, along with the men's soccer and tennis teams, would be eliminated as a result of a reduction in the athletic department's budget. Indiana University of Pennsylvania had an undergraduate enrollment of 44 percent men compared to 56 percent women, while the athletic department comprised 62 percent men and 38 percent women. After the elimination of these four teams, the percentage of male and female athletes would not change. Women students brought a lawsuit arguing violation of Title IX and sought the reinstatement of the two women's teams. In ruling in favor of the plaintiffs, the court applied the three-part test contained in the Policy Interpretation: comparison of athletic participation opportunities for each sex proportionate to their respective enrollments; whether the institution can show a history and continuing practice of program expansion; and whether the interests and abilities of the members of the underrepresented sex have been fully and effectively accommodated by the present program. The court found that Indiana University of Pennsylvania had failed to override the proportionality requirement of the test by failing to show a history of expanding the number of athletic opportunities for women or demonstrating that it had fully and effectively accommodated the interests and abilities of women students. The court ordered the immediate restoration of the two women's teams to their former status, with university backing and funding equivalent to that furnished during their last year as a varsity team.

2. In *Roberts, et al. v. Colorado State University*, C.A. No. 92-A-1310 (Colo. Dist. Ct., 1993), plaintiffs contend that a violation of Title IX occurred and/or has been occurring at Colorado State University after the women's softball team was terminated on June 1, 1992. The court used the same three-part "effective accommodation" test used in the *Brown* and *Favia* cases. The court stated that the plaintiffs had the burden of proving the first prong, that participation opportunities for male and female students are not proportionate to their respective enrollments. Once the plaintiffs established this lack of proportionality, then the defendants had the burden of proving either the second prong, that the institution could show a history and continuing practice of program expansion, or the third prong, that the institution can demonstrate that the interests and abilities of the underrepresented sex have been accommodated, existed. After the termination of the women's softball team, women

athletes made up approximately 38 percent of the athletes while enrollment of women at Colorado State University was 48 percent of the undergraduate student population. The court found that the percentage of female athletes was not substantially proportionate to the undergraduate enrollment percentage of females, and that the defendants could not show evidence of program expansion so that the interests and abilities of the female students were being effectively accommodated. The court, therefore, found a violation of Title IX and ordered Colorado State University to reinstate the women's softball team.

Ironically, Colorado State University had already gone through a Title IX compliance review conducted by the Office for Civil Rights in which the university had proposed a corrective action plan in 1983 which involved increasing female athlete participation up to 46.5 percent by the 1987–88 school year. This plan was not carried out, as evidence presented in this case showed that the athletic participation percentage for women at Colorado State University during the 1987–88 school year was 33.8 percent.

3. For further information, see Office for Civil Rights, *Title IX Athletics Investigator's Manual 1990.*

OCR TITLE IX COMPLIANCE REVIEWS AND ENFORCEMENT

The Office of Civil Rights is responsible for conducting compliance reviews of Title IX. The OCR selects schools at random to review for Title IX compliance and also reviews schools based on complaints brought by individuals. Educational institutions are required to keep and submit to the Department of Education accurate compliance reports to enable it to determine whether Title IX requirements have been satisfied. The educational institution is also required to permit access by the Department of Education to its books, records, accounts, and other sources of information, and its facilities, that may be pertinent to ascertaining compliance. Considerations of privacy or confidentiality will not restrict access. The OCR, in regards to Title IX violations in athletics, begins its investigations by notifying the schools and then collecting data on the overall athletic program. The information may include the number of teams, scheduling of games and practice times, travel and per diem allowances, compensation of coaches, provision of facilities, and amount of publicity (press releases and media guides, etc.). Aggrieved individuals may also sue an institution directly, without being required to rely on the enforcement mechanism of the Department of Education (see note 2). On the basis of a review of the data, the OCR will determine whether or not equivalent treatment, benefits, and opportunities as mandated by Title IX have been afforded to both sexes.

A finding of inequality in a single component of the program is not a basis in and of itself for the OCR to find a school in noncompliance with Title IX. The OCR's approach in investigating and determining compliance with Title IX has been to focus on the overall provision of equivalent opportunities in the athletic program. Therefore, the OCR will look to other components of the athletic program before it finds the school to be in noncompliance. In addition, Secretary Terrel H. Bell of the Department of Education adopted a nonconfrontation approach in 1981. Under this policy, the OCR may find schools in compliance with Title IX if the schools agree to rectify any violations of Title IX found through the OCR's investigation.

OCR officials will meet with the administrators of an investigated institution and review the OCR's proposed findings before a letter of noncompliance is issued. If the institution voluntarily forms a committee to adopt a plan to rectify its violations within a reasonable period, the institution will be granted a letter of compliance because it is implementing a corrective plan. The Department of Education is then responsible for monitoring the progress of the plan. If the plan is not implemented within the time specified or proves to be an inadequate remedy, the institution will be found in noncompliance and further legal action against the school could be taken.

If there is a failure to comply with Title IX, or a voluntary compliance agreement cannot be reached, or the violations cannot be corrected by informal means, compliance may be effected by the suspension or termination of, or refusal to grant or to continue, federal financial assistance. Additionally, the Department of Education may refer the matter to the Department of Justice, with a recommendation that appropriate proceedings be brought to enforce any rights of the United States.

Prior to suspending, terminating, or refusing to grant or continue federal financial assistance, an institution must be afforded the opportunity to a hearing before an administrative law judge. If the educational institution does not request a hearing within the time allowed, the right to the hearing is waived and a decision will be made on the basis of the information then on file.

After a hearing is held, the hearing judge will either make an initial decision on the institution's compliance or certify the entire record, including his or her recommended findings and proposed decision, to the appropriate reviewing authority for a final decision. Both the Department of Education and the institution may appeal that determination to the department's reviewing authority. If the reviewing authority affirms the administrative law judge's decision, the institution may request a review by the secretary of education.

If the Department of Education decides to withdraw funding, it must report that decision to the appropriate congressional committees thirty days prior to the termination of funds. Having exhausted its administrative remedies, the institution could then seek judicial review of the department's actions.

In the area of athletics, the Department of Education rarely applies the formal administrative process to terminate funds to enforce Title IX regulations. The formal enforcement process is usually avoided because institutions have typically developed voluntary compliance plans acceptable to the OCR.

NOTES ────────────────────────────────────

1. In *Office of Civil Rights Title IX Compliance Review of the University of Akron*, the OCR selected the University of Akron for a Title IX compliance review of the university's intercollegiate athletics program. Various complaints alleged that the university discriminated against female athletes in selection of sports and levels of competition. For example, the school had no varsity track team for women, and it offered no scholarships for women athletes.

The OCR found that the University of Akron provided men and women equivalent treatment in five areas: (1) provision and maintenance of equipment and supplies, (2) travel and per-diem allowances, (3) provision of housing and dining services and facilities, (4) publicity, and (5) support services.

The OCR found that benefits, opportunities, and treatment were not equivalent in the areas of (1) scheduling of games and practice times, (2) opportunity to receive coaching, (3) provision of locker rooms, practice, and competitive facilities, (4) provision of medical and training facilities and services, (5) recruitment of student-athletes, and (6) accommodation of student interests and abilities. The OCR concluded that these disparities violated Title IX. However, the University of Akron was implementing a plan that would remedy the disparities within a reasonable period of time. Therefore, the university was found to be in compliance with Title IX.

2. In *Office of Civil Rights Title IX Compliance Review of University of Iowa*, the OCR investigated the women's athletic program at the University of Iowa. The sports information director's (SID) staff for the University of Iowa's women's program consisted of a full-time director, a quarter-time graduate assistant, two part-time assistants, and a student volunteer. It was determined that the provisions of publicity personnel were not equivalent because the lack of professional, travel, and clerical support severely limited the ability of the women's sports information director to perform tasks critical to her job function.

The following problem areas in the Iowa SID operation also were addressed by the OCR:

(a) Men's basketball, football, and wrestling received radio and TV coverage. Women's team events were broadcast occasionally on local radio.

(b) A newsletter that provided information about men's programs was sent to local high schools from six to eight times a year. No such service was rendered for the women's program.

(c) All media guides for the women's programs were mimeographed on plain paper and contained limited data. No recruitment brochures were provided. Three of the media guides for the men's programs were printed books that contained color photographs. All guides contained a great variety of data on the individual players, the coaches, and the facilities. The disparity present in the provision of publications was found to be of concern because of the impact they have on recruiting and attendance figures.

The following remedial actions were taken by the University of Iowa:

(a) A commitment was made to provide equivalent services and publications.

(b) A centrally located SID office encompassing a women's SID, a men's SID, and a pooled staff of assistants was established.

(c) A marketing assistant for men's minor sports and women's athletics was hired.

3. In *Cannon v. University of Chicago*, 406 F. Supp. 1257 (N.D. Ill. 1976), *aff'd on rehearing*, 559 F.2d 1077 (7th Cir. 1979), *rev'd*, 441 U.S. 677 (1979), *cert. denied*, 460 U.S. 1013 (1983), the Supreme Court reversed the lower courts and held that a private right of action will be implied under Title IX. Also, the Court said that administrative remedies need not be exhausted before filing suit in federal court.

4. See Exhibit 8–1 for a Title IX compliance checklist from the perspective of the educational institutions.

NCAA GENDER EQUITY STUDY AND TASK FORCE

The National Collegiate Athletic Association has become involved in the issue of sex discrimination in athletics through the study of the concept of gender equity. Gender equity is defined as "an athletics program is gender equitable when either the men's or women's sports program would be pleased to accept as its own the overall program of the other gender" (NCAA Gender-Equity Task Force, 1993). Thus, such areas as scholarship dollars, operational budgets, coaches' compensation, along with total number of sport programs and athletic opportunities available to each sex are addressed.

In the summer of 1991, in response to a resolution submitted by the National Association of Collegiate Women Athletic Administrators (NACWAA), the NCAA conducted a Gender-Equity Study. The results from this study were published in March 1992 and generated a great deal of attention and concern among athletic administrators, coaches, and athletes interested in Title IX and gender equity. The following are some of the results for Division I institutions from this NCAA Gender-Equity Study:

- Ratio of male athletic participants to female athletic participants = 2.24:1

Exhibit 8–1
Title IX Compliance Checklist

- Determine whether Title IX applies to the educational institution.
- If Title IX is applicable to the educational institution, determine the specific programs or activities (including athletics) which must be conformed to Title IX requirements.
- Evaluate, from time to time, the athletic department's policies and practices and their effects concerning treatment of student-athletes, and employment of both athletic and non-athletic personnel working in connection with its program or activity.
- Modify any policies and practices of the athletic department which do not or may not meet the requirements of Title IX.
- Take appropriate remedial steps to eliminate the effects of any discrimination which may have resulted from adherence to policies and practices which did not conform to Title IX.
- When applying for federal financial assistance for any athletic program or activity, execute and deliver an assurance that each athletic program or activity to which Title IX applies will be operated in compliance with its requirements.
- Designate at least one employee to coordinate the athletic department's efforts to comply with and carry out its responsibilities under Title IX, including investigation of any complaint communicated to the department alleging noncompliance with Title IX.
- Adopt and publish grievance procedures providing for prompt and equitable resolution of student-athlete and employee complaints alleging any action which does not conform to Title IX.
- Implement specific and continuing steps to notify applicants for employment, student-athletes and parents of student-athletes, employees, sources of referral of applicants for employment, and all unions or professional organizations holding collective bargaining or professional agreements with the athletic department, that it does not discriminate contrary to Title IX.
- Prominently include a statement of the athletic department's non-discrimination policy in each announcement, bulletin, catalog, or application.
- Comply with Title IX in programs subject to its application, unless an exemption applies.
- Keep such compliance reports as required by the Department of Education, including data showing the extent to which members of each sex are beneficiaries of and participants in federally-assisted programs and activities of the athletic department.
- Recognize that a claim of sex discrimination may be based on grounds other than Title IX, including the equal protection clause of the Fourteenth Amendment to the United States Constitution.

- Ratio of male scholarship expenses to female scholarship expenses = 2.28:1
- Institutional average operating expenses for males = $612,206 compared to females = $179,078
- Average recruiting expenses for males = $139,152 compared to females = $28,840
- Of head coaches of male sports 98.6 percent are men, while 55.2 percent of the head coaches of female sports are men
- Institutional average for male head coach salaries = $272,057 while female head coach salaries = $149,740. (NCAA Gender-Equity Study, March 1992)

The results for just Division I-A institutions indicated more pronounced differences (i.e., ratio of male participants to female participants was 2.49:1).

As a result of this NCAA Gender-Equity Study and the information compiled, many people in the collegiate athletic community were alarmed, and the NCAA formed a Gender-Equity Task Force which was given the charge "to develop a definition of gender equity; to assure that no NCAA policy, practice or legislation could deter a member institution from compliance with Federal or state law relevant to gender equity; to examine the policies of the Association for gender bias; to attempt to correct any such policy, and to assist the member institutions in achieving gender equity" (NCAA Gender-Equity Preliminary Report, May 14, 1993). This committee released a preliminary report in May 1993 which included proposed legislation that would be put before the NCAA membership at the January 1994 Convention for possible adoption. This proposed legislation included the following:

a. Emerging Sports for Women
   (1) Recommended any two emerging sports be acceptable toward meeting the minimum sports-sponsorship requirements; further, established minimum contests and participants and maximum financial aid limitations in the following emerging sports: team sports—crew, ice hockey, team handball, water polo; individual sports—archery, badminton, bowling, and squash. Also, minimum number of contests and participants and maximum financial aid limits were established for each emerging sport.
   (2) Recommended that all of the identified emerging sports be countable for purposes of revenue distribution (i.e., for sports sponsorship and grants-in-aid).
b. Financial Aid
   (1) Recommended an increase in the maximum financial aid limitations for Divisions I and II women's sports. The subcommittee rec-

ommended no changes in the existing financial aid limitations for Divisions I and II men's sports.

(2) Recommended that the NCAA Council request the NCAA Committee on Financial Aid and Amateurism and the NCAA Special Committee to Review Financial Conditions in Intercollegiate Athletics to develop a new financial aid model to decrease the amount of available athletics aid to student-athletes that is not based on need. Legislation should be proposed no later than the 1995 NCAA Convention with a grandparent clause to exempt student-athletes who are already enrolled in collegiate institutions and receiving athletics aid from the application of such legislation. (NCAA Gender-Equity Preliminary Report, May 14, 1993)

Other recommendations put forth by the NCAA Gender-Equity Task Force included additional NCAA-sponsored championships for women; the exploration of the addition of one graduate assistant or volunteer coach, who must be a female, to the numbers of allowable coaches in men's and women's sports, not including football and basketball; and the recommendation that institutions conduct gender-equity self-studies and formulate strategies to address their inequities in a timely manner.

The issue of gender equity is in the forefront of serious issues being addressed in relation to collegiate athletics in the 1990s. With the increased awareness and involvement of major athletic organizations (National Collegiate Athletic Association, National Association of Collegiate Women Athletic Administrators, National Federation of State High School Associations, the United States Olympic Committee, etc.) across the country in regard to this issue, the area of sex discrimination in college athletics is undergoing a change. How institutions and college athletics deal with Title IX and gender equity may have far-reaching implications for athletics.

NOTES ————————————————————————————————

1. For more information see the "NCAA Gender-Equity Task Force Report," *NCAA News*, May 19, 1993, p. 16.

2. The *NCAA Gender-Equity Task Force Preliminary Report* was one step toward addressing the issue of gender equity in the collegiate athletic setting. Other steps include attention brought to this issue by conferences and individual institutions across the country. The Big Ten conference has instituted a mandate calling for 60/40 participation figures within five years for male and female athletes as well as identifying emerging sports for women that will be sponsored by the conference. The University of Iowa has gone a step further, proposing 50/50 participation figures and number of scholarships for male and female student-athletes within a five-year plan. The Southeastern Conference adopted a gender equity policy in June 1993 which requires schools to provide at least two more women's sports programs than the number

of sports programs for men. This policy is effective August 1, 1995, and also requires equitable funding of women's and men's programs in all areas, including equipment, scholarships, and coaches' compensation.

3. The State of Florida in 1993 passed legislation regarding gender equity which, among other things, requires school districts to sponsor sports for which athletic scholarships at the collegiate level are given, requires each state university to develop a gender equity plan, requires membership of each state committee to be balanced by gender (50/50 proportion), requires an equitable portion of athletics fees and admission fees to athletic events to be designated for women's intercollegiate athletics, and states that any public community college or school district found to be out of compliance with the rules of gender equity can be penalized through the forfeiture of state grants and general revenue funds.

SEX DISCRIMINATION CASES INVOLVING INDIVIDUAL ATHLETES

The subsections and cases that follow are discussed in terms of the presence or absence of teams available to either sex. Within each category, the subsections and cases are further divided into those dealing with contact and those dealing with noncontact sports. This was done because the approach taken—and sometimes the results reached—by the courts is different because of the type of sports involved.

The division of subsections and cases is not by legal theory, since very often the litigation makes use of one, two, or even three prominent theories—for example, equal protection, Title IX, and state equal rights amendments (in certain states). To distinguish between the cases would therefore entail too much repetition without sufficiently differentiating the decisions.

The courts view contact sports and noncontact sports differently. Thus, in cases involving sex discrimination in athletics, the arguments used will vary depending on whether or not the particular sport is designated a contact sport. Under Title IX, contact sports include boxing, wrestling, rugby, ice hockey, football, basketball, and other sports in which the purpose or major activity involves bodily contact. In some jurisdictions, baseball and soccer have also been labeled contact sports.

In a sport designated "contact," certain arguments are commonly propounded. The most frequent argument raised by defendants is that women, as a group, lack the physical qualifications necessary for safe and reasonable competition against men in a sport in which bodily contact is expected to occur. It is argued that women are more susceptible to injury because they have a higher percentage of adipose (fatty) tissues and a lighter bone structure. Because of these physiological differences, the argument goes, contact sports are dangerous for all women.

Plaintiffs counter this argument by insisting that determinations of physical capability should be made on a case-by-case basis. When there is no other opportunity for participation in a certain sport, a blanket prohibition is overinclusive and violates equal protection by assuming that all women have identical physical structures and that all men are stronger and more athletically capable than women. Indeed, the health and safety rationale behind such total exclusion may fail a court challenge, as has been demonstrated in some cases. In one case, a woman who was five feet nine inches tall and weighed over two hundred pounds was denied a chance to play football because her supposedly lighter bone structure would render her more susceptible to injury. There were, however, no height or weight requirements for men, and the court thus found exclusion from participation to be unacceptable. (See *Clinton v. Nagy* in the section Contact Sports.)

Although the most important consideration used to substantiate separate teams for contact sports is the health and safety of the participants, this argument does not apply to noncontact sports. Since there is no legitimate and important state interest for allowing exclusion from noncontact sports, citing sex as the sole exclusionary factor would constitute a violation of the U.S. constitutional guarantees of the equal protection clause. Thus, the arguments made by defendants in noncontact sports sex discrimination cases are different.

The most common argument is that if men and women are allowed to compete together and/or against each other, the psychological development of both would be impaired. This stance is generally based on a variation of the "tradition" argument, which says that allowing men and women to compete as equals will irreparably disturb the innate nature of relationships between the sexes.

Another commonly made argument is that if men and women are allowed to compete together, men will dominate the co-ed teams. The underlying rationale here is that since men are inherently stronger and more physically capable than women, co-ed teams will actually limit opportunities for women. Plaintiffs argue that a justification of this sort does not take into account individual differences among participants. It also does not recognize the argument that if women are given opportunities to compete against men from the beginning of their athletic careers, their capabilities would improve and men might not be able to totally dominate the athletic field.

Men's Team, No Women's Team

The general rule in both contact and noncontact sports is that when only one team is available, both sexes must be allowed to try out for and play on that team. Determinations as to the student-athlete's capability and risk of injury must be made on an individual basis, with the recognition that the contact or noncontact sports designations only make a difference if there is opportunity for athletes of both sexes to compete. If there is ample opportunity for women to compete on their own, courts appear to be less apt to allow women to compete with men in contact sports.

NOTE ————————————————————————————————

1. For further information, see the following law review articles.
   (a) Wien, "The Case for Equality in Athletics," 22 *Cleve. St. L. Rev.* 570 (1973).
   (b) Skilton, "The Emergent Law of Women and Amateur Sports: Recent Developments," 28 *Wayne L. Rev.* 1701 (Summer 1982).

Contact Sports

In cases in which contact sports are involved and there is no women's team, there is a split in decisions as to whether to allow a female to play on the men's team. In some cases, as represented by *Clinton v. Nagy* (see note 1), the courts uphold the women's sex discrimination claim and allow participation on the men's team. In other cases, the plaintiff female was not successful because of the lack of state action or because there was no violation of the sex discrimination laws (see note 2).

NOTES ————————————————————————————————

1. In *Clinton v. Nagy*, 411 F. Supp. 1396 (N.D. Ohio 1974), a twelve-year-old girl alleged that recreation and city officials deprived her of equal recreational opportunities in refusing to allow her the opportunity to qualify to play recreational league football because of her sex. Pursuant to 42 U.S.C. § 1983, the girl sought to prohibit the officials from denying her equal recreational opportunities on the basis of sex and to receive a declaratory judgment that "the policies, customs, and practices of the defendants are in violation of the Constitution." The court held that when a regulation is based on a sex-based classification, "the classification is subject to scrutiny under the Equal Protection Clause of the Fourteenth Amendment to ascertain whether there is a rational relationship to a valid stated purpose." The court therefore decided the case for the girl.

The court stated that organized contact sports are considered an opportunity and means of developing strength of character, leadership qualities, etc., "yet, although these are presumably qualities to which we desire all of the young to aspire, the opportunity to qualify to engage in sports activities through which such qualities may be developed has been granted to one class of the young and summarily denied to the other."

2. In *Junior Football Ass'n of Orange County, Texas v. Gaudet*, 546 S.W.2d 70 (Tex. Civ. App. 1976), the trial court granted a temporary injunction allow-

ing a girl to play football in the Junior Football Association until she reached puberty. This decision was based on Article 1, Section 3a of the Texas Constitution, which provides: "Equality under the law shall not be denied or abridged because of sex, race, color, creed or national origin."

The association appealed on the basis that there was no state action sufficient to authorize the injunction. The association complained that there was insufficient evidence of state involvement to authorize the temporary injunction and the court agreed. On appeal, the temporary restraining order was reversed and dissolved. Even though the association was chartered by the state of Texas as a nonprofit corporation, the players usually practiced on school grounds, and games were played in a park owned by the City of Orange, the court of appeals did not find state action or private conduct closely interrelated in function with state action.

3. In *Lavin v. Chicago Board of Education*, 73 F.R.D. 438 (1975), *Lavin v. Illinois High School Ass'n*, 527 F.2d 58 (7th Cir. 1977), a class action lawsuit for declaratory, injunctive, and monetary relief against the Chicago Board of Education was instituted because plaintiff Lavin was denied participation in interscholastic athletics based on her sex. Lavin and another classmate tried out for the varsity basketball team at their high school and were denied positions on the squad because of the Illinois State High School Association rules. Lavin contended that the Fourteenth Amendment guarantee of equal protection had been violated. The appeals court reversed and remanded the trial court's summary judgment for the board of education and awarded monetary damages to the athletes. On remand, the trial court denied the class action claim because Lavin was no longer a member of the "class" because of graduation. In addition, the trial court reasoned that she did not present an argument that showed she was qualified enough to make the boys' squad, and therefore was not a member of that particular "class" of girls either. The trial court allowed Lavin's individual claim for damages.

4. In *Muscare v. O'Malley*, Civil No. 76-C-3729 (N.D. Ill. 1977), an action was brought by a twelve-year-old girl who wanted to play *tackle* football in Chicago Park District football games. There was a *touch* football program available for girls. In ruling for the girl, the court reasoned that offering a sport for males, yet not to females, is a violation of equal opportunity rights under the Fourteenth Amendment.

5. In *Hoover v. Meiklejohn*, 430 F. Supp. 164 (D. Colo. 1977), an action was brought by plaintiff Hoover, who wanted to play on her high school soccer team. The Colorado High School Athletic Association limited interscholastic soccer team membership to boys. The district court held for Hoover, based on an equal protection analysis. The court held that the appropriate analysis requires a triangular balancing of the importance of the opportunities being unequally burdened or denied against the strength of the state's interests and the character of the group being denied the opportunity. The court found that a complete denial, as in this case, violated Hoover's rights to equal protection.

The court determined that the school had three options. It could allow coed teams, it could discontinue the sport for males, or it could field a second all-female team.

6. In *Leffel v. Wisconsin Interscholastic Athletic Ass'n*, 444 F. Supp. 1117

(E.D. Wis. 1978), plaintiff brought a class action suit charging that an inter-scholastic athletic association's rule limiting co-educational athletics violated her civil rights as guaranteed under the equal protection clause. The court granted summary judgment for the plaintiff, finding that:

> exclusion of girls from all contact sports in order to protect female high school athletes from unreasonable risk of injury was not fairly or substantially related to a justifiable government objective in the context of the Fourteenth Amendment, where demand for relief by plaintiffs would be met by establishing separate girls' teams with comparable programs.

The plaintiffs were granted the right to participate in a varsity interscholastic program in any sport in which only a boys' team was provided.

7. In *Simpson v. Boston Area Youth Soccer, Inc.*, Case No. 83-2681 (Mass. Super. Ct. 1983) (settled), an action was brought by a sixth-grade female soccer player. Defendant soccer association excluded the girl from the all-male soccer team in her town. The girl had played for three years on co-educational teams, and many of her former teammates were on the team. Although the soccer association also maintained a girls' league, no team in that league was readily accessible to the girl. The girl was also considered an above-average soccer player and maintained that the girls' league would present inferior compe-tition. The case was settled when defendant soccer league agreed to change its constitution and bylaws to allow females to play on male teams, with such teams being entered in the boys' league.

8. In *Force v. Pierce City R-VI School District*, 570 F. Supp. 1020 (W.D. Mo., 1983), a thirteen-year-old female plaintiff sought injunctive relief to allow her to play on the interscholastic football team. The court granted injunctive relief for the girl and held that:

> (1) no sufficiently substantial relationship was shown between blanket prohibi-tion against female participation on a high school football team and Title IX of the Educational Amendments of 1972, the high school activities association rules and regulations, and maintaining athletic educational programs which are as safe for participants as possible, or administrative ease, and (2) under the circum-stances, rules and regulations of high school activities association and manner of promulgation and enforcement thereof constituted "state action," thus subjecting association's actions to equal protection clause requirements and, as such, en-forcement of a rule which effectively prohibited members of the opposite sex from competing on the same team in interscholastic football was enjoined.

9. In *Lantz v. Ambach*, 620 F. Supp. 663 (S.D.N.Y. 1985), the court pro-hibited enforcement of a New York public high school regulation that pro-hibited mixed sex competition in football, as a violation of the Fourteenth Amendment, and permitted a sixteen-year-old healthy female student to try out for junior varsity football. Although the court acknowledged an important governmental objective in protecting the health and safety of female high school students, it found the regulation was overbroad and lacked reasonable relation to the objective.

10. In *Opinion of the Justices to the House of Representatives*, 371 N.E.2d 426 (1977), the Supreme Judicial Court of Massachusetts rendered an opinion that proposed legislation which would have disallowed participation of girls with boys on the following contact sports teams—football and wrestling—

would be unconstitutional under the state's equal rights amendment. The court specifically reserved the question whether a statute "more limited in its impact" would serve a compelling state interest—for example, whether females could be constitutionally excluded from male teams in a particular sport if they were provided with an equal team.

11. For further information, see the following law review articles.

(a) Note, "Irrebuttable Presumption Doctrine: Applied to State and Federal Regulations Excluding Females from Contact Sports," 4 *U. Dayton L. Rev.* 197 (1979).

(b) Comment, "Title IX of the Education Amendment of 1972 Prohibits All-Female Teams in Sports Not Previously Dominated by Males," 14 *Suffolk U. L. Rev.* 1471 (1980).

(c) Note, "Girls High School Basketball Rules Held Unconstitutional," 16 *J. Fam. L*: 345 (1978).

(d) Jacklin, "Sexual Equality in High School Athletics: The Approach of *Darrin v. Gould*," 12 *Gonz. L. Rev.* 691 (1977).

12. Review *Yellow Springs Exempted Village School District Board of Education v. Ohio High School Athletic Ass'n* concerning the scope and applicability of Title IX, and *Darrin v. Gould* concerning the legality of a state equal rights amendment.

13. See the section Injunctive Relief in Chapter 4, for an explanation of the standards required for an injunction.

14. See the section Waiver and Release of Liability in Chapter 7 for a discussion of waivers and releases of liability. The plaintiff in *Clinton v. Nagy* signed one before being allowed to participate.

15. In *Saint v. Nebraska School Activities Ass'n*, 684 F. Supp 626 (D. Neb. 1988), a female high school sophomore sought a temporary restraining order to restrain the Nebraska School Activities Association from refusing to permit her to wrestle on the high school boys' wrestling team during pendency of trial. The high school did not have a girls' wrestling team. U.S. district court judge ruled in favor of plaintiff, granting temporary restraining order. The judge reasoned that plaintiff showed a reasonable probability of success on the merits in the claim, and that plaintiff would suffer irreparable harm if the restraining order were denied.

16. In *Libby v. South Inter-Conference Association*, 728 F. Supp 504 (N.D. Ill., 1990), a female high school student brought a civil rights action against high school athletic association, challenging a rule prohibiting her from playing interscholastic soccer on the boys' team, where a girls' team did not exist. After a series of temporary restraining orders, which allowed her to compete in the state tournament, the case was dismissed as moot because the season had ended. Plaintiff was not awarded attorney's fees because she was not the prevailing party.

Noncontact Sports

In cases in which noncontact sports are involved and there is no women's team, the trend and majority of cases allow the women to participate on the men's team. Some cases (see notes 1 and 2) allowed women to participate on men's cross-country and tennis teams where there were no women's teams. Some courts have prevented females from participating on the men's teams (see notes 8 and 9). In cases where private organizations are involved, the plaintiff women also must prove state action (see notes 11b, c, and d).

NOTES _____

1. In *Gilpin v. Kansas State High School Activities Ass'n*, 377 F. Supp. 1233 (D. Kan. 1974), Gilpin, a junior at Southeast High School in Wichita, Kansas, brought a civil rights suit against the Kansas State High School Activities Association (KSHSAA). Gilpin claimed she was deprived of equal protection by a KSHSAA rule that prevented her from participating in interscholastic cross-country competition solely on the basis of her sex.

The court held that because Southeast High School offered no cross-country program for girls, the KSHSAA rule effectively deprived Gilpin of an opportunity to compete at all. The court held:

> Thus, although the Association's overall objective is commendable and legitimate, the method employed to accomplish that objective is simply overbroad in its reach. It is precisely this sort of overinclusiveness which the Equal Protection Clause disdains.

The district court determined that the KSHSAA rule prohibiting mixed competition was unconstitutional as applied to Gilpin and accordingly granted her the requested injunctive relief.

2. In *Brenden v. Independent School District 742*, 342 F. Supp. 1224 (D. Minn. 1972), *aff'd*, 477 F.2d 1292 (8th Cir. 1973), plaintiff high school student-athletes brought an action against Independent School District 742, alleging violation of their constitutional rights under the Fourteenth Amendment and Civil Rights Act (42 U.S.C. § 1983). The plaintiffs contended that the Minnesota State High School League (MSHSL) rule prohibiting girls from participating in boys' interscholastic athletic competition was arbitrary and unreasonable as applied to their particular situations and thus, constituted a violation of their rights under the equal protection clause of the Fourteenth Amendment.

Because of the circumstances—that is, the girls were capable of competing on the boys' team, that no girls' team existed at their respective schools in the sports in which they wished to participate, and that Brenden and St. Pierre were kept from participation solely on the basis of sex—the court found the application of the rule to be arbitrary and unreasonable. Since the classification by sex had no fair or substantial relation to the objective of the interscholastic league rule, its application to Brenden and St. Pierre was in violation of the equal protection clause of the Fourteenth Amendment. The district court granted the requested injunctive relief and prohibited the MSHSL from imposing sanctions on the schools or any of their opponents stemming from plaintiffs' participation on boys' interscholastic athletic teams.

3. In *Reed v. Nebraska School Activities Ass'n*, 341 F. Supp. 258 (D. Neb. 1972), plaintiff Reed, a student-athlete at Norfolk High School in Nebraska, brought an action which challenged a state high school athletic association's

practice of providing a public school golf program for boys, while providing none for girls and prohibiting girls from interscholastic participation with or against boys. Reed sought a preliminary injunction prohibiting the Nebraska School Activities Association and school officials from denying her membership on the boys' golf team. The court held for Reed and stated:

> For Debbie Reed, her benefits are fixed in time to the present golf season and when it ends, so will its benefits to her. The loss, whatever its nature or dimensions, will be irretrievable. It is true that defendant's interest in enforcement of the rules... will be similarly lost... however, that interest is less weighty than those of Debbie Reed in the context of this case.

4. In *Carnes v. Tennessee Secondary School Athletic Ass'n*, 415 F. Supp. 569 (E.D. Tenn. 1976), an action was brought by an eighteen-year-old girl who wanted to play on the boys' high school baseball team. Plaintiff Carnes sought a preliminary injunction from the court against the Tennessee Secondary Athletic Association rule barring mixed competition in contact sports. Baseball in this case was considered a contact sport.

In granting the preliminary injunction, the district court held that there was a likelihood that Carnes would prevail on the merits of the claim of invalidity of the association's rule and that a denial of injunction would result in irreparable harm to Carnes, whose last opportunity to play high school baseball was drawing to an end.

5. In *Morris v. Michigan State Board of Education*, 472 F.2d 1207 (6th Cir. 1973), plaintiff Morris brought an action against a state high school athletic association rule barring mixed competition in interscholastic sports. Morris and a female friend wanted to play on the high school boys' tennis team. There was no girls' team.

Morris contended a violation of equal protection under the Fourteenth Amendment. The lower court ruled for Morris. The appeals court affirmed the decision but remanded the suit to the lower court to have noncontact sports added to the wording of the order granting the injunction. As a result of the case, Michigan Laws Act 183 were enacted, which permitted women to participate with men on noncontact sports teams.

6. In *Haas v. South Bend Community School Corporation*, 259 Ind. 515, 289 N.E.2d 495 (1972), a suit was brought by a female who was seeking injunctive relief from a state high school athletic association rule barring mixed competition on sports teams. Plaintiff Haas had made the "B" golf team but was denied the opportunity to play with the "A" team because of the association's rule. The lower court held for the association. The decision was later reversed by the appellate court, which held that the rule was a violation of equal protection under the Fourteenth Amendment and the Civil Rights Act. The court found the association's arguments to be insufficient justification for barring girls from noncompetitive sports or from denying girls the chance to qualify.

7. In *Israel v. West Virginia Secondary Schools Activities Commission*, 388 S.E.2d 480 (W. Va. 1989), a female high school student brought a sex discrimination action against School Activities Association after she was refused the opportunity to play on the boys' high school baseball team. In reversing the lower court's decision, the appeals court held that the regulation

prohibiting girls' participation in baseball violated federal and state equal protection standards, and the games of baseball and softball are not substantially equivalent for purposes of determining whether equal athletic opportunities are provided to boys and girls in high school.

8. In *Gregoria v. Board of Educ. of Asbury Park*, Case No. A-1277-70 (N.J. Super. Ct. App. Div. 1971) (unreported), an action was brought by plaintiff Gregoria, who wanted to play on the high school boys' tennis team. There was no girls' team. The board of education would not permit her to play. The trial court ruled in favor of the board of education. The appeals court affirmed the lower court's ruling that the "psychological well-being of girls is a rational reason for exclusion."

9. In *Hollander v. Connecticut Interscholastic Athletic Conf., Inc.*, Civil No. 12-49-27 (Conn. Super. Ct. New Haven County, 1972), *appeal dismissed*, 295 A.2d 671 (Conn. Ct. App. 1972), an action was brought by plaintiff Hollander, who wanted to run on the boys' cross-country team at her high school. The Connecticut Intercollegiate Athletic Association barred mixed competition. The court worked out an agreement with the association to allow girls to compete on boys' teams in noncontact sports. Despite that, the court held for defendant association based on Fourteenth Amendment equal protection arguments. The court expressed the opinion that allowing girls to compete on the same teams with boys would bring into question the physical safeguard for girls and the "removal of challenge and incentive for boys to win."

10. In *Bednar v. Nebraska School Activities Ass'n*, 531 F.2d 922 (8th Cir. 1976), the mother of a high school student brought a civil rights action on behalf of her daughter, who had been denied the opportunity to participate on the boys' cross-country team because of her sex. There was no girls' team. The district court issued a preliminary injunction prohibiting the school from excluding Bednar from competition. The school association appealed the decision, but the court of appeals affirmed, finding that as Bednar was one of the top competitors in her event and her qualification for higher levels of competition was likely, she would be subject to irreparable harm if she were not allowed to compete.

11. The following cases involve suits against Little League Baseball:

(a) In *Rappaport v. Little League Baseball, Inc.*, 65 F.R.D. 545 (1975), a group of parents and plaintiff girl filed suit against the Little League because of its policy of excluding girls from participation. The Little League changed its policy after the complaint was filed. The court ruled the case moot.

(b) In *King v. Little League Baseball, Inc.*, 505 F.2d 264 (6th Cir. 1974), an action was brought by a twelve-year-old girl who wanted to play on a Little League team. The national Little League Baseball rules excluded girls from competing. However, the Little League Regional Board permitted plaintiff King to try out, and she made the team on the basis of her ability. The team was notified by the National Little League Association that if King continued to play or practice with the team, the team would lose its charter. King was dropped from the roster; the result was that the town revoked the team's privilege to use the municipal field for games. King was then put back on the roster, and the team lost its charter.

The case was dismissed and affirmed on appeal. The courts held that there was not sufficient state action involved in the defendants' enforcement of the "no girls" rule to bring it under the color of state law. The courts agreed that they did not have jurisdiction over the subject matter in the case.

(c) In *McGill v. Avonworth Baseball Conference,* 516 F.2d 1328 (3rd Cir. 1975), the court of appeals affirmed the trial court's decision for the conference because the girl had failed to show significant state involvement in the league's discrimination. The court reasoned that the waiver of a $25 fee for use of the public playing field was de minimus; that analysis of nature, value, and proportion of state aid to the conference did not end the court's inquiry; and that nexus between the state's and the conference's allegedly offensive policy was not sufficiently close so that the conference's action could be fairly treated as state action in that the conference was granted nonexclusive, scheduled use of four public playing fields, school buildings were used only for once-a-year registration purposes, and no government officials were involved in determining eligibility requirements.

(d) In *Fortin v. Darlington Little League, Inc.,* 376 F. Supp. 473 (D.R.I. 1974), *rev'd,* 514 F.2d 344 (1st Cir. 1975), an action was brought by a ten-year-old girl who was denied the opportunity to try out for Little League baseball solely because of her sex. Plaintiff Fortin argued that the baseball park where the team played was public property, a fact that supplied sufficient proof to find the required state action. The appeals court ruled for the girl, reversing the lower court's decision. The appeals court found that the league's preferred dependency on city baseball diamonds introduced significant state involvement to find state action. The appeals court also rejected the league's argument that the discrimination was appropriate because females would injure more easily than males, because it was not supported by the facts.

(e) In *National Organization for Women, Essex County Chapter v. Little League Baseball, Inc.,* 318 A.2d 33 (N.J. Ct. App. Div. 1974), the Essex County chapter of the National Organization for Women (NOW) filed suit on behalf of eight- to twelve-year-old girls who wanted to play Little League baseball. NOW contended this discrimination against girls was a violation of New Jersey's antidiscrimination laws. In affirming a lower court order for the girls, the superior court held that the evidence permitted the finding that girls of the particular age concerned were not subject to greater hazard of injury while playing baseball than boys of the same age group and that the Little League did not fall within any statutory exemptions.

12. In August 1983, Mary Decker, Grete Waitz, and 50 other leading female runners filed a sex discrimination suit against the International Olympic Committee (IOC), the Los Angeles Olympic Organizing Committee, the International Amateur Athletic Federation, The Athletics Congress, and others. The suit was filed in Los Angeles Superior Court and sought an order that

would force the defendants to include 5,000- and 10,000-meter runs for women at the 1984 Olympic Games in Los Angeles. These events were part of the men's events and were historically excluded from the women's program because of the belief that women could not physically handle the distances. (See *Martin v. International Olympic Committee* in Chapter 4 and "Female Runners Sue to Add Long Events," *New York Times*, August 12, 1983, p. A18, Col. 1.) The request for injunctive relief was denied by the court. The IOC later added these events to the women's program for the 1988 Olympic Games in Seoul, S. Korea.

Women's Team, No Men's Team

The all-women-no-men-type of case has arisen only with noncontact sports. Unlike the converse situations just covered, men are generally not allowed to play on all-female teams. To support this conclusion, courts often cite the theory that male participation would destroy any attempt to redress past discrimination.

Noncontact Sports

In cases in which there is a women's team and no men's team for noncontact sports, there is a split in decisions as to whether to allow a male to play on the women's team. In *Gomes v. Rhode Island Interscholastic League* (see note 1), the court upheld the male's sex discrimination claim and allowed him to play on the women's volleyball team. In *Clark v. Arizona Interscholastic Ass'n* (see note 2), the court refused to allow boys to compete on the girls' volleyball team. The plaintiff male may not be successful for a variety of reasons, including lack of state action when a private organization is involved (see note 3), prohibition of males on women's teams to redress disparate treatment of females in scholastic athletic programs (see note 4), promotion of athletic opportunities for females (see note 5), and the fact that males already have more athletic opportunities than females (see note 6).

NOTES _____

1. In *Gomes v. Rhode Island Interscholastic League*, 469 F. Supp. 659 (D.R.I. 1979), *vacated as moot*, 604 F.2d 733 (1st Cir. 1979), plaintiff Gomes, a senior at Rogers High School in Newport, Rhode Island, brought an action under the federal civil rights statute. He sought preliminary injunctive relief prohibiting school officials from preventing his participation on the girls' volleyball team since the school offered no separate male squad in this sport. Rogers High allowed Gomes to join the all-female team but did not use him in Rhode Island Interscholastic League competition for fear of league disqualification.

Consequently, Gomes brought suit against the league at the start of the volleyball season. He alleged that the rule against male participation in volleyball competition violated both the Fourteenth Amendment and Title IX. Without reaching the constitutional issues, the district court ruled in Gomes's favor. The district court found that the exception for separate-sex teams under Title IX was not applicable since defendants sponsored no men's volleyball teams and opportunities for boys to play the sport previously had been nonexistent. Since the district court decision was rendered in the middle of the volleyball season, the league persuaded the appeals court that implementation of the district court's order would disrupt the remainder of the season. The appeals court stopped the implementation of the order pending review. The merits of the case were never reached on appeal since the case was dismissed as moot (the season had ended and Gomes was graduating), the judgment vacated, and the case remanded for dismissal.

2. In *Clark v. Arizona Interscholastic Ass'n*, 695 F.2d 1126 (9th Cir. 1982), *cert. denied*, 104 S. Ct. 79 (1983), plaintiffs were Arizona high school students who demonstrated their prowess in volleyball by participating on national championship teams sponsored by the Amateur Athletic Union. The student-athletes were not, however, able to participate on their high school volleyball teams. Their schools only sponsored interscholastic volleyball teams for girls, and a policy of the Arizona Interscholastic Association (AIA) had been interpreted to preclude boys from playing on girls' teams, even though girls are permitted to participate on boys' athletic teams.

The trial court found that the rules and regulations of the AIA do not violate the equal protection clause of the Fourteenth Amendment. It held that the maintenance of a girls only volleyball team "is substantially related to and serves the achievement of the important governmental objective" of (1) promoting equal athletic opportunities for females in interscholastic sports, and (2) redressing the effects of past discrimination. On appeal, the trial court decision was affirmed, upholding the rule prohibiting boys from playing on the girls' volleyball team. The appeals court noted that

> in this case, the alternative chosen may not maximize equality, and may represent trade-offs between equality and practicality. But since absolute necessity is not the standard, and absolute equality of opportunity in every sport is not the mandate, even the existence of wiser alternatives than the one chosen does not serve to invalidate the policy here since it is substantially related to the goal. That is all the standard demands.... While equality in specific sports is a worthwhile ideal, it should not be purchased at the expense of ultimate equality of opportunity to participate in sports. As common sense would advise against this, neither does the Constitution demand it.

For further information on *Clark v. Arizona Interscholastic Ass'n* see the following law review articles.

(a) Carr, "Constitutional Law—Equal Protection—Sex Discrimination Against Males in Athletics—Physiological Differences Are Valid Reasons to Exclude Boys From Girls' Athletic Teams" (*Clark v. Arizona Interscholastic Ass'n*, 695 F.2d 1126 [9th Cir. 1982], *cert. denied*, 104 S. Ct. 79 [1983]), 6 *Whittier L. Rev.* 151 (1984).

(b) Note, "Equal Protection Scrutiny of High School Athletics" *Clark v. Arizona Interscholastic Ass'n*, 695 F.2d 1126 [9th Cir. 1982] *cert. denied*, 104 S. Ct. 79 [1983]), 72 *Ky. L. J.* 935 (1983–84).

3. In *White v. Corpus Christi Little Misses Kickball Ass'n,* 526 S.W.2d 766 (Tex. Civ. App. 1975), an action was brought by plaintiff White, a ten-year-old boy who was not allowed to register to play in the girls' kickball association, because of his sex. The district court held for the association, and the boy appealed. On appeal, the boy argued that denial of right to play because of his sex was a denial of equal protection under both federal and state constitutions. The appeals court denied his claim because he had failed to establish the requisite state action. His participation was denied by a private organization acting without any connection to government except that the games were played in a public park.

4. In *Forte v. Board of Education, North Babylon Union Free School District,* 431 N.Y.S.2d 321 (1980), an action was brought by plaintiff Forte on behalf of his son, a seventeen-year-old high school student who wanted to play on the North Babylon High School volleyball team, which was all female. The court held for the school district. The court reasoned that the rule the school district had enacted was a discernible and permissible means of redressing disparate treatment of females in interscholastic athletic programs.

5. In *Petrie v. Illinois High School Ass'n,* 75 Ill. App. 3d 980, 31 Ill. Dec., 653, 394 N.E.2d 855 (1979), an action was brought by plaintiff Petrie, who wanted to play on the girls' high school volleyball team since the school had no boys' team. The Illinois High School Association would not allow Petrie to play on the girls' team. The appeals court affirmed a lower court decision which upheld the association's rule. The court found no violation of state law and reasoned that the association's rule "substantially related to and served the achievement of the governmental objective of maintaining, fostering, and promoting athletic opportunities for girls."

6. In *Mularadelis v. Haldane Central School Board,* 427 N.Y.S.2d 458 (App. Div. 1980), an action was brought by plaintiff Mularadelis, a member of his high school's girls' tennis team, who was told by the school board that he could no longer play on the team. The appeals court reversed a lower court decision and held for the school board on the basis that Title IX allowed for the exclusion of boys from the girls' team when there were, overall, more athletic opportunities for boys in the community.

7. In *Atty. Gen v. Massachusetts Interscholastic Athletic Ass'n Inc.,* 393 N.E.2d 284 (Mass. S.J.C. 1979), an action was brought by the state attorney general, who claimed that an athletic association rule excluding boys from competing on a girls' team, even though a girl could play on a boys' team if that sport was not offered for girls, was discriminatory. Injunctive relief was sought.

The Massachusetts Supreme Judicial Court held that the discriminatory classification could not be justified by (1) the theory that the classification was based on inherent biological differences rather than sex, (2) the theory that absolute exclusion on the basis of gender was necessary to protect player's safety, and (3) the theory that such a discriminatory classification would protect "emergent girls' programs from inundation of male athletes." The court found that more of the above were applicable and held that any "rule prohibiting any boy from playing on a girls' team was invalid under the state equal rights amendment and statute barring sex discrimination in the educational sphere."

The case was remitted for declaration that the rule was invalid and an issuance of an injunction prohibiting its application.

8. In *B.C. v. Cumberland Regional School District*, 531 A.2d 1059 (N.J. Super. A.D. 1987), a male high school student challenged Athletic Association rule prohibiting him from competing on girls' field hockey team. In affirming the lower court's decision, the court held that a rule prohibiting boys from playing on girls' field hockey team is permissible under both the state and the federal Constitution. The court reasoned that were plaintiff permitted to compete on girls' team, his personal interest would be gained at the cost of denying females the right to have equality of athletic opportunities with their male counterparts.

9. In *Clark v. Arizona Interscholastic Association*, 886 F.2d 1191 (9th Cir. 1989), the brother of plaintiff in *Clark v. Arizona Interscholastic Ass'n*, 695 F.2d 1126 (9th Cir 1982), brought civil rights action challenging rule of the association prohibiting him from competing on girls' high school volleyball team. The appeals court affirmed the lower court's decision in favor of association. As in the earlier *Clark* case, the judge reasoned that the rule was substantially related to the goal of redressing past discrimination and promoting equality of athletic opportunity between the sexes.

Women's Teams and Men's Teams

Four different types of legal arguments are raised in cases in which there are teams for both sexes. The first type is in cases in which the plaintiff women argue that "separate but equal is not equal." In these situations the women sue to participate on the men's team because the competition may be better and the women are far superior to the participants on the women's teams. As *O'Connor v. Board of Education of School District 23* (see note 1 in the section Separate but Equal) illustrates, the court will generally approve "separate but equal" teams and rule against plaintiff females who want to play on boys' teams based on playing ability arguments.

The second type of argument is that the separate teams are not equal, especially with respect to the benefits and opportunities provided to the teams. In *Aiken v. Lieuallen* (see note 2 in the section Separate but Equal), plaintiff female athletes contended that they were discriminated against in the areas of transportation, officiating, coaching, and the school's commitment to competitive programs. In a similar situation, *Blair v. Washington State University* (see note 3 in the section Contact Sports), the court awarded damages to plaintiff female athletes and ordered equivalent funding for men's and women's athletic programs.

The third type of case occurs when two teams exist, but the women compete under different rules than the men (see the section Same Sport, Different Rules). These situations, challenged on equal protection grounds, have produced mixed results. The trend seems to be away from allowing different rules to exist when those rules are based purely on the gender of the athletes, especially when those rules place those who play under a disadvantage if they want to continue in the sport.

The fourth type of case involves different seasons for the same men's and women's sport (see the section Same Sport, Different Seasons). The courts have generally held that separate seasons of play are not a denial of equal protection of the law.

Separate but Equal

The sexes are generally separated when it comes to participation in sports, and the challenges to this practice have been largely unavailing. The doctrine of "separate but equal" remains applicable to sex distinctions, even though it has been rejected for distinctions based on race. Thus, if separate teams exist for men and women, there may be a prohibition against co-ed teams or against women competing against men. The doctrine of "separate but equal" raises the critical question of whether or not such separate teams are substantially equal. The fact that two teams exist does not necessarily satisfy the doctrine. "Separate but equal" is based on the concept that the exclusion of a group is not unconstitutional if the excluded group is provided with comparable opportunities. If women are excluded from the men's basketball team but are provided with an equal one of their own, the school district will not be in violation of Title IX under the "separate but equal" theory. When the sexes are segregated in athletics, there must be an overall equality of expenditures, coaching, and access to facilities. Without this substantial equality, the existence of separate teams and the prohibition of women competing with men may be unconstitutional.

Apart from these circumstances, the segregation of the sexes in athletics is generally upheld, although the court is careful to examine the specific circumstances in each case before making a determination. The court usually considers whether or not the particular sport in question is considered to be a contact or a noncontact sport. Physiological differences between the sexes have been found to be a valid reason for the exclusion of one sex from a contact sport. Contact sports include boxing, wrestling, rugby, ice hockey, football, basketball, and other sports in which the major activity involves bodily contact.

Contact Sports

In cases in which there are both women's and men's teams in contact sports, the courts have generally not allowed a female to participate on the men's team. In *O'Connor v. Board of Education of School*

District No. 23 (note 1), the court denied the sex discrimination allegation of a female who wanted to participate in better competition by playing on the men's team. The other issue which may be raised is whether the separate men's and women's teams are in fact equal. Both *Aiken v. Lieuallen* (note 2) and *Blair v. Washington State University* (note 3) deal with this issue.

NOTES ————————————————————————————

1. In *O'Connor v. Board of Education of School District No. 23*, 645 F.2d 578 (7th Cir. 1981), *cert. denied*, 454 U.S. 1084 (1981), an appeal was instituted in response to a district court order granting a preliminary injunction to restrain defendant school board from refusing to permit female plaintiff to try out for the boy's sixth grade basketball team. The plaintiff argued that the school board's policy of maximizing participation in sports by providing for separate but equal boys' and girls' interscholastic sports teams violated Title IX. The appellate court held that the trial court abused its discretion in granting a preliminary injunction restraining the school board because the plaintiff failed to show a reasonable likelihood of success on the merits.

2. In *Aiken v. Lieuallen*, 39 Or. App. 779, 593 P.2d 1243 (1979), an action was brought by plaintiff taxpayers and parents of student-athletes on the University of Oregon's women's varsity basketball team who appealed a determination by the chancellor of the State Board of Higher Education that the university was not violating state statue ORS 659.150, which prohibited discrimination on the basis of sex in state-financed education programs. The plaintiffs filed a complaint in March 1977, alleging that the following four areas of Oregon's athletic program were in violation of ORS 659.150: transportation, officiating, coaching, and commitment to competitive programs. A contested case hearing was held in October 1977, in which the hearing officer determined that the university was in violation of ORS 659.150.

The findings and recommendations were issued in March 1978 and were submitted to the Oregon chancellor of higher education for review and entry of an order. The chancellor reversed the hearing officer's decision and found that the university was not in violation of the statute. The appeals court reversed the chancellor's order and sent the case back for further proceedings. The court, after reviewing the plaintiffs' allegations of discrimination in the areas of transportation, officiating, coaching, and university commitment, stated that upon the second hearing, the chancellor should address these allegations to determine whether the university's actions have led to "unreasonable differentiation of treatment" under ORS 659.150. Determinations of the unreasonableness of actions should include evaluations of whether or not the action by the university had a disparate effect on the opportunity for women to participate in athletics.

3. In *Blair v. Washington State University*, 740 P.2d 1379 (Wash. Sup. Ct. 1987), female athletes and coaches of female athletes brought sex discrimination action under the State Equal Rights Amendment. Trial court ruled for plaintiffs and awarded damages, injunctive relief, attorney fees, and costs. On appeal, the Washington Supreme Court affirmed the lower court's conclusion

of sex discrimination but modified the lower court's calculations on comparative scholarships between male and female athletes and attorney fees.

4. In *Hutchins v. Board of Trustees of Michigan State University*, C.A. No. G79–87 (W.D. Mich. 1979) (unreported), the women's basketball team from the East Lansing campus of Michigan State brought a Title IX complaint against Michigan State University and the board of trustees, alleging that the men's team was receiving better treatment. The alleged better treatment included more money for traveling and better facilities. The court held for the women's basketball team and issued a temporary restraining order barring the better treatment of the men's team.

5. In *Petersen v. Oregon State University* (settled 1980), two student-athletes filed a complaint with the Board of Education of the State of Oregon, alleging that Oregon State University (OSU) offered athletic programs of lesser quality to female student-athletes than were offered to their male counterparts. A settlement reached in July 1980, entitled "OSU Conciliation Agreement for Sex Equality in Intercollegiate Athletics," implemented a five-year plan at OSU designed to put the men's and women's athletic programs on an equal competitive basis.

6. For further information on *Aiken and Petersen*, see Branchfield and Grier, "*Aiken v. Lieuallen* and *Petersen v. Oregon State University:* Defining Equity in Athletics," 8 *J. C. & U. L.* 369 (1981–82).

7. In *Michigan Department of Civil Rights, ex rel. Forton v. Waterford Township Department of Parks and Recreation*, 335 N.W.2d 305 (Mich. Ct. App. 1983), plaintiff brought a Civil Rights Act claim based on defendant's policy of maintaining a gender-based elementary-level basketball program. The appeals court reversed the district court's decision and ruled in favor of the plaintiff. The court reasoned that (1) separate leagues involved were not equal and could not withstand equal protection analysis, and consequently violated the Civil Rights Act, and (2) subsequent modification of policy to allow up to two girls to participate on each boys' basketball team and two boys on each girls' basketball team did not cure the statutory violation.

8. In *Lafler v. Athletic Board of Control*, 536 F. Supp. 104 (W.D. Mich. 1982), the court upheld the denial of a woman's application to box in the flyweight division of the Golden Gloves boxing competition under the Fourteenth Amendment, the state public accommodation statute, and the state equal rights amendment. The court cited Title IX regulations permitting establishment of separate male-female teams in contact sports and the Amateur Sports Act provisions providing for separate programs for females and males.

Noncontact Sports

In cases in which there are both women's and men's teams in noncontact sports, the courts have generally not allowed the female to participate on the men's team. The rationale is that separate but equal is equal, since this enhances athletic opportunities for females.

NOTES ——————————————————————————

1. In *Ritacco v. Norwin School District*, 361 F. Supp. 930 (W.D. Pa. 1973), a high school graduate and her mother filed a class action challenging the

Pennsylvania Interscholastic Athletic Association (PIAA) rule, which in effect required separate girls' and boys' teams for interscholastic noncontact sports. The district court ruled in favor of the defendant school district. It held that since the school district had not deprived Ritacco of her constitutional rights in violation of the Civil Rights statute, 42 U.S.C. § 1983, she was entitled to neither the declaratory judgment nor the injunctive relief. The court held that "separate but equal" in the realm of athletic competition is justifiable and permissible when a rational basis for the rule exists, and that sex, unlike race, is not an inherently suspect classification for purposes of determining a denial of equal protection. The court concluded that the PIAA rule forbidding co-educational noncontact sports teams did not invalidly and unfairly discriminate against females. In fact, the court observed that this rule had produced positive effects on girls' interscholastic athletics in Pennsylvania since its adoption in 1970. The court was convinced that "the prime purpose behind the no-mixed-sex competition rule is a valid one seeking to enhance the quality, quantity, and calibre of interscholastic sports opportunities for girls and boys in Pennsylvania."

2. In *Ruman v. Eskew*, 343 N.E.2d 806 (Ind. Ct. App. 1975), an action was brought by plaintiff Ruman, who wanted to play on the high school boys' tennis team, even though there was a girls' team at her school. The Indiana High School Athletic Association prohibited girls from playing on boys' teams if girls' teams in the same sport exist. The court held for the defendant, and relying on *Haas v. South Bend Community School Corporation* (see note 6, in the section Noncontact Sports), upheld the rule, since it was reasonably related to the objective of providing athletic opportunities for both males and females. The court of appeals affirmed the judgment of the trial court.

3. In *Gregoria v. Board of Education of Asbury Park*, Case No. A-1277-70 (N.J. Super. Ct. App. Div. 1971), the trial court refused to prohibit enforcement of the New Jersey Athletic Association rule prohibiting co-ed interscholastic sports, including noncontact sports such as tennis. Among the rational bases for the policy, the court cited the psychological impact on males, the need for additional female trainers, and the possibility of insufficient bathroom facilities. The appeals court affirmed the lower court's ruling that the "psychological well-being of girls is a rational reason for exclusion."

4. Deb Schiff, a sixteen-year-old student at West Essex Regional High School in New York, was initially barred from participating on the boys' fencing team because state regulations said she could not compete in view of the fact that the school offered a separate girls' division. Sabers were allowed in the boys' division, but they were not used by the girls' team. Schiff objected to the ban on the grounds that a nearby female high school student was allowed to play on the football team, while she was denied an opportunity to participate in a less violent sport.

The executive committee of the New York Interscholastic Athletic Association later granted Schiff a waiver of the rules in her favor. The decree may open the door to any other girl in the state who is deprived of competing on a boys' team. ("Schoolgirl Fencer to Duel with Boys," *New York Times*, February 19, 1986, p. 16, col. 5.)

Same Sport, Different Rules

Cases and issues in this section have traditionally arisen in basketball because of women's playing rules being different from men's rules. As evidenced by *Bucha v. Illinois High School Ass'n* (see note 1 in the section Noncontact Sports), the cases have also evolved from generally disparate treatment of student-athletes rather than from different rules of a sport.

Contact Sports

In cases in which there are different playing rules for women's and men's teams in contact sports, there is a split in decisions as to whether the women's rules should be changed to conform with the men's. The plaintiff women in these cases generally have alleged sex discrimination based on the rule differences with men's sports and also the reduced opportunity to compete against other women (who had the advantage of playing under men's rules) for college scholarships. In *Dodson v. Arkansas Activities Ass'n* (note 1), the court ruled for the plaintiff, while in *Jones v. Oklahoma Secondary School Activities Ass'n* (note 2) and *Cape v. Tennessee Secondary School Athletic Ass'n* (note 3), the courts ruled for the defendant athletic associations.

NOTES ————————————————————————————————

1. In *Dodson v. Arkansas Activities Ass'n*, 468 F. Supp. 394 (E.D. Ark. 1979), plaintiff Dodson, a junior high school basketball player in the Arkadelphia, Arkansas, public school system, brought an action in January 1977 against three defendants: the school district, the superintendent, and the Arkansas Activities Association (AAA). Her suit challenged the constitutionality of rules for girls' junior and senior high school basketball, which in Arkansas differed from those under which boys played. The court held that "none of the reasons proffered [for the rule differentiation] is at all relevant to a gender-based classification." The defendant stated that "no physiological differences between males and females ... prohibit females from playing five-on-five basketball," and the primary justification given for the sex-based distinction between rules was simply that of tradition. The court ordered that the defendants be permanently prohibited and restrained from enforcing different rules for girls and boys playing junior and senior high school basketball in Arkansas. However, after stating that the case was not about male-female competition or discrimination between programs, the court stated:

> The point here is that Arkansas boys are in a position to compete on an equal footing with boys elsewhere, while Arkansas girls, merely because they are girls, are not.... Arkansas schools have chosen to offer basketball. Having taken that step, they may not limit the game's full benefits to one sex without substantial justification.

2. In *Jones v. Oklahoma Secondary School Activities Ass'n*, 453 F. Supp. 150 (W.D. Okla. 1977), plaintiff Jones sought an injunction to suspend the

association's split-court basketball rules, arguing that they created an arbitrary and unreasonable distinction between boys and girls that violated her right to equal protection. The court held for the athletic association. Jones's Title IX arguments were dismissed because she did not follow administrative procedures. Her Fourteenth Amendment argument was seen as faulty because her allegations concerning her reduced opportunity to compete in the future and a reduced likelihood for college scholarships did not rise to the level of an equal protection interest. Her claims that such rules interfered with her enjoyment of the game as well as her physical development also did not establish a cognizable equal protection claim.

3. In *Cape v. Tennessee Secondary School Athletic Ass'n*, 424 F. Supp. 732 (E.D. Tenn. 1976), *rev'd per curiam*, 563 F.2d 793 (6th Cir. 1977), plaintiff Cape, a high school student, challenged the "split-court" rules used in women's basketball. These rules, she claimed, denied her the full benefits of the game as well as an athletic scholarship to college. The court held for the athletic association and dismissed Cape's arguments, which were based on a private right of action under Title IX and the Fourteenth Amendment. The court held that Cape, who sought to challenge the regulations, must first exhaust all administrative remedies within the Department of Health, Education and Welfare under Title IX before her suit could be addressed in federal court.

4. For further information, see Johnson, "Half Court Girls' Basketball Rules: An Application of the Equal Protection Clause and Title IX," 65 *Iowa L. Rev.* 766 (1980).

Noncontact Sports

The courts have allowed different rules for men's and women's noncontact sports. The courts can apply a rational relationship test and find that the physical and psychological differences between male and female athletes justify different rules.

NOTE ────────────────────────────────────

1. In *Bucha v. Illinois High School Ass'n*, 351 F. Supp. 69 (N.D. Ill. 1972), plaintiffs, two female students at Hinsdale Center Township High School, brought a class action challenging the Illinois High School Association (IHSA) bylaws placing limitations on girls' athletic contests that were not applicable to boys' athletics. The girls sought to have the court declare the IHSA rules in violation of the equal protection clause of the Fourteenth Amendment and to prohibit the enforcement of the bylaws. They also sought a judgment against all defendants in the amount of $25,000.

The court first determined that the named plaintiffs in this cause adequately represented all the members of their class and thus, their standing to bring a class action was affirmed. It stated:

> Although these two girls might have an interest in becoming members of presently all-boy teams, they also have an interest in seeking the development of a "separate but equal" program.... The fact that the named plaintiffs have interests which exceed those of some class members will not defeat the class action, so long as they possess interests which are coextensive with those of the class.

The defendants—IHSA, its directors, and the board of education of Hinsdale Township—based their motions to dismiss on three arguments:

1. The IHSA and the board of education were not persons within the meaning of 42 USC § 1983 (1970).
2. The challenged discrimination was not an action under color of state statute, ordinance, regulation, custom or usage.
3. The challenged discrimination did not constitute a deprivation of a right guaranteed by the U.S. Constitution and laws.

Concerning the defendants' first argument, the court held that "all defendants may properly be prohibited as persons under § 1983, but only the individual defendants can be liable for the damages sought." On the second argument, the court rejected defendants' contention that the acts of the IHSA did not amount to state action and therefore could not be reached under § 1983.

On the third and final argument, the court reviewed the girls' complaint that the athletic association had denied them equal protection, stating that the relevant inquiry was whether the challenged classification based on sex was rational. Because participation in interscholastic athletics is not a constitutionally guaranteed right and the Illinois courts do not interfere with the policies of a voluntary association such as the IHSA unless it acts "unreasonably, arbitrarily, or capriciously," the girls had asserted their claims based on an equal educational opportunity argument and not the right to interscholastic athletic participation.

The court analyzed the alleged denial of equal protection in this case using the traditional test that identifies the purposes or objective of a legislative scheme and then asks whether the challenged discrimination bears a rational relationship to one of those purposes.

The court found a factual basis for defendants' claims that the physical and psychological differences between male and female student-athletes would lead to male domination of co-ed interscholastic sports and result in decreased female athletic participation should unrestricted competition between the sexes be permitted. It held that

> the uncontroverted existence of a bona fide athletic program for girls coupled with the physical and psychological differences ... also support the rationality of the IHSA's decision to conduct girls' interscholastic sports programs different from boys'.

The district court entered summary judgment in favor of all defendants on the basis that the traditional equal protection standard

> requires this court to defer to the judgment of the physical educators of the IHSA once a rational relationship has been shown to exist between their actions and the goals of interscholastic athletic competition.

Same Sport, Different Seasons

The courts have allowed different seasons for men and women in the same sport as long as there is a rational basis for the difference. In one case, an athletic association scheduled men's swimming in a different season (e.g., fall) than the women's season (e.g., winter) and was challenged on sex discrimination grounds. The athletic association's decision was upheld. The court reasoned that there was a reasonable basis for the decision: the lack of available pool time for both women's and men's teams to practice during the same seasons.

NOTES _____

1. In *Striebel v. Minnesota State High School League,* 321 N.W.2d 400 (Minn. 1982), an action was brought by plaintiff female student-athlete against the Minnesota State High School League (MSHSL), challenging the constitutionality of a MSHSL rule which authorized "separate seasons of play for high school athletic teams separated or substantially separated according to sex." The MSHSL had established separate seasons for boys and girls in tennis and swimming. The district court held that the league's policy of establishing separate seasons for boys and girls was constitutional and in compliance with the statute. The court found that under the circumstances presented, separating teams by season was a "reasonable means of achieving maximum participation by both sexes in the high school athletic program." On appeal, the Minnesota Supreme Court held that "where limited athletic facilities made it necessary to schedule high school boys' and girls' athletic teams in two separate seasons, and neither was substantially better than the other, that scheduling decision was not a denial of equal protection of the law."

2. In *Ridgeway v. Montana High School Ass'n* 633 F. Supp. 1564 (D. Mont. 1986), the court decided not to overturn the decision of the Montana High School Association, which allowed the seasonal placement of girls' basketball (fall) and girls' volleyball (winter) to remain as is, contrary to the prevailing seasonal placement for the sports throughout the rest of the country. The court agreed with the reasoning advanced by the MHSA, which determined that a change in seasonal placement would not facilitate "the goal of maximizing participation in athletics by the most students."

Varsity Sport Versus Club Sport

Another trend that has been occurring in recent Title IX litigation involves the argument that a sport that has been operating under "club" status should be raised to "varsity" status when the counterpart sex operates a varsity team in that same sport. This argument has been used by women athletes who feel that denial of varsity status to their sport is a violation of Title IX, given that the men student-athletes operate a varsity team in the same sport. This argument is based on the area of proportional ratios of sport participation opportunities offered to men and women student-athletes. The raising of the women's team to varsity status would be one way the school would be in compliance with Title IX if they felt they were not in compliance because of these participation opportunities. The plaintiffs would have to prove initially that the school was out of compliance with Title IX and that adding this particular sport program as a varsity sport would constitute compliance with Title IX.

The plaintiffs could also argue a Title IX complaint based on equal benefits and opportunities provided to the sport programs. The plaintiffs' argument could revolve around the fact that if a school offers a varsity team in a particular sport for the men, then they must offer the same sport for women at the varsity level and provide it with the benefits and opportunities that the men's team receives. The plaintiffs would need to prove that student-athletes have the interest and ability to compete on the varsity level, and that there is ample competition to sustain a team. This type of argument was used in the *Cook, et al. v. Colgate University* case, Case No. 90-CV-411 (N.D. N.Y. 1992), in which the plaintiff female student-athletes argued that their club sport of women's ice hockey should be raised to varsity status and that failure to do so was a violation of Title IX (see note 1). This approach to Title IX compliance is relatively new and the courts have yet to rule on this type of complaint.

NOTE

1. In *Cook, et al. v. Colgate University,* Case No. 90-CV-411 (N.D. N.Y. 1992), the plaintiff female student-athletes argued that refusal by Colgate University to raise their club ice hockey team to varsity status was a violation of Title IX because they were being denied the benefits and opportunities that were afforded to their male ice hockey–playing counterparts. Shortly after women students were admitted into the university in 1970, a women's ice hockey club team was formed. In 1979, 1983, 1986, and 1988, the women's ice hockey club team applied for varsity status and was denied all four times by the university. Varsity status is important in that it provides the team with full-time coaches, designated schedules, rules and regulations, equipment, practice facilities, travel accommodations, and appropriate budgetary support. Colgate University argued that individual programs should not be looked at (a comparison in this instance involving the support received by the men's varsity ice hockey team versus the women's club ice hockey team) and that no evidence had been presented to show that Colgate's athletic program discriminates against women.

The district court ruled for the plaintiffs and ordered Colgate to grant the women's ice hockey team varsity status and to provide all the amenities that accompany such a designation. The court ruled that Title IX is designed to protect not only a particular class of persons (women as a whole within the athletic department), but individuals as well. Therefore, a separate team comparison is appropriate when analyzing Title IX compliance. The court stated that because Colgate sponsors separate ice hockey teams for each gender, the court has the authority to compare the two programs according to the Title IX equal opportunity and benefit areas.

Colgate University also set forth six reasons why rejection of varsity status for the women's team took place: women's ice hockey is rarely played on the secondary level; championships are not sponsored by the NCAA; the game is only played by approximately fifteen colleges in the East; hockey is expensive to fund; there is a lack of general student interest in women's ice hockey; and, there is a lack of ability among the members of the women's club team. The court stated that the only real reason why the requests for varsity status were denied was that hockey is expensive to fund and elevating the team to varsity status would have a dramatic financial impact on the university. The court went on to state that financial problems and funding shortfalls are not legitimate excuses for Title IX violations.

Colgate University appealed this decision. The U.S. Court of Appeals heard the case and vacated the lower-court decision by ruling that the case was moot because all five of the plaintiffs either had graduated or were scheduled to graduate in May 1993. In August 1993, a new class action suit was filed against Colgate bringing the same complaint against the institution. A class action suit is a lawsuit brought by a representative party on behalf of a group, all of whose members have the same or a similar grievance against the defendant. The five original plaintiff student-athletes are bringing this new lawsuit on behalf of all current and future female athletes at Colgate University. Therefore, this issue has yet to be resolved by the courts. This may be an important issue in future Title IX litigation. If the original district court's opinion was adopted, it could have changed Title IX analysis to a sport-by-sport comparison rather than an overall programmatic approach.

SEX DISCRIMINATION CASES INVOLVING ATHLETIC EMPLOYMENT

The following sections and cases focus on sex discrimination in the area of athletic employment. Sex discrimination in this context can best be defined as the imposition of any barrier to employment which affects one gender but not the other. The plaintiff is generally an employee who serves as a coach or physical education teacher. The courts favor coaches or instructors who can prove that school districts or universities have discriminated against them on the basis of sex. The rulings in these cases favoring coaches and teachers post a warning to school officials that the rights of coaches must be understood and considered.

Equal Pay Act and Title VII

Two separate statutes specifically pertain to discrimination in employment. The first is the Equal Pay Act, which was passed in 1963 (effective date was June 10, 1964). The second is Title VII of the Civil Rights Act of 1964. While the Equal Pay Act deals solely with wages paid to women and men within the same company, Title VII focuses on discriminatory hiring/firing practices and advancement policies within companies. Neither is specific to the issue of sex discrimination; however, they both encompass discrimination on the basis of race, religion, or national origin. Both of these statutes have been applied to interscholastic and intercollegiate athletics, primarily in suits brought by female coaches claiming sex discrimination.

The Equal Pay Act stipulates that an employer must pay equal salaries to men and women holding jobs that require equal skill, effort, and responsibility and that are performed under similar working conditions. The Equal Pay Act, 29 U.S.C. § 206(d)(1) (1982), provides that

> No employer having employees subject to any provision of this section shall discriminate, within any establishment in which such employees are employed, between employees on the basis of sex by paying wages to employees in such establishment at a rate less than the rate at which he pays wages to employees of the opposite sex in such establishment for equal work on jobs the performance of which requires equal skill, effort, and responsibility, and which are performed under similar working conditions. . . .

The basic theme underlying the act is "equal pay for equal work." The courts apply a "substantially equal test" for judging the equality of jobs under the Equal Pay Act. The courts interpret this standard as consistent with the middle course intended by Congress between a requirement that the jobs in question be exactly alike and a requirement that they merely be comparable. In conducting its inquiry, the court looks at overall job content. The plaintiff must show that any job differences are so insignificant that they do not contribute to the differences in pay. The courts will look behind job classifications to the substance of the work. Any differences in job duties and responsibilities must be real and not just indicated by a nominal title or designation. Consequently, the Equal Pay Act addresses only the most overt wage discrimination cases and does not apply to problems created by prior discrimination in the workplace.

The Labor Department's Division of Wages and Hours was initially responsible for enforcing the Equal Pay Act under the Fair Labor Standards Acts (29 U.S.C. § 201 et seq). In 1979, enforcement was moved to the Equal Employment Opportunity Commission (EEOC). By statute, the EEOC consists of five members and is empowered to receive complaints, intervene in certain civil actions, and otherwise administer the Equal Pay Act and Title VII. Enforcement procedures consist of routine checks as well as investigations in response to specific complaints. If an employer is discriminating and the EEOC determines that this cannot be corrected informally, the Department of Labor may file suit to enforce the law.

An individual party bringing a discrimination complaint must establish that his or her job is substantially equal to that of another employee of the opposite sex who is being paid more for performing similar services and tasks. The party must file the suit within two years of the alleged discrimination, or within three years if the discrimination is found to be willful. If a claim is substantiated and a violation is found, the complaining party may receive the differences between the wages paid to men and women for a maximum two-year period or three years plus a penalty if the discrimination is found to be willful. To remedy a violation of the act, an employer may not reduce the wages of the higher paid employee.

The other statute available to combat employment discrimination is Title VII of the Civil Rights Act of 1964 (42 U.S.C. § 2000e-2[a] 1976), which states that

> [i]t shall be an unlawful employment practice for any employer to fail or refuse to hire or to discharge any individual, or otherwise discriminate against any individual with respect to his compensation, terms, conditions, or privileges of employment, because of such individual's race, color, religion, sex, or national origin. . . .

Title VII was enacted as a comprehensive prohibition on private acts of employment discrimination. It forbids discriminatory employment practices based on the race, color, religion, sex, or national origin of the applicant. These categories may, however, be used to differentiate between applicants when sex, religion, or national origin is a bona fide occupational qualification (BFOQ). A BFOQ is very narrowly defined as an actual job requirement, not merely a customer or employer preference. For example, race is never considered a BFOQ.

Title VII also contains a "nonretaliation" provision which prohibits all employers defined in the act from discriminating against any employee or job applicant who has invoked his or her rights under Title VII or who has assisted with or participated in any proceeding brought by someone else.

In the analysis of the courts, the alleged sex discrimination action need not only be based upon a consideration of an unalterable characteristic (like gender) possessed by the discriminatee but which is not possessed by the discriminator. Thus, not only are acts such as terminating female employees when they marry or refusing to accept employment applications from any female actionable, but also acts taken by a member of one sex against a member of the same sex can be actionable. A demand for sexual favors directed by one male to another as a condition of employment can be just as discriminatory as a similar demand directed by a male to a female.

Title VII is applicable to all employers of more than fifteen persons, and it specifically covers almost all state and local government employees as well as employees of most educational institutions. It is enforced by the EEOC, which has the authority to process and investigate any complaints. The EEOC may also bring suits in federal court if necessary. A charge brought by the EEOC is based on what the EEOC perceives to be a pattern or practice of unlawful discrimination which adversely affects an entire class of individuals. The EEOC may also conduct industrywide compliance reviews. If the discrimination found by the EEOC in state or local government cannot be corrected informally, the EEOC may refer the matter to the U.S. Attorney General. In all other cases, the EEOC may go to federal court to enforce the law.

Enforcement of Title VII is not limited to EEOC actions, however, because the legislation also has individual and class causes of action. This type of charge originates from an individual or group of individuals who allege that they were adversely affected by some act of unlawful discrimination. Organizations can bring discrimination claims on behalf of their members if the alleged discriminatory action injured its members, if the claim can proceed without the participation of those injured members, and if the claim is relevant to the organization's purposes.

The requirements for filing a charge include the following:

1. The person filing the charge must be or represent an aggrieved person (must have a personal stake in the outcome of the controversy and must have suffered a personal injury), except in cases in which the charge is filed by the EEOC itself.
2. The charge must be directed against an "employer" as defined by Title VII.
3. The charge must be filed within the specified time limits.
4. The form of the charge must comply with certain procedural requirements.

Once these requirements are met, the EEOC will proceed with the charge.

The remedies of both injunctive and affirmative relief are available to the winning party in an employment discrimination suit. The prevailing party may be awarded back pay and attorney's fees as well as an injunction prohibiting the employer's unlawful action. In addition, the court may order the employer to cease its discriminatory practices, to reinstate employees, and to implement an appropriate affirmative action plan to eliminate existing discrimination and prevent its recurrence. These remedies are guided by the two goals of the act: (1) to achieve equality of employment opportunity by removing barriers based on race, color, religion, sex, or national origin, and (2) to make the victim of unlawful discrimination whole—to put the victim in the position he or she would have been in had the discrimination not occurred.

Both of these approaches have limitations. Even taken together, they are not sufficient to enforce a prohibition against sex discrimination. Although the Equal Pay Act applies to all employers, Title VII has been limited to employers of more than fifteen people. Thus, many smaller businesses are not subject to the mandates of Title VII. The Equal Pay Act is limited in other ways. For example, it is directed only to discrepancies in pay levels once on a job. It does not address the problem of discriminatory hiring or advancement policies. The basic weakness of these acts is that neither is all-encompassing. They fail to address the overall problems of sex discrimination that exist outside of the workplace. Thus, very few of the problems of discrimination encountered in athletics are addressed by either act. This legislation provides potential relief only in athletic employment.

Another major problem in pursuing litigation under these statutes is the cost. Neither statute provides any guaranteed basis for the eventual recovery of attorney's fees and/or double or triple damages. Thus, litigation is not an option for many of those who might wish to file claims. Cases are seldom pursued, and the effectiveness of the legislation diminishes as the chance that an employer will be punished lessens. One last problem is that courts have been reluctant to interpret the statutes broadly. This reluctance stems from the fact that hiring and salary decisions are well within the area of management prerogatives allotted to employers. The court is reluctant to interfere in any discretionary decision unless there has been a clear abuse of that discretion. Thus, it is very difficult to establish a case based on a complaint regarding practices in either of these areas. Usually, the evidence is open to a variety of interpretations. Such circumstances can make it difficult or even impossible for a plaintiff to prevail in a sex discrimination case under application of the aforementioned statutes.

NOTES ───

1. In *Kunda v. Muhlenberg College*, 621 F.2d 532 (3rd Cir. 1980), an action was brought which involved an employment discrimination case based on sex. The plaintiff was a female physical education instructor at a private college. She was denied tenure because she lacked a master's degree, whereas three male members of the physical education department who lacked master's degrees were promoted. The court issued an injunction requiring the college to promote the female instructor with tenure and back pay. The court of appeals affirmed the decision, stating that "Academic institutions' decisions are not *ipso facto* entitled to special treatment under federal laws prohibiting

discrimination." The court noted that although the interests of an educational institution in academic freedom are important, academic freedom is not implicated in every academic employment decision.

2. In *Caulfield v. Board of Education of City of New York,* 632 F.2d 999 (2nd Cir. 1980), the court upheld a decision that Title IX applies to athletic hiring practices because discrimination against women's access to supervisory positions has a discriminating effect on the institution's students, the direct beneficiaries of federal financial aid. Coaching and other supervisory positions in athletic programs must be assigned without discrimination, even if the program receives no direct federal aid for funding the positions.

3. In *Cannon v. University of Chicago,* 441 U.S. 677 (1979), the Supreme Court held that Title IX should be interpreted as being similar in intent to Title VII of the Civil Rights Act of 1964. The court cited cases in which plaintiffs suing officials of the federal government under Title VII secured orders requiring those officials either to aid recipients of federal funds in devising nondiscriminatory alternatives to presently discriminatory programs or to cut aid to those programs. The court held that these rulings applied to Title IX situations as well.

4. In *Shenefield v. Sheridan County School District No. 1,* 544 P.2d 870 (Wyo. 1976), plaintiff Shenefield, a female teacher in Wyoming, was passed over for a teaching position by the principal in favor of a man who could coach as well as teach and be hired for $2,600 less than Shenefield. The Wyoming Fair Employment Commission agreed that sex discrimination had taken place. The district court reversed the commission's decision, and the teacher appealed to the state supreme court.

The court, which analyzed the case under the State Fair Employment Practices Act, reasoned that a school board does not give up its freedom to choose the teacher (coach) it wants just because it advertises such a position. The court, in favoring the hiring of the male teacher, stated:

> If it turns out for reasons of economy, one applicant can fulfill the needs of a district at a cost substantially less than another applicant, even though the rejected applicant may on paper possess the greater qualifications, a selection of the less expensive teacher cannot be said by any board or court to have been the result of discrimination on the basis of sex.

The court concluded that a school board has the discretion of hiring a teacher who can also coach and should be able to select a teacher who is personally attractive to it without the threat of discrimination.

5. In *Civil Rights Division of Arizona Department of Law v. Amphitheater Unified School District No. 10,* 680 P.2d 517 (Ariz. App. 1983), defendant school district combined two positions, biology teacher and football coach, and advertised them as a single position. One of the female applicants filed this lawsuit under the Arizona Civil Rights Act, contending that this practice of coupling academic contracts with added contracts to coach football had a disparate impact on women applicants for academic teaching positions. The trial court, which examined the case under Title VII because of its similarity to the Arizona Civil Rights Act, ruled in favor of the school district on the theory that it had established the defense of business necessity in filling the

positions together. The court of appeals disagreed and held that this method of filling the dual teaching-coaching position had a disparate impact on females. The court held that the school district in this instance failed to prove that a business necessity existed which required them to couple the contracts.

6. In *Anderson v. City of Bessemer City, North Carolina*, 557 F. Supp. 412 (W.D.N.C.), *rev'd*, 717 F.2d 149 (4th Cir. 1983), *rev'd*, 470 U.S. 564 (1985), the Supreme Court upheld a claim of sex discrimination by a female applicant for position of city recreation director under Title VII. The Court agreed with the district court, which found that the female was more qualified than the male applicant who was offered the position and that the selection committee was biased.

7. In *Harrington v. Vandalia-Butler Board of Education*, 418 F. Supp. 603 (S.D. Ohio 1976), *rev'd*, 585 F.2d 192 (6th Cir. 1978), *cert. denied*, 441 U.S. 932 (1979), the court upheld a female retired physical education teacher's claim that unequal working conditions violated Title VII, but ruled that compensatory damages, except for back pay awards, were unavailable under Title VII. Because the teacher had been unable to recover damages, the court ruled that she was not a "prevailing party" and that she therefore was not entitled to attorney's fees.

8. In *Wynn v. Columbus Mun. Separate School Dist.*, 692 F. Supp. 672 (N.D. Miss. 1988), a female high school physical education teacher brought Title VII sex discrimination action, alleging discriminatory denial of her application for the position of athletic director. Defendants argued that the plaintiff was not qualified because the position was not simply athletic director but athletic director/head football coach. The court reasoned that the combined position unlawfully excluded the plaintiff from consideration. The court held that defendants discriminated against the plaintiff on basis of gender by refusing to appoint her athletic director.

9. In *Hooker v. Tufts University*, 581 F. Supp. 104 (1983), a female professor of physical education brought employment discrimination action under Title VII of the Civil Rights Act of 1964 for denial of tenure. The district court held that plaintiff failed to make a prima facie case of sex discrimination and ruled for the defendants.

10. In *Greer v. University of Arkansas Bd. of Trustees*, 544 F. Supp. 1085 (1982), female faculty members at state university brought class action claiming employment discrimination on basis of sex under Title VII of the Civil Rights Act of 1964. In ruling for the plaintiffs, the judge stated that the sex discrimination practices of the defendants were "too blatant to overlook," and thus permanently enjoined defendants from considering sex when making future job decisions.

11. Title VII of the Civil Rights Act of 1964, U.S.C. § 2000d, et. seq., prohibits discrimination on the basis of race, color, or national origin in connection with any program or activity which receives federal financial assistance. Title VII was designed to prevent the use of federal funds to promote discrimination and has been construed as protecting individual rights to be free from discrimination. Title IX was closely modeled after Title VII and adopts the same prohibitory language and procedural regulations of Title VII.

Coaching

Allegations of discrimination based on sex have often been made in the area of coaching. Many of the claims are based on a lack of pay parity between the coaches of male and female teams. Often coaches of women's teams—women, usually—are paid less than coaches of men's teams. The justification most often made by school districts for the pay differential is that coaches of men's teams and coaches of women's teams do not perform equivalent work. In order to redress the inequality in salary, women must prove they perform substantially equivalent work. Some factors that courts consider in making determinations are the nature of the game, the number of the players being supervised, the length of the playing season, the time taken up in practices, the amount of travel required, and any other responsibilities undertaken by the coach—recruiting, scouting, academic counseling, and so forth.

In cases in which it is difficult for the coach of a women's team to meet the standard of "equivalent work," the argument has been made that the work is more difficult. Plaintiff coaches of women's teams have argued that girls have not been as exposed to sports as boys; therefore, coaches of women's teams often spend much more time actually teaching their players. They do not have the luxury of merely retraining skills in a player who has participated in that sport for a number of years. Instead, they often coach women who have had little experience in the particular sport at all. However, as women's athletic programs proliferate at the youth levels, this argument is becoming less effective.

NOTES _____

1. In *McCullar v. Human Rights Com'n*, 511 N.E.2d 1375 (Ill. App. 4 Dist. 1987), female coach of girls' high school and junior high school volleyball teams appealed the decision of the Human Rights Commission that she was not a victim of employment discrimination on basis of her sex. Plaintiff cited example of male coaches with allegedly similar responsibilities and experiences who were paid higher salaries.

In deciding the case, the judge scrutinized the alleged discrimination using various legal statutes, including the Equal Pay Act and the Civil Rights Act of 1964. The court affirmed the commission's order that there was no employment discrimination on the basis of sex. First, the judge ruled that plaintiff failed to establish a prima facie case of employment discrimination because the position of boys' junior high school basketball coach, which plaintiff cited for comparison, did not involve approximately the same time commitment. The judge further held that pay differential between coaching positions for male and female sports at junior high school and high school was not based on the sex of the coaches but on the sex of the participants, which was considered a valid basis for differential.

2. In *EEOC v. Madison Comm. Unit School Dist. No. 12*, 818 F.2d 577 (7th Cir. 1987), the Equal Employment Opportunity Commission (EEOC) brought suit against school district under the Equal Pay Act, and female athletic coaches allegedly victimized by district's discrimination intervened and added Title VII counts. Plaintiffs claimed that female coaches at the school district were paid less than their male counterparts for performing equal jobs. Where male and female coaches of the same sport were compared, the judge affirmed the district court's ruling that the school district had violated the Equal Pay Act. However, in cases where the sports were different, the appellate judge vacated the findings of the district judge with respect to a violation of the Equal Pay Act. The court rejected the school district's defense that the unequal pay between women coaching girls' teams and men coaching boys' teams was due to the sex of the participant, not the sex of the coach because Madison School District had openly discouraged women from seeking coaching positions for boys' teams.

3. In *Burkey v. Marshall County Board of Education*, 513 F. Supp. 1084 (N.D. W. Va. 1981), plaintiff Burkey instituted a girls' basketball program at a junior high school in West Virginia during the 1971–72 school year. She posted a career mark of 31–5 in the four years she coached the team. In the 1973–74 season, Burkey received nominal remuneration for coaching. In keeping with school board policies, Burkey was paid one-half of the amount given to the coach of the junior high boys' team. Additionally, she was prevented from coaching the boys' team, solely on the basis of her sex. In 1977, HEW issued a finding that the school district's operation of the girls' athletic program violated the rights of women coaches and female student-athletes as protected under Title IX. The Equal Employment Opportunity Commission also found reasonable cause to believe the board's policies constituted unlawful sex discrimination against Burkey. She was removed as coach and transferred from the junior high to an elementary school after she filed a complaint with the West Virginia Human Rights Commission.

Burkey brought suit against the school board, alleging sexual discrimination in violation of rights granted to her by Title VII, the Civil Rights Act of 1971, and the Equal Pay Act. The court found for Burkey and awarded her $1,260 in lost back pay. It also ordered the school board to offer Burkey the next available vacant physical education teaching position in either the junior or senior high school, and to offer her the headcoach's position for girls' basketball at that school.

4. In *California Women's Coaches Academy v. California Interscholastic Federation*, Case No. 77-1270 LEW (C.D. Cal. 1980) (settled), the California Women's Coaches Academy and three individual members of the academy filed a class action on behalf of themselves and certain other female coaches and officials for girls' high school interscholastic athletic contests.

The plaintiffs made certain allegations of unlawful sex discrimination, including charges that the defendants (education officials):

(a) Excluded women from participating in the Federated Council.

(b) Established fewer interscholastic sports for girls than for boys.

(c) Established shorter seasons for girls than for boys.

(d) Discriminated on the basis of sex in the hiring of persons to appoint officials for girls' contests.

(e) Discriminated on the basis of sex in the hiring of officials for girls' contests.

(f) Established lower rates of pay for officials of girls' interscholastic athletics.

The plaintiffs reached out-of-court settlements with each group of defendants.

The following is a summary of the terms and conditions that were common in all parts of the settlement:

(1) The number of sports available to female athletes will equal approximately the same number of those available to male athletes.

(2) Levels of competition and scheduling will be determined without regard to the sex of the athlete.

(3) Facilities will be made available without regard to the sex of the athlete.

(4) The length of the season in identical sports will consist of an equal number of weeks.

(5) Appointments to officiate and rates of officials' pay for identical sports will be determined without regard to the sex of the athletes or the officials.

(6) Plaintiffs and class members will relinquish any claims they had for lost wages and lost employment opportunities due to past discrimination by defendants.

(7) Defendants need not schedule identical sports during the same season as long as it is not to the detriment of one sex over another.

5. In *Jackson v. Armstrong School District*, 430 F. Supp. 1050 (W.D. Pa. 1977), an action was brought by plaintiffs Jackson and Pollick, who were women's basketball coaches. They claimed the school district had violated Title VII and the Pennsylvania Human Relations Act by paying them significantly less than the male coaches of the men's basketball team. There were four men and four women within the district coaching women's basketball who were all paid equally. The court ruled in favor of the school district, finding that it lacked jurisdiction under the State Human Relations Act and that the coaches' claim was not valid.

6. In *Kenneweg v. Hampton Township School District*, 438 F. Supp. 575 (W.D. Pa. 1977), plaintiffs Kenneweg and Love sued the Armstrong School District on grounds of sex discrimination. They were both coaches and claimed they were paid less because of their sex. The court held that because the charge filed with the Equal Employment Opportunity Commission had dealt only with the question of pay, the complaint could not be amended to allege discrimination with respect to working conditions. The court also held that the actions of the school district in paying female coaches of female sports less than male coaches of male sports did not constitute discrimination based on sex. The court decided for the school district, stating that the claim was based on a Title VII argument and that "disparity in treatment not based on plaintiffs' sex was not a valid claim under Title VII."

7. In *State Division of Human Rights v. Syracuse City Teachers Ass'n*, 412 N.Y.S.2d 711 (App. Div. 1979), an action was brought by two female

coaches who had filed a complaint with the State Division of Human Rights. The women had agreed to coach the junior high girls' basketball team as volunteers and were not paid. The women later found that the male basketball coach was receiving $308 to coach the boys' team. The commissioner of the Human Rights Division found that the board of education had discriminated against the women and ordered equal payment. The appeals board affirmed the decision.

The court overturned the commissioner's decision and held for the teachers association. It found no discrimination in employment by the board. The court reasoned that both the male and female coaches were treated equally and that the unequal pay schedule was reasonable because the job responsibilities and time commitment differed.

8. In *United Teachers of Seaford v. New York State Human Rights Appeal Board*, 414 N.Y.S.2d 207 (App. Div. 1979), the court held that a union has the obligation to represent its member coaches fairly and impartially and may not discriminate on the basis of race or sex. The fundamental purpose of a union is to provide for its members the bargaining power that unity creates; when a union fails to exercise that power in the bargaining process and permits an employer to discriminate against union members, it discriminates against them as surely as if it proposed the inequitable agreement. Evidence proved that the union was aware of the unduly low salaries and that the union had settled for an agreement that grossly discriminated against female coaches.

9. In *Kings Park Central School District No. 5 v. State Division of Human Rights*, 424 N.Y.S.2d 293 (App. Div. 1980), the petitioners asked the court to review a decision of the State Division of Human Rights finding unlawful discrimination by the petitioner in paying coaches of boys' teams more than those of girls' teams. The court granted the petition and found no discrimination by the school district. Although the skill, effort, and responsibility were equal, coaching boys' teams required greater coaching time and travel.

10. In *Brennan v. Woodbridge School District*, 8 Empl. Prac. Dec. 9640 (D. Del. 1974), the court held that lower pay to a female coach of a girls' softball team constituted a violation of the Equal Pay Act, since she performed work equal to that of the male coach of the boys' hardball team.

11. In *Erickson v. Board of Education, Provise Township High School*, 458 N.E.2d 84 (Ill. Ct. App. 1983), the court held that the Equal Pay Act was not violated when compensation for coaches was set in accordance with the sex of the players rather than the sex of the coaches. The court ruled that no sex discrimination had taken place since the difference was explained by the application of a higher pay rate to all coaches who worked in male sports than to those coaches who worked in female sports.

12. In *Countiss v. Trenton State College*, 392 A.2d 1205 (N.J. Ct. App. 1978), the court held that the fact that eleven of thirteen male coaches and four of seven female coaches were tenured failed to establish that the university had demonstrated sex bias in awarding tenure to physical education instructors. However, the court held that the fact that female coaches received only four hours per year release time credit while male coaches received ten hours did constitute sex discrimination.

13. In *Pennsylvania Human Relations Comm'n v. School District of Town-*

ship of Millcreek, 368 A.2d 901 (1977), *rev'd,* 377 A.2d 156 (Pa. Ct. App. 1977), the court held that failure to pay equal supplemental wages to the coach of the girls' varsity tennis team (as opposed to the boys' team) constituted discrimination in violation of the state human relations statute.

14. For further information, see Notes, "Equal Pay for Coaches of Female Teams: Finding a Cause of Action under Federal Law," 55 *Notre Dame L. Rev.* 751 (June 1980).

Sports-Related Employment Discrimination

While Title IX has been available as a basis to contest sex discrimination in coaching, attacks on perceived inequalities in other sports-related employment have largely consisted of allegations of the denial of equal protection rights. Cases regarding discrimination in officiating, refereeing, and media coverage have stemmed from charges that employment practices, and specifically exclusionary rules, are arbitrary, are related to no legitimate purpose, and are, therefore, violations of the plaintiff's constitutional rights.

Officiating

Arbitrary height and weight requirements for umpires and referees may act unlawfully to discriminate against women. When such requirements are not sufficiently related to the job, they may be deemed to be arbitrary and thus impose unconstitutional restrictions.

One issue in particular—women athletes who wish to compete in professional wrestling—has produced a series of decisions in which state athletic commissions were named defendants. The courts, in most cases, have granted the commissions great latitude in granting licenses and have generally upheld their decisions.

NOTES _____

1. In *New York State Division of Human Rights v. New York-Pennsylvania Professional Baseball League,* 320 N.Y.S.2d 788 (App. Div. 1971), *aff'd,* 329 N.Y.S.2d 99 (Ct. App. 1972), the plaintiff Human Rights Division brought an action upon a complaint by a female umpire charging the defendant baseball league with a violation of a state statute (Sec. 296, Executive Law) prohibiting employment discrimination. The New York Supreme Court, Appellate Division, held that league rules requiring an umpire to stand at least 5 feet 10 inches tall and weigh at least 170 pounds "were not justified by the claim that umpires must command respect of big men or by factors relating to increased size of professional catchers, physical strain, travel conditions and length of games, and that the standards were inherently discriminatory against women." The league was ordered to cease and desist such discrimination.

2. In *State Division of Human Rights v. New York City Dep't of Parks and Recreation,* 326 N.Y.S.2d 640 (App. Div. 1971), the court invalidated the height requirement of 5 feet 6 inches and the weight requirement of 125 pounds for

lifeguards because of the discriminatory impact on women and the lack of proof of job relatedness.

Participation in Professional Sports

Although females have competed with males on all levels of amateur athletics, relatively few women have entered as participants into professional sports. Sex discrimination cases litigated in regard to female participation in professional sports have largely concerned professional wrestling. These cases have not centered on the right to participate with men but rather on the constitutionality of rules that refuse women the right to petition for and receive a professional wrestling license. Plaintiffs have relied on equal protection claims to challenge these exclusionary rules.

NOTES _____

1. In *Calzadilla v. Dooley,* 286 N.Y.S.2d 510 (App. Div. 1968), a discrimination suit was brought by a woman wrestler who alleged the refusal by the state's athletic commission to grant her a professional wrestling license constituted a violation of the Fourteenth Amendment's equal protection clause. In arguing that "a great deal of latitude and discretion must be accorded the State Athletic Commission," the court held that the commission's rule against granting wrestling licenses to women was not "an unjust and unconstitutional discrimination against women." The court reasoned that no one had an inherent right to participate in public wrestling exhibitions.

2. In *Hesseltine v. State Athletic Comm'n,* 126 N.E.2d 631 (S. Ct. Ill. 1955), plaintiff Hesseltine (also known as Rose Roman) applied through normal procedures for a permit to wrestle. The Illinois State Athletic Commission rejected her application. She appealed to the circuit court and won. The commission appealed. The appeals court affirmed the decision. The defendant's adoption of a rule excluding women from wrestling within the state was seen as arbitrary and therefore invalid.

3. In *State v. Hunter,* 300 P.2d 455 (S. Ct. Or. 1956), defendant Hunter, a female wrestler, was prosecuted for competing in a wrestling match that was held in violation of a statutory ban on women's wrestling. The court ruled in favor of the plaintiff, holding that the ban on women's participation in wrestling was not unconstitutional.

4. In *Whitehead v. Krulewitch,* 271 N.Y.S.2d 565 (App. Div. 1966), plaintiff Whitehead appealed a ruling of the New York Special Term Court denying her a professional wrestling license. The New York Supreme Court, Appellate Division, affirmed the decision.

5. In *Garrett v. New York State Athletic Comm'n,* 370 N.Y.S.2d 795 (Sup. Ct. 1975), the court held that a claim by a woman boxer of wrongful denial of a professional boxing license stated a cause of action under the Fourteenth Amendment. Thus, the athletic commission's motion to dismiss the case was denied. The court directed the woman to resubmit her application, and the commission would have to provide her with its answer.

6. In *Rubin v. Florida State Racing Comm'n,* Civil No. 6819113 (11th Cir.

Dade County, Fla., 1968), the court upheld the claim of a female plaintiff for an apprentice jockey license.

7. In *Kusner v. Maryland Racing Comm'n.*, Civil No. 37044 (Civil Ct.— Prince George's County, Md. 1968), the court upheld the claim of a female plaintiff for a jockey license.

8. For further information, see Kuhn, "Employment and Athletics Are Outside HEW's Jurisdiction," 65 *Georgetown L. J.* 49 (1976).

The Media

Barring members of the news media from locker rooms has been an area of concern for many sports organizations. If a barred reporter is female (see note 1, *Ludtke v. Kuhn*), and male members of the news media are not similarly restricted, she may allege a violation of equal protection of the laws under the Fourteenth Amendment. In all Fourteenth Amendment cases, the plaintiff must demonstrate that state action is involved before relief under the Fourteenth Amendment can be considered (see Chapter 4). The court in *Ludtke* found such state action because the New York Yankees had leased their stadium from the city of New York, a subdivision of the state. Private universities that lease stadiums from the state, municipal, or local governments could face a similar result. When public institutions such as state universities are involved, a court is likely to find state action without the need for such a relationship with a facility. A court is likely to have difficulty finding state action when a private institution (for example, the Boston Red Sox) does not lease from a governmental entity but instead owns its playing facility.

The *Ludtke* decision is the only reported case involving a rule barring female reporters from a male locker room. One important issue— the players' right to privacy—remains unanswered after *Ludtke*. In *Ludtke*, the court found that the players' right to privacy had been negated by the presence of television cameras in the locker room. If the right of privacy is not negated in a future case, the court will have to strike a balance between the players' right to privacy and the female reporters' right not to be discriminated against.

NOTES ───

1. In *Ludtke v. Kuhn*, 461 F. Supp. 86 (S.D.N.Y. 1978), a civil rights action suit was brought by plaintiff female reporter for *Sports Illustrated* magazine. The female reporter sought an order "enjoining defendants, the New York Yankees, from enforcing a policy determination made by Baseball Commissioner Kuhn, and approved by American League President MacPhail, which required that accredited female sports reporters be excluded from the locker room of the Yankee clubhouse in Yankee Stadium." Defendants admitted that accredited male sports reporters could enter the locker room after a ball game for the purpose of interviewing ballplayers and that such fresh-off-the-field

interviews were important to the work of sports reporters. The defendants argued that women reporters were excluded from the locker rooms "in order (1) to protect the privacy of those players who are undressed or in various stages of undressing and getting ready to shower; (2) to protect the image of baseball as a family sport; and, (3) preservation of the traditional notions of decency and propriety."

The court held "that defendants' policy of total exclusion of women sports reporters from the locker room at Yankee Stadium is not substantially related to the privacy protection objective and thus deprives plaintiff Ludtke of that equal protection of the law which is guaranteed her by the Fourteenth Amendment."

The court stated:

> The undisputed facts show that the Yankees' interest in protecting ballplayer privacy may be fully served by much less sweeping means than that implemented here. The court holds that the state action complained of unreasonably interferes with plaintiff Ludtke's fundamental right to pursue her profession in violation of the due process clause of the Fourteenth Amendment.

2. Counsel for Kuhn and Major League Baseball decided not to appeal *Ludtke v. Kuhn*, since they believed that the decision was not a damaging precedent. (See *NCAA Public Relations and Promotions Manual*, NCAA publication, Mission, Kansas, 1985, Appendix C.)

3. The NCAA requires that its championship teams open locker rooms to all certified members of the media after a ten-minute cooling-off period. See, for instance, *1992 Men's and Women's Soccer National Collegiate Championships Handbook*, NCAA publication, Mission, Kansas, 1983, p. 47.

4. For further information on media access to locker rooms, see Brennan, "Civil Rights in the Locker Room: *Ludtke v. Kuhn*," 2 *Journal of Communication and Entertainment Law*, 645 (Summer 1980).

Chapter 9

TELEVISION AND MEDIA BROADCASTING

INTRODUCTION

Amateur athletic associations, conferences, and individual schools have a property right in the accounts and descriptions of their games, whether the event broadcast is on the radio, television, or cable television. This property right has numerous legal ramifications and involves copyright, antitrust, and contract law. It is important for athletic administrators to be aware of these legal considerations when entering into contract negotiations for the broadcast rights to their organization's sporting events.

In order to detail these legal considerations some basic terminology relating to the broadcasting industry must be reviewed:

- *Standard Broadcast Television.* What most individuals consider "television." Local television stations broadcast programming which is received by local home television when the antenna picks up air transmission signals. Standard broadcast television is broadcast on channels 2–69, with channels 2–13 known as very high frequency (VHF) and channels 14–69 known as ultra high frequency (UHF).

- *Cable Television* (formerly known as CATV [community antenna television]). A service provided to consumers by which traditional television programming and/or other broadcast signals (e.g., pay cable) are brought into the home of the subscriber by way of cable transmission (as opposed to over-the-air transmission), usually for an initial installation charge and a monthly subscription fee.

- *Pay Cable.* Refers to a premium cable television service, by which special channels are provided to subscribers for an additional cost that provides unique programming such as sports. Examples of special channels are Sports Channel and HBO, among others. Standard broadcast stations can be brought into a subscriber's home or business by cable to give a better signal. In addition, cable can provide subscribers with stations which regular antennas would not be able to pick up.

- *Superstations.* Refers to a local independent distant signal television station whose programs, including sports, are carried via satellite to cable systems outside the station's local broadcast range. Distant signals are television stations outside a viewer's ordinary viewing area. Examples would be WTBS in Atlanta, WWOR in New Jersey, and WPIX in New York.

- *Satellites.* Serve as a space-based distribution system of program services for standard broadcast and cable television. Satellites relay television signals across the world.

- *Earth Station, Uplink, Downlink*, and *Transponder*. All are used in satellite transmissions of broadcast signals. The uplink is the ground-to-satellite transmission of a broadcast signal; a down-link is a satellite-to-earth-station transmission of a broadcast signal; and an earth station is a ground antenna designed to communicate with a satellite. A transponder is the part of the satellite that consists of the receiver to pick up the signals from the uplink, a processor to convert the signal's frequency and amplify its strength, and a transmitter to rebroadcast the signal on the downlink.
- *Fixation*. Recording all or parts of a broadcast on film, videotape, or replay tape for purposes of protecting the copyright and the manner in which it was recorded.

Chapter 9 begins with an explanation of why sports broadcasts are a protectable property right of the athletic organization sponsoring the event. Congress further strengthened this legal right with the passage of the Copyright Act of 1976, the topic of the next section. The chapter goes on to discuss issues and clauses that are unique to sports broadcast contracts.

In addition to the impact of the copyright laws on broadcast contracts, the antitrust laws have also had a major impact. In 1984, the Supreme Court declared that the NCAA 1982–85 football television plan violated the Sherman Antitrust Act. This ruling, which affected networks, producers, syndicators, advertisers, and NCAA member institutions, is examined next in Chapter 9. The final section of the chapter presents a broadcasting checklist for athletic administrators so that some of the legal problems surrounding television and media broadcasting can be avoided.

SPORTS BROADCASTS: A PROTECTABLE PROPERTY RIGHT

Since 1921 it has been held that an athletic organization has the right to control the dissemination of the accounts of its games. The early cases in this area dealt with unauthorized radio broadcasts of professional sports contests. In cases of unauthorized use, the courts held that such use was a misappropriation of a club's property right to control "descriptions or accounts" of games, and to allow broadcast stations to do so would be an "unjust enrichment" to a station. *Property* is generally defined as

that which belongs exclusively to one ... the unrestricted and exclusive right to a thing; the right to dispose of a thing in every legal way, to possess it, to use it, and to exclude everyone else from interfering with it. (*Black's Law Dictionary*)

This legal right was further strengthened when Congress enacted the Copyright Act of 1976. In enacting that law Congress extended copyright protection to live sports broadcasts. Copyright grants the owners of a copyrightable work the exclusive right to "perform the copyrighted work publicly." Since the enactment of copyright law, legal issues have arisen over who owns the copyright for a broadcast.

It was widely believed by broadcast networks that the copyright belonged to them. However, in 1978 the Copyright Royalty Tribunal concluded that, based on the legislative history of the 1976 legislation, the copyright belonged to the sports entity whose game or event is being telecast. This view was upheld by the courts.

For the sports administrator the importance of the above holding is that (1) the amateur sports organization or its parent institution has the ultimate right to decide whether it wants to have its sporting events (property) broadcast on one of the electronic media, and (2) for any subsequent rebroadcast of the sports entity's game the organization can expect to receive compensation.

Another interesting property issue raised in broadcasting revolves around who owns the rights to a game—the home team or the away team? Generally, this issue is resolved in the game contract, and such agreements usually give the property right to the home team or host sports entity. At least one court has ruled that, based on common law principles of misappropriation and contractual interference, a visiting team controls the right to broadcast a game back to its "home" city and surrounding area (see *Wichita State University Intercollegiate Athletic Ass'n v. Swanson Broadcasting Co.*, Case No. 81C130 Kan. Dist. Ct., Jan. 3, 1981]).

COPYRIGHT LAWS

As noted previously, the Copyright Act of 1976 gave sports organizations a right to copyright the broadcast of their games or contests, insuring a statutory property right. Amateur athletic organizations are most often impacted by the copyright laws in regards to retransmission of a broadcast of the organization's games or contests. This rebroadcasting most frequently occurs with cable television—for instance, when a local cable system broadcasts a game from a distant signal television station. Under the 1976 law, cable television companies were granted a compulsory license that exempts them from having to seek permission to retransmit any programming that a standard broadcasting television station is originating. This means that if a local television station is broadcasting a school's basketball game and if a cable system has the capability to pick up that transmission, the cable company can also broadcast it over its cable system without the permission of the school.

Cable systems do have to pay a royalty commission for telecasting the contest to a central fund. To distribute these royalty payments to deserving sports entities (and nonsports copyright holders), the 1976 Copyright Act established the Copyright Royalty Tribunal. The Tribunal was established so that each cable network and each rights holder would not have to negotiate for the rights to each game. The Tribunal is a governmental agency that must decide who gets royalties and how much they receive in the way of payments. With sports the Tribunal has devised a distribution formula that weighs relative marketplace values of the programming retransmitted against the value to the cable system for using the broadcast and the harm inflicted by its broadcast to the copyright holder. The cable companies pay a royalty fee that is based on a sliding scale relative to their overall revenues. When the first royalty fees were divided for the year 1978, it was determined that sports would receive 12 percent of the total pool, which amounted to $15 million. In 1979 and 1980 the split was 15 percent of the pool to sports. From 1983 to 1990 the split was 16.35 percent of the pool.

In intercollegiate athletics, the NCAA represents its membership collectively before the Copyright Royalty Tribunal. The association has filed a joint claim for cable royalty fees on behalf of its interested member institutions since the Tribunal was first convened in 1978. Initially, participation by NCAA member schools was quite extensive, but recently only a few hundred claims have been submitted by the NCAA.

This decrease is due to institutions and conferences negotiating their own cable network contracts which cannot be claimed for royalty fees. Participation in this program is voluntary for NCAA members, but it is in the best financial interest of the institution to collect any royalty fees they may be due.

The NCAA also has an elaborate annual system for collecting data from its membership concerning retransmissions of broadcasts. In June 1991 the NCAA distributed its data collection form for the 1990 calendar year, which noted in part the following:

It is now time to collect information regarding *nonnetwork 1990 football and basketball telecasts* that may qualify for cable copyright fees from all institutions and conferences that want the NCAA to file a joint claim in their behalf for a share of the 1990 fees. As in the past, this office will undertake the responsibility for initial data collection and organization, and the Association's Washington, D.C. legal counsel will file the formal claim with the Copyright Royalty Tribunal.

In order to participate, please complete the enclosed forms relating to your *nonnetwork football and basketball telecasts during the calendar year 1990,* and the authorization letter (a draft letter is enclosed) typed on your institution or conference stationery. These documents, completed, should be returned to Gina L. McNeal, Assistant Director of Communications, at the NCAA national office.

Please list the *call letters* of *all* stations on which each game was telecast. We will conduct the necessary research to determine whether the stations listed were carried by cable systems on a distant-signal basis. It is *very important* that every station is identified by its *call letters,* not by its channel number. *A claimed telecast that does not include the call letters of the station cannot be processed.*

Please note that network telecasts (telecasts produced by ABC, CBS, or NBC that are aired nationwide) and cable-originated programs (events produced and shown by ESPN, SportsChannel, Prime Sports Network, or local cable systems) do not qualify and *should not* be listed. Events produced by local over-the-air stations, including network affiliates and independent over-the-air stations, or by syndicators (e.g. Raycom) *do qualify and should be listed.*

In order to file a claim for statutory cable royalty fees, please complete the enclosed programming logs relating to nonnetwork football and basketball telecasts and the authorization letter (a draft letter is attached) typed on your institution or conference stationery.

This request concerns copyright ownership of "rights," *not* "rights to telecast." The transfer or sale to a station or production company of the rights (including exclusive rights) to telecast your games does not automatically affect copyright ownership.

All such copyright fees are paid by cable systems. There is no liability upon local broadcast stations. Each institution and/or conference simply is claiming compensation for use by cable systems of telecasts of events that originally were licensed only for local or regional television coverage broadcast over-the-air. Understandably, a member may not be aware that cable retransmission has taken place. If the NCAA does not receive information about your telecasts, however, it will not be possible to secure fees for events that are eligible. Please follow these instructions in filing a claim for statutory cable royalty fees.

1. Each member is requested to complete a programming log for football and basketball games that were televised in 1990. Both logs should be completed and returned to the NCAA by September 1, 1991.

2. Only nonnetwork (local or regional) over-the-air football and basketball telecasts qualify for statutory copyright royalty fees. Any games broadcast as national network programs by ABC, CBS or NBC, any games cablecast by ESPN, SportsChannel, New England Sports Network, Prime Sports Network, USA Network etc., for example, or produced and shown *only* by a local cable com-

pany, *should not* be listed. Regional over-the-air basketball and football telecasts or telecasts syndicated by a national or regional carrier, e.g. Turner Broadcasting System, Raycom, etc. should be included. Games carried by "superstations" (WGN, WTBS, WOR, etc.) also should be listed.

3. A local telecast by a station affiliated with a network *should* be listed.

4. Games broadcast by public broadcasting stations may qualify and should be included on the logs.

5. Please list the call letters of all stations on which each game was telecast. If all stations are not known, list those that can be verified. The NCAA will conduct the necessary research to determine if the station(s) listed was carried by a cable system on a distant-signal basis. *THE NCAA CANNOT PROCESS A CLAIM FOR A TELECAST THAT DOES NOT INCLUDE THE CALL LETTERS OF THE STATION; THE CHANNEL NUMBER OF THE STATION IS NOT SUFFICIENT.*

6. Please indicate if the game was telecast live or on a delayed basis.

7. Please indicate if the institution or the conference owned the copyright to the telecast. If no indication of ownership is made the claim will be awarded to the "home" team.

8. Please indicate if the telecast was preserved or "fixed" in some manner (i.e., all or parts of the telecast were recorded on film, videotape, replay tape or audiovisual logger by the station that produced the event at the time of the event). It is a common practice for television stations to preserve or "fix" a telecast. The institution and/or conference, however, should insist that the station record the method of "fixation" at the time of production and provide the institution that information.

9. If an event was telecast more than once, either by the same or different station(s), please list each telecast separately.

10. Please send to the NCAA, on your official stationery, a letter of authorization for the Association to file a joint claim on your behalf with the Copyright Royalty Tribunal. A sample letter is attached.

BROADCAST CONTRACTS

Copyright protection is just one area of contract language that must be scrutinized by amateur athletic administrators in order to ensure that all the broadcast rights of an athletic organization are protected. The basics of contract law, which were covered in Chapter 3, are just as important. Here, we will focus on contract issues and clauses that are unique to the broadcast business.

Rights Granted

In a broadcast contract, the sports organization grants the rights to broadcast the game in exchange for some specified benefit, generally a rights fee from the broadcast organization. The broadcast organization might be only one station, or it might consist of a number of stations that form a network. Usually, a broadcast organization seeks exclusive rights to telecast a game. *Exclusive rights* are defined as rights granted by the sports organization to one broadcaster for the purpose of setting up a single-station broadcast or an exclusive network, and such rights do not permit any other broadcast organization the right to broadcast the event. Exclusive rights are the opposite of *multioriginations*—that is, when many broadcast organizations are given the right to telecast the same event.

Exclusive rights may be granted for different technologies. Therefore, an organization might negotiate exclusive rights contracts for live standard broadcast television, delayed standard broadcast television, cable television, and/or radio. Often, in intercollegiate athletic broadcast contracts, exceptions are included, even in exclusive arrangements, to allow for an origination by a student radio or television station of a sports broadcast so that the students can gain experience in sports broadcasting. A contract clause with a broadcasting organization might specify as follows: "The parties acknowledge that notwithstanding this agreement, [name] University may grant to University's student-run radio station the right to broadcast any game."

In general, any broadcast contract would include at a minimum the following clauses:

1. Term and scope of contract, including event(s) to be broadcast
2. Definitions
3. Access and admission to events
4. Facilities furnished
5. Stipulations, requirements, and reservations
6. Rights fee and schedule of payments

Exhibit 9–1 is a typical radio contract, and Exhibit 9–2 is a typical television or cable television contract.

Broadcast Rights of a League or Conference

Beyond contractual matters with broadcasters, an amateur athletic administrator must also be concerned about the property rights to a broadcast between competing clubs, institutions, and within a league or conference arrangement. For instance, with any championship

Exhibit 9–1
Radio License Agreement

AGREEMENT made as of this _____ day of (month), 19_____ by and between CORPORATION on behalf of Radio Station WXXX-AM, (address) (Station) and _____ (Sports Organization).

The parties hereby agree as follows:

1.(a) Except as otherwise specified, (Sports Organization) grants (Station) the sole and exclusive right to broadcast and rebroadcast over the facilities of (Station), and to authorize the radio broadcast of, all (Sports Organization)'s games, including regular season and any post-season games to which (Sports Organization) has broadcast rights, (hereinafter the "Games") during the (name years) seasons. The parties acknowledge that notwithstanding this Agreement, (Sports Organization) may grant (i) to (Sports Organization's) student-run radio station the right to broadcast any Game and (ii) to any opponent of (Sports Organization) in any Game the right to broadcast or grant broadcast rights with respect to that Game to another radio station or cable radio station.

(b) Broadcasting may commence hereunder from the point of origin of a Game up to thirty (30) minutes prior to the scheduled commencement of a Game and continue up to thirty (30) minutes simultaneously with its playing. (Station) may in its discretion broadcast a pre-Game and post-Game show in connection with the broadcast of the Games. (Unless otherwise indicated, reference to "Game(s)" herein shall be deemed to include any post-Game or pre-Game show.) (Station) shall have the sole and exclusive right to sell or otherwise use all of the commercial time in the adjacencies prior to the pre-Game and subsequent to the post-Game Shows, together with all commercial time during the broadcast of each Game, and to retain all revenue derived therefrom.

(c) (Station) may terminate this Agreement effective (date) of any year while this Agreement is in effect upon prior written notice to (Sports Organization).

(d) (Station) and (Sports Organization) shall negotiate in good faith during the period beginning on (date) and ending on (date) (the "Negotiating Period") with respect to the possible renewal of this Agreement.

2. For all rights granted by (Sports Organization) herein and for the performance of all the terms and provisions of this Agreement on the part of (Sports Organization) to be performed, (Station) agrees to pay and agrees to accept the annual license fee as follows:

(Station) shall pay (Sports Organization) fifty percent (50%) of the "adjusted net profits" made by (Station) in selling commercial availabilities in and adjacent to broadcasts of the Games. As used herein "net profits" shall mean the (Station's) revenues (net of agency commissions) derived from said commercial availabilities for each Game less all of (Station's) reasonable and necessary costs attendant to producing and promoting the availabilities for each Game less all of (Station's) reasonable and necessary costs attendant to producing and promoting the broadcast of the Games and selling the said availabilities, including, without limiting the generality of the foregoing, out-of-pocket advertising and promotion costs, talent and announcer fees, production and technical costs, transmission costs to (Station's) facilities, travel costs for talent, production and technical personnel, rights fees, merchandising costs, coaches' show production costs including coaches' talent fee, Game statistical costs, and account executive commissions. (Station) shall retain the first five thousand dollars ($5,000) of net profits, for each Game, and the balance remaining shall be deemed to be "adjusted net profits."

(Station) shall pay (Sports Organization) each year's license fee in one payment on or before the date following thirty (30) days after the last Game played by (Sports Organization) team during that year's season. (Station) shall provide (Sports Organization) with a statement of revenues and costs at that time. At (Sports Organization's) request, (Station) shall produce supporting documentation for the figures set forth in the statement of revenues and costs provided to (Sports Organization).

3. The rights granted (Station) in subparagraph 1(a) are confined to radio and do not include motion picture or television broadcasting rights, all of which are reserved to (Sports Organization) for its sole use and benefit at any time. In the event (Station) is unable to obtain facilities to broadcast a Game through circumstances beyond its

Exhibit 9–1 continued

control, it may produce and broadcast transcriptions, recordings and recreations of any such Game.

4.(a) (Station) shall have complete control over the production (including pre- and post-production) and format of its broadcasts hereunder, including, without limitation, length of coverage. (Station) shall select and employ the "play-by-play" and "color analyst" announcers; provided, however, that (Sports Organization) shall have the right to require the selection of different announcers if (Station's) selection is unacceptable to (Sports Organization).

(b) (Sports Organization) shall make available to (Station) without charge at all home Games held at (sites) and shall take all reasonable steps at all away Games, which for purposes of this Agreement shall include (Sports Organization) home Games played at the Byrne Meadowlands Arena or Madison Square Garden, to make available to (Station) suitable space for (Station's) equipment and broadcasting and technical personnel, including access, provision for electrical power lines, cable lines and such other equipment and facilities as (Station) deems necessary or desirable. (Sports Organization) shall use its best efforts to obtain such away Game facilities without charge to (Station). (Station) shall have the right to display its name and trademark on any broadcasting booth and shall have the right to display the initials "WXXX-AM", and its frequency and trademark, on all equipment used in connection with broadcast of the Games; provided, however, (Sports Organization) cannot guarantee the foregoing with respect to the broadcast of away Games, as defined above.

(c) (Sports Organization) will and will cause its employees, and its head coach to cooperate with (Station) in all reasonable respects in all phases of the preparation, production and broadcast of the Games and attendant activities, including pre-Game and post-Game shows and at no additional charge; provided, however, that the head coach shall be paid reasonable compensation of $_____ per game by (Station) for appearances of any coach's show.

(d) So far as it is authorized to do, (Sports Organization) hereby grants to (Station), and (Station) may grant to others, the right to disseminate, reproduce, print and publish the names "(Sports Organization) Name" and the names, likenesses, voices and biographical material of (Sports Organization's) players and coaches, and of all persons connected with the attendant activities, as news or informative matter for publicity and or advertising purposes in connection with any Game, but not for any direct endorsement of any commercial product or service without (Sports Organization's) and any such person's written consent.

5. (Sports Organization) shall provide the following, at its own expense:

(a) A (Station) dinner, at a (Sports Organization) or other suitable facility, [ ] prior to commencement of each season listed in paragraph 1(a) above, arranged in consultation with (Station).

(b) A full page in each Game program which (Sports Organization) is responsible for producing to promote (Station)'s broadcast. (Station) shall provide (Sports Organization) printed copy for such ad.

(c) Four (4) public address announcements promoting (Station's) broadcast and acknowledging (Station's) sponsors at every home Game held at Arena. (Sports Organization) shall use its best efforts to have such public address announcements promoting (Station's) broadcast and acknowledging sponsors at each home game of (Sports Organization) held at the Byrne Meadowlands Arena and Madison Square Garden.

(d) Fifty (50) tickets to each (Sports Organization) home Game held at Arena. (Sports Organization) shall use its best efforts to provide such tickets at each home Game of (Sports Organization) held at the Byrne Meadowlands Arena and Madison Square Garden.

6.(a) (Station) has the right to preempt any Game, in whole or in part, and (Station) shall have fully discharged its obligations to (Sports Organization) with respect to the Games by payment of the applicable compensation set forth in paragraph 2 hereunder. If (Station) preempts any Game(s), (Station) shall either: (i) broadcast said Game(s) on another radio station at its expense; (ii) tape delay broadcast the Game(s); or (iii) broadcast a "split-feed" (as that term is commonly understood in the broadcast industry) of the Game(s).

(b) In the event that the broadcasting of any Game is prevented or omitted because of: suspension or disruption or termination of a Game for any reason, Act of God; inevitable accident; fire; lockout, strike or other labor dispute; riot or civil commotion; act of public enemy; enactment, rule, order or act of any government or gov-

Exhibit 9–1 continued

ernmental instrumentality (whether federal, state, local or foreign); failure of technical facilities; failure or delay of transportation facilities; or any other cause of a similar or different nature; the revenues derived from the sale of availabilities for the broadcast of said Game shall not be included in computing the net profits, and the total number of Games shall be reduced.

7. (Sports Organization) warrants that, to the best of its knowledge and ability:

(a) It has the full right and power to grant (Station) the rights hereby granted and to enter into and fully perform this Agreement; and that the exercise by (Station) of the rights herein granted as contemplated by this Agreement will not violate any rights of any person, firm or corporation.

(b) The Games are sanctioned by the National Governing Body and that the Games will be conducted in accordance with applicable National Governing Body rules. The Games shall be subject to and conducted in accordance with applicable National Governing Body rules. The Games shall be subject to and conducted in accordance with all applicable federal, state and local laws.

(c) All representations to (Station) by (Sports Organization) and all representations made by (Sports Organization) to third parties about any and all elements of the Games including without limitation, format, record of the participants, etc., are and shall be accurate and true in all material respects. (Sports Organization) further warrants that it has made and will make full disclosure to (Station) with respect to all such elements of the Games as soon as practicable after (Sports Organization) has knowledge thereof.

(d) All publicity which it issues or disseminates or otherwise makes available concerning all elements of the Games will be accurate and true in all material respects.

(e) All rights herein granted to (Station) in and to the Games are and will be free and clear of liens and encumbrances of every kind and character which are the result of actions by (Sports Organization)

(f) None of the Games will contain any defamatory, scandalous or obscene matter contrary to law or to the generally accepted standards of the radio broadcast standards or of the Federal Communications Commission.

(g) There is no outstanding contract, commitment or arrangement, and no pending or threatened claim or litigation which is or may be in conflict with this agreement or which may in any way limit, restrict, impair or interfere with either party's rights hereunder.

(h) No part or any of the Games will violate or infringe the copyright, trademark, performing patent, literary, intellectual, artistic or dramatic right, the right of privacy, or any other right or privilege or any third person or party.

8.(a) (Sports Organization) shall indemnify and hold harmless (Station) and any person, firm or corporation deriving rights from (Station) from all claims, damages, liabilities, costs and expenses (including reasonable counsel fees), arising out of or caused by, (i) any breach by (Sports Organization) of any warranty or agreement made by (Sports Organization) herein, (ii) any act or omission by (Sports Organization), or persons whose services are furnished by (Sports Organization) with regard to any Game or element furnished by (Sports Organization) to (Station) hereunder, or (iii) the use of any materials, persons or services furnished by (Sports Organization) in connection with (Station)'s production or broadcast of the Games.

(b) (Station) shall indemnify and hold harmless (Sports Organization) from and against any and all suits, claims, damages, liabilities, costs and expenses, including reasonable counsel fees, arising out of any breach by (Station) of any agreement made by it herein or out of the use of any materials or services furnished by (Station) or by any advertiser, if any, for and in connection with the broadcast of the Games.

(c) The indemnitee hereunder shall promptly notify the indemnitor of any claim, demand or litigation, and the indemnitor shall be solely responsible for the defense, settlement or payment thereof; provided that the indemnitee may, if it so desires, at its own cost and expense and by its own counsel, participate in any such defense, and in such event its counsel will cooperate with counsel for the indemnitor. Any settlement by an indemnitor under this Agreement which derogates from the rights of the indemnitee hereunder may be concluded only with the express approval of the indemnitee, which will not be unreasonably withheld. Indemnitor's liability hereunder shall be limited to any judgment or settlement approved by indemnitor. The foregoing indemnities shall survive this Agreement.

9.(a) (Sports Organization) will comply with the requirements of Section 507 of the Federal Communications Act of 1934, as amended, concerning broadcast matter and

Exhibit 9–1 continued

disclosures required thereunder, insofar as that Section applies to persons furnishing program material for radio broadcasting. (Sports Organization) warrants and represents that none of the Games or related activities include or shall include any matter for which any money, service or other valuable consideration is directly or indirectly paid, promised to, or charged or accepted by (Sports Organization). (Sports Organization) shall exercise reasonable diligence to inform its employees, players and other persons with whom (Sports Organization) deals directly in connection with the Games and related activities, of the requirements of the said Section 507; provided, however, that no act of any such employee, player or of any independent contractor connected with any of the Games or related activities shall constitute a breach of the provisions of this paragraph unless (Sports Organization) has actual notice thereof. As used in this paragraph, the term "service or other valuable consideration" shall not include any service or property furnished without charge or at a nominal charge for use in or in connection with the Games or related activities unless it is so furnished in consideration for an identification in such broadcast . . . of any person, product, service, trademark or brand name beyond and identification which is reasonably related to the use of such "service or property in such broadcast," as such terms are used in the said Section 507.

(b) (Station's) Program Practices Department policies and standards shall apply to the Games and to the sites of the Games; (Station) agrees to provide (Sports Organization) with a copy of its program policies and standards. (Sports Organization) shall comply with and shall use its best efforts to cause those persons controlling each site to comply with all such policies and standards.

10. Each party acknowledges that the rights and privileges granted to the other pursuant to this Agreement are special, unique, extraordinary and unusual in character, and that the breach by either party of any of the provisions contained in this Agreement will cause the other party irreparable injury. In the event of any such breach by either party, the non-breaching party will be entitled to injunctive relief or other equitable relief to enjoin and restrain such violation for a period ending not less than one (1) year after the expiration or any termination of this Agreement.

11.(a) Except as otherwise specifically provided herein, all notices hereunder shall be in writing and shall be given by personal delivery, registered or certified mail or telegraph (prepaid), at the respective addresses hereinabove set forth, or such other address or addresses as may be designated by either party. Such notices shall be deemed given when mailed or delivered into a telegraph office, except that notice of change of address shall be effective only from the date of its receipt.

(b) Nothing herein shall create any association, partnership, joint venture, or the relation of principal and agent between the parties hereto, it being understood that neither party shall have the authority to bind the other or the other's representatives in any way.

(c) This Agreement shall be construed in accordance with the laws of the State of _____ applicable to contracts made and fully performed therein.

(d) Neither party may assign, license or sublicense this Agreement or any of its rights hereunder to any person, firm or corporation, or any parent, subsidiary or affiliated corporation without the prior written consent of the other party. Any permitted assignment shall not relieve the assigning party of any of its obligations hereunder.

(e) If any provision of this Agreement, as applied to either party or to any circumstance, shall be adjudged to be void or unenforceable, the same shall in no way affect any other provision of this Agreement, the application of such provision in any other circumstance, or the validity or enforceability of this Agreement.

(f) No waiver by either party of the breach of any term or provision of this Agreement shall be construed to be a waiver of any prior or subsequent breach of the same or any other term or provision.

(g) This Agreement contains the entire understanding of the parties hereto relating to the subject matter herein contained, and this Agreement cannot be changed, rescinded or terminated orally.

IN WITNESS WHEREOF, the parties hereto have executed this Agreement as of the day and year first above written.

SPORT ORGANIZATION   STATION

By_____   By _____

Exhibit 9–2
Cable Television Agreement (Institutional Contract)

This Contract made as of this _____ day of _____, 19 _____, between

_____, with its

principal address at _____

_____ (hereinafter "Institution") and

the _____

(hereinafter "Station,") a ___(state)___ corporation with executive offices at

(address) _____

WITNESSETH:

1. (Institution) hereby grants to (Station) exclusive television rights (except as expressly hereinafter otherwise provided) to produce and to cablecast for distribution to subscription cable television systems, throughout the United States of America, each athletic event described in paragraph 2, below, subject to the terms and conditions of this Contract.

2. Each athletic event subject to this Contract (hereinafter "the event"), the participants in the event, the date or dates of the event, and the consideration payable within 15 days following the occurrence of the event by (Station) to (Institution) for all rights granted herein with respect to the event (hereinafter "rights fee") are as follows:

EVENT   DATE(S)   RIGHTS FEE

_____   _____   _____

_____   _____   _____

3. All arrangements with other participants in the event related to the cablecasting of the event, including but not limited to any required consent of an opponent or participant and any compensation to be paid to an opponent or participant therefor, will be made by (Institution).

4. (Institution) will make available to (Station) and any sponsors suitable space, as specified to (Institution) at the time of (Station's) advance technical survey of the site of the event, as shall be necessary for their participation in the production of the cablecast of the event. (Station) will have the right to install, maintain in, and remove from each site and the surrounding premises such wires, cables and apparatus as may be necessary for (Station's) participation in the production of the cablecast of the event and to use power at the site without additional charge; provided, however, that such facilities shall not substantially interfere with the use of the site or with any of the means of ingress or egress. Employees and agents of (Station) and of sponsors will be admitted to the site free of charge to the extent necessary to accomplish the pick up and cablecast of each event and of the commercial announcements, and (Institution) will provide to (Station) the credentials necessary for such purposes.

5. At least three (3) days prior to the date of the event, (Institution) will furnish to (Station) a list of all musical compositions to be played before, during and after the event and during any intermissions. If (Station) is unable to clear any musical composition for performance, (Station) will so notify the (Institution) and each composition which cannot be cleared will not be played.

6. (Station), each sponsor, its advertising agencies, and affiliated cable systems shall have the right and may grant to others the right to make appropriate references, including but not limited to the use of pictures, to (Institution), any opponent, and their respective teams, athletic personnel, and any and all other persons connected with the event, in promoting, advertising and cablecasting the event and the sponsorship of such cablecast by the sponsors.

7. Except as expressly limited by this Contract, the (National Governing Body), and (Station), with the (National Governing Body's) approval, may at any time use and

Exhibit 9–2 continued

reuse portions of films, tapes or other recordings of the event on news, documentry and other sports programs, highlights programs, anthologies, pre-event and post-event programs. The rights granted herein include such usage without additional charge or compensation to (Institution).

8. All rights granted to (Station) pursuant to this Contract, and all rights to be exercised by (Station) pursuant to this Contract, will be used only in connection with cablecasting by subscription cable television systems. Nothing herein contained shall be construed as granting to (Station) any right to produce, to broadcast, to cablecast, or to transmit television programs for presentation by broadcast television stations, subscription broadcast television stations, or pay-per-program cable television systems, and (Station) agrees to take reasonable and adequate security measures to prevent such presentations. Except as specifically required or authorized in this Contract, (Station) shall not use (present, exhibit, perform, exploit, lease, sell, license, or otherwise use by any means, method or process, now or hereinafter known), or authorize any other person to so use, any right herein granted to (Station).

9. (a) Except as expressly limited by this Contract, the television rights granted to (Station) hereunder shall be exclusive (limited, however, to use in cablecasting for distribution to subscription cable television systems), for the duration of the periods of exclusivity specified in this Contract, and, without limiting the generality of the foregoing, (Institution) shall not grant the right to produce or televise, whether for presentation by broadcast television stations, subscription broadcast television stations, pay-per-program cable television systems or otherwise, the event during such periods.

(b) In the event that a television broadcast station or a cable television system should fail to respect (Station's) program exclusivity or other rights hereunder pursuant to the rules of the Federal Communications Commission or other applicable law or regulation, (Station) shall notify (Institution) and the (National Governing Body) promptly of such fact and may institute such actions and proceedings as are proper under the rules of the Federal Communications Commission or any other applicable law or regulation in order to enforce its program exclusivity and other rights hereunder and to recover damages for the violation thereof. (Institution) or the (National Governing Body) may, but shall not be obligated to, join (Station) in such actions and proceedings and, if it so elects, (Institution) or the (National Governing Body) may institute and prosecute such actions and proceedings in its own name.

(c) Notwithstanding the foregoing or any other provision of this Contract, (Station) may use, and (Station) or (Institution) may permit any television broadcaster or cablecaster to use extracts of programs of events of the broadcast, or to televise extracts of such events by whomsoever produced, not to exceed two (2) minutes in running time, at any time (but not on a live basis) for telecasts or cablecasts within the framework of general newscasts and sports newscasts and such use shall not be a violation of (Station's) right of exclusivity or any other right of (Station) or (Institution) under this Contract.

10. (Institution) and (Station) hereby assign to the (National Governing Body) all copyright interest in all programs comprised of or relating to broadcast. (Station) will take all necessary steps to prevent all such copyright of all material from falling into the public domain. (Station) will fix all such television programs in a tangible form, affix appropriate notice of the copyright interest on all tape cassettes or film reels of such programs, and include in each cablecast, video tape, film, or other copy thereof an appropriate notice of copyright.

11. (Station) will not simultaneously cablecast and distribute any event of the broadcast to a cable television system, any part of the subscribers to which are located in the television market area of the site of the event, if, in (Institution's) opinion after consulting with (Station), such release of the cablecast would materially reduce attendance at such event. If simultaneous release of the cablecast of such event is not permitted at the site of the event, any delayed release of the cablecast of the event in such television market shall not be made until at least twenty-four (24) hours have elapsed after the conclusion of the event, unless (Institution) in writing authorizes earlier releases.

Exhibit 9–2 continued

12. All rights granted to (Station) pursuant to this Contract shall be limited in territorial scope to the United States of America.

13. Neither this Contract, nor any license or right herein granted by (Institution) to (Station) may be assigned by (Station), either voluntarily or by operation of law, without the written consent of (Institution) and the (National Governing Body) provided, however, that (Station) may assign to the (National Governing Body) or to any other person the right to produce any television program subject to this Contract. This Contract may not be assigned by (Institution).

14. Nothing herein contained shall in any way create any association, partnership, joint venture, or the relation of principal and agent between (Station) and (Institution), or be construed to evidence an intention to constitute such. Neither of the parties hereto shall represent that any such relationship exists contrary to the terms of this paragraph, by advertising or otherwise.

15. (Institution) warrants and represents that it has the authority to enter into this Contract and to grant the rights granted to (Station) hereunder, and that all required consents and authorizations of all opponents and other entities or persons having an interest herein have been obtained.

16. All notices hereunder shall be in writing and shall be by personal delivery, by registered or certified mail, or by telegraph, at the respective addresses of the parties.

17. This Contract constitutes the entire agreement of the parties hereto, and, except as herein otherwise specifically provided, may not be changed except by an agreement in writing signed by an officer or other authorized representative of the party against whom enforcement is sought.

18. The following attached provisions supplement, or if they contradict the foregoing shall supercede, the foregoing terms and conditions of this Contract (list attachments):

IN WITNESS WHEREOF, the parties have executed this Contract as of the day and year first above written.

STATION   INSTITUTION

By: _____ By: _____

Date: _____ Date: _____

Title: _____ Title: _____

sponsored by the NCAA, the association "owns all rights to each and all of its championships.... These rights include ... rights to television (live and delayed), radio broadcasting, filming and commercial photography" (*1993–94 NCAA Manual*, Bylaw 31.6.4). The NCAA grants rights to telecast its championships on a sliding scale that represents in part the attractiveness and marketability of the event. The NCAA, in awarding media rights, states that "television, radio and film rights shall be awarded in such a manner as to advance most fully the following interests: (a) gate attendance, (b) promotion of interest in the sport, (c) promotion of intercollegiate athletics as a part of collegiate education, and (d) promotion of the Association and its purposes and fundamental policy" (*1990–91 NCAA Manual*, Bylaw 31.6.4.1).

An allied conference within the NCAA may also have its own policies for broadcasting. In part, this will reflect how much power the individual conference member institutions have granted the conference to act as an agent for them in seeking broadcasting possibilities. An athletic administrator must always be aware of what rights have been granted to a conference and what rights an institution retains. At a minimum, most allied conferences have the rights to conference championship event broadcasts.

An example of an allied conference's television policy for NCAA Division IA football and Division I basketball would be that called for by the Big-10 Conference in 1992–93, a portion of which is reprinted here:

Television Policies

Football—The conditions and policies of the Conference's football television plan (broadcast and cable) shall be followed.

1. The fee for filming of a *non-televised* game to be used for a commercial highlights show shall be negotiated by each Conference member.
2. A fee shall not be assessed for the filming of a *non-televised* game to be used for a coach's television show and/or school highlights show.
3. A fee shall not be assessed for the filming of *non-televised* game action to be used on a regularly scheduled news program, with the footage used not to exceed two minutes in length.
4. The fee for a live or delayed telecast of a game not selected by the Conference's broadcast or cable network shall be negotiated by each Conference member. (*1992–93 Handbook of the Big-10 Conference*, Agreements for Men's Programs, V-C, 1991–92)

A typical allied conference agreement for delayed broadcast rights within the conference is that used by the Southwest Athletic Conference in 1992–93. It noted the following:

Delayed Football and Basketball Television Rights and Football and Basketball Radio Rights

The following policy regarding delayed telecasts of football and basketball games and radio broadcasts of basketball games is in effect.

(a) Delayed television rights for both football and basketball games will be disposed of by individual Conference members and funds derived from the sale of these rights shall be retained by the home institution. This policy is subject to the additional restriction that films, coaches' shows excepted, shall not be released for television purposes in the home area of the visiting institution without first obtaining the approval of such release from the visiting institution.

(b) Each member institution shall be permitted to dispose of its football and basketball radio rights and retain the fees therefrom.

Exception to this regulation is the Conference Post-Season Basketball Tournament.

By agreement of both institutions, radio rights as stated in (b) may be waived.

(c) The post-game film rights for the football season may be disposed of by individual Conference members and funds derived from the sale of these rights be retained by the home institution. This policy is subject to additional restriction that films shall not be released for television purposes in the home area of the visiting institution without first obtaining the approval of such release from the visiting institution.

Particular attention is called to the fact that before a film or tape of a game can be released in the home area of the visiting institution, permission for such release must be obtained from the visiting institution. Also, in accordance with NCAA Rules post-game films or tape cannot be shown on television earlier than 10:30 P.M. (local time) the night of the game. (*1992–93 Southwest Conference Handbook*, Appendix D)

To ensure that the above policy was followed, the Southwest Athletic Conference included the following clauses in its conference football contracts:

1. The home team shall own the exclusive live television, delayed television, and movie rights. Receipts derived from live regional or national telecasting by ABC, ESPN, CBS, NBC, WTBS, WGN, or USA shall be divided according to SWC rules and regulations which are in effect on the date of the game. The visiting team will be given an outlet and space in the press box, free of charge, for delayed television or movie coverage to the visiting team's own locale, and all revenue collected by the visiting team for these rights shall belong exclusively to the visiting team. Pay-per-view telecast rights and revenue collected from the sale of these rights shall belong to each team.

2. The home team shall own the live radio broadcasting rights. Proceeds from the home team's radio broadcasting shall belong to the home team. However, the visiting team will be given an outlet free of charge for radio coverage. Revenue collected by the visiting team shall belong exclusively to the visiting team. (*1992–93 Southwest Conference Handbook*

Allied conferences also need a policy for distribution of revenues, including broadcast revenue, among member institutions. In 1992–93, the Pacific 10 Conference used the following system for television revenue:

Football Television Rights Fees and Income Distribution
The rights fee for a live telecast or cablecast of a Pac-10 football game not a part of a Conference program shall be negotiated, respectively, by

each institution into whose home area the telecast is presented or by which the telecast is syndicated. Income from such home-area telecasts (per AR 2-1-e) shall be divided evenly between the two Pac-10 teams and per contract between the participants in a non-Conference game. If a Conference game is released beyond the home areas of the participants, then all income resulting from the telecast shall be subject to the Conference's revenue sharing formula (55 percent to the participants, 45 percent divided equally among the 10 members).

If coverage of a game between Pac-10 members A and B is televised by A in its home area and by B in and beyond its home area, institution A shall retain its rights fee income, but institution B must apply the Conference formula for sharing such income to all of its rights fees, those for the release in the home area and those for release beyond.

1. Income from Live Telecasts/Cablecasts. Television income resulting from an appearance by a member institution in a live telecast or cablecast which is presented on a Conference program or released by a Pac-10 institution beyond its home area will be divided according to the following formula:
   55% to Pacific-10 participant(s)
   45% to Pacific-10 members (divided 10 ways).
2. Income from ABC Pay-Per-View Agreement. Television income resulting from the ABC pay-per-view agreement shall be divided equally among the Conference's ten member institutions.
3. Determination of Rights Fee. In determining the per-game rights fee to which the formula is to be applied for a game in a Conference program, a national telecast appearance will be assigned twice the value of a split-national or regional telecast appearance.
4. Definition of National Game. See AR 2-1-b for definition of national game.
5. Conference Game Released Beyond Home Area. The rights fee for the live telecast or cablecast of a Conference game, which is not selected for presentation on a Conference television program but is released beyond the home areas of the participants, shall be subject to the Conference's revenue sharing formula as outlined in AR 2-2-d-(1).
6. Non-Conference Game Released Beyond Home Area. The rights fee for the live telecast or cablecast of a non-Conference game, which is not selected for presentation on a Conference television program but is released beyond the home area of the Pac-10 participant, shall be subject to the Conference's revenue sharing formula as outlined in AR 2-2-d-(1), regardless of whether it is a home game.
7. Home Area Telecasts.
   (a) Conference Game. Television income resulting from an appearance on a live home area telecast or cablecast of a Conference game that is shown only in the home areas of the competing teams shall be divided according to the following formula: 50% to each Pac-10 participant.

(b) Non-Conference Game. Television income resulting from an appearance on a live home area telecast or cablecast of a non-Conference game that is shown only in the home areas of the competing teams shall be divided between the competing institutions per the provisions of their game contract.

8. Income from Delayed Telecasts/Cablecasts. Income from a delayed telecast or cablecast of a Conference football game, or a delayed telecast or cablecast of a non-Conference game presented by a Pac-10 member, shall be retained by the institution which authorizes the telecast/cablecast and is not shared with its opponent institution.

9. Telecasts of Non-Conference Games by Non-Conference Institutions. To cooperate with football opponents which are not members of the Pac-10, the Conference has entered into agreements with other organizations, conferences and institutions specifying the conditions and terms under which live telecasts and cablecasts of non-conference games may be presented. The goal in reaching these agreements is to maximize the television exposure of college football and the participating institutions. In some cases, the telecasting of games covered by these agreements also may be affected by the game contract between the two participants. The contract shall govern telecasting of a game not covered by a Conference agreement.

If such a game is played at a Pac-10 site, the Pac-10 member must ensure that the visiting institution observes the restrictions in all applicable Pac-10 media contracts. If such a game is played at a non-Conference site, it is probable the Pac-10 member will face similar restrictions in the host institution's conference contracts, if it is a member of a conference. Income from the live telecasting of such a game by the Pac-10 institution beyond its home area shall be subject to Conference's revenue-sharing formula. Income from the telecasting by the opponent which is shared by the Pac-10 member shall be subject to the Pac-10's revenue sharing formula as applicable.

10. Incentive Fees. An incentive fee paid by the television networks for moving the site and/or date of a football game for television purposes shall be retained by the participating institution(s) and not included within the Conference's distribution of television revenue.

11. Expense Reimbursement. Reimbursement of expenses may be approved by the Athletics Directors Committee for a team which moves a football game to accommodate a national or other network telecast or a national cable presentation if the move adds to out-of-pocket costs. Detailed documentation of the actual, rather than estimated, expenses is required.

12. Fee for Sixth Appearance. Any fee paid by ABC Sports to the Conference for the rights to telecast a sixth appearance by a member institution's football team during a given season shall be

subject to the Conference's revenue-sharing formula as described in AR 2-2-d-(1).

13. Lighting Expenses. The cost for providing necessary lighting to make an appearance on the Conference's supplemental football television series shall be deducted from the television revenue for the series as an expense item and the remainder of the television revenues shall be distributed as per the formula set forth in this regulation.

14. Distribution of Receipts. Television income resulting from an appearance by a member institution in a telecast in a Conference program, or the income to be shared from a telecast not on a Conference program which is subject to one of the above formulae shall be sent to the Commissioner by the carrying media company, participating or host member institution. The Commissioner shall invest the pooled monies and the accrued interest shall be used to decrease the assessment for the Pacific-10 membership. The Commissioner then shall distribute the original monies as per the formulae set forth in this regulation to the member institutions.

Men's Basketball Television Income Distribution

The method of distribution of income received as the rights fee for a live telecast or cablecast of a men's basketball game of a member institution is to be based upon the source of the fee. If the fee is for a game telecast by a television network, the Conference distribution formula of 55 percent to the Pac-10 participants, 45 percent divided equally among the 10 members shall be applied. If the fee is derived from the Conference's syndicated series, it shall be divided evenly among all members.

1. Network Rights Fee. Each national network game involving two Conference teams shall be assigned a value of $233,334. Each national network game involving one Conference team shall be assigned a value of $116,667. Each regional network game involving either one or two Conference teams shall be assigned a value of $100,000. For each national or regional network game, 55% of the value shall be shared equally by the appearing institution(s) and 45 percent shall be shared equally among the 10 Conference members. Following payment for national and regional network telecasts, remaining rights fees, including fees for split regional telecasts, shall be divided equally among the 10 Conference members.

2. Definition of National Game. See AR 2-1-b for definition of national game.

3. National Television Game Where Television Rights Fees are Unidentified. When a basketball game is televised nationally but a television rights fee is not identified as a part of the fee for participation in the game, the portion of the participation fee equal to the established fee for a national network telecast of a

Pac-10 game on that network that season would be split per the Conference basketball television financial distribution formula (55–45) and the participating institution shall retain all income above that figure.

4. Extra Expenses. A member institution shall be compensated for the full cost of extra expenses it incurs in making adjustments to accommodate a presentation on the Conference's basketball television package(s). Detailed documentation of the actual, rather than estimated, expenses is required.

5. Lighting Expenses. The cost for providing necessary lighting to make an appearance on a Conference basketball television series shall be deducted from the gross income of that series rather than from the rights fee assigned to the specific game. If a single game is televised, such lighting costs would be deducted from the rights fee for it.

In representing the members of an athletic conference, the conference administration must grant many of the same rights to a broadcast company that an individual institution would usually grant. The Sun Belt Conference has a section with information on men's basketball television contracts in its handbook (*1992–93 Sun Belt Conference Handbook*):

7. Television Policies for Men's Basketball

7.1 Philosophy
The Sun Belt Conference shall attempt, as its top priority, to maximize regional and national television exposure for men's basketball.

7.2 Television Contracts

7.201 The Sun Belt Conference may employ a television syndicator. The contract with the syndicator will be legally binding with regard to the rights and responsibilities of the syndicator, the Sun Belt Conference, and the member institutions.

7.202 Conference members will not enter into agreements that conflict with the contractual rights of the syndicator and/or existing Conference policies without the approval of the Commissioner.

7.203 All Conference institutions must attach a television addendum to any non-conference basketball game contract, which states that the "non-conference game(s) contracted for in this agreement may be televised only with the expressed written consent of the Sun Belt Conference institution."

An exception to this policy is in the event a member institution is involved in a tournament hosted by a nonconference institution, or a third party. Any other exceptions to this game contract requirement must be approved in advance by the Commissioner.

Broadcast Rights of an Individual Institution

The *NCAA Radio Network Manual* noted in its 1984 edition that provisions should be made in contracts between individual institutions for radio broadcasts and suggested the following clause be included in game contracts:

> D. *Contracts Between Universities*—Radio language differs between institutions in terms of what radio broadcast rights are and what they should be. A suggested sample section concerning radio broadcasts in contracts between institutions could be as follows:
> The Radio Broadcast of the home game shall be under the control of the HOME TEAM. The rights of each team are as follows:
> The Visiting Team shall be allowed one free radio outlet for its official station or network. All other stations shall pay the established fee set by the Home Team. All stations from the Visiting Team's territory must be certified to the Home Team by the Visiting Team. The Visiting Team shall control radio rights and income in its home normal market area only.

In a nonconference game, an institution must also protect its broadcast rights. A typical contract clause would be like the one the University of Kentucky (UK) used in 1991–92.

> Broadcasting rights to UK games are assigned exclusively to Host Creative Communications, Inc., of Lexington. One reciprocal rights fee waiver is guaranteed opponent schools visiting Lexington.

Broadcast Rights of a Facility Owner

A facility owner may also have to specify broadcast rights for a contest held within a facility. For instance, for the 1985 Kickoff Classic held at Giants Stadium in East Rutherford, New Jersey, the New Jersey Sports and Exposition Authority used the following clause in its contract with Brigham Young University:

> ### Communication Rights
>
> (a) The parties agree that Katz Sports, Inc., a division of Katz Communications, Inc., shall have exclusive, world-wide television rights to broadcast the Game.
> (b) The parties agree that CBS Radio, Inc. shall have exclusive radio rights to broadcast the Game.
> Notwithstanding the above, BYU may designate a commercial radio station and/or network which originates its broadcast signal within the State of Utah to broadcast a live report of the Game, and for this privilege

the designated stations and/or network shall pay to the Authority a radio broadcast rights fee of $1,750.00.

Restrictions on the Use of Advertising

Finally, in any broadcast there may be restrictions placed on the use of certain types of advertising. An athletic administrator must be aware of any governing body's or institution's restrictions. For instance, the NCAA has the following regulations regarding advertisements during NCAA championships.

Advertising policies of the NCAA are designed to exclude those advertisements that do not appear to be in the best interests of higher education. The executive director shall have the authority to rule in cases where doubt exists concerning acceptable advertisers and advertising copy of game programs, broadcasts and telecasts of NCAA championships; however, the following expressly are prohibited: alcoholic beverages that exceed six percent alcohol by volume, cigarettes, smokeless and other tobacco products, professional sports organizations or personnel (except as specified hereafter) in games other than certified postseason football games, and organizations or individuals promoting gambling. Bona fide political advertisements are acceptable in game programs and on broadcasts and telecasts of NCAA championships.

Advertising of malt beverages, beer and wine products that do not exceed six percent alcohol by volume may be used in game programs. Such advertisements, however, shall not comprise more than fourteen percent of the space in the program devoted to advertising or not more than sixty seconds per hour of any telecast or broadcast (either a single sixty-second commercial and thirty-second commercial or three thirty-second commercials).

Advertisements featuring active professional athletes from the sport for which an NCAA telecast, broadcast or game program is being produced shall be prohibited. Advertisements featuring active professional athletes in other sports may not comprise more than seven percent of the space devoted to advertising in a game program or thirty seconds per hour of any telecast or broadcast. Parties representing the NCAA in advertising sales or involved in advertising sales for NCAA telecasts, broadcasts or game programs shall take every reasonable step to discourage the use by advertisers of active professional athletes from sports regulated by the NCAA, informing the advertisers of the NCAA's desire that such professional athletes not be used. Every potential sponsor shall be advised of the terms of this provision prior to contracting with such sponsor. Advertisements in telecasts, broadcasts or programs are not acceptable that contain references to or photographs of the games, personnel (except as noted above), broadcasts, telecasts or other activities of professional sports organizations.

Nontherapeutic drugs and, generally, other drugs and patent medicine advertisements are excluded; however, analgesics, cold remedies, antacids and athletics training aids that are in general use are acceptable. Institutional advertising by pharmaceutical firms also is acceptable.

No commercial or advertisement may relate, directly or indirectly the advertising company or the advertised product to the participating institutions or their student-athletes, or the Association itself, unless prior written approval has been granted by the NCAA executive director.

The NCAA reserves the right of final approval for all advertising in any championship.

Advertising content in a game program shall not exceed forty percent of the total pages in the program, including the cover pages. (*1992 National Collegiate Championship Manual*)

APPLICATION OF ANTITRUST LAW TO SPORTS BROADCASTING

Basic antitrust law principles are discussed in Chapter 13. In this section we discuss the basic application of antitrust law to sports broadcasting. For amateur athletic administrators that means being careful not to try to control the overall flow of their sports broadcasts, in a concerted action, such that a monopoly or other antitrust violations develop. It is always important to remember that the antitrust laws were designed to encourage the easy flow of any business activity into the general stream of commerce. In drafting such laws, legislators reasoned that it was important to have open and free market competition.

The major antitrust decision involving broadcasting and amateur athletics occurred on June 27, 1984. On that date, the Supreme Court of the United States, in a 7–2 decision (*NCAA v. Board of Regents of University of Oklahoma*, 468 U.S. 85 [1984]), struck down the NCAA's 1982–85 football television plan because it violated federal antitrust law. The ruling immediately impacted networks, producers, syndicators, advertisers, and NCAA member institutions, all of which had to scramble to implement broadcast schedules for the 1984 season. This decision, and its ramifications, continues to be a major factor today in the broadcast industry. (See note 5a.)

The reactions to the decision were predictably and decidedly mixed: "It's the worst possible thing that could have happened," said former University of Michigan athletic director Don Canham. Pennsylvania State University athletic director Jim Tarman reacted to the decision with concern, stating: "The worst scenario is that everyone is on their own. We don't feel that scenario is in Penn State's best interest or the best interest of college football." Other parties were delighted by the Supreme Court's decision: "The position of the universities has been vindicated. The property right theory has been upheld," said Chuck Neinas, executive director of the College Football Association (CFA).

The lawsuit brought by the University of Oklahoma and the University of Georgia against the NCAA is likely to have long-term repercussions within amateur athletic governance. Here we focus on the impact that the Supreme Court's decision will have on how amateur athletic organizations will meet their new responsibility to provide competition in broadcasting of their events.

An important group in the area of television and intercollegiate athletics is the College Football Association of America. The CFA is composed of sixty-three NCAA Division I-A member institutions and includes five of the major football-playing conferences: the Big 8, Southeast, Southwest, Atlantic Coast Conference, Western Athletic Conference, and major independents, such as Notre Dame. The only major football-playing schools which are not CFA members are the Pacific-10 and Big-Ten Conferences. The CFA was formed to promote the interests of its Division I-A member schools within the National Collegiate Athletic Association structure. Beginning in 1979, the CFA started to believe that its voice in the formulation of football television policy was diluted in the 800-plus institutions of the NCAA membership, and was not reflective of its own members' importance in obtaining a national television contract.

The CFA negotiated a contract of its own with the National Broadcasting Company (NBC) for the 1982 and 1983 football seasons. The NBC contract was more attractive to CFA members in terms of rights, fees, and appearances than the 1982–85 agreements that the NCAA had with ABC and CBS. While CFA member institutions were considering whether to accept the NBC pact, the NCAA indicated that doing so would be in violation of NCAA rules and that disciplinary sanctions would result. This caused many CFA members that originally had approved the CFA-NBC contract to vote against accepting it. As a result of the CFA's failure to contract with NBC and continued dissatisfaction with the NCAA's television policy, the University of Georgia Athletic Association and the University of Oklahoma brought suit in November 1981. They challenged the NCAA's exclusive control over televised football games and contended that the NCAA was violating the Sherman Antitrust Act by its exclusive television contracts with two major networks—ABC and CBS. The NCAA, since it was given authority by a vote of its membership at its annual convention in January of 1952, had administered the live telecasting of games for its member institutions. The details of the television plan have varied through the years. The plans have, however, consistently limited the number of live television appearances an NCAA member institution could make in a year; prevented individual member institutions from contracting on an individual basis with national, local, and cable television companies; fixed revenue amounts for rights fees allocated by the NCAA to member institutions whose teams appeared as part of the network television contract; and allocated a percentage of the total television contract for the NCAA's operating budget.

The NCAA argued that the television package was beneficial to its membership as a whole and accomplished two important purposes. First, it protected the live gate of college and high school football games, which resulted in higher attendance at games. In support of this argument, the NCAA pointed to an increase in total attendance for NCAA football games in all but one year during the period of 1953–1983.

Second, the NCAA contended that its plan had the positive effect of spreading television revenues and exposure to a greater number of member institutions. The NCAA also contended that limitations on the number of television appearances a member institution could make allowed a greater number of institutions to appear on television, which resulted in the schools receiving substantially higher rights fees. In addition to the revenues, these institutions received invaluable television exposure and extensive media attention. As a result, the recruitment efforts of these institutions were enhanced.

The NCAA maintained that uncontrolled televising of football games would result in the creation of a football *super* power group, since a limited number of institutions would be attractive to television broadcasters. With increased revenues and media attention to the super power group, the NCAA predicted that the disparity among the member institutions would be increased. This would be contrary to the policies and purposes of the NCAA, since it would place irresistible temptations for the development of winning teams, thereby threatening the future of the sport.

Judge Burciaga, a federal district court judge, ruled in favor of the University of Oklahoma and the Georgia Athletic Association on September 15, 1982, reasoning that the television contracts between the NCAA and ABC, CBS, and the Turner Broadcast System were in violation of the Sherman Antitrust Act and therefore void. The court held that "[t]he right to telecast college football games is the property of the institutions participating in the games, and that right may be sold or assigned by those institutions to any entity at their discretion." Judge Burciaga found that the NCAA's television football controls constituted price fixing, output restriction, a group boycott, and an exercise of monopoly power over the market of college football television. The court found that the membership of the NCAA agreed to limit production to a level far below that which would occur in a free market situation. In addition, Judge Burciaga was not persuaded that the televising of college football games would have any negative impact on game attendance at nontelevised games.

Judge Burciaga disagreed with the NCAA that the television controls helped maintain competitive balance among the football programs of various schools. In his reasoning, he compared the telecasting policies of NCAA football to NCAA basketball. The NCAA does not control the televising of regular season basketball games. The arrangements are left to the individual member institutions and conferences which have contracted with various national and local television and cable companies. Judge Burciaga rejected the NCAA's contention that televising football was distinguishable from televising basketball; in fact, he held "the market in television basketball to be persuasive evidence of how a free market in television football would operate." Judge Burciaga's decision rendered illegal the NCAA's television contracts with ABC and CBS for $131.75 million each and Turner Broadcasting System for $18 million. His decision voided a total of $281.5 million in television contracts.

The NCAA appealed the decision to the Court of Appeals for the Tenth Circuit, arguing that Judge Burciaga incorrectly concluded that there was price fixing in the awarding of television contracts, since there was vigorous competition among the networks in bidding for the national television contracts. The NCAA further argued that the court erred in its conclusion that the NCAA was not a voluntary association. In May 1983, the court of appeals upheld the district court's ruling.

As noted previously, in *NCAA v. Board of Regents of University of Oklahoma*, the U.S. Supreme Court upheld the decisions of the district court and court of appeals. The Supreme Court summarized its decision by noting:

> The NCAA plays a critical role in the maintenance of a revered tradition of amateurism in college sports. There can be no question but that it needs ample latitude to play that role, or that the preservation of the student-athlete in higher education adds richness and diversity to intercollegiate athletics and is entirely consistent with the goals of the Sherman Act. But consistent with the Sherman Act, the role of the NCAA must be to *preserve* a tradition that might otherwise die; rules that restrict output are hardly consistent with this role. Today we hold only that the record supports the District Court's conclusion that by curtailing output and blunting the ability of member institutions to respond to consumer preference, the NCAA has restricted rather than enhanced the place of intercollegiate athletics in the Nation's life.

In the wake of the Court's ruling a number of lawsuits related to the decision were filed. Unsatisfied with the CFA agreement, which forbid national appearances by member association teams or networks other than ABC or the Entertainment and Sports Programming Network (ESPN), the University of Southern California (USC), the University of California at Los Angeles (UCLA), along with the Pacific-10 and Big-Ten Conferences, brought suit against the ABC-CFA agreement which prevented two games—UCLA against Nebraska and USC against Notre Dame—from being telecast. The suit sought preliminary and permanent injunctions against the defendants because the ABC-CFA exclusive agreement, it was charged, prevented *crossover* games, which are games between CFA member schools and non-CFA member schools. In granting the injunction for UCLA and USC, a federal district court sitting in Los Angeles noted that if the exclusion was allowed to stand, the schools would be harmed by loss of revenue. "By issuance of this order, ABC and ESPN are not measurably harmed, other than by some perceived diminution of their ability quickly to dispatch CBS from the market for nationwide football telecasts." Soon afterwards, the parties to the suit settled their differences and dropped any further litigation involving this situation. In general, such questions of property broadcast ownership are now determined in the game contracts, as was discussed earlier. (See note 5b.)

Soon after the decision, the Association of Independent Television Stations (INTV) filed two suits in federal district court aimed at opening the college telecast market further to local broadcast stations. INTV is a coalition of stations not affiliated with the major networks (ABC, CBS, and NBC). The suits sought on antitrust grounds to open *protected* time frames that the major networks have arranged with the different football governing bodies, such as the CFA. INTV's first suit was filed in Los Angeles against CBS and the Big-Ten and Pacific-10 Conferences. The second suit was filed in Oklahoma City against ABC, ESPN, the CFA, and the Big Eight Conference.

In March 1986, Judge Burciaga rejected the arguments of INTV and ruled that CFA's plan granting some networks exclusivity in two time periods was allowable under the antitrust laws. Judge Burciaga noted:

> The CFA is a powerful entity. . . . Nonetheless, it remains to be demonstrated beyond reasonable factual dispute that the CFA can both control price and restrict entry to the college football television market. The market is a different one than the court analyzed in 1982. Unlike the NCAA, the CFA . . . have their rivals.

Important questions concerning the legality of any national or regional television plan that seeks to place controls and limitations on the marketplace remain. The CFA came under additional scrutiny by the Federal Trade Commission (FTC) in 1990. The FTC has jurisdiction over enforcement of antitrust laws. In September 1990 the FTC filed an administrative complaint against the CFA and Capital Cities-ABC, claiming that their national television contracts were anticompetitive. The complaint alleged that consumers had been deprived of the selection of college football games because of the limitation on teams and games selected to be televised by the CFA-Capital Cities contract. The CFA withstood this challenge when Judge James P. Timony, an administrative law judge, ruled that the FTC has no jurisdiction over the television agreement because colleges and universities are not considered profit-making corporations over which the agency has legal responsibility. The FTC had argued that major-college football programs are operated for commercial rather than educational objectives and therefore are subject to antitrust laws despite the CFA's nonprofit status. Judge Timony ruled, though, that the proceeds from the CFA's television rights to college football games go to the schools and have a nonprofit educational purpose.

The CFA withstood this FTC challenge to their television contract but received a setback when the University of Notre Dame seceded from the CFA television contract with ABC and entered its own agreement in January 1990 with NBC for $38 million. The original CFA-ABC contract was for $210 million but had to be scaled down by about $25 million when Notre Dame defected and entered into their own agreement. Notre Dame's athletic director Dick Rosenthal said the NBC contract was a result of Notre Dame's nonapproval of the ABC contract, which called for regional coverage. Rosenthal believed this would have denationalized the Fighting Irish, hurting their broad appeal. With the NBC contract, Notre Dame's home games are televised nationally. This contract is also more financially lucrative for the Fighting Irish, bringing in $1.2 million per game, which is divided equally between Notre Dame and their opponent. Under the CFA-ABC agreement, Notre Dame was paid $1.53 million during the 1988–89 season. The CFA seems to have no legal recourse against the University of Notre Dame because of the precedent of free and open competition in the television marketplace that the courts have found since the *NCAA v. Board of Regents of University of Oklahoma* decision.

In comparison to collegiate football television contracts, in which the NCAA is no longer a party, collegiate basketball is another story. The NCAA signed a $1 billion contract with CBS in November 1989 for the television rights to the Men's Basketball Tournament over the next seven years. This contract includes $1 billion to be paid to the NCAA over the seven-year life of the contract, with CBS maintaining rights to televise the Men's Basketball Tournament, Division I Women's Basketball Championship, College World Series, Division II

Men's Basketball Championship, and twelve other NCAA championship events. This contract has not been subject to litigation by the schools or conferences because the NCAA owns the right to their championship events and therefore has jurisdiction to enter into television contracts for these championships as they see fit.

NOTES _____

1. For further information on federal government regulation of television, see 47 C.F.R. § 1 et seq., which deals with the Federal Communications Commission.

2. For further information on cable television, see "Coping with the Complexity of Cable in the 80's," *Nielsen Station Index*, A.C. Nielson Co. (1979), which gives the reader an overview of the cable television industry and its technology; covers basic terminology, language, and legal issues involving rights and liabilities of individuals establishing a cable operation.

3. For further information on the legal aspects of telecasting sporting events, see the following law review articles.

(a) Hochberg and Horowitz, "Broadcasting and CATV: The Beauty and Bane of Major College Football," 38 *Law Contemp. Probls.* 112 (1973). Reviews the legal concerns surrounding the broadcasting of sporting events and other issues, such as the pirating of broadcast signals.

(b) Hochberg and Garrett, "Sports Broadcasting and the Law," 59 *Ind. L. J.* 155 (1984). Reviews the legal issues raised by the broadcasting of sports on the so called "Superstations"; details some of the economic concerns this poses to sports organizations.

(c) Cryan and Crane, "Sports on the Superstations: The Legal and Economic Effects," 3 *Entertainment and Sports L. J.* 35 (1986). Reviews the effect the Supreme Court's ruling had on the televising of intercollegiate football on the television and cable television broadcast media. It places particular emphasis on the public policy concerns of the Supreme Court, that such broadcasts should not be artificially restrained by sports organizations.

(d) Wong and Ensor, "The Impact of the U.S. Supreme Court's Antitrust Ruling on College Football," 3 *Entertainment and Sport Lawyer* 3 (1985).

4. For further information on the NCAA and the broadcast industries, see the following.

(a) *Cable Television and Other Alternatives to Conventional Television*, Briefing Book, NCAA Subcommittee on Non-network Television, NCAA Publications (Mission, Kan., 1981). Gives the reader an overview of cable television applications to intercollegiate athletics. The material is somewhat dated but does contain a good historical perspective of the NCAA relationship with the broadcast industries and the association's initial reaction to this new broadcast medium.

(b) Host, *NCAA Radio Network Manual*, NCAA Publications (Mission, Kan., 1984). Gives the reader an overview of how to establish and operate an intercollegiate football or basketball radio network. This is a comprehensive study which includes sample contracts and other documents.

(c) *NCAA Public Relations and Promotions Manual,* NCAA Publications (Mission, Kan., 1985). Gives the reader a comprehensive overview of the operation of a public relations office for intercollegiate athletics. It contains chapters on the broadcast industry.

5. The following major court cases involve amateur athletics and broadcasting.

(a) In *National Collegiate Athletic Ass'n. v. Board of Regents of University of Oklahoma,* 468 U.S. 85 (1984), two members of a college athletic association successfully brought an antitrust challenge to the association's plan for televising the college football games of member institutions for the 1981–85 seasons.

(b) In *Regents of University of California v. ABC,* 747 F.2d 511 (9th Cir. 1984), the court upheld a preliminary injunction to bar Nebraska and Notre Dame, members of the College Football Association, which had an agreement with ABC, from refusing to allow games with non-CFA members to be televised on CBS.

(c) In *Cox Broadcasting Corp. v. National Collegiate Athletic Ass'n,* 297 S.E.2d 733 (Ga. 1982), broadcasting companies filed action seeking to restrain athletic associations from alleged breach of contract concerning broadcasts of college football games.

(d) In *Colorado High School Activities Ass'n v. NFL,* 711 F.2d 943 (10th Cir. 1983), it was alleged that the telecast of professional football games within seventy-five miles of a "protected" high school game violated federal and state antitrust laws. The court ruled against the association because the association did not identify the specific stadium where the game was to be played. The association only identified the metropolitan area where the high school game was to be played, which was not sufficient to invoke the statute.

(e) In *Warner Amex Cable v. American Broadcasting Companies, Inc.,* 499 F. Supp. 537 (S.D. Ohio 1980), Warner Amex Cable sought a preliminary injunction against the NCAA and ABC which would have stopped the defendants from preventing the televising of football games which were not otherwise televised by commercial networks. The court denied the injunction, stating that the issuance of an injunction would potentially threaten the NCAA and its member institutions.

6. For further information on the Copyright Act of 1976, see 17 U.S.C. 101 *et seq.*

A BROADCASTING CHECKLIST

In addition to achieving a basic understanding of sports broadcasting rights, how sports broadcast contracts are written, and how the antitrust laws affect sports broadcasting, amateur athletic administrators can minimize legal problems that often accompany television and media broadcasts of athletic events by referring to the following broadcasting checklist:

1. Establish who has the property right in a broadcast.
2. Make sure the requirements of the 1976 Copyright Act are being followed, especially in regards to "fixing" the broadcast and in filing for any royalty fees due with the Copyright Royalty Tribunal.
3. Include proper broadcast rights clauses in any game or contest contract, including rights of opponents regarding broadcasts into their "home" territory.
4. Review conference or league rights to broadcast of applicable championships or individual games or contests.
5. Review all facility lease or rental contracts and facility third-party contracts for possible broadcast rights problems.
6. Review all contracts with television, cable, or radio broadcast stations to ensure proper clauses are included to protect the sports entity's property right in a broadcast.
7. Review all conference or league broadcast contracts for possible antitrust monopoly problems.

Chapter 10

TRADEMARK LAW

INTRODUCTION

The names, logos, and symbols associated with sports organizations have become very marketable items. Their primary purpose has historically been to create an identifiable image through which an athletic organization could promote the sale of its product or service. More recently, however, the sale of a name, logo, or symbol in association with caps, pennants, T-shirts, jerseys, and other souvenirs has become a significant revenue generator in and of itself for an athletic organization. As a result, these organizations have fought many legal battles to retain the exclusive right to dictate who will put their name, logo, or symbol on these salable items.

In addition to gate receipts, television, and other sources of income, the consumers' appetite for sport-related items with a team affiliation has created another revenue stream for many organizations. Most professional sports leagues, for example, have developed licensing programs to capitalize on the public demand. College athletic departments and other organizations, such as the U.S. Olympic Committee and the U.S. Tennis Association, have done likewise. In 1989 the merchandising arms of Major League Baseball, the NFL, and the NBA are reported to have grossed in excess of $1 billion, $750 million, and $500 million, respectively.

Not surprisingly, consumer demand for properties associated with professional and amateur athletic organizations has prompted a number of manufacturers to attempt to cash in on this lucrative opportunity by using names, logos, or symbols associated with a team or organization without authorization. Such attempts have, on a number of occasions, resulted in litigation where the athletic organization sought to protect its exclusive right to its name, logo, or symbol, usually on the basis of trademark law.

Chapter 10 first presents the principles of trademark law. The chapter then discusses trademark infrigement and ambush marketing. The chapter next ties trademark law to intercollegiate athletics. Some of the recent cases that have defined the crucial issues involved in the use of sports trademarks are discussed. The next section focuses on licensing programs and the increasing use of licensing agents by colleges and universities for the sale of products bearing school logos. Such items account for millions of dollars of sales. Therefore, controlling the school or organization trademarks can have favorable economic results. The last section contains a discussion of trademark law and the Olympic Games.

PRINCIPLES OF TRADEMARK LAW

The Federal Trademark Act of 1946, Lanham Act § 45, 15 U.S.C. §§ 1051–1127 (1946), commonly known as the Lanham Act, governs the law of trademarks, the registration of trademarks, and remedies for the infringement of registered trademarks. Many common law principles governing this area have also been incorporated into the act. The Lanham Act was passed to "simplify trademark practice, secure trademark owners in their goodwill which they have built up, and to protect the public from imposition by the use of counterfeit and imitated marks and false descriptions." The Lanham Act's definition of "trademark" was distilled from, and is consistent with, definitions appearing in court decisions both under prior trademark laws and common law.

A *trademark* is defined in the federal Lanham Act as "any word, name, symbol, or device or any combination thereof adopted and used by a manufacturer or merchant to identify his goods and distinguish them from those manufactured or sold by others." Trademarks refer to goods and can be distinguished from service marks and collective marks. The Lanham Act defines a *service mark* as "a mark used in the sale or advertising of services to identify the services of one person and distinguish them from the services of others." While a trademark identifies and distinguishes the source and quality of a tangible product, a service mark identifies and distinguishes the source and quality of an intangible service. The term *collective mark*, as defined in the Lanham Act, means a trademark or service mark used by the "members of a cooperative, an association, or other collective group or organization and includes marks used to indicate membership in a union, an association or other organization." League and sports teams' names and logos are, when used to identify the activities of the leagues and teams, service marks (see Exhibit 10–1). A league name or logo may even be considered a collective membership mark.

A trademark serves the following functions:

1. It designates the source or origin of a particular product or service, even though the source is unknown to the consumer.
2. It denotes a particular standard of quality which is embodied in the product or services.
3. It identifies a product or service and distinguishes it from the products or services of others.
4. It symbolizes the goodwill of its owner and motivates consumers to purchase the trademarked product or service.
5. It represents a substantial advertising investment and is treated as a species of property.
6. It protects the public from confusion and deception, ensures that consumers are able to purchase the products and services they want, and enables the courts to fashion a standard of acceptable business conduct.

Exhibit 10–1
Example of a Service Mark

Int. Cl.: 41

Prior U.S. Cl.: 107
United States Patent and
Trademark Office

Reg. No. 1,234,940

Registered Apr. 12, 1983

SERVICE MARK
Principal Register

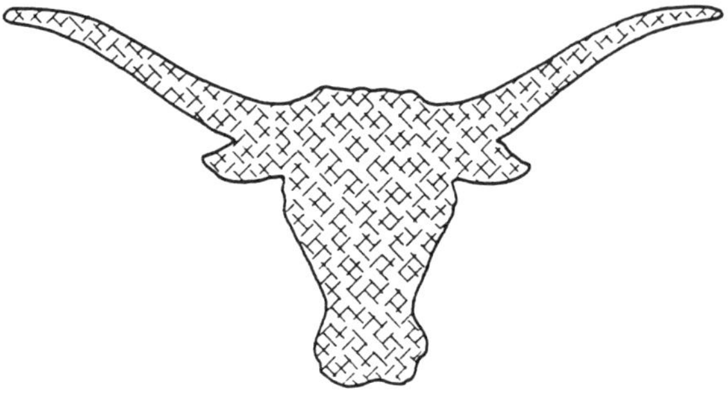

Board of Regents, The University of
Texas System (Texas agency)
201 W. 7th St.
Austin, Tex. 78701

For: ENTERTAINMENT SERVICES—
NAMELY, COLLEGE SPORT GAMES
AND EVENTS RENDERED LIVE AND
THROUGH THE MEDIA OF RADIO
AND TELEVISION, in CLASS 41 (U.S.
Cl. 107).

First use 1958, in another form 1914;
in commerce 1960, in another form,
1914.

The drawing is lined for the color
orange.

Ser. No. 322,001, filed Aug. 3, 1981.

KIMBERLY KREHELY, Examining Attorney

Identification Function of a Trademark

Although the trademark does not necessarily disclose on its face the origin of the goods, it does provide the purchaser with a way of recognizing the goods of a particular seller or manufacturer. When the seller or manufacturer has conveyed desirability of the goods to the purchaser through the trademark, the seller or manufacturer has something of value. This identification function of the trademark also serves as a symbol of the goodwill established by a business. Trademarks, therefore, "are the symbols by which goodwill is advertised and buying habits established." *Goodwill* is a business value, which arises from the reputation of a business and its relations with its customers. It is unique to the particular business. Goodwill has also been defined as "buyer momentum" and "the lure to return." Goodwill is an intangible asset of a business. An *intangible asset* exists only in connection with something else. A patent is an intangible asset. It is an idea or formula, not something that can be touched. A *tangible asset,* on the other hand, is something that can be touched. A car or truck is a tangible asset of a business.

Trademark or service mark rights continue indefinitely, since these marks identify the source of goods or services. A mark can be registered for twenty years and can be renewed for subsequent periods. This procedure is in contrast to other forms of intellectual property protection, such as patents, which have finite terms. However, to maintain rights in the mark, it must be used, must not be abandoned, and must be protected so as not to become generic.

Preying upon the fans' desire to identify with a favorite franchise or athletic organization, numerous businesses have exploited the goodwill and marketability of these organizations by producing anything from hats to T-shirts to jerseys to pennants which carry a team name, nickname, team player name or number, logo, or symbol of the organization without authorization. After being made aware of the infringement, the trademark owner can demand that the activity cease. If these demands are ignored, then the owner is left with no other recourse but to pursue legal remedies provided under the Lanham Act and the common law.

Secondary Meaning

Secondary meaning is a mental recognition in the buyer's mind, associating symbols, words, colors, and designs with goods from a single source. Secondary meaning "tests the connection in the buyer's mind between the product bearing the mark and its source." Secondary meaning in a commercial sense is buyer association, mental association, drawing power, or commercial magnetism. Secondary meaning is important when the trademark is nondistinctive. Nondistinctive marks may not be registered and protected under the Lanham Act as trademarks until they have become distinctive of the goods in commerce.

An example of a nondistinctive mark is a descriptive mark. A mark is descriptive if it describes the intended purpose, function, or use of the goods, the size of the goods, the class of users of the goods, a desirable characteristic of the goods, or the end effect upon the user. Some examples of descriptive marks are "Beer Nuts" for salted nuts, "Holiday Inn" motel, and "Raisin Bran" cereal made with raisins and bran. Descriptive marks are considered weak marks and, at most, are given narrow trademark protection. Barring descriptive marks reflects the Lanham Act's distinctiveness requirement. Thus, absent secondary meaning, nondescriptive marks are ineligible for trademark protection.

Secondary meaning does not have to be demonstrated when the trademark is distinctive. Distinctive marks may be registered and protected under the Lanham Act as trademarks. Some examples of distinctive marks are arbitrary and fanciful or suggestive marks, which are considered strong marks, and these are given strong trademark protection. *Arbitrary marks* are those "words, names, symbols, or devices" that are in common linguistic use but which, when used with the goods or services in issue, neither suggest nor describe any ingredient, quality, or characteristic of those goods or services. Some examples of arbitrary marks are "V-8" juice, "Stork Club," "Ivory" soap, and "Old Crow" whiskey. *Fanciful marks* are coined words that have been invented for the sole purpose of functioning as a trademark. Such marks comprise words that are either totally unknown in the language or are completely out of common usage at the time, as with obsolete or scientific terms. Some examples of fanciful marks are "Clorox" bleach, "Kodak" photographic supplies, and "Polaroid" cameras. Suggestive marks are legally indistinguishable from arbitrary marks. An example of a suggestive mark would be "Greyhound" for a bus line, a name that suggests speed and sleekness.

TRADEMARK INFRINGEMENT

The Lanham Act defines *trademark infringement* as the reproduction, counterfeiting, copying, or imitation, in commerce, of a registered mark "in connection with the sale, offering for sale, distribution, or advertising of any goods or services on or in connection with which such use is likely to cause confusion, or to cause mistake, or to deceive without consent of the registrant."

In order to be successful in a trademark suit, the trademark owner must first establish a protectable property right in the name or mark it seeks to defend, and, second, establish that the infringing party's use of a similar mark is likely to cause confusion, mistake, or deception in the market as to the source, origin, or sponsorship of the products on which the marks are used.

Under the Lanham Act, the registration of a mark with the United States Patent and Trademark Office (see Exhibit 10–2), constitutes prima facie evidence that the registrant owns the mark and has the exclusive right to use the mark and that the registration itself is valid. The burden is then placed on the one challenging the mark to rebut the presumption of validity.

In order to qualify for trademark protection, a "word, name, symbol, or device, or any combination thereof" must be distinctive—that is, able to be distinguished from the "word, name, symbol, or device" of other owners or manufacturers. Generic names of products and services do not qualify for trademark protection. Words such as "cola," "table tennis," and "photocopier" are examples of nondistinctive, or generic, terms. They represent the actual product and are not associated with the source or manufacturer of the product. Terms such as "Coca-Cola," "Ping-Pong," and "Xerox," however, are protected by the trademark laws. They clearly are identified with the manufacturer and qualify as being distinctive terms.

Certain nondistinctive words can qualify for trademark protection under the Lanham Act if they become distinctive—in other words, if they become associated with a single source. "McDonalds" is an example of a nondistinctive name that has become synonymous with fast-food restaurants. When nondistinctive words become distinctive and qualify for trademark protection, they are said to have acquired secondary meaning.

In addition to contending that the "word, name, symbol, or device" is indistinguishable from that of other owners or manufacturers, the alleged infringer may contend that the mark is functional and, therefore, not worthy of trademark status. This was one of the key issues in *Dallas Cowboys Cheerleaders, Inc. v. Pussycat Cinema, Ltd.* 604 F.2d 200 (2nd Cir. 1979), where the defendant alleged that cheerleading uniforms were a purely functional item necessary for the performance of cheerleading routines and, therefore, incapable of becoming the subject of a trademark.

Finally, the infringer may contend that the owner of the mark, though once possessed of a property interest in the mark, had abandoned or relinquished its right. Here, however, rather than relying on the owner's failure to prosecute alleged infringers or allowing the uncontrolled use of the mark for a period of time as evidence of aban-

Exhibit 10–2
Example of a Certificate of Trademark Registration

The State of Texas

SECRETARY OF STATE

Date of Registration <u>July 31, 1981</u>

Registration No. <u>36975</u>

CERTIFICATE OF REGISTRATION

I, GEORGE W. STRAKE, JR., Secretary of State of the State of Texas, hereby certify:

That the attached is the duplicate APPLICATION FOR REGISTRATION.

That in accordance with the provisions of CHAPTER 16, TEXAS BUSINESS AND COMMERCE CODE and the application filed in this office the MARK described below has been duly registered in this office on behalf of:

Name of Applicant <u>Board of Regents, The University of Texas System</u>

Address of Applicant <u>201 West 7th Street</u>

<u>Austin Texas 78701</u>

Description of Mark <u>Texas</u>

Class Number <u>Intl. 41 Education & Entertainment</u>

Dates of First Use: Anywhere <u>1914</u>   In Texas <u>1914</u>

The Term of Registration is for Ten Years and Extends to and

Includes <u>July 31, 1991</u>

IN TESTIMONY WHEREOF, I have hereunto signed my .name officially and caused to be impressed hereon the Seal of State at my office in the City of Austin, this

<u>31st</u> *day of* <u>July</u> *, A.D. 19* <u>81</u>

Secretary of State

donment, the infringer must establish both the intent of the owner to abandon the mark and the loss of all indication as to the source of the mark's origin.

Even though an alleged infringer may be unable to rebut the presumption of validity of a mark successfully, this does not settle the infringement issue under section 32(1) of the Lanham Act. The owner of the mark then bears the burden of establishing that the infringement is likely to cause confusion, mistake, or deception in the market as to the source, origin, or sponsorship of the products on which the mark is used. One might expect that the similarity or duplication of a registered mark would be sufficient to establish confusion; however, such has not been the case. Courts generally have required the production of evidence to establish that individuals do make the critical distinction as to sponsorship or endorsement, or direct evidence of actual confusion between the authentic and counterfeit product. The "likely to cause confusion" issue has proved to be the key question in the majority of sports trademark cases. Of paramount concern is whether there is a likelihood of confusion such that the public believes that the goods are endorsed or authorized by the trademark owner.

NOTES ——————————————————————————————

1. In *American Basketball Ass'n. v. AMF Voit, Inc.*, 416 U.S. 986 (1974), preliminary and permanent injunctions to prevent a sporting goods company from manufacturing for sale a red-white-and-blue basketball in the pattern used by the ABA were denied. The ABA had sought and was granted a trademark for the design of the basketball. The court held, however, that the colors were merely a decoration and did not constitute a distinctive design. Furthermore, the ABA had not established a secondary meaning in the ball.

2. In *WCVB-TV v. Boston Athletic Association, et al.*, 926 F.2d 42 (1st Cir. 1991), the Boston Athletic Association (BAA) appealed a district court's refusal to grant a temporary injunction which would have banned WCVB-TV, Channel 5, from televising the Boston Marathon. The BAA registered the words "Boston Marathon" as a trademark to signify the marathon run. As part of the trademark violation argument, the BAA stated that Channel 5, by broadcasting the words "Boston Marathon" in connection with the event, had violated federal trademark law. In addition, the Boston Marathon was licensed to Channel 4, another Boston television station, for broadcasting coverage. The district court ruled there was not sufficient evidence to prove a violation of trademark law. The court of appeals affirmed, holding that there was insufficient likelihood of consumer confusion to warrant granting an injunction. Subsequent to this decision, Channel 5 and the BAA reached a settlement with all broadcast rights protected and the BAA maintaining exclusive national and international rights. Both Channels 4 and 5 were allowed to air full coverage of the marathon.

3. In *United States Golf Ass'n. v. St. Andrew's Systems, Data Max, Inc.*, 749 F.2d 1028 (3d Cir. 1984), an amateur golf organization, the USGA, sought

to enjoin a computer company from using its mathematical formula for "handicapping" golfers. The court held that the mathematical formula was "functional" rather than an identifying feature of the USGA and was thus not protectable by trademark laws.

4. In *Augusta National, Inc. v. Northwestern Mutual Life Insurance*, 193 U.S.P.Q. 210 (S.D. Ga. 1976), owners of the mark *THE MASTERS* for the Masters Golf Tournament successfully prevented, by claiming unfair competition, the use of the mark in the Ladies' Masters Tournament.

5. In *Professional Golfers of America v. Bankers Life & Casualty Co.*, 186 U.S.P.Q. 447 (5th Cir. 1975), plaintiff golf association successfully enjoined the defendant from displaying the initials *PGA* on its clubhouse and golf courses by persuading the court that such use of a collective service mark falsely suggested an affiliation and constituted unfair competition and trademark infringement.

6. In *Boston Professional Hockey Ass'n. v. Reliable Knitting Works, Inc.*, 178 U.S.P.Q. 274 (E.D. Wisc. 1973), a preliminary injunction was entered barring defendant from manufacturing, selling, advertising, or distributing knit caps displaying the word *BRUINS* or the circled letter *B*. The plaintiff was successful in proving to the court that the hats bearing such marks had a high likelihood of confusing consumers about the Boston hockey team's approval of such merchandise.

7. *In re National Novice Hockey League, Inc.*, 222 U.S.P.Q. 638 (TTAB 1984), the Trademark Board refused to register the marks *National Novice Hockey League* and *NNHL* because of the likelihood of confusion with the National Hockey League.

8. In *National Football League Properties, Inc. v. Coniglio*, 554 F. Supp. 1224 (D.D.C. 1983), the NFL sought a temporary restraining order to prevent the sale of unauthorized souvenir merchandise in the District of Columbia after the Washington Redskins appearance in the Super Bowl. The court, however, refused to grant an injunction, noting that an injunction might hamper legitimate merchants as well as infringers. The court did state, however, that if the NFL could demonstrate injury it could sue in the future to recover damages.

9. In *Boston Professional Hockey Ass'n v. Dallas Cap & Emblem Mfg., Inc.*, 510 F.2d 1004 (5th Cir. 1975), the NHL and its member clubs were granted a permanent injunction restraining the defendant from making and selling emblems embodying the teams' registered and unregistered trademarks and service marks. In addition, the court found that even if the defendant included a disclaimer indicating that such use was not authorized by the trademark owner, the defendant would be violating the Lanham Act.

10. In *Boston Athletic Association v. Sullivan*, 867 F.2d 22 (1st Cir. 1989), the defendant sold T-shirts with the logos *Boston Marathon* and *B.A.A. Marathon* printed on them. Plaintiffs brought action against the defendant for infringement of plaintiff's trademark. In reversing the lower court's decision, the judge ruled that the shirts infringed on BAA's trademark, and that defendant would be enjoined from manufacturing and selling the shirts.

11. In *National Football League Properties, Inc. v. New Jersey Giants, Inc.*, 637 F. Supp. 507 (D. N. J. 1986), the defendant company exploited the fact

that the New York Giants football team play their home games in New Jersey. The company manufactured and sold T-shirts and other merchandise displaying the name *New Jersey Giants*. The New York Giants and NFL Properties, Inc., brought action against the company, alleging infringement of the New York Giants' trademark. In ruling for the plaintiffs, the judge permanently enjoined defendant from further use of the name *New Jersey Giants* on merchandise and as their company name.

12. In the important sports trademark case of *National Football League Properties, Inc. v. Wichita Falls Sportswear, Inc.*, 532 F. Supp. 651 (W.D. Wash. 1982), it was the court's scrutiny of the consumer confusion issue that led to the plaintiff's success in preventing a defendant sportswear company from manufacturing and selling NFL football jersey replicas which created the likelihood of confusion. NFL Properties alleged that its trademark rights were violated when Wichita Falls manufactured jerseys in the blue and green colors of the Seattle Seahawk uniforms. The court stated that NFL Properties had the burden of proving (1) that the secondary meaning of the descriptive term (e.g., Seattle) related the jersey to the NFL team and (2) that Wichita Falls's activities created a likelihood of confusion.

13. NFL Properties, the NFL's licensing operation, has successfully gained similar relief as granted in the *Wichita Falls* case in a number of state and federal courts.

(a) *National Football League Properties, Inc. v. Dallas Cap & Emblem Manufacturing Company*, 327 N.E.2d 247 (Ill. App. Ct. 1975).

(b) *National Football League Properties, Inc. v. Consumer Enterprises, Inc.*, 327 N.E.2d 242 (Ill. App. Ct. 1975).

(c) *National Football League Properties, Inc. v. James Gang Silk Screen Works, et al.*, Case No. 80-1929T (S.D. Cal. 1980).

(d) *National Football League Properties, Inc. v. Motwani and Various John Does, Jane Does, and XYZ Corporations*, Case No. 81-293 (E.D. La. 1981).

(e) *National Football League Properties, Inc. and Los Angeles Raiders v. Richard Lieber, et al., and Does One through One Hundred*, Case No. 424283 (Super. Ct. Cal., L.A. Co. 1982).

(f) *National Football League Properties, Inc. v. Eugene Robinson et al., and Does One through Four Hundred*, Case No. C 440022 (Super. Ct. Cal., L.A. Co. 1983).

(g) *National Football League Properties, Inc. and Miami Dolphins Ltd. v. Various John and Jane Does and ABC Companies*, Case No. 83-2830 (Cir. Ct. Dade Co. 1983).

(h) *National Football League Properties, Inc. v. Michael Yingling, Elliot Johnson, Nobuko Hamshalter and Various John and Jane Does and ABC Companies*, Case No. 84-839 (Cir. Ct. Hillsborough Co. 1983).

14. For further information on trademark law, see the following.

(a) Gilson, *Trademark Protection and Practice* (New York: Matthew Bender, 1982).

(b) McCarthy, *Trademarks and Unfair Competition*, 2nd ed. (New York: The Lawyers Cooperative Publishing Company, 1984).

(c) Callman, *Unfair Competition, Trade-Marks, and Monopolies*, 4th ed. (Wilmette, Ill.: Callaghan & Company, 1981).

(d) Kelly, "Trademarks: Protection of Merchandising Properties in Professional Sports," 21 *Duq. L. Rev.* 927 (Summer 1983).

Ambush Marketing

Within the sports industry, a recent trend related to trademark law has been in the area of "ambush marketing," defined as the intentional efforts of a company to weaken, or "ambush," a competitor's official association with a sports organization which was acquired through the payment of sponsorship fees. Companies have undertaken this ambush marketing tactic through the purchase of advertising time surrounding an "official" event. The purchasing of commercial time allows the ambushing company to associate itself with the sporting event without having to pay the official sponsor fees for that event.

Another form of ambush marketing is through the sponsoring of a contest surrounding a sporting event. The company engaged in the ambush marketing need only make sure the "official" name of the event is not used in their promotional materials. Such contests are difficult to challenge legally as long as the company takes steps to avoid creating the "likelihood of confusion" challenge under the Lanham Act that the sports organizations will raise (see note 1). Disclaimers are often used to communicate information to the consumer stating that the company sponsoring the contest is not a sponsor of the sporting event, is not affiliated with any such sponsors, and claims no ownership rights to the sporting event.

Ambush marketing has been costly to sports organizations trying to sell the rights to their sporting events to companies for sponsorship revenue. As more and more ambush marketing occurs, the value placed on "official sponsor" language decreases and the sports organizations lose out. It is extremely difficult for the sports organizations to challenge ambush marketing techniques. First, companies have become increasingly sophisticated and creative in their methods of testing the gray line between legal marketing activity covered by the commercial and free speech provisions of the First Amendment and the fair-use doctrine, versus promotion and advertising that could constitute trademark infringement and unfair competition. Sports organizations need to show that a "likelihood of confusion" exists in the consumer's mind, a very difficult thing to prove. Also, there are few decided cases that address the legal parameters of ambush marketing and fewer still that specifically refer to the term *ambush marketing*. In addition, most ambush marketing campaigns last only a brief period, making the time and cost of litigation prohibitive. Sports organizations are also fearful of the consequences of a negative ruling on ambush marketing which could open the floodgates to future problems. Ambush marketing seems certain to continue, as well as grow, until the courts become more involved in this issue and determine the course for interpretation of the Lanham Act and its relation to ambush marketing techniques.

NOTE _____

1. The following case shows how creative companies can be in marketing, while not violating the law, as well as showing the difficulty the court has in drawing the line. In *National Hockey League, et al., v. Pepsi-Cola Canada Ltd./Pepsi-Cola Canada Ltd.*, Supreme Court of British Columbia (Vancouver Registry) No. C902104 (1992), the National Hockey League filed a lawsuit alleging that Pepsi-Cola Canada, a company without rights to NHL trademarks, had engaged in misappropriation and unfair competition by using marks "confusingly similar" to those owned by the NHL. In spring 1990, Pepsi-Cola Canada conducted a consumer contest called the "Diet Pepsi $4,000,000 Pro Hockey Playoff Pool," whereby fans matching information under bottle caps with actual NHL Playoff results became eligible for prizes. In addition, Pepsi-Cola Canada sponsored the broadcasts of the NHL playoff games throughout Canada and used its commercial spots to advertise the promotion.

On all promotional materials connected with this contest and at the beginning of all commercials during the playoff games, Pepsi-Cola Canada displayed a disclaimer disassociating Pepsi-Cola Canada and its promotion from the NHL. The NHL claimed that not only was use of these disclaimers an admission by Pepsi-Cola Canada that it was aware of the misrepresentations contained in its advertising, but also that use of the words *National Hockey League* in the disclaimers was itself a trademark infringement.

The Supreme Court of British Columbia ruled against the NHL, holding that Pepsi-Cola Canada had used sufficient disclaimers in its promotional announcements and commercial advertising to make consumers aware that it was not officially associated with the NHL. The judge stated that Pepsi's product is soft drinks and the NHL's product is hockey, and therefore there can be no confusion in the consumer's mind as to which product belongs to which company. The judge refused to accept the arguments brought forth by the NHL about the disclaimers used by Pepsi-Cola Canada, stating that a company can use the trademark of another company in its disclaimers because this allows the company to convey it promotional offer to the consumers truthfully and accurately. The use of disclaimers by Pepsi-Cola Canada was found to be sufficient to alleviate any potential confusion among consumers.

TRADEMARK LAW AND INTERCOLLEGIATE ATHLETICS

The need for trademark protection in intercollegiate athletics is a relatively recent occurrence that reflects the growing popularity of intercollegiate athletics as a consumer product. Consumers purchase the intercollegiate sports product, for example, when they buy admission tickets to intercollegiate events, view commercial television, purchase periodicals and books relating to intercollegiate athletics, or subscribe to cable television channels devoted to sports. A by-product of the increased purchasing of intercollegiate athletic products is a desire by the consumer to be identified with an athletic program. This identification process often entails purchases of products with the consumer's favorite athletic team's logo or mascot printed on them. The dramatic increase in the purchases of such products over the past decade has led to an increased awareness of the need for trademark protection in intercollegiate athletics.

In *University of Pittsburgh v. Champion Products, Inc.*, 686 F.2d 1040 (3d Cir. 1982), *cert. denied*, 459 U.S. 1087 (1982), the United States District Court declined to extend the *Wichita Falls* holding to intercollegiate athletics, reversing on remand an appeals court decision that had applied the professional sports-related *Wichita Falls* rationale. The court of appeals had extended the *Wichita Falls* decision by holding that the University of Pittsburgh had a right of prospective injunctive relief against a manufacturer that allegedly infringed the university's trademark. This was seen as an especially important development in sports trademark law, given the previously unrestricted use of educational institutions' symbols, which manufacturers/sellers had enjoyed for years. Furthermore, the right to control a particular symbol would have allowed the institution not only to gain financial benefits but also to protect and cultivate its own reputation and good name.

However, the district court on remand from its original decision that dealt with an unrelated question found that "there is no likelihood of confusion, whether of source, origin, sponsorship, endorsement, or any other nature, between the soft goods of...Champion Products, Inc., emblazoned with Pitt insignia, and with...Pitt." The court declined to apply the *Wichita Falls* rationale which the appeals court had suggested might govern.

Since the 1930s, the school had goods with its insignia manufactured and sold by one company, initially for the school's athletic department, somewhat later for retail sales in the local area, and eventually for national distribution. In the mid-1970s the school registered its marks under state and federal trademark laws in order to protect what it believed were valuable rights. This was due to the increasing popularity and national prominence of Pitt's football team. School officials sought to enter into a licensing agreement with Champion for continued use of the insignia. Champion was the premier manufacturer of "soft goods" imprinted with the insignia of educational institutions and was reproducing emblems of more than 10,000 schools, colleges, and universities. The company was reporting annual sales in excess of $100 million. It had no such licensing agreement with any other schools, and it refused to enter into an agreement with Pitt.

Pitt went to court to stop Champion's unauthorized use of the school's insignia. The district court denied Pitt's request for a temporary injunction pending trial due to the doctrine of laches (neglect for an unreasonable time to take lawful action). The court of appeals, however, ruled that Pitt's delay in bringing infringement action did not prevent its right to future injunctive relief. The case was remanded to the district court.

In ruling against Pitt, the district court noted that Pitt, as the plaintiff in this case, had to prove four elements to be successful in its litigation. These elements, considered essential for success in any trademark case based on unfair competition, were likelihood of confusion, nonfunctionality, secondary meaning, and priority of use. In the opinion of the district court, Pittsburgh did not "provide any real evidence of confusion." The court held that the university's presentation was very weak, and instead of showing a likelihood of confusion, the university showed little chance of any confusion whatsoever. The district court, in discussing the functionality aspect of the case, noted: "The insignia on these soft goods serves a real, albeit aesthetic function for the wearers." Similarly, the court found no likelihood that in regards to secondary meaning the university was being associated with the manufacture of the product.

Finally, as to priority of use, Pitt had to show that it had priority "of trademark use in commerce." The district court ruled that the Pitt insignia was an ornament and not eligible for trademark protection. The court noted that Pittsburgh had failed to prove any of the elements necessary to make its case.

Other issues in the intercollegiate athletics area are raised in *Texas A & M University System v. University Book Store, Inc.*, Court of Appeals for the Tenth Supreme Judicial District of Texas at Waco, No. 10-84-088-CV (1984) (unreported decision). University Book Store, Inc. (UBC) and four other retail book stores filed suit against Texas A&M in August 1981. UBC operated stores near the university's campus in College Station and wanted to sell goods with the Texas A&M marks on them. Texas A&M refused to allow UBC to do so.

The case was tried without a jury, and a judgment was rendered for UBC; the trial court canceled Texas A&M's marks. The judgment was based on the trial court's finding that Texas A&M "is not the owner of the described marks" because it has not used the marks, and the conclusion that "the certificates of registration should be canceled pursuant to Art. 16.16(a)(4)(B), Tex. Bus. & C. Code."

Texas A&M appealed on two grounds, asserting that (1) the trial court erred in failing to dismiss this suit on their plea of sovereign immunity, and (2) the trial court's finding that Texas A&M does not own the service marks because of lack of use is not supported by any evidence.

The court of appeals reversed the district court's decision. It based its decision on sovereign immunity and also held:

> We disagree with appellees' contentions that the University is not the owner of the service marks and that the registrations are unlawful or invalid acts. The service marks carried rebuttable presumptions of the validity of the registrations, of the University ownership of the service marks, and of the University's exclusive right to use the mark in connection with higher education services.

The court of appeals reasoned that "there is no evidence rebutting the University's use of the marks in connection with its higher educational services."

A number of different considerations are raised in the *Texas A&M University System* case, in contrast to the *University of Pittsburgh* case. First, a retailer was involved instead of a manufacturer. Second, the plaintiff in *Texas A&M University System* challenged the marks and, as a plaintiff, could not successfully raise a laches argument, since laches is generally viewed to be a defense. And third, *Texas A&M University System* involved state institutions, which consequently raised sovereign immunity arguments.

While this chapter has focused on the legal issues involved, litigation may well be obviated by purely business considerations. On the intercollegiate level, despite its success on the merits in the *University of Pittsburgh* case, Champion Products settled the case and executed a licensing agreement with the university. There is clearly a trend for manufacturers to execute licensing arrangements with mark owners, despite the possibility of success on the merits in a trademark case on the intercollegiate level. There are a couple of reasons for the move to licensing agreements and away from litigation. First, the manufacturer that challenges the university faces litigation expenses. Second, a manufacturer may have other business dealings with a university which may be adversely affected by litigation. For example, Champion Products supplies uniforms for intercollegiate athletic programs at many universities, and the loss of this business would be costly.

When Champion settled the *University of Pittsburgh* case by executing a licensing agreement with Pittsburgh, many other major manufacturers decided to do the same as well. As a result, mark holders and manufacturers are presently on good terms (at least temporarily). However, this does not foreclose the possibility of future litigation, and there may be a licensee or a nonlicensed manufacturer waiting for the right time and fact situation to challenge the universities.

NOTES _____

1. In *University of Georgia Athletic Ass'n v. Latte,* 756 F.2d 1535 (11th Cir. 1985), a federal appeals court held that a beverage distributor could not sell "Battlin' Bulldog Beer" because the University of Georgia had the exclusive right to market and control Georgia Bulldog merchandise.

2. For further information, see Wong, "Recent Trademark Law Cases Involving Professional and Intercollegiate Sports," 1986 *Det. C. L. Rev.,* 87 (1986).

LICENSING PROGRAMS FOR INTERCOLLEGIATE ATHLETICS

In pursuance of the economic benefits to be reaped from the sale of caps, pennants, T-shirts, jerseys, and souvenirs bearing a team's name or logo, many universities have instituted licensing programs to merchandise properties associated with their athletic teams. What is developing is a situation analogous to that in the major professional sport leagues, in that a licensing agent handles the licensing program for one or more university athletic departments or school stores. One such agent, CCI/ICE–The Collegiate Licensing Company, currently represents over 105 colleges and universities, ten postseason bowl games, and the Southeastern Conference.

There are several reasons why a university or bowl game might use a licensing agent. For example, a university may not have the expertise or time to register the marks, negotiate licensing agreements with manufacturers, police licensed manufacturers for quality control, police for mark infringers, and litigate when necessary. Also, a licensing agent often packages marks to manufacturers on a state, regional, or conference basis.

Along with the advantages of using a licensing agent there are several potential disadvantages. One is that the university may prefer to control the selection of manufacturers and the quality of products. The university may also prefer to maintain flexibility in arranging licensing agreements. For example, universities that handle their own licensing programs may vary fees according to the type of product, the sales volume, whether the item is academically oriented, and other factors. A university that contracts with a licensing agent pays 40 to 50 percent of the royalty revenues generated, which reduces the university's net royalty revenues to 3 or 4 percent (instead of 6 to 8 percent). Another disadvantage is that the university may prefer to retain control of decision-making authority with respect to enforcement of mark infringement cases.

Economies of scale are linked with licensing agents who represent numerous clients. For example, the agents can negotiate with one manufacturer on behalf of all the schools they represent. A college athletic conference could, for instance, decide to arrange for all its member institutions to contract with one licensing agent and distribute revenues equally within the conference. Another advantage to using a licensing agent for all conference members and the conference itself is that it allows the licensing agent to market individual member institutions and the conference merchandise together.

Universities face a number of decisions and challenges in the area of trademarks and service marks. Initially, there is the decision of whether to begin a licensing program. If the answer is affirmative, the university must register the existing marks both on the state and federal level. The university may later be faced with the decision of whether to register a new mark, such as "Phi Slamma Jamma" at the University of Houston. The university must weigh the advantages and disadvantages of handling the licensing program itself or contracting with a licensing agent. In either situation, the university must establish public association with the mark, as used on various products, with the university's sponsorship. The university must decide whether and what collateral marks and products will be sold. Finally, the university must be able to enforce the marks. If the university undertakes its own licensing program, it must police the mark wherever the products are sold. This may be only on a local basis in the state or region of the university, or it may be on a national basis if the school has a national reputation and sells its products nationwide.

Policing marks against infringers is one of the key determinants of long-term success for intercollegiate licensing programs. This is a costly and timely consideration, and one that may well reduce the profitability of a licensing program for universities that do not realize great royalty revenues. It remains to be seen whether universities will be able to establish the expertise and spend the manpower and dollars necessary for effective enforcement of their marks. This issue alone may be the compelling reason for many universities to contract with a licensing agent, who, with tremendous economies of scale, can police and enforce marks (see Exhibit 10–3).

Regardless of whether the university decides to handle the licensing program by itself or to contract with a licensing agent, it must make some decisions regarding the distribution of royalty revenues. Among the alternatives to be considered in distributing royalty revenues are appropriating money for athletic scholarships, the general scholarship

Exhibit 10–3
Example of a Licensing Agent's Contract with a University

CCI/ICE REVOCABLE NONEXCLUSIVE LICENSE TO USE CERTAIN INDICIA OF UNIVERSITIES

This is an Agreement between _____
_____ , a corporation of the State of _____ ,
having its principal place of business at _____
_____ (hereafter
called "Licensee"), and International Collegiate Enterprises, Incorporated, a corporation of the State of California, whose address is 6312 Variel Avenue, Suite 205, Woodland Hills, CA 91367-2574 (hereafter called "ICE"), and Collegiate Concepts, Incorporated, a corporation of the State of Delaware, whose address is 4501 Circle 75 Parkway, Suite E-5180, Atlanta, GA 30339 (hereafter called "CCI"), a joint venture (hereafter called "CCI/ICE").

Whereas CCI/ICE represents certain licensing interests of the various universities listed in Appendix A attached hereto, pursuant to which, it has to the extent referred to in this agreement the exclusive right to license within the United States for commercial purposes the use of certain University designations, comprising designs, trademarks, service marks, logographics and/or symbols, and

Whereas Licensee desires to be licensed to utilize Licensed Indicia, as hereinafter defined in connection with the manufacture, sale, and/or distribution of certain articles of merchandise;

Now, therefore, in consideration of the premises and the mutual promises and covenants herein contained, the parties hereto agree as follows:

1. DEFINITION

For the purposes hereof:

(a) "Member Universities" or "Universities" means the universities listed on Appendix A attached hereto.

(b) "Indicia" means the designs, trademarks, service marks, logographics, and symbols which have come to be associated with the respective Member University.

(c) "Licensed Indicia" means Indicia which are set forth in Appendix B attached hereto.

(d) "Licensed Articles" means the articles of merchandise or products listed in Appendix C attached hereto and bearing one or more Licensed Indicia.

(e) "Retail Sales" means the sale of Licensed Articles directed to the ultimate consumer at retail outlets or through mail order, catalogs or any other forms of direct response.

(f) "Net Sales" means the amount of gross sales of Licensed Articles after deducting any credits for returns actually made and allowed as such. In computing Net Sales there shall be no deduction for costs incurred in manufacturing, selling, advertising (including without limitation cooperative or other advertising or promotional allowances) or distributing the articles covered by this agreement, nor shall any indirect expenses be deducted, nor shall any deductions be made for uncollectable accounts.

(g) "Premium" means any article given free or sold at less than the usual selling price for the purpose of increasing the sale, promoting, or publicizing any other product or any service, including incentives for sales force, trade or consumer.

2. GRANT OF LICENSE

(a) Grant: Subject to the limitations set forth in paragraph 2(e) below and other conditions of this agreement, CCI/ICE hereby grants to Licensee the nonexclusive right to utilize the Licensed Indicia on the Licensed Articles. This license applies only to indicia of the Universities listed in Appendix A which Licensee has selected pursuant to paragraph 4(a) hereof.

Exhibit 10–3 continued

(b) Territory: The license hereby granted extends to the United States of America, its territories and possessions, and the Commonwealth of Puerto Rico, as well as to United States military bases abroad.

(c) Term: This agreement shall begin effective the last date of signature below and shall continue for twelve (12) months, unless terminated sooner in accordance with the provisions of this agreement.

(d) Renewal: Provided that net royalties from the sale of Licensed Articles during the term of this agreement exceed the level required for payment of the advance fee prescribed in section 7(c) hereof, and set forth in Appendix C, Licensee shall be considered for renewal of this agreement for a period of one year, subject to a satisfactory performance of the requirements of Section 9(a). Such determination is at the sole discretion of CCI/ICE.

(e) Limitation on License: No license is granted hereunder for the use of Licensed Indicia for any purpose other than upon or in connection with the Licensed Articles. No license is granted to Licensee hereunder for the manufacture, sale or distribution of Licensed Articles to be used as premiums, for publicity purposes, for fund raising, as give aways, in combination sales, or to be disposed of under similar methods of merchandising. Licensee shall not use any of the Licensed Indicia in connection with any sweepstake, lottery, game of chance of any similar promotional or sales device, scheme, or program. In the event Licensee desires to sell Licensed Articles for such purposes, Licensee agrees to obtain written approval therefor from CCI/ICE.

(f) Licensee recognizes that any person who has collegiate athletic eligibility cannot have his or her name and/or facsimile utilized on any commercial product. Therefore, in conducting licensed activity under this agreement, Licensee shall not encourage or participate in any activity that would cause an athlete or a University to violate any rule of the National Collegiate Athletic Association (NCAA).

3. PROMOTIONAL PROGRAMS

(a) General: Licensee recognizes that promotions are inherent to the success of any licensing program and as such will assist CCI/ICE with such promotional efforts by its participation.

(b) Merchandising Catalog: CCI/ICE plans to produce annually, a merchandising catalog, in which participation by Licensee is anticipated. Licensee will provide all necessary Licensed Articles for display therein upon request of CCI/ICE. The display of Licensee's products and the cost of the development and promotion of such catalog and for periodic changes therein, presently contemplated to be annual, shall be agreed upon in advance by CCI/ICE and Licensee.

4. SELECTION OF MEMBER UNIVERSITIES AND PERFORMANCE GUARANTEE

(a) Selections: Prior to contract execution hereof, Licensee may select, by check marks to the list of Appendix A, those Member Universities, and the Licensed Indicia of Appendix B, which Licensee desires to utilize on Licensed Articles.

(b) Performance: With respect to each of the Member Universities selected by Licensee, Licensee undertakes to make and maintain adequate arrangements for the broadest possible distribution of Licensed Articles throughout the territory, consistent with its current marketing and distribution plans and objectives. Licensee agrees to maintain what it normally considers to be adequate inventories of Licensed Articles as an essential part of the distribution program.

5. NONEXCLUSIVITY

The license or licenses granted to Licensee by this Agreement are nonexclusive. Nothing in this Agreement shall be construed to prevent CCI/ICE or any Member University from licensing the use of any of the Licensed Marks to any party for any purpose including, without limitation, the grant of other licenses to other manufacturers during the term of this agreement for the use of the Licensed Marks upon the articles described in Appendix C, either within or outside the territory.

Exhibit 10–3 continued

6. MODIFICATION BY CCI/ICE OF LISTS OF UNIVERSITIES, INDICIA AND PRODUCTS

(a) The list of Universities in Appendix A hereto, the list of Indicia in Appendix B hereto, the list of University policies in Appendix B-1 hereto, and the list of products or goods in Appendix C hereto, may be changed by CCI/ICE when and if such changes are made necessary by changes in the contracts between the Universities and CCI/ICE. CCI/ICE shall give prompt written notice to Licensee of any additions to, deletions from, or changes in Appendices A, B, or C.

(b) By way of monthly advisory bulletins, CCI/ICE will inform Licensee of any new Member Universities for Appendix A, or changes in Indicia as set forth in Appendix B-1, or changes in policies by Member Universities as set forth in Appendix B-1. Such bulletins will constitute official notice. Licensee agrees to acknowledge all new Member Universities by written response indicating its desire to add or not add such Member University within 30 days of receipt of bulletin. Licensee further agrees that failure to respond will constitute a breach of Section 9(a).

(c) If there is any deletion from Appendices A, B, or C, Licensee agrees that it's permission to use the affected Indicia or to manufacture, distribute, or sell the affected products pursuant to this Agreement will cease on the effective date of the deletion. In such event those provisions of paragraph 20 relating to disposal of inventory will become effective for the affected Indicia or products unless Licensee obtains written permission from the University concerned, to continue to use the Indicia, or to sell the products directly or indirectly, as of the effective date of deletion.

7. RATE, ADVANCE, AND ADMINISTRATIVE FEES

(a) Rate: Licensee agrees that it will pay to CCI/ICE a royalty of _____ of Net Sales of all Licensed Articles sold during the term of this Agreement and during the period allowed pursuant to paragraph 20 hereof (said payments hereinafter called "Royalty Payments").

(b) For purposes of determining the Royalty Payments, sales shall be deemed to have been made at the time of invoicing or billing for said Licensed Articles or at the time of delivery thereof, whichever is earlier.

(c) Initial Advance Payment: Upon execution of this Agreement by CCI/ICE, Licensee will pay CCI/ICE, as a nonrefundable payment, the Initial Advance Payment under this Agreement, set opposite the Licensed Articles in Appendix C. Licensee may deduct this Initial Advance Payment from payments due under the terms of this Agreement.

(d) Administrative Fee: Upon execution of this Agreement by CCI/ICE, Licensee will pay CCI/ICE, as a nonrefundable payment, the Administrative Fee set opposite the Licensed Articles in Appendix C.

8. MULTIPLE ROYALTIES

CCI/ICE recognizes that Licensee may be subject to other License Agreements, which together with this License Agreement, would subject certain Licensed Articles to one or more additional Royalty Payments. CCI/ICE agrees that the Royalty Payments required to be paid to CCI/ICE hereunder for Licensed Articles, which are subject to other License agreements and additional Royalty Payments, may be reduced by the amount that the other Licensor or Licensors reduces its or their standard royalty, up to a total maximum reduction of three percent (3%) of Net Sales.

9. STATEMENT AND PAYMENTS

(a) On or before the twentieth (20) day of each month, Licensee shall submit to CCI/ICE full and accurate statements showing the quantity, description, and Net Sales of the Licensed Articles distributed and/or sold during the preceding calendar month, listed (1) by category or article and (2) by Member Universities and showing

Exhibit 10–3 continued

any additional information kept in the normal course of business by the Licensee, which is appropriate to enable an independent determination of the amount due hereunder with respect to the Licensed Indicia of each Member University. All payments then due CCI/ICE shall be made simultaneously with the submission of the statements. Such monthly statements shall be submitted whether or not they reflect any sales.

(b) Licensee shall, unless otherwise directed in writing by CCI/ICE send all royalty payments and accounting reports to

_____

_____

10. EXEMPT AREA

On or around each Member University campus, certain accounts or areas may be exempt from the obligations to pay any Royalty Payments required under paragraph 7(a) for sales made and delivered by Licensee to customers located within said identified exempt area. Appendix B-1 denotes those accounts or areas which are exempt from Royalty Payments. CCI/ICE reserves the right to add or to delete from Appendix B-1, by notification to Licensee in writing.

11. OWNERSHIP OF INDICIA AND PROTECTION OF RIGHTS

(a) Licensee acknowledges and agrees that each University owns each of its Indicia identified in Appendix B, and that each of said Indicia is valid, and that each University has the exclusive right to use each of its Indicia subject only to limited, nonexclusive, revocable permission granted to Licensee to use the Indicia pursuant to this Agreement. Licensee further acknowledges the validity of each state and federal registration, which each University may own for each Licensed Indicia as of the date of this Agreement or which each University may thereafter obtain or acquire. Licensee further undertakes that it shall not, at any time, file any application in the United States Patent and Trademark Office, or in any state, or in Puerto Rico, or in any territory or possession of the United States, or in any foreign country for the trademark or service mark registration of any mark or other Indicia of any of the Universities, whether or not such mark or Indicia is or are identified in Appendix B, and Licensee further undertakes that it shall not register or deposit any of the Universities' Indicia as, or as part of, a trademark, service mark, trade name, fictitious name, or company or corporate name anywhere in the world. Any trademark or service mark registration obtained or applied for, or obtained during this Agreement, affecting the Licensed Indicia, will be transferred to the Member University.

(b) Licensee undertakes and agrees that it will not, on the basis of any use by Licensee of any of the Licensed Indicia, oppose or seek to cancel, in any court or state or federal agency, including, but not limited to, the United States Patent and Trademark Office, any registration for any mark for which any of the Universities files an application or obtains a registration for any goods or services, and Licensee further undertakes and agrees not to object to, or file any action or lawsuit because of any use by any of the Universities of any Indicia of any of the Universities for any goods or services, whether such use be by any of the Universities directly or through different Licensees or authorized users.

(c) Licensee agrees to assist CCI/ICE in the protection of the several and joint rights of the Member Universities and CCI/ICE, in and to the Licensed Marks and shall provide, at reasonable cost to be borne by CCI/ICE, any evidence, documents, and testimony, concerning the use by Licensee of any one or more of the Licensed Indicia, which CCI/ICE may request for use in obtaining, defending, or enforcing any Licensed Indicia or its registration.

(d) Licensee agrees that nothing in this Agreement shall give to Licensee any right, title, or interest in any Licensed Indicia (except the right to use in accordance with the terms of this Agreement) greater than Licensee already has and all uses by Licensee of any Licensed Indicia associated with each Member University. The Licensee, upon specific request from CCI/ICE, shall provide the following to CCI/ICE for each Licensed Indicia and for each Licensed Article to the extent reasonably available to Licensee:

Exhibit 10–3 continued

(1) The date of first sale of each Licensed Article, description of the Licensed Article and Licensed Indicia thereon and name and address of the recipient of the initial distribution of the Licensed Article within the home state of the respective Member University.

(2) The date of the first sale of each Licensed Article, description of the Licensed Article and Licensed Indicia thereon and name and address of recipient of the initial distribution of the Licensed Article outside the home state of the respective Member University.

12. DISPLAY AND APPROVAL OF INDICIA

(a) Licensee shall use the Licensed Indicia properly on all labels, containers, packages, products, tags, and displays, in all print advertisements and literature, and in all television and radio commercials. On all visible material, the Indicia shall be emphasized in relation to surrounding material by using a distinctive type face, or color, or underlining, or other technique approved by the Universities. Any use of any Indicia shall conform to the requirements as specified on the Appendix B. Wherever appropriate, the Licensed Indicia shall be used as a proper adjective and the common noun for the product shall be used in conjunction with the Licensed Indicia and the proper symbol to identify the Indicia as a trademark, (viz, the circled "R" symbol if the Indicia is registered in the United States Patent and Trademark Office or the "TM" symbol if not so registered), shall be placed adjacent to each Indicia. Except when otherwise expressly authorized in writing by CCI/ICE, Licensee shall not use on any one product the Indicia of more than one University.

(b) CCI/ICE will provide to Licensee guidance on the proper use of the Licensed Indicia. A true representation or example of any proposed use by Licensee of any of the Indicia listed in Appendix B, in any visible or audible medium, and all proposed advertisements and promotional materials depicting any Indicia or referring thereto, shall be submitted at Licensee's expense to CCI/ICE for approval prior to such use. CCI/ICE shall have thirty (30) days from its receipt of the proposed material within which to approve or disapprove the proposed use. If CCI/ICE fails to disapprove the use within thirty (30) days, Licensee may use the Indicia in the form and on the material sent to CCI/ICE subject to the conditions of this Agreement. Licensee shall not use any Indicia in any form or in any material disapproved by CCI/ICE.

(c) Licensee shall display on each product or its container the trademark and license notices required by CCI/ICE's written instructions in effect as of the date of manufacture.

13. DISPLAY OF OFFICIAL TAG

Licensee agrees and undertakes to attach to each product or its container an "Officially Licensed Collegiate Product" tag or label in the form prescribed by CCI/ICE.

14. PROCEDURE FOR PRODUCT APPROVAL

(a) Licensee understands and agrees that it is an essential condition of this Agreement to protect the high reputation enjoyed by the Universities, and that the goods sold, promoted, or advertised in association with any of the Licensed Indicia shall be of high and consistent quality, subject to the approval and continuing supervision and control of the Universities.

(b) The standards, specifications, and characteristics of each product to be sold under each of the Licensed Indicia are set out in Appendix C annexed hereto, or in an attachment to Appendix C. Licensee agrees to adhere strictly to the agreed standards, specifications, and characteristics for each product sold under each of the Licensed Indicia.

(c) Prior to the production or sale of any product of which a physical sample has not already been inspected and approved by CCI/ICE, Licensee shall submit to CCI/ICE, at Licensee's expense, one sample of the product for each University

Exhibit 10–3 continued

checked in Appendix A and one sample of CCI/ICE files, as it would be produced for sale. CCI/ICE shall have thirty (30) days from the receipt of a sample within which to approve or disapprove the product or obtain additional time, up to thirty (30) days, by written notice thereof within the first thirty (30) day period. If CCI/ICE approves the product or fails to disapprove the product within thirty (30) days from the receipt thereof, or during said additional time, the product shall be accepted to serve as an example of quality for that item, and production quantities may be manùfactured by Licensee in strict conformity with the sample that was submitted. Only items manufactured in accordance with the corresponding sample accepted hereunder, and which have substantially the same relative quality position in the marketplace as do the sample thereof, may be manufactured.

(d) At least thirty (30) days prior to renewal in accordance with paragraph 2(d), in addition to any other requirement, Licensee shall submit to CCI/ICE such number of each product sold under the Licensed Indicia as may be necessary for CCI/ICE to examine and test to assure compliance with the quality and standard requirements for products bearing licensed Indicia, as set forth in Appendix D attached hereto. Each product shall be shipped in its usual container or wrapper, together with all labels, tags, and other material which usually accompany the product. Licensees shall bear the expense of manufacturing and shipping the required number of products to the destination designated by CCI/ICE. CCI/ICE shall have thirty (30) days from the receipt of each sample to approve or disapprove the product. Failure to approve by the end of said thirty (30) day period shall be deemed to be an approval.

(e) If CCI/ICE notifies Licensee of any defect in any product, or of any deviation from the approved use of any of the Indicia, Licensee shall have thirty (30) days from the date of notification from CCi/ICE within which to correct every noted defect or deviation. Defective products in Licensee's inventory shall not be sold under, or in association with, any of the Licensed Indicia, but if it is possible to correct all defects in the goods in Licensee's inventory, such goods may be sold under one or more of the Licensed Indicia after all defects are corrected.

(f) A product and the manner of use of Indicia on the product and on materials associated with the products shall be deemed to be approved for the purposes of paragraphs 12(b) and 14(c) and (d), with respect to any University, when Licensee regularly sells or supplies that product bearing the Indicia to the bookstore or any department of that University, so long as Licensee is not notified of any disapproval of a product or manner of use of Indicia by the University or by CCI/ICE. CCI/ICE shall have the right to require the submission of samples for inspection or testing at any time and Licensee shall promptly comply, at its expense, with such requirement, as provided in paragraph 14(d).

15. NO JOINT VENTURE OR ENDORSEMENT OF LICENSEE

Nothing in this Agreement shall be construed to place the parties in the relationship of partners or joint venturers or agents and neither Licensee nor CCI/ICE shall have the power to obligate or bind each other in any manner whatsoever. CCI/ICE is in no way a guarantor of the quality of any product produced by Licensee. Licensee agrees that it will neither state nor imply, either directly or indirectly, that the Licensee, or its activities, other than pursuant to exercise of the license herein, are supported, endorsed or sponsored by CCI/ICE or by any Member University and, upon the direction of CCI/ICE, shall issue express disclaimers to that effect.

16. INFRINGEMENT

Neither CCI/ICE nor any Member University shall be liable as the result of activities by Licensee under this agreement for infringement of any patent, copyright, or trademark belonging to any third party, or for damages or costs involved in any proceeding based upon any such infringement, or for any royalty or obligation incurred by Licensee because of any patent, copyright, or trademark held by a third party.

Exhibit 10–3 continued

17. INDEMNIFICATION AND INSURANCE

Licensee hereby agrees to be solely responsible for, to defend, and indemnify CCI/ICE, the Member Universities, and their respective officers, agents, and employees, and to hold each of them harmless from all liability claims, demands, causes of actions or damages, including reasonable attorney's fees caused by or arising from workmanship, material, or design of any Licensed Article or out of any action by the Licensee in using the Licensed Marks in connection with the manufacture, sale, distribution, or any other use of the Licensed Articles. Licensee will obtain, prior to the first sale of any Licensed Article, product liability insurance providing protection for CCI/ICE, Member Universities, and their respective officers, agents, and employees as insureds in amounts of coverage specified below, against any claims, demands, or causes of action and damages, including reasonable attorney's fees arising out of any alleged defects in such articles, or any manufacture or use thereof. Such insurance policy shall not be cancelled without at least thirty (30) days written notice to CCI/ICE. CCI/ICE shall be furnished with a certificate of such insurance. Licensee agrees that such insurance policy or policies shall provide coverage of One Million Dollars ($1,000,000) for personal injuries arising out of each occurrence and coverage of Three Hundred Thousand Dollars ($300,000) for property damage arising out of each occurrence. However, recognizing that the aforesaid amounts may be inappropriate with regard to specific classes of goods, it is contemplated that CCI/ICE and Licensee may agree upon reasonable adjustment to the foregoing amounts.

18. RECORDS AND RIGHT TO AUDIT

Licensee agrees to keep all books and accounts and records covering all transactions relating to the license herein in a manner such that the information contained in the statements referred to in Paragraph 9 can be readily determined. CCI/ICE and/or its duly authorized representatives shall have the right to examine such books of account and records and all other documents and material in Licensee's possession or under it's control, with respect to the subject matter and terms of this Agreement, and shall have a reasonable amount of freedom and access thereto for such purposes and for the purpose of making copies and/or abstracts therefrom. Should an audit indicate an underpayment of 10% or more of the royalties due in terms of the contract, the cost of audit will be paid by Licensee, along with the full amount of underpay, within fifteen (15) days from receipt of a memorandum of charge from CCI/ICE. All such books of account and records shall be kept available for at least four (4) years after the termination of this agreement.

19. CANCELLATION

(a) To the extent then permitted by law, this Agreement shall be deemed cancelled automatically, effective immediately, should any of the following occur:

(1) Any voluntary or involuntary act of insolvency on the part of Licensee, including, but not limited to, an adjudication of insolvency, any filing under any provision of the Bankruptcy Act, the appointment of a receiver or trustee, an assignment for the benefit of creditors, or any bulk sale by Licensee for the payment of debts; or

(2) Any attempt by Licensee to grant a sublicense or any attempt by Licensee to assign any right or duty under this Agreement to any person, corporation, partnership, association, or any other third party, without the prior written consent of CCI/ICE.

(b) CCI/ICE may cancel this Agreement, effective thirty (30) days from the date of written notice to Licensee, should any of the following occur.

(1) Any failure by Licensee to account for and to pay to CCI/ICE within twenty (20) days of the due date, the royalties due for the period prior to the date when such accounting and payment are due; or

(2) Any act or omission by Licensee for which any Clause or Paragraph of this Agreement provides for cancellation or termination; or

Exhibit 10–3 continued

(3) Any other breach by Licensee of any Clause or Paragraph of this Agreement for which cancellation or termination is not otherwise provided, unless, within thirty (30) days, Licensee fully remedies such omission or breach.

(4) Any act or omission by Licensee which should reflect unfavorably or embarrass or otherwise detract from the high reputation of any Member University.

20. EFFECT OF TERMINATION AND DISPOSAL OF INVENTORY

After termination of this Agreement, Licensee shall have no further right to manufacture, advertise, distribute, sell, or otherwise deal in any Licensed Articles, and Licensee shall not use any Licensed Indicia or any derivation thereof of any Indicia confusingly similar thereto, unless expressly authorized by a Member University or except as elsewhere herein provided. Upon such termination, unless the same shall occur pursuant to paragraph 14, hereof, Licensee may dispose of Licensed Articles which are on hand or in process at the time of such termination, for a period of one hundred eighty (180) days thereafter provided all payments then due are first made to CCI/ICE and statement of payments with respect to that one hundred eighty (180) day period are thereafter made in accordance with paragraph 9 hereof.

21. FINAL STATEMENT

If the Agreement is terminated by CCI/ICE pursuant to paragraph 19, Licensee will furnish to CCI/ICE a statement showing the number and description of Licensed Articles on hand or in process within thirty (30) days after notice of termination is given.

22. SURVIVAL OF RIGHTS

(a) The terms and provisions of this Agreement necessary to protect the rights and interest of the Universities in their marks, Indicia, copyrights, names, reputations, and goodwill shall survive the cancellation or termination of this Agreement for any reason, including licensee's obligation under paragraph 17.

(b) The terms and conditions of this Agreement providing for the furnishing to CCI/ICE of any reports, statements, or accounts and payment of monies due to CCI/ICE, and the right to examine and make copies of Licensee's books and records to determine or verify the correctness and accuracy of Licensee's reports, statements, accounts, or payments shall survive the cancellation of termination of this Agreement for any reason.

(c) All of the terms and conditions of this Agreement which provide for any activity following the effective date of cancellation or termination of this Agreement shall survive until such time as those terms and conditions will have been fulfilled or satisfied.

23. NOTICES

All notices and statements to be given and all payments to be made hereunder, shall be given or made to the parties at their respective addresses set forth above, Attention: President, unless notification of a change of address is given in writing. Any notice shall be sent by first class mail, or by mailgram, telex, TWX, or telegram, and shall be deemed to have been given at the time it is mailed or sent.

24. CONFORMITY TO LAW

(a) Licensee undertakes and agrees that the manufacturing and sale of all of the products described in Appendix C hereto shall be in conformity with all federal, state, and local laws, ordinances, regulations, and rules.

(b) Licensee undertakes and agrees to obtain and maintain all required permits and licenses at Licensee's expense.

(c) Licensee undertakes and agrees to pay all federal, state, and local taxes which may be due on or by reason of the sale of any products described in Appendix C.

Exhibit 10–3 continued

25. SEVERABILITY

In the event any portion of this Agreement is declared invalid or unenforceable for any reason, such portion is deemed severable herefrom and the remainder of this Agreement shall be deemed to be, and shall remain, fully valid and enforceable unless such validity or unenforceability tends to deprive either party of the benefits to be provided it by this Agreement, in which case said deprived party shall have the option of keeping this Agreement in effect or terminating.

26. MISCELLANEOUS

This Agreement and any rights herein granted are personal to Licensee and shall not be assigned, sublicensed, or encumbered without CCI/ICE's written consent. This Agreement constitutes the entire Agreement and understanding between the parties hereto and cancels, terminates, and supersedes any prior Agreement or understanding relating the subject matter hereof between Licensee and CCI/ICE and Member Universities. There are no representations, promises, agreements, warranties, covenants or understandings other than those contained herein. None of the provisions of this Agreement may be waived or modified, except expressly in writing signed by both parties. However, failure of either party to require the performance of any term in this Agreement or the waiver by either party of any breach thereof shall not prevent subsequent enforcement of such term nor be deemed a waiver of any subsequent breach. When necessary for appropriate meaning, a plural shall be deemed to be the singular and a singular shall be deemed to be the plural. The attached appendices are an integral part of this Agreement. Paragraph headings are for convenience only and shall not add to or detract from any of the terms or provisions of this Agreement. This Agreement shall be construed in accordance with the laws of the State of California, and shall not be binding on CCI/ICE until signed by an officer of CCI/ICE.

Licensee:

by: _____

title: _____

date: _____

Collegiate Concepts, Inc.
International Collegiate Enterprises, Inc.
A Joint Venture

by: _____

title: _____

date: _____

fund, or a general university fund, or returning the money to the campus bookstore.

There are other issues involving campus bookstores, such as whether the campus bookstore should receive a most favored status and be allowed to carry items that do not require royalty payments, since if the bookstore did not have a priority status, it would pass these additional costs to students at the university who purchase items at the bookstore and effectively increase the cost of going to school. There are also several compelling reasons against granting bookstores a most favored status. First, this would place outside competitors at a distinct disadvantage. The off-campus bookstores would have the increased overhead cost of royalty payments. Second, granting most favored status is economically inequitable to some university students. Those who benefit from the exemption are individuals who purchase items at the campus bookstore, which include some of the students but also nonstudents. A far more equitable and efficient economic model would require royalty payments from the goods sold at campus bookstores, which the consumers, the purchasers of the goods, would pay. This, in effect, would be a user tax, which is a far more efficient tax in that those who use the product pay the tax. The royalty revenues obtained from a licensing program that includes campus bookstores could then be distributed to a general university fund that would benefit all students at the university. Third, many purchasers are not university students, and if campus bookstores receive most favored status, then this group of purchasers would, in effect, be subsidized. The alumni of the university are probably the majority of these purchasers, and they may not need the subsidy. And fourth, potential antitrust issues are raised by giving campus bookstores the competitive advantage of selling items not requiring royalty fees.

NOTE

1. In fall 1983, Finus Gaston of the University of Alabama made a survey of collegiate licensing programs. His report, "Administrative Decision Making: A Study of Collegiate Trademark Licensing Programs" (May 1984), contained the following conclusions:

   1. Significant differences exist in the perceptions of college and university administrators on important issues associated with collegiate trademark licensing:
      a. All royalty income from the collegiate licensing program should be deposited into the university's general fund to be used as deemed appropriate by the university board of trustees.
      b. Colleges and universities that operate licensing programs should charge the same royalty fee for all license agreements.
      c. As the collegiate licensing movement develops there will emerge a need for all colleges and universities to standardize their license agreements and operating procedures.

      d. Colleges and universities that operate licensing programs should closely examine each product prior to licensing.

      e. Colleges and universities that operate licensing programs should actively promote the sale of their licensed products.

2. Agreement on the concept of collegiate trademark licensing exists among institutional leaders by their endorsement of the following principles:

      a. Collegiate licensing is a legitimate activity for institutions of higher education.

      b. Colleges and universities have a legal right to protect the use of their institutional names, logos, and insignia on commercial products.

      c. The payment of royalty fees to colleges and universities by product manufacturers will not unreasonably increase the cost of merchandise to consumers.

      d. The primary purpose for establishing a collegiate licensing program should not be to create a source of unrestricted income for the institution.

      e. Colleges and universities that operate licensing programs should be willing to engage in litigation to enforce their trademark rights.

3. Despite diversity in administrative structures and practices, the development of licensing consortia such as Collegiate Concepts, Incorporated, will force standardization of operating procedures and, possibly, organizational structures.

4. There is a need for more expertise in trademark law among university counsel, for more support of the licensing program from the university administration, for better enforcement procedures to prevent trademark infringement, and for more coordinated efforts among licensing professionals in program standardization and the promotion of collegiate licensing.

TRADEMARK LAW AND THE OLYMPICS

The Olympic Games, with the terminology and symbols used, have also been involved in trademark law litigation. In the United States, the United States Olympic Committee has pursued violators who have tried to use the protected marks and terminology of the USOC. In fact, protection has been provided not only through use of trademark law but also through the Amateur Sports Act of 1978, which contains a section devoted entirely to the protection of Olympic terminology and symbols (Sec. 36 U.S.C. 380).

    SEC. 110. (a) Without the consent of the Corporation, any person who uses for the purpose of trade, to induce the sale of any goods or services, or to promote any theatrical exhibition, athletic performance, or competition—

    1. the symbol of the International Olympic Committee, consisting of 5 interlocking rings;

    2. the emblem of the Corporation, consisting of an escutcheon having a blue chief and vertically extending red and white bars on the base with 5 interlocking rings displayed on the chief;

    3. any trademark, trade name, sign, symbol, or insignia falsely rep-

resenting association with, or authorization by, the International Olympic Committee or the Corporation; or

4. the words 'Olympic', 'Olympiad', 'Citius Altius Fortius', or any combination or simulation thereof tending to cause confusion, to cause mistake, to deceive, or to falsely suggest a connection with the Corporation or any Olympic activity;

shall be subject to suit in a civil action by the Corporation for the remedies provided in the Act of July 5, 1946 (60 Stat. 427; popularly known as the Trademark Act of 1946). However, any person who actually used the emblem in subsection (a) (2), or the words, or any combination thereof, in subsection (a) (4) for any lawful purpose prior to September 21, 1950, shall not be prohibited by this section from continuing such lawful use for the same purpose and for the same goods or services. In addition, any person who actually used, or whose assignor actually used, any other trademark, trade name, sign, symbol, or insignia described in subsections (a) (3) and (4) for any lawful purpose prior to enactment of this Act shall not be prohibited by this section from continuing such lawful use for the same purpose and for the same goods or services.

(b) The Corporation may authorize contributors and suppliers of goods or services to use the trade name of the Corporation as well as any trademark, symbol, insignia, or emblem of the International Olympic Committee or of the Corporation in advertising that the contributions, goods, or services were donated, supplied, or furnished to or for the use of, approved, selected, or used by the Corporation or United States Olympic or Pan-American team or team members.

(c) The Corporation shall have exclusive right to use the name 'United States Olympic Committee'; the symbol described in subsection (a) (1); the emblem described in subsection (a) (2); and the words 'Olympic', 'Olympiad', 'Citius Altius Fortius' or any combination thereof subject to the preexisting rights described in subsection (a).

The USOC has been involved in lawsuits by different organizations that believed they had a right to use a particular name or symbol (see *San Francisco Arts & Athletics, Inc., et al. v. United States Olympic Committee*, 483 U.S. 522 [1986]), and by doing so were not in violation of trademark or the Amateur Sports Act.

NOTES ⸻

1. In *United States Olympic Committee v. Intelicense Corp.*, 469 U.S. 982 (1984), the defendant, a Swiss corporation, had a license from the International Olympic Committee to market pictograms bearing the Olympic rings. Because the defendant did not have the consent of the USOC they were found to be in infringement of the trademark granted by the Amateur Sports Act and were enjoined from all further sales in the United States.

2. In *United States Olympic Committee v. Olymp-Herrenwasche-fabriken Bezner GmbH & Co.*, 224 U.S.P.Q. 497 (T.T.A.B. 1984), a German sportswear

manufacturer applied to register the mark *OLYMP* to be placed on shirts, blouses, and collars. The USOC objected to the registration of this mark because of the similarity with the word *Olympic,* which was already protected. This application was denied by the Trademark Board because of the likelihood of confusion of these products with the athletic uniforms and equipment bearing the registered mark of the USOC *OLYMPIC.*

3. In *United States Olympic Committee v. Union Sport Apparel,* 220 U.S.P.Q. 526 (E.D. Va. 1983), the Trademark Board enjoined the defendant sportswear manufacturer from marketing clothing bearing a logo of three interlocking rings and the letters *U.S.A.* The court determined that the defendant was trying to take advantage of the goodwill created by the USOC and thus infringed the trademark established in the Amateur Sports Act.

4. In *United States Olympic Committee v. International Federation of Bodybuilders,* 219 U.S.P.Q. 353 (D.D.C. 1982), the defendants were enjoined from using a seven-ring symbol similar to the Olympic interlocking ring symbol in their magazines or for purposes of advertising various products. This ruling was based on the trademark protection granted through the Amateur Sports Act. The term *MR. OLYMPIA,* used to refer to the winner of a professional bodybuilding contest, was allowed.

5. In *San Francisco Arts & Athletics, Inc., v. United States Olympic Committee,* 483 U.S. 522 (1986), the United States Olympic Committee (USOC) brought action against San Francisco Arts & Athletics, Inc. (SFAA), for using the word *"Olympics"* in their promotion of the "Gay Olympic Games." They alleged a trademark violation under the Lanham Act. The court of appeals affirmed the lower court's summary judgment for the USOC and issued a permanent injunction against SFAA from further using the word *"Olympics."*

Chapter 11

PROFESSIONAL CAREERS AND PLAYER AGENTS

INTRODUCTION

One of the most important responsibilities of athletic administrators at both the high school and college level is to provide guidance to student-athletes who are dealing with possible professional career opportunities. Performing this duty serves a dual purpose: It ensures the continued eligibility of the player and it prepares the athlete to deal with sports agents and the professional sports industry.

Chapter 11 examines eligibility issues and how contact with agents can affect the athlete's status. The chapter next addresses the structure and function of the professional leagues' drafts and collective bargaining agreements. In addition, salary and contract information is provided. The chapter then looks at player agents—their functions and how and by whom they are regulated. The information contained in this chapter will help the athletic administrator to understand the issues which may face the student-athlete who has the potential to be a professional athlete. Chapter 11 concludes with two brief sections on individual performer sports and the opportunities available to U.S. athletes who want to play in foreign leagues, as well as a brief section on endorsement contracts.

AMATEUR ELIGIBILITY ISSUES

The athletic administrator who deals with the college student-athlete must be aware of certain issues that might affect the eligibility of the athlete. The issues that will most likely affect the amateur status of a student-athlete are the payment to or employment of an athlete. These areas have already been addressed in Chapter 5; here we focus on how important it is that the athletic administrator understand why athletes are sometimes willing to sacrifice their eligibility for the opportunity to become a professional.

An athlete faces many pressures when deciding whether or not to turn pro. Peer pressure is often a factor in that the athletes think they must prove their worth to others who play at the same level. The signing of a professional contract may put to rest any questions their peers have about their ability. The money an athlete can earn as a professional also makes becoming a professional seem a very attractive proposition. The money may be viewed by the athlete as a way of becoming self-supporting and/or helping his or her family. A student-athlete may feel the pressure to secure these outstanding amounts before his or her amateur eligibility ends to avoid the risk that a career-threatening injury during his or her amateur career would limit the chances of ever earning the large salary.

Player agents may put pressure on an athlete to turn pro. Agents will try to recruit using various methods, both legal and illegal, and the athlete may have a hard time retaining amateur status in the face of attractive offers of a professional contract. From the agent's standpoint recruiting is a very competitive business, and signing a top prospect before someone else can be most rewarding. A final source of pressure on an athlete may come directly from the professional teams. They may try to lure the athlete into special deals with bonus money and high salary offers, although this has usually occurred only when there were competing leagues.

It is the athletes themselves who must ultimately make the critical decisions which will impact many areas of interest. They first must decide if they are ready to compete at the professional level. They then must try to establish which round they will be drafted in and, if drafted, whether or not it will be the right team for them. In professional basketball and football, the athletes usually do not have the luxury of picking a desired team, but they may have more flexibility in professional baseball. They must also decide whether they are physically and mentally prepared for the rigors of the game, both on and off the court or field. Another consideration is what will happen if they wait to turn pro. By waiting, will they sacrifice a large contract, or will they maybe attract an even larger contract?

Other issues also face student-athletes. Whether or not they can talk to an attorney or player agent must be considered. If they are able to talk to a player agent, they must decide whether it is possible for the agent to be a part of the marketing of their abilities. Athletes who are drafted must realize that they may lose their amateur eligibility by being drafted. And, if they are drafted, how long will the drafting team keep their rights?

Student-athletes who do not want to take the step of employing an agent need to know to whom they can turn for assistance. Will the league office give them some direction? Will the club that is interested in drafting them be helpful in giving some direction? And who from the club is best to talk to? Upon being drafted, the athletes will also want to talk with a representative of the players' union to obtain salary information and to find out about the procedures and applications of membership.

We will attempt to address several of these questions in this chapter. However, there is neither the time nor the space to address all of these issues, mainly because the rules and regulations differ for each professional league, for each sport (e.g., track and basketball differ), and for each amateur association (e.g., the NCAA and the USOC have different interpretations of "amateur"). In addition, the practices of the leagues and unions differ for each sport. Because there are so many combinations of rules, regulations, and league practices, to which are added the student-athlete's on-the-field accomplishments, potential, and maturity levels, each student-athlete's case should be handled individually. Another reason for individual treatment according to many general managers of professional teams is that both the draft and player evaluations are inexact sciences.

This chapter may raise more questions than it answers. What is important, however, is that it raise the level of awareness for athletic administrators and student-athletes in terms of their options and the information they should be striving to obtain so that they can make informed decisions. From the perspective of the athletic director, this area is often ignored; yet, the negative ramifications for an athletic program can be tremendous. Several programs, including Villanova's, Iona's, and Alabama's basketball programs, have been penalized because a student-athlete entered into a professional contract or agreed to be represented by an agent before the expiration of his collegiate eligibility. Such a step can result in the forfeiture of victories, finishes in a tournament, and the recall of television and/or tournament participation monies. From the student-athlete's perspective, the decisions concerning a professional career and representation are extremely important, because one mistake can bring about severe consequences. In pursuit of information about a professional career, student-athletes should be concerned about maintaining their eligibility. They should also be aware of the dire consequences to themselves and their institution of an incorrect decision.

PROFESSIONAL CAREERS

Professional careers can be very lucrative for an athlete. The status of being a "professional" represents a very high level of achievement. It also represents a challenge, for the athlete must maintain this status and avoid the premature dissolution of his or her professional career. The average time span of a professional career is short, and many athletes achieve their highest skill level only to fall from the professional ranks within a short period. Before entering the professional ranks the amateur athlete must become knowledgeable about the draft, player contracts, and the collective bargaining agreement for the sport in question.

Beginning with the draft, amateur athletes should know their options relative to the draft. After the draft, the two key legal documents are the standard player contract and the collective bargaining agreement. The end product of negotiations between an agent and the player's club will be the player's salary. Athletic administrators should have an understanding of these basic elements so that they are prepared to advise the student-athlete in the event that their advice is sought.

Professional Drafts

The draft is used by each sport as a means of distributing young talent among the various teams in the league. Generally, each team will make a selection in reverse order of finish from the previous season and can trade to improve its draft position. Another important purpose of the draft is to reduce to one the number of teams with which an incoming player can negotiate. This, in theory, has the effect of minimizing players' negotiating leverage and thereby reducing player salaries, but also equalizing talent among teams.

Each of the four major professional leagues holds an annual draft. The eligibility, duration of eligibility, and signing rules for the draft vary from one sport to another.

Major League Baseball

Major League Baseball has the most complicated rules of any of the professional drafts. Each year Major League Baseball conducts one amateur free agent selection meeting on or about June 10 (a January amateur free agent draft, as well as "secondary phases" of drafts, for previously selected players, was eliminated in 1986). The players eligible for the summer amateur free agent selection meeting consist of high school graduating seniors (or those without remaining eligibility); certain four-year college players; junior college (JUCO) players; and all other amateur players not previously selected.

A high school player who is drafted may sign with the professional club if his eligibility has expired prior to the student's graduation from high school because of (1) the student's age, (2) his completion of the maximum number of semesters of attendance, or (3) the ending of the maximum number of seasons in which he is eligible to participate in any major sport. A student who drops out of high school prior to expiration of his athletic eligibility and remains out for at least one year may thereafter be signed to a contract for immediate service. If he decides not to sign and instead enrolls in a four-year college, he becomes selectable at the next summer selection meeting at which he becomes eligible according to the Professional and College Players Rules of Major League Baseball. No player who is a member (or, if a freshman, a prospective member) of a baseball team which represents a college in intercollegiate competition may be signed by a Major League or a National Association club. There are, however, five exceptions:

1. The player who has reached age twenty-one and is currently between school years.
2. The player who has completed his junior year and is currently between school years.
3. The player who has completed the full period of eligibility for intercollegiate baseball.
4. The player whose association with the college has been terminated by reason of scholastic deficiency.
5. The player who withdraws from college and remains out for at least 120 days (including the date of withdrawal).

A junior college player is eligible for selection at any summer selection meeting. However, upon reentering junior college, such players cannot be signed until the completion of the college baseball season (signings during tournament time were allowed beginning in 1987).

Once a player is drafted, the onus is on the team to begin negotiations within fifteen days and offer the player a contract. Since initial minor league salaries have maximum ceilings of $850 per month at all class levels (AAA, AA, A, Rookie Leagues), the signing bonus is one of the major items of negotiation for selected players, especially those chosen in the earlier rounds.

Other relevant considerations include the following:

1. The summer amateur free agent selection meeting is not open to the press. The names of selected players are released alphabetically rather than by round of selection, and they are not released to the media until seven days following the selection meeting. The exception is Round 1 selections; those names and the order of selection are immediately released.
2. Each draft consists only of a regular phase (the "secondary phase" draft for previously selected but unsigned players was eliminated in 1986). Each club other than Rookie League clubs is entitled to select, at each selection meeting, the following number of players:
   Major League Club: one
   Class AAA Club: one
   Class AA Club: one
   Class A Club: no limit
   A club's right to select shall be terminated when (a) it has selected its limit of players as set forth above, (b) it has announced a "pass," or (c) it has failed to respond to a call.
3. The draft is conducted in reverse order of *league* finish.
4. Selected players are placed on a club's Negotiation List until the start of the next Closed Period (seven days preceding June

selection meeting) unless, at an earlier date:

(a) The player signs.

(b) The player is found to be not eligible.

(c) The player enters or returns to college.

(d) The club's negotiation rights are revoked (failure to tender contract within fifteen days).

5. A club cannot transfer its negotiation rights to another club.

6. A college or JC player selected at the preceding June draft whose team's intercollegiate schedule (including regional or national tournaments) extends past the start of the Closed Period, may be signed during the Closed Period, during the interim starting day after the team's last intercollegiate game and ending at 12:01 A.M. of the day on which the June draft commences.

7. An amateur player who is eligible for the summer free agent selection meeting but is not selected may be signed by *any* club from the conclusion of the summer selection meeting until the start of the next Closed Period, in compliance with the Professional and College Players Rules. However, a college player eligible solely because of age or completion of his junior year, but not selected, may be signed by *any* club *only* during summer recess between school years. If he returns to college, he becomes subject to the next summer's free agent selection.

8. A player who was not previously contracted with a Major League or National Association club, *who is not a United States resident,* and who is not subject to high school, college, JUCO, or American Legion draft eligibility rules may be signed by any club if (a) he is seventeen years old at the time of signing, or (b) if he is sixteen years old upon signing and will reach seventeen prior to either the conclusion of the effective season he signed for, or September 1 of the effective season, whichever date is later. An amateur player shall be considered a U.S. resident, for draft purposes, if he is enrolled in a U.S. high school or college or has been a resident of the United States for at least one year.

9. No player in high school may sign a contract during his period of eligibility for participation in high school athletics (there are exceptions for dropouts and Canadian and Latin American students).

10. Clubs and club representatives are prohibited from suggesting or influencing players to withdraw from high school or college, or to transfer.

A player's NCAA eligibility is not affected when he is drafted by a club.

National Basketball Association

The NBA holds its annual draft in June, after the completion of the playoffs. The draft consists of two rounds, with teams selecting in reverse order of finish for the previous year. The NBA developed a lottery in response to critics who claimed some teams were dumping games in order to gain a higher draft pick. All seven teams who do not make the playoffs participate to determine their draft order. However, the team with the worst record in the league is guaranteed a pick no worse than the fourth overall to try to ensure the availability of a quality player for the team that needs a player most. In addition, no team that acquires a lottery pick by trade can select higher than fourth if that team participated in the playoffs during the preceding season. All players whose college eligibility has expired are automatically included in the draft pool.

The notification and participation in the draft effectively renounces the athlete's remaining or future intercollegiate eligibility. If a player changes his mind, he must rescind his notification before the aforementioned deadline passes in order to maintain intercollegiate eligibility. Any college undergraduate may ask to be drafted by submitting his name to the NBA at least forty-five days prior to the draft. High school seniors can also be declared eligible for the draft by notifying the NBA. Once the player enters the draft, he loses NCAA eligibility whether selected by a team or not.

Once drafted, the NBA team must offer the athlete at least a minimum contract by September 5. The minimum salary for most NBA rookies is $140,000 per season. However, if the player is drafted in the first round the minimum salary is set at $180,000. If the player declines the offer, his rights are held by the team until the next draft. If a player signs a professional contract with another league (such as the Continental Basketball Association or European league) after being drafted by an NBA team, the NBA team retains the right to negotiate with the player within the period ending one year from the earlier of the following two dates: (1) the date the player notifies the NBA team that he is immediately ready to sign a contract or (2) the date of the college draft occurring in the twelve-month period from September 1 to August 30 in which the player notifies the NBA team of his availability and intention to play in the NBA during the season immediately following the stated twelve-month period.

National Football League

The NFL has perhaps the strictest and narrowest eligibility rules of the four major professional leagues. Only college players who have completed their eligibility or have submitted a letter to the NFL forfeiting their remaining college eligibility may be drafted. A player who graduates before his eligibility expires must submit a letter stating his intention to be graduated before the fall semester if he wants to be drafted. In this case, the team which selects this player cannot offer the athlete a contract until it receives word from the NFL office that he has in fact graduated. If the player fails to graduate, the club loses the selection and the player forfeits his college eligibility. The timing of the NFL draft usually falls between March and May and lasts seven rounds.

The NFL also has a supplemental draft for players who become eligible after the draft but before the start of the NFL season. Cleveland Browns quarterback Bernie Kosar took this route. Cleveland had to give up its first-round selection in the next NFL draft in this situation.

Players who have lost their intercollegiate eligibility due to improper conduct may request special permission from the commissioner to be included in the draft pool. This has become a concern for college administrators, because of players who have forfeited their eligibility due to receipt of payments from agents in violation of NCAA rules.

Any NFL draftee must be offered a minimum contract by June 7, or he is free to negotiate with any team. If he chooses not to sign, he is eligible for the next NFL draft, but once again is limited to one club in negotiations. However, if a drafted player does not play professional football for two years, he may then sign with any team. A player who plays professionally in the Canadian Football League or any other professional football league and whose rights are held by an NFL club can only negotiate with that club for two years. After that point the player may negotiate with any NFL team, but the team which held his original rights can match the offer and thereby retain the player. Exhibit 11–1 expands on the basic eligibility rules that are enforced by the NFL.

National Hockey League

The NHL holds its annual draft on the Saturday of the second full week in June. Any amateur player who will turn eighteen by September 15 is eligible. Any player who has gone undrafted previously may be selected until he is twenty as of the next September 15, after which he becomes a free agent able to negotiate with any team.

A drafted player must receive a bonafide offer by the next draft or he is eligible to be drafted again, or if he doesn't meet the age requirement, he becomes a free agent. There is no maximum age requirement for European players, who must be drafted before they can sign. Finally, any drafted player who enters college remains the prop-

Exhibit 11–1
NFL Rules: Eligibility for the Player Draft

ELIGIBILITY OF NEW PLAYERS

A member club cannot sign a player to an NFL Player Contract or select a player in a draft (principal or supplemental) until such player meets one of the following requirements:

COLLEGE ELIGIBILITY. All college football eligibility of such player has expired through participation in college football (expiration does not include a loss of college football eligibility through withdrawal from school, dismissal or signing of a professional contract in another football league). Or,

GRADUATION. Such player has been graduated and received a diploma from a recognized college or university prior to the beginning of the League's next regular season ("recognized college or university" means any institution listed in the Blue Book of College Athletics published by the Rohrich Corporation, 903 E. Tallmadge Avenue, Akron, Ohio 44310 and/or the *Education Directory, Colleges and Universities*, U.S. Dept. of Education, Washington, D.C.). A diploma of graduation issued by a recognized college or university to a student under an accelerated course or program is acceptable for eligibility purposes despite the fact that the student actually attended such institution for a period of less than four years. Or,

FIVE-YEAR RULE. Five League seasons have elapsed since such player first entered, attended, practiced football at, or participated in football games for a recognized junior college, college, or university ("recognized junior college, college, or university" means any institution listed in appropriate publications by the publishers cited in the above section). Special consideration is granted to those players whose college and or conference allow five years of football eligibility, during all of which a player may participate full-time, as distinguished from those who "red-shirt," *i.e.*, do not participate during one particular year. If a player under such circumstances has completed four years of participating football eligibility and elects not to avail himself of the fifth year, such player is eligible for selection in the League. Or,

NON-FOOTBALL COLLEGIANS. Such player did not play or otherwise participate in college football, and four League seasons have elapsed since the player first entered or attended college. Or,

SPECIAL ELIGIBILITY. Such player has been granted eligibility through special permission of the Commissioner.

OTHER ELIGIBILITY RULES

The following additional rules have bearing on the basic requirements listed above:

ANOTHER SPORT. The fact that a player has college athletic eligibility remaining in a sport other than football does not affect his eligibility for the League, provided such player meets all other applicable League eligibility requirements.

COMPLETION OF COLLEGE GAMES. Despite the fact that player may meet other League eligibility requirements stated here, a member club cannot sign a player to a player contract, select a player in a draft (principal or supplemental), or in any manner, directly or indirectly, engage the services of a player until completion of all football games, including postseason bowl games, in which the team of the school or college of such player is to participate and in which the player is to participate. If a club violates this section, it is subject to disciplinary action by the Commissioner.

COLLEGE AND NFL IN SAME SEASON. No person who plays college football after the opening date of the NFL training season in any year may be under

Exhibit 11–1 continued

contract to, practice with, or play games for a club in the League during the balance of that same football season.

REPEATED ELIGIBILITY. No person who has never been drafted in the League and who has a college *football* eligibility remaining and who registers at a college for the fall term or semester may be signed to a contract by a club in the League until the close of the next succeeding principal draft of the League, at which time he would be eligible for selection regardless of how many seasons in excess of five have elapsed since he first registered at a college and regardless of how many drafts for which he was eligible have transpired.

EARLY SIGNINGS. No person eligible for a draft (principal or supplemental) may be signed to a contract with a club in the League until completion of the draft for which he is eligible.

EARLY GRADUATION. Any player who expects to graduate before his college football eligibility expires may become conditionally eligible for the League's principal draft (i.e., the 12-round annual draft that includes approximately 336 choices) by declaring to the Commissioner in writing his intention to graduate before the League's next succeeding regular season, which declaration must· be in the Commissioner's office no later than 15 days before the date of the opening of the principal draft (for 1987, the deadline is Monday, April 13). The Commissioner has the authority to change the receipt date of the written declaration if he deems such change appropriate. If a player's written declaration· is received in timely fashion and the League Office determines that he has a reasonable opportunity to graduate before the next succeeding regular season of the League, all member clubs will be advised of his conditional eligibility for the principal draft. Any player so designated cannot be signed to an NFL Player Contract, regardless of whether he is selected in the draft, until the League office is advised by an appropriate authority at the player's college that he has graduated. Any player who makes such a declaration to graduate and who does not graduate before the next succeeding regular season of the League will be ineligible in the League for that season and postseason; and, if such player has been selected in the principal draft, the selecting club will forfeit its selection choice. Any player who fails to make a timely written declaration of his intent to graduate but does graduate before his college football eligibility expires and before the beginning of the next succeeding regular season of the League will be eligible for a supplemental draft.

ELIGIBLE PLAYER NOT SELECTED. A player eligible for a draft (principal or supplemental) who is not selected is a free agent and may be signed by any club in the League, provided, however, that if such player returns to college *to play football*, he is subject to the provisions of *REPEATED ELIGIBILITY* and/or *COLLEGE AND NFL IN SAME SEASON* above.

SUPPLEMENTAL SELECTION. Any player who is ineligible for the principal draft but who becomes eligible after such draft and prior to the beginning of the League's next regular season is not eligible to be signed as a free agent but is eligible for a supplemental selection procedure conducted by the Commissioner. The order of selection in any supplemental draft will be established by a weighted lottery (the weakest club will have its name in the drawing 28 times, the next weakest 27 times, etc., until the Super Bowl winner will have its name in once). The procedure proceeds by rounds, and any club selecting a player forfeits a selection choice in the next succeeding principal draft equal to that exercised in the supplemental draft.

erty of the drafting team until 180 days after he graduates or leaves school.

Unlike football and basketball, and similar to baseball, participation in the NHL draft is not detrimental to collegiate or high school eligibility. If a player is selected but decides not to sign, he can still participate on the amateur level.

The Standard Player Contract

Once an agent representing the player and management reach an agreement, it is then usually up to the athlete to give his approval to the agent, at which point the contract is formed. After consumation of the contract, the player is legally bound to perform to the best of his abilities during the term of the contract, and management must perform its part by remunerating the athlete as expressed in the agreement. Exhibit 11–2 contains an example of a standard player contract, also called a uniform player contract, for the National Basketball Association.

Although both sides are committed to the agreement legally, a recent trend in pro sports, particularly baseball, has been renegotiation of contracts. Renegotiation is almost always initiated by the athlete after a season in which he performed well beyond all expectations at the time of the original agreement. Management is in no way forced to even consider the athlete's request; however, teams are often compelled to do so in order to keep the player happy and motivated. Most clubs have established policies regarding renegotiation, which vary from firm non-renegotiation to frequent renegotiation. One of the most common alternatives used by many teams is to reward players by adding on years at the end of the contract at an increased salary.

It should also be pointed out that attorneys who represent players often face ethical concerns with respect to renegotiation. Many of these agents may advise a client not to renegotiate a contract because they believe in the sanctity of contracts. One way to circumvent this problem is to include a "reopener clause" in the original contract, which would allow renegotiation to take place if certain stated situations came about.

Another important aspect of the player contract for both the player and the club is the bonus clause. It is often the desire of both parties to include a bonus clause in the player's contract because it can provide for the contingency that the player will be worth more than current accomplishments or prospects indicate. In some instances, a bonus clause may be given to lure a player to sign. This signing bonus can serve more than one purpose. It can also provide up-front money that may be the only reward a marginal player receives under the

Exhibit 11–2
Sample Standard Player Contract

NATIONAL BASKETBALL ASSOCIATION
UNIFORM PLAYER CONTRACT

(ROOKIE OR VETERAN—TWO OR MORE SEASONS)

THIS AGREEMENT made this _____ day of _____, 19_____ by and between _____ (hereinafter called the "Club"), a member of the National Basketball Association (hereinafter called the "Association") and _____

whose address is shown below (hereinafter called the "Player").

WITNESSETH:

In consideration of the mutual promises hereinafter contained, the parties hereto promise and agree as follows:

1. The Club hereby employs the Player as a skilled basketball player for a term of _____ year(s) from the 1st day of September 19_____. The Player's employment during each year covered by this contract shall include attendance at each training camp, playing the games scheduled for the Club's team during each schedule season of the Association, playing all exhibition games scheduled by the Club during and prior to each schedule season, playing (if invited to participate) in each of the Association's All-Star Games and attending every event (including, but not limited to, the All-Star Game luncheon and/or banquet) conducted in association with such All-Star Games, and playing the playoff games subsequent to each schedule season. Players other than rookies will not be required to attend training camp earlier than twenty-eight days prior to the first game of each of the Club's schedule seasons. Rookies may be required to attend training camp at an earlier date. Exhibition games shall not be played on the three days prior to the opening of the Club's regular season schedule, nor on the day prior to a regularly scheduled

Exhibit 11–2 continued

game, nor on the day prior to and the day following the All-Star Game. Exhibition games prior to each schedule season shall not exceed eight (including intra-squad games for which admission is charged) and exhibition games during each regularly scheduled season shall not exceed three.

2. The Club agrees to pay the Player for rendering services described herein the sum of $_____ per year. (less all amounts required to be withheld from salary by Federal, State and local authorities and exclusive of any amount which the Player shall be entitled to receive from the Player Playoff Pool) in twelve equal semi-monthly payments beginning with the first of said payments on November 1st of each season above described and continuing with such payments on the first and fifteenth of each month until said sum is paid in full; provided, however, if the Club does not qualify for the playoffs, the payments for the year involved which would otherwise be due subsequent to the conclusion of the schedule season shall become due and payable immediately after the conclusion of the schedule season.

3. The Club agrees to pay all proper and necessary expenses of the Player, including the reasonable board and lodging expenses of the Player while playing for the Club "on the road" and during training camp if the Player is not then living at home. The Player, while "on the road" (and at training camp only if the Club does not pay for meals directly), shall be paid a meal expense allowance as set forth in the Agreement currently in effect between the National Basketball Association and National Basketball Players Association. No deductions from such meal expense allowance shall be made for meals served on an airplane. While the Player is at training camp (and if the Club does not pay for meals directly), the meal expense allowance shall be paid in weekly installments commencing with the first week of training camp. For the purposes of this paragraph, the Player shall be considered to be "on the road" from the time the Club leaves its home city until the time the Club arrives back at its home city. In addition, the Club agrees to pay $50.00 per week to the Player for the four weeks prior to the first game of each of the Club's schedule seasons that the Player is either in attendance at training camp or engaged in playing the exhibition schedule.

4. The Player agrees to observe and comply with all requirements of the Club respecting conduct of its team and its players, at all times whether on or off the playing floor. The Club may, from time to time during the continuance of this contract, establish reasonable rules for the government of its players "at home" and "on the road," and such rules shall be part of this contract as fully as if herein written and shall be binding upon the Player. For any violation of such rules or for any conduct impairing the faithful and thorough discharge of the duties incumbent upon the Player, the Club may impose reasonable fines upon the Player and deduct the amount thereof from any money due or to

Exhibit 11–2 continued

become due to the Player during the season in which such violation and/ or conduct occurred. The Club may also suspend the Player for violation of any rules so established, and, upon such suspension, the compensation payable to the Player under this contract may be reduced in the manner provided in the Agreement currently in effect between the National Basketball Association and National Basketball Players Association. When the Player is fined or suspended, he shall be given notice in writing, stating the amount of the fine or the duration of the suspension and the reason therefor.

5. The Player agrees (a) to report at the time and place fixed by the Club in good physical condition; (b) to keep himself throughout each season in good physical condition; (c) to give his best services, as well as his loyalty to the Club, and to play basketball only for the Club and its assignees; (d) to be neatly and fully attired in public and always to conduct himself on and off the court according to the highest standards of honesty, morality, fair play and sportsmanship; and (e) not to do anything which is detrimental to the best interests of the Club or of the Association.

6. (a) If the Player, in the judgment of the Club's physician, is not in good physical condition at the date of his first schedule game for the Club, or if, at the beginning of or during any season, he fails to remain in good physical condition (unless such condition results directly from an injury sustained by the Player as a direct result of participating in any basketball practice or game played for the Club during such season), so as to render the Player, in the judgment of the Club's physician, unfit to play skilled basketball, the Club shall have the right to suspend such Player until such time as, in the judgment of the Club's physician, the Player is in sufficiently good physical condition to play skilled basketball. In the event of such suspension, the annual sum payable to the Player for each season during such suspension shall be reduced in the same proportion as the length of the period during which, in the judgment of the Club's physician, the Player is unfit to play skilled basketball, bears to the length of such season.

(b) If the Player is injured as a direct result of participating in any basketball practice or game played for the Club, the Club will pay the Player's reasonable hospitalization and medical expenses (including doctor's bills), provided that the hospital and doctor are selected by the Club, and provided further that the Club shall be obligated to pay only those expenses incurred as a result of continuous medical treatment caused solely by and relating directly to the injury sustained by the Player. If, in the judgment of the Club's physician, the Player's injuries resulted directly from playing for the Club and render him unfit to play skilled basketball, then, so long as such unfitness continues, but in no event after the Player has received his full salary for the season in which the injury was sustained, the Club shall pay to the Player the compensation prescribed in paragraph 2 of this contract for such season. The Club's

Exhibit 11–2 continued

obligations hereunder shall be reduced by any workmen's compensation benefits (which, to the extent permitted by law, the Player hereby assigns to the Club) and any insurance provided for by the Club whether paid or payable to the Player, and the Player hereby releases the Club from any and every other obligation or liability arising out of any such injuries.

(c) The Player hereby releases and waives every claim he may have against the Association and every member of the Association, and against every director, officer, stockholder, trustee, partner, and employee of the Association and/or any member of the Association (excluding persons employed as players by any such member), arising out of or in connection with any fighting or other form of violent and/or unsportsmanlike conduct occurring (on or adjacent to the playing floor or any facility used for practices or games) during the course of any practice and/or any exhibition, championship season, and/or play-off game.

7. The Player agrees to give to the Club's coach, or to the Club's physician, immediate notice of any injury suffered by him, including the time, place, cause and nature of such injury.

8. Should the Player suffer an injury as provided in the preceding section, he will submit himself to a medical examination and treatment by a physician designated by the Club. Such examination when made at the request of the Club shall be at its expense, unless made necessary by some act or conduct of the Player contrary to the terms of this contract.

9. The Player represents and agrees that he has extraordinary and unique skill and ability as a basketball player, that the services to be rendered by him hereunder cannot be replaced or the loss thereof adequately compensated for in money damages, and that any breach by the Player of this contract will cause irreparable injury to the Club and to its assignees. Therefore, it is agreed that in the event it is alleged by the Club that the Player is playing, attempting or threatening to play, or negotiating for the purpose of playing, during the term of this contract, for any other person, firm, corporation or organization, the Club and its assignees (in addition to any other remedies that may be available to them judicially or by way of arbitration) shall have the right to obtain from any court or arbitrator having jurisdiction, such equitable relief as may be appropriate, including a decree enjoining the Player from any further such breach of this contract, and enjoining the Player from playing basketball for any other person, firm, corporation or organization during the term of this contract. In any suit, action or arbitration proceeding brought to obtain such relief, the Player does hereby waive his right, if any, to trial by jury, and does hereby waive his right, if any, to interpose any counterclaim or set-off for any cause whatever.

10. The Club shall have the right to sell, exchange, assign or transfer this contract to any other professional basketball club and the Player agrees to accept such sale, exchange, assignment or transfer and to faithfully perform and carry out this contract with the same force and

Exhibit 11–2 continued

effect as if it had been entered into by the Player with the assignee club instead of with this Club. The Player further agrees that, should the Club contemplate the sale, exchange, assignment or transfer of this contract to another professional basketball club or clubs, the Club's physician may furnish to the physicians and officials of such other club or clubs all relevant medical information relating to the Player.

11. In the event that the Player's contract is sold, exchanged, assigned or transferred to any other professional basketball club, all reasonable expenses incurred by the Player in moving himself and his family from the home city of the Club to the home city of the club to which such sale, exchange, assignment or transfer is made, as a result thereof, shall be paid by the assignee club. Such assignee club hereby agrees that its acceptance of the assignment of this contract constitutes agreement on its part to make such payment.

12. In the event that the Player's contract is assigned to another club the Player shall forthwith be notified orally or by a notice in writing, delivered to the Player personally or delivered or mailed to his last known address, and the Player shall report to the assignee club within forty-eight hours after said notice has been received or within such longer time for reporting as may be specified in said notice. If the Player does not report to the club to which his contract has been assigned within the aforesaid time, the Player may be suspended by such club and he shall lose the sums which would otherwise be payable to him as long as the suspension lasts.

13. The Club will not pay and the Player will not accept any bonus or anything of value for winning any particular Association game or series of games or for attaining a certain position by the Club's team in the standing of the league operated by the Association as of a certain date, other than the final standing of the team.

14. This contract shall be valid and binding upon the Club and the Player immediately upon its execution. The Club agrees to file a copy of this contract with the Commissioner of the Association prior to the first game of the schedule season or within forty-eight (48) hours of its execution, whichever is later; provided, however. the Club agrees that if the contract is executed prior to the start of the schedule season and if the Player so requests, it will file a copy of this contract with the Commissioner of the Association within thirty (30) days of its execution, but not later than the date hereinabove specified. If pursuant to the Constitution and By-Laws of the Association. the Commissioner disapproves this contract within ten (10) days after the filing thereof in his office, this contract shall thereupon terminate and be of no further force or effect and the Club and the Player shall thereupon be relieved of their respective rights and liabilities thereunder.

15. The Player and the Club acknowledge that they have read and are familiar with Section 35 of the Constitution of the Association, a copy of

Exhibit 11–2 continued

which, as in effect on the date of this Agreement, is attached hereto. Such section provides that the Commissioner and the Board of Governors of the Association are empowered to impose fines upon the Player and/or upon the Club for causes and in the manner provided in such section. The Player and the Club, each for himself and itself, promises promptly to pay to the said Association each and every fine imposed upon him or it in accordance with the provisions of said section and not permit any such fine to be paid on his or its behalf by anyone other than the person or club fined. The Player authorizes the Club to deduct from his salary payments any fines imposed on or assessed against him.

16. Notwithstanding any provisions of the Constitution or of the By-Laws of the Association, it is agreed that if the Commissioner of the Association, shall, in his sole judgment, find that the Player has bet, or has offered or attempted to bet, money or anything of value on the outcome of any game participated in by any club which is a member of the Association, the Commissioner shall have the power in his sole discretion to suspend the Player indefinitely or to expel him as a player for any member of the Association and the Commissioner's finding and decision shall be final, binding, conclusive and unappealable. The Player hereby releases the Commissioner and waives every claim he may have against the Commissioner and/or the Association, and against every member of the Association, and against every director, officer, stockholder, trustee and partner of every member of the Association, for damages and for all claims and demands whatsoever arising out of or in connection with the decision of the Commissioner.

17. The Player and the Club acknowledge and agree that the Player's participation in other sports may impair or destroy his ability and skill as a basketball player. The Player and the Club recognize and agree that the Player's participation in basketball out of season may result in injury to him. Accordingly, the Player agrees that he will not engage in sports endangering his health or safety (including, but not limited to, professional boxing or wrestling, motorcycling, moped-riding, auto racing, sky-diving, and hang-gliding); and that, except with the written consent of the Club, he will not engage in any game or exhibition of basketball, football, baseball, hockey, lacrosse, or other athletic sport, under penalty of such fine and suspension as may be imposed by the Club and/or the Commissioner of the Association. Nothing contained herein shall be intended to require the Player to obtain the written consent of the Club in order to enable the Player to participate in, as an amateur, the sport of golf, tennis, handball, swimming, hiking, softball or volleyball.

18. The Player agrees to allow the Club or the Association to take pictures of the Player, alone or together with others, for still photographs, motion pictures or television, at such times as the Club or the Association may designate, and no matter by whom taken may be used in any manner desired by either of them for publicity or promotional purposes. The

Exhibit 11–2 continued

rights in any such pictures taken by the Club or by the Association shall belong to the Club or to the Association, as their interests may appear. The Player agrees that, during each playing season, he will not make public appearances, participate in radio or television programs or permit his picture to be taken or write or sponsor newspaper or magazine articles or sponsor commercial products without the written consent of the Club, which shall not be withheld except in the reasonable interests of the Club or professional basketball. Upon request, the Player shall consent to and make himself available for interviews by representatives of the media conducted at reasonable times. In addition to the foregoing, the Player agrees to participate, upon request, in all other reasonable promotional activities of the Club and the Association.

19. The Player agrees that he will not, during the term of this contract, directly or indirectly entice, induce, persuade or attempt to entice, induce or persuade any player or coach who is under contract to any member of the Association to enter into negotiations for or relating to his services as a basketball player or coach, nor shall he negotiate for or contract for such services, except with the prior written consent of such member of the Association. Breach of this paragraph, in addition to the remedies available to the Club, shall be punishable by fine to be imposed by the Commissioner of the Association and to be payable to the Association out of any compensation due or to become due to the Player hereunder or out of any other monies payable to him as a basketball player. The Player agrees that the amount of such fine may be withheld by the Club and paid over to the Association.

20. (a) In the event of an alleged default by the Club in the payments to the Player provided for by this contract, or in the event of an alleged failure by the Club to perform any other material obligation agreed to be performed by the Club hereunder, the Player shall notify both the Club and the Association in writing of the facts constituting such alleged default or alleged failure. If neither the Club nor the Association shall cause such alleged default or alleged failure to be remedied within five (5) days after receipt of such written notice, the National Basketball Players Association shall, on behalf of the Player, have the right to request that the dispute concerning such alleged default or alleged failure be referred immediately to the Impartial Arbitrator in accordance with Article XXI, Section 2(h), of the Agreement currently in effect between the National Basketball Association and National Basketball Players Association. If, as a result of such arbitration, an award issues in favor of the Player, and if neither the Club nor the Association complies with such award within ten (10) days after the service thereof, the Player shall have the right, by a further written notice to the Club and the Association, to terminate this contract.

(b) The Club may terminate this contract upon written notice to the Player (but only after complying with the waiver procedure provided for

Exhibit 11–2 continued

in subparagraph (f) of this paragraph (20)) if the Player shall do any of the following:

(1) at any time, fail, refuse or neglect to conform his personal conduct to standards of good citizenship, good moral character and good sportsmanship, to keep himself in first class physical condition or to obey the Club's training rules; or

(2) at any time, fail, in the sole opinion of the Club's management, to exhibit sufficient skill or competitive ability to qualify to continue as a member of the Club's team (provided, however, that if this contract is terminated by the Club, in accordance with the provisions of this subparagraph, during the period from the fifty-sixth day after the first game of any schedule season of the Association through the end of such schedule season, the Player shall be entitled to receive his full salary for said season); or

(3) at any time, fail, refuse or neglect to render his services hereunder or in any other manner materially breach this contract.

(c) If this contract is terminated by the Club by reason of the Player's failure to render his services hereunder due to disability caused by an injury to the Player resulting directly from his playing for the Club and rendering him unfit to play skilled basketball, and notice of such injury is given by the Player as provided herein, the Player shall be entitled to receive his full salary for the season in which the injury was sustained, less all workmen's compensation benefits (which, to the extent permitted by law, the Player hereby assigns to the Club) and any insurance provided for by the Club paid or payable to the Player by reason of said injury.

(d) If this contract is terminated by the Club during the period designated by the Club for attendance at training camp, payment by the Club of the Player's board, lodging and expense allowance during such period to the date of termination and of the reasonable travelling expenses of the Player to his home city and the expert training and coaching provided by the Club to the Player during the training season shall be full payment to the Player.

(e) If this contract is terminated by the Club during any playing season, except in the case provided for in subparagraph (c) of this paragraph 20, the Player shall be entitled to receive as full payment hereunder a sum of money which, when added to the salary which he has already received during such season, will represent the same proportionate amount of the annual sum set forth in paragraph 2 hereof as the number of days of such season then past bears to the total number of days of such schedule season, plus the reasonable travelling expenses of the Player to his home.

(f) If the Club proposes to terminate this contract in accordance with subparagraph (b) of this paragraph 20, the applicable waiver procedure shall be as follows:

Exhibit 11–2 continued

(1) The Club shall request the Association Commissioner to request waivers from all other clubs. Such waiver request must state that it is for the purpose of terminating this contract and it may not be withdrawn.

(2) Upon receipt of the waiver request, any other club may claim assignment of this contract at such waiver price as may be fixed by the Association, the priority of claims to be determined in accordance with the Association's Constitution or By-Laws.

(3) If this contract is so claimed, the Club agrees that it shall, upon the assignment of this contact to the claiming club, notify the Player of such assignment as provided in paragraph 12 hereof, and the Player agrees he shall report to the assignee club as provided in said paragraph 12.

(4) If the contract is not claimed, the Club shall promptly deliver written notice of termination to the Player at the expiration of the waiver period.

(5) To the extent not inconsistent with the foregoing provisions of this subparagraph (f) the waiver procedures set forth in the Constitution and By-Laws of the Association, a copy of which, as in effect on the date of this agreement, is attached hereto, shall govern.

(g) Upon any termination of this contract by the Player, all obligations of the Club to pay compensation shall cease on the date of termination, except the obligation of the Club to pay the Player's compensation to said date.

21. In the event of any dispute arising between the Player and the Club relating to any matter arising under this contract, or concerning the performance or interpretation thereof (except for a dispute arising under paragraph 9 hereof), such dispute shall be resolved in accordance with the Grievance and Arbitration Procedure set forth in the Agreement currently in effect between the National Basketball Association and the National Basketball Players Association.

22. Nothing contained in this contract or in any provision of the Constitution or By-Laws of the Association shall be construed to constitute the Player a member of the Association or to confer upon him any of the rights or privileges of a member thereof.

23. This contract contains the entire agreement between the parties and there are no oral or written inducements, promises or agreements except as contained herein.

EXAMINE THIS CONTRACT CAREFULLY BEFORE SIGNING IT

IN WITNESS WHEREOF the Player has hereunto signed his name and the Club has caused this contract to be executed by its duly authorized officer.

Exhibit 11–2 continued

Witnesses: _____

_____   By _____
                                          Title:

_____   _____
                                          Player

                                    Player's Address _____

MISCONDUCT OF OFFICIALS AND OTHERS

35. (a) The provisions of this Section shall govern all members, and officers, managers, coaches, players and other employees of a member and all officials and other employees of the Association, all hereinafter referred to as "persons." Each member shall provide and require in every contract with any of its officers, managers, coaches, players or other employees that they shall be bound and governed by the provisions of this Section. Each member, at the direction of the Board of Governors or the Commissioner, as the case may be, shall take such action as the Board or the Commissioner may direct in order to effectuate the purposes of this Section.

(b) The Commissioner shall direct the dismissal and perpetual disqualification from any further association with the Association or any of its members, of any person found by the Commissioner after a hearing to have been guilty of offering, agreeing, conspiring, aiding or attempting to cause any game of basketball to result otherwise than on its merits.

(c) Any person who gives, makes, issues, authorizes or endorses any statement having, or designed to have, an effect prejudicial or detrimental to the best interests of basketball or of the Association or of a member or its team, shall be liable to a fine not exceeding $1,000, to be imposed by the Board of Governors. The member whose officer, manager, coach, player or other employee has been so fined shall pay the amount of the fine should such person fail to do so within ten (10) days of its imposition.

(d) If in the opinion of the Commissioner any other act or conduct of a person at or during a pre-season, championship, playoff or exhibition game has been prejudicial to or against the best interests of the Association or the game of basketball, the Commissioner shall impose upon such person a fine not exceeding $1,000 in the case of a member, officer, manager or coach of a member, or $10,000 in the case of a player or other employee, or may order for a time the suspension of any such person from any connection or duties with pre-season, championship, playoff or exhibition games, or he may order both such fine and suspension.

(e) The Commissioner shall have the power to suspend for a definite or indefinite period, or to impose a fine not exceeding $1,000, or inflict both such suspension and fine upon any person who, in his opinion, shall have been guilty of conduct prejudicial or detrimental to the Association.

Exhibit 11–2 continued

(f) The Commissioner shall have the power to levy a fine of $1,000 upon any Governor or Alternate Governor who, in the opinion of the Commissioner, has been guilty of making statements to the press damaging to the Association.

(g) Any person who, directly or indirectly, entices, induces, persuades or attempts to entice, induce, or persuade any player, coach, trainer, general manager or any other person who is under contract to any other member of the Association to enter into negotiations for or relating to his services or negotiates or contracts for such services shall, on being charged with such tampering, be given an opportunity to answer such charges after due notice and the Commissioner shall have the power to decide whether or not the charges have been sustained; in the event his decision is that the charges have been sustained, then the Commissioner shall have the power to suspend such person for a definite or indefinite period, or to impose a fine not exceeding $5,000, or inflict both such suspension and fine upon any such person.

(h) Any person who, directly or indirectly, wagers money or anything of value on the outcome of any game played by a team in the league operated by the Association shall, on being charged with such wagering, be given an opportunity to answer such charges after due notice, and the decision of the Commissioner shall be final, binding and conclusive and unappealable. The penalty for such offense shall be within the absolute and sole discretion of the Commissioner and may include a fine, suspension, expulsion and/or perpetual disqualification from further association with the Association or any of its members.

(i) Except for a penalty imposed under subparagraph (h) of this paragraph 35, the decisions and acts of the Commissioner pursuant to paragraph 35 shall be appealable to the Board of Governors who shall determine such appeals in accordance with such rules and regulations as may be adopted by the Board in its absolute and sole discretion.

EXCERPT FROM BY-LAWS OF THE ASSOCIATION

3.07 *(Waiver Right.)* Except for sales and trading between Members in accordance with these By-Laws, no Member shall sell, option or otherwise transfer the contract with, right to the services of, or right to negotiate with, a Player without complying with the waiver procedure prescribed by these By-Laws.

3.08 *(Waiver Price.)* The waiver price shall be $1,000 per Player.

3.09 *(Waiver Procedure.)* A Member desiring to secure waivers on a Player shall notify the Commissioner, and the Commissioner, on behalf of such Member, shall immediately notify all other Members of the waiver request. Such Player shall be assumed to have been waived unless a Member shall timely notify the Commissioner by telegram and telephone of a claim to the rights of such Player. Once a Member has notified

Exhibit 11–2 continued

the Commissioner to attempt to secure waivers on a Player, such notice may not be withdrawn. A Player remains the financial responsibility of the Member placing him on waivers until the waiver period set by the Commissioner has expired.

3.10 *(Waiver Period.)* If the Commissioner distributes notice of request for waiver at any time during the Season or within four weeks before the beginning of the Season, any Members wishing to claim rights to the Player shall do so by giving notice by telephone and telegram of such claim to the Commissioner within 48 hours after the time of the Commissioner's notice. If the Commissioner distributes notice of request for waiver at any other time, any Member wishing to claim rights to the Player shall do so by sending notice of such Claim to the Commissioner within ten days after the date of the Commissioner's notice. A team may not withdraw a claim to the rights to a Player on waivers.

3.11 *(Waiver Preferences.)* In the event that more than one Member shall have claimed rights to a Player placed on waivers, the claiming Member with the lowest team standing at the time the waiver was requested shall be entitled to acquire the rights to such Player. If the request for waiver shall occur between Seasons or prior to midnight November 30th, the standings at the close of the previous Season shall govern.

If the won and lost percentages of two claiming Teams are the same, then the tie shall be determined, if possible, on the basis of the Championship Games between the two teams, during the Season or during the preceding Season, as the case may be. If still tied, a toss of the coin shall determine priority. For the purpose of determining standings, both conferences of the Association shall be deemed merged and a consolidated standing shall control.

3.12 *(Players Acquired Through Waivers.)* A Member who has acquired the rights and title to the contract of a Player through the waiver procedure may waive such rights at any time, but may not sell or trade such rights for a period of 30 days after the acquisition thereof, provided, however, that if the rights to such Player were acquired between schedule Seasons, the 30 day period described herein shall begin on the first day of the next succeeding schedule Season.

3.13 *(Additional Waiver Rules.)* The Commissioner or the Board of Governors shall from time to time adopt such additional rules (supplementary to these By-Laws) with respect to the operation of the waiver procedures as he or it shall determine. Such rules shall not be inconsistent with these By-Laws and shall apply to but shall not be limited to the mechanics of notice, inadvertent omission of notification to a Member and rules of construction as to time.

Source: National Basketball Association

Exhibit 11–3
A Signing Bonus Used by the NFL

SIGNING BONUS

Between _____ and _____
              (Club)   (Player)

    As additional consideration for the execution of NFL Player Contract(s) for the year(s) _____, and for the Player's adherence to all provisions of said contract(s), Club agrees to pay Player the sum of $ _____.

    The above sum is payable as follows:

$ _____ upon execution of this rider (Player acknowledges receipt of said sum); and

$ _____ on _____ 19_____ ; and

$ _____ on _____ 19_____ ; and

$ _____ on _____ 19_____ .

    It is expressly understood that no part of the bonus herein provided is part of any salary in the contract(s) specified above, that said bonus will not be deemed part of any salary in the contract(s) specified above if Club exercises an option for Player's services in a season subsequent to the final contract year, and that such obligations of Club are not terminable if such contract(s) is (are) terminated via the NFL waiver system.

    In the event Player, in any of the years specified above or an option year, fails or refuses to report to Club, fails or refuses to practice or play with Club, or leaves Club without its consent, then, upon demand by Club, Player will return to Club the proportionate amount of the total bonus not having been earned at the time of Player's default.

Date: _____

Club: _____   Player: _____

By: _____

---

contract. If the player is released before the regular season begins because of failure to make the team, he at least gets to keep the signing bonus, even though the rest of the contract becomes null and void. Exhibit 11–3 is an example of a signing bonus that the NFL uses.

Bonus clauses are also used to compensate a player who has exceeded expectations. It is important to structure the bonus so that the proper salary escalation is allowed if the player fulfills or exceeds current prospects. Different leagues attach different names to the same types of bonus clauses. Generally, however, bonuses can be broken down based on status (the signing bonus), statistical performance, volume of play, awards and honors, and other contingencies. Exhibit 11–4 contains examples from actual statistical bonus provisions in those sports that allow them.

Exhibit 11–4
Examples of Statistical Bonus Provisions in Football, Basketball, and Hockey

---

FOOTBALL

Quarterback:	250 passing attempts	$
	150 completions	$
	Pass 1,000 yards	$
	Pass 1,500 yards	$
	Pass 2,000 yards	$
	Pass 5 touchdowns	$
	Pass 10 touchdowns	$
Running Back:	Rushes for 400 yards	$
	Catches over 40 passes	$
	Scores 6 touchdowns	$
	Scores 5 touchdowns rushing	$
	Scores 3 touchdowns rushing	$
	Leads NFC or AFC in scoring	$
Defense:	Leads team in total tackles	$
	Leads team in assists	$
	Leads NFL in tackles	$
	Leads NFC in tackles	$
	Leads or ties linebackers in interceptions	$
	Returns interception for touchdown (each)	$
	Leads or ties team in tackles for loss	$
	Fumble recoveries (each recovery)	$
	Ties or leads team in interceptions	$
	Leads NFL in interceptions	$
	Leads NFC in interceptions	$
	Leads or ties team linebackers for quarterback sacks	$
	Quarterback sacks (each sack)	$

BASKETBALL

In addition to other monies Player shall receive the following, if such are attained in any year under this contract:
For averaging over 20 points per game, the sum of $_____ .
For leading the team in scoring, the sum of $_____ .
For leading the NBA in assists or steals, the sum of $_____ .
For being in the top five in the NBA in scoring, the sum of $_____ .

HOCKEY

30 goals or 65 points .... $_____ , and
35 goals or 75 points .... $_____ , and
40 goals or 85 points .... $_____ , and
45 goals or 95 points .... $_____ , and
50 goals or 105 points .... $_____ .

Collective Bargaining Agreements

The players' union, an integral part of the professional athlete's career concerns, has a wide variety of functions. The union helps the players file grievances against management, it provides information to player agents to aid in negotiations with individual teams, and it generally looks out for the collective interests of the players, including the generation of revenues for the association through licensing and marketing programs using the particular association's logo. The primary function of the players' union, however, is to negotiate the collective bargaining agreement with the league (CBA), which sets forth the terms and conditions of employment for the players, including minimum salaries and other benefits.

Therefore, the CBA is valuable to professional athletes, and they must learn to recognize the importance of this agreement with the help of the player agent and team representative.

The categories negotiated in the CBA between the two parties include economic benefits and noneconomic concerns. Severance pay, which is awarded to athletes who have finished their careers, minimum wage scales, minimum rookie salaries, playoff money, all-star allotments, and preseason pay are all chiefly economic concerns. Disability compensation in the line of duty, permanent disability, widows' and survivors' compensation, life insurance, major medical insurance, injury protection (in MLB a player who is injured during a season is entitled to receive from the club the unpaid balance of the full salary for the year in which the injury was sustained), dental coverage, and joint control of insurance are concerns that are presented in the bargaining sessions that outline general benefits. There are also noneconomic concerns that the players' union will make known when negotiating a CBA. These include player contracts, regulation of player agents, players' medical rights, noninjury grievance procedures, rules impact, joint counseling programs, and drug-testing policies.

NOTE ───

1. The twenty-eight National Football League member clubs and their players had been operating since 1987 without a collective bargaining agreement. What resulted was a seemingly unbroken string of litigation for a six-year stretch which culminated in June 1993, when the NFL and NFLPA officially signed a new CBA which covers the 1993–99 seasons.

As a result of litigation begun by New York Jets running back Freeman McNeil, in *McNeil v. National Football League*, 790 F. Supp. 871 (D. Minn. 1992), the two sides reached an agreement in January 1993 which resulted in expanded free agency rights for the players and salary cap provisions for the owners aimed at keeping down total team salary expenses.

Key points in the settlement agreement and new CBA include the following:

(a) Free Agency—Open to five-year veterans with expired contracts. Free agent signing period: March 1–July 15.

(b) Salary guarantee—Players receive a minimum 58 percent of defined gross revenues (DGR) each year of the agreement that includes a salary cap.

(c) Salary cap—If player costs reach 67 percent of DGR, a salary cap is triggered and free agency begins after four years of NFL experience. If the cap is triggered, the team salary cap drops to 64 percent, 63 percent, and 62 percent of DGR in succeeding years.

(d) Free agency exceptions—Each team is able to exempt one "franchise player" from free agency for his career. By March 1, either the club must increase its minimum offer to the average of the five highest salaries at the player's position; or the club can maintain its original offer, but the player may seek proposals from other teams. If the original club does not match a new offer by another team, the original club receives two first round draft picks as compensation from the signing club. In addition in 1993 each club was able to place the right of first refusal status on two "transition players." The clubs were required to offer these players the average of the top ten salaries at their position, or 110 percent of their previous year's salary, whichever was higher. For the 1994 season, the number of "transition players" was cut to one per club, and discontinued altogether after 1994.

(e) Draft—Cut from twelve rounds to seven, plus a round for compensatory picks for teams losing free agents.

(f) Rookie salary cap—The rookie pool will include 3.5 percent of DGR, or an average of $2 million per club, whichever is greater. Rookie signing bonuses will be prorated over the length of the contract.

In addition to the restructured player system, the new CBA provides for each team to increase its spending on benefits from $4.04 million in 1993 to $6.6 million in 1999, including expanded severance, pension, life, medical, and dental coverage.

Salary Information

Contracts negotiated by agents can include a variety of salary items, including a base salary figure, signing bonus, training camp reporting bonuses, and even deferred compensation packages. Signing bonuses are popular with draft picks by giving the rookie a nice payout during the first year in the professional league. Exhibit 11–5 shows the bonus payments made during the first five rounds of the NFL player draft.

In terms of comparing the four major professional leagues—National Basketball Association, National Football League, Major League Baseball, and National Hockey League—the highest average salary is being paid in the sport of basketball (NBA) with Major League Baseball not far behind. Exhibits 11–6, 11–7, 11–8, and 11–9, and 11–10 contain information on average salaries or average team payrolls for each of the professional sport leagues.

Exhibit 11–5
Compensation Awarded to Players in First Five Rounds of 1990 NFL Player Draft

	First	Second	Third	Fourth	Fifth
Average Base Salary - First Year	$318,673	$183,839	$130,964	$93,315	$83,839
Average Signing Bonuses	1,355,385	307,232	135,786	79,537	44,018
Average Reporting Bonuses	29,900	15,364	9.357	11,045	10,188
Average Roster Bonuses	45,077	21,905	24,058	20,827	19,109

NOTE _____

1. In 1993, Major League Baseball had an average player salary of $1,116,946, with 262 players earning in excess of $1 million per season. In addition, there were 100 players earning $3 million or more per season. The Toronto Blue Jays led the Major Leagues with a team average of $1,708,000, while the Colorado Rockies' figure of $327,926 per player was the lowest.

Despite team salary caps set at 53 percent of defined gross revenues (DGR), the National Basketball Association had 110 players over the $1 million per season mark for 1993. Salary inflation and the complicated rules of the NBA salary cap system had by the 1993 season led twenty-one of the twenty-seven teams to find themselves over the salary cap. NBA teams, however, fully realize the effect of the restrictions designed to limit flexibility once they have exceeded this limit.

PLAYER AGENTS

A player agent, also called a player representative, is a person authorized by another person to act in his or her name. The promise of compensation is not required to establish the relationship, although such compensation is usually presumed. The NCAA constitution prohibits college student-athletes from using player agents:

> An individual shall be ineligible for participation in an intercollegiate sport if he or she ever has agreed (orally or in writing) to be represented by an agent for the purpose of marketing his or her athletics ability or reputation in that sport. Further, an agency contract not specifically

Exhibit 11–6
NBA Salary Cap and Average/Minimum Salary Amounts

N.B.A. Salary Cap

Season	Salary Cap	Average Salary
1984-85	$3.6 million	$325,000
1985-86	$4.233 million	$375,000
1986-87	$4.495 million	$440,000
1987-88	$6.164 million	$510,000
1988-89	$7.232 million	$600,000
1989-90	$9.802 million	$725,000
1990-91	$11.871 million	$925,000

Source: Sporting News, August 27, 1990

N.B.A. Salaries

Season	Average Salary	Minimum Salary
1980-81	$180,000	$37,500
1981-82	$200,000	$40,000
1982-83	$240,000	$40,000
1983-84	$265,000	$40,000
1984-85	$325,000	$65,000
1985-86	$400,000	$70,000
1986-87	$475,000	$75,000
1987-88	$580,000	$75,000
1988-89	$650,000	$100,000
1989-90	$750,000	$110,000
1990-91	$825,000	$120,000
1991-92	$1,050,000	$130,000

Source: National Basketball Players Association

limited in writing to a sport or particular sports shall be deemed applicable to all sports and the individual shall be ineligible to participate in any sport. (*1993–94 NCAA Manual,* Bylaw 12.3.1) Securing advice from a lawyer concerning a proposed professional sports contract shall not be considered contracting for representation by an agent under this rule, unless the lawyer also represents the student-athlete in negotiations for such a contract. (*1990–91 NCAA Manual,* Bylaw 12.3.2)

Because several player agents have represented student-athletes in contract negotiations under the guise of supplying legal advice, the NCAA Council issued a clarification concerning the use of legal coun-

Exhibit 11–7
NFL Salary Trends, 1970–1991

	Avg. Salary-- All	Avg. Salary-- Starters	Avg.Base Salary-- All	Avg.Base Salary-- Starters	Median Base Salary-- All
1970	$23,200				
1971	$24,600				
1972	$26,100				
1973	$27,500				
1974	$33,000				
1975	$39,600				
1976	$47,500				
1977	$55,300				$45,600
1978	$62,600				$53,700
1979	$68,900				$57,700
1980	$78,700				$70,000
1981	$82,400		$79,600		$75,000
1982	$95,800		$90,400		$80,000
1983	$133,800		$111,800		$90,000
1984	$177,400		$135,600		$110,000
1985	$193,900	$231,500	$164,300	$210,500	$140,000
1986	$197,800	$247,600	$183,100	$232,600	$150,000
1987	$203,500	$285,300	$189,300	$267,500	$175,000
1988	$238,500	$321,750	$209,000	$288,400	$180,000
1989	$300,000	$381,100	$254,500	$329,000	$200,000
1990	$350,000	$466,000	$300,000	$405,000	$236,000
1991	$425,000	$544,050	$347,650	$470,000	$250,000

Source: National Football League Players Association.

Exhibit 11–8
Salary Components for Draftees, 1989–1991

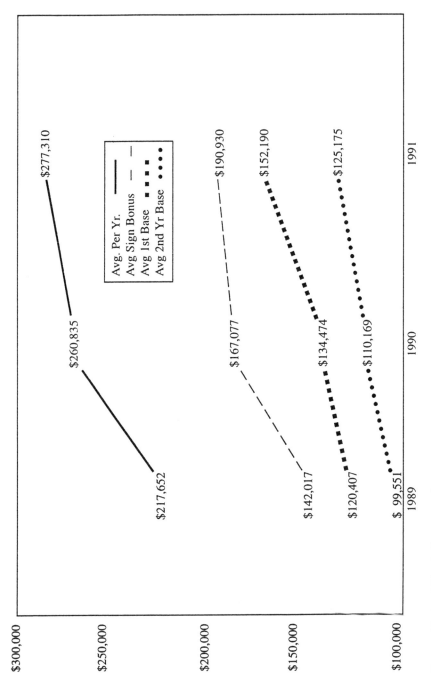

Source: National Football League Players Association.

Exhibit 11-9
Major League Baseball Average Salaries, 1967-1990

Average baseball salary as complied by the Major League Baseball Players Assocation and the minimum salary. Beginning in 1979, salary deferrals without interest are discounted at 9 percent per year. Beginning in 1987, signing bonuses are increased at 9 percent per year. Beginning in 1987, signing bonuses are increased at 9 percent per year:

Year	Minimum	Average
1967	$ 6,000	$ 19,000
1968	10,000	NA
1969	10,000	24,909
1970	12,000	29,303
1971	12,750	31,543
1972	13,500	34,092
1973	15,000	36,566
1974	15,000	40,839
1975	16,000	44,676
1976	19,000	51,501
1977	19,000	76,066
1978	21,000	99,876
1979	21,000	113,558
1980	30,000	143,756
1981	32,500	185,651
1982	33,500	241,497
1983	35,000	289,194
1984	40,000	329,408
1985	60,000	371,571
1986	60,000	412,520
1987	62,500	412,454
1988	62,500	438,729
1989	68,000	497,254
1990	100,000	597,537

Source: Major League Baseball Players Association.

sel by student-athletes. The council asserted that any student-athlete may retain counsel for the purpose of reviewing a contract offered by a professional team. However, the student-athlete who decides to have legal counsel contact a professional team concerning the contract offer has effectively hired counsel as an agent and is no longer eligible. Additionally, the NCAA specifies that a contract which is executed and does not specifically refer to a particular sport will be considered applicable to all sports. Also, any type of agency contract is prohibited, including present contracts for provision of future services. This rule

Exhibit 11-10
NHL Average Salary Per Team

Following is a breakdown of what each team in the NHL pays on an average to the top 20 players on its roster and its total payroll.

Los Angeles Kings	$375,000	$8.4 million
Pittsburgh Penguins	$305,000	$6.4 million
Edmonton Oilers	$280,000	$6.0 million
Calgary Flames	$275,000	$6.3 million
Montreal Canadiens	$270,000	$5.8 million
New York Rangers	$255,000	$6.3 million
Philadelphia Flyers	$255,000	$6.3 million
Vancouver Canucks	$245,000	$5.5 million
Detroit Red Wings	$240,000	$5.3 million
Chicago Black Hawks	$235,000	$5.4 million
Quebec Nordiques	$235,000	$5.1 million
Boston Bruins	$220,000	$4.8 million
Hartford Whalers	$210,000	$4.7 million
Toronto Maple Leafs	$210,000	$4.8 million
Winnipeg Jets	$210,000	$4.3 million
Minnesota North Stars	$205,000	$4.4 million
New Jersey Devils	$200,000	$4.4 million
Buffalo Sabres	$195,000	$4.5 million
New York Islanders	$197,000	$4.4 million
Washington Capitals	$188,000	$4.2 million
St. Louis Blues	$156,000	$3.5 million

Source: Sporting News, February 12, 1990.

applies at all times, and therefore includes those contracts made prior to matriculation at college.

At its 1984 convention, the NCAA approved a plan, recommended by its Special Committee on Player Agents, under which athletics career counseling panels would be established in individual institutions to assist student-athletes who are contemplating foregoing their remaining college eligibility to pursue a career in professional sports (*1993–94 NCAA Manual*, Bylaw 12.3.4). In addition, should the athlete opt for a professional career, the panel would assist in the selection of a competent representative or agent.

Player representatives are a relatively recent phenomenon in collegiate sports. The growth of professional leagues, teams, and salaries since the late 1960s has made athlete representation a very lucrative and extremely competitive business. Agents use a variety of methods to charge their clients for services rendered. The most common is for an agent to take a percentage of the total value of the player contract—anywhere from 3 to 10 percent. Some agents will represent a player in a contract negotiation for a predetermined fee, regardless of the time spent or the amount of the contract. Agents may also elect to charge an hourly rate for each hour spent working for the athlete—usually between $100 and $300. The other alternative is a combination of a stated percentage (usually less than 7 percent), plus a predetermined or hourly fee, whichever is less.

The disadvantage for the athlete in agreeing to pay an hourly fee to the agent is that the athlete is obligated to that agent if he or she doesn't make the team. However, if the athlete makes the team, the fee based on an hourly rate may be less than the contingency fee rate. If the athlete and agent have agreed to a contingency fee, however, there is no obligation to pay the agent if the athlete does make the team. On the other hand, the athlete may find paying an hourly fee to the agent a disadvantage if the agent extends the contract negotiations ad infinitum.

These agent fees can become enormous in view of the salaries paid to some of today's superstar athletes. The escalation of player salaries has made the percentage method very popular among agents. Because of the tremendous amount of money available, some agents are tempted to lure top athletes, even while they are still in school. In order to build or protect their own personal interests, some agents will contact, offer inducements to, and attempt to sign student-athletes with remaining college eligibility. They may also entice athletes to leave college early to join professional teams. Inducements may take the form of cash, "loans," and/or the use of a car or other benefits. This transfer and acceptance of money or other benefits by student-athletes are in direct conflict with the principles of amateurism and specifically violate rules related to receiving compensation or pay and limits on the amount and type of acceptable remuneration (*1993–94 NCAA Manual*, Bylaw 12.1.2).

The offer sheet is one method by which agents may attempt to circumvent NCAA rules. An offer sheet is presented by the player agent to the student-athlete, who often mistakes it for a contract. The student-athlete signs this form prior to the expiration of college eligibility, but the agent will not sign it until after the student-athlete's eligibility has expired. Since most student-athletes are not versed in the technicalities of the requirements for a binding contract, they often believe they have a contract with the agent and will discontinue dealing with other agents. Agents who use this tactic to reserve players claim the offer sheet is not an agency contract until the representative executes the document at the close of the student-athlete's playing season. Since no contract exists, there can be no violation of NCAA rules. The NCAA, however, disagrees, believing that the substance of its rules clearly prohibits any agreements to provide future services, even if the agreement does not constitute an enforceable contract.

NOTES

1. Some agents in the past have argued that because the NCAA does not govern player agents, members of the profession are not subject to the association's rules. Furthermore, some agents have gone as far as to publicly acknowledge that their business conduct as an agent is often in "constant and conscious violation of NCAA rules." (See "Some Offers They Couldn't Refuse," *Sports Illustrated*, May 21, 1979, p. 28.)

2. The player's responsibility to the agent upon signing an offer sheet may be an area of contention. In 1979, a suit was filed against O. J. Anderson, a former University of Miami football player. The suit alleged breach of contract and damages in the amount of $52,000. Anderson had signed an offer sheet with an agent before his eligibility had expired. Immediately upon Anderson's expiration of eligibility, the agent signed the offer sheet and had it notarized. Subsequently, Anderson decided that he did not want the agent to represent him, and the agent filed the suit in an attempt to enforce the offer sheet agreement. The suit was settled before trial.

3. When a coach acts as an adviser concerning a student-athlete's professional prospects, does this make the coach an agent? Is the coach's role thus incompatible with NCAA rules? Technically, any person who agrees to help a student-athlete deal with professional offers is an agent. Therefore, a coach who acts as a buffer between a student-athlete and agents or professional teams, when such action is done with the consent and knowledge of the student-athlete, is arguably an agent, even if no compensation or promise of compensation is involved.

This problem was the focus of an NCAA investigation involving George Rogers, a star running back at the University of South Carolina, and his coach, Jim Carlen. The NCAA decided that Carlen was not acting as Rogers's agent, even though the coach admitted acting as a buffer for Rogers. Carlen had done so to protect Rogers from tempting offers that might affect his playing eligibility. The NCAA did not further clarify the basis for the agent-buffer distinction.

4. In October 1984, Mike Rozier, former University of Nebraska star running back and 1983 Heisman Trophy winner, revealed that while still under NCAA eligibility regulations, he accepted money from an agent and negotiated a professional football contract with the USFL's Pittsburgh Maulers. Both acts were violations of NCAA regulations. Rozier accepted a total of $2,400 during his last intercollegiate season. His contract with the Maulers was finalized a few days before the Orange Bowl in Miami, and was signed hours after the completion of the game. Rozier claimed that he made his revelations because he was ashamed and hoped that young athletes could learn from his mistakes. For further details of this incident, see "The Year the Heisman Went to a Pro," *Sports Illustrated*, October 22, 1984, p. 21.

5. Leigh Steinberg, a leading sports agent and head of the Ethics Committee of the Association of Representatives of Professional Agents, in October 1984 alleged that "at least one third of the top athletes in college football and basketball are signing early every year. It is usually done in return for money payments. It is an open secret that no one wants to talk about. It is uncon-

scionable." Steinberg suggested that increasing scholarship monies awarded by the schools might take some of the pressure off the student-athletes to sign early with agents. For further information, see the following articles:

(a) "Steinberg: Early Signings Are Common Practice," UPI Wireservice, *Newark Star Ledger*, November 1, 1984, p. 58.

(b) "Agents Have Upper Hand with Top College Players," AP Wireservice, *Newark Star Ledger*, November 1, 1984, p. 109.

6. Agents have been accused of breaching their fiduciary duty to their clients.

(a) Detroit Lions free agent running back Billy Sims, under the guidance of his agent Jerry Argovitz, signed a contract with the Houston Gamblers on July 1, 1983. On December 16, 1983, Sims signed a second contract with Detroit, and filed a complaint in Oakland County Circuit Court seeking a determination that the July 1, 1983 contract between Sims and the Houston Gamblers was invalid because the defendant, Jerry Argovitz, breached his fiduciary duty when negotiating the Gamblers' contract. The court concluded that Argovitz breached his duty to Sims by having significant ownership interest in the Houston franchise, and not representing him properly in contract negotiations with Detroit. The contract between Sims and Houston was rescinded by the court. See *Detroit Lions, Inc. and Sims v. Argovitz*, 580 F. Supp. 542 (E.D. Mich. 1984).

(b) In *Brown v. Woolf*, 554 F. Supp. 1206 (S.D. Ind. 1983), a professional athlete brought action for constructive fraud and breach of fiduciary duty against the defendant agent. The athlete claimed the agent negotiated a contract for him with a new team of the National Hockey League. After reaching an agreement for compensation, the new team began to have financial difficulties and eventually defaulted on their contractual obligations. Plaintiff claimed he was only paid $185,000 of the total $800,000 contract, but the defendant agent received his full $40,000 fee (5 percent of the contract). Plaintiff also contended the agent breached his fiduciary duty to the plaintiff by failing to conduct any investigation into the financial stability of the new team. The district court denied the defendant's motion for a summary judgment.

7. The argument has also been reversed, as an agent recovered from being terminated by a player. Leo Zinn, the agent for Cincinnati Bengals' cornerback Lemar Parrish, was successful in recovering after Parrish terminated him in 1974 shortly after Zinn negotiated a four-year contract for Parrish. Zinn sought to recover his 10 percent commission on the 1974–77 Bengals' contracts and did so. The court ruled that Zinn fulfilled the terms of the contract to use reasonable efforts to procure professional football employment, despite failing to obtain jobs or contracts in many cases; it was not a failure to perform. See *Zinn v. Parrish*, 644 F.2d 360 (7th Cir. 1981).

8. Some agents have been accused of going far beyond the activities which resulted in the defenses raised by Lemar Parrish against Leo Zinn. Charges of outright fraud or embezzlement have been made and, at least in one instance, have been substantiated. Consider the following: Richard Sorkin's 1978 conviction for grand larceny represents an example of an agent's mis-

appropriating client funds. Sorkin allegedly misappropriated money from approximately fifty professional athletes he was representing, totaling more than $1.2 million. Acting as their agent and handling their funds, Sorkin had easy access to the athletes' monies and squandered their funds for his own uses, either through mob gambling or bad personal investments. See *People v. Sorkin*, No. 46429 (Nassau County, N.Y., Nov. 28, 1977), *sentence aff'd*, 407 N.Y.S.2d 772 (App. Div. 2d Dept., July 24, 1978). See also, "The Spectacular Rise and Ignoble Fall of Richard Sorkin, Pros' Agent," *New York Times*, October 9, 1977, Sec. 5, p. 1; *New York Times*, February 2, 1978, Sec. 4, p. 15.

9. For further information on player agents, see the following.

(a) "The Offer Sheet: An Attempt to Circumvent NCAA Prohibition of Representation Contracts," 14 *Loy. U. L. Rev.* 187 (1980).

(b) Ruxin, *An Athlete's Guide to Agents* (New York: The Stephen Greene Press, 1989).

(c) Grandall, "Agent-Athlete Relationship in Professional and Amateur Sports: The Inherent Potential for Abuse and the Need for Regulation," 30 *Buff. L. Rev.* 815 (1981).

(d) Ruxin, "Unsportsmanlike Conduct: The Student-Athlete, the NCAA, and Agents," 8 *J. C. & U. L.* 347 (1982).

(e) "Athletics Career Counseling Panels," Legislative Assistance (column), *NCAA News*, May 30, 1984, p. 3.

(f) "Attorneys and Professional Contracts," Legislative Assistance (column), *NCAA News*, May 9, 1984, p. 7.

(g) Fox, "Regulating the Professional Sport Agent: Is California in the Right Ballpark?" 15 *Pac. L. J.* 1231 (1984).

(h) Massey, "The Crystal Cruise Cut Short: A Survey of the Increasing Regulatory Influence over the Athlete-Agent in the National Football League," 1 *Entertainment & Sports Law Journal* 53 (1984).

Functions of the Player Agent

Attorneys and agents who represent professional athletes are called on to render a wide variety of services for their clients. The diversity of services, in fact, is such that it is unreasonable to expect one individual to master all the knowledge and skills necessary to accomplish the tasks demanded. Among other realities, this has led to a separation of the law and management functions, and player representatives are examining a number of devices that would allow them to use full-service operations.

The traditional role of the player agent has been to negotiate the player's contract and represent the athlete on any other legally-related issues with the club. Representation today may also include marketing of the player's name; soliciting personal appearances; and offering financial and investment advice, tax planning and tax return preparation, and personal, legal, and financial counseling. An athlete must consider either retaining independent advisers for legal, financial, and investment advice or a multifaceted management group that can provide all of these services. With demands for the full range of services coming to the fore, pressures are mounting to set up a business organization that will respond to the plethora of needs. The point to remember is that the player representative is in a business that demands a number of services. Before proceeding with other considerations, such as the legal and ethical constraints placed on player representatives, the functions themselves must be considered.

Negotiating

The player agent must be able to obtain the necessary background information, map the appropriate strategies, and have the flexibility to counter alternatives in order to represent the client effectively. When entering into a negotiation session, the agent must be prepared, not only in terms of the issues to be brought up, but also in regard to refuting or responding to management's claims. A good agent will know the market value of his client, based on salaries of comparable players (same position, ability). The agent should also have detailed information about the team with respect to his client's likelihood to succeed, chances of starting, depth at client's position, and historic negotiation outcomes. This type of preparation is of paramount importance to the agent if an optimal contract is to be negotiated.

One important point to remember in the sports context is that, in a sense, one rarely stops negotiating. The signed contract is usually only the first step. A number of occurrences during the term of the contract may call for even greater skill on the part of the negotiator, a point emphasized later in this chapter.

A second important point is the interconnections between the negotiating function and the functions described below. One cannot, and should not, attempt to isolate completely one from the others. As noted earlier, a single individual cannot effectively handle all functions, at least not in the great majority of situations. So, knowing how to deal with the overlaps while dividing the functions efficiently calls for careful thought, planning, and organizational structure.

Counseling

Counseling is an often overlooked function of vital importance, both during negotiations and after the contract is signed. Making certain the client understands what is at stake in a professional sports contract may prevent later disillusionments.

For the nonsuperstar, the contract may be largely illusory, in that it exists only if the player makes the team. There are no guarantees. Such rudimentary facts are not always grasped by the client. Making the team and contract rights are not always paired in the client's mind. Such information must be conveyed.

After the contract is signed, other problems call for counseling. For example, the player makes the team but is sitting on the bench. Personal frustrations become predominant. In this and many other contexts, the counseling function is crucial.

Managing

Many athletes come out of college with little self-discipline and an almost total lack of knowledge about financial matters. The money soon disappears if the client is left unsupervised.

Not all player representatives get into money management, and those who do not should advise the client as to where such assistance can be obtained. An ongoing relationship between the representative and a firm that deals in management and investments should be explored.

Marketing

There is a prevailing attitude, although a mistaken one, that most professional athletes do well because of lucrative endorsements and other types of outside income. In truth, such wealth is largely reserved for the top stars. Other athletes do what they can to supplement their income with personal appearances at local clubs, dinners, commercial establishments, and other less-than-top-dollar affairs. Even so, the possibilities for some types of outside income do exist. How aggressively they are sought on behalf of the client varies with the representative, but some willingness of the representative to assist the client in seeking supplementary income is demanded. With that in mind, a few rules and regulations should be noted.

First, chances are that either the player's contract with the club or the league's collective bargaining agreement will have some provisions regarding endorsements. These should be reviewed before any action is taken. Second, the other side of the marketing issue is being vigilant about protecting the player's name and image. These are property rights capable of protection under a variety of legal theories, including rights of privacy and publicity. Instances in which athletes have had to resort to the courts over alleged infringements are many, although in more than one case the player was held to have signed away his rights through the broad grant contained in an earlier contract. Noting these should be fair warning to the player agent about the careless granting of rights.

Cases in this area continue to appear, as athletes are more and more often viewed as celebrities whose names and images have commercial potential. Together with the ever-growing number of cases dealing with the rights of celebrities in other entertainment areas, these cases have brought about a substantial body of law revolving around rights or privacy and publicity.

Resolving Disputes

When things have gone awry under an existing contract, and the other side is believed to have done something that must be redressed legally, the player's representative basically has two possibilities for action: arbitration and litigation. Arbitration has preempted litigation in many situations in professional sports. A player agent must thus be aware of these instances because the time period in which complaints under arbitration must be filed is often short. Rights are easily waived. The arbitration process, which is usually initiated through the players' association, is specified in the collective bargaining agreement between the association and the league. This document has become indispensable in the player agent's library. Litigation is a feasible alternative in some situations. Alleged antitrust violations by a league or a club, for example, are still the province of the courts, although the leagues have become increasingly insulated from attacks by the labor exemption existing under the Sherman and Clayton acts. Even so, the cases still occur.

Planning

An athlete's career lasts but a short time. The average career for professional athletes, assuming they make the team in the first place, is in the four- to five-year range, varying only slightly by the sport played. Thus, for many, there is never anything beyond the first contract. For this reason, the player agent must prepare the client for what will occur in the not-too-distant future. Such a task is easy to describe but hard to carry out.

Athletes may claim that they realize theirs will not be a long career, but it is hard to grasp just how short a career can be. Most players are not really prepared for the end. Their attitude is invariably—"next year, perhaps, but not now."

The player agent may be unable to cushion the psychological blow completely. The hope is that the client has had sufficient time to produce enough income so that at least some preparations can be made for the financial transition. Achieving this goal relates to the managing function, but it adds the future ingredient of careful planning. The player agent needs to obtain professional assistance in order to maximize the client's financial resources so that a bridge can be built to span the time period needed to get the athlete into a new career. A player agent in this business for any period of time will have to confront this problem.

NOTE _____ _____

1. The following excerpts are from an information pamphlet that was sent to prospective professional athletes by a sports consulting firm that was attempting to establish itself.

What We Do

Contract negotiation: We deal directly with management to obtain the maximum commitment regarding salary, benefits and contract provisions.

Endorsements and appearances: We will seek to supplement our client's regular income by promoting product endorsements and personal appearances. We will both pursue appearance possibilities and negotiate on our client's behalf for endorsement fees.

Investments: We will review investment recommendations and proposals with our Investment Consultants. In addition, we will draw upon investment research from several investment banking and brokerage firms to augment our investment consultants.

Financial planning, insurance, legal and tax matters. We will also:
1. Evaluate our client's financial condition and establish a proper plan to insure maximum use of present and future earnings.
2. Have outside insurance consultants analyze our client's insurance programs and make recommendations as to adequacy of individual and group life, health and accident and disability insurance programs. We will make recommendations to our clients according to their needs after reviewing our consultants' proposals.
3. Provide complete legal advice in all areas of general law as they may affect our clients' needs.
4. Prepare personal Federal, State and other necessary tax returns—and—provide complete professional advice on Foreign Tax Matters, Tax-Sheltered Investments and other areas of tax specialization.

Our policy will be to care for the normal needs of the client and this effort will be incorporated into the negotiation fee.

Our clientele will be normally drawn from those who are not superstars and it is our feeling that we should not charge them excessively. We are sure that our fees are at least ½ to⅓ of those fees charged by other people in the athletic representative field.

We want to establish a feeling of honesty and fairness with our clients. We are sure that from our clients will come superstars with whom we will become more involved. But, we will always maintain a policy of providing low cost and honest service to the average professional athlete.

In most cases, our advice to the athletes will be to let their money grow in savings or in AAA bonds. Then, when they have reached superstar status and/or have a large enough cash base, we will have them diversify their investments.

Outside Consultants

Investment advisers. We will receive investment advice from professional investment counselors and investment banking and brokerage firms. Our investment counselors include:

Investment Banking and Brokerage Houses.

We work closely with several brokerage houses including [names of firms]. Investment research and recommendations which are acted upon by us will realize brokerage commissions to those firms. Therefore, there will be no outside fee expense in conjunction with such investments.

Attorneys and tax specialists. We receive legal and tax advice from several major law firms.

Insurance, pensions, profit sharing, etc. Our insurance consultants include representatives and managers of several major Insurance Companies—to include: [names of firms].

Advertising consultants. Our Advertising Consultants are creative directors, artists and copy writers at several Advertising Agencies and provide leads of client firms seeking professional athletes as well as advice on public relations, fee schedules and promotions.

Regulation of Player Agents

A good deal of notoriety has surrounded the relationship between player agents and their athlete clients. The publicity concerning those who represent players has been far from favorable. As a result, increasing scrutiny is being directed toward the player representative, leading in some instances to legal and other constraints being placed on the agent, obviously having an effect on the client relationship.

Government Regulation

Numerous states have enacted legislation to regulate the conduct and practice of sports agents. As of October 1993 twenty-nine states had addressed the issue of sports agents' conduct, and twenty-three states currently have laws dealing with sports agents and four states have pending legislation. These state laws are very diverse, but the common legislation followed by most states requires sports agents to register with the state and pay a registration fee. In addition, some states require sports agents to post a surety bond, which may be utilized to satisfy any damages caused to an athlete by the acts of an agent. Specified acts upon which an athlete can receive monetary payment due to an agent's misconduct include intentional misrepresentation, fraud, deceit, or any unlawful or negligent act.

NOTES

1. California was the first state to initiate agent regulation with the passage of the statute *Cal. Lab. Code 1500-1547.* This statute is applicable to any person engaged in athlete representation unless he or she is a member of the State of California bar and is acting as legal counsel. Sports agents are required to submit an application listing their experience in contract negotiations and complaint resolution, pay an application fee, pay an annual agent's fee, and pay a branch fee. Sports agents are also required to post a $25,000 surety bond. Player/agent contract forms must be approved by the Labor Commissioner, and sports agents, as part of their fee, are limited to 10 percent of the athlete's annual income. Sports agents who violate the statute or commit other violations are subject to financial penalties, imprisonment, or both.

2. The state of Texas was one of the early states to pass legislation specif-

ically aimed at controlling player representatives in their dealings with NCAA student-athletes. The following excerpts are from the *Texas Statutes,* Article 8871, §§ 1–13.

ART. 8871. REGULATION OF ATHLETE AGENTS

Definitions

Sec. 1. (a) In this Act:

(1) "Person" means an individual, company, corporation, association, partnership, or other legal entity.

(2) "Athlete agent" means a person that, for compensation, directly or indirectly recruits or solicits an athlete to enter into an agent contract, professional sports services contract, or financial services contract with that person or that for a fee procures, offers, promises, or attempts to obtain employment for an athlete with a professional sports team.

(3) "Agent contract" means any contract or agreement under which an athlete authorizes an athlete agent to negotiate to solicit on behalf of the athlete with one or more professional sports teams for the employment of the athlete by one or more professional sports teams.

(4) "Financial services contract" means any contract or agreement under which an athlete authorizes an athlete agent to provide financial services for the athlete, including the making and execution of investment and other financial decisions by the agent on behalf of the athlete.

(5) "Athlete" means an individual who resides in this state and who:

(A) is eligible to participate in intercollegiate sports contests as a member of a sports team of an institution of higher education located in this state that is a member of a national association for the promotion and regulation of intercollegiate athletics; or

(B) has participated as a member of such a sports team at an institution of higher education and who has never signed a contract of employment with a professional sports team.

(b) For purposes of this Act, execution by an athlete of a personal service contract with the owner or prospective owner of a professional sports team for the purpose of future athletic services is equivalent to employment with a professional sports team.

Registration Requirements; Renewal

Sec. 2. (a) An athlete agent must register with the secretary of state before the athlete agent may contact an athlete, either directly or indirectly, while the athlete is located in this state. A registered athlete agent may make those contacts only in accordance with this Act.

(b) An applicant for registration as an athlete agent must submit a written application for registration to the secretary of state on a form prescribed by the secretary of state. The applicant must provide the information required by the secretary of state, which shall include:

(1) the name of the applicant and the address of the applicant's principal place of business;

(2) the business or occupation engaged in by the applicant for the five years immediately preceding the date of application;

(3) a description of the applicant's formal training, practical experience, and educational background relating to the applicant's professional activities as an athlete agent;

(4) if requested by the secretary of state, the names and addresses of five professional references; and

(5) the names and addresses of all persons, except bona fide employees on stated salaries, that are financially interested as partners, associates, or profit sharers in the operation of the business of the athlete agent, except that an application for registration or renewal by any member of the State Bar of Texas must state only the names and addresses of those persons that are involved in the activities of the athlete agent and is not required to state the names and addresses of all persons who may be financially interested as members of a law firm or professional corporation but who do not become involved in the business of the athlete agent.

(c) If the applicant is a corporation, the information required by Subsection (b) of this section must be provided by each officer of the corporation. If the applicant is an association or partnership, the information must be provided by each associate or partner.

(d) A certificate of registration issued under this Act is valid for one year from the date of issuance. The secretary of state by rule may adopt a system under which certificates of registration expire on various dates during the year. For the year in which the registration expiration date is changed, the renewal fee payable on the anniversary of the date of issuance shall be prorated so that each registrant pays only that portion of the fee that is allocable to the number of months during which the registration is valid. On the renewal of the certificate of registration on the new expiration date, the total registration renewal fee is payable.

(e) A registered athlete agent may renew the registration by filing a renewal application in the form prescribed by the secretary of state, accompanied by the renewal fee. The renewal application must include the information prescribed by the secretary of state, which shall include:

(1) the names and addresses of all athletes for whom the athlete agent is providing professional services for compensation at the time of the renewal; and

(2) the names and addresses of all athletes not currently represented by the athlete agent for whom the athlete agent has performed professional services for compensation during the three years preceding the date of the application.

(f) The secretary of state by rule shall set all fees required for the administration of this Act. The secretary shall set the fees in amounts that are reasonable and necessary to cover the costs of administering this Act.

(g) When an application for registration or renewal is made and the registration process has not been completed, the secretary of state may issue a temporary or provisional registration certificate that is valid for no more than 90 days.

(h) Before the issuance or renewal of a certificate of registration, an athlete agent that enters into a financial services contract with an athlete must deposit with the secretary of state a surety bond in the sum of $100,000, payable to the state and conditioned that the person applying for the registration will comply with this Act, will pay all amounts due any individual or group of individuals when the person or the person's representative or agent has received those amounts, and will pay all damages caused to any athlete by reason of the intentional misrepresentation, fraud, deceit, or any unlawful or negligent act or omission by the registered athlete agent or the agent's representative or employee while acting within the scope of the financial services contract. The athlete agent shall maintain the bond until two years after the date on which the athlete agent ceases to engage in the provision of financial services for an athlete. This subsection does not limit the recovery of damages to the amount of the surety bond.

(i) If an athlete agent that has entered into a financial services contract with an athlete fails to file a new bond with the secretary of state not later than the 30th day after date of receipt of a notice of cancellation issued by the surety of the bond, the secretary of state shall suspend the certificate of registration issued to that athlete agent under the bond until the athlete agent files a new surety bond with the secretary of state.

(j) An athlete agent that enters into an agent contract only is not required to meet the bond requirements of this section.

Disciplinary Actions

Sec. 3. The secretary of state may suspend or revoke a certificate of registration issued under this Act for a violation of this Act or a rule adopted under this Act or may take other disciplinary actions. A disciplinary action under this Act is subject to the Administrative Procedure and Texas Register Act (Article 6252-13a, Vernon's Texas Civil Statutes).

Disposition of Fees

Sec. 4. Fees and other funds received under this Act by the secretary of state shall be deposited in the State Treasury to the credit of the General Revenue Fund.

Contracts: Cancellation Option

Sec. 5. (a) Any agent contract or financial services contract to be used by a registered athlete agent with an athlete must be on a form approved by the secretary of state.

(b) Each contract must state the fees and percentages to be paid by the athlete to the athlete agent and must include the following statements printed in at least 10-point boldface type:

NOTICE TO CLIENT

(1) THIS ATHLETE AGENT IS REGISTERED WITH THE SECRETARY OF STATE OF THE STATE OF TEXAS. REGISTRATION WITH THE SECRETARY OF STATE DOES NOT IMPLY APPROVAL OR ENDORSEMENT BY THE SECRETARY OF STATE OF THE COMPETENCE OF THE ATHLETE AGENT OR OF THE SPECIFIC TERMS AND CONDITIONS OF THIS CONTRACT.

(2) DO NOT SIGN THIS CONTRACT UNTIL YOU HAVE READ IT OR IF IT CONTAINS BLANK SPACES.

(3) IF YOU DECIDE THAT YOU DO NOT WISH TO PURCHASE THE SERVICES OF THE ATHLETE AGENT, YOU MAY CANCEL THIS CONTRACT BY NOTIFYING THE ATHLETE AGENT IN WRITING OF YOUR DESIRE TO CANCEL THE CONTRACT NOT LATER THAN THE 16TH DAY AFTER THE DATE ON WHICH YOU SIGN THIS CONTRACT.

(c) Each registered athlete agent shall file with the secretary of state a copy of each agent contract and financial services contract entered into with an athlete by the athlete agent. Such a contract must include a schedule of fees that the agent may charge to and collect from an athlete and a description of the various professional services to be rendered in return for each fee. The athlete agent may impose charges only in accordance with the fee schedule. Changes in the fee schedule may be made, but a change does not become effective until the seventh day after the date on which a copy of the contract as changed is filed with the secretary of state.

(d) If a multiyear professional sport services contract is negotiated by a registered athlete agent for an athlete, the athlete agent may not collect in any 12-month period for the agent's services in negotiating the contract a fee that exceeds the amount the athlete will receive under the contract in that 12-month period.

(e) In addition to filing with the secretary of state a copy of each contract made with an athlete, if the athlete is a student at an institution of higher education located in this state, the athlete agent must file a copy of the contract with the athletic director of the institution. The athlete agent must file the contract not later than the fifth day after the date on which the contract is signed by the athlete.

(f) An athlete may cancel an agent contract or financial services contract before the expiration of the 15th day after the date the contract is signed by notifying the athlete agent of the cancellation in writing.

Advertising Requirement; Prohibitions

Sec. 6. (a) In all forms of advertising used by the athlete agent, the agent shall disclose the name and address of the agent.

(b) A registered athlete agent may not:

(1) publish or cause to be published any false, fraudulent, or misleading information, representation, notice, or advertisement or give any false information or make any false promises or representations concerning any employment to any person;

(2) divide fees with or receive compensation from a professional sports league or franchise or its representative or employee;

(3) enter into any agreement, written or oral, by which the athlete agent offers anything of value to any employee of an institution of higher education located in this state in return for the referral of any clients by that employee;

(4) offer anything of value, excluding reasonable entertainment expenses and transportation expenses to and from the athlete agent's registered principal place of business, to induce an athlete to enter into an agreement by which the athlete agent will represent the athlete; or

(5) except as provided by Section 7 of this Act, directly contact an athlete who is participating in a team sport at an institution of higher education located in this state to discuss the athlete agent's representation of the athlete in the marketing of the athlete's athletic ability or reputation or the provision of financial services by the athlete agent, or enter into any agreement, written or oral, by which the athlete agent will represent the athlete, until after completion of the athlete's last intercollegiate contest, including postseason games, and may not enter into an agreement before the athlete's last intercollegiate contest that purports to take effect at a time after that contest is completed.

(c) This Act does not prohibit or limit an athlete agent from sending to an athlete written materials relating to the professional credentials of the agent or to specific services offered by the agent relating to the representation of an athlete in the marketing of an athlete's athletic ability or reputation or to the provision of financial services by the agent to the athlete. This Act does not prohibit an athlete or the athlete's parents, legal guardians, or other advisors from contacting and interviewing an athlete agent to determine that agent's professional proficiency in the representation of an athlete, in the marketing of the athlete's athletic ability or reputation, or the provision of financial services by the agent on behalf of the athlete.

Permitted Contacts With Certain Athletes

Sec. 7. (a) All institutions of higher education located in this state shall sponsor athlete agent interviews on their campuses before the athlete's final year of eligibility to participate in intercollegiate athletics, and a registered athlete agent may interview the athlete to discuss the athlete agent's provision of financial services and advice to the athlete or the athlete agent's representation of the athlete in the marketing of the athlete's athletic ability or reputation.

(b) All institutions sponsoring athlete agent interviews shall give public notice of those interviews not later than the 30th day before the date on which the period in which the interviews may be conducted begins. Institutions shall provide written notice of the time, place, and duration of the athlete agent interview program to those registered athlete agents who have previously furnished the athletic director of such institutions with their addresses.

(c) The athlete agent shall strictly adhere to the specific rules of each separate electing institution with regard to the time, place, and duration of the athlete agent interviews. The interviews must be conducted in the final year of eligibility during a period not to exceed 30 consecutive days.

Remedies for Violation; Criminal Penalty

Sec. 8. (a) A registered athlete agent who violates Subsection (a) of Section 2 or Section 6 of this Act may be subject to:

(1) a civil penalty, as provided by Section 9 of this Act;

(2) forfeiture of any right of repayment for anything of value either received by an athlete as an inducement to enter into any agent contract or financial services contract or received by an athlete before completion of the athlete's last intercollegiate contest;

(3) a refund of any consideration paid to the athlete agent on an athlete's behalf; and

(4) reasonable attorney's fees and court costs incurred by an athlete in suing and recovering against an athlete agent for a violation of this Act.

(b) Any agent contract or financial services contract that is negotiated by an athlete agent who has failed to comply with this Act is void.

(c) An athlete agent commits an offense if the agent knowingly violates Subsection (a) of Section 2 or Section 6 of this Act. An offense under this subsection is a Class A misdemeanor.

Civil Penalty

Sec. 9. (a) If the secretary of state determines that a person regulated under this Act has violated this Act or a rule adopted under this Act in a manner that constitutes a ground for disciplinary action under Section 3 of this Act, the secretary of state may assess a civil penalty against that person as provided by this section.

(b) The secretary of state may assess the civil penalty in an amount not to exceed $10,000. In determining the amount of the penalty, the secretary shall consider the seriousness of the violation.

(c) If after examination of a possible violation and the facts relating to that possible violation the secretary of state concludes that a violation has occurred, the secretary shall issue a preliminary report that states the facts on which the conclusion is based, the fact that a civil penalty is to be imposed, and the amount to be assessed. Not later than the 10th day after the date on which the secretary issues the preliminary report, the secretary shall send a copy of the report to the person charged with the violation together with a statement of the right of the person to a hearing relating to the alleged violation and the amount of the penalty.

(d) Not later than the 20th day after the date on which the report is sent, the person charged either may make a written request for a hearing or may remit the amount of the civil penalty to the secretary of state. Failure either to request a hearing or to remit the amount of the civil penalty within the time provided by this subsection results in a waiver of the right to a hearing under this Act. If the person charged requests a hearing, the hearing shall be conducted in the manner provided for a contested case hearing under the Administrative Procedure and

Texas Register Act (Article 6252-13a, Vernon's Texas Civil Statutes). If it is determined after hearing that the person has committed the alleged violation, the secretary shall give written notice to the person of the findings established by the hearing and the amount of the penalty and shall enter an order requiring the person to pay the penalty.

(e) Not later than the 30th day after the date on which the notice is received, the person charged shall pay the civil penalty in full or, if the person wishes to contest either the amount of the penalty or the fact of the violation, forward the assessed amount to the secretary of state for deposit in an escrow account. If, after judicial review, it is determined that no violation occurred or that the amount of the penalty should be reduced, the secretary shall remit the appropriate amount to the person charged with the violation not later than the 30th day after the date on which the judicial determination becomes final.

(f) Failure to remit the amount of the civil penalty to the secretary of state within the time provided by Subsection (e) of this section results in a waiver of all legal rights to contest the violation or the amount of the penalty.

(g) A civil penalty owed under this section may be recovered in a civil action brought by the attorney general at the request of the secretary of state.

(h) A penalty collected under this section shall be deposited in the State Treasury to the credit of the General Revenue Fund.

Records

Sec. 10. (a) An athlete agent shall keep records as provided by this section and shall provide the secretary of state with the information contained in the records on request. The records must contain:

(1) the name and address of each athlete employing the athlete agent, the amount of any fees received from the athlete, and the specific services performed on behalf of the athlete; and

(2) all travel and entertainment expenditures incurred by the athlete agent, including food, beverages, maintenance of a hospitality room, sporting events, theatrical and musical events, and any transportation, lodging, or admission expenses incurred in connection with the entertainment.

(b) The records kept by the athlete agent under Subdivision (2) of Subsection (a) of this section must adequately describe:

(1) the nature of the expenditure;

(2) the dollar amount of the expenditure;

(3) the purpose of the expenditure;

(4) the date and place of the expenditure; and

(5) each person on whose behalf the expenditure was made.

Rules

Sec. 11. The secretary of state may adopt rules necessary to carry out this Act. Acts 1987, 70th Leg., 2nd C.S., ch. 13. §§ 1 to 11, eff. Oct. 2, 1987.

Section 12(b) and (c) of the 1987 Act provides:

"(b) An athlete agent is not required to be registered and is not required to comply with this Act until January 1, 1988.

"(c) In addition to the information required under Subsection (b) of Section 2 of this Act, a person who is engaged in business as an athlete agent on the effective date of this Act must include in the registration application:

"(1) the names and addresses of all athletes for whom the applicant is providing professional services for compensation on the date the application is filed: and

"(2) the names and addresses of all athletes not currently represented by the athlete agent for whom the athlete agent has performed professional services for compensation during the three years preceding the date of the application."

Title of Act

An Act relating to the regulation of athlete agents: providing civil and criminal penalties. Acts 1987, 70th Leg., 2nd C.S., ch. 13.

Cross References

Punishment. Class A misdemeanor, see V.T. C.A. Penai Code, § 12.21.

3. The following states have passed legislation concerning sports agents: Alabama, Arkansas, California, Florida, Georgia, Indiana, Iowa, Kentucky, Louisiana, Maryland, Michigan, Minnesota, Mississippi, Nevada, North Carolina, Ohio, Oklahoma, Pennsylvania, South Carolina, Tennessee, Texas, Virginia, and Washington.

4. In *The Secretary of State of Texas v. TEAM America and Rodgers,* proceedings before the Secretary of State of Texas, 1990, TEAM America and its employee Johnny Rodgers were found to have failed to register as athlete agents in Texas and offered gifts, cash, and other inducements to Andre Ware prior to the expiration of his collegiate eligibility. Johnny Rodgers, an employee of TEAM America, contacted Joyce Ware, Andre's mother, when she was in New York to attend her son's Heisman Trophy award presentation. Rodgers purchased a fur coat and other clothing for her and spoke to her about her son's hiring TEAM America. A settlement agreement relieved Rodgers of personal liability but held TEAM America liable for a $10,000 penalty and barred them from signing Andre Ware.

5. In *Abernethy v. State,* 545 So. 2d 185 (Ala. Ct. App. 1988), sports agent Jim Abernethy was accused of tampering with a sports contest when he signed an Auburn University football player, prior to the player's senior year, and paid the player bonuses including $100 for every interception the player made while still playing in college. The court of criminal appeals reversed the circuit court's ruling and held that Abernethy did not violate the tampering statute because the number of interceptions made by the player did not influence the outcome of a sports contest.

6. In *United States v. Walters & Bloom,* a federal grand jury in Chicago in April 1989 found sports agents Norby Walters and Lloyd Bloom guilty of racketeering and fraud stemming from their dealing with college athletes. The two sports agents had signed forty-four college athletes secretly to pro contracts before their NCAA eligibility had expired. In September 1990, the 7th Circuit Court of Appeals overturned the convictions of Walters and Bloom on a legal technicality.

Ethical Constraints

The player representative who is also an attorney faces the constraints imposed by the canons of ethics. This can be particularly troublesome when competing with nonlawyers who do not face similar requirements. Issues relating to solicitation are foremost among these concerns.

Another ethical area is somewhat more subtle. This relates to dealing with student-athletes who still have remaining college athletic eligibility. Under the NCAA rules, any number of activities involving the athlete with a prospective representative may cause forfeiture of the athlete's remaining eligibility. While these regulations do not impose restrictions directly on the player representative, they do raise ethical issues for that person. It is also possible that a court might view a representative's activities, whereby the representative causes an athlete to lose eligibility, as constituting "unclean hands." This could affect the representative's legal remedies in certain situations.

NOTE _____

1. The American Bar Association's Ethical Code (EC) of Professional Responsibility states:

[A] lawyer should maintain high standards of professional conduct and should encourage fellow lawyers to do likewise. He should be temperate and dignified, and he should refrain from all illegal and morally reprehensible conduct....

EC 2-3 Advice is proper only if motivated by a desire to protect one who does not recognize that he may have legal problems or who is ignorant of his legal rights or obligations. Hence the advice is improper if motivated by a desire to obtain personal benefit, secure personal publicity, or cause litigation to be brought merely to harass or injure another.

EC 2-4 A lawyer who volunteers advice that one should obtain the services of a lawyer generally should not himself accept employment, compensation or other benefit in connection with that matter.

These considerations should be followed by all American Bar Association members. Nevertheless, the position of player representative allows for opportunities to violate some of these recommendations.

NCAA Regulations

The NCAA during the 1980s and into the 1990s has become more concerned with the actions of player agents, particularly as they relate to on-campus solicitation of student-athletes. Accounts of former college athletes stating that they had received illegal payments from agents while still in school have caused the NCAA to crack down in this area (see Chapter 5).

In 1982 the NCAA prepared a manual called "A Career in Professional Sports: Guidelines That Make Dollars and Sense." This booklet was designed to help students obtain competent representation. It provided a more general discussion of the NCAA's athlete-representation regulations.

During the 1984–85 academic year, the NCAA initiated two programs designed to increase the information available to student-athletes concerning player agents and the transition from collegiate to professional athletics. The first program permitted institutions to provide counseling on professional careers to student-athletes through a panel appointed by the institution's chief executive officer. The panel would consist of employees of the institution outside the athletics department. Each institution's panel was allowed to obtain information and expertise from a variety of sources (e.g., lawyers, financial consultants, professional sports teams, player associations, and player agents) in an effort to provide objective information about professional career opportunities and evaluate the various services and proposals extended by player agents.

The second program instituted by the NCAA was a player agent registration program. This was a voluntary program in which the player agent registered with the NCAA by supplying requested educational and professional information. The list of registered player agents was provided to the institutional career counseling panel, which would recommend agents on the list to the student-athlete. By registering the agent agreed to notify the director of athletics at the institution before the first contact with an enrolled student-athlete with remaining eligibility or with the student-athlete's coach. During 1985–86 the NCAA had over 400 agents registered in this program. The program was discontinued in August 1989.

Currently the NCAA still employs the career counseling panel program. The only change in this program involves the composition of the panel.

The counseling panels are organized by the institution. The panel consists of three people from the institution who will advise the student-athlete. The guidelines by which the three-member panel are selected are left to the discretion of the university. For the most part, it is suggested that the panel consist of employees from the institution. The committee can consist of a member of the bar, a law professor, or a teacher of business law; someone who deals with financial matters; and a person chosen at random. The NCAA also allows one full-time member of the athletic department staff to serve as a panel member. During the actual advising and counseling sessions, no agent or prospective agent may be present.

The institution decides whether or not to organize these panels; they are not required by the NCAA. In institutions that have set up counseling panels, the student-athletes are able to utilize the panel's services at any time. They do not have to wait for their eligibility to expire.

Some of the responsibilities of the panel are to establish policies that indicate the manner by which an agent can contact a student-athlete, to provide support and guidance during interviews with prospective agents, and to coordinate presentations by speakers for the benefit of the student-athlete.

College or University Regulations

Besides employing a career counseling panel, recommended but not required by the NCAA, a number of NCAA members have taken their own steps to ensure that student-athletes do not lose their eligibility as a result of infractions relating to agent representation. Duke University, for example, asks all agents to register prior to visiting any athlete. The university monitors the agents closely under its counseling committee (see Exhibit 11–11). The counseling committee recommends agents to student-athletes, but the student-athletes maintain the right to select any agent they wish.

Players Association Certification

Largely through the impetus of player unions, various sports leagues are moving to control the player-representative relationship. Baseball has for some time required that a signed authorization by the player be filed with a club before the club will deal with that player's chosen representative.

The National Football League, as a result of provisions inserted into the 1982 collective bargaining agreement, set a precedent for all professional sports leagues. The NFL Players Association, pursuant to those provisions, has imposed registration and other requirements, including maximum fee schedules, on all who wish to act as contract advisers for NFL players.

Other professional sports unions have followed the NFLPA's lead and established guidelines for the registration and regulation of agents. The National Basketball Association's Collective Bargaining Agreement contains the following restrictions on player agents.

ARTICLE XXXI
Player Agent Certification

Section 1. The NBA shall not approve any Player Contract between a player and a Team unless such player: (i) is represented in the negotiations with respect to such Player Contract by an agent or representative duly certified by the Players Association in accordance with the Players Association's Agent Regulation Program and authorized to represent him; or (ii) acts on his own behalf in negotiating such Player Contract.

Section 2. The NBA shall impose a fine of $1,000 upon any Team that negotiates a Player Contract with an agent or representative not certified by the Players Association in accordance with the Players Association's Agent Regulation Program if, at the time of such negotiations, such Team either (a) knows that such agent or representative has not been so certified or (b) fails to make reasonable inquiry of the NBA as to whether such agent or representative has been so certified. (1988 NBA Collective Bargaining Agreement)

Exhibit 11–11
Questionnaire for Registration as a Player Agent Representing Duke University Student-Athletes

PLEASE ANSWER ALL QUESTIONS THOROUGHLY

1. **General**
   a. Full name of applicant: _____
   b. Have you ever been known by any other name or surname (including a maiden name)?

   _____
   (Yes or No)
   If so, state all names used and when used:
   _____
   _____

   c. Date of birth ___/___/___　　　　　d. Birthplace _____

2. **Education**
   a. Law or other graduate school attended:

   _____
   (School)　　　　　　　　　　　　　　　　(City & State)
   Dates of Attendance: From: _____ To: _____
   　　　　　　　　　　　　　Month Year　　Month/Year
   Degree: _____ Date Awarded: _____

   b. Colleges or Universities attended:

(Name)	(City & State)	(Dates Attended)	(Degree)
(Name)	(City & State)	(Dates Attended)	(Degree)
(Name)	(City & State)	(Dates Attended)	(Degree)

   c. High School Attended:

(Name)	(City & State)	(Date Degree Received)

3. **Current Occupation/Employment**
   a. I am currently: (Check One)
      ____ Employed by:
      　　　　　　　　　　　　　　　　　　(　)
      _____
      (Name of Employer)　　(Address)　　(Telephone)

      _____
      (Dates of Employment)

      _____
      (Nature of Employment)
      ____ Self-Employed
   b. If self-employed, please state nature and location of business:

   _____
   _____

   c. Please list below the names of employers, addresses, positions held, and dates of all employment you have had for the past five years:

   _____
   _____

Exhibit 11–11 continued

_____

_____

_____

4.   **Lawyers and Law Graduates**

   a. Have you been admitted to the Bar in any jurisdiction? _____ If so, please list
       (Yes or No)
       jurisdictions and dates of admission:

   _____   _____
   (Jurisdiction)   (Date of Admission)

   _____   _____
   (Jurisdiction)   (Date of Admission)

   _____   _____
   (Jurisdiction)   (Date of Admission)

   b. Do you have any applications for Bar admission currently pending? _____ If yes,
       (Yes or No)
       please state where you have applied and the status of that application:

   _____

   _____

   _____

   c. Have you ever been disbarred, suspended, reprimanded, censured, or otherwise dis-
       ciplined or disqualified as an attorney, as a member of any other profession, or as a
       holder of any public office? _____ If yes, please describe each such action, the
       (Yes or No)
       dates of occurrence, and the name and address of the authority imposing the action
       in question:

   _____

   _____

   _____

   _____

   d. Are any charges or complaints currently pending against you regarding your conduct
       as an attorney, as a member of any profession, or as a holder of public office?

       _____ If yes, please indicate the nature of the charge or complaint and the name
       (Yes or No)
       and address of the authority considering it:

   _____

   _____

   _____

   _____

   e. Has your right to practice before any governmental office, bureau, agency, commission,
       etc. ever been disqualified, suspended, withdrawn, denied, or terminated? _____
       (Yes or No)
       If yes, please explain fully:

   _____

   _____

   _____

   _____

   _____

Exhibit 11–11 continued

5. **Other (Than Legal) Occupations**

    a. Are you a member of any business or professional organizations which directly relate to your occupation or profession? _____ If so, please list:
                         (Yes or No)

_____

_____

_____

_____

    b. Please list any occupational or professional licenses or other similar credentials (i.e., Certified Public Accountant, Chartered Life Underwriter, Registered Investment Advisor, etc.) you have obtained other than college or graduate school degrees, including dates obtained:

_____

_____

_____

    c. Have you ever been denied an occupational or professional license, franchise or other similar credentials for which you applied? _____ If yes, please explain fully:
                         (Yes or No)

_____

_____

_____

    d. Do you have currently pending any application for an occupational or professional license, franchise or other similar credentials? _____ If yes, please describe and
                         (Yes or No)
       indicate status of each such application:

_____

_____

_____

    e. Have you ever been suspended, reprimanded, censured, or otherwise disciplined or disqualified as a member of any profession, or as a holder of any public office?

       _____ If yes, please describe each such action, the date(s) of occurrence, and the
       (Yes or No)
       name and address of the authority imposing the action in question:

_____

_____

_____

_____

    f. Are any charges or complaints currently pending against you regarding your conduct as a member of any profession, or as a holder of public office? _____ If yes,
                                            (Yes or No)
       please indicate the nature of the charge or complaint and the name and address of the authority considering it:

_____

_____

_____

Exhibit 11–11 continued

g. Has your right to engage in any profession or occupation ever been disqualified, suspended, withdrawn, or terminated? _____ If yes, please explain fully:
(Yes or No)

_____

_____

_____

_____

_____

6. **All Applicants**

a. Have you ever been convicted of or pled guilty to a criminal charge, other than minor traffic violations? _____ If yes, please indicate nature of offense, date of convic-
(Yes or No)
tion, criminal authority involved, and punishment assessed:

_____

_____

b. Have you ever been a defendant in any civil proceedings, including bankruptcy proceedings, in which allegations of fraud, misrepresentation, embezzlement, misappropriation of funds, conversion, breach of fiduciary duty, forgery, or legal malpractice were made against you? _____ If yes, please describe fully and indicate results
(Yes or No)
of the civil proceeding(s) in question:

_____

_____

_____

_____

_____

c. Have you ever been adjudicated insane or legally incompetent by any court?

_____ If yes, please provide details:
(Yes or No)

_____

_____

_____

d. Were you ever suspended or expelled from any college, university, law school, or graduate school? _____ If so, please explain fully:
(Yes or No)

_____

_____

_____

e. Has any surety or any bond on which you were covered been required to pay any money on your behalf? _____ If so, please describe circumstances:
(Yes or No)

_____

_____

_____

f. Are there unsatisfied judgments of continuing effect against you (other than alimony or child support)? _____ If yes, provide full details:
(Yes or No)

_____

_____

Exhibit 11–11 continued

7. **References**

    a. Please list below the names, addresses, and telephone numbers of three persons, not related to you and not engaged in business with you, who have known you for at least the last three years and who can attest to your character.

    _____

    _____

    _____

    _____

    _____

    b. Please list below the names, addresses, and telephone numbers of at least two entities which can attest to your financial credit:

    _____

    _____

    _____

8. **Other Services**

    a. Please indicate what services you offer to athletes, in addition to contract negotiation services.

    _____

    _____

    _____

    _____

    _____

    _____

    b. Do you handle players' funds? _____
                                              (Yes or No)

    If so, are you bonded? _____ If yes, please provide details as to the amount of
                                  (Yes or No)
    the bond, the name and address of the surety or bonding company, etc.:

    _____

    _____

    _____

DUKE UNIVERSITY AGENT REGISTRATION

DUKE UNIVERSITY, relying upon an Application for Registration previously filed, hereby grants Registration to _____

_____to act as an agent pursuant to the Duke University Policy Concerning Student-Athletes of Duke University and Agents adopted September 1, 1985, and amended from time to time thereafter. This Registration is effective beginning as of the date hereof, and shall continue in full force and effect until and unless suspended, revoked, or terminated in accordance with this Policy.

Dated at Durham, N.C. this _____ day of _____, 19____.

DUKE UNIVERSITY

BY: _____
           Chairman, Student-Athlete
           Counseling Committee

NOTE ——————————————————————————————

1. The following are the addresses and telephone numbers of the player union offices and the various league offices.

Union Offices:

National Basketball Players Association
1175 Broadway, Suite 2401
New York, NY 10019
(212) 333-7510

Major League Baseball Players Association
805 3rd Avenue, 11th Floor
New York, NY 10022
(212) 826-0808

National Hockey League Players Association
Maitland House
37 Maitland Street
Toronto, Ontario, Canada M4Y 1C8
(416) 924-7800

Major Indoor Soccer League Players Association
2021 L Street, N.W.
Washington, DC 20036
(202) 463-2200

National Football League Players Association
2021 L Street, N.W.
Washington, DC 20036
(202) 463-2200

Canadian Football Players Association
1686 Albert Street
Regina Saskatchewan, Canada S4P 2S6
(306) 525-2158

Professional League Offices:

National Football League
410 Park Avenue
New York, NY 10022
(212) 758-1500

Canadian Football League
1200 Bay Street
12th Floor
Toronto, Ontario, Canada M5R 2A5
(416) 928-1200

National Hockey League—New York
650 Fifth Avenue
33rd Floor
New York, NY 10019
(212) 398-1100.

National Basketball Association
645 Fifth Avenue
New York, NY 10022
(212) 826-7000

The National League of Professional Baseball Clubs
350 Park Avenue
New York, NY 10022
(212) 339-7700

Major Indoor Soccer League
7101 College Boulevard
Suite 320
Overland Park, KS 66210
(913) 339-6011

The American League of Professional Baseball Clubs
350 Park Avenue
New York, NY 10022
(212) 339-7600

Baseball Commissioner's Office
350 Park Avenue
New York, NY 10022
(212) 339-7800

Representative-Player Agreements

The relationship established between the player representative and the client has traditionally varied greatly in terms of the formality of any agreement effectuated between the parties. The agreement has ranged from a handshake, to a letter of understanding, to a detailed contract. Increasingly, interested parties within professional sports are urging that greater formality and detail be introduced into the relationship in order to safeguard the rights of both parties. For example, the NBPA has suggested a contract form that might be used (Exhibit 11–12).

NOTE _____

1. For further information on the problems of those who represent the professional athlete, see the following articles and books.

(a) Garvey, *The Agent Game* (Washington, DC: Federation of Professional Athletes, AFL-CIO, 1984).

(b) Ruxin, *An Athlete's Guide to Agents* (New York: The Stephen Greene Press, 1989).

(c) Giulietti, "Agents of Professional Athletes," 15 *New Eng. L. Rev.* 545 (1980).

(d) Hearings Before the House Select Committee on Professional Sports, 94th Cong., 2d Sess. (1976).

(e) Weistart and Lowell, *The Law of Sports* (Indianapolis: Bobbs-Merrill, 1979). Note, particularly, pp. 319–333.

(f) Gallner, *Pro Sports: The Contract Game*, 1975.

Exhibit 11-12
Standard Representation Agreement Between NBPA Contract Advisor and Player

AGREEMENT made this _____ day of _____, 1986, by and

between _____ (hereinafter the "Agent")

and _____ (hereinafter the "Player").

WITNESSETH:

In consideration of the mutual promises hereinafter contained, the parties hereto promise and agree as follows:

1. General Principles

This agreement is entered into pursuant to and in accordance with the National Basketball Players Association's (hereinafter the "NBPA") Regulations Governing Player Agents (hereinafter "the Regulations") as promulgated effective March 7, 1986, and as may be amended thereafter from time to time The Agent represents that in advance of executing this Agreement, he has read and familiarized himself with the Regulations and has applied for and been certified as a Player Agent by the NBPA.

This Agreement shall apply only with respect to the Agent's performance of the services described below.

2. Contract Services

Commencing on the date of this Agreement, the Agent agrees to represent the Player — to the extent requested by the Player — in conducting individual compensation negotiations for the performance of the Player's services as a professional basketball player with the Player's NBA club.

[If the Agent will not be "conducting individual compensation negotiations," then insert in lieu of those quoted words: "in assisting, advising or counselling the Player in connection with individual compensation negotiations."] After a contract with the Player's club is executed, the Agent to continue to assist, advise and counsel the Player in enforcing his rights under that contract.

In performing these services the Agent is the NBPA's delegated representative and is acting in a fiduciary capacity on behalf of the Player. In no event shall the Agent have the authority to bind or commit the Player in any manner without the express prior consent of the Player and in no event shall the Agent execute a player contract on behalf of the Player.

3. Compensation for Services

The Player shall pay fees to the Agent for services performed pursuant to this Agreement in accordance with the following provisions:

(1) If the Player receives only the minimum compensation under the NBA-NBPA collective bargaining agreement applicable for the playing season or seasons covered by the individual contract, the Agent shall receive a $2,000 fee for each such season, unless any lesser amount has been

Exhibit 11–12 continued

agreed to by the parties and is noted in the space below;
[The parties hereto have agreed to the following lesser fee:

_____

_____

_____]

(2) If the Player receives compensation in excess of the minimum compensation applicable under the NBA-NBPA collective bargaining agreement for one or more playing seasons, the Agent shall receive a fee of four percent (4%) of the "compensation" received by the Player for each such playing season, unless a lesser percent (%) or amount has been agreed to by the parties and is noted in the space below.
[The parties hereto have agreed to the following lesser fee:

_____

_____

_____]

In computing the allowable fee pursuant to paragraph 3(1) and /or (2) above, the term "compensation" shall include base salary, signing bonus and any performance bonus actually received by the player; no other benefits provided in the player contract shall be taken into account in computing the fee — including, but not limited to, the fact that the contract guarantees compensation to the player for one or more seasons, the value of a personal loan, an insurance policy, an automobile, or a residence, etc.

4. Time for Receipt of Payment of Agent's Fee

The agent shall not be entitled to receive any fee for the performance of his services pursuant ot this Agreement until the Player receives the compensation upon which the fee is based; within fifteen (15) days of the Player's receipt of each compensation payment(s) (as defined in paragraph 3 above) during the term of this Agreement or any extension, renewal, or modification thereof, the Player shall make his fee payment to the Agent in an amount computed in accordance with paragraph 3 above.

The Player has the sole discretion to decide that it is in his best interest to make an advance fee payment(s) to his Agent, in which case the Agent is authorized to accept that advance payment; provided, however, that (a) the advance payment cannot exceed the fee prescribed in paragraph 3 above, and (b) with respect to any advance payment relating to deferred compensation the fee shall be based upon the present value of that compensation.

In no case shall the Agent accept, directly or indirectly payment of his fee from the Player's club. Further, the amount of the Agent's fee shall not be discussed with the NBA club with whom the Agent is negotiating on behalf of the Player, nor shall the Agent or Player secure an agreement from the NBA club respecting the amount of the Agent's fee.

5. Expenses

All expenses incurred by the Agent in the performance of the services hereunder shall be solely the Agent's responsibility and shall not be reimbursable by the Player, except that with respect to each player contract negotiated under this Agreement (irrespective of the number of playing seasons covered) the Player shall (i) reimburse the Agent for reasonable travel, living and communications expenses (e.g., telephone, postage) actually incurred by

Exhibit 11–12 continued

the Agent up to One Thousand Dollars ($1,000.00); provided, however, if the expenses exceed One Thousand Dollars ($1,000.00), the Player shall be obligated to reimburse the Agent for the amount of the excess only if he gave express prior consent to the Agent to incur those expenses, and the Player shall (ii) pay or reimburse the Agent for the fees and expenses of any attorney, accountant, tax consultant or other professional engaged by the Agent at the Player's express request to render services to the Player, but only if such services are other than in connection with the negotiation and execution of such player contracts. The Player shall promptly pay all expenses, fees and costs for which he is obligated under this paragraph 5 upon receipt of an itemized statement therefor.

6. Term

The term of this Agreement shall begin on the date hereof and shall continue in effect until the expiration date of any player contract executed pursuant to this Agreement or any extension, renewal or modification of the Player's contract, whichever occurs later; provided, however, that either party may terminate this Agreement effective fifteen (15) days after written notice of termination is given to the other party; and, provided, further, that if the Agent's certification is suspended or revoked by the NBPA or the Agent is otherwise prohibited by the NBPA from performing the services he has agreed to perform herein, this Agreement automatically shall terminate effective as of the date of such suspension or termination.

Upon being terminated pursuant to either of the above provisions, the Agent shall be entitled to be compensated for the reasonable value of the services he had already performed based upon the fee schedule contained in paragraph 3 above.

7. Arbitration: Resolution of All Disputes Arising Out of This Agreement

Any and all disputes between the Player and the Agent involving the meaning, interpretation, application, or enforcement of this Agreement or the obligations of the parties under this Agreement shall be resolved exclusively through the Arbitration prcedure set forth in Section 5 of the NBPA Regulations Governing Player Agents. As provided in Section 5 F of those Regulations, if any arbitration hearing takes place, the NBPA may participate and present, by testimony or otherwise, any evidence relevant to the dispute. Because of the uniquely internal nature of any such dispute that may arise under this Agreement, the Player and the Agent agree that the arbitrator's award shall constitute a final and binding resolution of the dispute and neither party will seek judicial review on any ground.

8. Notices

All notices hereunder shall be effective if sent by certified mail, postage prepaid, return receipt requested, as follows:

If to the Agent:

If to the Player:

Exhibit 11–12 continued

9. Entire Agreement

This Agreement sets forth the entire agreement between the parties. This Agreement cannot be amended or changed orally and any written amendments or changes shall be effective only to the extent that they are consistent with the Standard Form Agreement approved by the NBPA.

This Agreement replaces and supersedes any agreement between the parties entered into at any time on or after March 7, 1986 providing fees for services performed as defined in Sections 2 and 3 above.

10. Governing Law

This Agreement shall be construed, interpreted and enforced according to the laws of the State of New York.

11. Filing

This contract should be signed in triplicate. One copy must be promptly delivered by the Agent to the NBPA Committee on Agent Regulation within five (5) days of its execution; one copy must be promptly delivered by the Agent to the Player; and one copy should be retained by the Agent.

EXAMINE THIS CONTRACT CAREFULLY BEFORE SIGNING IT

IN WITNESS WHEREOF, the parties hereto have hereunder signed their names as hereinafter set forth.

_____

PLAYER AGENT

_____

PLAYER

_____

PARENT or GUARDIAN (if Player is
under 21 Years of Age)

(g) Woolf, *Behind Closed Doors* (New York: Atheneum, 1976).

(h) Jones, ed., *Current Issues in Professional Sports* (Durham: University of New Hampshire, 1980). Note particularly Shepherd, "Establishing the Contractual Relationship Between the Representative and the Athlete," pp. 13–29.

(i) Kohn, "Sports Agents Representing Professional Athletes: Being Certified Means Never Having to Say You're Qualified," 6 *The Entertainment and Sports Lawyer* 1 (1988).

(j) Needham, ed., *Counseling Professional Athletes and Entertainers*, 3rd ed. (New York: Practicing Law Institute, 1971).

(k) Blackman and Hochberg, *Representing Professional Athletes and Teams* (New York: Practicing Law Institute, 1990).

(l) Trope, *Necessary Roughness: The Other Game of Football Exposed by Its Most Controversial Super Agent* (Chicago: Contemporary Books, 1987).

(m) Fishoff, *Putting It on the Line* (New York: W. Morrow, 1983).

(n) Shropshire, *Agents of Opportunity: Sports Agents and Corruption in Collegiate Sports* (Philadelphia: University of Pennsylvania Press, 1990).

INDIVIDUAL PERFORMER SPORTS

The sports worlds of tennis, golf, boxing, track, horse and auto racing, and other events that largely have the athlete competing as an individual rather than on a team in a league, present far different vistas than those that have been considered to this point. The possibilities for exploration of issues are so great, in fact, that no attempt is made in this brief aside other than to suggest a few of the important considerations.

Obviously, the basic contract starting points differ. Gone, for example, is the uniform player contract. Even so, its influences are not missing. After all, in tennis and golf, there are players' associations—perhaps not unions in the full sense as in the league sports but important in terms of giving their blessings to certain activities, including the types of contracts tendered players. Thus, when it comes to tennis and golf tournaments, the Sponsor-Player Contract assumes great uniformity as to many of the terms.

Endorsement contracts are staples in individual performer sports. These are not discussed here, except to note their prevalence and importance. But they can comfortably be considered in tandem with league player endorsements.

Finally, for many of the individual performer sports, there are clubs or resorts that wish to have a player's name associated with the facility. Any of a number of deals are possible, ranging from straight money payments to trade-outs and other enticements.

A legal inquiry that is raised but not pursued in this part of the book is whether individual performer sports require variant legal standards in some instances. For example, is injunctory relief available when the athlete fails to honor a contract? When the specific situation is relevant in a court fashioning the relief to be awarded, it may be that a performer in individual sports stands in a position that is different from that of a team player. If so, that must be anticipated in the drafting of the initial agreements.

FOREIGN LEAGUES

Limited alternatives are available to U.S. athletes to play "professionally" in foreign countries. In football, there is the Canadian Football League or the World Football League. For baseball players, Japan offers opportunities, generally for former Major Leaguers. In basketball and hockey, leagues exist across Europe, with the quality of play varying substantially from country to country, and usually below the quality in the United States.

All foreign leagues limit the number of noncitizens who can play on any one team. This makes the scramble for spots by U.S. players an intense one, particularly in the better leagues. For example, the Italian basketball league is considered the strongest outside the United States. Top players can earn as much as $150,000 a year, even though the league is classified as amateur under international rules. Each Italian team is severely limited as to how many foreign players can make a squad. It takes a top U.S. player, one just below the NBA level, to secure a contract, unless the player can claim Italian citizenship, and not count against the team's foreign quota. Exhibit 11–13 contains a contract between a basketball player from the United States and an Italian basketball team.

ENDORSEMENT CONTRACTS

Athletes, because of their athletic talents and wide appeal to the public, can be of great interest to a company wanting to increase their exposure and promote their products. Endorsement contracts are entered into quite often in professional sports as the athlete allows the advertising agencies or company to use his or her name and image in product promotional activities. In entering into these endorsement contracts, the player must be careful to understand exactly how his or her name and image will be used. In addition, the professional team and league may have certain restrictions on the use of this athlete in the company's promotional activities (i.e., the athlete could be pro-

Exhibit 11–13
Basketball Contract Between U.S. Player and an Italian Team

This agreement made this day 19th of July, 1988, by and between _____ _____ (hereinafter referred to as PLAYER) and _____ _____ (hereinafter referred to as CLUB).

WITNESSETH:

In consideration of the mutual promises herein contained, the parties hereto promise and agree as follows:

I. - a) The CLUB hereby employs the PLAYER as a skilled basketball player for a term of one (1) season which shall begin the 20th day of August 1988 and shall end one week after the last official game (no option year). The PLAYER'S employment shall include attendance and participation in regular season games scheduled by or entered in by the CLUB.

b) Upon signing, this contract becomes fully guaranteed against skill and /or injury. Regardless of circumstances, excluding rule infractions, all monies contracted are due and payable to PLAYER in accordance to the rules of this contract.

II. - a) The CLUB agrees to pay the PLAYER for rendering services described herein, the salary of ONE HUNDRED FORTY THOUSAND ($140,000 USA) for the 1988-89 season, payable as follows:

Sept. 1	14,000 US	Feb. 1	14,000 US
Oct. 1	14,000 US	Mar. 1	14,000 US
Nov. 1	14,000 US	Apr. 1	14,000 US
Dec. 1	14,000 US	May 1	14,000 US
Jan. 1	14,000 US	June 1	14,000 US

CLUB also agrees to pay PLAYER a deferred signing bonus of THIRTY THOUSAND DOLLARS ($30,000 US) at the beginning of playing season.

All salary and bonus payments are net of Italian taxes.

b) Payments which are received later than the day noted shall be subject to an interest penalty of FIFTY DOLLARS ($50.00) per day. In the case of scheduled payments not being made by the CLUB within five (5) days of the payment date, the PLAYER shall be entitled to all monies due in accordance with the Agreement, but shall not have to perform in practice sessions or games until all scheduled payments have been made in full plus appropriate penalties.

c) The CLUB will pay the following bonuses to PLAYER:
    1) If Club finishes regular season:
        a) If Club finishes 5th-10th, an additional FIVE THOUSAND DOLLARS ($5,000 US)
        b) If Club finishes 1st-4th, an additional TEN THOUSAND DOLLARS ($10,000 US)
    (ACCUMULATIVE)
    2) PLAYOFFS:
        a) If Club wins 1st round, an additional FIVE THOUSAND DOLLARS ($5,000 US)
        b) If Club wins 2nd round, an additional SEVEN THOUSAND FIVE HUNDRED DOLLARS ($7,500 US)
        c) If Club wins 3rd round, an additional TEN THOUSAND HUNDRED DOLLARS ($10,000 US)
        d) If Club wins Italian League Championship, an additional TWENTY THOUSAND DOLLARS ($20,000 US)

Exhibit 11–13 continued

                        (all Playoff bonuses accumulative)
          3)   ITALIAN CUP
                        a) If Club reaches finals, an additional TWO THOUSAND FIVE HUNDRED
DOLLARS ($2,500 US)
                        b) If Club wins Italian Cup Championship, and additional FIVE
THOUSAND DOLLARS ($5,000 US)
                        (ACCUMULATIVE)

          4)   If Player finishes among the Top 4 (or is tied) in final Player Valuation, an
additional FIVE THOUSAND DOLLARS ($5,000 US)

All bonuses are net to PLAYER and must be paid in month earned. Same penalties as late
salary payments will apply here.

          e)   The salary will be paid to the PLAYER in lira at the Banco di Roma's last fixing
rate of the previous week.
                        If desired by the PLAYER, the CLUB will assist PLAYER in sending money to the
U.S., but always in accordance with the Italian rules on foreign currency.

          f)   The salary and bonuses are to be free and clear of all Italian taxes. Should the
payments of taxes be required it is of responsibility of the CLUB to pay them. PLAYER is to be
given a written verification that all of his Italian taxes has been paid prior to his departure.

III.   The CLUB agrees to provide the following to the PLAYER for each contract year:
          a) Three (3) round trip business class tickets and two (2) round trip coach tickets,
originating in from Inglewood, California and terminating in Rome, Italy and return.
          b) All medical, dental (non cosmetic), and hospitalization costs incurred by PLAYER
and/or his family in Italy or US.
          c) A minimum of three (3) bedroom, fully furnished apartment/house (all utilities
included). PLAYER pays his phone bills.
          d) Free use of one car (of Player's approval) of which Club will pay for all taxes, license &
registration fees, insurance and maintenance. Player will be responsible for gas and oil plus any
traffic fines.
          e) A $1 million Insurance policy against permanent disability and/or death. Player will
name all beneficiaries.
          f) All proper and necessary expenses of the PLAYER while playing for the CLUB on the
road and during training camp. The CLUB will pay the total cost of room and board in the
above cases.
          g) A $1,500 US maximum moving allowance between US and Italy for total year.

IV.   a) This will be a fully guaranteed contract after PLAYER has passed CLUB's medical
examination. Exam must be given no later than one (1) week after his arrival. After that time
has passed, with or without medical examination, all terms and conditions of this contract are
binding to both parties. The President of the CLUB as well as CLUB's sponsor's President will
guarantee this contract.
          b) If PLAYER is injured at any time during the effect of this contract and is unable to
continue to play, all monies are still due and payable plus reimbursement for medical expenses
incurred because of the injury.
          c) If PLAYER feels that his injury is serious enough to require surgery in the U.S.,
PLAYER will submit to the prevailing opinion of three (3) doctors (one chosen by CLUB, one by
PLAYER, both doctors agreeing on a third). If majority opinion concurs and surgery is required,
PLAYER will be flown to U.S. at CLUB's expense for the operation. After surgery is performed,
CLUB will submit to majority opinion of three (3) U.S. doctors (chosen as was done above) to
decide whether PLAYER can continue play that year. If it is agreed that PLAYER can, he must
rehabilitate in Italy under CLUB's supervision. If he cannot, PLAYER can remain in U.S. and
will be paid in accordance with the terms and conditions of this contract.

Exhibit 11–13 continued

V. a) The PLAYER agrees to observe and comply with the requirements of the CLUB, whether on or off the basketball court.
The CLUB may establish reasonable rules of behavior for the team and list of fines for the players which PLAYER must observe. PLAYER also agrees to obey his coach and to be prompt for all games, practices and CLUB meetings.

b) PLAYER and his agent must be supplied with a copy of all club rules and fines before paragraph 5 hereinabove is accepted. If some of the rules seem too vague, PLAYER will ask for clarification. If some of fines seem too excessive, PLAYER will seek reductions. All must be done before this paragraph is made a part of this agreement. PLAYER's agent must be notified of each infraction before any disciplinary action is taken by CLUB.

c) Failure to comply with CLUB's disciplinary policies may result in fines and/or suspension of PLAYER's employment.

VI. If PLAYER is forced to initiate legal action to insure payment of this contract and its provisions, both CLUB and CLUB's sponsor agree to bear all legal cost both incurred by PLAYER both in U.S. and Italy. This agreement will be governed by Italian Law, and CLUB and CLUB's sponsor agree to submit to Italian jurisdiction to resolve any dispute.

VII. a) In case of PLAYER's death for whatever reason during the term of this contract, CLUB will pay to PLAYER's designated beneficiary an amount equal to the compensation specified in Paragraph III. less all of the compensations received by the PLAYER prior to his death.

VIII. If the PLAYER should desire to play for another Club within Italy, Club can only ask up to a maximum of $75,000 US for transfer of Player's rights (Nulla-Oltra) to interested club(s).

IX. This contract contains the entire agreement between the parties and no other agreement, oral or otherwise regarding the subject of this contract shall be deemed to exist or bind any of the parties hereto.

IN WITNESS WHEREOF, the parties have hereto set their hands:

hibited from wearing the team's uniform unless an endorsement fee is also paid to the professional league).

Exhibit 11–14 contains an endorsement contract between a professional athlete and a widely known sporting goods manufacturer.

NOTE _____

1. In January 1992, Michael Jordan of the Chicago Bulls requested that the National Basketball Association not use his likeness on NBA official apparel. Michael Jordan has an endorsement contract with Nike giving them the exclusive right to use his image. The NBA complied with Jordan's request and expected other players who might also possess exclusive endorsement contracts with companies to follow.

Exhibit 11–14
Athlete Endorsement Contract

AGREEMENT

This Agreement, made and entered into this thirteenth day of November, 1989, by and between
_____ having its principal place of business at _____
(Company)   (Address)
_____ . _____ (hereinafter referred to
                                   (Player's Company)
as "Company"), and _____ (hereinafter referred to as

"Enterprises").

WITNESSETH

WHEREAS, Enterprises has the sole and exclusive right to provide the services of
_____ (hereinafter referred to as "Athlete") and to license the name
(Player)
_____ for the purposes of this Agreement as hereinafter set forth; and

WHEREAS, Athlete is recognized and widely known throughout the world as an expert
basketball player; and

WHEREAS, Athlete's name by virtue of his ability and extensive experience, has acquired
secondary meaning in the mind of the purchasing public important to the advertisement,
promotion, and sale of Endorsed Products as defined in Paragraph One (1) (d) below; and

WHEREAS, Company is engaged in the manufacture, distribution, and sale of Endorsed
Products and is desirous of acquiring the exclusive right to utilize Athlete's Endorsement (as
defined in Paragraph One (1) (a) below) and services in connection with the sale, advertisement,
and promotion of Endorsed Products;

NOW THEREFORE, in consideration of the mutual covenants as set forth herein and
for other good and valuable consideration, it is agreed as follows:

1.   Definitions. As used herein, the terms set forth below shall be defined as follows:

        (a) "Athlete's Endorsement" shall include only the right to use the name,
nickname, likeness, photograph, signature, initials, statements, facsimile, and
endorsement of Athlete;
        (b) "Contract Territory" shall mean the world;
        (c) "Contract Year" shall mean the twelve (12) month period commencing on
each thirteenth day of September during the Term of Agreement;
        (d) "Endorsed Products" shall mean any athletic footwear, athletic apparel, caps,
visors, and athletic bags as may now or hereinafter be manufactured, distributed, marketed,
licensed, and/or sold by Company or on Company's behalf.

2.   Term of Agreement. The Term of this Agreement shall commence September 13,
1989, and shall continue until September 12, 1993.

Exhibit 11–14 continued

3. Commercial Materials, In connection with this Agreement, "Commercial Materials" shall mean those materials produced pursuant to Paragraphs Six (6) and Fifteen (15) hereof, including, without limitation, radio and television commercials, video tapes, audio tapes, still photographs (including those lifted from television commercials or video tapes), billboards, all forms of print advertising, point-of-purchase materials, posters, product packaging, hang tags, the name(s) of product(s), all collateral materials, Company's Annual Report, materials produced for promotional purposes, materials used for trade contests, trade publications, and all internal and/or external sales and marketing pieces.

4. Grant of Endorsement Rights. Subject to the terms and conditions hereinafter set forth, Enterprises hereby grants to Company the exclusive right and license, within the Contract Territory and during the Term, to utilize the Athlete's Endorsement in connection with the advertisement, promotion, and sale of Endorsed Products.

5. Retention of Endorsement Rights. Subject to the provisions of Paragraph Four (4) above, Company agrees that Enterprises shall retain all rights in and to Athlete's name and endorsement and, whether during the Term or any extension thereof, Enterprises shall not be prevented from using, or permitting and licensing others to use, Athlete's name or endorsement in connection with the advertisement, promotion, or sale of any product or service other than the type of products included in the definition of Endorsed Products within the Contract Territory. However, Enterprises agrees that Athlete will not endorse any non-athletic footwear or apparel products which are sold under the trademark or tradename of a competitive manufacturer of performance athletic footwear. Enterprises agrees that it shall consult with Company prior to the grant of Athlete's Endorsement to any other Company, showing due regard for Company's considerations. Company, however, shall have no specific right of approval over Enterprises's other endorsement opportunities.

Company further agrees that upon the expiration or other termination of this Agreement, for any cause whatsoever, it will immediately cease using the Athlete's Endorsement, the Athlete's name or any facsimile thereof for advertising, promotional, or any other purpose whatsoever, except pursuant to the following paragraph.

However, Enterprises agrees that the Company shall have the right, for a period not to exceed ninety (90) days following the date of the expiration or earlier termination of this Agreement, to continue to sell and distribute all printed promotional materials and, in the event Enterprises has materially breached this Agreement and Company has purchased media time, broadcast materials featuring Athlete which have been produced by or for the Company and are in inventory prior to the date of such termination ("closing inventory").

6. Use and Ownership of Commercial Materials.
A. Commercials. During the Term of this Agreement, company shall have the exclusive right to broadcast, use, and reuse the television and radio commercial(s) and video and audio materials produced hereunder in the Contract Territory and in any and all media.
B. Print Commercial Materials. During the Term of this Agreement, Company shall have the right to use the Athlete's Endorsement, the Commercial Materials, or any part thereof in print for publication and display in the Contract Territory as Company, subject to the reasonable approval by Enterprises and its business representative, may determine, including all forms of print advertising, cooperative advertising, retail tie-in promotions, point-of-purchase materials, product(s) name(s), billboards, posters, company's Annual Report, materials produced for promotional purposes, Company's Annual Report, materials produced for promotional purposes, internal and/or external sales and marketing pieces, trade contests, trade publications, hang tags and generally to Company's employees and shareholders.

7. Protecting Athlete's Endorsement. Company agrees that it will take all necessary reasonable steps during the Term and any extension thereof to protect Athlete's Endorsement, the Athlete's name or any facsimile thereof, in connection with the promotion, advertisement, and sale of Endorsed Products.

Exhibit 11–14 continued

8. <u>Technical Features</u>. Company acknowledges that for Athlete to successfully compete on a championship level in professional basketball, his shoes may have to incorporate certain technical features that he requires. In this connection, company agrees to consult with Enterprises, its business representatives, Athlete, and/or technical advisor of Enterprises' choice, to make any modifications to the particular model of Company product which he will wear in competitive play. Enterprises agrees that Athlete and his business representatives and/or technical advisor will cooperate with Company with respect to design and technical features in order to facilitate and maximize the working relationship between Company and Enterprises. Enterprises further acknowledges the possibility that such modifications may be accomplished through the use of custom designed orthodic insert devices. Company agrees to furnish Enterprises, its business representatives, and/or technical advisor, for their inspection and review, samples of the model of Company shoes Athlete selects to wear in competitive play. Enterprises, its business representatives, and/or technical advisor agree to promptly notify Company of their evaluation of such sample model Endorsed Product submitted to them for review and Company shall use its genuine best efforts to incorporate Enterprises', its business representatives', Athlete's, and/or technical advisor's recommendations and suggestions into the final design of said shoes.

9. <u>Direction and Control</u>. Athlete's services, pursuant to the terms and conditions of this Agreement, may be on-camera or off-camera as Company may select and shall be rendered under Company's direction and control at such times and locations as shall be designated by Company, subject to reasonable prior notice to Enterprises and subject to Athlete's then existing professional commitments. The commercials to be produced hereunder may be taped, filmed, or recorded in such manner as Company may determine.

10. <u>Premier Spokesman</u>. The parties mutually agree that one of the major inducements for Enterprises to enter into this long term contract is Company's assurance that Athlete will be advertised and promoted as one of its premier "flagships" in basketball, particularly professional basketball, for as long as he continues to be an All-Star player. In this connection, Company agrees to utilize Athlete during the Term as one of its spokesmen and ambassadors in the advertising, promotion, and sale of Company's basketball products and basketball-related products, particularly the articles of Company product contained in the Endorsed Products. In achieving this goal and business purpose, Company agrees to consult with Enterprises and its business representatives, _____, regarding advertising and promotional campaigns and strategy featuring Athlete.

11. <u>Marketing Commitment</u>. The parties acknowledge that the successful introduction to the public and continued profitability of the Company's basketball products and the overall Company-Enterprises relationship mandates an aggressive marketing commitment by Company. It is the specific intent and understanding of the parties that Company will aggressively advertise and promote its relationship with Enterprises and the sale of the Endorsed Products in a manner consistent with Paragraph Six (6) of this Agreement in order to maximize the sales of the Endorsed Products.

12. <u>Use of Endorsed Products</u>. Athlete warrants and represents that he is a user of the Endorsed Products and that, during the Term of this Agreement, he shall continue to use the Endorsed Products exclusively. Enterprises further warrants and represents that all personal endorsements or representations made by or attributed to Athlete with his consent in the Commercial Materials produced hereunder are true and accurate.

13. <u>Athlete to Use Endorsed Products</u>. Enterprises agrees that during the Term and within the Contract Territory Athlete will exclusively wear Company athletic shoes and Company athletic apparel whenever he is playing competitive basketball, posing for basketball photographs, conducting basketball-related promotional interviews, or is otherwise engaged in basketball and athletic-related promotional activities, and shall not wear the athletic shoes and, where appropriate, the athletic apparel of a company competitive with Company.

Exhibit 11-14 continued

14. <u>Endorsed Products for Athlete's Use</u>. During the Term, Company shall supply Enterprises, at no charge, with such quantities of Endorsed Products as Athlete may reasonably request for his own personal use and for the personal use of his immediate family. In addition, company agrees to supply Enterprises at no charge such quantities of Endorsed Products as Athlete may reasonably request for gifts to others, up to an aggregate wholesale value of Four Thousand U.S. Dollars ($4,000) during each Contract Year.

15. <u>Athlete to be Available to Company</u>.

(a) If requested by Company, Enterprises agrees to make Athlete available, for up to twenty (20) days in each Contract Year, at times and places as designated by Company, subject to reasonable prior notice to Enterprises and subject to Athlete's then-existing professional commitments, to make personal appearances, pose for photographs, and otherwise assist Company in the preparation of advertising and promotional materials utilizing the Athlete Endorsement; provided, however, that such appearances shall include the production of radio and television commercials. Company and Enterprises agree that Athlete's obligations for the aforementioned twenty (20) days shall be allocated as follows:

(i)	Up to five (5) consecutive days may take place outside of the United States:
(ii)	Up to nine (9) days may be spent producing television and radio commercials, posing for photographs, and making elite level corporate appearances; and
(iii)	Up to six (6) days may be spent making personal appearances, within the United States.

Each such "day" as used herein, shall be defined as consisting of no more than eight (8) hours per appearance, excluding travel time, for the production of radio and/or television commercials, and no more than four (4) hours excluding travel time, for photography sessions or personal appearances.

(b) Company agrees to reimburse Enterprises for first class, round-trip travel as well as all other reasonable travel, hotel, meals, and expenses incurred by Athlete in connection with such appearances on behalf of Company. On all appearances, Athlete shall be accompanied by a representative of either Company or ProServ, at Company's expense.

16. <u>Optional Appearances</u>. "Optional Appearance" shall mean any appearance by Athlete requested by Company in excess of the twenty (20) appearances per Contract Year, as set forth in Paragraph Fifteen (15) above. For each Optional Appearance, Enterprises shall receive a mutually agreeable fee, payable within ten (10) days following each Optional Appearance. No appearance by Athlete shall be deemed an Optional Appearance unless made upon the prior written request of Company.

17. <u>Approval of Advertising and Promotional Materials</u>. Company agrees to submit to Enterprises and its business representatives, _____

(Name of Company)

for their approval, a copy of all advertising and/or promotional materials utilizing the Athlete's Endorsement at least five (5) working days prior to their release to the general public; and Company further agrees that the same shall not be released without the prior written approval of Enterprises or its business representatives. Enterprises and its business representatives agree, however, that they shall not unreasonably withhold or delay their approval of said materials and that in the absence of disapproval, within five (5) working days of receipt thereof, said advertising and promotional materials shall be deemed approved. Enterprises further agrees that once said materials are deemed approved, Company shall have the right to make multiple uses of said materials without submitting to Enterprises and its business representatives for approval for every such use.

18. <u>Annual Compensation</u>. In consideration for the rights and benefits granted to Company pursuant to this Agreement, Company agrees to pay Enterprises the following amounts as Annual Compensation in each Contract Year:

Exhibit 11–14 continued

	Contract Year	Annual Compensation
First	September 13, 1989 through September 12, 1990	$300,000 (Three Hundred Thousand US Dollars)
Second	September 13, 1990 through September 12, 1991	$300,000 (Three Hundred Thousand US Dollars)
Third	September 13, 1991 through September 12, 1992	$300,000 (Three Hundred Thousand US Dollars)
Fourth	September 13, 1992 through September 12, 1993	$300,000 (Three Hundred Thousand US Dollars)

The Annual Compensation due and owing Enterprises by Company in each Contract Year shall be paid quarterly on or before January 1, April 1, July 1, and October 1 of each Contract Year except that the initial quarterly payment hereunder shall be made on the first business day of January 1990 (i.e. Enterprises' Compensation for the first quarter shall cover the period commencing September 13, 1989 and ending December 31, 1989), and except that the final payment due hereunder shall be made on September 12, 1993, in lieu of the first business day of October 1993, in the amount of a full quarterly payment.

If Company decides, in its sole discretion, to manufacture and market Endorsed Products which bear the name, nickname, likeness, and/or initials of Athlete directly on the Product, or by means of decals or labels, or on packaging therefor (such Endorsed Products to be known as "Signature Products") at any time during the Term, Company agrees to pay Enterprises Royalty Compensation on the net sales of all such Signature Products in an amount to be mutually agreed upon by Company and Enterprises. Such Royalty Compensation shall be deemed to be full consideration for the use by Company of all trademarks owned and registered by Enterprises.

19.   Bonus Compensation. In addition to all other Compensation provided for herein, Company agrees to pay Enterprises the following Bonus Compensation in the applicable Bonus Years (as defined below) if the total amount of sales revenues, less returns, accrued by Company from the sale of (i) _____ brand men's basketball shoes (as
                    (Company)
designated in _____ product line catalogues, but not including children's
                    (Company's)
basketball shoes); and (ii) fifty percent (50%) of the sales revenues, less returns, of
_____ brand women's performance basketball shoes during the applicable Bonus Year equals or exceeds the amounts set forth in the table below, within thirty (30) days of the end of each Bonus Year:

Total Amount of Sales Revenues, Less Returns Accrued by Company From Sale of Products Defined in Paragraph Nineteen (19)	Amount of Bonus For Bonus For Bonus Years One and Two	Amount of Bonus For Bonus Years Three and Four
$250,000,000 through $349,999,999	$100,000	$150,000

Exhibit 11–14 continued

$350,000,000 through $499,999,999	$250,000	$250,000
$500,000,000 and above	$500,000	$500,000

For purposes of this section only, the First Bonus Year shall begin on March 1, 1990, and continue through February 28, 1991; the Second Bonus Year shall begin on March 1, 1991, and continue through February 28, 1992, the Third Bonus Year shall begin on March 1, 1992, and continue through February 28, 1993, and the Fourth Bonus Year shall begin on March 1, 1993, and continue through February 28, 1994.

20.   Reductions

(a) Company shall have the right to reduce the amount of the Annual Compensation payable to Enterprises in accordance with Paragraph Eighteen (18) hereof in the event Athlete plays in fewer than Seventy-Six (76) official NBA regular season games during each Contract Year by an amount equal to Three Thousand Three Hundred Thirty-Three U.S. Dollars ($3,333) for each game missed below Seventy-Six (76) games.

(b) Company shall have the right to reduce the amount of Bonus Compensation payable to Enterprises in accordance with Paragraph Nineteen (19) hereof, in the event Athlete plays in fewer than Fifty (50) official NBA regular season games during any Contract Year, by an amount equal to Fifty Percent (50%) of the Bonus Compensation otherwise payable to Enterprises in such Contract Year. In this connection, it is agreed that each Bonus Year, as described in Paragraph Nineteen (19) above, shall correspond to the same ordinal Contract Year, as defined in Paragraph 1(c) above. For example, the First Bonus Year shall correspond to the First Contract Year.

21. Active Basketball Professional. During the Term of this Agreement, Athlete shall remain active as a National Basketball Association ("NBA") professional basketball player. Company shall have the right, by written notice to Enterprises, to terminate this Agreement and to be relieved of all its obligations hereunder, including, without limitation, its obligation to pay any compensation to Enterprises, if for any reason during the Term of this Agreement, Athlete fails to be on either the active or injured reserve list of any NBA Team.

22. Payments to Enterprises. All payments to be made to Enterprises pursuant to this Agreement shall be made by check in U.S. Dollars and made payable to and mailed to it,

23. Time is of the Essence.

(a) Company acknowledges that time is of the essence in the payment of all compensation due Enterprises and Enterprises acknowledges that time is of the essence in the performance of his obligations. Company hereby agrees that in the event any payment due Enterprises is not received by Enterprises or its business representatives within thirty (30) days of the date set forth in this Agreement for such payment that, in the event written notice has been provided to Company and Company has failed to cure such nonpayment in five (5) days, Enterprises shall be paid interest at the rate of two percent (2%) per month or the maximum interest rate permissible by U.S. law, whichever is less, on the total balance due and owing Enterprises, calculated from the actual payment date set forth herein. In addition, Enterprises shall also have the right and option to terminate this Agreement, effective upon the expiration of thirty (30) days following written notice to Company of his election to so terminate for failure of Company to perform in accordance with the provisions hereof, unless such payment has been received by Enterprises or its business representative within such thirty (30) day period. The reservation of specific rights by Enterprises herein shall not preclude Athlete from exercising any other remedy it may have at law or in equity to enforce the terms of this Agreement.

Exhibit 11–14 continued

(b) Enterprises hereby agrees that if Athlete should fail to appear for the filming of a previously scheduled television commercial without providing Company at least one (1) day's prior notice of his inability to appear, and his failure to appear was not due to a strike, boycott, war, act of God, labor troubles, rift, delay of commercial carriers, restraint of public authority, or for any other reason, similar or dissimilar, he shall reimburse Company for an amount equal to twenty-five percent (25%) of Company's out-of-pocket production costs, for said commercial, not to exceed Seventy-five Thousand U.S. Dollars ($75,000).

24. Insurance. Company shall have the unrestricted right to obtain disability, life, and any other types of insurance policies covering Athlete if Company, in its sole discretion, so chooses, and Enterprises agrees that Company or its designee shall be the beneficiaries of such policies. Promptly following Enterprises's execution of this Agreement, Enterprises agrees that Athlete shall submit to physical examinations, undertake any other reasonable actions, and execute all documents required to assist Company in obtaining such insurance.

25. Special Right of Termination by Enterprises. Enterprises shall have the right to terminate this Agreement upon thirty (30) days prior written notice to Company in the event of the occurrence of any of the following:

(a)   If Company is adjudicated as insolvent, declares
        bankruptcy, or fails to continue its business of selling
        Endorsed Products; or

(b)   If Company fails to make payment to Enterprises of any
        sums due pursuant to this Agreement within the thirty
        (30) days following the receipt by Company of written
        notice from Enterprises that such payment is past due.

26. Special Right of Termination by Company. Enterprises agrees that Company shall have the right to terminate this Agreement upon written notice to Enterprises:

(a)   In the event of Athlete's death during the Term; or

(b)   In the event Athlete is convicted of a felony or other
        crime involving moral turpitude; or

(c)   In the event Athlete is permanently disabled; or

(d)   In the event the commercial value of Athlete is
        substantially impaired by reason of the commission by
        Athlete of any act or acts.

27. Breach.

(a)   By Enterprises: If Enterprises or Athlete at any time
        commits a material breach of any provision of this
        Agreement or at any time Enterprises or Athlete fails or
        refuses to fulfill his obligations hereunder, and fails to
        remedy the same within thirty (30) days after having
        received such notice, then Company may, by written
        notice to Enterprises specifying the default or breach by
        Enterprises or Athlete, terminate this Agreement
        forthwith. In the event this Agreement is terminated
        prior to the expiration of the Term of the Agreement, the
        Company's sole obligation shall be to pay to Enterprises
        the compensation that may be due to Enterprises as of
        the date of termination. Company shall have no further
        obligation or liability to Enterprises except as to any
        amounts due as a result of the use or reuse of any
        commercial(s) broadcast pursuant to this Agreement.

Exhibit 11–14 continued

(b) By Company: In the event Company fails to make any
payment due pursuant to Paragraphs Eighteen (18) and
Nineteen (19) hereof within thirty (30) days after having
received written notice from Enterprises or Enterprises'
representative and fails to remedy same within thirty
(30) days after having received such notice, or Company
at any time commits a material breach of this
Agreement, and fails to remedy the same within thirty
(30) days after having received notice from Enterprises
specifying the breach, then Enterprises may, in addition
to all other remedies available to it in law or equity,
terminate this Agreement by written notice to Company
specifying the default or breach by Company.

28. Right of First Negotiation. During the Term of this Agreement and for a period of
thirty (30) days following the expiration or earlier termination of this Agreement, Enterprises
shall negotiate in good faith only with Company and not with any third party or entity
concerning Athlete's endorsement of any products which are the same as or similar to or
otherwise compete with the Athlete's Endorsed Products. If, at the end of such thirty (30) day
period, Enterprises and Company are unable to reach an agreement concerning Athlete's
endorsement of the Endorsed Products, Company shall submit to Enterprises, in writing, its last
best offer for a new contract. Enterprises shall then be free to negotiate a new contract with
any company of its choice. However, Enterprises agrees that Company shall have the right of
first refusal to match any offer from a new company which is one hundred and twenty-five
percent (125%) or less of the total guaranteed compensation set forth in Company's last best
written offer.

29. No Disparagement. Enterprises agrees that at no time during and after the Term of
this Agreement shall Athlete disparage his association with Company, its products, employees,
advertising agencies or other connected with Company. The provisions of this paragraph shall
survive any termination of this Agreement.

30. Trademarks. In the event that Enterprises should desire to obtain at any time
during the Term a trademark or trademarks in any part of the Contract Territory which include
any part or all of the Athlete's Endorsement, Company, if so requested by Enterprises, shall
execute any and all documents which Enterprises reasonably believes to be necessary and/or
desirable for the successful registration and protection of such trademark or trademarks
registered in the name of Enterprises. Upon use of such trademark, if requested by Company,
Enterprises agrees to grant Company a license for the exclusive use of such trademark during
the Term in connection with the manufacture, advertisement, promotion, distribution, and sale
of Endorsed Products which license shall be coextensive and coterminous with the
endorsement rights granted pursuant to this Agreement with respect to the Athlete
Endorsement. Said license shall not require any increase in the Compensation payable to
Enterprises hereunder, but shall contain any additional provisions, not inconsistent herewith,
which Enterprises reasonably believes are necessary for the protection of such trademark
registered in the name of Enterprises. However, it is understood that Enterprises shall acquire
no interest whatsoever in the Company trade name.

31. Warranties. Company and Enterprises warrant that they are free to enter into this
Agreement and that the rights granted hereunder will not infringe upon the rights of any third
party. Enterprises' execution, delivery, and performance of this Agreement shall not violate the
rights of any third party or breach any agreement in which Enterprises is a party.

32. Indemnity.
(a) Company agrees to protect, indemnify, and save harmless Enterprises and/or
Athlete from and against any and all expenses, damages, claims, suits, actions, judgments, and
costs whatsoever, including attorney's fees, arising out of, or in any way connected with, any

Exhibit 11–14 continued

claim or action including but not limited to personal injury or death resulting from the advertisement, manufacture, distribution, sale, or use of Endorsed Products. The provisions of this paragraph shall survive any termination of this Agreement or any act or omission of Company.

(b) Enterprises and/or Athlete shall at all times indemnify and hold harmless Company and its officers and directors from and against any and all claims, damages, liabilities, costs, and expenses, including reasonable attorneys' fees, arising out of or related to any breach or alleged breach by Enterprises of any representation, warranty, or agreement made by Enterprises herein or any act or omission of Enterprises.

33. Force Majeure. If, for any reason, such as strike, boycott, war, act of God, labor troubles, riot, delay of commercial carriers, restraint of public authority or for any other reason, similar or dissimilar, beyond Company's control, Company shall be unable to use and/or reuse the Commercial Materials or the services of Athlete for any period of time during the Term of this Agreement, then Company shall have the right to extend the Term of this Agreement for an equivalent period thereof, without additional Compensation to Enterprises.

34. Assignment. Neither Enterprises nor Company shall have the right to grant sublicenses hereunder or to otherwise assign, alienate, transfer, encumber, or hypothecate any of its rights or obligations hereunder, except that Enterprises shall have the right to assign the financial benefits hereof and Company hereby consents to such assignment upon receipt by Company of written notice thereof from Enterprises or its business representative.

35. Waiver. The failure of Company and Enterprises at any time, to demand strict performance by the other of any of the terms, covenants, or conditions set forth herein shall not be construed as a continuing waiver or relinquishment thereof, and either party may, at any time, demand strict and complete performance by the other of said terms, covenants, and conditions.

36. Employer/Employee Relationship. Enterprises' and/or Athlete's relationship with Company shall be that of an independent contractor, and nothing contained in this Agreement shall be construed as establishing an employer/employee relationship, partnership, or joint venture between Company and Enterprises and/or Athlete. Accordingly, there shall be no withholding for tax purposes from any payment by Company to Enterprises herein.

37. Notices. All notices and/or submissions hereunder shall be sent via Certified Mail, Return Receipt Requested, to the parties at the following addresses, or such other addresses as may be designated in writing from time to time:

Company

Enterprises

Notices shall be deemed given upon deposit of same with the postal authority.

38. Terms of Agreement Confidential. It is hereby agreed that the specific terms and conditions of this Agreement, including, but not limited to, the financial terms and the duration, are strictly confidential,
and shall not be divulged to any third parties without the prior written consent of both Company and Enterprises, unless otherwise required by law.

39. Significance of Paragraph Headings. Paragraph headings contained hereunder are solely for the purpose of aiding in speedy location of subject matter and are not in any sense to be given weight in the construction of this Agreement. Accordingly, in case of any question

Exhibit 11–14 continued

with respect to the construction of this Agreement, it is to be construed as though paragraph headings had been omitted.

40. <u>Governing Law</u>. This Agreement shall be governed by and construed in accordance with the laws of the Commonwealth of Massachusetts regardless of the fact that any of the parties hereto may be or may become a resident of a different state or jurisdiction. Any suit or action arising shall be filed in a court of competent jurisdiction within the Commonwealth of Massachusetts.

The parties hereby consent to the personal jurisdiction of said court within the Commonwealth of Massachusetts.

41. <u>Severability</u>. If any provision of this Agreement or the application thereof shall be invalid or unenforceable to any extent, the remainder of this Agreement or the application thereof shall not be
affected, and each remaining provision of this Agreement shall be valid and enforceable to the fullest extent permitted by law.

42. <u>Service Unique</u>. The parties hereto agree that the services to be performed by Athlete and the rights granted to Company hereunder are special, unique, extraordinary and impossible to replace, which gives them a peculiar value, the loss of which could not be reasonably or adequately compensated in damages in an action at law, and that Athlete's failure or refusal to perform his obligations hereunder would cause irreparable loss and damage. Should Athlete fail or refuse to perform such obligations Company shall be entitled, in addition to any other legal remedies Company may have, to <u>ex parte</u> injunctive or other equitable relief against Enterprises to prevent the continuance of such failure or refusal or to prevent Athlete from performing services for, or granting rights to other in violation of this Agreement, and Company's exercise of such right shall not constitute a waiver of any other or additional rights at law or pursuant to the terms of this Agreement, it being understood that all such remedies shall be cumulative.

43. <u>Union Membership</u>. Enterprises warrants and represents that Athlete is, and will remain during the Term of this Agreement, a member in good standing of all unions, guilds, or other organizations having jurisdiction over Athlete's services as rendered under this Agreement. In the event Company is assessed or incurs any expense, including, without limitation, any fine or penalty, as a result of Athlete's failure to remain a member in good standing or otherwise comply with the regulations governing members of such union, guild, or other organization, then Enterprises shall immediately pay to such union, guild, or other organization any such expense, fine, or penalty assessed against Company as a result thereof, and if Company actually incurs and pays any such expenses, fine, or penalty, Enterprises will reimburse Company the full amount of any such expense, fine, or penalty, including attorneys' fees incurred or paid by Company.

44. <u>Entire Agreement</u>. This Agreement constitutes the entire understanding between Company and Enterprises and cannot be altered or modified except by an agreement in writing signed by both Company and Enterprises. Upon its execution, this Agreement shall supersede all prior negotiations, understandings, and agreements, whether oral or written, and such prior agreements shall thereupon be null and void and without further legal effect.

IN WITNESS WHEREOF, the parties hereto have caused this Agreement to be executed as of the date first above written.

ACCEPTED AND AGREED:

_____   _____
(Company)   (Player)

_____   _____
Date   Date

Exhibit 11–14 continued

ASSENT AND GUARANTEE

In order to induce   ("Company") to enter into the Agreement dated November 13, 1989 between Company and
("Athlete"), by his signature below, hereby assents to the execution of the Agreement and agrees to be bound by the terms and conditions thereof relating to Athlete. Athlete acknowledges, warrants and represents that he has read and understands the Agreement, that he is free to perform the provisions on his part to be performed pursuant thereto, that he shall comply with all of the provisions thereof which refer to him and that he shall not enter into commitments in conflict therewith. Athlete represents that all warranties and representations made by which concern him are true and that he will fully perform all of obligations under the Agreement. Further, Athlete personally guarantees that will perform all of the terms and conditions of the Agreement on its part to be performed. Finally, Company shall be under no obligation to make any payments whatsoever to Athlete in connection with the services and materials to be provided and/or rendered by Athlete pursuant to the Agreement, except as may be specifically provided in said Agreement.

Date:_____   _____
              (Athlete)

Source: National Basketball Players Association.

Chapter 12

DRUG TESTING IN AMATEUR ATHLETICS

INTRODUCTION

Drug abuse, one of the most emotionally charged and important issues facing athletics and society today, defies easy solutions. The problem of drug abuse has grown at all levels of athletic competition over the past twenty years at a frightening speed, from the interscholastic to the Olympic and intercollegiate levels of competition. In the United States, the increase of drug abuse in athletics reflects a like increase and, to a degree, acceptance of drugs among the general populace. It is a serious issue that includes health considerations, law enforcement problems, and moral/ethical questions for athletes, coaches, and athletic administrators.

The growing awareness of the presence of drug use in the world of athletics has produced drug and alcohol awareness programs. Another outcome has been drug testing of athletes, a topic surrounded by controversy and, more recently, by litigation. Extensive drug testing was implemented at the 1984 Summer Olympic Games in Los Angeles. Drug testing was also approved in 1986 by the NCAA for its championship events. Although the NCAA to date has not required its member schools to implement drug-testing programs, several colleges and universities have done so. Recently drug testing has been instituted at the interscholastic level.

Chapter 12 examines the legal principles in drug testing and takes a look at the general considerations that must be kept in mind by any institution or organization implementing a drug testing program. This chapter also examines the drug testing policies and procedures of the NCAA, NCAA member institutions, interscholastic organizations, and the United States Olympic Committee.

LEGAL PRINCIPLES IN DRUG TESTING

Drug testing in amateur sports organizations raises a number of legal issues, including concerns about an athlete's constitutional rights to due process, equal protection, and privacy, as well as protection against illegal search and seizure and self-incrimination.

The first legal principle Chapter 12 examines is *state action.* A plaintiff must be able to prove state action by a university, association, or other amateur governing body when attempting to invoke constitutional law protection in a drug testing challenge. The university, association, or other amateur governing body must be shown to be part of the federal government, a state government, or an arm or agency of a state government. Private entities are not subject to constitutional challenges.

Another legal principle prevalent in drug testing cases is *due pro-*

cess. Due process was reviewed earlier in this book in the discussion of the Fifth Amendment and the Fourteenth Amendment. Some of the potential claims a plaintiff may argue under the due process theory are an objection to the consent forms for drug testing to be signed by the student-athlete as prerequisite to participation; an appropriate hearing to rebut a positive test result as being inadequate or denied; or an argument that penalties assessed on the grounds of evidence brought forth by an unreliable test were unfair. Under the due process clause, the plaintiff needs to show the deprivation of a significant liberty or property interest. Legal precedent in this area has most often found that a student-athlete does not have a liberty or property interest in athletics.

A third legal principle is *equal protection.* Student-athletes may argue under this principle that they are being singled out, through a student-athlete versus non-student-athlete class distinction. An institution/organization cannot discriminate against a group, such as student-athletes, in a drug testing program unless they can establish a rational relationship for the existence of this classification in order to justify the drug testing program.

Invasion of privacy has also been a legal principle of concern in drug testing programs. This principle relates to excessive or unjustified intrusions into a person's life. The court considers whether an institution or organization has the right to infringe upon a person's right to privacy in order to obtain a urine sample to test. Some courts have found that the compelling state interest in drug testing an individual can outweigh the infringement upon the individual's right to privacy.

In developing a drug testing program one must also be aware of *unreasonable search and seizure.* The Fourth Amendment of the U.S. Constitution provides "[t]he right of the people to be secure in their persons, houses, papers, and effects against unreasonable searches and seizures." The testing of an athlete's urine or blood can constitute a search and therefore must be deemed "reasonable" in order to take place.

A final legal principle is the *Fifth Amendment protection against self-incrimination.* The Fifth Amendment provides that "[n]o person shall be compelled in any criminal case to be a witness against himself." Drug testing programs do not have to be very concerned with this legal principle as courts have consistently held that urine testing and blood testing do not amount to testimonial evidence and thus a student-athlete is not being a witness against himself, or herself in undergoing a drug test.

NOTES ————————————————————————————————

1. In *Shoemaker v. Handel,* 795 F.2d 1136 (3rd Cir. 1986), horse racing jockeys brought an action challenging the New Jersey Racing Commission

regulations which permitted a state racing steward to direct any official, jockey, trainer, or groom to submit to breathalyzer and urine testing to detect alcohol or drug consumption. The jockeys claimed this constituted illegal search and seizure and was a violation of their Fourth Amendment rights. The court of appeals affirmed the district court's decision upholding the regulations by stating the commission's concern for racing integrity warranted the tests, and that as long as the commission keeps the results of the tests confidential there is no violation of the jockeys' rights.

2. In *Horsemen's Benevolent and Protective Association, Inc. v. State Racing Commission*, No. S-4759 (Mass. Dist. Ct. 1989), the plaintiff association brought a case on behalf of trainers, jockeys, owners, blacksmiths, and stable employees challenging the drug testing program instituted by the State Racing Commission in 1986. The plaintiff stated that the drug testing program was an unreasonable search and seizure and therefore unconstitutional according to Massachusetts Constitution law. The burden of proof was placed on the racing commission to prove sufficient compelling reasons for the drug testing policies. The district court ruled for the plaintiff, stating that the racing commission did not present a strong interest in justifying the random testing and reasonable suspicion testing components of the drug testing program.

3. For further information regarding legal challenges to amateur drug testing programs, see the following law review articles.

> (a) Scanlan, "Playing the Drug-Testing Game: College Athletes, Regulatory Institution, and the Structures of Constitutional Argument," 62 *Ind. L. J.* 863 (1987).
>
> (b) Lock and Jennings, "The Constitutionality of Mandatory Student-Athlete Drug Testing Programs: The Bounds of Privacy," 38 *U. Fla. L. Rev.* 581 (1986).
>
> (c) Pernell, "Random Drug Testing of Student Athletes by State Universities in the Wake of *VonRaab* and *Skinner*," 1 *Marq. Sports L. J.* 41 (1990).
>
> (d) Pernell, "Drug Testing of Student Athletes: Some Contract and Tort Implications," 67 *Denv. U. L. Rev.* 279 (1990).

GENERAL CONSIDERATIONS IN DRUG-TESTING PROGRAMS

When an association, institution, or organization considers implementing a drug testing plan for its amateur athletes, a number of serious questions have to be answered:

- Should the organization implement a drug education program? If so, what type of program?
- Should the organization implement a drug testing program? If so, what type of program?
- If the organization has a drug testing policy, it is clearly defined and in writing?

- Does the organization's drug testing policy conform to conference and association rules and regulations?
- Who will conduct the tests?
- Who will be tested?
- Who will pay for the tests?
- Will the tests be random and mandatory, or only for probable cause or reasonable suspicion?
- What constitutes probable cause or reasonable suspicion?
- How much notice should be given before testing begins?
- What types of drugs are to be tested for, and how frequently?
- Should testing include "street drugs" such as marijuana and cocaine, or just performance-enhancing drugs, such as steroids?
- What actions will be taken when an athlete tests positive?
- Will there be an appeal process for a positive test result?
- Is there a method for retesting when the initial results are positive?
- What confidentiality and constitutional law issues does drug testing raise?
- Do the sanctions to be imposed adhere to federal and/or state constitutional law and statutes?

The answers to these critical questions, and many others like them, should provide the basis for a carefully designed drug testing program. A meaningful program should, at the very least, consider the following components:

1. A *policy statement*—The purpose(s) behind the implementation of a drug testing program must be clearly stated from the outset.
2. *Notification of testing*—Before starting a drug testing program it is imperative to give advance written notice to all who could be affected by its implementation. This information should include all policies and procedures utilized by the program, as well as the voluntary consent form, to be signed by the amateur athlete, which allows for urinalysis testing and for the release of test result information.
3. *Identification of banned substances*—The organization needs to decide what types of drugs the athlete will be tested for and provide a comprehensive list of these banned substances to its athletes.
4. A *testing component*—The organization needs to decide whether the drug testing program will be random, in that all athletes are mandatorily required to submit to testing on a periodic basis, or based on reasonable suspicion, so that only ath-

letes suspected of drug involvement are required to submit to testing.

5. *Accuracy of the tests*—No drug testing method is 100 percent accurate so the organization needs to address the problem of "false positives" before implementing a testing program. One sound method of dealing with the problem of false positives results is to conduct a second, more sensitive test on any positive test result. Another possible concern relates to the actual collection process and "chain of custody" used in testing. Detailed security procedures regarding the sample need to be followed, and documented maintenance of the specimen needs to be assured.

6. *Sanctions*—Decisions must also be made as to what action will be taken when an athlete tests positive.

7. *Due process considerations*—When implementing a program, consideration should also be given to an athlete's right to have a hearing in response to a positive test result or to challenge penalties imposed as a result of a positive test.

8. *Confidentiality issues*—Steps should be taken to be sure that the procedures outlined in the program will not violate the privacy of the athlete.

The NCAA Drug Testing Program was revised in January of 1989 with the addition of a voluntary off-season drug testing program. The testing program was revised again with the adoption of Proposal 53 at the 1990 NCAA Convention. Proposal 53 replaced the voluntary off-season testing program for schools that sponsor football in Divisions I-A and I-AA. Only athletes in the sport of football and indoor or outdoor track and field at Division I institutions are tested, and these athletes can be tested at any time from August until the end of their institution's spring term. The postseason testing program at NCAA championship events and football bowl games remains intact.

NOTE ───

1. For further information on drug testing in amateur athletics, see the following law review articles.

(a) Brock and McKenna, "Drug Testing in Sports," 92 *Dick. L. Rev.* 505 (1988).

(b) Cochran, "Drug Testing of Athletes and the United States Constitution: Crisis and Conflict," 92 *Dick. L. Rev.* 571 (1988).

(c) Rose and Girard, "Drug Testing in Professional and College Sports," 36 *Kan. L. Rev.* 787 (1988).

(d) Rose, "Mandatory Drug Testing of College Athletes: Are Athletes Being Denied Their Constitutional Rights?" 16 *Pepp. L. Rev.* 45 (1988).

(e) Note, "Does the National Collegiate Athletic Association's Drug

Testing Program Test Positive If It Is Subjected to Constitutional Scrutiny?" 37 *Drake L. Rev.* 83 (1987–88).

(f) Comment, "Random Urinalysis: Violating the Athlete's Individual Rights?" 30 *Howard L. J.* 93 (1987).

(g) Ford, "Drugs, Athletes, and the NCAA: A Proposed Rule for Mandatory Drug Testing in College Athletics," 18 *J. Marshall L. Rev.* 205 (1984).

(h) Comment, "An Analysis of Public College Athlete Drug Testing Programs Through the Unconstitutional Condition Doctrine and the 4th Amendment," 60 *S. Cal. L. Rev.* 815 (1987).

(i) Covell and Gibbs, "Drug Testing and the College Athlete," 23 *Creighton L. Rev.* 1 (1989–90).

(j) Note, "The Drug Testing of College Athletes," 16 *J. C. & U. L.* 325 (1988).

(k) Note, "Drug Testing: The Toughest Competition an Athlete Ever Faces," 13 *T. Marshall L. Rev.* 143 (1987–88).

(l) McBride, "The NCAA Drug Testing Program and the California Constitution: Has California Expanded the Right to Privacy?" 23 *U. S. F. L. Rev.* 253 (1989).

THE NCAA DRUG-TESTING PROGRAM

In January 1986, the NCAA membership at its annual convention agreed to begin a drug-testing program for NCAA-sanctioned championships and other events such as football bowl games.

The decision to implement a drug-testing policy was not easily reached. Chief among the dissenting views of the policy is that it singles out the student-athlete, who may or may not be a scholarship athlete, to undergo urine testing that is not required of any other student who lives on campus and participates in student activities. In other words, why should an athlete be treated any differently from a member of the band, drama society, or glee club? However, by passage of the drug-testing policy, the NCAA has made acceptance of a possible postseason mandatory urine test a requirement before a student-athlete can compete in his or her sport on an intercollegiate level. In fact, each year the student-athlete is required to sign a student consent form agreeing to this policy.

The NCAA drug-testing plan is expensive. In 1986–87 the testing program cost $950,000 for approximately 3,000 tests. In addition, $430,000 was budgeted for drug education programs for NCAA athletes. For the 1987–88 testing program, $1,965,000 was budgeted by the NCAA for drug testing and education, 2.5 percent of the NCAA's overall budget. For the 1990–91 drug testing efforts the NCAA budgeted a total of $3.2 million. Half of this amount was used in the NCAA championship events and postseason drug-testing program, and the other $1.6 million in the Proposal 53 year-round drug testing program. Additional costs accrue to individual schools that choose to implement their own programs.

Critics of the NCAA's drug-testing program claim that it does not:

1. Safeguard student-athletes' procedural rights, especially in re-gard to the appeal process for a positive test.
2. Safeguard the student's privacy rights, especially when the me-dia become aware of a test result.
3. Give the student-athletes sufficient information before they sign the mandatory consent form.
4. Ensure that the school will represent the student-athlete's in-terests and rights when an athlete tests positive.

In addition, many coaches have criticized the plan for the effect it has on a team when team members must participate in drug testing after an NCAA tournament or a championship victory. John Chaney, basketball coach at Temple University, noted that the NCAA drug-testing program is "just another example of their [NCAA] imposing themselves into becoming Big Brother." Chaney noted further:

> What they're trying to do is overcome something that is already inherent in our society, and there's no way they can do that. They are applying a tourniquet to a wound that requires a much greater covering.
>
> You can't take the evils of society at large and solve them through sports. The education has to come at a much lower level, in the grade schools. Drug testing here just diverts attention from the areas where we should be concentrating. We're dibbling and dabbling here. And what are we going to find? The majority of players are clean livers.

The NCAA drug-testing plan is constantly evolving and being mod-ified, but as offered presents the athletic administrator with the basic materials needed to make an informed decision when dealing with coaches, medical staff, student-athletes, and the NCAA about the plan. Remember, these policies apply only to the NCAA championships and sanctioned events.

Drugs Banned by the NCAA

The NCAA provides a list of banned substances to its membership. More than seventy drugs in six different categories are included in this list. These are drugs that the NCAA considers to be "performance-enhancing and/or potentially harmful to the health and safety of the student-athlete." The NCAA refers to the use of any of the banned substances as "doping." Any student-athlete who tests positive will be subject to disciplinary action, including being declared ineligible for further participation in postseason and regular season competition during the period ending one calendar year after the student-athlete's positive drug test result and until the student-athlete retests negative, and until restored to eligibility by the NCAA Eligibility Committee (*1993–94 NCAA Manual*, Bylaw 18.4.1.5.1). A brief description of the six categories follows. Examples of specific drugs in each of these categories are listed in Exhibit 12–1.

1. *Psychomotor and central nervous system stimulants:* Psychomotor stimulants prevent or delay fatigue, mask pain, and increase self-confidence and aggressiveness. The danger in masking pain is that serious injury can occur. Preventing or delaying fatigue can lead to heat exhaustion, heat stroke, and even death. Central nervous system (CNS) stimulants increase endurance because they stimulate respiration and heart rate. The danger associated with their use in sports is that by increasing heart rate they also increase blood pressure and can cause dehydration, cerebral hemorrhage, stroke, and other cardiac irregularities that could lead to heart arrest or even death.

2. *Anabolic steroids:* It has long been believed that anabolic steroids increase muscle mass. They are a derivative of the male hormone testosterone. Some serious side effects can occur, including cardiac disorders and bone growth damage in children.

3. *Substances banned for specific sports:* Alcohol is sometimes used in rifle competitions to minimize tremor in the shooter's arms. Beta blockers are sometimes used to decrease the heart rate and lower the blood pressure so that the shooter can get off a shot between heart contractions and pulsations in the arm. Both are banned by the NCAA. Beta blockers are known to affect the functioning of the cardiovascular system adversely.

4. *Diuretics:* Diuretics remove body fluids quickly and thus lower body weight. They are used by athletes who need to make weight classifications. They are also used to flush out other drugs that an athlete might have been taking prior to competition. The problem with their use is that electrolytes are removed along with body fluids and an upset electrolyte balance can lead to cardiac arrest.

5. *Street drugs:* Drugs such as cocaine, marijuana, heroin, and amphetamines are used mainly outside the sports setting. They bring about a sense of euphoria and relax inhibition. In the sports setting, they prevent or delay fatigue and mask pain. In or out of sports, the use of these substances can cause memory im-

Exhibit 12–1
NCAA Banned Drugs List

Bylaw 31.2.3.1 Banned Drugs. The following is the list of banned-drugs classes: (Revised: 8/15/89, 7/10/90, 12/3/90. 5/4/92)

(a)   Stimulants:

amiphenazole   meclofenoxate
amphetamine   methamphetamine
bemigride   methylphenidate
benzphetamine   nikethamide
caffeine (1)   pemoline
chlorphentermine   pentetrazol
cocaine   phendimetrazine
cropropamide   phenmetrazine
crothetamide   phentermine
diethylpropion   picrotoxine
dimethylamphetamine   pipradol
doxapram   prolintane
ethamivan   strychnine
ethylamphetamine   and related compounds
fencamfamine

(b)   Anabolic steroids:

boldenone   nandrolone
clostebol   norethandrolone
dehydrochlormethyl-testosterone   oxandrolone
dromostanolone   oxymesterone
fluoxymesterone   oxymetholone
mesterolone   stanozolol
methandienone   testosterone (2)
methenolone   and related compounds
methyltestosterone

(c)   Substances banned for specific sports:

Rifle: alcohol   pindolol
        atenolol   propranolol
        metoprolol   timolol
        nadolol   and related compounds

(d)   Diuretics:

acetazolamide   furosemide
bendroflumethiazide   hydrochlorothiazide
benzthiazide   hydroflumethiazide
bumetanide   methyclothiazide
chlorothiazide   metolazone
chlorthalidone   polythiazide
ethacrynic acid   quinethazone
flumethiazide   spironolactone
triamterene   and related compounds
trichlormethiazide

(e)   Street drugs:

heroin   THC (tetrahydrocannabinol) (3)
marijuana (3)

Exhibit 12–1 continued

(f)   Peptide hormones and analogues:

     growth hormone   corticotrophin (ACTH)
      (HGH, somatotrophin)   chorionic gonadotrophin
                                       (HCG - human chorionic gonadotrophin)
     All the respective releasing factors of the above-mentioned substances also are banned.
     erythropoietin (EPO)

(g)   Definition of positive depends on the following:

     (1) for caffeine - if the concentration in the urine exceeds 15 micrograms/ml.
     (2) for testosterone - if the administration of testosterone or the use of any other
          manipulation has the result of increasing the ratio of the total concentration of
          testoterone to that of epitestosterone in the urine to grater than 6:1.
     (3) for marijuana and THC - if the concentration in the urine of THC metabolite exceeds
          25 nanograms/ml.

Source: 1993–94 NCAA Manual

pairment, respiratory distress, convulsions, coma, and even death.

6. *Peptide hormones and analogues:* The NCAA added this category to be in agreement with banned drugs by the USOC. This group consists of chemically produced drugs which have similar effects to already existing substances in the body (i.e., growth hormone and other hormones which increase testosterone and other steroids) and increase the effects of these steroids in the body.

The NCAA bans these drugs for either of two reasons—because they illegally enhance performance or because they are potentially harmful to the student-athlete's health. The practice of blood doping; the intravenous injection of whole blood, packed red blood cells, or blood substitutes; as well as the use of growth hormone, human, animal, or synthetic, are also prohibited by the NCAA.

There are two general exceptions to the NCAA banned drug list. These exceptions involve the use of local anesthetics and asthma- or exercise-induced bronchospasm medications. As long as they are administered correctly and their use is medically justified, the NCAA approves them.

The NCAA drug testing program has come under scrutiny in the courts as a result of complaints filed by student-athletes that the program is an invasion of privacy, an infringement of their equal protection rights, and an unreasonable search and seizure. One noteworthy case, *Hill v. NCAA*, 273 Cal. Rptr. 402 (Cal. Dist. Ct. App. 1990), involved a student-athlete at Stanford University who complained that the NCAA's drug testing collection of the urine sample and consent form, which asked for disclosure of medical and sexual information from the student-athlete, were invasions of the right to privacy. The court concurred with the student-athlete and permanently enjoined the NCAA from enforcing its drug testing consent forms requirement for the student-athletes at Stanford University. See note 1.

Implementation of the NCAA Drug-Testing Program

The NCAA Executive Committee established a drug-testing committee to oversee the implementation of its drug-testing program. The committee conducts drug education programs for its member schools as was mentioned earlier. It also trains crew chiefs to conduct the actual tests at selected championship events. At these events, student-athletes may be chosen for drug testing in accordance with the following NCAA selection criteria:

4.0	*Championship, Institution and Student-Athlete Selection*
4.1.	The method for selecting championships, institutions or student-athletes to be tested will be recommended by the NCAA competitive safeguards committee, approved by the Executive Committee in advance of the testing occasion, and implemented by the NCAA staff and assigned crew chiefs. All student-athletes are subject to testing.
4.1.1.	Student-athletes competing in the sport of football or indoor or outdoor track and field at NCAA Division I institutions are subject to year-round testing according to the provisions of Section 1.3.1.1.
4.1.2.	All student-athletes are subject to NCAA testing at NCAA championships or in conjunction with postseason bowl events.
4.2.	At NCAA individual/team championships events, choice of student-athletes may be based on NCAA-approved random selection or position of finish. Crew chiefs will be notified which method or combination of methods have been approved by the Executive Committee or the executive director acting for the Executive Committee.
4.3.	At NCAA team championships, student-athletes may be selected on the basis of playing time, position, and/or an NCAA-approved random selection. Crew chiefs will be notified which method or combination of methods have been approved by the Executive Committee or the executive director acting for the Executive Committee.

4.4.	In nonchampionship testing events, student-athletes may be selected on the basis of position, athletics financial-aid status, playing time, an NCAA-approved random selection or any combination thereof.
4.4.1.	Student-athletes will be selected by the NCAA from the official institutional squad list.
4.4.1.1.	Students listed on the squad list who have exhausted their eligibility or who have career-ending injuries will not be selected by the NCAA.
4.5.	If the use of a banned substance is suspected, the NCAA will have the authority to select specific additional student-athletes to be tested.
4.6.	Persons who test positive and subsequently restore eligibility will automatically be tested at any subsequent NCAA championship at which they appear and at which drug testing is being conducted or at any subsequent nonchampionship NCAA testing event.
4.6.1.	It is the responsibility of the institution to notify the drug-testing crew chief that a student-athlete who is present must be tested to satisfy the retesting requirement as outlined in Section 4.6.
4.7.	Student-athletes may be tested prior to, during or after NCAA championships and certified postseason football bowl games. (*1992–93 NCAA Drug Testing Program Protocol*)

A student-athlete who has been selected for drug testing must undergo the following specimen-collection procedures as specified by the NCAA:

6.0.	*Specimen-Collection Procedures*
6.1.	Only those persons authorized by the crew chief will be allowed in the collection station.
6.1.1.	The crew chief may release a sick or injured student-athlete from the collection station or may release a student-athlete to return to competition or to meet academic obligations only after appropriate arrangements for having the student-athlete tested have been made and documented on the Student-Athlete Signature Form.
6.2.	Upon entering the collection station, the student-athlete will be identified by the crew chief or a designate and will record time of arrival and name on the Student-Athlete Roster Form.
6.2.1.	The student-athlete will provide the crew chief or a designate with the Student-Athlete Notification Form.
6.2.2.	When ready to urinate, the student-athlete will select a beaker that is sealed in a plastic bag from a supply of such and will record his/her initials on the beaker's lid.

6.2.3.   A crew member will monitor the furnishing of the specimen by observation in order to assure the integrity of the specimen until a specimen of at least 80 ml is provided.

6.2.4.   Fluids given student-athletes who have difficulty voiding must be from sealed containers (certified by the crew chief) that are opened and consumed in the station. These fluids must be caffeine- and alcohol-free.

6.2.4.1.   Drug-testing crews will not provide food to student-athletes. Student-athletes or their institutions may supply food subject to the approval of the crew chief.

6.2.5.   If the specimen is incomplete the student-athlete must remain in the collection station under observation of a crew member until the sample is completed. During this period, the student-athlete is responsible for keeping the collection beaker covered and controlled.

6.2.6.   Once a specimen (at least 80 ml) is provided, the student-athlete will select a numbered specimen-collection kit, which includes a Student-Athlete Signature Form, from a supply of such.

6.2.6.1.   The crew member who monitored the furnishing of the specimen by observation will sign the Student-Athlete Signature Form.

6.2.6.2.   The student-athlete will pour at least 60 ml of the specimen into the "A bottle" and most of the remaining amount in to the "B bottle," leaving a small amount in the beaker.

6.2.6.3.   The student-athlete will place the cap on each bottle; the crew member will then seal each bottle in the required manner under the observation of the student-athlete and witness (if present) and seal each bottle in a plastic security container.

6.2.7.   A crew member will check the specific gravity and the pH of the urine remaining in the beaker.

6.2.7.1.   This finding is recorded on the Student-Athlete Signature Form. If the urine has a specific gravity below 1.010 or is alkaline (greater than 7.5), the student-athlete must remain in the station until an adequate specimen is provided.

6.2.7.1.1.   The student-athlete will select a new beaker and new specimen-collection kit for each specimen collected.

6.2.8.   All specimens provided by the student-athlete will be sent to the laboratory. The final determination of specimen adequacy will be made by the laboratory.

6.3.   The student-athlete and witness (if present) will sign the Student-Athlete Signature Form, certifying that the procedures were followed as described in the protocol. Any deviation from the procedures must be described and recorded on the Student-Athlete Signature Form at that time. If deviations are alleged, the student-athlete will be required to provide another specimen.

6.3.1.	Failure to sign the Student-Athlete Notification Form or the Student-Athlete Signature Form, to arrive at the collection station at the designated time without justification or to provide a urine specimen according to protocol is cause for the same action(s) as evidence of use of a banned substance. The crew chief will inform the student-athlete of these implications (in the presence of witnesses) and record such on the Student-Athlete Signature Form. If the student-athlete is not available, the crew chief will notify the NCAA official responsible for administration of the event or an institutional representative. The student-athlete will be considered to have withdrawn consent and will be ineligible on that basis.
6.3.2.	The crew member will sign the Student-Athlete Signature Form, give the student-athlete or a designee a copy and secure all remaining copies. The compiled Student-Athlete Signature Forms constitute the "Master Code" for that drug testing.
6.3.2.1.	The laboratory's copy of the Student-Athlete Signature Form does not contain the name of the student-athlete.
6.4.	All sealed specimens will be secured in an NCAA shipping case. The crew chief will put the laboratory copy of the Student-Athlete Signature Form in the case, and prepare the case for forwarding.
6.5.	After the collection has been completed, the specimens will be forwarded to the laboratory, the remaining supplies returned, and all copies of all forms forwarded to the designated persons.

(*1992–93 NCAA Drug Testing Program Protocol*)

Once the testing has been completed and the urine samples have been sealed, they are shipped to an NCAA-approved laboratory for analysis. The laboratories adhere to the following strict NCAA procedures regarding notification of results:

8.0.	*Notification of Results and Appeal Process*
8.1.	The laboratory will use a portion of specimen A for its initial analysis.
8.1.1.	Analysis will consist of sample preparation, instrument analysis and data interpretation.
8.1.2.	The laboratory director or designated certifying scientist will review all results showing a banned substance and/or metabolite(s) in specimen A.
8.1.3.	By facsimile transmission, the laboratory will inform the NCAA group executive for administration and finance or a designate of the results by each respective code number. Subsequently, the laboratory will mail the corresponding written report to the NCAA group executive director for administration and finance or designate.

8.2.   Upon receipt of the laboratory report, the NCAA group ex-
             ecutive director for administration and finance or a designate
             will break the number code to identify any individuals with
             positive findings.

8.2.1.   For NCAA individual/team championships, if a member in-
             stitution has not heard from the NCAA within 30 days after
             the specimen was provided, the test results will be assumed
             to be negative.

8.2.2.   For student-athletes who have a positive finding, the NCAA
             group executive director for administration and finance or a
             designate will contact the director of athletics or a designate
             by telephone as soon as possible. The telephone contact will
             be followed by "overnight/signature required" letters
             (marked "confidential") to the chief executive officer and the
             director of athletics. The institution shall notify the student-
             athlete of the finding.

8.2.2.1.   The NCAA group executive director for administration and
             finance or a designate will, during the telephone conversa-
             tion, advise the director of athletics that specimen B must
             be tested within 24 hours after the telephone notification,
             that any appeal must be held on the same day that specimen
             B results become known and that the student-athlete may
             be present at the opening of specimen B.

8.2.2.2.   The institution will be given the option to have the student-
             athlete represented at the laboratory for the opening of spec-
             imen B. Notification by the institution of intent to have the
             student-athlete represented must be given to the NCAA
             within 12 hours of the initial notification.

8.2.2.3.   If the institution desires representation but cannot arrange
             for such representation in 24 hours, the NCAA will arrange
             for a surrogate to attend the opening of specimen B.

8.2.2.3.1.   The surrogate will not otherwise be involved with the anal-
             ysis of the specimen.

8.2.2.4.   The student-athlete, institution's representative or the sur-
             rogate will attest by signature as to the code number on the
             bottle of specimen B, that the security seals have not been
             broken, and that there is no evidence of tampering.

8.2.2.5.   Sample preparation for specimen B analysis will be con-
             ducted by a laboratory staff member other than the individual
             who prepared the student-athlete's specimen A.

8.2.2.6.   Specimen B findings will be final subject to the results of
             any appeal. By facsimile transmission, the laboratory will
             inform the NCAA of the results. Subsequently, the laboratory
             will mail the corresponding written report to the NCAA
             group executive director for administration and finance or
             designate.

8.2.2.7.   A positive finding may be appealed by the institution to the competitive safeguards committee or a subcommittee thereof. The institution shall notify the student-athlete of the positive test and of the right to appeal.

8.2.2.7.1.   The institution shall appeal if so requested by the student-athlete.

8.2.2.7.2.   Such an appeal will be conducted by telephone conference on the date that the laboratory's test results of specimen B are known, with the student-athlete being given the opportunity to participate therein. A technical expert may serve as a consultant to the committee in connection with such appeals. Notifications by the institution of intent to appeal must be given to the NCAA within 12 hours of the initial notification.

8.2.2.7.3.   The crew chief may serve as a consultant to the committee in appeal phone calls involving matters of collection protocol.

8.2.3.   Time constraints regarding notification of results, B specimen testing and appeal may be modified by the institution and by the NCAA upon mutual agreement of both.

8.3.   The NCAA will notify the institution's chief executive officer and director of athletics of the findings and the result of any appeal. This notification will be initiated by telephone to the director of athletics. This will be followed by another "overnight/signature-required" letter (marked "confidential") to the chief executive officer and the director of athletics. It is the institution's responsibility to inform the student-athlete. At this point, normal NCAA eligibility procedures will apply.

8.3.1.   The NCAA may release the results of a student-athlete's final positive test to the involved institution's conference office upon the approval of the institution.

8.4.   The NCAA group executive director for administration and finance or designate will send a confidential report of aggregate findings to the NCAA executive director for reporting to the NCAA Executive Committee. No report of aggregate data will be otherwise released without the approval of the Executive Committee.

                (*1992–93 NCAA Drug Testing Program Protocol*)

The process of sample collection and notification of results has been targeted in complaints against the NCAA regarding their drug testing program. In one particular case, *Premock v. Montana*, Case No. 74947/40 (Mont. Dist. Ct. 1991), the student-athlete challenged an NCAA drug test in which he was found positive for steroid use. The judge found that the NCAA's goal of extinguishing drugs from college sports

was commendable but that the drug testing method use in this case
was deplorable (see note 5).

NOTES _____

1. In *Jennifer Hill, et al. v. National Collegiate Athletic Ass'n*, 273 Cal.
Rptr. 402 (Cal. Dist. Ct. App. 1990), the California District Court of Appeals
affirmed a lower court's decision and ruled there was an invasion of privacy
against Stanford student-athletes Hill and McKeever in regard to certain
NCAA drug-testing policies and procedures. The court ruled that on the basis
of the California Constitution, the NCAA's monitored taking of urine samples
for drug testing along with its requirement of disclosure of medical and sexual
information were clearly invasions of the right to privacy. The NCAA is permanently enjoined from enforcing its requirement that Stanford obtain signed
drug testing consent forms from its athletes or requiring Stanford athletes to
participate in the NCAA drug testing program. The NCAA is appealing this
decision.

2. In *Bally v. National Collegiate Athletic Ass'n*, 707 F. Supp. 52 (D. Mass.
1988), the Superior Court of Massachusetts ruled that the NCAA consent form
did not infringe on any rights secured by the Massachusetts Civil Rights Act
and that the consent form by itself does not subject the plaintiff to an illegal
search and seizure or violate his or her right to privacy.

3. In *Barbay v. National Collegiate Athletic Ass'n*, No. 86-5697 (La. Dist.
Ct. 1987), the plaintiff, a football player at Louisiana State University, tested
positive for steroids prior to the January 1987 Sugar Bowl and was thus prohibited from competing in the bowl game by the NCAA. The plaintiff sought
a preliminary injunction preventing the NCAA from enforcing this penalty
based on a violation of his Fourteenth Amendment rights. The plaintiff stated
that the NCAA penalty prohibiting student-athletes from competing in postseason competition after testing positive for drugs was instituted after he had
taken steroids to help in his rehabilitation of a knee injury. He should not be
punished, therefore, for taking steroids prior to the establishment of this penalty. The district court first found that there was no state action; thus the
plaintiff had no claim against the NCAA. In addition, the plaintiff could not
demonstrate an irreparable harm if a ruling in his favor was not granted;
therefore, the court denied the plaintiff's petition for a preliminary injunction.

4. In *Mira v. National Collegiate Athletic Ass'n*, No. 87-55213 (Fla. Dist.
Ct. 1988), the plaintiff sought a temporary and permanent restraining order
preventing the NCAA from enforcing its drug testing program. The plaintiff
argued that the drug testing program violated the plaintiffs constitutional
rights. The district court ruled that there was no state action and therefore no
claim upon which it could base relief.

5. In *Premock v. Montana*, Case No. 74947/40 (Mont. Dist. Ct. 1991), the
student-athlete brought a complaint regarding the drug testing protocol that
was used, which resulted in a positive drug test result. The judge found that,
although the NCAA's "goal of drug-free sports is commendable, their methods
of achieving that goal are deplorable." The judge found that the drug testing
area lacked the control required for a credible collection process (Premock
had left the collection area for several minutes and his urine sample was left

unattended during that time); there were violations of the NCAA's chain-of-custody requirements (the NCAA could not account for the specimens from the time they reached the campus of UCLA, where there were to be tested, until they arrived at the drug-testing laboratory); the lab breached the protocol in the testing and retesting process (the urine analysis test on both samples was conducted by the same person and took more than twenty-four days to complete); and the NCAA failed to notify the university of Premock's test results until thirty-three days after the sample was collected. Premock won a restraining order from the district court judge restoring his eligibility, but Premock had already completed his eligibility and the case was settled out of court. The settlement means the case sets no official legal precedent.

6. Many athletic conferences have taken positions on the drug testing issue from providing statements regarding drug usage in their handbooks to implementing their own drug testing programs. The Southwest Conference (SWC) has listed drug testing protocols in three different testing program areas for its members. The first area is a steroid testing program for all sports conducted in the fall semester. Thirty student-athletes in the sport of football and twenty "top" returning athletes in all other sports are selected to undergo this test. The student-athletes are notified no more than forty-eight hours in advance of the test and the substances tested for include all NCAA-banned anabolic steroids. The second area includes a street drug testing program for SWC men's and women's basketball tournaments for NCAA-banned street drugs. The final area involves a spring steroid testing program for all sports. Twenty-four athletes from all sports are selected to be tested during the spring semester for NCAA-banned anabolic steroids.

INTERCOLLEGIATE DRUG-TESTING PROGRAMS

The NCAA, as previously discussed, passed legislation which allows it to test for drugs at events over which it has jurisdiction. This includes all NCAA-sponsored championships, such as the NCAA basketball tournament and the NCAA track and field championships. It also covers football bowl games which the NCAA is responsible for sanctioning. The NCAA, however, has not taken jurisdiction for drug testing of its member institutions for non-NCAA championship events, primarily the regular season events.

The NCAA has encouraged, but not mandated, that member institutions implement some type of drug-testing program. A 1990 NCAA Drug Education and Drug Testing survey, which was conducted by the NCAA Committee on Competitive Safeguards and Medical Aspects of Sports, showed that drug education and testing programs have been increasing at the collegiate level since 1984. Over half, 54 percent, of the schools surveyed responded that they had a drug/alcohol education program. An additional 10 percent of the institutions are actively planning to begin a program. The percentage of institutions that have instituted a drug testing program also increased dramatically from 10 percent in 1984 to 36 percent in 1990.

NCAA member institutions have taken a varied approach to the issue of drug testing. These approaches can be categorized as follows:

1. No drug-testing or drug education programs.
2. An educational program on the drug issue, but no drug testing.
3. Mandatory random drug testing.
4. Testing only for street drugs such as marijuana and cocaine.
5. Testing only for performance-enhancing drugs such as steroids.

The characteristics of a majority of institutional drug testing programs include the programs' being mandatory for student-athletes but exclude coaches and other staff from testing. The programs provide a specific written policy on testing to student-athletes and require the student-athlete to sign an institutional waiver or consent to testing form.

Institutional drug testing programs have come under scrutiny by student-athletes, much as the NCAA drug testing program has, for possible violations of the student-athlete's constitutional rights. Institutions will face challenges when they require athletes to sign a NCAA Drug-Testing Consent Form in order to compete, a requirement placed on the institution by the NCAA, when the student-athlete refuses to sign the form, claiming that drug testing is a violation of their constitutional rights.

NOTES —————————————————————————————————————

1. In *O'Halloran v. University of Washington*, 679 F. Supp. 997 (W.D. Wash. 1988), a student-athlete at the University of Washington claimed the NCAA and the school's drug testing program were violating her privacy and conducting an unreasonable search and seizure. The district court found that the collection of a urine sample was a "search" for purposes of the Fourth Amendment, but that the compelling interest of the university and the NCAA in implementing the drug testing program far outweighed the hardships on the student-athlete. The court ruled for the university.

2. In *Bally v. Northeastern University*, 532 N.E.2d 49 (Mass. Sup. Jud. Ct. 1989), a student-athlete challenged the university's drug testing program by claiming the university's policy of requiring student-athletes to consent to drug testing as a condition of participating in intercollegiate athletics was a violation of civil rights, and the right to privacy and constituted a breach of contract. The court ruled for the university and upheld the constitutionality of the drug testing program.

3. In *Derdeyn v. University of Colorado*, No. 86 CV 2245 (Colo. Dist. Ct. 1989), the plaintiff argued that the various tests performed on student-athletes as part of the University of Colorado's drug testing program were a violation of an individual's right against unreasonable search and seizure and were

therefore unconstitutional. The district court found that the drug testing program tests were in violation of constitutional rights by involving an unreasonable search because warrant and probable cause requirements of the Fourth Amendment were not met. Exceptions could be made in terms of warrant and probable cause requirements if the university could prove the drug testing program fulfilled a compelling special need, the court determined that the university failed to prove a compelling special need. The drug testing program at the University of Colorado was therefore declared unconstitutional.

INTERSCHOLASTIC DRUG-TESTING PROGRAMS

Throughout much of the 1980s, drug testing was almost nonexistent at the interscholastic level. However, as evidence on the use and abuse of "street drugs," alcohol, performance-enhancing drugs, and other substances in high schools (see note 1) mounted, increasing numbers of schools and school districts have turned to an education/testing alternative to combat this problem. As Robert Morris, executive director of the National High School Athletic Coaches Association, noted: "Schools are beginning to look at testing programs as a tool to rid their schools of these dangerous drugs. A complete program of education and testing can move us forward."

One of the earliest steps to fight the problem of drugs and alcohol at the interscholastic level was taken by the National Federation of State High School Associations with the formation of TARGET. This service to schools across the country was organized as a nonprofit corporation after the federation's National Council passed a resolution concerning mind-altering chemicals in 1984. TARGET was established to offer "a long-term commitment to help America's youth cope with alcohol and other drugs."

Set up as a multifaceted supplement and complement to programs in schools throughout the country, TARGET seeks to utilize the unique capabilities of the federation to offer a drug and alcohol resource center. The range of services extended by this clearinghouse include education/prevention programs, leadership training, audiovisual aids, speaker lists, and even drug and alcohol treatment insurance coverage for students. As an outgrowth of this response to problems of drugs and alcohol at the interscholastic level, many state associations and regional groups have established modified TARGET programs to aid in the prevention of drug abuse.

Some school systems have gone further, deciding to test student-athletes for drugs. Greeneville High School, in Greeneville, Tennessee, for example, has implemented an interscholastic drug testing program. The stated purposes of this drug education and testing program include the following:

1. To employ education, testing, and counseling *to deter drug use*, and where deterrence is unsuccessful, to terminate participation in athletics.
2. To educate students about the physiological and psychological dangers inherent in the misuse of alcohol and other drugs.
3. To protect students from the health-related risks inherent in the misuse of alcohol and other drugs.
4. To protect students, and others with whom they compete, from potential injury as a result of the misuse of alcohol and other drugs.
5. To provide a testing program to identify student-athletes who are misusing drugs and assist them, through education and counseling, before they injure themselves or others, or become physiologically or psychologically dependent.
6. To assure athletes, parents, and the community that the health and academic progress of each of its athletes is Greeneville High School's primary goal.
7. To reiterate to the entire school community that the misuse of alcohol and other drugs is not condoned by school officials.
8. To offer student-athletes additional incentives to say no to alcohol and other drugs.

Under the Greeneville program, all athletes are given urinalysis tests at the time of their preparticipation physical. The samples are tested for amphetamines, barbiturates, marijuana, cocaine, and PCP. Throughout the year, athletes are then subjected to random testing once a month. Any positive result is confirmed by use of the highly sensitive gas chromatography/mass spectrometry test. A first-time confirmed positive test result serves as a warning to the student-athlete, and the parents, coach, trainer, athletic director, and team physician are notified of the results. Drug-counseling options are also presented at this time. A second test is then conducted in thirty days. A positive result would initiate a similar notification process, as well as further counseling and an immediate suspension from the team. A student-athlete can apply for reinstatement only after a negative test result has been recorded and a drug-counseling program completed.

Along with alcohol and "street drug" use, steroid abuse has become a major issue at the high school level. In a pamphlet published by the National Federation of State High School Associations' TARGET Program, "Steroids—a Growing Concern," the dangers of steroid use are stated very clearly: "Anabolic-androgenic steroid use presents a very real health risk to those youth who have become involved or are contemplating its use.... The use of anabolic-androgenic steroids has invaded sport. The total integrity of sports is at risk. This risk can effect all who are involved in sports, including coaches, parents and, certainly, the athlete." In an attempt to make coaches and student-athletes more aware of the dangers associated with steroid use, the Coaches Association and the American Association for Clinical Chemistry prepared the "High School Coaches' Guide to Steroid Use and Detection." Along with educational information, this guide suggests, "the only way to conclusively prove steroid use is by detecting it in a test of an athlete's urine."

The evolution of programs, such as those advocated by the Coaches Association and implemented by Greeneville High School, increases the risk of potential litigation challenging the legality of drug testing at the interscholastic level. While legal challenges against high school programs have not been as numerous as those initiated against intercollegiate programs, such litigation does exist. The interscholastic drug testing programs face the same type of constitutionality claims as intercollegiate programs, including complaints of invasion of privacy, unreasonable search and seizure, and equal protection. The courts have taken a similar stand on interscholastic drug testing programs as on intercollegiate programs. Provided that the drug testing program fulfills a compelling need and the "reasonableness" requirement, then the objectives necessitating the implementation of a drug testing program will outweigh the potential invasion of privacy of the student-athletes.

NOTES

1. Thirty-nine percent of 16,000 high school seniors questioned about drug use acknowledged the use of an illicit substance during 1988, according to the fourteenth annual "Monitoring the Future: A Continuing Study of the Lifestyles and Values of Youth" survey conducted by the University of Michigan's Institute for Social Research. The study also found that 54 percent of this group had experimented with drugs at least once in their lifetime; 12 percent had used cocaine at least once; 5 percent had used crack-cocaine at least once; and 64 percent had taken one or more drinks in the preceding thirty days.

2. Seven percent of 3,400 male high school seniors in forty-six public and private schools across the country reported taking anabolic steroids, according to a 1988 Penn State University study. Forty-seven percent of those seniors using steroids stated that the main reason for taking them was to improve athletic performance, especially in football and wrestling.

3. In *Schaill by Kross v. Tippecanoe County School Corp.*, 864 F. 2d 1309 (7th Cir. 1988), two student-athletes alleged that the random urinalysis drug testing program instituted by the defendant violated their rights under the Fourth Amendment and the due process clause of the Fourteenth Amendment. The court determined that the urine collection was a "search" but that the Tippecanoe School Corporation had a substantial interest in enforcement of its random urinalysis program because of the evidence that drug use among

student-athletes is a problem with serious implications for their health and safety. The student-athletes claimed that the drug testing program violated their due process rights as the program was insufficient in allowing a student to challenge a positive result. The court found that the Tippecanoe School Corporation drug testing program provided sufficient due process to the student-athlete who tested positive. The constitutionality of this drug testing program was therefore upheld.

OLYMPIC DRUG-TESTING PROGRAMS

Drug testing is a primary area of concern among the International Olympic Committee, International Sport Federations, and National Olympic Committees. Tremendous advances have been made in the areas of testing procedures and sensitivity of tests. In addition, agreements between countries regarding drug testing procedures and sharing of information are becoming more prevalent.

Government intervention has also become a factor in drug testing issues. In response to the disqualification at the 1988 Summer Olympics of Ben Johnson, a Canadian sprinter who tested positive for steroid use after winning the gold medal in the 100-meter event, Canadian Prime Minister Brian Mulroney ordered the "Commission of Inquiry into the Use of Drugs and Banned Practices Intended to Increase Athletic Performance" to investigate the matter.

In any testing program, sports federations have to address the conflict-of-interest problem. Some federations have been accused of protecting their star athletes, and there have been suspicions of coverups to protect the athlete so as not to put the country at a competitive disadvantage, to prevent a drug scandal, and to avoid the risk of losing corporate sponsors and fans.

The International Olympic Committee (IOC) has been making strides with numerous countries in the testing of athletes. The major point of interest concerns unannounced testing or short-notice testing. When testing for anabolic steroids is done only at competitions, it is easy for athletes to avoid detection by stopping steroid use before competition. The IOC has moved to a program in which athletes are subject to testing at any time, in or out of training. Only a handful of countries, including Britain, Canada, Sweden, and Norway, previously had such programs. The unannounced testing program is seen as more difficult to implement in some countries, such as the United States, because of the laws protecting the privacy of citizens in this country.

The United States Olympic Committee (USOC) employs its own drug testing and drug education program for events involving national team tryouts and competitions. The USOC Drug Education Program includes three key components:

1. The *education* of athletes, coaches, and administrative and medical personnel about appropriate uses of medications and the problems associated with misuse and abuse.
2. Periodic drug *testing* of athletes for banned substances to deter tempted athletes from resorting to these substances.
3. Support of selected *research* that would allow more effective educational and testing programs.

Testing seeks to identify use of drugs in the following major categories:

1. Stimulants
2. Anabolic steroids
3. Narcotics and certain painkillers
4. Tranquilizers, sedatives, beta blockers, and alcohol, in certain sports
5. Diuretics
6. Peptide hormones and analogues

The USOC employs an out-of-competition testing program in which any athlete eligible to compete in events sanctioned by his or her sports federation or by the USOC will be subject to short-notice drug testing three times a year. The program also employs an independent auditor who oversees the program and an officer who investigates drug-related accusations.

The testing process begins with the collection of two specimens (A and B). Specimen A is tested; if a positive result occurs, another sample from A will be tested. If this second test of Specimen A results in another positive test, the athlete will be notified immediately by the USOC. This notification will also tell the athlete the time and date of the testing of Specimen B. The athlete may witness this testing, or a surrogate representative will be assigned to witness the testing of Specimen B. If Specimen B tests positive, the appropriate penalties will be imposed. The athlete has the right to request a hearing about the positive drug result. Penalties for a positive drug result are listed in Exhibit 12–2, and the USOC Hearing Process for a positive drug result is listed in Exhibit 12–3.

The USOC also operates a twenty-four-hour, toll-free drug hotline on which athletes, coaches, trainers, doctors, and administrators can call for more information on banned drugs, drug testing procedures, and the drug education program.

In 1989, the U.S. Olympic Committee and the National Olympic Committee of the USSR entered into an agreement designed to rid sport in the two nations of the use of performance-enhancing drugs by Olympic and other world-class athletes. The program features out-

Exhibit 12–2
U.S. Olympic Committee Penalties for a Positive Drug Result

3.0 Subject to the due process and appellate process of the respective entity, recommended sanctions shall be as follows:

1. Anabolic steroids, amphetamine-related and other stimulants, diuretics, beta-blockers, narcotic analgesics, and designer drugs:

   • 2 years for the first offense.

   • Life ban for the second offense.

2. Ephedrine, phenylpropanolamine, codeine, caffeine, and all other banned substances or practices (when administered orally as a cough suppressant or painkiller in association with decongestants and/or antihistamines):

   • A maximum 3 months for the first offense.

   • 2 years for the second offense.

   • Life ban for the third offense.

3.1 Sanctions will be imposed by the NGB who has jurisdiction over the event or occasion involved. In cases where the USOC has jurisdiction over the event, the USOC will conduct a hearing for the purpose of making recommendations to the NGB.

3.2 Failure to comply with policies and procedures of this program can be cause for the same action(s) as if found at that occasion to have used a banned substance. Refusal to be tested after signing a consent form to be tested shall result in the imposition of a sanction of two years if under USOC jurisdiction or, if under the jurisdiction of the NGB, for a period to be determined by the NGB.

3.3 Any physician, coach, athletic trainer, or other attendant to an athlete with a positive finding who is shown to have aided or abetted that offense, will be suspended from NGB and USOC programs by the NGB for at least the period that the athlete was suspended, subject to appropriate due process and appellate procedures.

3.4 The action of the NGB shall not prohibit the USOC from taking appropriate further action concerning the person's involvement in USOC programs.

Source: U.S. Olympic Committee Drug Education Handbook, 1989–92, p. 55.

of-competition testing on a forty-eight-hour, short-notice schedule for athletes selected by each nation and additional testing at selected competitions involving Soviet and American athletes. Under the agreement, scientists from each nation reside in the other country on a long-term basis, allowing joint analysis of drug tests.

National governing bodies have also entered the fight against drug use by athletes. The Athletics Congress (TAC), the national governing body for track and field in the United States, employs one of the most expensive drug testing programs among all NGBs. TAC conducts a year-round, short-notice testing program in which fourteen athletes are chosen randomly each week for testing. TAC notifies the athlete forty-eight hours prior to the actual testing. If the athlete cannot attend the testing, he or she must notify TAC immediately. TAC decides whether an athlete's extenuating circumstances warrant missing the test. Failure to appear for a test calls for an automatic two-year suspension.

The most recent step in the international drug testing arena involves challenge testing. This type of testing was presented by the executive director of TAC and an International Amateur Athletic Federation

Exhibit 12–3
U.S. Olympic Committee Hearing Process for a Positive Drug Result

According to policy adopted by the USOC Executive Board in October 1989, the principal ingredients of the hearing process for anabolic steroids and related substances will be as follows:

1. Upon determination of a "B" positive laboratory finding for substances, the athlete who tests positive shall have the right to request a hearing regarding the laboratory findings.

2. If the athlete requests such a hearing, a three-member hearing panel shall consist of a former Federal court or state district court judge selected from a pool of such persons provided by the American Arbitration Association. The person shall chair the hearing. Another member shall be selected from a pool of athletes designated for such purpose by the Athlete's Advisory Council. The third member shall be selected from a pool of individuals designated for such purpose by the National Governing Bodies.

3. The hearing shall be conducted in such a way as to provide all necessary ingredients of due process.

4. There shall be a presenter who shall be a full-time USOC employee and who shall present all information to the panel supporting the "B" positive finding.

5. There shall be a neutral medical review officer who shall have access to all details relating to the "B" positive finding. The expert will consult with the athlete regarding any defense to the "B" positive finding and shall assist the athlete in presenting information to the panel regarding his/her response to the "B" positive where such relates to medical issues.

6. After hearing all information relating to the "B" positive finding, the hearing panel shall reach a decision whether the "B" finding shall be confirmed.

7. The determination shall be reported to the National Governing Body which will take action regarding the athlete's eligibility according to its own Constitution and By-Laws.

Source: U.S. Olympic Committee Drug Education Handbook, 1989–92, p. 11.

(IAAF) vice president, Ollan Cassell, and was approved by track and field's international federation, the IAAF. In challenge testing the top five national federations in track and field have seventy-five challenges apiece of foreign athletes. This short-notice testing was seen as a positive step toward alleviating the use of drugs by the top athletes in this sport.

When dealing with drug testing during international competitions, complications can arise because of the various parties (and countries) that are involved. For instance, when Butch Reynolds, a United States athlete, challenged a positive drug test result which occurred at an international track and field meet in Monte Carlo, the organizations that were involved in this dispute included, the USOC, the Athletics Congress (the national governing body for track and field in the United States), the IAAF, and the court system in the United States (see note 2). The problem arises as to which organization and/or country has the final authority in disputes surrounding a drug testing program.

NOTES ──────────────────────────────────────

1. USOC Drug Education Program information is provided in the *U.S. Olympic Committee Drug Education Handbook*, 1989–92. For further infor-

mation, contact the USOC Drug Education Program, 1750 East Boulder, Colorado Springs, CO 80909.

2. In August 1990, Butch Reynolds, world record holder in the 400 meters and a 1988 Olympic silver medalist, allegedly tested positive for the anabolic steroid nandrolone after an international track and field meet in Monte Carlo. Shortly thereafter, the International Amateur Athletic Federation (IAAF), the world governing body for track and field, suspended Reynolds from competition for two years. Reynolds immediately filed suit in U.S. District Court in Ohio, claiming that the testing procedure was flawed and that he had not used steroids. The court ruled, however, that Reynolds must first exhaust all administrative remedies.

Reynolds next took his case before the American Arbitration Association, a procedure specified by the U.S. Amateur Sports Act and the U.S. Olympic Committee (USOC) constitution, and was exonerated. Both the IAAF and The Athletics Congress (TAC), however, refused to accept the decision because the USOC's administrative proceedings were inconsistent with the IAAF's adjudication process. In September 1991, however, the TAC also exonerated Reynolds after finding clear and convincing evidence that the test results were tainted. Once again, the IAAF refused to accept the decision.

In the three weeks preceding the 1992 U.S. Olympic trials, Reynolds once again turned to the courts in order to gain the right to compete for the U.S. Olympic team. The district court in *Reynolds v. International Amateur Athletic Federation,* Case No. C-2-92-452 (Ohio Dist. Ct. 1992), found that Reynolds had established a likelihood of success on the merits of his case, ruling that a breach of contract appeared to have occurred when evidence showed inconsistencies in the testing and that the IAAF, ignoring its own policy of confidentiality, released information that Reynolds had tested positive before granting him a hearing. The court issued a preliminary injunction on June 19, 1992, which allowed Reynolds to compete in all track and field competitions including the Olympic trials and Games.

TAC appealed the decision to the U.S. Sixth Circuit Court of Appeals, which overturned the lower court's decision, ruling that no U.S. court had the jurisdiction to allow Reynolds to compete in Barcelona. In addition, the court ruled that granting Reynolds an injunction would harm other athletes through the IAAF's threat to invoke their "contamination rule," which would bar any athlete from the Olympic Games should compete against Reynolds.

Reynolds appealed to the U.S. Supreme Court. On June 20, 1992, Justice John Paul Stevens reinstated the injunction, claiming that the IAAF's threatened harm to other athletes could not dictate the disposition of Reynolds's claim.

The issue of whether or not Butch Reynolds could compete in the Barcelona Olympiad was rendered moot on June 26, when he finished fifth in the 400-meter final and failed to qualify.

On December 3, 1992, a U.S. District Court in Ohio awarded Reynolds $27.3 million ($6.8 million in compensatory damages and $20.5 million in punitive damages) from the IAAF as a result of the $12.5 million civil lawsuit he filed against TAC and the IAAF citing lost earnings and personal anguish. Judge Joseph P. Kinneary stated in his ruling that the IAAF had "defamed"

Reynolds, had acted with "malice" and "a spirit of revenge," and had "purposefully avoided the truth" in the case.

The IAAF has maintained from the beginning that no court in the United States holds any legal jurisdiction over the federation and has thus far been unwilling to change this position. The IAAF even went so far as not to appear in court throughout the proceedings. Reynolds began the process of collecting his judgment by attacking funds owed to the IAAF by its U.S. sponsors.

In August 1993, a U.S. District Court judge ruled that the $691,667 sponsorship money owed to the IAAF from the Mobil Corp. for the period May 21–August 27 should instead be paid to Reynolds. The judge directed the Mobil Corp. to pay this money to an escrow account which will be held by the U.S. District Court for Eastern Virginia pending an appeal by the IAAF.

Chapter 13

ADDITIONAL LEGAL CONCERNS IN AMATEUR ATHLETICS

INTRODUCTION

Amateur athletic administrators should be aware of and concerned about three additional legal areas: the antitrust laws, the tax laws, and illegal gambling. These topics are not related. They are given brief mention in Chapter 13 for the purpose of providing an overview and some background information on potential legal problems in these areas.

THE ANTITRUST LAWS

Antitrust laws are designed to promote competition in the business sector through regulation "designed to control the exercise of private economic power" (Gellhorn, *Antitrust Law and Economics*, 1977). In athletics, antitrust law concerns have primarily involved professional sports, which are private economic business entities operated theoretically to make a profit. Increasingly, however, amateur athletic organizations have come under the scrutiny of antitrust laws, partly because of the transformation of many areas of amateur athletics into "big business." This is particularly true of intercollegiate athletics, primarily football and men's basketball. For example, the NCAA's Football Television Plan for 1984–85 was declared to be in violation of the antitrust laws because it prevented the free flow of televised intercollegiate football (see Chapter 9). The decision, upheld by the U.S. Supreme Court in 1984, disrupted the entire sports telecasting industry by allowing a glut of televised intercollegiate football to flood the market. The decision caused the financial rights fees for these televised games to drop significantly, causing many institutions to experience a shortfall in their annual budgets.

Two major antitrust laws form the underlying basis for court decisions: the Sherman Antitrust Act and the Clayton Act.

The Sherman Antitrust Act

The Sherman Antitrust Act was passed in 1890 during a period of U.S. history when business had gained domination over the delivery of goods and services to the detriment of the average citizen. The purpose of the law was to encourage free and open competition in business. The ultimate beneficiary was the consumer, who would not have to pay above-market prices for goods and services. The law, which was neither detailed nor overly focused, had two major sections. Section I, sometimes referred to as Sherman I, stated: "Every contract, combination in the form of trust or otherwise, or conspiracy in restraint of trade or commerce among the several states or foreign nations is declared to be illegal." Section II, or Sherman II, stated: "Every person who shall monopolize, or attempt to monopolize or combine or conspire with any other person or persons, to monopolize any part of the trade or commerce among the several states, or with foreign nations, shall be deemed guilty of a felony."

Federal antitrust laws seek to regulate competitive conduct involving interstate commerce. The Sherman Antitrust Act specifically covers transactions in goods, land, or services. Section I of the Sherman Act concerns agreements that restrain trade, such as a group of businesses attempting to fix prices among themselves. In determining what constitutes an impermissible restraint of trade, the courts use a "rule of reason" test, which weighs the alleged illegal practice against the anticompetitive effect it has on business to see if in balance the practice should be deemed improper and unlawful. Some conduct, such as price fixing, is by its nature deemed illegal and does not require a rule of reason analysis.

Section II of the Sherman Act attempts to prevent monopolistic action by a business or businesses, such as attempting to control all televised football so as to prevent another school or league from being telecast. It is all right for a monopoly to exist for natural reasons, as long as the monopoly then does not attempt to drive out competition through illegal means.

The Clayton Act

The Clayton Act was enacted in 1914 to tighten up some of the generalities of the Sherman Act. It was specifically designed to prevent certain practices in the sale of goods in interstate commerce. Specific sections of the Clayton Act deal with subjects involving corporate mergers, price discrimination, and other matters.

Antitrust Liabilities of Amateur Athletic Associations

In the past, amateur athletic organizations have not been subject to the antitrust litigation that the professional sports industry has faced. However, with the increased prominence associated with amateur athletics and the money now involved, organizations such as the NCAA are increasingly subject to antitrust litigation.

Historically, defendant amateur athletic associations had been successful in arguing that the antitrust laws were not applicable to them because amateur athletics are not "trade" or "commerce" as defined by the Sherman Act. Amateur organizations have traditionally argued that since their athletic associations are nonprofit organizations, their primary purpose is educational and noncommercial in nature, and hence cannot be defined as trade or commerce. However, in the cases discussed here, the courts seem to be defining amateur athletics, and especially the NCAA, as "trade" or "commerce," and therefore are declaring them subject to the antitrust laws.

In 1972 the federal antitrust laws were first applied to amateur athletics in *Amateur Softball Ass'n of America v. United States*, 467 F.2d 312 (10th Cir. 1972). In that case, the governing organization for softball in the United States was deemed not exempt from antitrust laws. The court reasoned that even though the primary purpose of the association was noncommercial, subsequent actions or operations of an amateur athletic association could trigger application of the Sherman Act.

A similar result occurred in *Tondas v. Amateur Hockey Ass'n of the United States*, 438 F. Supp. 310 (W.D.N.Y. 1977). The court held that the amateur hockey association had significant market and economic power to trigger possible antitrust law applications. However, in *Ass'n for Intercollegiate Athletics for Women v. National Collegiate Athletic Ass'n*, 558 F. Supp. 487 (D.D.C. 1983), 735 F.2d 577 (D.C. Cir. 1984), the courts held that the NCAA's dominance of the amateur sports television market does not by itself create a monopolistic practice against a rival association, since no illegal tying arrangement existed.

In *College Athletic Placement Services, Inc. v. National Collegiate Athletic Ass'n*, 1975 Trade Cases (CCH) ¶ 60,177 (E.D. Va.), the court found no violation of the Sherman Act for an amendment by the NCAA to its constitution which would render students who obtained information from services such as the plaintiff's ineligible for intercollegiate competition. The court applied the rule of reason test and found that the NCAA amendment was neither anticompetitive nor intended to damage the plaintiff. Instead, the amendment was consistent with the NCAA objective of preserving amateurism in college sports.

An important distinction between NCAA commercial and noncommercial rules was made by the court in *Justice v. NCAA*, 577 F. Supp. 356 (D. Ariz. 1983) (see note 6). In this case the court pointed out that the NCAA engages in two types of rule making: (1) noncommercial rules, which include limitations on the number of assistant coaches (*Hennessey;* see note 4) and eligibility rules (*Jones;* see note 2; and *Gaines;* see note 13), which are rooted in the NCAA's concern for the protection of amateurism; and (2) commercial rules (*NCAA v. Board of Regents*) (see also note 8), which have a discernible economic purpose in mind. In applying the rule of reason test to these two different types of rules, the courts have consistently upheld the NCAA rules when dealing with the noncommercial aspect. The courts have found these rules consistent with the NCAA objectives of preserving amateurism and not anticompetitive, as defined by the Sherman Antitrust Act. Rules falling into the commercial area, however, have encountered stricter scrutiny by the courts in terms of antitrust law violations.

While amateur organizations were successful in defending antitrust cases from 1972 to 1984, the NCAA was successfully challenged on antitrust grounds in *NCAA v. Board of Regents of University of Oklahoma and University of Georgia Athletic Ass'n*, 468 U.S. 85 (1984) (see note 8). This decision was important for three reasons: (1) it was the first successful challenge of an amateur organization based on antitrust theory; (2) it had a significant impact on the NCAA and intercollegiate athletic departments by reducing television revenues for most institutions; and (3) the U.S. Supreme Court rendered the decision, applying antitrust laws to an amateur organization, which may serve as a precedent for future cases.

Some of the antitrust litigation brought subsequent to *NCAA v. Board of Regents of University of Oklahoma and University of Georgia Athletic Ass'n* has attempted to clarify the court's decision (see *Regents of the University of California v. American Broadcasting Companies, Inc.*, note 9; and *Association of Independent Television Stations, Inc. v. CFA, Big-8, ABC, Inc., ESPN, Inc.*, note 10).

Other litigation has been brought on antitrust theory against amateur organizations by student-athletes who have been adversely affected by an organization's decision. In *McCormack v. National Collegiate Athletic Ass'n*, 845 F.2d 1338 (5th Cir. 1988), the court decided that the NCAA's eligibility rules placing restrictions on student-athletes' compensation did not constitute illegal price fixing and were not in violation of the Sherman Act. In *Banks v. NCAA* (see note 12) and *Gaines v. NCAA* (see note 13), football players unsuccessfully challenged the NCAA on antitrust theory with regard to eligibility rules. The Indiana federal district court in *Banks* ruled that the NCAA eligibility rules in question were subject to scrutiny under the Sherman Antitrust Act but concluded that the rules were procompetitive and, using the rule of reason test, were reasonable, on the basis of their intentions. In the *Gaines* case, however, the Tennessee federal district court ruled that the NCAA eligibility rules were not subject to scrutiny under the Sherman Antitrust Act. However, the court went on to state that, assuming the antitrust laws did apply to the NCAA eligibility rules, the rules were reasonable in terms of the rule of reason test.

Antitrust law may be an emerging avenue used by plaintiffs to challenge amateur organizations. The successful challenge by the plaintiffs in *NCAA v. Board of Regents of University of Oklahoma and University of Georgia Athletic Ass'n* suggests that amateur organizations may qualify as "trade or business" under the Sherman Antitrust Act. This decision opens up a plethora of potential claims based on antitrust theory. The move to the antitrust approach may be further encouraged by the NCAA's successful defense in the *NCAA v. Tarkanian* decision, 488 U.S. 179 (1988). This decision reduced the likelihood of success in challenging the NCAA on federal constitutional law theories, therefore encouraging plaintiffs to pursue lawsuits based on other legal theories, such as antitrust law.

In considering whether the antitrust laws apply to amateur athletic organizations, athletic administrators should ask the following questions:

1. Is the primary purpose of the amateur association commercial or noncommercial?
2. If the primary purpose is noncommercial, do certain aspects of the association's activities constitute commercial economic enterprises (e.g., radio/television telecasts, sales of goods or services, facility rentals, etc.)?
3. Does the association enjoy a dominant position in the marketplace or is it employing practices designed to drive all competition from the marketplace using undue influence derived from its dominant position?

NOTES

1. In *Samara v. National Collegiate Athletic Ass'n*, 1973 Trade Cases (CCH) ¶ 74,536 (E.D. Va. 1973), two track student-athletes from the University of Pennsylvania and Adelphi University were invited to participate in an AAU-sponsored Russian-American track and field meet. Under NCAA rules, such a meet is defined as an "extra event" and requires NCAA certification to prevent the athletes from being denied NCAA eligibility. This particular AAU meet was not certified by the NCAA. The plaintiffs sought relief on the basis of the Sherman Act to prevent the NCAA from imposing sanctions as a result of their participation. The court rejected the plaintiffs' claims.

2. In *Jones v. National Collegiate Athletic Ass'n*, 392 F. Supp. 295 (D. Mass. 1975), the plaintiff was an American ice hockey player who was compensated for five years while playing junior hockey in Canada prior to entering Northeastern University. Because of receiving compensation for playing, Jones was declared ineligible to compete at Northeastern. Jones argued that the NCAA violated the antitrust laws by declaring him ineligible to compete. With respect to the antitrust allegations, the court held that the Sherman Act does not apply to the NCAA or its members in the setting of the eligibility standards for intercollegiate athletics.

3. In *Board of Regents, University of Oklahoma v. National Collegiate Athletic Ass'n*, 561 P.2d 499 (Okla. Sup. Ct. 1977), Oklahoma University assistant football coaches asserted that an NCAA bylaw limiting the number of coaches a Division I school might employ was a violation of the Sherman Act by preventing coaches from practicing their lawful profession. The appellate

court overruled the decision of the trial court, stating that the NCAA rule appeared to be a reasonable one, rationally related to its announced objective of curtailing costs of NCAA members. The court concluded that the restraint did not prevent coaches from exercising their lawful profession, but merely limited the number of coaches any given member school could employ.

4. In *Hennessey v. National Collegiate Athletic Ass'n*, 564 F.2d 1136 (5th Cir. 1977), the district court found that NCAA Bylaw 12-1, which put a limitation on a school coaching staff, had sufficient impact on interstate commerce (as it curtailed the interstate flow of assistant coaching services) to fall within the Sherman Act. The court, however, ruled that the bylaw's fundamental objective was to preserve and foster competition in intercollegiate athletics, and that it was thus permissible under the rule of reason and was not a violation of the Sherman Act.

5. In *Warner Amex Cable Communications, Inc. v. ABC*, 499 F. Supp. 537 (S.D. Ohio 1980), the plaintiff objected to a change in the NCAA television plan which restricted its ability to cablecast Ohio State University football games when ABC did not broadcast them. The plaintiff had been permitted to cablecast these games in the past. The plaintiff alleged violations of the antitrust laws by both ABC and the NCAA. The court found that the NCAA's television plan did not violate antitrust laws and was within the rule of reason.

6. In *Justice v. National Collegiate Athletic Ass'n*, 577 F. Supp. 356 (D. Ariz. 1983), four members of the University of Arizona's football team asserted antitrust injury due to the loss of potential professional contracts after the NCAA imposed sanctions against the team, including prohibition from post-season play in 1983 and 1984 and prohibition from television appearances for 1984 and 1985. The court held that the loss of potential professional contracts and bonuses resulting from the denial of television and bowl game appearances could not be determined to be a direct result of the NCAA sanctions. The court also held that the NCAA restrictions were permissible under the rule of reason because the sanctions sought to preserve amateurism and enhance fair competition among the association's member institutions.

7. In *English v. National Collegiate Athletic Ass'n*, 439 So. 2d 1218 (La. Ct. App. 1983), a college football player, after transferring twice from a four-year college to a two-year college, was declared ineligible for another season of competition because of an NCAA transfer rule. The plaintiff's challenge to the NCAA transfer rule was based on Louisiana antitrust laws. The court held that Louisiana antitrust laws were inapplicable to the NCAA, because the NCAA is engaged in interstate commerce and therefore subject only to federal antitrust law. The court also ruled, however, that if the Louisiana antitrust laws were applicable to the NCAA, the court would still rule for the defendant, because the NCAA rules were reasonable and not a violation of the state antitrust laws.

8. In *National Collegiate Athletic Ass'n v. Board of Regents of University of Oklahoma and University of Georgia Athletic Ass'n*, 468 U.S. 85 (1984), the NCAA operated a college football television plan which limited the number of televised Division I college football games. The University of Oklahoma and the University of Georgia were members of the College Football Association (CFA), which negotiated an independent television contract allowing

for a larger number of appearances on television. When the NCAA announced that it would take disciplinary action in response to this independent contract, the University of Oklahoma and the University of Georgia filed suit, claiming that the NCAA's actions violated the Sherman Act. The Supreme Court affirmed the decisions of the district court and court of appeals, holding that the NCAA television plan violated antitrust laws through an unreasonable restraint of trade and also illegal price fixing (see Chapter 9).

9. In *Regents of the University of California v. American Broadcasting Companies, Inc.*, 747 F.2d 511 (9th Circuit, 1984), the plaintiffs claimed that the ABC-CFA television contract violated the antitrust laws. The plaintiffs, who were not part of the ABC-CFA television contract, entered into a television contract with CBS as part of the Pac-10/Big Ten package. The ABC-CFA contract stipulated that ABC had broadcast rights for all CFA member institution football games and broadcast rights to CFA versus non-CFA member games. The University of California was scheduled to play Nebraska, and the University of Southern California was scheduled to play Notre Dame; both Nebraska and Notre Dame were CFA members. The plaintiffs filed this antitrust suit stating that the ABC-CFA television plan, in effect, represented "group boycott," because of the CFA members' refusal to deal with non-CFA members on television broadcast coverage and "price-fixing," through the formation of a cartel restricting the output of televised games so as artificially to raise the value of the ABC-CFA contract. The district court granted a preliminary injunction for the plaintiffs, prohibiting Nebraska and Notre Dame from refusing to consent to the broadcast of one of their fall games solely on the basis of the exclusivity terms of their contract with ABC. The appeals court affirmed the district court ruling, stating that although the actual antitrust implications were not ruled on, the plaintiffs showed a likelihood of success on the merits and therefore should be granted a preliminary injunction.

10. In *Association of Independent Television Stations, Inc. v. CFA, Big-8, ABC, Inc., ABC Sports, Inc., ESPN, Inc.*, Civil No. 84-2283-JB (W.D. Okla. 1986), the plaintiff challenged the contracts the CFA entered into with ABC and ESPN after the NCAA television plan dissolved as a result of *NCAA v. Board of Regents of Oklahoma*. The Association of Independent Television Stations (INTV) challenged the contracts as a violation of the Sherman Act, alleging that the defendants fixed prices, limited output, divided markets, excluded competition, and restricted television viewers' choice among games. The court dismissed the plaintiff's claims, stating that the contracts were not in violation of antitrust laws.

11. In *United States v. Walters*, 1989 WL 42693 (N.D. Ill. 1989), two sports agents were charged with numerous criminal violations relating to their signing contracts with student-athletes who had not yet completed their eligibility. The defendants moved to dismiss the charges, stating that the NCAA's eligibility regulations restricting the compensation received by student-athletes violated the Sherman Act and constituted illegal price fixing. The court ruled that the NCAA's eligibility rules do not violate the federal antitrust laws.

12. In *Banks v. National Collegiate Athletic Ass'n*, No. S90-394 (N.D. Ind. 1990), the plaintiff was a football player at the University of Notre Dame who entered the April 1990 NFL draft. Because he entered the draft, the NCAA,

under Rules 12.2.4 and 12.3, declared Banks ineligible for future intercollegiate competition. When Banks was not selected by a team in the draft, he wanted to return to the University of Notre Dame for his last year of football eligibility. Accordingly, he filed suit, arguing that the NCAA rules forbidding him from competing violated the Sherman Antitrust Act. After a hearing on Banks's request for a preliminary injunction, the court ruled that the NCAA regulations at issue, whatever their wisdom or soundness as intercollegiate athletic policy, do not offend the federal antitrust laws. The court applied the rule of reason analysis and stated that the NCAA rules in question defined amateurism for purposes of intercollegiate athletic eligibility and were central to the pro-competitive purpose of the NCAA. Banks has appealed this ruling.

13. In *Gaines v. NCAA*, No. 3-90-0773 (M.D. Tenn. 1990), the facts were similar to those in the *Banks* case. The plaintiff was a football player at Vanderbilt University who entered the 1990 NFL draft. Gaines was not drafted by any NFL team and wanted to return to Vanderbilt to finish his eligibility. The NCAA declared Gaines ineligible because he had entered the NFL draft. Gaines filed suit in federal district court in Tennessee, stating that the NCAA, by preventing college football players like him from returning to college play (for which they are otherwise eligible) after an unsuccessful bid in the NFL draft, is engaged in an unlawful exercise of monopoly power in violation of section 2 of the Sherman Act. The district court ruled that the eligibility rules of the NCAA are not economic in nature and therefore are not subject to scrutiny under the Sherman Act. This was a different stance than the one taken by the Indiana federal district court in *Banks*. The court further stated that, even assuming the antitrust laws did apply to the NCAA eligibility rules, the rules are overwhelmingly pro-competitive and are justified by legitimate business reasons.

Although the *Gaines* court decided that the antitrust laws did not apply to the NCAA eligibility rules, it still analyzed the plaintiff's likelihood of success on the merits of the case. The *Gaines* court reached a conclusion similar to that in the *Banks* case: that under the rule of reason, the purpose of the rules justified their existence.

14. Currently the Federal Trade Commission (FTC) is investigating the College Football Association's (CFA) five-year $300 million television contract with Capital Cities/American Broadcast Corporation (ABC) for an alleged antitrust violation. The FTC is arguing that the CFA's program is operated as a commercial rather than an educational venture, and therefore is subject to antitrust laws despite its nonprofit status. Further the FTC claims that major college athletic programs, such as the CFA, operate as "independent business enterprises" rather than charitable programs. For further information see "FTC Probe Leads to Far-Reaching TV Subpeonas," *NCAA News*, May 22, 1991, p. 1.

15. See the following law review articles.

(a) Hochberg and Horowitz, "Broadcasting & CATV: The Beauty & The Bane of Major College Football," 38 *Law & Contemp. Probs.* 112 (1973).

(b) Note, "National Collegiate Athletic Association's certification requirement: A Section 1 violation of the Sherman Antitrust Act," 9 *Val. U. L. Rev.* 193 (1974).

(c) Bashinsky, "Antitrust Law—National Collegiate Athletic Association Held Subject to the Rule of Reason Test of the Sherman Antitrust Act," 7 *Cumb. L. Rev.* 505 (1977).

(d) Note, "Tackling Intercollegiate Athletics: An Antitrust Analysis," 87 *Yale L. J.* 655 (1978).

(e) Weistart, "Antitrust Issues in the Regulation of College Sports," 5 *J. C. & U. L.* 77 (1978–79).

(f) Kirby and Weymouth, "Antitrust and Amateur Sports: The Role of Noneconomic Values," 61 *Indiana L. J.* 31 (1985).

(g) McKenzie and Sullivan, "Does the NCAA Exploit College Athletes? An Economics and Legal Reinterpretation," 32 *Antitrust Bulletin* 373 (1987).

(h) Note, "Antitrust Issues in Amateur Sports," 61 *Indiana L. J.* (1985).

16. The Supreme Court's unusual antitrust approach in *National Collegiate Athletic Ass'n. v. Board of Regents of University of Oklahoma* has been the subject of many law review articles, including the following.

(a) Note, "Antitrust Law—NCAA Thrown for a Loss by Court's Traditional Antitrust Blitz: NCAA v. Board of Regents of the University of Oklahoma," 18 *Creighton L. Rev.* 917 (1984–85).

(b) Note, "NCAA Board of Regents of the University of Oklahoma: The NCAA's TV Plan Is Sacked by the Sherman Act," 34 *Cath. U. L. Rev.* 857 (1985).

(c) Note, "Antitrust and Nonmarket Goods: The Supreme Court Fumbles Again: National Collegiate Athletic Association v. Board of Regents," 60 *Wash. L. Rev.* 721 (1985).

(d) Note, "NCAA v. Board of Regents of the University of Oklahoma: Has the Supreme Court Abrogated the Per Se Rule of Antitrust Analysis?" 19 *Loy. L.A. L. Rev.* 437 (1985).

(e) Note, "The Commercialization of College Football: The Universities of Oklahoma and Georgia Learn an Antitrust Lesson in NCAA v. Board of Regents," 12 *Pepp. L. Rev.* 515 (1985).

(f) Note, "NCAA v. Board of Regents: The Supreme Court Intercepts Per Se Rule and Rule of Reason," 39 *U. Miami L. Rev.* 529 (1985).

(g) Greenspan, "College Football's Biggest Fumble: The Economic Impact of the Supreme Court's Decision in National Collegiate Athletic Association v. Board of Regents of University of Oklahoma," 33 *Antitrust Bulletin* 1 (1988).

THE TAX LAWS

Several of the tax issues facing the college and high school athletic administrator revolve around the status of most amateur organizations as tax-exempt. These organizations are also commonly referred to as nonprofit or not-for-profit organizations.

Internal Revenue Service Code section 501(a) governs organizations that seek to obtain an exemption from federal income tax. To qualify for the exemption, the athletic endeavor must be organized for one or more of the purposes set forth in section 501. Section 501(c)(3) of the code designates those organizations, which include religious, charitable, educational, scientific, literary, testing for public safety, fostering national or international amateur sports competition, or the prevention of cruelty to children or animals. State or municipal instrumentalities also fall under 501(c)(3), and these may include high schools and state universities. Therefore, activities such as the Olympics, national sports festivals, and state games may fall in the "national or international amateur sports competition" area. Athletic departments may be classified as "educational institutions" or "municipal instrumentalities." Booster clubs, Little Leagues, and Pop Warner Football may be classified as "charitable organizations."

Nonprofit Organizations

An organization seeking nonprofit status must file an application with the Internal Revenue Service. The purposes and proposed activities of the organization must be set forth in the corporate papers. In addition, a classified statement of receipts and expenditures, and a balance sheet for the current year and the three immediate prior years are needed for existing organizations. If a new organization is applying, a proposed budget for two full accounting periods and a current statement of assets and liabilities must be filed. After receipt of the necessary application materials, the IRS will issue a decision in a determination letter.

There are three main advantages to an organization which attains nonprofit status. The first and major advantage is the exemption from federal income tax liability. The organization is not subject to any tax on the income it generates as long as it is related to the organization's exempt purpose. The second advantage is that services performed in the employ of a nonprofit organization may be exempted from liability for the social security (FICA) taxes. This exemption could lower the operating costs of the organization. The third advantage is that contributions by an individual taxpayer or business to a nonprofit organization qualify as charitable contributions and are deductible by the donor for income tax purposes. This is an obvious incentive for individuals and businesses to contribute to a particular organization.

However, nonprofit status also has its disadvantages. The first is the amount of paper work that must be filed. The second is that the application for exemption and the supporting documentation are available for public scrutiny. However, there are procedures for withholding the information from the public if the IRS determines that the disclosure would adversely affect the organization.

A variety of other restrictions placed on nonprofit organizations should be considered before applying for the favorable tax treatment. For example, the assets of an organization must be permanently dedicated to the exempt purpose. This means that if the organization is dissolved, the assets must be distributed to another exempt purpose, or to the federal, state, or local government for a public purpose. Therefore, one cannot build profits through a nonprofit organization, then dissolve the business and take the profits. In addition, although employees of a nonprofit organization may be paid a salary, the salary cannot be tied to the profitability of the organization.

A not-for-profit organization is often incorrectly interpreted as a business that cannot make money in any tax year. This is untrue; the bottom line for a nonprofit organization may be in the black. However, the profits may not be used to benefit the organizers or employees.

Another topic of concern related to tax-exempt sports organizations is whether substantial broadcast receipts diminish the organization's tax-exempt status. In 1980 the IRS concluded in Revenue Ruling 80-294 that "the status of an organization exempt under Section 501(c)(6) of the Code created to promote interest in, elevate the standards of, and conduct tournaments in a certain professional sport will not be adversely affected merely because its primary support is derived from the sale of television broadcasting rights to the tournament it conducts." The taxability of broadcast receipts in exempt organizations has continued to be a controversial issue; it is discussed later in this chapter.

NOTES

1. In *Bohemian Gymnastics Association Sokol v. Higgins,* 147 F.2d 774 (2d. Cir. 1945), the court found an educational basis for exemption under 501(c)(3) for a gymnastics association.

2. In *Mobile Arts & Sports Association v. United States,* 148 F. Supp. 311 (S.D. Ala. 1957), the U.S. District Court held that an organization whose purpose was to present an annual senior college bowl football game made substantial civic, educational, and cultural contributions to the community and therefore qualified for exemption under Section 501(c)(3).

3. In *Hutchinson Baseball Enterprises, Inc. v. Commissioner,* 696 F.2d 757 (10th Cir. 1982), the court found that the promotion, advancement, and sponsoring of amateur athletes qualified as an exempt purpose.

4. For further details on nonprofit organizations, see the booklet "How to Apply for and Retain Exempt Status for Your Organization," *Internal Revenue Service Publication* 557.

5. For further information, see Moot, "Tax-Exempt Status of Amateur Sports Organizations," 40 *Wash. & Lee L. Rev.* 1705 (1983).

Unrelated Business Income

The tax on unrelated business income has become a major issue for athletic organizations. A tax-exempt organization may be held liable for taxes on unrelated business income, which is income from a trade or business, regularly carried on, that is not substantially related to the charitable, educational, or other purpose constituting the basis for its exemption (see Internal Revenue Code sections 511, 512, and 513).

Prior to the 1950 imposition of the unrelated business income tax by Congress, organizations would either be totally taxable or totally tax-exempt. This issue became controversial after World War II as colleges and universities began acquiring totally unrelated businesses, in areas such as automobile parts, food products, and oil wells. Income from these ventures was determined by the courts to be tax-exempt because they benefitted the nonprofit entity; the destination rather than the source of the income was the determining factor. Private companies complained that such treatment constituted unfair competition. Congress agreed, and in 1950 it implemented the unrelated business income tax, which targeted the source of the income rather than the destination. The question of college athletics and the unrelated business income tax was not directly addressed, but the issue has become more controversial in recent years as the financial stakes have increased.

It is important for the college athletics administrator to understand how the structure and function of a college athletics department or program relates to the IRS rules and regulations pertaining to unrelated business income and subsequent taxation. The unrelated business income tax was enacted to accomplish two objectives: (1) to eliminate unfair competition between charitable organizations and the taxed private sector and (2) to increase federal tax revenues.

Intercollegiate athletics today are characterized by schools with multimillion dollar athletic budgets, the desire to win and produce revenue to perpetuate those budgets, and an increasing gap between the goals of the educational institution and the goals of the athletic department. Because of the current climate in intercollegiate athletics, there is an increasing need for athletic administrators to deal intelligently with conflicts that arise from activities that, while within an educational and tax-exempt institution, take on the characteristics and function of an "unrelated business."

The IRS language relating to educational organizations, and specifically athletic organizations, reads as follows (Pub. 557, 1985, "Tax-Exempt Status for Your Organization"):

> The term *educational* relates to the instruction or training of individuals for the purpose of improving or developing their capabilities, or the instruction of the public on subjects useful to individuals and beneficial to the community....
>
> An athletic organization must submit evidence that it is engaged in

activities such as directing and controlling interscholastic athletic competitions, conducting tournaments, and prescribing eligibility rules for contestants. If it is not so engaged, your organization may be exempt as a social club.... Raising funds to be used for travel and other activities to interview and persuade prospective students with outstanding athletic ability to attend a particular university does not evidence an exempt purpose....

The issues surrounding the unrelated business income tax affect the following categories of income:

- Income from rental/admission fees for use of college athletic facilities for profit-making entertainment aimed primarily or solely at the general public (e.g., big-time football and basketball games, rock concerts, renting to professional franchises)
- Income from rental/admission fees for use of college athletics facilities by the general public, in which an admission or usage fee is charged
- Income from tuition for summer camps and clinics on campus (sports camps)
- Income from rental and user fees charged to private companies (e.g., health clubs) that operate on campus and under the auspices of the college athletic department
- Income from radio and television contracts
- Income from businesses sponsoring college athletic events and games
- Income from licensing agreements

The extent to which this income will be subject to the unrelated business income tax is subject to many conflicting interests. The fact that some university athletic departments operate independently of the rest of the university, both financially and administratively, only adds to the debate over what activities are to be classified as unrelated business activities separate and apart from the charitable, tax-exempt function of the educational institution.

Before looking closely at what constitutes unrelated business income according to IRS definition, let us take a general overview of the topic. In 1977 the IRS shocked the college athletics ranks when it issued a tax bill on the broadcast receipts of the Cotton Bowl. The tremendous backlash caused by this action pressured the IRS in 1978 to reverse its position, thus creating a de facto exemption for college/ university athletic programs—a decision that has since raised a few eyebrows from those who perceive university athletic programs largely as a profit-motivated entertainment industry subject to taxation.

These critics contend that, by and large, intercollegiate athletic programs are, both financially and philosophically, too far removed from the educational function of the institution to justify charitable, tax-exempt status.

The critical question in determining whether income is related or unrelated is whether the operation that produces money, whether it be a big-time college football game, an on-campus health club, or a summer sports camp, meets the three characteristics of unrelated business income within a charitable institution. Generally, an unrelated business is not taxable when it (1) fails to meet all three criteria outlined below, (2) is operated entirely by volunteers, or (3) is carried on "primarily for the convenience of the college's members, students, patients, officers, or employees." One also must consider whether the business is "in serious competition" with the private sector. For instance, if a university athletic department conducted a money-making tennis facility that competed with a local, privately operated tennis facility, the income from the university tennis facility may be taxable according to IRS rules.

An institution's "unrelated business taxable income" is defined by the IRS as the net income of any

1. trade or business that is
2. "regularly carried on" *and* is
3. "not substantially related (aside from the need of such organization for income or funds or the use it makes of the profits derived) to the exercise or performance" of the college's educational function.

Any activity having these three characteristics is an "unrelated business," the income from which, after customary business deductions are taken, is taxed at the regular corporate rates, without regard to whether the entity actually carrying on the business is a charitable corporation. In short, the test of whether an unrelated business is taxable looks to the *source* of the income, irrespective of its use. Proof of the funds' proper use is now irrelevant to the questions of their taxability; instead, the critical question is whether the operation that produces those funds is an "unrelated business." In addition, any organization whose "unrelated" activities become predominant to the overall charitable function and goals of the institution risks losing its basic tax exemption. An organization's activities must still be primarily charitable in nature for it to qualify as a tax-exempt organization in the first place. It is only the problem of primarily charitable entities (for example, educational institutions) engaging in some noncharitable activity that the unrelated business income tax addresses.

In order to better assess whether an athletic department activity is subject to unrelated business income taxation, it is important for the high school and college athletic administrator to understand the general principles and issues considered in determining whether the activity constitutes a trade or business regularly carried on and not substantially related to the exercise and performance of the institution's educational function. An activity will be classified as a trade or business if it "is carried on for the production of income from the sale of goods or the performance of services." The activity does not lose identity as a trade or business merely because it is carried on within the larger aggregate of similar activities. In other words, a business activity is not made otherwise by association with charitable (e.g., educational) operations. Additionally, the absence of profits does not necessarily eliminate the possibility of taxation. Instead, it is the *quest for profit* that is decisive.

The key considerations in an inquiry are the (1) existence of profits, (2) the activity's source of funding, and (3) other factors that give the activity a commercial flavor, including broadcast receipts (which alone may show athletic programs to be undertaken for profit purposes) and recruiting intensity. In general, the activity is a trade or business if it is *expected* to make money, even if it also has certain nonfinancial objectives, such as promoting the school's image, or pleasing alumni and state legislators.

Section 513(a) of the IRS Tax Code lists the general rule in defining an unrelated trade or business which is not "substantially related to the exercise or performance by such organization of its charitable, educational, or other purpose or function" which sets forth the basis for the trade or businesses exemption from tax.

Determining whether or not the activity is "substantially related" is the most difficult to analyze because of the broad definition of "education." Hence, the issue of substantial relatedness usually focuses on a second, more restrictive question: What is the activity's relationship to the exempt purpose? More specifically, does the activity *contribute importantly* to the accomplishment of the exempt purpose of the institution? These judgments are made on a case-by-case basis. Conversely, an activity is substantially related if it "contributes importantly" to the university's educational mission, even if the activity's principal purpose is financial or is otherwise unrelated to education. Under this analysis, university-operated summer sports camps and health clubs will generally fall into the tax-exempt category. How one measures an activity's contribution to education, and thus the contribution's importance, has not yet been clarified by the courts.

In addition to the "important contribution" yardstick, a second consideration is whether the size and extent of the activity is proportional to the nature and extent of the exempt function which it purports to serve.

The question of whether intercollegiate athletics, in general, contributes importantly to the institution's educational mission is problematic at best. Until the courts decide otherwise, intercollegiate athletic programs will remain shrouded in philosophical debate over the word "education" and will remain exempt from taxation as an unrelated business, despite the search-for-profits analysis and the commercial aspects of these activities (including broadcast receipts, independent funding, and the resulting pressures on athletic recruiting). In large part, this is because of legislative sympathy toward the educational institution and a hesitancy to tax college sports.

However, a change in attitude toward taxing college sports has been developing in recent years. Protests from the business community have pressured legislators to reconsider their position on taxing these enterprises. As of February 1987, eighteen states had enacted or had pending legislation to curb what many consider an unfair competitive advantage available to educational institutions. The IRS has become more aggressive toward college sports. In 1986, for example, it taxed the University of Michigan athletic department on money earned from the sale of advertising space in football game programs (see note 2). The same issue was addressed in *NCAA v. Commissioner* (see note 4). In reversing the Tax Court's decision, the 10th Circuit Court of Appeals ruled that the sale of advertising space in the programs of the 1982 NCAA basketball tournament was not a regularly carried on business, and thus was not taxable as unrelated business income. The IRS is currently investigating the taxability of money from title sponsors to the Cotton Bowl and the John Hancock Bowl (formerly the Sun Bowl), which could result in the loss of several million dollars to each (see note 3). In July 1992 both the U.S. House of Representatives and the Senate Committee on Finance approved respective bills that included provisions related to corporate-sponsorship payments that exempted them from the unrelated business income tax if the corporation received no substantial benefit other than the display of its name or logo. Unfortunately for the college bowl games, President Bush vetoed this bill and therefore confusion over accepted versus taxable corporate-sponsorship payments in connection with athletic events still exists.

NOTES _____

1. For further information on the unrelated business income tax, see Kaplan, "Intercollegiate Athletics and the Unrelated Business Income Tax," 80 *Colum. L. Rev.* 1430 (1980).

2. For details on the University of Michigan tax bill on the sale of adver-

tising space in its football programs, see "IRS Audit Leaves U. of Michigan $258,000 Poorer," *Chronicle of Higher Education*, September 7, 1988, p. A26.

3. For details on the IRS investigation of the Cotton Bowl and the John Hancock Bowl, see "Cotton Bowl vs. IRS: Are Sponsor Monies to Non-Profits Taxable?" *Amusement Business*, October 15, 1990, p. 1.

4. In *NCAA v. Commissioner of Internal Revenue*, 914 F. 2d 1417 (10th Cir. 1990), the NCAA challenged the IRS determination that the income derived from the sale of advertising space in the programs of the 1982 NCAA men's basketball tournament was taxable as unrelated business income. In reversing the lower court's decision, the court of appeals ruled that the sale of advertising space was not a regularly carried on business, and therefore was not taxable as unrelated business income.

Facility Rentals

The use of facilities on campus for university-related activities such as intercollegiate, intramural, and physical education programs clearly qualifies as tax-exempt activity. When the university leases a facility to an outside group, the income derived may be classified as unrelated business income. For example, a university's rental income from professional sports teams is not tax-exempt simply because the university uses the same facility itself at other times. Even when a university leases a facility for an unrelated business, issues may arise with respect to determining the amount of tax. In *RPI v. Commissioner* (see note 1), the method of allocating fixed costs between the unrelated business use of a collegiate facility and the tax-exempt use of the facility is discussed.

NOTE ――

1. In *Rensselaer Polytechnic Institute v. Commissioner of Internal Revenue*, 732 F.2d 1058 (1983), a college used its field house for both tax-exempt purposes and unrelated business purposes; therefore, income from the unrelated business use was taxable. However, in this case, a dispute regarding how to allocate the deductible expenses, such as depreciation, between the taxable and tax-exempt uses of the facility, arose. The plaintiff argued that the expenses should be divided in accordance with the relative amount of time the facility was used for each activity. For example, if the facility was used for tax-exempt purposes for five hours and for taxable purposes for five hours, half of the expenses could be used as a deduction for the taxable income. The commissioner, however, argued that the expenses should be allocated proportionally between the amount of time the facility was used for taxable purposes and the amount of time available for use, whether it was actually used or not. Therefore, even if it was used half for tax-exempt purposes and half for taxable purposes, they could not allocate half of the expenses to the taxable purposes because the time that the facility was dormant had to be factored into the equation. The judge ruled for the plaintiff college, holding that their method was "reasonable."

Broadcast Receipts

Broadcast receipts of tax-exempt organizations have long been of concern to many. The simple nature of broadcast receipts seems to imply a profit-making motive. However, this issue was directly addressed by the IRS in 1980 in Revenue Rulings 80-295 and 80-296. In these two rulings, the IRS concluded that revenue received by a tax-exempt athletic organization from the sale of broadcast rights to a radio or television network or to an independent producer does not constitute unrelated business. This issue came to the forefront when the IRS tried to tax the broadcast receipts of the Cotton Bowl in 1977. The IRS later reversed its decision and subsequently issued the two revenue rulings addressing this issue. It should be noted that while revenue rulings are given some weight by the courts, they are not law.

In January 1993, the IRS issued proposed regulations regarding the taxability of corporate sponsorships/revenues vis-á-vis tax-exempt organizations and, in particular, bowl games. The proposed regulations say that there is *no* tax liability provided that the sponsor is viewed as a donor. However, the proposed regulations further state that if the money is viewed as "doing advertising," then the sponsor is no longer considered a donor, but rather is viewed as an advertiser and hence this money is then taxable. Advertising is defined as "promoting products or services," or if it is tied to a Nielsen rating, then it is taxable. These are only proposed regulations which are not final. Hearings are being conducted and the final regulations are pending.

NOTE ————————————————————————————————————

1. For further information on broadcast receipts, see Thompson and Young, "Taxing the Sale of Broadcast Rights to College Athletics—An Unrelated Trade or Business?" 8 *J. C. & U. L.* 331 (1981–82).

Charitable Contributions, Luxury Box Rentals, and Scholarships

While most amateur athletic organizations pay no income taxes, the tax laws indirectly affect the way they operate. A significant source of funds for many athletic organizations is through the contributions of individuals and businesses. The attractiveness of these contributions for the contributor directly depends on the tax laws regarding itemized deductions. Athletic administrators should be aware of recent developments in the tax laws that have affected the attractiveness of contributions to athletic organizations.

Beginning in 1991, individual taxpayers with adjusted gross income (AGI) exceeding $100,000 faced reductions in their allowable itemized deductions. Taxpayers would have to reduce their total itemized deductions by 3 percent of the AGI exceeding $100,000. This reduction diminishes the attractiveness of contributing to athletic organizations.

Because of the heavy reliance of many athletic programs on contributions, athletic administrators have kept a close eye on Congress's treatment of certain charitable contributions. In October 1988 Congress arrived at a compromise on the issue of whether payments to athletic programs qualify as deductions for charitable contributions when the payments afford the right to purchase preferred seating at athletic events. Under the new provision, 80 percent of the fair market value of the preferred-seating privilege qualifies for a charitable deduction. Any amount contributed in excess of this fair market value remains fully deductible. This 80 percent rule of Congress reversed IRS Revenue Ruling 86-63, which provided that none of said fair market value is deductible. Such an arrangement required the taxpayer to determine what proportion of a given contribution actually purchased the privilege. In many cases the athletic scholarship program will provide this information.

Another recent development in tax laws relates to new limitations on the deductibility of entertainment expenses and luxury box rentals. Such limitations could cause businesses to seek alternatives to spending money on athletic events. As of January 1, 1994, only 50 percent of business meal and entertainment expenses could be deducted by the entity that incurred them. Furthermore, when a company rents a luxury skybox for more than one event per year, it may only deduct the actual cost of the tickets themselves, which is tied to the value of the highest priced nonskybox ticket available to the general public. As of 1989, any amount paid in excess of this ticket price was no longer deductible. The impact of this development on universities that have constructed skyboxes in their stadiums could be substantial.

Athletic administrators must also be concerned with the tax law's impact on scholarships and grants. In the past, all funds provided to a student as scholarships or grants were not included in the student's gross income. However, under the tax law, scholarships and grants awarded after August 16, 1986, for taxable years beginning after December 31, 1986, may contain certain amounts that must be included in the recipient's gross income.

The tax law defines qualified tuition and related expenses as tuition and fees required for enrollment, fees, books, supplies, and equipment required for courses of instruction. Scholarships and grants for these expenses are excluded from the recipient's gross income. However, amounts for room and board are not excludable. In addition, any portion of a scholarship or grant representing payment for teaching, research, or other services required as a condition for receiving the qualified scholarship is also included in the recipient's gross income.

This would require the grantor to file wage information returns regarding these amounts and also face the possibility of paying social security and employment taxes. In addition, IRS notice 87-31 urges the grantor to supply the recipient with a calculation of the appropriate amount to be included in his or her gross income.

The tax law is a constantly changing body of rules which seem to change without much publicity in some cases. Athletic administrators need to be aware of what effects the new law will have on their organizations so as to properly react and attempt to maintain the support they currently enjoy.

NOTE

1. For further information, see the following law review articles.
    (a) Jensen, "Taxation, The Student-Athlete, and the Professionalization of College Athletics," 1987 *Utah L. Rev.* 35 (1987).
    (b) Judge, "Student-Athletes As Employees: Income Tax Consequences," 13 *J. C. & U. L.* 285 (1986).

INTERCOLLEGIATE ATHLETICS AND GAMBLING

The problems associated with illegal gambling and the influence it may exert on intercollegiate athletics are of special concern to athletic administrators and others, since gambling affects the integrity of the games, the games themselves, and the public confidence in athletes and sports. Some argue that betting on games is encouraged by the press, which prints the "spread" on games in its sports pages, as well as advertisements on weekly tip sheets and betting aids. Although some contend that betting on athletics is enjoyable and is a form of entertainment, others contend that gambling has a negative impact on society and sports. Many athletic managers have taken steps to combat the dangers of illegal gambling in an effort to preserve the integrity of their schools, conferences, and leagues.

Estimates are that gambling on college athletics is a $1 billion a year industry. Problems associated with and arising from wagering have continually plagued college athletics. In 1945, five Brooklyn College basketball players were expelled from school after they admitted to accepting bribes to lose a game. In 1951, thirty-seven players at twenty-two schools were caught shaving points (trying to win by fewer points than bookmakers predict) in forty-four games. A gambling scandal at Boston College during the 1978–79 season led to the conviction of basketball player Rick Kuhn, who was sentenced to ten years in prison on federal gambling charges (see notes 8–10). In 1985, a gambling and drug scandal was uncovered at Tulane University. That incident, which involved a number of basketball players, led to Tulane

President Eamon Kelly's decision to drop the Division I men's basketball program "forever." However, just four years later, in 1989, the program was revived for competition in the Metro Conference.

The NCAA's disapproval of illegal gambling in intercollegiate athletics is clearly spelled out in the following bylaw:

10.3 Gambling Activities

Staff members of the athletics department of a member institution and student-athletes shall not knowingly:
  (a) Provide information to individuals involved in organized gambling activities concerning intercollegiate athletics competition;
  (b) Solicit a bet on any intercollegiate team;
  (c) Accept a bet on any team representing the institution, or
  (d) Participate in any gambling activity that involves intercollegiate athletics through a bookmaker, a parlay card or any other method employed by organized gambling. (*1993–94 NCAA Manual*, Bylaw 10.3)

The NCAA has continued to add to its investigating staff to keep up with the gambling problem. Many NCAA investigators are former FBI agents who attempt to maintain contacts with bookmakers, both in Nevada where sports gambling is legal and in other states where it is not. This unorthodox relationship between bookmakers and NCAA investigators is based on mutual concern that sporting events not be rigged to reach a predetermined outcome. The bookmakers cannot afford a rigged game for economic reasons, because their winning percentages and profit margins are based on a "point spread," which they formulate on the theory that the game is not rigged. The NCAA and the individual school's concerns are based on the integrity of the game and on their reputation.

The bookmakers usually alert investigators if there is a sizable change in the point spread on a particular game. Such a change is suspicious and may indicate that bettors have placed large wagers on a team. Of course, heavy betting may occur for other reasons, such as a coach's announcement of an injury to a key player. If no legitimate reasons are found, however, it increases the possibility that gamblers have "fixed" the game by bribing a coach, player, or official. Remember, bribes are not necessarily made to ensure that a team loses—just that it wins by fewer points than the predicted point spread. Once suspicions are aroused, college officials such as the president and athletic director are then informed by the NCAA. They may also be notified if investigators hear "street talk" about "something funny" going on somewhere in the institution's athletic program.

NOTES

1. John Thompson, basketball coach of the 1984 NCAA champion George-town University team, made the following remarks during an appearance before the District of Columbia Citizen's Gambling Study Commission:

> My opinion then, as now, is that it's not a question of whether gambling should be legal or not, but of being consistent. To legalize some forms of gambling, like lotteries, and to run betting lines in newspapers and broadcast them on television, is a kind of "entrapment."
>
> It's like putting heroin all over the street and advertising it in the newspapers, then arresting somebody for using it. By creating an atmosphere of permissiveness, it tells a kid it's okay to gamble because we've gone public with it.

2. Tony Vaccarino, an agent in the FBI's Criminal Investigations Division, says that coaches should study tapes of all games and talk with players to make sure they are all performing properly. He thinks a coach should get in touch with the FBI "if he feels his team is not performing the way it should." Vaccarino claims the FBI is opposed to legalizing sports gambling of any sort: "We say it would create situations where people get involved in gambling who would normally not get involved. It exposes them to involvement with organized-crime figures—with loan sharks, for instance, to pay off gambling debts."

3. In June 1985, at hearing held by the President's Commission on Organized Crime, John R. Davis, president of the NCAA, testified that the association would be in favor of a law that prohibited the printing of "point spreads" in newspapers, "were it not for apparent constitutional limitations." Davis also called for a federal law banning gambling on amateur sports. At the same hearings, Vince Doria, assistant managing editor for sports at the *Boston Globe*, testified:

> I think most newspapers have come to the conclusion that gamblers are readers too.... In fact, they are extremely avid readers of the sports pages. I think most of us believe that those readers deserve to be serviced.

See "Davis Gives Views at U.S. Hearing," *NCAA News*, July 3, 1985, pp. 1, 12.

4. For more information on gambling in intercollegiate athletics, see "Gambling on College Games Said to Be Up Dramatically," *Chronicle of Higher Education*, March 2, 1983, pp. 1, 16–18. The following excerpt is from that article:

> The Commission on the Review of the National Policy Toward Gambling recommended in its 1976 report, *Gambling in America*, "that there be an absolute prohibition against the inclusion of wagering on amateur sporting events [if betting on professional sports is legalized]. While the commission recognizes that some amateur events already are the objects of illegal wagering nationwide, it cannot condone the utilization for wagering purposes of educational institutions and similar organizations dedicated to the improvement of youth.
>
> This opinion is in part predicated on the fact that young athletes of high school and college age are far more impressionable and therefore are in greater danger of being subjected to the temptations of player corruption. Additionally, unlike professional sports leagues, particularly the [National Football League], amateur

athletic associations do not have enforcement or investigative capabilities which would enable them to maintain sufficient safeguards."

5. Billy Packer and Al McGuire, TV broadcast personalities, have produced a film called *Sell Out*, which warns athletes of the dangers associated with gambling. The film was produced by TPC Communication and financed by Nike, Inc.

6. Nevada, which is the only state in the nation to allow legal sports gambling, does not permit betting on college games involving public or private institutions located in the state, whether the contest is being played inside or outside state borders. The regulation was enacted in 1972 by the Nevada Gambling Control Board. The Nevada law had its most recent effect on the 1991 NCAA men's final four basketball tournament, which involved teams from UNLV, North Carolina, Duke, and Kansas. Legal wagering in Nevada was restricted to the Kansas-North Carolina semifinal and the Kansas-Duke final but was prohibited by law on the UNLV-Duke semifinal.

7. Most athletic conferences, if they address the problem of gambling at all, do so in a manner to disclaim responsibility. The following excerpt is from the *1992–93 Pacific-10 Conference Handbook*, Administrative Rule 3-8.

> Instructions Re: Gambling, Pro Contracts. Each member institution shall carry out its own procedures to inform and instruct its student-athletes on their responsibilities in protecting themselves and their sports from gambling interests....

8. In *United States v. Burke*, 700 F.2d 70 (2d Cir. 1983), *aff'd* 464 U.S. 816 (1983), Rick Kuhn, a former Boston College basketball player, was charged (along with four co-defendants) and convicted of racketeering by conspiring to fix at least six games, of sports bribery, and of violation of the Interstate Travel and Aid to Racketeering statutes. In sentencing Kuhn to a ten-year sentence, the court noted:

> The crimes in this case are especially significant in view of the ramifications which they have had on the world of sports, college basketball in particular. A group of gamblers and career criminals were able to band together and successfully bribe and influence college athletes. Their motivation was simple and clear—financial gain. The crime, however, reminds millions of sports fans that athletics can be compromised and are not always merely honest competition among dedicated athletes.
>
> While it is true that only one or possibly two athletes were compromised, the effect remains basically the same. Every college athlete may now come under suspicion by fans and coaches. This suspicion has existed previously due to earlier scandals dating back several years, and it is now renewed as a result of this offense.
>
> This 26-year-old defendant undoubtedly assumed one of the more essential roles in this offense. While it may be true that his performance during games was not particularly pivotal, his actions away from the basketball court are of significant importance. He was a member of the 1978–79 Boston College team who initially agreed to participate and thereafter recruited other players, maintained contact with the gamblers and accepted their payments.
>
> It is interesting to note that there was not testimony introduced at the trial which indicated a reluctance on the part of the defendant to participate (in point shaving) or a desire to terminate his involvement. Rather, he emerges as some-

what of a greedy individual who was more interested in collecting money from his criminal associates than he was in winning basketball games.

The defendant is a product of a stable and supporting working-class family. From a young age, he developed natural abilities in athletics and was essentially successful in signing a professional baseball contract in 1973 and in attending college on a basketball scholarship three years later. Various individuals who have been (associated) with the defendant in his home town of Swissville, Pennsylvania, have described him in very positive terms. The reasons therefore as to why he became involved in this offense remain unclear.

On final analysis, deterrence emerges as the most important sentencing objective. A strong argument can be offered that the substantial term of incarceration imposed on this defendant will be recalled in the future by another college athlete who may be tempted to compromise his performance.

9. The NCAA followed the *Burke* (*Kuhn*) case with great interest and followed up the conviction with a full account of the interaction with organized crime which led to Kuhn's ten-year sentence. See "Boston College: A Gamble That Didn't Pay Off," *NCAA News*, February 15, 1982, p. 3.

10. In 1984, a federal court acquitted Ernie Cobb, a teammate of Kuhn's, of charges arising out of the same violations as those which convicted Kuhn. Cobb admitted accepting $1,000 in 1979 from one of the men convicted but claimed it was not for fixing games but only for giving advice as to which teams Boston College was likely to beat. See "Former College Players Acquitted on Basketball Gambling Charge," *Chronicle of Higher Education*, April 4, 1984, p. 28.

11. In May 1983, in the wake of disclosures made to the FBI by Baltimore Colts quarterback Art Schlichter that while at Baltimore he had run up in four months gambling debts of $389,000, his alma mater, Ohio State, began an investigation into his alleged gambling while a student-athlete. "It would only be prudent administration for us to know what took place," said Ohio State associate athletic director James Jones. See "Collegiate Gambling," *Boston Globe*, May 6, 1983.

Schlichter later admitted he had been gambling for years, in high school, at Ohio State, and while with the Colts. See "Schlichter Enters the Next Phase Along the Way Back," *New York Times*, July 23, 1984, p. C1.

12. In March 1985, three Tulane University basketball players were arrested and charged with fixing the outcome of games, the first point-shaving scandal to involve intercollegiate athletics since the Boston College incident during the 1978–79 season. In the wake of the scandal all Tulane basketball coaches resigned, the basketball program was terminated, and the athletic director resigned. The case was closed in April 1987 with a final tally of eight people pleading guilty to felony or misdemeanor charges. Basketball was reinstated at the University for the 1989–90 season. For more information on this incident see the following articles.

(a) "Tulane U., Beset by Recruiting Violations, Gambling Allegations, to Drop Basketball," *Chronicle of Higher Education*, April 10, 1985, p. 31.

(b) "Blowing the Whistle on Men's Basketball at Tulane U.," *Chronicle of Higher Education*, April 17, 1985, pp. 27, 28.

(c) "Big Trouble at Tulane," *Sports Illustrated*, April 8, 1985, p. 36.

(d) "Tulane Ends Basketball," *New York Times*, February 19, 1985, p. A26.

(e) "NCAA Accepts Tulane Reforms," *New York Times*, January 22, 1987, p. D30.

(f) "Tulane Basketball Back," *New York Times*, April 22, 1988, p. A22.

13. In August 1985, the first of the Tulane basketball players to go on trial, John "Hot Rod" Williams, had a mistrial called after a few days of testimony when the judge ruled that the state's prosecutor had withheld valuable evidence from the defendant's attorney during pretrial discovery. In November 1985 a state appeals court ruled that Williams had to stand trial, reinstating the charges against him. In June 1986, Williams was acquitted by a jury of the five gambling-related charges against him. for further information, see the following articles.

(a) "Trial Starts Today for Tulane Star," *New York Times*, August 12, 1985, p. C8.

(b) "Tulane Trial Is Halted by Judge," *New York Times*, August 14, 1985, p. B9.

(c) "Mistrial Declared for Ex-Tulane Star," *New York Times*, August 16, 1985, p. A19.

(d) "Mistrial Order Opposed," *New York Times*, August 18, 1985, p. 12.

(e) "Ex-Tulane Player Denies Fixing Games," *USA Today*, June 11, 1986, p. 7C.

(f) "Jury Acquits Former Tulane U. Basketball Star of Charges He Shaved Points to Aid Gamblers," *Chronicle of Higher Education*, June 25, 1986, p. 26.

(g) "Not Guilty at Tulane," *Sports Illustrated*, June 30, 1986, p. 11.

14. The Tulane basketball players were charged under Louisiana's Bribery of Sports Participants law (L.S.A.—R.S. 14:118.1):

A. Bribing of sports participants is the giving or offering to give, directly or indirectly, anything of apparent present or prospective value to any professional or amateur baseball, football, hockey, polo, tennis or basketball player or boxer or any person or player who participates or expects to participate in any professional or amateur game or sport or any contest of skill, speed, strength or endurance of man or beast or any jockey, driver, groom or any person participating or expecting to participate in any horse race, including owners of race tracks and their employees, stewards, trainers, judges, starters or special policemen, or to any owner, manager, coach or trainer of any team or participant in any such game, contest or sport, with the intent to influence him to lose or cause to be lost, or corruptly to affect or influence the result thereof, or to limit his or his team's or his mount or beast's margin of victory in any baseball, football, hockey or basketball game, boxing, tennis or polo match or horse race or any professional or amateur sport or game in which such player or participant or jockey or driver is taking part or expects to take part, or has any duty in connection therewith.

The acceptance of, or the offer to accept directly or indirectly anything of apparent present or prospective value under such circumstances by any of the above named persons shall also constitute bribery of sports participants.

Whoever commits the crime of bribery of sports participants is guilty of a felony and shall be punished by a fine of not more than ten thousand dollars and imprisoned for not less than one year nor more than five years, with or without hard labor, or both.

B. The offender under this Section, who states the facts under oath to the district attorney charged with the prosecution of the offense, and who gives evidence tending to convict any other offender under that Section, may, in the discretion of such district attorney be granted full immunity from prosecution in respect to the offense reported, except for perjury in giving such testimony.

15. As a result of the investigation surrounding the Tulane University "point shaving" scandal, Memphis State University also became the target of a gambling probe. For further information, see the following articles.

(a) "Rumors Worry Head of Memphis State," *New York Times*, February 27, 1985, p. 42.

(b) "Probe by Memphis State U. Fails to Turn Up Any Evidence to Support Gambling Rumors," *Chronicle of Higher Education*, July 31, 1985, pp. 23, 26.

16. See also *Louisiana v. Angelo Trosclair III*, 443 So. 2d 1098 (La. Supp. Ct. 1984), for a Louisiana Supreme Court decision which examined the Louisiana Bribery Sports Participant law in relation to horse racing.

17. In March 1990, point-shaving allegations involving former North Carolina State basketball players surfaced. It was alleged that up to four players, including Charles Shackleford, had conspired with bookmakers to shave points on at least four North Carolina State basketball games. Shackleford and others denied the charges.

The allegations were yet another blow to the North Carolina State basketball program, which had been placed earlier in the 1989–90 season on two years' probation by the NCAA for recruiting violations. These controversies and other allegations of academic improprieties eventually led to the dismissal of head basketball coach Jim Valvano in April 1990.

GLOSSARY OF LEGAL AND SPORTS TERMS

Acceptance: The offeree's notification to the offeror that he agrees to be bound by the terms and conditions of the offer.

Accommodation: Adjustment or settlement.

Accrue: Increase, add to, become due.

Addendum: Addition and/or change.

Adjudicate: Have a court make a decision or decide a dispute.

Administrative law: Law which affects private parties, promulgated by governmental agencies other than courts or legislative bodies. These administrative agencies derive their power from legislative enactments and are subject to judicial review.

Advance: To give or grant funds.

Aff'd (affirmed): To affirm a judgment, decree, or order is to declare that it is valid and right and must stand as rendered by the lower court.

Affidavit: A written statement or declaration of facts sworn to by the maker, taken before a person officially permitted by law to administer oaths.

Agent: One who is authorized by the principal to make contracts with third parties on behalf of the principal.

Amateur Athletic Union (AAU): An amateur athletic association dedicated to the development of amateur sports and physical fitness for amateur athletes of all ages.

Amateur Sports Act: Passed by the U.S. Congress in 1978 to reorganize and coordinate amateur athletics in the U.S. and to encourage and strengthen participation of U.S. amateurs in international competition. The Act creates a governing structure for the USOC by empowering it to select one national governing body (NGB) for each Olympic or Pan-American sport.

American Bar Association: National association of lawyers in the United States.

American Basketball Association: Defunct corporation which operated a professional basketball league in the United States from 1966–

1970 and which eventually merged with the National Basketball Association.

American Football League: Defunct corporation which operated a professional football league in the United States from 1960–1966 and which eventually merged with the National Football League.

Amicus curiae: Friend of the court; a third party who presents a brief to a court on behalf of one or the other of the parties in a case.

Annotations: (1) Statutory: brief summaries of the law and facts of cases interpreting statutes passed by Congress or state legislatures which are included in codes; or (2) textual: expository essays of varying length on significant legal topics chosen from selected cases published with the essays.

Answer: The defendant's initial pleading on the alleged violation of criminal or civil law.

Antitrust law: Designed to promote competition in the business sector through regulation designed to control the exercise of private economic power.

Appeal: A request from the losing party in a case that the decision be reviewed by a higher court. Acceptance of the request and issuance by a writ of appeal is mandatory for the higher court.

Appeal denied: A refusal by the higher (or appellate) level court to review a lower court decision for error.

Appeal filed: A request for a higher (or appellate) level court to review a lower court decision for error.

Appellant: The party who appeals a decision from a lower to a higher court.

Appellate court: Court of appellate jurisdiction.

Appellate jurisdiction: Covers cases tried or reviewed by the individual state's highest court involving federal questions, including those bearing on the U.S. Constitution, congressional acts, or foreign treaties. It also covers cases tried or reviewed by the U.S. courts of appeals or the U.S. district courts.

Appellee: The party against whom an appeal is taken.

Arbitration: The hearing and settlement of a dispute between opposing parties by a third party. This decision is often binding by prior agreement of the parties.

Arraignment: The appearance of a defendant to a criminal charge before a judge for the purpose of pleading guilty or not guilty to the indictment.

Assault: An unlawful, intentional show of force or an attempt to do physical harm to another person. Assault can constitute the basis of a civil or criminal action. *See also* **Battery.**

Association of Intercollegiate Athletics for Women: Defunct amateur athletic association which governed women's intercollegiate athletics before the National Collegiate Athletic Association assumed those duties in the mid-1980s.

Assumption of the risk: Knowledge by one of the parties to an agreement of the risks to be encountered, and that party's consent to take the chance of injury therefrom.

Attorney general opinions: Opinions issued by the government's chief counsel at the request of some governmental body that interpret the law for the requesting agency in the same manner as a private attorney would for his client. The opinions are not binding on the courts but are usually accorded some degree of persuasive authority.

Authority: Refers to the precedential value to be accorded an opinion of a judicial or administrative body. A court's opinion is binding authority on other courts directly below it in the judicial hierarchy. Opinions of lower courts or of courts outside the hierarchy are governed by the degree to which it adheres to the doctrine of stare decisis. Authority may also be either primary or secondary. Statute law, administrative regulations issued pursuant to enabling legislation, and case law are primary authority and if applicable will usually determine the outcome of a case. Other statements of or about law are considered secondary authority, and thus not binding.

Battery: An unlawful use of force against another person resulting in physical contact (a tort); it is commonly used in the phrase "assault and battery," assault being the threat of force, and battery the actual use of force. *See also* **Assault.**

Bill: Refers to a legislative proposal introduced in the legislature. The term distinguishes unfinished legislation from directly enacted law.

Bona fide: Real, true, and actual.

Book value: The value at which a security is carried on the bank's balance sheet. Book value is often acquisition cost, plus or minus accretion or amortization, which can differ from market value significantly.

Branch banking: The right of banks headquartered in some states to take deposits, cash checks, and make loans at more than one location (branch) in the state. Where branch banking is not allowed, "unit banking" prevails.

Breach of contract: The failure to perform any of the terms of an agreement.

Brief: In American law practice, a written statement prepared by the counsel arguing a case in court. It contains a summary of the facts of the case, the pertinent laws, and an argument of how the law applies to the facts supporting counsel's position.

Buckley Amendment: Federal legislation which regulates the release and review of student-athletes' records concerning academic and financial aid information.

Business unit: A part of a bank managed and accounted for as a self-contained, independent business, serving customers outside the bank and/or other business units in the bank. These units are encouraged to innovate and contribute to corporate profits, while remaining consistent with corporate policies and objectives.

Case book: A textbook used to instruct law students in a particular area of substantive law. The text consists of a collection of court opinions, usually from appellate courts, and notes by the author(s).

Case law: The law of reported appellate judicial opinions as distinguished from statutes or administrative law.

Cause of action: A claim in law and in fact sufficient to bring the case to court; the grounds of an action. (Example: breach of contract.)

Certiorari: A writ issued by a superior to an inferior court requiring the latter to produce the records of a particular case tried therein. It is most commonly used to refer to the Supreme Court of the United States, which uses the writ of certiorari as a discretionary devise to choose the cases it wishes to hear. The term's origin is Latin, meaning "to be informed of."

Cert. (certiorari) denied: A decision by an appellate court to refuse to review a lower court decision.

Cert. (certiorari) granted: A decision by an appellate court to grant a hearing to review a lower court decision.

Charitable immunity: Similar to sovereign immunity in that it limits the liabilities of charitable organizations.

Citation: The reference to authority necessary to substantiate the validity of one's argument or position. Citation to authority and supporting references is both important and extensive in any form of legal writing. Citation form is also given emphasis in legal writing, and early familiarity with *A Uniform System of Citation*, published by the Harvard Law Review Association, will stand the law student in good stead.

Cited case: A case which is referred to in a court decision.

Civil law: (1) Roman law embodied in the Bode of Justinian, which presently prevails in more countries of Western Europe other than

Great Britain and which is the foundation of Louisiana Law; (2) the law concerning noncriminal matters in a common law jurisdiction; (3) one form of legal action for enforcement or protection of private rights and prevention or redress of private wrongs.

Civil Rights Restoration Act: Legislation enacted by Congress in 1988 which returned Title IX applicability to the "institutional approach"; therefore in a collegiate setting, athletic departments or any program within an institution that receives federal funding is subject to Title IX legislation.

Claim: (1) The assertion of a right, as to money or property; (2) the accumulation of facts which give rise to a right enforceable in court.

Class action: A lawsuit brought by a representative party on behalf of a group, all of whose members have the same or a similar grievance against the defendant.

Code: By popular usage a compilation or a revised statute. Technically, the laws in force are rewritten and arranged in classified order, with the addition of material having the force of law taken from judicial decrees. The repealed and temporary acts are eliminated and the revision is reenacted.

Collective bargaining: The process by which the terms and conditions of employment are agreed upon through negotiations between the bargaining representative of the employees (union) and the employer (management).

College Football Association (CFA): An amateur athletic association composed of NCAA Division IA members who compete in football.

Common law: The origin of the Anglo-American legal systems. English common law was largely customary law and unwritten, until discovered, applied, and reported by the courts of law. In theory, the common law courts did not create law but rather discovered it in the customs and habits of the English people. The strength of the judicial system in pre-parliamentary days is one reason for the continued emphasis in common law systems on case law. In a narrow sense, common law is the phrase still used to distinguish case law from statutory law.

Comparative negligence: Doctrine in the law of negligence by which the negligence of the parties is compared, and a recovery being permitted when the negligence of the plaintiff was less when compared to the negligence of the defendant.

Compensatory damages: A money award equivalent to the actual injury or loss sustained by plaintiff.

Complaint: The plaintiff's initial pleading and according to the Federal Rules of Civil Procedure, no longer full of the technicalities demanded by the common law. A complaint need only contain a short and plain statement of the claim upon which relief is sought, an indication of the type of relief requested, and an indication that the court has jurisdiction to hear the case.

Compromise: An agreement reached by each party giving up part of its claim(s), right(s), or property.

Congressional documents: Important sources for legislative histories, which are often necessary for proper interpretation of statute law. Congressional documents are most accessible through specialized indexes and include hearings before congressional committees, reports by or to House or Senate committees, and special studies conducted under congressional authority.

Consideration: Something to be done or abstained from, by one party to a contract in order to induce another party to enter into a contract.

Constitution: Contains the fundamental law of any organization possessing one. Most national constitutions are written; the English and Israeli constitutions are unwritten.

Continental Basketball Association: A corporation which operates professional basketball leagues in the United States.

Contract: An agreement between two or more parties, a preliminary step in making of which is an offer by one and acceptance by the other, in which minds of parties meet and concur in understanding of terms. The elements of an enforceable contract are competent parties, a proper subject matter, consideration, and mutuality of agreement and obligation.

Contributory negligence: The negligence of a plaintiff which contributes to or enhances the complaining party's injuries. Contributory negligence is a bar to recovery at common law in some jurisdictions.

Corporation: An artificial person or legal entity created under state corporation statutes.

Counterclaim: A claim made by the defendant against the plaintiff in a civil lawsuit; it constitutes a separate cause of action.

Counteroffer: The offeree's response to an offer, in which the offeree proposes different or additional terms than were contained in the original offer. A counteroffer is construed as a rejection of the original offer, and a new offer by the original offeree.

Covenant: An agreement of promise of two or more parties.

Criminal law: One form (division) of legal action by which the state (federal or state) treats crimes and their punishments, usually by imprisonment, fine, or both.

Damages: Monetary compensation awarded by a court for an injury caused by the act of another. Damages may be *actual* or *compensatory* (equal to the amount of loss shown), *exemplary* or *punitive* (in excess of the actual loss and which are given to punish the person for the malicious conduct which caused the injury), or *nominal* (less than the actual loss—often a trivial amount) which are given because the injury is slight or because the exact amount of injury has not been determined satisfactorily.

Data base: The accumulation of textual or other material available to the user of an on-line computerized information service.

Defamation: Anything published (libel) or publicly spoken (slander) which injures a person's character, fame, or reputation by false and malicious statements.

Defendant: The party against whom legal action is taken; particularly, a person accused or convicted of a criminal offense.

Deposition: The testimony of one witness taken out of court before a court reporter and under oath.

Direct Payment License: Program administered by USA Track &Field in which licensed athletes can receive endorsement fees, sponsorship monies, etc. directly and still maintain their amateur eligibility.

Discharge: To release, usually from an obligation.

Discovery: A method by which opposing parties may obtain information from each other, to prepare for trial and to narrow the issues to be presented at trial.

Diversity jurisdiction: That aspect of the jurisdiction of the federal courts which applies to suits between residents of different states.

Docket number: A number, sequentially assigned by the clerk at the outset to a lawsuit brought to a court for adjudication.

Due care: The legal duty one owes to another according to the circumstances of a particular case.

Due process of law: A term found in the Fifth and Fourteenth Amendments of the U.S. Constitution and also in many states constitutions. Its exact meaning varies from one situation to another and from one era to the next, but basically it is concerned with the guarantee of every person's enjoyment of his rights (e.g., the right to a fair hearing in any legal dispute).

Endorse: To sign.

Equal Pay Act: Passed in 1963 and stipulates that an employer must pay equal salaries to men and women holding jobs that require equal skill, effort, and responsibility and that are performed under similar working conditions.

Equal protection: The constitutional guarantee that no person shall be unreasonably discriminated against legally.

Equal Rights Amendment: A proposed amendment to the U.S. Constitution to guarantee equal rights to women which did not get ratified in the early 1980s but which certain states have adopted.

Equitable: Just; fair; reasonable.

Equity: Legal rules, remedies, customs, practices, and principles devised by courts of law to supplement those of the common law.

Et al.: And another; and others.

Evidence: Any form of proof presented at trial through the use of witness records, documents, and concrete objects, and used to assist the trier of fact in making his determination of the case.

Ex parte: A hearing or examination in the presence of only one of the parties to a case.

Ex rel.: On behalf of, in the name of; a legal proceeding instituted by a state on behalf of an individual who has a private interest in the matter.

Federal question: A case which contains a major issue involving the U.S. Constitution or a provision of an act of Congress or a U.S. treaty. The jurisdiction of the federal courts is governed, in part, by the existence of a federal question.

Felony: A serious criminal offense, as distinct from a misdemeanor. Typically, those crimes for which the punishment may exceed one year in jail.

Forbearance: Refraining from doing something which one has a legal right to do.

Governmental activity: One which can be performed only by the state.

Grievance arbitration: The submission of the parties grievance to a private unofficial person(s) who listens to the disputed question and contentions and then gives a decision regarding the dispute.

Health, Education and Welfare Department: A former cabinet department in the federal government that oversaw Title IX compliance.

Hearings: Extensively employed by both legislative and administrative agencies and can be adjudicative or merely investigatory. Adjudicative hearings can be appealed in a court of law. Congressional committees often hold hearings prior to the enactment of legislation; these hearings are then important sources of legislative history.

Hearsay evidence: Evidence not based on the personal knowledge of the witness but from the mere repetition of what one has heard another say.

Holding: The declaration of the conclusion of law reached by the court as to the legal effect of the facts of the case.

Immunity: A condition which protects against liability (tort) or prosecution (criminal law).

Incur: To take on or accept.

Independent contractor: One who contracts to perform work according to his own methods and without being subject to the control of the employer except for the result of the contractor's work.

Indictment: A formal accusation of a crime made by a grand jury at the request of a prosecuting attorney.

Induce: To urge on or to lead into.

Injunction: A judge's order that a person do or, more commonly, refrain from doing a certain act. An injunction may be preliminary or temporary pending trial of the issue presented, or it may be final if the issue has already been decided in court.

In loco parentis: Placed in the position of the parents of the child, such as a coach or teacher given this status within their relationship with the student-athlete.

In personam: Against a person. A legal proceeding instituted to obtain decrees or judgments against a person.

In re: In the matter of, concerning; usual method of entitling a judicial proceeding in which there are not adversary parties.

Instruction to the jury: A statement by the judge to a jury of the applicable law.

Instrument: Usually a document, such as a contract.

International Federations (IFs): An IOC-recognized body for each sport which sets its own rules and regulations governing eligibility of athletes for international competitions.

International Olympic Committee (IOC): World sanctioning body for the Olympic Games; it is located in Switzerland.

Interrogatories: Return questions directed to a party or witness, who must serve return answers to the questions under oath.

Jurisdiction: The power of a court to hear and determine a given class of cases; the power to act or a particular action.

Jurisprudence: (1) The science or philosophy of law; (2) a collective term for case law as opposed to legislation.

Knight Commission: Created in 1989 by the Knight Foundation to study collegiate athletics and devise a proposal for reform. The Knight Commission is comprised of university presidents, company CEOs, and a U.S. Congressman.

Laches: Wrongful or unwarranted delay.

Legislative history: Provides the meanings and interpretations (intent) of a statute as embodied in legislative documents. Also, citations and dates to legislative enactments, amendments and repeals of statutes are sometimes imprecisely identified as legislative histories. More accurate designations of these citations of legislative changes, as included in codes, are historical notes or amendatory histories.

Lexis: The pioneering computerized full text legal research system of Mead Data Central. The data base organizes documents into "libraries" and "files." Documents may be court decisions, statutory, or administrative provisions.

Liability: The condition of being responsible either for damages resulting from an injurious act or for discharging an obligation or debt.

Libel: Written defamation of a person's character.

Major Indoor Soccer League: Corporation which operates professional indoor soccer in the United States.

Majority opinion: An appellate court decision, in which the holding of the court is not unanimous.

Major League Baseball (MLB): Corporation which operates professional baseball in the United States and Canada; it is located in New York City.

Malfeasance: The doing of an act that is wrong and unlawful.

Malpractice: Professional misconduct or unreasonable lack of skill. This term is usually applied to such conduct by doctors and lawyers.

Misdemeanor: A minor criminal offense, as distinct from a felony.

Misfeasance: Performance of a legal act in an illegal manner.

Mitigation of damages: A requirement in contract law that a plaintiff alleviate the damages of the one who has breached a contract.

MLB Players Association: Represents professional union players in Major League Baseball.

Modified: Changed; a decision altered by the introduction of new elements or the cancellation of existing elements.

Moot question: A case which, because of changed circumstance or conditions after the litigation was begun, no longer contains a justiciable question.

Motion: A formal request made to a judge pertaining to any issue arising during the pendency of a lawsuit.

National Association for Intercollegiate Athletics (NAIA): An amateur intercollegiate athletic association for small-sized four-year colleges; it is located in Kansas City, Missouri.

National Basketball Association (NBA): Corporation which operates professional basketball in the United States; it is located in New York City.

National Collegiate Athletic Association (NCAA): The major intercollegiate athletic association for men and women in the United States; it is located in Overland Park, Kansas.

National Federation of State High School Associations (NFSHSA): Amateur athletic association for interscholastic athletics in the United States.

National Football League (NFL): Corporation which operates professional football in the United States; it is located in New York City.

National Governing Bodies (NGBs): Governing bodies for individual sports sanctioned by the U.S. Olympic Committee.

National Hockey League (NHL): Corporation which operates professional hockey in the United States and Canada; it is located in New York City.

National Junior College Athletic Association (NJCAA): Amateur intercollegiate athletic association for two-year colleges in the United States; it is located in Colorado Springs, Colorado.

National Reporter System: The network of reporters published by West Publishing Company; these reporters attempt to publish and digest all cases of precedential value from all state and federal courts.

NBA Players Association: A union which represents professional players in the National Basketball Association.

Negative covenant: An understanding in a deed or contract whereby a party obliges him or herself to refrain from doing or performing some act.

Negligence: The failure to exercise due care.

Negotiation: The deliberation, settling, or arranging of the terms and conditions of a possible transaction.

NFL Players Association: Union which represents professional union players in the National Football League.

NHL Players Association: Union which represents professional union players in the National Hockey League.

Nonfeasance: In tort law this term applies to nonperformance of some act which ought to be performed, omission to perform a required duty at all, or total neglect of duty.

North American Soccer League: Defunct corporation which operated professional outdoor soccer in the United States from 1968 to 1985.

Obligation: Debt or duty.

Offer: An act on the part of one person giving another the legal power of creating the obligation called a contract.

Offeree: One to whom a contract is made.

Offeror: One who makes a contract offer.

Opinion: An expression of the reasons why a certain decision (the judgment) was reached in a case. A *majority opinion* is usually written by one judge and represents the principles of law which a majority of the judge's colleagues on the court deem operative in a given decision; it has more precedential value than any of the following. A *separate opinion* may be written by one or more judges in which he or they concur in or dissent from the majority opinion. A *concurring opinion* agrees with the result reached by the majority, but disagrees with the precise reasoning leading to that result. A *dissenting opinion* disagrees with the result reached by the majority and thus disagrees with the reasoning and/or the principles of law used by the majority in deciding the case. A *plurality opinion* (called a "judgment" by the Supreme Court) is agreed to by less than a majority as to the reasoning of the decision, but is agreed to by a majority as to the result. A *per curiam opinion* is an opinion "by the court" which expresses its decision in the case but whose author is not identified. A *memorandum opinion* is a holding of the whole court in which the opinion is very concise.

Option clause: In sports law, the club's right to renew a contract for a one-year period under the same terms and conditions as the previous year of the contract, including another option year, except that the option year of the contract will not contain an option clause. The only term which may differ in the option year is the salary, which varies from league to league, according to provisions set forth in the contract and/or collective bargaining agreement.

Option contract: A contract which binds the offeror to hold his offer open for a specified period of time in which the offeree must give consideration for the option.

Ordinance: The equivalent of a municipal statute, passed by the city council and governing matters not already covered by federal or state law.

Original jurisdiction: Jurisdiction to take cognizance of a cause at its inception, try it, and pass judgment upon the law and facts. Covers two types of cases: those involving ambassadors, ministers, and consuls, and those involving a state as one of the parties to a lawsuit.

Parallel citation: A citation reference to the same case printed in two or more different reports.

Parol evidence rule: Prohibits the admission of oral statements, preliminary agreements, or writings made prior to or at the time of signing that would in any way alter, contradict, or change the written contract.

Per annum: Per year.

Per curiam: By the court. An opinion of the Court which is authored by the justices collectively.

Per diem: Per day.

Permanent injunction: An injunction intended to remain in force until the final termination of the particular suit.

Per se: By itself; inherently; in isolation.

Petitioner: The party who brings an action; the party who seeks a *writ of certiorari.*

Plaintiff: The party who brings an action; the complainant.

Precedent: A case which furnishes an example or authority for deciding subsequent cases in which identical or similar facts are present.

Preliminary injunction: An injunction granted at the institution of a suit to restrain the defendant from doing or continuing some act, and which may be discharged or made perpetual as soon as the rights of the parties are determined.

Presidents Commission of the NCAA: An advisory body comprised of university presidents within the NCAA's governing structure which can propose legislation to be voted upon by the NCAA membership.

Prima facie: At first sight; on the face of it; presumability; a fact presumed to be true unless disproved by some evidence to the contrary.

Proprietary activity: One which is done by the state but could be undertaken by the private sector.

Proximate cause: The act which is the natural and reasonably foreseeable cause of the harm or agent which occurs and injures the plaintiff.

Punitive damages: Compensation in excess of actual or consequential damages. They are awarded in order to punish the wrongdoer, and will be awarded only in cases involving willful or malicious misconduct.

Ratification: The adopting or confirming of an act which was previously executed without authority or an act which was voidable.

Reckless misconduct: An action which falls between the unintentional tort of negligence and the intentional torts of assault and battery. Behavior characterized by intent on the part of the defendant to commit the act but no intent to harm the plaintiff by the act.

Regional reporter: A unit of the National Reporter System which reports state court decisions within a defined geographical area.

Regulations: Orders issued by various governmental departments to carry out the intent of the law. Agencies issue regulations to guide the activity of their employees and to ensure uniform application of the law. Regulations are not the work of the legislature and do not have the effect of law in theory. In practice, however, because of the intricacies of judicial review of administrative action, regulations can have an important effect in determining the outcome of cases involving regulatory activity. U.S. government regulations appear first in the *Federal Register,* published five days a week, and are subsequently arranged by subject in the *Code of Federal Regulations.*

Relinquish: To give up, surrender, or turn over.

Remand: To send back for further proceedings, as when a higher court sends a case back to a lower court.

Reports: (1) *Court reports* are published judicial cases arranged according to some grouping, such as jurisdiction, court, period of time, subject matter or case significance; (2) *administrative reports* or *decisions* are published decisions of an administrative agency; (3) *annual statements of progress, activities or policy* are reports issued by an administrative agency, or an association.

Rescission: Canceling, annulling, voiding.

Reserve clause: In sports law, the club's right to renew a contract for a one-year period under the same terms and conditions as the previous year of the contract; the only term that may differ in the option year is the salary, which varies from league to league according to provisions set forth in the contract and/or collective bargaining agreement.

Res ipsa loquitur: Rebuttal presumption that defendant was negligent, which arises upon proof that instrumentality causing injury was not defendant's exclusive control, and that the extent was one which ordinarily does not happen in absence of negligence.

Res judicata: An adjudicated matter; a legal issue that has been decided by a court.

Respondent: The party against whom legal action is taken; the party against whom a writ of certiorari is sought.

Rev'd (reversed): A decision by an appellate court which voids a lower court decision based on some error made in the lower court. Often times the case is also remanded (sent back) to the lower court with instruction.

Right: That which a person is entitled to keep and enjoy, and to be protected by law in its enjoyment. A right constitutes a claim when it is not in one's possession. The word "right" also signifies an interest when used in regard to property. "Right" in this sense entitles a person to hold or convey his property at pleasure.

Shepardizing: A term that is the trademark property of Shepard's Citations, Inc. and is descriptive of the general use of its publications.

Slander: Oral defamation of a person's character.

Sovereign immunity: Certain protections afforded to the state against tort liability regardless of the circumstances when the state is engaged in a governmental function.

Specific performance: An equitable remedy, whereby the court orders one of the parties to a contract to perform his duties under the contract. Usually granted when money damages would be an inadequate remedy.

Standard of care: The level of caution that one should exercise.

Standing: The qualifications needed to bring legal action. These qualifications relate to the existence of a controversy in which the *plaintiff* himself has suffered or is about to suffer an injury to or infringement upon a legally protected *right* which a court is competent to redress.

Stare decisis: To stand on what has been decided; to adhere to the decision of previous cases. It is a rule, sometimes departed from, that a point settled in a previous case becomes a precedent which should be followed in subsequent cases decided by the same court.

State action: Legal principle consisting of the university, association, or governing body being shown to be part of the federal government, state government, or an arm or agency of a state government. State action must be proven to bring a constitutional law challenge.

Statutes: Acts of a legislature. Depending upon its context in usage, a statute may mean a single act of legislature or a body of acts which are collected and arranged according to a scheme or for a session of a legislature or parliament.

Statutes of limitations: Laws setting time periods during which disputes may be taken to court.

Strict liability: Liability regardless of fault. Under tort law, strict liability is imposed on any person who introduces into commerce any good that is unreasonably dangerous when in a defective condition.

Subpoena: A court order compelling a witness to appear and testify in a certain proceeding.

Summary proceeding: A judicial action, usually a judgment or decision, which is taken without benefit of a formal hearing. Summary decisions of the Supreme Court are those made without the Court having heard an oral argument.

Summons: Actual serving of notice to a person notifying the person that an action has been commenced against them and that they are required to appear in court and answer the complaint in such action.

Supreme Court: (1) The court of last resort in the federal judicial system. (It also has original jurisdiction in some cases.) (2) In most states, the highest appellate court or court of last resort (but not in New York or Massachusetts).

Temporary restraining order: An order, of limited time duration, restraining the defendant from doing the threatened act until the propriety of granting an injunction can be determined.

Terminate: To end or bring to an end.

The Athletics Congress: Amateur athletic organization that governs amateur (nonintercollegiate or interscholastic) track competition in the United States.

Title IX: Became law in 1972. This law specifically and clearly recognizes the problems of sex discrimination and forbids such discrimination in any program, organization, or agency that receives federal funds.

Title VII: Was passed in 1964 and focuses on discriminatory, on the basis of race, color, religion, sex, or national origin, hiring/firing practices and advancement policies within companies.

Tort: A civil wrong which does not involve a contractual relationship. The elements of a tort are a duty owed, a breach of that duty, and the resultant harm to the one to whom the duty as owed.

Trademark: A name, a device, or symbol which has become sufficiently associated with a good or has been registered with a governmental agency; once established, the manufacturer has a right to bring legal action against those who infringe upon the protection given the trademark.

Trial court: Court of original jurisdiction.

Unfair labor practice: Activities by management or the union under the National Labor Relations Act which the National Labor Relations Board determines to be in violation of the act.

United States Basketball League: Corporation which operates professional basketball in the United States during the spring and summer months.

United States Football League: Corporate organization that operates professional football in the United States.

United States Olympic Committee: Amateur athletic association that governs Olympic competition and eligibility in the United States. It is located in Colorado Springs, Colorado.

U.S.C.: United States Code. A compilation of Congressional statutes and their amendments organized into 50 subject titles.

U.S.C.A.: United States Code Annotated. A commercially published edition of the *United States Code.*

Vacated: Annulled, set aside, canceled, or rescinded; the canceling or rescinding of an entry of record or of a judgment.

Venue: The particular geographical area where a court with jurisdiction may try a case.

Vicarious liability: Imposes liability for a tortious act upon a person who is not personally negligent, but is held liable because of the relationship between the parties (i.e., a school may be held liable for a coach's tortious act because the school is the employer of the coach, employee).

Void: Having no legal effect and not binding on anyone.

Voidable: That which may be legally annulled at the option of one of the parties.

Waiver: The voluntary relinquishment of a known right.

Westlaw: A computerized data base and legal research system available through West Publishing Company. The data base contains statutory material and cases from components of the National Reporter System.

Women's Basketball Association: Defunct corporation which operated a professional women's basketball league in the United States from 1978 to 1982.

Worker's Compensation: Name commonly used to designate the methods and means created by statutes for giving greater protection and security to the worker and their dependents against injury or death occurring in the course of employment.

World Football League: Defunct corporation which operated a professional football league in the United States in the 1970s.

Writ: A written order, of which there are many types, issued by a court and directed to an official or party, commanding the performance of some act.

Writ of appeal: A suit or action brought before the Supreme Court on appeal. Usually involves a state supreme court holding a federal act to be unconstitutional or a state action to be constitutional, a lower federal court deciding against the United States in a criminal case, a suit brought by the U.S. under the Interstate Commerce Act, or a federal district court hearing a suit involving a restraint on enforcement of a state or federal statute on the grounds that it is unconstitutional.

Writ of certiorari: An appellate court reviewing an action of an inferior court.

INDEX

About the Author

GLENN M. WONG is an attorney who actively practices in sports law. He is a Professor, Department of Sports Management, University of Massachusetts-Amherst and Head of the Department.